What to Expect
The First Year

◆

ARLENE EISENBERG
HEIDI E. MURKOFF
SANDEE E. HATHAWAY, B.S.N.

Note: All children are unique and this book is not intended to subsitute for the advice of your doctor who should be consulted on infant matters, especially when a baby shows any sign of illness or unusual behaviour.

◆

First published in Great Britain by
Simon & Schuster Ltd in 1993
A Viacom Company
This edition published 1996

Copyright © 1989 by
Arene Eisenberg, Heidi E. Murkoff, and Sandee E. Hathaway
Book illustrations copyright © 1989 by Workman Publishing Company Inc.

Simon & Schuster UK Ltd
Africa House
64-78 Kingsway
London WC 2B 6AH

Simon & Schuster Australia
Sydney

A CIP catalogue record for this book is
available from the British Library
ISBN 0-684-81788-8

5 7 9 10 8 6

"What Your Baby May Be Doing This Month," adapted from DDST © 1978.
W.K. Frankenburg, M.D., by permission of the author.

Book Design: Jeanette Graham
Book Illustration: Marika Hahn

Typeset by Hewer Text Composition Services, Edinburgh
Printed and bound in Finland by WSOY Book Printing Division

Dedication

To Emma and Wyatt, Rachel and Ethan
for the magical, memorable first years each of you gave us.
To our partners in parenting, Howard, Erik and Tim
without whom we couldn't have made it through those first years.

A Million Thanks

If there's anyone who needs more help than parents during the first year of a baby's life, it's authors writing a book about the first year of a baby's life. We've been fortunate to be able to get all the help we've needed – from dozens of academics, doctors in practice, other professionals and parents. We thank them all for the valuable contributions they've made to this work.

Thanks particularly to paediatrician Henry Harris, M.D., and obstetrician Richard Aubry, M.D., our trusted medical advisers, for taking the time to read the manuscript and for giving us the benefit of their knowledge, wisdom and insight.

Very special thanks to very special doctors Max Kahn, Michael Levi, Michael Traister and Herb Lazarus, who among them waded heroically through the manuscript in their very spare, spare time. And to Kathy Lawrence and Eve Coulson, who took time out of their busy mothering schedules to read the manuscript and give us their comments.

Thanks, too, to the many other professionals and friends who read pertinent portions of the manuscript and/or offered their expertise, including Ronald L. Poland, M.D.; Michael Lewis, Ph.D.; Alfred T. Lane, M.D.; Irving J. Selikoff, M.D. and Jerrold Abraham, M.D.; Deborah Campbell, M.D.; Barbara Hogan; Judy Lee; Ken Gorfinkle and Doris Ullendorf; Dina Rosenfeld and Howard Berkowitz, M.D.; Richard Weisman, M.D.; Steven M. Silverman, American Red Cross (Greater Boston Region); John J. Caravollas, D.D.S.; Paul Leonard, EMTA; the other Sandy Hathaway, R.N.; Lisa Shulz; Phil Sherman; Bonnie Cowan; Mary Lewis, Consumer Product Safety Commission; Michelle Weber and Jeff Moulter; Mort Lebow; Bill Delay; Marvin Eiger, M.D., and Sally Wendkos Olds. And thanks to the American Heart Association, the March of Dimes, the American College of Obstetrics and Gynecology, the American Academy of Pediatrics, and *Contemporary Pediatrics,* for their invaluable help and mountains of information.

To David and Shana Roskies, Sarah Jacobs and David Kronfeld, Susan and David Kramer, Ann Wimpfheimer and Baruch Bokser, Herb and Judy Seaman, Bilick Shelly Bazes and Rueven Weiss, Nessa Rapoport and Toby Kahn, Linda and David Shriner-Kahn, Pearl Beck and David Fisher, Alan Nadler and Diane Sharon, Sharon and Michael Strassfeld, Betsy and David Teutsch, and countless other parents for sharing their concerns with us, so that we could share them with our readers.

To Marika Hahn for her lovely illustrations.

To the entire Workman Publishing crew, for their tireless support and good humour, but especially to Suzanne Rafer for caring as much as we do. And to Kathy Herlihy-Paoli, Mary Wilkinson, Lisa Hollander, Shannon Ryan, Barbara Scott-Goodman, Bert Snyder, Janet Harris, Ina Stern, Saundra Pearson, Steve Garvan, Linda Randel, Jim Joseph, Andrea Glickson, Chip Duckett, and all those who helped this book to come to fruition and get a good healthy start. And to Peter Workman, without whom none of this could ever happen.

To Elise and Arnold Goodman, our agents and friends, who had the good sense to bring us to Workman in the first place.

To Mimi and Gramps, who taught us the importance of love in parenting.

To the caring parents and good friends who participated in our classes and seminars and taught us so much. And, finally, to the many readers of *What to Expect When You're Expecting* who asked that we write this book.

Contents

—————————————————— PART THREE ——————————————————
Ready Reference

A Word From the Doctor

A new baby is fun and exciting, but anxiety provoking, too. At the outset, the responsibilities of new parenthood loom awesomely large. But that natural insecurity and concern are manageable with reassuring advice, down-to-earth information, and an occasional good night's sleep. *What to Expect the First Year* guarantees two out of three, and as such is a welcome extension of my role as counsellor to parents with a new baby.

I'm impressed with the authors' medical accuracy, and with the sensible way it's translated into useful mother-to-mother advice. Anticipatory guidance – on feeding, colic, crawling, safety, and day-to-day crisis control – is the heart of paediatrics. During pregnancy, you probably found the reassurance and easily accessed answers you needed in *What to Expect When You're Expecting*. This book picks up where that one left off, telling you what you need to know when you need to know it: as baby grows, one month at a time.

Paediatrics has changed dramatically since I began practising and teaching it at Albert Einstein Medical Center 25 years ago. Not just in hi-tech diagnosis, treatment and management of disease. The new mothers and fathers I see today are more advanced, too – more challenging, better informed, more searching and sophisticated in their questions. For them, this lively, comprehensive and well-organized book is just what the paediatrician ordered.

I was pleased when the American Academy of Pediatrics asked me as an AAP national media spokesman to review the manuscript. One of its three authors is a grandmother, and today's paediatrician, too, assumes that role. Solving a rare diagnostic dilemma may be the paediatric challenge we enjoy most. But in practice, the day-to-day essence of our work is surrogate grandparenting. With the old extended family virtually dismantled, grandmothers are jogging, sculpting, golfing, travelling and starting new careers. For the anticipatory guidance grandma once dispensed, parents now turn to their paediatricians.

That kind of guidance is so indispensable that in 1988, on a trip to China to evaluate paediatric practices, I was astonished at its absence. When I commented to my host paediatricians, 'I notice you don't give any advice on child development or mothers' everyday problems,' they looked at me oddly. 'That's true,' said the senior physician, 'We're too busy.' It wasn't until I was invited to his home for lunch and two sets of grandparents descended from their rooms to join us for tea that I understood. 'There's our answer,' I exclaimed to my wife. 'Chinese parents don't need paediatricians for advice on feeding and toilet training. They've got live-in grandmothers.'

The advice in *What to Expect the First Year*, I'm happy to say, is a lot more up-to-date, informative, and authoritative than grandma's. I've never seen a popular paediatrics book as strong on diet and nutrition. The recommendations of AAP committees on nutrition and early childhood – with the new concerns about cholesterol, obesity and fitness – receive excellent support on these pages. The information on 'What Your Baby Should Be Doing This Month' should be wonderfully helpful. And the guidance on the three major parent-child combat zones (sleeping, feeding and stool-gazing) deserves the thorough, well-balanced treatment it receives – more attention than many busy paediatricians can manage to give.

In short, I'm delighted that so thorough and useful a book – one which I suspect will be to parents of the 80s and 90s what Spock was to those of the 50s and 60s – has been published at last. How glad? I plan to hand a copy to every new mother who comes through my office door.

Read it. Enjoy it. You can rely on it. *What to Expect the First Year* – a book by mothers – is first-rate. It won't replace your paediatrician, but it will make his or her life easier, and its well-researched counsel will save you a lot of anxiety.

Henry Harris, M.D.,
Fellow of the American Academy of Pediatrics,
Albert Einstein Medical Center, New York

Why This Book Was Conceived

It seemed so simple and so certain. I would walk into the hospital pregnant and walk out a mother. The role that had come naturally to thousands of generations of women would surely come naturally to me – courtesy of my endocrine glands, which would magically endow me with all the expertise I needed to care for my baby and all the milk I needed to feed her.

Emma's cord had barely been cut when I tested the efficacy of that theory for the first time; it seemed faulty, to say the least. Not only were my feelings on cradling my brand new daughter, still damp from amniotic fluid and ruddy with my blood, less glowing than I'd expected, they were more ambivalent than I'd ever imagined. Why didn't I feel close to her? Why didn't she seem to feel close to me? And why – oh, why – didn't she stop crying? More faults surfaced as I lifted my gown and aimed Emma's swollen face at my breast. Instinct seemed sorely lacking on both sides. My attempts at manoeuvring my breast into her mouth were completely ineffectual; her attempts to take hold of the nipple and suckle (she invariably took hold and then let it go) were equally futile.

Nor did matters improve on our arrival home; my ineptitude was evident everywhere and all the time. When I changed her nappy, when I burped her, when I tried to get her to eat or sleep, when I bathed her and dressed her. In the next few weeks, I cried almost as much as Emma did. No mean feat, considering her colic.

Surely I was the most incompetent mother ever. Or so I thought – until I started talking to other mothers. Feelings of incompetence rivalling mine were, I discovered, rampant among those spending their first weeks as parents. As were the worries (I'd thought I had the market cornered on these, too). Worries that baby wasn't eating enough and was sleeping too much. Worries

about the blotchiness of baby's skin and the looseness of baby's bowel movements. Worries about the risks of exposing baby to strangers and their germs, and the risks of immunizing against disease.

Like other new mothers, I turned to every conceivable source for reassurance and guidance – baby books, magazines, more experienced family members, friends who'd been through it before. Each had something to offer, but the sum total of the information they could provide (most of which was contradictory anyway) couldn't answer a fraction of my questions. My baby's paediatricians probably could have answered most of them, but none of them was willing to move in with Emma, my husband Erik, and me.

And so, just as *What to Expect When You're Expecting* was born out of a need for practical, easily accessible, month-by-month information and day-to-day reassurance during the nine months of pregnancy, *What to Expect the First Year* was born out of the same needs during the first twelve months of parenting.

What to Expect the First Year is designed to make the first year easier (it will never be *easy*), to guide you – and your spouse and older children – through the hundreds of problems, crises and transitions that are an inevitable part of the first year, with the understanding and empathy of those who've gone through it themselves and the benefit of the latest medical information.[1] It strives to take into account the individual differences among mothers and among babies – as with pregnancies, wide ranges of 'normal' exist. It allows for variations in parenting styles, too, since far more often than not when it comes to baby-care

---

1. For the reader's convenience, we've repeated some material in chapters 1, 22, 23, 24, and 25 that previously appeared in *What to Expect When You're Expecting*.

What Your Baby May Be Doing This Month

All parents want to know if their babies are developing well. The problem is that when they compare their babies to the 'average' baby of the same age, they find that their own children are usually ahead or behind – few are exactly average. To help you determine whether your baby's development fits within the wide range of normal rather than just into the limited range of 'average', we've developed a monthly span of achievements into which virtually all babies fall, based on the Denver Developmental Screening Tests and on the Clinical Linguistic Auditory Milestones (CLAMS). In any one month, a full 90% of all babies will have mastered the achievements in the first category, 'What your baby should be able to do'. About 75% will have gained command of those in the second category, 'What your baby will probably be able to do'. Roughly half will have accomplished the feats in the third category, 'What your baby may possibly be able to do'. And about 25% will have pulled off the exploits in the last category,

'What your baby may even be able to do'.

Most parents will find their babies achieving in several different categories at any one time. A few may find their offspring staying constantly in the same category. Some may find their baby's development uneven – slow one month, making a big leap the next. All can relax in the knowledge that their babies are perfectly normal.

Only when a baby is not achieving what a child of the same age 'should be able to do' on a consistent basis, need a parent be concerned and consult the doctor. Even then, no problem may exist.

Use the What Your Baby May Be Doing sections of the book to check progress monthly, if you like. But don't use them to make judgments about your baby's abilities now or in the future. They are not predictive. If checking your baby against such lists becomes anxiety provoking rather than reassuring, by all means ignore them. Your baby will develop just as well if you never look at them – and you may be happier.

---

decisions, there is no one 'right' way to proceed.[2] It trusts a mother's instincts, but recognizes that she often doesn't trust them herself. And most of all it reassures that almost everything a mother feels and almost everything a baby does is normal – even if it's not what the mother next door is feeling or what the baby next door is doing.

I survived the first year. In fact, as my weeks on the job turned to months, and Emma and I settled into our roles more comfortably, I began to enjoy mothering. So much so that not long after, I decided to become a mother again. Five years later I

(and my co-author and sister, Sandee, who has also made the trip through the first twelve months twice during this time) realize how true it is that the good things in life – chief among them children – don't come easily, but that they are most emphatically worth the effort.

It is to that effort – and to you who are about to make it – that we dedicate *What to Expect the First Year*.

Heidi E. Murkoff
New York City

---

2. Of course, when it comes to medical decisions, mother doesn't always know best, and even with a book such as this, you should not attempt to be your baby's doctor. Consult the doctor who cares for your baby before making any decision concerning his or her health.

What to Expect The First Year

◆

ONE

Get Ready, Get Set

---◆---

After nearly nine months of waiting, there's finally a light at the end of the tunnel (perhaps, even, effacement and dilatation at the end of the cervix). But with just weeks to go before B-Day arrives, have you yet come to terms with your baby coming to term? Will you be ready for your baby's arrival when he or she's ready to arrive?

Even for a former Girl Guide, there's no way to be prepared completely, both physically and psychologically, for the time when baby makes three (or more). But there are myriad steps that can be taken – from selecting the right cot to selecting the right doctor, from deciding between breast and bottle to deciding between terry nappies and disposables, from preparing yourself for the new arrival to preparing the family dog – to make the transition a smoother one. The flurry of activity as you prepare for the birth will occasionally seem frenzied, but you'll find it good preparation for the even more hectic pace that awaits you afterwards.

Feeding Your Baby: Breast or Bottle?

For many women, there is no question. When they close their eyes and summon up a daydreamed snapshot of life with baby, they clearly see themselves suckling their infant-to-be at the breast or, just as clearly, cuddling their newborn as it feeds from the latest nursing bottle. Whatever their reasons – emotional, medical, practical – they made up their minds about baby feeding decisively and early in pregnancy, perhaps even before it began.

For other women, however, the picture is not well focused. Maybe they can't see themselves breastfeeding, but they've heard so much about how breast milk is better for baby that they can't see themselves bottle feeding either. Maybe their mother is encouraging them to use the bottle as she did, while friends are pushing for the breast. Maybe they'd really like to try breastfeeding but are afraid it's not practical because they'll be going back to work soon after baby arrives. Or maybe it's the expectant father's mixed feelings that are giving the mother-to-be second thoughts.

No matter what's causing the ambivalence or confusion, the best way to bring the picture into focus is to look at the facts while exploring the feelings of everyone involved. First of all, what are the facts?

Facts Favouring Breastfeeding

Paediatricians, obstetricians, midwives, even manufacturers of infant formulas, agree that breastfeeding is best. No matter how far technology advances, there will always be some things that Nature does better. Among them: formulate the best food and best food delivery system for babies – one that is at the same time good for mothers. As Oliver Wendell Holmes the Elder said well over a century ago, 'A pair of substantial mammary glands has the advantage over the two hemispheres of the most learned professor's brain in the art of compounding a nutritious fluid for infants.' Breastfeeding advantages include:

Milk that is individualized for your baby. Human breast milk contains at least a hundred ingredients that are not found in cow's milk and that can't be synthesized in the laboratory. Moreover, unlike formula, the composition of breast milk changes constantly to meet a baby's ever-changing needs: it's different in the morning than it is in the late afternoon; different at one month than it is at seven; different for a premature baby than for a term baby.

Better digestibility. Breast milk is designed for a human baby's sensitive and still-developing digestive system, rather than for a young calf's. Its protein (mostly lactalbumin) and its fat are more easily handled by the baby than are the protein (mostly caseinogen) and fat in cow's milk. The practical result: breastfed babies may be less likely to suffer from colic, gas and excessive spitting up.

Less sodium and protein. Since breast milk is lower than cow's milk in both of these nutrients, it puts less stress on the fledgling kidneys of the newborn.

Better absorption of calcium. This increased absorption is probably due, in part, to breast milk's lower levels of phosphorus, a mineral that, in excess, interferes with the utilization of calcium.

Less risk of allergy. Babies are almost never allergic to breast milk. Though an infant may be sensitive to something a mother has eaten that has passed into her milk (including cow's milk), he or she virtually always tolerates mother's milk, itself, well. On the other hand, better than 1 out of 10 infants, after an initial exposure, turn out to be allergic to cow's milk formula. (A switch to a soy or hydrolysate formula usually solves the problem – though such formulas stray even further from the composition of human milk than cow's milk.[1])

No problems with constipation or diarrhoea. Because of breast milk's naturally laxative effect, infants who nurse are often notoriously prolific when it comes to filling the nappy pail, and constipation is virtually unheard of among them. Also, though their movements are generally very loose, diarrhoea is rarely a problem. Breast milk appears to reduce the risk of digestive upset in two ways: first, by directly destroying a number of the causative harmful microorganisms; and second, by inhibiting their growth via encouraging the growth of the beneficial microorganisms that keep them in check.

Less risk of nappy rash. The breastfed baby's sweet-smelling movements are less likely to cause nappy rash, but this advantage (as well as the less objectionable odour) disappears once solids are introduced.

Better health for baby. Every time breastfed infants suckle at their mother's breasts, from the first time to the last, they are getting a healthy dose of antibodies to bolster their immunity to disease. In general, they will come down with fewer colds, ear infections, and other illnesses than do bottle-fed infants, and will usually recover more quickly and with fewer complications. They are also hospitalized less often. And one recent study suggests that there may also be a decreased risk of childhood cancer in breastfed babies.

Less obesity. Oftentimes, breastfed infants are less chubby than their bottle-fed peers. That is, in part, because breast-feeding puts baby's appetite in charge of consumption. With bottle feeding, on the other hand, baby may be urged to continue until the bottle is empty. In addition, breast milk is actually calorie controlled. The hind milk, the milk that a baby gets at the end of a nursing session, is higher in calories than that at the beginning, and tends to make a baby feel full – a signal to stop sucking. Be aware, however, that the breastfed baby who is offered the

---

1. Soy *milks*, however, are not nutritionally adequate and should not be used for infant feeding.

breast too often – every time he or she is cranky, for instance – can gain too quickly.

More sucking satisfaction. A baby can continue sucking at an empty breast, but not at an empty bottle, for optimum sucking enjoyment.

Possibly improved cholesterol metabolism. Studies are unclear, but there has been some evidence that breastfed babies have lower cholesterol levels as adults, perhaps because of improved metabolism.

Better mouth development. Mother's nipples and baby's mouth are a perfect match (though it often doesn't seem so the first time mother and baby try to work together). Even the most scientifically designed substitute nipple fails to give a baby's jaws, gums and teeth the workout he or she would get at mother's breast – a workout that ensures optimum oral development. And since there is no forward thrust of the tongue, as with sucking on a bottle, breastfed babies are less prone to orthodontic problems than those raised on the bottle.

Convenience. Breast milk is always in stock, ready to use, clean and consistently at the perfect temperature. It's the ultimate convenience food. No formula to run out of, shop for, or lug around, no bottles to sterilize or refill, no cans to open, no feedings to warm. Wherever you are – in bed, on the road, at a restaurant, on the beach – all the nourishment your baby needs is always ready and waiting. Should baby and mother be apart, for the night, the day, or even the weekend, breast milk can be expressed in advance and stored in the refrigerator or freezer for bottle feedings.

Lower cost. Breast milk is free, whereas bottle feeding can be an expensive proposition (and a wasteful one, since half-used bottles or opened cans often end up being dumped down the kitchen sink). Though it's true that a nursing mother needs slightly more food than a non-nursing one, the cost of this more ample diet needn't be high. If it's chosen with an eye towards nutrition, as it should be, it can in fact be a bargain. A carton of low-fat milk is less expensive than a bottle of cherry cola; a bowl of Shredded Wheat and fresh fruit is less expensive than a Danish pastry; a homemade juice lolly is less expensive than a store-bought, sugar-sweetened one.

Quicker recovery for mother. Breastfeeding is better for mother's body. All your motivations for breastfeeding needn't be selfless ones. Because breastfeeding is part of the natural cycle of pregnancy-child-birth-mothering, it is designed to be good not just for baby, but for you as well. It will help your uterus shrink back to prepregnancy size more quickly (that's the increased cramping a mother feels during the first postpartum days as her baby suckles), which in turn will reduce your flow of lochia (the postpartum discharge) more rapidly. And it will help you shed leftover pregnancy weight by burning upwards of 500 extra calories a day. Some of this weight, you may remember, was laid down in the form of fat reserves especially to help you produce milk; now's your chance to use them. (But beware of burning your fat too quickly; see page 526.)

Some protection against pregnancy. A nursing mother is generally granted a reprieve from 'that time of the month' problems for many months postpartum. Ovulation and menstruation are suppressed in most lactating women at least until their babies begin to take significant supplementation (whether in the form of formula or solids), often until weaning, and sometimes for several months afterwards. (Which is not, unfortunately, to say that you can't become pregnant. Since ovulation can quietly precede your first postpartum period, you can never be certain as to when the protection you've been receiving from breastfeeding will cease. See page 557 for birth control information.)

Possibly a reduction in the risk of breast cancer. Though breastfeeding does not seem to confer protection from breast cancer that occurs after menopause, there does seem to be some evidence to suggest that it may reduce the risk of breast cancer occurring earlier.

Enforced rest periods. Breastfeeding ensures frequent breaks in your day, especially at first (sometimes, more frequent than you'd like). Whether or not you feel you have the time to relax, your postpartum body needs the time off your feet that breastfeeding forces you to take.

Less complicated nighttime feedings. Even parents who can't get enough of their adorable infants during the day don't look forward to seeing them at 2 A.M. (or at any other time between midnight and dawn). But baby's nighttime waking can be a lot more tolerable (you may even enjoy it as a time of special closeness) when comfort is as close as your breasts, instead of far off in the kitchen refrigerator, needing to be warmed and poured into a bottle. (It's even easier on mum if dad completes the transfer of baby from cot to breast and back again.)

Strong mother-baby relationships. As almost any mother who's ever breastfed will tell you, the breastfeeding benefit you're likely to treasure most is the bond it builds between mother and child. There's skin-to-skin and eye-to-eye contact, and the opportunity to cuddle, baby-babble, and coo at your wonderful new arrival. True, you can reap the same pleasures when bottle feeding, but you've got to make more of a conscious effort (see page 55), since you may frequently be faced with the temptation to relegate the task to others when you're tired, for example, or to prop the bottle when you're busy.

Facts Favouring Bottle Feeding

If there were no advantages to bottle feeding, no one capable of breastfeeding would ever turn to formula. But there are some very real advantages, and for some mothers (and some fathers) they outweigh the many benefits of breastfeeding:

Longer satisfaction for baby. Infant formula made from cow's milk is more difficult to digest than breast milk, and the large rubbery curds it forms stay in a baby's stomach longer, giving a feeling of satiety that can last several hours, extending the period between feedings to three or four hours even early on. Because, on the other hand, breast milk is so easily and quickly digested, many nursing newborns feed so often that it sometimes seems as though they're permanently attached to their mothers' breasts. Though this frequent nursing isn't for naught – it stimulates the production of milk and improves the supply – it can be draining.

Easy monitoring of intake. You know just how much a bottle-fed baby is taking. Because breasts aren't calibrated to measure baby's intake, the inexperienced nursing mother often worries that her newborn isn't getting enough to eat. The bottle-feeding mother has no such problem – a glance at the bottle tells her exactly what she wants to know. (This can be a disadvantage, however, if anxious mothers push babies to take more than they want.)

More freedom. Bottle feeding doesn't tie a mother down. Want to take in dinner and a show with your husband? Or even get away for a romantic weekend? Grandmother will likely be more than happy to baby-sit and take charge of the feeding honours. Intend to go back to work part-time when baby is three months old? No weaning or expressing breast milk will be necessary. Just tell the baby-sitter where the bottles and formula are, and you're off.

More participation for father. Dads can share in the pleasures of baby feeding when baby is bottle fed in a way that's impossible with the breastfed infant. (Some dads of breastfed babies actually feel cheated.)

More participation for older siblings. There's little that gives an older child as much a feeling of taking care of 'his or her new baby' as giving a bottle.

Fewer demands. The woman exhausted by a difficult labour may be delighted to have the option of not getting up for middle-of-the-night feedings, or even those at 6 A.M. Father, grandmother, baby nurse – or anyone else on hand – can take those over until she's stronger. There is also less of a physical drain on mother's resources if she doesn't have to produce breast milk.

No interference with fashion. A bottle-feeding mother can dress as she pleases. The nursing mother's wardrobe is not quite as limited as it was when she was pregnant, but most of the time she won't be able to put fashion before practicality. Whenever she will be nursing, she'll have to forgo one-piece dresses that don't button up the front. (Try accommodating a hungry baby by lifting your dress over your head and you'll see why.)

Less restriction on birth control methods. While a breastfeeding mother has to limit her choice of contraception to those methods that won't hurt her baby (see page 557), the bottle-feeding mum has no such restrictions.

Fewer dietary demands and restrictions. A bottle-feeding mother can stop eating for two. Unlike the nursing mum, she can stop taking in extra protein and calcium, and she can forget about her antenatal vitamin supplements. (Though unless she's one of the rare women who has trouble eating enough to keep weight on, she may be less happy about having to relinquish the extra calories a nursing mother can keep enjoying until weaning.) She can have a few drinks at a party, take aspirin for headaches or medication prescribed by her doctor for allergies, eat all the spicy foods she wants – without worrying about the possible effect on her baby. After the first six weeks postpartum (though not before, when her body is still in the recovery phase), she can diet strenuously, but intelligently, to take off any pregnancy weight that lingers. This is something that the breastfeeding mother can't do until baby is weaned – though, because of the calories milk production requires, she may not have to diet at all to reach her goal.

Less stressful feeding in public. Bottle feeding can be done in public without embarrassment or dishabille. While the nursing mother may receive curious or disapproving glances when she chooses to breastfeed in public, no one will look twice or askance at a woman bottle feeding her baby. Neither will the bottle-feeding mother need to worry about the sometimes awkward procedure of redressing (refastening bra flaps, retucking in shirts, rebuttoning buttons) after the feeding is done.

No interference with lovemaking. After nine months of making love under somewhat less than ideal conditions, many couples look forward to picking up where they left off before conception. For the breastfeeding woman, a vagina left dry by the hormonal changes of lactation, teamed with sore nipples and leaky breasts, can sometimes make this an impossible dream for months to come. For the bottle-feeding mother, nothing (except for an unexpectedly awake and crying baby) need stand between her and her partner.

Factoring in Feelings

The facts are before you; you've read them and reread them, considered them and reconsidered them. And yet, perhaps, you're still left undecided. That's because, as with many other decisions you're making these days, the decision between breast and bottle doesn't just depend on facts. It depends a great deal on how you – and your partner – feel.

Do you feel that you really want to breastfeed, but believe it's impractical because you're planning to go back to work soon after your baby is born? Don't let circumstances deprive you and your baby of the experience. A few weeks of nursing are better than none at all; both of you stand to benefit from even the briefest encounter with it. And with a little extra dedication and planning, you may be able to work out a system for continuing to breastfeed even after you've returned to work (see page 166).

Do you feel fundamentally negative about breastfeeding, yet find the facts in favour of it too convincing to ignore? Here again, you might give nursing a try. If your feelings don't take a shift towards the positive, you can quit. At least your baby will have reaped the benefits of breastfeeding for a short time (which is better than no time at all), and you'll know that you tried, erasing those nagging doubts. (Don't quit before you've given nursing your best shot, however. A really fair trial should last at least a month, or better six weeks, since it usually takes that long to establish a good nursing relationship even under the best of circumstances.)

Do you have a deep-seated aversion to breastfeeding, feeling totally uncomfortable about every aspect of it, from having to bare your breast (not quite literally, of course) in public to the very idea of putting your child at your bosom to suckle? Or have you previously breastfed and not enjoyed it? If your feelings about breastfeeding are purely negative, and if, for you, these feelings far outweigh the facts favouring it, then bottle feeding will very likely be best for you and your baby. That may also be true if your feelings are *fairly* negative and the facts of your life (such as a planned early return to work) mitigate against breastfeeding. In either case, you should make the decision to turn to a bottle without feeling guilty.

Do you fear that you won't be able to nurse because of a high-strung (can't-sit-still) temperament, but agree that breast milk is best for baby? Again, you have

---

Breastfeeding Myths

- **MYTH: You can't breastfeed if you have small breasts or flat nipples**.
  Reality: In no way does outward appearance affect the production of milk or a mother's ability to dispense it. Breasts and nipples of all shapes and sizes can satisfy a hungry baby. Inverted nipples that don't become erect when stimulated may need some advance preparation to make them fully functional; see page 24.

- **MYTH: Breastfeeding is a lot of trouble**.
  Reality: Never again will it be so easy to feed your child. Breasts, unlike bottles, are ready when baby is. You don't have to remember to take them with you when you're planning a day at the beach, lug them in a tote bag, or worry about the milk inside them spoiling in the hot sun.

- **MYTH: Breastfeeding ties you down**.
  Reality: It's true that breastfeeding is naturally better suited to mothers who plan to be with their babies most of the time. But those who are willing to make the effort to express and store milk, or who prefer to supplement

with formula can satisfy their need to work – or see a film, or go to an all-day seminar – and their desire to breastfeed. And when it comes to stepping out with baby, it's the breastfeeding mother who is more mobile, always having an ample supply of food along no matter where she goes or how long she plans to stay.

- **MYTH: Breastfeeding will ruin your breasts**.
  Reality: Much to the surprise of many people, breastfeeding doesn't seem to permanently affect the shape or size of your breasts at all. Because of hereditary factors, age, poor support (going braless), or excessive weight gain during pregnancy, your breasts may be less firm after having a child. But breastfeeding won't be to blame.

- **MYTH: Breastfeeding excludes father**.
  Reality: A father who wants to be involved in the care of his nursing infant can find ample opportunity – for bathing, changing, holding, rocking, playing with and, once solids are introduced, sending 'trains through the tunnel'.

nothing to lose by trying, and you have everything to gain should your personality turn out to be more compatible with breast-feeding than you'd speculated. Don't judge the situation too early in the game, however. Even women ordinarily graced with Madon-na-like calm can find the first few weeks of breastfeeding a time of high anxiety. Many women, however, are surprised, once a smoothly working breastfeeding relation-ship is established, to find that nursing is relaxing – the hormones released as baby suckles actually enhance relaxation, and the experience itself is one of the healthiest routes to tension relief. (At the beginning, give yourself the best chance of success by using relaxation techniques before putting your newborn to breast.) Keep in mind that you can always switch to the bottle later, should your initial instincts prove correct.

Does your partner feel jealous or repelled at the thought of your breastfeeding – though you yourself would like to nurse? If he does, have him read the facts, too. They may persuade him that his loss, which, after all, is only a temporary one, or his distaste, which will also be temporary, will be baby's gain. Also have him read the section on breastfeeding in Chapter 25 (Becoming a Father). If his mind remains made up against breastfeeding, however, and yours resolved for it, you'll need to do some further nego-tiating to break the impasse and come up with a solution that suits you both.

As in the making of any important marital decision, there are two good approaches: one is compromise; the other is giving the decision to the partner who cares the most about or has the most at stake in a particular issue. A compromise might be for you to breastfeed, but only for three months. Or if it's your nursing in public that bothers your partner, you might agree to breastfeed in private only, and to supplement with a bottle when privacy isn't available. If compromise won't work, then try the other approach. If the chance to nurse means everything to you, ask him to concede this point. If he is the more adamant one (a less likely scenario), give in to him.

Some women find breastfeeding an over-whelmingly positive experience, joyful and exhilarating; when it comes time to wean baby (especially if it's the last baby), tears and a bout with depression are common. Others nurse their babies because they know it's best, but feel little more than ambivalence while they do it. Still others never learn to tolerate, never mind enjoy, breastfeeding. But you aren't likely to know where you fall along the spectrum until you've actually held your baby to your breast. Many women who begin to breast-feed out of duty continue to do it out of love. Many who, before baby arrives, are thor-oughly appalled at the thought of engaging in such an intimate act in the company of strangers live to eat their words and to lift their shirts with aplomb at the sound of baby's first cry – on an aeroplane, in a crowded park, at a ritzy restaurant.

In the end, however, if you opt not to breastfeed (with or without a trial run), don't feel guilty. Almost nothing you do for your baby is right if it doesn't feel right for you – and that includes breastfeeding. Even babies who were born yesterday are wise enough to sense feelings of uneasiness in their mothers; a bottle given lovingly can be better for your infant than a breast offered grudgingly.

When You Can't or Shouldn't Breastfeed

For some women, the pros and cons of breastfeeding and bottle feeding are aca-demic. They don't have the option of nur-sing their new babies, because of either their own health or their baby's. If your medical history includes any of the following, you will almost certainly be advised not to breastfeed:

- Serious debilitating illness (such as heart or kidney disease, or severe anaemia), or extreme underweight (your body needs fat stores to produce milk).

- Serious infection, such as AIDS or tuber-culosis, and possibly hepatitis B. (You may be able to nurse in spite of the

---

Adoption and Breastfeeding

Though few adopting mothers would consider it an option, it is indeed occasionally possible to breastfeed an adopted child. This can work only if plenty of advance planning and pre-paration is undertaken, and if the baby will be picked up within a few days after birth. See page 493 for tips on breastfeeding an adopted baby.

---

hepatitis if your baby is treated postpartum with gamma globulin and hepatitis B vaccine.)

- A condition requiring regular medication that passes into the breast milk and might be harmful to the baby, such as antithyroid, anticancer, or antihypertensive drugs; lithium, tranquillizers, or sedatives. (The need for temporary medication should not, however, interfere with breastfeeding; see page 542.)

- Present drug abuse – including the use of tranquillizers, amphetamines, barbiturates, or other pills, heroin, methadone, cocaine, marijuana, tobacco, and the moderate or heavy use of caffeine or alcohol.

- Inadequate glandular tissue in the breasts (this has nothing to do with the size of your breasts) or damage to the nerve supply to the nipple (as from injury or surgery). In some cases you may be able to attempt breastfeeding, under careful medical supervision to be certain your baby is thriving. If you've had surgery for breast cancer in one breast, ask your doctor about the possibility of nursing from the other. From present information it isn't clear whether it is safe or not, though it does appear that a mother does not transmit cancer-causing substances to her baby through breast milk. Future research may be able to tell us more about the safety of breastfeeding following cancer surgery.[2]

There are also conditions of the newborn that can interfere with breastfeeding:

- A metabolic disorder, such as phenylketonuria (PKU) or lactose intolerance, that makes the baby unable to digest human milk.

- A deformity, such as cleft lip and/or cleft palate, that makes suckling at the breast difficult or impossible. (However, in some instances a mother may be able to use a supplemental nutrition system or to express milk to feed a baby born with such a problem, and after corrective surgery, may even be able to breastfeed.

If you can't breastfeed, or if you just don't wish to, be assured that a commercial baby formula will almost certainly nourish your baby adequately (rare exceptions would include infants with multiple allergies who require special formulas). Millions of healthy, happy babies (possibly, you among them) have been raised on the bottle, and your baby can be, too, especially if you remember to make bottle feeding as loving an affair as breastfeeding.

---

2. Many experts recommend a woman wait three to five years after breast cancer surgery before becoming pregnant and breastfeeding because of the fear that the hormones stimulated might activate cancer cells during this period when the risk of the recurrence of the cancer is greatest.

What You May be Concerned About

Coping With Motherhood

*'Everything's ready for the baby –
except me. I just can't picture myself as
a mother.'*

Even those women who pictured themselves
as mothers from the first time they changed
a Betsy-Wetsy or dried Tiny Tears' eyes often
start to doubt the validity of their calling
when it threatens to become a round-the-
clock reality. Those who spurned dolls for
relationships with trucks and soccer balls,
mowed lawns instead of baby-sitting, and
rarely gave passing prams more than a
passing glance until the day their pregnancy
test came back positive may face delivery day
with even greater trepidation.

But not only is this ninth-month crumbling of confidence normal, it's healthy.
Strolling into motherhood blithely self-assured may only set you up for a swift and
unsettling comedown when the task turns
out to be more overwhelming than you'd
imagined. A little anxiety (a recognition that
life with baby will include some difficult,
even some seemingly impossible, days and
nights) and uncertainty will help you head
off postpartum reality shock.

So if you don't feel ready for motherhood
don't worry. But do prepare. Read at least
the first few chapters in this book and
everything else you can about newborns
and infants (always keeping in mind that
babies don't always go 'by the book').
Spend some time, if possible, with newborns or young babies; try holding them,
even change them; talk to their parents
about the pleasures and frustrations of caring for an infant. Take a parenting course, if
one's available in your area. Thousands have
been developed in recent years – by hospitals and medical groups, universities and
schools, religious institutions and private
entrepreneurs – in response to the demand
of parents wanting to learn more about the
toughest job they may ever have to handle.
Most of all, realize that mothers are not

born – they're created on the job. A woman
who's gained some experience with other
people's infants may be somewhat more
comfortable at first than the totally inexperienced new mother, but by the six-week
checkup it will be difficult to tell them
apart. And the still-pregnant women in the
waiting room will envy them both their skill
and poise as mothers.

Remember, too, that we all have gained
some experience in child rearing, if only
from observation. We have all watched
parents – our own as well as friends' and
strangers' – at work and silently programmed our own mental computers. A
mother slaps her toddler in the supermarket and you say to yourself, 'I'll never do
that', or another jogs with her baby in a
pushchair through the park and you say,
'That's what I'll do'.

A Changing Lifestyle

*'I really look forward to having my
baby. But I worry that the lifestyle my
husband and I have grown
accustomed to will be totally
disrupted.'*

For your mother's generation, a change in
lifestyle wasn't an issue. Most young couples
married and had children right out of
school or college; they had little chance to
develop a child-free adult lifestyle before
children appeared on the scene. Having
gone directly from their parents' home to
their own, the only lifestyle they knew was a
family-centred one. Today's mother-to-be is
likely to be many years out of school and
into an independent, *self*-centred lifestyle –
one that may include frequent lunches and
dinners out, spontaneous weekends of
skiing or boating, late nights of dancing
followed by long and leisurely mornings
in bed, and a cupboard full of dry-clean-
only clothes. She may also be accustomed to
making love when and where the spirit

moves (within the realm of good taste, of course).

This lifestyle needn't come to a crashing end. But, realistically, it will need to undergo some radical alterations. Some lunches and dinners may still be taken out, but less often at candlelit French bistros and more often at family-style eateries with high chairs and a high tolerance for peas and carrots ground into the carpeting. Weekends away will no longer be as spontaneous (planning becomes more vital and packing more complicated), but if you've got the will, you'll find the way to get away – usually with baby, occasionally without (if you're bottle feeding or once your breastfed baby is weaned). An early film or concert may have to replace late night dancing for a while, unless you think you can waltz in for the 2 A.M. feeding and be up again for the 6. And those silk dresses and wool trousers will probably have to be tucked away in the back of the wardrobe for baby-free occasions, so room can be made for washables that can weather baby's spitup and worse. Lovemaking needn't be entirely abandoned, but opportunity will become as critical a factor as mood in determining when you and your husband are intimate.

Nevertheless, if you're like most parents today you won't want to abandon your former style of living entirely and will try to fit baby into it, at least to some extent. Of course, you won't always succeed, especially as baby grows older. While a tiny infant may not object to being dragged hither and yon with mum and dad, a baby even a few months old begins to have social needs and personal preferences of his or her own, and these needs inevitably have to be taken into account as you plan your schedule.

Just how much your lifestyle will have to change will depend a lot on the individual needs of you, your partner, and your baby. And how well you adjust to the changes will depend to a great extent on your own attitudes. If you look at the changes as positive and exciting, then your life will be better and richer than ever. If, however, you're resentful of and resistant to every change mothering brings, then both you

and baby (and probably your spouse as well) are in for a very hard time.

Whether or Not to Go Back to Work

'Every time I talk to a friend or read an article on the subject, I change my mind about whether or not to go back to work soon after my baby is born.'

Today's expectant working woman has it all to look forward to: all the satisfaction of a fulfilling career, all the joy of raising a family – and all the guilt, anxiety and confusion inherent in deciding which of the two will hold priority in her life after delivery.

But while it seems as though this is a choice you should make now, it really isn't. Deciding while you're still pregnant whether you'll stay home or go back to work (and when) after baby is born is like deciding between a job you're familiar with and one you know nothing about. Instead, assuming you have the options, keep them open until you've spent some time at home with your baby. You may find that nothing you've ever done – including your job – has ever given you as much satisfaction as does caring for your newborn, and may postpone going back to work indefinitely. Or you may find that, as sweet and adorable as baby is, you're climbing the walls after a month, and may hasten your return to the 9-to-5 life. Or you may find that neither full-time mothering nor full-time working alone fills all your needs, and that you'd like to combine the best of both worlds – by taking a part-time position, if you're lucky enough to find one or savvy enough to create one. (See page 575 for some advice on making the decision once baby appears on the scene.)

Dad Taking Time Off

'My husband wants to take his holiday time when the baby is born. That means there'll be no holiday

*later in the year. Does this make
sense?'*

Someday – hopefully sooner than later – this
question won't be one that expectant parents will need to ask. Fathers and mothers
alike will automatically be granted paternity
or maternity leave upon the birth of their
babies – just as they already are in many
other industrialized nations.

But since that bright day has not yet
dawned, fathers-to-be who elect to spend
the immediate postpartum period at home
usually have to give up all or part of their
holiday time to do so. This is, of course, a
matter of choice and circumstance. While
changing nappies and doing laundry may
not seem like much of a holiday, to some
fathers enjoying those first days as a family
can offer more fun than a Mardi Gras, more
awe and inspiration than a view of the Grand
Canyon, and more memories to cherish than
a round the world cruise. If your partner
feels this way, by all means make the time
following baby's arrival holiday time. Be
sure, however, that he is fully acquainted
in advance with basic household mechanics:
laundry, simple cooking, vacuuming, and so
on. (Many husbands, of course, are already
at least as proficient as, and some are more
proficient than, their wives at these chores.)

On the other hand, if you've already
enlisted more help than you will need
(grandmother is coming, a younger sister
is moving in for two weeks, and/or a baby
nurse has been engaged), and the father-to-be would feel like a fifth wheel being around
the house during the day and would just as
soon get to know his new offspring in the
quiet of the night, it may make sense to save
those holiday days for a real holiday en
famille.

Don't, however, extend invitations to all
and sundry to come and help if you and your
husband would really rather do it yourselves;
it's a wonderful way for mummy, daddy and
baby to become a family.

Grandparents

*'My mother has her bags packed and is
ready to get in the car in the moment
the baby arrives "to give me a hand".
The idea makes me nervous because
my mother tends to take over, but I
don't want to hurt her feelings and tell
her not to come.'*

Whether it's loving and warm, distant and
frosty, or tottering on the brink somewhere
in between, a woman's relationship with her
mother (or mother-in-law) is one of the
most complicated in her life. It becomes
even more so when daughter becomes
mother, and mother becomes grand-mother. Though there may be hundreds
of situations in the next couple of decades
of parenting and grandparenting when your
wishes will come into conflict with your
parents', this is the one that will probably
set the precedent for those to come.

You and your husband are the ones who
should decide who will be around to help
out when baby arrives. If you both would
rather spend the first week or so alone with
your baby, then explain to your mother (and
your mother-in-law, too, if necessary) that
you and your husband want to get to know
the baby and to get more comfortable with
him or her before having houseguests. Assure her that you are very eager for her to
visit when the baby is a couple of weeks old,
reminding her, too, that the baby will be
more responsive, interesting, and awake
then, anyway. She may feel rejected temporarily, but once she holds her grandchild
in her arms, the hurt feelings are sure to melt
away, the episode forgotten. What won't be
forgotten is that you and your husband are
the ones who set the rules for your baby, an
important concept to relay to parents and in-laws early. As an old proverb goes: If God
had wanted the elderly to raise infants, He
would not have invented menopause.

Some new parents, of course, welcome
the experience and the extra set of hands
that come with a postpartum visit from
grandmother, particularly when they aren't
accompanied by an overbearing, take-

charge attitude. Just as those who feel the need to say, 'Mother, I'd rather do it myself', shouldn't be plagued by guilt, those who feel they need the help shouldn't have qualms about saying, 'I'd rather *not* do it myself'.

The expertise that grandparents bring with them is irreplaceable. Whether you feel your parents (or your husband's) did a great job raising you or just a fair one, there is always something to be learned from their experience, even if it's only what not to do. There's no point in reinventing the wheel – or child-care practices – in every generation.

Being open to suggestion, of course, puts you in the position of sometimes (maybe even most of the time) having to disagree. Don't let this stop you from talking over baby preparations, and later baby care, with your mother (or your husband's). She probably disagreed with her own mother (or mother-in-law) when you were born, too – something you can remind her of when she's upset by your rejections. What's *right* in baby care, as in almost any other area, changes from generation to generation, and you should both keep your sense of humour about that. (You'll need it again when your little newborn, twenty or thirty years from now, becomes a mummy or daddy and accuses you of being old-fashioned.)

If you disagree with grandmother on an issue – bottle feeding versus breastfeeding, for example – explain your point of view. She may come around when you talk about it, or at least understand why you feel the way you do. Even if she doesn't, your relationship will be better if you are open and share your thoughts and feelings than if you bottle them up.

And remember, if parenthood is a responsibility, grandparenthood is the reward – one you will someday want to enjoy yourself. Be sure you don't deprive your parents of theirs.

A Lack of Grandparents

'My husband's parents are deceased.

Mine are elderly and live in another country. Sometimes I feel the lack of having family to talk to about my pregnancy and about the baby. I think it will be worse when the baby arrives.'

You're not alone in feeling alone. Whereas in generations past the extended family rarely extended beyond the county line, millions of couples in today's mobile society live far from parents and family. Never is this separation more keenly felt than when a new generation is being added.

What helps – besides the telephone – is finding surrogates for family members who are far away or deceased. Churches or synagogues, especially those with a strong sense of community, are a good source of this kind of support. So are parent groups, which sometimes evolve out of childbirth education or exercise classes, or simply develop spontaneously among casual acquaintances. Then there are senior citizens who have as great a need for grandchildren as you do for grandparents. You can find one through seniors groups in your neighbourhood and 'adopt' each other. Weekly visits and joint outings can give you and your baby a sense of family and give an elderly person or couple a sense of being needed.

If you're worried about not having an experienced grandmother around when you come home from the hospital, consider a baby nurse.

Considering a Baby Nurse

'Some of my friends hired baby nurses when their babies were born. Do I need one, too?'

For many years, baby nurses were a fixture of the upper class; a new mother who could afford to have one wouldn't have thought of being without one. Today, even royalty are changing their share of nappies and taking charge of their share of feedings (though nannies are still employed to tend to the other share), and many new mothers who have the financial resources to hire a baby nurse don't have the desire to do so.

Once you've determined there's enough money in your budget for a baby nurse, you'll need to consider several other factors before deciding whether or not to hire one. Here are some reasons why you might opt for one:

- To get some hands-on training in baby care. If you haven't had experience or taken a parenting class, and feel you'd rather not learn from the mistakes you make on the job and on your baby, a good baby nurse will be able to instruct in such basics as bathing, burping, changing, and even breastfeeding. If this is your reason for hiring a nurse, however, be sure that the person you hire is as interested in teaching as you are in learning. Some won't tolerate novice mothers peeping over their shoulders; one with such a dictatorial take-charge attitude can leave you as inexperienced and unsure on her departure as you were on her arrival.

- To avoid getting up in the middle of the night for feedings. If you're bottle feeding and would rather sleep through the night, at least in the early weeks of postpartum fatigue, a baby nurse, on duty 24 hours a day or hired just for nights, can take over this feeding responsibility. (This chore can also be tended to by an obliging father or grandparent.)

- To spend more time with an older child. Some women hire a baby nurse so that they can be more available to their older children, and hopefully spare them the pangs of jealousy that are often provoked by new arrivals. Such a nurse might be hired to work just a few hours a day during the time you want to spend with your older child. If this is your major reason for hiring a nurse, however, bear in mind that her presence will probably only serve to postpone feelings of sibling jealousy; the older child will be in for a dose of reality shock when the nurse leaves and mummy starts her double

duty. See page 597 for other ways of coping with the sibling problem.

- To give yourself a chance to recuperate after a caesarean or difficult vaginal birth. Since you probably won't know if you're going to have a difficult time beforehand, it's not a bad idea to do some scouting around for nurses in advance, just in case. If you have the name of a potential nurse or two or at least have spoken to an agency, you can call shortly after you deliver and have a helper hired before you get home.

A baby nurse may not be the best solution to your postpartum needs if:

- You're breastfeeding. Since a nurse (unless she's a wet nurse) can't feed a nursing baby, and feeding is one of the most time-consuming tasks in the care of a newborn, she may not be much of a help. For the nursing mother, household help – someone to cook, clean, shop and do laundry – is probably a wiser investment, unless you can find a nurse who will do these chores and also offer breastfeeding instruction.

- You're not comfortable with a stranger living in your home. If the idea of having a non-family member sharing your bathroom, your kitchen and your table 24 hours a day makes you uneasy, hire a part-time nurse rather than a live-in, or opt for one of the other sources of help described below.

- You'd rather do it yourself. If you want to be the one to give the first bath, catch sight of the first smile (even if they say it's only wind), soothe your baby through the first bout of crying (even if it's at 2 A.M.), don't hire a nurse, hire household help to free you up for fun with baby.

- You'd like the father to do it, too. If you and your partner want to share baby care, a nurse may get in the way. Even if she is willing to grant mothers some rights, she may not be used to fathers doing anything more than handing out cigars. And may want to keep it that way.

If she is willing to share the baby-care workload with both of you, there won't be much left for her to do – except to collect her paycheque, which you could probably spend more sensibly on cleaning help.

If you decide that a baby nurse is right for you, the best way to go about finding one is to ask for recommendations from friends who've used one. Be sure to find out if the nurse in question has the qualifications and qualities you're looking for. Some cook, some don't. Some will do light housework and laundry, others won't. Some are gentle, motherly women who will nurture your innate mothering ability and leave you feeling more confident; others are bossy, cold, and patronizing, and will leave you feeling totally inadequate. Many are licensed practical nurses; some have also been trained specifically in caring for mother as well as baby, in mother-child relations, and in teaching breastfeeding and child-care basics. A personal interview is extremely important, since it's the only way to know whether you are going to feel comfortable with a particular individual. But excellent references (do check them out) are a must. It's also important that a nurse – or anyone else you hire who may come in contact with the baby – has been screened for TB.

Other Sources of Help

'With the loss of my income, we just can't afford the expense of a baby nurse. Since I may need a caesarean – my baby's in a breech position – I wonder if I will be able to manage without help.'

Just because you can't afford – or don't want to hire – a baby nurse doesn't mean you have to go it alone. Most women, in fact, rely on other sources of help, at least one of which is probably available to you:

The new father. If your partner can arrange

his schedule so that he can be with you both for the first week or so, he is probably your best baby helper. Together and without outside assistance or interference, you'll both learn more about your baby and baby care than you would any other way. No experience is necessary for the job; you'll both catch on quickly. Do take a baby-care class at your hospital if one is offered and read a child-care book or two before baby arrives to pick up some of the basics beforehand – and feel free to turn to family, friends, the baby's doctor, the hospital nursery staff, La Leche, and other sources of information and advice to fill in the blanks.

A grandmother. If you have a mother or mother-in-law whom you'd be comfortable having around on a live-in or come-in basis for the first weeks, this may provide another satisfactory solution. Grandmothers have at least a hundred and one uses: they can rock a crying baby, cook a splendid supper, wash and fold the laundry, do the shopping, and much, much more. This kind of arrangement can work particularly well if you can handle a little well-meant interference good-naturedly. Of course, if the grandmother in question has an already busy life and isn't interested in changing nappies, this won't be an option.

Your freezer. You won't be able to put baby on ice when you're tired, but you will be able to pull meals off the ice if you prepared some during the last weeks of pregnancy when, if you weren't working you may have had too much time on your hands anyway. A few nutritious casseroles, some chicken roasted and ready to reheat or a prepared pasta sauce will ease the pressure of having to feed the rest of your family nightly – so you can concentrate more on feeding baby (which you may find a full-time job for a while). Don't hesitate to stock up on frozen vegetables, too; they take little preparation time and are at least as nutritious as fresh.

Your favourite take-out. If you don't have the time or the opportunity to prepare meals in advance, you still won't have to cook in those busy postpartum days. Nearly every neighbourhood has one or more takeaway shops where you can get meats, chicken, sometimes fish, and side dishes ready to heat and eat – and increasingly, fresh salads that require only a fork and an appetite to enjoy. But don't take out fast foods very often. They offer little in the way of nutrition and much in the way of excess fat and sodium.[3]

Then, of course, there's the pizzeria (try to get whole-wheat crust for best nutrition), the Chinese restaurant (order brown rice if it's available), and the local salad bar (favour fresh items over prepared, which are usually slathered in high-fat dressings, and avoid establishments that add sulfites). Cold cereals, canned tuna and salmon, low-fat cottage cheese, hard cheese, yogurt, wholegrain breads, and fresh fruits will help to fill the gaps in your meals without any cooking or heavy preparation.[4]

Paper goods. When dinner is over, whether it was prepared in your kitchen or at your local eatery, there are always dishes to do unless you rely on paper plates, plastic flatware, and disposable cups. Disposables will also come in handy for serving snacks to visitors who have come to admire the baby. (Keep such entertaining to a minimum, however, if you want to survive the postpartum period.)

Cleaning help. If there's one job that most new mothers would gladly relinquish, it's cleaning. Give it up – to a cleaning service, a cleaning person, someone you've used before, or someone new – anyone who can vacuum and dust, mop floors and scour bathrooms, so that you can have more time and energy to devote to baby, your husband, any older children, and yourself. This is a good route for a woman who wants to do most of the newborn care herself (or with her hus-

band), but doesn't want a 'She tried to be Superwoman' label pinned to her chart when she's returned to the hospital suffering from complete and total exhaustion.

Remember, even if you hire help, and most especially if you don't, there will inevitably be things that don't get done during those early weeks. As long as getting everybody fed and getting rest for yourself aren't among them, don't worry – and do get used to it. Though a certain amount of order will eventually be restored to your home, life with children will almost always include living with at least a few untied ends.

Circumcision

'I thought that circumcision was routine nowadays, but the paediatrician says that it's not really necessary.'

Circumcision is probably the oldest medical procedure still performed. Though the most widely known historical record of the practice is in the Old Testament, when Abraham circumcized Isaac, its origins are lost in antiquity, probably going back to before the use of metal tools. Practised by Moslems and Jews throughout most of history as a sign of their covenant with God, circumcision became widespread in the late nineteenth century when it was theorized that the removal of the foreskin would make the penis less sensitive (it doesn't), thus making masturbation a less tempting pursuit (it didn't). In the years that followed, many other medical justifications for routine circumcision have been proposed – among others that it might prevent or cure epilepsy, syphilis, asthma, lunacy and tuberculosis – none of which it apparently does.

Circumcision does reduce the risk of infection of the penis, but careful attention to cleaning under the foreskin once it is retractable will do as well. It also eliminates the risk of phimosis, a condition in which the foreskin remains tight as the child grows and can't be retracted as it normally can in

---

3. Many fast-food chains now provide nutrition information on request; use these as your guide. Generally, stick to salads, grilled meats, poultry, fish or pizza, and avoid white buns, fried entrées and sides, other foods very high in sodium and fat and sugary sweets.

4. A lot of ready-to-eat foods, such as tuna and cottage cheese, are exceptionally high in sodium, so, when possible, look for the low-sodium varieties.

older boys. Phimosis can be extremely painful and sometimes interferes with erection. It is estimated that between 5 and 10% of uncircumcised males have to undergo the discomfort of circumcision some time after infancy because of infection, phimosis, or other problems.

Still, until recently, most of the medical community took the position that there were no 'absolute medical indications' that warranted exposing an infant to the surgery, minor though it is. But there are medical benefits and advantages to the procedure. New studies in the U.S. show that compared to circumcised infants, baby boys who are uncircumcised appear to have a 10 times greater risk of urinary tract infection, which can be severe enough to require hospitalization. The studies show a link to penile cancer (possibly because of a higher rate of infection with human papillomavirus) and sexually transmitted diseases, including AIDS, appear to be less conclusive.

Parents should make their decisions about circumcision in conjunction with their baby's doctor and based upon a full consideration of medical benefits and risks as well as on aesthetic, social, cultural and religious factors.

The most common reasons parents give for opting for circumcision, in addition to just 'feeling it should be done', include:

- Religious observance. The religious laws of both Moslems and Jews, rooted in the Bible, require circumcision of the newborn.

- Cleanliness. Since it's easier to keep a circumcised penis clean, cleanliness is next to godliness as a reason for circumcision in the West.

- The locker-room syndrome. Parents who don't want their sons to feel different from their friends or from their father or brothers often choose circumcision.

- Appearance. Some feel removal of the foreskin will make their son look better.

- Health. The hope of reducing the risk of infection, cancer or other future problems (including possible later circumcision) prompts many to elect to do the surgery immediately.

The reasons why more parents are deciding against circumcision include:

- The lack of medical necessity. Many question the sense in removing a part of an infant's body without good cause.

- Fear of bleeding and infection. Though complications, particularly when the procedure is carried out by an experienced doctor or a ritual circumciser with medical training, are very rare, many parents are nevertheless apprehensive about the possibility.

- Concern about pain. There is believed to be some pain connected with circumcision though it is probably of short duration. (Pain can be minimized by use of a padded restraint chair and a local anaesthetic and/or a sugar-coated dummy.)

- The wish for the child to be like his uncircumcised father. Another version of the like-father/like-son complex.

- A belief in children's rights. Some parents wish to leave the decision to the child at a later date.

- To allow optimal sexual enjoyment. Some still believe an uncircumcised penis is more sensitive, though there's no scientific support for this position.

- Less risk of nappy irritation. It's been suggested that the intact foreskin may protect against nappy rash on the penis.

The risks of circumcision are minimal, but complications can occur. To reduce the risk, be sure the person who is performing the procedure is experienced and, if he's a ritual circumciser, that he is well trained and comes highly recommended. Also be sure that the surgery is not done in the delivery room, but rather when your baby is stabilized, usually after at least 12 to 24 hours. And do not permit cauterization with a metal clamp, which could cause serious burns.

If you remain undecided about circumcision as delivery day approaches, read about circumcision care in Chapter Four and discuss the issue with the doctor you have chosen for your baby – and possibly with friends who have gone either route.

Which Nappies to Use

'Most of my friends are using disposable nappies, and they do seem a lot less of a mess than terry ones. But are they as good for baby?'

Ever since Eve, mothers have had to confront the problem of how to cover baby's bottom. Native American mothers, we are told, kept their babies (and their own backs) dry and comfortable by packing their papoose boards with the shredded, soft insides of cattails.

Luckily, as a mother, you won't have to wade daily into the marshes to choose the softest and most absorbent cattails to pad your Snugli. But you will have to choose among the plethora of ready-to-wrap-around-baby possibilities available, ranging from several types of terry nappies (to launder yourself or order from a nappy service) to a bewildering and ever-changing array of disposables.

The choice that's right for you and your baby may be different from the one that's right for your neighbour and her infant. Personal factors will be of major significance since, scientifically and economically, there's no conclusive winner in the nappy derby. Consider the following in making your choice:

Disposable nappies. Convenience is a major advantage – no dirty nappies to collect, tote around, and pile up for weekly pickup. Disposables also save a certain amount of time and effort; they're faster and easier to put on and take off and require no pins (especially important if your baby is a wriggler). Newer styles are increasingly more absorbent and theoretically less likely to cause nappy rash,

they're trimmer, and less apt to leak. These desirable features also add up to a distinct disadvantage: since disposables soak up so much urine and often 'feel' dry when they're far from it, parents are less likely to change them frequently enough – and too infrequent changes can lead to nappy rash. Additionally, the new superbreed of nappy keeps babies so comfortable when wet that toilet training may be made more difficult. Also on the minus side is the effect that paper nappies have on the environment (they aren't biodegradable and just add to the collection of clutter on our planet) and the inconvenience of having to shop and lug them home. This last drawback can be avoided if your local service or shop delivers disposables.

Home-delivered terry nappies. To those who are reluctant to encase their infants' bottoms in paper and plastic, soft, comfortable, sterilized, and possibly ecologically preferable cotton nappies are appealing, especially when they are delivered to the door weekly. Some studies (those nappy services are fond of quoting) show a lower incidence of nappy rash with such nappies; others (cited by disposables manufacturers) show super-absorbent disposables yielding a lower incidence of rash. If terry nappies are continued into toddlerhood (few parents manage this), toilet training may be easier to accomplish, because direct contact between a wet terry nappy and skin makes a child very uncomfortable and more aware of having wet.

There are disadvantages, however. Separate waterproof pants are needed to avoid having to change baby, cot, and often mother's clothes, every time baby wets. These pants increase the risk of rash by keeping air out and moisture in, though breathable pants or wraps made of cotton or wool (sometimes with airy mesh linings and/or absorbent foam fillings) can reduce or even eliminate this problem. Nappy changes, because of fussing with pins (unless fitted terry nappies or wraps with Velcro closings are used) and separate pants, are more trouble with terry nappies, particularly

as baby becomes more proficient at squirming. Because absorbency is more limited,
double nappies are usually needed at
night, and, for some heavy wetters, during
the day; boys, who concentrate their urine in
front, may need paper liners. And then there
are the plastic bags of soiled nappies to be
carried home from outings and the ever-
present pail of dirty nappies, which is never
truly odour free.

Home-laundered terry nappies. These
may be the clear loser compared to the other
two choices. Because they can't be adequately sanitized, home-laundered nappies
are, according to studies, more likely to
cause nappy rash. This is compounded by
the fact that, as with other terry nappies, they
are almost always used with waterproof pants
that further encourage the development of
nappy-area irritation. While, like other terry
nappies, they are more ecologically sound
than paper, they also present many of the
same disadvantages. And though they seem
to be far less expensive than either of the
other types they are, when one considers
the cost of soap, water and power used, only
slightly so. In addition, they demand a greater
expenditure of time and effort – to soak,
wash, dry and fold them between use.

Some parents decide to use terry nappies for
the first few months, a time when baby
usually spends more time at home than
on the go, and then move on to disposables. They will often, however, use disposables on outings and, sometimes, at night
(because their greater absorbency keeps
baby more comfortable longer and may
ensure a better night's sleep) from the start.
  Whichever nappy you decide on now you
may find that your baby develops nappy rash
frequently later. This could point to a sensitivity to your choice. If this occurs, don't fight
it – switch. Try a different type (go from terry
to paper or vice versa) or a different brand
of disposable. Also see the tips for treating
nappy rash on page 174.

Quitting Smoking

*'Except for the first few months of
pregnancy, when I couldn't smoke
because it made me queasy, I never
managed to give up smoking – and
neither has my husband. How much
does smoking around a baby affect him
or her?'*

Nothing you can buy in a baby department,
splurge on in a toy store, or put away into a
trust fund can match the gift to your newborn of growing up in a smoke-free environment. Smoking by parents has been
linked to an increase in respiratory illnesses
(colds, flu, bronchitis, asthma) and ear infections during the first year of life and
impaired lung function and reduced lung
capacity. Not only are the children of
smokers sick more often than children of
nonsmokers, but their illnesses last longer.
They are also more likely to be hospitalized
in the first three years of life. The more
smokers in the household, the more severe
the negative effects, since the level of coti-
nine (a by-product of the metabolism of
nicotine) in the blood is directly related to
the number of smokers a child is exposed to
on a regular basis.
  Smoking parents are also more likely to
have colicky babies (for the uninitiated, that
means a baby who cries, usually inconsolably, for at least two or three hours everyday), though the reasons for this aren't clear.
  Perhaps worst of all, children of smokers
are more likely to become smokers than
youngsters whose parents don't smoke. So
quitting before you deliver may not only
keep your child healthier in childhood, it
may also, by lessening the chance of smoking later in life, keep him or her alive and
well longer.
  If you haven't been able to quit up until
now, it obviously won't be easy. As they
would with any drug addiction, your body
and your mind will align against you. But if
you're determined to fight back – for your
sake and your baby's – you can triumph over
both. And the best time to do it is now,
before baby is born. Giving up smoking

before delivery will increase the oxygen available to your baby during childbirth; and your newborn will come home from the hospital to clean, breathable air and, if you're breastfeeding, to nicotine-free milk. If you are still in the early months of pregnancy, quitting now will also reduce the risk of premature delivery and of having a low birthweight baby.

There are many approaches to giving up the cigarette habit. Some are totally inappropriate for the pregnant mother (nicotine chewing gum, for example). Ideal are those that are designed for expectant mums. You can obtain free copies of *Passive Smoking*, and further information from: ASH (Action on Smoking and Health), 109 Gloucester Place, London WIH 3PH.

A Name for Baby

'I've always been unhappy with my name. How can we be sure our son won't be unhappy with the name we choose?'

What's in a name? To a newborn baby, not much. Feed him, clothe him, comfort and entertain him, and you can call him 'Rover' for all he'll care. Once friends and the outside world begin to supersede you and the rest of the family as the centre of your child's existence, however (usually early in primary school), antipathy to the name you selected may develop. Though there's no way to guarantee baby will love the name you choose for a life-time, careful and sensitive selection will lessen the chance of a name turning out to be Trouble.

- Make sure both you and your spouse like the name – the way it sounds and looks, and the connotations it carries. Ask yourselves, 'Would I like it if it were my name?'

- Select a meaningful name – name your baby after a loved family member, a respected historical or biblical character, a favourite character in literature, or after an important event. Such a name

gives the child a sense of belonging, of being part of an extended family or of the greater world.

- Select a fitting name – one that seems right for your baby. Melanie, for example, which means 'black' or 'dark', would be fitting for a dark beauty; Dustin, 'a fighter', might be appropriate for a boy who made it through a difficult delivery. Or one that symbolizes a quality you wish for him or her, such as Faith or Constance, or Isaac, which means 'he will laugh'. Or that reflects your feelings about the birth – Joy, for example, or Ian, 'gracious gift of God'. Such a name can make a child feel extra special – but the choice will often have to wait until your baby is born.

- How will the name sound to others? Are there any possible hidden meanings or sound-alike words that might someday make the name embarrassing to your child? Check the initials; do they spell something that could make your child the butt of jokes or teasing? The name Anne Sue Smith, for example, could be the source of frequent anguish for a child. What about possible nicknames? Could they trigger childish insults? If you choose a very ethnic name, will the child be living in, and going to school in, an environment in which such a name would be appreciated or made fun of? (If you do pick an unusual ethnic name, be sure it has a pleasing English equivalent in case your child wants to switch later.)

- Include a middle name so that if your child turns out to be unhappy with his or her first name, the middle name can be substituted.

- Choose a name that's easy to say and spell. A very unusual name that teachers are always mispronouncing or a very unusual spelling that's always being misspelled will bring your child grief, not compliments.

- Avoid the trendy or the political. Don't saddle your child with this year's hot name (after a TV or film star or politician who's making every magazine cover); when the famous namesake turns out to be a flash in the pan or worse, the name may become outdated or place your child in a light that is uncomfortable.

- Use a real name instead of a diminutive (Richard not Rick, Elizabeth instead of Liz). You can use the diminutive form throughout childhood, but your child then has the option of switching to the more dignified version when he or she ventures out into adulthood.

- If you don't want your child to be one of six Jasons or Jennifers in the class, avoid picking a name from the year's Top Ten. Many newspapers run an annual piece on the subject of popular names, so check the index or call the paper's library. Check out the most popular names by reading the birth announcements, or take a stroll in the playground and listen to the names mothers call their little ones.

- Consider family feelings, but don't let them dominate. If there's a family name that you don't love but they'd like to see perpetuated, out of either tradition or sentiment, try it as a middle name, alter it so that it's more appealing to you, choose another form of the same name (most names actually have several forms), or select a name with the same meaning. A good baby name book will be helpful here. And remember, no matter what names you choose, your parents and grandparents will come to love the children – even if they detest their names at first.

- Be sure the name or names are euphonic with the last name and with each other. A good general rule: a short last name goes well with a long first name (Susannah Jones) and vice versa (James Janofsky), while two-syllable firsts usually complement two-syllable lasts.

Preparing the Family Pet

'Our dog is intensely jealous of my affections – she always tries to come between me and my husband when we hug. I'm worried about how she'll react to the new baby.'

It's hard for a dog who's always been treated like a baby to roll over and play dog when real baby appears on the scene. But that's exactly what she'll have to do when her place in your heart – and, possibly, your bed – is taken over by that tiny but menacing new human you'll soon be bringing home from the hospital. Though a little initial moping around may be unavoidable you'll want to do whatever you can to prevent excessive jealousy and, of course, any aggressive reactions. Start now.

- Invest in an obedience training programme for your dog if she isn't trained already and even if you've never felt there was the need for it before. Friskiness and over enthusiasm aren't usually a problem in a childless home, but they could be in one with a new baby. Particularly because the baby's behaviour won't be controllable or predictable, your dog's must be. Obedience training won't take the spirit out of your pet, but it will make her more stable, and thus less likely to harm your baby.

- Get your dog used to babies now, if you can. Invite friends with babies over to the house, or let her (under careful supervision and if the parent is willing) sniff a baby in the park or be petted by a toddler, so that she can become familiar with their moves.

- Get your dog used to life with a baby in the house. Use a baby-size doll as a prop in her training (it'll also be helpful in yours). Change the doll, sing to it and rock it, swaddle it and carry it around the house with you, 'nurse' it, put it to bed in the cot, and take it for a walk in the pram (if you don't mind the neighbours staring). Now and then, play a tape of a crying baby.

- Get your dog used to sleeping alone, if that's what the postpartum arrangement will be, so that the change doesn't come as a shock. Fix up a comfortable doggie bed in a corner – with a favourite pillow or blanket for company. Everything in your pet's new bed should be washable because once your baby-to-be starts crawling, there's a good chance you will find baby curled up in doggie's space.

- Take your dog for a complete medical checkup. Be sure that your dog's rabies shots are up-to-date (even though the U.K. is rabies-free), that she is flea- and tick free (but don't plan on using a flea collar unless you are sure it doesn't carry chemicals poisonous to babies and don't use a flea bomb either during pregnancy or after your baby is born). Also be sure to check your dog for worms of any kind.

- If you have new puppies in your home, have them wormed as soon as possible since the worms, which are excreted in the stools (and can remain in the soil for years), can cause serious disease in babies and children.

- If your baby will have a separate room, train your dog to stay out of it while you're not there. A gate to block the doorway will help discourage unsolicited visits. If your baby's cot will be in your room or in a corner of the living room, train your dog not to go under it since she could accidentally unlock the cot side, letting it fall.

- If your dog's feeding station is one your baby will later be able to get to easily, move it to the cellar, garage, or some other area that a curious crawler can be kept out of, since even a pleasant dog can become vicious when her food is threatened. If you live in a small apartment, get your dog on a late-evening feeding schedule and remove her food dish during the day. Don't even leave her food around when the dog is safely outside, because those tasty nuggets taste good not only to canines – many babies love them, too. Use a non-tip water bowl unless you enjoy mopping the floor frequently.

- After delivery, but while you're still in the hospital, have your husband bring home an unwashed piece of clothing your newborn has worn so that your pet can become familiar with the baby's scent. When you arrive home, let your husband hold the baby while you greet your pet. Then to satisfy her curiosity, let the dog sniff the baby – who should be well swaddled, with head and face protected by your arms. Once the baby's snug in the cot, break out a special treat for the dog, and spend a little time alone with her.

- Be attentive to your new baby, of course, but don't act overprotective around your dog. This will only make the animal more jealous and insecure. Instead, as you would with a human sibling (though on a different level, naturally), try to get your pet involved with the new addition and let her know she's still a loved member of the family. Pet her while you nurse, walk her while you take the baby out in the pram, allow her into the baby's room while you're there. Try to make a point of spending at least five minutes a day with her alone. But should she show even the slightest aggression towards your baby, reprimand her immediately.

- If, despite your efforts to prepare and reassure her, your dog seems hostile towards the new arrival, keep her tied up and away from the baby until you're sure she's worked out her feelings. Just because a dog has never bitten before doesn't mean she's not capable of it under such duress. If tying the dog up only adds to her hostility, you may have to consider finding another home for her. (With male dogs, neutering may reduce aggressiveness.)

'I worry that our tomcat, who has always slept with us, may be jealous of the new baby.'

Even friendly cats can undergo personality changes when a baby arrives. And since cats are just as capable of harming an infant as dogs are, with their claws as well as with their jaws, it's as important to make sure that they are well prepared for the family expansion. Most of the above tips for preparing a dog can work for a cat, as well. Be particularly careful to reassure your cat – through plenty of attention – that he is still a family favourite. And because cats usually love to cuddle next to a warm body and can quickly scale the sides of a cot, be sure to attach a net securely over it to keep yours from bedding down with baby – a friendly gesture that could end in tragedy. Also keep a kitten from licking your infant's face or any broken skin.

Preparing your Breasts for Breastfeeding

'I have a friend who insists that I should massage my nipples to toughen them in preparation for nursing. Is that a good idea?'

Female nipples are designed for nursing. And, with very few exceptions, they come to the job fully qualified, without the need for prior preparation. In fact, in some cases the procedures recommended for readying

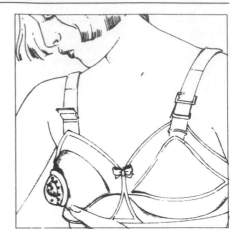

Breast shields are ventilated plastic devices that are available at maternity shops and chemists.

the nipples for breastfeeding can do more harm than good. For instance, applying alcohol, witch hazel, or tincture of benzoin can dry the nipples and make them more, rather than less, likely to crack and fissure; even soap can be drying, and its use on the nipples should be avoided during the last trimester of pregnancy and during lactation itself. Using a brush on nipples will also be counterproductive, irritating the tissues and making them more likely to crack under the pressures of nursing.

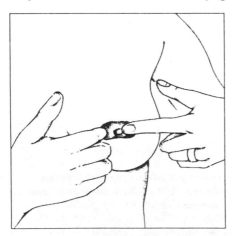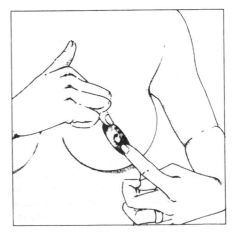

To draw out inverted nipples: Several times daily, place your forefingers at opposite locations on the margins of the areola, then pull outwards.

But while most nipples don't need any preparation for breastfeeding, many women feel more comfortable doing something to improve their chances of succeeding at it than doing nothing. If you feel you would like to do something constructive, have your breasts examined by your obstetrician to see if there are any anatomical features that might interfere with breastfeeding, such as inverted nipples or underdeveloped glandular tissue. Ask if it would be a good idea for you to wear breast shields (see illustration, page 24) to help draw out inverted nipples or to massage tender ones to toughen them. But don't undertake nipple massage during pregnancy without your doctor's approval, since nipple stimulation may trigger labour under certain conditions.

With your doctor's okay, you can try any of the following to ready your nipples for your baby's tough gums (though, again, preparation is usually not necessary): rubbing a towel *gently* across them after showering; exposing them to air by walking topless around the house for some time each day; allowing them to rub against your clothing as you go about braless (unless

your breasts are heavy and/or prone to sagging) or in a nursing bra with open flaps; rolling them between your thumb and forefinger a couple of times a day, then lubricating them with breast cream, salad oil or baby oil; expressing a few drops of colostrum, if you can, daily during the last three months; or having your husband stimulate your nipples during lovemaking (even if this doesn't work, you'll have fun trying). There's no solid evidence these practices make breastfeeding more comfortable, but they don't seem to do any harm either, and some women find them helpful. Massage and nipple rolling have the added advantage of reducing a woman's inhibitions about handling her breasts – necessary if she's going to be comfortable nursing.

More important than preparing your breasts for breastfeeding is preparing your head. Learn all you can about breastfeeding (take an antenatal course, if possible; read books on the subject), select a paediatrician who strongly advocates it, and find other women who will be able to support you and answer your questions when they arise.

WHAT IT'S IMPORTANT TO KNOW:
Selecting the Right Doctor

When you first became pregnant, it was hard to imagine there was actually going to be a baby to deliver. Now, with tiny but powerful fists, feet and knees regularly using you as a punching bag, you no longer have any doubts. Not only is there a baby in there – but it's eager to get out. And before it does, you want to ensure that you are happy with the doctor who'll care for it; delaying your decision might mean having a stranger care for your baby should you deliver early; no one to ask important questions of during those confusing first days; and no familiar face in case of an emergency.

Assuming you stay in the community and are relatively satisfied with the care, the

doctor you choose will be seeing baby – and you – through 16 to 18 years of runny noses, earaches, sore throats, high fevers, upset stomachs, bumps and bruises, maybe even broken bones, through dramatic physical and psychological developmental milestones that will both thrill and bewilder, through moments you can't now even imagine. You won't be living with your baby's doctor during those years (though there will be times, particularly nights and weekends, when you'll wish you were), but you'll still want someone you feel comfortable and compatible with. Someone you wouldn't hesitate to waken at 2 A.M. when your nine-month-old's fever hits a new high, someone you wouldn't be embarrassed to ask about your six-month-old's sudden fascination with his genitals, someone you would feel free to question when you aren't sure an antibiotic that's been prescribed is necessary.

Before you start securing names, you need to make some basic decisions about the type of doctor you want to care for your baby.

Paediatrician or GP?

When your mother had a runny nose or a bothersome case of nappy rash, her mother didn't bundle her up and take her to a paediatrician. Chances are she took her to the same doctor who brought her into the world, who treated her father's bursitis and her grandmother's arthritis, who removed her uncle's kidney stones and her cousin's tonsils: the family doctor, a general practitioner (GP). Today, though some rare runny noses and rashy bottoms are tended to by the paediatrician, a childcare specialist, most parents in the U.K. opt to have their babies cared for by a GP experienced with children – if not their own GP, usually one in the same surgery.

The paediatrician. Babies, children and, sometimes, adolescents are their business – their only business. Paediatricians in the NHS are hospital-based specialist consultants, available on referral for the baby with special problems. Private paediatricians are available, if you can afford it or have private insurance. The major advantage of selecting a paediatrician for your baby is obvious – since they see only children, and lots of them, they are more familiar than other doctors with what's normal, atypical and pathological in young patients. They are also more likely to have the answers to the questions that nag new parents, from 'Why does he want to nurse all the time?' to 'Why isn't she sleeping more?' to 'Why does he cry so much?'

A disadvantage is that since paediatricians see only younger members of a family, they may not be attuned to the whole family picture (though many are), and may not recognize when a child's problem is rooted in what's going on, either physically or emotionally, with a parent or other family member. Another negative: if the entire family comes down with something that requires medical treatment, it may be necessary to call upon the services of two doctors.

The general practitioner. Like the paediatrician, the GP has usually had three years of specialty training following medical school. But an GP residency programme is much broader than a paediatric one, covering internal medicine, psychiatry and obstetrics and gynaecology, in addition to paediatrics. The advantage of choosing a family doctor is that your entire family can be cared for by the same doctor, one who knows each of you clinically and personally and who can use this information in diagnosis and treatment. If you already have a GP, adding your baby to the register will have the added advantage of bringing the new family member to an old friend, not a stranger.

The disadvantage: because he or she has had less training and experience in paediatrics than a paediatrician has, a family doctor may be less helpful in dealing with the multitude of well-baby questions you may raise as well as less astute at picking up the obscure diagnosis. To minimize this disadvantage, look for a family doctor who sees a lot of babies, not just older children – most do.

What Kind of Practice is Perfect?

To some patients, the type of practice may be almost as important as the type of doctor. There are several options; the one most appealing to you will depend on your personal preferences and priorities.

The solo practitioner. Like the GPs of yesteryear, today's solo practitioners have the opportunity to build close one-to-one relationships with each of their patients. But unlike their predecessors, they aren't likely to be on call round the clock and round the calendar. They'll be around for scheduled appointments (unless called to an emergency), and on call most of the time; but they will take holidays and occasional nights and weekends off, leaving patients who require emergency care or consultation to a locum doctor who may be unfamiliar to them. If you do select a solo practitioner, ask about who will be covering at such times, and be sure that in an emergency your child's records will be available even when the doctor is not.

The partnership. Sometimes two doctors are better than one. If one isn't on call, the other almost always is. If you see them in rotation, you and your child often can, thanks to the frequent well-child visits during the first year, build good relationships with both. Though partners will probably concur on most major issues and will likely share similar philosophies of practice, they may occasionally offer different opinions. Having more than one opinion may in some instances be confusing, but hearing two approaches to a particularly confounding problem can be useful. (If one doesn't seem to be able to solve your baby's sleeping problems, maybe the other will.)

An important question to ask before deciding on a partnership: can you schedule appointments with the doctor of your choice? If not, and if you discover you like one but not the other, you may spend half your visits with a doctor you're not comfortable with. Even if you can choose the preferred doctor for checkups, sick children must usually be seen by whoever is available at the time.

The group practice. If two are good, will three or more be better? In some ways yes, in others no. A group is more likely to be able to provide 24-hour coverage by doctors in the practice, but less likely to ensure close doctor-patient relationships – again, unless you can select the same doctor (or two) for regular checkups. The more doctor a child will be exposed to on well-child and sick-call visits, the longer it may take to feel comfortable with each one, though this will be much less of a problem if all the doctors are warm and caring practitioners. Also a factor here: if you rotate doctors, contradictory advice can either enlighten or confound. In the long run, more important than the number of doctors in a group practice will be the confidence you have in them individually and as a group.

A practice that has a child health clinic. Any of the above types of practices may be associated with a clinic staffed by a health visitor or certified midwife. The health visitor is an RN with additional training (generally at the masters degree level) in her specialty area. She usually offers nutritional advice and handles well-baby checkups, and sometimes the treatment of minor illnesses as well, consulting with her doctor colleagues as needed. Problems beyond her scope are referred to one of them. You're likely to favour or object to your baby being cared for by a health visitor for many of the same reasons you favoured or objected to a nurse-midwife's caring for you during your pregnancy. Like the midwife, the health visitor will frequently spend more time with patients at each visit, often devoting as much attention to lifestyle questions as to medical ones. But because the level of training is not equal to that of the doctor, you may have less confidence in the care your baby is getting. This, however, isn't always a valid concern since many studies have shown that nurse-practitioners are, on the average, at least as successful as, and sometimes more successful than, doctors at diagnosing and treating minor illnesses.

Finding Dr. Right

For every patient, there is a Dr. Right. Once you know what kind of doctor in what type of practice you're looking for, you're ready to start tracking yours down. If your community doesn't have a computer service for matching doctors and patients (a few do), you'll have to rely on more traditional, but usually reliable, sources.

Your own GP, obstetric consultant or midwife. Doctors generally recommend other doctors whose style and philosophy are similar to their own, whose work they are familiar with and respect. So if you've been happy with your antenatal care, ask for a suggestion. On the other hand, if you've been disappointed, look elsewhere for a recommendation.

An obstetric or paediatric nurse. If you know a nurse or midwife who works with paediatricians, in either an office or hospital setting, she's sure to be a good source of information on which doctors are competent, conscientious, caring and relate well both to parents and children, and which are sloppy, brusque, humourless and unfriendly. If you don't know a nurse, consider phoning the nursing station on the paediatric floor at the hospital where you're going to deliver to seek recommendations.

Parents. No one can tell you more about a doctor's bedside manner than his or her satisfied (or dissatisfied) patients, or, in this case, parents of patients. Recommendations are best when they come from friends or acquaintances who mirror you in temperament and child-rearing philosophy. Otherwise, the very qualities that make them swear by their paediatrican may make you want to swear at him or her.

The local Family Health Services Authority (FHSA). While they won't recommend one doctor over another, they will be able to provide a selection of reputable doctors in your area for you to choose from.

Hospital or other referral services. Some hospitals, medical groups and entrepreneurs have set up referral services to supply the names of doctors in specific specialities. Hospitals may recommend doctors who have privileges at their own institution; a referral service may be able to provide additional information about a doctor's specialty, training and board certification.

Medical registers. The lists available at your public library are other bare-bones sources of prospects, providing a way to check credentials (education, training and affiliations are all listed).

La Leche League or National Childbirth Trust. If breastfeeding, for example, is a priority and you would particularly like support in this from your paediatrician, your local group may be able to suggest good doctors in your area.

Making Sure Dr. Right is Right for you

Procuring a list of names from any of the above sources is a good beginning in your search for Dr. Right. But to narrow down that list to a smaller one of potential candidates, and finally, to that one practitioner of your health-care dreams, will take a little more investigative phoning and legwork, and personal interviews with a few finalists.

Hospital affiliation. It's advantageous if the doctor you choose is affiliated with a nearby hospital, so that emergency treatment will be easily accessible. And it's nice if that doctor has privileges at the hospital where you are planning to deliver. But don't eliminate from the running a good candidate who doesn't have such an affiliation. Sometimes special permission will be granted for a non-affiliated doctor to see (but not treat) a baby. If not, a staff doctor can perform the hospital exam and arrange for discharge, and you can take baby to see the chosen doctor after you've left the hospital.

Credentials. Most important is a residency in paediatrics or family medicine. Paediatricians or family doctors who maintain their status in their professional organizations by sitting periodically for recertification exams are telling you that they are interested both in keeping current medically and in giving their patients the best possible care. Some private doctors charge a fee for a preliminary consultation, others don't. During your seventh or eighth month, make appointments with those on your list of finalists and arrive ready to evaluate your prospective baby doctor, taking into account the following:

Surgery location. Lugging a large belly with you everywhere you go may seem like a struggle now – but it's travelling light compared to what you'll be travelling with after delivery. Going unwalkable distances will no longer be as easy as hopping on a bus, the tube, or into a car, and the farther you have to go, particularly in foul weather, the more complicated outings will become. But though a nearby doctor's surgery is certainly a convenience, it can be more – when you're dealing with a sick or injured child, it can mean prompter care and treatment. But keep in mind, when you make your decision, that a truly one-of-a-kind doctor may be worth a lengthier trip.

Surgery hours. What constitutes convenient office hours will depend on your own schedules. If one or both of you have 9-to-5 jobs, some early morning, evening, or weekend hours may be a major requirement.

Atmosphere. You can tell a lot about the atmosphere of a surgery before you even see it. If you're treated curtly on the phone, chances are in-surgery experiences won't be any more pleasant. If, on the other hand, you're greeted by a cheerful welcoming voice, you're likely to be met with concern and kindness when you come in, panic-stricken, with a sick or injured baby. You can gain further insight when you make your first visit to the surgery for an interview with the doctor. Is the receptionist friendly, or is her manner as crisp and sterile as her hospital whites? Is the staff responsive to and patient with its young clients, or is communication with them limited to 'Get down', 'Don't touch', and 'Keep quiet'? Is the reception area separate from the waiting area, so you

can enjoy some measure of privacy when revealing concerns to and asking questions of surgery staff?

Decor. A baby doctor needs more than a couple of magazines on the table and a few Expressionist prints on the wall to make the 'Right' design statement in his waiting room. On your reconnaissance visit, look for features that will make waiting less painful for both you and your expected: a comfortable play area for toddlers as well as a waiting area for older children; a selection of well-maintained toys and books appropriate for a range of ages; low chairs or other sitting space designed for little bodies. Wallpaper in bold colours and intriguing patterns (orange kangaroos and yellow tigers rather than tastefully understated earth-tone pinstripes) and child-bright pictures (in both the waiting room and the examing rooms) will also give uneasy minds something comforting to focus on while anticipating or experiencing the poking and prodding of a checkup. (But keep in mind, not every good doctor is a Disney buff.) A welcome addition in the family doctor's surgery: separate waiting areas for adults and children.

Waiting time. A forty-five-minute wait when you're pacing with a fussy infant or trying to distract a restless toddler with yet another picture book can be a trying experience for all involved. Yet such waits are not uncommon. For some parents a long wait may merely be an inconvenience; for others it is something their schedules simply can't accommodate.

In trying to gauge the average waiting time in a particular surgery, don't go by how long *you're* kept waiting for your consultation. Such visits are a courtesy, rather than a medical necessity; screaming infants will (or should) take priority. Instead, ask the receptionist, and if her answer is vague or noncommittal, pose the question to a few waiting parents.

A long average wait can be a sign of disorganization, of overbooking, or of a doctor having more patients than he or she can handle. But it doesn't tell you much about the quality of medical care. Some very good doctors are not very good managers. They may end up spending more time with each patient than allotted (something you will appreciate in the examining room, but not in the waiting room) or may not like to turn down requests to fit ill children into an already full schedule (something you will appreciate when it's your child who's ill).

All waiting doesn't take place in the waiting room. The most uncomfortable wait is often in the examining room, holding an unhappy, undressed baby, with no space to pace, or trying to distract a frightened toddler without benefit of the toy collection just outside. While long waits in the examining room may not alone be sufficient reason for rejecting a doctor, if they do prove to be a problem, be sure to make a point of letting the nurse know that you would rather do all your waiting in the waiting room.

House calls. Yes, some paediatricians and GPs still make them. Most of the time, however, as your doctor will probably explain, house calls are not only unnecessary, they aren't best for baby. At the surgery, a doctor can use equipment and perform tests that can't be stashed in a little black bag. Still, occasions may arise when you will appreciate very much the doctor who is willing to put his or her bedside manner to work literally – as when junior is home from nursery school with a cold, baby's down with a fever and a cough, and you're on duty at home alone without a car.

Protocol for taking phone queries. If new mothers rushed to the doctor's every time they had questions about their babies' health or development, surgeries would be jammed day and night. That's why many queries are answered and worries assuaged via the telephone. And why you'll want to know in advance how your prospective baby doctor handles such calls. Some parents prefer the call-hour approach: a particular time is set aside each day, during which no patients are seen and distractions are few, for the doctor to field phone calls. This ensures almost immediate access to the doctor – though there may be several bouts with a busy signal or a brief wait for a call back. Other parents find it difficult to confine their worries to between 7 and 8 in the morning or 11 A.M. and noon, or worse, to wait until tomorrow's call-hour for relief of today's worries. They prefer the doctor call-back system: they call when a problem or question arises, and the doctor calls back when there's a free moment between patients. Even if the call back doesn't come for hours (in a non-emergency, of course), callers can at least unburden themselves on – and sometimes be reassured or counselled by – the person who takes the call. And there is the comfort of knowing they will talk to the doctor by the end of the day.

How emergencies are handled. When accidents happen – and they will – how your doctor handles emergencies will be of some consequence. Some doctors instruct parents to take emergencies straight to the emergency room at the local hospital, where the emergency staff can provide treatment. Others ask you to call the surgery first and, depending on the nature of the illness or injury, will see your baby at the surgery or meet you at the hospital. Some doctors are available (unless they're out of town) days, nights, and weekends for emergencies. Others use colleagues or partners to cover for them during off hours.

Matters financial. Some parents do opt to go private for their baby's first year. For all except the very wealthy and the very heavily insured, how financial matters are handled is a prime consideration. Some private doctors request payment at the time of a visit (unless other arrangements are made in advance); others issue bills. Some offer a package deal for first-year care that covers any number of visits. Though the package costs more than the sum of fees for the year's scheduled number of checkups, it is usually a good gamble: you will break even with two or three visits for illness. Insurance reimbursement for sick visits, package deal or no, will be handled according to the terms of your coverage.

You might also want to ask whether routine lab work is done in the surgery; if so it will probably cost you less than tests sent to an outside laboratory.

Style. When you're looking for the right doctor, as when you're shopping for baby furniture, the style that's best will depend on your style. Do you prefer a doctor who is easygoing and informal, rigid and businesslike, or somewhere in between? Are you most comfortable with a father (or mother) figure who expects to have the last word on everything, or with a doctor who accepts you as a partner and is interested in your opinions? Do you want a doctor who gives the impression of having all the answers, or one who is willing to admit, 'I don't know.'

Just as there are certain features all parents look for in a cot or a pram (quality, workmanship, value), there are certain traits they all want in a prospective baby doctor: the ability to listen (without eyeing the next name in the appointment book); an openness to questions and a willingness to respond to them fully and clearly (without becoming defensive or feeling threatened); and, most of all, a genuine fondness for children.

Philosophy. Even in the best of marriages partners don't always agree, and even in the best of doctor-patient relationships there may be points of difference. But, as with marriages, doctor-patient relationships are most likely to succeed if both partners agree on most major issues. And the ideal time to find out whether you and your prospective baby doctor mesh philosophies is before you make a commitment, at your consultation interview.

Ask about the doctor's positions on any of the following that you consider important:

- Breastfeeding. If you're eager to nurse, a doctor who is only lukewarm towards or confesses to little knowledge of the subject may not provide the support and assistance novice nursers need.

- Nutrition. If good nutrition matters to you, beware of the doctor who dismisses the topic with a 'don't worry, most kids eat a balanced diet'.

- Circumcision. Whether you've decided for or against, you'll want a doctor who won't belittle your choice.

- Antibiotics. It's a good idea to select a doctor who doesn't prescribe them for every sniffle.

- Vegetarianism. If you and your family are non-flesh eaters, it's useful to have a doctor who not only respects that, but knows something about meeting a growing child's nutritional needs on a vegetarian diet.

- Preventive medicine. If you believe in more than an ounce of prevention, beware the doctor who is grossly overweight, has an ashtray full of cigarette butts on the desk, and nibbles chocolate as you speak.

The doctor who has been in practice for any length of time has probably developed some pretty set ideas about child rearing. If you, on the other hand, are new at the game, you may have only the vaguest notion about how you will want to play it (and you will probably make drastic changes in your strategy once the game is underway). With you unsure about your own philosophy and having to judge the doctor's from a short interview, making a perfect match may prove difficult. Still, it's sensible to weed out any candidate whose philosophy seems blatantly contrary to the ideas that have been gestating in your mind during your baby's gestation in your womb.

The Antenatal Interview

Once you've settled on a doctor for your baby, there are probably a number of issues – many of which are examined in this chapter and the next – that you'll want to discuss in a consultation, among them:

Your obstetrical history and family health history. How will these impact on the forthcoming delivery and on your new baby's health?

Hospital procedures. What medication will be used in baby's eyes to prevent infection? Which tests are routine after birth? How will jaundice be handled? What are the criteria for early discharge?

Circumcision. What are the pros and cons? Who should perform the procedure and when, if you do opt for it?

Bottle feeding. What type of bottles, teats and formula does the doctor recommend?

Breastfeeding. How can your baby's doctor help you get a good start? Can a surgery visit at one or two weeks postpartum be arranged if you're having difficulty nursing or to assess your progress?

Baby supplies and equipment. Get recommendations on such health supplies as paracetamol, thermometer, and nappy rash ointment, and on equipment such as cots, car seats, and pushchairs.

Suggested reading. Are there any books the doctor would like to specifically recommend, or to steer you away from?

Surgery etiquette. What should you know about the way the doctor's surgery operates – for instance, the times that calls are taken or how emergencies are handled?

Your Partnership with Dr. Right

Once you've chosen Dr. Right, you can't just drop your baby's health care into his or her lap, sit back with a waiting room magazine, and relax, assured of the right results. As parents, you, and not your doctor, have the most significant impact on your baby's health. If you don't hold up your part of the partnership, even the best of doctors won't be able to provide the best of care for your baby. To be the right patient-parent for Dr. Right, you have a long list of responsibilities of your own.

Follow surgery etiquette. Arrive for appointments on time, or if the surgery perpetually runs late, call half an hour in advance of a scheduled appointment and ask how much later you can safely arrive; try to give at least 24 hours notice when cancelling. Remember, patients (or in this case, parents of patients) are partly responsible for the smooth operation of a doctor's surgery.

Practice prevention. Though it's wise to select a baby doctor who believes in preventive medicine and concentrates on well-baby care, the burden for keeping baby healthy will fall more heavily on you than on the doctor. It's you who must see that baby gets proper nutrition, enjoys a wholesome balance of rest and active play, is not exposed unnecessarily to infection or cigarette smoke, and is kept as safe as possible from accidental injury. It's you who must help your baby establish good health and safety habits (ideally, through your shining example) that can last and give benefit for a lifetime.

Put your worries on paper. Many of the questions you'll come up with between checkups are worthy of your concern without being worthy of a special phone call ('Why doesn't my baby have any teeth yet?' or 'How can I get him to enjoy his bath?'). Jot these down as they occur to you, before they have a chance to escape in the course of a typically hectic day with baby.

Take notes. The doctor gives you instructions about what to do if your baby has a reaction to her first shots. You get home, she has a fever, and you panic. What was it he said? It's not surprising you've forgotten – the baby was crying after the shot and you could barely hear the instructions as you struggled to redress her, never mind remember them. The remedy for parental memory loss: always bring a pencil and paper to your doctor visits and jot down diagnoses, instructions, and any other information you may want to refer to later. This may not be easy while balancing baby on your lap (that's why two-parent visits are ideal), but it's worth the contortions that may be involved.

Take notes at telephone 'visits', too. Though you're positive you'll remember the name of the over-the-counter ointment the doctor recommended for baby's rash or the dosage of paracetamol prescribed for teething pain, these details can easily drift from your head when you hang up the phone to the sight of baby smearing potatoes all over the kitchen wall.

Pick up the phone. The relief for your worries is only a phone call away. But don't use your baby's doctor as a ready reference; before making a call, try to find the answers to your questions in this or in another baby book on your shelf. If you're unsuccessful, however, don't hesitate to call for fear of abusing your telephone privileges. In the early months, baby doctors expect a lot of telephone calls, especially from first-time mothers. Don't call cold, however. Go over the Before Calling the Doctor check list on page 399 and call prepared.

Follow doctor's orders. In any good partnership, both sides contribute what they know or do best. In this partnership, your baby's doctor will be contributing years of training and experience. To get the most benefit from those contributions, it makes sense to take the doctor's advice when feasible, and to inform him or her when you don't intend to or, for some reason, can't. This is particularly vital in medical situations. Say an antibiotic has been prescribed for baby's cough. The baby spits up the medication and won't touch another drop. Since the cough seems a little better anyway, you give up trying to force it down his little throat and don't bother to let the doctor know. Then, two days later, baby's temperature is up, the cough is worse, and playing your baby's doc-

tor has turned out to be a dangerous game. What the doctor would have told you, had you called, is that once the medication is begun the baby may start to improve, but that unless the full course of treatment is completed, the illness can return with greater force. He or she would also have been able to advise you on better ways of getting the medication down or of alternative ways of medicating.

Speak up. To say that it's important to follow doctor's orders is not to say that mother (or father) doesn't sometimes know best — even better than doctor. If you sense the doctor's diagnosis is off or you're afraid the cure prescribed may be worse than the illness, say so, but not in a challenging way. Give the reasons for your concern and ask the doctor to explain the rationale behind his or her position. You may learn something from each other.

Speak up, too, if you've heard about a new form of immunization, a new treatment for colic, or anything else that might benefit your baby. If it's something you've read, bring in the source when possible. Perhaps the doctor has already heard about this advance and can give you additional information for or against it. If the doctor is unfamiliar with it, he or she will probably want to learn more about it before offering an opinion. Be aware however, that medical reporting is notoriously uneven. With your doctor's help, you should be able to sort out the useful from the useless.

Sever an intolerable relationship. Divorcing your baby's doctor (like any divorce) can be very unpleasant. But it's less unpleasant than living with an unsatisfactory relationship — and better for the children. When possible, try to talk out your disagreements and problems with the doctor before severing ties entirely; you may find a misunderstanding rather than serious philosophical differences behind the rift, in which case you may be able to make a fresh start with the same doctor. If the doctor you've chosen turns out to truly be Dr. Wrong, you will begin the search for a new doctor a lot wiser and, hopefully, end up with better results. To make sure you don't leave your baby uncovered by a doctor while you shop around again, avoid terminating your relationship with Dr. Wrong until you've found a replacement. When you have, be sure all of your child's medical records are transferred promptly.

TWO

Buying for Baby

♦

You've resisted the temptation for months. Passed wistfully by the Baby Department on your way to Maternity, not daring to run as much as a finger over the lacy rompers and handknit blankets, casting no more than a longing glance at the musical mobiles and cuddly teddies. But now, at long last, with delivery only weeks away, it's not only okay to stop resisting and start buying, it's absolutely necessary.

Do, however, resist the urge to belly up to the counter and put yourself in the hands of the grandmotherly saleswoman who's waiting to sell you everything she has in stock and several other things she's ready to order at the drop of a credit card. Her voice-of-experience sales pitch may make you forget that you'll be getting some hand-me-downs from your sister-in-law, that dozens of gifts will soon come pouring in, and that you will be doing laundry frequently. And you may end up with shopping bags loaded with more tiny outfits, toys, and paraphernalia than your baby will ever be able to use before outgrowing them.

Instead, do your homework before starting your shopping. Calculate your minimum needs (you'll always be able to fill in later) using the shopping list on page 37, and face that salesperson armed with these basic guidelines:

- Don't buy a complete layette as espoused by the store or any list; use lists merely as a guide.

- Keep in mind how many times a week you (or someone else) will be doing the laundry. If you will be washing almost every day, buy the smallest suggested number of items on the list; if you will have to lug loads down to the launderette and can only do it weekly, then buy the largest number.

- Check off items borrowed or handed down before finalizing your shopping list.

- If friends and family ask what you'll need, don't be embarrassed to tell them. They really would rather buy you something you'll use than something you'll have to carry back to the store postpartum. Suggest a few items in various price ranges to give them freedom of choice, but don't suggest the same items to different people.

- Hold off on buying items you won't need right away (a high chair, a baby seat for the bathtub, toys too advanced for infants) and items you may end up not needing (the full quota of pajamas, towels, T-shirt sets) until you've received all your gifts. When they stop coming in, recalculate your needs, and head out for the store once more.

- Buy mostly 6- to 9-month sizes. You may want a couple of 3-month-size shirts and maybe an outfit or two for dress-up that fit just right, but for the most part it's more practical to roll up sleeves and endure a slightly blousy look for a few weeks until baby starts to fill out the larger sizes. And as irresistible as it may be to unpack your purchases into baby's new dresser, don't do so. Keep all baby clothes (even the set you're planning to take baby home in) tagged or in their original packages. That way, if baby checks in at 4.67kg (10 pounds 6 ounces), your husband, mother, or a friend can exchange at least some of them for 6-month sizes while you're still in the hospital, and the others soon after. Likewise, if your baby arrives early, weighing just 2.3kg (5 pounds), some of the larger sizes can be exchanged.

In general, buy at least one size ahead (most six-month-old babies wear 9- or 12-month sizes, some even wear 18-month sizes), but eyeball before purchasing because some styles (particularly imported ones) can run much larger or smaller than average.

- Keep the season in mind as you shop. If baby is expected on the cusp of a season, buy just a few tiny items for the immediate weather and larger ones for the weather expected in the months ahead. Continue to consider the seasons as baby grows. That adorable appliquéd sunsuit at half price may be difficult to pass up, but if it's a 12-month size and your baby will be a year old next June, it's a purchase you'll regret.

- When selecting baby clothes, consider convenience and comfort first, fashion second. Tiny buttons at baby's neckline may be darling, but the struggle to fasten them with baby squirming on the changing table won't be. An organdy party frock may look fetching on the hanger – but may have to stay there if it irritates baby's delicate skin. An imported sailor suit may look smart – until you have to change baby and find no access to the nappy area. Always look for outfits made of soft, easy-care fabrics, with snaps instead of buttons (inconvenient, and should baby manage to chew one off, unsafe), head openings that are roomy (or have snaps at the neck), and bottoms that open conveniently for nappy changing. Shun long strings or ribbons, which are potentially hazardous, and rough seams, which are potentially uncomfortable. Room for growth is another important feature:

adjustable shoulder straps, stretch fabrics, undefined waistlines on one-piece garments, elasticized waistlines, double rows of snaps on sleepwear, trousers that can be rolled up, wide hems that can be taken down, tucks, pleats, or yokes. Pajamas with 'feet' should be the right length, or should have elasticized ankles to keep them in place.

- If you haven't learned the gender of your baby through ultrasound or amniocentesis, don't buy everything in yellow or green (unless you're mad about those colours), particularly since many infants don't have the complexion to carry off these shades. Both boys and girls can wear reds, blues, and navys. If you wait on some purchases until baby arrives, you'll be able to indulge in some dainty pinks for a daughter or some more distinctly masculine styles for a son. At some stores, you can order a layette and not pick it up until after the baby is born – at which time you can specify the colour. This will work only if dad, grandmother, or a friend can pick up your order while you're in the hospital, or if it can be delivered before you arrive home.

- When buying baby furniture, practicality and safety should supersede style. An antique cradle, either purchased or passed down, may lend that heirloom look to the nursery – but you could be setting your baby up for a fall should the bottom not prove strong enough to support his or her weight, or for a lead overdose if the paint job, too, is antique. If you have a dog, a cradle may be too close to the ground for comfort. A plush Rolls-Royce of prams may evoke a lot of smiles when you walk down the street, but a lot of frowns when you hold up the bus queue while struggling to fold it and lug it, baby and nappy bag, up the steps. For other features to favour in baby furniture, see page 40.

- When buying toiletries for baby, buy only what you need (see list on page 38), rather than one of everything you see. When comparing products, look for those that are alcohol-free (alcohol is drying to a baby's skin) and contain the fewest artificial colours, preservatives and other chemical additives. Do not buy baby powders. They serve no medical purpose, can cause irritation if they collect in baby's cracks and crevices, can be dangerous if inhaled and, if they contain talc, may even cause lung cancer down the road.

• When stocking the medicine chest, however, err on the side of excess, filling it, just in case, with everything you might need in an emergency and hope you'll never have to use. Otherwise, you may find yourself helpless when your baby wakes in the middle of the night burning up with fever and you have no medication on hand to bring it down. Or when he or she is found nibbling on the lovely but poisonous Christmas holly plant a guest has brought and you have nothing in the medicine chest to induce vomiting.

First Wardrobe

3 to 7 vests. Open-front, side-snap styles are easiest to use with newborns, but pullovers are smoother and more comfortable; snap-bottom body shirts don't ride up, keeping tummies covered in cold weather.

3 to 8 nightgowns with drawstring bottoms. Drawstrings should be removed as baby becomes more active.[1]

2 to 3 blanket sleepers, for late autumn or winter babies. Do not use the bag types once your baby can pull up.

3 to 4 waterproof pants, nappy covers, or nappy wraps, if you're planning to use terry

---

1. Clothing for babies and children to sleep in must meet CE standards for flame resistance; they are usually made of synthetic fibres that do not flame up.

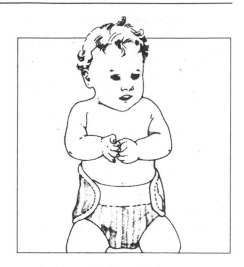

Nappy wraps eliminate the need for pins or rubber pants; they are made of cotton or wool and 'breathe,' reducing the risk of rash.

nappies. If you're using disposables, just one dress-up pair for special occasions.

2 to 3 pairs of booties or socks. Select those that won't kick off easily.

3 to 6 babygros with feet, for an autumn or winter baby, but just 2 or 3 for a late spring or summer arrival.

3 to 6 rompers (one-piece, short-sleeved, snap-at-the-crotch outfits), for a late spring or summer baby.

2 washable bibs, or a pack of disposables. Even before solids are introduced, you'll need these to protect clothes from spitup.

1 to 3 jumpers. 1 lightweight jumper will do in summer; heavier ones will be needed in cold weather.

1 to 3 hats. Lightweight with brim (for sun protection) for a summer baby; heavier-weight, and shaped to cover the ears snugly but not too tightly, for a winter baby.

1 bunting or snowsuit bag with attached mittens, for a late autumn or winter baby.

Linen Wardrobe

3 to 6 cotton, flannel or cellular blankets, depending on season.

3 to 4 fitted sheets each, for cot, cradle, bassinet, and/or pram.

2 quilted mattress pads, if desired.

2 to 6 waterproof pads, for protecting cot, pram, laps and furniture.

2 washable cot or bassinet blankets or comforters. Lightweight for summer; heavier for winter. Avoid long fringes and loose threads.

1 to 2 blankets for pram or pushchair. Just 1 lightweight one for a summer baby.

2 to 3 terry cloth towels, with hoods.

2 to 3 soft washcloths.

1 dozen square terry muslins, for protecting your shoulders when burping baby, to protect sheets when baby spits up, for emergency bibs, and much more.

Nappy liners for cloth nappies if you like, for heavy wetters or extra nighttime protection.

Nappies. Purchase 2 to 5 dozen prefolded terry ones, if you are washing your own, or several dozen disposables, if you are using them exclusively (a couple dozen if you will use them only for outings and emergencies). If you are planning on using a nappy service, sign up in the eighth month and they will be ready to deliver as soon as you do.

Toiletries

Items needed for nappy changes should be kept on a shelf high enough above the changing table to prevent baby's grabbing for them, but low enough for you to reach easily.

Baby soap or bath liquid, to be used sparingly.

Baby shampoo. For young infants, baby bath can be used for shampoo.

Baby oil, if desired. This is not a necessary item, unless the doctor prescribes it for cradle cap, and salad oil will often serve as well.

Baby cornflour, if desired. Not necessary, but nice for warm weather use.

Ointment for nappy rash. Ask the doctor or midwife for a recommendation.

Petroleum jelly, such as Vaseline, for lubricating rectal thermometers. Do not use to self-treat nappy rash.

Wipes, for nappy changes, hand washing, and a dozen other uses. But use cotton wool and plain water for cleansing baby's bottom during the first few weeks and whenever nappy rash is a problem.

Sterile cotton wool, for cleaning baby's eyes, for daubing alcohol on the umbilical stump, and for nappy changes in the first few weeks and when baby has a rash.

8 nappy pins, if you're using terry nappies. Metal heads are better than plastic, which can crack.

Baby nail scissors or clippers.

Baby brush and comb. Use only a wide-toothed comb on wet hair.

Medicine Chest

Have these supplies on hand rather than waiting to buy them as needed. Ask baby's doctor for recommendations. Store them out of reach of infants and children.

Liquid aspirin substitute, such as Baby Calpol, Tempra, Panadol (all are brands of paracetamol).

Liquified charcoal, if recommended by your doctor.

Syrup of Ipecac, in case of accidental poisoning (but do not use without medical advice; see page 441).

Liquid decongestant, infant formula, to be used only if prescribed by the doctor (it is not usually recommended for babies).

Antiseptic cream, such as bacitracin or neomycin, for minor cuts and scrapes.

Hydrogen peroxide, for cleaning cuts.

Calamine lotion or hydrocortisone cream (½%), for mosquito bites and itchy rashes.

Rehydration fluid, if the baby's doctor recommends it for treatment of diarrhoea; it's not usually needed for breastfed infants.

Sunscreen cream or lotion. Do not use until baby is six months old, unless the doctor suggests otherwise.

Rubbing alcohol, for cleaning thermometers, but not for rubdowns.

Calibrated spoon, dropper, and/or oral syringe, for administering medications.

Sterile band-aids and gauze pads, in a variety of sizes and shapes.

Adhesive tape, for securing gauze pads.

Tweezers, for pulling out tiny splinters.

Nasal aspirator, a bulb syringe for clearing a stuffy nose (see page 412).

Ear syringe, for removing wax buildup, if baby's doctor recommends it.

Cold mist vaporizer/humidifier. The old-fashioned, hot steam humidifier is not recommended because it can lead to burns.

A standard rectal thermometer. This old standby is preferred to the sometimes less accurate digital thermometer and the usually inaccurate temperature strips.

Small penlight, to check throat for inflammation or pupils for signs of concussion.

Tongue depressors, for examining the throat.

Heating pad and/or hot-water bottle, for soothing a colicky tummy or relieving sore muscles.

Feeding Supplies

1 bottle with teat, for water or an emergency supplementary feeding, if you're breastfeeding exclusively.

4 bottles, 100-ml (4-fl ounce) size, and 10 to 12 bottles, 250-ml (8-ounce) size, with teat units, if you're bottle feeding; 4 to 6, if you're supplementing. Glass bottles are easiest to clean, but are breakable, and are not recommended for use with breast milk. Plastic bottles come in two types: traditional-style reusable and the newer reusable holders with disposable liners, which collapse as baby feeds, minimizing air swallowing.

Teats come in several shapes (including the more natural orthodontic) and with different hole sizes (smaller for formula and younger babies, larger for juice and older babies). Silicone teats are odour and taste free, don't get gummy, are dishwasher safe and see-through (so you can see if they're clean). You may want to try several types to see which work best for your baby.

Utensils for formula preparation, if you're bottle feeding. Exactly which items you'll need will depend on the type of formula you plan to use, but the shopping list will usually include bottle and teat brushes, large Pyrex measuring jug, Pyrex measuring cup, long handled mixing spoon and tongs. All should be boilable.

A sterilizer, if you will be bottle feeding, or supplementing early on.

A dummy, if you decide to use one. Look for sturdy one-piece construction, newborn size, a shield with ventilation holes, and orthodontic shape. Like teats, they also come in easy-to-clean silicone. *Warning*: Never attach a cord or ribbon to a dummy.

Furnishings

On all items. *Look for*: lead-free paint, if painted; sturdy non-tip construction; smooth edges and rounded corners; safety restraint straps at crotch and waist, where appropriate. *Avoid*: rough edges, sharp points, or small parts that might break loose; exposed hinges or springs; attached strings, cords, or ribbons. Be sure to follow the manufacturer's directions for use and maintenance of all items and to regularly check baby's cot, pram and other equipment for loose screws, frayed straps, supports that have snapped, and other signs of wear.

Cot. *Look for*: A label stating European Certification (CE) standards have been met; bars no more than 6 cm (2⅜ inches) apart, with no splinters or cracks in the wood; mattress level adjustability; minimum rail height of 56 cm (22 inches) when the mattress is at its highest position and the rail is at its lowest setting; steel stabilizing bars; plastic covering on teething rails, if any, tightly secured and unbroken; casters for mobility. *Avoid*: posts or knobs that protrude; crossbars.

Cot mattress. *Look for*: firmness; pocketed-coil innerspring or, if there's a family history of allergy, dense foam (or put an airtight cover over an innerspring); snug fit in cot (with no more than two adult-finger widths between cot and mattress).

Cot bumpers. *Look for*: snug not floppy fit around entire perimeter of cot; at least 6 ties or sets of snaps for fastening to cot rails.

Moses basket or cradle. Optional, but useful in the early weeks when baby may enjoy the cozy quarters and you may appreciate its mobility (though a pram can serve the same purpose). *Look for*: firm mattress; sturdy stable base; adequate size to hold your baby (a fragile antique may collapse under the weight of a heavy baby).

Changing space. This can be a table or dresser top designed especially for baby changing, or a makeshift unit put together from things you already have. *Look for*: a comfortable height; washable padding; restraining straps; nappy storage within your reach, toiletry storage out of baby's reach.

Nappy bucket, if you will be doing your own nappies (nappy service will provide one, if you use their nappies). *Look for*: easy washability; a tight fitting top that a baby or toddler can't pry open (babies have drowned in water-filled buckets and been poisoned by tasting the cake of deodorant).

Chest of drawers, or other storage unit for baby's clothes.

Baby bath. *Look for*: non-skid bottom or use a towel or stick-ons to keep baby from slipping); easy washability; roomy size (large enough for your baby at four or five months, as well as now); support for baby's head and shoulders; easy portability; easy drainage. *Avoid*: non-removable sponge pads.

Tub seat, for when baby graduates to the big tub. *Look for*: restraining straps; a suction bottom.

Infant seat. *Look for*: wide, sturdy, stable base; non-skid or suction bottom; crotch and waist restraint straps; adequate size (some are too small for any but the tiniest infants); convenient carry handle. *Also nice*: a rocking mechanism; adjustability. Never leave an infant, even a very young one, in such a seat at the edge of a table or counter or near something (such as a wall) he or she could push off from, and never use an infant seat as a car seat unless it is certified as such.

Toy chest. *Look for*: lightweight lid, removable or with a support mechanism that will keep it from slamming down on a child; smooth edges and corners on metal chests, and no splinters on wooden ones; ventilation holes in lid and sides; no lock or latch. An open bin or toy shelves are preferable for toy storage.

Outings Equipment

Pushchair. *Look for*: CE certification seal; a reclining seat, so it can be used when baby is very young as well as for naps when baby is older; a broad non-tip base; large wheels for better manoeuvrability; good brakes; secure and easy-to-fasten restraining straps; easy foldability (try it); lightweight, if you plan to carry it onto buses or other vehicles often; sun and rain shields; hinges that won't catch curious fingers; comfortable handle height; package rack. When using it, be sure the folding mechanism is properly locked in the open position and don't overload handles with bags or other items, since they could tip it over.

Combination pram-pushchair. This has some of the advantages of both, but is not as lightweight as a pushchair.

Pram. Many families, especially those living in cramped quarters, or who take most of their outings in a car, don't need or want a pram. If you do, *look for*: smooth rocking motion; foldability (if that is important to you); manoeuvrability (be sure it will fit through the doors in your home); a package rack; secure locking devices if top is removable for use as a bassinet. Always be sure a foldable unit is properly locked open when in use; once your baby can sit, propped, always use a baby harness.

Car seat. Even if you don't own a car, you will need a seat if you plan on taking baby for drives in anyone else's car. If you rent a car, you can rent a seat along with it, but keep in mind it may not be the best seat available. There are three types – the infant seat, the

Infant car seat. *This rear facing seat is suitable for infants up to about 9kg (20 pounds). Some models work for those weighing more: check labels. Some seats can be removed and installed with baby in them and can be used as infant seats indoors. Never place any rear-facing infant seat in the front seat of a car equipped with passenger-side airbags. All children under 14 are safer in the back seat.*

convertible seat, and the toddler seat – and you should *look for* the following when selecting one: a seat manufactured recently, conforming to CE standards (don't borrow an older one, or one that's already restrained a child in an accident); ease of installation (preferably without a tether): a one-latch harness, which makes fastening and releasing baby easier (test it yourself to be sure you can handle these manoeuvres quickly); comfort and roominess for baby, with adequate visibility and ease of movement for an older infant; adjustability, so that seat will still be safe and comfortable as baby grows.

Baby carrier. Convenient for carrying a young baby at home or away, leaving your hands free for chores or carrying bundles. *Look for*: a front carrier model (a baby is too young for a back carrier until he or she can sit independently) that is easy to hook up and detach without help; adjustable, padded straps that don't bind; easy washability; head and shoulder support for baby, and a wide

Convertible car seat. This unit is designed for children from birth to 18 kg (40 pounds). It faces the rear in a semi-reclining position when used for an infant, then can be switched to an upright, front-facing position when baby is older and interested in looking out (see seat at right).

Older babies are ready for **toddler seats,** *designed for children over a specific height and weight (see product label). Secured by the car seat belt, these provide more mobility and visibility. Children should not ride a booster seat until they are at least 18 kg (40 pounds).*

bottom that supports bottom and thighs. A carrier that allows baby to be held face outward when awake is ideal. A sling carrier that puts most of the weight on your hips is better for your back when baby is heavier. Never use a carrier instead of a car seat.

Nappy bag. *Look for:* multiple compartments, at least one waterproof; shoulder strap or rucksack style; a zip closing for main compartment. A detachable changing pad is a plus. See page 83 for how to pack a nappy bag.

Nice to Have

Rocking chair. Great for feeding and calming a baby. *Look for:* sturdy rockers; a comfortable fit (try it).

Intercom. Ideal if baby's room is out of earshot of your bedroom or other parts of the house. *Look for:* portability and safety (no exposed parts that can cause electrocution).

Baby swing. Can often soothe an unhappy baby. *Look for:* secure restraining straps; smooth edges and surfaces; sturdiness; a seat that reclines for a young infant; an activity tray

for diversion. *Avoid:* a swing with hinges that can catch little fingers, or small parts that can break off. If the swing is to be attached to a doorway, be sure it will fit yours. Do not use for a baby younger than six weeks.

Portable cot, if you plan on travelling often to places where such equipment will not be available. *Look for:* safety features listed for playpens below.

You Will Need, or May Want, Later

Feeding chair. Available in both high and low models, but high are presently more popular. *Look for:* wide, sturdy, nontip base; a tray that can be easily removed or locked in place with one hand; a wide lip to catch spills; washability; a seat back high enough to support baby's head; an adjustable foot rest; restraining straps; a secure locking device if the chair folds; CE certification.

Portable feeding seat. These are useful when visiting and at restaurants, as well as at home. *Look for:* a locking mechanism to prevent falls; a comfortable seat; a crotch guard to prevent baby's slipping out. Never use such a seat on a glass or pedestal table, or with a chair under it. (For other safety tips, see page 228.)

Playpen. Wooden playpens are better for learning to pull up, but mesh pens are softer if baby falls against the sides. *Look for:* CE certification seal; slats no more than 6 cm (2⅜ inches) apart on a wooden pen; fine netting on a mesh pen (it won't catch fingers or buttons); tough vinyl pads that won't tear easily (babies can choke on the torn plastic or on exposed filling); padded metal hinges; a baby-proof collapse mechanism. *Do not* use an accordion-type playpen or leave a mesh pen with the sides down.

Safety gate, for doorways or stairs. *Look for:* rigid mesh or swinging metal construction (not accordion-type, unless it is of a post-1985 design and has safety certification) and a latch that is easy to open and close (or you may neglect to close it).

Walker. Some babies enjoy this piece of equipment, but it must be used under careful supervision (see page 224). *Look for:* wide, sturdy, non-tip base; secure locking mechanism to safeguard fingers; protective covers for any accessible coil springs; wide three-sided tray for play and protection.

What to Take to the Hospital

Use this as a checklist.

En Route

☐ Your antenatal notes/'co-operation' card

☐ Cash for the taxi fare or parking garage

☐ Watch or clock with a second hand for timing contractions

☐ Notebook and a pen for recording contractions and emotional and physical symptoms

For the Labour or Birthing Room

☐ Plenty of change for telephone calls and snack machines

☐ Hospital information

☐ Lotion for massages

☐ Small paper bag to remedy hyperventilation

☐ Tennis ball or rolling pin for countermassage during back labour

☐ Sugarless sweets to keep your mouth moist

☐ Heavy socks for cold feet

☐ Coloured flannel

☐ Champagne labelled with your name, for celebrating

☐ Sandwiches or other snacks for dad

☐ Your address book or a list of family and friends to be called

☐ *What to Expect When You're Expecting*[2]

For Your Hospital Room

☐ This book

☐ Robe and two to three nightgowns (not your best, since they may end up stained by lochia; alternatively, you can use the hospital's)

☐ Bed jacket, slippers

☐ Perfume, powder, cosmetics, toothbrush, toothpaste

☐ Soap, deodorant, skin lotion, shampoo, conditioner

☐ Hair brush, hair dryer, curling iron

☐ Glasses or contact lenses (with necessary paraphernalia)

☐ Sanitary towels

☐ Playing cards, books, magazines, other distractions

---

2. The first book in this series contains valuable information about what you can expect to happen in the hospital.

- A baby name book, if you haven't made that decision yet

- Packets of raisins, nuts, whole-wheat crackers

- Clothes and nappies for baby, if not provided by the hospital

For Going Home: Mum

- A roomy outfit to go home in

- Bra (nursing bra if you plan to breastfeed)

- Panties and slip

- Shoes and hosiery

- Coat or sweater, if necessary

- Shopping bags to bring home gifts

For Going Home: Baby

- 2 disposable nappies, or 4 terry nappies with pins and waterproof pants or wrappers

- 1 undershirt

- 1 babygro or nightgown

- Socks or booties

- 1 cotton blanket

- Sweater and cap in cool weather

- Bunting or heavy blanket in cold weather (if bunting won't fit in the car seat, strap the baby in, then cover with a blanket)

- Infant car seat

Going Home

In the 1950s, new babies came home from the hospital after ten days, in the '80s after two days. Today you may bring your new infant home within hours of delivery. It's scary, controversial, and not always appropriate. the decision is best made on a case-by-case basis with a consultant's input. Early discharge is safest when an infant is full-term; is an appropriate weight; has started feeding well; is going home with a parent (or parents) who knows the basics and is well enough to provide care; and will be seen by the doctor at two or three days after birth. If for any reason you have concerns about early discharge, speak to your child's doctor, but take comfort from the fact that you and the baby will be visited by a community midwife for the next ten days.

If you and your baby are discharged early, a doctor's visit should be booked within the next 48 hours. Also be on the lookout for problems typical of newborns, such as yellowing of the skin* and the whites of the eyes (a sign of jaundice); refusal to eat; dehydration (fewer than six wet nappies in 24 hours, or dark yellow urine); constant crying or moaning instead of crying; fever; red or purple dots anywhere on the skin.

---

*To check for jaundice, press your baby's arm or thigh with your thumb. If the area beneath the pressure turns yellowish rather than white, jaundice may be present.

THREE

Your Newborn Baby

◆

What Your Baby May Be Doing

Your baby within a few days of birth will probably be able to:

- lift head briefly when on the tummy

- focus on objects within 20 to 25 cm (8 to 15 inches)

- move arms and legs on both sides of the body equally well

What You Can Expect at the Hospital Checkups

Your baby's very first checkup will be in the delivery or birthing room. Here, or later on in the nursery, you can expect that a doctor or nurse will do some or all of the following:

- Clear baby's airways by suctioning his or her nose (which may be done as soon as the head appears or after the rest of the baby is delivered)

- Clamp and cut the umbilical cord (antibiotic ointment may be applied to the cord stump, and the clamp is usually left on for at least 24 hours)

- Check the placenta to be sure it's complete and evaluate its condition

- Assign baby an Apgar score (rating of baby's condition at one and five minutes after birth; see page 47)

- Administer eyedrops or ointment (silver nitrate or antibiotics; see page 65) to prevent gonococcal or chlamydial infection

- Count fingers and toes, and note if baby's observable body parts and features appear normal

- Record passage or lack of passage of urine and/or stools, (to help rule out an elimination problem)

- Administer vitamin K injection, to enhance the clotting ability of baby's blood

- Weigh baby (average weight is 3.4 kg/7½ pounds; 95% of new babies weigh between 2.5 and 4.5 kg/5½ and 10 pounds)

- Measure baby's length (average length is 51 cm/20 inches; 95% of newborns are between 46 and 56 cm/18 and 22 inches)

- Measure head circumference (average is 35 cm/13.8 inches; normal range is from 33 to 37.5 cm/12.9 to 14.7 inches)

- Obtain blood from infant's heel, to be screened for phenylketonuria (PKU) and hypothyroidism; from the umbilical cord for the Coombs test, to screen for antibodies that would indicate Rh sensitization has occurred; for any other necessary metabolic screening tests (for

Portrait of a Newborn

Most first-time parents are unprepared for the appearance of the bundle of joy that is handed them at delivery. Despite the oohs and aahs from excited friends and families, most newborns are not cute. The typical new arrival has a head that looks too large for its body (it's about one quarter of the total length), skinny 'chicken' legs, and often, unless delivered by caesarean, a battered countenance.

Newborn hair may be sparse or full, it may lay flat or stand up straight in what looks like the latest punk style. When hair is thin, blood vessels in the scalp may appear very prominent and the pulse may be visible at the soft spot, or fontanel, on the top of the head.

A newborn's eyes may appear squinty because of the folds at the inner corners and because of swelling from delivery and infection-protecting eye drops. They may also be blood-shot from the pressures of labour. The nose may be flattened and the chin unsymmetrical or pushed in from being squeezed through the pelvis. If it was a particularly tight squeeze, the head may have moulded to a point, looking as though baby were wearing a dunce cap.

And/or a bruise, or cephalohaematoma, may have been raised on the scalp. (Most of these effects of labour will diminish in a few days, or at most a few weeks.)

Because a newborn's skin is thin, it usually has a pale pinkish caste (even in black babies) from the blood vessels just beneath it. The skin is most often covered with the remains of the vernix caseosa (a cheesy coating) that protects the foetal skin during the time spent soaking in the amniotic fluid, though the later a baby arrives, the less of this coating there is. Many babies, particularly those born early, are also covered with lanugo, a downy prenatal fuzz, usually on the shoulders, back, forehead, and cheeks, that will disappear within the first weeks of life. Because of an infusion of female hormones from the placenta just before birth, many babies, both boys and girls, have swollen breasts and/or genitals. There may even be a milky discharge from the breasts and, in girls, a vaginal discharge (sometimes bloody).

These newborn features will begin to disappear in the weeks to come. And pretty soon, your baby will be picture pretty.

low blood sugar, for example); for sickle-cell screening[1]

- Assess gestational age (time spent in the uterus) in babies born before term

Before your baby leaves the delivery or birthing room, ID bands will be placed on both you and your baby. The baby's doctor, usually of your choosing, will give baby a more complete examination sometime during the next 24 hours; if you (with or without your spouse) can arrange to be present, this is a good time to ask questions. The doctor will check the following:

- Weight (it will probably have dropped since birth, often by as much as 10% of body weight), head circumference (may be larger, as any molding of the head rounds out), and length (which won't actually have changed, but might seem to have because measuring a baby, who can't stand or cooperate, is a highly inexact procedure)

1. Some tests are more accurate when performed after the first day of life. Sickle-cell testing is usually limited to high-risk groups but some experts are calling for universal screening. In the U.K., tests for PKU and hypothyroidism are usually done by a midwife or health visitor, when baby is 6–10 days old and established on milk feeds.

- Heart sounds and respirations
- Internal organs, such as kidneys, liver, and spleen, by palpation (examining by touch, externally)
- Newborn reflexes
- Hips, for possible dislocation
- Hands, feet, arms and legs
- Genitals
- The umbilical stump

Apgar Test

The first test most babies are given – and which most pass with good scores – is the Apgar, developed by anaesthesiologist Virginia Apgar. The scores, recorded at one minute and again at five minutes after birth, reflect the newborn's general condition and are based on observations made in five assessment categories. Babies who score between 7 and 10, are in good to excellent condition, and usually require only routine postdelivery care; those scoring between 4 and 6, in fair condition, may require some resuscitative measures; and those who score under 4, in poor condition, will require immediate and maximal lifesaving efforts. It

APGAR Table

SIGN	POINTS		
	0	1	2
Appearance (colour)*	Pale or Blue	Body pink, extremities blue	Pink
Pulse (heartbeat)	Not detectible	Below 100	Over 100
Grimace (reflex irritability)	No response to stimulation	Grimace	Lusty cry
Activity (muscle tone)	Flaccid (no or weak activity)	Some movement of extremities	A lot of activity
Respiration (breathing)	None	Slow, irregular	Good (crying)

* In non-white children, the colour of mucous membranes of mouth, of the whites of the eyes, of lips, palms, hands, and soles of feet will be examined.

was once believed that babies whose scores remained low at five minutes were destined to have future neurological problems, but recent research shows that most of these babies turn out to be normal and healthy.

Your Newborn's Reflexes

Startle, or Moro, reflex. Sudden or loud noise or the sensation of falling causes a young baby to extend legs, arms, and fingers, arch back, and draw head back, then draw arms back, fists clenched, into chest.
Duration: Four to six months.

Babinski reflex. When the sole of the foot is gently stroked from heel to toe, the toes flare upward and foot turns in.
Duration: Between six months and two years, after which toes curl downward.

Rooting reflex. A newborn whose cheek is gently stroked will turn in the direction of the stimulus, mouth open and ready to suckle.
Duration: About three to four months, though it may persist when baby is sleeping.

Walking, or stepping, reflex. Held upright on a table or other flat surface, supported under the arms, a newborn (this works best after the fourth day of life) may lift one leg and then the other taking what seem to be 'steps'.
Duration: Variable, but typically about two months. (Existence of this reflex does not forecast early walking.)

Palmar grasping reflex. With baby facing forward, arms flexed, an index finger pressed against his or her palm will cause a flexing of the hand in an attempt to grasp the finger. A newborn's grasp may be powerful enough to support full body weight.
Duration: Three or four months.

Tonic neck reflex. Placed on the back, a young baby will assume a 'fencing position', head to one side, with arms and legs on that side extended and opposite limbs flexed.
Duration: It may be present at birth or may appear at about two months, and disappears at about six months.

You can try to elicit these reflexes from your baby, but keep in mind that your results may be less reliable than those of a doctor or other trained examiner and that the response may be affected by factors such as fatigue and hunger. If you fail to induce an appropriate response to one or more of these tests when done at home, chances are

---

The Brazelton Neonatal Behavioural Assessment Scale

More complex and more time-consuming to administer than the Apgar test, the Brazelton, developed in America by baby doctor T. Berry Brazelton, is believed by some to be a better predictor of future development. The thirty-minute assessment – often carried out over several days – uses a variety of stimuli (bells, colours, shapes, rattles, lights) to test the way newborns respond to and cope with their environment. It looks at four types of behaviour: interactive (how the baby relates to people, including alertness and cuddliness); motor (including reflexes, muscle tone, hand-mouth activity); control of physiological state (including how well the baby can self-console or be consoled after being upset); and reaction to stress (including the startle reflex). Rather than a baby's average performance during the test, the Brazelton uses the baby's best performance in scoring, and testers make every effort (often enlisting the mother's help) to bring out the best in the newborn subject. Most doctors reserve this test (or ones similar in the U.K.) for occasions when they suspect a problem, such as with low birthweight babies or those who show signs of neurological problems.

the fault lies more with your technique or timing than with your subject. Try again another day, and if you still can't elicit a response, mention the fact to baby's doctor, who probably has already tested your baby successfully and will be happy to repeat them for you at the next surgery visit. The verified absence of a reflex or its lingering beyond the usual age of disappearance requires further assessment.

Feeding Your Baby: Getting Started

Whether you decide to nourish your infant at bottle or breast, you'll soon realize that feeding time isn't just a time for giving your baby sustenance. It is a time for getting to know and love each other.

Getting Started Breastfeeding

They make it look so easy, those nursing mothers you've seen. Without skipping a beat of conversation or a mouthful of salad, they lift their shirts and put their babies to breast. Deftly, nonchalantly, as though it were the most natural process in the world.

Yet the first time you put your baby to your breast, nothing seems to come naturally. Even with all your concentration and most concerted efforts, you can't seem to get the baby to hold on to your nipple, never mind to suck on it. The baby's fussy; you're frustrated; soon you're both in tears. If you're failing at the most basic of mothering functions, you wonder, can failure at the rest of motherhood be far behind?

Don't throw in the nursing bra yet. You're not failing – you're just getting started. Nursing, like most other fundamentals of mothering, is learned, not instinctive. Give yourself and your baby a little time, and it won't be long before you're making it look easy, too. Keeping these pointers in mind will help.

Get an early start. If both you and baby are up to it, and baby isn't whisked off to the nursery, try to nurse in the birthing or delivery room. But don't fret if you and baby aren't successful right off. Trying to force the feeding to happen when you're both exhausted from a difficult delivery only sets the stage for a disappointing experience. Cuddling at the breast can be just as satisfying as nursing in the first few moments of your baby's life. If you don't get around to feeding on the delivery bed, ask to have the baby brought to your room for nursing as soon as possible after all necessary nursery procedures have been completed. Remember, however, that although an early start is ideal, it doesn't guarantee instant success. Plenty of practice will be needed before you and your baby make perfect.

Beat the system. Hospitals are usually run for the greater good – which doesn't always coincide with the needs of the breastfeeding mother and baby. To be sure you aren't thwarted in your efforts by insensitivity, ignorance, or arbitrary regulations, ask your doctor *in advance* to make your preferences (demand feeding, no bottles, no dummies) known to the staff or explain them to the nurses in a friendly way. Winning a nursery nurse to your side may be your best route to success. You will, however, need the doctor's support if you have a fever and still want to nurse.

Get together. Breastfeeding can't happen if you and your baby are apart. Thus sharing a room, or rooming-in, can be ideal for a nursing mother, since it doesn't leave her dependent on the nursery staff to bring her baby to her for nursing and ensures that no one will sneak a bottle of plain or glucose water into the infant instead. If you're tired out from a difficult delivery, or don't feel confident enough yet to deal with the baby on a 24-hour basis, partial rooming-in (having baby with you during the day and in the nursery at night) may be preferable.

Breastfeeding Basics

- Have a drink. A glass of milk, juice, or water just before or during each feeding will give you the extra fluids you need to produce breast milk. Something stronger (alcoholic, that is) is okay only occasionally, and doesn't count towards your fluid intake.

- Get comfortable. For the first few feedings, lying on your side may work best (see illustration). Later, sitting up in bed or in a chair may be better. But don't lean forward to get the nipple in baby's mouth; instead place a pillow across

The side hold, good for small babies.

your lap to support the arm cradling baby, and to bring him or her up to, and directly facing, your breast. Experiment to find the position most comfortable for you, one you can hold for a long period of time without feeling strained or stiff.

- Take hold of your breast with your free thumb and forefinger (thumb on top) just above the areola. Holding it this way, bring the nipple towards your baby's lips and tickle them, going from top lip to bottom and back. This should tease the mouth open. But don't tickle or squeeze the cheeks to force the mouth open because baby won't know which way to turn. Once the mouth is open, gently place the nipple in its centre so baby can latch on. If necessary, repeat the sequence until baby takes the nipple in his or her mouth. Don't force. Given the chance, your baby will eventually take the initiative.

- Be sure your baby has a hold on the areola as well as the nipple. Sucking on just the nipple will not only leave your child hungry (because the milk glands that secrete the milk won't be compressed), but it will also make your nipples sore. Be sure, too, that your baby hasn't missed the mark and

A position that lets you nurse and rest.

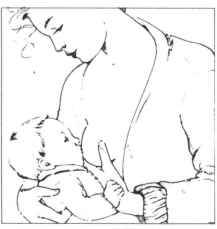

Use your free hand to guide your nipple.

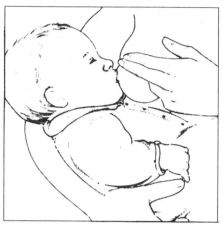

Use fingers to give baby breathing room.

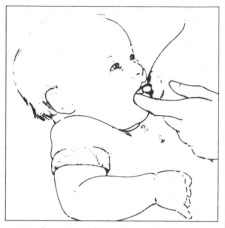

Break suction safely with your forefinger.

started sucking on another part of the breast entirely. Newborns are eager to suck even if no milk is forthcoming and can cause a painful bruise by gumming sensitive breast tissue.

- Be sure your baby isn't sucking his or her own lower lip or tongue. You can check by pulling the lower lip down while nursing. If it does seem to be the tongue that's being suckled, break the suction with your finger, remove your nipple, and make certain the tongue is lowered before you start again. If it's the lip, gently ease it out while baby suckles.

- Once your baby has a good grip, be sure that his or her nose isn't blocked by your breast. If it is, use your finger to press the breast out of the way and give baby plenty of space to breathe.

- Watch for a strong, steady, rhythmic motion in baby's cheek, a sign that suckling is in progress. Later, when your milk comes in, you'll want to listen for the sound of swallowing (sometimes even gulping) that assures baby is not suckling in vain. If the milk seems to be coming out so quickly that it is flooding baby's mouth, causing gagging or choking, stop nursing and express a little milk by hand or with a pump to reduce the surplus. If either swollen (engorged) breasts or sore nipples are interfering with your nursing, see pages 511 and 544.

- Nurse for no more than 5 minutes per side at each feeding the first day, 10 the next day, and 15 or more the third. (Some experts okay nursing for as long as baby likes from the start.) Once the milk is in, nurse for 10 minutes on the first breast, and as long as baby wants to on the second, switching back to the first if baby still seems hungry after emptying the second. If baby falls asleep before you switch, a good burp may have him or her sniffing for more.

Start each feeding with alternate breasts. As a reminder, you can fasten a safety pin to your nursing bra on the side you started with at the previous feeding, or you can tuck a nursing pad or tissue in the bra cup on that side. The pad will also absorb any leakage from the breast you're not nursing on.

- When baby is finished, pat your nipples dry; then, when possible, expose them to the air for ten or fifteen minutes. This will help toughen them, and won't be necessary once nursing is well established.

- When your milk comes in, nurse often – at least eight or ten times in 24 hours, giving baby both breasts and emptying at least one at each feeding. If baby doesn't nurse vigorously or long enough at any one feeding, and a breast isn't emptied, it may be a good idea to express the remainder (see page 92), especially if your milk supply is scant. The expressed milk can be saved in the refrigerator or freezer for supplementary feedings.

With this system you can feed your baby on demand during the day, and on the nursery's schedule at night.

If rooming-in isn't available, isn't possible, or doesn't appeal to you, you can ask to have the baby brought to you when he or she is awake and hungry rather than at the nursery's convenience. Since this is considered a tall order in some hospitals, you may have to make arrangements in advance. Even then, baby may be brought to you by the midwife only sporadically, particularly if the nursery is crowded and, as is often the case, understaffed.

If all else fails, you can opt for early discharge so you and baby can room-in at home. If that's not possible, and requests for demand feeding are denied altogether, nurse on the hospital schedule until you do receive your walking papers. But don't let your baby sleep through visits with you. If you're handed a sleepyhead, awaken him or her and get in a few minutes of nursing.

Practise, practise, practise. Consider the feedings before your milk comes in as 'dry runs', and don't be concerned that baby is getting very little in the way of nourishment. Your milk supply is tailored to your baby's needs. Right now those needs are minimal – in fact, the newborn stomach can't tolerate a lot of food – and the tiny quantity of colostrum you're producing is just right. Use those initial feeding sessions to work on your nursing technique rather than to fill baby's belly, and be assured that he or she isn't starving while you're both learning.

Take requests. Feeding on demand – when baby is hungry – is always best for a nursing infant. It may only be possible, however, if you're rooming-in, or if the baby nursery is well staffed enough to allow nurses to deliver babies whenever they are hungry. If neither is the case, you'll have to feed whenever you get the chance, which may mean not letting a sleeping babe lie.

Ban the bottle. Consider supplementary feedings of glucose water – routinely offered in some hospitals to breastfed new-

borns – as sabotage to your nursing efforts. Even a few sips of sugar water will satisfy tender appetites and early sucking needs, leaving baby more sleepy than hungry when brought to you later. You may also find your baby reluctant to struggle with the breast nipple after a few encounters with an artificial nipple, which yields results with a lot less effort. If your baby doesn't nurse, or nurses only briefly or half-heartedly, your breasts won't be stimulated to produce milk, and a cycle almost certainly destined to undermine breastfeeding will have begun.

Though you may be told that breastfeeding newborns need the extra fluids bottled water supplies (since all they're receiving from their mothers is a few teaspoons of colostrum), this is so only if dehydration or hypoglycaemia – both very rare – are problems. The practice of giving water or formula is most likely to benefit the harried postnatal ward staff; it's less time-consuming to put a bottle in a crying baby's mouth at night than to cart the bassinet down the hall to mummy, or to assist at length when breastfeeding does not come easily.

Give it time. No successful breastfeeding relationship was built in a day. Baby is certainly inexperienced, and you are, too, if this is your first time. You both have a lot to learn, and you'll both have to be patient while you learn it. There will be plenty of trial and even more error before supplier and demander are working in concert.

Keep in mind that things may go even more slowly if one or both of you had a difficult time during labour and delivery, or if you had anaesthesia; drowsy mothers and sluggish infants may not be up to tackling the art of breastfeeding just yet. Sleep it off (and let baby do the same) before getting serious about the task ahead of you.

Don't go it alone. A hundred years ago, mothers and babies facing first attempts at breastfeeding had a lot of help. Mothers, aunts and grandmas were usually on hand to pass on their experience; midwives were around to augment the family support.

But just because your baby's been delivered in a hospital instead of in a four-poster and because it's likely your mother and aunts are not only not living nearby but have no breastfeeding experience, you don't have to confront those first breastfeeding encounters alone and unaided. Some hospitals offer breastfeeding classes or individualized instruction, and/or provide written materials. If no one offers help postpartum, ask for it – from a midwife, from your doctor, a health visitor, or from a lactation consultant affiliated with the hospital. If you don't get any help, or you don't get enough, call your local La Leche League or National Childbirth Trust group for advice or referrals. An early visit (at one or two weeks postpartum) to the baby's doctor to go over your breastfeeding progress is often helpful and reassuring. Talking to mothers who are nursing successfully is too.

Keep your cool. This isn't easy to do when you're a brand-new mother, but it's vital if you want to succeed at breastfeeding. Tension can inhibit the let-down of milk, which means that even if you are producing milk, it may not be dispensed until you relax. If you're feeling edgy, banish visitors from the room fifteen minutes before you're scheduled to feed your baby, or if you're feeding on demand, ask guests to leave as soon as baby begins to appear hungry. Do relaxation exercises if you feel they might help, pick up a book or magazine, switch on the TV, or just close your eyes and listen to soft music for a few minutes. Though wine or beer has often been recommended to enhance relaxation and assist let-down, there is no evidence that this works. And because a recent study suggests that as little as one glass of wine a day consumed by a nursing mother could slow motor development in her baby, daily alcohol isn't advisable.

Getting Started Bottle Feeding

Bottle feeding, oddly enough, comes more naturally – or at least more easily – than breastfeeding. Babies have little difficulty learning to suckle from an artificial teat, and mothers (and fathers, too) have little difficulty at the delivery end. Preparing formula and sterilizing bottles are a little more complicated, but even these skills are mastered without much effort. (See page 39 for information on the types of bottles and nipples available, and for bottle-feeding supplies you will need.)

Selecting a Formula

With the help of your baby's doctor, select a formula that is closest to human milk in composition – types and proportions of proteins, fats, sugars, sodium and other nutrients should be as similar as possible to those in breast milk. Iron-fortified formula (or a nutritional supplement containing iron) is not necessary until four months; fluoride fortification is not needed until six months and then only if you live in an area without fluoridated water, will not be mixing the formula with fluoridated water, or will not be giving a fluoride supplement. Special formulas are available for babies with milk allergies or metabolic disorders, such as PKU. Commercial formulas come in the following forms:

Ready to use. This comes in 100- and 250-ml (4- and 8-fl ounce), single-serving bottles and is ready for baby with the addition of a sterilized teat.

Ready to pour. Available in cartons of various sizes, this liquid formula need only be poured into sterilized bottles to be ready for use.

Ready to mix. Less expensive, but a little more time-consuming to prepare, this concentrated liquid or powder is diluted in bottles of plain or sterilized water. It's available in tins or single-serving packets.

Do not use homemade formula. Formula made from evaporated or fresh milk plus sugar and water will not approximate either human milk or commercial formula, will not adequately nourish your baby, and may impose a severe strain on immature kidneys. *Do not* use any formula or formula-substitute without the approval of your baby's doctor. At least one company has put out a soya beverage that they claimed was a suitable replacement for mother's milk but was later found to be nutritionally inadequate.

Safe Bottle Feeding

At one time, giving a baby a bottle was a risky proposition. Because of poor sanitation and inadequate formulas, bottle-fed babies often didn't thrive and frequently fell ill or even died from infection. Today's commercial baby formulas are designed to imitate mother's milk as much as is scientifically possible and are a safe and appropriate choice in baby feeding. But proper sanitation and correct mixing in the home must be followed in order to be sure the milk you feed your baby is safe.

- Always check the expiration date on formula; do not buy or use any formula that has expired. Do not buy or use dented, leaky, or otherwise damaged cans or other containers.

- Wash your hands thoroughly before preparing formula.

- Before opening, wash the tops of formula cans with detergent and hot water; rinse well and dry. Shake, if required.

- Use only a sharp, clean can opener, preferably reserved only for opening formula, to open tins of dry formula (a rotary blade is most efficient); wash the opener after each use and check for food or rust deposits before using again. Use a clean punch-type opener to open cans of liquid formula, making two openings – one large, one small – on opposite sides of the tin to make pouring easier. Wash after each use.

- When preparing bottles of formula, also prepare a bottle or two of sterilized water for use as needed between feedings.

When your baby is between one and two months old, your doctor may okay giving water that hasn't been boiled.[2]

- Wash everything used for baby feeding in a clean bowl reserved for this purpose, scrubbing with bottle brushes, detergent and hot water. (New items should be boiled before first use.) Squeeze soapy water through teat holes, then squeeze hot rinse water through several times. If the holes seem blocked, pierce with a nappy pin. (Clear silicone teats are easiest to clean.) Rinse all utensils under hot running water.

- Follow the manufacturer's directions precisely when mixing formula. If they differ from those given by the nursery or your doctor, be sure to ask why before preparing the formula; it may be that the instructions you were given were for a different formula. *Always check cartons to see if formula needs to be diluted – diluting a formula that shouldn't be diluted, or not diluting one that should be, could be dangerous.* Continue sterilizing for as long as the doctor recommends – most suggest two or three months, though a few feel washing with hot soapy water is sufficient from the very first. See page 56 for the most common sterilizing techniques.

- Heat a bottle of formula before using, if necessary, by running hot water over it. (Most babies, however, are just as happy with their formula unheated.) Check the temperature frequently by shaking a few drops on your inner wrist; it's ready for baby when it no longer feels cold – it needn't be warm, just body temperature. Once warmed, you should use formula immediately, since bacteria multiply rapidly at lukewarm temperatures. Do not heat formula in a microwave oven – the liquid may warm unevenly or the container may remain cool when the formula

2. If the safety of the tap water in your home is questionable (see page 232), use bottled water that's not distilled (valuable minerals are removed in the distillation process) for preparing formula and for drinking.

has got hot enough to burn baby's mouth or throat.

- Do not reuse leftover formula. Any formula remaining after a feeding should be discarded – it's a potential breeding ground for bacteria.

- Rinse bottles and teats right after use for easier cleaning.

- Opened cartons or bottles of liquid formula should always be covered tightly and stored in the refrigerator for *no longer* than the times specified on the labels. Tins of dry formula should be covered and stored in a cool, dry place for use within the month.

- Don't store liquid formula, opened or unopened, at temperatures below 0°C (32°F) or above 35°C (95°F). Ideally store it between 7.2°C (45°F) and 32.2°C (90°F). Don't use formula that has been frozen (soya products freeze more quickly) or that shows white specks or streaks even after shaking.

- Keep prepared bottles of formula refrigerated until ready to use. If you are travelling away from home, take along ready-to-use bottled formula or bottles of sterile water and single-serving formula packets to mix with them; or store previously prepared bottles in an insulated container or in a plastic bag with a small ice pack or a dozen ice cubes (the formula will stay fresh as long as most of the ice is frozen); or pack the bottles with a small box or can of juice that you've prefrozen (when you or an older child is ready for a snack, the juice will have defrosted and the formula will still be fresh). Do not use formula that is no longer cold to the touch.

Bottle Feeding with Love

No matter how inept a first-time breastfeeder may be in her attempts to hook her baby up to her nipples, she's not likely to have trouble giving her newborn enough skin-to-skin contact – a built-in feature of the breastfeeding system. Unfortunately, it is possible to bottle feed a tiny infant with a minimum of such contact, and many well-meaning but harried bottle-feeding mothers have given in to feeding shortcuts that compromise closeness for convenience. So if there's one area in which beginning bottle feeders have to try harder than novice nursers, it's in making sure they don't lose touch with their babies at feeding time. The following tips will help you to make bottle-feeding sessions as rewarding to both participants as breastfeeding ones:

Don't prop the bottle. For a young baby, who is as hungry for emotional gratification in the form of cuddling as for oral gratification in the form of food, propping is very unsatisfying. And propping has physical as well as emotional drawbacks. Babies are more susceptible to choking when feeding on their backs – a very serious problem when mum isn't around to help. They may also be more susceptible to ear infections in this feeding position, and because they may fall asleep with bottle in mouth, to tooth decay once the first teeth come in.

Limit baby feeders at first. Your baby is just getting used to the idea of sucking on a rubber teat for nourishment. Because every adult has a different way of holding, handling, and talking to a baby, having many different people (mother, father, grandparents, nurses, other children) give bottles can hamper good feeding adjustment and mother-baby bonding. Initially, try to do most of the feeding yourself with, if necessary, assistance from one other person. Later, when baby becomes proficient, you can let others share in the fun of feeding baby.

Go skin to skin, when possible. There's something special about a baby's cheek touching his mother's breast – for both participants. Even as a bottle feeder you can achieve this by opening your shirt and placing baby next to your chest as you give the bottle. Of course this isn't practical in public, but it works well in private. Or you might want to try a supplemental nutrition system, which allows women who can't nurse but crave the breastfeeding experience to put their infants to the breast (see page 100).

Switch arms. Give your baby a chance to see the world from different perspectives by switching arms at midfeeding. This gives you a chance to relieve the ache that can develop from staying in one position for so long.

Sterilizing Techniques

The terminal-heating method for use with concentrated liquid or powder formula. Prepare the formula according to directions in a clean measuring cup or mixing bowl, then pour it into clean bottles. Loosely top bottles with teats, caps, and collars. Place them on a rack or folded towel in a sterilizer or large pot, and add 7.5 cm (3 inches) of water. Heat to boiling, then cover and boil for 25 minutes. Remove from the heat. Tighten caps when they are cool enough to handle, and refrigerate until needed. (Refrigerating before cooling may cause film to form on the formula, clogging the teats at feeding time.) Use within 48 hours.

The aseptic method for use with concentrated liquid or powder formula. Place clean bottles, teats, collars, caps, mixing spoon, tin opener, measuring jug, measuring cup and tongs (be sure all these items are boilable) in a rack or on a folded towel in a sterilizer or large pot. Add water to cover and put the lid on the sterilizer or pot. Heat to boiling and boil for five minutes. In another saucepan, measure the amount of water needed for formula. Cover, bring to a boil, and boil for five minutes. Remove from the heat and allow both to cool to room temperature while still covered. Measure formula in a sterilized measuring jug and add it to the sterilized water in the saucepan. Pour the blended formula into sterilized bottles; add teats, collars and caps using sterilized tongs to avoid contaminating with your hands. Store in a refrigerator for up to 48 hours. Shake before using.

The single-bottle method for use with concentrated liquid or powder formula.

Add specified amounts of water to each clean nursing bottle, then loosely top with teats and caps. Place on a wire rack or folded towel in a sterilizer or large saucepan. Add water to level of the water in the bottles. Bring to a boil, cover, and boil for 25 minutes. Remove from the heat. When cool to the touch, remove bottles, tighten caps, and store at room temperature. Use within 48 hours. At feeding time, remove the cap and teat from one bottle, add the specified quantity of concentrated liquid or powder, replace the cap, and shake well to mix. (Powdered formula will dissolve better in warm water, so you might want to reheat slightly before mixing.)

Ready-to-use-formula methods.
Ready-to-use formula requires no mixing. When it comes in ready-to-use bottles, all you need to do is boil the teats, caps and collars, tongs and teat jar and lid on a wire rack or folded towel in a sterilizer or large covered pot for five minutes. Remove from the heat. When cool, use the tongs to place the teat units in the sterilized jar or in clean plastic bags. Keep them covered until ready to place on bottles of formula. If formula is stored at room temperature, warming is unnecessary. Shake well and use immediately after opening.

Ready-to-use formula that comes in 250-ml or 1 litre (8-fl ounce or 2-pint) tins requires sterilization of bottles with teat units lightly attached. Follow the aseptic method above. When bottles are cooled, tighten collars, and store in a clean place. Add formula when ready to feed, or prepare a full day's supply of bottles, filling them all, and refrigerate. Shake well before using.

Let baby call it quits. If you see only 75 ml (3 fl ounces) have been emptied when the usual meal is 6 ounces, you may be tempted to push more. Don't. A healthy baby knows when to stop. And it's this kind of pushing that leads to bottle-fed babies being much more likely than breastfeds to become too plump.

Take your time. A nursing baby can keep suckling on a breast long after it's been emptied, just for comfort and sucking satisfaction. Your bottle-fed baby can't do the same with an empty bottle, but there are ways you can supply some of the same satisfactions. Extend the pleasure of the feeding session by socializing once the bottle is drained – assuming the little tyke hasn't dropped off into a milk-induced sleep. If your baby seems to want to continue sucking after each feeding, try using teats with smaller holes, which will make it necessary to work harder and longer for the same meal, or offer a bottle of water or a dummy for brief periods. If your baby seems to be fussing for more at meal's end, consider whether you're offering enough formula. Increase it 30 ml or 50 (a fl ounce or two), with the doctor's permission, to see if it's really hunger that's making your baby fretful.

Feel good about bottle feeding. If you were eager to breastfeed and couldn't for some reason, don't feel guilty or frustrated. You can give your baby good nutrition and just as much loving and cuddling with bottle feeding. And your guilt and frustration are feelings you don't want to pass on to your baby.

Bottle Feeding with Ease

If you've had some experience bottle feeding a young infant – either a sibling, a baby-sitting charge, or friend's baby – the correct technique will come back to you virtually the moment you hold your baby in your arms. If not, you need to know a few bottle-feeding basics:

- Let baby know that 'formula's on' by stroking his or her cheek with your finger or the tip of the teat. That will encourage your baby to turn in the direction of the stroke. Then place the teat gently between baby's lips and, hopefully, sucking will begin.

- Tilt the bottle up so that formula always fills the teat completely. If you don't, and air fills part of it, baby will swallow the air and may become windy – which may make both of you miserable. This precaution isn't, however, necessary if you are using disposable bottle liners, which automatically deflate, eliminating air pockets.

- Don't be concerned if your baby doesn't seem to take much formula the first few days. The newborn's need for nutrition is minimal at first – a breastfed baby, on orders from Mother Nature, is now getting only a few teaspoonsful of colostrum at each feeding. The nursery will probably give you full 100-ml (4-fl ounce) bottles, but don't expect them to be drained. A baby who falls asleep after taking just half an ounce or so is probably saying, 'I've had enough'. But a baby who fusses after taking only a small amount, turns his or her head away, or

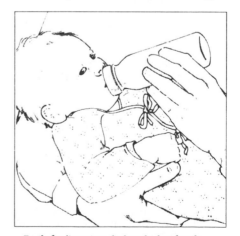

Bottle feeding gives dad and other family members the chance to get close to baby, to use the time for cuddling and interaction; nourishment needn't come from the breast to come with love.

Tips for Successful Feeding Sessions

Feeding a baby in the early weeks isn't an effortless process, no matter what the source of milk. But whether it's a breast or a bottle that will be your newborn's ticket to a full tummy, the guidelines that follow should help make the trip a smoother one:

Minimize the mayhem. You and your baby will both have to concentrate in these early feeding sessions and will fare better with as few distractions as possible. If visitors are banished at feeding times in the hospital, regard the rule a blessing since it will give you the quiet time you need with your baby. If they aren't, consider banishing them yourself. When you get home, try to continue minimizing distractions at baby's mealtimes, at least until you feel comfortable and competent nursing or giving a bottle. Retire to the bedroom to feed baby when you have guests or when the general atmosphere in the living room rivals that of a three-ring circus. Turn off the phone or put on the answering machine at baby's mealtimes; if you have other children, divert their attentions to some quiet activity, or take this opportunity to read them a story.

Make a change. If your baby is relatively calm, you've time for a change. A clean nappy will make for a more comfortable meal and reduce the need for a change right after – a definite plus if your charge has nodded off to dreamland and you'd rather he or she stay there for a while. But don't change during the night if it's not necessary; such a disruption makes falling back to sleep more difficult.

Wash up. Even though you won't be doing the eating, it's your hands that should be washed with soap and water before your baby's meals. If you're breastfeeding, your nipples needn't be washed before each feeding; a once-a-day soapless wash in the shower or tub is sufficient.

Get comfy. Muscular aches and pains are an occupational hazard for new parents who use unaccustomed muscles to carry growing babies around. Feeding baby in an awkward position will only compound the problem. So before putting baby to breast or bottle, be sure you're comfortable, with adequate support for your back and for the arm under baby.

Loosen up. If your baby is tightly swaddled, unwrap him or her so you can cuddle while you feed.

Cool down a screaming baby. A baby who's upset will have trouble getting down to the business of feeding, and even more trouble with the business of digesting. Try a soothing song or a little rocking.

Sound reveille. Some babies are sleepy at mealtimes, and a concerted effort is required to rouse them to the task of nursing at breast or bottle. If your little one is a dinner dozer, try the wake-up techniques on page 59.

Make contact. Cuddle and caress your baby with your hands, your eyes and your voice. Remember, meals shouldn't fill your baby's daily requirements just for nutrients, but for mother love as well.

Break for a burp. Between breasts or half-way through the bottle, routinely burp your baby. Also try burping if baby seems to want to stop eating prematurely – it may be wind, not food, that's filling the little tummy.

lets go of the teat and refuses to take it back again may be in need of a burping. If after a good bubble the teat is still rejected, the meal is probably over.

How much your baby takes at a feeding will increase as his or her weight does, from just a few millilitres/fl ounces up to as many as 250 ml (8 full fl ounces), or a total of approximately 900 ml (32 fl ounces) a day by the time the twelfth week is reached. Don't be concerned if your baby takes a little more or less at each feeding, or each day, as long as weight gain is good.

• Be certain that formula is coming through the teat at the right speed. You can check by giving the bottle, turned upside down, a few quick shakes. If milk pours or spurts out, it's flowing too quickly, if just a drop or two escapes, too slowly. If you get a little spray, and then some drops the flow is just about right. You can also get a clue from observing your baby suck. If your baby seems to work very hard at suckling for a few moments, then seems very frustrated, possibly letting go of the teat to complain, the flow's too slow. If, on the other hand, there's a lot of gulping and sputtering and milk is always leaking out of the corners of the mouth, it's too fast.

The problem could simply be in the way the cap is fastened. A very tight cap inhibits flow by creating a partial vacuum, and loosening it makes milk flow more easily. If adjusting the cap doesn't seem to correct the flow, the problem is probably in the size of the teat opening. If the milk is flowing too quickly, the opening is too big. Boiling the teat for a few minutes may reduce the size of the opening, but if it doesn't, you will have to discard the teat or put it aside until your baby is much older, and substitute a teat with a smaller hole. If the flow is too slow, the opening is too small. You can enlarge it by poking the tip with a nappy pin or wide-diameter needle heated to red hot, or by forcing a round wooden toothpick into the opening and boiling the teat for five minutes. Or make a new hole.

• Make night feedings less of an ordeal by investing in a bedside bottle holder, which keeps baby's bottle chilled until ready to use and then warms it to room temperature in minutes. Or keep a bottle on ice in baby's room, ready to serve cold or to warm under the bathroom tap when baby starts fussing for a feeding.

What You May Be Concerned About

Sleeping through Meals

'The doctor says I should feed my baby every three or four hours, but sometimes I don't hear from him for five or six. Should I wake him up to eat?'

Some babies are perfectly happy to sleep through meals, particularly during the first few days of life. If yours is one of these, try this arousal technique at mealtime: set him in a sitting position on your lap, one hand holding up his chin, the other supporting his back. Now, bend baby forward at the waist. The moment he stirs, assume a nursing position. If he drifts back to sleep before

you have the chance to get things started, repeat the sequence. Also try removing swaddling, or even all clothing except for the nappy (very young babies usually don't like being naked); a nappy change; rubbing the area under baby's chin with your finger; tickling his feet; a burp.

If your baby wakens, takes the nipple, then promptly falls asleep, try jiggling the breast or bottle, stroking his cheek, jostling him, or adjusting his position or yours to get the sucking action going again. You may find that in the course of a feeding period you have to jiggle several times to get a full feeding in – some young babies suckle and doze alternately from the start of the meal to the finish. If you're unsuccessful at restarting sucking, try some of the wake-up techniques above. If nothing works, give up and let sleepyhead dream a bit longer. But don't let him go more than five hours between meals yet.

It's okay to let your baby sleep if he drops off to dreamland after only a brief appetizer and attempts at encouraging him to resume sucking fail; a five-minute meal may be all he wanted this time around. It's not, however, a good idea to let your baby nip and nap at fifteen- to thirty-minute intervals all day long. If that seems to be the trend, go all out in your attempts to waken him as soon as he dozes off mid-meal, and try to get in a full-course meal before you let him succumb to sleep once again.

If chronic sleepiness interferes with eating and threatens your baby's well-being (see page 98 for signs of failure to thrive), consult the doctor immediately.

Not Sleeping after Meals

'I'm afraid my baby is going to turn into a little blimp. Almost immediately after I put her down, she's up again crying for food.'

Your baby may indeed be destined to be plump if you feed her again immediately after she's had an adequate meal. Babies cry for reasons other than hunger, and it may be that you are misreading her. Consider that she may just be having a little difficulty getting into a deep sleep. Allowed to fend for herself for a couple of minutes, she may accomplish this all by herself. Or maybe your baby isn't ready for sleep after all, is crying out for companionship, and would like to be frolicked with, not fed. Try a little socializing. Or maybe she's just having trouble calming down. Help her by rocking her or try some other soothing technique. Consider, also, that your baby's problem may be wind. In that case, more feeding would only compound it. Try eliciting a burp by putting her over your lap or shoulder and gently rubbing her back. (Be sure to burp her at frequent intervals during feedings.)

The problem could also be the way you put her into her cot (see page 118 for tips on how to put a sleeping baby down so she'll stay asleep). Or the problem may just be temporary; she may be going through a growth spurt and need more food.

If you offer your daughter food every time she cries right after eating, even when not particularly hungry, not only will she be likely to blimp out, but she may develop a snack and snooze habit that will be difficult to break later.

Do be sure, however, that your baby is gaining weight at an adequate rate. If she isn't, she may indeed be crying out of hunger – a sign that you may not be producing enough milk. See page 98 to find out what to do if baby doesn't seem to be thriving.

Birthweight

'My friends all seem to be having babies that weigh 3.5 and 4 kg (8 and 9 pounds) at birth. Mine weighed in at a little over 3 kg (6½ pounds) at full term. She seems so small.'

Healthy babies come in all kinds of packages – long and lanky, big and bulky, slight and slender. Though a birthweight of under 2.5 kg (5½ pounds) full term can mean that baby was not well nourished during gestation, or that growth was otherwise interfered with (for unknown and uncontrollable reasons or because the mother drank, smoked, or took drugs), a petite 3-kg baby (6½-pounder) can be as vigorous and sound as a chubby 4-kg baby (9-pounder).

Many factors affect a baby's size, among them:

The mother's diet during pregnancy. Too little food or too little of the right kinds of food can produce a small baby; too much food, an overly large one.

The mother's pregnancy weight gain. A bigger weight gain may yield a bigger baby, but if the weight was gained on junk food, the baby may be tiny and the mother fat.

The mother's antenatal lifestyle. Smoking, drinking and drug abuse can all stunt foetal growth.

The mother's health. Poorly controlled diabetes (even the gestational type) can be responsible for an extra-large baby. Toxaemia (preeclampsia or eclampsia) or a placenta that is inadequate can interfere with foetal growth, with a tiny newborn the result.

The mother's weight before pregnancy. Heavier women tend to have heavier babies; slight women, lighter ones.

The mother's own birthweight. If the mother weighed in at around 3.2 kg (7 pounds), her first baby is likely to, also. If she was very small or very large, her baby will often follow the same pattern.

Genetics Large parents usually have large babies. If the mother is small and the father is large, the baby is more likely to be on the small side – nature's way of trying to decrease the odds of a difficult delivery. If baby is genetically destined to take after the father, rapid growth spurts during the first year and later on will make up for small birth size.

Baby's sex. Boys, on the average, tend to be a little heavier and longer than girls.

Birth order. First babies are often smaller than subsequent ones.

The number of foetuses. Babies of a multiple pregnancy generally weigh less than singletons.

Race. Oriental, black and Indian babies are generally smaller than Caucasian babies (although the size differences between black and white babies may be due more to socioeconomic factors than race; middle-class black babies and middle-class white babies are more evenly matched in weight).

Bonding

'I had an emergency caesarean and they whisked my baby away to the SCBU before I had a chance to bond with her. I worry that this will affect our relationship.'

Bonding at birth is an idea whose time has come – and, by now, should be gone. The theory that a mother-baby relationship will be better when the two spend 16 hours of the first 24 in close loving contact was first suggested in the 1970s. Though recent research has not substantiated it, and even the original propounders of the theory have expressed concern that the concept has been misused, it continues to be popular.

The consequences have been mixed. On the one hand, many hospitals now permit new mothers (and often fathers) to hold their babies moments after birth, to cuddle and nurse them for anywhere from ten minutes to an hour or more, instead of dispatching the newborn off to the nursery the instant the cord is cut. This encounter gives mother and baby a chance to make early contact, skin to skin, eye to eye – certainly a positive change. On the other hand, many mums who've had surgical deliveries or traumatic vaginal births or whose babies arrived in need of special care, and who consequently didn't get to hold their babies immediately after birth, are led to believe that they've missed the chance of a lifetime to foster a close relationship with their offspring. Some become so frantic about the necessity for instant bonding that they demand it even at risk to the health of their infants.

Many experts dispute the idea that parent-child bonding can take place at birth. They believe that the newborn infant is too primitive a creature to bond instantly with anyone; a week or more usually passes before the baby is able to recognize its mother, never mind form a lifelong bond with her. And though the mother isn't too primitive to be capable of initiating an attachment with her baby, there are many reasons why she may not be ready for bonding: exhaustion from a long labour and delivery, grogginess from medication, pain from cramping or an incision, or simply lack of preparation for the experience of holding and caring for a newborn. In addition, there's no solid evidence that a mother-infant attachment has to be firmly established (or even begun) on the first day of life. And there are some who suggest that it doesn't actually take place until somewhere in the second half of the baby's first year.

Bonding at birth may indeed be part of a long process of mother-baby attachment, but it is only the beginning. And this beginning can just as well take place hours after birth in a hospital bed, or through the portholes of an incubator, or even weeks later at home. When your parents were born, they probably saw little of their mothers and even less of their fathers until they went home (usually ten days after birth), and the vast majority of that 'deprived' generation grew up with strong, loving family ties. Mothers who have the chance to bond at birth with one child and not with another usually report no difference in their feelings toward the children. And adoptive parents, who often don't meet their babies until hospital discharge (or even much later), manage to foster strong bonds.

The kind of love that lasts a lifetime can't magically evolve in a few hours, or even a few days. The first moments after birth may become a cherished memory for some, but for others they may turn out to be a disappointment they'd rather forget. Either way, these moments don't indelibly colour the character and quality of your future relationship.

The complicated process of parent-child bonding actually begins for parents during pregnancy, when attitudes and feelings towards the baby start developing. The relationship continues to evolve and change all through infancy, childhood and adolescence, and even into adulthood. So relax. There's lots of time to tie those bonds that bind.

'I've been told that bonding at birth brings mother and baby closer

together. I held my new daughter for nearly an hour right after delivery, but she seemed like a stranger to me then, and still does now three days later.'

Love at first sight is a concept that flourishes in romantic novels and movies, but rarely materializes in real life. The kind of love that lasts a lifetime usually requires time, nurturing, and plenty of patience to develop and deepen. And that's as true for love between a newborn and parents as it is between a man and woman.

Physical closeness between mother and child immediately after birth does not (in spite of what supporters of 'bonding at birth' may tell you) guarantee instant emotional closeness. Those much-touted first postpartum moments aren't automatically bathed in a glow of maternal love. In fact, the first sensation a woman experiences after birth is far more likely to be relief than love – relief that the baby is normal and, especially if her labour was difficult, that the ordeal is over. It's not at all unusual to see that squalling and unsociable infant as a stranger with very little connection to the cozy, idealized baby you carried for nine months – and to feel little more than neutral towards her. One study found that it took an average of over two weeks (and often as long as nine weeks) for mothers to begin having positive feelings towards their newborns.

Just how a woman reacts to her newborn at their first meeting may depend on a variety of factors: the length and intensity of her labour; whether she received medication during labour; her previous experience (or lack of it) with infants; her feelings about having a child; her relationship with her husband; extraneous worries that may preoccupy her; her general health; and probably most important of all, her personality.

Your reaction is normal for *you*. And as long as you feel an increasing sense of comfort and attachment as the days go by, you can relax. Some of the best relationships get off to the slowest starts. Give yourself and your baby a chance to get to know and appreciate each other, and let the love grow unhurriedly.

If you don't feel a growing closeness after a few weeks, however, or if you feel anger or antipathy towards your baby, discuss these feelings with your doctor. It's important to work them out early on, to prevent lasting damage to your relationship.

Rooming-in

'Having the baby room-in with me sounded like heaven before I gave birth. Now it seems more like hell. I can't get the baby to stop crying – yet what kind of mother would I be if I asked the midwife to take her at night?'

You would be a very human mother. You've just completed the Herculean task of giving birth, and are about to undertake an even greater challenge: child rearing. Needing a few days of rest in between is nothing to feel guilty about. Now that 'rooming-in' is the rule, rather than the exception, some new mothers handle it with ease. They may have had deliveries that left them feeling exhilarated instead of exhausted. Or they may have had prior experience caring for newborns, their own or other people's For these women, an inconsolable infant at 3 A.M. may not be a joy, but it's not a nightmare, either. For a woman who's been without sleep for 48 hours, however, whose body has been left limp from an enervating labour, and who's never been closer to a baby than a nappy ad, such predawn bouts can leave her wondering tearfully: Why did I ever decide to become a mother?

Playing the martyr can raise motherly resentments against the baby, feelings the baby will be likely to sense. If, instead, the midwife takes the baby to the nursery between feedings at night, mother and child, both well rested, may find getting acquainted easier when morning comes. And morning is a good time to take advantage of one of the major advantages of rooming-in: the chance to learn how to take care of your new baby in a safe environment with experienced help

there to advise and assist you if necessary. Even though you will have the baby with you all day, you shouldn't feel you can't call upon the midwives for help. That's what they're there for.

When night falls again, try keeping the baby and see how things go; she may surprise you. Or if you're ready for a baby-break, ask a midwife if she can take the baby while you sleep. You are *not* a failure or a bad mother if you don't enjoy, or if you feel too tired for, 24-hour rooming-in.

Be flexible. Focus on the quality of the time you spend with your baby in the hospital rather than the quantity. Round-the-clock rooming-in will begin soon enough at home – with hospitals discharging postpartum patients earlier and earlier, nowadays it could be within 24 to 48 hours. By then, if you don't overdo now, you should be emotionally and physically ready to deal with it.

Baby's not Getting Enough to Eat

'It's been two days since I gave birth to my little girl, and nothing comes out of my breasts when I squeeze them, not even colostrum. I'm worried that she's starving.'

Not only is your baby not starving, she isn't even hungry yet. Babies aren't born with an appetite, or even with immediate nutritional needs. And by the time your baby begins to get hungry for a breast full of milk, usually around the third or fourth postpartum day, you will very likely be able to oblige. (Occasionally, especially in second-time mothers, breast milk comes in earlier. Rarely, it comes in as late as the seventh day. In such a case, the doctor may recommend giving the baby formula after each nursing as a precaution.)

Which isn't to say that your breasts are empty now. Colostrum (which provides your baby with nourishment and with important antibodies her own body can't yet produce, while helping to empty her digestive system of meconium and excess mucus) is almost certainly present, though in very tiny amounts (first feedings average less than a half-teaspoon; by the third day, less than three tablespoons per feeding over ten feedings). But until your breasts begin to swell and feel full, indicating your milk has come in, it's not that easy to express manually – and for some mothers, it isn't easy even then. Even a day-old baby, with no previous experience, is better equipped to extract this premilk than you are.

Baby's Sleepiness

'My new son seemed very alert right after he was born, but ever since he's been sleeping so soundly I can hardly wake him to eat, much less to socialize.'

You've waited nine long months to meet your baby; and now that he's here, all he does is sleep. But he's just doing what comes naturally. Wakefulness for the first hour or so after birth followed by a long stretch, often 24 hours, of very sound sleep is the normal newborn pattern (which probably gives him a chance to recover from the fatiguing work of being born).

Don't expect your newborn to become much more stimulating company immediately upon awakening from this beneficial sleep. In the first weeks, his two- to four-hour-long sleeping periods will end abruptly with crying. He will rouse to a semi-awake state to eat, drifting back to sleep when satiated. He will probably even doze while feeding, and it will take a shake of the nipple in his mouth to get him sucking again. He will finally fall more soundly asleep, managing a few last-ditch nibbles at the nipple as you remove it.

He will be truly alert for only about three minutes of every hour during the day, and less (you hope) at night. That allows a total of about an hour a day for active socializing. He's not mature enough to benefit from longer periods of alertness, and his periods of sleep, particularly of REM for dream state)

sleep, apparently help him to mature. Gradually, his periods of wakefulness will grow longer. By the end of the first month, most babies are alert for about two to three hours every day, most of it in one relatively long stretch, usually in the late afternoon. And some of their naps, instead of being two or three hours long, may last as long as six or six and a half hours.

In the meantime, you may continue to be thwarted in your attempts to get to know your baby. But instead of standing over his cot waiting for him to wake up so you can play with him, use his sleeping time to store up some sleep of your own. You'll need it for the days (and nights) ahead, when he'll probably be awake more than you'd like.

Pain Medication

'I've been having some pretty bad pain from my caesarean incision. My obstetrician has prescribed some pain medication, but I'm afraid to take it because I don't want to drug my little girl with my breast milk.'

You're doing your baby more harm if you don't take needed medication than if you do. The tension and exhaustion that can result from unrelieved post-caesarean pain will only hamper your ability to establish a good nursing relationship with your baby (you need to be relaxed) and a good milk supply (you need to be rested). Besides which, the medication will appear only in very minuscule amounts in your colostrum; by the time your milk supply comes in, you probably won't need narcotic pain relief. And if your baby does receive a small dose of medication, she'll sleep it off easily, with no ill effects.

Baby's Looks

'People ask me whether the baby looks like me or my husband. Neither one of us has a pointy head, puffy eyes, an ear that bends forward, and a

pushed-in nose. When will he start looking better?'

There's a good reason why two- and three-month-old babies are used to portray newborns in movies and television commercials: most newborns are not exactly photogenic. And though parental love is blinder than most, even parents who are head over heels can't help but notice the many imperfections of their newborn's appearance. Fortunately, most of the newborn characteristics that will keep your baby from co-starring in films and selling nappies on TV are temporary.

The features you're describing weren't inherited from some distant pointy-headed, puffy-eyed, flap-eared relative. They were acquired during your baby's stay in the cramped quarters of your uterus, during the stormy passage through your bony pelvis in preparation for birth, and during his final traumatic trip through the narrow confines of your birth canal during delivery.

If it weren't for the miraculous design of a foetus's head – with the skull bones not fully fused, allowing them to be pushed and moulded as the baby makes its descent – there would be many more surgical deliveries. So be thankful for the pointy little head that came with your vaginal delivery, and rest assured that the skull will just as miraculously return to cherubic roundness within a few days or so.

The swelling around your baby's eyes is also due, at least in part, to the beating he took on his fantastic voyage into the world. (Another contributing factor, in babies who have had silver nitrate drops instilled into their eyes, is the irritating effect of this infection-preventing drug.) Some have postulated that this swelling serves as natural protection for newborns, whose eyes are being exposed to light for the first time. The worry that puffy eyes may interfere with a baby's ability to see mummy and daddy, making bonding impossible, is unfounded. Though he can't distinguish one from another, a newborn can make out blurry faces at birth – even through swollen lids.

The bent ear is probably another outcome of the crowding your baby experienced in the uterus. As a foetus grows and becomes more snugly lodged in his mother's cozy amniotic sac, an ear that happens to get pushed forward may stay that way even after birth. But this is only temporary. Taping it back won't help, say the experts, and the tape might cause irritation, but you can speed the return to normal ear positioning by being sure the ear is back against the head when putting baby to sleep on his side. Some ears, of course, are genetically destined to stand out somewhat. Hair will eventually help camouflage this cosmetic problem, and plastic surgery is available for those who wish to eliminate it. (Though it certainly needn't be considered a handicap – remember Clark Gable?)

The pushed-in nose is very likely a result of a tight squeeze during labour and delivery, and should return to normal naturally. But because baby noses are so different from the adult variety (the bridge is broad, almost nonexistent, the shape often nondescript), it may still be a while before you can tell whose nose your baby has.

Eye Colour

'I was hoping my baby would have green eyes like my husband, but her eyes seem to be a dark greyish colour. Is there any chance that they'll turn?'

The favourite guessing game of pregnancy – will it be a boy or a girl? – is replaced by another in the first few months of a baby's life – what colour will her eyes turn out to be?

It's definitely too early to call now. Most Caucasian babies are born with dark blue or slate-coloured eyes; most black and Oriental infants with dark, usually brown, eyes. While the dark eyes of the darker-skinned babies will stay dark, the eye colour of white babies may go through a number of changes (making the betting more lively) before becoming set somewhere between three and six months, or even later. And since pigmentation of the iris may continue increasing during the entire first year, the depth of colour may not be clear until around baby's first birthday.

Gagging and Choking

'When they brought my baby to me this morning, he seemed to gag and choke and then spit up some liquidy stuff. I hadn't nursed him yet, so it couldn't have been spitup. What's wrong?'

Your baby spent the last nine months, more or less, living in a liquid environment. He didn't breathe air, but he sucked in a lot of fluid. Though a nurse or doctor probably suctioned his airways clear at birth, there may have been additional mucus and fluid in his lungs, and this gagging and choking is your baby's way of clearing out what remains. This is a perfectly normal occurrence.

Startling

'I'm worried that there's something wrong with my baby's nervous system. Even when she's sleeping, she'll suddenly seem to jump out of her skin.'

Assuming your baby hasn't been overdoing the black coffee, the jumpiness you notice is due to the very normal startle reflex. Also known as the Moro reflex, it may occur for no obvious reason, more frequently in some babies than in others, but most often in response to a loud noise, jolting, or a feeling of falling – as when a young infant is picked up without adequate support. Typically, the baby stiffens her body, flings her arms up and out symmetrically, spreads her usually tightly clenched fists wide open, draws her knees up, then finally brings her arms, fists clenched once again, back to her body in an embracing gesture – all in a matter of seconds. She also may cry out. The Moro is just another of the many protective reflexes with which babies are born, likely a primitive attempt to regain perceived loss of equilibrium.

While the sight of a startled baby often worries parents, a doctor is more likely to be concerned if a baby doesn't startle. Newborns are routinely tested for this reflex, the presence of which is one reassuring sign that the neurological system is functioning well. You'll find that your baby will gradually startle less frequently, and that the reflex will disappear fully somewhere between four and six months. (Your baby may occasionally startle, of course, at any age, but not with the same pattern of reactions.)

Quivering Chin

'Sometimes, especially when he's been crying, my baby's chin quivers.'

Though your baby's quivering chin may look like another one of his ingenious inborn ploys for playing at your heartstrings, it's actually a sign that his nervous system, like those of his peers, is not fully mature. Give him the sympathy he's craving, and enjoy the quivering chin while it lasts – which won't be for long.

Birthmarks

'The first thing I noticed about my baby after I saw that she was a girl was the raised bright red blotch on her thigh. Will it ever go away?'

Long before your daughter starts petitioning parental powers for her first bikini, that strawberry birthmark – like most birthmarks – will be a part of her childish past, leaving her thigh ready (even if her father isn't) for beach baring. Of course, looking at a newborn's birthmark, this often seems hard to believe. Sometimes the mark grows a bit before fading, or sometimes it doesn't even appear until some time after birth. And when it does begin to shrink or fade, the changes from day to day are often difficult to see. For that reason, many doctors document birthmark changes by photographing and measuring the lesion periodically. If your baby's doctor doesn't, you can do so just for your own reassurance.

Birthmarks come in a variety of shapes, colours and textures and are usually categorized in the following ways:

Strawberry haemangioma. This soft, raised, strawberry red birthmark, as small as a freckle or as large as a coaster, is composed of immature vascular materials that broke away from the circulatory system during foetal development. It may be visible at birth or may seem to appear suddenly during the first few weeks of life, and is so common that 1 out of 10 babies will probably have one. Strawberry birthmarks may grow for a while, but eventually will start to fade to a pearly grey and almost always finally disappear completely, sometime between ages five and ten. Although parents may be tempted to demand treatment for a very obvious strawberry mark, particularly on the face, such birthmarks are best left untreated unless they continue to grow or interfere with a function, such as vision. Treatment apparently can lead to more complications than a more conservative let-it-disappear-on-its-own approach.

If your child's doctor determines treatment is advisable, there are several options. The simplest are compression and massage, both of which seem to hasten involution. More aggressive forms of therapy for strawberry haemangiomas include the administration of steroids, surgery, X-ray or laser therapy, cryotherapy (freezing with dry ice), and injection of hardening agents (such as those used in treating varicose veins). Many experts believe no more than 0.1% of these birthmarks require such radical therapies. When a strawberry, reduced by either treatment or time, leaves a scar or some residual tissue, plastic surgery can usually eliminate it.

Occasionally a strawberry mark may bleed, either spontaneously or because it was scratched or bumped. Applying pressure will stem the flow of blood.

Cavernous haemangioma. This birthmark is less common than the strawberry haemangioma – only 1 or 2 out of every 100 babies

has one. Often combined with the strawberry type, it is composed of larger, more mature vascular elements and involves deeper layers of skin. The usually bluish or bluish red lumpy mass, with less distinct borders than strawberry marks, may appear almost flat initially. It grows rapidly in the first six months, then more slowly in the next six. By twelve to eighteen months, it begins to shrink. Fully 50% are gone by age five, 70% by seven, 90% by nine, and 95% by the time the child is ten or twelve. Most often no blemish remains, but occasionally there is a residual scar. The range of possible treatment modes is similar to that for strawberry birthmarks.

Salmon patch or nevus simplex. These salmon-coloured patches can appear on the forehead, the upper eyelids, and around the nose and mouth, but are most often seen at the nape of the neck. They invariably become lighter during the first two years of life, becoming noticeable only when the child cries or exerts himself. Since more than 95% of the lesions on the face fade completely, these birthmarks cause less concern cosmetically than other birthmarks.

Portwine stain or nevus flammeus. These purplish red birthmarks, which may appear anywhere on the body, are composed of dilated mature capillaries. They are normally present at birth as flat or barely elevated pink or reddish purple lesions. Though they may change colour slightly, they don't fade appreciably over time and can be considered permanent. Treatment with pulse-dyed laser, any time from infancy to adulthood, can improve appearance. Water-resistant cosmetic creams can be used to cover them, and at about age twelve, laser treatment may be effective in removing them. Rarely, these lesions are associated with an overgrowth of the underlying soft tissue or bone, or when on the face, with abnormalities of brain development. Ask your baby's doctor if you have any concerns.

Café au lait spots. These flat patches on the skin, which can range in colour from tan (coffee with a lot of milk) to light brown (coffee with a touch of milk), can turn up anywhere on the body. They are quite common, apparent either at birth or during the first few years of life, and don't disappear. If your child has a large number of café au lait spots (six or more), point this out to his or her doctor.

Mongolian spots. Blue to slate grey, resembling bruises, Mongolian spots may turn up on the buttocks or back, and sometimes the legs and shoulders, of 9 out of 10 children of black, Oriental, or Indian descent. These ill-defined patches are also fairly common in infants of Mediterranean ancestry, but are rare in blond-haired, blue-eyed infants. Though most often present at birth and gone within the first year, occasionally they don't appear until later and/or persist into adulthood.

Congenital pigmented nevi. These moles vary in colour from light brown to blackish and may be hairy. Small ones are very common; larger ones, 'giant pigmented nevi', are rare, but carry a greater potential for becoming malignant. It is usually recommended that large moles, and suspicious smaller ones, be removed if removal can be accomplished easily, and that those not removed be followed carefully by a doctor familiar with their treatment.

Complexion Problems

'My baby seems to have little white pimples all over his face. Will scrubbing help to clear them?'

The mother expecting peaches-and-cream smoothness may be dismayed to find a sprinkling of tiny whiteheads across her newborn's face, particularly around the nose and chin, an occasional one or two on the trunk or extremities, or even on the penis. The best treatment for these milia, which are caused by clogging of the newborn's immature oil glands, is no treatment at all. As tempting as it may be to squeeze or scrub them, don't. They'll disappear spontaneously, usually within a few weeks.

'I'm worried about the red blotches with light centres on my baby's face.'

Rare is the baby who escapes the neonatal period with skin unscathed. The newborn complexion woe that caught your baby is also one of the most common: toxic erythema. Despite its ominous-sounding name and alarming appearance – blotchy, irregularly shaped, reddened areas with pale centres – toxic erythema is completely benign and short lived. It looks like a collection of insect bites and will disappear without treatment.

Mouth Cysts or Spots

'When my baby had her mouth wide open screaming, I noticed a few little white bumps on her gums. Could she be getting teeth?'

Don't alert the media (or the grandparents) yet. While a very occasional baby will sprout a couple of bottom centre incisors six months or so before schedule, little white bumps on the gum are much more likely to be tiny fluid-filled papules, or cysts. These cysts are common in newborns and will soon disappear, leaving gums clear in plenty of time for that first toothless grin.

Some babies may also have yellowish white spots on the roof of their mouths at birth. Like the cysts, they are neither uncommon nor of any medical significance in newborns. Dubbed 'Epstein's pearls', these spots will disappear without treatment.

Early Teeth

'I was shocked to find my baby was born with two front teeth. The doctor says she'll have to have them pulled, which is very upsetting to my husband and me.'

Every once in a while, a newborn arrives on the scene with a tooth or two. If these teeth are not well anchored in the gums, they may have to be removed to avoid baby choking on or swallowing them. Early teeth may be preteeth, or extra teeth, which, after they've been removed, will be replaced by primary teeth at the usual time. But more often they are primary teeth, and if they must be extracted, temporary dentures may be needed to stand in for them until their secondary successors come in.

Thrush

'My baby seems to have a white curd in her mouth. I thought it was spitup milk, but when I tried to brush it away, her mouth started to bleed.'

There's a fungus among you – or, more accurately, between you. Though the fungus infection known as thrush is causing problems in your baby's mouth, it probably started its dirty work in your birth canal as a monilial infection – and that's where your baby picked it up. The causative organism is *Candida albicans*, which is a normal inhabitant of the mouth and vagina. Kept in check by other microorganisms, it usually causes no problem. But should this arrangement be upset – by illness, the use of antibiotics, or hormonal changes (such as in pregnancy) – conditions become favourable for the fungus to grow and cause symptoms of infection.

Thrush appears in elevated white patches that look like cottage cheese or milk curds on the insides of a baby's cheeks, and sometimes on the tongue, roof of the mouth, and gums. If the patches are wiped away, a raw red area is exposed, and there may be bleeding. Thrush is most common in newborns, but occasionally an older baby, particularly one taking antibiotics, will become infected. Call the doctor if you suspect thrush.

Though the yeast infection itself is not dangerous, it is painful and can interfere with baby's feeding. Rarely there may be complications if the condition goes untreated by anti-fungal agents.

Weight Loss

'I expected my baby to lose some weight in the hospital, but she dropped from 3.4 kg (7½ pounds) to 3.1 kg (6 pounds 14 ounces). Isn't that excessive?'

New mothers, eager to start issuing reports on their baby's progress in the weight-gain department, are often disappointed when their babies check out of the hospital weighing considerably less than when they checked in. But nearly all newborns are destined to lose some of their birth weight (usually between 5% and 10%) in the first five days of life – not as a result of fad dieting in the nursery, but because of normal post-delivery fluid loss, which is not immediately recouped since babies need and take in little food during this time. Breastfed babies, who take in only teaspoons at a time of the premilk colostrum, generally lose more than bottle-fed babies. Most newborns have stopped losing by the fifth day and have regained or surpassed their birth weight by ten to fourteen days of age – when you can start issuing those bulletins.

Jaundice

'The doctor says my baby is jaundiced and has to spend more time under the bili-lights before she can go home. She says it isn't serious, but anything that keeps a baby in the hospital sounds serious to me.'

Walk into any newborn nursery, and you'll see that more than half the babies have begun to yellow by their second or third days – not with age, but with newborn jaundice. The yellowing, which starts at the head and works its way down to the toes,[3] tinting even the whites of the eyes, comes from an excess of bilirubin in the blood. Bilirubin, the yellow end product of the normal breakdown of oxygen-carrying red

---

3. The process is the same in black- and brown-skinned babies, but the yellowing is visible only in the palms of the hands, the soles of the feet, and the whites of the eyes.

blood cells, is usually removed from the bloodstream and processed by the liver, then passed along to the kidneys for elimination. But newborns often produce more bilirubin than their immature livers can handle. As a result, the bilirubin builds up in the blood, causing the yellowish tinge and what is known as normal, or physiologic, newborn jaundice (or icterus).

In physiologic jaundice, yellowing usually begins on the second or third day of life and starts diminishing when the baby is a week or ten days old. It appears a bit later (about the third or fourth day) and lasts longer (often fourteen days or more) in premature babies because of their extremely immature livers. Jaundice is more likely to occur in boys, or in babies who lose a lot of weight right after delivery, in babies who have diabetic mothers, and in babies who arrived via induced labour.

Sometimes a doctor will keep a baby with physiologic jaundice in the hospital a few extra days for observation and treatment. In most cases, the bilirubin levels (determined through blood tests) will gradually diminish, and the baby will go home with a clean bill of health. Rarely, there will be a rapid increase in bilirubin, suggesting that the jaundice may be abnormal, or pathologic.

Pathologic jaundice is extremely uncommon. It usually begins either earlier or later than physiologic jaundice, and levels of bilirubin are higher. When it is present at birth or develops rapidly during the first day of life, it may indicate haemolytic disease, caused by blood group incompatibility (as when the baby has a different Rh factor from the mother). Jaundice that doesn't develop until later (usually between one and two weeks after birth) could indicate obstructive jaundice, in which an obstruction in the liver interferes with the processing of bilirubin. Pathologic jaundice can also be caused by other, often hereditary, blood or liver diseases and by a variety of intrauterine and neonatal infections. Treatment to bring down abnormally high levels of bilirubin is important to prevent a buildup of the substance in the brain, a condition known as kernicterus. Signs of kernicterus are weak crying, sluggish reflexes, and poor sucking in a jaundiced infant; untreated, it can lead to permanent brain damage or even death.

Mild physiologic jaundice usually requires no treatment. More severe cases can be treated effectively with phototherapy under an ultraviolet lamp, often called a bili-light. During the treatment, babies are naked and their eyes are covered to protect them from the light's rays. They are also given extra fluids to compensate for the increased water loss through the skin, and may be restricted to the nursery except for feedings. New units, using a fibre-optic pad wrapped around baby's middle, allow more flexibility, sometimes permitting baby to go home with mum.

The treatment of pathologic jaundice will depend on the cause, but may include phototherapy, exchange blood transfusions, or surgery to remove obstructions. New drug therapy with a substance that inhibits bilirubin production, may also be used.

In an older baby or child, jaundice, or yellowing, can indicate anaemia, hepatitis, or some other infection or liver malfunction, and should be reported to the doctor as soon as possible.

'I've heard that breastfeeding causes jaundice. My baby is a little jaundiced – should I stop nursing?'

Blood bilirubin levels are, on the average, higher in breastfed babies than in bottle-fed infants and they may stay elevated longer (as long as six weeks). This is believed to be just an exaggerated form of physiologic jaundice and not medically significant. Continuation of breastfeeding is usually recommended, since interrupting it and/or giving glucose water feedings seems to increase rather than decrease bilirubin levels and can also interfere with the establishment of lactation. It's been suggested that breastfeeding in the first hour after birth can reduce bilirubin levels in nursing infants.

True breast-milk jaundice is suspected when levels of bilirubin rise rapidly *late* in the first week of life and other causes of pathologic jaundice have been ruled out. It's believed to be caused by a substance in the breast milk of some women that interferes with the breakdown of bilirubin and is estimated to occur in about 2 out of every 100 breastfed babies. The diagnosis is confirmed by a dramatic drop in bilirubin levels when formula is substituted for breast milk for approximately 36 hours (during which time mum continues to empty her breasts by expressing the milk at feeding times to keep up her milk supply). When breastfeeding is resumed, bilirubin levels usually rise again, but not to previous highs. The condition usually clears up within a few weeks.

Dummy Use

'In the hospital, many mothers stick a dummy in their babies' mouths every time they cry. I've always hated seeing older kids with dummies, and I'm afraid that will happen to my daughter if she gets started on one now.'

Being quieted with a dummy during her two or three days of life will not get her hooked on them. There are, however, some sound reasons why you might prefer that she not be given a dummy right now:

- If you're nursing, it might cause nipple confusion (sucking on the artificial teat requires a different motion than suckling at the breast) and interfere with the establishment of breastfeeding.

- Whether you're breast or bottle feeding, your baby may get sufficient sucking satisfaction from the dummy and refuse to suckle at feeding times.

- Your newborn is better off having her needs attended to when she cries than having a dummy plugged in.

If you decide you'd rather not give your baby a dummy, tell the night staff at the hospital as well. If she's crying and there's no one available to comfort her in the nursery, ask them to bring her to you for a little tender loving care, and perhaps a feeding, which should satisfy sucking needs. Or keep her

with you at night. If your baby seems to need more sucking once you're at home, and you're considering dummy use, see page 115.

Stool Colour

'When I changed my baby's nappy for the first time, I was shocked to see that his stools were greenish black.'

This is only the first of many shocking discoveries you will make in your baby's nappies during the next year or so. And for the most part, what you will be discovering, though occasionally unsettling to the sensibilities, will be completely normal. What you've turned up this time is meconium, the tarry greenish-black substance that gradually filled your baby's intestines during his stay in your uterus. That the meconium is now in his nappy instead of his intestines is a good sign – now you know that his bowels are unobstructed.

Sometime after the first 24 hours, when all the meconium has been passed, you will see transitional stools,[4] which are dark greenish yellow and loose, sometimes 'seedy' in texture (particularly among breastfed infants), and may occasionally contain mucus. There may even be traces of blood in them, probably the result of a baby's swallowing some of his mother's blood during delivery (save any nappy containing blood to show to the midwife or doctor, just to be sure no problem is indicated).

After three or four days of transitional stools, what your baby starts putting out will depend on what you've been putting into him. If it's breast milk, the movements will be golden yellow (like mustard), sometimes loose, even watery, sometimes seedy, mushy, curdly, or the consistency of mustard. If it's formula, the stool will be soft but better formed than a breastfed baby's

---

4. If all meconium in the bowels is passed before a baby is born, as may happen when the foetus is in distress during labour and delivery, the first stools after birth may be transitional.

and anywhere from pale yellow to yellowish brown, light brown, or brown-green. If the formula is iron-fortified, especially if it is whey rather than casein based, or if baby is taking vitamin drops with iron, the stool may be green, greenish, dark brown, or black.

Whatever you do, don't compare your baby's nappies to those of the baby in the next bassinet. Like fingerprints, no two stools are exactly alike. And unlike fingerprints, they are different not only from baby to baby, but from day to day (even movement to movement) in any one baby. The changes, as you will see when baby moves on to solids, will become more pronounced as his diet becomes more varied.

Eye Discharge

'There's a crusty yellowish discharge on my baby's eyes. Is this an infection?'

This discharge isn't likely to be an infection, but rather the result of the hospital's efforts to prevent a gonococcal infection in your baby's eyes. Once the major cause of blindness, it has been virtually eliminated by this prophylactic treatment. When silver nitrate drops are instilled into a newborn's eyes at birth, however (as they routinely are in many delivery rooms), a chemical conjunctivitis, characterized by swelling and a yellowish discharge that disappears by the fourth or fifth day, develops in about 1 in 5 newborns. Many hospitals now prefer to use antibiotic ointment or drops, which are less likely to trigger an adverse reaction (or to cause a temporary grey stain on the cheek from the drops dripping, another disadvantage of silver nitrate) and can prevent not only gonococcal infection but neonatal chlamydial conjunctivitis as well.

If the swelling and discharge don't clear up, or if they begin any time after the first 24 hours following the administration of the silver nitrate, they may be caused by an infection. So report the symptoms immediately to a midwife or to your baby's doctor. Tearing, swelling, or infection that begins once you are home from the hospital may also be caused by a blocked tear duct (see page 107).

WHAT IT'S IMPORTANT TO KNOW:
The Baby Care Primer

Put the nappy on backwards? Take five minutes to get baby in a productive position for a burp? Forget to wash under the arms at bathtime? Don't worry. Babies are not only forgiving – they usually don't even notice. Nevertheless, every new parent wants to do everything, or at least as much as possible, right. This Baby Care Primer will help guide you to that goal. But remember, these are only suggested ways to care for baby. You may come up with some of your own that are even better.

Bathing Baby

Until a baby starts getting down and dirty on all fours, a daily bath isn't a necessity. As long as adequate spot cleaning is done during nappy changes and after feedings, a bath two or three times a week in the precrawling months will keep baby sweet smelling and presentable. Such a light bathing schedule can be particularly welcome in the early weeks when the ritual is often dreaded by both bather and bathee. Babies who don't soon become fond of the bath can continue to be bathed two or three times a week, even when dirt begins to accumulate. Daily spongings, in such critical places as face, neck, hands and bottom, can stand in between dunks (see page 244 for tips on reducing fear of the bath). For those babies, however, who find it a treat, a daily bath becomes an indispensable ritual.

Just about any time of the day can be the right time for a bath, though bathing just before bedtime will help induce a more relaxed state conducive to sleep. Avoid baths just after or just before a meal, since so much handling on a full tummy could result in spitting up, and baby may not be cooperative on an empty one. Allot plenty of undivided time for the bath, so it needn't be hurried and you won't be tempted to leave baby unattended even for a second to take care of something else. Turn on the telephone answering machine, if you have one, or simply plan on not answering the phone during the bath.

While you are using a portable tub, any room in the house can accommodate the procedure, though with all the splashing and dripping, the kitchen or bathroom provides the most suitable setting. Your work surface should be at a level that's easy for you to manoeuvre at, and roomy enough for all the paraphernalia it must hold. For baby's comfort, especially in the early months, turn off fans and air conditioners until the bath is over, and be sure the room you choose is warm (23.9° to 26.7°C/75° to 80°F, if possible) and draught free. If you have a hard time achieving such a temperature range, try warming the bathroom first with shower steam or invest in a safe space heater.

The sponge bath. Until the umbilical cord and circumcision, if any, are healed (a couple of weeks, more or less) tub baths will be taboo, and a flannel will be your baby's only route to clean. For a thorough sponge bath, follow these steps:

1. Select a bath site. The changing table, a kitchen work surface, your bed, or the baby's cot (if the mattress is high enough) are all suitable locations for a sponge bath; simply cover your bed or the cot with a waterproof pad or the work surface with a thick towel or pad.

2. Have all of the following ready *before* undressing baby:

- baby soap and shampoo, if you use it
- two flannels (one will do if you use your hand for soaping)
- sterile cotton wool for cleaning the eyes
- towel, preferably with a hood
- clean nappy and clothing
- ointment for nappy rash, if needed
- rubbing alcohol and cotton wool or alcohol pads for the umbilical cord
- warm water, if you won't be within reach of the sink

3. Get baby ready. If the room is warm,

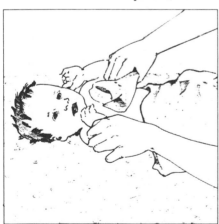

Covering baby's bottom while you wash baby's top keeps baby warm and comfortable while you work; and it protects you, particularly if baby is a boy, from a sudden spurt.

The nappy area will require the most concentrated cleaning effort, and should be saved for last so any germs harboured in the region won't be spread to other parts of the body.

you can remove all of baby's clothing before beginning, covering him or her loosely with a towel while you work (most babies dislike being totally bare); if it's cool, undress each part of the body as you're ready to wash it. No matter what the room temperature, don't take off baby's nappy until it's time to wash the bottom; a naked baby should always be considered armed and dangerous.

4. Begin washing, starting with the cleanest areas of the body and working toward the dirtiest, so that the flannel and the water you're using will stay clean. Soap with your hands or a flannel, but use a clean cloth for rinsing. This order of business usually works well:

- Head. Once or twice a week, use soap or baby shampoo, rinsing very thoroughly. On interim days, use just water. A side hold (see illustration, page 50) at the sink's edge can be the easiest and most comfortable way to rinse baby's head. Towel-dry baby's hair (for most babies this takes just a few seconds) before proceeding.

- Face. First, using a sterile cotton wool ball moistened in warm water, clean baby's eyes wiping gently from the nose outwards. Use a fresh ball for each eye. No soap is needed for the face. Wipe around the outer ears, but not inside. Dry all parts of the face.

- Neck and chest. Soap is not necessary, unless baby is very sweaty or dirty. Be sure to get into those abundant creases. Dry.

- Arms. Extend the arms to get into the elbow creases, and press the palms to open the fist. The hands will need a bit of soap, but be sure to rinse them well before they are back in baby's mouth. Dry.

- Back. Turn baby over on the tummy with head to one side, and wash back, being sure not to miss those neck folds. Since this isn't a dirty area, soap probably won't be necessary. Dry, and dress the upper body before continuing if the room is chilly.

- Legs. Extend the legs to get the back of the knees, though baby will probably resist being unfurled. Dry.

- Nappy area. Follow special directions for care of the circumcised penis and the umbilical stump (pages 86 and 105) until healing is complete, and instructions for care of the uncircumcised penis on page 84. Wash girls front to back, spreading the labia and cleaning with soap and water. White vaginal discharge is normal; don't try to scrub it away. Use a fresh section of the flannel and clean water or fresh water poured from a cup to rinse the vagina. Wash boys carefully, getting into all the creases and crevices with soap and water, but don't try to retract the foreskin. Dry the nappy area well, and apply ointment if needed.

5. Change nappy and dress baby.

The baby-tub bath. A baby is ready for a tub bath as soon as both umbilical cord stump and circumcision, if any, are healed. If baby doesn't seem to like being in the water, go back to sponge baths for a few days and try again. Be sure the water temperature is comfortable and that baby is held firmly to combat any innate fear of falling.

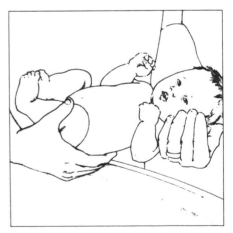

Most babies are very tentative, even tearful, the first few times they're in a tub. So go out of your way to offer support – with reassuring words and a strong, steady grip.

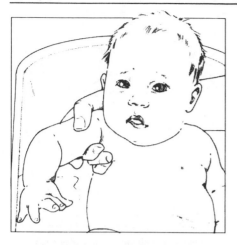

If the tub doesn't offer adequate support for your baby's slippery body and floppy head, you'll need to do so. Gently but firmly does it.

Until baby's neck gains more control over the head, you'll have to hold it steady with one hand while you use your other hand to wash the back.

1. Select a site for the portable baby tub. The kitchen or bathroom sink or work-surface or the big tub (though the man-oeuvring involved when bathing a tiny baby while bending and stretching over a tub can be tricky) are all good candidates. Be sure you will be comfortable and have plenty of room for the tub and bath paraphernalia. The first couple of times you give a tub bath, you might want to omit the soap – soapy babies are slippery babies.

2. Have all of the following ready *before* undressing baby and filling the tub:

- tub, basin, or sink, scrubbed and ready to fill[5]

- baby soap and shampoo, if you use it

- two flannels (one will do if you use your hand for soaping)

- sterile cotton wool for cleaning the eyes

- towel, preferably with a hood

- clean nappy and clothing

- ointment for nappy rash, if needed

---

5. If you use a sponge pad at the bottom of the tub, be sure to dry it between uses in the sun or in your dryer. Check with the manufacturer for the proper temperature. Towels spread on the bottom of the tub should be washed and dried between baths.

- as a nice addition, a bath apron of terry cloth with a plastic lining to keep you dry.

3. Run 5 cm (2 inches) of water into the baby tub; test with your elbow to be sure it's comfortably warm. Never run the water with baby in the tub because a sudden tem-perature change might occur. Don't add baby soap or bubble bath to the water, as these can be drying to baby's skin.

4. Undress baby completely.

5. Slip baby gradually into the bath, talking in soothing and reassuring tones to minimize fear, and holding on securely to prevent a startle reflex. Support the neck and head with one hand unless the tub has built-in support, or if your baby seems to prefer your arms to the tub's support, until good head control develops. Hold baby securely in a semi-reclining position – slipping under suddenly could provide a bad scare.

6. With your free hand, wash baby, working from the cleanest to the dirtiest areas. First, using a sterile cotton wool ball moistened in warm water, clean baby's eyes, wiping gently from the nose outwards. Use a fresh ball for each eye. Then wash face, outer ears and neck. Though soap won't usually be necessary elsewhere every day (unless your baby tends to have all-over

'accidents'), do use it on hands and the nappy area daily. Use it every couple of days on arms, neck, legs and abdomen as long as baby's skin doesn't seem dry – less often if it does. Apply soap with your hand or with a flannel. When you've taken care of baby's front parts, turn him or her over your arm to wash back and buttocks.

7. Rinse baby thoroughly with a fresh washcloth.

8. Once or twice a week, wash baby's scalp using mild baby soap or baby shampoo. Rinse very thoroughly and towel dry.

9. Wrap baby in a towel, pat dry, and dress.

Burping Baby

Milk isn't all baby swallows when sucking on a nipple. Along with that nutritive fluid comes nonnutritive air, which can make a baby feel uncomfortably full before he or she's finished a meal. That's why burping baby to bring up any excess air that's accumulated – every 50 ml or so (couple of fl ounces) when bottle feeding, and every five minutes or so (or at least between breasts) when breast-feeding – is such an important part of the feeding process. There are three ways this is commonly done – on your

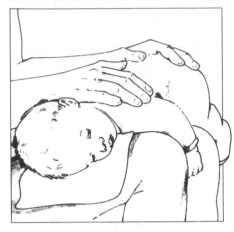

The lap-burp position has the added benefit of being soothing to some colicky infants.

shoulder, face-down on your lap, or sitting up – and it's a good idea to try them all to see which works most efficiently for both you and baby. Though a gentle pat or rub may get the burp up for most babies, some need a slightly firmer hand.

On your shoulder. Hold baby firmly against your shoulder, firmly supporting the buttocks with one hand and patting or rubbing the back with the other.

Face-down on your lap. Turn baby face-down on your lap, stomach over one leg, head resting on the other. Holding him or

An over-the-shoulder burp yields best results for many babies, but don't forget to protect your clothes.

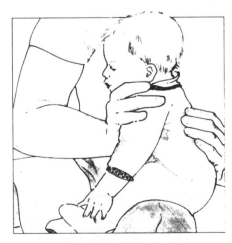

Even a newborn can sit up for a burp – but be sure the head gets adequate support.

her securely with one hand, pat or rub with the other.

Sitting up. Sit baby on your lap, head leaning forward, chest supported by your arm as you hold him or her under the armpit. Pat or rub, being sure not to let baby's head flop backwards.

Changing Nappies

Especially in the early months, the time for a change can come all too often – sometimes hourly during baby's waking hours. But as tedious a chore as it can be for both baby and you, frequent changing (taking place, at the very least, before or after every feeding and whenever there's a bowel movement) is the best way to avoid irritation and nappy rash on baby's sensitive bottom. If you're using disposables, you won't be able to use wetness as a gauge; since they absorb so well, disposables don't feel wet until they're seriously saturated. You needn't wake a sleeping baby to change a nappy, however, and unless baby's very wet and uncomfortable or has had a bowel movement, you don't need to change nappies at nighttime feedings; the activity and light involved can interfere with baby's getting back to sleep.

To ensure a change for the better whenever you change your baby's nappy.

1. Before you begin to change a nappy, be sure everything you need is at hand, either on the changing table or, if you're away from home, in your nappy bag. Otherwise, you could end up removing a messy nappy only to find out you have nothing to clean the mess with. You will need all or some of the following:

- a clean nappy

- cotton wool and warm water for babies under one month (or those with nappy rash) and a small towel or dry flannel for drying; wipes for older babies

- a change of clothes if the nappy has leaked (it happens with the best of them); clean nappy wraps or waterproof pants if you're using terry nappies

- ointment, if needed, for nappy rash; lotions and powders are unnecessary, and the latter can be dangerous and can also interfere with the sticking power of the tabs on disposables

- cornflour, if needed, to keep baby drier, particularly in hot weather

2. Wash and dry your hands before you begin, if possible, or give them a once-over with a wipe.

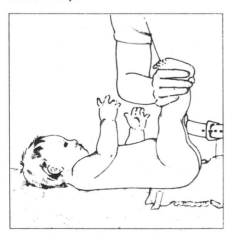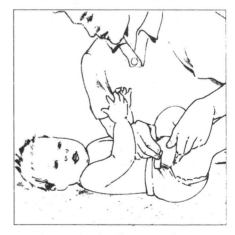

Disposables make quick work of changing as long as you avoid placing baby's bottom on the adhesive tabs. Once baby is in place, simply bring the front of the nappy through baby's legs and fasten, making sure the tabs are pressed down securely.

Safe Seating

New parents taking their babies out for the first time are always careful to bundle them up (often over-bundling them) against the elements, fearful of the consequences of a sudden gust of wind or sprinkle of rain. Yet millions of these same parents fail to protect their offspring where it counts – in the car. Though brief exposure to adverse weather conditions will usually have no ill effect on a newborn, riding unprotected by a safety seat or riding in a safety seat that is improperly anchored can. It is not disease that parents should fear most, but car accidents – which kill and maim more children yearly than all of the major childhood illnesses combined.

So for that first ride home from the hospital, be sure an infant safety seat is *properly* installed in your car, and baby properly secured in it whenever the car is in motion. Even if your home is literally minutes from the hospital, use the seat (most accidents occur within 25 miles of home and not, as is often believed, on motorways). Don't rely on the fact that you will be driving slowly (a crash at 30 miles per hour creates as much force as a fall from a third-storey window). Nor should you rely on your arms to secure your baby, even if you're using a seatbelt (in a crash, your baby would be whipped from your arms and could also be crushed by your body). And remember, too, that you needn't actually crash for severe injury to result – many injuries occur when a car stops short or swerves to avoid an accident.

Getting your baby used to a safety seat from the very first ride will make later acceptance of it almost automatic. And children who ride in safety restraints regularly are not only safer but better behaved during drives – something you'll appreciate when you're riding with an active toddler.

In addition to buying a seat that meets EC safety standards, be sure that you install and use it correctly:

- Follow manufacturer's directions for installation of the seat and securing of your baby. Check before each ride that the seat is properly secured and the belts or tethers holding it are snugly fastened. Use locking clips, available with most seats, to secure lap/shoulder belts that don't stay tight.

- Infants should ride in a rear-facing car seat (at a 45° angle) until they weigh at least 9kg (20 pounds) or are one year old. Over 9kg, they can ride face forward; over 13.5kg (30 pounds), they can ride in a booster designed for car use.

- When possible, the infant should ride in the middle of the back seat, the safest spot in the car; if the driver is alone with the baby, it's okay to relocate the child to the centre of the front seat for better observation and communication. (Note: it is dangerous to move a baby in a rear-facing seat to the front if there is an airbag.) Whenever possible, avoid placing a child seat at either side of the car because these positions are most vulnerable to side impact and because the seat belts on the sides can be difficult to use with a child safety seat.

- Be sure that large or heavy objects, such as suitcases, are firmly secured so that they can't become hazardous flying objects during a short stop or crash.

- Adjust the shoulder harness on the car seat, if it's adjustable, to fit your baby. Be sure all straps fit snugly, and do not use a shield, if any, without the harness straps. For very young babies, pad the sides of the car seat and the area around the head and neck with a rolled blanket or towel to provide support (special cushioned inserts are available for this purpose). If the seat is very deep, placing a rolled towel between baby and the crotch strap will also make baby more comfortable.

- For older babies, attach soft toys to the seat with plastic links or very short cords – loose toys tend to be flung around the car or dropped, upsetting baby and distracting the driver. Or use toys designed specifically for baby car seat use.

3. Have baby entertainment available – live or otherwise. Live shows can be provided by the nappy changer or by siblings, parents, or friends on hand. Other entertainment can come from a mobile hanging over the changing table, a stuffed toy or two in baby's range of vision (and later, within reach), a music box, a mechanical toy – whatever will hold your baby's interest long enough for you to take off one nappy and put on another. But don't use such items as powder or lotion containers, since an older baby may grab and mouth them.

4. Spread a protective terry nappy or a changing cloth if you are changing baby anywhere but on a changing table. Wherever you make the change, be careful not to leave baby unattended, not even for a moment. Even strapped to a changing table, your baby shouldn't be out of arm's reach.

5. Unfasten the nappy (pins on terry nappies, tabs on paper ones), but don't remove it yet. First survey the scene. If there's a bowel movement, use the nappy to wipe most of it away, keeping the nappy over the penis as you work if your baby is a boy. Now fold the nappy under baby with the unsoiled side up to act as a protective surface, and clean baby's front thoroughly with warm water or a wipe, being sure to get into all the creases; then lift both legs, clean the buttocks, and slip the soiled nappy out and a fresh nappy under before releasing the legs. (Keep a fresh nappy over a penis for as much of this process as possible, in self defence.) Pat baby dry if you used water. If you note any irritation or rash, see page 174 for treatment tips.[6]

6. If you're using terry nappies, they're probably prefolded and ready to use. But you may have to fold them further until your baby is a bit bigger. The extra fabric should be in the front for boys and the back for girls. To avoid sticking baby when using pins, hold your fingers under the layers of nappy as you insert the pin. Sticking the pins

in a bar of soap while you're making the change will make them slip more smoothly through the fabric. Once a pin becomes dull, discard it.

If you're using disposables, follow the manufacturer's directions (they vary a bit from one brand to another) in order to get the best coverage and protection. Be careful not to let the tape stick on baby's skin.

Nappies and protective pants should fit snugly to minimize leaks, but not so snugly that they rub or irritate baby's delicate skin. Tell-tale marks will warn you that the nappy is too tight.

Wetness will be less likely to creep up to drench vest and clothing on boys if the penis is aimed downwards as the nappy is put on. If the umbilical cord is still on, fold the nappy down to expose the raw area to air and keep it from getting wet.

7. Dispose of nappies in a sanitary fashion. When possible, drop any formed stool (there probably won't be any in the nappies of breastfed babies until solids are introduced) into the toilet. Used disposables can be folded over, tightly retaped, and tied in a plastic bag for disposal in a dustbin. (Using one plastic bag for disposing of an entire day's nappies is sounder ecologically.) Used terry nappies should be kept in a tightly covered nappy pail until pickup or wash day. If you are out, they can be held in a plastic bag until you get home.

8. Change baby's clothing and/or bed linen as needed.

9. Wash your hands with soap and water, when possible, or clean them thoroughly with a wipe.

Dressing Baby

With floppy arms, stubbornly curled-up legs, a head that invariably seems larger than the openings provided by most baby clothes, and an active dislike for being naked, an infant can be a struggle to dress and undress. But there are ways of making these chores less onerous for both of you:

---

6. Baby boys often get erections during changes; this is perfectly normal, and not a sign that they're being over-stimulated.

1. Select clothes with easy-on, easy-off features in mind. Wide neck openings or necks with snap closings are best. Sleeves should be fairly loose and a minimum of fastening (particularly up the back) should be necessary. Clothes made of stretch or knit fabrics are often easier to put on than garments with less give.

2. Make changes only when necessary. If you find the odour from frequent spitups offensive, sponge the spots lightly with a wipe rather than changing outfits every time baby has a productive burp. Or try guarding against such incidents by putting a large bib on baby during and after feedings.

3. Dress baby on a flat surface, such as a changing table, bed, or crib mattress. And have some entertainment available.

4. Consider dressing time a social time, too. Light, cheerful conversation can help distract baby from the discomforts and indignities of being dressed and make cooperation more likely. Making a learning game out of pulling on clothes will team distraction with stimulation.

5. Stretch neck openings with your hands before attempting to get baby into a garment. Ease, rather than tug, them on and off, keeping the opening as wide as possible in the process, and trying to avoid snagging the ears or nose. Turn the split second during which baby's head is covered, which might

otherwise be scary or uncomfortable, into a game of peekaboo ('Where is mummy? Here she is!' and then, as baby gets old enough to realize that he or she is equally invisible to you, 'Where is Janey? Here she is!').

6. With sleeves, try to reach into them and pull baby's hands through, rather than trying to shove rubbery little arms into limp cylinders of cloth. A game here, too ('Where is baby's hand? Here it is!'), will help distract and educate when baby's hands temporarily disappear.

7. When pulling a zip up or down, draw the garment away from baby's body to avoid pinching the skin.

Ear Care

The old adage 'Never put anything smaller than your elbow in your ears' is advocated not only by grandmothers, but by modern medical authorities as well. They agree that putting anything in the ear that fits – whether it's a coin inserted by a mischievous toddler or a cotton swab inserted by a well-meaning adult – is dangerous. Do wipe your baby's outer ears with a flannel or cotton wool ball, but don't try to venture into the ear canal itself with swabs, fingers, or anything else. The ear is naturally self-cleaning, and trying to remove wax by probing may only force it further into the ear. If wax seems to be accumulating, ask the doctor about it at the next visit.

Lifting and Carrying Baby

For those who have never carried a tiny baby, the experience can, at first, prove very unnerving. But it can be equally unnerving for the baby. After months of being moved gently and securely in the snug uterine cocoon, being plucked up, wafted through the open air, and plunked down can come as quite a shock. Particularly when adequate support isn't provided for the head and neck, this can result in a frightening sensation of falling for baby, and, consequently, a startle reaction. So a good infant carrying technique aims not only at carrying baby in a way that *is* safe, but also in a way that *feels* safe.

You'll eventually develop techniques of carrying your baby that are comfortable for both of you, and carrying will become a completely natural experience. Baby will be casually slung over your shoulder or under your arm as you sort laundry, push the vacuum cleaner, or read labels in the supermarket, yet feel as secure as he or she did in utero. In the awkward interim, however, these tips will help:

Picking baby up. Before you even touch your baby, make your presence known through voice or eye contact. Being lifted unawares by unseen hands to an unknown destination can be unsettling.

Let baby adjust to the switch in support from mattress to arms by slipping your hands under him or her (one under head and neck, the other under bottom) and keeping them there for a few moments before actually lifting.

Slide the hand under baby's head down the back so that your arm acts as a back and neck support, and your hand cradles the buttocks. Use the other hand to support the legs, and lift baby gently towards your body, caressing as you go. By bending over to bring your body closer, you will limit the distance your baby will have to travel in midair – and the discomfort that comes with it.

Carrying baby comfortably. A small baby can be cradled very nicely in just one arm (with your hand on baby's bottom, and your forearm supporting back, neck and head; see illustration) if you feel secure that way.

With a larger baby, you may both be more comfortable if you keep one hand under legs and buttocks and the other supporting back, neck, and head (your hand encircling baby's arm, your wrist under the head).

Some babies prefer the shoulder carry all the time or some of the time. It's easy to get

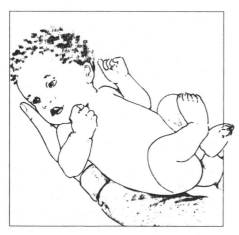

Be sure to carefully support the neck and back with your arm when lifting a baby who is lying face up.

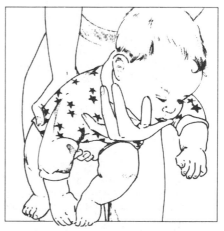

Slip one hand under the chin and neck and the other under the bottom to pick up a baby lying face down.

The hip carry leaves the carrier with a free hand.

The front carry is a favourite with babies since it allows them a view of the world.

baby up there smoothly with one hand on the buttocks, the other under head and neck. Until baby's head becomes self-supporting, you will have to provide the support. But this can be done even with one hand if you tuck baby's bottom into the crook of your elbow and run your arm up the back with your hand supporting the head and neck.

Even fairly young babies enjoy the front-face carry, in which they can watch the world go by, and many older babies prefer it. Face

your baby out, keeping one hand across his or her chest, pressed back against your own, and the other supporting baby's bottom.

The hip carry gives you freedom to use one hand for chores while carrying an older baby resting on your hip. (Avoid this hold if you have lower-back problems.) Hold baby snugly against your body with one arm, resting his bottom on your hips.

Putting baby back down. Hold baby close to your body as you bend over the cot or pram (again to limit the midair travel distance), one hand on baby's bottom, one supporting back, neck and head. Keep hands in place for a few moments until baby feels the comfort and security of the mattress, then slip them out and adjust his or her position for sleeping (usually on the tummy). A few more pats on the back or a bit of gentle hand pressure (depending on what seems to please your baby most), a few parting words if baby's awake, and you're ready to make the break.

Nail Trimming

Although trimming a newborn's tiny fingernails may make most new mothers nervous, it's necessary, nevertheless, because little hands with little control can do a lot of scratching, usually of baby's own face.

An infant's nails are often overgrown at birth, and so soft that cutting through them is nearly as easy as cutting through a piece of paper. Getting your baby to hold still for the procedure won't be so easy, however. Cutting a baby's nails while he's sleeping may work if you've got a sound sleeper or if you don't mind waking him or her. When baby's awake, it's best to trim the nails with the help of an assistant who can hold each hand as you cut. Always use a special baby nail scissor, which has rounded tips – if baby starts to bolt at the wrong moment, no one will be jabbed with a sharp point. To avoid nipping the skin as you clip the nail, press the finger pad down and out of the way as you cut. Even with this precaution you may, however, occasionally draw blood – most mothers do at one time or another. If you do, apply pressure with a sterile gauze pad until bleeding stops; a band-aid probably won't be needed.

Nose Care

As with the inside of the ears, the inside of the nose is self-cleaning and needs no special care. If there is a discharge, wipe the outside, but do not use cotton swabs, twisted tissues, or your fingernail to try to remove material from inside the nose – you may only push the matter back further into the nose, or even scratch delicate membranes. If baby has a lot of mucus due to a cold, suction it out with an infant nasal aspirator (see page 412).

Outings with Baby

Never again will you be able to leave the house empty-handed – at least not when baby's along. In general, you will need some or all of the following whenever you venture forth:

A changing bag. Don't leave home without it. It can be a bag designed specifically for this purpose or any tote bag you find convenient. Some helpful features include: a built-in changing pad, multiple pockets (including room for your money, credit cards), an insulated pocket for bottles, and at least one waterproof compartment. Keep the bag packed and ready, restocking it regularly, so you can just pick up and go.

A changing pad. If your bag doesn't have one, pack a waterproof pad. You can use a towel or a terry nappy in a pinch, but they won't protect carpeting, beds, or furniture when you're changing baby during a visit.

Nappies. How many depends on how long your outing will be. Always take at least one more than you think you'll need – you'll probably need it. Most people use disposa-

bles for outings, but you can use terry nappies if you prefer.

Wipes. A small convenience pack is easier to carry than a full-size container, but it must be refilled frequently. Or you can use a small plastic sandwich bag to tote a mini-supply. Wipes are handy, incidentally, for washing your own hands before feeding baby and before and after changes, as well as for removing spitup and baby-food stains from clothing or furniture.

Small plastic bags. You'll need these for disposing of dirty disposables, particularly when no bin is available, as well as for carrying wet and soiled baby clothes home.

A formula feeding. If you are going to be out past the next feeding with a bottle-fed baby, or might be, you'll have to bring a meal along. No refrigeration will be necessary if you take along an unopened bottle of ready-to-use formula (carry a sterilized teat in a clean plastic bag) or a bottle of sterilized water to which you will add powdered formula. If, however, you bring along formula you've prepared at home, you will have to store it in an insulated container along with a small ice pack or ice cubes.

A shoulder protector. Your friends may enjoy holding your baby, but not being spit up on. A handy terry nappy or muslin square will prevent embarrassing moments and smelly shoulders.

A change of baby clothes. Baby's picture perfect in a brand-new outfit and you're off to a special family gathering. You arrive, lift your heir from the car seat, and find a pool of loose, mustardy stools has added the 'finishing touch'. Just one reason why you need to carry along an extra – and for extended outings, two extra – sets of clothing.

An extra blanket or sweater. Particularly in transitional seasons, when temperatures can fluctuate unpredictably, the additional covering will come in handy.

A dummy, if baby uses one. Carry it in a clean plastic bag.

Entertainment. Something to provide visual stimulation is appropriate for very young babies – particularly for the car seat or pushchair. For older babies, lightweight toys they can swat at, poke at and mouth will fit the bill. Toddlers like books, trucks, dolls, stuffed animals and small pull-toys.

A sunscreen. Once baby is six months old, a sunscreen is a must year-round (in winter, snow and sun can combine to cause serious burns).

A snack for mum. If you're breastfeeding or will be out for a long stretch and may not be able to find a nutritious snack easily, take one along: a piece of fruit; some rounds, sticks, triangles, or cubes of cheese; some whole-grain crackers or bread; a bag of dried fruit. A container or can of fruit juice or a thermos containing a hot or cold drink is a nice addition if your outing will be to a park where no liquid refreshment is available.

A snack (or two, or three) for baby. Once solids are introduced, bring along jars of baby food (no refrigeration is needed before they're open, no heating up is needed before serving) if you'll be out during meal-time; a spoon stashed in a plastic bag (save the bag to bring the dirty spoon home in); a bib; and plenty of paper towels. Later, a selection of finger foods (nonperishable if you'll be out in hot weather) such as fresh fruit, crackers, bread and breadsticks will ward off hunger between meals, while providing baby with a wholesome activity during your outing. Beware, however, of using snacks to ward off boredom or to keep baby from crying – the pattern of eating for the wrong reasons in childhood can continue as an undesirable habit later on.

Miscellaneuos toiletries and first aid items. Depending on any particular health needs your child may have as well as on where you are going, you may also want to carry: nappy rash ointment; baby or regular cornstarch (in hot weather); adhesive strips and antibiotic ointment (especially if your child has begun to get around); medication your baby is taking (if you will be out when the next dose is due; if refrigeration is required, pack with an ice pack in an insulated container).

Penis Care

The penis is comprised of the cylindrical shaft (most of its length) with a rounded end called the glans. The shaft and the glans are separated by a groove called the sulcus. At the tip of the glans is an opening, the meatus, through which semen and urine flow, though not at the same time. The entire penis – shaft and glans – is covered by a continuous layer of skin, called the foreskin, or prepuce. The foreskin itself is made up of two layers: the outer skin, and a lining similar to a mucous membrane.

At birth, the foreskin is firmly attached to the glans. Over time, foreskin and glans begin to separate, as cells are shed from the surface of each layer. The discarded cells, which are replaced throughout life, accumulate as whitish, cheesy 'pearls' that gradually work their way out via the tip of the foreskin.

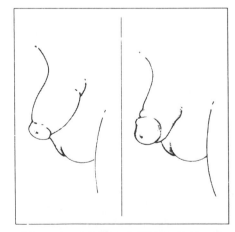

The uncircumcised penis (left) requires meticulous hygiene; the circumcised penis, from which the foreskin has been removed, requires no special care.

Usually by the end of the second year for 9 out of 10 uncircumcised boys, but sometimes not until five, ten, or more years after birth, foreskin and glans become fully separated. At this point the foreskin can be pushed back, or retracted, away from the glans.

Care of the uncircumcised penis. Contrary to what was once believed, no special care is needed for the uncircumcised penis in infancy – soap and water, applied externally, just as the rest of the body is washed, will keep it clean. It is not only unnecessary to try to forcibly retract the foreskin, or clean under it with cotton swabs, irrigation, or antiseptics – it can actually be harmful. Once the foreskin has clearly separated, you can retract it occasionally and clean under it. By the age of puberty most foreskins will be retractable, and at that time a boy can learn to retract his and clean under it himself.

Care of the circumcised penis. The only care the circumcised penis will ever need, once the incision is healed, is ordinary washing with soap and water. For care during the recovery period, see page 132.

Shampooing Baby

This is a fairly painless process with a young baby. But to help forestall future shampoo problems, avoid getting soap or shampoo in your baby's eyes from the first. Shampoo only once or twice a week, unless cradle cap or a particularly oily scalp requires more frequent head cleanings.

1. Wet baby's hair with a gentle spray from the sink or by pouring a little water from a cup. Add just a drop of baby shampoo or baby soap (more will make rinsing difficult), and rub in lightly to produce a lather.

2. Rinse thoroughly with a gentle spray or two or three cupfuls of clean water.

Older babies, who can stand on their own and have moved up to the big tub, can be

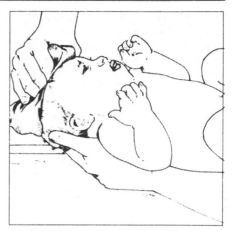

Sometimes rinsing off shampoo is best done with a few gentle wipes with a flannel.

shampooed in the tub, but only after the bath is over if your child is a girl, since bathing in dirty shampoo water can lead to vaginal infection. The problem, however, is that most children do not like to put their heads back for the shampoo – it makes them feel too vulnerable – and trying to shampoo them this way often ends in tears and tantrums. A spray nozzle, if your tub has one, will give you more control and can be fun for some babies, though others will find it too frightening. A specially designed shampoo visor (available in juvenile-furnishing and toy stores and from mail-order houses) that guards the eyes from flowing water and soap, but leaves the hair exposed for washing, is ideal if your child will wear it – some won't. If your baby resists both sprays and visors, you can continue shampooing (or at least rinsing, after doing the lathering in the tub) at the sink until he or she is more cooperative in the tub. Though the process isn't perfect (and it can grow awkward as the child grows larger), it's quick and consequently minimizes the period of suffering for both of you.

Swaddling Baby

For some babies, swaddling is soothing and may even reduce crying; others dislike the lack of freedom. If your baby seems to like it, here's how the wrapping's done:

1. Spread a cotton blanket on a cot, a bed, or a changing table, with one corner folded down about 15 cm (6 inches). Place baby on the blanket diagonally, head above the folded corner.

2. Take the corner near baby's left arm and pull it over the arm and across the baby's body. Lift the right arm, and tuck the blanket corner under baby's back on the right side.

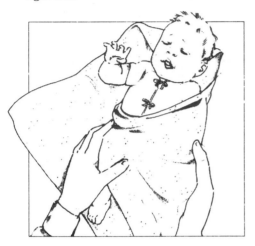

3. Lift the bottom corner and bring it up over baby's body, tucking it into the first swathe.

4. Lift the last corner, bring it over baby's right arm, and tuck it in under the back on the left side.

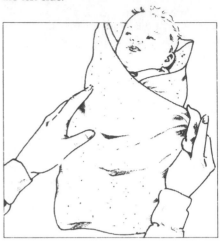

If your baby seems to prefer more hand mobility, do the wrapping below the arms, leaving them free. Because swaddling is confining and can interfere with development in older babies, do not use it once your baby is a month old.

Umbilical Stump Care

The last remnant of a baby's close attachment to its mother in the uterus is the stump of the umbilical cord. It turns black a few days after birth and can be expected to drop off anywhere between one and four weeks later. You can hasten healing and prevent infection by keeping the area dry and exposed to air. The following will help accomplish this:

1. When putting on baby's nappy, fold the front of it down below the navel to keep urine off and let air in. Fold the shirt up.

2. Skip tub baths and avoid wetting the navel when sponging until the cord falls off.

3. Dab the stump with alcohol (on sterile absorbent cotton balls, sterile gauze squares, or alcohol pads) to help keep the site clean and to hasten drying.

4. If the area around the navel turns red, or the site oozes, call the doctor.

Baby Business

There are two very important documents that your baby will need periodically throughout life. One is a birth certificate – which will be needed as proof of birth and citizenship when registering for school and applying for a driver's licence, passport, marriage licence, or benefits. Usually, the hospital will notify your local registry office of the baby's birth. One parent should register the birth within six weeks of the birth date (three weeks in Scotland).

When you do receive the birth certificate, examine it carefully to be sure it's accurate – mistakes are sometimes made. If you find errors after you get home, call the registry office for instructions on how to make the necessary corrections or additions. Once you have a correct birth certificate, make a few copies and file them in a safe place.

The second document that your baby will need is a National Health Service card. When you register the birth, you will be given a pink card with your baby's NHS number on it. Take it to the doctor's surgery when you register your baby with the GP. If your baby needs to see the GP before you have registered the birth, you can fill in an NHS registration form at the GP's surgery.

FOUR

The First Month

◆

What Your Baby May Be Doing

By the end of this month, your baby . . . should be able to (see Note):

- lift head briefly when on stomach on a flat surface

- focus on a face

Note: If your baby seems not to have reached one or more of these milestones, check with the doctor. In rare instances the delay could indicate a problem, though in most cases it will turn out to be normal for your baby. Premature infants generally reach milestones later than others of the same birth age, often achieving them closer to their adjusted age (the age they would be if they had been born at term), and sometimes later.

. . . will probably be able to:

- respond to a bell in some way, such as startling, crying, quieting

- follow an object moved in an arch about 15 cm (6 inches) above face to the midline (straight ahead)

. . . may possibly be able to:

- on stomach, lift head 45 degrees

- vocalize in ways other than crying (e.g.: cooing)

- follow an object moved in an arch about 15 cm (6 inches) above face *past* the midline (straight ahead)

- smile in response to your smile

. . . may even be able to:

- on stomach, lift head 90 degrees

- hold head steady when upright

- bring both hands together

- smile spontaneously

- laugh out loud

- squeal in delight

- follow an object in an arc about 15 cm (6 inches) above the face for 180 degrees (from one side to the other)

By the end of this month, a baby should be able to focus on a face.

What You Can Expect At This Month's Checkup

Each doctor, midwife or health visitor will have a personal approach to well-baby checkups. The overall organization of the physical exam, as well as the number and type of assessment techniques used and procedures performed will also vary with the individual needs of the child. But in general, you can expect the following at a checkup when your baby is between 10 days and four weeks old. The first visit may take place earlier under special circumstances, such as when a newborn has had jaundice, was premature, or when there are any problems with the establishment of breastfeeding; in the U.K., a community midwife will visit you at home for 10 days postpartum.

- Questions about how you and baby and the rest of the family are doing at home, and about baby's eating, sleeping and general progress.

- Measurement of baby's weight, length and head circumference, and plotting of progress since birth.

- Vision and hearing assessments.

- A report on results of neonatal screening tests (for PKU, hypothyroidism and other inborn errors of metabolism), if not given previously. If the doctor doesn't mention the tests, the results were very likely normal, but do ask for them for your own records. If your baby was released from the hospital before these tests were performed, or if they were done before he or she was 72 hours old, they will probably be performed or repeated now.

- A physical exam. The doctor or midwife will examine and assess all or most of the following, although some evaluations will be carried out by the experienced eye or hand, without comment:

☐ heart sounds with a stethoscope, and visual check of the heartbeat through the chest wall (ideally, baby shouldn't be crying for this part of the exam)

☐ abdomen, by palpation and/or stethoscope, for any abnormal masses

☐ hips, checking for dislocation by rotating the legs

☐ hands and arms, feet and legs, for normal development and motion

☐ back and spine, for any abnormalities

☐ eyes, with an opthalmoscope and/or a penlight, for normal reflexes and focusing, and for tear duct functioning

☐ ears, with an otoscope, for colour, fluid, movement

☐ nose, with otoscope, for colour and condition of mucous membranes and abnormalities

☐ mouth and throat, using a wooden tongue depressor, for sores, bumps, colour

☐ neck, for normal motion, thyroid and lymph gland size (lymph glands are more easily felt in infants, and this is normal)

☐ underarms, for swollen lymph glands

☐ the fontanels (the soft spots), by palpating with the hands

☐ respiration and respiratory function, by observation, and sometimes with stethoscope and/or light tapping of chest and back

☐ the genitalia, for any abnormalities, such as hernias or undescended testicles; the anus for cracks or fissures; the femoral pulse in the groin, for a strong steady beat

☐ the skin, for colour, tone, rashes and lesions, such as birthmarks

☐ reflexes specific to baby's age

☐ overall movement and behaviour, ability to cuddle and relate to adults

- Guidance about what to expect in the next month in relation to feeding, sleeping, development and infant safety.

- Recommendations about fluoride supplementation if needed in your area, and vitamin D supplementation if your baby is breastfed.

Before the visit is over, be sure to:

- Ask for guidelines for calling when baby is sick. (What would necessitate a call in the middle of the night? How can the doctor be reached outside of regular calling times?)

- Express any concerns that may have arisen over the past month – about baby's health, behaviour, sleep, feeding and so on.

- Jot down (or even tape record) information and instructions (you're sure to forget them, otherwise).

When you get home, record all pertinent information (baby's weight, length, head circumference, blood type, test results, birthmarks) in a permanent health record.

Feeding Your Baby This Month
Expressing Breast Milk

You see them in lavatories all over the country. During intermission at the opera and half time at sporting events; in airports, bus depots, and train stations; in offices, factories and shops; in restaurants and department stores; in schools and hospitals. Wherever women work, play, travel, or study, you'll find mothers expressing milk.

Why Mothers Express Milk

Unlike mothers in primitive societies, who carry their babies in slings at their breasts for convenient round-the-clock nipping, busy mothers in our fast-paced industrialized society can't always count on their babies and their breasts being in the same place at the same time. For this, and a host of other reasons, virtually every woman who breastfeeds expresses milk or pumps her breasts at one time or another. Most commonly, breasts are pumped to:

- Draw out inverted nipples late in pregnancy.

- Induce lactation in an adopting mother, or in a biological mother whose milk is slow in coming in.

- Relieve engorgement when the milk comes in.

- Increase or maintain the milk supply.

- Collect milk for interim feedings when working or away from home.

- Prevent clogging from over-full breasts.

- Provide milk for bottle or tube feeding when a baby (premature or otherwise) is too weak to nurse, or has an oral defect that hinders nursing.

- Provide breast milk for a hospitalized sick or premature baby.

- Prevent engorgement and maintain milk supply when nursing is temporarily halted because of illness (mother's or baby's).

- Stimulate relactation, if a mother changes her mind about nursing or if a baby turns out to be allergic to cow's milk after early weaning.

Techniques for Expressing Breast Milk

At one time, the only way to express milk was by hand, a long and tedious process that often failed to produce significant quantities of milk. Today, spurred by the resurgence of breastfeeding, manufacturers are marketing a variety of breast pumps – ranging from simple hand-operated models that cost a few pounds to sophisticated electric ones costing hundreds of pounds – to make pumping easier and more convenient. Though an occasional mother will still express by hand, at least to relieve engorgement, most will invest in one of the following:

- A bulb or 'bicycle-horn' pump, which suctions milk from breasts with each squeeze of the bulb. These are inexpensive – but inefficient, difficult to clean (which could lead to unsanitary milk collection), and uncomfortable to use, often causing sore nipples. Impractical for regularly expressing milk for infant feedings, they can be used to relieve occasional engorgement.

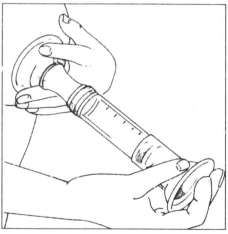

Though tough on the arm that's doing the pumping, the syringe pump is one of the least expensive yet convenient instruments for expressing milk.

- A trigger-operated pump, which creates suction with each squeeze of the trigger. More expensive than the bulb type, but still very affordable, it has the advantage of requiring only one hand to operate. But, because it requires a great deal of dexterity and strength, women who don't

have large strong hands may have trouble using such a pump, and many women may find it difficult to empty the breast opposite their non-dominant hand. Another drawback: the glass construction. Not only are these pumps breakable, but certain immunity-conferring factors from the breast milk may adhere to the glass (they don't adhere to plastic), depriving baby of their benefits.

- A syringe pump, which is composed of two cylinders that fit inside one another. The inner cylinder is placed over the nipple and the outer, when pushed in and pulled out, creates suction that draws milk into it. This type is the most popular because it's fairly simple to use, is moderate in price, easy to clean, portable, and can also double as a feeding bottle. Some allow pressure to be adjusted to more closely mimic an infant's suckling, making expressing milk more comfortable.

- A convertible manual pump, which can be connected, when desired, to an electrical system. This versatile model offers faster, more efficient operation when electricity is available as well as portability for use away from a power source.

- A battery-operated pump, which promises portability and efficient operation, but not all models deliver. Moderately priced, they are less powerful than electric models; and the speed at which some eat batteries makes them expensive to use and of questionable practicality. Check with your local La Leche League for the latest on these.

- An electric pump, which is powerful, fast, and easy to use, leaves a mother's hands free for nursing (on the other breast) or other activities during pumping. They are usually very expensive, often costing from a hundred to £500 or more, but if time is an important consideration, one may be well worth the investment. If portability of a unit will affect your choice, keep in mind that an electric pump is unwieldy at best, but that you can buy a second more portable pump for the road and still get a lot of mileage out of your electric model at home.

Many women rent electric pumps, from either hospitals, or La Leche or NCT groups; some buy or rent jointly with other women, or buy them, use them, and then sell them. Insurance plans may cover the cost of purchase or rental if breast milk is prescribed and nursing is not possible, usually when a baby is premature or sick. Personal pump kits (with shield, cup, lid and tubing) are available, disposable or sterilizable, to make sharing a pump or using a hospital pump more practical.

Before selecting a pump, talk to friends, to someone at La Leche League, a child-birth educator, a lactation consultant, or your baby's doctor (if he or she is conversant with the subject) to learn the pros and cons of various models. If possible, try the one you are considering – by borrowing or renting – before making a purchase. You will want a pump that is easy and convenient to operate, clean, relatively comfortable to use, and, if you will be using it away from home, portable.

How to Express Breast Milk

Basic preparations. No matter what method of expressing you choose, you may find it difficult to express milk for the first few days. Making these preparations before getting started will help:

• Choose a time of the day when your breasts are ordinarily fullest – for most women, that's the morning. Plan on expressing milk for collection about once every three or four hours. Each collection can take from 20 to 40 minutes, and sometimes even longer.

• Make sure that all your equipment is clean and sterilized according to the manufacturer's directions; washing your pump immediately after each use will

make the difficult job of keeping it clean easier. If you use your pump away from home, carry along a bottle brush, detergent, and paper towels for washup.

• Especially while you are still a novice, select a quiet, comfortably warm environment for pumping, where you won't be interrupted by phones or doorbells, and where you will have some privacy. At work, a private office, an unoccupied meeting room, or the women's lounge can serve as your pumping headquarters. If you're at home, it's ideal if someone else can care for the baby, leaving you free to concentrate on the job at hand.

• Wash your hands with soap and water, your breasts with water only – don't use soaps, creams, ointments, or anything else on your nipples.

• Drink a full glass of water, juice, milk, decaffeinated tea or coffee, or soup just before beginning. A warm drink may be more helpful than a cold one for stimulating let-down.

• Make yourself comfortable, with your feet up, if possible.

• Relax for several minutes before beginning. Use meditation or other relaxation techniques, music, TV or whatever you personally find helps you unwind.

• Think about your baby and about nursing or look at baby's photo to help to stimulate let-down. Otherwise, having baby in the room just before you start pumping could do the trick, though ideally someone else should be around to care for baby once you begin. If you're using an electric pump, which leaves your hands free, you can even hold the baby – though many babies balk at being so near and yet so far from being fed. Applying hot soaks to your nipples and breasts for five or ten minutes, taking a hot shower, doing breast massage, or leaning over and shaking your breasts are other ways of enhancing let-down.

• If you find you have a lot of difficulty

getting results, ask your doctor about an oxytocin nasal spray, which encourages letdown. Use it only as directed.

To massage your breast, place one hand underneath your breast, the other on top. Slide the palm of one or both hands from the chest gently toward the nipple and apply mild pressure. Rotate your hands around the breast and repeat in order to reach all the milk ducts.

Expressing milk by hand. To begin place your hand on one breast, at the edge of the areola, with your thumb opposite the other fingers. Press your hand in toward your chest, gently pressing thumb and forefinger together. (Keep your fingers on the areola only; don't let them slip onto the nipple.) Repeat rhythmically to start milk flowing, rotating your fingers to get to all milk ducts. Repeat with the other breast, massaging in between expressions, as needed. Repeat with the first breast, then do the second again.

If you want to collect the milk expressed, use a wide-topped, sterilized cup under the breast you are working on. You can collect whatever drips from the other by placing a sterilized milk cup over it inside your bra. Collected milk should be poured immediately into sterilized bottles and refrigerated as soon as possible.

Expressing milk with a hand-held or electric pump. Simply follow the directions for the pump you are using. Be patient; it often takes a while to become proficient at pumping. If you want to use a hand pump on one breast while nursing your baby on the other, either prop the baby on a pillow (being sure he or she can't tumble off your lap), or have someone else to do the pumping as you hold baby. Since you don't have to use your hands to operate an electric pump, you can nurse your baby on one side and pump on the other with ease.

Expressing breast milk by hand is a slow, sometimes painful process. This method is best for expressing only small amounts, as when the breast is too engorged for baby to get a comfortable mouthful.

Collecting and Storing Breast Milk

Plastic containers are better than glass for collecting and storing breast milk, not only because glass is breakable, but also because disease-fighting white blood cells in mother's milk have been shown to cling more to glass than to plastic, making them less available to baby. Many pumps come with containers that can be used as storage and feeding bottles; others allow you to use a standard feeding bottle to collect the milk. 100-ml (four-fl ounce) bottles are practical for young babies, whose appetites are still small, 250-ml (8-fl ounce) ones for older babies. A thermos, packed with ice until it is ready to be filled, can be used to keep breast milk fresh when you're away from home – but it may have the drawback of being glass-lined.

Sterilize containers and bottles, or wash them in a dishwasher with temperatures that reach at least 82°C (180°F), if milk is going to be kept at room temperature for longer than 30 minutes or stored for more than 48 hours in the refrigerator or freezer. Otherwise, washing thoroughly with hot soapy water and a bottle brush should be sufficient.

Refrigerate expressed milk as soon as you can; if that's not possible, use a sterile container, in which it will stay fresh at room temperature (but away from radiators, sun, or other sources of heat) for as long as six hours. You can store breast milk for up to 48 hours in the refrigerator, or chill for 30 minutes, then freeze. Fill containers for the freezer only three-fourths full to allow for expansion, and label with the date (always use the oldest milk first). Breast milk will stay

fresh in the freezer for anywhere from a week or two in a single-door refrigerator, to about three months in a two-door frost-free model that keeps foods frozen solid, to six months in a freezer that maintains a –18°C (0°F) temperature.

To thaw breast milk, shake the bottle under lukewarm tap water, then use within 30 minutes. Or thaw in the refrigerator and use within three hours. Do not thaw in a microwave oven, on the top of the stove, or at room temperature; and do not refreeze. When your baby has finished feeding on a bottle, discard the remaining milk. Also discard any milk that has been stored for periods longer than those recommended above.

If you are going to transport breast milk regularly, invest in an insulated bottle bag, a thermos, or an insulated bag that can hold the bottle and a frozen ice pack.

What You May Be Concerned About

'Breaking' Baby

'I'm so afraid of handling the baby – he's so tiny and vulnerable looking.'

Newborn babies may look as fragile as china dolls, but they're not. In fact, they're really pretty sturdy. As long as their heads are well supported, they can't be harmed by normal handling – even when it's a little clumsy and tentative, as is often the case when the handling is being done by a first-time parent. You'll gradually learn what's comfortable for your baby and for you, since handling styles vary greatly from parent to parent. Soon you'll be toting your baby as casually as a bag of groceries – and often *with* a bag of groceries.

Infant Acne

'I thought babies were supposed to have great complexions. But my two-week-old seems to be breaking out in a terrible case of acne.'

As unfair as it might seem, some babies go through bouts with 'adolescent' skin before they're days old, let alone teenagers. And actually, many of their complexion problems have the same cause as many of the complexion problems of teenagers: hormones. Except in the case of newborns, it's not their hormones that are causing the problems, but those of their mothers that are still circulating in their systems. Another reason pimples are likely to crop up is that the pores of newborns aren't completely developed, making them easy targets for infiltration by dirt and the resultant blossoming of blemishes.

Don't squeeze, scrub, slather with lotions, or otherwise treat your newborn's acne. Just wash it with water two or three times daily, pat it dry, and it will clear within a few months, leaving no lasting marks.

Hearing

'My baby doesn't seem to react much to

noises. In fact, he sleeps right through the dog's barking and my older daughter's tantrums. Could his hearing be impaired?'

It's probably not that your baby doesn't hear the dog barking or his sister screaming, but that he's used to these sounds. Although he saw the world for the first time when he exited your uterus, it wasn't the first time he heard it. Many sounds – from the music you played on the stereo to the honking horns and screeching sirens on the street – penetrated the walls of his peaceful uterine home, and he became accustomed to them.

Most babies will react to loud noise – in early infancy by startling, at about three months by blinking, at about four months by turning toward the source of the sound. But those sounds that have already become a part of the background Muzak of a baby's existence may elicit no response – or one so subtle the untrained eye misses it, such as a change in position or activity.

If you're concerned about your baby's hearing, try this little test: clap your hand behind his head and see if he startles. If he does, you know he can hear. If he doesn't, try again later; children (even newborns) have a wonderful way of ignoring or blocking out their environment at will, and he may have been doing just that. A repeat test may elicit the response you want. If it doesn't, try to observe other ways in which your baby may react to sound: is he calmed or does he otherwise respond to the soothing sounds of your voice, even when he isn't looking directly at you? Does he respond to singing or music in any way? Does he startle when exposed to an unfamiliar loud noise? If your baby seems never to respond to sound, discuss this with his doctor as soon as it's practical. The earlier a child's hearing deficit is diagnosed and treated, the better the long-range outcome.

Experts disagree on the cost effectiveness of audiological screening of all newborns but all agree high risk infants should be evaluated. These include children who weighed in under 2.5 kg (or 5½ pounds), or who experienced serious complications during or shortly after birth (such as asphyxia, seizures, or intracranial haemorrhage); those exposed prenatally to drugs or infections known to affect hearing (such as rubella); those with a family history of unexplained or inherited deafness; those with visible abnormalities of the ears; and those who are mentally retarded, blind, autistic, or have cerebral palsy.

Vision

'I put a mobile over my baby's cot, hoping the colours would be stimulating. But he doesn't seem to notice it. Could something be wrong with his vision?'

It's more likely there's something wrong with your mobile – at least with where it's hung. A newborn baby focuses best on objects that are between 20 and 35 cm (8 and 14 inches) away from his eyes, a range that seems to have been selected by nature not randomly, but by design – it being the distance at which a nursing infant sees his mother's face. Objects closer or farther away from a baby lying in his cot will be nothing but a blur to him, although he will fixate on something distant that is bright or in motion if there is nothing worth looking at within his range of vision.

In addition, he will spend most of his time looking to his right or to his left, rarely focusing straight ahead in the early months. A mobile directly above his cot is not likely to catch his fancy, whereas one hung to one side or the other may. Few babies, however, show any interest at all in mobiles until they are three to four weeks old, and many not until even later.

So your newborn can see, but not the way he will in three or four months. If you want to evaluate your baby's vision, hold a penlight to one side of his line of vision, about 25 to 30 cm (10 to 12 inches) from his face. During the first month, a baby will generally focus on the light for a brief period, long enough for you to know he's seeing it. By the end of the first month, some babies will follow as you move the light slowly towards the centre of their field of vision. Generally, not until three months will a baby begin to follow an object in a full 180° arc, from one side to the other.

Your baby's eyes will continue maturing during the first year. He probably will be farsighted for several months and not be able to perceive depth well (which may be why he's a perfect candidate for falling off changing tables and beds) until nine months. But though his vision isn't perfect now, he does enjoy looking at things – and this pastime is one of his most important avenues to learning. So provide him with plenty of visual stimuli. But don't overload his circuits – one or two eye-catchers at a time are about all he can handle. And because his attention span is short, change the scenery frequently.

Most young babies like to study faces – even crudely drawn ones. They prefer black-and-white patterns to bright colours; complex objects to simple ones. They love looking at light: a chandelier, a lamp, a window (especially one through which light is filtered via the slats of vertical or horizontal blinds), will all attract their rapt scrutiny; and they are usually happier in a well-lit room than in a dim one.

Vision screening will be part of your baby's regular checkups. But if you feel that your baby doesn't seem to be focusing on objects or faces or doesn't turn towards the light, mention this to his doctor at the next visit.

Spitting Up

'My baby spits up so much that I'm worried she's not getting enough nourishment.'

Although it may seem all that's going into your daughter is coming back up, that's not likely to be the case. What looks like a mealful of milk to you is probably no more than a tablespoon or two, mixed with saliva and mucus – certainly not enough to in-terfere with your baby's nourishment. (To see how much a little bit of liquid can look like, spill a couple of tablespoons of milk on your kitchen table.) The material your baby spits up will be relatively unchanged from the form in which it entered baby's mouth if it only went as far as the oesophagus before coming back up. But if it travelled down to the stomach before its return trip, it will look curdled and smell like sour milk.

Most babies spit up at least occasionally; some spit up with every feeding. The process in newborns may be related to an immature sphincter between the oesophagus and the stomach and to excess mucus that needs to be cleared. In older babies, spitting up occurs when milk mixed with air is regurgitated with a burp. Sometimes a baby wisely spits up because she's eaten too much.

There are no sure cures for spitting up. But you can try to minimize the air gulping around mealtimes that can contribute to it: don't feed her when she's crying (take a break in the action to calm her down); keep her as upright as possible while feeding and for a while afterwards; be sure bottle teats are neither too large nor too small and that bottles are tilted so that formula (not air) fills the nipple. It may also be helpful to keep your baby from making a pig of herself, and to avoid bouncing her around while she's eating or just afterwards (when possible, strap her in a baby seat or pushchair for a while). And don't forget to burp her during a meal, instead of waiting until the end of the meal when one big bubble may bring up the works.

Accept, however, that no matter what you do, if your baby's a spitter, she's going to spit – and you're going to have to live with it for at least six months. (The living will be a little neater, however, if you keep a precautionary nappy on your shoulder or lap whenever you're on baby duty.) Most babies ease up on their spitting when they start sitting upright, although a few will continue causing malodorous mayhem well up until their first birthdays.

Ordinary spitting up usually presents no hazards (other than to clothes and furniture).[1] But because a small infant can choke on regurgitated material if she lies on her back, a baby who is a spitter should be placed on her stomach to sleep or play.

Some kinds of spitting up do, however, signal possible problems. Call the doctor if your baby's spitting up is associated with poor weight gain or prolonged gagging and coughing, or if her vomit is brown or green in colour or shoots across the room (projectile vomiting). These could indicate a medical problem, such as an intestinal obstruction (treatable by surgery).

Swaddling

'I've been trying to keep my baby swaddled, like they showed me in the hospital. But she keeps kicking at the blanket, and it gets undone. Should I stop trying?'

The first few days of life on the outside can be a little disorienting – and even a little scary. After spending nine months snugly enveloped in the uterine cocoon, a newborn must adjust to the suddenly wide-open spaces of her new environment. Many child-care experts feel the transition can be made more comfortable if the security and warmth of the newborn's former home is simulated by swaddling, or bundling, her in a receiving blanket. Swaddling also keeps the infant from being disturbed by her own jerky movements while she sleeps, and keeps her warm in the early days when her thermostat is not at peak efficiency. But don't swaddle in a warm room because overheating is a cot-death risk factor.

Just because all babies are swaddled in the hospital, however, doesn't mean all babies need to be swaddled at home. Many babies will continue to derive comfort from swaddling (and hence will sleep better) for a few weeks, some even longer. It may also

help calm some colicky infants. But all eventually outgrow the need for swaddling, usually once they become more active, and make this clear by trying to kick off the wrapping. Some seem not to need it from the start, perfectly content without it or obviously disturbed with it. A good rule: if swaddling seems to feel good to your baby, do it; if it doesn't, don't.

Having Enough Breast Milk

'When my milk came in, my breasts were overflowing. Now that the engorgement is gone, I'm not leaking any more, and I'm worried I don't have enough milk for my son.'

Since the human breast doesn't come equipped with millilitre/fl ounce calibrations, it's virtually impossible to discern with the eye how adequate your milk supply is. Instead, you'll have to use your baby as a guide. If he seems to be happy, healthy and gaining weight well, you're producing enough milk. You don't have to spray like a fountain or leak like a tap to nurse successfully; the only milk that counts is the milk that goes into your baby. If at any time your baby doesn't seem to be thriving, more frequent nursing plus the other tips on page 98 should help you produce more milk.

'My baby was nursing about every three hours and seemed to be doing very well. Now, suddenly, she seems to want to nurse every hour. Could something have happened to my milk supply?'

Unlike a well, a milk supply is unlikely to dry up if it's used regularly. In fact, quite the contrary is true: the more your baby nurses, the more milk your breasts will produce. A much more plausible explanation for your baby's frequent trips to the breast is a growth or appetite spurt. These occur most commonly at three weeks, six weeks and three months, but can occur at any time during an infant's development. Sometimes,

---

1. Keep a small plastic bottle of water mixed with a little baking soda handy for spitup spot cleaning. Rubbing a cloth moistened with the mixture on spots will keep them from setting and will eliminate most of the odour. Or use a pre-moistened wipe.

much to parental dismay, even a baby who has been sleeping through the night begins to wake for a middle of the night feeding during a growth spurt. In this case, a baby's active appetite is merely nature's way of ensuring that her mother's body increases milk production to meet her growth needs.

Just relax and keep your breasts handy until the growth spurt passes. Don't be tempted to give your baby formula (or even worse, solids) to appease her appetite, because a decrease in frequency of nursing would have the side effect of cutting down your supply of milk, which is just the opposite of what the baby ordered. Such a pattern – started by baby wanting to nurse more, leading to mother becoming anxious about the adequacy of her milk supply and offering a supplement, followed by a decrease in milk production – is one of the major causes of breastfeeding being abandoned prematurely.

Sometimes a baby begins to demand more daytime feedings temporarily when she begins to sleep through the night, but this too shall pass with time. If, however, your baby continues to want to nurse hourly (or nearly so) for more than a week, check her weight gain and see below. It could mean she's not getting enough to eat.

Your Breastfed Baby not Thriving

'At three weeks, my baby seems skinnier than when he was born. He seems to nurse a lot, so I can't imagine he isn't getting enough milk. What could be wrong?'

If there's anything capable of producing more anxiety than the course of pregnancy weight gain, it's the course of baby's weight gain during the first few months of life. Except, in most cases, pregnant women worry about gaining too much weight, while new mothers worry about their babies gaining too little.

Occasionally, an infant who had a lot of facial swelling at birth begins to look thinner as the swelling goes down. Most, however, have started to fill out by three weeks, looking less like scrawny chickens and more like rounded babies, though those who see a baby every day may be less aware of the change than those who see him less often. In most cases, you can expect a breastfed baby to regain his birthweight by two weeks and then gain roughly 170 to 225 g (6 to 8 ounces) a week for the next couple of months. If you have some doubt about your baby's progress, you might borrow a baby scale and weigh him. Most likely, you will be reassured by your findings. If you still have concerns about your baby's progress, or you can't locate a scale, ask the doctor if you could bring your baby in for an impromptu weighing – to make you feel better and to catch and correct any problems if they turn out to exist.

The fact that your baby is nursing frequently isn't in itself assurance that he's getting all the food he needs; it may, in fact, indicate the opposite. A baby who isn't being satisfied may nurse almost continuously, trying to get enough nourishment. This may be temporary, as when an infant going through a growth spurt is trying to increase his milk supply (see page 97). Or it may indicate a truly inadequate supply. But there are signs you can look for to reassure you that this isn't so for your baby:

He's having at least five large, seedy, mustardy bowel movements a day. Breastfed newborns may have a movement after every feeding, sometimes as many as a dozen a day. Fewer than five movements a day in the early weeks could indicate inadequate food intake.

His nappy is wet when he's changed before each feeding and the urine is colourless. If a baby urinates fewer than eight to ten times a day or passes urine that is yellow, possibly fishy-smelling, and/ or contains urate crystals (these look like powdered brick, give the wet nappy a pinkish red tinge, and are normal before the mother's breast milk comes in but not later), he is not getting enough fluids. Such signs of dehydration may not, however, show up until the problem has become severe.

You hear a lot of gulping and swallowing as your baby nurses. If you don't, he may not be getting much to swallow. Don't worry, however, about relatively silent eating if baby is gaining well.

He seems happy and content after most feedings. A lot of crying and fussing or frantic finger sucking after a full nursing could mean a baby is still hungry. Not all fussing, of course, is related to hunger – after eating, it could also be related to wind or an attempt to push out a bowel movement.

You experienced breast engorgement when your milk came in. Engorgement is a good sign you can produce milk. And breasts that are fuller when you get up in the morning and after four or five hours without nursing than they are after nursing indicate they are filling with milk regularly – and also that your baby is emptying them. If baby is gaining well, however, lack of engorgement need not concern you.

You notice the sensation of let-down and/or experience milk leakage. Different women experience let-down differently (fullness, tingling, tightening, stinging, cramping, lumpiness, with or without actual dripping or spraying), but feeling it, when you start nursing, hear your baby cry, or even just think about him, indicates that milk is coming down from the storage ducts to the nipples ready to be enjoyed by your baby. Not every woman notices let-down when it occurs, but its absence (in combination with signs of baby's failure to thrive) should raise a warning flag in your mind.

You don't start menstruating during the first three months postpartum. The menses usually doesn't return in a woman who is exclusively breastfeeding, particularly in the first three months. Its premature return may be due to lowered hormone levels, reflecting inadequate milk production.

In addition to routine weighing, the doctor may want you to weigh your baby before and after nursing, without changing his nappy in between. That would tell you how many millilitres/ fl ounces he's taking at a feeding – at least at that feeding – something a bottle-feeding mother knows automatically.

If the doctor's exam shows your baby isn't thriving on breastfeeding, there are a wide range of possible reasons. Some can be remedied:

You are not feeding baby often enough. In this case, increase feedings to at least eight, even ten, in 24 hours. Don't go more than three hours during the day or five at night between feedings (four-hour schedules were devised for bottle-fed babies, not those on the breast). That means waking up a sleeping baby so that he won't miss dinner or feeding a hungry one even if he just finished a meal an hour earlier. If your baby is 'happy to starve' (some newborns are) and never demands feeding, it means taking the initiative yourself and setting a busy feeding schedule for him. Frequent nursings will not only help to fill baby's tummy (and fill out his frame), they will also stimulate your milk production.

You're not emptying at least one breast at each feeding. Nursing for at least ten minutes at the first breast should empty it; if your baby accomplishes this task, let him nurse for as long (or as little) as he likes on the second. Remember to alternate the starting breast at each feeding. Switching breasts every five minutes works better for some women (and their babies), because the baby gets the lion cub's share of milk from each before satiety sets in – but be sure to provide a total of at least ten minutes on the first breast. If baby doesn't do the job, empty the breast with a pump to improve milk production.

Your baby is a lazy or ineffective suckler. This may be because he was preterm, is ill, or has abnormal mouth development (such as a cleft palate or tied tongue). The less effective the suckling, the less milk is produced, setting baby up for failure to thrive. Until he's a strong suckler, he will need help stimulating your breasts to provide adequate milk. This can be done with a breast pump, which you can use to empty the breasts after each feeding (save any milk you collect for future use in bottles). Until milk production is adequate, your doctor will very likely recommend supplemental feedings of formula via bottles or the supplemental nutrition system shown on this page which has the advantage of not causing nipple confusion by introducing the artificial nipple) following breast feedings.

If your baby tires easily, you may be advised to nurse for only five minutes on each

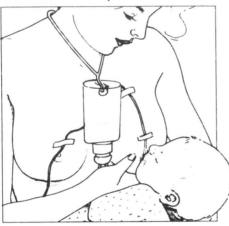

Supplemental Nutrition System: *This vastly useful bit of apparatus can supply baby with supplementary feedings while stimulating mother's milk production. A feeding bottle hangs around the mother's neck; slim tubes leading from the bottle are taped down her breasts, extending slightly past the nipples. The bottle is filled with mother's own milk, collected with a breast pump; with breast milk from a milk bank; or with the formula recommended by the baby's doctor. As baby nurses at the breast, he takes the supplement through the tube. This system avoids the nipple confusion that arises when supplementary feedings are given in a bottle (a baby must learn to suck differently at bottle than at breast) and stimulates the mother to produce more milk even as she is supplementing artificially.*

breast, then follow with a supplement of expressed milk or formula given by bottle or the supplemental nutrition system, both of which require less effort by the baby.

Your baby hasn't yet learned how to coordinate his jaw muscles for suckling. This ineffective suckler will also need help from a breast pump to stimulate his mother's breasts to begin producing larger quantities of milk. In addition, he will need lessons in improving his suckling technique; the doctor may even recommend physical therapy for him. While your baby is learning, he may need supplemental feedings. For further suggestions on improving suckling technique, call your local La Leche League or NCT Breastfeeding Counsellor.

Your nipples are sore or you have a breast infection. Not only can the pain interfere with your desire to nurse, reducing nursing frequency and milk production, it can actually inhibit milk let-down. So take steps to heal sore nipples or cure mastitis (see pages 545 and 546). But do not use a nipple shield, as this can interfere with your baby's ability to latch on to your nipples, compounding your problems.

Your nipples are flat or inverted. It's often difficult for a baby to get a firm hold on such nipples. This situation sets up the negative cycle of not enough suckling, leading to not enough milk, to even less suckling, and less milk. Help baby get a better grip during nursing by taking the areola between your thumb and forefinger and compressing the entire area for his sucking. Use breast shells between feedings to make your nipples easier to draw out, but avoid breast shields during nursing, which, though they can draw nipples out, can prevent baby from properly grasping your nipple and set up a longer-term problem.

Some other factor is interfering with milk let-down. Let-down is a physical function that can be inhibited as well as stimulated by your state of mind. If you're embarrassed or anxious about breastfeeding in general, or in a particular situation, not only can let-down be stifled, but the volume and calorie count of your milk can be affected. So try to feed baby where you are most at ease – in private, if nursing around other people puts you on edge. To help you relax, sit in a comfortable chair, play soft music, have something non-alcoholic to drink (see page 537), try some of the relaxation techniques you learned in childbirth education classes. Massaging the breasts or applying warm soaks just before nursing also encourages let-down. If these aren't effective, ask your baby's doctor about prescribing an oxytocin spray. Though this spray won't increase your milk supply, it will help get the milk you do produce down and out to your baby.

Your baby is getting sucking satisfaction elsewhere. If your baby is getting most of his sucking satisfaction from a dummy or other non-nutritive source, he may have little interest in the breast. Toss out the dummy and nurse baby when he seems to want to suck. And don't give him supplementary bottles of water, which not only supply non-nutritive sucking, but can dampen appetite, and in excess alter blood sodium levels (see page 134).

You're not burping baby between breasts. A baby who's swallowed air can stop eating before he's had enough because he feels uncomfortably full. Bringing up the air will give him room for more milk. Be sure to burp baby between breasts whether he seems to need it or not, more often if he fusses a lot while nursing.

Your baby is sleeping through the night. An uninterrupted night's sleep is great for mum's looks, but not necessarily for her milk supply. After she undergoes several days of uncomfortable engorgement as baby begins to go seven or eight (or even ten) hours a night without nursing, her milk may begin to diminish, and supplementation may eventually be needed. To avoid this, you may have to wake baby once in the middle of the night. He shouldn't be going longer than five hours without a feeding at this time.

You've returned to work. Returning to work – and going 8 to 10 hours without nursing during the day – can also decrease the milk supply. One way to prevent this is to express milk at work at least once every four hours you're away from baby.

You're doing too much too soon. Producing breast milk requires a lot of energy. If you're expending yours in other ways and not getting adequate rest, your breast milk supply may diminish. Try a day of almost complete bed rest, followed by three or four days of taking it easy, and see if your baby isn't more satisfied.

You're sleeping on your stomach. When you sleep on your stomach, something a lot of women are eager to do after the later months of pregnancy when they couldn't, you also sleep on your breasts. And the pressure on your breasts could cut down on your milk production – almost as a binder used to prevent lactation would. So turn over, at least partway, to take the pressure off your mammary glands.

You're harbouring placental fragments in your uterus. Your body won't accept the fact that you've actually delivered until all the products of pregnancy have been expelled, including all of the placenta. Until it's thoroughly convinced, it may not produce adequate levels of prolactin, the hormone that stimulates milk production. If you have any abnormal bleeding (see page 505) or other signs of retained placental fragments, contact your obstetrician at once. A dilatation and curettage (D and C) could put you and your baby on the right track to successful breastfeeding, while avoiding the danger a retained placenta can pose to your own health.

Even with your best efforts, under the best conditions, with ample support from your doctors, your husband, and your friends, it may turn out that you're still unable to breastfeed successfully. In spite of assurances they may have heard to the contrary, a small percentage of women are simply unable to

Double the Trouble, Double the Fun

In previous generations, when the stethoscope was an obstetrician's most sophisticated method of antenatal diagnosis, twins often took parents by surprise in the delivery room, leaving no time for the necessary extra preparations. Today, when most expectant parents of twins see double on the ultrasound screen early in pregnancy, mad postpartum dashes to the store for a second set of everything are rare. Though, even with seven or eight month's notice, it may be impossible to prepare completely for the day when babies make four (or if siblings are already on the scene, more). Knowing more about how to plan and what to expect can provide a greater sense of control over what may seem a fundamentally uncontrollable situation.

Be doubly prepared. Since double blessings often come before they're expected, it's a good idea to start organizing for the babies' arrival well in advance of due day. Try to have every childcare item in the house and ready for use before you go to the hospital. (All the preparations suggested in Chapter One for expectant mothers, are doubly important for you.) But while it makes sense to devote a lot of time to preparations, it doesn't make sense to exhaust yourself (particularly if your doctor has given you specific orders to the contrary). Get plenty of rest before the babies arrive – you can expect it to be a rare luxury once they do.

Double up. Do as much as possible for your babies in tandem. That means waking them at the same time so they can be fed together, putting them in the bath (once they're able to sit in a tub seat) together, walking them in the stroller together. Double bubble the babies together across your lap, or with one on your lap and the other on your shoulder. When you can't manage to double up, alternate. Bathe one one night, the other the next. Or cut down. Bathe them every second or third nights (at an early age daily bathes aren't necessary) and sponge in between.

Split up. The work, that is. When daddy is around, divide the household chores (cooking, cleaning, laundry, shopping) and the babies (you take over one baby, he the other). Be sure that you alternate babies so that both children get to know both parents well, and vice versa.

Try the double-breasted approach. Nursing twins is a physical strain, but eliminates fussing with dozens of bottles and endless millilitres/fl ounces of formula. Nursing simultaneously will save time and avoid a daily breastfeeding marathon. You can hold the babies, propped on pillows, in the side position with their feet behind you, or, with one at each breast, their bodies crossed in front of you. Alternate the breast each baby gets at every feeding to avoid creating favourites (and to avoid mismatched breasts, should one baby turn out to be a more proficient sucker than the other). If your milk supply doesn't seem adequate for two, you can nurse one while you bottle feed the other – again alternating from feeding to feeding. To keep up both your energy and your milk supply, be sure to get super nutrition (including 400 to 500 extra calories per baby) and adequate rest.

Plan to have some extra hands on hand, if you're bottle feeding. Bottle feeding twins requires either an extra set of hands or great ingenuity. If you find yourself with two babies and just two hands at feeding time, you can sit on a sofa between the babies with their feet towards the back and hold a bottle for each. Or hold them both in your arms with the bottles in bottle-proppers raised to a comfortable height by pillows. You can also occasionally prop the bottle for one in a baby seat (but never lying down), while you feed the other the traditional way. Feeding them one after the other is another possibility, but one which will significantly cut into the already tiny amount of time you'll have for other activities. Such a procedure will also put the babies on somewhat different napping schedules if they sleep after eating, which can be good if you'd like some time alone with each, or bad if you depend on that tandem sleeping time to get things done for yourself and around the house.

Do half the work. Cut corners on non-essentials. Use paper plates and take-out food, ignore dust and disorder, rely on disposables or a nappy service, and easy-care clothes for everyone in the family. Use bibs and rubber pants (if you're determined to use terry nappies) to protect clothing and cut down on laundry.

Keep twice as many records. Who took what at which feeding, who was bathed yesterday, who's scheduled for today? Unless you keep a log (in a notebook, posted on the nursery wall, or on a blackboard), you're sure to forget. Also make note in a permanent record book of immunizations, illnesses and so on. Though most of the time, the babies will both get everything that's going around, occasionally only one will – and you may not remember which one.

Sneak sleep. Sleep will necessarily be scarce for the first few months, but it will be scarcer if you allow your babies to waken at random during the night. Instead, when the first cries, wake the second and feed them both. Any time that both your little darlings are napping during the day, catch a few winks yourself – or at least put your feet up.

Double the help. All new mothers need help – you need it twice as much. Accept all the help you can get, from whatever source: spouse, parents, other relatives, friends, local teenagers, paid baby-sitters. If you can afford it, hire two baby-sitters when you leave your babies during the day. Or sign up two friends or relatives or neighbourhood teens. That way, when you take a few hours off, you will know that each of your babies is getting individual attention.

Learn to tune out some of the fussing and crying. You can't be in two places at once, and both you and your twins will have to learn to accept that fact. Pretty soon they will be entertaining each other, giving you more time for other chores.

Double up on equipment. When you don't have another pair of hands around to help, utilize such conveniences as baby carriers (one in the carrier, one in your arms), baby swings (but not until your babies are six weeks old), and infant seats. A playpen is a safe playground for your twins as they get older, and because they'll have each other for company, they will be willing to be relegated to it more often and for longer periods than a singleton. Select a twin pushchair to meet your needs (if you will be traversing narrow grocery aisles, for example, a back to front model will be more practical than a side by side one); you will probably find a pram a waste of money. And don't forget that you will need two car seats. (Put one in centre front, one in centre back, if possible.)

Join a twins network. Parents of twins who've already survived the first few months and more will be your best source of advice and support; be sure to tap them. Find a parents of twins support group in your neighbourhood, or if one is lacking, start one – locating members via a notice on your doctor's bulletin board. But avoid becoming too clannish, socializing with only the parents of twins and having your babies participate in twins-only playgroups. Though there's something indisputably different about being a twin, excluding your children from relationships with singletons will discourage normal social development with peers – the majority of whom, of course, will not be twins.

Be doubly alert, once your twins are mobile. Any trouble one baby can get into, two babies can get into – and more often. You'll find, as your babies begin crawling and cruising, that what one of them doesn't think of in the way of mischief, the other will. Consequently, they will need to be watched twice as carefully.

Expect things to get doubly better. The first four months with twins are the hardest; though it never gets easy, handling your twins will become more manageable as you become more adept. Keep in mind, too, that twins are often each other's best company – many have a way of keeping each other busy that mothers of demanding singletons find enviable, and which will free you up more and more in the months and years to come.

breastfeed their babies without supple-mentation, and a very few can't breastfeed at all. The reason may be physical, such as a prolactin deficiency, insufficient mammary glandular tissue, markedly asymmetrical breasts, or damage to the nerves to the nipple caused by breast surgery. Or it could be psychological, due to negative feelings about breastfeeding that can inhibit let-down. Or, occasionally, it may not be pinpointed at all. An early clue that your breasts may not be able to produce adequate milk is their failure to enlarge during pregnancy – though it's not an infallible clue, and may be less reliable in second and subsequent pregnancies than in first ones.

If your baby isn't thriving, and unless the problem appears to be one that can be cleared up in just a few days, his doctor is almost certain to prescribe supplemental formula feedings. Don't despair. What's most important is adequately nourishing your baby, not whether you give breast or bottle. In most cases, when supplementing, you can have the benefits of the direct mother-baby contact that nursing affords by letting baby suckle for pleasure (his and yours) after he's finished his bottle, or by using a supplemental nutrition system.

Ardent breastfeeding advocates may frown at your use of formula; they may recommend that you, instead, radically change your diet, add brewer's yeast, drink beer, or try some other panacea. Though getting the Breast-feeding Daily Dozen (see page 526) is im-portant for keeping up your strength and the quality of your milk, there is no scientific evi-dence that any dietary manipulations will cure your breastfeeding woes. Try them if you like, but don't let your baby starve while you do.

Once a baby who is not doing well on the breast is put on formula, he almost in-variably thrives. In the rare instance that he doesn't, a return trip to the doctor is ne-cessary to see what it is that is interfering with adequate weight gain.

The Fontanels

'I'm so nervous when I handle my

baby's head – that soft spot seems so vulnerable. Sometimes it seems to pulsate, which is very scary.'

That 'soft spot' – actually there are two and they are called fontanels – is tougher than it looks. The sturdy membrane covering the fontanels is capable of protecting the new-born from the probing of even the most curious sibling fingers, and certainly from everyday handling.

These openings in the skull, where the bones haven't yet grown together, aren't there to make new parents nervous about handling baby, but for two important rea-sons. During childbirth, they allow the foetal head to mould to fit through the birth canal, something a solidly fused skull couldn't do. Later, they allow for the tremendous brain growth of the first year.

The larger of the two openings, the anterior fontanel, is on the top of the newborn's head; it is diamond shaped and may be as wide as 5 cm (2 inches). It starts to close when an infant is six months old and is usually totally closed by eighteen months. The fontanel normally appears flat, though it may bulge a bit when baby cries, and if baby's hair is sparse and fair, the cerebral pulse may be visible through it. A depressed anterior fontanel is usually a sign of dehy-dration, a warning that the baby needs to be given fluids promptly. (Call the baby's doctor immediately to report this symptom.) A fontanel that bulges persistently may in-dicate increased pressure inside the head and also requires immediate medical atten-tion.

The posterior fontanel, a smaller trian-gular opening towards the back of the head less than 1 cm (half an inch) in diameter, is much less noticeable, and may be difficult for you to locate. It is generally completely closed by the third month.

Nursing Blisters

'Why does my baby have a blister on her upper lip? Is she sucking too hard?'

For a baby with a hearty appetite, there's no such thing as sucking too hard – although a new mother with tender nipples may disagree. And though 'nursing blisters', which develop on the centre of the upper lips of many newborns, both breast and bottle fed, are caused by vigorous sucking, they have no medical significance, cause the infant no discomfort, and will disappear without treatment within a few months. Sometimes, they even seem to disappear between feedings.

Healing of the Umbilical Cord

'The cord still hasn't fallen off my baby's belly button, and it looks really awful. Could it be infected?'

Healing belly buttons almost always look and smell worse than they actually are. What constitutes 'perfectly normal' in medical terms can actually send the weak-of-knee to the floor as fast as the climatic scene in a chain-saw horror film.

If you've been taking fastidious care of the cord stump (see page 86), infection is unlikely. If, however, you note redness in the surrounding skin (which could be due to irritation from alcohol applications as well as infection) or a discharge from the navel or from the base of the umbilical cord, particularly a foul-smelling one, check with your baby's doctor. If infection is present, antibiotics will probably be prescribed to clear it up.

The cord, which is shiny and moist at birth, usually dries up and falls off within a week or two, but the big event can occur earlier, or even much later – some babies don't seem to want to give them up. Until it does, keep the site dry (no tub baths), exposed to air (turn nappy down and shirt up), and cleaned with alcohol (but try to protect the surrounding skin, perhaps coating it with a baby lotion prior to swabbing the cord).

Umbilical Hernia

'Every time she cries, my baby's navel seems to stick out. Our baby nurse says it's a hernia and wants to wrap a belly band around the baby's middle.'

The diagnosis is probably correct, but the treatment is definitely wrong. Antenatally, all babies have an opening in the abdominal wall through which blood vessels extend into the umbilical cord. In some cases (for black babies more often than white) the opening doesn't close completely at birth. When these babies cry or strain, a small coil of intestine bulges through the opening, raising the umbilicus, and often the area around it, in a lump that ranges from fingertip to lemon size. While the appearance of such a lump (especially when it's tagged with the ominous-sounding term 'hernia') might be alarming, it's actually no cause for concern. Unlike other hernias, the intestine almost never strangulates in the opening, and in most cases, the hernia eventually resolves without intervention. Small openings usually close spontaneously or become inconspicuous within a few months, larger ones by a year and a half or two.

Belly bands (or binders), band-aids, and adhesive-taped coins are outdated and ineffective remedies, and the tape can irritate skin. The best treatment is usually no treatment at all. Though surgery to correct umbilical hernias is simple, safe and sure, it isn't recommended unless the opening in the abdomen is very large, is growing larger, bothers baby, or upsets mother. Often the paediatrician will suggest waiting until the child is six or seven before considering surgery, because most hernias will have closed by then. If, however, you see signs of strangulation – the lump does not recede after crying, can't be pushed in, suddenly becomes larger and tender, baby is vomiting – go to Emergency. Immediate surgery may be needed.

Don't confuse a navel that protrudes temporarily (before the cord drops off) or permanently (an 'outie') with a hernia. A hernia expands with crying, a normal protruding navel doesn't.

Sneezing

'My baby sneezes all the time. He doesn't seem sick, but I'm afraid he's caught a cold.'

Hold off on the chicken soup. What your baby's caught isn't likely to be a cold, but some amniotic fluid and excess mucus in his respiratory passages, very common in young babies. And to clear it out, nature has provided him with a protective reflex: sneezing. Frequent sneezing (and coughing, another protective reflex), also helps the newborn to get rid of foreign particles from the environment that make their way to his nose – much as sniffing pepper makes many adults sneeze.

Crossed Eyes

'The swelling is down around my baby's eyes. Now she seems cross-eyed.'

Babies are very obliging: they always give their mothers something new to worry about. And most mothers worry plenty when they notice their babies' eyes appear to be crossed. Actually, in most cases, it's simply extra folds of skin at the inner corners of the eyes that make the babies look cross-eyed. When the folds retract as baby grows, the eyes begin to seem more evenly matched.

During the early months, you may also notice that your baby's eyes may not work in perfect unison all the time. These random eye movements mean she's still learning to use her eyes and strengthening her eye muscles; by three months, coordination should be much improved. If it isn't, or if your baby's eyes always seem to be out of synch, then talk to her doctor about the problem. If there is a possibility of strabismus, or true crossed eyes (in which the baby uses just one eye to focus on what she's looking at, and the other just seems aimed anywhere) consultation with a paediatric ophthalmologist is in order. Early treatment is important, because so much that a child learns she learns through her eyes; and because ignoring crossed eyes could lead to amblyopia or 'lazy' eye (in which the eye that isn't being used becomes lazy and consequently weaker, from disuse).

Teary Eyes

'At first, there were no tears when my baby cried. Now her eyes seem filled with tears even when she's not crying. And sometimes they overflow.'

Tearless crying is common in newborns. It is not until near the end of the first month of life that the fluid that bathes the eye (called tears) begins to be produced in the lacrimal glands over the eyeballs. The fluid normally drains through tiny lacrimal ducts, located at the inner corner of each eye, and into the nose, which is why a lot of crying can make your nose run. The ducts are particularly tiny in infants and in 1 in 100 babies, one or both are blocked at birth.

Since a blocked tear duct doesn't drain properly, tears fill the eyes and often spill over, producing the perpetually 'teary-eyed' look even in happy babies. Most clogged ducts will clear up by themselves by the end of the first year without treatment, though your baby's doctor may recommend massaging the ducts to hasten the clearing. (If you do use massage and the baby's eyes become puffy or red, stop massaging and inform the doctor.)

Sometimes there is a small accumulation of yellowish white mucus in the inner corner of the eye with a tear duct blockage, and the lids may be stuck together when baby wakes up in the morning. Mucus and crust can be washed away with cooled boiled water and sterile absorbent cotton wool balls. A heavy, darker yellow discharge and/or reddening of the whites of the eye, however, may indicate infection and the need for medical attention. The doctor may prescribe antibiotic ointments or drops, and if the duct becomes chronically infected, may refer your baby to an ophthalmologist. The eye doctor may recommend probing the duct with a very thin wire to establish normal tear flow, or may suggest continuing to wait it out, possibly until your child is a year old or so. Very, very rarely, probing doesn't work and surgery is needed.

First Smiles

'Everybody says that my baby's smiles are "just wind", but he looks so happy when he does it. Couldn't they be real?'

They read it in books and magazines. They hear it from mothers-in-law, friends with children, their paediatricians, perfect strangers in the park. And yet, no new mother wants to believe that her baby's first smiles are the work of a passing bubble of wind, rather than of a wave of love meant especially for her.

But alas, it appears from scientific evidence so far to be true: most babies don't smile in the true social sense before four to six weeks of age. That doesn't mean that a smile is always 'just gas'. It also may be a sign of comfort and contentment – many babies smile as they are falling asleep, as they urinate, or when their cheeks are stroked.

When baby does display his first real smile, you'll know it, and you'll melt accordingly. In the meantime, enjoy those glimpses of smiles to come – undeniably adorable no matter what their cause.

Keeping Baby the Right Temperature

'It seems too hot out for a jumper and hat, but when I bring my baby out in just his T-shirt and nappy, everyone on the street complains that he's underdressed.'

As far as well-meaning strangers on buses, in shops, and on the street are concerned, new mothers (even if they are on their second or third child) can do no right. So get used to the criticism. But for the most part, don't let it affect how you take care of your baby. Grandmothers and grandmotherly types will go to their graves claiming otherwise, but once a baby's natural thermostat is properly set (within the first few days of life), you needn't dress him any more warmly than you dress yourself. (And in fact, prior to that, too much clothing can be as taxing to the newborn's heat-regulating mechanism as too little.)

So in general, use your own comfort (unless you're the kind of person who's always warm when everybody else is cold, or always cold when everybody else is warm) as a gauge in determining whether baby is comfortable. If you're unsure, don't check his hands for confirmation (as those 'well-meaners' will, with disapproving clucks of 'See! His hands are cold!'). A baby's hands and feet are usually cooler than the rest of his body, again due to an immature circulatory system. Don't take the fact that your baby sneezes a few times to mean he's cold either, he may sneeze in reaction to sunlight or because he needs to clear his nose. If it's warm out, your baby is not underdressed.

While you needn't listen to strangers, do listen to your baby. Babies will tell you that they are cold (as they tell you most everything else) by fussing or crying. When you get such a message, check the nape of the neck, arms, or trunk (whichever is easiest to reach under baby's clothing) with the back of your hand for a temperature reading. If baby feels comfortably warm, maybe it's a hungry or tired cry you're hearing. (And if he's sweaty, he's probably overdressed.) If he's cool, add clothing or covering, or turn up the thermostat. If a young baby seems extremely cold, get him to a warm place right away because his body probably can't produce enough heat to rewarm himself even if he has a lot of covering. In the meantime, put him close to the warmth of your body, under your shirt if necessary.

The one part of a baby that needs extra protection in all kinds of weather is his head; partly because a lot of heat is lost from the uncovered head, and partly because most babies have very little protection in the way of hair. On even marginally cool days, a hat is a good idea for a baby under a year old. In hot, sunny weather a hat with a brim will protect baby's head, face, and eyes – but even with this protection exposure to full sun should be no more than fleeting.

A young baby also needs extra protection from heat loss when he's sleeping. In deep sleep his heat-producing mechanism slows down, so in cooler weather bring along an extra blanket or covering for his nap. If he sleeps in a cool room at night, a blanket sleeper or warm quilt will help him stay warm.

When it comes to dressing baby in cold weather, the layered look is not only fashionable, it's sensible. Several light layers of clothing retain body heat more efficiently than one heavy layer, and the outer layers can be peeled off as needed when you walk into an overheated store or board a stuffy bus, or if the weather takes a sudden turn for the warmer.

An occasional baby falls outside the norm for body temperature control – just as the occasional adult does. If your baby seems cooler than you do, or warmer, all the time, then accept that fact. You may find in talking to your in-laws that your spouse was the same way as a baby. That means, for the cooler baby, more coverings and warmer clothes than you would usually need. For the warmer baby (you'll probably discover this because of heat rash even in the winter), it means fewer coverings and lighter clothes.

Taking Baby Out

'It's been ten days since I brought my baby home from the hospital, and I'm starting to go stir-crazy cooped up in the house. When can I take her out?'

Unless your hospital and your home are connected by subterranean tunnel, you've taken your baby outside already. And barring a blizzard, a rainstorm, or significantly subfreezing temperatures, you could have conceivably continued to take her outside every day since. Old wives' tales (which continue to be perpetuated by even not-so-old mothers and mothers-in-law) that have kept newborns and new mothers captives in their own homes for two weeks postpartum and more are completely invalid. Any baby hardy enough to leave the hospital is hardy enough to weather a stroll through the park, a trip to the supermarket, even a lengthy excursion to visit grandmother (though in flu season, you might want to limit baby's exposure to indoor crowds, especially for the first month). Assuming you're up to the exercise (you're more likely to need rest than your baby, and should spend a lot of time off your feet for at least the first postpartum week), feel free to plan that first escape from the confines of your home.

When you take baby out, dress her appropriately and always take along an extra covering if there's a possibility of a change for the cooler in the weather. If it's windy or rainy, use a weather shield on the stroller or carriage; if it's very chilly or extremely hot and humid, limit the amount of time your baby spends out of doors – if you're freezing or sweltering, she is too. Avoid more than brief exposure to direct sunlight, even in mild weather. If your outing is in a car, be sure your baby is properly harnessed in her infant safety seat.

Exposure to Outsiders

'Everybody wants to touch our son. The doorman, the clerk in the supermarket, old women in stores, visitors we have in our home. I'm always worried about germs.'

There's nothing that cries out to be squeezed more than a new baby. Baby cheeks, fingers, chin, toes – they're all irresistible. And yet resist is just what most mothers would like outsiders to do when it comes to their newborns.

Your fear of your baby picking up germs this way is a legitimate one. A very young infant is more susceptible to infection because his immune system is still relatively immature and he hasn't had a chance to build up immunities. So, for now at least, politely ask strangers to look but don't touch – particularly the hands, which usually end up in baby's mouth. You can always blame it on the doctor. 'The paediatrician said not to let anyone outside the family handle him yet.' As for friends and family, ask them to wash their hands before picking up baby, at least for the first month. This should continue indefinitely when those who have a communicable illness handle your baby. And skin-to-skin contact should be avoided with anyone who has a rash or open sores.

No matter what you do or say, expect that every once in a while your baby will have some contact with strangers. All is not lost. If a friendly checker in the supermarket tests your child's grasp on his finger, just pull out a wipe and wash off baby's hands – discreetly, of course.

As your baby gets older, however, he needn't – and shouldn't – be raised in a plastic bubble environment. He needs to be exposed to a wide variety of 'bugs' in order to start building up immunities to those common in your community. So loosen up a little and let the germs fall where they may after the first month.

Skin Colour Changes

'My baby suddenly turned two colours – reddish blue on the bottom and pale on top. What's wrong with her?'

There's probably little more frightening than watching your baby turn colour before your eyes. And yet there's virtually nothing to fear when a newborn suddenly takes on a split-colour appearance, either side to side or top to bottom. As a result of her immature circulatory system, blood has simply pooled on half of your baby's body. Turn her upside down (or, if the colour difference is side by side, over) momentarily, and normal colour will be restored.

You may also notice that your baby's hands and feet appear bluish, even though the rest of her body is pink. This, too, is due to immature circulation and usually disappears by the end of the first week.

'Sometimes when I'm changing my new

baby I notice bis skin seems to be mottled all over. Why?'

Purplish (sometimes more red, sometimes more blue) mottling of a tiny baby's skin is sure to raise questions in his parents' minds. But mottling when a baby is chilled or crying is not at all unusual. These transient changes are yet another sign of an immature circulatory system, visible through baby's still very thin skin. He should outgrow this phenomenon in a few months. In the meantime, when it occurs, check the nape of his neck or his midsection to see if he is too cool. If so, increase his clothing or covering. If not, just relax and wait for the mottling to disappear, as it probably will in a few minutes.

Feeding Schedule

'I seem to be nursing my new daughter all the time. Whatever happened to the four-hour schedules I've heard about?'

Unfortunately, your baby (and all the other nursing babies you'll notice nipping at their mother's breasts almost continuously in the first few months of life) hasn't heard about the four-hour schedule. Hunger calls and she wants to eat – a lot more often than most 'schedules' would permit her to.[2]

Let her – at least for now. Three- and four-hour schedules are based on the needs of bottle-fed newborns, who usually do very well on such regimens. But most breastfed babies need to eat more often than that. First of all, because breast milk is digested more quickly than formula, making them feel hungry again sooner. Second, because frequent nursing helps establish a good milk supply – the foundation of a successful breastfeeding relationship.

Nurse as frequently as baby seems to want

2. Do remember, however, that like labour contractions, intervals between feedings are timed from the beginning of one to the beginning of the next. So a baby who nurses for forty minutes starting at 10 A.M., then sleeps for an hour and twenty minutes before eating again, is on a two-hour schedule, not a one-hour-and-twenty-minute one.

to during the early weeks. But if your baby is still demanding food every hour at three weeks of age or so, check with the doctor to see if her weight gain is normal. If it isn't, seek advice from the doctor, and see 'Your Breastfed Baby not Thriving', page 98. If she seems to be thriving, however, it's time to start making demands of your own. Hourly nursing is not only too much of an emotional strain for you, it's a physical strain as well, and will probably result in sore nipples and fatigue. Neither is it best for your baby, since she needs longer periods of sleep and longer periods of wakefulness when she isn't eating and when she should be looking at something other than a breast.

Assuming your milk supply is well established, you can start thinking about fitting your baby into a schedule of sorts. Try stretching the periods between feedings (which may also help your baby sleep better at night). When baby wakes crying an hour after feeding, don't rush to feed her. If she still seems sleepy, try to get her back to sleep without nursing her. Before picking her up, pat or rub her back, turn on a musical toy, and see if she'll drift back off. If not, pick her up, sing softly to her, walk with her, rock her, again with the goal of getting her back to sleep. If she seems alert, don't rush to feed her. Change her, talk to her, distract her in some other way, even take her for a stroll out of doors. She may become so interested in you and the rest of the world that she actually forgets about your breasts – at least for a few minutes.

When you finally do nurse, don't accept the snack-bar approach some babies try to take; encourage her to nurse at least ten minutes on each side – twenty would be even better. If she refuses to nurse this long, start with five minutes on each side so that she fills up with most of the milk from both breasts in ten minutes, then return her to the first breast to continue for as long as she likes. If she falls off to sleep, try to waken her to continue the meal. If you can manage to stretch the periods between nursings a little more each day, eventually you and baby will be on a more reasonable schedule: two to three hours, and eventually four or so. But it

should be a schedule based on her hunger, not the clock.

Hiccups

'My baby gets the hiccups all the time – and for no apparent reason. Do they bother him as much as they do me?'

Some babies aren't just born hiccupers, they're hiccupers before they're born. And chances are, if your baby hiccuped a lot inside of you, he'll hiccup plenty in the first few months on the outside, too. But a newborn's hiccups, unlike the adult variety, don't have a known cause. They are believed to be another of baby's reflexes, though they're frequently triggered by giggling later on. And also unlike adult hiccups, they're not bothersome, at least not to baby. If they are to you, try letting your baby nurse or suck on a bottle of water which may quell the attack.

Bowel Movements

'I expected one, maybe two bowel movements a day from my breastfed baby. But she seems to have one in every nappy – sometimes as many as ten a day. And they're very loose. Could she have diarrhoea?'

Your baby isn't the first breastfed infant ever who seemed to be aiming to beat the Guinness World Record for dirtying nappies. Not only is such an active elimination pattern not a bad sign in a breastfed newborn, it's a good one. Since the amount that's coming out is related to the amount going in, any breastfeeding mother whose newborn has five or more movements daily can be assured that her baby is getting sufficient nourishment. (Mothers of nursing newborns who have fewer movements should see page 98.) The number of movements progressively decreases and may dwindle down to no more than one a day, or every other day, next month, though some babies continue to have several movements a day for the entire first year. It's not necessary to keep count – the number may vary from day to day, and that's perfectly normal, too.

Normal, too, for breastfed infants is a very soft, sometimes even watery, stool. But diarrhoea – frequent stools that are liquidy, smelly, and may contain mucus, often accompanied by fever and/or weight loss – is rare among children who dine on breast milk. If they do get it, they have fewer, smaller movements than bottle babies with diarrhoea and recover more quickly, probably because of the antibacterial properties of breast milk.

Constipation

'I'm worried that my baby is constipated. He's been averaging only one movement every two or three days. Could it be his formula?'

Constipation has been flippantly defined as having movements less often than your mother. But that's an unreliable gauge, since each individual has a personal pattern of elimination, and it's not necessarily a case of 'like mother, like child'. Some bottle-fed babies go three or four days between movements. But they're not considered to be constipated unless those infrequent movements are firmly formed or come out in hard pellets, or if they cause pain or bleeding (from a fissure or crack in the anus as a result of pushing). If your baby's movements are soft and cause no problems, don't worry. But if you suspect constipation, consult his doctor. It's possible a change in formula or the addition of a couple of tablespoons of diluted prune or other fruit juice to the baby's diet might help. (Citrus juices should not be introduced at this early age, since they are highly allergenic and very acidic.) But don't take any steps such as giving laxatives (especially mineral oil), enemas, or herbal teas without medical advice.

'I thought breastfed babies were never constipated – but my daughter grunts and groans and strains whenever she has a bowel movement.'

It's true that breastfed babies are rarely constipated because breast milk is just the right match for the human baby's digestive tract. But it's also true that some have to push and strain to get their movements out, even though the movement comes out soft and seems as though it should have been easy to pass.[3] Why this is so isn't certain. Some have theorized it's because the soft stool of the breastfed baby doesn't put adequate pressure on the anus. Others speculate that the muscles of the anus are neither strong enough nor coordinated enough to eliminate any stool easily. Still others point to the fact that young babies, who usually have bowel movements lying down, get no help from gravity.

Whatever the reason, the difficulty should ease up when solids are added to your baby's diet. But in the meantime, don't worry. And don't use laxatives (especially not mineral oil), enemas, or any other home remedies for the problem – because it really isn't one. When an adult is constipated, walking often helps alleviate the problem; you might try flexing and extending your baby's legs in a bicycling motion while she's on her back to assist her when she seems uncomfortable. And once she starts eating table foods, be sure she gets plenty of whole grains and legumes, fruits, and vegetables – and eventually, exercise.

Explosive Bowel Movements

'My son's bowel movements come with such force and such explosive sound, I'm worried that he has some digestive problem. Or maybe something's wrong with my breast milk.'

Breastfed newborns are rarely discreet when

---

3. If your breastfed baby has very infrequent bowel movements and is not gaining well, then see page 98 and check with your doctor. It's possible she isn't getting enough to eat and thus has not much to eliminate.

it comes to making bowel movements. The noisy barrage that fills the room as they fill their nappies can often be heard in the next room, and can alarm first-time parents. Yet these movements and the surprising variety of sounds that punctuate their passing are normal, the result of gas being forcefully expelled from an immature digestive system. Things should quiet down in a month or two.

Passing Wind

'My baby passes wind all day long – very loudly. Could she be having stomach troubles?'

The digestive exclamations that frequently explode from a newborn's tiny bottom, at least as emphatically as the grownup variety, can be unsettling – and sometimes embarrassing – to parents. But, like explosive bowel movements, they are perfectly normal. Once your newborn's digestive system works out the kinks, the wind will pass more quietly and less frequently.

Milk Allergy

'My baby is crying a lot, and a friend suggested that he might be allergic to the milk in his formula. How can I tell?'

Though friends are likely to blame excessive crying on a milk allergy, and mothers are so anxious to blame the crying on something other than themselves that they're likely to accept that explanation, doctors are less quick to do so. Milk allergy is the most common food allergy in infants, but it is less common than most people believe. Most doctors believe it an unlikely possibility in a child whose parents don't have allergies, and in one whose only symptom is crying. A baby who is having a severe allergic response to milk will usually vomit frequently and have loose, watery stools, possibly tinged with blood. (It's important to uncover the cause of such symptoms promptly since

they can lead to dehydration and a serious chemical imbalance.) Less severe reactions may include occasional vomiting and loose mucous stools. Some babies who are allergic to milk may also have eczema, hives, wheezing, and/or a nasal discharge or stuffiness when exposed to milk protein.

Unfortunately, there's no simple test to determine hypersensitivity (allergy) to milk with any degree of accuracy, except through trial and error. If you suspect milk allergy, discuss the possibility with your baby's doctor before taking any action. If there is no history of allergy in your family, and if there are no symptoms other than the crying, then it is likely the doctor will suggest you treat the crying spells as ordinary colic (see page 120).

If there are family allergies or symptoms other than crying, a trial change of formula – to hydrolysate (in which the protein is partly broken down or predigested) or soya – may be recommended. A rapid improvement in the colicky behaviour and the disappearance of other symptoms, if any, would suggest the possibility of an allergy to milk – or it could just be a coincidence. Reinstating the milk formula is one way of verifying the diagnosis; if the symptoms return with the milk, allergy is likely.

In many cases there's no change when a baby is switched to a soya formula. This may mean he's also allergic to soya, has a medical condition that has nothing to do with milk and that needs to be diagnosed, or simply has an immature digestive system. A switch from soya to hydrolysate formula should help if the baby seems to be sensitive to both soya and milk. In some cases, goat's milk may be recommended, but because it lacks folic acid, look for the type that is fortified with that vitamin.

Very rarely, the problem is an enzyme deficiency – the infant is born unable to produce lactase, the enzyme needed to digest the milk sugar lactose. Such a child has persistent diarrhoea from the start, and fails to gain weight. A formula containing little or no lactose will usually resolve the problem. Unlike a temporary lactose intolerance that sometimes develops during a bout with an intestinal bug, a congenital lactase deficiency is usually permanent. The afflicted baby will probably never be able to tolerate ordinary milk products – though he will probably be fine on those that are lactose-reduced.

If the problem is not traced to milk allergy or intolerance, you should probably switch back to a cow's milk formula, since it is better breast milk substitute.

Infant allergy to cow's milk is usually outgrown by the end of the first year, and almost always by the end of the second. If your baby is taken off cow's milk formula, his doctor may suggest trying it again after six months on a substitute formula, or may suggest waiting until the first birthday.

Using Detergent on Baby's Clothes

'I've been using baby soap flakes to wash my daughter's clothes. But nothing seems to come clean, and I'm also getting tired of doing her loads separately. When can I start using detergent?'

Although manufacturers of special baby laundry soaps wouldn't want it to get around, many babies probably don't need their clothes washed separately from the rest of the family's. Even the kind of high-potency detergents that really get clothes clean, eliminating most stains and odours, aren't irritating to most babies when they're well rinsed. (Rinsing is most thorough, and stain-fighting powers are most effective, with liquid detergents.) An added advantage of using detergents: since they aren't taboo on fire-retardant garments, as soap products are, all of baby's clothes can be tossed in together.

To test your baby's sensitivity to your favourite laundry detergent, add one garment that will be worn close to baby's skin (such as a T-shirt) to your next family load, being careful not to overdo the detergent or underdo the rinse. If baby's skin shows no rash or irritation, feel free to wash her clothes with yours. If a rash does appear, try another detergent, preferably one without colours and fragrances, before deciding you have to stick with soap flakes.

Restless Sleep

'Our baby, who shares our room, tosses and turns all night. Could our being near be keeping him from sleeping soundly?'

Although the phrase 'sleeping like a baby' is often equated with enviably peaceful and restful sleep, particularly by the manufacturers of mattresses and sleep aids, babies' sleep isn't restful at all. Newborns do sleep a lot, but they also wake up a lot in the process. That's because most of their sleep is REM (rapid eye movement) sleep, an active sleep with dreaming and a lot of movement. At the end of each REM sleep period, the sleeper usually awakens briefly. When you hear your baby fuss or whimper at night, it's probably because he's finishing a REM period, not because you share a room with him.

As he gets older, his sleeping patterns will mature. He will have less REM sleep and longer periods of the much sounder 'quiet sleep', from which it's harder to rouse him. He will continue to stir and whimper periodically, but less frequently.

Though your being in the same room with baby probably isn't disturbing his sleep at this stage (though it may soon), it certainly is disturbing yours. Not only do you waken at every moan, but you also are tempted to pick him up more often than necessary during the night. Try to ignore your baby's midnight murmurings; pick him up only when he begins to cry steadily and seriously. You'll both sleep better. If you find that difficult, then perhaps you should consider separate sleeping quarters – if you have the space.

Do be alert, however, for sudden waking and crying, unusual restlessness, or other changes in sleeping patterns that don't seem to be related to events in baby's life (such as teething or an overstimulating day). If you note them, check for such signs of illness as fever, appetite loss, or diarrhoea (see Chapter 17). Call your doctor if the symptoms persist.

Sleeping Patterns

'I thought newborns were supposed to sleep all the time. Our three-week-old daughter hardly seems to sleep at all.'

Newborns often seem not to know what they're 'supposed to do'. They nurse erratically when they're 'supposed to' be on a three- or four-hour schedule, or they sleep 12 hours a day (or 22) when they're 'supposed to' sleep 16½ hours. That's because they know what we often forget – that there's almost nothing a baby is supposed to do at any specific time. 'Average' babies, who do everything by the book, do exist. But they are in the minority. The 16½ hours that is the average sleeping time for babies in their first month of life takes into account babies who sleep 10 hours a day and others who sleep 23, as well as all those in between. The baby who falls at either end of the spectrum is no less normal than one who falls near the average. Some infants, like some adults, appear to need more sleep than others, some less.

So assuming your baby seems healthy in every way, don't worry about her wakefulness, but do get used to it. Infants who sleep very little tend to grow into children who sleep very little – with parents who, not coincidentally, also sleep very little.

'My baby gets up several times a night. My mother says if I don't get her into a regular sleeping pattern now, she may never develop good sleep habits. She says I should let her cry it out instead of feeding her all night.'

Any experienced mother, particularly one who's had difficulty with a baby who wouldn't sleep through the night or who had trouble falling asleep, knows the importance of fostering good sleep habits in

children at an early age. But the first month of life is too early. Your baby is just beginning to learn about the world. The most important lesson she needs to learn now is that when she calls, you will be there – even at 3 A.M., and even when she's up for the fourth time in six hours. 'Crying it out', has its place in helping a baby figure out how to fall asleep by herself, but not for several months yet – not until she begins to feel more secure and more in control of her environment.

If you're breastfeeding, trying to institute a sleeping schedule now could also interfere with establishing a good milk supply – and with your baby's growth. Breastfed newborns need to eat more frequently than bottle-fed babies, often every two hours, which generally prevents them from sleeping through the night until somewhere between the third and sixth months. Like the time-honoured four-hour feeding schedule, the belief that babies should sleep through the night by two months is based on the developmental behaviour of bottle-fed infants, and is often unrealistic for those who are nursing.

So, as your mother advises, do think ahead about building some discipline into your child's sleeping habits, but don't let her cry it out just yet.

Noise when Baby is Sleeping

'I have a friend who turns off the phone when her son is sleeping, has a note on the door asking people to knock instead of ring, and tiptoes around the apartment at nap time. Isn't this a little extreme?'

Your friend is programming her child to be unable to sleep except under controlled environmental conditions, conditions that she will find virtually impossible to maintain on a permanent basis – unless her baby's bedroom is a padded cell.

And what's more, her efforts will probably be counterproductive. Though a sudden loud sound may waken some babies, others can sleep through fireworks, wailing sirens, and barking dogs. For most, however, a steady hum of background noise – from TV or stereo, a fan or air conditioner, musical toy or one that imitates uterine sounds, or from a white-noise machine – appears to be more conducive to restful sleep than perfect silence, particularly if the baby has fallen asleep to the beat of such sounds.

Just how much noise, as well as what kinds of noise, a baby can sleep through depends in part on the sounds he became accustomed to before birth and partly on individual temperament. So parents have to take their cues from their babies in determining how far they must go to protect them from unnecessary interruptions to sleep during naps and at night. If a baby turns out to be especially sound sensitive during sleep, it's probably wise to turn the phone down to low, to change the doorbell to a less abrasive ring, and to play the radio or TV more softly. Such tactics are unnecessary, however, if a baby sleeps through everything.

By attempting to turn off all the sound in her baby's life, your friend is very likely going to make it difficult for her child to get a good night's sleep later on, when he has to sleep in the real world.

Dummies

'My baby has crying jags in the afternoon. Should I give him a dummy to comfort him?'

In the long run, it's probably best for babies to learn, to some extent, to comfort themselves rather than to rely on artificial aids such as a dummy. A thumb (or a fist) can do the job of providing extra sucking for comfort as well as a dummy, but it's in the baby's control, not the parents'. It's there whenever he needs it; can be plucked out when he wants to smile, coo, cry, or otherwise express himself; and it won't cause nipple confusion, as a dummy can in young infants just learning to suckle at the breast.

Because of nipple confusion, it's not a good idea to introduce a breastfeeding baby to the dummy until lactation is well established. It shouldn't be used at all for a baby who isn't gaining weight at an adequate clip or one who is a poor nurser, because it may give him so much sucking satisfaction that he loses interest in suckling at the breast.

Occasionally a dummy may be warranted temporarily for a baby who cries a lot and is soothed by nothing else, or for one who wants more sucking satisfaction but hasn't yet figured out how to get his fingers to his mouth. But be aware that dummy use easily slips into dummy abuse. What starts out as the baby's crutch can easily become the mother's. There is the ever-present temptation to use the dummy as a convenient substitute for the attention she herself should be providing to her child. The well-meaning mother who offers the dummy to make sure her baby has adequate sucking experience may soon find herself popping in a dummy the moment he becomes fussy, instead of trying to determine the reason for the fussing or if there might be other ways of placating him. She may use it to get the baby off to sleep instead of reading him a story, to ensure quiet while she's on the phone intead of picking him up and consoling him while she's chatting, to buy his silence while she's picking out a pair of new shoes instead of involving him in the interaction. The result is often a baby who can only be happy with something in his mouth, and who is unable to comfort himself, entertain himself, or get himself to sleep.

Used at night, a dummy can interfere with a baby's learning to fall asleep by himself, and can also interrupt his sleep when he loses it in the middle of the night and can't get back to dreamland without it – and who do you think will have to rise to put it back in his mouth?

Another drawback, albeit a temporary one: as with thumb sucking, sucking on a dummy can distort the mouth, but this distortion is corrected if the habit is abandoned before the permanent teeth appear.

If you feel you must use a pacifier occasionally for your baby, do so wisely. Be sure the dummy you buy has air holes and is all of a piece, so a part won't break off and become a choking hazard. (Those made of silicone are softer than those made of rubber, are long lasting, dishwasher safe, and don't become sticky.) *Never* attach a pacifier to the cot, pram, playpen, or pushchair, or hang it around your baby's neck or wrist with a ribbon, string, or cord of any kind – babies have been strangled this way. If you wish to avoid your baby developing a strong dummy habit that may be hard to break later, begin withdrawing the dummy by the time he is three months old. Until then, each time you consider plugging it in, ask yourself first whether it's the dummy or you the baby needs.

Checking Baby's Breathing

'Everybody always jokes about sneaking into the baby's room to hear if he's breathing. Well, now I find myself doing just that– even in the middle of the night. Sometimes you can hardly hear his breathing, other times it's very noisy.'

A new parent neurotically checking a baby's breathing does seem like good grist for a joke mill – until you become a new parent. And then it's no laughing matter. You wake in a cold sweat to complete silence after putting baby to bed five hours earlier. Could something be wrong? Why didn't he wake up? Or you pass his cot and he seems so silent and still that you have to shake him gingerly to be sure he's still alive. Or he's grunting and snorting so hard you're sure he's having trouble breathing. You – and millions of other new parents.

Not only are your concerns normal, but your baby's varied breathing patterns when he snoozes are, too. A major part of a newborn's sleep is spent in REM (rapid eye movement) sleep, a time when he breathes irregularly, grunts and snorts and twitches a lot – you can even see his eyes moving under the lids. The rest of his slumber is spent in quiet sleep, when he breathes very deeply and quietly and seems very still, except for occasional sucking motions or startling. As he gets older he will experience less REM sleep, and the quiet sleep will become more like the non-REM sleep of adults. You will eventually become less panicky about whether or not he's going to wake up in the morning, and more comfortable with both you and him sleeping eight hours at a stretch.

Still, you may never totally be able to abandon the habit of checking on your child's breathing (at least once in a while) until he's off to college and sleeping in a dorm – out of sight, though not out of mind.

Mixing up of Night and Day

'My three-week-old sleeps most of the day and wants to stay up all night. How can I get her to reverse her schedule so my husband and I can get some rest?'

Babies who work (or play) the night shift, getting most of their sleep by day, can turn normally active, alert parents into barely functioning zombies. Happily, this blissful ignorance of the difference between day and night isn't a permanent condition. The newborn who, before her arrival in the world of daytime light and nighttime darkness, was kept in the dark for nine months just needs a little time to adjust.

Chances are your baby will stop mixing up her days and nights within the next few weeks on her own. If you'd like to help speed the process, try limiting her daytime naps to no more than three or four hours each. Although waking a sleeping infant – except when you don't want to – can be tricky, it's usually possible. Try holding her upright, eliciting a burp, stripping off her clothes, rubbing under her chin, or tickling her feet. Once she's somewhat alert, try to further stimulate her: talk to her, sing lively songs, dangle a toy within her range of vision, which is about 20 to 35 cm (8 to 14 inches). (For other tips on keeping baby

Better Sleep for Baby

Whether a good sleeper or a poor one, your baby can be helped to sleep to potential with some or all of the following sleep enhancers, many of which help re-create some of the comforts of home in the womb:

Cozy sleeping space. A cot is a great modern invention – but in the early weeks many newborns somehow sense its vastness and balk when sentenced to solitude, smack in the centre of its mattress, so clearly removed from its distant walls. If your baby seems uncomfortable in the cot, an old-fashioned cradle, a moses basket or a pram can be used for the first few months to provide a snugger fit that's closer to the nine-month-long embrace in the uterus. For added security swaddle baby, tuck bedding in snugly, and use a gown that ties at the bottom, or a baby sleeping bag instead of a blanket.

Controlled temperature. Being too warm or too cold can disturb a baby's sleep. For tips on keeping baby comfortable in warm weather, see page 378; for tips in cold weather, see page 385.

Soothing movement. In the uterus, babies are most active when their mothers are at rest; when their mothers are up and on the go they slow down, lulled by the motion. Out of the womb, movement still has a soothing effect. Rocking, swaying and patting will all contribute to contentment – and sleep.

Soothing sound. For many months your heartbeat, the gurgling of your tummy, and your voice entertained and comforted your baby. Now sleeping may be difficult without some background noise. Try the hum of a fan or an air cleaner, the soft strains of music

from a radio or stereo, the tinkling of a music box or musical mobile, or one of those baby soothers that imitate uterine or car sounds.

Isolation. Babies sleep better when they are in a room of their own. At this stage it's not so much that they're disturbed by your presence, but that you're more likely to pick them up at the least little whimper, breaking up their sleep unnecessarily. You should, however, be close enough to hear your baby's cries before they turn into frantic ear-piercing wails – or install an intercom between baby's room and yours.

Routine. Since your newborn will fall asleep most of the time while nursing or bottle feeding, a bedtime routine might seem unnecessary. But it's never too early to begin such a routine, and certainly by the age of six months it should top off every evening. The ritual of a warm bath, followed by being dressed in night clothes, a little quiet playtime on your bed, a sing-song story or nursery rhyme from a picture book, can be soothing and soporific for even the youngest babies. The breast or bottle can be last on the agenda for babies who still fall asleep that way, but can come earlier for those who have already learned to go to bed on their own.

Adequate daytime rest. Some mothers try to solve the nighttime sleeping problems of their babies by keeping them awake during the day, even at times when their baby wants to sleep. This is a big mistake (though it's all right to limit the length of daytime naps a little in order to maintain the contrast between day and night) because an overtired baby sleeps more fitfully than a well-rested one.

awake, see page 59.) Don't, however, try to keep her from napping at all during the day, with the hope that she'll sleep at night. An overtired, and perhaps overstimulated, baby is not likely to sleep well at night.

Making a clear distinction between day and night may help. During the day have baby sleep in a pram or pushchair, perhaps

out of doors. If she naps in her room, avoid darkening it or trying to keep the noise level down. When she wakens, ply her with stimulating activities. At night, do the opposite. Put your baby to bed in her cot or bassinet and strive for darkness (use room-darkening shades), relative quiet and inactivity. No matter how tempting it may be, don't play with or talk to her when she wakens; don't turn on the lights or the TV while you're feeding her; keep communications to a whisper or softly sung lullabies; and be certain when she's back in her bed that sleeping conditions are ideal (see Better Sleep for Baby, page 117).

Although it may seem like a dubious blessing, consider yourself lucky that your baby sleeps for long stretches – even if it is during the day. It's a good sign that she's capable of sleeping well and that once she's got her internal clock set correctly, she will sleep well at night.

Sleeping Positions

'We were told our first baby should sleep on his tummy. Now the doctor says our new baby should sleep on her back. I'm confused.'

It's getting harder and harder to keep up with the pendulum swings. For years the experts advised putting newborns to sleep on their tummies (prone) rather than on their backs to avoid the risk of their choking on spit up. But now many experts believe that the back (supine) or side (lateral) positions may be safer. Recent studies suggest that though there has been little evidence that inhaling vomit is a major problem there is an increased risk of cot death or SIDS (Sudden Infant Death Syndrome) when babies sleep on their tummies. Putting infants to sleep on their backs or sides can, some studies show, reduce cot death rates by 50%. This research has prompted the American Academy of Pediatrics and the UK Foundation for the Study of Infant Deaths to recommend the back or side sleeping position for all healthy, full term babies. There are some exceptions, however, such as infants with respiratory problems, those who spit up a lot, or those with upper airway malformations.

Ideally, you should start your baby sleeping on her back right away – so that she will get used to and feel comfortable that way. If she seems to fuss a lot in that po-

sition, try propping her on her side (with a tightly rolled up blanket or towel as support). Of course, many babies slide down onto their stomachs or backs after a brief time on their sides, especially if they aren't swaddled. If your baby is unhappy on her back or side talk to her doctor about letting her sleep prone (but on a firm surface). The slightly increased risk with tummy sleeping may not be great enough to warrant you both being miserable.

You will probably find that your baby startles more often lying on her back, which may lead to slightly more frequent wakings. It is also possible that she will develop a flat or bald spot from always facing in the same direction – usually because she is focusing on the same spot (often a window) – while lying on her back. To minimize this problem, alternate her position (head at one end of the cot one night, the other the next). If in spite of your efforts her head flattens or a bald spot develops, don't worry. These problems will gradually correct themselves as she gets older.

Putting her on her tummy to play when she's awake (and watched) will also minimize head malformations and is important for normal muscle development. Remember: *back to sleep, tummy to play.*

Moving a Sleeping Baby to Bed

'I'm a nervous wreck when I try to put my sleeping baby down in her cot. I'm always afraid she'll wake up – and she usually does.'

She's finally asleep – after what seems like hours of nursing on sore breasts, rocking in aching arms, lullabying in an increasingly hoarse voice. You rise ever so slowly from the armchair and edge cautiously to the crib, holding your breath and moving only the muscles that are absolutely necessary. Then, with a silent but fervent prayer, you lift her over the edge of the cot and begin the perilous descent to the mattress below. Finally you release her, but a split second too soon. She's down – then she's up. Turning her head from side to side, sniffing and whimpering softly, then sobbing loudly. Ready to cry yourself, you pick her up and start all over.

The scenario's the same in almost every home with an infant. If you're having trouble keeping a good baby down, wait ten minutes until she's in deep sleep, then try:

A high mattress. If you were a gorilla, you might be able to set your baby down in a cot with a low mattress without having to scale the rail or, alternatively, drop her the last 15 cm (6 inches). Since you're only human, you will find it much easier if you set the mattress at the highest possible level (but at least 10 cm/4 inches from the top of the rail), but be sure to lower it by the time your baby is old enough to sit up. Or, for the first few weeks, use a cot substitute such as pram, bassinet, or cradle, all of which may be easier to lift a baby into and out of. Often these offer the important plus of being rockable, so the rocking motion that started in your arms can continue after you bed baby down.

The right light. Though it's a good idea to get baby to sleep in a darkened room, be sure there's enough light (a night-light will do) for you to see your way to the cot without bumping into a dresser or tripping over a toy – which is sure to jar both of you.

Close quarters. The longer the distance between the place where baby falls asleep and the place where you are going to put her down, the more opportunity for her to awaken on the way. So feed or rock her as close to the cradle or cot as possible.

A seat you can get out of. Always feed or rock your baby in a chair or sofa that you can rise from smoothly, without disturbing her.

A ready bed. Prepare the landing site before bedtime, unless you're coordinated enough to turn down the bed or extract a teddy with your toes. Baby will be less likely to stay asleep if you have to do a lot of juggling to clear the way for touchdown.

A warm bed. The shock of cold sheets on warm cheeks can rouse the best of little sleepers. Warm the sheets on cold nights with a warm hot-water bottle or a heating pad set on low, but be sure to remove it and check the bedding temperature before putting baby down. Or use flannel or knit sheets, which stay more comfortable than a flat weave.

The right side. Or the left. Feed or rock baby in whichever arm will allow you to put her in the cot without first having to turn her around. If she falls asleep prematurely on the wrong side, gently switch sides and rock or feed some more before attemtpting to put her down. Alternatively, position her cot away from the wall or arrange the bedding so that you can put your sleeping angel down from either side.

Constant contact. When baby is comfortable and secure in your arms, suddenly being dropped into open space, even for an inch or two, startles – and awakens. Cradle baby all the way down, easing your bottom hand out from under (and gently flipping her over as you do if she's a tummy sleeper) just before you reach the mattress. Maintain a hands-on pose for a few moments longer, gently patting if she starts to stir.

A lulling tune. Hypnotize your baby to sleep with a traditional lullaby (she won't object if you're off key) or an improvised one with a monotonous beat (aah-ah-aah-ah ba-by, aah-ah ba-by). Continue as you carry her to her cot, while you're putting her down, and for a few moments afterwards. If she begins to toss, croon some more, until she's fully quieted.

Crying

'We congratulated ourselves in the hospital on having such a good baby. We were home hardly 24 hours when she started howling.'

If one- and two-day-old babies cried as much as they were destined to a couple of weeks later, new parents would doubtless think twice about checking out of the hospital with their newborns. Once they're safely ensconced at home, babies don't seem to hesitate to show their true colours, with all doing some crying, and many doing a considerable amount. Crying is, after all, the only way infants have of communicating their needs and feelings – their very first baby talk. Your baby can't tell you that she's lonely, hungry, wet, tired, uncomfortable, too warm, too cold, or frustrated any other way. And though it may seem impossible now, you will soon be able (at least part of the time) to decode your baby's different cries and know what she's asking for.

Some newborn crying, however, seems entirely unrelated to basic needs. Four out of every 5 babies (some studies indicate 9 out of 10), in fact, have daily crying sessions of from 15 minutes to an hour that are not easily explained. These crying spells, like those associated with colic, a more severe and persistent form of unexplained crying, most often occur in the evening. It may be that this is the most hectic time of day in the home, with dinner being prepared, father coming home from work, parents trying to eat, other children, if any, vying for attention, and that the hustle-bustle is more than the baby can tolerate. Or that after a busy day of taking in and processing all the sights, sounds, smells and other stimuli in her environment, a baby just needs to unwind with a good cry.

Some perfectly happy babies seem to need to cry themselves to sleep, possibly because of fatigue. If your baby cries for five or ten minutes before going off, don't be concerned. She will eventually outgrow this, and picking her up to calm her or providing a dummy will only make it more difficult for her to get to sleep on her own when she's older. What may help is a regular pre-bedtime ritual and enough rest during the day so she isn't overtired at night.

Meanwhile, hang in there. Though you'll be drying some tears for the next eighteen years or so, these probably tearless newborn crying spells are likely to be a thing of the past by the time your baby is three months old. As she becomes a more effective communicator and a more self-reliant individual, and as you become more proficient at understanding her, she will cry less often, for shorter periods, and will be more easily comforted when she does cry.

A sudden bout of crying, however, in a baby who hasn't cried a lot before could signal illness or early teething. Check for fever and other signs that baby isn't well or might be teething, and call the doctor if you note anything out of the ordinary.

Colic

'My husband and I haven't had dinner together since our baby was three weeks old. We have to take turns gulping our food and carrying him around while he cries for hours every evening.'

For the parents of a colicky baby, even a steak dinner becomes fast food, choked down to the accompaniment of indigestion-provoking screams. That the doctor promises baby will outgrow colic offers little consolation for their misery.

And if misery likes company, parents of colicky babies have plenty of it. It's estimated that 1 in 5 babies has crying spells, usually beginning in late afternoon and sometimes lasting until bedtime, that are severe enough to be labelled colic. Colic differs from ordinary crying (see above) in that the baby seems inconsolable, crying turns to screaming, and the ordeal lasts for two or three hours, sometimes much longer, occasionally nearly round-the-clock. Most often colicky periods recur daily, though some babies take an occasional night off.

The baby with a textbook case of colic pulls his knees up, clenches his fists, and generally increases his activity. He closes eyes tightly or opens them wide, furrows his brow, even holds his breath briefly. Bowel activity increases and he passes wind. Eating

Prescription for Colic

The desperate parents of a colicky baby often turn to the doctor for a magic potion to cure the crying. Unfortunately, there is no medicine that is known to completely cure colic in all infants, and because all prescription medications have side effects, most doctors prefer not to pick up their prescription pad when treating these chronic criers. There is, however, one medicine, widely used to treat colic in Europe, that does seem to help reduce or alleviate symptoms in many colicky infants. Its active ingredient is simethicone, the same anti-gas ingredient found in many adult preparations. Though there is no agreement that gas is the cause of infant colic, it is recognized that many colicky infants do seem gassy (whether this is a cause of the crying or an effect isn't clear), and studies show that reducing the gas seems to reduce the discomfort for many. Because the product isn't absorbed by the body, it is completely safe and has no side effects. If your colicky baby seems gassy, ask the doctor about simethicone drops.

and sleeping patterns are upset by the crying – the baby frantically seeks a nipple only to reject it once sucking is begun, or dozes for a few moments only to awaken screaming. But few infants follow the textbook description exactly. No two babies experience exactly the same pattern and intensity of crying and associated behaviour, and no two parents respond in exactly the same way.

Colic generally begins during the second or third week of life (later in preterm infants), and usually gets as bad as it's going to get by six weeks. For a while the nightmare seems as though it will stretch on interminably, but by twelve weeks the problem usually begins to diminish, and at three months (again, later in preterm babies) most colicky infants appear miraculously cured – with just a few continuing their problem crying through the fourth or fifth month. The colic may abate suddenly or gradually, with some good and some bad days, until they are all good.

Though these daily screaming periods, whether marathon or of more manageable duration, are usually dubbed 'colic', there is not a clear definition of exactly what colic is or how it differs, if it does, from other types of problem crying, such as paroxysmal or periodic irritable crying. Definitions and differences, however, matter very little to parents who are desperately trying to calm their infant.

What causes colic remains a mystery.

Theories, however, abound. Many of the following now have been totally or partially rejected: colicky babies cry to exercise their lungs (there is no medical evidence of this); they cry because of gastric discomfort triggered by allergy or sensitivity to something in their mothers' diet if they are breastfeeding or in their formula if they are bottle fed; (this is only occasionally a cause of colic); they cry because of parental inexperience (colic is no less common in second or subsequent babies, though parents may handle the crying with more aplomb); colic is hereditary (it does not appear to run in families); colic is more common in babies whose mothers had complications in pregnancy or childbirth (statistics don't bear this out); exposure to fresh air stirs up colic (in practice, many parents find that fresh air is the only way they can quiet their crying babies).

The theory that babies are colicky because their mothers are tense is a more controversial one. Though many experts believe it's more likely that it's the baby's crying that makes a mother tense, some insist that a mother who is very anxious may unconsciously communicate this to her baby, making him cry. It may be that although maternal anxiety doesn't cause colic, it can make it worse.

One current theory is that crying is merely a normal manifestation of a newborn's physiological immaturity: all babies cry, and colic is just an extreme form of this normal behaviour. Another suggests that the immature digestive tract contracts violently when wind is passed, causing the pain of colic. A third, that painful intestinal spasms occur because of progesterone withdrawal as the level of maternal hormones in an infant's body drops off. Still another explanation: the baby's immature nervous system has not yet learned to inhibit unwanted behaviour, such as crying.

Perhaps most plausible of all is the theory that newborns, who don't usually cry a lot, have a built-in blocking mechanism that shuts out stimuli, allowing them to sleep and eat without giving much attention to their surroundings. Around the end of the first month (when colic usually begins), this mechanism disappears, leaving them more alert and interested in the world around them. Bombarded with sensations (sounds, sights and smells) all day long, and unable to tune them out when overload begins, they reach the early evening hours overstimulated and overwhelmed. The result: unexplained crying and, in extreme cases, colic. By the time the baby reaches three or four months, or occasionally five, the theory continues, these babies have acquired the ability to tune out the environment before overload occurs, and bouts of colic end.

One environmental factor that does seem to contribute to an increase in colicky behaviour, though the reason for it isn't clear, is tobacco smoke in the home. And the more smokers in a household, the greater the likelihood of colic and the worse the colic will be.

What's reassuring about colic and paroxysmal crying is that babies who have these crying spells do not seem to be any the worse for the wear (though the same can't always be said for their parents), either emotionally or physically – they thrive, usually gaining as well as or better than babies who cry very little, and display no more behavioural problems than other children later on. Children who cry vigorously as infants appear, in fact, more likely to be vigorous and active problem solvers as toddlers than those with limp cries. And

most reassuring of all is the certainly that the condition won't last for ever. In the meantime, the tips on pages 124 and 125 should help you deal with the problem.

Helping Siblings Live with Colic

'Our new baby's constant crying seems to really upset our three-year-old daughter. What can I do?'

If there's an innocent victim in a household with a colicky newborn, it's an older sibling. Here's this baby she probably didn't ask for, and is likely to be feeling somewhat threatened and replaced by, making a terrible racket during what was once one of her favourite times of the day – dinner with mummy and daddy. Not only is the crying unbearable for her, so is the upheaval that comes with it. Instead of being a time for eating, sharing and quiet play, early evening turns into a time of disrupted meals, frantic pacing and rocking, and distracted parents. Worst of all, perhaps, is the helplessness the little victim feels. While the adults are able to at least take some action against the colic (though it may not help) and commiserate with each other about it, she can only sit by, powerless.

You can't make colic easy on your older child any more than you can make it easy on yourself. But you can help her cope better, if you:

Talk it out. Explain, on your older child's level, what colic is. Reassure her that it won't last, that once the baby gets used to being in his new and strange world, most of the crying will stop. If she, too, was a colicky infant, tell her – this should make it easier for her to believe that these screaming monsters actually do grow up to be nice, and relatively quiet, children.

Let her know it's not her fault. Little children tend to blame themselves for everything that goes wrong in a household, from mummy and daddy's arguing to great-grand-father's dying to a new baby's crying. They need to be reassured that no one is at fault here, least of all them.

Show and tell her you love her. Dealing with a colicky baby can be so distracting, and taking care of the basic food, clothing and shelter needs of the rest of the family so time consuming, that you may forget to do those special little things that show a toddler or older child you care. So make a point of doing at least one of those things (fix her hair a new way, play 'swimming' in the bath, bake cakes with her, help her paint a mural on an extra-large piece of paper) every day – and of course remember to tell her several times a day how terrific she is and how much you love her.

Save some time for her alone. Even if it's only half an hour, try to find some time every day to spend with your older child without baby sibling tagging along. Snatch the time when the baby is napping (this is more important than catching up with the dusting), when your husband is walking the floor with him, when your mother comes by to visit – or, if you're able to afford it – when you have a baby sitter for the baby.

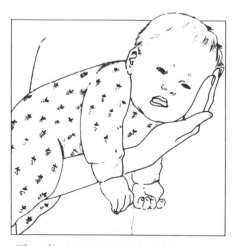

The colic carry. *Some colicky babies are soothed by the pressure applied to their abdomen when they are carried in this position.*

Surviving Colic

'This is our first baby and she cries all the time. What are we doing wrong?'

Relax. You're not guilty. The theory that colic in a baby is somehow the fault of the parents just hasn't held up. And in fact, the situation would probably be just the same if you were doing everything right (of course no parent does; and what's right varies from baby to baby and parent to parent). And it probably wouldn't be much worse if you were doing a lot of things wrong (no parent does *everything* wrong). Colic, the latest research indicates, has to do with baby's development and not yours.

The 'rightest' thing you can do is to try to cope with your baby's crying as calmly and rationally as possible. As anyone who's had a colicky baby knows, that's not easy, but the tips on page 124 should be helpful. Though you're not responsible for baby's crying, remaining calm may help her to calm down too.

'Sometimes when I'm rocking the baby through his third hour of colic, and he won't stop screaming, I have this terrible urge to throw him out the window. Of course I don't – but what kind of mother am I to even think such a thing?'

You're a perfectly normal mother. Even those otherwise qualified for sainthood couldn't survive the agony and frustration of living with a baby who won't stop crying without experiencing some feelings of anger – even momentary hatred – towards him. And though few would admit it freely, many parents of chronic criers have to regularly fight off the same kinds of horrifying impulses you've been feeling. If you find such feelings are more than momentary, and/or if you're afraid that you might really hurt your baby, get help immediately.

There's no question that parents get the worst of colic. Though it can safely be said that the crying doesn't seem to hurt baby, it certainly does leave its mark on mum and dad. Listening to a crying baby is irritating and

Coping with Crying

No medication, pharmaceutical or herbal remedy, or treatment approach is a sure cure for a baby's crying, and some may actually worsen it. But there are a number of things parents can do about their baby's crying; none will work all of the time, some won't work at all, sometimes none will work, but all are worth trying.

Try prevention. In societies where babies are carried papoose style, long periods of crying or fussiness in healthy children are unknown. A recent U.S. study showed that babies who were carried, in the arms or in a baby carrier, for at least three hours every day cried much less than those who were carried less. Not only does carrying give a baby the pleasure of physical closeness to mother (something that was enjoyed in the uterus), but it may help a mother tune in better to her baby's needs.

Respond. Crying is your baby's only way of wielding any control over a vast and bewildering new environment, of making things happen: 'When I call, someone answers.' If you regularly fail to respond, the baby may feel not only powerless, but worthless ('I'm so unimportant that no one comes when I call'). Though it may sometimes seem that you're responding in vain because no matter what you do, nothing helps, responding to your baby's calls promptly will eventually reduce crying. And, in fact, studies show that babies whose mothers responded to them promptly in infancy cry less as toddlers. In addition, crying that's been left to intensify for more than a few minutes becomes harder to interpret – the baby becomes so upset, even he or she doesn't remember what started all the fuss in the first place. And the longer baby cries, the longer it takes to stop the crying. Of course, you needn't drop everything to answer baby's call if you're in the middle of taking a shower, draining the spaghetti, or answering the doorbell. Baby's being left to cry for a couple of extra minutes now and then won't prove detrimental – as long as the infant can't get into trouble while waiting for you.

Don't worry about spoiling your baby by responding promptly. You can't spoil a young infant. And babies who get a lot of attention in the early months are more precocious. Those who don't hang on to dependency and become more demanding.

For particularly difficult cases of inconsolable crying, some experts suggest setting up a routine where you let baby cry for ten or fifteen minutes in a safe place like his cot, pick him up and try to soothe him for another fifteen minutes, then put him down and repeat. If you're comfortable with this, it apparently won't cause any long-term problems.

Assess the situation. Before deciding your baby is crying just for crying's sake, determine if there's a simple and remediable underlying cause. If you think it may be hunger, try breast or bottle, but don't make the mistake of invariably responding to tears with food. Even at this tender age, food should be a response to a need for food, not attention. If you suspect fatigue, try rocking baby to sleep – in your arms, a carriage, a cradle, or a baby carrier. If a wet nappy may be triggering the crying, change it (of course, if you use pins, check for an open one). If baby seems too warm (perspiration is a clue), take off a layer or two of clothing, open the window, or turn on a fan or air conditioner. If cold may be the problem (neck, arms, or body feel cold to the touch), add a layer or turn up the heat. If baby began to cry when clothes were stripped off for a bath (most newborns dislike being naked), quickly cover him with a towel or blanket. If you think his being in the same position for a while may be causing discomfort, reposition baby. If he's been staring at the same view for the last half hour, try changing it.

Ritualism. For babies who thrive on routine, having as regular a schedule as possible (feeding, bathing, changing, going out, and so on up to bedtime ritual) may reduce crying. Be consistent even to the method you use for soothing baby or reducing crying – don't go for a walk one day, ride around in the car the next, and use a baby swing the third. Once you find what works, stick with it most of the time.

Try a little comfort. Sometimes this is all a baby needs and is crying for: being separated from your mummy after nine months of constant contact can be a lonely business. Try the techniques in the box on page 126, Comforting the Crier.

Sucking satisfaction. Babies often need sucking for its own sake, rather than simply for nourishment. Some babies appreciate your help in getting their fingers (particularly their thumbs) to their mouths for their sucking enjoyment. Others prefer grown-up pinkies – but with clean nails, please, carefully and closely clipped. Still others find pleasure in a dummy, but be sure it's an orthodontic style; that you *never* attach a string to it (which could wrap around baby's neck); that you give it only to calm baby after you've attended to other needs; and use it only as long as the colic continues.

A fresh face and a new set of arms. A parent who's been struggling for an hour to soothe a sobbing newborn will almost invariably start to show signs of stress and fatigue, which the infant is certain to sense and respond to with more crying. Hand baby over to someone else – the other parent, a relative or friend, a baby-sitter – and the crying may cease.

Fresh air. A change to an outdoor locale will often change a baby's mood miraculously. Try a trip in the car, the baby carrier, or the pushchair. Even if it's dark out, baby's sure to find distraction in the twinkling of street and car lights.

Air control. A lot of newborn discomfort is caused by swallowing air. Babies will swallow less of it if you keep them upright as much as possible during feeding and burping. The right-size teat hole on a bottle will also reduce air intake; be sure it isn't too large (which promotes gulping of air with formula) or too small (struggling for formula also promotes air swallowing). Hold the bottle so that no air enters the teat (see page 58), and be sure the formula is neither too hot or too cold (though most babies do fine with unheated formula, a few seem disturbed by it). Be sure to burp baby frequently during feedings to expel swallowed

air. One suggested pattern for burping: every 15 or 30 ml (½ to 1 fl ounce) when bottle feeding, every five minutes when breastfeeding, and in both cases, after feeding.

Less excitement. Having a new baby can be a fun time – everyone wants to see the baby, and you want to take him or her everywhere to be seen. You want to expose baby to new experiences, to stimulating environments. That's fine for some babies, *too* stimulating for others. If your baby is colicky, limit excitement, visitors and stimulation, particularly in the late afternoon and evening.

A diet check. Some babies cry a lot because they aren't getting enough to eat. If your bottle baby isn't gaining well, you should talk to the doctor about increasing the amount of formula you are offering. If your breastfed baby seems underweight, see page 98 for tips on assessing and dealing with failure to thrive. Don't, however, add solids, since this isn't a technique that works or is good for a very young baby. Occasionally, allergy or sensitivity to something in formula or breast milk may trigger discomfort and crying, but usually there are other symptoms as well.

Live entertainment. In the early months, some infants are content to sit and watch the world go by, while others cry out of frustration and boredom because there is, as yet, so little they are able to do on their own. Toting them around and explaining what you're doing as you go about your business, and making an extra effort to find toys and other objects in the environment for them to look at and later swat at and play with, may help keep them busy.

Outside relief. This is one time it doesn't make sense to say, 'I'd rather do it myself'. Take advantage of any and every possibility for sharing the burden (see page 16).

Acceptance. Have the wisdom to accept what you can't change. You can't cure your baby's colic and, very often, you may not even be able to quiet the screaming at all. Your only other choice, and perhaps not an easy one to accept: live with it.

Comforting the Crier

Comfort for a newborn comes in many packages, and what may be soothing to one baby may increase squalling in another. Use one method at a time, being careful to give each a fair trial before switching to another, or you may find you are trying, trying, trying and baby is crying, crying, crying. Switching back and forth or using several methods at the same time could overstimulate and increase misery, though you can usually combine soft crooning with rocking or another motion activity. Try the following steps:

- Rhythmic rocking, in your arms, a pram, a cradle, or an automatic baby swing (but not before the baby is six weeks old). Some babies respond better to fast rocking than to slow – but don't rock or shake your baby vigorously, since this can cause serious whiplash injury. For some babies rocking side to side tends to stimulate, rocking up and down to calm. Test your baby's response to different types of rocking.

- A ride in a pushchair, pram, or the family car. An alternative, recently devised: a device that makes the cot feel like an car going 55 miles an hour, complete with wind sounds as a soothing accompaniment. According to studies the product, SleepTight, works.

- Walking the floor with baby in a carrier or sling or simply in your arms. Tried and true, it's tiring but it often works.

- Swaddling baby. Being tightly wrapped is very comforting to some young infants.

- Cuddling in your arms. Like swaddling, cuddling gives many babies a sense of security; hold baby pressed close to

your chest, encircled snugly by your arms. Patting is optional.

- A warm water bath. But only if your baby likes the bath; some babies will scream more as soon as they hit the water.

- Singing. Learn whether your baby is soothed by soft lullabies, sprightly nursery rhymes, or pop tunes, and whether a light, high-pitched voice or a deep, strong one is more pleasing. If you hit on a tune your baby likes, don't hesitate to sing it over and over – most babies love repetition.

- Rhythmic sounds. Many babies are calmed, for example, by the hum of a fan or vacuum cleaner, a tape recording of uterine gurglings, or a record that plays soothing nature sounds, such as waves breaking on the beach or wind blowing through trees.

- Laying on the hands. For babies who like to be stroked, massage can be very calming; but it can cause increased screaming in those who don't. Invest in a baby massage book if you want to perfect your technique, or simply try rubbing your baby's back, belly, arms and legs in a firm but gentle, loving way. But be careful not to be so gentle you tickle. You may find it relaxing to both of you to administer the massage lying on your back, baby face down on your chest.

- Pressure tactics. Lying across an adult lap, tummy down, back being patted, is a favourite position for many colicky babies and one that often makes them more comfortable. Some prefer being upright on the shoulder, but again with pressure on their abdomens and their backs being patted or rubbed.

anxiety provoking. Objective studies show that everyone, even a child, responds to the constant crying of a young infant with a rise in blood pressure, a speeding up of the heartbeat, and changes in blood flow to the skin. If the baby was born prematurely, was poorly nourished in the uterus, or if the mother had toxaemia (preeclampsia/

eclampsia), the pitch of his cry may be unusually high and particularly hard to tolerate.[4]

In order to survive with some semblance of sanity the two or three months of colicky behaviour try the following:

---

4. If a baby's cry is inexplicably high pitched, check with the doctor; such a cry could indicate illness.

When to Check Crying with the Doctor

Odds are your baby's daily screaming sessions are due to normal colic or paroxysmal crying. But just in case there might be some medical problem underlying them, be sure to mention the crying, its duration, intensity, pattern and, especially, any variations from what has been your baby's norm, to the doctor. As the medical community learns more about crying, they are finding that certain aspects of crying (pitch, for example) may provide clues to illness.

An occasional baby does cry because of something his mother is eating or because of allergy to formula. If there is a family history of allergy, ask your baby's doctor about this possibility. He or she may suggest eliminating a food in your diet (often milk products) if you're breastfeeding, or changing the formula if you're bottle feeding. If a change reduces the colic significantly, then it's possible that allergy may be the cause. To prove it more conclusively (if you've got iron nerves and a scientific bent), you could reintroduce the offending food or formula and see if crying resumes. Crying that persists beyond three months may also point to allergy. And sudden sustained crying, in a baby who hasn't cried a lot previously, could indicate illness or pain. Check with the doctor.

Take a break. If you're the only one that has to cope with your baby seven nights a week at colic time, the strain is going to take its toll not only on your mothering, but on your health and your relationship with your husband as well. So take a break at least once a week, daily if possible, during your baby's crying time, relying on paid help if you can afford it, or imposing on grandma or other relatives or friends if you can't. (But avoid friends or relatives who drop direct or indirect hints that the crying is your fault – it's not.)

If you and your husband never have a peaceful dinner thanks to your little screamer, then have dinner out once in a while. It's not difficult to squeeze dinner in between baby's feedings, though more extensive outings may be tough if you're breastfeeding. If dinner out isn't practical, try going for a walk, visiting a friend (preferably one who doesn't have a tiny baby), playing tennis, or getting a massage.

Give baby a break. Sure, it's important to respond to baby's crying. But once you've met all his needs (feeding, burping, changing, comforting and so on) without perceptibly altering his level of screaming, you can give him a break from you – by putting him down in his cot or bassinet for a while. It won't hurt him to cry in his bed instead of your arms for ten or fifteen minutes while you do something relaxing, such as lying down, washing the dishes, baking, watching television, or reading a few pages of a book. In fact, it will do him good to have a mother who is refreshed rather than ragged.

Tune out. To lessen the impact of your baby's wails, use earplugs – they won't block out the sound entirely, just dull it so it will be more tolerable. Tucked in your ears, they can help you relax during a break from baby, or even while you're walking the floor with him.

Get physical. Exercise is a great way to work off tension, something you've got plenty of. Work out at home with baby early in the day (see page 516), swim or exercise at a health club (wallop a punching bag if they have one) that has child-care services, or take the baby for a brisk walk out of doors in his carriage when he's fussy (which may help calm him while it calms you).

Call for help. Since the main burden of baby care may fall on you if you are on maternity leave or have elected to stay home while your husband goes about business as usual, you may soon want to give up mothering as a bad job unless you get some help. The first line of assistance should be your spouse. Most fathers are very good at quieting a baby if they just give themselves a chance – though a minority can't deal with a crying baby at all. If you're lucky enough to have other relatives nearby, call on them, too. Many grandmothers, thanks to years of experience, seem to have a magic touch with babies – though as with fathers, a few may have trouble with a squaller. A sister, sister-in-law, or good friend can also make a fine relief person. If she has children of her own she can bring, at the least, experience to the task. If she has none she can bring enthusiasm, excitement and freshness to it.

If you can't get willing volunteers, you will have to turn to paid help – an experienced baby-sitter or baby nurse, for instance, who can take over walking your crying baby for an hour or so once a week, or more. A teenager who is comfortable with babies is often an inexpensive yet effective helper who can take your baby out in the push-chair, or carry him around the house while you shower and prepare dinner or even while you eat.

Talk about it. Do a little crying yourself – on any willing shoulder: your husband's, the baby's doctor's, your family doctor's, a cleric's, a family member's, a friend's. Talking about it may not cure the colic but you may feel a little better after sharing your sorry story. Most beneficial may be discussing your situation with other parents of colicky babies, particularly those who have weathered the storm successfully and are now sailing on clear waters.

If you really feel violent, get help. Almost everyone is irritated by a constantly crying baby. But for some people, such crying finally becomes more than they can bear. The result is sometimes child abuse. If your thoughts of throwing baby out the window are more than fleeting, if you feel about to give in to the urge to strike or shake your baby or harm him in any way, get help *immediately*. Go to a neighbour's, if you can, and hand the baby over until you can collect yourself. Then call someone who can help you – your husband, your mother or mother-in-law, a close friend, the baby's

doctor or your own, or the local child-abuse hotline. Even if your powerful feelings don't lead to child abuse, they can start eroding your relationship with your baby and your confidence in yourself as a mother unless you get counselling quickly.

Spoiling Baby

'We always pick our baby up when she cries. Are we spoiling her?'

Not sparing the comfort won't spoil the baby, at least not until she's at least six months old. In fact, studies show pouring on the comfort now – by picking her up within a couple of minutes whenever she cries and catering to all her needs – not only won't turn out a spoiled brat, it will turn out a happy, more self-reliant child who in the long run will cry less and demand less attention. She will also have a closer attachment to you (or to whoever it is who responds to her), and be more trusting. An additional plus: since she'll come to breast or bottle calm, without a bellyful of air swallowed while screaming, she will have better feeding sessions.

Of course, all isn't lost if once in a while you can't pick your baby up immediately – you might be in the bathroom, on the phone, or taking the casserole out of the oven. There's no harm done as long as you get to her as soon as possible. Nor will the results be catastrophic if you periodically take 15-minute breaks from a colicky baby.

Blood in Spitup

'When my two-week-old spit up today, there were some reddish streaks in with the curdled milk. I'm really worried about her.'

Any blood that seems to be coming from a two-week-old baby, particularly when it's found in her spitup, is bound to be alarming. But before you panic, try to determine if it's your blood, which it most likely is, or the baby's. If you're breastfeeding and your nipples are cracked, even very slightly, your baby could be sucking in some blood along with the milk each time she nurses. And since what goes into a baby must come out – sometimes in the form of spitup – such a situation could definitely account for the blood you've noticed.

If your nipples aren't obviously the cause (they may be, even if you can't see the tiny cracks), then call your doctor to help you solve the mystery.

Changing your Mind about Breastfeeding

'I had decided not to breastfeed my daughter, and I let my milk dry out. Now, seeing other mothers nursing their babies makes me have second thoughts. Is it too late to get my milk back?'

Nature allows for a change of heart – at least most of the time. This early in the game, particularly when their babies are between four and seven weeks old, women who want to breastfeed after allowing their milk to dry up (or women who've weaned their babies only to have regrets a few weeks later) can be reasonably successful at relactating.

Before you consider trying, however, be sure your change of heart is wholehearted. Success won't come easily and you'll need to be at least doubly dedicated in order to achieve it. You can expect that for the first several weeks relactation will take a great deal of time (you'll need to nurse your baby very frequently at first) and effort (you may also have to engage in some manual or mechanical expression of milk), and will produce a great deal of stress for both you and your baby (who may initially resist this new form of feeding). Even if you succeed in producing milk, you may not be able to supply all your baby's nutritional needs, and formula supplementation may be necessary.

If you decide breastfeeding is something you really want to try, or give another try to, switch to the Best-Odds Breastfeeding Diet (page 524) and follow the suggestions for inducing lactation on page 493. For many women – and their babies – the results are well worth the effort.

'I've been breastfeeding my son for three weeks, and I'm just not enjoying it. I'd like to switch to a bottle, but I feel so guilty.'

There's no reason to feel guilty about your decision, or even to regret it – as long as you're sure you've made it for the right reasons. Beginning breastfeeding is usually a series of trials and errors. As far as enjoyment goes, it can be elusive on both sides of the breasts in this early adjustment period. If you're certain that your dissatisfaction with breastfeeding isn't just the result of a bumpy start (which almost always turns into a smooth ride by the middle of the second month), and that you've given nursing your all in both time and effort, continuing is not likely to be a positive experience. But do try to wait it out until your baby is six weeks old (two months would be even better), by which time he will have received the most important health benefits of breastfeeding. Then, if you're still not enjoying nursing, feel free – and free of remorse – to wean him.

Photo Flashes

'I've noticed that our baby blinks when the flash from our camera goes off. Could it be hurting his eyes?'

Only the most sought-after celebrities are as hounded by the popping of flashbulbs as a newborn baby whose paparazzi parents are determined to capture in pictures every detail of his first days of life. But unlike celebrities, infants can't hide behind dark glasses when the bulbs start flashing. To protect your baby's eyes against the possibility of injury from a flashbulb exploding near him and from too intense and too close exposure to the camera lights, it's a good idea to take a few precautions during photo sessions. Try to keep the camera at least

100 cm (3 feet 4 inches) from baby, and use a diffusion screen over the flash unit to keep glare to a safe minimum. If your photographic equipment allows, bounce the light off a wall or ceiling instead of in baby's face. If you failed to take such precautions during previous shoots, don't worry. The risk of damage is exceedingly small.

Loud Music

'My husband likes to play loud rock music on the stereo. I'm afraid that it might damage our daughter's ears.'

All ears, young and old, have a lot to lose when they're exposed for long periods of time to loud music (whether rock, classical, or any other type) – namely, a certain amount of their hearing capacity. Though some ears are more naturally sensitive and prone to damage than others, in general the hearing of babies and small children is most susceptible to the harmful effects of overly loud sound. Damage to the ears can be either temporary or permanent, depending on the noise level and the duration and frequency of exposure.

How loud is dangerously loud? While a baby's crying might signal that music (or another noise) is too loud for her, don't wait for her protests before turning the volume down; a baby's ears don't have to be 'bothered' to suffer damage. The maximum noise level that is safe for adults is 90 decibels – a level that can easily be exceeded by a stereo set. If you don't have the equipment to measure the decibels your stereo is putting out when your husband plays his rock music, you can set the volume safely by maintaining a level that can be easily talked over – if you have to shout, it's too loud.

Vitamin Supplements

'Everybody we talk to has a different opinion on vitamins for babies. We can't decide whether or not to give them to our new son.'

Your great-grandmother probably never heard of vitamin supplements when she was a young mother, or even of vitamins (they weren't given that name until 1912); your grandmother was probably told to give her children cod liver oil 'for its vitamins'; your mother may not have been told to give you any supplements at all. With the science of nutrition still in its infancy, you can expect that the recommendations will continue to change as new information is uncovered. Considering the constant state of flux in the scientific community, it isn't surprising that there's a lot of confusion among lay people as to just what makes sense.

Current research indicates that healthy newborns usually do not need a multi-vitamin supplement. They get most of the vitamins and minerals they are believed to need from breast milk if their mothers are eating a good diet and taking a pregnancy-lactation supplement daily; or from formula if it is a medically approved commercial brand and not a home brew. Exceptions are those babies who have health problems that compromise their nutritional status (those who are not able to absorb certain nutrients well from their foods and/or are on restricted diets, for example) and babies of breastfeeding vegetarians who eat no animal products and take no supplements themselves. The latter should receive, at the very least, vitamin B^{12}, which may be totally absent in their mother's milk, and probably folic acid as well; but a complete vitamin-mineral supplement with iron is probably a good idea.

Whether a supplement is necessary for a baby who is a few months old is less clear. A commercial formula with iron will continue to supply all the nutrients a baby is known to need – everything that might be in the drops and more. Breast milk, on the other hand, is variable and much less easy to analyze; its nutrient makeup depends partly on the mother's diet, partly on her health, and partly on factors we don't even understand.

Once solids are introduced, a baby's diet becomes even less easy to evaluate and control. One day he takes a big bowl of nutrition-packed cereal for breakfast, a couple of tablespoons of yogurt for lunch, then turns down his nighttime carrots and peas. The next, he may reject anything but his bottle. The following day the oatmeal ends up on the floor, most of the yogurt appears to be smeared on the high chair tray, and the evening offering of baby meat is tentatively tasted, then spat out.

So though it's true that some of the vitamins you drop carefully in baby's mouth may on some days be excreted in his urine (it's been said that Americans have the world's healthiest urine, thanks to the vast quantities of vitamin supplements they take), some doctors nevertheless recommend giving the drops daily, as health insurance. Others claim this is unnecessary. If yours is one who insists, 'All babies need is a balanced diet', but you'd feel more comfortable knowing your baby is nutritionally 'insured' against day-to-day dietary lapses, there's no harm, and probably some good, in giving an over-the-counter supplement that supplies *no more* than the recommended daily allowance of vitamins and minerals for your baby.

There are some individual nutrients, however, that it is widely agreed do need to be supplemented:

Vitamin D. At least thirty minutes of sunshine per week, just over four minutes a day, while clad in only a nappy, or two hours a week, about seventeen minutes daily, fully clothed but hatless, is the estimated amount of sunshine an infant would need to prevent rickets. But because getting adequate vitamin D this way is not only chancy (a run of nasty weather can block out the sun for a week, and letting baby go hatless in very hot or cold weather is not possible) but also potentially dangerous (see the risks of sunning an infant on page 379), many doctors recommend vitamin D supplementation for babies beginning at two to four weeks of age. Such supplementation is found in commercial baby formulas (and in the fortified whole cow's milk your baby will graduate to later), but it's unclear whether or not there is adequate vitamin D in breast milk, even if the mother takes a supplement. So if you are breastfeeding, it is possible your doctor will recommend supplementation via vitamin drops. Do *not* give a baby (or anyone else, for that matter) more than the RDA for this vitamin (400 IU) – it is very toxic at levels not much above this level. A baby getting a formula containing vitamin D should *not* get additional supplementation.

Iron. Since iron deficiency during the first eighteen months of life can cause serious developmental and behavioural problems, mothers should make certain that iron intake is adequate. Your newborn, unless premature or low birth weight, probably arrived with a considerable iron reserve, but this will be depleted by somewhere between four and six months of age.

Many doctors recommend that some source of iron should be introduced into the infant's diet at no later than two months of age. Iron fortified formula (but not ordinary cow's milk) will fill the bill for bottle-fed babies, but for those on breast alone, another source will be needed. An option, once solids are begun, is iron-enriched cereals, but the doctor may also suggest an iron supplement (ferrous sulfate in doses based on your child's weight is cheap and effective), either alone or as part of a baby vitamin-mineral supplement.

Adequate vitamin C intake will improve iron absorption, and once your baby begins taking a lot of solids, it's a good idea to give a vitamin C food at each meal so that the benefits of any iron taken are maximized (see page 352). In spite of what you may hear, clinical studies show that iron supplements don't cause stomach upset in babies. But remember that the mineral can be toxic in large doses. To be safe, you may want to keep no more than a one-month supply in your home at any time and store it well out of the reach of babies and children.

Fluoride. This mineral provides excellent protection against tooth decay. If local water fluoride levels are low, you may be advised to give your baby and baby or child the following supplement: 0.25mg for children six months to three years; 0.50mg for three-to six-year-olds. When levels are between 0.3 and 0.5 ppm, no supplementaion for those under three; 0.25mg for three- to six-year-olds. When levels are 0.6 ppm or above, no supplement is needed for any child.

If you're uncertain of the fluoride levels in your tap water, your baby's doctor may be able to advise you. Or you can call your local health department. If your water is from a well or other private source, you can have its fluoride content checked by a lab (ask the health department how to have this done).

If your tap water turns out to be adequately fluoridated (0.3 parts per million is the minimum recommended for protection), try any of the following after six months to ensure your baby's intake.

• Prepare liquid or powdered ready-to-mix (*not* ready-to-serve, which should not be diluted) formula with the tap water. When you give juice, dilute it with tap water.

• After six months, get your baby in the habit of drinking water daily, preferably from a cup.

• Ask the doctor about prescribing fluoride or vitamin-mineral drops with fluoride if your baby doesn't get tap water in any form.

Once the teeth emerge, topical supplementation with rinses and toothpastes can also be used. The dose will be tailored to the percentage of fluoride in your area's water supply.

With fluoride, as with most good things, too much can be bad. Excessive intake while the teeth are developing in the gums, such as might occur when a baby drinks heavily fluoridated water *and* takes a supplement, can cause 'fluorosis,' or mottling. The lesser forms of mottling (white striations) are not noticeable or aesthetically unattractive. More serious mottling, however, is not only disfiguring, but the pitting can predispose the teeth to decay.

Babies and children, because of their small size and because their teeth are still developing, are particularly susceptible to fluorosis. So be wary of overdose. Before

you give fluoride supplementation, be sure your water supply is not already adequately fluoridated. Once brushing is started, don't use toothpaste unless your baby insists (and then use a thin smear of unfluoridated baby toothpaste). Cap the paste when it's not in use, and put it out of baby's reach – some babies love to eat the stuff.

Although giving your baby a vitamin-mineral supplement that provides no more than the RDA for infants once he's no longer solely dependent on breast milk or formula may be a good idea, it's not a good idea to give any additional vitamins or mineral supplements in any form. A 'nutritionist' should *not* prescribe vitamins, minerals, or herbs for your baby without the doctor's approval. Severe illness has been reported in children overdosed with vitamins or given herbal medicines by caring parents who thought they were doing good.

If your baby is one who hates the daily dose of liquid drops, try the tips for helping the medicine go down on page 403.

Circumcision Care

'My son was circumcised yesterday and there seems to be oozing around the area today. Is this normal?'

A body can't lose a part – even a small and largely unnecessary flap of skin such as the foreskin of the penis – without reacting to the loss. In this case there is usually soreness, sometimes a little bleeding, and oozing at the site of the surgery after circumcision has been performed – a sign the body's healing fluids are rushing to the area.

Using double nappies for the first day will help to cushion the penis and also to keep the baby's thighs from pressing against it; this isn't usually necessary later. Usually the penis will be wrapped in gauze by the doctor or mohel (a ritual circumcisor of the Jewish faith). You'll be asked to put a fresh gauze pad, dabbed with petroleum jelly or other ointment, on the penis with each nappy change and to avoid getting the penis wet in a bath (you

Keeping Baby Safe

Babies are, despite their fragile appearance, pretty hardy sorts. They don't 'break' when you pick them up, their heads don't snap off when you forget to support them, and they weather most falls without major injury. But they can be vulnerable. Even very young ones, who seem too innocent to get into trouble, do – sometimes the very first time they turn over or reach for something. To protect your baby from accidents that don't have to happen, be sure to follow *all* of these safety tips *all* of the time:

- Always use a car seat for your baby when you go for a drive. Wear a seat belt yourself, and make sure whoever's doing the driving does, too; no one's safe unless the driver is. And never drink and drive, or let baby ride with anyone who does.

- If you bathe baby in a large tub, put a small towel or cloth at the bottom to prevent slipping. Always keep one hand on baby during the bath.

- Never leave your baby unattended on a changing table, bed, chair, or sofa – not for a moment. Even a newborn who can't roll over can suddenly extend his or her body and fall off. If you don't have safety straps on your changing table, you should always keep one hand on baby.

- Never put a baby in an infant (or car) seat or carrier on a table, counter or any elevated surface, never leave baby unattended in a seat on *any* surface, even the middle of a soft bed – suffocation is a risk.

- Never leave a baby alone with a pet, even a very well-behaved one.

- Never leave baby alone in a room with a sibling who is under five years old. A game of peekaboo affectionately played by a toddler could result in tragic suffocation for an infant. An overly enthusiastic bear hug could crack a rib.

- Don't leave the baby alone with a baby-sitter who is younger than fourteen, whom you don't know well, or whose references you haven't checked. All baby-sitters should be trained in infant CPR and aware of your safety rules.

- Never jiggle or shake your baby vigorously or throw him or her up into the air.

- Never leave baby alone at home, even while you move the car, or check the laundry in the apartment building basement; it takes only seconds for a fire to blaze.

- Never leave a baby or child alone in a car. In hot weather even keeping the windows down might not prevent the baby from succumbing to heat stroke. In any weather the brakes might slip, sending the baby careering off, or a child-snatcher on the prowl could quickly make off with the car's precious cargo.

- Never take your eyes off your baby when you're shopping, going for a walk, or sitting at the playground. A pushchair or pram makes an especially easy target for a child-snatcher.

- Avoid using any kind of chain or string on baby or on any of baby's toys or belongings – that means no necklaces, strings for dummies or rattles, no religious medals on chains, no ribbons longer than 13 cm (5 inches) on cots or cradles. Make sure the ends of strings in hoods, gowns and pants are knotted so they can't slip through, and never leave cords, string, ropes, or chains of any kind around where baby might get to them. Be sure, too, that baby's cot, playpen and changing table are not within reach of electric cords (which present double danger), telephone cords, or venetian blind or drapery cords. All of these items can cause accidental strangulation.

- To prevent accidental suffocation, don't place film plastics, such as those used by dry cleaners, on mattresses or anywhere baby can get at them. Don't leave an unattended infant (awake or asleep) within reach of pillows, stuffed toys, or other plush items. Don't let a baby sleep with them or on a sheepskin, plush-top mattress, waterbed or a bed wedged up against the wall.

- Do not place a baby on any surface next to an unguarded window, even for a second, and even asleep.

- Use smoke detectors in your home and install them according to the recommendations of your local fire department. Keep them maintained.

probably won't be dunking your baby yet anyway, because the umbilical cord is not likely to have fallen off at this point) until healing is complete.

Swollen Scrotum

'It almost looks as though our new son has three testicles.'

Your son's testicles are encased in a protective pouch called the scrotum, which is filled with a bit of fluid to cushion them. Sometimes a child is born with an excessive amount of fluid in the scrotal sac, making it appear swollen. Called hydrocele, this condition is nothing to worry about since it gradually resolves during the first year, almost always without any treatment.

You should, however, point out the swelling to your son's doctor to be sure what you see isn't an inguinal hernia (more likely if there is also tenderness, redness and discolouration; see page 150), which can either resemble a hydrocele or occur along with it. By illuminating the scrotum, the doctor can determine if the scrotal swelling is due to excess fluid or if there is a hernia involved.

Hypospadias

'We were very disturbed to learn that the outlet in our son's penis is in the middle instead of the end.'

Every so often, something goes awry during antenatal development of the urethra and the penis. In your son's case, instead of the urethra (the tube that carries both urine and semen, but not at the same time) running all the way to the glans, or tip, of the penis, it opens elsewhere. This abnormality is called hypospadias. First-degree hypospadias, where the urethral opening is at the end of the penis but not in exactly the right place, is considered a minor defect and requires no treatment. Second-degree hypospadias, where the opening is along the underside of the shaft of the penis, can be corrected with reconstructive surgery. Third-degree hypospadias, where the opening is near the scrotum, can usually be corrected, but in such cases two operations are often needed.

Because the foreskin may be used for the reconstruction, circumcision, even ritual circumcision, is not performed on a baby with hypospadias.

Occasionally, a girl is born with hypospadias, with the urethra opening into the vagina. This, too, is usually correctable with surgery.

Supplementary Water

'A neighbour keeps suggesting that I give our daughter bottles of water instead of nursing her so often.'

Though a bottle-fed baby may require a little extra water (up to 100 ml/4 fl ounces in 24 hours) during very hot weather, healthy infants who are fed exclusively on breast milk or formula do not need additional water under ordinary circumstances. Too much water, especially commercially bottled water, can cause a drop in sodium levels in the blood, which can lead to seizures. Giving an older infant small sips of water from a cup, however, is okay. Children on solids can handle more water.

WHAT IT'S IMPORTANT TO KNOW:
Babies Develop Differently

From the day a baby's born, the race is on – and it's a sure bet that most parents, rooting their offspring on from the starting line, will be disappointed if their entry doesn't make a good showing. If the child-development chart shows that some babies start turning over at ten weeks, why hasn't their baby accomplished it by twelve weeks? If the baby in the next pushchair at the park grabbed an object at three and a half months, why hasn't their baby done it by then? If grandmother insists all of her children sat up by five months, why is theirs still slumping pathetically at six?

But in this race, the child who comes in first in mastering early developmental skills doesn't necessarily finish in the money, while the one who moseys along developmentally doesn't necessarily finish out of it. Though the very alert baby may indeed turn out to be a bright child and a successful adult, attempts to measure infant intelligence and correlate it with intelligence in later years have not been fruitful. The baby who seems to be a little slow, it appears, can also turn out to be bright and successful. Studies have shown, in fact, that 1 in 7 children gains 40 IQ points from the middle of the third year to the age of 17. That means an 'average' toddler can become a 'gifted' teenager.

Part of the difficulty, of course, is that we don't know how intelligence manifests itself in infancy, or even if it does. And even if we did know, it would be difficult to test for it because infants are nonverbal. We can't ask questions and expect answers, we can't assign a passage for reading and then test for comprehension, we can't present a problem to assess reasoning power. About all we can do is evaluate motor and social skills – and these just aren't equatable with what we later think of as intelligence. Even when we evaluate early developmental skills, our results are often in question; we never know whether a baby is not performing because of inability, lack of opportunity, or a momentary lapse in interest.

Anyone who's spent any time at all around more than one baby knows that children develop at different rates. Probably these differences are due more to nature than to nurture. Each individual seems to be born programmed to smile, lift his or her head, sit up, and take first steps at a particular age. Studies show that there is little we can do to speed up the developmental timetable, though we can slow it down by not providing an adequate environment for development, by lack of stimulation, by poor diet, by poor health care (certain medical or emotional problems can hamper development), and by simply not giving enough love.

Infant development is usually divided into four areas:

Social. How readily your baby learns to smile, coo and respond to the human face and voice tells you something about him or her as a social being. A serious delay in this area could indicate a problem with vision or hearing, or with emotional or intellectual development.

Language. The child who has a large vocabulary at an early age or who speaks in phrases and sentences before the usual time is probably going to have a way with words. But the child who makes requests with grunts and gestures into the second year may catch up and do just as well or even better later on. Since receptive language development (how well baby understands what is said) is a better gauge of progress than expressive language development (how well baby actually speaks), the child who 'understands everything' but says very little is not likely to be experiencing developmental delay. Again, very slow development in this area occasionally indicates a vision or hearing problem and should be evaluated.

Large motor development. Some babies seem physically active from the first kicks in the womb; once born, they hold their heads up early, sit, pull up and walk early, and may turn out to be more athletic than most. But there are slow starters who end up excelling on the football field or tennis court, too. Very slow starters, however, should be evaluated to be certain there are no physical or health impediments to normal development.

Small motor development. Early eye-hand coordination, and reaching for, grasping and manipulating objects before the average age *may* predict a person will be good with his or her hands. However, the baby who takes longer to become skilled in this area is not necessarily going to be 'all thumbs' later on.

Most indicators of intellectual development – creativity, sense of humour and problem-solving skills, for example – don't usually become apparent until toward the end of the first year at the earliest. But eventually, given plenty of opportunity, encouragement and reinforcement, a child's various inborn abilities will combine to create the adult who is a talented painter, a resourceful mechanic, an effective fund-raiser, a savvy stockbroker, a sensitive teacher, an all-star athlete.

The rate of development in the various areas is usually uneven. One child may smile at six weeks but not reach for a toy until six months, while another may walk at eight months but not talk until a year and a half. When an occasional child does develop evenly in all areas, this may provide a clearer clue to future potential. A child who does everything early, for instance, is likely to be brighter than average; the child who seems extremely slow in every area may have a serious developmental or health problem, in which case professional assessment and intervention is necessary.[5]

Though children develop at different rates, each child's development – assuming no environmental or physical barriers exist – follows the same three basic patterns. First, the child develops from the top down, from head to toes. Babies lift their heads up before they can hold their backs up to sit, and hold their backs up before they can stand on their legs. Second, they develop from the trunk outwards to the limbs. Children use their arms before they use their hands, and their hands before they use their fingers. Development moves, not surprisingly, from the simple to the complex.

Another aspect of infant learning is the deep concentration directed towards learning a particular skill. A child may not be interested in beginning to babble while practising to pull up. Once a skill is mastered another moves to centre stage, and the baby may seem to forget the old, at least for a while, so involved is he or she in the new. Eventually your baby will be able to integrate all the various skills and use each spontaneously and appropriately. But in the meantime, don't despair when he or she seems to forget what was recently learned or looks at you blankly when called on to perform the most recently acquired skill.

No matter what your child's rate of development, what is accomplished in the first year is remarkable – never again will so much be learned so quickly. Enjoy this time and let your baby know you're enjoying it. By accepting your baby's timetable as okay, you will be letting your child know that he or she is okay, too. Avoid comparing your child with other babies (yours or anyone else's) or with norms on developmental charts. Babies should be compared only to themselves, a week earlier or a month ago.

---

5. The Denver Developmental Screening Test, or one similar, is often used to assess infant development. If a child isn't able to accomplish a particular skill by the age at which 90% of other children do, there is a developmental delay in that area. If there is a delay in two or more areas, it's probably time to seek the underlying cause and to take remedial action. Early intervention can sometimes make a remarkable difference in the future lives of children who are developing slowly.

FIVE

The Second Month

❖

What Your Baby May Be Doing

**By the end of this month, your baby
. . . should be able to (see Note):**

- smile in response to your smile
- follow an object in an arc about 15 cm (6 inches) above the face to the midline (straight ahead)
- respond to a bell in some way, such as startling, crying, quieting (by 1½ months)
- vocalize in ways other than crying (e.g. cooing)

Note: If your baby seems not to have reached one or more of these milestones, check with the doctor. In rare instances the delay could indicate a problem, though in most cases it will turn out to be normal for your baby. Premature infants generally reach milestones later than others of the same birth age, often achieving them closer to their adjusted age (the age they would be if they had been born at term), and sometimes later.

. . . will probably be able to:

- on stomach, lift head 45 degrees
- follow an object in an arc about 15 cm (6 inches) above the face *past* the midline (straight ahead)

. . . may even be able to:

- hold head steady when upright
- on stomach, raise chest, supported by arms
- roll over (one way)
- grasp a rattle held to backs or tips of fingers

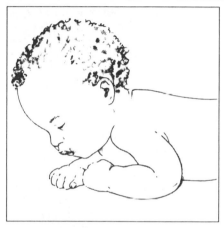

By the end of this month, most babies are able to lift their heads to a 45 degree angle.

- pay attention to a raisin or other very small object
- reach for an object
- say ah-goo or similar vowel-consonant combination

. . . may possibly be able to:

- smile spontaneously
- bring both hands together (2⅔ months)
- on stomach, lift head 90 degrees (2¼ months)
- squeal in delight (2¼ months)
- follow an object in an arc about 15 cm (6 inches) above the face for 180 degrees (from one side to the other)

What You Can Expect At This Month's Checkup

Each doctor, midwife or health visitor will have a personal approach to well-baby checkups. The overall organization of the physical exam, as well as the number and type of assessment techniques used and procedures performed, will also vary with the individual needs of the child. But in general, you can expect the following at a checkup when your baby is about two months old.

- Questions about how you and baby and the rest of the family are doing at home, and about baby's eating, sleeping and general progress. About child care, if you are planning to return to work.

- Measurement of baby's weight, length and head circumference, and plotting of progress since birth.

- Physical exam, including a recheck of any previous problems.

- Developmental assessment. The examiner may actually put baby through a series of 'tests' to evaluate head control, hand use, vision, hearing and social interaction or may simply rely on observation plus your reports on what baby is doing.

- First round of immunizations for diphtheria, tetanus and pertussis (DTP),

polio (TOPV) and Haemophilus type b (Hib) if baby is in good health and there are no contraindications.

- Guidance about what to expect in the next month in relation to such topics as feeding, sleeping and development, and advice about infant safety.

- Recommendations about fluoride supplementation if needed in your area, and vitamin D supplementation if your baby is breastfed. Recommendations about iron supplementation for babies not on iron-fortified formula.

Questions you may want to ask, if the doctor hasn't already answered them:

- What reactions can you expect baby to have to the immunizations? How should you treat them? Which reactions should you call about?

Also raise concerns that have arisen over the past month about baby's health, feeding problems, or family adjustment. Jot down information and instructions from the doctor. Record all pertinent information (baby's weight, length, head circumference, birthmarks, immunizations, illnesses, medications given, test results and so on) in a permanent health record.

Feeding Your Baby This Month: Supplementary Bottles

The kangaroo mummy doesn't have much choice. Her baby emerges from the birth canal, climbs into her pouch, latches onto a breast, starts suckling and continues as needed until it's ready for weaning. The system is much the same in many primitive cultures; babies are slung in a carrier of some sort next to their mothers' breasts and

suckle as often as they wish. There's never a need for supplementary feedings. In our society, where we revere independence, even young babies are often apart from their mothers at a long enough distance and for a long enough time to require one or more supplementary feedings. With more and more mothers of infants reentering the work force early, such supplementation is becoming increasingly common; but thanks to the development of good infant formulas and easy-to-use breast pumps, providing these feedings is becoming increasingly easier.

Why Supplement?

A breastfeeding mother may begin supplementary feedings for one or more of a variety of reasons:

- Plans to return to employment or to school while her baby is young.

- Plans to wean before her baby is able to get needed milk from a cup (usually eight or nine months at the earliest).

- The desire to be able to have an occasional afternoon or evening out without baby (alone, or with spouse, friend, or another child), keep appointments (with doctor, dentist, clients and so on), or attend meetings or classes without taking the child along.

- The wish to be prepared in case of emergency – you become ill and can't nurse, you get stuck at a meeting and can't get home in time for a regular nursing, you have to leave town for a day or two.

Mothers who decide not to supplement are more tied down than those who do, but most find it possible, on occasion, to go out to dinner between feedings, or to a movie after baby is bedded down for the night. Among the reasons for not supplementing:

- Fear that if baby becomes dependent on a bottle, weaning will have to be accomplished twice: first from the breast, then from the bottle. These mothers usually start their babies on a cup as soon as they can sit supported, and use a cup for supplementary feedings of formula or breast milk.

- The desire not to interfere in any way with the breast milk supply.

- Having a baby who rejects the bottle. Mothers who see no real need for insisting on it may decide not to press the issue.

How to Supplement

When to begin. Some babies have no difficulty switching from breast to bottle and back again right from the start, but most do best with both if the bottle isn't introduced until five or six weeks. Earlier than this, supplementary feedings may interfere with the successful establishment of breastfeeding, and babies may experience nipple confusion because dining at breast and bottle call for different sucking techniques. Much later than this, many babies reject rubber nipples in favour of their beloved mamma's familiar fleshy ones.

What to use. Since cow's milk isn't appropriate fare for a young baby, the two options available to mothers who want to supplement are breast milk and formula.

- Breast milk. This has the advantage of being free after the cost of pumping paraphernalia (which can range from nominal for most hand pumps to very high for electric models). But a great deal of time must often be invested in expressing breast milk (as much as 45 minutes to an hour at first, perhaps 15 minutes to half an hour later, though some women manage to empty both breasts in under 10 minutes once they become experienced). Breast milk has the advantage, of course, of offering optimum nutrition and disease resistance; though an occasional bottle of formula won't detract from that, frequent bottles of formula could.

- Formula. Expenditure of time and money will vary depending on the type of formula you choose. Ready-to-use formula is costly, but it takes virtually no time to prepare; it's often favoured by those who give supplementary formula only occa-

---

Emergency Cache

Even if you don't plan on giving supplementary bottles, it may be a good idea to express and freeze enough breast milk to fill six bottles – just in case. This will give you a backup supply if you become sick, you're temporarily taking medication that might pass into your milk, or you're called out of town unexpectedly. Even if your baby has never taken a bottle, it will be easier for him or her to accept one if it's filled with familiar breast milk rather than with unfamiliar formula.

---

sionally. Formula that requires mixing is less expensive, but requires more time to prepare. Formula is less perfect nutritionally than breast milk, but is certainly an adequate supplement.[1]

Whether you choose to supplement with breast milk or formula, you should keep in mind that it will probably be necessary for you to express milk if you will be away from your baby for more than three or four hours, to help prevent clogging of milk ducts, leaking and a diminishing milk supply. The milk can be either collected and saved for future feedings or disposed of. If you're planning to use formula at all, give it in the introductory bottles to accustom baby to its taste.

How much to use. One of the beauties of breastfeeding is that you need never worry about how much or how little your baby is taking. As soon as you start using a bottle, it's easy to succumb to the numbers game. Resist. Tell your baby's caretaker to give your baby only as much as he or she wants, with no prodding or pushing to finish any particular amount. The average 4-kg baby (9-pounder) may take as much as 175 ml (6 fl ounces) at a feeding, or less than 50 ml (2). Remind her, too, that you will be fitting in a couple of extra

---

1. Very rarely a baby who was sensitized to milk in the uterus or when he was given it unwittingly in the hospital nursery has a bad reaction to the first sips of cow's milk (in formula or straight). If your baby cries as if in pain, or if you notice swelling of the lips, tongue and mucous membranes of the mouth, or wheezing within minutes of having milk, call the doctor immediately. Call 999 if you notice the baby is having difficulty breathing. If you give formula only occasionally, do not use the iron-fortified type.

breastfeedings when you're at home so that she needn't feel obligated to overfeed, which could lead to an overweight baby – or one who doesn't want to nurse when the opportunity presents itself.

Winning baby over. Wait until your baby is both hungry (but not frantically so) and in a good mood before attempting to initiate the bottle. The first few bottles are more likely to be accepted if the nipples have been brought to body temperature under warm tap water and if they are offered by someone other than you – preferably when you're not in the same room for baby to complain to. The substitute feeder should cuddle and talk to the baby during the feeding, just as you would when nursing. If you have to do it yourself, it may help to keep your breasts well camouflaged (don't bottle feed braless or in a low cut blouse) and to distract the baby with background music, a toy, or another form of entertainment. Too much distraction, however, and your baby may want to play, not drink. If your baby tries out the teat, then drops it with seeming disapproval, try a different type of teat the next time. For a baby who uses a dummy, a teat that is similar in shape may work.

Getting down to a regular schedule. If your schedule will require your regularly missing two feedings during the day, switch to the bottle one feeding at a time, starting at least two weeks before you plan to go back to work or school. Give your baby a full week to get used to one bottle feeding before going on to two. This will help not only baby adjust gradually, but your body as well, if you are planning to supplement with formula rather than breast milk. The wonderful supply and demand mechanism that controls milk production will cut back as you do, making you more comfortable when you're finally back on the job.

Dealing with the occasional bottle. If you plan to give a bottle only occasionally, nursing fully on both breasts before going out will make fullness and leakage less of a problem. (But do insert breast pads in your bra, just in case.) Be sure your baby won't be fed too close to your return (less than two hours is probably too close) so that, if you are uncomfortably full, you can nurse as soon as you get home.

Supplementing when Baby isn't Thriving

Occasionally, formula supplementation is recommended because baby isn't doing well on breast milk alone. This often leaves a mother feeling unsure of what to do. On the one hand, she hears that giving a bottle in such a situation may totally wipe out her chances of breastfeeding successfully; on the other, she is told by the doctor that if she doesn't start supplementing her baby's diet with formula, the health consequences could be serious. The best solution in many such cases is the supplemental nutrition system, shown on page 100, which provides a baby with formula while stimulating mum's breasts to produce more breast milk.

What You May Be Concerned About

Cradle Cap

'I wash my daughter's hair every day, but I still can't seem to get rid of the flakes on her scalp.'

Don't pack away those dark-shouldered outfits yet. Cradle cap, a seborrhoeic dermatitis of the scalp common in young infants, doesn't doom your daughter to a lifetime of dandruff. Mild cradle cap, in which greasy surface scales appear on the scalp, often responds well to a brisk massage with mineral oil or petroleum jelly to loosen the scales, followed by a thorough shampoo to remove them and the oil. Tough cases, in which flaking is heavy and/or brownish patches and yellow crustiness are present, may benefit from the daily use of an anti-seborrheic shampoo and/or ointment that contains sulfur salicylates (make sure you keep it out of baby's eyes) after the oil treatment. (Some cases are aggravated by the use of such preparations. If your baby's is, discontinue use and discuss this with the doctor.) Since cradle cap usually worsens when the scalp sweats, keeping it cool and dry may also help – so don't put a hat on

baby unless absolutely necessary, and then remove it when you're indoors or in a heated car.

When cradle cap is severe, the seborrhoeic rash may spread to the face, neck, or buttocks. If this occurs, your baby's doctor will probably prescribe a topical ointment.

Occasionally, cradle cap will persist through the first year – and in a few instances, long after a child has graduated from the cradle. Since the condition causes no discomfort and is therefore considered only a cosmetic problem, aggressive therapy (such as use of topical cortisone, which can contain the flaking for a period of time) isn't usually recommended, but is certainly worth discussing with your child's doctor as a last resort.

Smiling

'My son is five weeks old, and I thought he would be smiling real smiles by now, but he doesn't seem to be.'

Cheer up. Even some of the happiest babies don't start true social smiling until six or seven weeks of age. And once they start smiling, some are just naturally more smiley than others. You'll be able to distinguish the first real smile from those tentative practice ones by the way the baby uses his whole face – not just his mouth. Though babies don't smile until they're ready, they're ready faster when they're talked to, played with and cuddled a lot. So smile at your baby and talk to him often, and very soon he'll be smiling back.

Cooing

'My six-week-old baby makes a lot of breathy vowel sounds, but no consonants at all. Does this mean she might have a speech defect?'

With young babies, the 'ayes' – and the a's, e's, o's, and u's – have it. It's the vowel sounds they make first, somewhere between the first few weeks and the end of the second month. At first the breathy, melodic (and adorable) cooing and throaty gurgles seem totally random, and then you'll begin to notice they're directed at you when you talk to your baby, at a stuffed animal who's sharing her playpen, at a mobile up above that's caught her eye, or even at a flower on the sofa upholstery. These vocal exercises are often practised as much for her own pleasure as for yours; babies actually seem to love listening to their own voices. They are also educational; baby is discovering which combinations of throat, tongue and mouth actions make what sounds.

For mummy and daddy, cooing is a welcome step up from crying on the communication ladder. And it's just the beginning. Within a few weeks to a few months baby will begin adding laughing out loud (usually by three and a half months), squealing (by four and a half months), and a few consonants to her repertoire. The range for initiating consonant vocalizations is very broad – some make a few consonant-like sounds in the third month, others not until five or six months, though four months is about average.

When babies begin experimenting with consonants, they usually discover one or two at a time, and repeat the same single combination (ba or ga or da) over and over and over. The next week, they may move on to a new combination, seeming to have forgotten the first. They haven't, but since their powers of concentration are limited, they usually work on mastering one thing at a time.

Following the two-syllable, one-consonant sounds (a-ga, a-ba, a-da), come sing-song strings of consonants (da-da-da-da-da-da) called 'babble,' at six months on the average. By eight months, many babies can produce word-like double consonants (da-da, ma-ma, ba-ba), usually without associating any meaning with them until two or three months later. (To fathers' delight, da-da generally comes before mama.) Mastery of *all* the consonants doesn't come until much later, often not until four or five years of age. A few perfectly normal youngsters have difficulty with certain consonants (often l's or s's) into their school years.

'Our baby doesn't seem to make the same kind of cooing sounds that his older brother made at six weeks. Should we be concerned?'

Some normal babies develop language skills earlier than average, some later. About 10% of babies start cooing before the end of the first month and another 10% don't start until nearly three months. Some start with strings of consonants before the 4½-month mark; others don't string consonants until past eight months. The early verbalizers may end up very strong in language skills (though the evidence isn't that clear); those who lag far behind, in the lowest 10%, may have a physical or developmental problem, but this isn't clear either. Certainly, it's too early to be concerned that this might be the case with your baby, since he's still probably well within the norm.

If it seems to you over the next several months that your baby consistently, in spite of your encouragement, falls far below the monthly milestones in each chapter, speak to his doctor about your concerns. A hearing evaluation or other tests may be in order. It may turn out that you are so busy that you aren't really noticing your baby's vocal achievements (this sometimes happens with second children). In the less likely case that there actually is a problem, early attention may be able to remedy it.

Crooked Feet

'Our son's feet seem to fold inwards. Will they straighten out on their own?'

The answer is almost certainly yes. Most babies appear bowlegged and pigeon-toed. This is because of the normal rotational curve in the legs of a newborn and because the cramped quarters in the uterus often force one or both feet into odd positions. When he emerges at birth, after spending several months in that position, the feet are still bent or seem to turn inwards.

In the months ahead, as your baby's feet enjoy their freedom and as he learns to pull up, crawl and then walk, his feet will begin straightening out. They almost always do without the early casting or special shoes and bars that were once routine treatments. Which is probably why these treatments, most of which are now deemed to be completely ineffective, usually appeared to 'cure' the problem.

Just to be sure that an abnormality isn't the cause of your baby's foot problems, express your concerns at his next well-baby visit. The doctor probably has already checked your baby's feet for abnormalities, but another check won't hurt. The doctor will also want to keep an eye on the progress of the feet as your baby grows. If your baby's feet don't appear to be straightening out on their own, casting or special shoes may be required at a later date. At just what point this becomes necessary will depend on the type of problem and on the doctor's point of view.

Comparing Babies

'I get together regularly with a group of other new mothers and inevitably they all start comparing what their babies have been doing. It makes me crazy – and worried about whether my daughter is developing normally.'

If there's anything more anxiety-provoking than a roomful of pregnant women comparing bellies, it's a roomful of recently delivered women comparing babies. Just as no two pregnant bellies are exactly alike, neither are any two babies. Developmental norms (such as those found in each chapter in this book) are useful for comparing your baby to a broad range of normal infants in order to assess her progress and identify any lags. But comparing your baby with someone else's child, or with an older one of your own, can only result in a lot of unnecessary fears and frustrations. Two perfectly 'normal' babies can develop in different areas at completely different clips – one may forge ahead in vocalizing and socializing, another in physical feats, such as turning over. Differences between babies become even more marked as the first year progresses – one baby may crawl very early but not walk until fifteen months, another may never learn to crawl at all but suddenly start taking steps at ten months. Then, too, a mother's assessment of her baby's progress is highly subjective – and not always completely accurate. One mother may not even recognize her baby's frequent coos as the beginnings of language, while another may hear one coo and swear, 'She said "mama"!'

All of this said, it's easier to intellectualize that comparing babies isn't a good idea than to actually stop doing it or avoid those who do. Many compulsive comparers can't sit anywhere near another mother-with-baby on a bus, in a doctor's waiting room, or at the park without assaulting her with outwardly innocent queries that lead to the inevitable comparisons ('What an adorable baby! She's sitting already? How old is she?'). The best advice, if you can't completely manage to 'mind your own baby', is to keep in mind how meaningless these comparisons really are. Your baby, like your belly before her, is one of a kind.

Using a Baby Carrier

'We usually carry our son around in a baby carrier. Is this a good idea?'

Although baby carriers – cloth sacks that harness infants to their caregivers – have become popular only recently, they have, in one form or another, been helping transport babies in other cultures since prehistoric times. There are at least three good reasons. First, babies are usually happy riding in a carrier; they enjoy the steady gentle movement and the closeness to a warm body. Second, babies tend to cry less during the rest of the day if they are carried around a lot, something made easier by the use of a carrier. And third, carriers provide mothers, dads and other caregivers with the freedom to attend to their daily chores while carrying baby.

But if baby carriers are a boon to today's parents, they can also be a bane. If you elect to continue using one, keep these risks in mind:

Overheating. On a very warm day, even a scantily clothed baby can simmer in a baby carrier – particularly one that encloses the baby's legs, feet and head or is made from a heavy fabric such as corduroy. Such overheating can lead to prickly heat and even heat stroke. If you use a carrier in warm weather or in overheated rooms or vehicles, check your baby frequently to be sure he isn't sweating and his body doesn't feel warmer than yours. If he does appear to be overheated, remove some clothing or take him out of the carrier completely.

Understimulation. A baby who's always cooped up in a baby carrier, with his visual perspective limited to a chest, and if he looks up, a face, doesn't have the opportunity he needs to see the world. This is not a major problem in the first few weeks of life,

when a baby's interest is usually limited to the most basic creature comforts, but it can be now, when he's ready to expand his horizons. Look for a convertible carrier in which baby can face in for a nap or out for viewing the world, or limit baby's sojourns to times when he will be sleeping or will be pacified only by being carried and you need your arms for other purposes. At other times, use a pushchair or baby seat.

Too much sleeping. Babies who are toted in baby carriers tend to sleep a lot – often a lot more than they need to. With two less-than-desirable results. First, they get used to catnapping (fifteen minutes when you run out to the grocery store, twenty when you walk the dog) rather than taking longer naps in their cots. Second, they may become so well rested during the day that they don't rest much at night. If your baby immediately falls asleep when placed in a carrier, use it only at naptime, and for the duration of the nap.

Risk of injury. A young infant's neck isn't strong enough yet to support his head when he's jiggled and jostled a lot. Though securing your baby in a baby carrier while you jog may seem like an ideal way of getting your exercise and keeping your baby happy too, the bouncing could be risky. Instead, strap him in a pushchair when you go for a jog. Also be careful to bend at the knees, *not the waist*, when wearing the carrier – or your baby could slip out.

While judicious use of a baby carrier can work well at this age, your baby won't be ready for a back carrier until he can sit by himself.

Immunization

'My baby's doctor says that immunization is perfectly safe. But I've heard a lot of horror stories about serious – even fatal – reactions, and I worry about letting him give my daughter the shots.'

We live in a society that considers good news to be no news. A story on the positive effects of immunizations cannot compete with one on the extremely rare instances of fatal complications associated with them. So it is likely that today's parents have heard more about the risks of immunization than the benefits. And yet, as your doctor has doubtless told you, for most infants those benefits continue to far outweigh the risks.

Not too many years ago, in the West, the most common causes of infant death were infectious diseases, such as diphtheria, typhoid and smallpox. Measles and whooping cough were so common that all children were expected to get them, and thousands, especially infants, died or were permanently handicapped by these illnesses. Parents dreaded the coming of summer and the infantile paralysis (polio) epidemics that seemed invariably to arrive with it, killing or disabling thousands of infants and children. Today, smallpox has been virtually eliminated, and diphtheria and typhoid are extremely rare. Only a small percentage of children are stricken with measles or whooping cough each year, and infantile paralysis is a disease young mothers are not only no longer afraid of, but often aren't even familiar with. Immunization is the reason.

Immunization is based on the fact that exposure to weakened or dead disease-producing microorganisms (in the form of vaccines) or to the poisons (toxins) they produce, rendered harmless by heat or chemical treatment (then called toxoids), will cause an individual to produce the same antibodies that would develop if the person had actually contracted the disease. Armed with the special memory that is unique to the immune system, these antibodies will 'recognize' the specific microorganisms, should they attack in the future, and destroy them.

Even the ancients recognized that when someone survived a particular disease, they weren't likely to contract it again; those who had recovered from the plague were sometimes used to care for new victims.

Although some societies attempted crude forms of immunization, it wasn't until Edward Jenner, a Scottish doctor, decided to test the old belief that a person who contracted the lesser disease cowpox would never get smallpox, that modern immunization was born. In 1796, Jenner smeared pus from the sores of a milkmaid infected with cowpox on two small cuts in the arm of a healthy eight-year-old boy. The child developed a slight fever a week later, then a couple of small scabs on his arm. Subsequently, he was exposed to smallpox and remained healthy. He had become immune.

Today, immunization saves thousands of lives each year in this country. But it's not perfect. Though most children have only a mild reaction to immunization, some become ill, a very few seriously so. With some types of vaccine, there may be an extremely slight risk of serious or permanent damage, even death. But as the benefits of crossing the street or going for a ride in the family car outweigh the very real risks involved in these activities, so do the benefits of protection from serious disease outweigh the risks of the immunization for all but high-risk children (see page 147). And as you take precautions to decrease risks when crossing the street (by crossing with the light and looking both ways) or riding in a car (by driving carefully and using car seats and seat belts), so should you take precautions when having your child vaccinated (by watching for and reporting side effects and being sure your child is in good health before being given a shot).

The first widely administered type of immunization, the smallpox vaccination, was so successful that it is no longer necessary. The disease seems to have been eradicated from the entire globe. It's hoped that immunization will someday wipe out other serious scourges as well. For now, your baby will probably receive the following immunizations, beginning at two months and continuing throughout childhood. (To reduce momentary pain, ask about a sugar solution just before the shot or an anaesthetic cream an hour earlier.)

What you Should Know About DTP

Common Reactions to DTP

The following reactions to DTP are listed in order of frequency, with the first three most common, occurring in about half of immunized children. All usually last only a day or two.

- Pain at the injection site

- Mild to moderate fever (37.8° to 40°C/100° to 104°F, rectally)

- Fussiness

- Swelling at the site

- Redness at the site

- Drowsiness

- Loss of appetite

- Vomiting

Baby paracetamol can be given for fever and pain – administered right after the immunization as a prophylactic measure, it appears to significantly reduce reactions. Warm compresses on the injection site may also help to reduce baby's discomfort. Fever and local soreness may be more of a problem with each subsequent dose of DTP, but fussiness and vomiting may be less frequent.

When to Call the Doctor

If your baby exhibits any of the following within 48 hours of a DTP injection, call the doctor's surgery.

- High-pitched persistent crying for more than three hours

- Excessive sleepiness (baby may be difficult to wake)

- Unusual limpness or paleness

- Rectal temperature of 40.5°C (104.9°F) or higher

- Convulsions

Symptoms of brain inflammation, such as convulsions or changes in consciousness, may not occur until as long as a week after the immunization. (A recent study indicated that even such a severe reaction is unlikely to cause significant permanent neurological damage.)

When to Omit the Pertussis Vaccine

Under certain conditions the Department of Health recommends that either

---

Diphtheria, Tetanus, acellular Pertussis vaccine (DTP). The first shot your baby is likely to be given is the DTP, which contains diphtheria and tetanus toxoids and pertussis (whooping cough) vaccine. While reactions to either toxoid are extremely rare, reactions to the pertussis vaccine are quite common (see box, above). Fortunately, most of these reactions are mild to moderate and present no serious hazard. Though there has been much concern about the possibilty that the pertussis vaccine could cause serious brain damage or even death, the most recent studies have led experts to the conclusion that there is no evidence of a link between the vaccine and brain damage. A new acellular pertussis vaccine, which appears less likely to cause adverse reactions, has recently been released in the U.S. for the fourth and fifth doses (at 15 to 18 months and then between 4 and 6 years). In the meantime, minute as the risk may be, it's wise to take the following steps to make certain your baby is safely vaccinated:

- Be sure the doctor gives your baby a thorough checkup before a DTP inoculation to be certain no illness is developing that isn't yet apparent.

- Observe your baby carefully for 72 hours after the vaccination (especially during the first 48), and report severe reactions to the doctor *immediately*. Continue observing for possible brain inflammation (see box, above) for 7 days.

- Ask the doctor to enter the vaccine manufacturer's name and the vaccine lot/

immunization be delayed or the anti-pertussis component of the DTP vaccine not be given to children in the following categories, and that DTP containing just the antidiphtheria and tetanus components, be susbtituted for children:

- With a past history of convulsions or seizures, unless or until neurological disease has been ruled out.

- With confirmed or suspected neurological disease, such as epilepsy.

- Who have had severe allergic reactions to a previous DTP shot, convulsions, a rectal temperature of 40.5°C (104.9°F) or more, or serious brain problems.

- Who, on a case-by-case basis, reacted to a previous shot with unusually high-pitched crying, uncharacteristically persistent crying for more than three hours, excessive sleepiness, limpness, unusual paleness. Discuss the significance of such reactions with your baby's doctor.

- Who are taking drugs or undergoing other treatments that lower the body's resistance to infection (cortisone, prednisone, certain anti-cancer drugs, or radiation therapy).

Policies for the administration of DTP vary slightly from doctor to doctor, and you should ask your baby's doctor about his or hers. Most will postpone the shot for a baby who has a fever, and some will do so even for a mild cold. Many wait as much as a month following a fever to administer the DTP. Vaccination is generally not postponed if a child suffers from frequent allergy-caused nasal congestion that has been traced to allergy rather than infection.

During an epidemic even high-risk children are generally immunized, since the danger from whooping cough itself, which kills 1 in 100 infected children under six months of age, is much more serious than the danger from the vaccine.

It's usually recommended that booster shots given after age seven not contain pertussis vaccine, since the disease is both less risky and less common after this age and the danger of the vaccine is greater. A reduced dose of diphtheria vaccine is also suggested after this age, when reactions tend to be more severe. The combined vaccine for older children is labelled Td, and boosters are recommended every seven to ten years throughout life.

batch number in your child's records, along with any reactions you report. Ask for a copy of the information for your own records.

- When the next DTP is scheduled, remind your baby's doctor about *any* previous reactions to the vaccine.

- If you have any fears about vaccine safety, discuss them with your baby's doctor.

Taking any possible precautions when your child is being immunized makes sense, but panicking and refusing to have your low-risk child immunized against diphtheria, tetanus and pertussis clearly doesn't. If parents began a widespread boycott of DTP, we would soon see a return of these diseases in epidemic proportions, with the death and disability that often accompanies them.

Polio Vaccine (OPV or TOPV). The polio vaccine has now been saving lives for more than thirty years. There are two types of polio vaccine: OPV, a live vaccine given by mouth, and IPV, an inactivated vaccine given by injection directly into the bloodstream. Both are effective. Children usually get a total of four doses before they go off to school: at two, three and four months, and between three and five years. Some doctors give an additional dose – either because the child lives in a high-risk area or because of the possibility that an infant lost part of a dose earlier (maybe he or she spat or vomited the vaccine up, drooled it out, or passed it in diarrhoea).

The vaccine has proven to be quite safe and children rarely have any reactions following a dose. But there is a minuscule risk (about 1 in 8.7 million) of paralysis and a slightly greater (about 1 in 5 million) risk that a susceptible parent or other household member might contract polio from a child immunized with OPV. For that reason IPV, which doesn't enter the digestive tract, is recommended when either the child or a family member has cancer or has an immune system depressed either by illness or medical treatment.

When the live oral polio vaccine (OPV) is used, meticulous care should be taken in cleaning up the recently vaccinated child after a bowel movement or vomiting; careful handwashing is essential.

Measles, Mumps, Rubella (MMR). You may not have been immunized against these common childhood diseases in your infancy, but your baby almost certainly will be – usually with a combination vaccine at thirteen months of age, because it is less effective earlier.[2] Measles, though often joked about, is in reality a serious disease with sometimes serious, potentially fatal, complications. Rubella, also known as German measles, on the other hand, is often so mild that its symptoms are missed. But because it can cause birth defects in the foetus of an infected pregnant woman, immunization in infancy is recommended – both to protect the future foetuses of girl babies and to reduce the risk of infected children exposing their pregnant mums. Mumps rarely presents a serious problem in childhood, but because it can have severe consequences (such as sterility or deafness) in adulthood, early immunization is recommended.

Reactions to the MMR vaccine are fairly common, but are generally very mild and usually don't occur until a week or two after the shot. About 1 in 5 children will get a rash or slight fever lasting a few days from the measles component. About 1 in 7 will get a rash or some swelling of the neck glands,

and 1 in 20, aching or swelling of the joints from the rubella component, sometimes as long as three weeks after the shot. Occasionally, there may be swelling of the salivary glands from the mumps component. Much less common are tingling, numbness, or pain in the hands and feet, all difficult to discern in infants, and allergic reactions. It is also possible (but experts aren't sure) that the MMR vaccine may be responsible for encephalitis (inflammation of the brain), convulsions with fever, or nerve deafness in very rare cases.

Caution should be taken in administering the vaccine to a child who is sick with anything but a mild cold, anyone with cancer or a disease that lowers the body's resistance to infection, anyone taking a drug that lowers resistance, or anyone who has had gamma globulin within the preceding three months. The vaccine could also be dangerous to those who have had a *severe* allergic reaction to neomycin; it can be safely given to children allergic to eggs. (Still some doctors prefer to observe such children for 90 minutes following MMR to be sure there is no serious reaction).

Varicella vaccine. Varicella, or chicken pox, is usually a mild disease without serious side effects. There can be complications, however, such as Reye's syndrome and bacterial infections; and the disease can be fatal to high-risk children, such as those with leukemia or immune deficiencies, or whose mothers were infected just prior to their birth. A varicella vaccine, which appears to provide long-term protection, is now licensed by the FDA in the U.S., but is not yet recommended for routine use in the U.K.

Haemophilus b vaccines. By October 1992, more than 25,000 children under the age of one will have been immunized against Hib in the U.K. These vaccines are aimed at thwarting the deadly haemophilus influenzae b (Hib) bacteria that are the cause of a wide range of very serious infections in infants and young children. Hib is responsible

---

2. Occasionally, because of a high incidence of cases in a community, this vaccine will be given at one year – on the theory that a little protection is better than none.

Immunization Recommendations

AGE	DTP	Td	OPV or TOPV	TB test	MMR	Hib	HBV
birth				x*			x*
1 to 2 months							x**
2 months	x		x			x	
3 months	x		x			x	x***
4 months	x		x*			x	
6 to 18 months							x**
12 to 18 months					x	x	
3 to 5 years	x		x				
11 to 12 years					x****		
14 to 16 years	x						

*In high-risk areas. **Infants whose mothers test positive for HBV should be vaccinated at birth, at 1 month and at 6 months. ***If first dose not given at birth. ****If measles vaccination is given for school admission, it is not usually repeated.

for about 13,000 cases of meningitis in the U.K. annually (70% in children under 2 years; 5% of them fatal) and for nearly all epiglottis (a potentially fatal form of croup that obstructs the airways). It is also the leading cause of septicaemia (blood infection), cellulitis (skin and connective tissue infection), osteomyelitis (infection of the membrane surrounding the heart) in young children. Children under four are at greatest risk.

A trial Hib vaccine appears to have few, if any, side effects. The Department of Health recommends the vaccine be given at two, three and four months, at the same time as the DTP. Children already 13–48 months will receive only one dose of the vaccine.

As with other vaccines, Hib vaccines should not be given to a child who is ill with anything more than a mild cold, or who might be allergic to any of their components (check with the doctor). Though adverse reactions are rare, a very small percentage of children may have fever, redness and/or tenderness on the site of the shot, diarrhoea, vomiting and crying after receiving the conjugate Hib vaccine.

Hepatitis B vaccine. Hepatitis B is a serious liver disease which can lead to cancer later in life. Children, unless living in homes with infected adults where they can pick up the disease through exposure to infected blood or other body fluids, are not likely become infected. The main purpose of the U.S. vaccination programme (not routine in the U.K.) is to have children immune once they reach adulthood, as adult immunization efforts have failed.

If for some reason any of your baby's vaccinations are postponed, there's no cause for concern. Immunization can pick up where it left off; starting over isn't necessary.

Flu Immunization

'Everybody's talking about a big influenza epidemic coming and about getting shots. Should my two-month-old son have them?'

Generally, influenza is a mild disease with few serious complications in healthy people, and one that doesn't attack everyone, even during an epidemic. Because of this, and because immunization is short term and protects only against this year's strain of virus and not next year's, flu shots are recommended only for children who are highly susceptible: those with serious heart or lung disease, those with depressed immune systems, and those with sickle-cell anaemia or similar blood diseases. Though newborns are particularly susceptible to influenza, immunization against it isn't presently recommended for them because little is known about the benefits and risks of giving flu shots to children under six months of age.

If your baby is healthy, it's very likely your doctor will tell you that flu shots are unnecessary. Do, however, follow the suggestions on page 567 for avoiding the spread of illness in your home if someone does come down with flu. If your doctor does suggest that your baby be immunized against flu, only the 'split-virus' form of the vaccine should be used. A spray vaccine, now under study, may make flu immunizations easier in the future..[4]

Don't confuse a flu (or influenza) shot with immunization for haemophilus influenzae type b (Hib), which is routinely recommended.

Undescended Testicles

'My son was born with undescended testicles. The doctor said that they would probably descend from the abdomen by the time he was a month or two old, but they haven't yet.'

The abdomen may seem a bizarre location for testicles, but it isn't. The testicles (or testes) in males and the ovaries in females both develop in the foetal abdomen from the same embryonic tissue. The ovaries, of course, stay put. The testes are scheduled to descend down through the inguinal canals in the groin, into the scrotal sac at the base of the penis, somewhere around the eighth month of gestation. But in 3 to 4% of full-term boys and about one third of those that are preterm, they don't make the trip before birth. The result: undescended testicles.

Because of the migratory habits of testicles, it's not always easy to determine that one hasn't descended. Normally, the testicles hang away from the body when they are in danger of overheating (protecting the sperm-producing mechanism from temperatures that are too high). But they slip back up into the body when they are chilled (protecting the sperm-producing mechanism from temperatures that are too low) or when they are handled (again protective, to avoid injury). In some boys the testes are particularly sensitive and spend a lot of time sheltered in the body. In most, the left testicle hangs lower than the right, possibly making the right seem undescended (and making a lot of young boys worry). The diagnosis of undescended testicle or testicles is therefore made only when one or both have never been observed to be in the scrotum, not even when the baby is in a warm bath.

An undescended testicle causes no pain or difficulty with urinating and, as your doctor assured you, usually descends on its own. By age one, only 3 or 4 boys in 1,000 still have undescended testicles. In the rare cases that remain stubbornly in the abdomen by age five, surgery is recommended and is generally successful.

Hernia

'I was very upset when the doctor said

---

4. Influenza vaccine should not be given to anyone who has had a severe allergic reaction to eggs. High-risk children may, instead, be given antiviral medicines to prevent flu developing.

that my twin boys have inguinal hernias and will have to have surgery.'

A hernia is often thought of as something that occurs in a grown man who has lifted too heavy a load. But hernias are not unusual in newborns, particularly boys, and especially those born prematurely (as twins often are).

In an inguinal hernia, a part of the intestines slips through one of the inguinal canals (the same channels through which the testes descend into the scrotum) and bulge into the groin. The defect is often first noted as a lump in one of the creases where the thigh joins the abdomen, particularly when a baby is crying or very active; it often retracts when he is quiet. When the section of the intestines slips all the way down into the scrotum, it can be seen as an enlargement or swelling in the scrotum, and may be referred to as scrotal hernia.

Though most of the time an inguinal hernia causes no problems, occasionally it becomes 'strangulated'. The herniated section becomes pinched by the muscular lining of the inguinal canal, obstructing blood flow and digestion in the intestines. Vomiting, severe pain, even shock can result. For this reason, any parent who notices a lump or swelling in their baby's groin or scrotum should report the finding to the doctor as soon as possible. Since strangulation of an inguinal hernia is most common in babies under six months of age, doctors usually advise repair as soon as the hernia is diagnosed – assuming the baby is fit for surgery. Such surgery is usually simple and successful, with a very short (sometimes one-day) hospitalization. Only very rarely does an inguinal hernia recur following surgery, though in some children a hernia occurs on the opposite side at a later date.

Because of the usually prompt treatment of diagnosed infant inguinal hernia, most cases of strangulated hernia turn up in babies whose hernias haven't been previously diagnosed. So parents who note a baby suddenly crying in pain, vomiting and not having bowel movements should check for a lump in the groin. If one is found, an immediate call to the doctor is necessary. If the doctor can't be reached, the baby should be taken to the nearest emergency room. Elevating the baby's bottom slightly and applying an ice pack while en route to the ER may help the intestine to retract, but don't try to push it back in by hand. And don't offer a breast or bottle to comfort the baby, since surgery will probably be necessary and an empty digestive tract will be best.

Inverted Nipples

'One of my daughter's nipples sinks in instead of standing out. What's wrong with it?'

This sounds like her nipple is inverted, not at all uncommon in infants. Often, a nipple that is inverted at birth corrects itself spontaneously later. If it doesn't, it poses no functional problem until she's ready to nurse her own baby, at which point there will be steps she can take to draw the nipple out.

Rejection of the Breast

'My baby was doing very well at the breast – now suddenly, he's refused to nurse for the past eight hours. Could something be wrong with my milk?'

Something is probably wrong – though not necessarily with your milk. Temporary rejection of the breast is not unusual, and almost always has a specific cause, the most common of which are:

Mother's diet. Have you been indulging in pasta al pesto or another dish redolent with garlic? Feasting your chops and chopsticks on barbecue chicken? If so, your baby may simply be protesting the spicy and/or strong flavours your diet is imparting to his milk. If you figure out what turns your baby off, avoid eating it until after you've weaned him.

A cold. Babies who can't breathe through stuffy noses can't nurse and breathe through their mouths at the same time; understandably, they opt for breathing. Use a cool mist vaporizer, gently suction nostrils with an infant nasal aspirator, or ask your baby's doctor about nose drops.

Teething. Though most babies don't begin the struggle with teeth until at least five or six months, a few babies begin teething much earlier, and a very occasional two-month-old actually sprouts a tooth or two. Nursing often puts pressure on swollen gums, making suckling painful. When teeth are the cause of breast rejection, a baby usually starts nursing eagerly, only to pull away in pain.

An earache. Because ear pain can radiate to the jaw, the sucking motions of nursing can make discomfort worse. See page 416 for other clues to ear infection.

Thrush. If your baby has this fungal infection in his mouth, nursing may be painful. Be sure the condition is treated so that the infection isn't passed on to you through cracked nipples, or spread elsewhere on the baby (see page 69).

Slow let-down. A very hungry baby may grow impatient when milk doesn't flow immediately (in some women let-down may take as long as five minutes to occur), and may push away the nipple in a fury before let-down begins. To avoid this problem, express a little milk before you pick him up, so that he'll get something for his efforts the moment he starts to suck.

A hormonal change in you. A new pregnancy (very unlikely now if you're nursing exclusively, more possible if you've started your baby on solids and/or numerous supplemental formula feedings) can produce hormones that change the taste of the breast milk, causing baby to reject the breast. So can the return of menstruation, which again isn't usually an issue until partial weaning begins.

Tension in you. If you're worried or upset you may be communicating your tension to your baby, making him too agitated to nurse. Relax.

Readiness for weaning. An older baby who rejects the breast may be saying, 'Mummy, I've had it with nursing. I'm ready to move on.' Ironically, babies seem to do this when their mothers are not the least bit interested in weaning, rather than when mother is ready to quit nursing.

Once in a while, there appears to be no obvious explanation for a baby's turning down the breast. Like an adult, a baby can be 'off his feed' for a meal or two. Fortunately, this kind of hiatus is usually temporary. If disinterest in nursing continues, or if it occurs in connection with other signs of illness, speak to his doctor.

Favouring one Breast

'My little girl hardly ever wants to nurse on my left breast and it's shrunken to be considerably smaller than the right.'

Some babies play favourites. Why a baby prefers one breast over another isn't certain. It could be that she's more comfortable cradled in her mother's favoured, and probably stronger, arm, so she develops a taste for the breast on that side. Or that her right-handed mother tends to place her on the left breast, so that the right hand is free for eating, holding a book or the phone, or handling other chores, leaving the right to dwindle in size and production. Perhaps one breast is the better provider, due to the mother or baby favouring one side early on in the nursing relationship, for reasons as diverse as the location of the pain from a caesarean incision and the location of the TV set in your bedroom.

Whatever the reason, preferring one breast over the other is a fact of nursing for some babies, and lopsidedness a fact of life for their mothers. Though you might try to increase production on the less favoured side by pumping daily and/or starting every feeding with it (if your baby will cooperate), these efforts may not do the trick. In many cases, mothers go through the entire nursing experience with one breast larger than the other. The lopsidedness will diminish after weaning, though a slightly greater-than-normal difference may continue. The only sure solution in the interim: stuffing the roomier bra cup to make the breasts look even and clothes fit better.

Very rarely the baby rejects a breast because it harbours a developing malignancy. So do mention your baby's penchant to your doctor.

Difficult Baby

'Our little girl is adorable, but she seems to cry for the least little reason. If it's too noisy, or too bright, or even if she's a little wet. My husband and I are going crazy. Are we doing something wrong?'

No parent expects to have a difficult baby. Pregnant daydreams are pink-and-blue collages of a contented infant who coos, smiles, sleeps peacefully, cries only when she's hungry, and grows into a sweet-tempered cooperative youngster. Bawling, inconsolable babies and kicking, screaming toddlers belong to others – parents who did it all wrong and are paying the price.

And then, for parents like you, just weeks after your perfect baby is born, reality shatters the fantasy. Suddenly, it's your baby who's crying all the time, who won't sleep, or who seems perpetually unhappy and dissatisfied. Why shouldn't you wonder. 'What did I do wrong?'

The answer is probably nothing, except perhaps pass on some unfortunate genes to your offspring, for a baby's temperament appears to have much more to do with heredity than environment. How the childhood environment is structured, however, can make a difference as to how inborn temperament affects future development.

With more attention to stimulation, for example, difficult children often turn out to have higher IQs than average. And the child who, with help from mummy and daddy, learns to direct and develop inborn personality traits, transforming them from liabilities into assets, can go from impossible problem infant to successful adult.[5]

The parental role in this metamorphosis is critical. The first step is to identify which of several different types of personalities that have been linked to difficult behaviour your own baby displays (some display a combination). Your baby seems to be a what is known as a low-sensory threshold baby. A wet nappy, a starched dress, a high neckline, a bright light, a staticky radio, a scratchy blanket, a cold cot – any or all of these may unduly upset a baby who seems to be extra sensitive to sensory stimulation. In some children, all five senses – hearing, vision, taste, touch and smell – are very easily overloaded; in others, just one or two. Dealing with the low-sensory-threshold child requires keeping the general level of sensory stimulation down, as well as avoiding those specific things that you notice bother baby, such as:

- Sound sensitivity. Lower the sound level in your home by keeping the radio, stereo and TV low or off, adjusting your telephone ring to low, asking people to knock instead of ringing the doorbell, and installing carpeting and curtains, where possible, to absorb sound. Speak or sing to your baby softly and have others do the same. Be sure any musical or other sound-producing devices aren't disturbing to baby. If outside noises seem to be a problem, try a whitenoise machine or air cleaner in baby's room to block them out.

- Light or visual sensitivity. Use room darkening shades or curtains so baby can sleep later in the morning and nap during the day, and avoid very bright

5. For valuable help in dealing with a difficult baby, see *The Difficult Child* by Stanley Turecki, M.D.

Do you Have a Difficult Baby?

The active baby. Babies often send the first clue that they're going to be more active than most right from the uterus; suspicions are confirmed soon after birth when coverings are kicked off, changing and dressing sessions become wrestling matches, and baby always ends up at the opposite end of the cot after a nap. Active babies are a constant challenge (they sleep less than most, become restless when feeding, and are always at risk of hurting themselves), but they can also be a joy (they're usually very alert, interested and interesting, and quick to accomplish). While you don't want to squelch such a baby's enthusiasm and adventurous nature, you will want to take special protective precautions as well as learn ways to quiet him or her for eating and sleeping. The following tips should help:

- Use a sleeping bag in cold weather, lightweight sleepers in cool weather, for a baby who kicks off the covers.

- Be especially careful never to leave an active baby on a bed, changing table, or any other elevated spot even for a second – they often figure out how to turn over very early and sometimes just when you least expect it. A restraining strap on the changing table is useful, but should not be relied upon if you're more than a step away.

- Adjust the cot mattress to its lowest level as soon as the active baby starts to sit alone for even a few seconds – the next step may be pulling up and over the sides of the cot. Keep all objects a baby might climb on out of cot and playpen.

- Don't leave an active baby in an infant seat except in the middle of a double (or larger) bed or on the floor – they are often capable of overturning the seat. And of course, baby should always be strapped in.

- Learn what slows down your active baby – soft music (either your own singing or a record or tape), a warm bath (but never leave him or her alone in it), or looking at a picture book (though active children may not be ready for this as early as quieter children). Build such quieting activities into your baby's schedule before feeding and sleeping times.

The irregular baby. At about six to twelve weeks, just when other babies seem to be settling into a schedule and become more predictable, these babies seem to become more erratic. Not only don't they fall into schedules on their own, they aren't interested in any you may have to offer.

Instead of following such a baby's lead and letting chaos take over your home life, or taking the reins yourself and imposing a very rigid schedule that is contrary to the infant's nature, try to find a middle ground. For both your sakes, it's necessary to put at least a modicum of order in your lives, but try as much as possible to build a schedule around any natural tendencies your baby seems to exhibit. You may have to keep a diary to uncover any hints of a recurring time frame in your child's days, such as hunger around 11 AM every morning or fussiness after 7 PM every evening.

Try to counter any unpredictability with predictability. That means trying, as much as possible, to do things at the same times and in the same ways every day. Nurse in the same chair when possible, give baths at the same time each day, always soothe by the same method (rocking or singing or whatever works best). Try scheduling feedings at roughly the same times each day, even if your baby doesn't seem hungry, and try to stick to the schedule even if he or she is hungry between meals, offering a small snack if necessary. Ease rather than force your baby into more of a structured day. And don't expect true regularity, just a little less chaos.

Nights with an irregular baby can be torture, mostly because the baby doesn't usually differentiate them from days. You can try the tips for dealing with sleep problems (page 114) and night-day differentiation problems (page 115), but it's very possible they won't work for your baby, who may want to stay up throughout the night. To survive, mummy and daddy may have to alternate night duty or share split shifts until things get better, which they eventually will if you are persistent and stay cool. In extreme situations, the doctor may recommend a sedative (for the baby, not for you) to calm your child enough to allow you to work on establishing some sort of sleeping routine.

The poor-adaptibility or initial-withdrawal baby. These babies consistently reject the unfamiliar – new objects, people, foods. Some are upset by change of any kind, even familiar change such as going from the house to the car. If this sounds like your baby, try setting up a daily schedule with few surprises. Feedings, baths and naps should take place at the same times and in the same places, with as few departures from routine as possible. Introduce new toys and people (and foods, when baby is ready for them) very gradually. For example, hang a new mobile over the cot for just a minute or two. Remove it and bring it out again in a short while, leaving it up for a few minutes longer. Continue increasing the time of exposure until baby seems ready to accept and enjoy the mobile. Introduce other new toys and objects in the same way. Have new people spend a lot of time just being in the same room with your baby, then talking at a distance, then communicating close up, before they make an attempt at physical contact. Later, when you introduce solids, add new foods very gradually, starting with tiny amounts, and increasing portion size over the span of a week or two. Don't add another food until the last is well accepted. Try to avoid unnecessary changes when making purchases – a new feeding bottle with a different shape or colour, a new gadget on the pushchair, a new blanket on the cot. If an item wears out or breaks, try to replace it with an identical or similar model.

The high intensity baby. You probably noticed it right at the beginning – your baby cried louder than any other child in the hospital nursery. The loud crying and screaming, the kind that can frazzle even the steadiest of nerves, continued when you got home. Unfortunately you can't flip a switch and turn down the volume on your baby – but turning down the volume of noise and activity in the environment may help tone down your child a bit. Also, you will want to take some purely practical measures to keep the noise from bothering family and neighbours. If possible, soundproof your baby's room by insulating the walls with insulating board or padding, adding carpeting, curtains and anything else that will absorb the sound. You can try earplugs, a whitenoise machine, a fan or air conditioner to reduce the wear and tear on your ears and nerves without totally blocking out your baby's cries. As crying lessens in the months ahead, so will this problem, but your child will probably always be louder and more intense than most.

The negative or 'unhappy' baby. Instead of smiling and cooing, some babies just seem miserable all the time. This is no reflection on the parents (unless, of course, they've been neglectful), but it can have a profound impact on them. They often find it difficult to love their unhappy babies, and sometimes they even reject them. If nothing seems to satisfy your baby (and no medical explanation is uncovered), then do your best to be loving and caring anyway, secure in the knowledge that one of these days, when your baby learns other ways of expression, the crying and general unhappiness will diminish, though he or she may always be the 'serious' type.

How do you Talk to a Baby?

The roads to communication with a baby are endless and each parent travels some more than others. Here are some you may want to take, now or in the months ahead:

Do a running commentary. Don't make a move, at least when you're around your baby, without talking about it. Narrate the dressing process: 'Now I'm putting on your nappy . . . here goes the T-shirt over your head . . . now I'm buttoning your overalls.' In the kitchen, describe the washing of the dishes, or the process of seasoning the spaghetti sauce. During the bath, explain about soap and rinsing, and that a shampoo makes the hair shiny and clean. It doesn't matter that your baby hasn't the slightest inkling of what you're talking about. Blow-by-blow descriptions help get you talking, and get baby listening – thereby starting him or her on the path to understanding.

Ask a lot. Don't wait until your baby starts having answers to start asking questions. Think of yourself as a reporter, your baby as an intriguing interviewee. The questions can be as varied as your day: 'Would you like to wear the red pants or the green overalls?' 'Isn't the sky a beauti-ful blue today?' 'Should I buy string beans for dinner or broccoli?' Pause for an answer (one day your baby will surprise you with one), and then supply the answer yourself, out loud ('Broccoli? Good choice.')

Give baby a chance. Studies show that infants whose parents talk *with* them rather than *at* them learn to talk earlier. Give your baby a chance to get a coo, a gurgle or a giggle in edgewise. In your running commentaries, be sure to leave some openings for baby's comments.

Keep it simple – some of the time. Though right now your baby would probably derive listening pleasure from an animal assessment of the economy, as he or she gets a bit older, you'll want to make it easier to pick out individual words. So at least part of the time, make a conscious effort to use simple sentences and phrases: 'See the light', 'Bye-bye', 'Baby's fingers, baby's toes', and 'Nice doggie'.

Put aside pronouns. It's difficult for a young baby to grasp that 'I' or 'me' or 'you' can be mummy, or daddy, or gran, or even baby – depending on who's talking. So most of the time, refer to yourself as 'mummy' (or 'daddy' or 'gran') and to

lights in rooms she frequents. Don't expose her to too much visual stimulation at once – hang just one toy in the cot, or put just a couple in the playpen at a time. Select toys that are soft and subtle in colour and design rather than bright and busy.

- Taste sensitivity. If your baby is breastfed and has a bad day after you eat garlic or onions, consider that the unfamiliar taste of your milk may be the cause; if she's bottle fed and seems cranky a lot, try a formula with a different taste. When you introduce solids, recognize the fact that your baby may not relish every taste sensation and may reject some entirely.

- Touch sensitivity. Some babies lose their composure as soon as they wet their nappies, become frantic when they're too warm or dressed in rough fabrics, scream when they're dunked in the tub or put down on a too-cold mattress, or, later, when you buckle their shoes over wrinkled socks. So keep clothing comfortable (cotton knits with smooth seams and buttons, snaps, labels and collars that won't irritate because of size, shape, or location are ideal), bath water and room temperatures at levels she seems your baby by name: 'Now mummy is going to change Jason's nappy.'

Raise your pitch. Most babies prefer a high-pitched voice, which may be why women's voices are usually naturally higher-pitched than men's, and why most mother's voices climb an octave or two when addressing their infants. Try raising your pitch when talking directly to your baby, and watch the reaction. (A few infants prefer a lower pitch; experiment to see which appeals to yours.)

Stick to the here and now. Though you can muse about almost anything to your baby, there won't be any noticeable comprehension for a while. As comprehension does develop, you will want to stick more to what the baby can see or is experiencing at the moment. A young baby doesn't have a memory for the past or a concept of the future.

Imitate. Babies love the flattery that comes with imitation. When baby coos, coo back; when he or she utters an 'ahh', utter one, too. Imitation will quickly become a game that you'll both enjoy, and which will set the foundation for baby's imitating your language.

Set it to music. Don't worry if you can't carry a tune – little babies are notoriously undiscriminating when it comes to music. They'll love what you sing to them whether it's an old show standard, a new Top-40 hit, or just some nonsense you've set to a familiar tune. If your sensibilities (or your neighbours') prohibit a song, then sing-song will do. Most nursery rhymes entrance even young infants (invest in an edition of Mother Goose if your memory fails you). And accompanying hand gestures, if you know some or can make some up, double the delight. Your baby will quickly let you know which are favourites, and which you'll be expected to sing over and over – and over – again.

Read aloud. Though at first the words will have no meaning, it's never too early to begin reading some simple children's rhymes to your baby. When you aren't in the mood for baby talk and crave some adult-level stimulation, share your love of literature (or recipes or gossip or politics) with your little one by reading what you like to read, aloud.

Take your cues from baby. Incessant chatter and song can be tiresome for anyone, even an infant. When your baby becomes inattentive to your word play, closes or averts his or her eyes, becomes fussy or cranky, or otherwise indicates that saturation point has been reached, give it a rest.

happiest at, and nappies changed frequently (absorbent disposables may be better accepted than cloth).

A small percentage of babies are so oversensitive to touch that they resist being held and cuddled. Don't overhandle such a baby; do a lot of your caressing and interacting with words and eye contact rather than actual physical touching. When you do hold your baby, learn which way seems least annoying (tight or loose, for example).

- Smell sensitivity. Unusual odours aren't likely to bother a very young infant, but some children begin to show a negative reaction to certain odours before the end of the first year. The aroma of frying onions, the smell of a nappy rash ointment, the fragrance of mother's new perfume or father's new after-shave lotion, can all make such a baby restless and unhappy. If your baby seems sensitive to smells, limit strong odours when you can.

- Stimulation sensitivity. Too much stimulation of any kind seems to trigger trouble for some infants. These babies need to be handled gently and slowly. Loud talk, hurried movements, too many playthings, too many people around, too much activity in day – these can all be upsetting. To help such a baby sleep better, avoid active play just before bedtime, substituting a soothing, warm bath followed by quiet storytelling or lullabies. Soft recorded music can often help such a baby to settle down, too.

Living with a difficult baby isn't easy, but with plenty of love, patience and understanding it is possible, and in the long run it can even be rewarding. Before you decide your baby is one of the difficult ones, however, you should be sure that there isn't some underlying physical cause of his or her troubling behaviour. Describe it to the doctor so that any possible medical explanation – illness or allergy, for example – can be ruled out. Sometimes a baby who seems to be difficult is simply allergic to her formula, is teething, or is ill. For descriptions of other types of difficult babies, see the box on page 157.

A Second Language

'My husband is French and he wants to speak French to our baby exclusively; I speak English. I think it would be wonderful for her to speak a second language, but wouldn't it be confusing at this age?'

It's generally agreed that teaching a child a second language gives her an invaluable skill, may help her to think in different ways, and may even improve her self-image. If the language is one that her forebears spoke, it also gives her a significant link with her roots.

There is less agreement on just when to introduce the second language, however. Some experts suggest beginning as soon as a baby is born, but others believe that this puts the child at a disadvantage in both languages – though probably for only a while. They generally recommend waiting until a child is two and a half or three before putting on the Berlitz. By this time she usually has a pretty good grasp of English but is still able to pick up a new language

easily and naturally. It is generally agreed that waiting to introduce the second language until after a child can read will impede her fluency in it.

Whether you start now or in a couple of years, there are several approaches to encouraging a child to pick up a second language. One parent can speak English and the other the foreign tongue (as your husband suggests), or both parents can speak the foreign language (with the expectation the child will pick up English in school and elsewhere), or a grandparent, baby-sitter, or *au pair* girl can speak the foreign language and the parents English (usually the least successful of the methods). None of the methods of teaching a second language is particularly successful if the 'teacher' isn't fluent in the language.

Experts recommend you forget about 'teaching' a second language and instead immerse your child in it – play games in it, read books in it (many popular children's books have been translated from English into other languages, including Dr. Seuss books, Spot books, and Sesame Street books), sing songs in it, listen to tapes and watch videos in it, visit with friends who are fluent in it and, if possible, visit places where the language is spoken. Whoever is speaking the second language should speak it exclusively to the child, resisting the temptation to resort to English or to translate if the child seems to be struggling with comprehension. During the school years the child should be taught to read and write in the second language in order for it to take on greater usefulness and significance. If classes aren't available at school, tutoring or computer-programmed learning may be a good idea.

Baby Talk

'Other mothers seem to know how to talk to their babies. But I don't know what to say to my six-week-old son and, when I try, I feel like an absolute idiot. I'm afraid that my inhibitions will slow down his language development.'

They're tiny. They're passive. They can't talk back. And yet, for many novice mothers and fathers, newborn babies are the most intimidating audience they'll ever face. The undignified, high-pitched baby talk that seems to come naturally to other parents eludes them, leaving them tongue tied – and feeling guilty over the awkward silence that envelops the nursery.

Though your baby will learn your language even if you never learn his, his speech will develop faster and better if you make a conscious effort at early communication. Babies who aren't communicated with at all suffer not just in language development but in all areas of growth. But that rarely happens. Even the mother who is bashful about baby talk communicates with her baby all day long – when she cuddles him, responds to his crying, sings him a lullaby, says 'It's time for a walk', or mutters 'Oh, not the phone again', just as she's settled down to nurse. Parents teach language when they talk to each other as well as when they talk to their baby; babies pick up almost as much from second-hand dialogue as they do when they're part of a conversation.

So although it's not likely that your baby is going to spend the next year in the company of a silent mum, there are ways to expand your baby-word power, even if you're the kind of adult to whom baby talk doesn't come naturally. The trick is to start practising in private, so the embarrassment of gurgling and babbling to your baby in front of other adults won't cramp your conversation style. If you don't know where to begin, use the tips on page 156 as a guideline. As you grow more comfortable with baby talk, you'll likely find yourself slipping into it unawares, even in public.

WHAT IT'S IMPORTANT TO KNOW:
Stimulating Your Baby in the Early Months

In our achievement-oriented society, many parents worry about turning out babies that can compete – and they begin worrying early. They worry that if he doesn't smile by the time he's three weeks old, he may not get into the right preschool programme. They worry that if she hasn't turned over by two months, she may not make the prep-school tennis team. And then they worry that unless they do everything right they won't be successful in turning the basically unresponsive lump they brought home from the hospital into a candidate for Oxford.

Actually, they have little reason to worry. Babies – even those destined for greatness – develop at different rates, and those who get off to a somewhat slower start often excel later. And parents – even those who are chronically insecure – usually do a thoroughly competent job of stimulating their offspring, often without making a conscious effort.

Yet, as comforting as this knowledge should be, it doesn't always stop the worry.

For many parents, there is the nagging fear that doing what comes naturally when it comes to parenting may not be quite enough. If you'd like to check what you've already been doing instinctively to see if you're on the right track, the following tips for creating the right atmosphere for learning and for supplying sensory stimulation should be helpful to you.

Creating a Good Environment

Love your baby. Nothing helps a baby grow and thrive as much as being loved. A close relationship with a parent, or parents, and/or a substitute parent is crucial for normal development.

Relate to your baby. Take every opportunity to talk, sing, or coo to your baby – while you're changing a nappy, giving a bath, shopping for groceries, or driving the car.

These casual but stimulating exchanges go further in making a brighter baby than forcing flash cards. And even the best toys in the world are useless if baby doesn't have you to play with part of the time. Your goal isn't to 'teach' your baby, but to be involved with him or her.

Get to know your baby. Learn what makes your baby happy or miserable, excited or bored, soothed or stimulated, paying more attention to what you learn from your baby than from any book or adviser. Gear attempts at stimulation to your unique baby, rather than to some typical textbook child. If loud noises and/or roughhousing upset your child, then entertain with soft sounds and gentle play. If too much excitement makes your baby frantic, limit the length of playtimes and the intensity of activity.

Take the pressure off – and have fun. Neither you nor your baby will benefit from your preoccupation with his or her level of performance. Learning and development aren't hastened by pressure, and they may be hindered. Harmful to baby's self-esteem is the message – no matter how carefully camouflaged – that you're not satisfied with his or her progress up the developmental ladder. Instead of thinking of the times you spend stimulating your baby as intensive cramming sessions, relax and enjoy – for both your sakes.

Give your baby space. Adequate attention is vital; too much can be suffocating. Though children need to know that help is available when they need it, they also need to learn how to seek it out. Your constant hovering will also deprive your baby of the chance to look for and find diversion elsewhere – in the friendly looking teddy bear who's sharing the cot, in the pattern of light cast by the venetian blinds, in his or her own fingers and toes, in the sound of an aeroplane overhead, a fire engine down the street, the dog barking next door. It may also hamper your baby's ability to play and learn independently later on – and a dependent baby will make it difficult for you to turn

your attention to anything else. By all means, play with your child and spend quality time, but sometimes just get baby and toy together and then move off while they get acquainted.

Follow the leader. And make sure your baby, not you, is in the lead. If he or she is fascinated by the mobile, don't bring out the activity board; instead, focus on the mobile together. Allowing baby to take the wheel once in a while not only enhances learning by taking advantage of the 'teachable moment', but also reinforces baby's budding sense of self-esteem by communicating that his or her interests are worthy of mummy's attention.

Let your baby take the lead, too, in deciding when to end a play session – even if it's before the rattle is grasped. Your baby will tell you, 'I've had enough', by turning away, fussing, crying, or otherwise showing disinterest or displeasure. Ignoring the message and pressing on deprives a baby of a sense of control, turns off interest in the subject (at least for a while), and ultimately makes playtime a whole lot less fun for both of you.

Time it right. A baby is always in one of six states of consciousness: (1) deep, or quiet, sleep; (2) light, or active, sleep; (3) drowsiness; (4) active wakefulness with interest in physical activity; (5) fussiness and crying; and (6) quiet wakefulness. It's during active wakefulness that you can most effectively encourage physical development, and during quiet wakefulness that you can best foster other types of learning. Also keep in mind that infants have very short attention spans. A baby who turns you off after two minutes of looking at a book isn't rejecting intellectual pursuits, but has simply run out of concentration.

Provide positive reinforcement. When your baby starts achieving (when he or she smiles, swats at a rattle, lifts shoulders and arms off the mattress, turns over, or grasps a toy successfully) show your approbation. Do it with hugs, cheers, applause –

what ever is comfortable for you and gets the message across to your baby: 'I think you're terrific.'

Practical Tips for Learning and Playing

Some parents, without ever reading a book about or taking a course in infant stimulation, seem to have an easier time than others initiating learning-playing activities with their babies. And some babies, because they are unusually responsive, are easier to engage in such activities. But any parent-baby team can be successful at learning-playing with a little guidance.

The areas to nourish and encourage are:

The sense of taste. Right now you don't have to go out of your way to stimulate this sense. Your baby's taste buds are titillated at every meal on breast or bottle. But as baby gets older, 'tasting' will become a way of exploring, and everything within reach will end up being mouthed. Resist the temptation to discourage this, except, of course, when what goes into the mouth is poisonous, sharp, or small enough to swallow or choke on.

The sense of smell. In most environments, the keen smelling apparatus of infants gets plenty of exercise. There's breast milk, mum's perfume, Rover scampering nearby, the roasting chicken. Unless your baby shows signs of being overly sensitive to odours, think of the various scents as additional opportunities for your baby to learn about the environment.

The sense of sight. Though we once believed that babies were sightless at birth, we now know that they can not only see, but begin learning from what they see. Through their sense of sight, they learn very quickly to differentiate between objects and human beings (and between one object or human being and another), to interpret body language and other nonverbal cues, and to understand a little bit more every day about the world around them.

Decorate your baby's room or corner with the goal of supplying stimulating visual surroundings, rather than satisfying your own tastes. When selecting wallpaper, quilts, wall hangings, toys, or books, keep in mind that babies like sharp contrasts, and that designs that are bold and bright rather than soft and delicate are more appealing (black-and-white patterns are favoured for the first six weeks or so, bright colours later). Limit playthings in the cot, playpen, and baby seat to one or two at a time – too many can lead to confusion and overstimulation.

Many objects, toys among them, can stimulate baby visually:

- Mobiles. Figures on a mobile should be fully visible from below (the baby's perspective), rather than from the side (the adult's perspective). A mobile should be no more than 30 to 38 cm (12 to 15 inches) over the baby's face, and should be hung to one side or the other of the child's line of vision, rather than straight above (most children prefer to gaze towards the right, but observe your child to discover a preference).

- Other things that move. You can move a rattle or other bright toy across baby's line of vision to encourage tracking of moving objects. Take a field trip to a pet shop and position baby in front of a fish tank or bird cage to view the action. Or blow bubbles for baby.

- Stationary objects. Babies spend a lot of time just looking at things. This isn't idle time, but learning time. Geometric patterns or simple faces in black-and-white, hand drawn or store bought, are early favourites. Bright colours and sharp contrasts are preferred over pale, more delicate designs.

- Mirrors. Mirrors give baby an ever-changing view and most love them. Be sure to use safe metal baby mirrors rather than glass ones; hang them on the cot, in the pram, over the changing table.

- People. Babies delight in looking at faces close up, so you and other family members should spend plenty of time in close proximity to baby. You can also show baby family portraits, pointing out who's who.

- Books. Show baby simple pictures of babies, children, animals, or toys and identify them. The drawings should be clear and sharply defined without a lot of extra (for a baby) detail.

- The world. Very soon your baby is going to take an interest in seeing beyond his or her nose. Provide plenty of opportunity to see the world – from the pushchair, pram, car seat, or by carrying your baby face forward. Now and then point out cars, trees, people, and so on. But don't ramble on non-stop during every outing; you'll become bored, and baby will start tuning you out.

The sense of hearing. It's through hearing that infants learn about language, about rhythm, about danger, about emotions and feelings – and about so much else that goes on around them. Auditory stimulation can come from almost any source.

- The human voice. This, of course, is the most significant type of sound in a new infant's life, so use yours – talk, sing and babble to your baby. Try lullabies, nursery rhymes, nonsense ditties you create yourself. Imitate animal sounds, especially ones your baby regularly hears, such as the barking of a dog or the meowing of a cat. Most importantly, play back for your baby the sounds he or she makes.

- Household sounds. Many young babies are captivated by either soft or lively background music, the hum of the vacuum or the blender, the whistle of the tea kettle or the splash of running water, the crinkling of paper (but don't offer newspaper for crinkling, since the newsprint could be poisonous), or the tinkling of a bell or wind chime – though they may become fearful of many such sounds later in the first year.

- Rattles and other toys that make gentle sounds. You don't have to wait until your baby is able to shake a rattle independently. In the early months, either do the shaking yourself, put the rattle in baby's hand and help shake it, or attach a wrist rattle. Coordination between vision and hearing will develop as baby learns to turn towards sound.

- Music boxes. You'll be surprised at how quickly your baby will learn to recognize a tune; especially nice are music boxes that have visual appeal, but if one is placed within reach, be sure it doesn't have small pieces that can be broken off and mouthed by your baby.

- Musical toys. Be sure that keys or other parts are child-safe. Toys that make music and also provide visual stimulation and practice with small motor skills (such as a bunny that moves and makes music when baby pulls a string) are particularly good. Avoid toys that make loud noises that can damage hearing, and don't place even moderately noisy ones right by baby's ear.

- Children's records and tapes. Try to give them a spin before buying to be sure they're good listening. Infancy is also an ideal time to start exposing your child to classical music (play it softly during play time in the cot, or during dinner or bathtime), although many babies seem to prefer the livelier rhythms of rock or country music. Always watch your baby for reactions to music; if he or she seems disturbed by what you're playing, turn it off.

The sense of touch. Touch, though often underrated, is actually one of a baby's most valuable tools for exploring and learning about the world. It's through touch that a baby learns the softness of mummy, the relative hardness of daddy, that rubbing a teddy bear feels wonderful, that rubbing a stiff brush doesn't feel that good, and most important of all, that those who take care of him are loving – a message you send every time you bathe, change feed, or rock your baby.

You can provide more varied touching experiences for your baby with:

- A loving hand. Try to learn how your baby likes to be handled – firmly or lightly, quickly or slowly. Most babies love to be caressed and kissed, to have their tummies tickled or razzed by your lips, to have you blow gently on their fingers or toes. They love the difference between mummy's touch and daddy's, the rough way a sibling hugs or tickles them and the expert ease with which grandmother rocks them.

- Massage. Premies who are massaged for at least twenty minutes daily gain weight faster and do better overall than those who aren't (whether it's the massage or the fact that they're handled more is unclear), babies who aren't touched at all don't grow at a normal pace. Discover the kind of strokes your baby enjoys most, and avoid those that seem to annoy.

- Textures. Try rubbing a baby's skin with different textures (satin, terry, velvet, wool, fur, or absorbent cotton) so he or she gets to know how each feels; later encourage independent exploration. Let baby lie face down on surfaces with different textures: the living room carpet, a terry towel, grandmother's fur coat, your corduroy skirt, dad's wool sweater, the marble-topped coffee table – the possibilities are limitless.

- Playthings with texture. Offer toys that have interesting textures to baby. A plush teddy bear and a coarse-haired doggy; hard wooden blocks and soft stuffed ones; a rough wooden spoon and a smooth metal bowl: a silky pillow and a nubby one.

Social development. Your baby becomes a social being through watching you, through interacting with you and the rest of the family, and later with others. This isn't the time to begin teaching your baby how to throw a successful party or make interesting small talk over the onion dip but it is time to begin teaching by example how people should behave towards one another. A few years from now, when your growing child talks to friends, teachers, neighbours, or begins 'playing house', you'll often hear your example echoed in that tiny voice; hopefully, you'll be pleased (and not shocked or disappointed) by what you hear.

Toys that help babies with social development are stuffed animals, animal mobiles and dolls. Though it will be many months before they'll be able to hug them and play with them, even at this point they can and do begin to socialize with them – just watch an infant converse with animals prancing on the cot bumpers or revolving on a mobile. Later, books and opportunities for make-believe and dress-up play will also help children to develop social skills.

Small motor development. Right now your baby's hand movements are totally random, but in a couple of months, those tiny hands will move with more purpose and control. You can aid in the development of purposeful movement by giving your baby's hands plenty of freedom; don't keep them swaddled or tucked under a blanket (except outdoors in cold weather). Provide a variety of objects that are easy for small hands to pick up and manipulate, that don't require fine dexterity. And since young babies usually won't grasp objects that are directly in front of them, offer these objects from the side.

Give your baby ample opportunity for 'hands-on' experience with the following:

- Rattles that fit small hands comfortably. Those with two handles or grasping surfaces allow a baby to pass the rattle from hand to hand, an important skill, and those that baby can mouth will help bring relief when teething begins.

- Cradle gyms (they fit across pram, playpen, or cot) that have a variety of parts for baby to grab hold of, spin, pull and poke. Beware of those, however, with strings more than 15 cm (6 inches) long, and take any gym down once your baby is able to sit up.

- Activity boards that require a wide range of hand movements to operate, many of which your baby won't be able to intentionally manoeuvre for a while, but some of which even a young infant can set in motion accidentally with a swipe of a hand or foot. Besides the spinning, dialing, pushing and pressing skills these toys encourage, they also teach the concept of cause and effect.

Gross motor development. Putting your baby through the paces of an infant exercise video won't increase muscular strength or speed motor development. Good motor skills, well-developed bodies and physical fitness for infants depend instead on the following: good nutrition; good health care (both well-baby and sick-baby); and plenty of opportunity for self-motivated physical activity. Babies kept cooped up in a swing or baby seat, harnessed in a pram, or pushchair, or swaddled in a blanket or bunting will have little opportunity to learn about how their bodies work. Those who are never put down on the tummy will be slow to learn to lift their head and shoulders or turn over front to back. Change your baby's position often during the day (propping him up in a sitting position, placing her sometimes on stomach and other times on back) to maximize the opportunities for physical activity.

Encourage physical development by pulling your baby to a sitting position, letting him or her 'fly' (allowing exercise of arms and legs) or 'ride', (lying face down, lengthways on your shins). Motivate rolling over by putting an interesting object to one side as baby lies on his or her back; if baby turns a bit, then give a little help in going all the way. Encourage creeping by letting baby push off against your hands when lying belly down.

Intellectual development. Encouraging the development of all the senses, as well as small and large motor control, will contribute to your baby's intellectual growth. Talk to your infant a lot, right from the start. Give names to objects, animals and people your baby sees, point out body parts, explain what you're doing. Read nursery rhymes and simple stories, showing your baby the illustrations as you go. Expose your child to a variety of settings (the supermarket, your church or synagogue, a department store, the museum). Travel on buses, in cars, in taxicabs. Even at home, vary your baby's point of view: place the baby seat by a window (but *only* if it has a window guard) or in front of a mirror, lay baby in the middle of the living room carpet to survey the action or in the middle of the bed to watch you fold the laundry, or park the bassinet or stroller in the kitchen while you prepare dinner.

Whatever you do, however, don't put yourself or your baby under pressure to perform. The play's the thing, and it should be fun – the learning that comes with it is a bonus, though an important one.

SIX

The Third Month

◆

What Your Baby May Be Doing

By the end of this month, your baby . . . should be able to (see Note):

- on stomach, lift head up 45 degrees (2⅔ months)
- follow an object in an arc about 15 cm (6 inches) above the face past the midline (straight ahead) (by 2½ months)

Note: If your baby seems not to have reached one or more of these milestones, check with the doctor. In rare instances the delay could indicate a problem, though in most cases it will turn out to be normal for your baby. Premature infants generally reach milestones later than others of the same birth age, often achieving them closer to their adjusted age (the age they would be if they had been born at term), and sometimes later.

. . . will probably be able to:

- laugh out loud
- on stomach, lift head up 90 degrees
- squeal in delight
- bring both hands together
- smile spontaneously
- follow an object in an arc about 15 cm (6 inches) above the face for 180 degrees – from one side to the other (3¼ months)

. . . may possibly be able to:

- hold head steady when upright
- on stomach, raise chest, supported by arms
- roll over (one way)

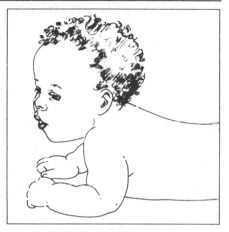

Many, but not all, three-month-olds can lift their head to a 90 degree angle.

- grasp a rattle held to backs or tips of fingers (3½ months)
- pay attention to a raisin or other very small object (3½ months)

. . . may even be able to:

- bear some weight on legs when held upright
- reach for an object (3⅔ months)
- keep head level with body when pulled to sitting
- turn in the direction of a voice, particularly mummy's
- say ah-goo or similar vowel-consonant combination
- razz (make a wet razzing sound)

What You Can Expect At This Month's Checkup

Each doctor, midwife health visitor will have a personal approach to well-baby checkups. The overall organization of the physical exam, as well as the number and type of assessment techniques used and procedures performed will also vary with the individual needs of the child. But in general you can expect the following at a check-up when your baby is about three months old.

- Questions about how you and baby and the rest of the family are doing at home, and about baby's eating, sleeping and general progress. About child care, if you are working.

- Measurement of baby's weight, length and head circumference, and plotting of progress since birth.

- Physical exam, including a recheck of any previous problems.

- Second round of immunizations for diphtheria, tetanus and pertussis (DTP), polio (TOPV) and for Haemophilus type B (Hib) if baby is in good health and there are no other contraindications. Be sure to discuss any reactions to the first round of immunizations beforehand.

Questions you may want to ask, if the doctor hasn't already answered them:

- What reactions can you expect baby to have to the second round of immunizations? How should you treat them? Which reactions should you call about?

Feeding Your Baby This Month: Nursing While Working Outside The Home

There's an added responsibility that's not included in any job description, but which many employed mothers are electing to take on. It's time consuming, and it can be arduous, even tedious. It cuts into coffee breaks and lunch hours, and makes the hectic times before and after work even more hectic. And yet most of the women who've added nursing to their workday are glad they have – and they'd do it again.

The reasons are powerful. First of all, employed mothers who nurse continue to give their babies many of the physical benefits of breastfeeding (fewer illnesses, decreased risk of allergy), and all of them if no supplementary formula is given. Second, they can feel less guilty about leaving their babies during the day because they know they are doing something important for them even while they are away. Third, because employed nursing mothers must

nurse before going to work and again when they get home, they have the opportunity to spend time in close contact with their babies at least twice a day. No matter how busy, they can't prop a bottle or have someone else give it while they shower or get dinner ready. And finally, and perhaps most importantly, mothers who continue to nurse when they go back to their jobs can, along with their babies, enjoy the emotional benefits of breastfeeding for a longer time.

Making Nursing and Employment Work

As with everything else that's related to going back to work when you have a young infant, plenty of forethought is necessary. To make nursing and employment work, keep the following in mind:

- Don't start giving bottles until your milk supply is well established. It's tempting to start very early so the bottle won't be rejected. But starting too early can lead to both nipple confusion (see page 101) and an inadequate milk supply. Wait to introduce the bottle until you've worked out any problems with nursing (such as sore nipples) and feel confident about the adequacy of your milk supply. For most women, that's somewhere around six weeks – though some women find things going smoothly a bit sooner or later.

- Introduce the bottle well in advance of return-to-the-job day. Though you won't want to bring on the bottle much before six weeks, don't wait much longer either, even if you won't be returning to your job for a while. The older and smarter babies get, the less easy it is to persuade them to take a bottle. Work towards getting your baby used to taking at least one supplementary bottle a day – preferably at a time of day when you'll usually be working – by the time you are ready to start collecting paycheques. Use formula or breast milk, depending on which you plan to use later.

- If you intend to supplement with breast milk rather than formula, become proficient at expressing your milk well before you return to work. Freeze a few bottles of excess milk so you'll have an emergency stash for those first frenzied days back on the job. If you plan on using formula, you will probably still have to learn to pump your breasts, since it will probably be necessary to express milk at work to avoid clogged milk ducts and a diminishing milk supply.

- Wait, if possible, until your baby is at least sixteen weeks old before you return to work outside your home. In general, the older a baby is when a mother takes this step, the more successful the continuation of breastfeeding – probably because both breastfeeding and mother-baby relationships have had more time to become well established.

- Work part-time if you can, at least at first. More hours with your baby will strengthen breastfeeding links. Working four or five half-days is more practical than two or three full ones for several reasons. Working half-days, you may in some cases not have to miss any feedings, and certainly no more than one daily. You will have little trouble with leakage and probably won't have to pump milk at work at all. And you will spend most of each day with your baby, which many experts believe is more beneficial. Working nights is another option that interferes very little with breastfeeding, especially if baby is sleeping through the night, but it can interfere with both rest and romance.

- Stay faithful to your Best-Odds Breastfeeding Diet; you'll need it not only for milk production, but also to keep your energy up and your emotions on an even keel.

- Enlist support at your workplace. If your employer and/or coworkers don't understand and support your decision to continue nursing while you work, your odds of success will drop dramatically. Try to arrange in advance a time and place for expressing milk, and for refrigeration for storage if you'll need it. If you have no way to store and/or transport what you pump, you will have to discard it and depend on breast milk pumped and stored while you are at home mornings, nights and weekends, or on formula, for feedings.[1]

- When you arrange for a caregiver for your baby, be sure it is a person who understands and supports your plan to continue breastfeeding. If not, you may find your baby recently fed and fully satiated when you arrive home eager to nurse. Give the baby-sitter a quick course in the whys and ways of breastfeeding

---

1. Recent studies indicate that breast milk can remain fresh for as long as six hours at room temperature; but to be extra safe, store your milk in sterilized bottles or containers and refrigerate, if possible.

and breastfed babies, if she's unfamiliar with them; explain the differences in feeding schedules and bowel movements, as well as the importance of frequent nursing to keep the milk supply up. Leave strict instructions not to give bottles of milk (or juice or water) for at least two hours before you're expected home to nurse.

- Enlist support from your husband, too. He'll have to share some of the household burdens so that you will be able to spend the necessary time nursing when you're at home.

- Keep your priorities straight. You won't be able to do everything and do everything well. Keep your baby and your relationship with your spouse (and any other children you have) at the top of the list, and cut corners everywhere else – except, of course, at your job if it means a lot to you, either financially, emotionally, or professionally.

- Stay flexible. A calm and happy mother is more valuable to your baby's well-being than a diet made up exclusively of breast milk. Though it's entirely possible you'll be able to continue providing all of your baby's milk (if that's what you want to do), it's also possible that you won't be able to. Sometimes the physical and emotional stresses of holding a job and nursing curtail a woman's milk supply. If your baby isn't thriving on breast milk alone, try nursing more frequently when you're at home and, if it's feasible, returning home during your lunch break to breastfeed and help rebuild your milk supply. If this doesn't work, it will probably be necessary to supplement with formula.

- Dress for breastfeeding success. To keep leakage from being visible and from staining your best outfits, wear loose blouses or shirts in colourful prints on easy-care opaque cottons or blends. Avoid pale colours, clingy fabrics and sheers, as well as tight tops that might either trigger let down (by rubbing against your nipples) or inhibit it (by acting as a binder). Be sure your top can be lifted or opened easily from the front for pumping at work, and that it won't be stretched out of shape or badly wrinkled by being pulled up. Line your nursing bra with breast pads to further protect your clothing, and carry an extra supply of pads in your bag as replacements for wet ones.

- Do a couple of trial runs. Rehearse your workday game plan, doing everything as you would if you were really going to work (including expressing milk away from home), but leave the house for just a couple of hours the first time, longer the next. Note what problems arise, and figure out how they can be handled.

- If you're going back to a full-time job you might also try returning on a Thursday or Friday to give yourself a chance to get started, see how things go, and evaluate the situation over the weekend. It will also be a little less overwhelming than starting out with five days ahead of you.

- Arrange your schedule to maximize the number of nursings. Squeeze in two feedings before you go to work, if possible, and two or three (or more) in the evening. If you work near home and can either return during lunchtime for nursing or have the nanny meet you somewhere with the baby consider doing this. If you leave your baby at a childminder's house, nurse when you arrive there, or in your car before you go in, if that works better. Also try nursing your baby at pickup time, instead of waiting until you get home.

- Try taking home any work that can be done out of the office or shop (with your employer's blessing, of course). This will give you more flexibility and allow you to be home more of your baby's waking hours. Though you will probably have to relegate most of baby's care to someone else when you're home working, you should be able to nurse as needed.

- If your job entails travel, try to avoid trips that take you away from home for more than 1 day until your baby is weaned; if you must travel, do try to express and freeze enough milk for the duration of your trip in advance or get your baby accustomed to formula before you plan to go. For your own comfort and to keep up your milk supply, take along a breast pump (or rent one where you'll be) and express milk every three or four hours. When you get home you may find your milk supply somewhat diminished, but more frequent-than-usual nursings, along with extra-special attention to diet and rest, may replenish it. If it doesn't you will probably have to use formula, at least for the worktime feedings.

- If, to ensure your baby gets the proper nutrition needed for growth and development, you must use formula supplements for home feedings, breastfeed before giving the formula feedings rather than after, so as to interfere as little as possible with what milk you are producing.

- Do what works and seems right for you and your baby, whether it's supplementing with formula or feeding your baby exclusively on breast milk, working part-time or full-time, giving up nursing altogether – or even giving up your job.

What You May Be Concerned About

Establishing a Regular Schedule

'I know that the old idea of fitting a baby into a schedule is frowned upon. But I'm exhausted trying to fit into my baby's schedule. He demands and I nurse nearly every hour, all day long.'

Women of this generation are vocal in demanding their rights in the workplace, but they sometimes forget that they also have rights where their children are concerned. And as your baby gets older, you can begin demanding yours from him.

Before you do, however, be certain his seemingly gluttonous nursing pattern isn't his way of trying to get adequate nourishment – either because you're not producing enough milk or because he's unusually active or going through a growth spurt. Does he seem to be growing as he should? Is his body filling out nicely? Is he outgrowing his newborn sleepers? If not, see page 98 for tips on improving your breast milk supply. If they don't work, talk to the doctor about supplementing your baby's diet with formula.

Once you've determined that your baby is thriving, and that it isn't hunger that's motivating his frequent pleas of 'Please, mum, can I have some more', then it's time to start making some changes to ensure that you thrive, too. Hourly nursing sessions are too much of a strain on you, both physically and emotionally, are likely to cause sore nipples, and may understandably result in your feeling resentment towards your baby for taking up so much of your day and night with his greedy habit. As for your baby, overnursing isn't only unnecessary – it's unhealthy. It interferes with his sleep, which he needs in longer stretches now, and with his development while he's awake. Having a breast in his mouth all day long doesn't give him a chance to do much of anything else.

By three months, many babies will have established a pretty regular daily rhythm. Typically, it's something like this: he wakes about the same time each morning, feeds, perhaps stays awake for a short period, takes a nap, wakes again for lunch, follows with another nap, feeds, then perhaps has a fairly long period of wakefulness late in the afternoon, capped off by a meal and a nap in the early evening. If this nap tends to run past the parents' bedtimes, they may wake him to eat before they retire, maybe about

11 P.M. At this point he may go back to sleep again until early morning, since babies this age can often sleep six hours at a stretch, and sometimes more.

Some babies have a more idiosyncratic schedule. One, for example, may wake up at 6 A.M., feed, and go back to sleep for an hour or two. Upon awakening, he may be content to play for a while before nursing, but once he starts nursing, he wants to do so nonstop for the next three hours. After a twenty-minute nap, however, he wakes up ready to play happily all afternoon with just one nursing period and another five-minute nap. He nurses again at about 6:00 and by 7:00 is sound asleep, and he stays that way until mum wakes him for a nightcap before she retires. His isn't the traditional four-hour schedule, but it is one a mother can plan her day around.

Many babies, unfortunately, don't fall smoothly into any schedule at all, even past three months. They wake, eat and sleep in a totally random pattern, eating frequently or infrequently, sometimes combining the two unpredictably. If your baby is one of these, it's up to you to take the initiative by trying to make the parts of his life you do have some control over as organized as possible. Baths, outings and bedtime should come at roughly the same times every day. Try to stretch the periods between feedings by talking to, singing to, or playing with your baby before putting him to the breast or bottle. Put him in a baby swing for a few minutes, or in his cot with his musical mobile or cradle gym for entertainment – anything that he enjoys and that will successfully keep him from getting his next meal as early as he'd like. Be sure, too, that he has enough to do between feedings. His frequent nursings may have more to do with boredom than with anything else. He's no longer a newborn and needs a more active lifestyle (see page 159 for tips on stimulating him).

Once you've successfully cut down on nursings and developed some sort of daily routine you will have more time for your own life and more control over your baby.

'People think I'm strange or remiss when they hear I don't have any particular schedule for my baby – no special bedtime or eating times or bath time for her. But that's the way I'm comfortable.'

Though much of our society is run on schedules – train schedules, work schedules, class schedules, parking schedules – there are those of us who function perfectly well without them. And if baby doesn't have any serious sleep problems at night and seems perfectly contented, active and interested by day, a laissez-faire attitude towards scheduling may be fine for the time being.

There are, however, certain pitfalls in raising children in an unstructured environment. Watch out for these problems if you choose such a lifestyle:

- Some babies crave schedules right from the start. They become cranky when feedings are late or overtired when naps and bedtimes are delayed. If your baby reacts unhappily to your unscheduled days and nights, it may be that she needs a little more structure, even if you don't.

- Schedules become increasingly important to family stability and to a baby's well-being as time goes by. Many children seem to do perfectly well without a schedule in early infancy, when they're extremely portable and can fall asleep or be fed anywhere. Later they often begin to respond to irregular mealtimes and sleep times with regular crying and crankiness.

- Without a regular bedtime for their babies, parents often find they never spend any time alone. They enjoy their threesome so much in the evening, they often forget the fun two can – and should – have.

- Families that omit regular sleep and mealtimes sometimes shortchange their babies by unthinkingly also omitting the sleep and mealtime rituals that most babies seem to need.

- For mothers who plan to go back to a paid job sometime within the first two years of their baby's life, not having a schedule for a child-care provider to work with will mean their baby not only won't have mummy around all day, but also won't have a familiar routine to cling to that would help with adjustment.

- For all babies, the absence of structure in their lives early on can interfere with their developing, and then exercising, self-discipline later in life. Getting to school on time, completing homework and getting papers in on schedule can be inordinately difficult for children who have never been exposed to any kind of structure previously.

In spite of the pitfalls babies can, and do, thrive in families where a schedule, even a loose one, is nonexistent. And in fact, an extremely strict schedule can be as stifling as a too-lax one can be disorienting. How much structure you put in your baby's life should depend on your baby's natural eating and sleeping patterns, her inborn personality (does she seem to need more structure or less), and the needs of the rest of the family. What works best for other people, as in most things, may not work best for you. If it's your baby who objects to schedules, see page 154.

Putting Baby to Bed

'My baby always falls asleep nursing. I've heard that this is a bad habit for her to get started on.'

It's an idea that looks good in print: put a baby to bed when she's awake, not already asleep, so that later, once she's weaned, she'll be able to get to sleep on her own, without the breast or a bottle. In practice, as any mother who's tried to keep her baby from falling asleep while nursing or tried to rouse a baby who's konked out while sucking knows, it's an idea that's not necessarily compatible with reality. There's just very little you can do to keep a nursing baby

awake if she wants to sleep. And if you could wake her up, would you really want to?

Teaching your baby to fall asleep without assistance from breast (or bottle) can more practically wait until baby is older – between six and nine months – and nursing less often. And if the habit hangs on, breaking it can certainly be accomplished fairly quickly after your baby has been weaned.

Whenever the opportunity presents itself, however, do try to put your baby down for a nap or at bedtime awake – not so awake that sleep will be elusive, but in a state of drowsy readiness. A little rocking, nursing, or lullabying can usually bring a baby to this state (but try not to prolong the comforting action to the point of sound sleep).

Not Sleeping Through the Night

'My friend's baby has been sleeping through the night since he got home from the hospital, but mine is still waking up and eating as often as he did when he was first born.'

Babies are creatures of habit. Create a habit for them and they're likely to cling to it, particularly if it's one that gets them food and attention.

In young infants, the habit of feeding frequently at night is often a nutritionally necessary one. Though some babies, such as your friend's, no longer need night feedings by the third month (and sometimes sooner), most two- or three-month-old babies, particularly breastfed ones, still need to eat once or twice during the night. If the night-waking habit continues into the fifth or sixth month, however, you can begin to suspect that your baby is waking not because he *needs* to eat during the night, but because he's become *accustomed* to eating then; a stomach that's used to being filled at regular intervals around the clock will cry 'empty' even when it's sufficiently full to last a lot longer.

Although it may be legitimate for your baby to get one middle-of-the-night feeding, he certainly doesn't need three or four of them. You'll need to gradually reduce the number of late-show feedings he's getting now as a first step in preparing him to sleep through the night later. Here's how:

- Increase the size of the bedtime feeding. Many sleepy babies nod off before they've totally filled their tanks for the night; restart yours with a burp or a jiggle or some other ploy, and continue feeding until you feel he's had enough. In a month or two, when baby is ready for solids, you may want to build up the evening feeding further with cereal or another food – though it isn't scientifically proven that this helps babies sleep through the night, it does sometimes work.

- Wake your baby up to feed him before you retire at night; this may fill him enough to last him through your own six or eight hours of sleep. Unfortunately, some babies are too sleepy when they are awakened to take a lot, but sometimes even a small latenight feeding will hold them one or two hours longer than would have been the case with none at all. (Of course, if your baby begins waking more often once you've instituted this procedure, discontinue it. It could be that being awakened by you makes him more prone to waking himself.)

- Be certain your baby is getting enough to eat all day long. If he isn't, he may be using those night feedings to catch up on calories. If you think this is so, consider nursing more frequently during the day to stimulate milk production (also check the tips on page 98). If your baby's on the bottle, increase the amount of formula you give at each feeding. Be aware, however, that for some babies feeding every couple of hours during the day sets up a pattern of eating every two hours, a pattern they continue around the clock.

- If he's waking and demanding food every two hours (maybe necessary for a newborn, but not for a thriving two- or three-month-old), try to stretch the time

between feedings, adding half an hour each night or every other night. Instead of jumping to get him at the first whimper, give him a chance to try to fall asleep again by himself – he may surprise you. If he doesn't, and fussing turns to screaming, try to soothe him without picking him up – pat or rub his back, sing a soft, monotonous lullaby, or turn on a musical cot toy. If the crying doesn't stop after a reasonable time (give it a good fifteen minutes at this age), pick him up and try soothing him in your arms by rocking, swaying, cuddling, or singing. If you're breastfeeding, the soothing tactics have a better chance of success if dad's in charge; a breastfeeding infant who sees, hears, or smells his source is not easily distracted from eating. Keep the room dark, and avoid a lot of conversation or stimulation.

If, after all your efforts, baby doesn't fall back to sleep and still demands feeding, feed him – but by now you've probably stretched the interval between feedings by at least half an hour from the previous plateau. The hope is that baby will reach a new plateau within the next few nights and sleep half an hour longer between feedings. Gradually try to extend the time between meals until baby is down to one nighttime feeding, which he may continue to need for another two or three months.

- Cut down the amounts at the nighttime feedings you want to eliminate. Reduce the number of millilitres/fl ounces in your baby's bottle by 30 ml/1 fl ounce or the number of minutes he nurses by a couple. Continue cutting back a little more each night or every other night. With a bottle-fed baby it may work to dilute the formula, gradually adding a little more water and a little less formula each night until you're down to all water at the unwanted feedings. At that point, some babies will decide that getting up for a bottle of water isn't worth the effort, and will choose to sleep instead. Most, however, will prefer water to no bottle at all, and will continue to waken for this bottle. But since a baby's hunger can't be satisfied with water, you will at least have eliminated the hunger-feeding cycle, making it easier to eventually drop the feeding entirely. (Check with your baby's doctor before diluting the formula to be sure you won't be cutting out needed calories.)

- Increase the amount offered at the night feeding you are most likely to continue. If your baby is getting up at midnight, two and four, for example, you may want to cut out the first and last of these feedings. This will be easier to do if you increase the amount your baby takes at the middle one, either from bottle or breast. A nip from the breast or 60 ml/a couple of fl ounces from the bottle is not likely to knock him out for long. See the tips for keeping a sleepy baby awake for feeding on page 60.

- Don't change your baby's nappy during the night unless it's absolutely necessary – a quick sniff can usually tell you when it is. (Of course, the fewer midnight snacks you indulge him in, the less necessary nighttime changing will become). If he wears terry nappies (which become very soggy and uncomfortable), consider using paper liners at bedtime, or switching to super absorbent disposables at night. If your baby is between sizes, using the next larger size, snugly wrapped to prevent leakage (unless he's prone to nappy rash), will provide extra surface area for absorption. Also consider that if you do have to change him, it will be swifter and less disruptive to fasten on a fresh disposable than to fuss with a terry set.

- If you're sharing a room with your baby, now's a good time to think about splitting up (see page 181). Your nearness may be the reason he's waking so often and why you're picking him up so often.

Still Using a Dummy

'I was planning to let my daughter use a dummy only until she was three months old, but she seems so

dependent on it, I'm not sure I can take it away now.'

Babies are also creatures of comfort. The comfort they crave can come in a number of packages – a mother's breast, a bottle, a soothing lullaby, or a dummy. And the more accustomed they become to a particular source of comfort, the more difficult it becomes for them to do without it. If you don't want to run into the problems that may later be associated with dummy use, now is an ideal time to make a break. For one thing, at this age her memory is short and she will easily forget the dummy when it disappears from her life. For another, she is more open to change than an older baby – more likely to accept an alternative route to pacification. A toddler not only won't forget her dummy, but will probably demand it with a storm of will and temper. And of course a habit of three months is easier to break than one that has been building for a year or more.

To comfort your baby without a dummy, try rocking, singing, a clean knuckle for sucking (or help her to find her own fingers), or some of the other techniques listed on page 126. Admittedly, all of these take more time and effort on your part than tucking a dummy in her mouth, but they'll be better for baby in the long run, especially if they are gradually eliminated in favour of letting baby learn to comfort herself. (See page 71 for the pros and cons of using a dummy.)

Spastic Movements

'When my son tries to reach for something he doesn't succeed, and his movements seem so spastic I'm worried that there's something wrong with his nervous system.'

There's probably nothing wrong with his nervous system – it's just very young and inexperienced. Though it has come a long way from the days when you felt little twitches in your uterus, your baby's nervous system still hasn't worked out all the kinks.

When his arm whips out at a toy that's caught his eye but doesn't land anywhere near its target, the lack of coordination may be worrisome to a new parent, but it's actually a normal stage in infant motor development. Soon he will gain more control, and the purposeful, clumsy batting will be replaced with skillful reaching movements. And once he gets to the stage when nothing within that cunning reach is safe again, you may look back fondly on a time when he looked, but wasn't able to touch.

If you'd like some additional reassurance, check with your baby's doctor at his next checkup.

Giving Baby Cow's Milk

'I'm breastfeeding and would like to give my baby a supplement, but I don't want to use formula. Can I give him cow's milk?'

Cow's milk is a great drink for little cows – but it just doesn't have the right mix of nutrients for human babies. It contains more salt (much more) and protein than breast milk or commercial formula, and these excesses put a strain on young kidneys. It is also lacking in iron. Babies who are fed cow's milk exclusively, as well as those who receive iron-poor formulas, require iron supplementation in the form of vitamin-mineral drops (later, iron-fortified cereal can also supply iron needs). The composition of cow's milk also varies from that of breast milk in a variety of other ways. In addition, it causes mild intestinal bleeding in a small percentage of infants. Though the blood lost in the stool is generally not visible to the naked eye, the bleeding is significant because it can lead to anaemia.

So if you're planning to supplement your breastfeeding, it's best to use expressed breast milk or a formula recommended by the doctor – preferably until your baby is a year old. Easiest are ready to-use formulas, which require no preparation other than the screwing on of a clean teat. If, once you start solids, using a bit of formula or breast milk for such purposes as mixing baby cereal is cumbersome, ask your baby's doctor about using small amounts of whole cow's milk.

Nappy Rash

'I change my baby frequently, but she still gets nappy rash – and I have trouble getting rid of it.'

There's a good reason why your baby (and 7 to 35% of her comrades-in-nappies) isn't sitting on a pretty bottom. Exposed as it is in the nappy area to high moisture, little air, a variety of chemical irritants and infectious organisms in urine and faeces, and oftentimes the rubbing of nappies and clothing, it's an easy target for a wide variety of problems. Nappy rash can remain a problem as long as a baby is in nappies, but incidence usually peaks between seven and nine months when a more varied diet is reflected in the more irritating nature of her stools, and then starts to diminish as baby skin toughens.

Unfortunately, nappy rash tends to repeat in some babies – perhaps because of an inborn susceptibility, allergic tendencies, an abnormal stool pH (an imbalance between acidity and alkalinity), excessive ammonia in the urine, or simply because once skin becomes irritated, it is more susceptible to further irritation.

The exact mechanism responsible for nappy rash isn't known, but it is believed that it probably begins when a baby's delicate skin becomes irritated by chronic moisture. When the skin is further weakened by friction from a nappy or clothing, or by irritating substances in stool or urine, it is left open to attack by germs on the skin or in the urine or stool. Aggressive and frequent cleansing of the nappy area with detergents or soaps can increase the susceptibility of an infant's skin, as can very tight nappies or rubber pants, which keep air out and moisture in. The ammonia in urine, once thought to be the major culprit in nappy rash, doesn't appear to be a primary cause, but can irritate already damaged skin. But the rashes do tend to start where urine concentrates in the nappy, toward the bottom with girls and the front with boys.

The term 'nappy rash' describes a number of different skin conditions in the nappy area. Just what distinguishes one nappy rash from another is not widely agreed on in the medical community (maybe the subject just hasn't aroused enough interest to stimulate serious study and clearer definitions), but they are often described this way:

Perianal dermatitis. Redness around the anus usually is caused by the alkaline stools of a bottle-fed baby and does not usually occur in breastfed infants until after solids have been introduced.

Chafing dermatitis. This is the most common form of nappy rash and is seen as redness where friction is greatest, but not in a baby's skin folds. It generally comes and goes, causing little discomfort if not complicated by a secondary infection.

Atopic dermatitis. This rash is itchy, and may turn up in other parts of the body first. It usually begins to spread to the nappy area between six and 12 months.

Seborrhoeic dermatitis. This deep red rash, often with yellowish scales, usually starts on the scalp as cradle cap, though it sometimes begins in the nappy region and spreads upward. Like most nappy rashes, it's usually more bothersome to parents than to baby.

Candidal dermatitis. Bright red and tender, this uncomfortable rash appears in the inguinal folds (the creases between the abdomen and the thighs), with satellite pustules spreading from that point. Nappy rashes that last more than 72 hours often become infected with candida albicans, the same yeast infection responsible for thrush. This type of rash may also develop in a baby on antibiotics.

Impetigo. Caused by bacteria (streptococci or staphylococci), impetigo in the nappy area occurs in two different forms: bullous, with large, thin-walled blisters that burst and leave a thin yellow-brown crust, or non-bullous, with thick, yellow, crusted scabs and a lot of surrounding redness. It can cover thighs, buttocks, and lower abdomen, and spread to other parts of the body as well.

Intertrigo. This type of rash, which manifests itself as a poorly defined reddened area, occurs as a result of the rubbing of skin on skin. In infants it is usually found in the deep inguinal folds between the thighs and the lower abdomen, and often in the armpits. Intertrigo rash may sometimes ooze white to yellowish matter, and may burn when urine touches it, causing baby to cry.

Tidemark dermatitis. This is an irritation precipitated by friction from the edge of a nappy rubbing against the skin.

The best cure for nappy rash is prevention – though it isn't always possible. Keeping the nappy area dry and clean is one of the most important principles of prevention. See page 77 for practices that will help you to do this. If preventive measures don't work, the following may help eliminate your baby's simple nappy rash, and will be helpful in warding off recurrences:

Less moisture. To reduce moisture on the skin, change the nappy often, even in the middle of the night if your baby's awake. Put any plans to train her to sleep through the night on hold until the rash has cleared up. For persistent nappy rash, change baby as soon as you're aware that she's wet or had a bowel movement. Less superfluous liquid should go into baby, too. Drinking bottle after bottle of juice leads to excessive urination and more rash. Better, use a cup only for juice, to avoid overdosing.

More air. Keep baby's bottom bare part of the time, placing her on a couple of folded terry nappys or cotton cellular blankets over a plastic or waterproof pad or sheet to protect the surface below. If necessary let her sleep the same way, but be sure the room is warm enough so she won't be chilly. If she's in terry nappies, use nappy wraps instead of rubber pants, or leave the pants off altogether and put her on a waterproof pad. If she's wearing disposables, poke a few holes in the waterproof outer cover. This will allow some air in, and it will also allow some moisture to seep out – which will encourage more frequent nappy changes.

Fewer irritants. You can't limit the natural irritants such as urine and stool except by changing nappies frequently, but you can limit those that you apply to baby's bottom. Soap can dry and irritate the skin, so use it only once daily. Baby soaps are generally recommended (most so-called 'gentle' soaps aren't), or ask the doctor for a suggestion. For changes when the infant has had a bowel movement, wash skin thoroughly (for about thirty seconds to one minute) with warm water and cotton wool balls instead of 'wipes'. Wipes may contain substances that irritate your baby's skin (different babies are sensitive to different substances); those that contain alcohol are particularly drying. If the ones you're using seem to cause a problem, switch – but don't use wipes at all when your baby has a rash. A really messy movement may be best cleaned by a dip in the tub or sink, when that's convenient. Be careful to pat baby dry thoroughly after washing. A baby who is merely wet needn't be cleaned up at all – just changed.

Different nappies. If your baby has a recurrent rash, consider switching to another type of nappy (from terry to disposables or vice versa, from one type of disposable to another) to see if the change makes a difference. If you home-launder nappies, rinse them with ½ cup of vinegar or a special nappy rinse, and if necessary boil them in a large pot for ten minutes.

Blocking tactics. Spreading a thick protective layer of ointment (A & D, Desitin, zinc oxide, Sudocrem, Eucerin Nivea, Kamillosan or whatever your baby's doctor recommends) on baby's bottom after washing it at changing time will prevent urine from reaching it. If you buy these products in the largest sizes, you'll save money and be more likely to use them liberally – which is best. But don't use the ointment when you're airing baby's bottom.

Do not use boric acid or talc when treating the rash. Though boric acid may help relieve simple nappy rash, it is very toxic when taken internally and most doctors suggest not using it around infants, or even having it in the house. The talc may also help by absorbing moisture and keeping baby drier, but it can be inhaled by an infant and cause pneumonia, and it is also carcinogenic. Cornflour is an effective and safer substitute. And don't use medications around the house that have been prescribed for other family members; some combination ointments (those that contain steroids and antibacterial or antifungal agents) are a major cause of allergic skin reactions, and you could sensitize your baby by using them.

If your baby's nappy rash doesn't clear up or improve in a day or two, or if blisters or pustules appear, call her doctor, who will try to uncover its cause and then treat it. For seborrhoeic dermatitis, a steroid cream may be necessary (but it should not be used long-term); for impetigo, antibiotics given by mouth; for intertrigo, careful cleansing plus a hydrocortisone cream and protective ointments; and for candida, the most common nappy infection, a good topical antifungal ointment or cream. Ask how long it should take for the rash to clear, and then report back to the doctor if it isn't better by then or if the treatment seems to make it worse. If the rash persists, the doctor may check for dietary or other factors that may be contributing to it. In rare cases, the expertise of a paediatric dermatologist may be needed to unravel the mystery of a baby's nappy rash.

Penis Sore

'I'm very concerned about a red raw area at the tip of my son's penis.'

What you see is very likely nothing more than a localized nappy rash. It is common and can sometimes cause enough swelling to prevent a baby from urinating. Because spread to the urethra could eventually cause scarring, you should do everything you can to get rid of the rash as soon as possible. If you've been using home-laundered nappies, switch to a nappy service or disposables until the problem has resolved, and follow the other tips for treating rash given above, adding warm soaks if your baby is having trouble urinating. If the rash persists after two or three days of home treatment, call the doctor.

If you return to using home-laundered nappies, be sure to use a special nappy rinse to sanitize them.

Sudden Infant Death Syndrome

'Since a neighbour's baby died of cot death, I'm so nervous that I've been waking my baby up several times a night to make sure she's okay. Would it be a good idea to ask my doctor about a monitoring machine?'

The fear that a baby might die suddenly in the middle of the night has plagued mothers probably from the beginning of time – long before such deaths were given a medical name: Sudden Infant Death Syndrome (SIDS). Ancient writings mention such deaths; the baby described in the Book of Kings as being 'overlaid' by his mother was very likely a victim of cot death.

But unless your baby has experienced an actual life-threatening episode in which she stopped breathing and needed to be revived (in which case, see page 179), the chances of her actually succumbing to SIDS are less than 2 in 1,000. And preoccupation with the idea that your child will be one of the two is more harmful than helpful – to both of you.

For most mothers, no reassurance will totally obviate the need they feel to check their baby's breathing occasionally at night.

Many, in fact, don't breathe easily themselves until their babies have passed the one-year mark, the age when infants seem to outgrow the problems that cause SIDS. And that's okay as long as you don't let worry pervade your every activity.

Though investing in a monitor, an apparatus that can signal if your baby suddenly stops breathing, may seem like an ideal (if expensive) way of easing your fears, monitoring a normal baby can cause more problems than it solves. It upsets family dynamics and often adversely affects the way a mother and child interact. And the false alarms that are common with monitors result more in worry than relief. Monitors are recommended only for babies who have had life-threatening episodes of apnea (cessation of breathing), who have heart and lung problems that make them particularly susceptible to SIDS, or who have two or more siblings who died of SIDS or had near misses.

What can make you (and every other mother) feel more secure is learning infant CPR, and being sure that dad, baby-sitters, housekeepers, and anyone else who spends time alone with your baby also knows this lifesaving technique – so that if your baby ever does stop breathing, for whatever reason, resuscitation can be attempted immediately (see page 441). If gnawing fears continue to plague you, you might talk to your baby's doctor about doing an evaluation of his lung and heart functions – usually reserved for cases where there have been previous indications of a problem – to give you some reassurance. If an evaluation shows your baby not to be at high risk for SIDS, relax. If you can't relax, talk to a therapist who is familiar with SIDS and can help to allay your fears.

'Yesterday afternoon I went in to check on my baby, who seemed to be taking a very long nap. He was lying in the cot absolutely still and blue. Frantic, I picked him up and shook him and he was okay. Now his doctor wants to put him in the hospital for tests and I'm terrified.'

What is SIDS?

Cot death, SIDS, or Sudden Infant Death Syndrome, is defined as the sudden death of an infant that is unexplained either by the baby's history, a postmortem exam, or the examination of the scene of death. Although rare, it's the major cause of infant death between the ages of two weeks and twelve months. Though it was once believed that victims were 'perfectly healthy' babies stricken suddenly without reason, researchers are now convinced that SIDS babies only *appear* healthy, and actually have some underlying defect – one that hasn't as yet been identified – that predisposes them to sudden death.

The risk of the average baby dying of SIDS is very small – about 1.7 in 1,000. It's even lower for the majority of healthy babies. But it is higher for certain small groups of infants. At high risk are those who have survived a very serious life-threatening event unrelated to injury or accident during which they stopped breathing, turned blue and required resuscitation. (Babies who have had brief spells of apnea lasting under twenty seconds appear not to be at increased risk.) At lesser risk, but still more susceptible than 'normal' babies, are small and/or premature infants, and those from multiple births. SIDS strikes males more often than females.

The theory that the root of the problem may go back to antenatal foetal development is supported by the fact that babies of women who had poor antenatal care or who smoked during pregnancy, and possibly of smokers who had severe anaemia during pregnancy, are also at somewhat increased risk. Babies of young mothers (under twenty) are, too, but this may be as much (or more) because of the poor antenatal care as because of age.

Suspicion that heredity is a major factor in SIDS hasn't been borne out by research, but there does seem to be a very slight increase in risk among siblings of SIDS victims, possibly because the same factors that contributed to the first event – poor medical care or maternal smoking, for example – are present during both pregnancies. Racial differences – in the US SIDS occurs more often among blacks than whites, most often among Native Americans and least often among Orientals – seem to point to a genetic factor. But it isn't clear whether these differences are partly or entirely due to economic inequalities and/or cultural differences, since SIDS is more common among the poor.

There does *not* seem to be a correlation between SIDS and the use of anaesthesia or pain medication in labour, the length of first or second stages of labour, caesarean deliveries, urinary tract infections, vaginitis, or STDs in the mother. Letting baby sleep in parent's beds does not reduce the risk.

A great deal of research is being done to try to determine just what it is that causes SIDS; it may turn out that there is more than one type of SIDS, each with a different cause, or that several factors combine to cause the syndrome. A leading theory is that delay in maturation of the brain stem predisposes a baby to SIDS. Another suggests an occasional case may be related to child abuse. Recent studies point to sleeping prone (face down), particularly on a soft surface in which recesses can form, as a major factor. A mild cold or other infection, swaddling and overheating may compound the risk when an infant sleeps tummy down. Information is being collected on the characteristics that SIDS babies have in common (which include certain types of tissue changes and signs of unexplained asphyxiation) and on other common factors in the deaths (they are most likely to occur between the second and fourth months of life, at home, in the cot, more often in cold weather, and mostly between midnight and 8 A.M.).

As terrifying as the experience may have been for you, you can actually consider yourself very lucky that it occurred. Not only did your baby survive, but he gave you a very good warning that this kind of event might happen again (though it usually doesn't), and that you should get medical help to prevent a more serious recurrence.

Your doctor's suggestion that your baby, who experienced what is called 'apnea of infancy', be hospitalized is a good one. This kind of episode does put an infant at increased risk for SIDS, though the chances are 99 to 1 on his side. A brief stay at the hospital will enable the staff to evaluate your baby's health through a complete health history and physical exam, diagnostic testing and, possibly, monitoring for further spells of prolonged apnea (when a baby stops breathing for more than twenty seconds), in order to try to find an underlying cause for the event. Sometimes it's something fairly simple – such as an infection, a seizure disorder, or an airway obstruction – that can be treated, eliminating the risk of future problems.

Unfortunately, no test will always accurately predict the infant at risk for SIDS. But a comprehensive evaluation will tell the doctor whether or not a baby should be monitored at home or possibly put on medication.

This kind of evaluation may also be done on an infant who has no history of apnea, but who has had two or more siblings who succumbed to SIDS or one who died and others who suffered apparent life-threatening events and possibly on one with cousins who were SIDS victims.

For more information on SIDS or cot death, contact the Foundation for The Study Of Infant Deaths, 35 Belgrave Square, London SW1X 8QB, or telephone 0171–235–0965 (or The 24-hour helpline on 0171–235–1721).

If it is discovered that an illness caused your baby's apnea, it will be treated. If the cause is undetermined, or if heart or lung problems that put him at high risk for sudden death are discovered, the doctor may recommend putting your baby on a device that monitors breathing and/or heartbeat at home. The monitor is usually attached to the baby with electrodes, or is embedded in his cot, playpen, or bassinet mattress. You, and anyone else who cares for your baby, will be trained in connecting the monitor as well as in responding to an emergency with CPR. The monitor won't give your baby absolute protection against SIDS, but it will help your doctor learn more about his condition and help you feel you are doing something, rather than sitting helplessly by waiting for the worst to happen.

Don't, however, let your baby's problem and his monitor become the focus of your life. Doing so could be very destructive, turning your probably normal baby into an invalid, interfering with his growth and development, and damaging your relationship with him and others in the family. Seek help from your doctor or a qualified counsellor if a monitor seems to add to family tension rather than reduce it.

Though criteria may vary from doctor to doctor and community to community, babies who've had no critical episodes since their first usually come off a monitor when they have been free of events requiring prolonged and vigorous stimulation or rescue for two months. More stringent requirements for going off the monitor are usually set for those who have had a second critical episode. Though babies are rarely removed from the monitor until they pass six months, when the peak period for SIDS is over, a total of 90% are off their monitors by the time they reach one year.

'My premature baby had occasional periods of apnea for the first few weeks of her life, but her doctor says that I shouldn't worry, that she doesn't need to be monitored.'

Apnea is very common in premature babies; in fact, about 50% of those born before 32 weeks gestation experience it. But this 'apnea of prematurity', when it occurs before the baby's original due date, appears totally unrelated to SIDS; there is no increased risk of SIDS or of apnea, itself, later. So unless your baby has serious apneic episodes after her original due date, there's no cause for concern or follow-up.

Even in full-term babies, brief lapses in breathing without any blueness or limpness or need for resuscitation are not believed by most experts to be a predictor of SIDS risk, few babies with such apnea are lost to SIDS, and most babies who do die of SIDS weren't observed to experience apnea previously.

'I've heard that DTP immunizations can cause SIDS, and I'm really worried about having my baby immunized.'

The theory has been put forth that SIDS may be related to DTP injections – though of course, even if this were so, it would only be one cause, since sudden infant death considerably predates the use of immunization. But to date, the only large controlled case study found no relationship between SIDS and DTP. It isn't surprising, of course, that some babies who get DTP shots also die of SIDS, since these shots are routinely administered at two and four months of age, and SIDS is at its peak between two and four

months. But if you're still concerned, talk to your baby's doctor. His or her reassurance will doubtless make you more comfortable about going ahead with DTP shots.

Early Weaning

'I'm going back to work full-time at the end of the month, and I'd like to give up nursing my daughter. Will it be hard on her?'

A three-month-old is, in general, a pretty agreeable and adaptable sort. Though well past the newborn-as-blob stage, with a budding personality all her own, she's still far from the opinionated (and sometimes tyrannical) toddler she'll eventually turn into. So if you're going to pick a time for weaning from the breast that's going to be easiest for her, this may be it. Though she may thoroughly enjoy nursing, she probably won't cling to it as stubbornly as a six-month-old who's never had a bottle and is suddenly subjected to weaning. All in all, you'll probably find that weaning at three months is less difficult for your baby than it is for you.

Reporting Breathing Emergencies to your Doctor

Though very brief (under twenty seconds) periods of breathing lapse can be normal, longer periods, or short periods accompanied by the baby turning pale or blue or limp and having a very slowed heartbeat, require medical attention. If you have to take steps to revive your baby, call the doctor or emergency squad immediately. If you can't revive your baby by gentle shaking, try CPR (see page 441), and call or have someone else call 999. Try to note the following to report to the doctor.

- Did the breathing lapse occur when baby was asleep or awake?
- Was baby sleeping, feeding, crying,

spitting, gagging, or coughing when the event occurred?

- Did baby experience any colour changes; was he or she pale, blue, or red in the face?
- Were there any changes in baby's crying (higher pitch, for example)?
- Did baby seem limp or stiff or was he or she moving normally?
- Does your baby often have noisy breathing (see the discussion of stridor on page 407); does he or she snore?
- Did baby need resuscitation? How did you revive him or her, and how long did it take?

Ideally, mothers who want to wean their babies early should begin giving supplementary bottles, using either expressed milk or formula, by around five or six weeks so the infants become adjusted to suckling on the bottle as well as on the breast. If you haven't, your first step is to get baby acclimatized to an artificial nipple; silicone teats may be more appealing than rubber, and you may have to try several different styles to find one your baby likes. At this point it would be best to use formula, so that your present breast milk supply will begin to diminish. Be persistent, but don't force the teat. Try giving the bottle before the breast; if your baby rejects the bottle the first time, try again at the next feeding. Bottles may be more acceptable to baby if someone other than the mother gives them. (See page 139 for more tips on introducing the bottle.)

Keep trying until she takes at least 30 to 60 ml/a fl ounce or two from the bottle. Once she does, substitute a meal of formula for a nursing at a midday feeding. A few days later, replace another daytime breastfeeding with formula. Making the switch gradually, one feeding at a time, will give your breasts a chance to adjust without uncomfortable engorgement. Eliminate the evening breastfeeding last, as this will give you and your baby a quiet and relaxing time together when you get home from work. If you like, you may – assuming your milk supply doesn't dry up entirely, and assuming your baby is still interested – be able to continue this once-a-day feeding for a while, postponing total weaning until a later date, or until your milk is gone.

Sharing a Room with Baby

'Our ten-week-old has been sharing our room since birth. When should we move him to his own room?'

In the first weeks of life, when baby's at the breast or bottle as much as he's in bed, and nights are a blur of feedings, changes and rocking sessions interrupted only occasionally by snatches of sleep, having him within a weary arm's reach makes sense. Once he outgrows the physiological need for frequent feedings during the night (anywhere from about two weeks to three months, or sometimes later), having your baby for a roommate raises a number of serious problems.

Less sleep for parents. Being in the same room with your baby all night, you're tempted to pick him up every time he whimpers. And even if you resist picking him up, you're sure to lie awake waiting for the whimper to turn to a howl. You may also lose a few good nights' sleep over his tossing and turning; babies are notoriously restless sleepers.

Less sleep for baby. The fact that you pick him up more often at night if he's in your room not only means less sleep for you, but for him, too. In addition, during his lighter phases of sleep, your son is likely to be wakened by your activity, even if you tiptoe around in soft slippers and climb silently into bed.

Less lovemaking. Sure, you know (or at least you hope) your baby is sleeping when you start to make love. But how uninhibited can you really be in your ardour when you've got company (breathing loudly, tossing his head back and forth, moaning softly in his sleep) so close by?

More problems adjusting later. In societies where whole families sleep in one room, there's no need to socialize children to sleep alone. But in our culture, where most children are expected to do so, having your baby in your room for a lengthy period will make it more difficult when you finally do move him to a room of his own.

Of course, 'a room of his own' isn't possible in every household. If you live in a one-bedroom apartment or a small house with several children, there may be no option but for your baby to share. If that's the case, consider a divider – either a screen, or a heavy curtain hung from a ceiling track (the curtain is also a good sound insulator). Or give your bedroom up to the baby and invest in a sofabed in the living room for you. Or partition off a corner of the living room for the baby and do your late night TV watching or talking in the bedroom.

If your baby will have to share with another child, how well the sleeping arrangement will work out will depend on how well the two sleep. If either one or both are light sleepers with a tendency to awaken during the night, you may all be in for a difficult period of adjustment until each has learned to sleep through the other's wakings. Again, a partition or curtain may help muffle the sounds, while providing the older child with privacy.

Sharing a Bed

'I've heard a lot about the benefits of children sharing a bed with their parents. And with all the night waking our daughter has been doing, it seems like such an arrangement would mean more sleep for everyone.'

Co-sleeping, parents and children sharing a bed at night, does work well – but chiefly, it seems, in other societies. In a society like ours, which stresses the development of independence and the importance of privacy, co-sleeping is associated with a wide range of problems:

Sleep problems. Probably most significant for overtired parents is the fact that bed sharing seems to increase the incidence of sleep disorders in children. One study of those six months to four years of age showed that sleep problems were present in 50% of co-sleepers, compared with only 15% of those who slept in their own beds; another showed that 35% of toddlers who slept with parents had sleep problems compared to 7% of those who slept alone. It's theorized that co-sleeping deprives children of the chance to learn how to fall asleep on their own – an important lifelong skill.

Dental problems. It appears that co-sleeping encourages, rather than discourages, the chronic nighttime feeders greedy habit. And for the nursing baby who is allowed to use the co-sleeping arrangement for convenient nipping and napping all night long, dental caries (the decay is caused, as in baby-bottle mouth, by milk that stays in baby's mouth while she sleeps) can be an unfortunate result – particularly if nighttime nursing continues past the first birthday.

Developmental problems. Though more research is required to analyze the effects of co-sleeping on a child's emotional development, some experts have speculated that the arrangement may interfere with a child developing a strong sense of being a separate person, a feeling of independence, and a sense of privacy. It may also lead to separation anxiety lasting longer than normal; a child may feel lonely and insecure whenever she's without her parents.

Peer problems. If co-sleeping continues into the school years, children who share a bed with their parents may be ridiculed by friends.

Marital problems. If sleeping in the same room with a baby is inhibiting to the parents' sexual relationship, having a baby in the same bed can be fatal to it. And though there's no evidence that a very young baby can be emotionally scarred if she accidentally wakes up and views her parents making love, that may not be true for an older child.

Safety problems. Potential risks include: plush mattresses, pillows, duvets, waterbeds; a crevice between bed and wall; a bed that doesn't meet cot safety standards, a sound sleeping or drug/alcohol impaired parent who rolls over on the infant.

Drawing-the-line problems. It's one thing to have an infant, or even a toddler, in bed with you – but where do you draw the line? And when you do, how will you teach a child who has always slept with you to suddenly sleep in her own bed? And is it fair to accustom a child to having a warm body beside her at night, only to suddenly banish her to a cold and lonely bed? Even if you deem it fair, you may find it next to impossible. A child who's formed a habit of sleeping with parents will return as surely as a swallow to Capistrano.

Though the evidence seems stacked in favour of separate beds and bedrooms for babies once they've passed the three-month birthday (when excessive nighttime crying has usually subsided), the issue is still a personal one. It's true that co-sleeping has worked in countless societies for countless generations, and that children do experience a special warmth and comfort when they sleep with their parents. Some families will decide that they don't want to give in to social pressures, and will opt for the 'family bed'. That's fine, as long as they are aware of the possible risks. And those who elect to sleep alone can achieve some family togetherness by bringing baby into bed, some mornings or every morning, for a feeding or some cuddling.

Roughhousing

'My husband loves to roughhouse with our twelve-week-old, and she loves when he does it. But I've heard that shaking an infant too much, even in fun, can cause injury.'

Watching the glee in a young baby's face as she's tossed up in the air by her adoring dad, it's hard to imagine that such fun could end in tragedy. And yet it could. There are two kinds of damage that can occur during such roughhousing. The first is a detached retina, which can cause serious vision problems or even blindness. The second is whiplash, which in an infant, whose neck is very unsteady, could lead to serious brain damage, and in rare cases, even to death.

Such injuries occur most often when a baby is being shaken in anger, but they can happen at play. So avoid roughhousing that vigorously shakes or jostles your baby's unsupported head or neck. Also avoid jogging or other 'bouncing' activities with a young infant in a baby carrier (do your running while pushing baby in a pushchair, instead). That doesn't mean no fun at all – babies love a good, smooth 'fly' through the air supported by a pair of strong hands, and other non-jarring physical games.

Although roughhousing should be avoided in the future, don't worry about any your baby has been treated to in the past. If damage had been done, it would have been apparent.

Fewer Bowel Movements

'I'm concerned that my breastfed baby may be constipated. She always had six or eight bowel movements a day, and now she rarely has more than one, and sometimes even misses a day.'

Don't be concerned – be grateful. This slowdown in production is not only normal, but will send you to the changing table less often. Definitely a change for the better.

It's normal for many breastfed babies like yours to start having fewer bowel movements somewhere between one and three months of age. Some will even go several days between movements. Others will continue their prodigious production rates as long as they are nursing. That's normal, too.

Constipation is rarely a problem for breastfed babies, and infrequency isn't a sign of it; hard, difficult-to-pass stools are (see page 111).

Leaving Baby with a Baby-Sitter

'We'd love a night out alone, but we're afraid of leaving our daughter with a baby-sitter when she's so young.'

Go to town – and soon. Assuming you're going to want to spend some time alone together (or just alone) during the next eighteen years, getting your baby used to being cared for occasionally by a non-parent will be an important part of her development. And in this case, the earlier she starts making the adjustment, the better. Infants two and three months old may recognize their mothers, but out-of-sight usually means out-of-mind. And as long as their needs are being met, young babies are generally happy with any attentive person. By the time babies reach nine months (much sooner in some babies), most begin experiencing what is called separation or stranger anxiety – not only are they unhappy being separated from mother or father, they're also very wary of new people.

At first you'll probably want to take only short outings, especially if you're nursing and have to squeeze your dinner in between baby's meals. What shouldn't be short, however, is the time you spend choosing and preparing the baby-sitter, to ensure your baby will be well cared for. The first night, have the sitter come at least half an hour early so you can fully acclimatize him or her to the eccentricities of your child's needs and habits and so baby and baby-sitter can meet. (See the Baby-Sitter Checklist, page 185 and What It's Important to Know, page 186.)

'We almost always take our baby with us when we go out; we only leave her with a baby-sitter when she's asleep, and then only for a few hours. Friends say this will make her too dependent.'

A lot of people today seem more concerned about the child whose mother or father never leaves her than the one whose parents regularly do. But there's no evidence to support such concern. Though there are some advantages to getting your baby adjusted to a baby-sitter now (before stranger anxiety rears its unfriendly head), and to not feeling so tied down yourself, a baby whose mummy is always around doesn't necessarily become overly dependent. Often, in fact, the child who spends a majority of the time in early infancy with one or both parents turns out to be very secure and trusting. She has unswerving faith that she is loved, that any

baby-sitter her parents leave her with will take good care of her, and that when her parents go out they will return when they say they will.

So do what makes you most comfortable, not what will satisfy your friends.

Being Tied Down by a Nursing Baby

'I was happy with my decision not to give our little boy supplementary bottles until I realized it's almost impossible to have a long evening out.'

Nothing's perfect, not even the decision to breastfeed exclusively. It has its advantages, of course, but there are occasions when it can bring regrets. Many women, however, have survived the decision and managed to retain some semblance of a social life in spite of it. First of all, though it may be difficult to get out now, it will get easier once your baby begins to go to sleep for the night at 8 or 9 P.M., allowing you to head out for a late night on the town. Also, once solids are introduced, a baby-sitter will have something to offer your baby should he awaken hungry. And finally, once you've introduced the cup, your baby will even be able to have a drink if he's thirsty.

In the meantime, if you have a special event you'd like to attend that will keep you from home for more than a couple of hours, try these:

- Take baby and baby-sitter along, if there's some place for them to stay, such as a lobby. It may be cumbersome, but it will allow baby to nap in a stroller or carriage while you enjoy the affair. Should he awaken, the baby-sitter can notify you and you can slip out and nurse in the ladies' room or another suitable area.

- If the event is out of town, take the family along. Either bring your own baby-sitter or hire one where you will be staying. If the place where you are staying is near enough to the reception, you can pop in at feeding time.

Baby-Sitter/Nanny Check List

Even the best nanny needs instructions. Before you leave your baby with anyone, make certain that he or she is familiar with the following:

- How your baby is most easily calmed (rocking, a special song, a favourite mobile, a ride in the baby carrier)

- What your baby's favourite toy is

- How your baby likes to sleep (on back, tummy, side)

- How your baby is best burped (over the shoulder, on the lap, after feeding, during feeding)

- How to change and clean baby (Do you use wipes or cotton wool balls? A double nappy or single? Rubber pants? An ointment for nappy rash?) and where nappies and supplies are kept

- Where extra clothing is kept in case those baby is wearing get soiled

- How to give the bottle, if your baby is bottle fed or is to get a supplement of formula or expressed milk

- What your baby can and can't eat or drink (making it clear that no food, drink, or medicine should be given to your baby without your okay, or the doctor's)

- The setup of your kitchen, the baby's room and so on, and any other pertinent facts about your house or apartment (such as a burglar alarm that might go off, and where fire exits are located)

- Any habits or characteristics of your baby that the baby-sitter might not expect (spits up a lot, has a lot of bowel movements, cries when wet, falls asleep only with a light on, can roll off the changing table)

- The habits of any pets you may have that the baby-sitter should be aware of, and rules concerning your baby and pets

- Baby safety rules (see page 133); you might want to photocopy rules and post them in an obvious place for the baby-sitter

- Where the first aid kit (or individual items) is located

- Where a flashlight (or candles) is located

- What to do in case the fire alarm goes off or smoke or fire is observed, or if someone who hasn't been cleared by you rings the doorbell

- Who is cleared by you to visit when you are not at home, and what your policy is on a baby-sitter's having visitors

You should also leave the following for the baby-sitter:

- Important phone numbers (the baby's doctor, where you can be reached, a neighbour who will be home, your parents, the hospital, the ambulance, the building superintendent, a plumber or handyman), and a pad and pencil for taking messages

- The address of the nearest emergency room and the best way to get there

- Cab fare in case of an unexpected emergency (such as the need to take the baby to the emergency room or the doctor's office), and the number to call for a cab

It's helpful to combine all the information necessary for caring for your baby – phone numbers, safety and health tips, and whatever else you deem necessary – in a small loose-leaf binder. Information can easily be changed or added as required, and everything is always at close hand for the sitter. The 'mad money' can be stashed in an envelope taped to the cover of the binder.

• Adjust baby's bedtime, if possible. If your baby usually doesn't go to bed until after nine, and you need to leave at seven, try to get him to skip his afternoon nap and put him to bed a couple of hours early. Be sure to give him a full nursing before you leave, and plan on feeding him again when you return home, if necessary.

• Leave a bottle of expressed milk or water and hope for the best. If your baby wakes up and is really hungry, he may take the bottle. At this stage nipple confusion won't interfere with his nursing, so you needn't worry on that score. If he doesn't take it, he may scream for a while, but will very likely fall back to sleep eventually. When you get home, feed him if necessary. Of course, if the baby-sitter feels he is so upset that you should return, you should be ready to do so.

WHAT IT'S IMPORTANT TO KNOW:
The Right Caregivers for Baby

Leaving your child with a baby-sitter for the first time is traumatic enough without worrying about whether you're leaving him or her with the right person in the right place. And finding child care that you're confident about is no longer as easy – at least, not for most – as picking up the phone and enlisting grandmother or the grandmotherly next-door neighbour. With extended family often extending several hundred miles, and many grandmothers working themselves, the mother who needs a baby-sitter usually must depend on a stranger.

When grandmother was the baby-sitter, a mother's biggest worry was whether her child would be plied with too many biscuits. Turning your baby over to a stranger (or group of strangers) raises a great many more concerns. Will she be responsible and reliable? Attentive and responsive to your baby's needs? Capable of providing your baby with the kind of play-learning stimulation that will help develop mind and body to their fullest potential? Will her child-care philosophies mesh comfortably with yours, and will she accept your ideas and respect your wishes? Will she be warm and loving enough to act as mother substitute without presuming to take your place as a mother?

Separating from your baby – whether for a 9-to-5 job or a Saturday night dinner and a show – will never be easy, especially not the first few times. But separating satisfied that you've left your baby in the best possible hands will help ease both your anxiety and your guilt.

In-Home Care

Most experts agree that if a mother can't be with her baby all of the time (because of work, school, or other commitments), the next best option is a mother substitute (a nanny, baby-sitter, au pair) who cares for the child at home.

The advantages are many. Baby is in familiar surroundings, with his or her own cot, high chair and toys; is not exposed to a lot of other babies' germs; and doesn't have to be transported to and fro. He or she also has the complete attention of the caregiver, assuming she hasn't been assigned a multitude of other tasks, and there is a good chance for a strong relationship to develop between baby and caregiver.

There are some disadvantages, however. If the caregiver is ill, unable to come to work for other reasons, or suddenly quits, there is no automatic backup person. A strong attachment between nanny and baby can lead to a crisis if the nanny leaves suddenly, or if the mother develops more than a mild case of envy. For some parents, the loss of privacy if the caregiver lives in is an added complication. And home care can be costly, probably more so if you choose a professionally trained nanny, probably less so if you choose a student, an au pair, or someone with little experience – or if you can find someone who wants to share a nanny. Though sharing is an increasingly popular option, you must be prepared to take into account (and often compromise for) the needs of the other parents involved, and the capacity of the nanny.

STARTING THE SEARCH

Finding the ideal caregiver can be a time-consuming process, so allow as much as two months for the search. There are several trails you can take to track her down:

The baby's doctor. Probably no one else you know knows as many babies – and their mothers and fathers – as your baby's doctor. Ask him or her for recommendations, check the suregry bulletin board for notices put up by care providers seeking employment (some doctors require that references be left at the reception desk when such notices are posted), or put up a notice of your own. Ask around the waiting room, too.

Other parents. Don't pass one by – at the playground, at a baby exercise class, at parties and business meetings – without asking if they've heard of, or have employed, a good caregiver.

Your church or synagogue. Here, too, the bulletin board can be an invaluable resource. So can your minister, priest, or rabbi, who may know of congregants who would be interested in caring for your child.

Teachers of nursery-age children. Nursery school teachers often know of, or employ part-time in their programmes, experienced child-care workers. They sometimes are available themselves evenings and weekends.

Parents' organizations. Groups such as the National Childbirth Trust, Parents at Work or Gingerbread (for one-parent families) can offer information, advice and new contacts for childcare-sharing arrangements.

Domestic staffing agencies and registries. Trained and licensed (and usually expensive) nannies are available through these services; selecting a caregiver this way eliminates a lot of guesswork and legwork. (But check references yourself, anyway.)

Baby-sitting services. Screened baby-sitters are available through these services, listed in your local classified phone book, for full-time, part-time, or occasional work.

A local hospital or nanny-training school. At hospitals, nursing schools and nanny-training schools, students may be available for baby-sitting jobs.

Local newspapers. Check daily papers and specialized publications, such as *The Lady*, for ads run by caregivers seeking employment and/or run an ad yourself.

College employment offices. Part-time or full-time, year-round or summer help may be found through local colleges.

Senior citizen organizations. Lively seniors can make terrific baby-sitters – and surrogate grandparents at the same time.

Au pair or nanny organizations. These services can provide families with a live-in au pair, usually a young woman from a foreign country who wants to visit or study in the U.K. for a year or so, or with a well-trained foreign nanny.

SIFTING THROUGH THE POSSIBILITIES

You won't want to spend endless days interviewing obviously unsatisfactory candidates, so sift them out either through c.v.'s that have come in the mail or phone conversations. Before you begin talking to people, develop a detailed job description so you know just what you are looking for. This may include such things as shopping and laundry responsibilities, but be wary of overloading with activities that will distract a caregiver's attention from your baby. In a preliminary phone interview, ask the person's name, address, telephone number, age, education, experience (this is actually less important than some other qualities, such as enthusiasm and natural ability), salary requirements (check beforehand to see what the going rate is in your area), and why she wants the job. Explain what the position will entail, and see if she is still interested. Set up a personal interview with those applicants who sound promising.

During interviews, look for clues in a candidate's questions and comments ('Does the baby cry a lot?' might reflect impatience with normal infant behaviour) as well as in her silence (the woman who never says anything about liking children and never comments on yours may be telling you something) to learn what she's like. To learn more, ask questions such as the following, phrasing them so that they require more than a yes or no answer (it doesn't mean much when you get a 'yes' to 'Do you like babies?'):

- Why do you want this job?

- What was your last job, and why did you leave it?

- What do you think a baby my child's age needs most?

- How do you see yourself spending the day with a baby this age?

- How do you see your role in my baby's life?

- What is your position on breastfeeding? (This is important, of course, only if you are breastfeeding and intend to continue – which will require her support.)

- When my baby starts getting more active and getting into trouble, how will you handle it? How do you discipline young children?

- How will you get to work in inclement weather?

- Do you have a driver's licence and feel comfortable behind the wheel? (If driving will be necessary on the job.)

- How long do you envision staying with this job? (The nanny who leaves as soon as your baby becomes adjusted to her can create a multitude of problems for your entire family.)

- Do you have children of your own? Will their needs interfere with your work? (Allowing a caregiver to bring her children along has some benefits and some draw-backs. On the one hand, it gives your child the chance to be exposed to the companionship of other youngsters on a daily basis. On the other hand, it gives your child more of a chance to be exposed to all of the youngsters' germs on a daily basis; and having other children to care for may also affect the quality and quantity of attention the caregiver can give your own baby. It may also result in greater wear and tear on your home.)

- Do you cook or do housework? (Having some of these chores taken care of by someone else will give you more time to spend with your baby when you're at home. But if the caregiver spends a lot of time with these chores, your baby may be neglected.)

- Are you in good health? Ask for evidence of a complete physical exam and a recent negative TB test, as well as about smoking habits (she should be a non-smoker), alcohol and drug use. This last information will probably not be forthcoming from a drug abuser, but be alert for clues, such as restlessness, talkativeness, nervousness, agitation, dilated pupils, poor appetite (stimulants, such as amphetamines or cocaine); slurred speech, staggering, disorientation, poor concentration, and other signs of drunkenness with or without the odour of alcohol (alcohol, barbiturates and other 'downers'); pinpoint pupils and craving for sweets (early heroin addiction); euphoria, relaxed inhibitions, increased appetite, loss of memory, possibly dilated pupils and bloodshot eyes, even paranoia (marijuana). A nanny who is trying not to use drugs or alcohol at work may exhibit signs of withdrawal of the abused substance, such as watery, runny eyes, yawning, irritability, anxiety, tremours, chills and sweating. Of course, many of these symptoms can be signs of illness (mental or physical) rather than drug abuse. In either case, should they show up in a caregiver, they should concern you. You will also want to avoid someone with a medical condition that could interfere with regular attendance at work.

• Have you recently had, or are you willing to take, CPR and baby first-aid training?

Though you'll be asking the questions, the job applicant shouldn't be the only one answering them. Ask these questions of yourself, based on your observations of each candidate, and answer them honestly:

• Did the candidate arrive for the interview well groomed and neatly dressed? Though you may not require a freshly starched nanny's uniform on the job, soiled clothes, unwashed hair, and dirty fingernails are all a bad sign.

• Does she seem to have a sense of orderliness that's compatible with your own? If she has to rummage through her handbag for five minutes for her references and you're a stickler for organization, you'll probably clash. On the other hand, if she seems compulsively neat and you're compulsively messy, you probably won't get along either.

• Does she seem reliable? If she's late for the interview, watch out. She may be late every time she's due to work. Check this out with previous employers.

• Is she physically capable of handling the job? A frail older woman may not be able to carry your baby around all day now, or chase your toddler later.

• Does she seem good with children? The interview isn't complete until the appli-

cant spends some time with your baby so that you can observe the interaction, or lack thereof. Does she seem patient, kind, interested, really attentive and sensitive to your baby's needs? Find out more about her aptitude for child care from previous employers.

• Does she seem intelligent? You'll want someone who can teach and entertain your child the way you would yourself, and who will show good judgment in difficult situations.

• Are you comfortable with her? Almost as important as the rapport the candidate has with your baby is the rapport she has with you. For your baby's sake, there needs to be constant, open, comfortable communication between a chosen caregiver and you; be certain this will be not only possible, but easy.

If the first series of interviews doesn't turn up any candidates you feel good about, don't settle – try again. If it does, the next step in narrowing down your selection is to check references. Don't take the word of a candidate's friends or family on her abilities and reliability; insist on the names of previous employers, if any, or if work experience is limited or nonexistent, those of teachers, clergy, or other more objective judges of character.

GETTING ACQUAINTED

You'd probably be very unhappy left to spend the day with a perfect stranger. You can expect your baby, who will experience the added stress of missing mummy, to be unhappy, too. To minimize the misery, introduce baby and caregiver in advance. If it's a baby-sitter-for-the-evening, have her come at least half an hour earlier the first time (an hour if your baby is more than five months old), so that your baby will have some time to adjust. Make the introduction gradually, starting baby off in your arms, moving him or her next to an infant seat or swing, so the sitter can approach on neutral territory then, finally, as baby becomes more comfortable with the newcomer, into the baby-sitter's arms. Then, once the initial adjustment has been made, stay away for just an hour or two. The next time, have the baby-sitter arrive half an hour ahead of your departure once again, and stay out a little longer. By the third time, a fifteen-minute period with you still at home should suffice, and after that baby-sitter and charge should be bosom buddies. (If they aren't, consider whether you've chosen the right baby-sitter.)

The daily nanny needs an even greater introduction period. She should spend at least a full day with you and the baby, becoming familiar not only with your baby, but also with your home, your child-care style, and your household routines. That will give you a chance to make suggestions, and her a chance to ask questions. It will also give you a chance to see the her in action – and a chance to change your mind about her if you don't like what you see. (Don't judge her on baby's reaction, but rather on how the she responds to it. No matter how good a nanny is, children – even very young children – often protest being with one as long as mummy is around.)

Your baby, incidentally, will probably adjust to a new caregiver most easily before the age of six months, before stranger anxiety appears on the scene.

THE TRIAL PERIOD

Always hire a child-care person on a trial basis so that you can evaluate her performance before deciding whether you want to keep her on for the long term. It's fairer to her and to you if you make clear in advance that the first two weeks or month on the job (or any specified period) will be probationary. During this time, observe your baby. Does he or she seem happy, clean, alert when you come home? Or more tired than usual, and more cranky? Does it seem a nappy change has been made fairly recently? Important, too, is the caregiver's frame of mind at day's end. Is she relaxed and comfortable? Or tense and irritable, obviously happy to be relieved of her charge? Is she eager to tell you about her day with the baby, reporting the infant's latest achievements, as well as any problems she's noted, or does she routinely tell you only how long the baby slept and how many millilitres/fl ounces of the bottle were emptied – or worse, how long the baby cried? Does she keep in mind that this is still *your* baby and accept the idea that you make the major decisions about her care? Or does she seem to feel that she's in charge now?

If your evaluation shows the new caregiver is less than the best, start looking anew. If you're not certain, you might try arriving home early and unannounced to get a look at what's really happening in your absence. Or you could ask friends or neighbours who might see the her in the park, at the supermarket, or walking down the street how she seems to be doing. If a neighbour reports your usually happy baby is doing a lot of crying while you're away, that should be a red flag.

If, from your point of view, the right full-time nanny or childminder seems not to have been born yet, perhaps you should reconsider your decision to go back to work rather that subject your baby to a series of incompetent or uncaring caregivers. If you decide to 'share' a nanny with other parents, you will have to work out an assessment between you – preferably having discussed your needs in advance.

Childminders

Many parents feel more comfortable leaving a baby in a family situation in a private home with just a few other children than in a more 'sterile' day nursery, and for those who can't arrange for a nanny in their own homes, childminders are often the choice.

There are many advantages to such care. Childminders, often mothers themselves, can often provide a warm, homelike environment at a lower cost than other forms of care. Because there are fewer children than in a day-care nursery, there is less exposure to infection and more potential for stimulation and individualized care (though this potential is not always realized). Flexible scheduling – early drop-off or late pickup when that's necessary – is often possible. Registered childminders in the U.K. are checked by the social services to ensure that they can offer a good standard of care in a safe environment.

The disadvantages vary from situation to situation. Some facilities are unregistered, giving little protection in the way of health and safety. The care provider is often un-trained, lacking in professional child-care experience, and may have a child-rearing philosophy that differs from the parents'. If she or one of her children is ill, there may be no backup. And though the risk may be lower than in a larger day-care facility, there is always the possibility of germs spreading from child to child, especially if sanitation is lax.

Contact your local social services for a list of registered childminders in your area.

Day Nurseries

Though it's not considered the ideal situa-tion for infants, and places are limited, some mothers nevertheless turn to group nur-series because they have no other choice.

A good nursery, however, can offer some significant advantages. In the best of them, trained personnel provide a well-organized programme specifically geared to a baby's development and growth, as well as op-portunities for play and learning with other babies and children. Because such facilities are not dependent on one person, as in home care is, there is generally no crisis if a teacher is sick or leaves, though the baby may have to adjust to a new one. And, in communities where day nurseries are li-cenced, there may be safety, health and in some cases, even educational monitoring of the programme.

The disadvantages for babies can also be significant. First of all, not all day nurseries are created equally good. Even in a good one, care is less individualized than it is in a baby's own home, there are more children per caregiver, and teacher turnover may be high. There is less flexibility in scheduling

than in a more informal setting, and if the nursery follows a school calendar, it may be closed on holidays when you're working. The cost is usually fairly high, unless sub-sidized by government or private sources, but may be less expensive than good in-home care. Possibly the greatest dis-advantage is the increased rate of infection among children in day-care situations. Since many employed mothers don't have another option when their children have colds and other minor ills, they often send them to the nursery anyway.

Certainly there are some excellent day-care facilities; the trick is to find such a fa-cility that has space for your baby.

WHERE TO LOOK

You can get the names of local day-nursery facilities (which may be non-profit, co-operative, or for profit) through recom-mendations from friends and acquaintances, or by calling your social services depart-ment; by asking at your church or synago-gue, or checking the phone book for child-care referral services or nurseries them-selves.

WHAT TO LOOK FOR

Day nurseries range in quality from top-of-the-line to bottom-of-the-barrel, with most falling in the mediocre middle. If you'll ac-cept only the best for your baby, you'll have to examine every aspect of each possibility. Look for:

Licencing. Some licenced facilities are checked for sanitation and safety, but *not* for the quality of care. Still, a licence does provide some safeguards.

A trained and experienced staff. The 'head' teachers, at least, should have de-grees in early childhood education; the entire staff should be experienced in caring for infants. Too often, because of the low pay, some nursery workers are people who are in the job because they are qualified for nothing else; in that case, it's likely they aren't qualified for child care, either. The staff turnover should be low; if there are several new teachers each year, beware.

A healthy and safe staff. All nursery workers should have had complete medical checkups, including a TB test. Background checks should have ascertained that they have not previously been involved in anything unsavoury.

A good teacher-to-baby ratio. There should be at least one staff person for every three infants. If there are fewer, a crying baby may have to wait until someone is free to met his or her needs.

Moderate size. A huge nursery facility might be less well supervised and operated than a smaller one – though there are exceptions to this rule. Also, the more children, the more chance for the spread of illnesses. Whatever the size of the facility, there should be adequate space for each child. Crowded rooms are a sign of an inadequate programme.

Separation of age groups. Infants under one year should not be mixed with toddlers and older children.

A loving atmosphere. The staff should seem to genuinely like children and caring for them. Children should look happy, alert and clean. Be sure to visit the facility unannounced in the middle or towards the end of the day, when you will get a more accurate picture of what the nursery is like than you would first thing in the morning. (Be wary of any school that does not allow unannounced parental visits.)

A stimulating atmosphere. Even a two-month-old can benefit from a stimulating atmosphere, one where there is plenty of interaction – both verbal and physical – with caregivers, and where age-appropriate toys are available. As children become older and able to handle objects more effectively, there should be plenty of opportunity for manipulation of toys, as well as exposure to books and music and the out-of-doors. The best programmes include occasional 'field trips': three to six children along with one or two teachers go to the supermarket, the dry cleaners, or other places a baby might go with a stay-at-home mother.

Parent involvement. Are parents invited to participate in the programme in some way; is there a parent board that makes policy?

A compatible philosophy. Are you comfortable with the centre's philosophy – educationally, religiously, ideologically?

Adequate opportunities for rest. Most infants, in day care or at home, still take a lot of naps. There should be a quiet area for such napping in individual cots, and children should be able to nap according to their own schedules – not the school's.

Strict health and sanitation rules. In your own home, you needn't be concerned with your baby putting everything in his or her mouth; in a nursery, with a convergence of children, each with his or her own set of germs, you should be. Day-care centres can become a focus for the spread of many intestinal and upper respiratory illnesses. To minimize germ spreading and safeguard the health of the children, a well-run day-care centre will have a medical consultant and a written policy that includes:

- Caregivers must wash hands (with liquid soap) thoroughly after changing nappies or helping children use the toilet, wiping runny noses or handling children with colds, and before feedings.

- Changing and food preparation areas must be entirely separate, and each should be cleaned after every use.

- Nappies should be disposed of in a covered container out of reach of children.

- Toys for infants must be rinsed with a sanitizing solution between handling by different children, or a separate box of toys must be kept for each child.

- Stuffed animals should not be shared and should be machine-washed frequently.

- Teething rings, dummies, flannels, towels, brushes and combs should not be shared.

- Feeding utensils must be washed in a dishwasher or, better still, must be disposable (infant bottles should be labelled with their owners' names so they aren't mixed up).

- Food preparation for infants on solids must be carried out under sanitary conditions (see page 224).

- Immunizations must be up to date for all babies.

- Children who are moderately to severely ill, particularly with diarrhoea, vomiting, high fever and certain types of rashes, must be kept at home (this isn't necessary with colds, since the cold is most contagious before it is evident) or in a special infirmary section of the facility.

- Medication for attending children should be administered according to a written policy of the nursery.

- When a baby has a contagious disease, all the parents of children in the nursery must be notified. In cases of haemophilus influenzae, immunization or medication may be given to prevent spread of the disease.[2]

Also check with the local health authority to be sure there are no outstanding complaints or violations against the nursery.

---

2. A particular problem for mothers who are planning to become pregnant again shortly is the possibility of the transmission of cytomegalovirus (CMV), spread easily among babies because of the more frequent contact with virus-laden urine and saliva. In an expectant mother who is not immune, the CMV poses a risk to her unborn child. CMV, which studies show spreads to 1 in 5 parents without immunity, usually causes no symptoms in adults or children. Because of the risk to the unborn, women who are considering another pregnancy and who are not immune might want to consider another type of child care.

Strict safety rules. Injuries, mostly minor, are not uncommon in day-care facilities. The top hazards are climbers, slides, hand toys and blocks, other playground equipment, doors and indoor floor surfaces. Even a crawling baby can get into trouble with these; all babies can get into trouble with small objects (that can be choked on or swallowed), sharp objects, poisonous materials and so on. A child-care nursery should meet the safety requirements you maintain in your own home. Particular attention should be paid to open stairways, doors that can slam on little fingers or can open on little faces, windows above ground level (they shouldn't be able to be opened more than 15 cm/6 inches and/or should have window guards), radiators and other heating devices, electrical outlets, cleaning materials and medications (often teachers have to dispense medication for several recovering children or those with chronic health problems), and to floors (they should not be littered with toys, which can trip a caregiver carrying an infant). Materials used by older children (paints, clay and so on, as well as toys with small or sharp parts) should be kept out of reach of babies. Smoke detectors, clearly marked fire escape routes, fire extinguishers and other fire safety precautions should be in evidence. Staff should be trained in CPR and first aid, and a fully equipped first-aid kit should be readily available.

Careful attention to nutrition. All meals and snacks should be healthy, safe and appropriate for the ages of the children being served. Parental instructions regarding formula (or breast milk), foods and feeding schedules should be followed. Bottles should never be propped.

Corporate Crêches

A common option in many European countries for many years, day-care facilities in or adjacent to a parent's place of work are too rarely offered in the U.K. It's an option many parents would choose if they had it.

Your Child as a Barometer of Child Care

No matter which child-care alternative you select for your baby, be alert to signs of discontent: sudden changes in personality or mood, clinginess, fretful-ness that doesn't seem attributable to anything else. If your baby seems unhappy, check into your child-care situation; it may need altering.

The advantages are attractive. Your child is near you in case of emergency; you can visit during your lunch hour or coffee break, even breastfeed; and since you commute with your child, you spend more time together. Such facilities are usually staffed by professionals and very well equipped. Knowing your child is nearby and well cared for allows you to give fuller attention to your work. The cost for such care, if any, is usually low.

There are some possible disadvantages. If your commute is a difficult one, it may be hard on your child. In some cases, seeing you during the day, if that's part of the programme, may make each parting more difficult for your baby, especially during times of stress. And visiting may take your mind from your work.

Corporate crèches, of course, should meet all the educational, health and safety standards of any child-care facility. If the one set up by your employer doesn't, then speak to those responsible for the facility about what can be done to rectify the deficiencies.

Babies on the Job

Very occasionally, a mother is able to take her baby to work with her even when no day care is provided. And very occasionally, it works. It works best before a baby is mobile and if colic is not a problem – and, of course, when the mother has the space for a portable cot and other baby paraphernalia near her work area and the support of her employer and those who work around her. Ideally, she also has a nanny on the spot, at least part of the time. This kind of situation is perfect for the nursing mum, or for any mum who wants her job and her baby, too.

When your Child is Ill

No mother likes to see her baby sick, but the working mother particularly dreads that first sign of fever or upset stomach. She knows that caring for her sick baby may present a great many problems, the central ones being who will take care of the baby and where?

Ideally, either you or your spouse should be able to get sick leave when your child is ill so that you can administer care yourself at home. Next best is having a trusted and familiar baby-sitter or another family member you can call upon to stay with your baby at home. Some day-care nurseries have a sick-child infirmary or satellite, where a child is in familiar surroundings with fa-miliar faces. There are also special sick-child day-care facilities, both in homes and in larger freestanding centres sprouting up to meet this need; but in these, of course, the child has to adjust to being cared for by strangers in a strange environment when he's least able to handle change. Some corporations, in order to keep parents on the job, actually pay for sick-child care, such as space in a sick-child day nursery or a baby nurse to stay with the child at home (which will also require adjustment to an unfamiliar caregiver).

These options are better than no care at all, of course. But as anyone who's ever been an ill child knows, there's nothing quite the same as having your mummy to hold your hot little hand, wipe your feverish brow and administer specially prescribed doses of love and attention. And because of an ill child's special needs, there should be more liberal leave for parents of ill children, so that they can have parental care during ill-ness.

SEVEN

The Fourth Month

◆

What Your Baby May Be Doing

**By the end of this month, your baby ...
should be able to (see Note):**

- on stomach, lift head up 90 degrees
- laugh out loud (3⅔ months)
- follow an object in an arc about 15 cm (6 inches) above the face for 180 degrees (from one side to the other)

Note: If your baby seems not to have reached one or more of these milestones, check with the doctor. In rare instances the delay could indicate a problem, though in most cases it will turn out to be normal for your baby. Premature infants generally reach milestones later than others of the same birth age, often achieving them closer to their adjusted age (the age they would be if they had been born at term), and sometimes later.

... will probably be able to:

- hold head steady when upright
- on stomach, raise chest, supported by arms
- roll over (one way)
- grasp a rattle held to backs or tips of fingers
- pay attention to a raisin or other very small object (4¼ months)
- reach for an object
- squeal in delight
- razz (make a wet razzing sound by 4½ months)

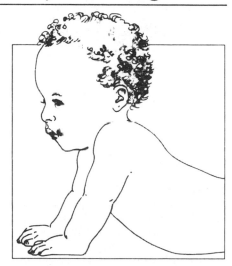

Many, but not all, four-month-olds can raise their body on their arms.

... may possibly be able to:

- keep head level with body when pulled to sitting (4¼ months)
- turn in the direction of a voice, particularly mummy's
- say ah-goo or similar vowel-consonant combinations

... may even be able to:

- bear some weight on legs when held upright
- sit without support
- object if you try to take a toy away
- turn in the direction of a voice

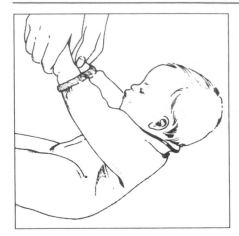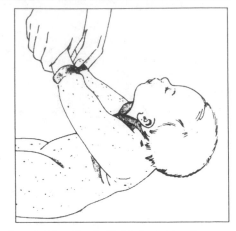

At the end of the fourth month, most babies still cannot keep their head level with their body when they are pulled to a sitting position (left). Their head usually falls backwards (right).

What You Can Expect At This Month's Checkup

Each doctor, midwife or health visitor will have a personal approach to well-baby checkups. The overall organization of the physical exam, as well as the number and type of assessment techniques used and procedures performed will also vary with the individual needs of the child. But in general, you can expect the following at a checkup when your baby is about four months old.

• Questions about how you and baby and the rest of the family are doing at home, and about baby's eating, sleeping and general progress. About child care, if you are working.

• Measurement of baby's weight, length and head circumference, and plotting of progress since birth.

• Physical exam, including a recheck of any previous problems. The posterior fontanel, on the back of the head, may have closed by now; the anterior, on the top of the head, may have grown since last visit.

• Developmental assessment. The examiner may actually put baby through a series of tests to evaluate head control, hand use, vision, hearing and social interaction, or may simply rely on observation plus your reports on what baby is doing.

• Third round of immunizations for diphtheria, tetanus and pertussis (DTP), polio (TOPV) and Haemophilus type B, if baby is in good health and there are no other contraindications. Be sure to discuss any reactions to the first round of immunizations beforehand

• Guidance about what to expect in the next month in relation to such topics as feeding, sleeping, development and infant safety.

• Recommendations about fluoride supplementation if needed in your area, and vitamin D supplementation if your baby is breastfed. Recommendations about iron supplementation for babies not on iron-fortified formula.

Questions you may want to ask, if the doctor hasn't already answered them:

• What reactions can you expect baby to have to the third round of immunizations?

How should you treat them? Which reactions should you call about?

• When is it suggested that you introduce your baby to solids?

Also raise concerns that have arisen over the past month. Jot down information and instructions from the doctor (you're sure to forget them, otherwise). Record all pertinent information (baby's weight, length, head circumference, birthmarks, immunizations, illnesses, medications given, test results and so on) in a permanent health record.

Feeding Your Baby This Month: Thinking About Solids

The messages that today's new mother receives about when to start feeding solids are many and confusing. Her mother declares, 'I started *you* at two weeks. What are you waiting for?' Buttressing her argument, she points to the obvious: '*You're* healthy, aren't you?' The doctor gives instructions to wait until her baby is five or six months old. For corroboration, he points to what little research there's been in the area. A well-meaning friend insists that starting solids earlier will help any baby sleep through the night. Her proof positive: a baby who's slept through since his first spoonful of cereal.

Whom do you listen to? Does mother know best? Or doctor? Or friends? Actually, your baby does – nobody can tell you when to start giving solids better than he or she can. And recent research indicates that an infant's individual development, rather than arbitrary age parameters, should be the deciding factor in promoting a baby to a more varied diet.

Very early introduction to solids (fashionable when your mother was mothering) isn't believed to be physically harmful in most cases. But medical research indicates that a very young baby's digestive system – from a tongue that pushes out any foreign substance placed on it, to intestines lacking many digestive enzymes – is developmentally unready for solids. It does not appear, however, to support the idea that because solid foods interfere with some of the beneficial aspects of breast milk and with the absorption of iron, they should postponed for most children until the end of the first year.

Picking the right time to introduce foods – neither too early nor too late – is important. Extremely early introduction of solids isn't harmful physically, but it can undermine future eating habits. When the infant who isn't ready for solids rejects them, frustration on both sides of the cereal bowl can set the stage for mealtime hassles later in childhood. Yet, waiting too long to introduce food (until late into the second half of the first year) can also lead to difficulties. An older baby may resist being taught the new tricks of chewing and swallowing solids if he or she has been too long accustomed to getting nourishment and oral satisfaction from nursing. And like habits, tastes may be tough to change at this point; unlike the more malleable four- to six-month-old, the year-old child may not be open to new gastronomic experiences.

To decide if your baby is ready for the big step into the world of solid foods (most will be between four and six months), look for the following clues, then consult the doctor.

• Your baby can hold his or her head up well. Even strained baby foods should not be offered until a baby holds his head up well when propped to sit; chunkier foods should wait until a baby can sit well alone, usually not until seven months.

• The tongue thrust reflex has disappeared. This is a reflex that causes young infants to push foreign matter out of their mouths (an inborn mechanism that protects them from choking on foreign bodies). Try this test: place a tiny bit of infant rice cereal thinned with breast milk or formula in your baby's mouth from the tip of a demitasse or baby spoon, or your finger. If the food comes right back out again with the tongue and continues to after several tries, the thrust is still present and baby isn't ready for spoon feeding.

● Baby reaches for and otherwise shows an interest in table foods. The baby who grabs the fork out of your hand or snares the bread from your plate, who watches intently and exhibits excitement with every bite you take, is telling you he's eager to try more grown-up fare.

● The ability to execute back-and-forth movements with the tongue, as well as up-and-down ones, is present. You can discover this by observation.

● Baby is able to draw the lower lip in so that food can be taken from a spoon.

There are instances, however, when even a baby who seems developmentally ready for solids may have to wait – most often because there is a strong history of allergy in the family. Until more is known about the development of allergies, it is generally recommended that children in such families be breastfed exclusively for most of the first year, with solids added very cautiously, one at a time, thereafter.

What You May Be Concerned About

Wriggling at Changing Time

'My daughter won't lie still when I'm changing her – she's always trying to turn over. How can I get her to cooperate?'

As far as cooperation when changing your daughter is concerned, you can expect to receive less and less as the months go by and her physical development continues to spurt ahead of her moral development. The indignity of changing, teamed with the turtle-on-its-back frustration of being temporarily immobilized, will set off a battle with each change. The trick: be quick (have all the paraphernalia ready and waiting before you lay baby on the table), and provide distractions (a mobile above the changing table, a music box, preferably one that's also visually tempting, a rattle or other toy to occupy her hands and, hopefully, her interest).

Propping Baby

'I had my baby propped up in his pram and I was scolded by two older women who insisted he was too young to sit up.'

If your baby wasn't old enough to sit up, he'd tell you so. Not in so many words, of course, but by slumping down or sliding off to one side when you tried to prop him.

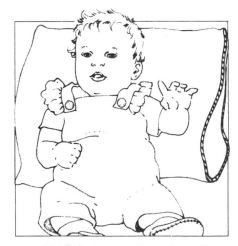

Propping baby up to a sitting position will not only offer him or her a welcome change of perspective, but it will also help build the muscles and experience needed for unassisted sitting.

Though you shouldn't attempt to prop a younger infant whose neck and back need more support than he would get with propping, a three- or four-month-old who holds his head up well and doesn't crumble when propped up is ready for such a position. (Specially designed head supports are available to keep babies' heads upright when propped.) Babies will usually signal when they've had enough of sitting by complaining or beginning to slump.

Besides providing a welcome change of position, sitting allows a baby an expanded view of the world. Instead of just the sky, or the inside of the pram an upright baby can see passersby (including those who are sure to upbraid you), shops and homes, trees, dogs, other babies in pushchairs, children walking home from school, buses, cars – and all the other marvellous things that inhabit his growing universe. He's also likely to stay happy longer than he would lying down, which will make outings more pleasant for both of you.

Baby's Standing

'My baby likes to "stand" on my lap. She cries if I make her sit down. But my grandmother insists that letting her stand so early will make her bowlegged.'

Babies usually know what they're ready for even better than their great-grandmothers do. And many babies of your daughter's age are ready, and eager, for supported lap 'standing'. It's fun, it's good exercise, it's an exciting change from lying on her back or slumping in an infant seat – and it most assuredly does not cause bowleggedness.

On the other hand, any baby who doesn't seem to want to stand shouldn't be pushed into doing so until she's ready. A baby who's allowed to set her own developmental pace will be happier and healthier than one whose parents try to set it for her.

Thumb Sucking

'My son has taken to sucking his thumb. At first I was happy because it was helping him sleep better, but now I'm afraid it's going to become a habit I won't be able to break him of later on.'

It isn't easy being a baby. Every time you latch on to something that gives you the comfort and satisfaction you're searching for, somebody wants to take it away from you. Sometimes without good reason.

Virtually all babies suck on their fingers at some time during the first year of life; many even begin the habit in the uterus. That's not surprising. The mouth in the infant is an important organ not just for eating, but for exploration and pleasure, too (as you will soon discover, to your dismay, when everything baby picks up goes into his mouth, whether it's a rattle or a long-deceased insect he's unearthed at the bottom of a closet). But even before a baby can reach for objects, he discovers his hands – and how natural to put the newly discovered hands into that wonderful sensory cavity, the mouth. The first time the hands may make it to the mouth by random chance, but the baby quickly learns that the fingers in the mouth provide a pleasurable sensation. Soon he's mouthing his fingers regularly. Eventually, many babies decide that the thumb is the most efficient and satisfying finger to suck on (maybe it's the most succulent) and switch from finger mouthing to thumb sucking. Some stick with one or two fingers, or even a whole fist.

At first you may think the habit is cute, or even be grateful that your baby has found a way to pacify himself without your intervention. Then, as the weeks pass and the habit intensifies, you begin to worry, envisioning your little boy trooping off to school with his thumb firmly implanted in his mouth, ridiculed by his classmates, reprimanded by his teachers. Will you have to paint his thumbnails with bitter solutions to make them unpalatable, then nag and plead when that doesn't work? Will you have to make monthly trips to the orthodontist for the work necessary to straighten the bite deformed by thumb sucking, or worse, weekly trips to the therapist to try to uncover the underlying emotional problems that made him suck on his thumb in the first place?

Well, stop worrying and start letting your baby indulge himself. There is no evidence that thumb sucking is in itself 'dangerous' or a sign of emotional illness. Nor, if it ceases by age five, does it appear to do damage to the alignment of permanent teeth; any distortion of the mouth that does occur before that time returns to normal when the habit is ended. Most experts agree that, since it is a developmental behaviour that usually is put aside as a child gets older anyway, attempts to wean a child from the thumb shouldn't begin before age four.

Some studies show that nearly half of all children do some thumb or finger sucking past infancy. The behaviour peaks on average between 18 and 21 months, though some have already abandoned the habit by then. Nearly 80% give it up by age five, and 95% by age six, usually on their own. Those who use it to help themselves get off to sleep hang on to the habit longer than those to whom it is simply a form of oral gratification.

As the child nears the time for permanent teeth to come in, a time when thumb sucking could hinder proper development of the mouth and lead to deformity, he is also mature enough to take an active part in eliminating the habit. And since most thumb sucking is not the result of emotional disturbance, thumb suckers are more likely to be weaned from their habit with specially designed dental appliances than through psychological counselling. (A few children do seem to suck their thumbs for emotional support and can benefit from counselling.)

In the meantime, let your baby suck away. Be sure, however, that if he is breastfed, he isn't sucking his thumb to compensate for suckling he isn't getting at the breast; if he seems to want to nurse a little longer at each feeding, let him (he won't get too much milk because the breast will have been emptied, or nearly so, at this point). And if thumb sucking seems to become the focus of his

daily activities, preventing him from using his hands for other explorations, occasionally remove his finger from its station long enough to distract him with toys, with finger or hand games ('this little piggy,' 'patty-cake', or 'so big', for instance), or by holding his hands and letting him stand, if he likes that.

If your baby does continue to suck his thumb into toddlerhood, you can expect some unfavourable comments, particularly from your parents' generation – many of whom have been thoroughly programmed to demonstrate disdain for thumb sucking. If you feel obliged to, explain to them that recent research indicates that thumb sucking is not harmful and doesn't mean a child is emotionally deprived.

If you yourself are disturbed by the thumb sucking because of prior programming, try to psych yourself out of it. If that doesn't work, you might want to substitute a dummy for your baby's thumb temporarily – assuming you don't also have an aversion to that. But, of course, that will leave you with a new habit to break.

Chubby Baby

'Everybody admires my chubby little daughter. But I am secretly afraid she's getting too fat. She's so round, she can hardly move.'

With dimples on her knees and her elbows, a belly to rival any Buddha's, several chins to chuck and an endearing amount of pinchable flesh on her cheeks, she's the picture of baby cuteness from head to chubby toes. Yet is the plump baby also the picture of health? Her grandparents probably think so. Her mother, on the other hand, convinced that slim is in, is likely to be concerned that her plump baby is on the way to being an unhappy fat child and a miserable obese adult. Most doctors, however, take a position somewhere in between. They agree that fat is not fit, but are less concerned with chubbiness in babies since it became clear that an increase in fat cells in infancy doesn't necessarily lead to obesity later. Only 1 in 5 fat babies are destined, in fact, to become fat adults.

Still there are disadvantages to extreme chubbiness early on. The baby who is too plump to budge may become a victim to a vicious cycle of inactivity and overweight. The less she moves, the fatter she gets; the fatter she gets, the less she can move. Her inability to move makes her frustrated and fussy, which may lead her mother to overfeed her to keep her happy. If she stays overweight through age four, a problem that is becoming more and more common among American and British children, the odds she will be an overweight adult increase.

Before you make a reservation at the fat farm for your baby, however, be certain she is indeed overweight and not just nicely rounded (remember, since babies haven't yet developed much in the way of muscle even a slim one will sport a certain amount of soft padding). Compare her growth with the curve on the height-weight chart on page 638. If her weight seems consistently to be moving upwards faster than her height discuss this with her doctor.

Unlike the prescription for a fat adult the prescription for a fat baby is not usually a diet. Instead of trying to get an overweight baby to lose weight, the goal is to slow down the rate of gain. Then as she grows taller, she will slim down – something many babies do without intervention as they become more active. Some of the following tips may help not only if your baby is already overweight, but also if you're afraid she's on her way:

- Use feeding only to assuage hunger, not to meet other needs. A baby who's fed for all the wrong reasons (when she's hurt or unhappy, when her mother's too busy to play with her, when she's bored in the pushchair) will continue to demand food for the wrong reasons and, as an adult, will eat for the same wrong reasons. Instead of nursing her every time she cries, comfort her with a hug or a soothing song. Instead of propping her up with a bottle, prop her in front of a mobile or a music box when you're too busy to play with her, or let her watch what you're doing (slice the carrots or fold the laundry on the floor beside her infant seat). Instead of always plying her with teething biscuits to quiet her in the supermarket, attach a toy to her stroller to keep her occupied while you shop. In spite of what your mother may have believed, constantly pushing food on your baby is not a sign of love.

- Make dietary adjustments, if necessary. One reason that breastfed babies are less likely to become overweight is that breast milk automatically adjusts to a baby's needs. The lower-fat, lower-calorie 'fore' milk, which comes at the beginning of a feeding, encourages the hungry baby to suckle. The higher-fat, higher-calorie 'hind' milk, which comes at the end of a feeding, tends to dampen the appetite, sending the message, 'You're feeling full'. If that isn't discouragement enough, and baby continues to nurse away, the breast is eventually emptied. Suckling for suckling's sake can go on without an excess of calories being consumed. Though baby formulas aren't customized in the same way, if your baby is gaining weight too quickly and is extremely overweight, her doctor may recommend switching to a lower-calorie formula. Before you make such a switch, however, be certain you are not underdiluting the ready-to-mix formula you are presently using – which could increase its calorie count considerably. Don't decide to overdilute it, either, without the doctor's okay. Or to switch to skimmed or lowfat milk. Babies, even overweight ones, need the cholesterol and fat in breast milk and formula (or when they're older, in whole cow's milk).

- Try water, the ultimate calorie-free beverage. Most of us tend to drink too little water. Infant diets (because they are entirely, or almost entirely, liquid) don't absolutely require supplementation with water. But water can be very useful for the overweight baby who wants to keep sucking after her hunger is satisfied, or who is thirsty rather than hungry in hot weather. Instead of breast or formula, offer a bottle or cup of plain tap water (with no sugar or other sweetening added) when your baby seems to be looking for a nibble between meals – that is, within an hour or two of a previous feeding. (Getting your baby used to the taste, or rather the non-taste, of water early on will make it more likely that she'll have the healthy habit of drinking water later.)

- Don't give solids prematurely as a way to encourage sleeping through the night – it rarely works and may lead to overweight. (Instead, try the tips for helping baby to sleep through the night on page 171.)

- Evaluate your baby's diet. If you've already started your baby on solids (on

your own, or on your doctor's recommendation) and she's taking more than just a few spoonfuls of cereal, check to see if she seems to be drinking as much breast milk or formula as before. If she is, this is probably the reason for excessive weight gain. Cut back on solids if you've started them prematurely, or cut them out entirely for a month or two (most experts recommend not beginning solids until four to six months anyway). A young infant does not need the nutrients in solid foods (except for iron, which can come from a supplement). Later, as more solids are added, the amount of breast milk or formula should usually be gradually reduced and the emphasis placed on solids such as vegetables, yogurt, fruits, cereals and breads. If baby is taking juices, dilute

How Does Your Baby Grow?

How does a baby grow? Quite contrary to the fears of nervous parents who scan weight and height charts frantically for signs that all is not well, usually in a pattern that's normal for him or her.

A baby's future height and weight are to a great extent preprogrammed at conception. And assuming antenatal conditions are adequate, and neither love nor nutrition is lacking after birth, most babies will eventually realize that genetic potential.

The programming for height is based primarily on the midpoint between the father's height and the mother's. Studies show that, in general, boys seem to grow up to be somewhat taller than this midpoint, girls somewhat shorter.

Weight also seems to be preprogrammed. A baby is usually born with the genes to be slim, stocky, or a happy medium. But the eating habits learned in infancy can help a baby to fulfill this destiny or defeat it.

Growth charts, like the one in the Ready Reference section in the back of this book, shouldn't become a source of

anxiety for parents – it's too easy to misread or misinterpret them. But they are useful in telling parents and doctors when a baby's growth is departing from the norm, and when an evaluation, taking into account parental size, nutritional status and general health, is necessary. Since growth often comes in spurts during the first year, one measurement that seems to show too little growth or too much may not be significant. It should, however, be viewed as a red flag. A two-month halt to weight gain may indicate only that baby is slowing down because he or she is genetically destined to be small (particularly if growth in the height department is also easing off), but it can also indicate that baby is being underfed or is ill. A weight gain that is double what is normal during the same two months (if it is not accompanied by a similar jump in height) may just be baby's way of catching up if birth weight was low or weight gain has been slow so far, but it can also be a sign that baby is on the way to creeping obesity later in life.

them half-and-half with water. And don't put thin cereal or other solids in a bottle for feeding – babies take too much that way.

- Get your baby moving. If your baby can 'hardly move', encourage activity. When you change her nappy, touch her right knee to her left elbow several times, then the reverse. With her grasping your thumbs and your other fingers holding her forearms, let her 'pull up' to a sitting position. Let her stand on your lap – and bounce, if she likes. (See page 164 for other tips on getting your baby moving.)

Thin Baby

'My friends' babies are all roly-poly; mine is long and thin – the 75th percentile in height and the 25th in weight. The doctor says he's doing just fine and I shouldn't worry, but I do.'

Thin continues to be in – everywhere but in the nursery. While the lean look is favoured on adults, plumpness is what many look for and love in babies. And yet, though they might not win as many nappy commercial roles as their roly-poly peers, slender babies are usually as healthy.

In general, if your baby is alert, active and basically content, is gaining weight steadily, and if his weight, though on the low side of average, continues to keep pace with his height, there is, as the doctor has pointed out, no cause for concern. There are often factors that affect a baby's size about which you can do very little. Genetic factors, for example – if you and/or your husband are thin and small boned, your baby is likely to be, too. And activity factors – the baby-on-the-go is usually thinner than the inactive one.

There are, however, a few reasons for thinness that do need remedying. A major one is underfeeding. If a baby's weight curve keeps dropping off for a couple of months, and if the loss isn't compensated for by a jump the following month, the doctor often

will consider the possibility that the child is not getting enough to eat. If you're breast-feeding and this is the case, the tips on page 98 should help get baby gaining again. If you're bottle feeding, you can supplement baby's diet with solids *if* the doctor okays them, or you can try diluting the formula a little less – again with the doctor's approval.

And don't underfeed intentionally. Some parents, eager to get their babies started on the path towards a future of slimness and good health, limit calories and fat in infancy. This is a very *dangerous* practice, since infants need both for normal growth and development. You can start them on the road to good eating habits without depriving them of the nourishment they need now.

Be sure, too, that your baby isn't one who is either so sleepy or so busy that he forgets to demand his meals regularly. Between three and four months old, an infant should be eating at least every four hours during the day (usually at least five feedings), though he may sleep through the night without waking to eat. Some breastfed babies may still be taking more feedings, but fewer feedings could mean your baby isn't eating enough. If your baby's the kind who doesn't make a fuss when he's not fed, take the initiative yourself and offer meals to him more often – even if it means cutting short a daytime nap or interrupting a fascinating encounter with his cot gym.

Rarely, a baby's poor weight gain is related to the inability to absorb certain nutrients, a metabolic rate that is out of kilter, or an infectious or chronic disease. Such illness, of course, requires prompt medical attention.

Heart Murmur

'The doctor says my baby has a heart murmur, but that it doesn't mean anything. Still, it's scary.'

Anytime the word 'heart' is part of a diagnosis, it's scary. After all, the heart is the organ that sustains life; any possibility of a defect is frightening, particularly to the parents of an infant whose life is just beginning. But in the case of a heart murmur there is, in the vast majority of cases, really nothing to worry about.

When the doctor tells you your baby has a heart murmur, it means that on examination abnormal heart sounds, caused by the turbulence of the flow of blood through the heart, are heard. The doctor can often tell just what kind of abnormality is responsible for the murmur by the loudness of the sounds (from barely audible to almost loud enough to drown out normal heart sounds), by their location, and by the type of sound (musical or vibratory, a twang, a click, or a rumble, for example).

Most of the time, as is likely in your baby's case, the murmur is the result of irregularities in the shape of the heart as it grows. This kind of murmur is called 'innocent' or 'functional', and can usually be diagnosed by the baby's doctor by simple surgery examination with a stethescope. No further tests or treatments or limitations of activities are necessary. But the existence of the murmur will be noted on your baby's record so other doctors who examine him at a later date will know it has always existed. Very often, when the heart is fully grown, the murmur will disappear.

There are, however, heart murmurs that do require follow-up. Some will cure themselves, but others may require surgical or medical treatment, and a few may become worse. If your baby's murmur is a problem, the doctor will tell you so and recommend a course of therapy. In most cases children with murmurs can – and should – maintain regular activities. The exceptions are those who become breathless or turn blue on exercising, or who are not growing well.

If you're worried no matter what anyone says, you can ask your baby's doctor to tell you exactly what type of murmur your baby has and whether or not it can be expected to cause any problems, now or in the future, and to explain just why you have nothing to worry about. If the answers aren't reassuring enough, ask for referral to a paediatric cardiologist for consultation.

Black Stool

'My daughter's last nappy was filled with a black stool. Could she be having a digestive problem?'

More likely she's been having an iron supplement. In some children, the reaction between the normal bacteria of the gastrointestinal tract and the iron sulfate in a supplement causes the stool to turn dark brown, greenish, or black. There's no medical significance in this change, no need to be concerned by it, and no need to discontinue the iron. Studies show that the iron doesn't increase digestive discomfort or fussiness. If your baby has black stools and isn't taking a supplement or a formula with iron, check with her doctor.

Baby Massage

'I have a friend who uses massage on her baby and says it's necessary for good mother-baby bonding, among other things. But I'm not sure I'd feel comfortable doing it. Should I anyway?'

Any mother-baby activity – be it looking at a book, singing a nursery rhyme, or sharing a hug – increases bonding. Massage is no exception. We also know that massage (gentle stroking) can actually improve the growth and development of premature infants. Whether it can have a similar effect on term infants, who have a lot more stimulation in their lives, are a lot more physically active, and may not require the added stimulation massage provides, isn't known.

Probably the best that can presently be said is that parents who enjoy massaging their infants should continue to do so, if not for the possible benefits, then simply for the pure pleasure of it. On the other hand, parents who are uncomfortable with the idea can safely skip it without worrying about harming their infants. There are plenty of other ways to get close to baby.

Exercise

'I've heard a lot about the importance of exercising your baby. Is it really necessary for me to take my little girl to an exercise class?'

Western parents tend to be extremists. Either they're totally sedentary, getting all their exercise turning on the TV and reaching for a beer, or they embark on a overly rigorous jogging programme that lands them in the sports specialist's surgery with aches and pains. And either they confine their babies to a stationary life in high chairs, pushchairs and playpens, or they rush out and enroll them in exercise classes the moment they can lift their heads, in hopes of creating a fit-for-life infant athlete.

But extremism in the pursuit of good health tends to be ineffective, and is usually doomed to failure. Moderation is a much better goal to aim for, in your lifestyle and your baby's. So instead of ignoring your baby's physical development or pushing her beyond her abilities, take the following steps to start her on the road to fitness:

Stimulate body as well as mind. We tend to like to teach our children intellectual matter from the cradle, but often figure the physical will take care of itself. And for the most part, it will – but paying a little extra attention to it will remind both you and your baby of its importance. Try to spend some part of your playtime with your baby in physical activity. At this stage, it may be nothing more than pulling her to a sitting position (or a standing one, when she's

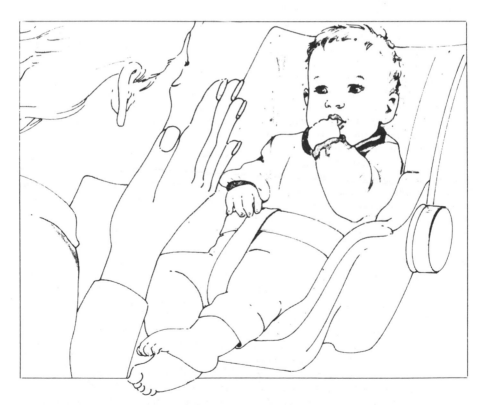

For a baby, playtime is learning time. Not only will a game of peekaboo elicit delighted giggles from a three- or four-month-old, it will help teach the important lesson of object permanence: when mummy or daddy hides their face behind their hands, they're still there.

ready), gently raising her hands over her head, bending her knees up to meet her elbows in a rhythmic way, or holding her up in the air with your hands around her middle, making her flex her arms and legs.

Make the physical fun. You want her to feel good about her body and about physical activity, so be sure she enjoys these little sessions – and certainly don't be grim about them yourself. Talk or sing to her and tell her what you're doing. She'll come to identify little rhythmic ditties (such as 'exercise, exercise, how I love my exercise') with the fun of physical activity.

Don't fence her in. A baby who's always strapped safely into a pram or an infant seat or snuggled into a baby carrier, without opportunity for physical explorations, is well on her way to becoming a sedentary – and unfit – child. Even an infant who's too little to crawl can benefit from the freedom to move that a blanket on the floor or the centre of a large bed (with constant supervision, of course) can offer. On their backs in such a position, many three- and four-month-olds will spend great stretches of time attempting to turn over (help them practice by slowly turning them over and back again). On their bellies, many will inch around, exploring with their hands and mouths, pushing their bottoms up in the air, raising their heads and shoulders. All of this activity naturally exercises tiny arms and legs – and is impossible to duplicate in a confined space.

Keep it informal. Exercise classes or taped programmes for infants are not necessary for good physical development, and in fact can be detrimental. Babies, given the opportunity, get all the exercise they need. Classes or tapes that have parents doing exercises to children will not, in spite of what you may have heard, speed development, improve muscle tone, or teach children to love exercise. Their basic value is that they encourage your playing with your child and, if in class form, provide exposure to other children. If you do choose to take your baby to

an exercise programme, check the programme first for the following:

• Do teachers have good credentials? Is the programme paediatrician-approved? (Though this can sometimes be misleading; an uninformed paediatrician can attach his or her name to a programme that isn't the best.) Any programme that encourages exercises that jostle or shake babies is a dangerous one (see page 281). Beware, too, of classes that are high pressure, rather than fun, encouraging competition instead of individual growth.

• Do babies seem to be having fun? If an infant isn't smiling or laughing while exercising, she isn't enjoying it. Beware especially if the babies seem confused or frightened, or pressured to do things that make them uncomfortable.

• Is there a lot of age-appropriate equipment for your baby to play with – things like carpeted steps, miniature slides and rockers?

• Are babies given plenty of opportunity for free play – explorations made on their own and with you? Most of the class should be devoted to this, rather than structured group activities.

• Is music an integral part of the programme? Babies like music and rhythmic activities, such as rocking and singing, and the two go together well in an exercise programme.

Let baby set her pace. Pushing a baby to exercise, or to do anything else she isn't ready for or in the mood for, can set up very negative attitudes. Begin exercise with your baby only when she seems receptive, and stop when she tells you, by her disinterest or fussiness, that she's had enough.

Keep her energized. Good nutrition is as important to your baby's good physical development as exercise. Once solids are introduced (with the doctor's permission of course), start her on the Best-Odds Diet for

Beginners (page 214) so that she has the energy needed for fun and games and the nutrients for optimal development.

Don't be an unfit mother. Teach by example; the family that exercises together stays fit together. If your child grows up watching you walking half a mile to the shops instead of driving, doing daily aerobics in front of the TV instead of munching chips, swimming laps in the pool instead of sunbathing alongside it, she'll enter adulthood with good feelings about fitness that she can pass on to her own offspring.

WHAT IT'S IMPORTANT TO KNOW:

Playthings for Baby

Walking baby into a store is like walking into a carnival in full swing. With every aisle vying for attention with its selection of eye-catching wares, bombarding the senses and sensibilities with an endless array of colourful boxes and displays, it's hard to know where to start. And though such trips can bring out the child in any adult, for parents several responsibilities come along with the joys of choosing toys.

To make sure you don't succumb to the prettiest packages and the most alluring gimmicks the toy industry has to offer, and end up with a vast selection of the wrong toys for your baby, consider these questions when contemplating a purchase – or when deciding whether to keep out, shelve, or return to the store playthings that have come as gifts:

Is it age appropriate? The most obvious reason for making sure a toy you purchase is age appropriate is so that your baby will appreciate it and enjoy it fully now. A less apparent reason, though, is just as important. Even an advanced baby who might be interested in a toy that's classified as appropriate for older children, and who might even manage to play with it on a primitive level, could be harmed by it since age appropriateness also takes safety into consideration. Giving your baby toys before he or she is ready for them has another disadvantage, as well; it's possible that by the time baby is ready for them, he or she will also be bored by them.

How can you tell if a toy is appropriate for your baby? One way is the age range listed on the packaging, though your baby may be able to appreciate a particular toy a little earlier or a little later than average. Another is to observe your child with the toy – if you have the toy already or can try it out at a friend's house or the store. Is he or she interested in it? Does he or she play with it the way it's meant to be played with? The right toy will help your baby to perfect skills already learned or promote the development of new ones just about to be tackled. It will be neither too easy (which encourages boredom), nor too difficult (which promotes failure).

Is it stimulating? Every toy doesn't have to bring your baby one step closer to that acceptance letter; babyhood (and childhood) are times for just plain fun, too. But your baby will have more fun with a toy if it's stimulating to the sense of sight (a mirror or a mobile), hearing (a music box or a clown with a bell in his belly), touch (a cradle gym or activity board), or taste (a teething ring, or anything else that's mouthable) than if it's merely cute or pretty. As your baby grows, you will want toys that help a child learn eye-hand coordination, large and small motor control, the concept of cause and effect, colour and shape identification and matching, auditory discrimination, spatial relationships, and that stimulate social and language development, imagination and creativity.

Is it safe? This is perhaps the most significant question of all, since toys (not including bikes, sledges, skates and skateboards, which cause hundreds of thousands of injuries of their own) are responsible for over 100,000 injuries a year in the U.S. In selecting playthings for your baby, look for the following:

- Sturdiness. Toys that will break or fall apart easily can often cause injury to a young child.

- Safe finish. Be sure that the paint or other finish isn't toxic.

- Safe construction. Toys with small pieces, sharp edges, or breakable parts are usually unsafe for babies.

- Washability. Toys that can't be washed can become breeding places for germs – a problem with infants who put everything in their mouths.

- Safe size. Toys that are tiny enough to be swallowed (smaller than baby's fist), or have removable or breakable parts that are that small, present a serious hazard.

- No strings attached. Toys (or anything else) with strings, cords, or ribbons longer than 15 cm (6 inches) should never be left anywhere near a baby because of the strangulation risk. Toys can be attached to cots, playpens and elsewhere with plastic links that are not only safe, but bright and attractive playthings in themselves.

- Safe sound. Loud sounds, such as those from toy guns, model planes and motorized vehicles, can damage baby's hearing, so look for toys that have musical or gentle sounds rather than sharp, loud, or squeaky ones.

Do you approve of it philosophically? This is less of a problem in infant toys than it will be later, but it's not too early to think about the subliminal message a toy is sending, and to consider whether that message agrees with your values. Don't let society – at least the part of society that creates some of the TV toy mayhem for children – decide what values will be passed on to your child. Even in infant toys, you will find some junk, and before you know it your innocent babe will be begging for a popular toy that you should not buy unless you truly approve. And should your child end up with a toy you wouldn't have bought (it happens), then explain to him or her what your feelings about that toy are. If, for example, you're uncomfortable with the tyke-size machine gun Uncle Bill gave your child for a birthday gift, explain when your baby is old enough to understand that it's a toy, that real guns are dangerous, that they hurt people.

EIGHT

The Fifth Month

◆

What Your Baby May Be Doing

**By the end of this month, your baby . . .
should be able to (see Note):**

- hold head steady when upright (by 4⅓ months)

- on stomach, raise chest, supported by arms (by 4⅓ months)

- roll over (one way)

- pay attention to a raisin or other very small object

- squeal in delight (4⅔ months)

- reach for an object

- smile spontaneously

- grasp a rattle held to backs or tips of fingers

Note: If your baby seems not to have reached one or more of these milestones, check with the doctor. In rare instances the delay could indicate a problem, though in most cases it will turn out to be normal for your baby. Premature infants generally reach milestones later than others of the same birth age, often achieving them closer to their adjusted age (the age they would be if they had been born at term), and sometimes later.

. . . will probably be able to:

- bear some weight on legs (5¼ months)

- keep head level with body when pulled to sitting

By the month's end, a few babies will be able to manage unassisted sitting when propped up by their hands, but most will still tumble forward in this position.

- say ah-goo or similar vowel-consonant combinations

- razz (make a wet razzing sound)

. . . may possibly be able to:

- sit without support (5½ months)

- turn in the direction of a voice

. . . may even be able to:

- pull up to standing position from sitting

- stand holding on to someone or something

- feed himself or herself a cracker

- object if you try to take a toy away

- work to get to a toy out of reach

- pass a cube or other object from one hand to the other

- look for dropped object

- rake a raisin and pick it up in fist

- babble, combining vowels and consonants such as ga-ga-ga-ga, ba-ba-ba-ba, ma-ma-ma-ma, da-da-da-da

What You Can Expect At This Month's Checkup

Most doctors do not schedule regular well-baby checkups this month. Do call the doctor if there are any concerns that can't wait until next month's visit. You may want to attend the well-baby clinic for a routine weight check and/or advice on starting solids.

Feeding Your Baby This Month: Starting Solids

It's the moment you've been waiting for, and you're giddy with anticipation. As daddy stands by with the video camera, ready to capture the momentous event, baby is decked out in party clothes and freshly laundered bib, propped up and secured in that spanking new high chair. As the camera rolls, baby's first bite of solid food – heaped on the engraved sterling silver spoon from Great-Aunt Alice – is lifted from the bowl to baby's mouth. Baby's mouth opens, then, as the food makes its bizarre first impression on inexperienced tastebuds, screws itself into a knot of displeasure, and spews the unfamiliar offering onto chin, bib and high chair tray. Cut!

The challenge to get your child to eat (or at least, eat what you'd like him or her to eat), a challenge that's likely to continue as long as you share the same dining table, has begun. But it's more than a matter of promoting good nutrition; it's one of instilling healthy attitudes towards mealtimes and snack times. As important as ensuring that the food that goes into your baby's mouth is wholesome is ensuring that the atmosphere in which the food is eaten is pleasant and noncombative.

In the first few months of solid feedings, the actual quantity of food consumed is not of great significance as long as breast or bottle feeding is continued. Eating at first is less a matter of gaining sustenance than of gaining experience – with eating techniques, with different flavours and varying textures, with the social aspects of dining.

Opening Night – and Beyond

Getting the video equipment set up isn't the only preparatory step you'll have to take to ensure a memorable first eating experience. You'll also want to pay attention to the timing, setting and props to make the most of this feeding – and future ones.

Time it right. If you're breastfeeding, the show should go on when your milk supply is at its lowest (in most women this is late in the afternoon or early in the evening). Evening is also a good choice if your baby awakens at night hungry and might be sustained longer by a more substantial evening meal. If, on the other hand, your baby seems hungriest in the morning, you might offer solids then. Don't worry if the menu is cereal and the serving time is 6 P.M. – baby will hardly be expecting steak.

Humour your headliner. You've slotted a 5:00 P.M. performance only to find that the star is cranky and overtired. Postpone the show. You can't introduce your baby to anything new, food included, when he or she is in this condition. Schedule meals for times when your baby is usually alert and happy.

Don't open to a full tummy. Whet baby's appetite before offering the solids, but don't drown it. Start off with an appetizer of a small amount of formula or breast milk. That way your baby won't be too ravenous to put up with the new experience, and won't be so satiated that the next course will have no appeal. Of course, babies with small appetites may do better starting solids hungry; you'll have to see which works best for yours.

Be ready for a long production. Don't try to schedule baby's meals in five-minute segments between other chores. Baby feeding is a time-consuming process, so be sure to leave plenty of time for it.

Set the stage. Holding a squirming baby on your lap while trying to deposit an unfamiliar substance into an unreceptive mouth is a perfect script for disaster. Set up a sturdy high chair or feeding seat (see page 229) several days before the first feeding experience and allow your baby to become comfortable in it. If your baby slides around or slumps in it, pad it with a small blanket, quilt, or some towels. Fasten the restraining straps for baby's safety and your peace of mind. If your baby can't sit up at all in such a chair or seat, it's probably a good idea to postpone solids for a bit longer.

Also be sure you have the right kind of spoon. It doesn't have to be a family heirloom or baby spoon, but it should have a small bowl (perhaps a demitasse or iced-tea spoon) and, possibly, a plastic coating, which is easier on baby's gums. Giving baby a spoon of his or her own to hold and attempt to manoeuvre discourages a tug-of-war over each bite, and also gives your budding individualist a sense of independence. A long handle is good for your feeding baby, but choose a short one with a curved handle for baby's use to avoid unintended pokes in the eye. If your young gourmand insists on 'helping' you with your feeding spoon, let a little hand hold on to the spoon as you firmly guide it to the target – most of the time you'll get there.

Finally, use a big, easy-to-clean, easy-to-remove, comfortable bib. Depending on your preference, it can be firm or soft plastic that can be wiped or rinsed off, cloth or plastic that can be tossed into the wash, or a paper disposable. You may not be concerned about your baby getting cereal stains on almost-outgrown sleepers now, but if the bib habit isn't instilled early, it is often difficult (if not impossible) to instill later. And don't forget to roll up long sleeves. An at-home alternative (room temperature permitting) to the bib is to let baby eat topless. You'll still have to do some wiping off, but stains won't be a problem.

Play a supporting role. If you give your baby a chance to run the show, your odds of succeeding at feeding are much improved. Before even trying to bring the spoon to the baby's mouth, put a dab of the food on the table or high chair tray and give your child a chance to examine it, squish it, mash it, rub it, maybe even taste it. That way, when you do approach with the spoon, what you're offering won't be totally foreign. Though offering new food in a bottle (with a large-holed teat) might seem like a good way to give baby a chance to self-feed, it's not recommended for several reasons. First, it can cause a baby to choke. Second, it reinforces the bottle habit and doesn't teach a baby how to eat like the rest of us, which after all is what early feedings are all about. And third, because babies tend to eat too much this way, it can lead to overweight.

Start with coming attractions. The first

several meals won't be real meals at all, but simply introductions for those to come. Start with a quarter to a full teaspoon of the selected food. Slip just the tiniest bit of it between baby's lips and allow some time for baby to react. If the morsel finds favour, the mouth will probably open more for the next bite, which you can place farther back for easier swallowing. Even if baby seems receptive, the first few tries may come sliding right back out of the mouth; in fact the first few meals may seem like total washouts. But a baby who is ready for solids will quickly start taking in more than he or she is spitting out. If the food continues to slide out, baby is probably not developmentally prepared for the big time yet. You can continue wasting time, effort and food at this fruitless pursuit – or wait a week or two, then try again.

Know when to end the show. Never continue a meal when your baby has lost interest. The signals will be clear, though they may vary from baby to baby and meal to meal: fussiness, a head turned away, a mouth clamped shut, food spit out, or food thrown around.

If your baby rejects a previously enjoyed food, taste it to be sure it hasn't gone bad. Of course there may be another reason for the rejection. Maybe your baby's tastes have changed (babies are very fickle about food), or maybe he or she is out of sorts or just not hungry. Whatever the reason, don't force the issue or the food. Try another selection, and if that doesn't go over, bring down the curtain.

Foods to Begin with

Though everyone agrees that the perfect first liquid for baby is mother's milk, there is not total agreement – even among paediatricians – about what the perfect first solid is. The reason is that there is little substantial scientific evidence that points to any single, best first solid food, and babies seem to do as well as on another (assuming it's appropriate fare for an infant). If your baby's doctor has no specific recommendations, try one of the following. Keep in mind that you won't be able to accurately assess baby's reaction to first-time foods by his or her expression – most babies will initially screw up their mouths with shock no matter how pleased they are with the offering, particularly if the taste is tart. Instead go by whether baby opens up for a refill.

Rice cereal. Because it is easily thinned to a texture not much thicker than milk, is very easily digested by most infants, is not likely to trigger an allergic reaction, and provides needed iron, iron-enriched baby rice cereal is probably the most commonly recommended first food. Mix it with formula, breast milk, water, or whole cow's milk (once your baby's doctor approves; many will allow small amounts of cow's milk before six months for mixing in cereal). Resist the temptation to stir in mashed bananas, apple purée, or fruit juices, or to buy ready-prepared cereal with fruit, or your baby will quickly come to accept only sweet foods, rejecting all else.

A food similar to milk. On the theory that a baby will most easily accept something familiar, a food that is close to milk in consistency and/or taste (such as plain, unsweetened, whole milk yogurt) is a popular starter. Whether you give yogurt first or add it later, don't serve it with fruit or sugar to make it what you deem more palatable; most babies will lap it up straight, and many will develop a taste for the tart and unsweetened that will serve them well later on. Babies who are allergic to or intolerant of milk products, of course, should begin with something else.

Something sweet. Many babies are started off on finely mashed or strained banana (thinned with a bit of formula or breast milk if necessary) or apple purée. True, most take to these foods eagerly, but they also then tend to refuse less sweet foods, such as vegetables and unsweetened cereals, when they are offered later. This is not usually an ideal choice.

Good Early Foods to Offer Baby

All of the following are usually enjoyed and tolerated well by young babies. But before introducing the selections from the sweeter fruit list, do try getting your baby acclimatized to several foods from the first three categories. Meat and poultry are usually introduced later – somewhere around seven or eight months. The foods, which can be prepared at home or purchased ready to use, should at first be very smooth in texture – strained, puréed, or finely mashed, and thinned with liquid if necessary to the consistency of thick cream. The texture should continue to be smooth until the sixth or seventh month, becoming progressively thicker as baby becomes a more experienced eater. Babies usually take less than half a teaspoon at first, but many work up to 2 to 3 tablespoons, sometimes more, in a short time. Food can be served at room temperature (which most babies prefer) or slightly warmed, though heating is usually done more for the adult's taste than the baby's.

Rice cereals	Squash	Yogurt (unsweetened)	Apples purée	Beef
Barley Cereals	Sweet Potato		Bananas	Chicken
Oat Cereals	Carrots		Peaches	Turkey
	Green beans		Pears	Lamb
	Peas			
	Avocado			

Note: Spinach, which is very high in oxalic acid, is often not recommended until a baby is older.

Vegetables. Vegetables are, in theory, a good first food – nutritious and not sweet. But their strong, distinctive flavours make them less appealing to many babies than cereal or yogurt, so they may not create a positive attitude towards the gastronomic experience. It's wise, however, to introduce them before fruit, while baby's palate is more receptive to new tastes. The 'yellows', such as sweet potatoes and carrots, are usually more palatable (as well as more nutritious) than 'green' such as peas or green beans.

Expanding Baby's Repertoire

Even if your baby devours her very first serving of breakfast cereal, don't plan on presenting her with a lunch of yogurt and string beans and a dinner of strained meats and sweet potatoes. Each new food you introduce to your baby, from the first one on, should be offered alone (or with foods that have already passed muster) so that if there's a sensitivity or allergy to it, you will recognize it. If you're starting with cereal, for example, give it exclusively, at least for the next three or four days (some doctors recommend five days). If your baby has no adverse reactions to it (excessive bloating or gassiness; diarrhoea or mucus in the stool; vomiting; a rough rash on the face, particularly around the mouth, or around the anus; a runny nose and/or watery eyes or wheezing that doesn't seem to be associated with a cold; unusual night wakefulness or daytime crankiness), you can assume he or she tolerates the food well.

If you spot what you think is a reaction, wait a week or so and try the food again. The same reaction two or three times is a good indication that your baby has a sensitivity to the food. Wait several months before introducing it again, and in the meantime try the same procedure with a different new food. If your baby seems to have a reaction to several foods or if there is a history of allergy in your family, wait a full week between new foods. If every food you try appears to cause a problem, talk to the baby's doctor about waiting a few months before reintroducing solids.

Introduce each new food in the same cautious manner, keeping a record of the food, the approximate amounts taken, and any reactions (memory can fail). Be sure to begin with single foods – just strained carrots or strained peas, for example. Most baby food companies make special single-food beginner lines for this purpose (which also come in small jars to avoid waste). Once a baby has taken both peas and carrots without any ill effects, it's fine to serve them up as a combo. Later, as baby's repertoire expands, a new food that isn't packaged solo (tomato, for example) can be introduced in a medley along with already accepted vegetables.

Some foods, because they are more allergenic than others, are introduced later. Wheat, for example, is usually added to the infant diet after rice, oats and barley have been well accepted. Occasionally this happens as late as the eighth month, although the okay is usually given earlier for babies with no signs and no family history of food allergy. Citrus juices and fruits are introduced after other fruits and juices, seafood after meat and poultry. Egg yolks (scrambled, or hard cooked and mashed) usually aren't given until at least the eighth month; the whites, which are much more likely to provoke an allergic reaction are often not given until near the end of the year. Chocolate and nuts are not only highly allergenic, but inappropriate infant fare and aren't usually given at all during the first year.

Best-Odds Diet for Beginners

Right now your baby is only dabbling in solids; he or she is still getting most nutritional requirements from breast milk or formula. But from the sixth month on, breast milk or formula alone won't be enough to meet all your baby's needs, and by the end of the year, most of baby's nutrition will come from other sources. So it's not too early to start thinking in terms of the Nine Basic Principles of Good Nutrition (page 349) when planning your baby's meals now, and a simplified Daily Dozen (below) once your baby begins taking a variety of foods – usually at about eight or nine months. Since a prudent diet is the best prevention for heart disease and many forms of cancer, the eating habits you help your baby develop in the high chair now may be life-saving later in life. Optimum nutrition started early will optimize your child's physical, emotional, intellectual and social development. It will help make him or her a better student and a happier person.

Over the next few months, you can start introducing the Infant Daily Dozen, gradually adding new foods and increasing quantities to those below. As baby's first birthday approaches, the Toddler Daily Dozen will be more appropriate. Additional Daily Dozen choices are listed beginning on page 351.

The Infant Daily Dozen

Calories. You don't need to count your baby's calories to tell if he or she is getting

---

No Honey for Your Little Honey

Honey not only offers little more than empty calories, it also poses a health risk in the first year. It may contain the spores of *Clostridium botulinum*, which in this form is harmless to adults but can cause botulism (with constipation, weakened sucking, poor appetite, and lethargy) in babies. This serious though rarely fatal illness can lead to pneumonia and dehydration. Some doctors okay honey at eight months; others recommend waiting till year's end. Because corn syrup may also contain these spores, it, too, should not be given to babies; it's safe, however, in infant formulas.

Double-Duty Jars

Use empty baby food jars, thoroughly washed in a dishwasher or by hand with detergent in very hot water, for heating and/or serving small portions of baby foods. Heat by placing the open jar in a small amount of hot water rather than in the microwave oven (it may heat foods unevenly).

---

enough – or too many. Is he or she unpleasingly plump? Too many calories are the likely reason. Or is your baby very thin or growing too slowly? Then caloric intake is probably insufficient. Right now most of the calories that keep baby thriving come from breast milk or formula; gradually more and more of them will come from solid foods.

Protein. Two or three tablespoons a day of egg yolk (once it has been approved), meat, chicken, fish, cottage cheese, or yogurt, or 25 g/1 ounce of cheese or 50 g/2 ounces of tofu will do while the greater share of protein is still received from formula or breast milk.

Calcium foods. Breast milk and/or formula supplies adequate calcium for an infant, but as these are decreased and solids increased, other calcium foods such as hard cheeses, yogurt, whole milk and tofu coagulated with calcium nigari should be added to the diet. The total requirement can be met with about two cups of whole milk or the equivalent in breast milk, formula, other milk products, or other calcium foods, until baby reaches a year (see page 351 for equivalents).

Whole grains and other concentrated complex carbohydrates. Two to four servings of grain foods, legumes, or dried peas a day will add essential vitamins and minerals, as well as some protein, to baby's diet. One serving equals 35 g (1¼ ounces) baby cereal, a half-slice of whole-grain bread, or 25 g (1 ounce) of cooked whole-grain cereal or pasta, 75 g (2½ ounces) of dry whole-grain cereal, or 25 g (1 ounce) cup puréed lentils, beans, or peas, but don't expect this intake for months.

Green leafy and yellow vegetables and yellow vegetables and yellow fruits.

Two or three tablespoons of winter squash, sweet potato, carrots, broccoli, kale, apricots, yellow peaches (puréed at first, chunky later) or 45 g (1½ ounces) ripe cantaloupe, mango, or peach cubes, when baby moves on to finger foods, will provide adequate vitamin A.

Vitamin C foods. Just 50 ml (2 fl ounces) of baby fruit juice fortified with vitamin C or orange or grapefruit juice (which are usually not introduced until after the eighth month) will provide enough vitamin C. So will 45 g (1½ ounces) cantaloupe or mango cubes, or 45 g (1½ ounces) puréed broccoli or cauliflower.

Other fruits and vegetables. If your baby has room for more food in his or her diet, add one of the following daily: one or two tablespoons of apple purée, mashed banana, puréed peas or green beans, or mashed potatoes.

High fat foods. The baby on formula or breast milk entirely gets all the fat and cholesterol needed. But as the switch to a more varied diet takes place and a baby spends less time at bottle or breast, it's important to be sure that fat and cholesterol intake remains adequate. Most dairy products served should be full-fat or made from whole milk. If you add instant nonfat dry milk to foods as part of your baby's protein and calcium allowance, add 2 tablespoons of half-and-half to each 25 g (1 ounce) dry milk to replace the fat. If you use low-fat cottage cheese for the rest of the family, you can use the same for baby if you add a bit of sweet or sour cream, or be sure baby also gets some full-fat hard cheese (such as Swiss or Cheddar, preferably low in sodium), which is very high in fat, daily.

Though it's important not to remove dairy fats from the diet, it's equally important not to load a baby's diet with large quantities of other fats or fried foods, which can add unneeded pounds, be difficult to digest, and set up poor eating habits.

Iron foods or supplementation. To help prevent iron-deficiency anaemia, your baby should have one of the following daily: iron-fortified cereal or formula, or a vitamin supplement with iron. Additional iron can come from such iron-rich foods as meat, egg yolks, wheat germ, whole-grain breads and cereals, and dried peas and, other legumes, as they are introduced into the diet.

Salty foods. Since a baby's kidneys can't handle large quantities of sodium, and because developing a taste for salt early in life can lead to problems with hypertension later on, baby's foods should not have added salt. Most foods contain some sodium naturally, particularly dairy foods and many vegetables, so baby can't possibly come up short even if you don't add salt to the menu.

Fluids. During the first four or five months of life virtually all of a baby's fluids come from bottle or breast. Now small amounts will come from other sources, such as juices, milk from a cup, and fruits and vegetables. As the quantity of formula or breast milk taken begins to decrease, it's important to be sure that the total fluid intake doesn't. In hot weather it should increase, so offer water and fruit juices diluted with water when temperatures soar.

Vitamin supplement. As a simple nutrition insurance policy, give vitamin and mineral drops especially formulated for infants. These drops should contain iron, if your baby does not take an iron-fortified formula, and no more than the Recommended Daily Allowance of vitamins and minerals for babies. Do not give any other vitamin or mineral supplements without the doctor's approval.

What You May Be Concerned About

Teething

'How can I tell if my baby's teething? She's biting on her hands a lot, but I don't see anything on her gums.'

When the teething fairy visits, there's no telling how extended or how unpleasant her stay will be. For one child it may be a long, drawn-out, painful affair. For another it may seem to pass with a single wave of the wand in the middle of a restful night. Sometimes a lump or a ridge seems visible in the gum for weeks or months; sometimes there seems to be no visible clue at all until the tooth itself appears.

On average the first tooth arrives sometime during the seventh month, although it can rear its pearly white head as early as three months, as late as twelve, or in rare instances, even earlier or later. Tooth eruption often follows hereditary patterns, so if you or your husband teethed early or late, your baby may do likewise. Symptoms of teething, however, often precede the tooth itself by as much as two or three months. These symptoms vary from child to child, and opinions as to exactly what these symptoms are and how painful teething actually is vary from physician to physician. But it's commonly accepted that a teething baby may experience any or all of the following:

Drooling. For a lot of babies, starting at anywhere from about ten weeks to three or four months of age, the tap's on. Teething stimulates drooling, more in some babies than in others.

Chin or face rash. In a prolific drooler, it's not unusual for a dry skin rash or chapping to develop on the chin and around the mouth because of irritation from constant contact with saliva. To help prevent this, gently wipe the drool periodically during the daytime, and place a towel under the cot sheet to absorb the excess while your baby sleeps. Should a patch of dry skin appear, keep it well lubricated with a mild skin cream (ask the doctor for a recommendation).

A little cough. The excess saliva can cause baby to gag or cough occasionally. This is nothing to worry about, as long as your baby seems otherwise free of cold, flu, or allergy symptoms. Often babies will continue the cough as an attention getter or because they find it an interesting addition to their vocalization repertoires.

Biting. In this case, taking a nip is not a sign of hostility. A teething baby will gum down on anything she can get her mouth on – from her own tiny hand, to the breast that feeds her, to a perfect stranger's unsuspecting thumb – the counterpressure from any of which will help relieve the pressure from under the gums.

Pain. Inflammation is the protective response of the tender gum tissue to the impending tooth, which it considers an intruder to fend off. It causes seemingly unbearable pain in some babies, but almost none in others. Discomfort is often worst with the first teeth (apparently most babies become accustomed to the sensations of teething and learn to live with them) and with the molars (which, because of their greater size, seem to be more painful, but which, fortunately, you won't have to worry about until sometime after baby's first birthday).

Irritability. As inflammation increases and a sharp little tooth rises closer to the surface, threatening to erupt, the ache in baby's gum may become more constant. Like anyone with chronic pain, she may be cranky, out of sorts, not 'herself'. Again, some babies (and their parents) will suffer more than others, with irritability lasting weeks instead of days or hours.

Refusal to feed. A teething baby may appear fickle when it comes to nursing. While she craves the comfort of something in her mouth – and may seem to want to 'nurse all the time' – once she begins to suck, and the suction created increases her discomfort, she may reject the breast or bottle she so passionately desired only moments before. With each repetition of this scenario (and some babies repeat it all day long when they're teething), she (and mother) becomes more frustrated and more out of sorts. A baby who's started solids may lose interest in them for the time being; this needn't be a source of concern, since your baby is still getting almost all of her necessary nutrition and needed fluids from nursing or formula, and her appetite will pick up where it left off once the tooth comes through. Of course, if your baby refuses more than a couple of feedings or seems to be taking very little for several days, a call to the doctor is in order.

Diarrhoea. Whether this symptom actually has a relationship to teething or not depends on whom you ask. Some mothers insist that every time their babies teethe, they have loose bowel movements. Some doctors admit that there appears to be a connection – perhaps because the excess saliva swallowed loosens the stool. Other doctors refuse to acknowledge this link, at least for the record – probably not because they are entirely sure it doesn't exist, but because they fear that legitimizing the theory could cause mothers to overlook possibly significant gastrointestinal symptoms, attributing them to teething. So though it may be that your baby will have looser movements with teething, you should report actual diarrhoea that lasts more than two bowel movements to her doctor whenever it occurs.

Low-grade fever. Fever, like diarrhoea, is a symptom that doctors are hesitant to link to teething. Still, some acknowledge that a low-grade fever (under 38.3°C/101°F, rectally) can occasionally accompany teething as a result of inflammation of the gums. To play it safe, treat fever with teething as you would low-grade fever at any other time, calling the doctor if it persists for three days.

Wakefulness. Babies don't teethe only during the daylight hours. The discomfort that has her fussing during the day can keep her awake at night. Even the baby who has been sleeping through the night may suddenly begin night waking again. To avoid her lapsing back into old habits, don't rush to comfort or feed her. Instead, see if she can settle back down herself. Night waking, like many other teething problems, is more common with first teeth and with molars.

Gum haematoma. Occasionally, teething initiates some bleeding under the gum, which may appear as a bluish lump. Such haematomas are nothing to worry about, and most doctors recommend allowing them to resolve on their own without medical intervention. Cold compresses may lessen discomfort and speed the resolution of gum haematomas.

Ear pulling; cheek rubbing. Pain in the gums may travel to the ears and cheeks along nerve pathways they share, particularly when the molars begin pushing their way in. That's why some babies, when they are teething, pull at an ear or rub a cheek or the chin. But keep in mind that babies also tug at their ears when they have ear infections. If you suspect an ear infection (see page 416), teething or no, check with the doctor.

There are probably as many home-tested treatments for teething discomfort as there are grandmothers. Some work, some don't. Among the best that old wives and new medicine have to offer are:

Something to chew on. This is not for nutritive benefits, but for the relief that comes from counterpressure against the gums – which is enhanced when the object being chewed is icy cold and numbing. A frozen bagel, a frozen banana (albeit messy), a clean flannel with an ice cube tightly wrapped and secured inside with a rubber band, a chilled carrot with the thin end sliced off (but don't use carrots once teeth are actually in and can chip off chokable bits), a bumpy rubber teething ring or other teething toy, even the plastic railing of a cot or playpen will all provide a wholesome chew. Health food stores sell nutritious teething biscuits that are fine before the teeth erupt, but afterwards, with their high carbohydrate content, could cause a decay problem if kept constantly in the mouth. Whatever food you use to soothe a teething baby, she should have it only in a sitting position and while under adult supervision.

Something to rub against. Many babies appreciate a grownup finger rubbed firmly on the gum. Some will protest the intrusion at first, since the rubbing seems to hurt at the start, and then calm down as the counterpressure begins to bring relief.

Something cold to drink. Offer your baby a bottle of icy cold water. If she doesn't take a bottle or is bothered by the working, offer the soothing liquid in a cup – but remove any ice cubes first. This will also augment the teething baby's fluid intake, important if she is losing fluids through drooling and/or loose movements.

Something cold to eat. Apple purée, puréed peaches, or yogurt, chilled in the freezer, may be more appealing to a teething baby than warm or room-temperature foods, and they offer more nutrition than a chilled teething ring.

Something to relieve the pain. When nothing else spells relief, paracetamol should do the trick. Check with your doctor for the right dose, or see page 615 if he or she is not available. Avoid giving any other medication by mouth or rubbing anything on baby's gums unless recommended by the doctor. This caveat includes brandy or any other alcoholic beverage. Alcohol is a dangerous poison to infants – and even a touch could encourage your baby to develop a taste for it.

Chronic Cough

'For the last three weeks my baby has had a little cough. He doesn't seem sick, and he almost seems to be coughing on purpose. Is this possible?'

Even as early as the fifth month, many babies have begun to realize that all the world's a stage, and that nothing beats an admiring audience. So when a baby discovers that a little cough – either triggered by excess saliva or stumbled upon in the ordinary course of vocal experimentation – gets a lot of attention, he often continues this affectation purely for its effect. As long as he's otherwise healthy, and seems in control of the cough rather than vice versa, ignore it. And though your little Olivier-in-training may never lose his flair for the dramatic, he will probably give up this attention-getter as he (or his audience) becomes bored with it.

Ear Pulling

'My daughter has been pulling at her ear a lot. She doesn't seem to be in any pain, but I'm worried that she might have an ear infection.'

Babies have a lot of territory to conquer – some of it on their own bodies. The fingers and hands, the toes and feet, the penis or vagina, and another curious appendage, the ear, will all be subjects of exploration at one time or another. Unless your baby's pulling and tugging at her ear is also accompanied by crying or obvious discomfort, fever, and/or other signs of illness (see page 416 if it is), it's very likely that it's only a manifestation of her curiosity, not a symptom of an ear infection. Some babies may also fuss with their ears when teething. Redness on the outside of the ear isn't a sign of infection, just a result of constant manipulation. If you suspect a problem, do check with the doctor.

Peculiar mannerisms such as ear pulling are common and fairly short-lived; they are replaced by newer and more exciting ones once baby outgrows or grows tired of them.

Naps

'My baby is awake more during the day now and I'm not sure – and I don't think he is either – how many naps he needs.'

It's inevitable. The first couple of weeks home from the hospital the proud mum and

---

Teething Chart

This is the most common pattern of tooth eruption, but there are many individual variations. Very rarely a tooth (or pair of teeth) never comes in – in which case the doctor will probably refer your baby to a paediatric dentist or to a general dentist who treats a lot of children. If your baby is an early or late teether now, the same pattern is likely to apply when the second set of teeth comes in.

dad, eager to begin active parenting, stand forlornly over their new baby's crib, waiting for him to wake from what seems like endless slumber. Then, as he spends more time awake, they begin to wonder, 'Why doesn't he ever sleep?'

Though the typical baby in the fifth month takes three or four pretty regular naps of an hour or so each during the day, some babies thrive on five or six naps of about twenty minutes each, and others on two longer ones of an hour and a half or two. The number and length of naps your baby takes, however, are less important than the total amount of shut-eye he gets (about $14\frac{1}{2}$ hours a day on average during the fifth month, with wide variations). Longer naps are more practical for you because they allow you longer stretches in which to get things done. In addition, the baby who gets into catnapping during the day may follow the same pattern during the night, waking up frequently.

You can try to encourage longer naps by:

• Offering a comfortable place to nap. Letting baby sleep on your shoulder will not only result in a stiff shoulder for you, but also in a shorter nap for him. A cot, pram, or even a sofa (with a chair or a low table padded with pillows alongside in case baby inches towards the edge) is preferable.

• Keeping the room temperature comfortable, neither too hot nor too cold, and coverings appropriate. But remember that we all need a little extra covering during sleep, when we're inactive.

• Not letting your baby fall asleep just before mealtime (when his empty stomach is likely to rouse him prematurely), when his nappy needs changing (he won't sleep as long if his bottom's drenched), when company (and noise) is expected, or any other time when you know the nap is destined not to last.

• Avoiding predictable disturbances. You will quickly learn what disturbs your baby's sleep. Maybe it's wheeling his pram into the supermarket. Or moving him from car seat to cot. Or the dog's shrill bark. Or the telephone in the hallway near his room. By trying to control the circumstances under which your baby sleeps, you may be able to eliminate these disturbances.

• Keeping baby awake for longer periods between naps. Your baby should now be able to stay awake for about three and a half hours at a stretch. If he does, he's more likely to take a longer nap. Try any of the infant-stimulating ideas on pages 159 and 256 to increase stay-awake time.

Though many babies regulate themselves pretty well when it comes to getting their quota of sleep, not every baby gets as much as he needs to. It may be that yours isn't napping enough or getting enough total sleep if he frequently seems cranky. If you believe your baby needs more sleep, you will have to intervene to increase sleeping time. But if your baby sleeps very little and seems perfectly happy, you will have to accept the fact that he's one of those babies who doesn't need a lot of shut-eye.

Eczema

'Just after I weaned my baby from breast to bottle, she began to break out in a red rash on her cheeks. It must be itchy, because she keeps trying to scratch it and is making the skin raw.'

This sounds like a classic case of infantile eczema, also known as atopic dermatitis. A skin disorder that sometimes arises when a baby is put on solids or switched from breast milk to formula or from formula to cow's milk, eczema is believed to be a type of allergic reaction. It's rare in babies who are breastfed exclusively, and more common in those with family histories of eczema, asthma, or hay fever. In formula-fed babies, the rash usually first appears around three months of age.

A bright red scaly rash commonly starts on the cheeks and often spreads elsewhere, most frequently to the area behind the ears, to the neck, arms and legs. (It usually doesn't spread to the nappy area until between six and eight months.) Small papules, or pimples, develop and fill with fluid, then ooze and crust over. The severe itching causes children to scratch, which can lead to infection. Except for the very mildest, self-limiting cases, eczema requires medical treatment to prevent complications. It clears by eighteen months in about half the cases, and usually becomes less severe by age three in the others. Approximately 1 in 3 children with eczema, however, will develop asthma or other allergies later.

The following are all-important in the handling of eczema:

Clip nails. Keep your baby's fingernails as short as possible to minimize the damage caused by scratching her rash. You may be able to prevent her from scratching by covering her hands with a pair of socks or mittens, particularly while she's sleeping, but she may still rub her face against the bed-sheets to get relief.

Curtail bathing. Since contact with soap and water increases skin dryness, limit baths to no more than 10 or 15 minutes, three times a week. Though no soap should be used on affected areas, you can use an extra mild soap (liquid baby soap, for example) on dirty hands and knees and napy area. Use the same soap, rather than shampoo, for hair washing. And keep your baby out of chlorinated pools and salt water, though fresh-water dips are okay.

Lubricate lavishly. Spread plenty of rich skin cream (one that her doctor recommends) on affected areas after baths while the skin is still wet. Do not use vegetable fats or oils or petroleum jelly (such as Vaseline).

Control the environment. Since excessive heat, cold, or dry air can worsen eczema, try to avoid taking your baby out of doors in extremes of weather; keep your home neither too warm nor too cold, and, if necessary, use a humidifier to keep the air moist.

Keep it cotton. Since perspiration can make eczema worse, avoid synthetics, wool and overdressing. Also avoid itchy fabrics and clothing with rough seams or trim, all of which can exacerbate the condition. Soft cotton clothing, loosely layered, will be most comfortable and least irritating. When your baby plays on carpeting, which can irritate the skin, too, place a cotton sheet under her.

Institute a limited quarantine. Not to protect other children from your baby (eczema isn't contagious), but to protect your baby from other children who might pass a virus (particularly herpes) or other illness that could lead to a serious secondary infection of the skin, which is open and vulnerable.[1]

Control diet. Under the doctor's supervision, eliminate any food that seems to trigger a flare-up or a worsening of the rash.

Get medical treatment. Eczema that comes and goes in infancy usually leaves no lasting effects. But if the condition continues into childhood, affected skin can become thickened, depigmented and cracked. Therefore treatment – which will usually include a steroid cream to spread on the affected areas, antihistamines to reduce the itching, and antibiotics if a secondary infection develops – is essential.

Using a Back Carrier

'Our baby is getting too big to lug around in a front baby carrier. Is it safe to use a back carrier?'

Once your baby can sit independently, even briefly, he's ready to graduate to a back

---

1. Though it is highly unlikely that your child will come into contact with anyone who has recently had a smallpox vaccination, you should be aware that such contact – or actual smallpox vaccination – is very risky for a child with eczema.

carrier – assuming it suits you both. Some parents find the conveyance a comfortable and convenient way to carry their babies, others find it awkward and a strain on the muscles. Some babies are thrilled by the height and view a back carrier afford them, others are frightened by the precarious perch. To find out whether a back carrier is right for you and your baby, take him for a test ride in a friend's or in a store floor sample before buying.

If you do use a back carrier, always be certain baby is fastened in securely. Also be aware that the position allows a baby to do a lot more behind your back than sightseeing – including pulling cans off the shelves in the supermarket, knocking over a vase in the gift shop, plucking (and then eating) leaves of shrubs in the park. Keep in mind, too, that acquiring this appendage will require you to judge distances differently – when you back into a crowded lift or go through a low doorway, for example.

Gratuitous Advice

'Every time I go out with my son, I have to listen to at least a dozen stra gers tell me that he's not dressed warmly enough, what I should do for his teething, or how I could make him stop crying. How am I supposed to handle all this unwanted advice?'

Although it's true that if you're very discriminating you can occasionally benefit from the voices of experience that chorus around the pram every time you leave your home, most of what you'll hear from these well-meaning strangers is best passed swiftly, without processing, in one ear and out the other.

You could come back with a smart retort or spend fifteen frustrating and fruitless minutes trying to persuade advice givers of the wisdom of your ways. But wiser in most situations is to plaster on a smile, extend a perfunctory thank you, and move on as speedily as possible. By letting them speak their piece without letting what they have to

say get under your skin, you'll make their day without ruining yours.

If the advice that's been proferred seems as if it might have some validity, but you're not sure, check it out with your baby's doctor or with another reliable source.

Starting the Cup

'I don't give my baby a bottle, but the doctor said I can give her juice now. Is it too early to start her on the cup?'

Whether she is started on the cup in the fifth month, the tenth month, or the eighteen-month, there's certainty in the fact that your baby will eventually get all of her fluids from one. But teaching her to drink from a cup early offers certain important advantages. For one, she learns that there's a route to liquid refreshment other than the breast or bottle, an alternative that will make it easier to wean her from either or both. For another, it provides an additional way to give fluids (water, juice and, after six months, milk) when a mother can't or doesn't want to nurse or isn't available, or when a bottle isn't handy.

Another advantage of early cup training: a five-month-old infant is markedly malleable. But wait until your baby's first birthday to introduce a cup, and you'll likely encounter considerable resistance. Not only will she be stubbornly set in her ways, but she's apt to sense that giving in to a cup will lead to her having to give up her bottle or breast. And even if she accepts the cup, it may be a while before she becomes skilled at using it, which means that it could be weeks or months before she will be able to drink significant amounts from it – hence, weeks or months before you can wean her.

To ease your baby into using the cup early and successfully:

Wait until she can sit supported. Babies as young as two months can be started on the cup, but gagging will be less of a problem once a baby can sit up with support.

Choose a safe cup. Even if you're holding the cup, baby may knock it down or swat at it impatiently when she doesn't want any more, so be sure the cups you use are unbreakable. A cup that is weighted at the bottom will not tip over easily. A paper or plastic cup, though unbreakable, won't work for training because – much to baby's delight – it's crushable.

Choose a compatible cup. The type of cup preferred differs from child to child, so you may have to experiment with several to find one your child really likes. Some children favour a cup with one or two handles they can grip; others prefer a cup without handles. (If such a cup tends to slip from baby's wet little hands, wrap a couple of strips of adhesive tape around it, changing the tape when it becomes ratty.) A cup with a spouted lid theoretically offers a nice transition from sucking to sipping (probably more so for babies who've taken a bottle than for those who are used to a human nipple), but some children just don't like it – perhaps because they find the liquid more difficult to extract from it, perhaps because they want to drink from a cup that's just like mummy's or daddy's. And though there will be fewer major spills at the start with a spouted lid, baby will eventually have to face the hurdle of learning to do without its protection – which may result in more spills later on.

Protect all concerned. Teaching your baby to drink from a cup won't be a neat affair; for quite some time you can expect more to drip down her chin than down her gullet. So until she becomes proficient, keep her covered with a large absorbent or waterproof bib during drinking lessons. If you are feeding her on your lap, protect it with a waterproof square or apron.

Get baby comfortable. Seat her so she feels secure – on your lap, in an infant seat, or propped up in a high chair.

Fill the cup with the right contents. It's easiest and least damaging to start with water. You can then also try expressed breast milk or formula (but not regular cow's milk until your doctor has okayed it), or diluted juice; some children will initially accept only juice in a cup and not milk, others only take milk.

Use the sip-at-a-time technique: Put just a small amount of fluid in the cup. Hold the cup to baby's lips and pour a few drops into her mouth. Then take the cup away, giving her a chance to swallow without gagging. Stop each session when your baby signals she's had enough by turning her head, pushing the cup away, or starting to fuss.

Even with this technique, you can still expect that almost as much liquid will exit your baby's mouth as enters it. Eventually, with plenty of practice, patience and perseverance, more will make its mark than escape it.

Encourage participation. Your baby may try to grab the cup from you, with an 'I'd rather do it myself' attitude. Let her try. A very few babies can manage a cup even at this early age. Don't worry if she spills it all – that's part of the learning process. She can also learn by sharing the job, holding the cup along with you.

Take no for an answer. If your baby resists the cup, even after a few tries, and even after you've tried several different liquids and several different types of cups, don't pressure her to accept it. Instead, shelve the project for a couple of weeks. When you try again, use a new cup and a little fanfare ('Look what mummy has for you!') to try to generate excitement. Or you might try letting your conscientious objector handle an empty cup as a toy for a while.

Food Allergies

'Both my husband and I have a lot of allergies. I'm worried that our son may have them, too.'

Unfortunately, it isn't just the better traits –

Feeding Baby Safely

With millions of cases occurring each year, food poisoning is one of the most common illnesses. And it's also one of the most easily prevented. Other hazards that originate at the feeding table (glass splinters, passing of cold germs) can also be avoided. To make sure you do everything you can to make eating safe for your baby, take the following precautions every time you prepare food:

- Always wash your hands with soap and water before feeding baby; if you touch raw meat, poultry, fish, or eggs (all of which harbour bacteria) during the feeding, wash them again. Wash your hands, too, if you blow your nose or touch your mouth. If you have an open cut on your hand, cover it with an adhesive strip before feeding your baby.

- Store dry baby cereals and unopened baby food jars in a cool dry place away from extremes of heat (over the stove, for example) or cold (as in an unheated cellar).

- Wipe the tops of baby food jars with a clean cloth or run them under the tap to remove dust before opening.

- If a jar is hard to open, run warm tap water over the neck or pry the side of the lid open with a bottle opener until you hear a pop; don't tap the top as this may splinter glass into the contents.

- Don't feed baby directly out of a baby food jar unless it's the last meal from that jar, and don't save a bowl of food baby's eaten from for the next meal, since enzymes and bacteria from baby's saliva will begin – 'digesting' the food, turning it watery and causing it to spoil more quickly.

- Make sure the button is down on safety lids before opening a jar for the first time; when opening listen for the 'pop' to make sure the seal was intact. Discard or return to the store any jar that has a raised button or that doesn't pop. If you use ordinary canned foods for an older baby (or anyone else), discard cans that are swollen or leaky. Don't use foods in which a liquid that should be clear has turned cloudy or milky.[2]

- Whenever you use a can opener, make sure it's clean (wash it after each use, scrubbing gears with a toothbrush set aside for this purpose), and discard it when it begins to look rusty or you can't get it clean.

- Remove one serving at a time from a jar of baby food with a clean spoon. If baby wants a refill, use a fresh spoon to scoop it out.

- After you've taken a serving out of a jar, recap the remainder and refrigerate until it's needed again; if it hasn't been used within three days for juices and

lustrous locks, long legs, musical ability, mechanical aptitude – that are inheritable. The less desirable ones are, too, and having two parents with allergies does make a baby much more likely to develop them than if he has two allergy-free parents. But that doesn't mean your baby is doomed to a lifetime of hives and sneezing. It does mean you should discuss your concerns with your baby's doctor, and if necessary with a specialist in paediatric allergies.

A baby becomes allergic to a substance when his immune system becomes sensitized to it by producing antibodies. Sensitization can take place the first time his body encounters a substance or the hundreth time. But once it does, antibodies rev into action whenever the substance is en-

2. Canned foods are less nutritious than frozen or fresh and often are high in salt and/or sugar, so use them sparingly, if at all, for baby.

fruits, and two days for everything else, discard it.

- It's not necessary to heat baby food (adults may have a preference for warm meats and vegetables, but babies have developed no such gustatory bias), but if you do, heat only enough for one meal and discard any unused heated portion. Do not heat baby's food in a microwave oven; though the container may stay cool, the inside continues cooking for a few minutes after you take it out, and may get hot enough to burn baby's mouth. Heat instead in an electric feeding dish or in a heat-resistant glass bowl over simmering water (hot water feeding dishes won't heat foods, but will keep them warm). When testing the temperature, stir up the food, then splash a drop on the inside of your wrist rather than taking a taste from baby's spoon; if you taste, use a fresh spoon for baby.

- When preparing fresh baby foods, be certain utensils and work surfaces are clean. Keep cold foods cold and warm foods warm; foods spoil fastest between 15.5°C and 48.9°C (60° and 120°F), so don't keep baby's food at those temperatures for more than an hour. (For adults, the safe period is closer to two or three hours.)

- When the doctor okays egg whites for your baby, be sure they are cooked thoroughly before serving. Raw egg whites can harbour salmonella.

- When tasting during food preparation, use a fresh spoon each time you taste, or wash the spoon between tastings.

- *When in doubt* about the freshness of a food, *throw it out.*

- On an outing, take unopened jars or dehydrated baby food (to which you can add fresh water). Carry any open jars or containers of anything that needs refrigeration in an insulated bag packed with ice or an ice pack, if it will be more than an hour before you serve it. Once the food no longer feels cool, don't feed it to the baby.

Another source of danger in baby's foodstuffs is chemical contamination pesticides on fruits and vegetables, additives in prepared foods, accidental or incidental contaminants in meat, poultry and fish (see page 235). Though for the most part, avoiding these chemicals means not buying foods containing them, you can also get rid of some of them in the kitchen:

- Peel vegetables and fruit, when possible, unless they are certified organically grown.

- Wash all fruits and vegetables that you don't peel in washing-up liquid and water, scrubbing with a stiff brush when practical. Rinse well to remove all traces of detergent.

---

countered, causing any one of a wide range of physical reactions, including runny nose and eyes, headache, wheezing, eczema, hives, diarrhoea, abdominal pain or discomfort, violent vomiting and, in severe cases, anaphylactic shock. There is even some evidence that allergy may also manifest itself through behavioural symptoms, such as crankiness.

The most common food offenders include milk, eggs, peanuts, wheat, corn, shellfish, berries, true nuts, peas and beans, chocolate and some spices. In some cases even a tiny amount of a food causes a severe reaction; in others, small amounts don't seem to cause a problem at all. Children often outgrow food allergies, but later develop hypersensitivities to other substances in the environment, such as household dust, pollens and animal dander.

Not every adverse reaction to a food or other substance, however, is an allergy. In fact in some studies of children, specialists were able to confirm allergy in fewer than half the subjects – all of whom had been previously diagnosed as 'allergic'. What appears to be an allergy may sometimes be an enzyme deficiency. Children with insufficient levels of the enzyme lactase, for example, are unable to digest the milk sugar lactose, and thus react badly to milk and milk products. And those with coeliac disease are unable to digest gluten, a substance found in many grains, and thus appear to be allergic to those grains. The workings of an immature digestive system or such common infant problems as colic may also be misdiagnosed as allergy.

For infants in families with a history of allergy, doctors generally recommend the following precautions:

Breastfeeding. Bottle-fed babies are more likely to develop allergies than breastfed infants – probably because cow's milk is a relatively common cause of allergic reaction. If you are nursing your baby, continue, if possible, for the entire first year. The later cow's milk becomes a mainstay of his diet, the better. Using a soya-based formula when a supplement is needed is often suggested in allergic families, but some babies turn out to be allergic to soya, too.[3] For those babies, a protein hydrolysate formula will be needed.

Delaying solids. It's now believed that the later a baby is exposed to a potential allergen, the less likely it is that sensitization will take place. So most doctors recommend postponing solids in allergic families – starting no earlier than five months, often not until six, and sometimes later.

More gradual introduction of new foods. It's always wise to introduce new foods to a baby one at a time, but this is especially important in allergic families. It may be recommended that you give each new food every day for an entire week before starting

another. If there is any kind of adverse reaction – looser movements, gassiness, rash (including nappy rash), excessive spitting up, wheezing, or runny nose – it's generally advised that the food be discontinued immediately and not be resumed for several weeks at least – at which time it may be accepted without distress.

Introduction of less allergenic foods first. Baby rice cereal, the least likely to cause allergy, is usually recommended as a starter food. Barley and oats are less allergenic than, and are generally given before, wheat and corn. Most fruits and vegetables cause no problems, but parents are often advised to hold off on introducing berries and tomatoes. Shellfish and peas and beans can also wait. Most of the other highly allergenic foods (nuts, peanuts, spices and chocolate) are not appropriate for babies anyway and can be introduced after two years of age.

Elimination diets and special liquid diets can be used to diagnose allergy, but they are complicated and time-consuming. Skin tests for food allergies are not highly accurate; a person can have a positive skin test to a particular food, yet have no reaction at all when he eats it. 'Food sensitivity' screening tests that claim to diagnose allergies from blood samples are even less accurate, and extremely expensive.

Happily, many childhood allergies are outgrown. So even if your baby is hypersensitive to milk or wheat now, he may no longer be in a few years – or even less.

For more on allergies and allergy testing, see page 406.

Walkers

'My daughter seems very frustrated that she can't get around yet. She's not content to lie in her cot or sit in her infant seat, but I can't carry her all day. Can I put her in a walker yet?'

Both the baby (who is all revved up with no place to go) and the parent (because the only options seem to be either to carry baby

---

3. Occasionally, recent research indicates, babies can have an allergic reaction to egg or cow's milk protein in their mothers' milk. More study is needed to confirm this.

around or listen to her cry) are frustrated in a situation like yours. Such frustrations are often at a peak from the time a baby begins to sit fairly well until she can get around on her own (by crawling, cruising, or whatever method she's devised). The obvious solution, until recently, was to get a walker – a seat set inside a stable framework, on four, wheeled legs. But because walkers are the cause annually of thousands of infant injuries that require medical treatment, and thousands more that are kissed-and-made-better at home, they are no longer recommended. Safer choices: a stationary walker or one that only goes around in circles; these give a certain amount of flexibility, though with less true freedom of movement than a walker.

If you nevertheless elect to use an ambulatory walker, keep in mind that it doesn't grant *you* freedom of movement – you must stay nearby and supervise closely. You should also see page 43 for tips on selecting a safe walker and:

Take your baby for a test drive. The best way to assess your baby's readiness for a walker is to let her try one out. If you don't have a friend whose baby has one, go to a store and let your baby try out a floor model. As long as she seems happy and doesn't slump pitifully in it, she's ready for a walker. Don't expect her to be able to go far yet; she may not go anywhere at first, and she's likely to take many steps backwards before she takes one forward.

Don't walk out while she's 'walking'. Your baby should *never* be left unsupervised for even a moment when she's in a walker, even if she hasn't yet demonstrated any great mobility in it. A push off the wall and a couple of quick strides, and she could end up at the other end of the room – and out the door or down the stairs.

Do your childproofing early. Most any trouble a crawling or walking baby can get into, a baby in a walker can get into, too. So even if your baby can't get around without the help of a walker, she should be considered as hazardous to her own health as a mobile baby. Read 'Making Home Safe for Baby' (page 285), and make all necessary adjustments before you let baby loose in her walker.

Keep dangers out of walker's way. The most potentially dangerous place for a baby in a walker to be is at the top of a flight of stairs; don't let your baby roam freely near a stairway in her walker, even if it is protected with a closed safety gate. Although most walker/stairway accidents occur on staircases where there is no safety gate or where a gate is left open, some do take place when a gate is not fastened to the wall securely. It's best, therefore, when your baby is in her walker, to block off entirely – with chairs or other heavy obstacles – areas leading to staircases. Other hazards to the walker-walking baby, which should be removed or blocked off before letting her loose, include room thresholds, changes in grade (as from carpet to linoleum or blacktop to grass), toys left on the floor, loose area rugs, and other low obstructions that can topple the walker.

Don't let her walk around the clock. Limit baby's time in the walker to thirty minutes per session. The walker gives a baby an artificial means of mobility, which might make her lazy about achieving mobility on her own. Every baby needs to spend some time on the floor, practising skills that will eventually help her to crawl, such as lifting her belly off the ground while on all fours. She needs the opportunity to pull up on coffee tables and kitchen chairs in preparation for standing and, later, walking. She needs more chances to explore and handle safe objects in her environment than a walker allows. And, too, she needs the interaction with you and others that free play requires and allows.

Don't wait until she can walk before you take away the walker. As soon as your baby can get around some other way – crawling or cruising, for instance – put away the walker. Its purpose, you remember, was to ease your

Safety Tips for Feeding Chairs

Feeding baby safely doesn't just mean introducing new foods gradually and being scrupulous about avoiding contamination from spoilage. In fact, feeding baby safely begins even before the first spoon is filled – when baby's placed in a feeding chair. To help make sure every mealtime passes safely, follow these rules:

All Feeding Chairs

- Never leave a young baby unattended in a feeding chair; have the food, bib, napkins, utensils and anything else necessary for the meal ready so that you don't have to leave your child alone while you fetch them.

- Always secure the safety or restraining straps, even if your baby seems too young to climb out. Be sure to fasten the strap at the groin to prevent him or her from slipping out the bottom.

- Keep all chair and eating surfaces clean (wash with detergent or soapy water and rinse thoroughly); babies have no compunctions about picking up a decaying morsel from a previous meal and munching on it.

High Chairs and Low Feeding Tables

- Always be certain slide-off trays are safely snapped into place; an unsecured one could allow a lunging and unbelted baby to go flying out head-first.

- Check to be sure that a folding-type chair is safely locked into the open position and won't suddenly fold up with baby in it.

- Place the chair away from any tables, counters, walls, or other surfaces that baby could possibly kick off from – causing the chair to tumble.

- To protect baby's fingers, check their whereabouts before attaching or detaching the tray.

Hook-On Seats

- Use the seat only on a stable wooden or metal table; do not use on glass-topped or loose-topped tables, tables with the support in the centre (baby's weight could topple it), card tables, aluminium folding tables, or on a table leaf.

- If a baby in a hook-on seat can rock the table, the table isn't stable enough; don't attach the seat to it.

- Avoid using placemats or tablecloths, which can interfere with the gripping power of the seat.

- Be certain any locks, clamps, or snap-together parts are securely fastened before putting your baby in the seat; always take your baby out of the seat before releasing or unfastening them. Be sure the clamps are always clean and functioning properly.

- Don't put a chair or other object under the seat as a safeguard should baby fall, or position the seat opposite a table brace or leg; a baby can push off against such surfaces, dislodging the seat. And don't allow a large dog or older child under the seat while baby is in it, because they might also dislodge it from below.

baby's frustration at being immobile. Keeping her in the walker not only won't help her to walk sooner, but its constant use may cause 'walking confusion' (much a giving a baby a bottle before she's learned to suck at the breast can cause nipple confusion) because walking in a walker and walking solo require different body movements. The walker doesn't require learning to balance or learning how to fall, both absolute necessities for walking independently. And travelling in it is, after all, easier, more fruitful, and less risky than those first few unassisted steps will be.

Bouncers

'We received a bouncing device, which hangs in the doorway, as a gift for our baby. He seems to enjoy it, but we're not sure if it's safe.'

Most babies are ready and eager for vigorous exercise long before they're independently mobile. Which is why many enjoy the acrobatics they can perform in a baby bouncer. But there are potential problems associated with the use of such devices. Some paediatric orthopaedic specialists warn that certain kinds of injuries to the bones and joints can occur to babies using a bouncer. In addition, baby's exhilaration with the freedom of movement afforded by the bouncer can quickly turn to frustration as he discovers that no matter how or how much he moves his arms and legs, he's destined to stay put in the doorway.

If you do opt to use the bouncer, check with the doctor about safety considerations. As with any baby-busying device (a walker, a swing, a dummy, for example), be sure that you use it to meet your baby's needs, not yours; if he's unhappy in it, take him out immediately. And never leave your baby, even thoroughly contented, unattended in the bouncer – even for a moment.

Feeding Chairs

'So far I've been feeding my baby on my lap, but it's getting very messy. When can I put her in a high chair?'

Though there's no perfectly neat way to feed a baby (both of you will need washable wardrobes for some time to come), using a feeding chair of some sort does minimize the mess while maximizing the efficiency of the feeding process. While a baby still needs support to sit, an infant seat (with baby strapped in and under your *constant* supervision) can double as a feeding seat. Once she can sit up fairly well by herself, it's time to change to a high chair or other type of feeding table.

Most babies will slip, slide and slump in their new seat at first. Small pillows, rolled towels, or a baby quilt or blanket can be used to wedge a novice sitter in snugly, and fastening the safety belt or tether (which should be fastened in any case) should help, too.

WHAT IT'S IMPORTANT TO KNOW
Environmental Hazards and Your Baby

What effect does growing up in a world of questionable safety, filled with contaminants and pollutants and suspected and proven carcinogens (things that cause cancer) and mutagens (things that cause changes in the genes), have on the young and vulnerable bodies of babies? How vigilant do parents have to be to protect their children from such dangers?

Fortunately life is not quite as perilous as many mothers fear or many journalists suggest. And, as during pregnancy, there are far more factors influencing a child's long-term health that are within a mother's control than are not. Ensuring adequate well-baby and sick-baby care from birth. Getting her baby off to the best nutritional start possible. Encouraging healthy lifestyle habits, such as exercise, and discouraging unhealthy ones, such as smoking and alcohol abuse, through example.

But there are some hazards in our environment that we control only partially or indirectly. And though they are believed to present a smaller risk than those things we can control, they do pose some perils. They are of particular concern to parents of young children because children are more susceptible to damage by the environment than adults. One reason is their smaller body size

- the same dose of a hazardous substance could do considerably more damage. Another is the fact that their organs are still in the process of maturation, and thus are more vulnerable to insults of various kinds. Still another is the longer life span a child is looking forward to; since the damage often takes many years to develop, it has more time to develop in a child. Clearly then, it makes sense to know what the potential risks are and what, if anything, you can do about them.

But it is also important to keep in mind that there is no possibility of a risk-free world, only a less risky one. We are constantly in the position of having to weigh risks against benefits: penicillin saves millions of lives but in a rare instance takes a life (the benefit is clearly worth the risk); tobacco gives a great deal of pleasure to smokers, but is responsible for hundreds of thousands of premature deaths annually (most would agree the benefit is not worth the risks); tens of thousands of people die in car accidents annually, but the car provides the benefit of needed transport for billions of passenger miles (here, most seem to agree that the benefits outweigh the risks).

We can't eliminate all risks, but we can reduce them to a greater or lesser extent in most instances. In the case of penicillin, for example, we can reduce risks by not giving the drug to anyone who has shown an adverse reaction to it previously. In the case of tobacco use, smokers can somewhat reduce their risks by not inhaling (though they increase the risks of those around them that way), or by using low-tar or low-nicotine cigarettes (though smokers often smoke more to compensate for the lost chemicals) or by smoking fewer cigarettes (though they then often smoke more of each one). And in the case of car use, we can cut risks tremendously by careful and sober driving, avoiding excessive speeds, choosing safer cars, and using such safety equipment as infant car seats and seat belts.

All of the following present both risks and benefits, but reducing the risks is almost always possible.

Household Pesticides

Household pests carry and transmit disease, are aesthetically unappealing and, in the case of rodents, can inflict painful and dangerous bites. But most home pesticides are dangerous poisons, particularly in the hands (or mouths) of infants and toddlers. You can minimize the risk while achieving the benefits of keeping home and hearth free of infestation with the following:

Blocking tactics. Use window screens and screen or otherwise close off entry points for insects and vermin.

Sticky insect or rodent traps. Not dependent on killer chemicals, these trap crawling insects in enclosed boxes (roach traps) or containers (ant traps), flies on old-fashioned fly paper, mice on sticky rectangles. Because human skin can stick to these surfaces (often the separation can be painful), these traps, when open, must still be kept out of the reach of children or put out after they are in bed at night and taken up before they are up and around in the morning. And they have the disadvantage of prolonging the death of rodents.

Box traps. The tenderhearted can catch rodents in box traps and then let the victims loose in fields or woods far from residential areas, though this isn't always easy. Because these rodents can bite, the traps should be kept out of the reach of children or put out when children are not around.

Safe use of chemical pesticides. Virtually all, including the much-touted boric acid, are highly toxic not just to pests but to humans as well. If you opt to use them, *do not* spread them (or store them) where babies or children can get to them or on surfaces where food is prepared. Always use the least toxic substance (check with your local health authority). If you use a spray, keep the children out of the house while spraying and for the rest of the day, at least. Better still, have the spraying done while you're on holiday, visiting grandmother, or otherwise away from home. When you return, open all the windows to air out the house or apartment.

Lead

For years it has been known that large doses of lead can cause severe brain damage in children. Now it is also recognized that even in relatively small doses, lead can reduce IQ, alter enzyme function, retard growth, damage the kidneys, as well as cause learning and behaviour problems, hearing and attention deficiencies. It may even have negative effects on the immune system.

It makes sense, then, for parents to know what the sources of lead are in their baby's environment and what can be done to minimize exposure.

Lead paint. In spite of legislation prohibiting its use, lead paint continues to be the major source of lead exposure in children. Many older homes still harbour lead paint, often containing very high concentrations of lead beneath layers of newer applications. As paint cracks or flakes, microscopic lead-containing particles are shed. These end up on baby's hands, toys, clothing – and eventually in the mouth. If there is the possibility of lead in your housepaint, have all the paint professionally removed – while the family, especially children and any pregnant women, are out. And be certain that any painted object – toy, cot, or anything else your baby comes in contact with – is lead free. Be particularly wary of items that are imported or were purchased outside the U.K., as regulatory standards vary.

Petrol emissions. Lead in petrol is a major source of lead in our environment. Thanks to the legislation in the U.K. and other developed countries, lead levels in the air and in exposed individuals have been dramatically reduced. Catalytic converters (which will soon be compulsory on new cars in EC member countries) and the use of unleaded petrol help to reduce the poisonous fumes produced by car exhausts.

Drinking water. The water in tens of millions of homes is probably contaminated with lead. The lead usually leaches into the water in buildings where there are lead pipes or where pipes are soldered with lead, especially where the water is particularly corrosive. Since most of the contamination occurs once the water has entered individual buildings rather than in the public water supply, most communities haven't made major efforts to correct the problem. If you fear your drinking water may be contaminated by lead (or other hazardous substance), have it tested by the local water health authority, if they do such testing, or by a private testing agency they recommend. If lead is found, there are several approaches to reducing or eliminating it, including: installing water purifier systems; asking your water company to reduce the corrosiveness of the water it delivers; using only cold water for cooking (hot leaches more lead from pipes); and replacing pipes in your building. Until your tap water is safely drinkable, use bottled water for cooking and drinking.

Soil. Lead housepaint that flakes off, industrial residue, dust from the demolition of houses that have been painted with lead can all end up contaminating the soil. Though you needn't be fanatic, do try to keep your baby from ingesting fistfuls of the stuff.

Newspapers and magazines. Because of the high level of lead in printing inks, particularly those used in four-colour illustrations, these reading materials should not be a regular part of your baby's diet. When baby stops skimming headlines and starts mouthing, it's time for a change of activity.

In addition to keeping your child away from known sources of lead, you should also try to increase his or her resistance to lead poisoning with good nutrition, particularly adequate levels of iron and calcium. And ask the doctor about screening tests for lead, particularly if you live in a possibly high risk area.

Otherwise Contaminated Water

Most tap water in the U.K. is fit to drink, but a small percentage of community water supplies contain substances that pose significant health risks. Water systems purified with activated charcoal rather than chlorine are believed to provide safer water, but only a few water districts presently use this type of purification. If you suspect your water is not safe, check with your local water authority about how to have it tested. Should it turn out to be contaminated, a water purifier can often make it safe to drink. Which type of purifier will be best for your home will depend on the contaminants in your water and how much you can spend.

Polluted Indoor Air

Most babies spend a great deal of time indoors, so the quality of the air they breathe there is extremely significant. Because the air in a home can, on occasion, be as polluted as that on a busy highway, be alert for the following indoor air risks:

Nonstick cookware fumes. Apparently safe for cooking purposes, the fumes given off by Teflon or Silverstone coatings when they are overheated or burning can be extremely toxic. There have been numerous reports of birds dying from exposure to such fumes and of adults coming down with 'polymer fume fever'. The long-term effects of Teflon toxicosis are unknown, but may include such potentially serious changes in the lungs as fibrosis and scarring. Nor are the effects on children known. To prevent any possible problems in your home, never use nonstick drip pans on your grill (they overheat rapidly), never use any nonstick cookware at high temperature settings (on grill or in oven, especially to catch drips on the oven bottom), and never leave such cookware unattended (so that liquids could cook out, allowing burning of the surface).

Carbon monoxide. This colourless, odourless, tasteless, but treacherous gas (it can cause lung ailments, impair vision and brain functioning, and is fatal in high doses) that results from the burning of fuel can seep into your home from many sources: improperly vented wood stoves or kerosene heaters (have the fire department check venting); slow-burning wood stoves (speed up burning by keeping the damper open); poorly adjusted or unvented gas stoves or other appliances (have adjustment checked periodically – the flame should be blue – and install an exhaust fan to the outside to remove fumes); gas ranges each time they are turned on (an electric ignition reduces the amount of combustion gases released); fireplaces with residue-blocked chimneys (fires should never be left to smoulder, and chimneys should be cleaned regularly); an attached garage (never leave a car idling, even briefly, in a garage that shares a wall or ceiling with your home, since the fumes can seep through).

Benzopyrenes. A long list of respiratory illnesses (from eye, nose and throat irritation to asthma and bronchitis to emphysema and cancer) can be attributed to presence of the tarlike organic particles that result from the incomplete combustion of tobacco or wood. To prevent your baby's exposure, allow no tobacco smoking in your home (let smoking guests step out to light up), be sure the flue that vents smoke from a wood fire does not leak, vent combustion appliances (such as driers) to the outdoors, change air filters on various appliances regularly, and increase ventilation in your home. Tight weatherstripping will keep heat in more efficiently, but will also trap potentially dangerous fumes.

Particulate matter. A wide variety of particles, invisible to the naked eye, can fill the air in our homes and present a hazard to our children. They come from such sources as household dust (which can trigger allergies in susceptible children), tobacco smoke, wood smoke, unvented gas appliances, ker-

Unsafe Play Sand

Bad news for tiny sand lovers. Recent evidence indicates that an occasional batch of play sand may be contaminated with a type of asbestos called tremolite. The tremolite fibres float in the air and if breathed can cause serious illness. The problem is more severe indoors, where sand tends to be dry and dusty, than outdoors, where it is often damp. Though it's virtually impossible for you to learn if the sand your baby digs in (at home or at a daycare nursery or in the playground) is contaminated, you can determine if it is dusty, and possibly risky to breathe. Return or get rid of the sand if it makes a cloud of dust when you dump a pailful, or if when you mix a spoonful in a glass of water the water remains cloudy once the sand settles. Find another source, preferably ordinary beach sand (a lot of play sand is ground up stone or marble).

osene heaters and asbestos construction materials (which contribute to a wide variety of diseases including some cancers and heart disease). The same precautions (no smoking, proper venting, filter changing) discussed above can minimize this threat. Air filter units can often remove many of these particles and are particularly useful if someone in the family has allergies. If you find asbestos in your home that may need removal, get professional assistance in dealing with it before particles begin to fly.

Miscellaneous fumes. Fumes from cleaning fluids, from some aerosol sprays (if they contain fluorocarbons, they can also be hazardous to the environment), and from turpentine and other painting-related materials can be highly toxic. If you use these substances at all, always use the least toxic product (water-based paints, beeswax floor waxes, paint thinners made from plant oils), use it in a well-ventilated area (even better, out of doors), and never use it when infants or children are nearby. Store these, like all other household products, safely out of reach of curious little hands. They are best stored in outdoor storage areas where, if they begin to evaporate, fumes won't seep into living areas.

Formaldehyde. With so many products in our modern world containing formaldehyde (from the resins in particle-board furniture to the sizing in decorator fabrics and the adhesives in carpeting), it isn't surprising that the gas, which has been found to cause nasal cancer in animals and respiratory problems, rashes, nausea and other symptoms in humans, is everywhere. The levels of formaldehyde gas released are highest when an item is new, but the gases can continue to be released for years. To minimize the potential damage, look for products that are formaldehyde-free when building, restoring or furnishing your home. To reduce the effects of formaldehyde already in your home, seal such materials as particle-board with an epoxy sealer, or even simpler and nicer, invest in a small indoor garden. Fifteen or twenty houseplants can apparently absorb the formaldehyde gas in an average-size house. If you suspect high levels of formaldehyde in your home, contact the 3-M Corporation, which produces a testing device.

Radon. This colourless, odourless, radioactive gas, a naturally occurring product of the decay of uranium in rocks and soil in parts of the U.K., increases the risk of lung cancer. Breathed in by unsuspecting residents of homes in which it has accumulated, it bombards the lungs with radiation. Such exposure over many years can lead to cancer.

Accumulation occurs when the gas seeps into a home from decaying rocks and soil beneath it and is retained because of poor ventilation in the structure. Taking the following precautions can help prevent the serious consequences of radon:

☐ Check before you buy a home in a contamination zone. The National Radiological Protection Board can give you information on where to turn for testing in the U.K. (see below).

☐ If you live in a high-radon area, or suspect your home may be contaminated, have it tested. Ideally testing should take place over a several month period to obtain an average. Levels are usually higher in seasons when windows are closed.

☐ If your home turns out to have high levels of radon, consult the NRPB for help in locating a radon abatement company in your community and ask them for any written material they might have on the subject of radon reduction. The first step will probably be to seal cracks and other openings in the foundation walls and floors. More important will be increasing ventilation by opening windows, installing vents in crawl spaces, attics and other closed spaces, and eliminating airtight weatherstripping and air-to-air heat exchangers. In some cases, a special house-wide ventilation system may be needed.

☐ For more information, write to:

Radon Leaflets,
Department of the Environment
Room A518, Romney House,
43 Marsham Street,
London SW1P 3PY.

Contaminants in Food

In this world of mass production, manufacturers have learned to use chemicals of various sorts to make the foods they produce look better, feel better, taste better (or at least more like the real thing), and last longer. But even foods that haven't passed through a manufacturing plant are often

contaminated – by pesticides or other chemicals used in growing or storing, or picked up incidentally from water or soil. In many cases, the risks from such chemicals to humans is either unknown or believed to be small, sometimes smaller than the risks from 'natural' foods such as coconut oil (which can contribute to heart disease) or spoiled peanuts (the aflatoxins in them can cause cancer). Nevertheless, it's prudent to protect your baby by following these basic rules when selecting and preparing foods:

• Don't buy processed foods with a lot of chemical additives. Such foods, in addition to their chemical content, are usually less nutritious than fresh, and thus make poor choices for a child's diet. Though many common food additives are believed to be safe, there are also many of questionable safety. Be particularly wary of foods containing any of the following: brominated vegetable oils (BVO), butylated hydroxyanisole (BHA), butylated hydroxytoluene (BHT), caffeine, monosodium glutamate (MSG), propyl gallate, quinine, saccharin, sodium nitrate and sodium nitrite, sulfites, and artificial colours and flavours. Questionable are carrageenan, hyptyl paraben, phosphoric acid and other phosphorus compounds (not because phosphorus is dangerous, but because excesses could cause dietary imbalance, particularly of calcium).

• Don't give your baby foods containing artificial sweeteners. Saccharin has been shown to cause cancer in animals and remains on the market only because it is believed to be a valuable weight control aid. Since infants do not need – and should not be put on – calorie-restricted diets, the sweetener doesn't belong in a baby's diet. And though the sweetener aspartame (Equal Nutrasweet) does appear to be safe for normal individuals,[4]

---

4. Aspartame should not be used by those with Phenylketonuria (PKU) or anyone else who has difficulty metabolizing phenylalanine, one of the constituents of the sweetener.

What to Keep Out of the Mouths of Babes

- Smoked or cured meats, such as hot dogs, bologna and bacon. Usually high in fat and cholesterol as well as in nitrates and other chemicals, and sometimes containing bone meal (which can be contaminated with lead and other substances), these should be served to babies rarely, if at all.

- Smoked fish, such as smoked salmon or whitefish. Usually cured with nitrites to protect freshness, they are not ideal infant foods.

- Fish from contaminated waters. Your local department of health should be able to give you information on which fish are safe and which aren't at any particular time in your community, and which can be served occasionally.

- Foods or beverages such as coffee, tea, cocoa and chocolate that contain caffeine or related compounds. Caffeine can make a baby jittery or worse, can interfere with absorption of calcium, and can replace worthwhile dietary items.

- Imitation foods, such as non-dairy creamers (full of fat, sugar and chemicals), frozen tofu desserts (ditto), citrus or other fruit drinks or beverages (contain unneeded sugar and, sometimes, chemicals). Feed food, not chemical cocktails, to your baby.

- Herbal teas. These often contain questionable substances (comfrey tea, for example, contains a carcinogen) and frequently have unwanted, even dangerous, effects on the body.

- Vitamin supplements, other than those designed for infants (and given as directed). Excessive vitamins can be particularly harmful to babies, whose bodies don't process them as quickly as adult bodies do. The acid in chewable vitamin C can damage tooth enamel and should be avoided by both adults and children.

- Raw fish, such as in sushi. Young children don't chew well enough to destroy the parasites that might dwell therein and that could cause serious illness.

- Alcoholic beverages. No one would put this on a baby's regular diet, but some folks do think it's fun to give a baby a sip – a dangerous game, both because alcohol can be poisonous for a baby and because it can give the infant a taste for the stuff.

- Tap water that is contaminated with lead, PCBs, or any other hazardous material. Check with your local health or water department, or have your water tested privately if you suspect contamination.

- Fruits or vegetables known to be contaminated. When news stories announce that a particular fruit or vegetable may be hazardous, avoid buying it until its name has been cleared or until you can buy an uncontaminated variety.

- Unpasteurized apple juice.

and may even be for infants (extensive testing has not taken place in the very young), it doesn't belong in a baby's diet either, again because calorie restriction is inappropriate.

- Buy fruits and vegetables that are free of chemicals, when possible. (But don't worry when it's not possible, since risks from such chemicals are believed by many scientists to be small.) Locally grown produce in season tends to be safest, since large quantities of chemicals aren't needed to preserve it during shipping or storage. Also safer are foods with heavy protective husks, leaves, or skin (such as corn, cauliflower, and bananas) that keep out pesticides. Food

Food Hazards in Perspective

Though it makes sense to limit chemicals in your family's diet when you can, fear of additives and chemicals can so limit the variety of foods your family eats that it can interfere with good nutrition. It's important to remember that a well-balanced nutritious diet, high in whole grains and fruits and vegetables (especially cruciferous ones like broccoli, cauliflower and Brussels sprouts, and those high in vitamin A, such as green leafies and deep yellows) will not only provide the nutrients needed for growth and good health, but will also help to counteract the effects of possible carcinogens in the environment. So wash food throughly, and limit chemical intake when practical, but don't drive yourself and your family crazy in the process.

that doesn't look perfect (has blemishes and black spots) may also be safer, since it's usually chemical protection that keeps foods looking beautiful. Buying foods that are labelled 'organically grown' may help, but it isn't always a guarantee of freedom from chemicals (see page 237).

- Peel fruits and vegetables before using (particularly those with a waxy finish), or wash with water and washing-up liquid, scrubbing with a stiff brush when feasible. Don't try the brush on lettuce or strawberries; do use it on apples and courgettes. This, unfortunately, won't remove systemic chemical residues, but does offer some protection.

- Keep baby's diet as varied as possible once a wide range of foods have been introduced. Variety adds more than spice to life – it adds a measure of safety (not to mention better nutrition by providing a wide range of vitamins and minerals from different sources). Instead of always offering apple juice, vary the juices from day to day (apple one day, orange the next, apricot the third, and pear the fourth). Vary the protein foods, cereals and breads, and fruits and vegetables you serve, too. Though this won't always be easy – many children fall into, and won't budge from, food ruts – it's important to make the effort.

- Limit your baby's intake of animal fat (other than that in milk or formula)

because the fat is where chemicals (antibiotics, pesticides and so on) are stored. Cook with oil or margarine instead of butter (better for the heart, too), trim fats from meat, trim fat and skin from poultry. And keep portions of beef, pork and chicken small. When possible, choose meat and poultry labelled as having been raised without chemicals or antibiotics.

- Never feed your baby fish caught in possibly contaminated waters (see page 235).

- Don't use foods of questionable freshness. Some of the greatest dangers in the food supply are from spoiled foods. Not only can they cause food poisoning (see page 224 for prevention of this problem), but certain ones, such as spoiled peanuts, corn, or other grains on which aflatoxins have formed, can actually contribute to the development of cancer.

- Keep abreast of the latest in food safety through reading your local newspapers, subscribing to a sensible, non-alarmist food-health publication, and adjusting your family's diet accordingly.

- Feed foods that are believed to have an anti-cancer effect, such as cruciferous vegetables (broccoli, Brussels sprouts, cauliflower, cabbage), dried peas and beans, foods rich in beta carotene (carrots, pumpkin, sweet potatoes, broccoli, cantaloupe), and those high in fibre (whole grains, fresh fruits and vegetables).

- Remember that while it's sensible to be cautious, hysteria is unwarranted. Even by the most pessimistic estimates, only a small percentage of cancers are caused by chemical contamination of foods. The risks to your child's health from tobacco, alcohol, poor diet, lack of immunization, or ignoring such safety precautions as seat belts are considerably greater.

Your Role as a Consumer

Taking all the precautions we can in safeguarding our children against environmental threats isn't enough. To protect their future, and the future of their children, we need to reach out and put pressure on those who control those things we don't have total control of: the outdoor air, the food we eat, the water we drink – and the government that regulates them. In the long run, making your appeal heard may be one of the most important things you can do for your baby. Pressurize your representatives – local and national – to legislate stricter regulations of chemicals used in growing and processing foods, and clear labelling of foods containing chemical residues (such as antibiotics in chickens, Alar on apples).

Organic Foods – Growing Availability

Organically grown foods are appearing more often in health food stores and supermarkets. But for most of us it still isn't possible to fill our shopping carts with nothing but the purest organic foods. Not enough of them are being produced, and what is available is expensive. But as demand grows and as farmers discover that organic farming is not only better for their customers, their environment and themselves, as well as the fact that it can also be lucrative, more acreage will be ploughed and planted without the use of chemicals. And we will continue to find a growing supply of organic food at the grocery.

Foods labelled 'organic' in the U.K. are governed by strict U.K. and EC standards, so look for certification.

Fortunately for young children and their parents, more and more jarred organic baby foods – preparations that are untainted by chemicals, as well as having no added sugar or salt – are turning up at the supermarket and local chemist as well as at health food stores. Many foods a fledgling eater can desire can be found in an organic line, from beginner cereals and strained fruits, vegetables and meats, to combination main courses. Toddler foods are increasingly available.

Buying organic, when you can find what you need and can afford the often higher prices, serves a couple of purposes. One, of course, is protecting your family from unwanted chemicals. Though there is no hard evidence linking chemically treated foods with illness in humans, there certainly has not been enough study to prove beyond a doubt that there aren't any long term effects. The second purpose is to encourage markets to stock organic products. If organic foods are not available in your neighbourhood, ask your supermarket or produce store to carry them; consumer interest will help bring the supply up and the prices down. And, again, don't worry if you can't find or can't afford organic produce – the risks involved with serving up other produce are small.

For more information you can contact the United Kingdom Register of Organic Food Standards (UKROFS) c/o Ministry of Agriculture, Fisheries and Food, Nobel House, 17 Smith Square, London SW1P 3JR.

An Apple a Day – Back in Style

The furore raised about the use of Alar (daminozide) in the late 1980s is an example of how, on the one hand, extremist pronouncements can confuse consumers and, on the other hand, of how public pressure can affect public policy. Used to hasten the ripening of fruit (mostly apples, grapes and peanuts), Alar raised concern because some studies showed it might be a cancer threat, particularly for small children, who tend to consume gallons of apple juice weekly. There was so much fear raised in the minds of concerned parents, that many banned apples and all apple products from their homes and their children's diets. Some even began to limit fruits and vegetables of all kinds. This extremism was unwarranted, and may have deprived children temporarily of needed vitamins and minerals. But the fact that consumers did raise their voices, did refuse to buy Alar-tainted products, and did question store managers and manufacturers, helped to bring about an immediate drop in the use of the chemical and subsequent legislation (in the U.S.) to ban it from the orchards entirely. The moral: Don't panic in the face of food threats, but do make your voice heard.

NINE

The Sixth Month

◆

What Your Baby May Be Doing

**By the end of this month, your baby . . .
should be able to (see Note):**

- keep head level with body when pulled to sitting (6⅓ months)

- say ah-goo or similar vowel-consonant combinations

Note: If your baby seems not to have reached either of these milestones, check with the doctor. In rare instances the delay could indicate a problem, though in most cases it will turn out to be normal for your baby. Premature infants generally reach milestones later than others of the same birth age, often achieving them closer to their adjusted age (the age they would be if they had been born at term) or sometimes later.

. . . will probably be able to:

- bear some weight on legs when held upright

- sit without support (by 6½ months)

. . . may possibly be able to:

- stand holding on to someone or something

- feed self a cracker (5⅓ months)

- object if you try to take a toy away

- work to get to a toy out of reach

- pass a cube or other object from one hand to the other

- look for dropped object

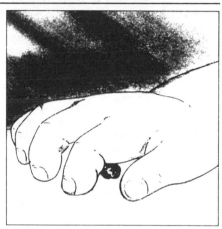

Some babies can pick up small and possibly dangerous objects with their fists– so be wary of leaving such things within reach.

- rake a raisin and pick it up in fist (5½ months)

- turn in the direction of a voice

- babble, combining vowels and consonants such as ga-ga-ga, ba-ba-ba, ma-ma-ma, da-da-da (by 6⅓ months)

. . . may even be able to:

- pull up to standing position from sitting

- get into a sitting position from stomach

- pick up tiny object with any part of thumb and finger

- say mama or dada indiscriminately

What You Can Expect At This Month's Checkup

Each doctor, midwife or health visitor will have a personal approach to well-baby checkups. The overall organization of the physical exam, as well as the number and type of assessment techniques used and procedures performed will also vary with the individual needs of the child. But, in general, you can expect the following at a checkup when your baby is about six months old.

- Questions about how you and baby and the rest of the family are doing at home, and about baby's eating, sleeping and general progress, and about child care, if you are working.

- Measurement of baby's weight, length and head circumference, and plotting of progress since birth.

- Physical exam, including a recheck of any previous problems. The mouth will probably be checked now and at future visits for the arrival, or imminent arrival, of teeth. The posterior fontanel, on the back of the head, will have closed by now; the anterior fontanel, on the top of the head, will probably now begin to grow smaller.

- Developmental assessment. The examiner may rely on observation plus your reports on what baby is doing, or may actually put baby through a series of evaluation 'tests', such as head control when pulled to sitting; vision; hearing; ability to reach for and grasp objects, to rake at tiny objects, to roll over and bear some weight on legs; and social interaction and vocalization.

- Possibly, a haemoglobin or haematocrit test to check for anaemia (usually by means of a pin prick on the finger), particularly for low-birthweight babies.

- Guidance about what to expect in the next month in relation to such topics as feeding, sleeping, development and safety.

- Recommendations about fluoride supplementation if needed in your area, and vitamin D supplementation if your baby is breastfed. Recommendations about iron supplementation for babies not on iron-fortified formula.

Questions you may want to ask, if the doctor hasn't already answered them:

- What foods can be introduced to baby now? Can baby get milk in a cup?

Also raise concerns that have arisen over the past month. Jot down information and instructions from the doctor. Record all pertinent information (baby's weight, length, head circumference, immunizations, illnesses, medications given, foods that can now be introduced and so on) in a permanent health record.

Feeding Your Baby This Month: Commercial or Home-Prepared Baby Foods

When baby foods made their debut on supermarket shelves in the 1930s, they were met gratefully by harried and weary mothers eager to stow away their food mills, proud to enter the age of modern convenience. Today, still at least as harried and weary and even more short on time, many mothers are shunning the commercial baby food products and returning instead to shifts at the food mill (or, more likely, the blender or food processor). And those who do opt for convenience often do so with embarrassment.

Do commercial baby foods deserve the bad label they've been plastered with lately? Are they any less wholesome than home made? Is homemade more nutritious – and safer? Read on before you decide.

Commercial Baby Food

The turn-around in attitudes towards commercial baby foods came about in the 1970s when it was discovered that the foods mothers were buying because they thought they were especially good for their babies might be especially harmful. They contained added sugar and salt, non-nutritive fillers and thickeners, and questionable additives such as MSG. With this discovery came improvements in commercial baby food formulations, partly due to pressure from consumers and the medical community, and partly due to the industry's desire to improve both its product and its image.

Today's commercial baby foods usually contain no added salt or chemicals, and sugar and fillers are rarely added to single-ingredient varieties. The convenience that was always a plus still is; foods come in ready-to-serve, baby-portion jars, reclosable for refrigerated storage of leftovers. But there are many other pluses as well. Since the fruits and vegetables are cooked and packed soon after picking, they retain a reliably high proportion of their nutrients.

The foods are consistent in texture and taste, and are safe and sanitary. They are also relatively economical, particularly if the time you save by using them is valuable to you, and when you consider that less food is likely to be wasted than when you prepare large batches.

The advantages of using commercial baby foods are greatest in the early months of feeding solids. The strained varieties are the perfect consistency for beginners, and single-ingredient starter foods make it easy to screen for allergies. Although major manufacturers do offer graduated textures for use as babies are ready for them, many families dispense with commercially prepared foods as soon as their young are able to handle softly cooked, mashed, coarsely chopped, or flaked foods from the family menu. They may still find ready-to-eat convenient for travel, however, and good to have on hand for emergencies or when they're going to be eating out.

Of course, not everything sold as 'baby food' is good for babies. Read labels and avoid such ingredients as sugar or corn syrup, salt, modified food starch and other thickeners, partially or completely hydrogenated shortening or fat, monosodium glutamate (MSG), artificial flavours or colours, and preservatives. The sugar added to some cereals, fruits and other desserts is just not necessary for an infant, whose taste buds are unspoiled and completely content with the natural sweetness of such foods. (If you want to occasionally treat baby to something extra sweet, use the recipes beginning on page 605 or purchase products sweetened only with fruit juice concentrates.) A few custards and puddings contain eggs; if your baby hasn't been introduced to them yet, avoid these desserts.

'Instant', or dehydrated, baby foods offer great convenience because they're lightweight, don't need refrigeration after opening, and can be mixed with liquids other than water to increase nutritive value. But they have some drawbacks: first of all, some of them contain partially hydrogenated or saturated vegetable oils and/or starchy fillers, ingredients your baby doesn't need. Second, the nutritive value of the instant as compared to the jarred foods is sometimes lower. Finally, the taste of a rehydrated dehydrated food is unavoidably different from the fresh, possibly confusing baby's taste buds when he or she moves on to table foods. So while dehydrated baby foods may be extremely handy on a trip, they probably aren't the best for your baby all of the time.

'Organic' baby foods are new on the market, but are expensive and not as widely available. These offerings are safe and provide good nutrition, but don't worry if you can't find or afford them. Commercial varieties, while not organic, are usually free of known potential hazards (such as MSG, Alar, preservatives and colourings) and present no risk to your baby.

Home-Prepared Baby Foods

If you have the time, the energy and the motivation, there's nothing wrong, of course, with making your own baby foods – assuming you follow these rules:

- When introducing a new food, prepare and serve it without any other ingredients.

- Don't add sugar or salt. If you're cooking for the whole family, remove baby's portion before adding salt and spices.

- Don't add fat to baby's food, either in cooking or at the table.

- Don't cook in copper pots, as this may destroy vitamin C.

- Don't cook acidic foods (such as tomatoes) in aluminium, since this can cause small quantities of aluminium to dissolve and be absorbed into the food.

- Steam, pressure cook, or waterless-cook vegetables, exposing them to a minimum of light, air, heat and water.

- Boil, microwave, or bake potatoes in their skins and peel after cooking.

- Never add baking soda; it may preserve colour, but it depletes vitamins and minerals.

- Don't soak or boil dried legumes (peas or beans) overnight; bring to a *full* boil, boil them for two minutes, then let them stand for an hour, and cook in the soaking water.

- Follow the principles of safe food preparation in Feeding Baby Safely on page 224.

For the first several weeks of feeding solids or at least until baby is six months old, the food you serve should be finely puréed and strained or sieved (though you can mash bananas and thin with liquid). For convenience, you can prepare a batch of carrots, peas, or other vegetables, then freeze in ice cube trays. Keep individual cubes stored in airtight freezer bags. Before using, thaw in the refrigerator, in a double boiler, in a microwave (at defrost, not cooking, settings), or under cold water (still in the plastic bag) – not at room temperature.

What You May Be Concerned About

Changes in Bowel Movements

'Since I started my breastfed baby on solids last week, his bowel movements have been more solid – which I would expect – but they are also darker and smellier. Is this normal?'

Alas, the time when everything that passed through your baby came out sweet and innocent is past. For the breastfeeding mother, the change from soft, mustardy, nonoffensive stools to thick, dark, smelly ones can be something of a shock. But, though the change may not be aesthetically pleasing, it is normal. Expect your baby's stools to become increasingly adult-like as his diet does – though a breastfed baby's may remain somewhat softer than a bottlefed's up until weaning.

'I just gave my baby carrots for the first time, and his next bowel movement was bright orange.'

What goes in must come out. And in babies, with their immature digestive systems, it sometimes doesn't change very much in the process. Once they start solids, stools seem to vary movement to movement, often reflecting the most recent meal in colour or texture. Later, foods not chewed thoroughly, especially those that are harder to digest, may come out whole or nearly so. As long as bowel movements don't also contain mucus and aren't unusually loose, which might signal gastrointestinal irritation (and the need to withhold the offending food for a few weeks), you can continue his newly varied diet without concern.

Bottle Rejection

'I'd like to give my baby an occasional supplementary bottle of expressed milk to free me up a little, but she refuses to drink it. What can I do?'

Your baby wasn't born yesterday. And unlike a relative newcomer she's developed a strong sense of what she wants, what she doesn't want, and how she can best go about getting things her way. What she wants: your nice, soft, warm breasts. What she doesn't want: a fabricated rubber or plastic teat. How she can best go about getting things her way: crying for the former, and rejecting the latter.

Waiting this long to introduce a bottle into your baby's life has turned the odds against you; the introduction is better made at about six weeks (see page 138). But it's still possible that you'll be able to win her over by following these tips:

Feed her on an empty stomach. Many babies will be more receptive to the bottle as a source of nourishment when they're in the market for something nourishing. So try offering the bottle when your baby is really hungry, not when she's recently nursed.

Or, feed her on a full stomach. With some babies, offering a bottle when they are looking for a breast makes them feel hostile towards the imposter and perhaps a little betrayed by the bottle giver. If this is the case with your baby (and you'll only find out through trial and rejection), don't offer the bottle when she's at her hungriest; instead, offer it casually between nursings – when she may be more in the mood to experiment and she might be ready for a snack.

Feign indifference. Instead of acting as though there's a lot at stake when you give her the bottle (even if there is), remain nonchalant no matter what her response.

Let her play before she eats. Before attempting to get down to business, let her play with the bottle. If she's had a chance to explore it on her own, she may be more likely to let it into her life and, hopefully, into her mouth. She may even decide to put it in her mouth herself – as she does everything else.

Banish your breasts. And the rest of you, when the bottle is first introduced. A breastfed baby is more likely to accept a bottle given by father, grandmother or another caretaker when mother is well out of smelling distance. At least until supplementary feeding is well established, even the sound of your voice may spoil baby's appetite for a bottle.

Try a favourite fluid. It's possible it's not the bottle baby's objecting to, but the fluid inside it. Some infants will take to a bottle better if it's filled with familiar breast milk, but others, reminded of breast milk's original source, are more comfortable with another drink. Try formula or diluted apple juice instead, or when the doctor okays it, whole cow's milk.

Know when to surrender – temporarily.
Don't let the bottle become the object of a
battle, or your side doesn't stand a chance
of winning the war. As soon as your baby
raises objections to the bottle, take it away
and try again another day. Perseverance –
while retaining your nonchalant attitude –
may be all that's necessary. Try the bottle
once every few days for at least a couple of
weeks before you consider admitting defeat.

Should defeat become a reality, however,
don't give up hope. There's another alternative to your breasts: the cup. Most babies
enjoy drinking from a cup, even at four or
five months of age, and happily take supplementary feedings from it (see page 222);
many become proficient enough cup drinkers by the end of the first year (sometimes
as early as eight or nine months) to be
weaned directly from the breast to the cup –
which saves their mothers the extra step of
weaning from the bottle.

Shoes for Baby

*'My baby's not walking yet, of course,
but I don't feel she's completely dressed
without shoes.'*

Although socks or booties or, weather
permitting, bare feet are best for your baby
at this stage of development, there's nothing
wrong with outfitting her little tootsies in
snappy footwear on special occasions – as
long as it's the right kind. Since your baby's
feet aren't made for walking (at least not
yet), the shoes you buy shouldn't be, either.
Shoes for infants should be lightweight,
made of a breathable material (leather or
cloth, but not plastic), with soles so flexible
that you can feel baby's toes through them
(hard soles are absolutely out). Shoes with
stiff ankle support (high-tops) are not only
unnecessary and unhealthy for feet now, but
will be when baby starts walking, too. And
considering how quickly first shoes will be
outgrown, it makes sense that they also be
inexpensive.

To check for proper length, press down
on the toe of each shoe with your thumb. If
there is a full thumb's width between your
baby's longest toe (usually the big toe, but
sometimes the next one) and the end of the
shoe, the length is right and there is room
for growth. To check width, try to pinch a bit
of shoe at the widest part of the foot. If you
can, there's enough room. Do not put shoes
on your baby that are too small – now or
later.

Bathing in the Big Bathtub

*'My son's far too big now for his infant
tub, but I'm afraid of washing him in
our bathtub.'*

Taking the plunge into the family bathtub
may seem a frightening prospect for both
you and the baby; he is, after all, such a
little – and slippery – fish for such a big
pond. But if care is taken both to prevent
accidents and to alleviate baby's fears, the
big tub can turn into a veritable water
wonderland for the six-month-old, and
bathtime into a favourite, if wet, family
ritual. To ensure a happy water baby, see
the basic tips on bathtub bathing in the
Baby-Care Primer, page 72, and try the
following:

Wait until he's a sitting duck. You'll both
be more comfortable with big-tub bathing if
your baby's capable of sitting alone, or with
only minimal support.

Ensure safe seating. A wet baby is a slippery baby, and even a baby who sits well
(even an adult, for that matter) can slip in
the tub. If he should go under the water
momentarily, it won't be hazardous, but the
scare could create a long-term fear of baths.
(Of course, if he slips and you're not there,
the consequences could be much more
serious.) Fortunately, today's parents have
an alternative to having to keep one hand on
baby at all times during bathing: the bath
seat with rubber suction cups that attach it
securely to the bottom of the tub. The seat

can be as simple as a ring for baby to sit within, or as elaborate as a large plastic seahorse for him to sit on. Some seats have foam pads to place under baby so he won't slide around. If yours doesn't, put a clean flannel or small towel under baby's bottom to achieve the same effect. Rinse, squeeze and hang the cloth to dry, or use a fresh one each bathtime to prevent the multiplication of germs in the damp material. If the seat has a foam pad, dry it in the dryer between uses for the same reason.

Let your baby test the waters in a familiar boat. For a few nights before he graduates from it, bathe him in his baby tub placed in the empty grownup bathtub. This way the new tub won't seem quite so formidable when it's filled with water – and him.

No swimming after eating. Whether your mother's ubiquitous summer chant was medically sound is debatable. But it may make sense not to bathe your baby directly after meals, because the increase in handling and activity could cause spitting up.

Avoid the big chill. Babies dislike being cold, and if they associate being chilled with being bathed, they may rebel against bathing. So be sure that the bathroom is comfortably warm. If your bathroom isn't adequately heated, you might want to warm the room with a small space heater or a heating unit in the ceiling (heed safety precautions, page 292). Don't remove baby's clothes until the tub is filled and you are ready to slip him into it. Have a large, soft towel, preferably with a hood, ready to wrap him in as soon as you lift him from the water. In cold weather, warming the towel on a radiator is a nice touch, but be sure the towel doesn't get too hot. Dry baby thoroughly, being sure to get into the creases, before unwrapping and dressing him.

Be prepared. Towel, flannel, soap, shampoo, tub toys and anything else you'll need for baby's bath should be on hand *before* you put baby in the tub. If you do forget

something and you have to get it yourself, *bundle baby in a towel and take him with you*. Also prepare by removing everything from tubside that's potentially dangerous, such as soap, razors and shampoo.

Do the elbow test. Your hands are much more tolerant of hot water than is a baby's sensitive skin. To make sure the temperature of the water you're running is just right, test it with your elbow or wrist before dunking baby. While it should be comfortably warm, it should not be hot. Turn the hot water tap off first, so that any drips from the tap will be cold and baby won't be scalded. A safety cover on the spout will protect baby from burns and bumps.

Be there. Your baby needs adult supervision every moment of every bath – and will continue to for his first five years of bathing. *Never leave him in the bath unattended*, even in a baby seat, even for a second.

Have entertainment on hand. Make the bathtub a floating playpen for your baby so that he'll be diverted while you tend to the more serious task of washing him. Specially designed bath toys (particularly those that bob atop the water) and plastic books are great, but so are plastic containers of all shapes and sizes. To avoid mildew buildup on toys, towel off after use and store in a dry container.

Let baby make a splash. But don't make one yourself. For most babies, splashing is a large part of bathtime fun, and the wetter a baby can make you, the happier he'll be (wear a plastic apron if you mind getting very wet). But while he almost certainly will like to make a splash, he may not like to be the target of one. Many a baby has been turned off to baths with a single playful splash.

Don't pull the plug until baby is out of the bath. Not only can it be a physically chilling experience to be in an emptying bath, it can be a psychologically chilling one, too. The gurgling sound can frighten even a young infant, and an older baby who sees the water rushing down the drain may fear that he's going down next.

Bath Fears

'My daughter is so terrified of being bathed in the bathtub that she screams irrationally and we have to force her to stay in the tub.'

Though it may seem irrational to an adult who's taken countless baths, a baby's fear of the bath is very real, looming larger than the tub itself at every bathtime. And forcing your baby to face the source of her fear won't help her to overcome it. Your goal should be to gradually, with patience and understanding, reverse her feelings about bathing – to make the tub a friendly place to visit and water a friendly companion within it.

Take well-travelled roads to clean. Until your baby's completely willing to take a tub bath, don't force her to. Continue bathing her in her familiar infant tub, or if she's wary of that, too, or has outgrown it entirely, give her sponge baths instead.

Try a dry run. If she's willing, put her in the tub (on a large bath towel or a bath seat to minimize slipping) without water and with a pile of toys, so she can become accustomed to the scenery and discover she can have fun playing in that locale. If the room is nice and warm and she's a baby who's comfortable being naked, let her play in there unclothed. Otherwise, keep her clothes on. As in any bathtub situation, don't leave her side for a moment.

Use a stand-in. While someone else holds your baby, give a demonstration bath to a washable doll or stuffed animal in the bathtub, with a running commentary each step of the way. When your baby is old enough, let her help with the bath if she likes, or bathe her 'baby' in a small basin as she sits in the dry tub.

Try some good wet fun. For the sitting baby, fill a plastic tub (you can use her infant tub or a dish basin) with warm water and bubbles made with liquid baby soap, and a couple of water toys. Put it in a towel-lined empty bathtub, or on the kitchen or bathroom floor if your baby refuses to get into the tub at all. Place your baby, clothed or unclothed, next to it and let her explore under your constant supervision. For the baby who's not sitting well yet, fill a smaller basin or bowl and put it on the tray of her feeding chair or walker for water play.

Dressed or not, she may try to climb into the smaller tub herself – a clue that she's ready to try a bath again. If she doesn't, you'll have to take the lead, dunking her toys and fingers in the water in the hope that she will follow. If she doesn't, give her a little more time.

Use the buddy system. Some babies are more amenable to a bath if they've got company. Try bathing with your baby, but at bath temperatures geared to her comfort. Once she becomes adjusted to these duet baths you can try her solo.

Be patient. Eventually your baby will take to the tub again. But she'll do it faster if she's allowed to do it at her own pace, and without parental pressure.

Brushing Baby's Teeth

'My daughter just got her first tooth. A neighbour, said I should start brushing it now, but that seems silly.'

Those tiny pearls that bring so much pain before they arrive and so much excitement when they first break through the gums are destined for extinction. They can all be expected to fall out during the early and mid school years, to be replaced by permanent teeth. So why take good care of them now?

There are several reasons: first of all, since they hold a place for the permanent teeth, decay and loss of these first teeth can deform the mouth permanently. Then, too,

Baby's First Toothbrush

Bristles should be soft and, when they become ragged, it's time for a change. Even a toothbrush that still looks new should be changed after six or eight weeks (some recommend as frequently as every three weeks) because over time bacteria from the mouth accumulate on the brush. Favourite cartoon character toothbrushes make brushes more appealing, but check their quality with your dentist.

---

your baby will need these primary teeth for biting and chewing for many years; bad teeth could interfere with nutrition. And healthy teeth are also important for the development of normal speech and appearance – both important to a child's self-confidence. The child who can't speak clearly because of faulty teeth, or who keeps her mouth shut to hide rotten or missing teeth, doesn't feel good about herself. Finally, if you start your child brushing early, she is likely to develop good dental habits.

The first teeth can be wiped with a clean damp gauze pad or flannel or brushed with a very soft, tiny (with no more than three rows of bristles) infant toothbrush moistened with water, after meals and at bedtime. Ask your dentist or pharmacist to recommend a brush. The gauze pad will probably do a more thorough job until the molars come in, but using the brush will get baby into the habit of brushing, so a combination of the two is probably best.[1] But be gentle – baby teeth are soft. Lightly brush or wipe the tongue, too, since it harbours germs.

No toothpaste is necessary for baby's teeth, though you can flavour the brush with a tiny bit of toothpaste if it makes her more interested in brushing. But don't use more than a pea-size dab until she can spit it out – most babies like to eat the stuff and could overdose on the fluorides, especially if the water is fluoridated. Most babies are eager to 'do it themselves'. Once she has the dexterity, which won't be for several months yet, you can let your baby brush on her own

after meals, adding a more thorough cleaning with a gauze pad yourself before she goes to bed as part of the bedtime ritual. Also let her watch you care for your own teeth. If mummy and daddy set a good dental-care example, she's more likely to be meticulous about brushing and, later, flossing.

Though brushing and flossing will continue to be important throughout your baby's life, proper nutrition will have equal impact on her dental health, starting now (actually, it started before she was born). Ensuring the adequate intake of calcium, phosphorus, fluoride and other minerals and vitamins (particularly vitamin C, which helps to maintain the health of gums) and limiting foods high in refined sugars (including commercial teething biscuits) or sticky natural sugar (such as dried fruit, even raisins) can help prevent the miseries that accompany a mouthful of decaying teeth and bleeding gums. Ideally, limit sweets (even healthy ones) to once or twice a day, since the more sugar intake is spread out over the day, the greater the risk to the teeth. Serve them with meals, when they do less damage to the teeth, rather than between meals. Or brush baby's teeth right after the sweets are eaten.

When your baby does have sweets or snacks high in carbohydrates between meals and a brush isn't available, follow them with a piece of cheese (such as Swiss or Cheddar), which seems to be able to block the action of tooth-decaying acids produced by the bacteria in plaque. For further tooth insurance, get your baby used to drinking juice from a cup now, and never let her go to sleep with a bottle.

---

1. A paediatric dentist may be able to tell you where you can purchase disposable cloth finger slips that are even more effective for cleaning tiny teeth than a gauze pad.

In addition to good home care and good nutrition, your baby will need good professional dental care to ensure healthy teeth in healthy gums. Now, before an emergency arises, ask your baby's doctor to recommend a reliable paediatric dentist or a general dentist who treats a lot of children and is good with them. If you have a question about your baby's teeth, call or make an appointment as soon as it comes up. If not, you won't need to arrange for a checkup until somewhere between her second and third birthdays. Some infant dental problems, such as a bad bite or the decay caused by baby-bottle mouth, need to be corrected early. Others, such as widely spaced teeth, which usually move closer later, are rarely a cause for early intervention.

Giving Baby Cow's Milk

'I'm breastfeeding, and want to wean my baby. I don't want to start with formula – can I give him cow's milk?'

Though small amounts of cow's milk are not likely to be a problem for a child in the first year of life, it is now becoming clear that weaning a breast- or formula-fed baby entirely to cow's milk before the first birthday is not a good idea. Doctors now recommend that when possible, continue breastfeeding until the end of the first year. When that isn't possible, an *iron-fortified* infant formula should be the choice. There are several reasons. First of all, cow's milk contains inadequate stores of iron, linoleic acid and vitamin E, and excessive levels of sodium, potassium and protein. Secondly, the composition of cow's milk may also interfere with a baby's absorption of iron from other foods, such as cereals. And thirdly, cow's milk can cause intestinal bleeding in some babies.

Because the nutritional needs of a six month old differ from those of a newborn, ask the doctor about the possibility of weaning your child to one of the formulas designed for older babies.

When you switch to cow's milk at a year be sure you use whole milk, rather than skimmed (nonfat) or low-fat. Whole milk is usually recommended until age two though some doctors okay using semi-skimmed milk after 18 months.

Baby-Bottle Mouth

'I have a friend whose baby's front teeth had to be pulled because of baby-bottle mouth. How can I prevent this from happening to my little boy?'

There's nothing cuter than a child whose grin reveals a charming space where his two front teeth used to be. But there's nothing cute about a toddler whose two front teeth have been lost years before their time to baby-bottle mouth. And yet this becomes the fate of a large number of babies every year.

Fortunately, baby-bottle mouth is completely preventable. It occurs most often in the first two years of life, when teeth are most vulnerable, and most frequently as a result of a baby's falling asleep regularly with a bottle in his mouth. The sugars in whatever beverage he's imbibing (cow's milk, breast milk, formula, fruit juice, or sugar drinks) combine with bacteria in his mouth to decay the teeth. The dirty work is abetted during sleep when the production of saliva, which ordinarily dilutes food and drink and promotes the swallowing reflex, slows dramatically. With little swallowing occurring, the last sips baby takes before falling asleep pool in his mouth and remain in contact with his teeth for hours.

To avoid baby-bottle mouth:

- Never give glucose (sugar) water, even before baby's teeth come in, so that he won't become 'addicted'. The same applies to such sugary drinks as cranberry juice cocktail, fruit punches, fruit drinks, or fruit-juice drinks.

- Once your baby's teeth come in, don't put him to bed for the night or down for a nap with a bottle of milk or juice. An occasional lapse won't cause a problem, but repeated lapses will. If you must give him a bottle to take to bed, make it a bottle of plain tap water, which will not harm the teeth and if it is fluoridated will help strengthen them.

- Don't let your baby use a bottle of milk or juice as a pacifier, to crawl or lie around with and suck on at will. All-day nipping can be as harmful to the teeth as night-time sucking. Bottles should be considered part of a meal or snack and like these should routinely be given in the appropriate setting (your arms, a baby seat and, later, a high chair) and at appropriate times.

- Don't allow a baby who sleeps in your bed to remain at your breast all night and nurse on and off. Breast milk can cause decay this way, particularly after the twelfth month.

- Wean your baby from breast or bottle at about 12 months.

Anaemia

'I don't understand why the doctor wants to test my son for anaemia at the next visit. He was premature, but is very healthy and active now.'

At one time many children became anaemic somewhere between six and twelve months of age, and many in poor families still do. Screenings for anaemia became routine because babies with mild anaemia usually seem to be healthy and active, not exhibiting the kinds of symptoms that often appear in adults,[2] and the only way to uncover their problem is with a test to determine the proportion of haemoglobin in the blood. When haemoglobin (the protein in red blood cells that performs the important function of distributing oxygen) is in low supply, anaemia is diagnosed.

Today, thanks to more attention to iron supplementation, only 2 or 3 in 100 middle-class infants become anaemic, and a routine screening is no longer deemed absolutely necessary. Still, many doctors continue to perform the test (between six and nine months for low-birthweight infants and between nine and twelve months for others) as a precaution.

Babies are occasionally born anaemic, usually because of a loss of red blood cells due to bleeding, destruction of cells due to a blood incompatibility problem, or an inherited illness such as sickle-cell disease or thalassaemia (see pages 485 and 488). They may become anaemic later in infancy because of hidden bleeding (such as might develop from drinking cow's milk at too early an age) or because of an infestation of parasites (often hookworms). Anaemia may strike, too, because an inadequate intake of folic acid or vitamin B_{12}, both of which are insufficient in the breast milk of strict vegetarian mums, or of vitamin C is interfering with the production of haemoglobin.

But it's iron that's the most essential building block of haemoglobin, and iron deficiency is the most common reason for babies to develop anaemia. Full-term babies are generally born with stores of iron built up during the last few months of pregnancy that carry them for the first few months. After that, as babies continue to require the mineral in large quantities to help expand their blood volume to meet the demands of rapid growth, they need a source of iron in the diet, such as a vitamin and mineral supplement with iron, iron-fortified baby cereal, or iron-fortified formula (for bottle-fed babies).[3] And though breastfeeding exclusively for the first four to six months is generally considered the best way to nourish your baby, and the iron in breast milk is very

---

2. Symptoms of anaemia in adults or older children include: initially, paleness, irritability, weakness, lack of appetite, little interest in their surroundings; and later, waxiness and sallowness of the skin, and susceptibility to infection.

3. Phytates in the grains, which normally bind iron, making it unusable by the body, once made iron fortification in infant cereal ineffective. This problem has been overcome with new production methods, however, and these cereals are now a good source of iron.

well absorbed, breastfeeding does not ensure adequate iron intake once his antenatal iron stores have been depleted.

Iron-deficiency anaemia is most common in babies born with poor iron stores, such as premature infants who didn't have time before birth to lay down sufficient reserves and those whose mothers didn't have enough iron during pregnancy. It often develops later in infants with intestinal problems (such as diarrhoea) or metabolic problems (such as coeliac disease) that interfere with the absorption of iron. But anaemia can also develop in babies without absorption problems who start out with good iron stores but who don't receive any form of supplementary iron when their stores run out.

Just when iron supplementation should begin is a matter of medical opinion, and you should rely on your baby's doctor for a recommendation.

Typically, the baby who develops iron-deficiency anaemia is one who depends mainly on breast or cow's milk or iron poor formula for nourishment, and takes very few solids. Because the anaemia tends to slacken his appetite for solids, his sole source of iron, a cycle of less iron/less food/less iron/ less food is set up, worsening matters. Prescribed iron drops usually corrects the situation.

To help prevent iron-deficiency anaemia in your baby, try the following:

- Be sure that if bottle-fed, your baby is getting a formula fortified with iron.

- Be sure that if breastfed, your baby is getting iron in some supplementary form, such as an iron-fortified cereal or vitamin drops containing iron. And feed a vitamin C food (see page 352) at the same time, when possible, to improve iron absorption.

- As your baby increases his intake of solids, be sure to include foods rich in iron.

- Avoid feeding bran to your baby, since it can interfere with iron absorption.

Vegetarian Diet

'We're vegans – strict vegetarians – and plan to raise our daughter the same way. Can vegetarianism provide enough nutrition for her?'

There are millions of vegetarians who raise their children as vegetarians with little or no effect, except slightly lower childhood weights. But there are risks to limiting all animal products, both for children and for adults. What's good for the goose and gander can be good for the gosling, if you:

- Breastfeed your baby. Since soya milk formulas are an imperfect substitute for breast milk, the vegan mother who can breastfeed should do so, to ensure her infant gets all the necessary nutrients for the first six months and most of them for the first year – assuming she's getting all the nutrients she needs (including folic acid and vitamin B_{12} in a supplement) to produce high-quality breast milk. If she can't breastfeed, she should be certain that the soya formula she uses is one recommended by her baby's doctor.

- Give your breastfed baby an infant vitamin-mineral supplement that contains iron, vitamin D (other than sunshine, the only major source is milk, to which vitamin D is routinely added), folic acid and vitamin B_{12} (found only in animal products). (See page 130 for more on vitamin supplements.) Give a supplement, too, when your baby is weaned from formula or breast milk.

- Serve only whole-grain beans and cereals once your baby graduates from beginner baby cereals. These will provide more of the vitamins, minerals and protein ordinarily obtained from animal products than would their refined counterparts.

- Use tofu and other soya-based products to provide added protein when your baby moves on to solids. Near the end of the first year, brown rice cooked fairly soft, mashed chickpeas or other legumes (beans and peas), and high-protein or whole-grain pastas can also be added to the diet as sources of protein. (See page 352 for a more complete list of vegetable proteins).

- Once you wean your baby, be sure that she gets adequate calcium in her diet to promote strong and healthy bones and teeth. Good vegetarian sources include tofu prepared with calcium (but beware the many soyabean beverages and frozen desserts that contain little or no calcium), broccoli and other green leafies, and finely ground almonds and pine nuts (ground so baby won't choke on them). Since these foods are not standard favorites with infants, you may also have to add a calcium supplement to your daughter's diet if you prefer not to give her milk. Check with her doctor.

Vegetarians who do use milk products have a much easier time ensuring good nutrition for their babies and children than those who don't. Dairy products provide the protein and calcium needed for growth and good health, as well as adequate amounts of vitamins A, B_{12} and D. If egg yolks are also part of the diet, they provide an additional source of iron – but, as for most children, iron supplementation may still be a good idea. (And, of course, as your baby gets older, eggs shouldn't be an everyday food.) Again, check with the doctor.

Salt Intake

'I'm pretty careful about how much salt my husband and I get. But how careful do I have to be about the salt in my daughter's diet?'

Infants, like all of us, do need some salt. But also like the rest of us, they don't need a lot of salt. In fact, their kidneys cannot handle large quantities of sodium, which is probably why Mother Nature made breast milk a very low-sodium drink (with only 5 milligrams of sodium per 250 ml (8 ounces), as compared to 120 milligrams per 250 ml (8 ounces) of cow's

milk). And there is growing evidence that too much salt too soon, especially when there is a family history of hypertension, can set the stage for high blood pressure in adulthood. Studies also show that babies do not have an inherent preference for things salty, but may develop a preference for them if they are fed a diet high in sodium – a preference that can prove deadly later in life.

In response to the mounting evidence that an excess of sodium is not good for babies, major baby food manufacturers have eliminated salt from their recipes. Mothers who prepare their own baby foods should do likewise. Don't assume that string beans or mashed potatoes won't appeal to your child unless they've been sprinkled with salt just because you like them that way. Give her taste buds a chance to learn what foods taste like when not adulterated with salt, and she'll develop a taste for food au naturel that'll last a lifetime.

To be sure that your baby doesn't pick up the high-salt habit and to help the rest of the family reduce salt intake, read labels routinely. You'll find large amounts of sodium in the most unlikely products, including cottage cheese and hard cheeses (choose the low-sodium varieties), breads and breakfast cereals, cakes and biscuits. Since a baby between the ages of six months and one year requires no more than 250 to 750 milligrams of sodium a day, foods that contain 300 or more milligrams per serving will quickly push the intake over this level. When buying for baby, opt for foods with under 50 milligrams per serving most of the time.

The Whole-Grain Habit

'I know that wholemeal bread is best for my baby, but I don't like it and I don't think she will either. Isn't it better for her to eat her white bread than not to eat her wholemeal?'

What was the first bread your mum gave you in the high chair? What kind of toast did you have with your eggs when you were growing

Sodium Content of Foods Fed to Babies

Food	Amount	MG of Sodium
Breast milk	250 ml (8 fl oz)	5 mg
Formula	250 ml (8 fl oz)	Varies, but usually approximates breast milk
Whole cow's milk	250 ml (8 fl oz)	120 mg
Baby cereal	4 tbl.	0 mg
Baby fruits (range)	½ jar	2–10 mg
Baby sweet potatoes	½ jar	20 mg
Baby carrots	½ jar	35 mg
Baby peas	½ jar	7 mg
Whole milk yogurt	2 tbl.	20 mg
Whole milk cottage cheese	2 tbl.	110 mg
Cottage cheese, unsalted*	2 tbl.	15 mg
Wholemeal bread	½ slice	90 mg
Wholemeal bread, unsalted	½ slice	5 mg
Rice cakes, salted	1 whole	28 mg
Rice cakes, unsalted	1 whole	0 mg

* If you use unsalted cottage cheese, which is usually available only in low-fat varieties, be sure baby gets adequate fat from other sources such as breast milk, formula, hard cheese and plain yogurt. Or add a tablespoon of light sweet or sour cream to each 4 tablespoons of cottage cheese.

up? What kind of bread sandwiched the cheese salad in your lunch box? It's a pretty good bet the answer to all three questions is 'white' – and it isn't any wonder that you prefer it. The food preferences we develop early stay with us for life (unless we make a concerted effort to change them), and that's exactly why it's important to give your baby *only* whole grains now and throughout childhood. If you do, not only will she grow up liking whole grains, but she'll prefer them – with white bread tasting bland and pasty by comparison. If the rest of the family jumps on the wholemeal wagon with her, it won't be long before you all favour the darker and healthier loaves.

Early Rising

'At first we were grateful that our daughter was sleeping through the night. But with her waking up like clockwork at 5:00 every morning, we almost wish she'd wake up in the middle of the night instead.'

With a night waker, at least there's the promise of another few hours of sleep once baby beds down again. But with a baby who greets her parents with infuriating alertness and energy, ready and eager to start every day when even the roosters are still snoozing, there's no hope of further rest until night falls once more. And yet this rude awakening is faced daily by countless parents.

Often, parents have no choice but to learn to live with this problem. But in some cases, it is possible to reset such a wayward little alarm:

Keep out the dawn's early light. Some babies (like some adults) are particularly sensitive to light when they're sleeping. Especially when the days are longer and it becomes light earlier, keeping baby's room dark can help her stay asleep longer. Invest in room-darkening shades or lined curtains, or hang a heavy blanket over the window at night.

Keep the traffic out. If your baby's window faces a street that carries a lot of traffic in the early morning hours, the noise could be waking her prematurely. Try keeping her window closed, hanging a heavy blanket or curtains at the window to help muffle sound, or moving her, if possible, to an off-street room. Or use a fan or a white-noise machine to drown out street noises.

Keep baby up later at night. It's possible that your baby is getting up earlier than she should because she's going to bed too early. Try putting her to bed ten minutes later each night until you've gradually postponed her bedtime an hour or more. To make this work, it will probably help to move her naps and meals forward simultaneously and at the same pace.

Keep baby up later during the day. Some early risers are ready to go back to sleep in an hour or two. To discourage this, postpone her return to the cot by ten minutes more each morning until she's napping an hour or so later, which may eventually help her to extend her night's sleep.

Keep daytime sleeping down. A baby needs only so much total sleep – an average of $14\frac{1}{2}$ hours at this age, with wide variations in individual babies. Maybe yours is getting too much sleep during the day and thus

needs less at night. Limit daytime naps, cutting one out or shortening all of them. But not to the point of your baby's being fatigued by the end of the day.

Keep her waiting. Don't rush to greet her at the first call from the cot. Gradually lengthen the time before you go to her, starting with five minutes – unless of course, she's screaming. If you're lucky, she may roll over and go back to sleep, or at least amuse herself for a while.

Keep a stash of toys in the cot. If keeping the room dark doesn't help, try letting the light seep through and keeping a supply of safe toys (activity centres attached to the side of the cot, stuffed but not plushy animals, which might pose a suffocation risk, and other cot-safe toys) around for your baby to play with before you rise.

Keep her waiting for breakfast. If she's used to eating at 5:30, hunger will regularly call at that time. Even if you're getting up with her then, don't feed her right away. Gradually postpone breakfast, so that she's less likely to wake up early for it.

All these efforts may, unfortunately, be in vain. Some babies just need less total sleep than others, and if yours turns out to be one of them, you may have to rise and shine early until she's old enough to get up and make her own breakfast. Until then, turning in earlier yourselves, and sharing the predawn burden by taking turns getting up with your baby (this will work only if mummy's presence isn't required for nursing), may be your best survival technique.

Still not Sleeping Through the Night

'My baby's still getting up twice a night, and she won't go back to sleep without nursing no matter how much we rock her or soothe her. Will we ever get any sleep?'

Your baby will continue to awaken several times a night for the rest of her life, as we all do. But until she learns how to fall back to sleep on her own, neither you nor she will be able to get a good night's sleep.

Helping her to fall back to sleep – with a breast, a bottle, a dummy, rocking, patting, rubbing, singing, sleep tapes – will only postpone her learning how to do it herself. But the inevitable moment will come when it will no longer be practical or possible for you to be her sandman. If you make that moment now, not only will you get more sleep, so will she.

Your first step should be to review the tips on page 117 for reducing the number of night wakings and for cutting down daytime naps. Then pick one of the following approaches to getting your baby started on the road to sleeping independence:

Cold turkey. If your baby generally wakes for a feeding once or twice a night, don't respond – let her cry it out.

Gradual withdrawal. If your baby is in the habit of waking three or four times a night, or more, or if you are just uncomfortable with cold-turkey tactics, move more slowly. Respond when she calls, but not by feeding her. Instead attempt to help her get back to sleep some other way (patting, singing, rocking). Once she can do without night feedings, start a gradual programme of letting her cry it out.

If in spite of your elaborate machinations your baby still doesn't sleep through the night, the problem probably lies with how she falls asleep at the beginning of a nap or at night. While some babies can drift off at the bottle or breast at naptime and bedtime and still manage to go back to sleep without these aids in the middle of the night, others can't. If your child is one of these, you will also have to change her going-to-bed patterns. Give feedings well before an intended nap or bedtime and then later, when she seems sleepy, try to put her into her carriage or cot drowsy but awake. Most babies will have trouble getting to sleep this way at first,

but almost all will succeed after a few chances to cry it out.

Sounds sensible – but is it possible? What if your baby invariably falls asleep feeding, whether you plan it that way or not? In these circumstances, it probably makes more sense to postpone your crusade rather than to try to rouse your babe in arms after every meal so she can fall asleep again on her own. Fortunately, as babies get older they are less likely to doze off while feeding, and you will have more opportunities to put your baby down awake. Take the opportunity whenever it comes up and eventually you will have a baby who knows how to get herself to sleep.

There are some breastfed babies who continue waking and feeding at night well into toddlerhood, not because they need the food, but because night after night they're presented with an offer they can't refuse: the comfort of nursing. And they usually continue to awaken nights as long as the offer stands. Their mothers are usually willing to sacrifice unbroken sleep to serve as round-the-clock milk dispensers until their children are weaned (at which time they apparently begin sleeping through the night, as if by magic), but it's not clear whether prolonged nighttime nursing is of any benefit to children. The babies most likely to have night waking problems are those breastfeeders who sleep with their mothers – a practice more common than most of us realize and one which can contribute, through frequent night feedings once teeth appear, to tooth decay.

Crying it Out

'Everyone is urging me to let my baby cry it out when he wakes in the night. But it seems so cruel.'

To a caring parent, programmed to respond to her baby's every need, 'crying it out' may indeed seem cruel and inhuman punishment, especially when his only crime is wanting mummy or daddy in the middle of the night. But it is actually the best way, sleep

Another Route to Sleeping Through the Night?

If you're among the softhearted or weak-nerved parents who just can't or won't listen to their babies crying it out, you may have another choice besides sleepless nights. A recent study showed that a programme called 'systematic awakening' may work as well as crying it out, though perhaps a bit more slowly. There are still a great many unanswered questions about systematic awakening – chief among them is why it works. Still, it's certainly worth a try.

Here's how: keep a diary of your baby's nighttime awakenings for a week so you will have an idea of the usual times. Then, set your alarm clock for about half an hour before you expect the first howl. At the alarm, get up, wake the baby, and proceed with what you usually do when the waking is spontaneous (change, feed, rock, or whatever). Anticipate each usual waking in the same way. Gradually expand the time between these systematic wakings and then begin to eliminate them. Within a few weeks you should be able to begin phasing them out entirely.

experts tell us, to respond to a baby's need to learn how to fall asleep on his own. Still, if you're philosophically opposed to the idea, don't try it. You probably won't stick to the game plan and the mixed signals you send will only confuse your baby, not help him sleep. Instead, let him use a back-to-sleep crutch (preferably one other than midnight snacking) for as long as necessary.

For hardier – or more desperate – souls, letting baby cry it out almost invariably works. You can use one of two approaches:

Crying it out all the way. If you can tolerate an hour or more of vigorous crying and screaming, don't go to baby, soothe him, feed him, or talk to him when he wakes up in the middle of the night. Just let him cry until he's exhausted himself – and the possibility, in his mind, that he's going to get anywhere, or anyone, by crying – and has fallen back to sleep. The next night do the same; the crying will almost certainly last a shorter time. Its duration should continue to diminish even further over the following few nights, until finally it ends completely. Your baby will have learned something that neither you nor he would have believed before: that he can go back to sleep without a nipple in his mouth or a pair of arms to rock him.

Until the dawn of that momentous morning when you awaken at 6:00 and realize you've slept through the night and that your baby seems to have, too, your nerves will probably be screaming as frantically as your baby. You may find that earplugs, the whir of the fan, or the hum of voices or music on the radio or TV can take the edge off the crying without blocking it out entirely. If you have an intercom from baby's room, the magnified crying may be particularly grating. You can reduce that problem by turning it off when the crying starts. If baby is truly hysterical, you may hear him anyway. If you can't hear him at all, set a minute timer for twenty minutes. When the buzzer rings, turn the intercom back on to see if he's still at it. Repeat this every twenty minutes until the crying stops.

If at any time your baby's crying changes and he sounds as though he might be in trouble, do check to be sure he isn't tangled in his covers or hasn't pulled up and found himself stranded, unable to get down. If he does have a problem, make him comfortable again, give him a loving pat and a few gentle words, and leave.

Crying it out, a little at a time. If you don't have the constitution to tolerate an hour's worth of heartrending pleas, let your baby cry for a few minutes (or as long as you can stand it), then go to him (or, if you're the feeding connection, have daddy go to him), reassure him with a pat and a whispered 'I love you' (without picking him up), and leave him again. Don't stay with him long enough for him to fall asleep while you're calming him. Repeat the process, extending the time you leave him alone by five minutes or more each time, until he falls asleep. The next night, extend the periods he spends by himself by a few more minutes, and continue extending them over several nights until he falls asleep after the very first period. There is a problem, however, with this approach: some babies may be unsettled by the parental visits and actually be stimulated to cry more heartily, increasing the time it will take them to fall back to sleep.

Unhappily for their parents, a few babies will not learn to fall back to sleep on their own, even when a programme of crying it out is followed with stalwart determination. Some may not be getting enough food during the day and wake up because they're really hungry in the middle of the night. For these babies, increased daytime feedings, particularly late in the day, may help. (Remember, if your baby was premature or small for gestational age, he may continue to need night feedings longer than other babies.) Others may be suffering from allergy or illness. For these babies, and any for whom night waking seems an insoluble problem, a consultation with the doctor is a must. Still others may be hypersensitive, disturbed by stimuli other babies wouldn't even notice at the normal wakings, and unable to fall back to sleep. For these babies, a carefully controlled environment – with noise, light, temperature and clothing all comfortable and conductive to sleep – can often do the trick. Others just don't need a lot of sleep and find 2 A.M. a great time to play. With these babies, parents can only hope that soon their offspring will be able to enjoy their middle-of-the-night play sessions alone.

An occasional baby always cries for a few minutes before falling asleep and also when waking at night. That's nothing to be concerned about – unless it invariably awakens you.

WHAT IT'S IMPORTANT TO KNOW:
Stimulating Your Older Baby

If stimulating a baby in the first few months of life takes ingenuity, stimulating a baby who's approaching the half-year mark takes sophistication. No longer is baby physical, emotional and intellectual putty in your hands. Now he or she is ready and able to take an active role in the learning process and to coordinate the senses – seeing what's being touched, looking for what's being heard, touching what's being tasted.

The same basic guidelines discussed in Stimulating Your Baby in the Early Months (page 159) will continue to apply as you approach the second half of baby's first year, but the kinds of activities you can provide are greatly expanded. Basically, they will be directed at these areas of development:

Large motor skills. The best way to help baby develop the large motor strength and

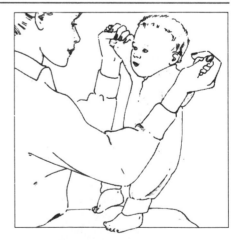

Babies love a lap to stand on. Pulling baby up to this position not only entertains, but also helps develop the leg muscles baby will need to pull up, and later stand, unassisted.

coordination necessary for sitting, crawling, walking, throwing a ball and riding a tricycle is to provide plenty of opportunity. Frequently change your baby's position – from tummy to back, from propped up to prone, from the cot to the floor – to provide the chance to practise feats of physical prowess. As your baby seems ready (which you may not know until you try), provide the opportunity to do the following:

- Stand on your lap and bounce
- Pull to sitting
- Sit in a 'frog' position
- Sit upright, propped with pillows if necessary
- Pull to standing, holding on to your fingers
- Pull to standing in a cot or playpen, or on other furniture
- Lift up on all fours
- 'Fly' through the air

Small motor skills. Developing the dexterity of baby's little fingers and hands will eventually lead to the mastering of many essential skills, such as self-feeding, drawing, writing, brushing teeth, tying shoelaces, buttoning a shirt, turning a key in a lock and so much more. Proficiency develops more quickly if babies are given ample opportunity to use their hands, to manipulate objects of all kinds, to touch, explore and experiment. The following will help hone small motor skills:

- Activity boards – a variety of activities give baby plenty of practice with small motor skills, though it will be months before most babies can conquer them all.
- Blocks – simple cubes of wood, plastic, or cloth, large or small, are appropriate at this age.
- Soft dolls and stuffed animals – handling them builds dexterity.
- Real or toy household objects – babies usually love real or toy telephones (with cords removed), mixing spoons, measuring cups, strainers, pots and pans, paper cups, empty boxes.

- Balls – of varying sizes and textures, to hold, to squeeze; they are especially fun once baby is able to sit up and roll them or crawl after them.
- Finger games – at first you'll be the one to play clap hands, patty-cake, the itsy bitsy spider and similar games, but before you know it baby will be performing some of them independently. After you do a demonstration or two, assist baby with the finger play while you sing along.

Social skills. The middle of the first year is a very sociable time for most babies. They smile, laugh, squeal and communicate in a variety of other ways and are willing to share their friendliness with all comers – most haven't yet developed 'stranger anxiety'. So this is a perfect time to encourage socialization, to expose your child to a variety of people of different ages – from other babies to elderly people. You can do this at church or synagogue, while shopping, when having friends over or while visiting them, even by having baby fraternize with his or her image in the mirror. Teach a simple greeting like 'hi' and some of the other basic social graces, such as waving bye-bye, blowing a kiss, and saying thank you.

Intellectual and language skills. Comprehension is beginning to dawn. Names (mummy's, daddy's, sibling's) are recognized first, followed by basic words ('no', 'bottle', 'bye-bye', for example), and soon thereafter, simple, often heard sentences ('Do you want to nurse?' or 'Make nice to the doggy'). This receptive language (understanding what you say) will come before spoken language. Other types of intellectual development are also on the horizon. Though it won't seem so at first, your baby is taking the first steps towards acquiring the skills of rudimentary problem solving, observation and memorization. You can help by doing the following:

How do you Speak to Your Baby Now?

Now that your baby hovers on the brink of language development, what you say to him or her takes on new meaning. It will provide the foundation for learning language, both receptive (understanding what is heard), which comes earlier, and expressive (speaking), which is slower to evolve. You can help your baby develop both kinds of language in the following ways:

Slow down. When your baby is starting to try to decode our confusing jargon, fast talk will slow his or her efforts. To give baby the chance to begin picking out words, you must speak more slowly, more clearly and more simply most of the time.

Focus on single words. Continue your running commentaries, but begin emphasizing individual words. Follow 'Now we're going to change your nappy', with 'nappy – this is your nappy', as you hold it up. At feeding time, when you say 'I'm putting juice in the cup', hold up the juice and add 'Juice, here is the juice', and the cup, and say 'cup'. In general, keep your phrasing shorter and less complex and focus primarily on words commonly used in baby's everyday life. Always pause to give baby plenty of time to decipher your words before going on to say more.

Continue to downplay pronouns. Pronouns are still confusing for your baby, so stick to 'This is mummy's book', and 'That is Jamie's doll'.

Emphasize imitation. Now that the number of sounds your baby makes is growing, so is the fun you can have imitating each other. Whole conversations can be built around a few consonants and vowels. Baby says, 'Ba-ba-ba-ba', and you come back with a profound, 'Ba-ba-ba-ba'. Baby replies, 'Da-da-da-da', and you respond, 'Da-da-da-da'. You can continue such stimulating dialogue for as long as you're both enjoying it. If baby seems receptive, you can try offering some new syllables

'Ga-ga-ga-ga', for example), encouraging imitation. But if the role reversal seems to turn baby off, switch back again. In not too many months, you'll find your baby will begin trying to imitate your words – without prompting.

Build a repertoire of songs and rhymes. You may find it tedious having to repeat the same nursery rhyme or little ditty a dozen times a day every day. Your baby, however, will not only love the repetition, but learn from it. Whether you lean on Mother Goose, Dr. Seuss, or your own creativity matters not; what counts is consistency. Now is also the time to expand the variety of music baby listens to on a record or tape player.

Use books. Baby's not ready for listening to stories yet, but simple rhymes in books with vivid pictures often catch even a young infant's attention. Do plenty of pointing out of single objects, animals, or people. Start asking, 'Where is the dog?' and eventually baby will surprise you by placing a pudgy finger right on Spot.

Wait for a response. Though baby may not be talking yet, he or she is starting to process information and often will have a response to what you say – even if it's just an excited squeal (when you've proposed a walk in the pushchair) or a pouty whimper (when you've announced it's time to come off the swing).

Be commanding. It's important for your baby to learn to follow simple commands such as 'Kiss gran', or 'Wave bye-bye', or 'Give mummy the dolly' (add 'please' if you want the word to come naturally with your baby's own requests). It won't happen right away, but don't show disappointment when baby doesn't perform. Instead, help your child to act out your request, and eventually he or she will catch on. Once that happens, beware of treating your baby like a trained seal, demanding performances of the latest 'trick' whenever there's an audience.

- Play games that stimulate the intellect (see page 312), that help baby observe cause and effect (fill a cup with water in the tub and let baby turn it over), that explain object permanence (cover a favourite toy with a cloth and then have baby look for it, or play peekaboo).

- Continue sharpening baby's auditory perception. When a plane goes by overhead or a fire engine speeds down the street, sirens screaming, point them out to baby: 'Is that an aeroplane?' or 'Do you hear the fire engine?' will help tune your child in to the world of sounds. Emphasizing and repeating the key words (aeroplane, fire engine) will also help with word recognition. Do the same when you turn on the vacuum or the water in the bathtub, when the tea kettle whistles or the doorbell or phone rings. And don't overlook those favourite funny noises – razzes on baby's belly or arm, clicks with your tongue and whistles are all educational, too, encouraging imitation, which in turn encourages language development.

- Introduce concepts. This teddy is soft, that coffee is hot, the car goes fast, you got up early, the ball is under the table. The broom is for sweeping, the water is for washing and drinking, the towel is for drying, the soap is for washing. At first your words will be meaningless to baby, but eventually, with lots of repetition, you will get the ideas across.

- Encourage curiosity and creativity. If your child wants to use a toy in an unusual way, don't be discouraging or disparaging. (Where would we be today if the parents of Edison, Einstein and Marie Curie had objected to their children doing things differently?) Give your child a chance to experiment and explore – whether that means pulling up tufts of grass in the garden or squeezing out a wet sponge in the tub. A baby will learn much more through experience than through being told.

- Encourage a love of learning. Though teaching specific facts and concepts to your child is important, equally important is teaching how to learn and imparting a love of learning.

TEN

The Seventh Month

◆

What Your Baby May be Doing

By the end of this month, your baby . . . should be able to (see Note):

- sit without support

- feed self a cracker (6¼ months)

- razz (make a wet razzing sound by 6½ months)

Note: If your baby seems not to have reached one or more of these milestones, check with the doctor. In rare instances the delay could indicate a problem, though in most cases it will turn out to be normal for your baby. Premature infants generally reach milestones later than others of the same birth age, often achieving them closer to their adjusted age (the age they would be if they had been born at term), or sometimes later.

. . . will probably be able to:

- bear some weight on legs when held upright

- object if you try to take a toy away

- work to get to a toy out of reach

- pass a cube or other object from one hand to the other

- look for dropped object

- rake a raisin and pick it up in fist

- turn in the direction of a voice (by 7⅓ months)

- babble, combining vowels and consonants such as ga-ga-ga-ga, ba-ba-ba-ba, ma-ma-ma-ma, da-da-da-da

- play peekaboo (by 7¼ months)

. . . may possibly be able to:

- stand holding on to someone or something

. . . may even be able to:

- pull up to standing position from sitting

- get into a sitting position from stomach

- play patty-cake (clap hands) or wave bye-bye

- pick up tiny object with any part of thumb and finger

What You Can Expect At This Month's Checkup

Most doctors do not schedule regular well-baby checkups this month. Do call the doctor if there are any concerns that can't wait until next month's visit. In the U.K., in most areas, a hearing test is routinely scheduled around 7–8 months, as part of a developmental check or separately.

Feeding Your Baby This Month: Moving Up From Strained Foods

Whether baby's passage to solids has been smooth sailing or bumpy and fraught with mishaps so far, another channel awaits crossing: between strained foods and coarser textures. And whether baby has proven to be an eager and adventurous gourmand or a hard-to-please, fussy eater, whether he or she is a veteran solids feeder or a newcomer to the high chair, that crossing is better made now than later on in the first year, when new experiences are more likely to encounter obstreperous rebuffs.

But the time has not yet arrived for a family junket to your favourite steak house. Even when the first couple of teeth are in place, babies continue to chew with their gums – which are no match for a hunk of meat. For now, coarsely puréed or mashed foods, which have just a touch more texture than strained, will fill the bill of baby's fare.

You can use the commercial 'junior' or 'stage 2' foods, or mash baby's meals from what you serve the family, as long as they have been prepared without added salt or sugar. You can try homemade porridge thinned with milk (but remember, unlike baby porridge, it usually has no added iron); mashed small-curd cottage cheese (preferably unsalted, see footnote on page 252); scraped apple or pear (scrape tiny bits of fruit into a dish with a knife); mashed or coarsely puréed cooked fruit (such as apples, apricots, peaches, plums); and vegetables (such as carrots, sweet and white potatoes, cauliflower, squash). By seven months, you can usually add meat and skinless poultry (puréed, ground, or minced very fine) and small flakes of soft fish. When the doctor okays starting egg yolk (it will probably be suggested you wait on the white, which is very allergenic), serve it hard-cooked and mashed, scrambled, or as French toast or pancakes, and serve it at the same meal as a vitamin C food, such as orange juice, to facilitate iron absorption. Watch out for strings from fruits (such as bananas and mangos), vegetables (such as broccoli, string beans and kale) and meats. And be sure to check fish very carefully for bones that might be left after mashing.

Some babies can also handle bread and crackers by seven months, but make your selections carefully. They should be whole grain, prepared without added sugar or salt, and have a melt-in-the-mouth texture. Ideal starters are wholemeal bagels that have been frozen (they're hard, but whatever baby manages to scrape off will be mushy) and unsalted rice cakes (they crumble easily but dissolve on the tongue, and though not very tasty are loved by most babies). Once these are handled well, baby is ready for whole-grain breads. To decrease the risk of choking, remove crusts and serve sliced bread in cubes and rolls or loaves in hunks; avoid commercial white breads, which tend to turn pasty when wet and can cause gagging or choking. Give bread and crackers – and all finger foods – only when your baby is seated and only under your supervision. And be sure you know how to deal with a choking incident (see pages 447 and 448).

What You May Be Concerned About

Biting Nipples

'My daughter now has two teeth and seems to think it's fun to use them for biting my nipples during nursing.'

There's no need to let your baby have her fun at your expense. Since a baby can't bite while actively nursing (her tongue comes between teeth and breast), biting usually signals that she's had enough milk and is now just toying with you. It's possible the fun began when she accidentally bit down on your nipple, you let out a yelp, she giggled, you couldn't help laughing, and she continued the game – biting you, watching for a reaction, smirking at your mock 'no', and seeing through your feeble attempts to keep a straight face.

So resist the temptation to laugh, and let her know that her biting you is not acceptable by issuing a firm but not harsh 'no' and by removing her from the breast. If she tries to hang on to your nipple, use your finger to break her grip. After a few such episodes, she'll catch on and give up.

It is important to nip the biting habit now, to avoid more serious biting problems later. It's not too soon for her to learn that while teeth are made for biting, there are things that are appropriate to clamp down on (a teething ring, a piece of bread, a banana) and things that are not (mother's breast, brother's finger, daddy's shoulder).

Spoiling Baby

'I pick my baby up the minute he cries, and end up carrying him around with me much of the day. Am I spoiling him?'

Though sparing the rod won't spoil your child (in fact, experts recommend that it be spared almost without exception), carrying him around with you all day at this age may. By the seventh month babies are already expert mummy manipulators; mothers who play 'baby taxi' – picking the little ones up the moment they are hailed by a pathetic wave of the arm – can count on being 'on duty' throughout their baby waking hours.

There are societies where babies are carried around, usually strapped to mummy, round the clock, but ours is not one of them. Here, a baby is expected to gain some measure of independence early on – through learning to entertain himself for at least short periods of time. This not only gives his mother a chance to attend to her own needs or other responsibilities, but also increases a baby's self-esteem by reinforcing the idea that he is good company. It also begins to teach him that other people have rights and needs, another important concept to grasp early on.

Assuming you don't want to spoil your baby, or that you want to unspoil him, now's the time to start a little manipulating of your own. Try the following, staying casually cool throughout. If your baby senses that you expect this to be an anxiety-provoking experience, he will try all the harder to fulfill your prophecy:

- First of all, determine if your baby is nagging to be carried because he really isn't getting quality attention. Have you actually sat down to play with him several times during the day – to read a book, play with an activity toy, or practice pulling up – or has most of your interaction consisted of dropping him in the playpen with a toy, strapping him in the car seat and driving to the shops, leaving him in the baby swing while you start dinner, picking him up in response to his crying and carting him around while you go about your business? If so, your baby has probably come to the conclusion that being carried around all day by you, while not very stimulating, is better than getting no attention at all.

- Next, see if your baby has physical needs. Is his nappy soiled? Is it time for lunch? Is he thirsty? Tired? If so, satisfy his needs, then go on to the next step.

- Move him to a new location: the playpen, if he was in the cot; the walker, if he was in the playpen; the floor, if he was in the walker. This may satisfy his wanderlust.

- Be sure he has toys or objects to entertain him – pots and pans, a cuddly stuffed animal, or an activity board – you know what he likes. Since his attention span is short, have two or three playthings within reach; too many toys at his disposal, however, will overwhelm and frustrate him. Provide a fresh selection when he seems to be getting restless.

- If he continues to complain, try distracting him, getting down on his level for a moment, but not picking him up. Show him how to bang on a pot with the wooden spoon, point out 'eyes-nose-mouth' on the stuffed animal, spin the cylinder and turn the dial on the busy box to get him started and challenge him to do the same.

- If he's momentarily diverted, and even if he's still voicing halfhearted objections, tell him you have work to do and move off to do it without hesitation. Stay within view, chatting or singing to him if it seems to help; but move out of eyeshot (but not earshot and only if he's in a safe playpen or cot) if your presence increases his dissatisfaction. Before you do, poke your head around a corner, playing peekaboo, to show him that when you disappear, you return.

- Leave him to his own devices a little longer each time, letting him object a little longer if necessary. But always return to his side before he starts screaming, to reassure him, and start the process over. Postpone picking him up for as long as you can, but don't get into a battle of wills – he'll almost always win. If you wait until he's screaming to pick him up, he'll conclude that that's the way to get attention.

- Don't feel guilty or anxious about not picking him up or playing with him every minute of the day. If you do, you'll be transmitting the message that playing alone is punishment and can't be fun, that there's something wrong with solitude. As long as you do spend plenty of time playing with him, some time apart will actually benefit both of you.

Baby's Still not Sleeping Through the Night

'My baby seems to be the only one of her peers who's not sleeping through the night yet. Will she ever?'

All babies wake up during the night and most, by this time, have acquired the ability to fall back to sleep on their own. Unfortunately, this is not something you can teach your daughter to do, the way you teach her to play peekaboo or wave bye-bye; it's something she must learn by herself. And the only way she'll be able to learn is if you give her the chance. That means not nursing her, giving her a bottle, rocking her, or using any other method to help her get back to sleep when she wakes up crying at night, but letting her struggle to fall back to sleep without your help. It may take her a few nights, even a week, to learn this skill – but rarely more than that.

If you've never tried the tips for helping baby sleep through the night on page 253, or if you tried them earlier and they didn't work or you caved in before baby did, now is the time to try or try again. The odds are very good that if you do, you'll all be sleeping as soundly as the rest of the neighbourhood very soon.

Grandparents Spoiling Baby

'My parents live nearby and see my daughter several times a week. When they do, they stuff her with sweets and give in to her every whim. I love them, but I don't love the way they spoil her.'

Grandparents have the best of all worlds: they can have the joy of spoiling a baby without the misery of living with the consequences. They can watch with pleasure as their grandchild relishes the sugary biscuits they've plied her with, but don't have to struggle with a fussy – and unhungry – baby come mealtime. They can keep her up through her naptime, so they'll have more time to play, but don't have to deal with her crankiness afterwards.

Is it an inalienable right of grandparents to spoil their grandchildren? To some extent, yes. They've paid their dues as the heavies during your childhood, weaning you from your precious bottle, cajoling you to eat the spinach you despised, battling with you over curfews. Now that it's your turn to play the heavy, they've earned the cushy job of spoilers. There should, however, be some sensible guidelines agreed upon by all:

● Wider latitude can be given to grand-parents whose longitude is distant from yours. Occasional grandparents – those who see your baby only two or three times a year, on holidays or special oc-casions – can't possibly spoil her, but should be given almost every opportu-nity to try. If baby misses a nap or stays up past her bedtime when your folks are on a one-day, half-birthday visit, or if she is toted around royally much more than you'd prefer while visiting them for the holidays, don't worry. Let everyone enjoy these infrequent lapses and rest assured that your daughter will quickly return to her normal routine afterwards.

● Grandparents who live near Rome should do as the Romans do – most of the time. It is possible for grandparents who live in the same town, and especially for those who live in the same house, to spoil a baby, making life miserable not only for the baby's parents, but for baby as well. Mixed signals – mother won't pick her up at every whimper, grand-mother will – make for a confused and unhappy baby. On the other hand, a baby will readily learn that the ground rules can vary with the territory: she can mush the food all over the table at grandmother's, but not at home. So some leeway, in areas of lesser con-sequence, needs to be allowed even close-by grandparents.

● Certain parental rules must be inviolate. Since it's the parents who live with their child on a 24-hour-a-day basis, it's the parents who must lay down the law on more significant issues – and it's the grandparents, near or far, who must abide by those rules, even if they don't necessarily agree with them. In one fa-mily, a bone of contention may be the bedtime hour; in another, sugar and junk foods in the diet; in yet another, what the children are permitted to watch on TV (not an issue yet with a seven-month-old but one that will enter the picture soon enough). Of course, if the parents wish to stand firm on every issue, then the grandparents should be allowed to ne-gotiate on occasion.

● Certain grandparental rights must be inviolate. The right to give gifts, for ex-ample, that the parents might not have chosen – either because they're very expensive, or frivolous, or, in the parents' opinion, tasteless. And to give them more often than mummy and daddy might. (Though gifts that are unsafe should be taboo and those that violate parental values should be negotiated prior to purchase.) In general, to indulge (yes, spoil) their grandchildren with a little extra of everything – love, time, material things. But not to the point where this spoiling regularly violates parental rules.

What if grandparents overstep the bound-aries of fair grandparenting? What if they ignore or openly flout all the rules you have so thoughtfully set up and try consistently to follow? Then it's time to open an honest dialogue. Keep the exchange on a loving and light level – but if any of your differ-ences centre on life-and-death issues (your father refuses to recognize the importance of using the car seat to go around the corner, your mother-in-law smokes while holding the baby in her arms), emphasize the seriousness of the problem. Explain (even if you have before) how much you want them to spend time with the baby, but how their breaking the rules you've estab-lished is confusing her and upsetting her schedule and the family equilibrium. Tell them you are willing to be flexible on certain issues, but that on others they will have to do the bending. If that doesn't work, leave this book, open to 'Grand-parents Spoiling Baby', in a place where they can't miss it.

Is My Baby Gifted?

'I don't want to be a pushy mother. But I don't want to neglect my daughter's talents if she's gifted. How can you tell an ordinary bright baby from a gifted one?'

Every child is gifted in some way. Musically. Socially. Athletically. Artistically. Mechanically. And whatever talent emerges in a child, it's important for parents to encourage its development, to praise the child for it, and not to wish it could be a talent they valued more. This encouragement should come as soon as the gift becomes apparent – which might even be in the first year. But encouraging is very different from demanding and pushing, neither of which is good for your child.

When most people talk about the 'gifted' child, however, they mean a child who excels intellectually. Even among those who are blessed with exceptional intellectual ability, there are differences. Some children are good with numbers, others with spatial relations, still others with words. Some are creative; others are great at organization. Many, but not all, of these talents can later be measured by intelligence testing, but all are difficult to recognize in infancy. Tests of motor development, most often used to evaluate IQ in the first year, do not correlate well with a child's IQ later on. Tests that evaluate a baby's ability to process information and manipulate the environment do correlate, but are not widely available. Still, there are clues to intelligence in the first year that you can look for in your own baby:

Uniformly advanced development. A baby who does everything 'early' – smiles, sits, walks, talks, picks up objects with a pincer grasp and so on – is probably going to continue to develop at an advanced clip, and may turn out to be truly gifted. Though early language ability, particularly the use of unusual words before the end of the first year, is the trait noted most frequently by parents in their gifted children, and is probably indicative of high intelligence, some gifted children are not verbal until fairly late.

Good memory and powers of observation. Gifted children often amaze their parents with the things they remember, often long before most babies have exhibited much memory at all. And when things differ from what they recollect (mummy's had her hair cut, daddy's wearing a new coat, grandad's wearing a patch on his eye after surgery), they notice immediately.

Creativity and originality. Though most babies under a year are not competent problem solvers, the gifted child may surprise parents by being able to figure out a way to get to a toy that's stuck behind a chair, reach a high shelf in the bookcase (pile up books from lower shelves to climb on, perhaps), or use sign language for a word that's beyond their linguistic abilities (such as pointing to her own nose to indicate that the animal in the book is an elephant, or to her ears if it's a rabbit). The baby on the way to being a gifted child may also be creative in play, using toys in unusual ways, using non-toys creatively as playthings, enjoying playing 'pretend'.

Sense of humour. Even in the first year, a bright child will notice and laugh at the incongruities in life: grandmother wearing her glasses on top of her head or daddy tripping over the dog and spilling his glass of juice, for example.

Curiosity and concentration. While all babies are intensely curious, the very gifted are not only curious, but have the persistence and concentration to explore what it is they are curious about.

Ability to make connections. The gifted child, more so and earlier than other children, will see relationships between things and will be able to apply old knowledge to new situations. A baby nine or ten months old may see in the store a book that daddy's been reading at home and say, 'Dada'. Or, accustomed to pushing the button for the lift in her apartment house, she sees a lift in a store and looks for the button.

Rich imagination. Before a year, the gifted child may be able to pretend (to drink a cup of coffee or to rock a baby) and soon after that may become heavily involved in making up stories, games, pretend friends and so on.

Difficulty sleeping. Gifted children may be so involved in observing and learning that they have trouble tuning out the world so they sleep – a trait that can exasperate parents.

Perceptiveness and sensitivity. Very early the gifted child may notice when mummy is sad or angry, may note that daddy has a boo-boo (because he's wearing a band-aid on his finger), may try to cheer up a crying sibling.

Even if your baby displays many or all of these traits, it's much too early to tag her with the 'gifted' label. What she needs now is not to be labelled, but to be loved. You can, of course, encourage her growth and development by being certain you raise her in a stimulating environment. Read to her, talk to her, play with her. But don't just pay attention to the talents you would like to see her develop – linguistic or musical, perhaps. Rather concern yourself with her overall development – physical and social as well as intellectual. As she grows, let her know that you love her not because of her special gifts, but because she's your child, and that you would never withdraw that love if she stopped being 'smart'. Encourage her to be kind and caring and to appreciate others, including those with fewer or different gifts.

Snacking

'My baby seems to want to eat all the time. How much snacking is good for her?'

With their own mothers' pronouncements about snacking ('Not before dinner, dear – it'll spoil your appetite!') still ringing in their ears, today's mothers are often reluctant to dole out between-meal goodies to their children on demand, even as they them-selves choose to graze through their day's nutritional requirements. Yet snacks, in moderation, do play an important role in the lives of babies and children.

Snacks are a learning experience. At mealtimes, baby usually is spoon-fed from a bowl; at snacktime she has the opportunity to pick up a piece of bread or cracker with her fingers and get it to and into her mouth herself – no small accomplishment considering how tiny her mouth is and how primitive her coordination.

Snacks fill a void. Babies have small stomachs that fill quickly and empty quickly, and can rarely last from meal to meal, as adults can, without a snack in between. And as solids become the most significant part of your baby's diet, snacks will be needed to round out nutritional requirements. You'll find it almost impossible to give baby her Daily Dozen in just three meals a day.

Snacks give baby a break. Like most of us, babies need a break from the tedium of work or play (their play *is* their work), and a snack provides this breather.

Snacks provide oral gratification. Babies are still very orally oriented – everything they pick up goes right to the mouth. Snacking gives them a welcome chance to put things in their mouths without being chastised.

Snacks smooth the way for weaning. If you didn't offer your baby a snack in the form of solids, the odds are good she would insist on one in the form of a breast or a bottle. Snacks will lessen the need to nurse frequently and eventually help to make weaning a reality.

For all its virtues, however, snacking can have some drawbacks. To reap the benefits of snacking without stumbling into the pit-falls, remember these pointers:

Snacks by the clock. Mum was right – snacks that come too close to mealtime can interfere with a baby's appetite for meals. Make an attempt to schedule snacks about midway between meals to avoid this problem. Non-stop snacking gets baby accustomed to having something in her mouth all the time, a habit that could be hazardous to the waistline should it be perpetuated into childhood and adulthood. And having the mouth continuously full of food can also lead to tooth decay – even a healthy starch like wholemeal bread turns to sugar when exposed to saliva in the mouth. One snack in the morning, one in the afternoon, and if there's a long span between dinner and bedtime, one in the evening should suffice. Make an exception, of course, if a meal is going to be delayed longer than usual.

Snack for the right reasons. There are good reasons to snack (as discussed above) and not-so-good reasons. Avoid offering snacks if baby's bored (distract her with a toy), hurt (soothe her with a hug and a song), or has accomplished something that should be rewarded (try verbal praise and an enthusiastic round of applause).

Snack in place. Snacking should be treated pretty much as seriously as mealtime eating. For reasons of safety (a baby eating lying on her back, crawling around, or walking can choke too easily), etiquette (good table manners are best learned at the table), and consideration to the housekeeper (you, or whoever does the cleaning, will appreciate not finding crumbs and spills in every nook and cranny), snacks should be given while baby is sitting, preferably in her feeding chair. Of course, if you're out and baby is in her pushchair or car seat at snacktime, you can serve it up there. But don't give her the idea that a snack is her compensation for serving time in these confining quarters; getting into pushchair or car should not be a signal to bring on the crackers.

Grazing

'I've heard that grazing is the healthiest way for anyone to eat, particularly a young child. Should I feed my son this way?'

Long before grazing became fashionable among adults, it was the preferred way of gastronomic life for young children. Presented with the option, many babies would choose to snack the day away, nibbling crackers and sipping juice as they play and never actually sitting down to a square meal. But though some experts propose that this is a healthier choice than the conventional one of three substantial meals supplemented by light snacks, others disagree. Consider the following:

Grazing interferes with proper nutrition. A heifer who grazes in fields of clover gets most of the nourishment she needs that way. But while it's possible that a baby who does nothing but graze all day on favourite finger foods will get his Daily Dozen, it's not likely. Nutritional requirements are filled much more efficiently when meals are taken, along with two or three nutritious snacks.

Grazing interferes with play. Always having a cracker or breadstick in hand (like always having a bottle) limits the amount and kind of playing and exploring a baby can do. And as baby becomes mobile, crawling or toddling around with food becomes dangerous because of the risk of choking.

Grazing interferes with sociability. A baby who's always got food in his mouth can't practice his social skills or his language skills and also misses out on the social experience of mealtime.

Grazing interferes with the development of good table manners. Children won't learn table manners munching a biscuit on the sofa, sipping milk on the bed, or savouring cheese on the carpet.

Not Sitting Yet

'My baby hasn't started sitting up yet, and I'm worried that she's slow for her age.'

Because normal babies accomplish different developmental feats at different ages, there's a wide range of 'normal' for every milestone. Though the 'average' baby sits unsupported somewhere around six and a half months, some normal babies sit as early as four months, others not until nine. And since your child has a long way to go before she reaches the outer limits of that range, you certainly needn't worry about her lagging behind.

A child is programmed by genetic factors to sit, and to accomplish other major developmental skills, at a certain age. Though there may not be much a parent can do to speed up the timetable, there are ways to avoid slowing it down. A baby who is propped up often at an early age, in either an infant seat, a pushchair, or a high chair, gets a lot of practice in a sitting position before she's able to support herself and may sit sooner. On the other hand, a baby who spends a majority of her time lying on her back or harnessed in a baby carrier, and is rarely propped to sit, may sit very late. In fact, babies in primitive countries who are carried constantly in baby carriers at their mothers' breast often stand before they sit, so accustomed are they to the upright position. Another factor that might interfere with the development of early sitting (and other large motor skills) is overweight. A roly-poly baby is more likely than a leaner child to roll over when attempting a sitting position.

As long as you're giving your baby plenty of opportunity to reach her goal, chances are she will sometime during the next two months. If she doesn't, and/or if you feel she's developing slowly in several other ways, consult her doctor.

Tooth Stains

'My daughter's two teeth seem to be stained a greyish colour. Could they be decaying already?'

Chances are what's keeping your baby's pearly whites a dismal grey isn't decay, but iron. Some children who take a liquid vitamin and mineral supplement that contains iron develop staining on their teeth. This doesn't harm the teeth in any way and will disappear when your child stops taking liquid and begins taking chewable vitamins. In the meantime, brushing your baby's teeth or cleaning them with gauze (see page 246) right after giving her supplement will help minimize staining.

If your baby hasn't been taking a liquid supplement, and especially if she's been doing a lot of sucking on a bottle of formula or juice at bedtime, the discolouration might suggest either decay, trauma, or a congenital defect in the tooth enamel. Discuss this with her doctor or a paediatric dentist as soon as possible.

Baby's Misbehaving with You

'The baby-sitter tells me that my baby is just wonderful with her, but he always starts to act up the minute I walk in the door after work. I feel like I must be a terrible mother.'

Like most babies his age, your baby's already learning how to be manipulative. And like most good mummies, you're falling right into his trap. Even at this tender stage, albeit at a very fundamental level, your baby is shrewd enough to see that playing the abandoned and neglected victim is the best way to guarantee that he'll get an extra dose of love and attention when you arrive home. He plays on your insecurities, instills the guilt, and gets what he wants – which is probably what you'd give him anyway, but he's not taking any chances.

The fact that most babies and toddlers, and even older children, are more likely to act up with their parents than with other caretakers is a sign that they are more comfortable and secure with their parents. They know they can let their emotions show without risking loss of love. But this acting up isn't always random – it often has a purpose. Not only does it get and keep parental attention, but it also is a way of testing limits: 'How far can I go before mummy (or daddy) explodes or gives in?' The baby who cries for a middle-of-the-night feeding is doing that. So is the one who smears the mashed carrots in his hair, or keeps dropping toys out of his playpen. And the one who repeatedly manoeuvres his walker to the brink of the stairway – the one area he's forbidden to explore.

A certain amount of manipulation is not only normal, it's probably healthy, giving a child a chance to exercise some control over his environment. But when it gets out of hand, it can be detrimental to emotional growth. So go along with your baby when it seems to make sense – when he really needs your attention and he's letting you know you're not giving it. But do set the limits you think are important for his health and safety and for your sanity, and stick to them.

WHAT IT'S IMPORTANT TO KNOW:
Raising A Superbaby

We've seen their photographs on the covers of major magazines and watched them perform on television talk shows. With an odd mixture of curiosity, disapproval and envy we've listened as their proud parents described their incredible accomplishments: reading words at six months, books at a year, *The Times* at two. We wonder how anyone could push their baby so intensely. And we wonder whether we should be doing the same with our own.

The Superbaby concept has undeniably made a significant splash in the media, even a few waves among the general public, and in some communities has reached tidal proportions. Programmes and books that dedicate themselves to the raising of these tiniest of wunderkinds have proliferated – there is even an institute devoted to this purpose. But among the most reliable experts in the field of child development, the proposition that babies and children should be pushed to achieve way beyond their normal rate of development has yet to make a ripple. That's because scientifically there's no evidence that such programmes are beneficial, or even that they work. Though it's possible to teach an infant a wide variety of skills long before they are ordinarily learned, including how to recognize words, there is no proven consistent method for doing so. Nor is there any evidence that intense early learning actually provides a long-term advantage over more traditional

learning patterns. Studies of extremely successful adults in such vastly different fields as music, athletics and medicine have shown that not only did their acquisition of skills in their fields not begin early in childhood, but when it did begin, it was more likely to have taken the form of play than serious, high-pressured activity.

Babies have lots to learn in the first year of life – more, in fact, than they'll be expected to learn in the first year of school. During these twelve busy months, their agenda will include building attachments to others (mummy, daddy, siblings, baby-sitter and so on), learning to trust ('When I'm in trouble, I can depend on mummy or daddy to help me'), and grasping the concept of object permanence ('When mummy hides behind the chair, she's still there, even though I don't see her'). They'll also need to learn to use their bodies (to sit, stand, walk), their hands (to pick up and drop, as well as to manipulate), and their minds (solving problems such as how-to-get-that-truck-from-the-shelf-I-can't-reach); the meanings of hundreds of words and how to reproduce them using a complicated combination of voice box, lips and tongue; and something about who they are ('What kind of person am I, what do I like, what don't I like, what makes me happy or sad?'). With such a heavy course load lined up already, it's probable that adding supplementary learning material would force one or more of these critical scheduled developmental areas to be neglected.

Though few parents would force a child to stand before he appeared ready and eager, many wouldn't hesitate to push a mental accomplishment such as reading. Why? Maybe because it's easier to imagine injury to a leg pushed too far than injury to an overworked mind. Or maybe because, in some homes, more value is placed on intellectual than on physical achievement.

Parents who are tempted to try to produce a superbaby, in spite of the clear stack of sentiment against early learning programmes in the child development community, should ask themselves the following questions:

- What's my goal? To make my child feel superior to other children? (Will such a feeling serve him or her well through life?) To provide early access to education – university at twelve? (And then what? What of the emotional impact and psychological stigma of being a child in college?) There is no evidence that the lives of child prodigies are richer and more fulfilling than those of children who are not pushed (in fact, there have been instances where the lives of child 'geniuses' have been disastrous). Even early on, parents and others tend to judge these superbabies by their success at learning what they are taught rather than for who they are as individuals.

- Am I motivated by fear that my child will not do well in today's highly competitive academic world without such early preparation? While it's true that children who learn to read before starting school often continue to read ahead of their age group, a child with a rich reading preparation background (exposure to the alphabet, songs and stories, and a variety of enriching experiences), who doesn't start deciphering words until formal education begins, can catch up quickly and do equally well.

- Am I uncomfortable with babies and children? Some people, unable to bring themselves down to the level of their babies (because they don't have the knack for baby talk, for example), want to bring their children up to their own level as soon as possible. But babies need their babyhood, and with some effort, it may be fairer for you to meet them down where they are than to drag them up to you.

- How would pushing one area of my child's development language, for example, through reading – impact on other areas? Will you have time to help your child develop socially (through playgroups or at the playground) and physically (with opportunities to climb a slide, throw a ball, jump down a step), and to encourage his or her growing curiosity (about everything from a dust ball on the floor to clouds in the sky)? Not every adult is 'well-rounded' or needs to be – but children need to understand their strengths and weaknesses, to uncover and explore every possible avenue to personal fulfillment, before sorting out those dimensions of self they most want to develop. This is a selection that should be made by the child, not the parents, and certainly not in the first year.

Even the parent who decides not to try to create a superbaby can produce a pretty terrific child, one who reaches his or her maximum potential at a rate that's personally appropriate, by offering ample stimulation and assistance in the ordinary tasks of infancy; by exposing him or her to a variety of settings (stores, zoos, museums, gas stations, parks and so on); by talking about people you see ('That lady is very old', 'That man has to ride around in a chair because he has a boo-boo on his leg', 'Those children are going to school'); and by describing how things work ('See, I turn on the tap and water comes out of the spout'), what they are used for ('This is a chair – you sit in a chair'), and how they differ ('The horse has a long flowing tail and the pig has a little curly one'). It's more important for your baby to know that a dog barks, eats, can bite, has four legs and has hair all over than to be able to recognize that the letters d-o-g spell dog.

If your baby does show an interest in words, letters, or numbers, by all means nurture that interest. But don't suddenly forsake trips to the playground so you and baby can spend all your time with flashcards. Learning – whether it's how to recognize a letter or how to throw a ball – should be fun. But there is little fun for either of you in a pressurized environment in which you're faced with a never-ending list of goals that must be met. Take your cues from your baby, let him or her set the pace, and if your little scholar seems unhappy at any activity, it's time to switch gears.

Children gain confidence from learning what is important to them, not what's important to their parents. The message that what mummy (or daddy) wants me to do is more important than what I want to do can deal a major blow to self-respect. So can failure to perform up to mummy's or daddy's expectations, realistic or not. In the long run, whether children learn to like and respect themselves is much more important than whether they learn to read or play piano in toddlerhood.

ELEVEN

The Eighth Month

◆

What Your Baby May Be Doing

By the end of this month, your baby . . . should be able to (see Note):

- bear some weight on legs when held upright

- feed self a cracker

- pass a cube or other object from one hand to the other (usually by 8½ months)

- rake a raisin and pick it up in fist

- turn in the direction of a voice (by 8⅓ months)

- look for a dropped object

Note: If your baby seems not to have reached one or more of these milestones, check with the doctor. In rare instances the delay could indicate a problem, though in most cases it will turn out to be normal for your baby. Premature infants generally reach milestones later than others of the same birth age, often achieving them closer to their adjusted age (the age they would be if they had been born at term) or sometimes later.

. . . will probably be able to:

- stand holding on to someone or something (8½ months)

- object if you try to take a toy away

- work to get a toy out of reach

- play peekaboo

- get into a sitting position from stomach

By the eighth month, a few babies can pick up small objects using the thumb and forefinger.

. . . may possibly be able to:

- pull up to standing position from sitting

- pick up tiny object with any part of thumb and finger

- say mama or dada indiscriminately

. . . may even be able to:

- play patty-cake (clap hands) or wave bye-bye

- walk holding on to furniture

- stand alone momentarily

- understand the word no (but not always obey it)

What You Can Expect At This Month's Checkup

Most doctors do not schedule regular well-baby checkups this month. Do call the doctor if there are any concerns that can't wait until next month's visit.

Feeding Your Baby This Month: Finally – Finger Foods

For most mothers, the novelty of feeding their babies soon wears as thin as the rice cereal they've been struggling to direct into those little mouths. The lips clenched willfully, the head turned away just at the critical moment (splat!), the pudgy hand grabbing the spoon and overturning it just before it reaches its destination, and the sheer tedium of repeating this messy ritual three times a day, every day, makes these mothers ready to relinquish the role they couldn't wait to take on a few months earlier. Fortunately, the opportunity to do so presents itself fairly quickly. Most babies are not only eager but able to begin finger foods by the time they are seven months old, some even earlier.

The transition is more sudden than gradual. Once babies discover they can get food into their mouths independently, the number of foods that they can expertly express to the mouth increases rapidly. At first, most babies hold the rice cake or piece of bread in the fist and munch on it that way, not having learned yet to coordinate individual fingers for pickup and transport. When the problem of how to get that last piece of food wrapped tightly in the palm into the mouth arises, they may demonstrate their frustration with a tearful outburst. The solution for some is to open the hand flat against the mouth, for others to put the food down and pick it up again with more of it exposed.

The ability to position an object between thumb and forefinger in the pincer grip doesn't develop in most babies until between nine and twelve months of age – though some perfect their pincers earlier and others later. Once this skill is mastered, it allows a baby to pick up very small objects, such as peas and pennies, and bring them to the mouth, considerably expanding the dining repertoire – and the risk of choking.

Learning to handle finger foods is usually the first step on the road to dinner-table independence. At first, finger foods merely supplement a young child's diet; as facility with self-feeding grows, a large proportion of the daily intake will be delivered by baby's own hand. Some will learn to wield a spoon respectably well by the middle of the second year or even sooner, and will switch to this more civilized style of eating; others will continue to get most of their meals to their mouths (even such dubious finger fare as cereal and cottage cheese) via the fingers for a long time to come. A few, usually those who were never allowed to 'do it themselves' because of the time or mess involved, will insist on being fed long after they are capable of feeding themselves.

The foods that qualify for first finger-food honours are those that baby can gum to swallowable consistency or that will dissolve in the mouth without chewing, and that have been well received in puréed form on earlier tries. Most of these foods should be cut into manageable cubes or chunks – pea-size for firmer items, marble-size for softer foods. Good choices include a wholemeal bagel, wholemeal bread or toast, rice cakes or other crackers that become mushy in the mouth; oat cereals (best are the varieties made without added salt or sugar, found in health-food stores), corn and wheat puffs;

tiny cubes of natural cheese, such as baby Swiss, Cheddar, Edam, Havarti; chunks of ripe banana, very ripe pear, peach, apricot, cantaloupe, honeydew, or mango; small chunks of cooked-to-very-tender carrot, white or sweet potato, yam, broccoli or cauliflower (flowerets only), peas (cut in half or crushed); flakes of grilled, baked, or poached fish (but screen *carefully* for bones); soft meatballs (cook in sauce or soup so they don't get crusty); well-cooked pasta of various sizes and shapes (break up before or cut after cooking, as necessary) if they contain no ingredients that baby isn't allowed yet; scrambled or hard-cooked egg yolk, and whole eggs once baby can have the whites; cubes of soft-cooked French toast or wholemeal pancakes (again, made at first with yolk only, then as whites are introduced, with whole eggs). About the same time you add finger foods, you can add more texture to the other foods baby is eating by using commercial toddler foods, or table foods that are chopped or mashed but that contain small, soft chunks baby can gum.

To serve finger foods, scatter four or five pieces on to an unbreakable plate or directly on to baby's feeding tray, and replace as baby eats them. Beginner eaters, confronted by too much food, especially all in one spot, may respond either by trying to stuff all of it in their mouth at once or by sending it all to the floor with one deft swipe. As with other foods, finger foods should be fed only to a baby who is seated, and not to

one who is crawling, cruising, or toddling around.

Because of the danger of choking, don't give your baby foods that won't dissolve in the mouth, can't be mashed with the gums, or can be easily sucked into the windpipe – such as uncooked raisins, popcorn, nuts, whole peas, raw firm-fleshed vegetables (carrots, peppers) or fruits (apples, unripe pears), chunks of meat or poultry, or hot dogs (which, with their high sodium and additive content, aren't meant for babies anyway).

Once the molars come in (the first teeth are for biting, and don't improve your child's ability to chew), somewhere around the end of the year for early teethers, some foods that require real chewing can be added, such as raw apples and other firm-fleshed raw fruits and vegetables, small slices of meat and poultry (cut across the grain), uncooked raisins (soft and fresh, squashed at first), and seedless or seeded grapes (skinned and halved). But hold off for many months on such frequent troublemakers as carrots, popcorn, nuts and hot dogs. Introduce them only when your baby is chewing well.

No matter what the texture, there are some types of food that should not be introduced to your baby at all, now or later: junk foods that offer no nutrition, foods prepared with added sugar or salt, and refined breads or cereals. They will certainly be introduced eventually outside the home, but by then your child will know they aren't acceptable everyday fare.

What You May Be Concerned About

Baby's First Words

'My baby has started saying "ma-ma" a lot. We were all excited until my neighbour said that she's just making sounds without understanding their meaning. Is she right?'

Only your baby knows for sure, and she isn't telling, at least not yet. Just when a baby makes the transition from sounds that mimic

real words but have no meaning to meaningful speech is difficult to pinpoint exactly. Your baby may just be practising her 'm' sounds now, or she may be calling for mummy, but it really doesn't matter which. The important thing is that she's vocalizing and attempting to imitate sounds she hears. Many babies, of course, say 'da-da' first – not a sign of favouritism, just a reflection of the consonant a baby has found easiest to pronounce initially.

In many languages the informal words for male and female parents sound very similar. Daddy, pappa, papa, abba. Mummy, mama, mommy, imma. It's a good bet that they all developed from babies' earliest mouthing of syllables, picked up on by eager parents trying to recognize their baby's first word. When, long ago, a young Spanish baby uttered her first 'maa-maa', complaining in the fashion typical of babies, her proud mother probably was certain she was calling 'madre'. And when an early Hebrew infant first vocalized 'ah-ba', his father probably puffed up his chest and said, 'He's trying to say av'.

When the first real word is spoken varies a great deal – and is, of course, subject to less-than-objective parental interpretation. According to the experts, the average baby can be expected to say what she means and mean what she says for the first time anywhere between ten and fourteen months. A small percentage of children start a couple of months earlier and some perfectly normal babies don't utter a single recognizable word until midway through their second year, at least as far as anyone can tell. Often, however, a baby may already be using syllables, alone and in combination, to represent objects, 'ba' for bottle, 'ba-ba' for bye-bye, or 'daw' for dog), but her parents may not be tuned in enough to notice until the enunciation becomes clearer. A child who is very busy developing motor skills – one who, perhaps, crawls and walks early, is involved in learning to climb stairs and ride a fire engine – may be slower than less active babies in starting to vocalize. This is nothing to worry about as long as it's clear from her behaviour that she understands a lot of the familiar words she hears.

Long before your baby utters her first word, she will be developing her linguistic skills. First, by learning to understand what is said. This receptive language starts developing at birth, with the first words your baby hears. Gradually, she begins to sort out individual words from the jumble of language around her, and then one day, about the middle of the first year, you say her name and she turns around. She's recognized a word. Pretty soon thereafter she should begin to understand the names of other people and objects she sees daily, such as mummy, daddy, bottle, juice, bread. In a few months, or even earlier, she may begin to follow simple commands, such as 'Give me a bite,' or 'Wave bye-bye' or 'Kiss mummy.' This comprehension moves ahead at a much faster pace than speech itself and is an important forerunner to it. You can encourage both receptive and spoken language development every day in many ways (see page 258).

Baby's not Crawling Yet

'My friend's baby started crawling at six months. My son's almost eight months, and he hasn't shown any interest in crawling. Is he delayed developmentally?'

When it comes to crawling, a baby's prowess shouldn't be compared to that of other babies. Crawling is not a skill that babies accomplish by a certain age and by which we

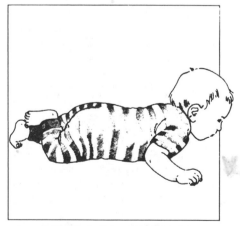

Some babies start off dragging themselves around on their belly. While many graduate to hands-and-knees crawling, a few will cling to creeping until they're up on their feet.

can gauge their overall development. Moving about on the belly, or creeping, is usually a precursor to moving about on the hands and knees, or crawling. Some babies crawl as early as six months, but 7½ to nine months is more typical. A few babies never crawl at all – they just pull up, start cruising (from chair to coffee table to sofa), and then take off and walk. Because crawling, unlike sitting or pulling up, is not a predictable part of every child's developmental pattern, it isn't included on most assessment scales.

Even among babies who do crawl, styles vary. Many begin crawling backwards or sideways, and don't get the hang of going forward for weeks. Some scoot on one knee or on their bottom, and others travel on hands and feet, a stage that many babies reach just before walking. The method a baby chooses to get from one point to another is much less important than the fact that he's making an effort to achieve independent locomotion.

Before a baby can crawl, he has to be able to sit well. Whether or when he begins to crawl after that is an individual matter and not one for concern unless he's behind in at least a couple of developmental areas (social, large or small motor, language and so on) or if he does not seem to be using both sides of his body (arms and legs) equally – in which case, check with his doctor. Good crawlers are often late walkers, while children who never take to crawling may walk early.

Some babies don't crawl because they haven't been given the chance. A baby who passes most of his day confined in a cot, pushchair, baby carrier, playpen, and/or walker won't learn how to raise himself on all fours or put his hands and knees in motion. Be sure your baby spends plenty of supervised time on the floor (don't worry about dirt as long as the floor has been swept or vacuumed free of small particles and cleared of dangerous objects). To encourage him to move forward, try putting a favourite toy or interesting object a short distance ahead of him. Do cover his knees, however, since bare knees on a cold, hard floor or a scratchy carpet can be uncomfortable and might even discourage your baby from attempting to crawl. Wean him from the walker if he's using one, and limit playpen exile to times when you can't supervise him.

One way or another, in the next few months your baby will be taking off – and off into trouble – and you'll be left wondering, 'Why was I in such a hurry?'

Hands-and-knees locomotion is the classic crawling technique. Some babies are so content zipping around this way that they don't bother with walking for months to come.

A cross between crawling and walking, the hands-and-feet posture may be one that baby settles on at first and sticks with, or one that he or she evolves into as a precursor of walking.

Scooting

'Our little girl scoots around on her bottom instead of crawling. She gets around, but looks a bit strange.'

For a baby eager and determined to get from one place to another, form and grace are of little consequence. And they should be to you, too. As long as your baby is attempting to get around independently, it doesn't matter how. You need only be concerned if your baby seems unable to coordinate both sides of her body, can't move her arms and legs in sync. This could be a sign of a learning disability, for which early treatment can be very helpful.

Messy House

'Now that my son is crawling around and pulling up on everything, I can't keep up with the mess he makes. Should I try to control him – and the mess – better, or give up?'

Clutter may be your worst enemy, but it's an adventurous baby's best friend. A home that is kept compulsively tidy provides about as much interest and challenge to a baby who's newly mobile as a wading pool would to Christopher Columbus or a suburban parking lot to Nigel Mansell. Within the parameters of reason (you needn't let baby dismantle your chequebook or reorganize your Filofax) and safety, your child needs to flex and extend his curiosity as he exercises his muscles. Letting him roam – and mess – freely is as important to his intellectual growth as it is to his physical development. Accepting this reality is important to your mental health; parents of young children who fight it, struggling to keep the house as neat as it was pre-baby, are in for a disappointment – as well as overwhelming frustration and anxiety.

You can, however, take some steps to make coping with the reality easier:

Start with a safe house. While it may be okay for him to scatter underwear on the bedroom floor or build a house of napkins on the kitchen linoleum, it isn't okay for him to clang wine bottles together to see what happens or to empty the floor cleaner on the rug. So before you let your baby loose, be sure to make the house safe for him and from him (see page 285).

Contain the chaos. The compulsive side of you will be a lot happier if you try to confine the mess to one or two rooms or areas in the home. That means letting your baby have free run only in his own room and perhaps the kitchen, family room, or living room – wherever you and he spend the most time together. Use closed doors or baby-safe gates to define the areas. If you have a small apartment, of course, you may not be able to place such restrictions on your baby; instead, you may have to resign yourself to daily messes and nightly cleanups.

Also reduce the potential for mess by wedging books in tightly on shelves accessible to your baby, leaving a few of his indestructible books where he can reach them and take them out easily; sealing some of the more vulnerable cabinets and drawers (especially those that contain breakables, valuables, or hazards) with childproof safety locks; keeping most knickknacks off low tables, leaving only a few you don't mind his playing with. Set aside a special drawer or cabinet for him to call his own, and fill it with such fun items as paper cups and plates, wooden spoons, a metal cup or pot, empty boxes and plastic hair curlers.

Don't feel guilty about not letting your baby adorn the bathroom with your lipstick, tear the pages out of your favourite books, empty boxes of cereal all over the kitchen floor, and generally redecorate your home as he pleases. Setting limits will not only help save your sanity but also help your baby's development – children really do thrive when limits are set for them – and teach him the important lesson that other people, even parents, have rights too.

Restrain yourself. Don't follow your baby

around as he wreaks havoc, putting away everything he takes out. This will frustrate him, giving him the sense that everything he does is not only unacceptable but totally in vain. And it will frustrate you if he immediately redoes the damage you've just undone. Instead, do the serious cleaning up twice a day, once at the end of his morning play period while he's napping or in his playpen or high chair, and once at the end of the afternoon or after he's in bed.

Teach him a lesson in neatness – over and over again. Don't do your intensive clean-ups with him around. But do pick up a couple of things with him at the end of each play session, making a point (even if he's not old enough to get the point) of saying, 'Now, can you help mummy pick this toy up and put it away?' Hand him one of the blocks to put back into the toy chest, give him a pot to return to the cabinet or some crumpled paper to throw into the waste-basket, and applaud each effort. Though he will be messing up a lot more often than he'll be cleaning up for years to come, these early lessons will help him to understand – eventually – that what comes out must go back in.

Let him make a mess in peace. Don't deliver continuous monologues of exasperated criticisms to your baby ('Oh, what a bad boy you are. I'll never get that crayon off the wall!'). Don't make him feel that expressing his natural and healthy curiosity ('If I turn this cup of milk over, what will happen?' 'If I take all these clothes out of the drawer, what will I find underneath?') is bad or means that he is bad. If it was something you would rather not see happen again, let him know – but as a teacher, not a judge.

You can't beat him, but don't join him. Don't decide that since you're fighting a losing battle anyway, you might as well let the mess mount and learn to ignore it. Living that way won't help your morale and will be of no benefit to your baby. Though it's healthy for a baby to be allowed to make a mess, it isn't healthy for him to always be surrounded by disorder. It will give him a sense of security to know that even though he leaves an untidy world at bedtime, it will be returned to order come morning. And it will also make making a mess more fun and more fulfilling – what challenge is there, after all, in messing up a room that's already a mess?

Set aside a sanctuary. You won't always be able to keep up with damage left behind by your junior hurricane, but do try to preserve a place of calm in the midst of the storm – your bedroom or the den or living room, for instance – either by not permitting baby to play there or by making sure that it invariably gets picked up in the afternoon or evening. Then at the end of every day, you and your husband will have a haven to escape to.

Play it safe. The exception to a laissez-faire attitude towards disorder is when it presents a threat to safety. If baby spills his juice or empties the dog's water bowl, wipe it up immediately – fresh spills turn an uncarpeted floor into a skating rink where falls are inevitable. Also pick up sheets of paper and magazines as soon as baby is through with them, and keep traffic lanes (stairways especially) clear of toys, especially those with wheels, at all times.

Eating off the Floor

'My baby's always dropping her cracker on the floor and then picking it up and eating it. It seems so unsanitary – is it safe?'

Even if you don't keep your floors 'clean enough to eat off', it's safe for your baby to picnic on them. There are germs on the floor, but not in significant numbers. And for the most part, they're germs your baby has been exposed to before, particularly if she frequently plays on the floor. The same is generally true of floors in other people's homes, supermarkets and department stores, although if your child's recycling a cracker off a foreign floor offends your aesthetic sense, there's nothing wrong with throwing it in the rubbish bin and replacing it with a fresh one.

There are exceptions, however. Although bacteria don't have a chance to multiply much on dry surfaces, they can multiply very rapidly on those that are damp or wet. If you have the choice, don't let her eat food that's been dropped in the bathroom, in puddles, or on other damp or wet surfaces. Moisture on food itself can also be a problem. A cracker or any food that's been mouthed for a time, then left (even in a clean place) for a few hours while bacteria multiply, isn't fit for consumption. So don't leave wet discards lying around where your baby can pick them up again. You won't always have the choice, of course; babies often reclaim long-lost foodstuffs and thrust them in their mouths before you can stop them. Fortunately, they rarely become ill as a result.

Out-of-doors, too, you need to be vigilant. Though many a baby has dropped a bottle in the street and then returned it to her mouth without ill effect, there is certainly more risk of picking up nasty germs where dogs defecate and urinate and thoughtless people expectorate. Replace or rinse any food, bottle, dummy, or toy that has fallen into the street, especially if the ground is damp. Use wipes to clean a teat or toy when running water is not available. In playgrounds, where dogs aren't allowed and where adults usually have more sense than to spit, there's probably less to worry about as long as the ground isn't wet – a quick brush-off of surface dirt should suffice. But even there, puddles can harbour dangerous disease-causing germs, and babies as well as their toys and snacks should be kept away from them. To avoid having to choose between appeasing a screaming baby and playing it safe by discarding a snack that you aren't sure is sanitary, always carry extras.

Eating Dirt – and Worse

'My son puts everything in his mouth. Now that he plays on the floor so much,

I have less control over what goes in. What's safe and what isn't'?

Into the mouths of babes goes anything and everything that fits: dirt, sand, dog food, roaches and other insects, cigarette butts, rotten food, even the contents of a soiled nappy. Though it's obviously best to avoid his sampling from such a smorgasbord, it's not always possible. Few babies get through the crawling stage without at least one oral encounter with something his parents consider revolting; some can't even get through a single morning.

But you've got a lot less to fear from what's unsanitary than from what's used to sanitize. A mouthful of dirt rarely hurts anyone, but even a lick of some cleansers can cause serious damage. You can't keep everything out of baby's inquisitive grasp, so concentrate on substances with the most harmful potential (see page 287 for a list), and concern yourself less with the occasional bug or clump of dog hair that finds its way into his mouth. If you do catch him with the cat-that-is-about-to-swallow-a-canary look, squeeze his cheeks with the thumb and forefinger of one hand to open his mouth, and sweep the object out with a hooked finger.

Of most concern – in addition to obviously toxic substances – are foods that are in the process of spoiling. Illness-causing bacteria or other microorganisms can multiply rapidly at room temperature, so be sure to keep food that's gone bad or is about to – which can most often be found in pet feeding bowls, in the kitchen rubbish, and on an unswept kitchen or dining room floor – out of baby's reach.

You should also be very careful not to let your baby mouth items small enough to swallow or choke on – buttons, bottle caps, paper clips, safety pins, coins and so on. Before you put your baby down to play, survey the floor for anything that's less than 3 cm (1⅜ inches) in diameter and remove it. Also put out of reach items that are potentially toxic, such as newspapers and lead-painted furniture. See Making Home Safe for

Baby, (page 285) for additional tips on what should be kept away from baby.

Erections

'When I'm changing my baby, he sometimes gets an erection. Am I handling his penis too much?'

As long as you're handling his penis only as much as it needs to be handled to be cleansed at nappy changes and bathtimes, you're not handling it too much. Your son's erections are the normal reaction to touch of a sensitive sexual organ – as are a little girl's clitoral erections, which are less noticeable but probably as common. A baby may also have an erection when his nappy rubs against his penis, when he's nursing, or when you're washing him in the bath-tub. All baby boys have erections sometimes (though their mothers may not be aware of them), but some have them more often than others. Such erections require no particular notice on your part.

Discovering Genitals

'My daughter has recently started playing with her genitals whenever her nappy is off. Is this normal at such an early age?'

If it feels good, humans do it. Which is what Mother Nature banked on when she created genitals; if she made them pleasurable to touch, they would be touched, at first by their owner and eventually, when the time was ripe, by a member of the opposite sex – thereby ensuring the perpetuation of the species.

Babies are sexual beings from birth, or more accurately, from before birth – male foetuses have been observed having erections in the uterus. Some, like your baby, begin fledging explorations into their sexuality in the middle of the first year, others not until year's end. This interest is as inevitable and healthy a part of a baby's

development as fascination with fingers and toes was earlier. Trying to stifle such curiosity (as generations past have felt obliged to do) is as misguided as stifling her interest in fingers and toes.

No matter what anyone may tell you, there is no harm – either physical or psychological – in babies or children handling their own genitals (this play can't be called masturbation until a later age). Making a baby or child feel that she's 'dirty' or 'bad' for engaging in such play, however, can be harmful and have a negative effect on future sexuality and self-esteem. Making self-stimulation taboo can also make it more inviting.

The fear that fingers that touch their genitals aren't clean enough to go into their mouths is also unfounded; all the germs that are in a baby's genital area are her own and pose no threat. If, however, you see your little girl probing with very dirty hands, it would be a good idea to wash them, to avoid the possibility of infection. A boy's genitals are not susceptible in the same way, but both boys and girls should have their hands washed after they've touched a soiled nappy area.

When your baby gets old enough to understand, you will want to explain that this part of her body is private, and that though it's okay for her to touch it, it isn't okay for her to touch it in public or to let anyone else touch it.

Getting Dirty

'My daughter would love to crawl around at the playground if I let her. But the ground is so dirty. . . .'

Break out the all-fabric bleach, and break down your resistance to letting your daughter get down and dirty. Babies who are forced to watch from the sidelines when they'd really like to be in the scrimmage are likely to stay spotless but unsatisfied. Children are eminently washable. The most obvious soil can be removed with wipes or premoistened towelettes while you're still at the playground or in the garden, and ground-in dirt will come off later in the bath. Even the dirt that ends up in their mouths – babies who spend any amount of time outdoors will inevitably consume some soil and sand – won't be harmful; you may get sick from watching her eat dirt, but she's not likely to. So ignore the slight to your sensibilities and, checking first to be sure there's no broken glass or dog droppings in her path, allow your little sport a carefully supervised crawl around. If she gets into something really dirty, give her hands a once-over with a wipe and send her on her way again.

Not all babies enjoy getting dirty; some would rather be spectators than players. If yours is one of these, be sure she isn't hesitating because she thinks you don't want her to get dirty. Encourage her to gradually become more active, but don't force her.

Soft shoes or sneakers will protect her feet when she's crawling on concrete; on grass in warm weather, bare feet are fine. It will be easier on her knees (but a challenge to your laundering skills) if she wears trousers or overalls during these excursions. If you take pride in her looking fresh and clean in public, keep a set of playclothes in your nappy bag and change her into them before handing her her travelling papers; then wash her up and put her back into clean clothes before you set off again.

Rough Play

'My brother-in-law likes to roughhouse with our son, throwing him in the air and catching him, and that sort of thing. The baby seems to love it, but we wonder if it's safe.'

It isn't. In most cases you can trust your baby to tell you when his body's not ready for something – starting solids, for instance, or standing, but not when it comes to this kind of roughhousing. Many babies enjoy the sensation of being whirled through the air or tossed up and caught (though some are terrified of it), but such handling – whether in fun or in anger – can be extremely dangerous for children under two years of age.[1]

There are several types of injuries that can result from throwing a baby in the air or shaking or vigorously bouncing him (as when jogging with him in a front or back baby carrier). One is a whiplash type of injury (such as an adult can get when rearended in a car accident). Because the baby's head is heavy in proportion to the rest of his body and his neck muscles are not fully developed, support for the head is poor. When the baby is shaken roughly, the head whipping back and forth can cause the brain to rebound again and again against the skull. Bruising of the brain can cause swelling, bleeding, pressure and, possibly, permanent neurological damage with mental or physical disability. Another possible injury is trauma to the delicate infant eye. If detachment or scarring of the retina or damage to the optic nerve occurs, lasting visual problems, even blindness, can result. The risk of damage is compounded if a baby is crying or being held upside down during the shaking, because both increase blood pressure in the head, making fragile blood vessels more likely to rupture. Such injuries are relatively rare, but the damage can be so severe that the risk is certainly not worth taking.

Don't spend time worrying about past roughhousing sessions. If your child hasn't exhibited any symptoms of injury, he's probably escaped unscathed thus far. If you have any concerns, consult your baby's doctor.

Some other kinds of roughhousing are also unsafe at this age. Because of a baby's (or even a young child's) still rather loose joints, don't swing him by the hands or suddenly twist or tug an arm (to get him moving when he's recalcitrant). The result could be a very painful (if easy-to-repair) dislocated elbow or shoulder.

1. Some parents shake rather than spank a baby when they are angry because it seems the preferable way of disciplining, or they shake a baby to let off steam and frustration, assuming it won't hurt. Neither assumption is true; any parent who feels compelled to 'punish' an infant needs help dealing with his or her feelings and caring for a child.

This doesn't rule out roughhousing completely; it only dictates more careful rough play. Many babies love 'flying' as they are held securely midtrunk and glided gently through the air, participating in ticklefests (though stop when baby is winded) and 'wrestling' matches, and being chased when they are old enough to crawl. There are some babies, however, both male and female, who dislike any kind of rough handling, and they have the right to more gentle treatment – even from exuberant uncles and grandpas.

Playpen Use

'When we bought our playpen a couple of months ago, our baby couldn't seem to get enough time in it. Now he screams to get out after only five minutes.'

A couple of months ago, the playpen didn't seem confining to your baby; on the contrary, it seemed his own personal amusement park. Now he's beginning to realize that there's a whole world or at least a living room – out there, and he's game to take it on. The four walls that once enclosed his paradise now represent frustrating barriers, keeping him on the inside looking out.

Take your baby's hint and start using the playpen for emergency duty only, for those times when he needs to be penned in for his own safety or, briefly and infrequently, for your convenience – while you mop the kitchen floor, put something in the oven, answer the phone, go to the bathroom, or straighten up for last-minute company. Limit the time he's sentenced to the pen to no more than five to fifteen minutes at a stretch, which is about as long as an active eight-month-old will tolerate it. Vary the company he has to keep, rotating his stock of toys frequently so he won't become bored prematurely. If he prefers to be able to see and hear you as he plays, keep the pen near you; if he seems contented longer when you're out of sight, keep it in the next room (but check him frequently). If he protests before he's done his time, try giving him some novel playthings – a few pots and pans, perhaps, or an empty plastic bottle or two (without the cap) – anything he doesn't usually play with in this setting. If that doesn't work, parole him as soon as you reasonably can.

Be alert to the possibility of a jailbreak. The extremely agile and resourceful baby may be able to escape by climbing on large toys – so keep them out of the playpen; and avoid hanging toys across the top.

'My daughter could stay in the playpen all day if I let her, but I'm not sure I should.'

Some placid babies seem perfectly happy to stay in the playpen for hours on end, even late into the first year. Maybe they just don't know what they're missing, or perhaps they're not assertive enough to demand their freedom. But though such a situation lets a mother accomplish much, it prevents a baby from accomplishing enough, intellectually or physically. So encourage your baby to see the world from a new perspective. She may be hesitant at first to leave the playpen, a little uneasy about losing the security of its four walls. Sitting with her on the wide-open floor, playing with her, giving her a favourite toy or a favourite blanket, or cheering on her attempts at crawling will make the transition easier.

Reading to Baby

'I'd like my son to develop an interest in reading. Is it too early to start reading to him?'

In an age when television seduces children away from books easily and early, it's probably never too soon to start reading to a child. Some believe there's value to reading to a baby still in the uterus, and many begin their babies on books shortly after birth. But it isn't until about some time in the second half of the first year that a baby becomes an active participant in the reading process – at first, by chewing on the corners of the book. Soon he begins to pay attention to the words as you read them (at this point, to the rhythm and sounds of the words rather than their meanings) and to the illustrations (enjoying the colour and patterns, but not necessarily relating the pictures to known objects).

To make sure your baby catches the book worm early, use the following strategies:

Read to yourself. Reading to your baby will have less impact if you yourself spend more time in front of the TV than behind a book (or newspaper, or magazine). Though it's hard for parents of young children to find a spare moment for a quiet read, it's worth the effort; as with any behaviour, desirable or undesirable, children are much more likely to do as you do than to do as you say. Read a few pages from a propped-up book while you nurse or give your baby a bottle, read a book in his room while he plays, keep a book on your nightstand for reading before you fall asleep and for showing your baby ('this is mummy's book').

Start a juvenile collection. There are thousands of children's books on the shelves of bookshores, but only a limited number are appropriate for a beginner. Look for the following:

• Sturdy construction that defies destruction. Sturdiest are books with laminated cardboard pages with rounded edges, which can be mouthed without disintegrating and turned without tearing. Laminated cloth books are good, too, but books of soft cloth, though indestructible, are pretty useless – they don't lie flat, babies can't turn their pages, and they bear little resemblance to real books. A spiral binding on a board book is a plus, since not only does it allow a book to lie flat when open, but baby can play with the fascinating spiral design. Vinyl books are good for bathtime, one of the few times some children sit still long enough for a reading session. To keep these free of mildew, dry thoroughly after each bath, and store in a dry place.

• Illustrations that include bold, bright, realistic pictures of familiar subjects, particularly animals, vehicles, toys and children. The pictures shouldn't be cluttered, so that baby won't be overwhelmed at a glance.

• Text that is not too complicated. Rhymes have the best chance of holding a baby's attention when you're reading to him since he's listening largely for ear appeal, not comprehension, and it'll be many months before he'll be able to follow a story line. One-word-on-a-page books are good, too, since they help him to increase his comprehension vocabulary, and eventually his spoken vocabulary.

• Activity tie-ins. Books that stimulate games like peekaboo, touch-and-feel books that encourage learning about textures, and books that have surprises hidden under little flaps encourage audience participation.

• Discardable reading matter. Babies also like to handle and look at magazines with a lot of full-colour illustrations, so instead of discarding old ones, keep a rainy-day collection for your baby. Of course, when he's through with them, you'll have to discard them.[2]

Learn to read parent-style. Most people think they know how to pick up a volume of Mother Goose and read it aloud. But there's more to reading to a baby. Tone and inflection are important; read slowly, with a lilting sing-song and exaggerated emphasis in the right places. Stop at each page to stress salient points ('Look at the little boy falling down the hill', or 'See the baby doggie laughing?') or to show him animals or people ('That's a cow – a cow says "moo",' or 'There's a baby in a cradle – the baby's going "rockabye baby"').

2. Be sure, however, that your baby doesn't mouth the pages of a magazine or newspaper. Both can contain high levels of lead, and frequent ingestion could result in dangerous levels for your baby. (Burning will also release lead into the air, so don't use newspapers or magazines for kindling.)

Make reading a habit. Build reading into baby's agenda – a few minutes at least twice a day, when he's quiet but alert, and when he's already been fed. Before nap-time, after lunch, after bath and before bed are all good reading times. But keep to the schedule only if baby's receptive; don't push a book on him when he's in the mood to practise crawling or to make music with two pot covers.

Keep the library open. Store precious destructible books on a high shelf for parent-supervised reading sessions, but keep a small (to prevent baby from being overwhelmed), rotating (to prevent baby from becoming bored) library of baby-proof books where he can reach and enjoy them. Sometimes a baby who resists being sat down for a reading session with mummy or daddy will be happy to 'read' to himself turning pages and looking at pictures at his own pace.

Left- or Right-Handedness

'I've noticed that my baby picks up and reaches for toys with either hand. Should I try to encourage him to use his right?'

We live in a world that treats minorities unequally; the left-handed, a minority of about 10%, are no exception. Most doors, irons, potato peelers, scissors and table settings are designed for righties. And lefties are destined to bump elbows at the dinner table and to shake with what to them is the 'wrong' hand. Many parents, reluctant to relegate their children to this minority status, try to force right-handedness on to lefty-prone offspring.

Experts once believed that such parental pressure to change what is thought to be a genetically determined trait led to stuttering and a variety of learning disabilities. Now, though they still don't recommend trying to change a child's natural-handedness, they suspect that several traits – both positive and negative – are genetically intertwined with

left-handedness. Many of these appear to be related to differences between lefties and righties with respect to development in the right and left hemispheres of the brain. In lefties the right side of the brain is dominant, making them excel in such areas as spatial relations, which may be why they are overrepresented in such fields as sports, architecture and art. Since more boys than girls are left-handed, it is also theorized that levels of testosterone, a male hormone, somehow affect brain development and handedness. Much more study is needed before we fully understand what makes a person left- or right-handed and just how handedness affects various areas of one's life.

Most babies use both hands equally at first; some show a preference for one hand or the other within a few months, others not until they reach their first birthdays. Some seem to favour one hand at first, and then switch. What's important is letting baby use the hand he's most comfortable with, not the one you would like him to use. Since about 70% of the population is strongly right-handed (the other 20% is ambidextrous), you can assume, until he demonstrates otherwise, that your baby will be, too. Offer things to his right hand. If he reaches over and grabs them with his left, or takes them with his right and then passes them to his left, he may be on his way to football stardom or to designing the world's tallest building.

Childproofing your Home

'I always said that a baby wasn't going to change the way we live. But with our daughter's crawling around, many of the valuable things we've collected over the years are at risk. Should I pack them away, or try to teach her to stay away from them?'

Many china shops would be as happy to host a bull as a seven- or eight-month-old baby. And indeed, your breakable valuables might stand as much of a chance of surviving in a living room with your baby as they would in a ring with El Toro.

So if you don't want to see the Baccarat bowl you picked up in Paris or the Wedgwood vase your best friend gave you for a wedding gift shattered at your baby's feet, put them well out of reach until she's old enough and responsible enough to treat them with respect – which may not be for a couple of years. Do likewise with objects (of art or otherwise) that are heavy enough to hurt her should she pull them down.

Still, your family shouldn't spend the next years in a house stripped bare of ornamentation – for your child's sake as much as for yours. If you want her to learn to live with the fine and fragile things in life, she should be exposed to some even at this age. Leave a few of the sturdier and less valuable pieces in your collection within your baby's reach. When she reaches, sternly tell her, 'No, don't touch that. That's mummy and daddy's.' Hand her a toy and explain that it is *hers*. If she persists in reaching for the forbidden object, take it away (too many no's begin to lose their effect) and put it out another day. Though you can't count on compliance now (young babies have short memories), eventually your child will understand – and you can bring on the Baccarat and Wedgwood.

WHAT IT'S IMPORTANT TO KNOW
Making Home Safe for Baby

Put a fragile day-old baby next to a sturdy seven-month-old and the newborn will seem, in comparison, so helpless, so much more vulnerable to harm. But in reality, it's the older baby who's more vulnerable. Newly acquired skills unmatched by good judgment, in fact, make babies in the second half of their first year extremely hazardous to their own health.

Once a baby is able to get around alone (or is getting around in a walker), the average home becomes a wonderland as dangerous as it is exciting, replete with potential booby traps capable of causing injury or even death. Newborn or toddler, the only protection for your baby during what the Metropolitan Life Insurance Company has called the 'risky first year of life' is your good sense, foresight and eternal vigilance.

It usually takes a combination of factors to trigger an accident, including a dangerous object or substance (in the case of a baby, perhaps a staircase or drug), a susceptible victim (your baby), and possibly, environmental conditions (ungated steps, an unlocked medicine chest) that allow victim and danger to come together. In the case of baby accidents, it may also hinge on the faltering vigilance – sometimes only for a moment – of a parent or caretaker.

To minimize the possibility of an accident, all of these factors must be modified in some way. Dangerous objects and substances must be removed from reach, the susceptible baby has to be made less susceptible by gradual safety training, the hazardous environment must be modified (with gates on stairs, locks on cabinets), and, possibly most important of all, caretakers must be ever on the alert, especially at times of stress, when most accidents occur. Because a great many accidents occur at the homes of others – particularly the homes of grandparents – you should extend many of these safety measures to homes baby visits often and offer this chapter as reading material to those who frequently care for your child.

Here's how to modify the factors that contribute to accidents.

CHANGE YOUR WAYS

Since modifying baby's behaviour will be a long, slow educational process, which can begin now but won't be complete for many years, it's your behaviour that will have the most impact on the safety of your child at this stage.

- Be eternally vigilant. No matter how carefully you attempt to childproof your house, remember that you can't make it completely accident-proof. Your attention, or that of another caretaker, must be continuous, especially if yours is a particularly resourceful child.

- Don't let your attention be diverted in mid-activity when using household cleaning products, medicines, electrical appliances, power tools, or any other hazardous object or substance when your baby is on the loose. It takes no more than a second for baby to get into serious trouble.

- Be particularly alert during times of stress and stressful times of day. It's when you're distracted that you're likely to forget to take the knife off the table, strap baby into the high chair, or close the stair gate.

- Do not leave baby alone in your house or apartment at any time, nor alone in a room except in a playpen, cot, or other safe enclosure – and then only for a few minutes, unless he or she is sleeping. Do not leave a baby alone, even 'safely' enclosed in a cot or playpen, awake or asleep, with a toddler (they often don't know their own strength or realize the possible consequences of their actions) or with a pet (even a docile one).

- Make baby less susceptible with appropriate clothing. Use only flame-retardant sleepwear (and wash it properly); be sure that pajama feet aren't too floppy, trouser cuffs too long, or socks or slippers too slippery for a baby who is pulling up or starting to walk. Avoid long scarves or sashes that can trip baby up, and always shun strings that can strangle (those over 30 cm/12 inches long).

- Become familiar, if you aren't already, with emergency and first-aid procedures (see page 427). You can't always prevent accidents, but knowing what to do if a serious one occurs can save lives and limbs.

- Give your baby plenty of freedom. Once you've made your baby's environment as safe as possible, avoid hovering. Though you want your child to be safety conscious, you don't want to discourage the normal experimentation of childhood. Children, like the rest of us, learn from their mistakes; never allowing them to make a mistake can prevent growth. And a child who is afraid to run, climb, or try new things misses out not only on the education that comes through free play, but on a lot of the fun of childhood as well.

CHANGE YOUR BABY'S SURROUNDINGS

Until now, your baby has seen the world – and your home – mostly from your arms, at your eye level. Now that he or she is beginning to get a look at it from down on all fours, you will have to begin looking at it from that perspective, too. One way to do this is to actually get down on the floor yourself; from there, you will see a multitude of dangers you may not have even realized existed. Another way is to examine everything that is within one metre (three feet) above the floor – the usual range of a baby's reach.

Changes throughout the home. As you tour your home, these are the things you should look at and alter as necessary:

- Windows. If they are above ground level, install window guards according to manufacturer's directions; or adjust them so they can't open more than 15 cm (6 inches).

- Cords to blinds or curtains. Tie them up so baby can't become entangled in them; do not place a cot or playpen, or a chair or bed baby can climb on, within reach.

- Electrical cords. Move them out of reach, behind furniture so that baby won't mouth them, risking electric shock, or tug at them, pulling lamps or other heavy items down.

Poison Control

Every year tens of thousands of children are victims of accidental ingestion of hazardous substances. That's sad, but not surprising. Children, particularly very young ones, do a lot of their discovery of the world orally. Virtually anything they pick up will go right to the mouth. They haven't yet learned to categorize substances or objects as 'safe' or 'unsafe' – everything is merely 'interesting'. Nor are their tastebuds sophisticated enough to warn them, as ours do, that a substance is dangerous because it tastes terrible.

To protect your innocents from perils, follow these rules without fail:

- Lock all potentially poisonous substances out of reach and out of sight of your baby – even crawlers can climb up on low chairs and stools or cushions.

- Follow all safety rules for administering or taking medicines (see page 403).

- Avoid buying brightly coloured or attractively packaged household cleansers, laundry detergents, and other substances. They will attract your baby. If necessary, cover illustrations with black tape (but don't cover instructions or warnings). Also avoid toxic substances with attractive food fragrances (such as mint, lemon, or apricot).

- Purchase products with childproof packaging, when possible.

- Make it a habit to return hazardous items to safe storage immediately after each use; don't put a spray can of furniture polish or a box of mothballs down 'just for a minute' while you answer the phone.

- Store food and non-food items separately and never put nonedibles in empty food containers (bleach in an apple juice bottle, for example, or lubricating oil in a jelly jar). Babies learn very early to identify where their food comes from, and won't understand why they can't drink what's in the juice bottle or lick what's in the jelly jar.

- Avoid using non-foods that look like foods (such as wax fruit).

- When discarding potentially poisonous substances, empty them down the drain, rinsing the containers before discarding unless the label instructs otherwise, and putting them out in a tightly closed dustbin immediately. *Never* dump them in a wastebasket or kitchen rubbish bin.

- Choose the less hazardous product over the one with a long list of warnings when possible. Among those household products generally considered less hazardous: non-chlorine bleaches, vinegar, borax, washing soda, lemon oil, beeswax, olive oil (for furniture), non-chemical flypaper, mineral oil (for lubrication, not internal use), compressed air drain openers (rather than corrosive liquids or granules).

- To help you think 'poison' whenever you see one, put 'poison' labels on all possibly poisonous products. If you can't locate such labels, simply put an 'X' of black tape on each product (but don't cover instructions or warnings). Eventually your child will also come to recognize that these products are unsafe.

- Think of all of the following as potentially perilous:
  Alcoholic beverages
  Ammoniated mercury (not useful medicinally)
  Aspirin
  Boric acid (not useful medicinally)
  Camphorated oil (not useful medicinally)
  Chlorine bleach
  Cosmetics
  Dishwasher detergents
  Drain cleaners
  Furniture polish
  Insect or rodent poisons
  Iron pills (even baby's own)
  Kerosene
  Lye (better not to have in the home at all)
  Medicines of all kinds
  Mothballs
  Turpentine (not useful)
  Oil of wintergreen (not useful medicinally)
  Sleeping pills
  Tranquillizers
  Weed killers

- Electrical outlets. Cover with caps or shields or place heavy furniture in front of them to prevent baby from inserting something (such as a hairpin) or probing with a drooly finger and getting a shock.

- Unstable furnishings. Put rickety or unstable chairs, tables, or other furniture that might topple if baby pulls on it out of the way for the time being; securely fasten to the wall bookcases or other structures that baby could pull down.

- Dresser drawers. Keep them closed so baby won't climb in them and pull the dresser down; if the dresser isn't stable, consider fastening it to the wall.

- Painted surfaces within baby's reach. Be sure they are lead free; if they aren't or if you aren't sure, repaint or wallpaper. If testing shows lead in the paint, it is best to remove it entirely.

- Ash trays. Put them out of reach so baby won't touch a hot butt or sample a handful of ashes and butts; better still, for your baby's health as well as safety, banish tobacco from your home entirely.

- Houseplants. Keep them out of baby's reach, where baby can't pull them down on him- or herself or nibble on them; be especially wary of poisonous plants (see page 295).

- Loose knobs on furniture or cabinets. Remove or secure any that are small enough to be swallowed (smaller than baby's fist) or cause choking.

- Radiators. Put barriers around them or radiator covers over them during the heating season.

- Stairs. Put a gate at the top and another three steps up from the bottom.

- Bannisters and railings. Be sure the gap between upright posts on stairs or balconies is less than 13 cm (5 inches), and that none are loose.

- Fireplaces, heaters, stoves, floor furnaces. Put up protective grills or other barriers to keep small fingers from hot surfaces (even the grill on a floor furnace can get hot enough to cause second-degree burns) as well as fire. Unplug space heaters when not in use, and whenever possible store them where children can't get at them. (For information on the environmental risks of space heaters, see page 232.)

- Tablecloths. If they hang over the side of the table and are not well anchored, remove them until your baby knows not to pull up on them or, alternatively, keep baby off the floor when you have a cloth on the table.

- Glass-topped tables. Either cover with a heavy table pad or put them out of reach temporarily.

- Sharp edges or corners on tables, chests and so on. If baby can bump into them, cover them with homemade or purchased cushioned strips and corner guards.

- Scatter rugs. Be sure they have nonskid backings; don't place them at the top of stairs or allow them to remain rumpled.

- Floor tiles and carpets. Repair all loose areas to prevent tripping.

- Heavy knickknacks and bookends. Place them where baby can't reach out and pull them over; babies have more strength than you may think.

- Toy chests. These should have lightweight lids with safety closing mechanisms (or no lids at all), as well as ventilation holes (in case baby should become locked in). In general, open shelves are safer for toy storage.

- Cot. Once your baby starts showing interest in pulling up (don't wait until the feat has been achieved), adjust the mattress to its lowest position and remove bulky toys, pillows, bumper pads, and anything else that can be used as a stepping stone to freedom – and disaster. When your baby is 89 cm (35 inches) tall, it's time for a bed.

Safety Equipment

Cabinet locks (to keep kitchen cabinets and drawers safe from prying fingers)

Cabinet latches (to do likewise)

Stove guards

Doorknob guards (to make it difficult for little ones to open doors)

Clear plastic corner cushioning (to soften corners of tables)

Edge cushions (to do same for sharp edges)

Outlet plugs or covers (in addition to snap-in caps, there are hinged shields that can be used even when appliances are plugged in)

Bathtub spout safety cover

Non-skid decorations for bathtub bottoms

Skid-resistant step stool (when baby walks)

Child-proof patio door locks

Potty proofer (suction cups or latch to keep lid down when not in use)

- Floor clutter. Try to keep it out of traffic lanes to prevent tripping. Wipe up spills and pick up papers immediately.

- Garage, basement and hobby areas. Lock securely and keep children out, since these areas usually contain a variety of hazardous implements and/or poisonous substances.

- Other areas with hazardous or breakable objects, such as a living room housing a collection of fine teacups. Put up a gate or other barrier to keep baby out.

Also be alert to the host of hazardous items found in the typical home and see that they are safely stored, generally in childproof drawers, cabinets, or chests or on absolutely out-of-reach shelves (you'd be surprised at how high some babies can manage to climb). When you're using such items, be sure baby can't get at them when you turn your back, and always be sure to put them away as soon as you've finished with them or as soon as you spot one that has been left out. Be particularly careful with:

- Sharp implements such as scissors, knives, letter openers, razors (don't leave these on the side of the bathtub) and blades.

- Swallowable notions such as marbles, coins, safety pins and anything else smaller than 3 cm (1⅜ inches) in diameter.

- Pens, pencils and other writing implements (substitute chunky non-toxic crayons).[3]

- Sewing and knitting supplies, particularly pins and needles, thimbles, scissors and buttons.

- Lightweight plastic bags such as produce bags, dry cleaning bags and packaging on new clothing (babies can suffocate if such a bag is placed over the face).

- Incendiary articles such as matches and matchbooks, lighters and hot cigarette butts.

- Tools of your trade or hobbies – paints and thinners, if there's an artist in the house; pins and needles if there's a dressmaker, woodworking equipment if there's a carpenter; and so on.

- Toys (if they belong to older siblings, they generally should not be played with by babies or toddlers under three; this includes building sets with small pieces, trikes and scooters, miniature cars and trucks, and anything with sharp corners, small pieces, removable or breakable small parts, or electrical connections).

- Button batteries – the disc-shaped type used in watches, calculators, hearing

---

3. Some children enjoy using pencils or pens just like mummy and daddy; if your baby does, allow such use only when he or she is safely seated and you can supervise closely.

aids, cameras and so on (they are easy to swallow and can release hazardous contents into baby's oesophagus or stomach).

- Food fakes of wax, papier-mâché, rubber, or any other substance that isn't safe for a baby or child to mouth (a wax apple, a candle that smells and looks like an ice-cream sundae, a child's eraser that smells and looks like a ripe strawberry).

- Cleaning materials.

- Glass, china, or other breakables.

- Light bulbs, especially small ones, such as those in night lights, that a baby can mouth and break.

- Jewellery, particularly beads, which can be pulled apart; and small items such as rings (all are attractive to baby and easily swallowed).

- Mothballs (they're poisonous).

- Shoe polish (besides making a mess, it can make baby sick).

- Perfumes and all cosmetics (they are potentially toxic); vitamins and medicines.

- Toy whistles (baby can choke on them, and on the small ball inside should it come loose).

- Balloons (uninflated or burst, they can be inhaled and cause choking).

- Small, hard finger foods, such as nuts or raisins, popcorn or hard sweets that may be left around in dishes (baby can choke on them).

- Lye and acid (better not to have these in your home at all).

- Alcoholic beverages (an amount that merely relaxes you could make your baby deathly ill).

- Strings, cords, cradle gyms, tape cassettes, or anything else that could get tangled around a baby's neck and cause strangulation. (Babies shouldn't sleep with dolls or stuffed animals that hold audio tapes.)

- Anything else in your home that would be dangerous if mouthed or swallowed by a baby. See list of poisons, page 287.

Fire-safety changes. Hearing that a child or children perished in a fire is distressing enough. To know that the fire could have been prevented, or could have been discovered before it spread, is even more disturbing. Check every corner of your home for possible fire hazards to be sure 'it can't happen here':

- If smoking is permitted in your home (and everyone will be better off if it isn't), dispose of all cigar or cigarette butts, ashes, pipe ashes and used matches carefully and never leave them where a baby can get at them. Any smokers in your home should make a habit of disposing of butts immediately, and you should empty ashtrays promptly when you have smoking guests.

- Do not permit anyone (visitors included) to smoke in bed.

- Keep matches and lighters out of the reach of children and babies.

- Do not allow rubbish to accumulate (especially combustibles such as paint or paint rags).

- Avoid using flammable liquids, kerosene as well as commercial products, for spot removal on clothing or furniture.

- Don't let anyone (adult or child) near a fireplace, wood stove, or space heater with trailing sleeves, dragging scarves, or hanging shirttails, any of which could accidentally catch fire.

- Cover halogen bulbs with a safety shield.

- Be sure your baby's sleepwear meets CE standards for flame resistance.

- Have your heating system checked annually, be careful not to overload electrical circuits, always remove plugs from sockets properly (don't jerk the cord), and check electric appliances and cords regularly for wear and/or loose connections.

- If you use space heaters, be sure they turn off automatically if toppled or if something is placed against them.

- Place extinguishers in areas where fire risk is greatest, such as in the kitchen or furnace room, and near the fireplace or wood stove. In an emergency, bicarbonate of soda can be used for putting out kitchen fires. Try to put out a fire only if it is small and contained (such as in your oven, a frying pan, or a wastebasket). If it is not contained, get out of the house instead.

- Install fire and smoke detectors as recommended by your local fire department, if you haven't already. Check periodically to see that they are in good working order and that batteries haven't run down.

- Install chairs and rope ladders at selected upper floor windows to facilitate escape; teach older children and adults how to use them. Practise getting down holding a baby doll.

- Hold fire drills periodically so that everyone who lives or works in your household will know how to get out safely and quickly in an emergency and know where to meet other family members. Assign parents and other adults to evacuate specific children. Be sure everyone (including baby-sitters) knows that the priority in case of fire is to evacuate the premises immediately – without worrying about dressing, saving valuables, or putting out the fire.[4] Most deaths occur from suffocation or burns due to hot fumes and smoke, not from direct flame. The fire department should

be called as soon as possible from a street phone or a neighbour's house.

Changes in the kitchen. Make a special tour of the kitchen, one of the most intriguing places in the house to your newly mobile baby – and also one of the most dangerous. You can make it safer by taking the following steps:

- Attach child-guard latches to drawers or cabinets that contain anything off limits to little ones, such as breakable glass items, sharp implements, hazardous cleaning compounds, medicines, or dangerous food-stuffs (such as peanuts, peanut butter – on which a baby could choke – and hot peppers). If your baby figures out how to unlatch the safety latches (some very wily ones do), you will have to relegate all dangerous items to out-of-reach storage areas or just keep your baby out of the kitchen entirely with a gate or other barrier. What is truly out of reach will change as your baby gets older, so your storage arrangement may have to as well.

- Set aside at least one cabinet (baby is less likely to catch his or her fingers in a cabinet than in a drawer) for your little explorer to enjoy freely. Some sturdy pots and pans, wooden spoons, strainers, tea towels, plastic bowls and so on can provide hours of entertainment and may satisfy your baby's curiosity enough to keep him or her out of forbidden places.

- Keep the handles of pots and pans that are on the stove turned towards the rear and out of baby's reach. If controls are on the front of the range, erect some sort of barrier to keep them untouchable or snap on stove knob covers. An appliance latch will keep conventional and microwave ovens inaccessible.

- Don't sit baby on a countertop near electrical appliances, the stove, or anything else that might be hazardous – or you may find him or her with fingers in the toaster, hands on a hot pot, or a knife

---

4. The only exception is a well-contained fire that can be put out with a fire extinguisher.

heading for an open mouth the moment you turn your back.

- Don't carry baby and hot coffee – or any hot liquid – at the same time. It's just too easy for the baby to suddenly bolt and spill it, possibly burning you both. Also be sure not to leave a hot beverage or a bowl of soup at the edge of a table where your baby can reach it.

- Keep rubbish in a tightly covered container that baby can't open or under the sink behind a securely latched door. Children love to rummage through waste, and the dangers – from spoiled foods to broken glass – are numerous.

- Clean up all spills promptly – they make for slippery floors.

- Follow the safety rules for selecting, using, and storing kitchen detergents, scouring powders, silver polishes and all other kitchen supplies (see page 287).

Changes in the lavatory. Nearly as alluring to a baby as the kitchen, and equally dangerous, is the lavatory. One way to keep it off limits is to put a hook and eye or other latch high up on the door, and to keep it latched when not in use. Baby-safe the bathroom by taking the following precautions:

- Keep all medications (including over-the-counter ones such as antacids), mouthwashes, toothpaste, vitamin pills, hair preparations and sprays, skin lotions and cosmetics safely stored out of baby's reach. (Actually, medicines and vitamins are better kept in the bedroom, where there is less exposure to moisture, than in the bathroom.)

- Don't leave a sunlamp or heater where baby can turn it on; if you can't store it out of the way, remove sunlamp bulb and unplug the lamp when it is not being used.

- Don't use, or let anyone else use, a hair dryer near your baby when he or she is in the bath or playing with water.

- Never leave small electrical appliances plugged in when you aren't using them. A baby could dunk a hair dryer in the toilet and get a fatal electric shock, switch on a razor and get cut, or get burned on a curling iron. Unplugging appliances won't be enough if your child has good manual dexterity (those little whizzes often figure out how to plug in an appliance, with possibly disastrous results) or if the appliance is a hair dryer (which can cause shocks even when not connected to a power source). Better not to leave these appliances out at all.

- Keep water temperature in your home set at between 49° and 52°C (120° and 125°F) to avoid accidental scalding, and always turn off the hot water tap before the cold. Routinely test bath water temperature with your elbow before putting baby in the tub. If your tub doesn't have a nonskid finish, add some skidproof stick-ons.

- When not in use, keep the toilet lid closed with suction cups or another device made expressly for this purpose. Most babies see the toilet as a private little swimming pool, and love to play in it any chance they get. Not only is this unsanitary, but an energetic toddler could topple in headfirst, with catastrophic results.

- Invest in a protective cover for the tub spout to prevent bumps or burns should baby fall against it.

- Do not leave your baby in the tub unattended, even once he's sitting well, and even in a special tub seat. This rule should be in force until your child is five years old.

- Never leave water in the tub when it's not in use; a small child may topple into the tub at play, and a drowning can occur in as little as *2.5 cm (an inch)* of water.

Changes for a safer out-of-doors. Though the home is the most dangerous environment for a baby, serious accidents can also occur in your own garden – or someone else's – as well as in the local streets and the community playground. Many of these accidents are relatively easy to prevent:

- Never let an infant or toddler play out-of-doors alone. Even a baby in a safety harness, napping in a pram or pushchair, needs to be watched almost constantly – he or she could suddenly wake and become tangled in the harness while struggling to be free. A sleeping baby who is not strapped in needs to be under someone's watchful eye full-time.

- Keep swimming or wading pools and any other water catchments (even if filled with only 2.5 cm/an inch of water) inaccessible to babies and toddlers – whether they are crawling, walking independently, or navigating in a walker. If you have a swimming pool, fence it in and keep gates or doors to the pool locked at all times; empty and turn wading pools upside down, and drain any other areas where water can accumulate before allowing baby to play nearby.

- Check public play areas before letting your baby loose. Though it's fairly easy to keep your garden free of dog droppings (they can harbour worms), broken glass and other dangerous debris, park attendants may find it more difficult to do so.

- It's not enough to beseech: 'Please don't eat the daisies!' You've got to be sure that your baby knows it's not okay to eat *any* plants, indoors or out. Avoid planting, or at least fence in, poisonous plants (see box, page 295).

- Be sure that outdoor play equipment is safe. It should be sturdily constructed, correctly assembled, firmly anchored, and installed at least 2 metres (6 feet) from fences or walls. Cap all screws and bolts to prevent injuries from rough or sharp edges, and check for loose ones periodically. Avoid S-type hooks for swings (the chains can swing out of them), and rings anywhere on the equipment that are between 13 and 26 cm (5 and 10 inches) in diameter, since a

child's head might become entrapped. Swings should be of soft materials (such as leather or canvas rather than wood or metal) to prevent serious head injuries. The best surfaces for outdoor play areas are sand, sawdust, wood chips, bark, rubber composition, grass, or other shock-absorbent material.

CHANGE YOUR BABY

Accidents are much more likely to happen to those who are susceptible to them – and of course, babies easily fall into that category. But it isn't too early to begin accident-proofing your baby even as you accident-proof your home. Teach your baby about the dangers. Pretend to touch the point of a needle, for example, saying 'Ouch', and pulling your finger away quickly in mock pain. Build and use a vocabulary of warning words 'Ouch', 'Boo-hoo', 'Hot', 'Sharp') and phrases ('Don't touch', 'That's dangerous', 'Be careful', 'That's an ouch', 'That will give you a boo-boo'), so that your baby will automatically come to associate them with dangerous objects, substances and situations. At first your little dramatizations will seem to be going right over your little one's head – and they will be. But gradually the brain will begin storing the information and one day it will be apparent that your lessons have taken hold. Begin teaching your baby now about the following:

Sharp or pointed implements. Whenever you use a knife, scissors, razor, or letter opener in front of your baby, be sure to mention that it is sharp, that it's not a toy, that only mummy and daddy or other grownups can touch it. As your child becomes older and gains better small motor control, teach cutting with a child's safety scissors and a butter knife. Finally, advance to supervised use of the 'adult' versions of these implements.

Hot stuff. Even a seven- or eight-month-old will begin to catch on when you consistently warn that your coffee (or the stove, a lit match or candle, a radiator or heater, a fireplace) is hot and shouldn't be touched. Very soon the word 'hot' will automatically signal 'Don't touch' to your baby. Illustrate your point by letting him or her touch something hot, but not hot enough to burn – the very warm outside of your coffee cup, for example. When a child is old enough to strike a match or carry a cup of coffee, he or she should be taught the safe way to do so.

Steps. Parents are often advised to put up safety gates at stairways in homes where there are babies who are beginning to be mobile – either independently or in walkers. On the one hand, this is an important safety precaution and one that too few families take. On the other hand, the baby who knows nothing about steps save that they are off limits is the one who is at greatest risk of accident the first time an open stairway is discovered. So put a gate at the top of every stairway of more than three steps in your home – getting down is much trickier, and thus much more hazardous, for a baby than getting up. But also put a gate three steps up from the bottom so that baby can practise going up and down under safe conditions. When he or she becomes proficient, open the gate occasionally to let baby tackle the full flight as you stand or crouch a step or two below, ready to lend support if a little foot or hand slips. Once going up is mastered, teach baby how to come down safely – a much more challenging task and one that may take several months to achieve. Children who know how to climb up and down steps are much safer should they happen upon an unprotected stairway, which every child does now and then, than those with no climbing experience. But continue to keep the gates in place, fastening them when you're not around to supervise, until your child is a very reliable step climber (somewhere around two years of age).

Electrical hazards. Electrical outlets, electric cords and electrically operated appliances all have great appeal for curious little minds and hands. It's not enough to distract a baby on the way to probing an unprotected outlet or to hide all the visible cords in your home; it's also necessary to repeatedly remind the baby of their dangerous potential ('ouch!'), and to teach older children respectful use of electricity and the risks of mixing it with water.

Bathtubs, pools and other watery attractions. Water play is fun and educational; encourage it. But also teach a baby not to get into the bathtub, a pool, a pond, or any other body of water without mummy or daddy or another grownup – and that includes babies and children who have gone through swimming classes. You can't sufficiently 'waterproof' a young child, so you can never leave one alone near water – but you can begin to teach some water safety rules.

Poisonous substances. You're always careful about locking away household cleansers, medicines and so on. But your parents are visiting and your dad leaves his heart medicine on a living room table. Or you're at your single sister's house and she has chlorine bleach and dishwasher detergent under the kitchen sink. You're asking for trouble if you haven't begun to teach your baby the rules of substance safety. Repeat these messages over and over again:

- Don't eat or drink anything unless mummy or daddy or another grownup you know gives it to you (this is a difficult concept for a baby, but an important one for all children to learn eventually).

- Medicine and vitamin pills are *not* sweets, though they are sometimes flavoured to taste that way. Don't eat or drink them unless mummy or daddy or another grownup you know gives them to you.

- Don't put anything in your mouth if you don't know what it is.

- Only mummy or daddy or another grownup can use aspirin, scouring powder, spray wax, or any other potentially poisonous substance. Repeat this every time you take or give a medication, scrub the tub, polish the furniture and so on.

Red Light on Greenery

Many common house and garden plants are poisonous when eaten. Since plant leaves and flowers are no exception to a baby's everything-in-the-mouth-that-fits rule, poisonous varieties must be off limits for babies. Place houseplants high up, where leaves or flowers can't fall on the floor below, and where baby can't get to them by pulling up, crawling, or climbing. Better still, give poisonous houseplants to childless friends. Label with the accurate botanical name any houseplant you do keep, so that if your baby accidentally ingests some leaves or flowers, you will be able to supply the accurate information to the poison centre or your baby's doctor. Place all plants, even nonpoisonous ones, where they can't be toppled with a tug.

The following houseplants are poisonous, some in very small doses:

Dumb cane, English ivy, foxglove, hyacinth bulbs (and leaves and flowers in quantity), hydrangea, iris rootstalk and rhizome, lily of the valley, philodendron, Jerusalem cherry.

Outdoor plants that are poisonous include:

Azalea, rhododendron, caladium, daffodil and narcissus bulbs, daphne, English ivy, foxglove, holly, hyacinth bulbs (and leaves and flowers in quantity), hydrangea, iris rootstalk and rhizome, Japanese yew seeds and leaves, larkspur, laurel, lily of the valley, morning glory seeds, oleander, privet, rhubarb leaves, sweet peas (especially the 'peas,' which are the seeds), tomato plant leaves, wisteria pods and seeds, yews.

Holiday favourites holly and mistletoe, and to a lesser extent poinsettia, are also on the danger list.

There are dangers outside your home, too, that your baby needs to be prepared for:

Street hazards. Begin teaching street smarts now. Every time you cross a street with your baby, explain about listening and watching for cars, about crossing at the green and not in between, and waiting for the Walk light. If there are driveways in your neighbourhood, then you should explain that it's necessary to 'stop, look, and listen' at them, too. Once your child is walking, teach him never to cross without holding on to an adult's hand – even if there's no traffic. It's a good idea to hold hands on the pavement, too, but many toddlers love the freedom of walking on their own. If you permit this (and you probably will have to at least some of the time), you will have to keep an eye on your child literally every second – that's all it takes for a child to dart into the path of an oncoming car. Infractions of the don't-go-in-the-street-alone rule deserve a sharp reprimand.

Be sure, too, that your baby knows not to leave the house or apartment without you or another adult. Every once in a while a toddler toddles alone out the front door and into trouble.

Car safety. Be certain that your baby not only becomes accustomed to sitting in a car seat, but understands the reason why it's essential. Also explain other car safety rules, such as no throwing toys around, no grabbing the steering wheel, and no playing with door locks or window buttons. Teach older children how to open the locks, in case they should become locked in alone.

Playground safety. Even a baby can begin learning playground safety rules. Teach yours not to twist a swing (when they or someone else is on it, or even if it's empty), push an empty swing, or walk in front of a moving one. Observe these rules yourself, and regularly mention them to your baby. Also explain that it's necessary to wait until the child ahead of you is off the slide before going down, and that it is unsafe to climb up from the bottom.

The best way you can teach your baby about safe living is to practise it. You can't expect a child to be happy about being strapped into a car seat when you don't buckle up yourself, to obey traffic signals if you dash across the street in spite of a Don't Walk light, or to respect fire if you leave the fireplace unscreened and burning cigarette butts all over the house.

TWELVE

The Ninth Month

— — — — — — — — — — ◆ — — — — — — — — — —

What Your Baby May Be Doing

By the end of this month, your baby . . . should be able to (see Note):

- work to get to a toy out of reach
- look for dropped object

Note. If your baby seems not to have reached either of these milestones, check with the doctor. In rare instances the delay could indicate a problem, though in most cases it will turn out to be normal for your baby. Premature infants generally reach milestones later than others of the same birth age, often achieving them closer to their adjusted age (the age they would be if they had been born at term) or sometimes later.

. . . will probably be able to:

- pull up to standing position from sitting (by 9½ months)
- get into a sitting position from stomach (by 9⅓ months)
- object if you try to take a toy away
- stand holding on to someone or something
- pick up tiny object with any part of thumb and finger (by 9¼ months)

- say mama or dada indiscriminately
- play peekaboo

. . . may possibly be able to:

- play patty-cake (clap hands) or wave bye-bye
- walk holding on to furniture (cruise)
- understand word 'no' (but not always obey it)

. . . may even be able to:

- 'play ball' (roll ball back to you)
- drink from a cup independently
- pick up a tiny object neatly with tips of thumb and forefinger
- stand alone momentarily
- stand alone well
- say dada or mama discriminately
- say one word other than mama or dada
- respond to a one-step command with gestures (give that to me – with hand out)

What You Can Expect At This Month's Checkup

Each doctor or health visitor will have a personal approach to well-baby checkups. The overall organization of the physical exam, as well as the number and type of assessment techniques used and procedures performed will also vary with the individual needs of the child. But in general, you can expect the following at a checkup when your baby is about nine months old:

- Questions about how you and baby and the rest of the family are doing at home, and about baby's eating, sleeping and general progress. Questions about child care, if you are working.

- Measurement of baby's weight, length and head circumference, and plotting of progress since birth.

- Physical exam, including a recheck of any previous problems. The fontanel on top of baby's head is smaller now and may even have closed.

- Developmental assessment. The examiner may actually put baby through a series of 'tests' to evaluate baby's ability to sit independently, to pull up with or without help, to reach for and grasp objects, to rake at and pick up tiny objects, to look for a dropped or hidden object, to respond to his or her name, to recognize such words as mummy, daddy, bye-bye and no-no, and to enjoy social games such as patty-cake and peekaboo, or may simply rely on observation plus your reports on what baby is doing.

- Immunizations, if not given before and if baby is in good health and there are no other contraindications. Be sure to discuss previous reactions, if any, beforehand. Tuberculin skin test may be administered now in high-risk areas, or may wait until fifteen months. It may be given prior to, or at the time of, the MMR (measles/mumps/rubella) immunization.

- Possibly, haemoglobin or haematocrit test to check for anaemia (usually by means of a pinprick on the finger).

- Guidance about what to expect in the next month in relation to such topics as feeding, sleeping, development, and infant safety.

- Recommendations about fluoride, iron, and vitamin D, or other supplementation, as needed.

Questions you may want to ask, if the doctor hasn't already answered them:

- What are positive and negative reactions to the tuberculin test, if one was administered? When should you call if there is a positive reaction?

- What new foods can be introduced to baby now? Can baby have milk in a cup? When can citrus, fish, meats, egg whites, be introduced, if they haven't been already?

- When should you consider weaning from the bottle, if your baby is bottle fed, or from the breast, if you haven't already weaned to cup or bottle?

Also raise concerns that have arisen over the past month. Jot down information and instructions from the doctor (you're sure to forget them, otherwise). Record all pertinent information (baby's weight, length, head circumference, immunizations, foods introduced, test results, illnesses, medications given and so on) in a permanent health record.

Feeding Your Baby this Month: Establishing Good Habits Now

We've all met her. The mother of a toddler who moans when her child gorges on ice cream, cake and sweets at a party, howls for chips instead of a sensible lunch in a restaurant, or insists on a soft drink instead of juice at dinner. Who groans when he refuses the sandwich on wholemeal offered at a friend's house and rolls her eyes when the playgroup reports that he won't drink milk at snacktime. She talks a lot about how she wishes she could get him to eat more nutritiously, but deep down inside she's convinced she'd be fighting a losing battle. Aren't kids, after all, born with a preference for junk foods?

The answer, though our well-meaning but misguided mum might be astonished to hear it, is no. A child's palate is born a clean slate; the tastes that develop depend on the foods introduced – even in those first months of eating. A Szechuan child, after all, doesn't favour cold noodles with sesame sauce, or an Indian child raita, because of genetic fate, but because of what he's exposed to at the dinner table. And how your child will eat – whether he or she will choose sandwiches on white bread or wholemeal, find snack satisfaction in a bag of carrot chips or a box of chocolate chip cookies, clamour for plain dried apricots or candied ones – will be primarily influenced by the foods you set on his or her high chair tray now.

So that you don't end up bemoaning your child's eating habits later, start feeding your baby right, right from the start.

Keep white out of sight. A disdain for white bread, rolls, pancakes, biscuits, cakes and crackers is a form of colour discrimination that's actually good to teach young children. A child who never develops a taste for bland, refined baked goods will never balk at the whole-grain varieties. Select only whole-grain products at the supermarket, bake with only whole-grain flours at home, and order only whole-grain breads, when possible, in restaurants.

Don't cut that sweet tooth yet. The longer you hold off on introducing really sweet foods, the better. Don't assume that baby won't eat cottage cheese or plain yogurt unless it's been mixed with mashed ripe banana, or cereal unless it's been sweetened with apple purée or strained peaches; babies whose taste buds haven't been corrupted will not only accept such foods 'straight', they'll learn to love them. Limit fruits, serving them only after your baby's had something that isn't sweet, and serve vegetables often, early on. Although it's okay to gradually introduce fruit-juice-sweetened biscuits, cake and jams as treats, don't get into the habit of doling out the biscuits instead of fresh fruit in the afternoon, topping off every meal with a sweet, or spreading jam on every cracker you hand your baby. When there is no older sibling, the introductions can often wait until baby's first birthday or later.

Keep baby sugar-free. Banning sugar from your baby's diet entirely – at least for the first year, and preferably for the first two – is actually a lot easier than trying to moderate sugar intake. If you allow sugar-sweetened puddings from the start, it will be difficult to restrict them later. It's better to forbid all such dubious treats until your baby understands such concepts as 'just one' and 'special occasion'. Such a restriction will have two important benefits. First, it will modify his or her taste for sugar later – studies show babies who were exposed to sugar early developed a significantly stronger taste for it than those who weren't. And second, it will provide the chance for developing a taste for treats that are nutritionally sound.

Expose your child to germs. The germ of the wheat, that is. Not only will sprinkling wheat germ on your baby's cereal, yogurt, cottage cheese, apple purée, or pasta supply a whopping measure of vitamins and minerals and extra protein found together in few other foods, it will help to nurture a taste for this versatile staple. In not too many months, you may find your toddler banging on the table demanding 'more wheat germ' on breakfast cereal while your neighbour's child is demanding another spoonful of sugar. In later years, when you no longer select what your child eats, this preference may help ensure good nutrition.

Eschew the mashed. Even a completely toothless baby needs something to sink his or her gums into. By now, strained foods should be a thing of the past, with coarsely mashed and finger foods having taken their place in baby's diet (see page 273). Babies who continue too long on strained foods tend to reject lumpier textures when they are finally offered and become very lazy about chewing. This pattern could severely hamper their getting a nutritionally adequate variety of foods later.

Serve the milk straight. When the doctor okays cow's milk – sometimes only in small amounts at this age – give it to your baby unadulterated. Not only does chocolate milk contain lots of sugar, but the chocolate somewhat diminishes the absorption of the calcium in milk (though recent studies indicate this may not be to a significant degree) and can also trigger allergic reaction in some children. In addition, any time you disguise the flavour of milk (even if it's in a juice-sweetened shake), you'll be sabotaging your baby's taste for the pure thing. Save such techniques for the inevitable 'I don't want my milk' rebellion of the preschool years.

Save the salt. Babies don't need salt in their foods beyond what is found there naturally. Don't salt food you prepare for baby and be particularly careful not to serve up salty snacks, which can give your child an unhealthy taste for foods high in sodium.[1]

Spice baby's diet with variety. It's not surprising that so many children turn their noses up when confronted with an unfamiliar food. In most cases, their parents have served up the same cereal every morning for breakfast and the same varieties of baby food for lunch and dinner day in and day out, never offering a change of pace or a chance to taste anything different. Be adventurous in feeding your baby – without, of course, overstepping any boundaries set by the doctor or mandated by your baby's age. Try different types of whole-grain cereals, hot and cold; varieties of whole-grain breads (oatmeal and rye, as well as wheat) in different forms (rolls, bagels, loaves, crackers and later pittas); different shapes of wholemeal or high-protein pastas; dairy products in different forms (yogurt, cottage cheese, kefir, pot cheese, such hard cheeses as Swiss and Cheddar, lower-fat cream cheese); vegetables and fruits beyond carrots, peas and bananas (sweet potato cubes, kale creamed with evaporated milk, ripe cantaloupe and mango slivers, split fresh blueberries and so on).

Variety now is no guarantee that your child won't go through a peanut-butter-and-jelly-only phase – most children do at one time or another. But a familiarity with a wider range of foods will make for a broader diet base and, in the long run, better nutrition.

Brainwash. Don't just practice good nutrition in your home, preach it as well. Even a very young child can learn that sugar is 'bad', white bread isn't good, whole wheat is best. That doesn't mean, of course, that your toddler will never ask for sugar or white bread and will always insist on whole wheat. Children test their parents, and yours is sure to test you by asking for a taste of such forbidden fruit. Don't buckle under. If you're wishy-washy once, then your baby

---

1. Some older children like to shake salt on their palms and then lick it off. Check with your doctor if your child does this. Though in most cases it's no more than a habit, there is a very small possibility that the craving for salt is related to a metabolic disorder.

will be even more persistent the next time, anticipating your giving in once again.

Make exceptions. If junk food is totally forbidden, your baby will come to crave it. Instead of a permanent ban, allow such foods as treats once in a while, when your baby is old enough to understand the idea of treats for special-occasions. Of course, if you've got his or her taste buds properly acclimated, these treats may not taste as good as expected.

Do it yourself. All the above efforts are doomed to failure if the preacher is lax in her own practices. If you breakfast on Danish, lunch on white bread and sausages, and nibble the rest of the day away on crisps and chocolate, you can't expect more from your child, now or ever. So if you haven't already switched to the Best-Odds Diet (see page 524), now is the time for you – and everyone else in your household, young and old – to do so.

Don't cave in to guilt. The reason most mothers end up giving their babies the kinds of things they know aren't good for them is guilt. Reluctant to deprive their children of what they themselves consider to be the just desserts (and chocolate milk and hot dogs) of childhood, they give in, and give up. If you think you might find yourself doing just that, consider these two points: First, at a tender age, a baby doesn't really know what he or she is missing. If you're at a party and ice cream and cake is being served up, your baby will probably be just as happy if you pull out a fruit-juice-sweetened biscuit for him or her to munch on. And second, though you are very likely to begin hearing complaints once the age of enlightenment dawns (so cottage cheese isn't the same as ice cream after all?), and can be sure your child will try very hard to stir up your guilt when you limit the goodies at a birthday party or treats at Halloween, in the long run your child will thank you. If you must feel guilty, better to feel it now than when the dentist announces your child has a mouthful of cavities, or when your teenager has a weight problem, or when, as an adult, blood pressure is high as a result of poor dietary habits.

What You May Be Concerned About

Feeding Baby at the Table

'We've been feeding our son separately, and putting him in the playpen while we eat. When should he start eating with us?'

Feeding themselves and their babies at the same time is a juggling feat most parents can't master – at least not gracefully, or without having to pop a couple of antacid tablets after every meal. So until your baby is a competent self-feeder, continue to give him his meals separately. But that doesn't mean he shouldn't begin to sit in on adult meals (as long as your schedules permit) for practice in table manners and sociability. Whenever it's practical and desirable, draw his high chair up to the table at your mealtime, or set him up in a hook-on dining seat, give him his own place setting (non-breakable dishes and a spoon only) and some finger foods, and include him in the table conversation. On the other hand, do reserve some late dinners for adults only in order to keep (or put back) the romance in your lives.

Walking too Early

'Our daughter wants to walk all the time, holding on to the hands of any willing adult. Several relatives have warned that we shouldn't let her, saying walking before she's ready will damage her legs.'

It's more likely to damage your backs than her legs. If your daughter's legs weren't ready for this kind of pre-walking activity, she wouldn't be clamouring for it. Like early standing, early walking (assisted or unassisted) can't cause bowleggedness (actually a normal characteristic of babies under two) or any other physical problem. In fact, both these activities are beneficial, as they exercise and strengthen some of the muscles used in walking solo. And if she's barefoot, they will help strengthen her feet as well. So as long as your backs hold out, let her walk to her legs' content.

A baby who doesn't want to walk at this stage, of course, shouldn't be pushed into it. As with other aspects of development, just follow your half-pint-size leader.

Pulling Up

'Our baby has just learned to pull up. He seems to love it for a few minutes but then starts screaming. Could standing be hurting his legs?'

If your child's legs weren't ready to hold him, he wouldn't be pulling up. He's screaming out of frustration, not pain. Like most babies who've just learned to stand, he's stranded in this unfamiliar position until he falls, collapses, or is helped down. And that's where you come in. As soon as you notice frustration setting in, gently help him down to a sitting position. Slowly does it – so that he can get the idea of how to do it himself, which should take a few days, or at most, a few weeks. In the meantime, expect to spend a lot of time coming to the rescue of your baby-in-distress.

'My baby is trying to pull up on everything in the house. Should I keep her in the playpen for safety?'

The more our children learn to do, the more nervous we become – and rightly so. As they learn to pull up, then cruise and finally walk, they enter a stage when they have more brawn than their brains can be responsible

for – and are at high risk of accidental injury. But banishment to the playpen (except for brief periods when no one is available to closely supervise) is not the solution. Nerve-racking as it may be to you, your almost-toddler needs plenty of opportunity to explore the world outside the playpen. And you need to make that world as safe as possible.

Be especially certain now that anything she might attempt to pull up on (get down on her level if necessary to determine what that might be) is secure. Unstable tables, bookcases, chairs and floor lamps should be put away or out of reach for the time being. Corners and sharp edges on remaining coffee or end tables should be cushioned in case baby falls against them (she probably will, and often). Be sure that breakable or dangerous knickknacks she couldn't reach before are put away. If you have a dishwasher, don't leave it open when she's on the loose. To prevent slips and trips, be sure that electrical cords are out of the way, that papers are not left lying around on the floor, and that spills on smooth-surfaced floors are wiped up quickly. And to be sure her feet won't sabotage her, keep her barefoot or in skid-proof socks or slippers, rather than in smooth-soled shoes.

When a child begins pulling up, cruising around the room – from chair to table to wall to sofa to daddy's legs, for example – can't be far behind. Which means that if you put her down in one spot in the room, you should be prepared to see her move to a totally different spot, or even to another room. So every corner of every room in your home (except those behind always-closed doors) has to be baby-proofed. If you didn't attend to this when your baby began crawling, or if she never crawled, see page 284 for tips on making home safe for baby.

Fear of Strangers

'Our little girl has always been friendly and outgoing. But when my in-laws – with whom she always loved to play – came in from out of town

yesterday, she broke into tears every time they came near her. What's come over her?'

Maturity – of a very immature sort. Though she'll show a definite preference for her mother and father after the first couple of months, a baby under six months or so will generally respond positively to almost any grownup. Whether they are familiar adults or strangers, she lumps them pretty much into the category of people who are capable of taking care of her needs. Often, as a baby approaches eight or nine months (though 'stranger anxiety', the official term for this phenomenon, can begin at six months or even earlier), she begins to realize which side her bread is really buttered on; that mother and father, and possibly another familiar person or two, are her primary caretakers; and that she ought to stick close to them and steer clear of anyone who might try to separate her from them (strangers). During this time, even once-beloved grandmothers and baby-sitters may be suddenly rejected, as baby clings desperately to her parents (particularly the parent who provides the most care).

Wariness of strangers may disappear quickly or not peak until somewhat past a year; in about 2 in 10 babies it never develops at all (possibly because these babies adjust easily to new situations of all kinds) or passes so quickly it isn't noticed. If your baby does exhibit stranger anxiety, don't pressure her to be sociable – she'll come around eventually, and it's best that she does on her own terms. In the meantime, warn friends and family that she's going through a shy stage (which they shouldn't take personally) and that quick advances will frighten her. Suggest that instead of trying to hug her or pick her up immediately, they try to break down her resistance slowly – by smiling at her, talking to her, offering her a plaything – while she sits securely on your lap. Eventually she may warm up, and even if she doesn't, at least there won't have been any tears and bad feelings along the way.

If it's a longtime nanny or childminder your child suddenly doesn't want to go to,

the odds are that once you leave the house – no matter how hysterical she may be in your presence – she will quiet down. If it's a new nanny, you may have to spend some additional orientation time before your baby will be willing to stay with the newcomer. If your baby is truly inconsolable when left with a caregiver, new or old, then it's time to re-evaluate your child-care situation. Maybe the nanny is not giving your baby the kind of attention and love she needs, even if she seems caring when you're around. Or it may simply be a case of extreme stranger anxiety. Some infants, particularly those who are breastfed, can cry for hours when mummy is gone, even when daddy or grandmother is the baby-sitter. In such a case, you may have to limit time away from your child, if possible, until this 'missing-mummy' phase has passed.

Security Objects

'For the last couple of months our baby has become more and more attached to his blanket. He even drags it around when he's crawling. Does this mean he's insecure?'

He is a little insecure, and with good reason. In the last couple of months he's discovered he's a separate person, not an extension of his parents. The discovery is undeniably exciting (so many challenges!), yet more than a little frightening (so many risks!). Many babies, when they realize that mummy and daddy may not always be available to lean on from now on, become attached to a transitional comfort object (a soft blanket, a cuddly stuffed animal, a bottle, a dummy as a sort of stand-in. Like parents, the object offers comfort – particularly appealing when a baby is frustrated, sick, or tired – but unlike parents, it's under the infant's control. For the baby who has trouble separating from his parents, taking the security object to bed makes going to sleep alone easier.

Sometimes a baby who hasn't become attached to a security object earlier will do so suddenly when confronted with a new and unsettling situation (a new nanny, a day nursery, moving to a new home and so on). The transitional comfort object is usually given up sometime between the ages of two and five (about the same time that thumb sucking is abandoned), but often not until it is lost, disintegrates, or in some other way becomes unavailable. Some children mourn for a day or two, but then get on with their lives; others hardly note the passing of their old friend.

Though parents (or other caregivers) should never tease or scold a baby or child about a security object or pressure him to give it up, it is often possible to set some limits early on that will make the habit less objectionable and help to prepare a baby for the inevitable separation:

- If the habit is in its early stages and is not yet deeply entrenched, try to head off future hassles by limiting its use to home or to bedtime. But don't forget to take it along on overnights and holidays.

- Before the object begins to take on a grubbiness that your baby can smell, wash it. Otherwise, he may become attached as much to the odour as to the object itself, and complain strenuously if it returns from the wash smelling like springtime. If you can't get it away from him during waking hours, wash it while he's asleep.

- If the object is a toy, you might want to invest in a duplicate. This will give you a ready replacement in case of loss, let you wash them alternately, and allow you to rotate the items so that neither becomes too grimy. If it's a blanket, you might consider cutting it into several sections so that lost or thread-worn pieces can be replaced as needed.

- Though the less said about the object, the better, you can remind your child now and then that when he's more grownup he won't need his blanket (or other object) any more.

- Although an empty bottle or a bottle of water is acceptable, don't let your baby use a bottle of juice or milk as a comfort object. Sucking on such liquids for long periods at a time – particularly at night – can cause dental decay and interfere with a baby's getting adequate solids.

- Make sure your baby is getting the comfort (and love and attention) he needs from you, including plenty of hugs and kisses, if he enjoys them, and frequent talking and playing sessions in which you give him your undivided attention.

Though attachment to a comfort object is a normal developmental step for many infants, a baby who becomes so obsessed with the object that he doesn't spend enough time interacting with people, playing with toys, or practising physical feats may have some emotional needs that aren't being met. If this seems to be the case with your baby, check with his doctor.

Flat Feet

'My baby's arches look totally flat when he stands up. Could he have flat feet?'

In babies, flatness is the rule, not the exception. And it's a rule that you're not likely to find an exception to. There are several reasons: first of all, since young babies don't do much walking, the muscles in their feet haven't been exercised enough to fully develop the arches. Second, a pad of fat fills the arch, making it difficult to discern, particularly in chubby babies. And when babies begin to walk, they stand with feet apart to achieve balance, putting more weight on the arch and giving the foot a flatter appearance.

In most children, the flat-footed look will slowly diminish over the years, and by the time full growth is attained, the arch will be well formed. In only a small percentage will the feet remain flat (not a serious problem, anyway), but that's something that can't be predicted now.

No Teeth

'Our baby is almost nine months old and still doesn't have a single tooth. What could be holding her teething up?'

Enjoy those toothless grins while you can, and be reassured that there are many nine-month-olds who are all gums – even a few who finish their first year without a single tooth with which to bite into their birthday cake – but that teeth come to every baby eventually. Though the average baby cuts a first tooth at seven months, the range is from two months (occasionally earlier) to twelve (sometimes later). Late teething is usually hereditary and is no reflection on your baby's intelligence or development. (Second teeth will come in later, too.) Toothlessness needn't interfere, incidentally, with a baby's moving on to chunkier foods; the gums are used for chewing in toothed and toothless babies alike until molars arrive in the middle of the second year.

Still Hairless

'Our daughter was born bald and still has little more than peach fuzz. When will she get some hair?'

To a mother tired of hearing 'Oh, what a cute little boy' whenever she's out with her daughter, and eager to make a definitive gender statement with ribbons and bows, baldness or near baldness that persists well into the second half of the first year can be frustrating. But, like toothlessness, hairlessness at this age is not unusual – and not permanent. The problem is most common among fair babies with light hair and is not a forecast of baldness later in life. In time your daughter's hair will come in (though perhaps not in quantity until sometime late in the second year). For now, be thankful that you don't have to wrestle with a tangled headful of hair during shampoos and comb-outs.

Loss of Interest in Nursing

'Whenever I sit down to breastfeed my son, he seems to want to do something else – play with my buttons, pull up on my hair, look at the television screen, anything but nurse.'

In the early months, when a breastfeeding baby's whole world seems to revolve around his mother's breasts, it seems implausible that a time will ever come when he will be disinterested in nursing. And yet, though some babies remain passionate about nursing until weaning, many display waning interest and concentration somewhere around the ninth month. Some simply begin to refuse the breast entirely; others nurse seriously for a minute or two and then pull away; still others are easily distracted during nursing, either by what's going on around them or by their desire to practise their new-found physical prowess. Sometimes the boycott is just transient. Maybe baby is going through a readjustment in his nutritional needs, or perhaps he's put off by the altered taste of your breast milk brought on by hormonal changes during your menstrual period or from the garlicky *pasta al pesto* you dined on the previous night. Or maybe he's lost his appetite to a virus or a bout of teething.

But if your baby regularly rejects the breast, it's possible he's telling you he's ready for weaning, because he either has a decreased need for sucking, is taking more solids and milk from a cup or bottle, or doesn't like being held and/or lying still for lengthy feedings. Before you decide, however, that weaning is imminent, be sure the problem isn't a feeding environment that is so distracting your baby can't concentrate on the task at hand. To rule out this possibility, try nursing in a quiet room with lights dimmed, no television or radio blaring, no older children playing and no adult conversation being carried on. If your baby still seems lackadaisical about nursing, he may truly be on the verge of giving up the breast. Of course, *you* may not be ready for this – but as many mothers before you have learned, you can lead a baby to the breast, but you can't make him drink.

Still, you should try to keep the weaning gradual – for your baby's health as well as your own comfort. Gradual weaning will allow baby time to increase his intake of a nutritional replacement, such as cow's milk or formula, before he gives breast milk up entirely. And it will give your breasts the chance to reduce production slowly to avoid painful engorgement. (See page 335 for tips on weaning; if your baby absolutely refuses to take any breastfeedings, see page 336 for making abrupt weaning easier.)

Ask his doctor if you should give your baby whole cow's milk (not skimmed or low-fat) now, or if you should stick with formula until he's a year old. If he's been taking a bottle, it's likely he will be able to get enough milk from this source – unless, as sometimes happens, he is no longer interested in sucking on a bottle either. In that case, or if he's never accepted a bottle at all, or if you'd rather not face the task of weaning him from the bottle later, milk from a cup is the alternative. Babies who were started on the cup earlier are often very proficient by this age; those who weren't often catch on quickly. Plain whole-milk yogurt or hard cheeses can be given as a calcium supplement for children who won't drink enough milk or formula straight.

Fussy Eating Habits

'When I first introduced solids, my daughter seemed to love everything I gave her. But lately, she won't eat anything but bread.'

To hear their parents tell it, some children (up until adolescence, when a week's worth of groceries lasts three days) live on nothing but air, love and the occasional crust of bread. But in spite of parental concerns, even picky eaters manage to drink, nibble and nosh enough during the day to thrive. Children are programmed to eat what they need to live and grow – unless something

happens to alter that programming early in their eating history.

At this stage of development, most babies are still getting a major portion of their needed nutrition from breast milk, formula, or whole milk and this is usually rounded out sufficiently by whatever bits of solid foods they get during the day. Vitamin drops with iron provide added insurance. But at nine months, nutritional requirements are beginning to increase and the need for milk begins to decrease. To be sure that your baby's intake continues to meet her requirements, incorporate the following into your feeding strategy:

Let them eat bread . . . Or cereal, or bananas, or whatever food they favour. Many babies and toddlers seem to be on a food-of-the-week (or -month) plan, refusing to eat anything but a single selection during that time. And it's best to respect their dietary preferences and aversions, even when taken to extremes: cereal for breakfast, lunch and dinner, for example. Eventually, if given a chance to do so on her own, a child will expand her repertoire of tastes.

. . . but make sure it's whole wheat. Of course, if your baby's eating only one or two foods (and actually, even if she's eating a variety), make sure that they provide high-quality nourishment. So if it's bread, bagels, crackers, or cereal she craves, give her only whole-grain varieties. If it's fruit or fruit juice, be sure it's unsweetened and try to encourage the more nutritious types, such as apricots, yellow peaches, cantaloupes, mangos and oranges.

Add on when you can. While you shouldn't push food on your baby, there's nothing wrong with trying to sneak it by her. Spread the bread with whipped or thinned cream cheese,[2] mashed banana, puréed pumpkin sweetened with apple juice concentrate and cinnamon, or cottage cheese,

---

2. Fat-reduced cream cheeses have more protein than the regular varieties and are thus more nutritious for baby. But read labels to be sure of what you're buying.

or melt some Swiss cheese on it. Or turn it into French toast, or 'eggie bread', served whole or cut into small pieces. Or try baking and buying breads that incorporate other Best-Odds requirements, such as pumpkin, carrot, cheese, or fruit. If it's cereal your baby craves, sprinkle cereal with wheat germ, and slip in a serving of fruit in the form of a diced banana, apple purée, cooked diced peaches or other fruit, or some iron in the form of diced cooked dried fruit. If bananas are her sole passion, try dipping slices in milk and rolling in wheat germ, serving them conspicuously with a small amount of cereal or cottage cheese, or mashing them on bread.

Omit the mush. Your baby's recent rebellion may simply be her way of telling you that she's had it with the mushed and the mashed and is ready for more grownup fare. Changing to chunky foods and finger foods that are soft enough for her to manage but intriguing enough in taste and texture to satisfy her maturing palate may turn her into the epicure you seek.

Vary the menu. Maybe your baby's just tired of the same old meals; a change may be what she needs to spark her appetite. If she lacks interest in cereal at breakfast, offer yogurt and toast instead. If cottage cheese with mashed baby peas and carrots for lunch seems to bore her, toss some buttered noodles with finely minced cooked cauliflower and broccoli and grated or shredded Cheddar. If minced meat and mashed potatoes doesn't appeal at dinner, try poached fish and baked yams. (See Best-Odds listings for additional ideas, page 349.) Also consider, when you plan your baby's menus, that she may enjoy eating what everyone else is eating rather than being an outcast. (If you are introducing new foods your baby hasn't had before, see page 213.)

Turn the tables. Perhaps it's just a newly emerging streak of stubborn independence that's keeping her mouth clenched at mealtime. Hand her the responsibility of feeding,

and she may open her mouth eagerly to a wide range of food experiences she would never take from the spoon you offer. (For appropriate choices for the self-feeding baby, see page 273.)

Don't drown her appetite. Many babies (and toddlers) eat very little because they're drinking too much juice, formula, or breast milk. Your baby should have no more than two Best-Odds fruit servings in the form of juice (preferably one of juice and one of whole fruit) and no more than three of formula (or later, milk) a day. If she wants to drink more than that, give her water or watered-down juice, spreading the servings out over the day. If you're breast-feeding, you don't know exactly how much milk she's taking, but you can be pretty sure that nursing her more than three or four times a day will interfere with her appetite; cut back.

Attack snacks. What does mum do when baby refuses breakfast? Plies her with snacks all morning, of course, which means she isn't likely to have any appetite for lunch. And what happens after lunch is missed? Baby's hungry again in the afternoon, snacking continues, and there's no room for dinner. Avoid this cycle, depressing to both baby's appetite and your spirit, by strictly limiting snacks to one mid-morning and one mid-afternoon, no matter how little your child eats at mealtimes. You can, however, increase the amount fed at snacktime by a bit in order to tide baby over from a light or skipped meal to the next feeding time.

Keep smiling. The easiest way for you to lay the foundation for a permanent feeding problem is to frown with displeasure when your baby turns her head away from the oncoming spoon, to comment unhappily when she comes out of the high chair as empty of food as when she went in, or to spend half an hour trying to get a couple of spoonfuls of food into her closed mouth with cajoling, pleading, or tricks 'here comes the choo choo train into the tunnel'). She needs to feel she's eating because she's hungry, not because you want her to. So at all costs – even at the cost of some missed meals – don't make eating (or not eating) an issue. If she clearly doesn't want any more, or doesn't want to eat at all, remove the dish and end the meal without further ado.

Short-term appetite loss, of course, can accompany colds and other acute illnesses, particularly when fever is present. Rarely, a baby will show a chronic lack of appetite due to anaemia (see page 255) or malnutrition (both uncommon among middle-class babies) or other illness. If your baby's loss of appetite is accompanied by lack of energy, lack of interest in her environment, a slowdown in development, insufficient weight gain, or a marked change in personality (sudden irritability or nervousness, for instance), check with her doctor.

Self-Feeding

'Every time the spoon comes near my baby, she grabs for it. If her bowl is near enough, she dips her fingers in and makes a mess trying to feed herself. She's getting nothing to eat and I'm getting frustrated.'

It's clearly time to pass the spoon to a new generation. Your baby is expressing her desire to be independent, at least at the table. Encourage rather than discourage her. But to minimize the mess and keep her from going hungry until she can pass muster with Miss Manners, pass the responsibility on gradually – if possible.

Begin by giving her a spoon of her own while you continue feeding her. She may not be able to do much more than wave it around at first, and when she does fill it and get it to her mouth it will usually be upside down. Still, wielding a spoon may keep her content enough to let you take care of most of the meal, at least for a while. The next step is to provide finger foods that she can feed herself while you spoon feed her. The combination of finger foods and a personal spoon (and/or a covered cup to take swigs from) usually keeps a baby occupied and

happy enough for mum or dad to get the rest of the meal into her, but not always. Some babies insist on doing it all themselves; if this is the only way your baby will eat, let her. Mealtimes will take longer and be messier at first, but the experience will make your child a more proficient self-feeder sooner. (Spreading newspaper on the floor beneath baby's chair will at least make cleanup easier.)

Whatever you do, don't let mealtime become battle time, or you'll risk setting her up for permanent eating problems. When self-feeding degenerates into all play and no eating (some play is normal), you can try picking up the spoon and taking over the feeding yourself. If your baby balks, it's time to wipe the carrots off the chin and the cottage cheese from between the fingers and call it quits until the next meal.

Changes in Sleep Patterns

'Suddenly my daughter doesn't want to nap in the morning. Is one nap a day enough for her?'

Though one nap a day may not be enough for the exhausted parents, it is all many babies need as they approach their first birthday. A few babies even try to give up both naps at this time. Most often it is the morning nap that goes first, but occasionally it's the after-lunch siesta. The babies of some lucky parents continue to nap twice a day well into the second year, and this is perfectly normal, too, as long as it doesn't seem to be interfering with a good night's sleep. If it does seem to be, baby should be weaned down to one nap (see page 219).

How much a baby sleeps is of less consequence than how well she functions on the sleep she's getting. If your baby refuses to go down for a nap or naps but seems cranky and overtired by dinnertime, it may be that she needs the extra sleep but is protesting because she doesn't want to waste precious time – that she could use for activity and exploration – on sleep. Not getting needed naps makes for a less happy, less cooperative baby during the day, and often one who goes to bed less easily and sleeps less well at night; being overtired and overcharged, she has a difficult time settling down and staying down.

If your baby doesn't seem to be getting the naps she needs, make a special effort to encourage her. Try putting her down – fed, changed and relaxed by a little quiet play and quiet music – in a dark room with no distractions. If that doesn't work, you may need to resort to walking her in the push-chair or driving around with her in the car. (Many city babies do all their napping in the pushchair, suburban babies in the car.) If necessary, try letting your baby – 'cry it out' before giving up on getting her to nap, but not for as long as you would at night. More that twenty minutes of crying and there goes her naptime.

'We thought we'd done everything right. Our baby always went to sleep without a fuss. Now he seems to want to stay up and play all night.'

It's something like making a sudden move from a small town to London. A couple of months ago, there wasn't much to keep your baby up at night. Now, with so many dis-coveries to make, toys to play with, people to interact with and physical accomplish-ments to fine-tune (who wants to lie down when you're just learning to stand up?), your baby doesn't want to take time out to sleep.

Unfortunately, in this case baby doesn't know what's good for him. As with not sleeping enough during the day, going to sleep too late at night can make him over-tired, which, in turn, can keep him from settling down well at all. Children who aren't getting adequate sleep are more likely to have trouble falling asleep and to wake up during the night. They may also be cranky during the day and more prone to accidents.

If your baby isn't going to sleep readily at night, be sure he's napping sufficiently during the day (see page 219). Next, establish a bedtime routine – or if you've already established one but have been adhering to it halfheartedly, enforce it. If a baby-sitter or grandparents will be putting baby to bed occasionally, make sure they are familiar with the rituals.

If you aren't certain what to include in a bedtime routine, you can try some or all of the following:

A bath. After a day of cleaning the floor with his knees, massaging his scalp with mashed banana, and rolling in the sand-pit, a baby needs a bath. But the evening bath does more than get a baby clean – it relaxes him. Warm, soothing waters wield magical, sleep-inducing powers; don't waste them by giving baby his bath earlier in the day.

A sleep-inducing atmosphere. Dim the lights, turn the TV off, send older children from the room, and keep other distractions to a minimum.

A story, a song, a cuddle. After your baby's been changed and pajama-ed, settle down together into a comfortable chair or sofa, or on baby's bed once he's graduated to one. Read him a simple story, if he will sit still for one, in a soft monotone rather than a lively, animated voice. Or if he prefers, let him look at some picture books himself. Sing quiet songs and lullabies, hug a little, but save rougher fun (such as wrestling matches and tickling ses-sions) for other times. Once baby's motor is turned on, it's hard to turn off.

A light for the wary. Some babies are afraid of the dark. If yours is one of them, give him a night light to keep him company.

Goodbyes. Put a favourite toy or animal to bed. Encourage your baby to wave bye-bye to it, as well as to stuffed animals, siblings, mummy and daddy. Share goodnight kisses all around, tuck baby into his cot and make your departure.

If he cries when you leave the room, return for a moment to be sure he's okay, kiss him again, then leave. If he continues crying, you will probably have to resort to letting him cry it out. The tried-and-usually-true technique, described on page 261, is likely to work, but it may be harder on you now that he's not only older but wiser. At this age, he will probably know how to get you back into the room, or at least how to make you feel guilty if you don't return. He may repeatedly pull up and scream until you help him to get down again. Or he may start calling 'ma-ma' or 'da-da', making it difficult for you not to respond. And rather than being calmed by a visit, as a younger baby might, he will probably be all the angrier when you leave him again. Your best bet with such a little wise guy is to try to stay away entirely while he gets himself back into the habit of going to sleep on his own.

'We haven't been able to set up a bed-time routine for our baby because he always falls asleep nursing before we start.'

If your baby routinely falls asleep with the last nursing of the evening, go through the entire go-to-bed routine – including the good-nights – before settling down to nurse. Or, if you'd like to try to break him of the nursing-to-sleep habit, try nursing him before his bath under conditions not conducive to sleep – with plenty of noise, light, and activity, and the promise of a bath and story ahead. If he falls asleep in spite of all your efforts, try waking him for the bath. If that doesn't work, go back to nursing after the bedtime rituals and try again in a couple of weeks.

'I think my baby's having trouble sleeping because she's cutting teeth. Even though there's nothing I can do for her, I feel guilty letting her cry at night.'

Better guilty now than sleepless from now on. As parents know all too well, there's very little you can do to comfort a baby who's experiencing severe teething pain. And in the middle of the night, there's no use trying. Stay up with her during these teething bouts, and you'll get her so used to having your presence at night that she'll demand it long after the new tooth (or teeth) comes

through. Teething pain usually keeps a baby up sporadically, for only a few nights at a time; knowing that a parent will appear when she cries can keep her up indefinitely. So resist the temptation to go to her and let her settle back down by herself – though you might want to peek in to be sure she hasn't pulled up and stranded herself, unable to get back down again, become uncovered, or otherwise got into trouble. If it makes either or both of you happier, go to her, pat her for a minute or two, tell her to go back to sleep, and then leave.

If she seems inconsolable, ask her doctor about the possibility of giving her a dose of baby paracetamol before she goes to bed. Do be sure, however, that your baby's night waking isn't prompted by illness – an ear infection, for example, the pain of which often worsens at night – which such pain medication could mask.

Slow Development

'We're worried because our baby has begun only recently to sit well by himself – much later than our friends' babies.'

Each baby's rate of development is predetermined primarily by his genes, which determine how quickly his nervous system develops. He is programmed to sit, pull up, stand, walk, smile his first smile and say his first word at a certain age. Few develop at a uniform rate in all areas; most are faster in some and slower in others. One baby might, for example, be quick to smile and talk (social and language skills), but not pull up until nearly a year (a gross motor skill). Another might walk (a gross motor skill) at eight months, yet not exhibit a pincer grasp (a fine motor skill) until after his first birthday. The rate at which motor skills develop is in no way related to intelligence.

Doing even most things later than other children, as long as development falls within the wide range considered normal and progresses from one step to the next, is not usually a matter for concern. When a child routinely reaches developmental milestones long after other children, however, a consultation with his doctor is in order. In most cases, such a consultation will put a parent's fears to rest. Some children mature slowly, yet are perfectly normal. Occasionally, further checks will be necessary to determine whether or not a problem really exists, which of course it sometimes does.

Once in a great while, the baby's doctor is not concerned but the parents have some lingering doubts in spite of every reassurance. Their best route to peace of mind: a referral to a developmental specialist. Sometimes the baby's doctor, who sees him only for brief evaluations, misses signs of poor development that a parent sees or senses and that an expert doing a lengthier check can pick up. The consultation serves a dual purpose. First, if parental concern turns out to be truly unnecessary, worry, at least about development, can be cast aside. Second, if there does turn out to be a problem, early intervention may improve the child's chances of living up to his full potential.

Strange Stools

'When I changed my baby's nappy today I was really puzzled. Her stool seemed to be filled with grains of sand. But she never plays in a sand-pit.'

Just when you're getting bored with changing nappies, another surprise turns up in one. Sometimes it's easy to figure out what went into baby to produce the change in her stools. Frightening red colour? Usually innocent beetroot or beetroot juice. Black specks or strands? Bananas. Small dark foreign objects? Maybe blueberries or raisins. Light green pellets? Perhaps peas. Yellow ones? Corn. Seeds? Very likely tomatoes, cucumbers, or melon from which the seeds were not completely removed.

Because babies don't chew thoroughly and their digestive tracts are not fully mature, what goes in often comes out largely unchanged in colour and texture.[3] Sandy stools, such as those in your baby's nappy,

are fairly common, not because babies snack from the sand-pit (though they do), but because certain foods – particularly oat cereals and pears – often appear sandy once they've passed through the digestive tract.

Odd changes in the stool come not just from natural items in your baby's diet, but also from those synthesized in the food lab (most of which aren't appropriate for babies, but nevertheless sometimes find their way into small tummies). Such products have been known to colour stools such dramatic hues as fluorescent green (from a grape-flavoured beverage) and shocking pinkish red (from a berry-flavoured breakfast cereal).

So before you panic at the sight of what's been filling your baby's nappy, stop and think about what's been filling her.

Baby and Biking

'My husband and I are ardent cyclists. Is it safe to take our baby along?'

Cycling may seem like the perfect way to combine quality family time and exercise, but child-safety experts now believe that bike riding with a baby involves too many risks. So if you really want to play safe, do your cycling solo.

If, in spite of this warning, you decide to hit the bike trails with your child, faithfully observe these vital rules:

- Don't even consider taking your baby along unless your child is at least a year old, you're a very competent cyclist and your bike is in perfect condition.

- Never bicycle unless you are both wearing approved and appropriate safety helmets.

- Have your child ride in an approved child bicycle seat that protects her feet and hands from being caught in the spokes and minimizes both the impact of a fall and the risk of injury should you take a

---

3. Squashing, mashing, or splitting raisins, berries, peas and corn kernels will make them not only easier to digest but safer.

tumble. Be sure the seat is properly installed and that your child is securely
belted before you start off.

- Or use a bicycle 'trailer' to pull your child
  behind you. The advantage is that even if
  you and your bike take a spill, the trailer
  and your baby will remain upright. The
  disadvantage: because it is below wind-
  shield levels of most vehicles, it may leave
  your child more vulnerable in traffic. So
  it's probably safest to use such a trailer
  only on bike paths.

- Restrict your bike outings to safe areas,
  such as parks, bicycle trails, quiet streets
  or roads. Avoid busy roundabouts;
  snowy, icy, or wet roads; and roads
  strewn with wet leaves. Walk your bike
  when you come to a downhill gradient –
  on a slope, dangerous speeds can be
  reached without even trying and braking
  becomes surprisingly difficult.

Better yet, hire a baby-sitter, take turns cycling, or wait until your child is old enough
to ride alongside you.

WHAT IT'S IMPORTANT TO KNOW:
Games Babies Play

When it comes to baby care, a lot has
changed since our mothers' mothers were
mothers. The trend is now towards breastfeeding, instead of away from it. Dirty nappies are tossed into the rubbish instead of
scrubbed and boiled on the stove for reuse.
Schedules are less by the book and more by
the baby. Yet with all the changes, some
things have remained the same. The sterling
silver teething ring too precious to allow
baby to teethe on it. The handmade cradle
that has helped rock three generations to
sleep. And the games that babies love.

Time-honoured as any heirloom, the
peekaboos and this-little-piggies that
brought squeals of delight to your grandmother's baby are guaranteed to do the
same for yours. But such games do more
than entertain; they improve socialization
skills, teach such concepts as object permanence (peekaboo), coordination of
words and actions (the itsy-bitsy spider),
counting skills (one, two, buckle my shoe),
and language skills (eyes, nose, mouth).

Chances are that even if you haven't heard
a nursery game in decades, many your mother played with you will come back to you
now that you're in her shoes. If they don't, ask
your mother for a replay of her favourites (a
mother never forgets). Tap, too, the resources of other relatives for venerable folk
songs, nursery rhymes and games that might
otherwise be lost, and your husband's side of
the family for their favourites.

Refresh your memory or learn a few new
games from the list below.

Peekaboo. Cover your face (with your
hands, the corner of a blanket, a piece of
clothing, a menu in a restaurant, or by hiding
behind a curtain or the foot of the cot and
say, 'Where's mummy?' (or daddy). Then
uncover your face and say, 'Peekaboo, I
see you'. Be ready to repeat and repeat
until you collapse; most babies have a vor-
acious appetite for this game. Or say 'Peekaboo' when you cover your face, 'I see you'
when you uncover it.

Clap hands. While you sing – 'Clap hands,
clap hands, till daddy comes home, 'cause
daddy has money and mummy has none' is
the traditional verse – take your baby's
hands and show him or her how to clap.
At first, your baby's hands will probably not
open wide, but the ability to hold the hands
flat will finally come, though maybe not until
the end of the year; don't push it. It may also
be a while before your baby can clap independently, but that, too, will come. During
the interim, he or she may enjoy holding
your hands and patting them together.

You can modernize the ditty, if you like: 'Clap hands, clap hands, till mummy comes home, 'cause mummy has money and baby has none.' Or you can try clapping feet, for a change of pace. Or you can use this rhyme: 'Patty-cake, patty-cake, baker's man, bake me a cake as fast as you can. Pat it, and prick it, and mark it with "B," and put it in the oven for baby and me.'

The itsy-bitsy spider. Use your fingers – the thumb of one hand to the pointer finger of the other – to simulate a spider climbing up an invisible web, and sing: 'The itsy-bitsy spider climbed up the water spout.' Then, use your fingers to imitate rain falling, and continue: 'Down came the rain and washed the spider out.' Throw your arms up and out for 'Out came the sun and dried up all the rain.' And then back to square one, the spider goes back up the web and you end with, 'And the itsy bitsy spider went up the spout again.'

This little piggy went to market. Take baby's thumb or big toe and start with, 'This little piggy went to market.' Move on to the next finger or toe, 'This little piggy stayed home.' And the next, 'This little piggy had roast beef' (or if you're a vegetarian, 'pizza'), fourth finger, 'This little piggy had none.' As you sing the final line, 'This little piggy cried wee, wee, wee, all the way home,' run your fingers up baby's arm or leg to under the arms or neck, tickling all the way.

So big. Ask, 'How big is baby?' (or use child's name, the dog's name, or a sibling's name), help your child to spread his or her arms as wide as possible, and exclaim, 'So big'.

Eyes, nose, mouth. Take both baby's hands in yours, touch one to each of your eyes, then both to your nose, then to your mouth (where you end with a kiss), naming each feature as you move along: 'Eyes, nose, mouth, smooch.' Nothing teaches these body parts faster.

Ring-a-ring roses. Try this one once your baby is walking. Hold hands with him or her (invite a sibling, playmate, or other adult to join the circle, when possible) and walk around in a circle, singing, 'Ring a-ring roses, a pocket full of posies, atishoo, atishoo, we all fall down' – at which point you all collapse down on the floor. One variation is to substitute 'hopscotch, hopscotch' for 'atishoo, atishoo,' and to jump up at each one.

One, two, buckle my shoe. When climbing stairs or counting fingers, sing: 'One, two, buckle my shoe. Three, four, knock at the door. Five, six, pick up sticks. Seven, eight, close the gate. Nine, ten, start again.'

Pop goes the weasel. You can turn slowly in a circle with baby if you're standing, or rock him or her back and forth if you're seated, as you sing, 'All around the mulberry bush, the monkey chased the weasel. The monkey thought it was all in fun. . . .' Then, 'Pop goes the weasel!' as you bounce baby with the pop. Once baby is familiar with the song, wait a moment before bouncing to give him or her a chance to do the popping.

THIRTEEN

The Tenth Month

◆

What Your Baby May Be Doing

By the end of this month, your baby . . . should be able to (see Note):

- stand holding on to someone or something

- pull up to standing position from sitting

- object if you try to take a toy away

- say mama or dada indiscriminately

- play peekaboo

Note: If your baby seems not to have reached one or more of these milestones, check with the doctor. In rare instances the delay could indicate a problem, though in most cases it will turn out to be normal for your baby. Premature infants generally reach milestones later than others of the same birth age, often achieving them closer to their adjusted age (the age they would be if they had been born at term), or sometimes later.

. . . will probably be able to:

- get into a sitting position from stomach

- play patty-cake (clap hands) or wave bye-bye

- pick up tiny object with any part of thumb and finger

- walk holding on to furniture (cruise)

- understand word 'no' (but not always obey it)

. . . may possibly be able to:

- stand alone momentarily

- say dada (by 10 months) or mama (by 11 months) discriminately

. . . may even be able to:

- indicate wants in ways other than crying

- 'play ball' (roll ball back to you)

- drink from a cup independently

- pick up a tiny object neatly with tips of thumb and forefinger

- stand alone well

- use immature jargoning (gibberish that sounds like baby is talking in a made up foreign language)

- say one word other than mama or dada

- respond to a one-step command with gestures (give that to me – with hand out)

- walk well

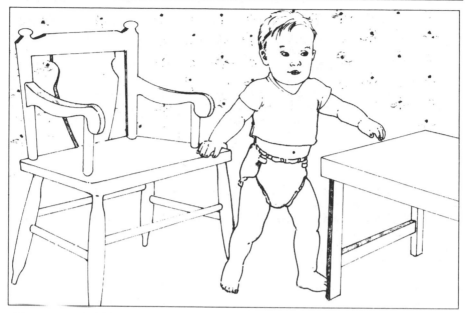

Many ten-month-olds have gained 'cruise control', the last step before unassisted walking. With one hand holding cautiously on to home base, they reach first with their other hand, then with a foot, towards another piece of furniture. Ensure sure footing by letting baby cruise only around steady chairs and tables.

What You Can Expect At This Month's Checkup

Most doctors do not schedule regular well-baby checkups this month. Do call the doctor if there are any concerns that can't wait until next month's visit.

Feeding Your Baby This Month: Thinking About Weaning

In most of the rest of the breastfeeding world, definite cultural norms – for either early or late weaning – have evolved. But in many parts of the West, where breastfeeding is in its own infancy after a recent rebirth, no such patterns exist. Some women breastfeed for six weeks, some six months, some three years or longer. The intended time of weaning may be set long before a baby is born, based on a scheduled return to work or simply a notion of what seems right. Or it may be spurred by the moment when baby or mother suddenly loses interest in nursing, for example.

When deciding how long you are going to breastfeed, you will probably want to consider many personal factors, as well as the few scientific ones available.

The facts. We have already stated that nursing even for just a few weeks is beneficial to an infant, since it's at this time that babies receive important antibodies to fight disease. But babies thrive better – with less illness and fewer allergies – if they are on breast milk for the first six months. And in fact, though it's acceptable to begin solids once a baby is four months old, breastfed babies can usually live quite well by breast milk alone during their first six months of life. Beyond the half-year mark, breast milk can continue to be the major source of a breastfed baby's nutrition (as formula can be for a bottle-fed infant), but it becomes necessary to augment it with solids.

By the end of the first year, however, scientists tell us that breast milk ceases to be adequate – not only is its protein content insufficient for the older baby, but it suffers from a decline in several vital nutrients including zinc, copper and potassium. In the second year, infants require the nutrients in cow's milk and the mother who is still breastfeeding should recognize that although both she and her baby may still be enjoying the experience, breast milk can't be considered a major source of nutrition for her baby. Nor do babies past a year appear to need the sucking breastfeeding provides.

In spite of much speculation, there's no solid evidence that nursing past the first year – or even well into the second or third or beyond – hinders a child's emotional development. But it does seem that prolonged breastfeeding, like prolonged bottle feeding, can lead to dental decay because during sucking (from breast *or* bottle) there is steady pooling of milk in the mouth that doesn't occur with drinking from a cup, which encourages a sip-and-swallow pattern. Another possible drawback to continuing either breast or bottle feeding much past the end of the first year is the increased risk of ear infection from feeding lying down, which many children do while suckling, especially just before bedtime.

Your feelings. Are you still enjoying breastfeeding, or are you starting to grow weary of hauling your breasts in and out of your shirt all day (and perhaps all night) long? Are you beginning to yearn for some of the freedom and flexibility that seem unattainable while

you're still nursing? Are you uncomfortable about the prospect of nursing an older child? If your feelings about your breastfeeding relationship have soured, your baby's radar will certainly pick this up. He or she may even take it as a personal rejection, rather than a rejection of the nursing experience. So weaning is probably in order.

Your baby's feelings. Some babies are self-weaners. Through their actions and reactions (restlessness and indifference at the breast, nursing that is erratic and brief) they show that they're ready to move on to other ways of obtaining nourishment. Be aware, however, that it's possible to misinterpret a baby's signals. At five months, disinterest in nursing may be only a sign of your baby's growing interest in the environment; at seven months, it may suggest a craving for physical activity that outweighs any craving for food; at nine months or later, it often signifies growing independence and maturity. At any age, it could be a response to illness or teething. At no age should it be construed as a rejection of you, only of the milk you provide.

A baby is most likely to self-wean somewhere between nine and twelve months. If your baby's attachment to the breast doesn't show any signs of letting up by the age of eighteen months (and this is not uncommon), it's not likely that he or she will ever be the one to take the initiative in weaning.

Your situation. Even mothers who at first thrive on nursing often begin to find breastfeeding onerous as inconveniences multiply, and as it begins to interfere more and more with work, school, sports, love-making, or other activities (be they necessities or luxuries) in their lives. When that happens, their negative feelings are easily transmitted to their babies, making nursing more problem than pleasure for both. Weaning is an appropriate step in such cases, but be wary of attempting it concurrently with other major changes in your lives. When possible, give yourself and your baby a chance to adjust to each change separately. Illness or the need for travel may also call for weaning, sometimes even sudden weaning.

Your baby's situation. The best time to wean a baby is when all's quiet on the home front. Sickness, teething, moving, travelling, your return to work, a change of nannies, or any other kind of change or stress in a baby's life suggests putting weaning on hold, so that an additional strain won't be imposed.

Your health. If you're perpetually exhausted and there seems to be no explanation other than the physical and emotional demands of nursing, you may want to discuss with your doctor the advisability of weaning so that you can recoup your strength. Before you do, however, be sure that it isn't some easily remedied problem, such as inadequate nourishment and/or insufficient rest, that's laying you low.

Your baby's health. Sometimes the supply of breast milk seems to diminish excessively as a baby gets older. If your baby is gaining weight poorly, is lethargic, irritable, or shows other signs of failure to thrive (see page 98), your breast milk may not be meeting all of his or her nutritional needs. Consider adding solids, supplementing with formula, or weaning completely. Often a weaned baby takes a sudden interest in other forms of nourishment that didn't appeal when the breast was available and begins to thrive anew.

Your baby's other sources of nourishment. If your baby has been accepting bottles all along, weaning to a bottle at any point will be relatively easy. Likewise, if your baby has learned to take fluids from a cup with fair skill, weaning directly to a cup will be possible – though not usually until about nine or ten months. If, on the other hand, your baby won't take milk from any source but your breast, weaning will have to be postponed until either bottle or cup is mastered.

Your baby's age. Even if they don't take the initiative, most babies are weanable sometime between nine and twelve months – they're less interested in and have less need for sucking, resist being held or sitting still for feedings (some even prefer to nurse standing up), and are generally more independent. They are also less attached to the breast at this age than they seem to be later on, and less opinionated, making them easier to wean than they will be when they become toddlers.

Making the decision to wean is only a step in the long process of switching a baby from the breast to other sources of nourishment, which begins with the first sip from the bottle or the first spoonful of solids. For some women the decision is easier than the weaning; for others it's the decision that causes the most turmoil. Whenever and however it comes, weaning is a time of mixed emotions for many women. They're relieved to no longer be completely tied down by their babies' needs, and they're proud that their offspring have achieved a new step on the road to growing up. But, at the same time, they're saddened by the loosening ties and by the fact that their babies don't depend on them as much as they did – and never will again.

Whether early or late, weaning is an inevitable step in a child's development. Babies (even the really ardent nursers) rarely end up missing it for more than a brief time, and mothers do survive – though they may experience pangs when they watch other mothers nurse, even years later.

What You May Be Concerned About

Messy Eating Habits

'My son doesn't eat anything until he's mushed it, smashed it, and rubbed it into his hair. Shouldn't we try to teach him some table manners?'

Eating with the average ten-month-old is enough to make anyone lose her appetite. There's as much playing with the food as eating it, and it's not unusual for more of it to end up *on* baby (and his clothes, his high chair and the family dog who's waiting eagerly below) than *in* him.

But that's because mealtimes are no longer just for nourishment, but for exploring and discovering as well. As in the sand-pit and the bathtub, he's finding out about cause and effect, about textures, about temperature differences. When he squeezes yogurt in his fist, mashes sweet potatoes into the table, slings a glob of oatmeal from his high chair tray, rubs banana into his T-shirt, blows bubbles in his cup of juice, crumbles crackers with his fingers – it's a mess for you, but a learning experience for him.

Expect the mealtime mayhem, and your need for paper towels by the caseful, to continue for months to come until your child has learned everything he can about the fascinating physical properties of food and is ready to move on to something else. That doesn't mean you have to grin (if you can) and bear it without taking some steps in defence of your sensibilities and your home and preparing your baby for a future of respectable (well, at least somewhat respectable) table manners:

Use coverups. An ounce of protection is worth a pound of paper towels. Use all the protective measures available to you: newspaper spread all around the base of the high chair or table, to be dumped after the meal; a wipe-clean bib that covers baby's front and shoulders, but which is comfortable enough so that he won't balk at wearing it; sleeves rolled up past the elbow to keep them dry and relatively clean. (Room temperature permitting, it may be more sensible to feed baby seriously messy foods in a nappy only.)

Thwart unwanted advances. You don't want to inhibit your baby's experimentation, but you also don't want to make it too easy for him to make a mess. So give him his food in a bowl, rather than a flat plate from which food can be pushed off easily. Or put it directly on his high chair tray (making sure that it's completely clean). Using a bowl that attaches to table or tray with suction gives additional protection, but will work only on a non-porous surface such as plastic. To minimize spills, give beverages in a tumbler or cup with a snap-on lid if your baby will drink from such a spout. If he won't, put just 30 ml (a fl ounce) or so of liquid in a regular cup and hand it to him whenever he's ready for a drink, but keep it out of reach between sips. Don't offer more than one bowl of food at a time, and don't serve more than two or three items in the bowl – babies tend to be overwhelmed by too many choices and react by playing and tossing instead of eating. All utensils and dishes should be nonbreakable, for both safety and economy.

Remain neutral. As you have probably already learned, babies are natural-born performers. If you respond by laughing at their antics in the high chair, you'll only encourage more of the same. They also don't take well to criticism. So scoldings and warnings to 'stop that now!' not only won't curb the behaviour – they will increase it. The best policy: don't comment on poor manners. If, however, your baby does take a few neat bites, with either the spoon or his fingers, praise him generously. Let him know whenever possible that neatness counts.

Retaliate with silverware. Even though he may do nothing with it but wave it through the air (while he continues to use his other hand for the transport of food), put a spoon in your baby's hand at the beginning of the meal, and also periodically during the proceedings. Eventually he'll get the idea of actually using it to eat with.

Don't resort to a hostile takeover. Desperate mothers tend to take desperate actions – in this case taking the feeding, and thus the ability to mess, completely out of their baby's control. But while such a takeover will result in neater mealtimes, it will also result in a baby who's delayed in learning how to feed himself and who, as a result, is also slow to develop polite table manners and good eating habits.

Be a model leader. It's not lectures and warnings that will teach your baby good table manners in the long run, but what he observes at family meals. If other family members eat with their fingers, shovel food in without a breath, chew loudly, reach for food instead of asking for it to be passed – if everyone talks with their mouths full, or worse, no one talks at all during the meal – your baby will cultivate these habits instead of the ones you hope to instill.

Know when to call a cease-fire. When the amount of time spent playing with the food begins to significantly outweigh the time spent eating it, it's time to call it a day. Clear the table and remove your baby from his high chair as soon as this moment arrives. It's unlikely that baby will protest (boredom with mealtime has prompted this behaviour in the first place), but if he does distract him with a toy or activity.

Head Banging, Rocking and Rolling

'My son has taken to banging his head on the wall or the side of his cot. Though it's painful for me to watch him, he doesn't seem to be in pain at all – in fact, he seems quite happy.'

It sounds as though your son has discovered

that he's got rhythm and this is his way of expressing it – at least until he takes to dancing or playing his Fisher-Price drum set. Head banging (like head rolling, rocking and bouncing, all of which are also common at this age) is a rhythmic movement, and rhythmic movements, especially of their own making, are fascinating to babies. Though most infant rock 'n' rollers rock when they hear music during waking hours, there seems to be more to such pursuits than simple fun. It's suspected that some of these children may be trying to reproduce the feeling of being rocked by mummy or daddy. Or that teething infants may be trying to cope with the pain – in which case rocking continues only as long as the teething, unless by that time it has become a habit. For those who bang, rock, or roll at naptime, bedtime and when they awaken in the middle of the night, these activities appear to be an aid to sleep, and perhaps may be a way of releasing tensions built up during the day. The behaviour is sometimes triggered, or increased, by stress (weaning, learning to walk, getting a new nanny and so on) in a child's life. Though boys and girls are equally likely to rock or roll, head banging is much more common in boys.

Rocking usually begins somewhere around six months, banging usually not until about nine months. These habits can last a few weeks or months, or a year or more. But most children abandon them by the time they are three years old without parental intervention. Scolding, teasing, or otherwise drawing attention to the behaviour not only does no good, it may make the problem worse.

Though it may be hard to believe, rocking, rolling and even head banging are not ordinarily hazardous to your baby's health. Neither are they, in a normally developing child, associated with neurological or psychological disorders. If your baby seems otherwise happy, isn't banging his head in anger, and isn't constantly bruising himself (an occasional black-and-blue mark isn't a cause for concern), there is nothing to worry about. But if these activities are taking up a good deal of your baby's time, if he seems to display other unusual behaviour, is developing slowly, or seems unhappy most of the time, do talk to his doctor about the problem.

You can't force a baby to give up one of these habits before he's ready, but the following tips may make it easier for both you and your baby to live with the habit and to eventually ease him out of it:

- Give your baby extra love, attention, cuddling and rocking during the day and at bedtime.

- Supply other – and to you, more acceptable – rhythmic activities for your baby during the day. Possibilities include: rocking in a rocking chair with him or showing him how to rock in a child-size one of his own; giving him one or more toy instruments, or just a spoon and pot, from which to elicit sounds; pushing him on a swing; and playing patty-cake or other finger or hand games, especially to music.

- Allow your baby plenty of time for active play during the day and ample opportunity to wind down before bedtime.

- Establish a regular, soothing presleep routine that includes quiet games, hugging, and perhaps some rocking (though not to the point of sleep).

- If your baby does most of his head banging in the cot, don't put him down until he's sleepy.

- If your baby rocks or bangs in his cot, minimize the danger to furniture and walls (which is usually much more serious than any damage to baby) by setting the cot on a thick rug and removing the casters so the cot won't bounce across the floor. Place the cot as far from the wall or other furniture as possible and, if necessary, pad the sides of the cot to soften the impact.

- You can try to protect your baby's head by placing bumper pads in the cot and a mat on the floor where he likes to bang if it isn't already carpeted – but the odds

are good he won't be satisfied with the cushioned blows and will make his way to a harder surface.

Blinking

'For the last couple of weeks, my daughter has been blinking a lot. She doesn't seem to be in any discomfort, and she doesn't seem to have trouble seeing, but I can't help worrying that there's something wrong with her eyes.'

It's probably more likely that there's something right with her curiosity. She knows what the world looks like through open eyes, but what if she closes her eyes partially, or if she opens and shuts them quickly? The results of her experimentation may be so intriguing that she may keep the 'blinking' up until the novelty wears off. (When she gets older, somewhere around age two, she will probably try similar experiments with her ears, putting her fingers in them or covering them with her hands to see what happens to sound.)

Of course, if your baby seems to have difficulty recognizing people and objects, or to have trouble focusing, call her doctor immediately. If not, and if the mannerism hasn't run its course by the time your baby goes for her next checkup, mention it to the examiner.

Squinting is another temporary habit that some babies cultivate, also for the change of scenery. Again, it shouldn't concern you unless it's accompanied by other symptoms or is persistent. In which case, check with her doctor.

Hair Rolling and Pulling

'When my daughter is sleepy or cranky, she pulls at a lock of her hair.'

Hair stroking or pulling is another way that a baby or a young child releases tension or tries to re-create the soothing comfort she received as an infant during nursing or bottle feeding, when she would stroke her mother's breast or cheek or pull at her hair. Since she's more likely to crave this comfort during times of stress, especially when she's overtired or cranky, she's more likely to indulge in such a mannerism during those times.

Occasional hair twirling, stroking, or pulling, which is often accompanied by thumb sucking, is common, and can linger into childhood without ill effect. Continuous or vigorous tugging at the hair, or hair pulling that results in lost patches of hair should, obviously, be stopped. These tips may help:

- Provide your child with more comfort and attention, especially at times of increased stress.

- Get her hair cut in a short style, so she won't be able to get a good grip on it.

- Give her something else to pull on – a long-haired stuffed animal, for instance.

- Engage her in other activities that keep her hands occupied.

If all else fails, seek advice from her doctor.

Teeth Grinding

'I often hear my son grinding his teeth when he's down for a nap. Is this harmful in any way?'

Like head banging or rolling, hair pulling or thumb sucking, teeth grinding is a way some babies discharge tension. To minimize grinding, reduce the tension in your baby's life when possible, and be sure that he has plenty of other outlets for releasing it – such as physical activity and toys that encourage banging. Lots of love and attention before nap or bedtime can also decrease the need for teeth grinding by helping a baby unwind. In most cases the habit is relinquished as a baby's coping skills improve, and before any damage is done to the teeth.

Tension isn't always the cause of teeth grinding. Sometimes a baby accidentally discovers the mannerism when experimenting with his new teeth, enjoys the sensation and sound of it, and adds it to his growing repertoire of skills. But before long, the thrill is gone and he loses interest in his dental orchestra.

If you find that your baby's teeth grinding is becoming more frequent, rather than diminishing, and you fear that he might begin to do damage to his teeth, consult his doctor or a paediatric dentist.

Breath Holding

'Recently my baby has started holding his breath during crying spells. Today he held it so long he actually passed out. Could this be dangerous?'

Invariably it's the parents who suffer most when a child holds his breath. While the adult witnessing the ordeal is likely to remain shaky for hours, even a baby who turns blue and passes out during a breath holding session recovers quickly and completely, as automatic respiratory mechanisms click into place and breathing resumes.

The breath holding is usually precipitated by anger, frustration, or pain. The crying, instead of letting up, becomes more and more hysterical, baby begins to hyperventilate, then finally stops breathing. In mild events, the lips turn blue. In more severe instances, baby turns blue all over and then loses consciousness. While unconscious, his body may stiffen or even twitch. The episode is usually over in less than a minute – long before any brain damage can occur.

About 1 in 5 infants holds his breath at one time or another. Some have only occasional episodes, others may have one or two a day. Breath holding tends to run in families and is most common between six months and four years, though it can occasionally begin earlier or run later. It can usually be distinguished from epilepsy (to which it is in no way related) by the fact that it is preceded by crying and the fact that

baby turns blue before losing consciousness. In epilepsy, there is usually no pre-
cipitating factor and the child doesn't
ordinarily turn blue before a seizure.

No treatment is necessary for a child who
has passed out due to breath holding. And
though there's no cure for the habit – other
than the passing of years – it is possible to
head off some of the temper tantrums that
result in these tactics:

- Be sure your baby gets enough rest. A
  baby who is overtired or overstimulated
  is more susceptible than a well-rested
  one.

- Don't make every issue a battleground.
  There's no question that you're the authority figure, and that you're bigger and
  wiser, you don't have to prove it constantly.

- Try to calm baby before hysteria sets in,
  using music, toys, or other distractions
  (but not food, which will create another
  bad habit).

- Try to reduce the tension around baby –
  yours and everyone else's – if this is at all
  possible.

- Respond calmly to breath-holding spells;
  your anxiety can make them worse.

- Don't cave in after a spell. If your baby
  knows he can get what he wants by
  holding his breath, he will repeat the
  behaviour frequently.

If your baby's breath-holding spells are severe, last more than a minute, are unrelated
to crying, or have you worried for any other
reason, do discuss them with his doctor as
soon as possible.

Toilet Training

*'My mother insists my sister and I were
toilet trained at ten months. Today, I
see children in nappies at three years
of age. When's the right age to start
training my son?'*

From the stories we hear from our mothers,
it would seem that babies thirty years ago –
all fully toilet trained before the first birthday, or at least soon after – were a more
precocious breed than today's tots. But it
wasn't the babies who were trained – it was
their mothers. It is possible to achieve early
bowel training with a baby who is very
regular (has a movement every morning
after breakfast, for instance) or who gives
clear warning of an impending movement
(by squatting, for example). It's much
harder to predict urination, though an occasional baby does cry before wetting his
nappy. But 'catching' a baby this way is but a
small victory, as the cooperation is purely
reflexive and the baby has little or no understanding of what he's doing and why.
And it often turns into a defeat later, when
the baby who seemed trained suddenly
balks at even going near the potty, or holds
back when put on the seat and becomes
constipated.

Training is far more successful, is accomplished much more quickly, and is far
less taxing on the trainer and far less traumatic for the trainee when the following
signs of readiness are exhibited: the child
becomes aware of elimination (first, that
he's just had a bowel movement, then that
he's having one, and finally that he's about to
have one); he can stay dry for two or three
hours at a stretch; he can dress and undress
himself for toileting; and he is able to understand and follow directions.

But just because your baby isn't ready for
potty training doesn't mean he can't start
becoming familiar with potty protocol right
now:

Let him know what he's doing. It's often
very obvious that a baby's having a bowel
movement; he may stop what he's doing,
squat, grunt, strain, get red in the face, or
simply turn very serious suddenly. When you
catch your baby in the act, tell him what he's
doing, using the same word or phrase to
describe his efforts and their yield each time
(poo, doodoo, or whatever's your family's
traditional favourite). Then use the full nappy
as a visual aid when you're cleaning him up.

It's virtually impossible to know when your baby's urinating, of course, unless he's bare bottomed. But when the opportunity presents itself – when he releases a stream in the bathtub, while you're changing his nappy, or when he's romping naked in the garden – do point out what is happening. Again, use the same term each time (pee-pee, wee-wee, urine, or whatever you're comfortable with). And when you change his wet nappy, explain to him why it's wet.

Let him see what you're doing. Children are great imitators, particularly of people they look up to, such as parents or older siblings. So instead of barring baby from the bathroom while you use the toilet, invite him in for a live demonstration, accompanied by a running commentary on the goings-on. If you have an older child willing to admit an audience (some will demand privacy), encourage baby to attend some of these performances, too. Explain to your baby that mummies and daddies, and big boys and girls, go on the potty and that when he is big, he will too. If the sound doesn't frighten him and he can manage the handle, let him flush; then, together, watch the contents swirling down and out. If he seems eager to sit on the toilet himself, buy a potty that fits on the regular seat or a separate children's potty (which is safer, more comfortable, less intimidating, and easier to push on), and let him try it out. But *don't* leave him unattended, and take him off as soon as he tires of the position. Becoming comfortable on the potty now – as long as it's his idea and not yours – may make it a less fearful place later on.

Make him feel good about the products of elimination. Positive self-image is very important to the success of any kind of training. So don't make baby feel that what comes out of him is offensive ('Oh, what a smelly mess!'), even if you find it so. Resist making faces and unfavourable remarks when you clean up his nappies. Instead, be positive and matter-of-fact in demeanour and comments.

While the end of the first year, when a baby is curious and still fairly malleable, is a good time to familiarize him with the potty, don't push your child at any age to perform on the potty. Encourage him, enlighten him, but wait until he's fully ready – probably somewhere around his second birthday, but possibly not until he's closer to his third – before beginning serious training.[1]

Starting Classes

'I see so many advertisements for classes for babies that I feel as if I'm depriving my daughter if I don't enroll her in at least one.'

You probably didn't take a class until you went to playgroup, unless you were one of the few in your generation who went to nursery school at three or four. You certainly didn't study art, music, or swimming before you could walk or talk – and you probably don't consider yourself deprived. And in spite of the enthusiasm of today's parents for getting their children involved in organized activities as early as possible, your baby won't be deprived if she isn't signed up for classes soon, either.

In fact, formal classes are not only unnecessary for infants, they can sometimes be harmful. What babies need to develop well is plenty of time to explore the world on their own and to learn about it at their own pace, with just a little help from their adult friends. Being required to explore or learn at a predetermined time, place and pace, as in a classroom, can dampen a child's natural enthusiasm for new experiences and damage her self-esteem. This doesn't mean that you should automatically reject all opportunities for group activities for your

---

1. One reason why the new generation is becoming trained so late is the disposable nappy. These modern miracles absorb urine so well and keep it away from baby's skin so successfully that children hardly notice when they are wet. It's no wonder that they are in no hurry to be trained – unlike previous generations of children who were perpetually uncomfortable in sopping wet terry nappies.

baby. It's nice for your child to play near other children – she probably isn't yet ready to play *with* them – and to spend time with and get to know other adults. It's even nicer for you to have a chance to talk to other mothers, sharing common concerns and experiences and picking up some new ideas for playing with your child.

There are some ways for you to reap group benefits for your baby without premature matriculation:

- Take her to a local playground. Even if she isn't walking, she will enjoy the baby swings, small slides and the sand-pit – and she will especially enjoy watching other children.

- Start or join a mother and baby group. If you don't know other mothers with babies your daughter's age, post recruitment notices in the doctor's surgery, in your church or synagogue, even in the supermarket. Such groups, which usually meet weekly in homes or at playgrounds, are often very informal, have frequent turnover, and provide an ideal introduction to group activities.

- Enroll her in an informal baby exercise class, observing the guidelines on page 205.

Shoes for Walking

'Our daughter has just taken her first steps. What kind of shoes does she need now?'

The best shoes for a new walker are no shoes. Doctors have discovered that the feet, like hands, develop best when they are bare, not covered and confined; walking barefoot helps build arches and strengthen ankles. And just as your baby's hands don't need gloves in warm weather, her feet don't need shoes indoors and on safe surfaces outdoors, except when it's cold. Even walking on uneven surfaces, such as sand, is good for her feet since it makes the muscles work harder.

But for safety and sanitation (you wouldn't want her to step on broken glass or in dog droppings) as well as appearance, your baby will need shoes for most excursions, as well as for special occasions (what's a party dress without Mary Janes?). Choose shoes that are closest to no shoes at all by looking for the following:

Flexible soles. Shoes that bend fairly easily when the toe is bent up will interfere least with the foot's natural motion. Many doctors recommend canvas shoes for their flexibility, but some maintain that traditional first-walker shoes are even more flexible and babies are therefore less likely to fall in them. Ask your baby's doctor for a recommendation, and test those available at your local store before making your selection.

Low cut. Don't buy the high-top shoes your mother probably bought for you when you started stepping out. Even though such shoes may stay put better than low ones, most experts believe they are too confining and interfere with ankle movement. They certainly shouldn't be used to prop up a baby who is not yet ready to walk.

Porous and flexible uppers. To stay healthy, feet need to breathe and to get plenty of exercise. They breathe best, and have the most freedom of movement, in shoes of leather, cloth, or canvas. Plastic or imitation leather is usually stifling and sometimes stiff, and tends to cause the feet to sweat excessively. Avoid 'running' shoes with wide bands of rubber around them since they can also increase sweating. If you purchase rain shoes or boots that are made of plastic or rubber for your baby, use them only when needed and take them off as soon as she is indoors.

Flat, non-skid bottoms with no heels. A beginner walker has enough difficulty maintaining her balance without having to contend with slippery soles. Rubber or composition soles, particularly when they are grooved, usually provide a less slippery surface than leather, unless it is scored or grooved. If an otherwise appropriate pair of shoes is too slippery, rough up the soles a bit with sandpaper or a few strips of adhesive tape.

Firm counters. The back of the shoe (behind the heel) should be firm, not flimsy. It's best if the top edge is padded or bound, and the back seam smooth with no irregularities that could cause irritation to the back of your baby's heel.

Roomy fit. Shoes are better too large than too small, but of course 'just right' is best of all. Though shoes can't provide as much foot freedom as going bare, too-tight shoes provide no freedom at all. If shoes are to be worn with thick socks, be sure to try shoes on with such socks. Have feet measured and test new shoes (both of them) for size when the baby is standing with her full weight on her feet. The top of the shoe shouldn't gap open while she's standing (though it's okay if it does when she walks), nor should her heels slip up and down with each step. To check the width, try to pinch the shoe at its widest point. If you can grasp a tiny bit of it between your fingers, the width is fine; if you can pinch a good piece of shoe, it's too wide; and if you can pinch none at all, it's too narrow. To check the length, press your thumb down between your baby's toes and the end of the shoe. If there's a thumb's width (or about 1 cm/half an inch), the length is right. There should also be room for your pinky at the back of the shoe. Once you've purchased a pair of shoes for your baby, check the fit every few weeks since babies outgrow shoes quickly, sometimes within six weeks, often within three months. When that distance at the toe shrinks to less than half a thumb's width, start to think about new shoes. Reddened areas on baby's toes or feet when shoes are removed are also a sign of poor fit.

Standard shapes. Unusual styles – such as cowboy boots or pointy-toed party shoes – can distort the foot as it grows. Look instead for a shoe with a broad instep and toe and a flat pancake heel.

Durability is not a requirement in children's shoes because they are rapidly outgrown. Though the temptation is great – because of the high price of children's shoes and their brief life span with each child – to pass shoes on from child to child, resist. Shoes mould to the shape of the wearer's foot, and wearing shoes moulded by someone else is not good for little feet. Make an exception only for those shoes (such as dress-up shoes) that are no more than lightly worn, have held their shape, and aren't run down at the heels.

A good shoe is only as good as the sock in it. Socks, like shoes, should fit well and be of a material (such as cotton or Orlon) that allows feet to breathe. Socks that are too tight can cramp foot growth; those that are too long can wrinkle and cause irritations or blisters, though neatly folding up the tip of a too long sock before putting on the shoe can often solve the problem of wrinkling. Stretch-to-fit socks usually do fit well, but be alert for the point at which they become too small and begin squeezing, usually indicated by marks left on baby's feet.

Biting

'My baby has started biting us playfully – on the shoulder, the cheek, any soft, vulnerable area. At first we thought it was cute. Now we're beginning to worry that he's developing a bad habit – and besides, it hurts!'

It's only natural for your baby to want to test his new set of chompers on every possible surface, you included. But it's also only natural for you not to want to be bitten – and only fair that you be allowed to put a stop to the biting, which can become a bad habit and, as more teeth come in, increasingly painful for its victims.

The biting at first is playful and experimental; baby has absolutely no idea he's hurting anyone with it. After all, he's bitten down on many a teething ring, sucked on many a stuffed toy and chewed on many a cot rail with nary a complaint. But then, when he gets a human reaction, he's often encouraged to continue in order to elicit more reactions. He finds the expression on mummy's face when he bites down on her shoulder funny, the startled look and mock 'Ouch!' from daddy hilarious, and the 'Isn't that darling, he's biting me', from grandmother a definite sign of approval. Oddly enough, even an angry 'Ouch!' or stern reprimand can reinforce the biting habit, because the baby either finds it amusing or sees it as a challenge to his emerging sense of independence, or both. And biting him back can make matters worse; not only is it cruel, but there's the not so subtle implication that what's good for the goose is fair play for him. For the same reason, love bites from parents or grandparents can also trigger biting.

The most effective way to respond is to remove the little biter calmly and matter-of-factly from the part he's biting, with a firm 'No biting'. Then quickly divert his attention with a song, a toy, or other distraction. Do this each time he bites and he will eventually get the message.

Hair Care

'Our daughter was born with a headful of hair and it's got quite straggly and hard to manage.'

To the parents of countless hairless nine-month-olds, yours would seem an enviable problem. But handling an unruly head of superfine hair, particularly when it belongs to a squirming, uncooperative baby, could make even Vidal Sassoon want to throw in his comb. Things will probably get worse before they get much better; for some toddlers, every shampoo and comb-out is an excuse for a tantrum. But short of resorting to a short haircut (which, if you're brave enough, may be the best way to go), you can best minimize the travail while keeping your baby's hair healthy and well groomed by using the following tips:

- Untangle hair before beginning to shampoo to prevent even worse tangles afterwards.

- Use a baby conditioner after shampoos if your baby will sit still for this double procedure. If not, use a combination shampoo-conditioner, or a spray-on cream rinse that doesn't need to be rinsed out. This will make comb-outs much easier.

- Use a wide-tooth comb or a brush that has bristles with plastic-coated tips for comb-outs on wet hair. A fine-tooth comb tends to tear the ends and also pulls more.

- Untangle from the ends up, keeping one hand firmly on the roots as you work to minimize the pulling on baby's scalp and the pain that comes with it.

- If you must use a hair dryer, use a low or cool setting to avoid damaging baby's delicate hair or burning her sensitive scalp.

- Don't braid baby's hair or pull it tightly into a ponytail or pigtails, since these styles can lead to patches of baldness or thinning of hair. If you do make ponytails or pigtails, make them loose and tie them with special protective clips or coated bands rather than with regular rubber bands or barrettes, both of which can pull out and damage hair.

- Trim hair (or have it trimmed at a salon that specializes in children's cuts) at least every two months, for healthier growth. Trim bangs when they reach the brows.

- If your baby has a parting in her hair, change it every few days to avoid the hair thinning around it.

- Plan hair grooming for a time when your baby isn't tired, hungry, or cranky. Make it more pleasant by getting her occupied with a toy before beginning, possibly a doll and a comb. Or set her up in front of a mirror so she can watch you work on her hair; eventually she may learn to appreciate the end result, making the sessions more tolerable.

Fears

'My baby used to love to watch me turn on the vacuum cleaner; now he's suddenly terrified of it – and anything else that makes a loud noise.'

When he was younger your baby wasn't frightened by loud noises – though they may have momentarily startled him – because he didn't perceive the possibility they might present a danger. Now, as his understanding of the world grows, it's likely, especially if he's had a few 'boo-boos,' that he's beginning to realize the perils and the potential for injury that surround him.

There are any number of things in a baby's everyday life that, though innocuous to you, can cause debilitating fear in him: sounds, such as the roar of a vacuum cleaner, the whir of a blender, the barking of a dog, the whine of a siren, the flushing of a toilet, the gurgle of water draining from the bathtub; having a shirt pulled over his head; being lifted high in the air (especially if he's begun to climb, pull up, or otherwise develop depth perception); being plunked down in a bath; the motion of a wind-up or mechanical toy.

Probably all babies experience fears at some point, though some overcome them so quickly their parents are never aware of them. Children who live in a lively, active environment, particularly when there are older siblings, tend to experience these fears earlier.

Sooner or later, most children leave the fears of late babyhood behind and burst forth as brash, and sometimes foolishly brave, toddlers. Till then, you can help your baby deal with his fears in these ways:

Don't force. Making your baby come nose to nozzle with the vacuum cleaner not only won't help, it may intensify his fear. Though his phobia may seem irrational to you, it's very legitimate to him. He needs to wait and

confront the noisy beast on his own terms and in his own time, when he feels it's safe.

Don't resort to ridicule. Making fun of your child's fears, calling them silly or laughing at them, will only serve to undermine his self-confidence and his ability to deal with them. Take his fears seriously – he does.

Do accept and sympathize. By accepting your baby's fears as real, and comforting him when his personal demons are about, you will lessen his burden and help him to cope. If he wails when you switch on the vacuum cleaner (or flush the toilet, or turn on the blender) be quick to pick him up and give him a great, big, reassuring hug. But don't overdo the sympathy or you may reinforce the idea that there is something to be afraid of.

Do reassure and support, then build confidence and skills. Though you should sympathize with his fears, your ultimate goal is to help him overcome them. He can only do this by becoming familiar with the things he fears, learning what they do and how they work, and gaining some sense of control over them. Let him touch or even play with the vacuum when it's turned off and unplugged – he is probably as fascinated with the machine as he is afraid of it.

Once he becomes comfortable playing with the vacuum when it's off, try holding him securely in one arm while you vacuum with the other – if this doesn't upset him. Then show him how to turn the machine on himself, with a little help from you if the switch is tricky. If it's the toilet's flush he fears, have him throw some paper in and encourage him to flush it down himself when he feels ready. If it's the draining tub, let him watch the water drain when he is safely out of it, fully dressed and, if need be, in your arms. If dogs are his nemesis, try playing with one while your baby watches from a distance – perhaps from daddy's lap. When he's finally willing to approach a dog, encourage your baby (while you hold him) to make 'nice doggy' to a dog you know is gentle and won't suddenly snap.

WHAT IT'S IMPORTANT TO KNOW:
The Beginnings of Discipline

You applauded wildly your baby's first successful attempt at pulling up and cheered proudly from the sidelines as creeping finally became crawling. Now you're wondering what all the celebration was about. Along with the new mobility has come a talent for getting into trouble to rival Dennis the Menace. If your baby's not adroitly turning off the VCR while your favourite show is being taped, he or she is triumphantly removing the tablecloth (along with the fruit bowl atop it) from the dining room table, gleefully unravelling whole rolls of toilet paper into the toilet, or industriously emptying the contents of drawers, cabinets and bookshelves on to the floor. Before, all you had to do to keep both baby and home from harm was to deposit your child in a safe spot; now, no such haven exists.

For the first time, you're likely to be upset by rather than proud of your offspring's exploits. And for the first time the question of discipline has probably come up in your home. The timing is right. Waiting to introduce discipline into a child's life much later than ten months could make the task much more difficult; trying to have done so much earlier, before memory was developed, would have been futile.

Why discipline a baby? First of all, to instill a concept of right and wrong. Though it'll be a long time before your child will fully grasp it, it's now that you should begin to teach right from wrong by both example and guidance. Second, to plant the seeds of self-control. They won't take root for a while, but unless they do eventually, your child won't be able to function effectively. Third, to teach respect for the rights and feelings of others, so that a child will grow from a normally self-centred baby into a sensitive and caring child and adult. And finally, to protect your baby, your home and your sanity – now and in the months of mischief ahead.

As you embark on a programme of child discipline, keep the following in mind:

- Though the word 'discipline' is associated with structure, rules and punishment in many minds, it actually comes from the Latin word for 'teaching'.

- Every child is different, every family is different, each situation is different. But there are universal rules of behaviour that apply to everyone, at all times.

- Until infants understand what is safe and what is not, or at least which actions are permissible and which are not, their parents have total responsibility for keeping the environment safe, as well as for safeguarding their own belongings and those of others.

- Withdrawal of parental love threatens a child's self-esteem. It's important to let children know that they are still loved, even when their behaviour is disapproved of.

- The most effective discipline is neither uncompromisingly rigid nor overly permissive. Strict discipline that relies entirely on parental policing rather than encouraging the development of self-control usually turns out children who are totally submissive to their parents but totally uncontrollable once out of reach of parental or other adult authority. But overly permissive parents aren't likely to turn out well-behaved children, capable of coping in the real world, either. Their overindulged children are often selfish, rude and unpleasant, quick to argue, slow to comply.

Both extremes of discipline can leave a child feeling unloved. Strict parents may seem cruel and thus unloving; permissive parents may seem uncaring. A more nurturing brand of discipline falls somewhere in between – it sets limits that are fair and enforces them firmly but lovingly.

That's not to say that there aren't normal variations in discipline styles. Some parents are simply more relaxed and some more rigid. That's okay as long as neither goes to the extreme.

- Effective discipline is individualized. If you have more than one child, you almost certainly noticed differences in personality from birth. Such differences will affect how each child is best disciplined. One, for instance, will refrain from playing with an electric outlet after a gentle remonstrance. Another won't take your warning seriously unless there is a toughness – or perhaps fear – in your voice. A third may need to be physically removed from the source of danger. Tailor your style to your child.

- Circumstances can alter a child's response to discipline. A child who ordinarily requires strong admonitions may be crushed if scolded when tired or teething. Switch gears, if need be, to meet your child's immediate needs.

- Children need limits. They often can't control themselves or their impulses and become frightened at the loss of control. Limits, set by parents and lovingly enforced, provide a comforting tether to keep children secure and steady while they explore and grow. Stretching those limits because he or she's 'just a baby' isn't fair to your child or to those whose rights are being violated. Tender age – at least after ten months – shouldn't guarantee carte blanche to pull a sibling's hair or tear up mummy's magazine before she's read it.

Just which limits you set depends on your priorities. In some homes, keeping shoes off the sofa and not eating in the living room are paramount issues. In others, staying out of mummy's or daddy's desk is of vital importance. In most families, common courtesy and simple etiquette – using 'please' and 'thank you', sharing, respecting other people's feel-

ings – are primary expectations. Set rules you will enforce carefully and limit their numbers.

Learning to live with limits from an early age can help calm some of the turmoil of the terrible twos. It will also be necessary for survival in a society that is full of limits – at school, work and play.

It's easier, of course, to talk about setting limits for babies than to actually enforce them. It's tempting to give in to an adorable kid who gives you an impish smile when you say 'no!' or to a sweet, sensitive one who breaks into tears at the very sound of the word. But steel yourself and remember it's for your child's own good. It may not seem vital now to stop your baby from taking the crackers into the living room, but if he or she doesn't learn to follow at least a few rules now, it will be harder to handle the many that will be faced later. You can continue to expect protestations, but gradually you will find that more and more, your child will accept limits matter of-factly.

- A baby who gets into trouble isn't 'bad'. Babies and young toddlers don't know right from wrong, so their follies can't be considered wicked. They learn about their world by experimenting, observing cause and effect, and testing the adults in it. What happens when I turn over a glass of juice? Will it happen again? And again? Or what's inside the kitchen drawers, and what will happen if I take it all out? What will mummy's reaction be?

Repeatedly telling your child that he or she is bad can damage the ego and interfere with self-confidence and achievement down the road. And the child who hears 'You're bad!' over and over may fulfill the prophecy in later years ('If they say I'm bad, I must be bad'). Criticize your baby's actions, but not your baby ('Biting is bad,' not 'You're bad').

- Consistency is important. If shoes on the sofa are forbidden today but permitted tomorrow, or if hand washing before dinner was compulsory yesterday but overlooked today, the only lesson learned is that the world is confusing and rules are meaningless. If you fail to be consistent, you lose credibility.

- Follow-through is crucial. Looking up from your book long enough to mutter 'no' to a baby who's tugging at the television wires but not long enough to make sure that he or she stops is not effective discipline. If your actions don't speak at least as loud as your words, your admonitions will lose their impact. When the first 'no' is ineffective, take immediate action, especially in such a dangerous situation. Put down your book, pick up your baby, and move him or her away from the tempting TV wires – preferably far away, into another room. Then take your baby's mind off the television with a favourite plaything. For most babies, what's been taken out of sight is quickly out of mind – though a few may try to return to the scene of the crime, in which case you may have to block it off. Distraction, when it works, also allows a baby who feels that 'no' is a challenge to his or her ego to save face.

- Babies and young toddlers have limited memories. You can't expect them to learn a lesson the first time it's taught, and you can expect them to repeat an undesirable action over and over again. Be patient, and be prepared to repeat the same message – 'Don't touch the VCR' or 'Don't eat the dog food' – every day for weeks before it finally sinks in or the fascination is lost.

- Babies enjoy the 'no game'. Most babies love the challenge of a parent's 'No!' as much as the challenge of climbing a flight of stairs or fitting a circle into a shape sorter. So no matter how your baby goads you, don't let your 'No!' deteriorate into a game or a fit of laughter. Your baby won't take you seriously.

- Too many 'No's' lose their effectiveness and are demoralizing. You wouldn't want to live in a world ruled by an unforgiving dictator whose three favourite words were 'No! No! No!' And neither should you want your baby to live in one. Limit the no's to those things in which baby's well-being or that of another person or of your home is threatened. Remember that not every issue is worth a fight. Fewer no's will be needed if you create a childproof environment (see page 284) in your home, with plenty of opportunities for exploration under safe conditions.

  Along with each 'No', always offer a 'Yes' in the form of an alternative: 'No, you can't play with daddy's book, but you can look at this one', or 'You can't empty the cereal cabinet, but you can empty the saucepan shelves'. Instead of 'No, don't touch those papers in mummy's desk' to the baby who already has emptied several items on the floor, try 'Let's see if you can put those papers back in mummy's drawer and close the drawer'. This face-saving approach gets the message across without making your baby feel 'bad'.

  Once in a while, when the stakes aren't high or when you realize you've made a mistake, let baby win – an occasional victory will help make up for the many losses he or she must take each day.

- Children need to be allowed to make some mistakes, and to learn from them. If you make it impossible for your child to slip up (stashing away all knickknacks, for instance), you won't have to say no very often, but you will also miss important chances to teach. Allow room for errors (though you'll want to avoid those that are dangerous and/or expensive through prudent childproofing), so that your baby can learn from them.

- Correction and reward work better than punishment. Punishment, always of questionable value, is particularly useless for young children since they don't understand why they're being punished. A baby is too young to associate being 'grounded' in the playpen with having just dumped the salt out of the salt shaker, or to understand that a bottle is being withheld because he or she bit a sibling. Instead of punishing misbehaviour, catch your baby being good. Positive reinforcement, rewarding and praising good behaviour, works much better. It builds, rather than smashes, self-confidence and reinforces good behaviour. Another productive approach, one that teaches that actions have consequences, is to have the perpetrator help remedy the results of the crime – wipe up the spilt milk, pick up the scattered tea towels, hand you the books to put back on the shelf.

- Anger triggers anger. Indulge in an angry outburst when your baby breaks a favourite sweet dish by tossing it like a ball across the room, and he or she's likely to follow in fury, rather than respond with remorse. If necessary, take a few moments to calm down before addressing the guilty party – leave the scene of the crime briefly, if that will help you temper your temper. Once your cool is collected, explain to your baby that what he or she did was wrong, and why. ('That wasn't a toy, it was mummy's dish. You broke it and now mummy's sad.') This is important to do even if the explanation seems to be sailing clear over your baby's head, or if distraction has already set in.

Try to remember at moments of high anxiety (it won't always be easy) that your long-term goal is to teach right behaviour, and that screaming or smacking will teach wrong behaviour, setting poor examples of what's appropriate when one is angry.

Don't worry if you occasionally find it impossible to put the brakes on your anger. As a human mother, you're allowed your share of frailties, and your baby needs to know that. As long as your tirades are relatively few, far between, and short-lived, they won't interfere with effective parenting. When they occur, be sure to apologize. 'I'm sorry I yelled at you, but I was very angry.' Adding 'I love you' will not only be reassuring, but will let your baby know that sometimes we get angry at people we love and that such feelings are okay.

- Discipline can be a laughing matter. Humour is the leavening of life – and a surprisingly effective disciplinary tool. Use it liberally in situations that would otherwise lead you to exasperation – for instance, when baby refuses to allow you to put a snowsuit on him. Instead of doing fruitless combat over shrill screams of protest, head off the tantrum and the struggle with some unexpected silliness. Suggest, perhaps, that you put the snowsuit on the dog (or the cat, or the dolly, or on mummy), and then pretend to do so. The incongruity of what you are proposing will probably take your baby's mind off objections to wearing the garment long enough for you to accomplish your goal.

Humour can be brought into a variety of disciplinary situations. Give orders while pretending you're a dog or a lion, Big Bird, or another of your child's favourites; perform unpopular chores with silly-song accompaniments ('This is the way we wash the face, wash the face . . .'; carry baby to the dreaded changing table upside down; make silly faces in the mirror with baby instead of chiding, 'Don't cry, don't cry'. Taking each other less seriously more often will add sunshine to your days, particularly as the stormy second year approaches. Stay serious, however, when a dangerous situation is involved, since then even a smile can be fatal to the effectiveness of the lesson you are trying to impart.

- Accidents require different treatment from intentional wrongdoings. Remember, everyone's entitled to mistakes, but babies, because of their emotional, physical and intellectual immaturity, are entitled to a great many more of them. When yours knocks over a glass of milk while reaching for a slice of bread, 'Oops, the milk spilled. Try to be more careful, darling' is an appropriate response. But when the cup is upended intentionally, 'Milk is to drink, not to spill. Spilling makes a mess and wastes the milk – see, now there's no more' is more fitting. In

To Smack or not to Smack

Though smacking has been passed on from generation to generation in many families, most experts agree that it is not, and never has been, an effective way to discipline a child. Children who are smacked may refrain from repeating a misdemeanour rather than risk another smacking, but they obey only as long as the risk is there. They often don't like or respect the people who hit them and frequently don't learn to differentiate right from wrong (only what they get smacked for and what they don't get smacked for) – a prime goal of discipline.

Smacking also has many negative aspects. For one, it teaches violence. Child beaters and wife beaters are almost always former victims of beatings themselves, and many a child who whacks a peer and is asked, 'Where did you learn that?' will respond with 'From my mummy (or daddy)'. For another, smacking teaches children that the best way to settle disputes is with force, and denies them the chance to learn alternative, less hurtful, routes to dealing with anger and frustration. It also represents an abuse of power by a very large, strong party against a very small, weak one. And it can lead to serious injury of a child, often unintentionally, particularly when it is done in anger. Smacking after the anger is cooled, though it may do less physical damage, seems even more questionable than lashing out in the heat of the moment. It is certainly more cruelly calculated, and it is even less effective in correcting behaviour.

If it's inadvisable for a parent to smack a child, it is even more inadvisable for another person to do so. Though with a parent a child is usually secure in the knowledge that the smack is being administered by someone who cares; with another person there's generally no such security. Nannies, teachers and others who tend to your child should be instructed *never* to strike him or her or administer any form of physical punishment.

Most experts (and parents) would agree that a sound smack on the hand or the bottom may be warranted in a dangerous situation to get a serious message across to a child too young to understand words – for example, when a toddler wanders out into the street or approaches a hot stove and a stern reprimand doesn't do the trick. Once comprehension is established, however, physical force is no longer justifiable.

either case, it also helps to hand baby a paper towel to help in the cleanup, to fill cups with only small amounts of liquids in the future, and to be sure that your baby has plenty of opportunity to pursue his or her experiments with pouring fluids in the tub or other acceptable surroundings.

• Parents have to be the adults in the family. If you expect your child to act responsibly, you'll have to, too: You promised baby a trip to the playground, but then would rather watch the afternoon soaps. A mature mummy would keep her promise, anyway. If you expect your child to admit mistakes comfortably, you'll have to lead the way: you made baby cry over spilled milk and learn later that it was daddy who spilled it. A mature mummy would apologize, and try to avoid jumping to conclusions next time. If you often find yourself getting down to your baby's level, following his or her tantrum, for example, with one of your own, or demanding things your way when they could just as easily be done your baby's way, it may be time to reevaluate your own behaviour.

• Children are worthy of respect. Instead of treating your baby as an object, a possession, or even 'just a baby', treat him or her with the respect you would accord any other person. Be polite (say please, thank you and excuse me), offer explanations (even if you don't think they'll be understood) when you forbid something, be understanding of and sympathetic to your baby's wants and feelings (even if you can't permit acting them out), avoid embarrassing your baby (by scolding in front of strangers) and listen to what he or she is saying. In this preverbal stage, when grunts and pointing are the main modes of communication, listening is a challenge and it continues to be so until speech becomes clear and language is well developed (somewhere around four or five) – but making that effort is important. Remember, it's frustrating for baby, too.

- There should be a fair distribution of rights between parents and child (or children). It's easy, when a baby is young, for inexperienced parents to err in this area, going to one extreme or the other. Some abrogate all their rights in favour of their child – they base their lives on the baby's schedule, never go out, forget the value of adult friends. Others live their lives as though they were still childless, heedless of their infant's needs – they drag an overtired baby to parties, skip baby baths in favour of a football game, and miss doctor appointments because of a big sale at a favourite store. The latter abuse their power (and it's tremendous when you compare it to that of an infant); the former don't use theirs at all. A balance is what's needed.

- Nobody's perfect – and nobody should be expected to be. Avoid setting unattainable standards for your baby. Children need all the years childhood provides to develop to the point at which they can behave as adults. And they need

to know that you don't expect perfection. Praise particular achievements rather than make sweeping pronouncements about your child's nature. 'You were very good today' rather than 'You're the best baby in the world'. Since no one can be 'good' all the time, such overlavish praise on a regular basis can make a child fear that your expectations can't possibly be lived up to.

Neither should you expect perfection from yourself. Parents who never lose their temper, never yell and never even have the remotest desire to slug a difficult toddler don't exist. And letting it out and clearing the air once in a while may be better than keeping your anger and frustration bottled up inside. Bottled-up anger has a way of bursting out inappropriately, often far out of proportion to the crime of the moment.

If, however, you find yourself losing your temper at your baby too often, try to determine the underlying cause. Are you angry about being responsible for all the child-care chores? Are you really angry at yourself or someone else, and taking it out on the most convenient and defenceless target, your baby? Have you set too many limits or provided too many opportunities for baby to get into trouble? If so, try to remedy the situation.

- Children need to know they have some control over their lives. For good mental health, everyone – even a baby – needs to feel as though he or she calls at least some of the shots. It won't always be possible for baby to have his or her way, but when it is, allow it. Give your baby a chance to make choices – the cracker or the piece of bread, the swing or the baby slide, the bib with the elephant or the one with the clown.

FOURTEEN

The Eleventh Month

◆

What Your Baby May Be Doing

By the end of this month, your baby . . . should be able to (see Note):

- get into a sitting position from stomach

- pick up a tiny object with any part of thumb and finger (by 10½ months)

- understand the word 'no' (but not always obey it)

Note: If your baby seems not to have reached one or more of these milestones, check with the doctor. In rare instances the delay could indicate a problem, though in most cases it will turn out to be normal for your baby. Premature infants generally reach milestones later than others of the same birth age, often achieving them closer to their adjusted age (the age they would be if they had been born at term), or sometimes later.

. . . will probably by able to:

- play patty-cake (clap hands) or wave bye-bye

- walk holding on to furniture (cruise)

. . . may possibly be able to:

- pick up a tiny object neatly with tips of thumb and forefinger

- stand alone momentarily

- say dada or mama discriminately

- say one word other than mama or dada

. . . may even be able to:

- stand alone well

- indicate wants in ways other than crying

- 'play ball' (roll ball back to you)

- drink from a cup independently

- use immature jargoning (gibberish that sounds like baby is talking a foreign language)

- say three or more words other than mama or dada

- respond to a one-step command without gestures (give that to me – without hand out)

- walk well

What You Can Expect At This Month's Checkup

Most doctors do not schedule regular well-baby checkups this month. Do call the doctor if there are any concerns that can't wait until next month's visit.

Feeding Your Baby This Month: Weaning Your Baby From The Breast

As the task of weaning your baby looms as large as any child-care challenge you've faced so far, it may be comforting to know that you've probably already begun the process. The first time that you offered your baby a sip from a cup, a nip from a bottle, or a nibble from a spoon, you took a step towards weaning.

Weaning is basically a two-phase process:

Phase One: Getting baby accustomed to taking milk or formula from a source other than your breasts. Since it can take a breastfeeding baby a while to catch on to drinking from a bottle or a cup, and some a considerable time to be willing to even try such alternative methods of feeding, it's best to introduce them well before you hope to complete weaning.[1]

If you don't introduce either bottle or cup early on, weaning may be slower and more difficult. In some cases, it may even be necessary temporarily to 'starve' your baby into submission by skipping one breastfeeding each day for three or four days and offering only your chosen alternative. Though a stubborn baby may reject a substitute at first, all eventually switch from the breast.

Use expressed breast milk, formula, or water for bottle or cup practice before six months; after that, most doctors will okay giving small amounts of whole cow's milk, or fruit juices diluted with water. Since your baby is more likely to be receptive to receiving these feedings from daddy than from mummy, this is a great time for him to get in on the baby-feeding act.

Phase Two: Cutting back on breastfeedings. Unlike a smoker giving up cigarettes or a chocoholic giving up chocolate, cold turkey isn't the best route for a baby giving up

the breast. Nor is it best for the mother whose breasts are being retired. For the baby, it's much too traumatic, physically and emotionally. For the mother, leaking, engorgement, clogged ducts and infection are all more likely if nursing stops suddenly. So unless illness or some other event in your lives makes hurried weaning necessary, wean gradually, beginning at least several weeks before your targeted weaning completion date. Postpone the process entirely at a time of change (major or minor) in your baby's life – such as when a new nanny is taking over, mummy is returning to work, or the family is moving to a new house.

The most common approach to weaning is to begin dropping feedings one at a time, waiting at least a few days, but preferably a week, until your breasts and your baby have adjusted to that loss before imposing another. Most mothers find it's easiest to first omit the feeding baby seems least interested in and takes the least amount at, or the one that most interferes with her own day. In the case of an employed mother, that's often the midday feeding. With babies under six months, who are mostly dependent on milk for their nourishment, each breastfeeding dropped should be replaced by formula. With older babies, a snack or meal can replace the nursings, as appropriate.

If you've been breastfeeding your baby on demand, and demand has been quite erratic, you may have to become more strict, getting down to a fairly regular schedule and a reduced number of feedings before you can get serious about weaning.

No matter what a mother's schedule, the early morning and late evening feedings – which provide the most comfort and pleasure for both mother and baby – are usually the last to go. Some women, in fact, continue to give one or both of these feedings to their otherwise weaned babies for weeks or even months, just for the joy of it. (This option isn't available for everyone; some women

---

1. If you do decide to wean *to* a bottle, remember that it's a good idea to wean *from* the bottle by the first birthday or shortly after, in order to avoid the problems of tooth decay from baby-bottle mouth (see page 248).

Keeping Yourself Comfortable

Gradual weaning is likely to prevent any serious discomfort, though occasionally, especially if your baby is still very young when you wean and has been exclusively breastfed, you may suffer some engorgement. If you do, express just enough milk to relieve it; expressing too much could stimulate further milk production. Gradual weaning will also lessen the emotional impact on you, but it probably won't eliminate it entirely. Weaning, like menstruation, pregnancy, childbirth and the postpartum period, is a time of hormonal upheaval and the result is often mild depression, irritability and mood swings. The feelings are often exaggerated by a sense of loss and sadness over giving up this most special relationship with your baby, especially if you don't plan on having any more children. (In a few women, postweaning depression can be severe and requires immediate professional help; see page 534 for the warning signs).

A few weeks after weaning, your breasts may seem totally empty of milk. But don't be surprised if you're still able to express small amounts of milk months, even a year or more, later; this is perfectly normal. It's also normal for breasts to take time to return to close to their former size – often they end up somewhat larger or smaller, and they are frequently less firm, due as much to heredity factors and pregnancy as to nursing.

If weaning must be accomplished suddenly, especially in the early months when the milk supply is at its most copious, discomfort for the mother can be considerable. Extreme engorgement accompanied by fever and flulike symptoms may result, and the chance of infection and other complications is much greater than with gradual weaning. Hot compresses and/or hot showers plus aspirin may relieve some of the pain from engorgement, and cutting back on fluids may help decrease the milk supply. Expressing just enough milk to relieve engorgement, but not enough to stimulate renewed production, may also help. Check with your doctor if symptoms don't diminish after 24 hours.

Sudden weaning can also be stressful to a baby. If you must wean without any prior preparation, be sure to give your infant plenty of extra attention, love and cuddling, and try to minimize other stresses in his or her life. If you have to be away from home, see that daddy, grandma, another relative, or a doting baby-sitter remembers to do likewise.

find that their milk supply depletes rapidly once they cut nursing back that far.)

For some women, particularly those who are at home full-time, cutting back on all feedings, rather than cutting out individual feedings, is a method that works well. To start, the baby is given 30 ml/1 fl ounce of milk from cup or bottle prior to each breastfeeding, and then allowed less time at the breast. Gradually, over the course of several weeks, the amount in the cup or bottle is increased and time at the breast for each feeding is decreased. Eventually the baby is taking adequate quantities of cow's milk or formula and weaning is accomplished.

Occasionally illness, a bout of painful tee-

thing, or a disorienting change of locale or routine (such as on holiday) can lead to backsliding, with baby demanding the breast more often. Be understanding and don't worry – such a setback will only be temporary. Once baby's life is back to normal, you can begin your mission anew.

Keep in mind that nursing is only one part of your relationship with your baby. Giving it up won't weaken the bond or lessen the love between you; in fact, some women find that the relationship is enhanced as they spend less time nursing and more time actively interacting.

Your baby may take to other sources of comfort, such as the thumb or a blanket, when the breast is taken away, and this is normal and healthy. He or she may also hunger for extra attention from you; give it freely. Such attention gives young children the security they need to become independent later on.

Don't be concerned that your baby might pine away indefinitely for the breast after weaning. That won't happen. Babies seem to have a built-in survival mechanism whereby even those with the best of memories appear to quickly forget the breastfeeding experience, or, at least, cease to crave it.

What You May Be Concerned About

Bowed Legs

'My daughter just started taking steps and she seems to be terribly bowlegged.'

Bowed until two, knock-kneed at four, a small child's legs certainly couldn't give Betty Grable's a run for their money. But even Betty's were probably bowed when she took her first steps. Almost all children are bowlegged (their knees don't touch when they stand with feet together) during the first two years of life. Then, as they spend more time walking, they become knock-kneed (their knees meet, but their ankles don't). Not until the teen years do the knees and ankles align and the legs appear to be shaped normally. Special shoes or orthotics (bars, braces, or other orthopaedic appliances) aren't needed and won't make a difference in this normal progression.

Occasionally, a doctor will note a true abnormality in a child's legs. Perhaps just one leg is bowed, or one knee turns in, or perhaps the baby is knock-kneed (though sometimes a baby only *looks* that way because of very chubby thighs), or normal bowing becomes progressively more pronounced once walking begins. In such cases, or if there is a history of bowlegs or knock-knees in adults in the family, the baby may need further evaluation, either by the baby's doctor or by a paediatric orthopaedist. Depending upon the particular case, treatment may or may not be recommended (see page 143). Fortunately, rickets, once the most common cause of permanent bowed legs, is fairly rare today, thanks to the fortification of formula, some milk and other dairy products with vitamin D, and to vitamin D supplements for breastfed babies.

Unclear Speech

'Our little girl says several words, but only my husband and I understand them. She seems to have trouble with a lot of consonants, says "b" for "f" and "d" for "k" and so on. Does this mean she'll need speech therapy?'

It's much too early to start thinking about sending your Eliza off to Professor Higgins. There are, after all, 21 consonants in the English language, which alone and in combination represent at least 23 different sounds, and it's usually not until well into the third or fourth year, sometimes much later, that a child learns to pronounce all of them skillfully. (Many children are still having trouble with 'th' sounds in the sixth and seventh year.) Multisyllabic words are especially difficult to handle at first. Though some children speak clearly enough to be understood by adults outside the family by age two, many don't until they reach age four or five.

It's not unusual for outsiders to be completely baffled by toddler talk that is easily deciphered by a child's own parents, whose ears have become accustomed to the child's language patterns. It takes time and plenty of exposure to toddlers to be able to tune in to them, just as it takes time and plenty of exposure to a new language to be able to tune in to it.

Don't keep correcting your child when she says 'frow' for throw, or 'dee' for key.

And don't withhold favours because of poor pronunciation, refusing to give her her bottle if she requests a 'ba-ba', or denying her a cup of water if she asks for 'wa-wa'. That approach will only make her hesitant about trying new words or even about saying old ones. But don't echo her words, use them when talking to her ('da-da's coming home soon'), or let her know you think her pronunciation's cute (even though it is). If she gets the idea that her mis-pronunciations are charming, she'll use them far longer than she would have without the encouragement.

What you can do, however, is accept and applaud her efforts, and at the same time teach correct pronunciation by example. When she points to the lamp and says 'wight', respond (displaying proper parental pride, of course) with 'Very good – that's the light'. When she asks for 'bana' in her cereal, say, 'Oh, you want some ba-na-na in your cereal. Here's some ba-na-na'. She may not be able to say 'banana' for months, or even a couple of years, but she will appreciate that you accept her present way of saying it, and she will get the subtle message that her pronunciation is not yet perfect. Of course, proud as you will be when she finally says bottle, water, daddy, light and banana as clearly as you do, you will doubtless experience a twinge or two of regret for the loss of her adorable baby talk.

Parental Nudity

'I sometimes dress in front of my baby, but I'm a little worried that seeing me naked might be detrimental in some way to his development.'

You've got some time before you'll have to start retreating behind closed doors to do your dressing and undressing. Experts agree that up until the preschool years parental nudity won't disturb a child in any way. Beyond the age of three or four, however, the consensus changes. At that point, some believe, it may be less healthy for children to see parents of the opposite sex fully un-dressed. Certainly, an infant under a year is too young to be stimulated by seeing his mother undressed (unless he's a breast-feeder) – and he's also too young to re-member, years later, what he's seen. In fact, he's as unlikely to notice anything special about mum's birthday suit as he is about her best dress, and will probably largely ignore it.

If your baby is curious about what he views, however, and wants to touch your pubic hair or pull at your nipples, feel free to end any explorations that bother you. Be matter-of-fact, and don't overreact. His in-terest in the private parts of your body is, after all, no less wholesome than his interest in the public parts, such as your nose or ears. 'That's mummy's' is a response that will help a baby begin to understand the con-cept of body privacy and help him keep his private parts private later on – but one that won't instill guilt.

Falls

'I feel as though I'm living on the brink of disaster ever since my little boy started to walk and climb. He trips over his own feet, bangs his head on table corners, topples off chairs . . .'

This is an age that many parents fear neither they nor their babies will survive. Split lips, black eyes, bumps, bangs, bruises and countless close calls for baby. Frazzled nerves and skipped heartbeats for mummy and daddy.

Yet babies keep going back for more. And a good thing, too, or they'd never learn to get around on their own – or, in fact, learn much of anything at all. Though horseback riding can be mastered, according to the old adage, with just seven falls, mastery of walking and climbing takes a good deal more – with seven or more falls not being uncommon in the space of a single morning. Some chil-dren learn caution fairly quickly; after the first topple off the coffee table, they retreat for a few days and then proceed more carefully. Others seem as though they will never learn caution, never know fear, never feel pain; five minutes after the tenth topple, they're back for number eleven.

Learning to walk is a matter of trial and error – or more accurately, step and fall. You can't, and shouldn't try to, interfere with the learning process. Your role, other than that of proud but nervous spectator, is to do everything possible to ensure that when your baby falls, he falls safely. While taking a tumble on the living room rug can bruise his ego, tumbling down the stairs can bruise a lot more. Bumping into the rounded edge of the sofa may draw some tears, but colliding with the sharp corner of a glass table may draw blood. To decrease the chance of serious accidents, be sure that your house is safe for your baby (see page 284). And even if you have removed the most obvious hazards from your toddler's path, remember that the most important safety feature in your home is you (or whoever else is minding your child). While your child needs plenty of freedom for exploration of the world around him, it should be permitted only under very close and *constant* adult supervision.

Even in the most conscientious of homes, however, serious accidents can happen. Be prepared for this possibility by knowing just what to do if one should occur; take a baby-resuscitation course and learn the first-aid procedures beginning on page 427.

Parental reaction often colours a baby's response to mishap. If each fall brings one more panicked adults rushing to his rescue, chorusing 'Are you okay? Are you okay?' between gasps and shudders, your fallen soldier is likely to overreact as much as those around him – shedding as many tears when he's not really hurt as when he really is – and may soon become over-cautious or lose his sense of adventure, perhaps even to the point of hesitating to attempt normal physical developmental hurdles. If, on the other hand, the adult's reaction is a calm 'Oops, you fell down! You're all right. Up you go,' then the child is likely to turn out to be a real trooper, taking minor tumbles in his stride and getting right back on his feet without missing a beat.

Not Pulling up Yet

'Although she's been trying for some time, my baby hasn't yet pulled up to stand. I'm worried that she's not developing normally.'

For babies, life's a never-ending series of physical (and emotional and intellectual) challenges. The skills that adults take for granted – rolling over, sitting up, standing – are for them major hurdles to be confronted and scaled with no small effort. And no sooner is one challenge met than another looms ahead.

As for pulling up, there will be babies who will master this skill as early as five months and those who will wait until well after the first birthday, though most will fall (or rather, stand) somewhere between the two developmental extremes. A baby's weight may have an impact on when she first pulls up; a heavier baby has more baggage to take with her than does a lighter one, and so the effort needed may be greater. On the other hand, a strong and well-coordinated baby may be able to pull up early no matter how much she weighs. The baby who's cooped up in a pushchair, baby carrier, or mesh playpen much of the day won't be able to practise her pull-ups. Nor will a baby want to practise if she is surrounded by fragile furniture that buckles under her every attempt to steady herself. Slippery shoes or socks can also hamper efforts to pull up and can cause falls that dampen enthusiasm for the activity – bare feet or slipper-socks with nonskid soles give baby a better foot to stand on. You can encourage your baby to try to pull up by putting a favourite toy in a place where she has to stand to get to it. Also, help her to pull up in your lap frequently, which will build her leg muscles as well as her confidence.

The average age for passing the pulling-up milestone is nine months; and most, but certainly not all, children have accomplished the skill by twelve months. Of course, it's a good idea to check with the doctor if your child hasn't successfully pulled up by her first birthday, just to rule out the possibility of a physical problem. Right now, all you need to do is sit back and wait for her to stand – in her own good time. Children gain confidence from being allowed to progress at their own pace, from discovering 'I can do it myself'. Trying to force a child to stand or walk before she's ready could set her back rather than move her forward.

Cholesterol in Baby's Diet

'My husband and I are very careful about cholesterol in our diets, but when we asked our paediatrician whether we should start our son on skimmed milk, he said no. Does this mean we don't have to worry about his cholesterol at all?'

A child in the first year of life, and probably in the second year as well, is in an enviable position – at least from the point of view of parents who miss their daily steak and eggs. Not only are fat and cholesterol not hazardous to a baby's health, they're believed to be essential for proper growth and for development of the brain and the rest of the nervous system. In addition, skimmed and low-fat milks are not appropriate fare for infants because their high ratio of protein to fat and high sodium levels put too great a strain on the kidneys. Most doctors recommend formula or breast milk for at least the first six months to a year, and whole milk after weaning. Some say it's okay to switch to 2% milk at fifteen months and skimmed at eighteen months; others hold out for whole milk until baby's second birthday.

Lack of sound scientific evidence makes it difficult to say precisely how much fat is too much or not enough in childhood. Moderation probably makes the most sense.[2]

---

2. Apparently strict limitations on fat and cholesterol for children with a hereditary tendency to produce excess cholesterol is helpful in lowering cholesterol levels and appears not to hamper growth and development. If there is such a tendency in your family, and especially if there is also a history of premature heart attack, stroke, or other vascular disease, speak to your baby's doctor about doing a blood cholesterol test soon.

Though it may not be necessary, or even wise, to strictly limit your baby's intake of fat and cholesterol, it is necessary to be sure that the eating habits he develops now will lay the foundation for a lifetime of healthy eating. Studies show that toddlers in the US are already beginning to get buildups in their arteries of the atherosclerotic plaque that leads to heart disease in adulthood, and that by age four, the average Western child has a blood cholesterol level much higher than levels in children in countries where heart disease is uncommon. These disturbing statistics, which don't bode well for the coronary futures of our children, are due largely to the typical diet consumed in the West. Begun in the high chair, it is high in saturated fat and cholesterol and low in fibre. In addition to cardiovascular diseases, it has been linked to several types of cancer, including some of the most pervasive: breast, colon and rectal.

So while you should continue to include whole milk in your baby's diet for a while yet, and needn't rigidly limit eggs or hard cheese, you should take steps to reduce his future risk of premature illness or death by instilling prudent eating habits now.

Ban the butter. If your baby becomes accustomed to bread, pancakes, vegetables, fish and other foods without added butter now, he won't have to undergo the ordeal of trying to cut back later. And if, when he's older, he wants to butter his bread or butter-sauté his broccoli, a smidgen will doubtless satisfy.

Forgo the frying. Fried foods aren't good for anyone – little children included. Serve or order baked potato instead of chips for your baby (and the rest of your family), grill the chicken instead of frying it, pan-fry the fish in a non-stick frying pan or bake it in the oven.

Be choosy with your cheese. High in protein and calcium, hard cheeses such as Swiss, Gouda, mozzarella, and Cheddar would be a balanced diet's best friend – if it weren't for their very high saturated fat and

Raising a Healthy Heart

It's never too early to start reducing your baby's risk of heart attack later in life. The following will help:

- Feed a diet low in saturated fat and cholesterol from the end of the second year, but introduce prudent diet habits earlier. If there is a family history of hypercholesteraemia (very high cholesterol), have your child's cholesterol monitored by the doctor.

- Feed a diet low in salt from infancy on.

- Feed a diet high in omega-3 fatty acids, which are found in plentiful supply in oily fish (salmon, shad and mackerel, for example). Don't use omega-3 fish-oil capsules, as their effectiveness and safety have not been proven.

- Watch your child's weight, and take action if it begins to shoot up much faster than his or her height (see page 200). An overweight baby may become an overweight child, who will almost certainly become an overweight adult.

- Don't smoke or permit smoking in your home. Parents who smoke are more likely than nonsmokers to have children who smoke. Educate your child from infancy about the dangers as well as the unpleasantness of tobacco and he or she is not likely to ever light up.

- Teach your child early on the value and pleasure of exercise and physical activity; don't be sedentary yourself, and don't let your child be.

- If your child's blood pressure is high or borderline, follow the doctor's instructions for controlling it.

- Keep consumption of sugar low. Sugar increases chromium needs and it may increase the chance of diabetes developing, which is a heart attack risk factor.

---

cholesterol counts, high even for babies, for whom a diet moderately high in cholesterol appears necessary. So look for the lower-fat cheeses (such as semi-skimmed mozzarella, Emmenthaler, or other skimmed-milk cheese) with no more than 5 to 7 grams of fat per 25 g (ounce), and use them in moderation since even they cannot truly be considered 'low-fat'.

Since the high sodium content of most cheeses is neither good for babies now nor for heart health later, choose cheeses that are relatively low in sodium – for example, those that contain no more than 35 milligrams per 25 g (ounce).

If children develop a taste for lower-fat, low-sodium cheeses when they're very young, they may even prefer them over the higher-fat and higher-salt varieties when they're older.

Defat other dairy products. Though you won't be switching your baby to skimmed milk yet, you can start weaning to lower-fat cream cheeses, yogurts and cottage cheese (choose salt-reduced or salt-free varieties of the latter) by the end of the first year (assuming your baby is getting adequate quantities of whole milk and/or hard cheeses and some eggs), so baby won't crave the richer kind. Because they contain large amounts of sugar as well as fat, commercial ice creams and other frozen desserts (including tofu desserts, which contain little nourishment and much sugar) shouldn't be given to babies at all; for nutritious home-made frozen dessert recipes, see page 605.

Be picky with your protein. Protein in adequate amounts is important for your entire family, but it's wise to select the sources that are low in cholesterol and fat, such as: fish, skinless poultry, dried beans and peas, tofu (bean curd). If your baby learns to enjoy fish and chicken now, he's less likely to spurn 'anything but hamburger' later. Serve red meat no more than three times a week, and then buy lean cuts and trim fat well. It's okay to avoid red meat entirely, but then be certain your baby has other sources of iron in his diet.

Fill out your menu with fibre. If fat increases blood cholesterol levels and the risk of heart attack, certain types of fibre, such as pectin and oat bran, decrease both. Be sure your baby's diet frequently contains pectin-rich fruits such as apples and oats in some form.

Favour fish. Like fibre, fish in the diet seems to have the effect of lowering blood cholesterol levels, probably thanks to the omega-3 oils found in it. Introduce your baby early to a variety of fresh fish, most of which have a pleasingly mild taste and an easily chewable texture, and which are low in fat and sodium. But check very carefully for bones.

Look at the label. Most of the fat and cholesterol in the diets of both adults and children is hidden in prepared foods. Cakes and pastries are, not surprisingly, major sources of dietary fat, bypassing butter and margarine. To avoid hidden fat, read labels carefully and don't buy products that contain fats from the 'bad' column on the facing page. Look instead for those made either without fat or with preferred fats or oils. The farther down 'fat' is on the list of ingredients, the less total fat a product contains, and the less the threat to your family's health.

Cut fat in cooking. When cooking, you can reduce the fat called for in most recipes without otherwise altering them. Using non-stick pans and cookware as well as vegetable cooking sprays will allow you to greatly reduce the amount of fat used in sautéing or pan-frying. When baking, reduce the fat and replace it with an equivalent amount of liquid.

Divide the eggs and conquer cholesterol. All of the roughly 280 milligrams of an egg's cholesterol are in the yolk. Use whites for all or some of the eggs called for in recipes (two egg whites equal one whole egg) when

baking and cooking for the entire family. In general, children and adults should have no more than three yolks a week; those with high cholesterol levels should have fewer. Your baby can still have an egg daily now, but start cutting back on the number of yolks he gets at about eighteen months. Remember, eggs used in cooking count in the quota.

Go on a family fast-foods fast. Most fast foods are very high not only in fat and cholesterol, but in salt as well. They are also usually lacking in many nutrients. So take the family to fast-food restaurants rarely – and then select those items that are lower in fat (pizza, baked fish, grilled chicken, plain baked potatoes, undressed vegetables from the salad bar). Though burgers at home are okay for baby, the fast-food variety are usually too high in sodium and fat, and the white-flour bun is nutritionally superfluous.

Once your baby is over two years old, he can join the rest of the family on a diet in which 50 to 55% of calories come from carbohydrates (whole-grain breads and cereals, legumes such as dried beans and peas, vegetables, fruits), 15 to 20% from protein (fish, poultry, meat, dairy products, legumes, tofu), and only 30% from fat (no more than 10% should be saturated and 10% should be in the form of polyunsaturated oils or olive oil).[3] Total daily intake of cholesterol (found in large quantities in animal products such as butter, whole milk, cheese, meat and especially eggs), according to prudent-diet guidelines, should not exceed 100 milligrams per 1,000 calories consumed up to a maximum of 250 to 300 milligrams a day. Consider that one large egg contains approximately 280 milligrams of cholesterol; one pat of butter, 10 milligrams; 250 ml (8 fl ounces) of whole milk, 33; 25 g (1 ounce) of

---

3. Do *not* reduce your child's intake of fat below this level without medical advice. Fats, particularly those (such as breast milk, safflower, corn and soya oils) containing linoleic acid, an essential fatty acid, are an absolute requirement for a good diet. And a diet that is extremely low in fat is inherently deficient in certain essential nutrients.

Cheddar cheese, 30; an 85-g (3-ounce) hamburger, 76; and that a two year-old consumes about 1,000 to 1,300 calories a day, a typical adult 1,800 to 2,400.

Growth Swings

'The doctor just told me that my son has dropped from the 90th to the 50th percentile in height. She said not to worry, but I'm afraid something might be wrong with his development.'

When a doctor assesses a child's developmental progress, she looks at more than the curve of his growth chart. Are both height and weight keeping pace fairly closely? Is baby passing developmental mileposts (sitting, pulling up, etc.) at about the right time? Is he active and alert? Does he appear happy? Does he seem to relate well to mummy? Are hair and skin healthy looking? Apparently your baby's doctor found your child to be developing normally and you should take your cue from that.

The most common reason for such a growth shift at this time is that a baby who was born on the large side is just moving closer to his genetically predestined size. If you and your husband are not very tall, you shouldn't expect your son to stay in the 90th percentile – chances are he won't. Height, however, isn't inherited through a single gene. So a child with a 1.8-metre (6-foot) father and a 1.5-metre (5-foot) mother isn't likely to reach adulthood exactly the same height as one or the other. More likely, he will end up somewhere in between. (Each generation is, however, on average, a little taller than the previous one.)

Occasionally a measuring error has been made, either at the present time or on a previous visit. Babies are usually measured while they're lying down and a baby's wriggling can easily yield inaccurate results. When a child graduates to upright measurement, he may appear to lose 2.5 cm (an inch) or so in height because his bones settle a little when he stands.

Do be certain, of course, that your baby is well nourished, and continues to be as he grows older. And bring any health concerns to the attention of his doctor. After that, record your baby's checkup statistics and forget about them. As you will soon realize, children grow up too fast anyway.

Fats: the Good, the Best and the Bad

The oils you select when preparing food for your family will have a major impact on their health. Whenever possible, choose those from the 'The Good' or 'The Best' list, rather than from the 'The Bad'.

The Good	The Best	The Bad
Margarine with a polyunsaturated to saturated fat ratio of 2:1 or better	Avocado oil	Palm and palm kernel oil
	Olive oil	Coconut oil
	Canola oil (rapeseed)	Cocoa butter
	Safflower oil	Hydrogenated vegetable fat or shortening
Peanut oil	Sunflower oil	Chicken or other poultry fat
Cottonseed oil (a little higher in saturated fats)	Corn oil	
	Soya oil	Suet (beef fat)
	Other oils high in polyunsaturates	Lard (pork fat)
		Butter*
		Partially hydrogenated fats

* If your family prefers the taste of butter as a spread, using small amounts (no more than a pat – 1 teaspoon – per person per day) will not appreciably increase cholesterol intake.

WHAT IT'S IMPORTANT TO KNOW:
Helping Baby To Talk

Your baby's come a long way, mummy. From a newborn whose only way of communicating was crying and who understood nothing but his or her own primal needs; to a six-month-old who was beginning to articulate sounds, comprehend words and express anger, frustration and happiness; to an eight-month-old who was able to convey messages through primitive sounds and gestures; and now, to an eleven-month-old who's uttered (or will soon utter) his or her first real words. And yet with all the accomplishments already behind your baby, still more astounding growth is up ahead. In the months to come, your baby's comprehension will increase at a remarkable rate; by around a year and a half, there will be a dramatic expansion in expressive language.

Here's how you can help your baby's language development:

Label, label, label. Everything in your baby's world has a name – use it. Verbally label objects in baby's home environment (bathtub, toilet, kitchen sink, cooker, cot, playpen, lamp, chair, sofa and so on); play 'eyes-nose-mouth' (take baby's hand and touch your eyes, your nose and your mouth, kissing the hand at the last stop) and point out other body parts; point to birds, dogs, trees, leaves, flowers, cars, trucks and aeroplanes while you're out walking. Don't leave out people – point out mummies, daddies, babies, ladies, men, girls, boys. Or baby – use his or her name often to help develop a sense of identity.

Listen, listen, listen. As important as what you say to your baby is how much you let your baby say to you. Even if you haven't identified any real words yet, listen to the babble and respond: 'Oh, that's very interesting', or, 'Is that so?' When you ask a question, wait for an answer, even if it's just a smile, excited body language, or undecipherable babble. Make a concerted effort to pick out words from your baby's verbal ramblings; many 'first words' are so garbled that parents don't notice them. Try to match baby's unrecognizable words with the objects they may represent; they may not even sound remotely correct, yet if the child uses the same 'word' for the same object consistently, it counts. When you have trouble translating what your baby's asking for, point to possible candidates ('Do you want the ball? The bottle? The puzzle?'), giving him or her a chance to tell you whether you've guessed right. There will be frustration on both sides until baby's requests become more intelligible but continuing to attempt to act as interpreter will help speed language development as well as provide baby with the satisfaction of being at least somewhat understood.

Concentrate on concepts. So much of what you take for granted, baby has yet to learn. Here are just a few concepts you can help your baby develop – you can probably think of many more.

- *Hot and cold:* let baby touch the outside of your coffee cup, then an ice cube; cold water, then warm water, warm porridge, then cold milk.

- *Up and down:* gently lift baby up in the air, then lower to the ground; place a block up on the dresser, then put it down on the floor, take your baby up on the see-saw, then down.

- *In and out:* put blocks in a box or bucket, dump them out; do the same with other objects.

- *Empty and full:* fill a container with bath water, then empty it; fill a bucket with sand, then empty it.

- *Stand and sit:* hold baby's hand, stand together, then sit down together; play ring-a-ring roses.

- *Wet and dry*: compare a wet flannel and a dry towel; baby's just-shampooed hair with your dry hair.

- *Big and little*: set a large ball beside a small one; show baby that 'mummy's big and baby's little' in the mirror.

Explain the environment and cause and effect. 'The sun is bright so we have light.' 'The refrigerator keeps food cold so it will taste good and stay fresh.' 'Mummy uses a little brush to brush your teeth, a medium brush to brush your hair, and a big brush to scrub the floor.' 'Flip the wall switch up and the room becomes light, down and it's dark.' 'If you tear the book, we won't be able to read it any more.' And so on. An expanded awareness and understanding of his or her surroundings, as well as sensitivity to other people and their needs and feelings, is a far more important step towards your baby's eventual mastery of language and reading than learning to parrot a lot of meaningless words.

Become colour conscious. Start identifying colours whenever it's appropriate. 'See, that balloon is red, just like your shirt', or 'That truck is green; your buggy is green, too', or 'Look at those pretty yellow flowers'.

Use double-speak. Use adult phrases, then translate them into baby shorthand: 'Now you and I are going for a walk. Mummy, Amy, go bye-bye.' 'Oh, you've finished your snack. Baby made all gone.' Talking twice as much will help baby understand twice as much.

Talk like a grown-up. Using simplified grown-up talk, rather than baby talk, will help your baby learn to speak correctly faster: 'Benjy wants a bottle?' is better than 'Baby wanna baba?' Forms like 'doggie' or 'dolly,' however, are okay to use with young children – they're naturally more appealing.

Introduce pronouns. Though your baby probably won't be using pronouns correctly for a year or more, now is a good time to start developing familiarity with them by using them along with names. '*Mummy* is

going to get *Josh* some breakfast – *I'm* going to get you something to eat.' 'This book is *mummy's* – it's *mine* – and that book is *Nina's* – it's *yours*.' This last also teaches the concept of ownership.

Urge baby to talk back. Use any ploy you can think of to try to get your baby to respond, in either words or gestures. Present choices: 'Do you want bread or crackers?' or 'Do you want to wear your Mickey Mouse pajamas or the ones with aeroplanes?' and then give baby a chance to point to or vocally indicate the favoured selection, which you should then name. Ask questions: 'Are you tired?' 'Would you like a snack?' 'Do you want to go on the swing?' A shake of the head will probably precede a verbal yes or no, but it's still a legitimate response. Get baby to help you locate things (even if they aren't really lost): 'Where's the ball? Can you find Raggedy Ann?' Give baby plenty of time to turn up the item, and reward with cheers and hugs. Even looking in the right direction would count – 'That's right, that's Raggedy Ann!'

Don't force the issue. Encourage your baby to talk by saying 'Tell mummy what you want' when he or she uses nonverbal communication (pointing, grunting) to indicate a need. If baby grunts or points again, offer a choice; for instance, 'Do you want the ball or the truck?' If you still get a nonverbal response, name the item yourself, 'Oh, it's the ball you want', and then hand it over. *Never* withhold something because your child can't ask for it by name or because he or she pronounces the name incorrectly. But do try to elicit the name of the item again next time – in the same patient, non-demanding way.

Keep directions simple. Most babies at this age can follow only simple commands, so give directions one step at a time. Instead of 'Please pick up the spoon and give it to me', try 'Please pick up the spoon', and when that's been done, add 'Now, please, give the spoon to mummy'. You can also help your baby enjoy early success in following commands by giving commands that he or she is about to carry out anyway. If, for example, your baby is reaching for a cracker, say 'Pick up the cracker'. These techniques will help develop comprehension, which must precede speech.

Correct carefully. Very rarely will a young child say even a single word perfectly and none say everything with adult precision. Many consonants may be beyond your baby's capability for the next several years or more and the ends of words may be omitted for at least many more months ('mo mi' may mean 'more milk and 'go dow' 'go down'). When your baby mispronounces a word, don't correct with schoolmarmish brusqueness – too much criticism could prompt a baby to give up trying. Instead, use a more subtle approach, teaching without preaching to protect your baby's tender ego. When baby looks up at the sky and says, 'moon, tar', say 'That's right. There's the moon and the stars'. Though baby mispronunciations are adorable, your repeating them will be confusing (baby knows the way they should sound).

Expand your reading repertoire. Rhymes are still favourites with babies entering their toddler years, as are books with pictures of animals, vehicles, toys and children. A few children are ready for very simple stories, though most won't be willing to sit still for them for several months yet. Even those who are ready usually can't handle more than three or four minutes with a book at this age – their attention span is still short. Children tolerate reading better if they can participate actively. Stop to discuss the pictures ('Look, that cat is wearing a hat!'), ask your child to point to familiar objects (naming them will come later) and name those he or she hasn't seen before or doesn't remember. Eventually (fairly soon for some children), your child will be able to fill in last words of rhymes or sentences in favourite books.

Think numerically. Counting is a long way off for baby, but the concept of one and many isn't. Comments like 'Here, you can have one biscuit', or 'Look, see how many birds are in that tree', or 'You have two kitty cats' will start to inculcate some basic mathematical concepts. Count, or recite 'One, two, buckle my shoe', as you climb the stairs with your baby, particularly once he or she can walk up while you hold both hands. Sing number rhymes, such as 'Baa, baa black sheep' (when you get to the 'three bags full' hold up three fingers, then bend down one finger at a time as you 'distribute' the bags), 'This old man, he played one, he played knickknack on my thumb', and 'ten little Indians', using your fingers to indicate the numbers. Integrate counting into your baby's life: when you do your sit-ups, count them out in one through tens; when you're baking count out the ingredients one by one as you add them; when you're adding banana to your baby's cereal count out the slices.

FIFTEEN

The Twelfth Month

◆

What Your Baby May Be Doing

By the end of this month, your baby . . . should be able to (see Note):

- walk holding on to furniture (by 12⅔ months)

Note: If your baby seems not to have reached this milestone, check with the doctor. In rare instances the delay could indicate a problem, though in most cases it will turn out to be normal for your baby. Premature infants generally reach milestones later than others of the same birth age, often achieving them closer to their adjusted age (the age they would be if they had been born at term), or sometimes later.

. . . will probably be able to:

- play patty-cake (clap hands) or wave bye-bye (most children accomplish these feats by 13 months)

- drink from a cup independently (many can't do this until 16½ months)

- pick up a tiny object neatly with tips of thumb and forefinger (by 12¼ months; many babies do not accomplish this until nearly 15 months)

- stand alone momentarily (many don't accomplish this until 13 months)

- say dada or mama discriminately (most will say at least one of these by 14 months)

- say one word other than mama or dada (many won't say their first word until 14 months or later)

. . . may possibly be able to:

- indicate wants in ways other than crying (many don't reach this stage until past 14 months)

- 'play ball' (roll ball back to you; many don't accomplish this feat until 16 months)

- stand alone well (many don't reach this point until 14 months)

- use immature jargoning (gibberish that sounds like a foreign language; half of all babies don't start jargoning until after their first birthday, and many not until they are 15 months old)

- walk well (3 out of 4 babies don't walk well until 13½ months, and many not until considerably later; good crawlers may be slower to walk; when other development is normal, late walking is rarely a cause for concern)

. . . may even be able to:

- say three words or more other than mama or dada (a good half of all babies won't reach this stage until 13 months, and many not until 16 months)

- respond to a one-step command without gestures (give that to me – without hand out; most children won't reach this stage until after their first birthday, many not until after 16 months).

What You Can Expect At This Month's Checkup

Each doctor, midwife or health visitor will have a personal approach to well-baby checkups. The overall organization of the physical exam, as well as the number and type of assessment techniques used and procedures performed, will also vary with the individual needs of the child. But in general, you can expect the following at a checkup when your baby is about twelve months old:

- Questions about how you and baby and the rest of the family are doing at home, and about baby's eating, sleeping and general progress. About child care, if you are working.

- Measurement of baby's weight, length and head circumference, and plotting of progress since birth.

- Physical exam, including a recheck of any previous problems. Now that baby can pull up, feet and legs will be checked when standing supported or unsupported, and walking if baby walks.

- A haemoglobin or haematocrit test to check for anaemia (usually by means of a pinprick on the finger), if not performed earlier.

- Developmental assessment. The examiner may actually put baby through a series of 'tests' to evaluate baby's ability to sit independently, to pull up and to cruise (or even walk), to reach for and grasp objects, to pick up tiny objects with a neat pincer grasp, to look for dropped or hidden objects, to respond to his or her name, to do some self-feeding, to use a cup, to cooperate in dressing, to recognize and possibly say such words as mummy, daddy, bye-bye, and no-no, and to enjoy social games such as patty-cake and peekaboo; or he or she may simply rely on observation plus your reports on what baby is doing.

- Immunizations, if not given before and if baby is in good health and there are no contraindications. Be sure to discuss previous reactions, if any, *beforehand* if not given shortly after birth, a tuberculin skin test to measure contact with TB may be administered now in high-incidence areas, or may not be given until 15 months. It may be given before, or at the same time as, the MMR (usually given before 15 months)

- Guidance about what to expect in the next month in relation to such topics as feeding, sleeping, development and infant safety.

- Recommendations about fluoride, iron and vitamin D, or other supplementation, as needed.

You may want to ask these questions if the doctor hasn't already answered them:

- What are positive and negative reactions to the MMR or to the tuberculin test, if one was administered? When should you call about a positive reaction? (Redness during first 24 hours is common, but redness or swelling after 48 to 72 hours is considered positive.)

- What new foods can be introduced to baby now? Can baby get milk in a cup? When can whole milk, citrus fruits, fish, meats and egg whites be introduced, if they haven't been already?

- When should you consider weaning from the bottle, if your baby is bottle fed, or from the breast, if you haven't already weaned?

  Also raise concerns that have arisen over the past month. Jot down information and instructions from the doctor (you're sure to forget them, otherwise). Record all pertinent information (baby's weight, length, head circumference, immunizations, test results, illnesses, medications given and so on) in a permanent health record.

Feeding Your Baby This Month: The Best-Odds Toddler Diet

With little but mashed bananas and strained sweet potatoes under his or her gastronomic belt, your toddler's palate is basically a clean plate waiting to be filled with a whole world of as yet undiscovered eating experiences. Exactly what it will be filled with now and in the next few formative years will have a great influence on what will please it in later years – which, of course, will have a significant impact on your child's future health and longevity. But good nutrition will also provide more immediate benefits. As your excellent diet antenatally gave your baby the best odds of being born alive and well, an excellent diet during early childhood will assure him or her of the best odds of staying healthy, as well as adequate energy to fuel a busy toddler's explorations.

The Best-Odds Nine Basic Principles

The basic principles for nutritious eating are very much the same for your toddler as they are for the rest of the family, though there are slight variations because of your child's age.

Every bite counts. This was an important principle when you were feeding your baby through the placenta, and then with your milk, if you breastfed; it's likewise important now that you're doing the feeding with spoons, cups and bowls and it's baby who's taking the bites. For young children, whose capacities and appetites are limited and whose tastes are often more so, bites wasted on non-nutritious fare are not likely to be made up. Empty treats (such as sugary biscuits, cakes and sweets) should be rare – though healthy treats (such as juice-sweetened whole-grain biscuits, and cakes) can be a mainstay of the diet.

All calories are not created equal. The 100 calories in a square of chocolate aren't nutritionally equivalent to the 100 calories in a small banana; plan meals and snacks accordingly.

Meal skipping is risky. Skipped meals deprive babies and young children of nutrients they need for growth and development. Not eating at regular intervals during the day saps children of energy, as well as making them cranky and irrational, sometimes because of low blood sugar. And because of their small capacities, toddlers usually need snacks in addition to their three squares. Of course, toddlers sometimes reject a meal or a snack – and you shouldn't push if they do. As long as you provide regular meals, you can let your baby skip a few now and then.

Efficiency is effective. Weight problems often begin in childhood. But if a toddler is gaining unwanted weight, dieting isn't in order, careful food selection is. Favour items that offer a lot of nutrition for few calories, such as fresh fruits and vegetables and wholemeal bread without butter. If a toddler is underweight or gaining too slowly, efficient food selection means choosing foods that provide bountiful nutrition in combination with a lot of calories and not too much bulk (peanut butter, bananas, avocado, cheese). Whether or not weight is an issue, selecting foods that fill more than one nutrient requirement at a time (broccoli for vitamin C and vitamin A, yogurt for protein and calcium) is always efficient and makes particularly good sense where small appetites are concerned.

Carbohydrates are a complex issue. Carbohydrates, starches and sugars are childhood favourites, and very young children – particularly those who refuse 'protein' foods such as meat or fish – often seem to live on nothing else. But there are carbohydrates, and there are *carbohydrates*. Some, known as complex carbohydrates, provide vitamins, minerals, protein and fibre, as well as calories (whole-grain breads and cereals, brown rice, peas, beans, whole-grain or high-protein pasta, fruits and vegetables); others, known as simple sugars and refined starches, provide little or nothing else besides calories (sugar, honey, refined grains, and foods made with them). Serve the right carbohydrates at home and allow others only rarely (at parties, when visiting, or at other times when there's no choice).

Sweet nothings are nothing but trouble. Sugar provides nothing but empty calories, and sugary foods often fill children up, leaving no room for needed nutrients. In addition, sugar contributes significantly to tooth decay, probably by encouraging the growth of the bacteria that do the dirty work. It may also be involved, indirectly, in the development of diabetes (by increasing the body's need for chromium). The jury is still out on whether or not sugar is a cause of hyperactivity. One study found that children who ate a lot of sugar were more active than those who didn't; other studies have not linked sugar to hyperactivity.

Almost all children seem to favour the sweet over the nonsweet right from the start, but research shows that children who eat a lot of sugary foods early on are more likely to crave them later. Keep sugar (including brown sugar, raw sugar, turbinado sugar, fructose, maple syrup, corn syrup and honey) out of your kitchen and offer sugar-sweetened foods as treats only rarely, if at all. Many mothers find it fairly easy to ban sugar entirely, at least until their children reach the age of two or begin socializing more with other children. No sugar doesn't, however, mean no sweets. Children in a sugar-free household should be able to enjoy cakes, biscuits, and muffins. And they can if you supply them with such goodies, home-made or from the increasing selection commercially available, sweetened with fruit and fruit juice concentrates.

Serve foods that remember where they

came from. The closer to its natural state a food is, the more likely it is to have retained the nutrients it started out with. But what is often added to processed foods – questionable chemicals, accidentally or incidentally – may be even more threatening than what might be lost. Because children process and dispose of foreign chemicals more slowly (thus retaining them longer), have smaller body sizes, and theoretically have a lot more years to live during which the chemicals can do their damage, they are more susceptible to the dangers of chemical contamination than adults. So serve foods that stay close to their roots, allowing highly processed foods rarely if at all, opting for the unrefined over the refined, choosing fresh meats and cheese over the processed varieties, and selecting fresh or fresh-frozen fruits and vegetables over heavily processed canned, frozen, or dehydrated ones. Then tamper with them as little as possible – don't overcook, store for long periods, or expose unnecessarily to air, water, or heat.

Make good eating a family affair. Junior won't eat carrots, forgo sugary sweets, or prefer wholemeal over white if dad's always leaving his carrots on his plate, mum is always breakfasting on donuts or snacking on sweets, and an older sibling lives on peanut butter on white bread. Having to eat virtuously alone is unfair; having company is fun. And cleaning up the family's dietary act for the sake of the youngest will benefit not only him or her, but everyone who sits at the family table.

Watch out for diet sabotage. Your toddler isn't likely to start undermining his or her diet with tobacco, excess alcohol or caffeine, or other drugs at any time soon. But excess junk food can sabotage the diet, too, by replacing more nutritious fare. And if a child learns at home that tobacco or illegal drugs in any amount and excess amounts of alcohol and caffeine are acceptable, those kinds of diet sabotage may come sooner than you'd imagine.

Milk Sense

If you've weaned your baby, or are about to, it's important to select the right milk to replace breast milk or formula. Most doctors recommend whole milk because skimmed milk has too much protein and sodium content for infants and toddlers, and because very young children seem to continue to need the extra fat and cholesterol for optimal brain and nervous system development probably until age two, although some doctors recommend switching to skimmed milk at eighteen months. Discuss the matter with your baby's doctor.

It is also urged that the milk be pasteurized. Though it is true that pasteurization does rob milk of some of its nutritive value, experts believe the risk of illness from the drinking of raw milk is too great to warrant its use.

You may be wondering how you can be sure your baby is getting enough milk now that you've abandoned clearly calibrated baby bottles. One way is to measure out the day's requirements – 700 ml/ 25 fl ounces (adding some to allow for spillage) – each morning, pour it into a clean jar, and refrigerate. Serve all your baby's milk (for cereal, drinking, mashing with potatoes or other vegetables) from this supply. If it's all gone at the end of the day, and baby didn't spill or leave over a great deal, the milk requirement was probably met. If a lot is left in the jar or lost to the high-chair tray or to the floor several days in a row, fit some

additional calcium in baby's diet this way:

- If your baby has been drinking only about 350 ml (12 fl ounces) of milk a day, add 30 g (1 ounce) nonfat dry milk plus 1 tablespoon single cream or 2 tablespoons half-and-half to that amount of fluid milk and use the mixture as baby's daily allotment. If baby has been drinking about 500 ml (16 fl ounces), add 20 g (¾ ounce) nonfat dry milk plus 1 tablespoon single cream or 2 tablespoons half-and-half.

- Switch to calcium-added milk, which your baby needs less of (500 ml/fl ounces) to fill the calcium requirement. But add 1 tablespoon of single cream or 2 tablespoons of half-and-half to each serving.

- Add one of the following to your baby's diet for each 75 ml (3 fl ounces) of whole milk your baby doesn't drink: about 15 g (⅜ to ½ ounce) lower-fat hard cheese (such as mozzarella); 20 g (⅔ ounce) higher-fat hard cheese (such as Cheddar); about 4 tablespoons yogurt; 85 g (3 ounces) calcium-coagulated tofu; 55 g (2 ounces) calcium-enriched orange juice; or half of any other toddler calcium serving.

Don't be concerned if some days your baby misses a calcium serving or two. He or she will probably make up for it the next day.

The Best-Odds Daily Dozen – for Toddlers

The Daily Dozen was first developed as an easy-to-follow outline for Best-Odds prenatal nutrition. In this modified form, it is the easiest way to nourish your toddler. Since children usually take small portions, feel free to mix and match partial servings to reach the needed requirements – remembering, too, that many foods can be counted for more than one requirement, (cantaloupe for

vitamin C and a yellow fruit, for instance). The amounts need not be exact, but you may want to measure or weigh until you feel pretty comfortable judging 25 g (an ounce) of cheese or 55 g (2 ounces) of carrots with the naked eye. Routinely using measuring spoons to scoop foods from containers to serving dishes is a painless way of keeping track of portions.

Calories – an average of 900 to 1,350. No calculations are necessary. You'll know if your toddler is getting the right number of calories simply by following his or her weight at checkup times. If it's staying on approximately the same curve, caloric intake is sufficient but not excessive, though there may occasionally be a jump or dip as a thin baby fills out or a chubby one slims down. The amount of food a child needs to eat to maintain that curve will depend on individual size, metabolism and level of activity. But keep in mind that too few calories can seriously hamper a toddler's growth and development.

Protein – four toddler servings (about 25 milligrams). One toddler serving equals any of the following: 175 ml (6 fl ounces) milk; 15 g (½ ounce) dried skimmed milk; 60 ml (2½ fl ounces) yogurt; 3 tablespoons cottage cheese; 20 g (¾ ounce) hard cheese; 1 whole egg or 2 egg whites; 20 to 25 g (¾ to 1 ounce) fish, poultry, or meat; 55 g (2 ounces) tofu; 1½ tablespoons peanut butter; 25 g (1 ounce)

high-protein pasta; 1 toddler vegetarian protein combination (see below).

Vitamin C foods – two or more toddler servings.[1] Spreading out these servings over the day – giving orange juice at breakfast, a sliver of cantaloupe at lunch, and broccoli at dinner – will enhance the absorption of iron from any iron-containing foods served. One toddler serving equals any of the following: ½ small orange or ¼ medium grapefruit; 45 g (1½ ounces) fresh strawberries; ⅛ cantaloupe or 1/12 small honeydew; 50 ml (2 fl ounces) fresh or frozen reconstituted orange juice; ¼ large guava or 45 g (1½ ounces) papaya; ½ large plantain; 55 g (2 ounces) broccoli or Brussels sprouts; 115 g (4 ounces) cooked greens; ¼ medium green or ⅙ medium red bell pepper; 1

---

1. Increase to four toddler servings when your child has a cold or flu.

Vegetarian Protein Combinations for Toddlers

It's preferable for your child to get some of his or her protein from animal sources: meat, fish, poultry, eggs, or dairy products. If your dietary practices make this wholly impossible, or if you occasionally like to serve purely vegetarian meals, the following food combinations will each provide an adequate serving of protein.

For a full toddler protein serving (about 6 grams), combine one portion from the Legumes column with one from the Grains column.

LEGUMES*
3 tablespoons lentils, split peas or chickpeas (garbanzos), soyabeans, mung, lima, or kidney beans
45 g (1½ ounces) cowpeas, black-eyed peas, white, broad, or Great Northern beans
35 g (1¼ ounces) green peas
25 g (1 ounce) tofu

GRAINS
15 g (½ ounce) soya or high-protein pasta

25 g (1 ounce) whole-wheat pasta
1½ tablespoons wheat germ
3 tablespoons (before cooking) oats
4 tablespoons cooked wild rice
*55 g (2 ounces) cooked brown rice, bulgur, kasha (buckwheat groats), or millet***
1 slice whole-grain bread
1 small (25 g/1 ounce) wholemeal pitta
½ wholemeal muffin or bagel
¾ tablespoon peanut butter

* Beans and peas should be split or lightly mashed so they won't be a choking hazard.
** These grains are protein poor; when serving them, routinely add 1½ teaspoons wheat germ per portion.

Note: Nuts are high in protein and can also be combined with legumes to provide vegetable protein servings. But do not serve them to toddlers unless they are finely ground, since nuts are a choking hazard.

Dairy Protein Combinations for Toddlers

Combine one of the following with one portion from the Legumes or Grains list in the Vegetarian Protein Combinations for Toddlers box (see page 353) for a Dairy Protein Combination.

2 tablespoons cottage cheese
75 ml (3 fl ounces) milk
2 tablespoons dried skimmed milk

30 ml (1 fl ounce) evaporated milk
50 ml (2 fl ounces) yogurt
½ egg or 1 egg white
10 g (⅓ ounce) lower-fat hard cheese (such as Swiss or mozzarella)
15 g (½ ounce) high-fat cheese (such as blue or Camembert)
1 tablespoon Parmesan cheese

---

small tomato, skinned; 175 ml (6 fl ounces) tomato sauce or 100 ml (4 fl ounces) juice; 80 ml (3 fl ounces) vegetable juice.

Calcium foods – four toddler servings. One toddler serving equals any of the following: 150 ml (5 fl ounces) milk; ⅓ glass milk enriched with 8 g (¼ ounce) dried skimmed milk; 15 g (½ ounce) dried skimmed milk; 100 ml (4 fl ounces) calcium-added milk[2]; 60 ml (2½ fl ounces) yogurt; about 20 to 25 g (¾ to 1 ounce) lower-fat hard cheese; 45 g (1⅓ ounces) high-fat cheese; 100 g (4 fl ounces) calcium-fortified orange juice.

One-half a toddler calcium serving equals 85 g (3 ounces) tofu prepared with calcium, 55 g (2 ounces) cooked broccoli, 45 g (1½ ounces) cooked kale or turnip greens, 35 g (1⅓ ounces) canned salmon with the bones (mashed), 25 g (1 ounce) sardines with the bones (mashed).

Green leafy and yellow vegetables and yellow fruits – two or more toddler servings daily.[3] One toddler serving equals any of the following: 1 medium fresh apricot or 2

2. Using nonfat dry or calcium-added milk is an easy way of adding calcium to your baby's diet, but don't use them frequently unless you add 1 tablespoon of light cream or 2 of half-and-half to each serving – your baby still needs the fat. Also add cream to calcium-added milk if it is less than 4% fat.
3. Excessive amounts of carotene, the form in which vitamin A appears in fruits and vegetables, can tint a child's skin yellow (and an adult's, at much higher doses). Don't overdo in this category – three or four carrots a day, for example, are too many.

small dried halves; a sliver of cantaloupe, or about 55 g (2 ounces) cubed; ⅛ large mango; 1 medium nectarine, peeled; ½ large yellow (not white) peach, peeled; ½ medium plaintain; 6 asparagus spears; 45g (1½ ounces) cooked broccoli; 75 g (2½ ounces) peas; 2 to 3 tablespoons chopped cooked greens; ½ small carrot; ½ tablespoon unsweetened pumpkin purée; 2 tablespoons cooked mashed winter squash; 1 tablespoon orange sweet potato; 1 small tomato, skinned; 115 g (4 ounces) cooked tomatoes or purée; 175 ml (6 fl ounces) tomato or 75 g (3 ounces) vegetable juice; ¼ large red pepper.

Other fruits and vegetables – one to two, or more, toddler servings. One toddler serving equals any of the following: ½ apple, peeled; ½ pear, peeled; ½ white peach, peeled; 1 medium plum, peeled; 1 small banana; 3 tablespoons apple purée; 55 g (2 ounces) cherries, berries, or grapes; 1 large fig; 2 dates; 3 dried peach halves; 1 dried pear half; ½ slice pineapple; 2 tablespoons raisins, currants, or dried apple rings; 2 or 3 asparagus spears; ¼ medium avocado; 55 g (2 ounces) green beans; 85 g (3 ounces) beetroots, aubergine, or diced turnip; 20 g (¾ ounce) sliced mushrooms, yellow summer squash, or courgettes; 5 okra pods; 35 g (1¼ ounces) peas; ½ small ear of corn. Cut corn kernels in half by slicing each row lengthwise, and peel fruit with tough skin before serving to a toddler.

Whole grains and other concentrated complex carbohydrates – five or more toddler servings. One toddler serving equals any of the following: 1 tablespoon wheat germ; ½ slice whole-grain bread; ½ small (25 g/1 ounce) pitta; ¼ wholemeal bagel or muffin; 1 toddler serving (or ½ adult serving) Best-Odds muffin or other baked good; 3 to 4 wholemeal bread sticks or 2 to 3 whole-grain crackers; 20 g (¾ ounces) brown or wild rice; ½ serving whole-grain breakfast cereal, unsweetened or fruit sweetened; 15 g (½ ounce) wholemeal or high-protein pasta; 25 g (1 ounce) cooked lentils, chick-peas, pinto or kidney beans (cooked until soft, and split).

Iron-rich foods – some every day. Good sources include: beef; treacle; baked goods made with carob or soya flour; whole grains; wheat germ; dried peas and beans, including soyabeans; dried fruit; liver and other organ meats (serve infrequently because they are high in cholesterol and are storehouses for the many chemical contaminants found in livestock today); sardines; spinach (serve infrequently because of high nitrate and oxalic acid levels). The iron in these foods will be better absorbed if a vitamin C food is eaten at the same meal. If your baby doesn't eat a lot of high-iron foods, or if he or she is anaemic, the doctor may recommend an iron supplement.

High-fat foods – six to seven toddler servings daily. One toddler serving equals any of the following: 8 g (¼ ounce) butter or margarine; ½ tablespoon polyunsaturated oil, olive oil, or mayonnaise; 1½ tablespoons cream cheese; 1 tablespoon peanut butter; ¼ small avocado; 1 egg; 150 ml (5 fl ounces) whole milk; 100 ml (4 fl ounces) whole-milk yogurt; 3 tablespoons half-and-half; 1 tablespoon double cream; 2 tablespoons sour cream; 20 g (⅔ ounce) hard cheese; 6 slices whole-grain bread or 75 g (2½ ounces) wheat germ; 1½ ounces lean beef, lamb, or pork. This allowance provides about 30% of daily calories from fat. For the toddler who is drinking whole milk (or eating the equivalent in other listed dairy products) and eating several eggs a week, additional animal fats are unnecessary; the remainder of the high-fat food requirement should be met with those vegetable fats high in polyunsaturates (safflower or sunflower oil, for example) or

monounsaturated oil (olive oil) rather than saturated fats (coconut oil or hardened vegetable shortening). A typical toddler might get fat this way: 500 ml (16 fl ounces) milk; 20 g (⅔ ounce) cheese; 1 egg; 3 slices wholemeal bread; and 45 g (1½ ounces) ground beef. No added fats are needed.

Salty foods – restrict added salt. All human beings require the sodium in sodium chloride (better known as salt) for survival, but most Westerners, including infants and toddlers, consume much more than they need. Since sodium is found naturally in or added in preparation to most of the foods children eat (milk, cheese, eggs, carrots, bread and most other baked goods), the requirement for salt in the diet is easily met, and easily exceeded. To avoid excessive salt intake, salt foods only lightly or not at all when cooking for children, and limit the consumption of presalted foods such as salted crackers, potato crisps, pretzels, pickles, green olives and so on (nuts of any kind are not safe for toddlers unless ground first). All salt you do use should be iodized to guard against iodine deficiency.

Fluids – 900 to 1,300 ml (32 to 48 fl ounces) daily. Your toddler will get a portion of his or her fluid requirement in food, particularly fruits and vegetables, which are 80 to 95% water. But 900 to 1,300 ml (32 to 48 fl ounces) of fluid should be consumed in fruit juices (preferably diluted with seltzer or water), vegetable juices, soups, seltzer, or straight water. Milk (which is ⅓ milk solids) provides only ⅔ of a fluid serving per 250 ml (8 fl ounces). Extra fluids are needed in hot weather or when baby has a fever, cold, or other respiratory tract infection, or diarrhoea or vomiting.

Supplements. Some doctors do not believe supplements are necessary for healthy babies one year or older. But others recommend an infant vitamin-mineral supplement with iron be continued past one year as an insurance policy. Considering the bizarre and erratic eating habits of toddlers, this makes good sense. However, giving your child a vitamin tablet each day doesn't give you license to abandon your commitment to providing him or her with a good diet. And the formulation you choose should be appropriate for a toddler and *not* contain more than 100% of the RDA for your child's age. (Some vitamins are toxic in levels not much higher than the RDA). Continue a liquid preparation until your child's molars are in, then switch to sugar-free chewable tablets.

What You May Be Concerned About

The First Birthday Party

'Everyone in the family is gearing up for my daughter's first birthday. I want the party to be special, but I don't want it to be too much for her.'

Many parents, caught up in the excitement of planning a party for baby's first birthday, seem to lose track of the fact that baby is still a baby. And the gala they so painstakingly stage is rarely suitable for the guest of honour, who is likely to end up cracking under the pressure and spending much of her fête in tears.

To plan a first-birthday-party-to-remember, instead of one you'd rather forget, follow this strategy:

Keep the invites light. A room too crowded with even familiar faces will probably overwhelm your birthday pixie, with the undesirable but probable result of clinging and weeping. Save the long guest list for her wedding and keep this crowd intimate, limiting it to a few family members and close friends. If she spends time with other babies her age, you may want to invite two or three; if she doesn't, the occasion of her first party probably isn't a good time to launch her social career.

Ditto the décor. A room decorated with all that your local party store has to offer, and then some, may be your dream but your baby's nightmare. Too many balloons, streamers, banners, masks and hats, like too many people, may prove too much for a toddler to handle. So decorate with a light hand, perhaps in a theme you know she'll appreciate (Noddy, if he's a favourite, or Mickey Mouse, or teddy bears). And if

balloons will round out your party picture, remember that tiny tots can choke on the rubber scraps left after balloons go pop.

Let her eat cake . . . But make sure it's not the kind of cake she shouldn't eat (one with chocolate, nuts, sugar, or honey). Instead serve up a Best-Odds carrot cake topped with unsweetened fresh whipped cream or fruit juice-sweetened cream cheese frosting – shaped like, or decorated with, a favourite character if you're feeling artistic. Serve your confection à la mode if you like, with homemade or store-bought ice cream.[4] Cut the cake at your baby's usual snacktime, if possible, keeping toddler portions small to avoid waste. And if the cake you've selected is nutritious enough to pass for a meal, it won't really matter if your child surprises you, really digs in, and is too full (or too tired) to eat much dinner later on. Finally, if you choose to put out party nibbles, choose them with safety as well as nutrition in mind. A birthday party's no time to risk a baby's choking on popcorn, peanuts, grapes, or small, chunky pretzels. Also for safety's sake, insist that all young guests do their eating sitting down.

Don't send in the clowns. Or magicians, or any other paid or volunteer entertainment that might frighten your baby or a playmate. One-year-olds are notoriously sensitive and unpredictable; what delights them one minute may terrify them the next. Also don't try to organize the toddler set into formal party

---

4. The good news: ice cream sweetened with fruit juices is available in most health food stores; it's delicious and all natural. The bad news: some of it is made with double cream and egg yolks. So consider it special occasion, rather than daily, fare, or look for the 'light' varieties.

games – they're not ready for that yet. If there are several young guests however, do have a selection of toys out for non-structured play, with enough of the same items to avoid competition. Simple, safe favours such as brightly coloured rubber balls, board books, or bath toys are a fun extra and can be handed to young guests just before the gifts are opened.

Don't command a performance. It would be nice, of course, if baby would smile for the camera, take a few steps for the company, open each present with interest and coo appreciatively over it – but don't count on it. She might learn to blow out the candles if you give her enough practice during the month before the party, but don't expect complete cooperation, and don't put the pressure on. Instead, let her be herself – whether that means squirming out of your arms during that party pose, refusing even to stand on her own two feet during the step-taking exhibition, or opting to play with an empty box rather than the expensive gift that came in it.

Time it right. Scheduling is everything when it comes to a baby's party. Try to orchestrate the big day's activities so that baby is well rested, recently fed (don't hold off her lunch figuring she'll eat at the party), and on her usual schedule. Don't plan a morning party if she usually naps in the A.M., or an early afternoon party if she usually conks out after lunch. Inviting a tired baby to participate in the festivities is tantamount to inviting disaster. And keep the party brief – an hour and a half at the most – so she won't be a wreck when the party's over or, worse, in the middle of it all.

Record it for posterity. The party will be over much too quickly, and so will your baby's childhood. Recording the occasion in snapshots, on videotape, or on film will be well worth the effort.

Not Yet Walking

'Today is my son's first birthday, and he hasn't even attempted to take his first step. Shouldn't he be walking by now?'

It may seem appropriate for a baby to take his first steps at his first birthday party (and great adult entertainment, to boot), but few babies are willing or able to oblige. Though some start walking weeks, or even months, earlier, others won't totter towards the momentous milestone until much later (sometimes when mum and dad aren't around). And while passing the first birthday without a step may be a disappointment to the relatives, and especially those who've dragged out the video equipment to capture history in the making, it in no way signals a developmental problem.

The majority of children, in fact, don't start walking until after their first birthday, with various studies placing the average age for first step-taking between thirteen and fifteen months. And the age at which a child first steps out, whether nine months, fifteen months, or even later, is no reflection on his intelligence.

When a baby walks is often related to his genetic makeup – early (or late) walking runs in families. Or to his weight and build – a wiry, muscular baby is more likely to walk earlier than a placid, plump one, and a child with short, sturdy legs before one with long, slender ones that are difficult to balance on. It may also be related to when and how well he learns to crawl. A child who is an ineffective crawler or who doesn't crawl at all sometimes walks sooner than the baby who is perfectly content racing about on all fours.

Poor nutrition or a non-stimulating environment can also delay walking. So can a negative experience – perhaps a bad fall the first time a tentative toddler let go of mummy's hand. In such a case, the child may not take a chance again until he's very steady, and then he may take off like a pro rather than with the stiff awkwardness of an amateur. The child who's been forced by overeager parents to endure walking practice sessions several times daily may rebel (particularly if he has a stubborn streak) and walk independently later than he would have if he had been allowed to do it on his own terms and at his own pace. The first steps of a baby who's had his energy sapped by an ear infection, the flu, or other illness may be delayed until he's feeling better. A child who's been virtually waltzing from room to room may suddenly regress to the two-step-and-tumble when under the weather, only to rebound just as quickly once he's feeling himself again.

A baby who's always corralled in a mesh playpen (in which he may not be able to pull up to a standing position), strapped in a pushchair, or otherwise given little chance to develop his leg muscles and his confidence through standing and cruising may walk late – in fact, may develop slowly on other fronts as well. Likewise, an older baby who's in a walker a good deal of the time is likely to be delayed in his independent walking rather than given an edge. Give your baby plenty of time and space for practising pulling up, cruising, standing and stepping in a room that doesn't have scatter rugs or a slippery floor to slip him up, and which has plenty of safe-for-pulling-up-on furniture arranged close enough together for confident transfers or very short toddles. He'll do best if he's barefoot, since babies use their toes for gripping when they take their first steps; socks are slippery, shoes too stiff and heavy.

Though many perfectly normal, even exceptionally bright, babies don't walk until the second half of their second year, particularly if one or both parents didn't, a baby who isn't walking by eighteen months should be examined by his doctor to rule out the possibility that physical or emotional factors are interfering with walking. But even at that age – and certainly at twelve months – a child's not walking yet isn't cause for alarm.

Attachment to the Bottle

'I was hoping to wean my son from the bottle at a year, but he's so attached to it I can't even get it away from him for a minute, much less permanently.'

Like a favourite teddy bear or blanket, a bottle is a source of emotional comfort and gratification for a small child. But unlike a teddy or blanket, a bottle can be harmful if used improperly or much past a baby's first birthday.

The most serious threat bottle drinking poses is to a baby's teeth, both those that have already erupted and those yet to come, including the permanent set. Baby-bottle mouth can lead to tooth loss and poor mouth development, and interfere with good eating habits. Another threat is to the ears; babies who continue on the bottle past the first year are more likely to suffer ear infections. Bottles also pose a threat to baby's nutrition. Sucking from a bottle of milk or juice all day long can satisfy his hunger and suppress his appetite for other foods, interfering with a balanced diet. And if those threats aren't sufficient to warrant a switch to a cup about now, factor in the effect the ever-present bottle can have on development. A toddler who's constantly toting a bottle has only one hand free for playing, learning and exploring; and one who's always sucking on a bottle (or on a dummy) has a mouth too full to speak out of.

For these reasons, many paediatricians recommend weaning from the bottle by the first birthday or soon after. And though weaning of any kind at any time is rarely easy, particularly when a strong attachment has formed, it will be easier now than later, when negativity and stubbornness become more pronounced. The weaning tips given on page 335 should ease the process further.

If you don't feel your baby is ready to give up the bottle entirely at this age, at least try to limit when, where, and how often he has it. Offer the bottle only two or three times a day, supplementing between meals with snacks and drinks from a cup. Filling the bottle with water rather than juice or milk may also reduce your child's interest in it while protecting his teeth. Don't allow your baby to take the bottle to bed, walk or crawl around with it, or suck on it casually as he plays. Instead, insist he drink from it on an adult's lap. When he wants to get down, put the bottle in the refrigerator if it isn't empty. Eventually, he should become restless enough with the lap feedings to be willing to give the bottle up. And even if that day is a long way off, restricting the use of the bottle this way will limit the amount of harm it can do in the meantime.

Putting the Weaned Baby to Bed

'I've never put my daughter to bed awake – she's always been nursed to sleep. How am I going to get her to sleep at night once she's weaned to a cup?'

How easy it's always been for your baby to suck her way blissfully into dreamland. And how easy for you to nurse your way hassle-free to a peaceful evening. From now on, however, if you're serious about weaning your baby from her nightcap, bedding her down is going to take a little more effort on both sides of the cot rail.

Like an addiction to any sleep aid – from pills to late-night talk shows – an addiction to bedtime nursing can be broken. And once it is, your child will have mastered one of life's most valuable skills: the ability to fall asleep on her own. To make this goal a reality, follow this plan:

Keep the old rituals. A bedtime routine, with each item on the agenda carried out in the same order each evening, can work its soporific magic on anyone, adult or child. If you haven't instituted such a ritual yet for your baby, do so at least two weeks before you plan to wean her off the nighttime feeding. Also make sure environmental conditions are conducive to sleep: the bedroom dark unless baby prefers a nightlight, neither too warm nor too cold, and quiet; the rest of the house maintaining a business-as-usual hum that lets her know you're there if she needs you. (See page 117 for more tips on making a baby sleepy.)

Add a new twist. A few days to a week before W-Day, add a bedtime snack to your baby's ritual, one she can eat after she's in pajamas and while you're reading to her. Keep it light but satisfying (a juice-sweetened biscuit and a half cup of milk, perhaps, or a piece of cheese), and let her enjoy it on your lap if she likes. Not only will the mini-meal eventually come to take the place of the nursing she'll be giving up, but the milk will have a sleep-inducing effect. Of course, if you've been brushing baby's teeth earlier in the evening, you will now have to move this part of the routine to after her snack. If she's thirsty once her teeth have been cleaned, offer her water.

Break the old addiction, but don't replace it with a new one. If there's anything a sleep-aid addict craves, it's an easy route to slumber. Supply your baby with another crutch (rocking, patting, singing, or music) to help her fall asleep and you'll only create another habit to break. Total sleeptime self-sufficiency develops only when a child is left to her own devices. So utilize cuddling, music and such in your baby's prebedtime routine if you like, but not to the point of sleep. Put her down dry, happy, snug, cuddly – and drowsy but awake.

Expect some crying. And, possibly, lots of it. Chances are your baby will resist this bold new approach to bedtime – vociferously. Few babies will accept the switch without a fight. But fortunately, the crying should tone down and lessen considerably within a few nights, and soon subside altogether. (See page 254 for the cold turkey and gradual methods of letting baby cry it out.)

Waking up at Night

'Our baby used to sleep through the night, but suddenly he started waking up once or twice. He gets very upset when I leave him alone in his bedroom, too, so I'm reluctant to let him cry.'

Separation anxiety, the familiar gremlin of

the daylight hours that usually peaks between twelve and fourteen months, can also come out at night. In fact, since separating at night leaves a baby completely alone, it can become a source of even more emotional trauma than daytime separation. The result for many babies: anxious, restless nights and sleep problems.

Nighttime separation anxiety is often worse among the children of employed mothers (the child who doesn't see much of his mother during the day may be fearful of losing her at night as well), particularly if there's a new carer on the scene. Whether you're with your baby during the day or not, try to alleviate some of his apprehension with some pre-bedtime reassurance in the form of some extra cuddling and undivided attention (leave those dinner preparations or dishes for later). A concentrated dose of mother and/or father love before you separate for the night can help make parting easier.

If your baby is having trouble falling asleep or if he awakens fearful in the middle of the night and 'crying it out' isn't working or seems too heartless, try sitting beside his cot for ten minutes or so, soothing him with a soft 'Shhhh' and a gentle hand on his back. But don't stay with him until he's asleep; he'll only become dependent on your presence for falling off. Instead, leave him drowsy and, hopefully, calm – and try not to return if he cries.

If baby begins waking because of molar pain, see page 409. When all else fails, ask his doctor about a milk-free diet; milk intolerance sometimes causes sleeplessness.

Shyness

'My husband and I are very social, and it upsets us to see how shy our daughter is.'

As sociable as you and your husband are, your daughter's shyness, if she's truly shy, comes from you. Not from the example you set, but from the genetic mould you created. Shyness, like a knack for figures or a flair for writing, is an inherited trait. Even if it's a trait parents don't display themselves, it's one that they carried to their child's conception. Though it's possible to modify shyness, it's rarely possible to eradicate it entirely. Nor should parents want to, if it's part of their child's personality.

Though many shy children retain an inner core of reserve all their lives, most turn out to be fairly gregarious adults. It's not parental prodding and pressure that brings them out of their shells, but a great deal of loving, nurturing and support. Drawing attention to a child's shyness as a shortcoming will only undermine her self-confidence, which in turn will only make her more bashful. On the other hand, helping her feel more comfortable with herself will help her feel more at ease with others and eventually diminish her shyness.

It's also possible that what seems to be shyness in your child is just a toddler's normal lack of sociability. One-year-olds and often even two-year-olds are not ready to make friends. As she approaches her third birthday, she may surprise you by her rapid progress in the art of socializing.

Social Backwardness

'We've been involved in a play group for the last few weeks, and I've noticed that my baby doesn't play with the other children. How can I get her to be more sociable?'

You can't, and you shouldn't try. A child under the age of two is not a social being and no amount of programming will change that. This lack of sociability wasn't an issue for previous generations, since most children were not exposed to group-play situations until at least three or four years of age, more often five. But it raises a great many concerns for today's parents, who often enroll their youngsters in play groups and group day care before their first birthdays, and nursery school by their second or third.

Though no harm (apart from a few extra

colds and other viruses) can come to babies from early exposure to their peers, emotional damage can result from parental pressure to perform socially. That's because children under three just aren't ready. They are rarely capable of more than parallel play – they'll play side-by-side, but not together. It's not that they're selfish, it's just that they're not yet able to recognize that other children might be worthy of their time and attention.

Remember that your baby doesn't need or know how to handle playmates, and that her behaviour is age appropriate. Pushing her to play with other children in her group will only make her withdraw from such situations altogether. For best results, you'll have to accept your baby's very normal social shortcomings and be prepared to let her set her own pace with her peers, not just now, but in the years to come as well.

Sharing

'My little boy belongs to a play group. He and the other children seem to spend most of their time fighting for the same toys. When will things get better?'

Not for a while. It's not until two, or more often three, years of age that children begin to understand the concept of sharing. Right now their own needs and desires are the only ones that matter to them – peers are treated as objects, not people. Not surprisingly, each child in the play group believes that his right to play with any and all toys whenever he wants is absolute. It will take a great deal of explaining and cajoling (never force) over the next couple of years to bring your child to the point of being able to share. And of course it's important for him to reach that point. But it's also important to keep your perspective when your two- or three-year-old refuses to let a guest so much as touch his trucks or teddy bears, won't share his biscuits with a child in the park, and howls when his younger cousin is given a ride in his pushchair. How often do you, after all, let a friend, much less a stranger, drive your car, have half of your hot fudge sundae, or take your place in a favourite armchair?

Hitting

'My son is in a play group with a few children who are slightly older than he is. Some of them hit when they don't get their way and my son has started doing it, too. How should I handle this?'

The right hook of a toddler rarely packs enough punch to do any real damage; playground shiners won't be brought home for many years to come. But just because a baby's hitting rarely harms doesn't mean it should be allowed to continue. Though a child under two may be incapable of understanding that others have feelings (he is the only little boy in his universe who does), he is capable of understanding that hitting is unacceptable.

When your child hits (or bites, or displays another form of undesirably aggressive behaviour), respond immediately, firmly and calmly. Anger is likely to put your child on the defensive and elicit more angry behaviour. Slapping or spanking him will only teach him that violence is an appropriate way of expressing anger. And overreacting to the incident will probably encourage a repeat performance in a quest for more attention. Take your child away from the scene of the crime while explaining (though the explanation may well be beyond his comprehension) that hitting is bad and that it can hurt people. Once the reprimand's over, use distraction to change the subject. Use this approach as many times as it proves necessary and eventually he'll get the idea.

In the meantime, always make sure that play sessions with other children are carefully supervised, since there's always the chance that a child might use more than a fist to strike with, and there's much more risk of injury from a foot, a toy, a rock, or a stick.

'Forgetting' a Skill

'Last month my daughter was waving bye-bye all the time, but now she seems to have forgotten how. I thought she was supposed to move forward developmentally, not backwards.'

She *is* moving forward developmentally, on to other skills. It's very common for a baby to practise perfecting a skill almost continuously for a while – to her delight and everyone else's – and then, once she's mastered it, to put it aside while she takes on a new challenge. Though your baby has tired of her old trick of waving bye-bye, she's more than likely excited by those she's rehearsing now, perhaps barking every time she sees a four-legged animal and playing peekaboo and patty-cake. All of which she will eventually temporarily retire once they, too, lose their attraction. Instead of worrying about what your baby seems to have forgotten, tune in to and encourage her in whatever new skills she's busy developing.

You need to be concerned only if your baby suddenly seems unable to do many things she did formerly, and if she isn't learning anything new. If that's the case, check with the doctor.

A Drop in Appetite

'All of a sudden, my son seems to have no interest in his meals – he only picks at his food and can't wait to get out of the high chair. Could he be sick?'

More likely Mother Nature has placed him on a maintenance diet. Because if he continued eating the way he did during the first year of life, and continued gaining at the same rate, he would soon resemble a small blimp instead of a toddler. Most babies triple their birthweight in the first year; in the second year they add only about a quarter of their weight. So a decline in appetite now is your baby's body's way of ensuring this normal decline in weight gain.

There are also other factors that may affect your baby's eating habits now. One is increased interest in the world around him. During most of his first year of life, mealtimes – whether spent in mummy's arms or in a high chair – were highlights of his existence. Now they represent an unwelcome interruption in 'a day in the life of a fledging toddler', who'd rather be on the go (so many things to do, so many places to see, so much trouble to make – so little time in a day!).

Growing independence can also influence a child's reaction to the food placed in front of him. The baby in the throes of becoming a toddler may decide that he, not you, should be the arbiter of the dinner table. Wide taste swings may be the rule – peanut butter on everything one week, rejection of anything vaguely resembling it the next. And it's better to accept baby's dictatorial menu planning (as long as what he chooses is nutritious) than to fight it. Eventually, eating eccentricities will diminish.

Maybe your baby's not eating because he dislikes being exiled to the high chair; if so, try seating him at the family table in a clip-on dining chair. Or maybe he can't sit still as long as the rest of the family; in which case, don't put him in the seat until his food is served, and release him as soon as he starts to get restless.

Some babies lose their appetites temporarily during teething bouts, particularly when they're cutting their first molars. If your baby's loss of appetite is accompanied by irritability, finger chewing and other symptoms of teething, you can be pretty sure that it will pass once the discomfort eases. If it's accompanied by signs of illness, however, such as fever, listlessness, or fatigue, check with his doctor. Also seek medical advice if his weight gain stops altogether, if he looks very thin, if he seems weak, apathetic and irritable, or if he has particularly dry, brittle hair and dry skin with little tone.

Though there's nothing you can do (or should do) about an appetite that's falling off as a result of your baby's normal growth slowdown, there are ways to make sure he eats what he needs to grow (see below).

Baby's Getting Adequate Nutrition

'I'm afraid my son's not getting enough protein or vitamins because he won't eat meat or vegetables.'

It may seem to parents that a one-year-old who eats sporadically and fussily couldn't possibly get his Daily Dozen of nutrients from the dribs and drabs of food he consumes over the course of a day, but, because the nutritional requirements for a one-year-old are surprisingly small, he can quite easily. And the requirements don't just come in the most obvious packages (protein in meat and fish, vitamin A in spinach), they also come in some unexpected and unexpectedly delicious ones.

- Protein. Your baby can get adequate protein without ever tasting meat or poultry or fish. Cottage cheese, hard cheeses, milk, milkshakes, yogurt, eggs, whole-grain cereals and breads, wheat germ, dried beans and peas and pastas (especially high-protein brands) all provide protein. The Daily Dozen requirement for a one-year-old can be met with 600 ml (21 fl ounces) of milk and 2 slices of bread *or* 500 ml (16 fl ounces) of milk and 25 g (1 ounce) of Swiss cheese *or* 250 ml (8 fl ounces) of milk, 140 ml (5 fl ounces) of yogurt, 1 bowl of porridge, and 1 slice of whole-wheat bread *or* 500 ml (16 fl ounces) of milk, 35 g (1¼ ounces) of cottage cheese, 1 bowl of baby cereal, and 2 slices of bread.

  If your baby doesn't like protein foods straight, try a little sleight of hand. Make pancakes with dried skimmed milk, eggs, and wheat germ; French toast with whole-grain bread, eggs, and milk; fish pancakes with fish and eggs; high-protein pasta with grated cheese. See recipes beginning on page 605, and the toddler vegetable protein combinations on page 352.

- Vegetable vitamins. You can serve up all of the vitamins in vegetables in a variety of tempting disguises: pumpkin muffins, carrot cake, tomato-broccoli sauce on pasta, veggie pancakes, vegetables tossed with cheese sauce or in a noodle casserole. Many taste favourites, including cantaloupe, mangoes, yellow peaches and sweet potatoes, provide the vitamins found in less-loved green leafies and yellows. See the list of green leafy and yellow vegetables and yellow fruits for more sources. And try the recipes on page 605.

Also keep the following points in mind when feeding the picky eater:

Let baby's appetite be your guide. Let him eat heartily when he's hungry and let him pick when he's not. Never force. But do sharpen his appetite for meals by limiting snacking between them.

Avoid the spoilers. Even small amounts of empty, or almost empty, calorie junk foods (sugary sweets, fried foods, refined grains) can fill a baby up, leaving no room for the nutritious foods he needs. So make foods that offer little more than a full tummy strictly taboo.

Don't give up. Just because your baby won't eat his meat (or chicken or fish) and spinach (or broccoli or carrots) today doesn't mean he won't eat them tomorrow. Make them available to him at the family table – but don't ever force him to eat them – in various forms regularly. One day he may surprise you by helping himself.

And even if he ends up eating nothing all day but orange juice, cereal with banana, pumpkin muffins and milk, or cantaloupe, pancakes, bread with cheese and apple juice – and he drinks some water and takes his vitamin-mineral supplement – you'll have the satisfaction of knowing that he's satisfied his Daily Dozen.

Increase in Appetite

'I thought a one-year-old's supposed to experience a drop in appetite. My daughter's has seemed to increase substantially. She's not fat, but I can't help worrying that she will be if she keeps eating at this rate.'

Chances are she's eating more because she's drinking less. Babies who are either just, or just about, weaned from the breast or bottle to the cup are likely to be getting less of their total caloric intake from milk and other liquids and may compensate by stepping up their intake of solids. Though it may seem that your daughter is taking in more calories, she probably is taking the same number or less, only in a different form. Alternatively, it could be that she's eating more because she's going through a growth spurt, or because she's become more active – possibly because she's walking a lot – and her body needs the extra calories.

Healthy babies, when allowed to eat as dictated by their appetites, hearty or not, continue to grow at a normal rate. And if your daughter's weight and height curves aren't suddenly parting company, there's no need to worry that she's overeating. Pay more attention to the quality, rather than the quantity, of her intake; and be sure that her robust appetite isn't squandered on nutritionally frivolous foods and that her diet isn't overloaded with high-fat fare (which could lead to obesity). Be aware, too, of her motivation for eating. If she seems to be eating out of boredom, for instance, instead of hunger, you can help by making sure she has plenty to keep her busy outside the kitchen between meals (see page 266 for more tips on keeping snacking under control). Or if you suspect she's eating out of a need for emotional gratification, make sure she gets enough attention and tender loving care.

Refusing to Self-Feed

'I know my son is perfectly capable of feeding himself – he's done it several times. But now he absolutely refuses to hold his bottle, pick up a cup, or try a spoon.'

The inner struggle between wanting to remain a baby and wanting to grow up has only just begun for your baby. For the first time he's capable of taking care of one of his needs, but he's not sure he wants to if it means giving up the secure and cushy role of baby. Instinctively, he senses that if he becomes less of a baby, you will become less of a mummy.

Don't force your baby to grow up too soon. When he wants to feed himself, let him. But when he wants to be fed, feed him. Eventually the big boy will triumph over the baby, if you let the two of them battle it out in the natural course of things – although the inner conflict will recur in every stage of his development into adulthood. In the meantime, present him with every opportunity to be self-sufficient – make the bottle, the cup and the spoon available to him without insisting he use them. Offer him finger foods often, at meals as well as snacktimes. Few children at this age are really competent with a spoon and most will make their first ventures into self-feeding with the five-pronged utensils that are conveniently attached to their wrists.

When he does feed himself, reinforce his decision by sticking around to give him plenty of encouragement, praise and, especially, reassuring attention. He needs to know that giving up being fed by mummy doesn't have to mean giving up mummy.

Unpredictability

'My little girl can't seem to make up her mind what she wants. One minute she's chasing me around the house, banging on my legs while I'm trying to get work done. The next, she's trying to get away from me when I sit down to hug her.'

Your daughter's not schizophrenic – she's a normal one-year-old. Like the baby who refuses to self-feed, she's split between a craving for independence and a fear of paying too high a price for that independence. When you're busy with something other than her, especially when you're moving about faster than she can follow, she worries that she's losing her hold on you and the love, sustenance, comfort and safety that you represent, and she responds by clinging. On the other hand, when you make yourself more available, she's able to play hard-to-get and to test out her independence in the security of your presence.

As she becomes more comfortable with her independence and more secure in the fact that you'll be her mummy no matter how grown-up she becomes, she'll be less clingy. But this split in her personality will manifest itself repeatedly for years to come, probably even when she's a mum herself. (Don't you sometimes wish you could be mummy's little girl again, if only for a moment, at the same time resenting her smallest interference in your life?)

In the meantime, you can help her to strike out on her own by making her feel more secure. If you are in the kitchen peeling carrots and she's across the divider in the living room, chat with her, stop periodically and visit with her, or invite her to help you, stationing her high chair next to you at the sink, for example, and giving her some carrots and a vegetable scrub brush. Support and applaud your baby's steps towards independence, but be patient and understanding when she stumbles and rushes back to the solace of your arms.

Also be realistic in terms of the amount of time you can humanly supply in response to her demand. There will be moments when you'll have to let her hang on your feet crying while you get dinner on the table and moments when you will be able to provide only intermittent bursts of attention while you balance your chequebook. As much as it's important for her to know that you'll always love her and will meet her needs, it's important for her to know that other people – you included – have needs, too.

Increased Separation Anxiety

'We've left our baby with a baby-sitter before. But now he makes a terrible fuss if he sees us getting ready to go out and we feel very guilty.'

That's exactly what he's aiming to make you feel. Next to getting you to change your mind entirely and stay home, getting you to feel guilty about going out is his primary objective. And though you should remain understanding throughout his desperate attempts at mummy and daddy manipulation, you should also try not to let him succeed at it. Heightened separation anxiety is normal at this stage of development and is rarely a result of anything parents have or haven't done – as many parents dealing with this problem fear it might be. It's due partly to the fact that your child now has a much better memory. He recalls what your putting on your coat, picking up your handbag and going 'bye-bye' without him means, and he's able to anticipate that you will be gone for some indefinite length of time when you walk out the door. And in fact, if you haven't left him with a baby-sitter often in the past, he may have some doubt that you'll return.

But although the guilt baby has succeeded in burdening his parents with may last the whole evening, the histrionics that created it generally subside soon after the goodbyes are over, the door is shut and the baby realizes that further carrying on will be futile.

To minimize baby's upset and your guilt, and to maximize his adjustment to being left with a sitter, follow these steps before stepping out:

- Make sure you're leaving your baby with someone who not only is reliable, but also will be understanding, patient, responsive and loving, no matter how difficult he becomes.

- Have the baby-sitter arrive at least fifteen minutes before you're planning to leave (earlier if it's her first time sitting for your baby), so that the two of them can get involved in an activity (crayoning, watching Playdays, looking out the window, building with blocks, putting dolly to bed) while you're still bustling around. Don't worry if your baby refuses to have anything to do with the sitter while you're still home; this is a shrewd child telling his parents he won't accept substitutes. Once you've left, he'll almost certainly consent to her advances.

- Give your baby advance notice of your departure. If you try to avoid a scene this time by sneaking out of the house while he's not looking, he may begin to fear that you'll leave without warning at any time and respond with excessive clinginess. Instead, tell him ten to fifteen minutes before you leave that you'll be going out. Give him more time than that and he might forget, less and he won't have a chance to adjust.

- Make a happy ritual out of leaving, with a hug and kiss from both of you. But don't prolong the goodbyes, or make them overly sentimental. Keep a smile on your face, even if he's tearful – and try to look as if you're taking it all in your stride. If there's a window, he can watch you leave; ask the baby-sitter to take him there so you can wave to him.

- If your baby is crying when you leave, be comforting. Instead of telling him to be grown-up and not to cry, tell him that you understand that he'll miss you and that you'll miss him, too.

- Reassure him you'll be back. 'See you later, alligator' is a good light phrase to use that he can begin to associate with your leaving and coming back. And one day he'll be able to respond happily with 'After a while, crocodile'.

If your baby screams for the entire time you're gone, consider that you may have the wrong baby-sitter, that you may not be giving your baby enough reassurance and attention when you're with him, or that you may need to give him some extra help adjusting to your going out. To do the latter, begin by leaving your baby with someone he

knows well, for fifteen minutes at a time, on several occasions. Once he's confident that you will return, he may be comfortable enough with these short outings to be ready for longer ones. Increase the time you spend away by fifteen-minute increments until you can stay away for several hours at a time.

Nonverbal Language

'Our little girl says very few words, but seems to have developed a system of sign language. Could her hearing be bad?'

It probably isn't that your child's hearing is bad, but that her resourcefulness is good. As long as your child seems to understand what you say and tries to imitate sounds even unsuccessfully, her hearing is almost certainly normal. Her use of sign language or other, more primitive, ways of expressing needs and thoughts (such as grunting) is merely an inventive way of coping with a temporary handicap: a limited comprehensible vocabulary. Some children simply have more difficulty forming words at this age than others; for many the difficulty continues, usually well into their preschool years and sometimes into nursery and primary school. They may be saying 'wove' for 'love' or 'toof' for 'tooth' when most of their age mates are speaking very clearly.

To compensate for the inability to communicate verbally, many of these children develop their own forms of language. Some, like your child, are good at talking with their hands. They point to what they want and push away what they don't. A wave is bye-bye, a finger pointed up is up, a finger pointed down is down. They may bark to indicate a dog, point to their nose to 'say' elephant or to their ears for rabbit. Some hum songs to communicate: 'Rockabye baby' when they are sleepy, 'Rain Rain Go Away' when it's pouring out, the Playdays theme when they want to watch TV.

Since this takes a lot of creativity and a strong desire to communicate – both good qualities to cultivate – you should do your best to decipher your child's special language and to show her you do understand. But don't forget that the ultimate goal is real speech. When she hums a lullaby, say, 'Do you want to go to sleep?' When she points to the milk, respond, 'You'd like a glass of milk? Okay.' And if she points to her ears when she sees a rabbit in her storybook, reply, 'Very good. That's a rabbit. A rabbit has long ears.'

If, however, she doesn't seem to hear you calling from behind her or from another room, or to understand simple commands, then you should ask the doctor about testing her hearing.

Gender Differences

'We're trying very hard not to raise our children in a sexist way. But we find that no matter how we try, we can't induce our eleven-month-old son to be nurturing with dolls – he prefers to throw them against a wall.'

You're making the same discovery that many well-meaning parents, determined to avoid moulding their offspring into homemade sexual stereotypes, make. Sexual equality is an ideal whose time has come, but sexual sameness is an idea whose time can never come – at least as long as Mother Nature continues to have some say in the matter. Boys and girls, it appears, are, for the most part, moulded in the womb, not in the playroom and garden.

The differences between the sexes, scientists now believe, begin in the uterus when sex hormones such as testosterone and oestradiol begin to be produced. Male fetuses receive more of the former and females more of the latter. This apparently makes for somewhat different brain development and different strengths and approaches to life.

Though much more work needs to be done before scientists can spell out all the differences precisely, we are aware of some differences that exist from birth on. Even

before they've come home from the hospital, girls may focus longer on faces, particularly talking faces. Girls react more to touch, pain and noise; boys react more to visual stimuli. Girls are more sensitive, but are more easily soothed and comforted; boys tend to cry more and be more irritable. These differences, of course, apply for groups of boys and girls and not necessarily for individuals; some girls may have more 'masculine' traits than some boys, and some boys more 'feminine' traits than some girls.

It's also apparent early on that boys have more muscle mass, larger lungs and hearts, and a lower sensitivity to pain, while girls have more body fat, a different shape to their pelvises and a different way of processing oxygen in their muscles, giving them less stamina than boys later in life. Girl babies, however, are definitely not the weaker sex – they tend from the start to be healthier and hardier than boys.

As physical development progresses, it becomes clear that most boys are more physically active than most girls. Girls generally show more interest in people, boys in things – which may be why girls like dolls and dress-up play, while boys prefer trucks and fire engines. Girls acquire language skills earlier and faster, possibly because, as a result of the hormonal environment in the uterus, both hemispheres of their brains are similar in size and function in harmony. Boys, on the other hand, are better at tasks that require spatial and mechanical skills, possibly because their right hemispheres are more developed than their left. Interestingly, though, boys are as kind as girls, even as infants, and girls are no more fearful than boys, though they may show their fears more readily – probably a learned trait.

By the time children play with others (at this age they engage in parallel play), it becomes clear that, in general, boys are much more aggressive, both physically and verbally, while girls are more compliant. Boys come to like group play, girls one-on-one. In school, girls continue to excel in language areas (spelling, reading comprehension, vocabulary, creative writing) and boys in spatial skills (depth perception, solving mazes and geometric puzzles, map reading) and in maths in the teen years (though it's not clear whether this is the result of nature or nurture). Girls tend to mature earlier – though there is overlap.

Psychological and emotional differences become more obvious as children grow. Boys are more vulnerable psychologically – it's they who are more likely to have difficulty handling a parental divorce. Moral development also seems to differ: boys appear to make moral judgments on the basis of justice and law, while girls make them on the basis of caring.

Does the fact that most girls dote on dolls while most boys career around with trucks mean that their destinies are preordained? Partly, yes – girls will grow up to be women and boys will grow up to be men. But much in their attitudes will depend on the attitudes their parents display and on the examples they set. You can raise children who are not 'sexist' in their points of view, who have respect for both males and females, who enjoy being the gender they were born into, who will choose their future life roles not on the basis of stereotypes (of any kind), but on the basis of their own personal strengths and desires. Following these tips will help you meet those goals:

- Remember that the fact that there are innate differences between males and females in no way means that one sex is in any way better or worse, stronger or weaker. Differences are enriching, sameness is stultifying. Pass this attitude on to your children.

- Treat your children as individuals. While as a group men have more muscles and are more aggressive than women, there are some women who have more muscle and are more aggressive than some men. If you have a daughter who has more 'male' traits or a son with more 'female' ones, don't berate or belittle them. Accept, love, and support your child as he or she is.[5]

- Modify extremes. Accepting your child as he or she is doesn't mean never using

your good sense to make some alterations. If a child is overly aggressive, you should teach him to tone the aggression down. If, on the other hand, he is overly passive, you can encourage assertiveness.

- Select toys not because you're trying to either make or break a stereotype, but because you truly believe your child will enjoy them and benefit from them. If a child uses a toy differently from the way you expect (boys and girls will use the same toys in different ways, and even within each sex the use will vary), accept that.

- Don't fall unconsciously into sexist traps. Don't tell your sobbing toddler not to cry because he's a big boy and then cuddle his sister when she's tearful. Don't limit your compliments to a daughter to 'How pretty you look', and to a son to 'Oh, how strong you are', or 'What a big boy you are'. Say these things, by all means, when appropriate. But also compliment a boy on his being sweet to his sister, and a girl for throwing a ball well. Do this not because you're trying to switch your children's sex roles – you're not – but because a child's personality is made up of many facets, all of which need nurturing.

- Try to avoid making value judgments about different types of skills or roles in life. If, for example, you give your children the impression that child care is a job that commands low respect, neither boys nor girls will come to value it as adults. If you give them the idea that going to an office to work is somehow more worthwhile than working as a full-

5. Boys who display feminine traits early in childhood, like to play with dolls and avoid rough sports are more likely to become homosexual in later life if their parents (particularly fathers) try to force them to 'be a man', either through teasing, subtle pressure, withdrawal of affection, or physical punishment. These boys become estranged from their fathers and, it is speculated, may ever hunger for male love and companionship in adulthood. If a child seems truly unhappy with his or her sexual assignment and doesn't enjoy playing with children of the same sex, professional consultation may be a good idea.

time parent or working in a non-office environment, they won't value the latter choices, either.

- Apportion family chores according to abilities, interests and time, rather than according to a preconceived stereotype or in order to break such a stereotype. That means the best cook should do most of the cooking (the other partner can do the dishes and clean up) and the best bookkeeper should balance the chequebook. If one parent has a less time-consuming job or no work outside the home at all, that parent should spend more time with the children and the other parent should make spending time with the children, whenever possible, a priority. Jobs no one wants to do can be rotated, apportioned by agreement, or relegated on the spur of the moment '(Darling, can you take out the rubbish, please?') but this latter system can fail miserably unless it's carefully monitored (as when nobody takes out the rubbish).

- Set an example. Decide which qualities in both males and females you and your husband value most and try to cultivate them in yourselves as well as in your children. Be a model of the sex roles you want to see your children adopt. Giving a little boy dolls to play with can be much less effective in teaching him to be nurturing than giving him a daddy who is nurturing himself. Having a bat and ball can be much less effective in encouraging a little girl to develop her physical aptitude than having a mother who jogs daily. Young children develop their gender identity partly through play with those of their own sex and partly through identification with the parent of the same sex; if you're unsure of what your sex role is, they may be, too.

Switching to a Bed

'We're expecting a second baby in six months. When and how should we switch our son from his cot to a bed?'

Whether or not your child is ready for a bed depends more on his age and size than on whether or not there's a new sibling on the way. The generally accepted rule: if a child is 92 cm (3 feet) tall or can climb out of a cot on his own, he's ready for a bed. Some particularly agile children can climb out of a cot before they reach the 92-cm (3-feet) cutoff; others, less adventurous, may never even try.

If you feel your older child isn't yet ready for a bed, and that he may not be even once the new baby arrives, buy him a new cot that converts into a youth bed. This way you can move him to the new cot now, so he won't feel displaced by the baby later on. When he meets the criteria for the youth bed or seems mature enough for it, simply convert his cot. Be prepared for the possibility of his climbing out of bed in the middle of the night by keeping his door closed or gated and by keeping his room as child-safe by night as by day, free of such hazards as open windows and electric fans within the reach of small hands. If you are afraid you won't hear him from your own bedroom, install an intercom to signal you of activity in his room. For restless sleepers who tend to topple out of bed, a guard rail is a good precaution.

If your firstborn can understand, tell him you are going to get him a special new bed. Add a strategic, 'The baby won't be able to sleep in it because it's a big-boy bed.' Have him participate in its selection, if this is possible, or if you plan on transferring him to a bed you already have, let him choose new linens and blankets. Make an occasion of the move to the new bed, supplying a festively wrapped new toy or doll for company in it and perhaps a few 'grown-up' decorative touches for the room, along with plenty of pomp and circumstance. Ideally, you should then take the cot down for a few weeks, not readying it until the new baby arrives or at least not much more than two weeks before the due date. This way the older child will feel less directly displaced. The new baby can sleep in a pram, cradle, or Moses basket the first few weeks, giving your toddler even more time to adjust to the change. When it's time for the cot takeover, explain to your older child that it's time to get out the cot for his new brother or sister ('Remember when you were a baby, and you slept in the cot?'). Don't ask his permission to use it; if he says 'no,' you will have a major problem. Do ask him to help you attach some toys to the cot for the baby, and perhaps to help select some pictures or other decorations for the room or corner.

Watching TV

'I feel very guilty because I have begun turning on the television for my baby when I start to prepare dinner. She seems to love it, but I'm concerned she'll become addicted to TV.'

That's a sound concern. According to the Nielsen Index, children two to twelve years of age watch an average of 25 hours of television a week. If your daughter becomes one of these, she will have spent 15,000 hours glued to the set by the time she leaves school – about 4,000 hours more than she will have spent in school. And if her viewing isn't carefully screened, she will, research suggests, have witnessed 18,000 murders, countless other crimes from robberies and rapes to bombings and beatings, and more casual sex than you could imagine (13.5 suggestive moments an hour). She will also have been the innocent target of thousands of commercials trying to sell her (and through her, you) products of dubious value.

Excessive TV viewing by children has other drawbacks. It's linked to obesity and poor school performance. And because it can reduce interaction among familiy members, it can interfere with family life. Perhaps worst of all, it creates a picture of the world that is distorted and inaccurate, and confuses a child's developing value system by establishing norms of behaviour and belief that are not accepted in the real world.

The TV problem for parents is compounded by the fact that even children's television often presents little decent programming (cartoons, often violent, standard fare). There are, of course, programmes that aim to teach such positive attributes as self-control, sharing, cooperation, racial tolerance and kindness towards others. But even these are not usually recommended for children under 10 months, for whom a television screen is believed to be nothing more than a confusing and hypnotic montage of lights and colours; they have no inkling of what is going on.

When your toddler does seem to be ready for some television (she jumps up and down when Playdays comes on the screen or claps her hands excitedly when she hears the Pingu theme, for example), limit her viewing to a single, non-commercial show of redeeming value. Even when she's older, television viewing should be limited. Such restrictions may be hard to enforce, however, if either you or someone else in the family watches TV all day long. A young child's attention span is usually very short, so she may watch only a brief segment before losing interest, or she may watch in spurts. But if the TV is on all the time, she'll think that's the way it's supposed to be and miss it when the screen is blank. Try to keep the television off during mealtimes, especially during the family dinner hour, or much time for family interaction will be lost to the monotonous, mesmerizing effect of the television.

Resist as much as possible (realistically, you won't always be able to) the temptation to use the TV as a convenient baby-minder. Instead, watch TV with your baby and participate in the viewing by pointing out familiar objects, animals and people, and by explaining what's going on. When your child is older, expand these explanation-and-discussion sessions. If your child's TV time is your time to get things done, try to get them done in view of the set so that you'll be able to throw in occasional comments.

Rather than relying on TV as the only audiovisual entertainment for your toddler, turn to audio tapes and records for stimulating her imagination and providing plenty of musical activity as well. And supplement with quality video tapes (Disney classics are

popular during the second year and beyond), which allow you more control over
when and what your child views and, in
addition, are commercial-free.

Hyperactivity

*'My daughter is on the go all day long—
crawling, walking, climbing, always
moving. I'm afraid she may turn out to
be hyperactive.'*

Observing the frenetic pace that the average
toddler sets, it's easy to see why so many
mothers of one-year-olds share the concern
that their child is hyperactive. Yet the vast
majority have nothing to worry about. What
seems an abnormally high activity level to
someone relatively inexperienced with
toddlers is much more likely to be a normal
one. After many months of frustration, the
mobility your child struggled so hard to
attain is finally hers. It's no wonder that she's
off and running (or toddling, or crawling, or
climbing) every chance she gets. As far as
she's concerned, the day's too short for all
the expeditions she wants to take.

True hyperactivity – officially labelled
'Attention Deficit Disorder with Hyperactivity (ADD)' and ten times more common
in boys than in girls – is characterized by
excessive activity that is both inappropriate
and unproductive, by a very brief attention
span, and by impulsiveness. As any parent
knows, these qualities are common among
all young toddlers; but it is only when they
are exaggerated to the point that they interfere with functioning that a problem is
signalled.

If worrisome hyperactive behaviour
continues and your child's attention span
doesn't grow as she does, do speak to her
doctor; there are several approaches to
controlling true hyperactivity that can help.
Since ADD is occasionally associated with
mental retardation, brain damage, hearing
loss, or emotional difficulties, these problems should be ruled out before treatment
begins.

In the meantime, do be sure your child
gets adequate amounts of rest – an overtired
child tends to speed up rather than slow
down. Entice her into quiet activities (such
as reading books, doing puzzles and sorting
shapes), but keep in mind her normally
short attention span and remember that, at
this age, such play usually requires adult
participation. Try a warm bath to calm her
when she seems to be getting out of control.
Also be sure she is well nourished and that
she's not getting a high-sugar diet – the
evidence isn't conclusive, but a small percentage of children may react to sugar, and
possibly some other foods, food dyes and
additives, with hyperactive behaviour.

Negativism

*'Ever since my son learned to shake his
head and say "No," he's been
responding negatively to everything –
even to things I'm sure he wants.'*

Congratulations – your baby is becoming a
toddler. And with this transition comes the
beginning of a behaviour pattern you're
going to see a lot more of, with increasing
intensity, in the next year or so: negativism.

As hard as it is on parents, negativism is a
normal and healthy part of a young child's
development. For the first time, he's able to
be his own person rather than your malleable baby, to exert some power, test his
limits and challenge parental authority. Most
importantly, he's able to express opinions of
his very own clearly and distinctly. And the
opinion, he's discovered, that has the most
impact is 'no!'

Fortunately, at this stage of negativism,
your child isn't likely to mean 'no' as fiercely
as he expresses it. In fact, he's often likely
not to mean it at all – as when he says 'no'
to the banana he was just clamouring for,
or shakes his head when you offer the ride
on the swing that you know he really wants.
Like pulling up or taking steps, learning
how to say 'no' and how to shake his head
are skills – and he needs to practise them,
even when they're not appropriate. That
babies invariably shake their heads 'no'

long before they shake their heads 'yes' has less to do with negativism than with the fact that it's a less complex, more easily executed movement, which requires less co-ordination.

Negativism can sometimes be avoided with a little clever verbal manipulation on your part; if you don't want to hear a 'no', don't ask a question that can be answered with one. Instead of 'Do you want an apple?' try 'Would you like an apple or a banana?' Instead of 'Do you want to go on the slide?' ask 'Would you like to go on the slide or the swing?' Be aware, however, that some children will answer even multiple-choice questions with a 'no'.

Occasionally, a twelve-month-old will even act out a primitive version of the 'terrible-twos' tantrum. These are usually laughable, though laughing at them (or at the vigorous use of 'no' and of head shaking) will only prolong the behaviour and encourage repetition. Though it won't work later on (an older toddler can keep a tantrum going full steam until he – or his parent – drops), ignoring a year-old baby's tirade will usually result in his giving up the struggle and sheepishly picking himself up to go play with a toy.

The 'no's' will probably have it in your household for at least another year – and they'll probably intensify before they taper off. The best way to weather this stormy period is to pay little mind to negative behaviour; the more you fuss over baby's 'no's', the more you'll hear. Keeping negativism in perspective while keeping your sense of humour may not help check the 'no's', but it may aid your ability to cope with them.

WHAT IT'S IMPORTANT TO KNOW:
Stimulating the Toddler

First words. First steps. With these two feathers in the toddler's cap, or nearly so, the learning game becomes more exciting than ever before. The world is growing by leaps and bounds; give your toddler a chance to explore and learn about it, and promote his or her continued physical, social, intellectual and emotional development, by offering the following:

Safe space to walk in – both indoors and out. The learner walker usually objects to being strapped in a pushchair or back pack, so use these only when absolutely necessary. Encourage baby to walk as often as possible, but keep an eagle eye out for dangers, especially near streets, roads and driveways. For the baby who isn't quite walking yet, put some enticing objects up out of reach, to provide incentive for pulling up and/or cruising.

Safe space for supervised climbing. Babies love to climb steps (when you're not supervising, a gate is a must), clamber up a slide (stay right behind, just in case), manoeuvre on to a low chair or off the bed. Let them – but stand by and be ready to come to the rescue if need be.

Encouragement to be physically active. The inactive baby may need a little cajoling to become more active. You may need to get down and crawl yourself and challenge such a child to come crawling or running after you ('Try and catch me!') or feign a threatening 'I'm going' get you' to encourage baby's moving away from you. Put toys or other favourite objects out of reach and encourage some sort of locomotion to retrieve them. The fearful baby may need some moral – and physical – support. Try to persuade such a baby to try, but don't ever force the issue or belittle him or her for not trying. Climb up and slide down the slide with a timid child until he or she is comfortable enough to go it alone. Stroll with the tentative walker, lending a hand (or two) for

Safety Reminder

Your baby is getting cleverer all the time – but it will be a long while before judgment catches up with intelligence and motor skills. So as baby enters the second year of life, be sure to continue your constant vigilance as well as all the safety precautions you have already put into effect, and then some – taking into account the fact that your toddler can now, or will soon be able to, climb with great skill. This means that virtually nothing in your home that is not behind lock and key or safety latch is safe from tiny hands – and that baby can get into even more trouble even faster than before. So do a second safety inventory, taking stock not only of those things that your toddler can reach from the floor, but also anything he or she could conceivably get to by climbing, and remove any hazards as well as anything you want to protect from baby. And be forewarned that toddlers have been known to show great resourcefulness in getting at what they want, piling up books or pulling a chair or toy over to reach a shelf they want to get to, for example. Also be sure that anything baby might climb on – chairs, tables, shelves – is sturdy enough to hold his or her weight. Continue setting limits ('No, you can't climb on that') but don't, just yet, depend on your young child to remember today's prohibition tomorrow.

support. Go on a 'big kid' swing together until your little kid is willing to risk the 'baby' swing solo.

A varied environment. The baby who sees nothing but the inside of his or her own home, the family car and the supermarket is going to be a very bored baby (not to mention how bored the caretaker will be). There's an exciting world outside the door, and your baby should see it daily. Even going out in the rain or snow (barring flooding or blizzard conditions) can be a learning experience. Give your baby a tour of area playgrounds, parks, museums (toddlers are usually fascinated by paintings and statues; on slow days, roomy galleries are terrific arenas for toddling or crawling), toy stores (where supervision is essential), restaurants (pick those that welcome children), pet shops and shopping malls or other busy business areas with lots of store windows to peer into and lots of people to see.

Pull-and-push toys. Toys that need to be pushed or pulled provide practice for those who've just begun to walk, and confidence (and physical support) for those just tottering on the brink. Riding toys babies can sit astride and propel with their feet may help some children walk, though others find walking independently easier. The use of a walker at this stage, on the other hand, will hinder, not help.

Creative materials. Scribbling with crayons provides tremendous satisfaction for many year-old babies. Taping the paper to a table, the floor, or an easel will keep it from sliding all over, and confiscating the crayons as soon as they are applied where they shouldn't be or if baby decides to chew on one will help teach their proper use. Don't allow pens and pencils, except under close supervision, since the sharp points can spell disaster if baby falls on either one. Finger painting can be fun for some, while others are uncomfortable with the dirty fingers that are an occupational hazard of the art. Though hand washing demonstrates that the condition is only temporary, some children continue resisting the medium. Musical toys can be fun, too – but look for those with fairly good quality sound. Baby can also learn to improvise musically, with a wooden or metal spoon on a pot bottom, for instance, if you demonstrate first.

Putting-and-taking toys. Babies love to put things in and take them out although the latter skill develops before the former. You can buy putting-and-taking toys, or just use objects around the house such as empty boxes, wooden spoons, measuring cups, paper cups and plates and napkins. Fill a basket with a variety of small items (but not small enough for baby to mouth and choke on) for starters. Be ready to do most of the putting in until baby becomes much more proficient. Sand (see page 233; in the house, many parents prefer to use raw rice) and water (you can limit its indoor use to the tub and baby's high chair) allow for putting in and taking out in the form of pouring – and most toddlers love both materials, but they require constant supervision.

Shape sorters. Usually long before babies can say circle, square, or triangle, they have learned to recognize these shapes and can put them in the proper opening in a shape sorter toy. These toys also teach manual dexterity and, in some cases, colours. Be aware, however, that baby may need many demonstrations and much assistance before mastery of shape sorters is achieved.

Dexterity toys. Toys that require turning, twisting, pushing, pressing and pulling encourage children to use their hands in a variety of ways. Many parental demonstrations may be needed before babies are able to handle some of the more complicated manoeuvres, but once mastered, these toys provide hours of concentrated play.

Bath toys for water play. These teach many concepts and allow the joy of water play without a mess all over the floor or furniture. The tub is also a good place for blowing bubbles – but you'll probably have to do the blowing yourself for a while yet.

Follow-the-leader play. Daddy starts clapping, then mummy. Baby is encouraged to follow suit. Then daddy flaps his arms and mummy does, too. After a while, baby will follow the leader without prodding and eventually will be able to take the lead.

Books, magazines, anything with pictures. You can't have a live horse, elephant and lion in your living room – but you can have all of them, and more, visit your home in a book or magazine. Look at and read books with your baby several times during the day. Each session will probably be short, maybe no more than a few minutes, because of your child's limited attention span, but together they will build a firm foundation for later enjoyment of reading.

Materials for pretend play. Toy dishes, kitchen equipment, pretend food, play houses, trucks and cars, hats, grown-ups' shoes, sofa cushions – almost anything can be magically transformed in an imaginative toddler's world of make-believe. This kind of play develops social skills as well as small motor coordination (putting on and taking off clothing, scrambling eggs or cooking soup), creativity and imagination.

Patience. Though the skills babies on the brink of toddlerhood display are much advanced over what they were at six months, their attention spans haven't expanded very much. They may be able to play with some toys for extended periods, but when you try to read a story or involve them with other toys, they may not be able to sit still for much longer than five minutes. Be understanding of these limitations, and don't despair – as babies grow, so do their attention spans.

Applause. Cheer your baby on as new skills are mastered. Achievement, while satisfying, often means more when accompanied by recognition.

PART TWO

Of Special Concern

SIXTEEN

A Baby for All Seasons

◆

Unless you're raising your baby in a climate-controlled plastic bubble, the vagaries of weather will have some impact on your lives. As the seasons change, and as sun, wind, heat, cold, snow and rain come and go with them, a wide range of new questions arise in the minds of parents – particularly first-timers. Questions about feeding, dressing and playing, about sunburn and frostbite, about window screens and fireplace screens, about swimming lessons and holiday decorations.

Feeding Your Baby: 'Round the Calendar

Your baby's nutritional needs are pretty much the same year-round, but seasonal temperature extremes do dictate some variations:

In cold weather. If your baby spends a lot of time outdoors in cold weather, extra calories are needed to fuel the body to provide extra heat. And because during the chillier months babies aren't exposed to much direct sunlight, you need to be sure enough vitamin D comes from the diet, either in the form of fortified formula, milk and other dairy products or, for babies who are getting almost all of their milk from the breast, in a multiple vitamin supplement.[1] A switch to comfortably warm (never hot) cereals may be more satisfying than a cold breakfast on wintry mornings. Most children, however, will prefer drinking milk or formula cold, which is best anyway since heating destroys some of the nutrients. To keep the immune system strong, and ensure that those illnesses that do strike don't strike

hard, provide your baby with plenty of vitamin A via green leafy and yellow vegetables and yellow fruits and vitamin C through vitamin C foods (see page 352).

In warm weather. In the summer, or in an ever-warm climate, your baby will sweat more and may feel like eating less. To compensate for the fluids lost through perspiration, increase fluid intake. For the very young baby, offer water frequently between feedings of breast milk (if a bottle is taken; if it isn't, nurse more frequently) or formula. For older children, add diluted fruit juices in bottles or cups, and once they've been introduced, juicy fruits such as melons, peaches and tomatoes. Do not serve drinks that are sweetened with sugar, such as sodas, juice drinks, or punches, since they increase thirst (and are inappropriate for babies, anyway), or drinks that contain added salt (such as special athletic drinks), since contrary to popular theory, large quantities of sodium are not only unnecessary in hot weather, they can be harmful.

To overcome a heat-dampened appetite, do not feed your baby immediately after

---

1. Your baby's doctor may recommend year-round vitamin D supplementation, since too much exposure to the sun's rays is inadvisable, especially for infants.

coming inside on a hot day. Allow time to cool off first, then, if possible, feed baby in a room that is air-conditioned or cooled by a fan. If solids have been introduced, serve smaller meals and larger snacks when baby doesn't seem to want to eat a lot at any one time, and stick to favourite fare. Provide foods that are nutrition dense (such as carrots, cantaloupe, mango, broccoli, cheese) and avoid empty-calorie items. Sprinkle wheat germ on cereals, desserts and pastas, or stir it into juice or a milk shake if your baby doesn't seem to be taking enough grain foods. If milk or formula is being rejected in favour of juices, ensure calcium intake by adding nonfat dry or whole evaporated milk to cereals and desserts, serving cubes of cheese at snack time, making homemade frozen desserts (see page 604) and serving commercial juice-sweetened ice cream, which will cool, refresh, delight and provide plenty of nutrition.

What You May Be Concerned About In Summer Or Summery Weather

Keeping Baby Cool

It's summertime – and the dressing is easy. Or is it? A common sight: a mother in sundress and sandals, hair lifted off her neck in a cooling pony tail, pushing a carriage holding an infant dressed for an arctic winter. What such well-intentioned mothers fail to realize is that in warm weather babies, even very new babies, needn't be dressed any more warmly than adults. Not only is adding extra clothing unnecessary, it can lead to undesirable consequences such as prickly heat and, in extreme cases, heat-stroke.

Unless you've got an unreliable personal thermostat (you're always warm when everyone else is cool, or you're always cool when everyone else is warm), feel free to dress your baby as you would yourself. If you're comfortable in shorts and a tank top, your baby will be fine in the junior equivalent. If you're sweltering in a swea-ter, your baby will be, too. Lightweight, loose-fitting, light-coloured clothing will be most comfortable when temperatures soar; a lightweight porous cap, hat, or bonnet will protect baby's head without overheating it. Materials should be absor-bent to soak up perspiration, but when clothing becomes damp, it should be changed – so routinely carry along an extra set of clothes for baby. Don't use a baby sling constructed of heavyweight fabric that totally covers baby, head to toe. Lack of ventilation in combination with your body warmth and a high outdoor temperature could add up to excessive heat within the confines of the carrier. If baby is to be in direct sun, protection from its damaging rays needs to be considered in selecting clothes.

Indoors in hot weather, your baby will enjoy the cooling effects of an air conditioner or fan as much as you do. Just be sure neither blows directly on the baby, that the room temperature doesn't drop much below 22.2°C (72°F), and that cooling equipment and its electrical cords are out of baby's reach. A nappy alone will do for sleeping on hot nights, but a lightweight sleeper and, possibly, a light cover may be needed if the air conditioner is running.

Cool hands or feet are not a sign that your baby is chilly; but perspiration (check the neck, head, underarms) is a sign of being too warm.

Heatstroke

Though mothers commonly worry about their babies being too cold, they often don't realize that being too hot can be just as dangerous. In the first year of life babies are particularly susceptible to heat because their temperature-regulatory systems aren't yet perfected and it's difficult for them to cool themselves effectively. As a result, overheating can lead to serious, even fatal, heatstroke. Heatstroke typically comes on suddenly. Signs to watch for include hot and dry (or, occasionally, moist) skin, very high fever, diarrhoea, agitation or lethargy, confusion, convulsions and loss of consciousness. Should your baby exhibit such symptoms, summon emergency medical help immediately and follow the first aid procedures on page 431.

As with most other medical emergencies, the best treatment is prevention. You can prevent heatstroke in these ways:

- Never leave an infant or child in a parked car in hot weather. Even with the windows open, the interior temperature can rise rapidly and dangerously. When the outdoor temperature is 35.5°C (96°F), for example, temperatures in the car can shoot up to more than 40.5°C (105°F) within fifteen minutes with the windows rolled halfway down, and to nearly 65.5°C (150°F) if the windows are closed.

- Don't bundle up a baby who has a fever with blankets or heating pads. A child with a fever needs cooling down, not heating up. 'Sweating it out' is not a recommended treatment in any type of weather.

- Dress baby lightly in hot weather and avoid direct sunlight. Beware of overheating in a baby sling.

- Always be sure that your child gets extra fluids in hot weather.

- Limit outdoor exercise for active toddlers in very hot or humid weather to no more than thirty minutes at a stretch, preferably in the shade.

Too Much Sun

There was a time when we considered youngsters who were tanned brown as berries, frolicking in the hot sun of a summer afternoon, healthy; 'sickly' children were those who were pale from too much time spent indoors. The sun's rays, we believed, were as wholesome as apple pie and as restorative as chicken soup. Unfortunately, we were wrong. As we now know, nothing is more likely to cause skin cancer (including the potentially fatal melanoma), brown spots and premature wrinkling and aging of the skin later in life. Though a tan looks 'healthy', it's actually a sign of injury to the skin and is that sensitive organ's way of trying to protect itself against further damage.

Excessive exposure to the sun's rays has also been strongly linked to the development of cataracts (they are much more common in sunny climes), and has recently been found to reduce body levels of betacarotene (a substance in the body believed to be protective against cancer). If that's not enough to make you take a dim view of bright sunshine, consider this: it can also precipitate certain other diseases, or make them worse, among them herpes simplex and some other viral skin diseases; vitiligo (white, or depigmented, spots on the skin); PKU; and photosensitive eczema. And for those taking certain antibiotics (such as tetracycline) or other medications, it can cause serious side effects. A pretty long rap sheet for an all-purpose panacea.

At least a few minutes of direct sunshine a day *was* once crucial to healthy growth and development in childhood – for it was the only available source of vitamin D, needed for building strong bones. Today, infant formulas, some milk and many other dairy products are fortified with the vitamin, and it is also found in baby vitamin supplements; you needn't sacrifice the future of your children's skin to ensure them the required dose of vitamin D.

To be certain your baby doesn't suffer the consequences of too much sun, keep in mind the following sun-safety facts and sun-safety tips.

SUN-SAFETY FACTS:

- The sun's intensity is greatest, thus its

rays most dangerous, between 10 A.M. and 3 P.M.

- Fully 80% of the sun's radiation penetrates cloud cover; so protection is needed on hot, cloudy days as well as on clear ones.

- Water and sand reflect the sun's rays, increasing the risk of skin damage and the need for protection.

- Wet skin allows more ultraviolet rays to penetrate than dry skin – so extra protection is needed in the water.

- The shade of sun umbrellas and trees is not reliable protection against the sun's rays, particularly at the beach.

- Extreme heat, wind, high altitude and closeness to the equator also accentuate dangers of the sun's rays, so take extra precautions under such conditions.

- Snow on the ground can reflect enough of the sun's rays on a bright day to cause a sunburn.

- Infants are particularly susceptible to sunburn because of their thin skin. A single episode of severe sunburn during infancy or childhood doubles the risk of the most deadly of skin cancers, malignant melanoma. And even seemingly innocent tanning without burning in the early years has been linked to basal cell and squamous cell carcinomas, the most common types of skin cancer, as well as to premature aging of the skin. The sun is believed responsible for at least 90% of all skin cancers, most of which could have been prevented.

- Fair-skinned individuals with light eyes and hair are most susceptible, but no one is immune from the hazardous effects of the sun's rays.

- There is no such thing as a safe tan, no matter how gradually acquired. Nor does a base tan protect the skin from further damage.

- The nose, lips and ears are the parts of the body most susceptible to sun damage.

SUN-SAFETY TIPS:

- Avoid exposing babies under six months to strong sunlight, particularly at the height of the sun's intensity in summer or in climates that are warm year-round. Protect these young infants with a sunshade or parasol on pushchairs or prams but do not use a sunscreen without a doctor's okay.

- At least fifteen (but preferably thirty) minutes before exposing an older baby or young child to the sun, apply sunscreen to all areas of the body not covered by clothing – though a dark-skinned child can tolerate brief exposures without sun protection. Avoid getting sunscreen into baby's mouth or eyes, or on the eyelids. For extra protection on very sensitive areas, such as lips, nose, and ears, ask the doctor about using a sun-blocking lip balm or stick, or zinc oxide.

- Initial exposures to the sun should be no more than a few minutes and can gradually be increased, by a couple of minutes a day, up to twenty minutes.

- Once your baby is six months old, carry a sunscreen in your nappy bag in case you should need it unexpectedly.

- In the sun, all babies and children should wear light hats with brims to protect eyes and face, and shirts to protect the upper body, even when they're in the water. Clothing should be of lightweight, tightly woven fabrics. Two thin layers may protect better than one, since the sun's rays can pass through some fabrics – but be wary of overdressing.

- During hot weather, try to schedule most outdoor activity for early morning or late afternoon. Keep children out of the midday sun whenever possible.

- Apply waterproof sunscreen all over little ones who are cooling off under sprinklers or in wading or swimming pools. After water play, towel-dry, then reapply sunscreen.

What to Look for in Selecting a Sunscreen

High SPF. Sunscreens are labelled with a sun protection factor, or SPF, from 2 to 30 (or rarely, as high as 50). The higher the number, the greater the protection. An SPF of at least 15 is recommended for babies and children, though a 30 is best for those with very fair or sensitive skin. Do not use tanning products on babies or children; they don't protect at all.

Effectiveness. Look for a product that contains ingredients that screen out both the short ultraviolet (UVB) rays of the sun that burn and can cause cancer as well as the longer ultraviolet (UVA) rays that tan, can cause long-term skin damage, and enhance the carcinogenic effects of the UVB rays.

Safety. Some sunscreen ingredients are irritating to or cause allergic reactions in some people, particularly infants with tender skins. Most common offenders are PABA (para-aminobenzoic acid) and forms of PABA (padimate O or octyl di methyl PABA, for example), fragrances, and colourings. So test a product out with a 24-hour patch test before smearing it all over your baby. Apply a small amount of sunscreen to the inside of baby's arm and cover with a band-aid. Remove the band-aid 24 hours later, and expose the area to fifteen minutes of sunlight while the rest of the body is protected by a hat and clothing. If the test patch reddens or swells, try a different product. If, once you've begun using a product, your baby develops an itchy red rash or any other kind of skin reaction, or if his or her eyes seem irritated, try another product, preferably one that is designed for use by infants or is hypoallergenic.

Protection in the water. When your baby is going to be in the water, select a product that is waterproof (which means it will retain its effectiveness after four 20-minute dunkings) or water resistant (it will retain effectiveness after two such dunkings).

And remember, even with a sunscreen, exposure to the sun should be limited.

- Avoid artificial tanning devices such as sun lamps, since they, too, contribute to premature aging and skin cancer and are inappropriate for babies.

- If your child is taking any medication, be sure that it doesn't cause photosensitivity (increased sensitivity to sunlight) before allowing sun exposure.

- Set a good example by protecting your own skin from the ravages of the sun's rays.

SIGNS OF SUNBURN

Many parents assume their babies are fine in the sun as long as there is no reddening of the skin. Unfortunately, they're mistaken. You can't see sunburn when it's occurring, and when you do see it, it's too late. It's not until two to four hours following exposure that the skin becomes red, hot and inflamed, and the colour doesn't peak at lobster red until ten to fourteen hours after exposure. A bad sunburn will also blister and will be accompanied by localized pain and, in the most severe cases, headache, nausea, chills and prostration. Redness usually starts to fade and symptoms diminish after 48 to 72 hours, at which point the skin, even in fairly mild cases, may start to peel. Occasionally, however, discomfort may continue for a week to ten days. See page 431 for tips on treating sunburn.

Insect Bites

Though most insects are harmless, their bites and stings almost always cause pain or uncomfortable itching and can occasionally transmit serious disease or cause a severe allergic reaction. So it makes sense to protect your baby from bugs and their bites whenever you can. (For treating insect bites, see page 427.)

BITE PROTECTION

Bees and other stinging insects. Keep baby out of areas where bees congregate, such as clover or wildflower fields, fruit orchards, or near birdbaths. Protect baby even in your own garden, especially on bright, warm days or after a heavy rain. If you discover a beehive or a wasp nest in or near your home, have it removed by an expert. To avoid attracting bees, dress your family for outdoor play in white or pastels rather than dark or bright colours or flowered prints. Don't use fragrant powders or lotions, cologne, or scented hair spray. Keep a light piece of fabric handy in your car to trap insects.

Mosquitoes. They breed in ponds, drain puddles, rain barrels and other areas that collect water. If in a mosquito area, keep baby indoors at night when mosquitoes swarm, and be sure windows have screens kept in good repair.

Deer ticks. Before outings in high tick areas, apply an insect repellent containing low concentrations (preferably 10% or less) of deet to clothing – *not* skin. Check family, pets and gear frequently for the pinheadsize ticks. (They are easier to spot on light-coloured clothing and cling less to tight weaves.) To prevent Lyme disease, remove ticks promptly (see page 427).

All biting or stinging insects. Keep arms, legs, feet and head covered in areas where such insects might be lurking. Where ticks are prevalent, tuck trousers into socks.

Summer Safety

The arrival of summer signals a whole new set of accident possibilities. The following

precautions will help minimize the chance that the possibilities will become realities:

• Because warm weather often means open windows, be sure to install window guards on all windows in your home. Don't depend on screens, since they can be pushed out by a vigorous baby. If window guards aren't in place in your home, or where you're visiting, open windows no more than 15 cm/6 inches (and be sure they can't be pushed open farther), or open them only from the top. Don't put furniture, or anything else a baby can climb, under windows.

• Doors, too, are often left open in warm weather, inviting crawlers to crawl and toddlers to toddle out and into trouble. Be sure to keep all doors, including sliding doors and screens, locked.

• Out of doors, never take your eyes off the baby who can crawl or toddle, and be especially watchful around swings and other playground equipment. Be sure any equipment in your own garden is at least 2 metres (6 feet) from fences or walls, and that there is protective surfacing (rubber, sand, sawdust, wood chips, or bark) under it. Always insist that your baby hold on with both hands when in a swing, sit in the centre, and not try to get out unless it has stopped moving. Discourage head-first sliding down the slide, and teach your child to watch for other children at the bottom or top. Don't use metal slides in warm weather without feeling them first – in the sun they can get hot enough to cause burns.

• Don't put baby down in deep grasses or anywhere there could possibly be poison ivy, poison oak, or poison sumac, or where he or she might get a hand on or nibble at other poisonous flowers, shrubs, or trees. When in wooded areas, be sure your baby is protected with cover-up clothing. If your baby accidentally has contact with poison ivy, oak, or poison sumac, remove all clothing while protecting your own hands with gloves or paper towels. Wash baby's skin thoroughly with soap (preferably yellow) and water immediately – wait five minutes and it may be too late to ward off a reaction. Anything else that might have touched the plants (clothing, pushchair, even the dog) should be washed, too. Shoes should be swabbed with cleaning fluid. Should a reaction occur, apply calamine or another soothing lotion to relieve itching (see page 406).

- Since warm weather also brings out the barbecues, take steps to protect babies from accidental burns. Keep grills out of reach of small hands; be sure there are no chairs or anything else on which a baby can climb to reach these hot attractions. Tabletop grills should be placed only on stable surfaces. Remember that coals can stay hot for a long time. To reduce the risk of accidental burns, drench the coals with water when the cooking is complete, then dispose of them where your child can't get to them.

Water Babies

Parents, eager to 'waterproof' their babies as well as to give them a competitive edge over their pint-size peers, are often enticed to enroll their babies in swim classes. But according to many experts, swim classes are not a good idea for babies. Though it is easy to teach crawlers to float – young children float naturally because they have a higher proportion of body fat than adults – it isn't possible to teach them to use this skill in a life-threatening situation. Nor do infant swim lessons make children better swimmers in the long run than do lessons taken later on in childhood. There is, in fact, some question as to whether children under three can benefit at all from swimming classes. In addition, there has been some suggestion that such early exposure to public pools could increase the risk of such infections as diarrhoea (because of germs swallowed along with pool water), swimmer's ear (because of water entering the ear) and swimmer's itch and other skin rashes.

That doesn't mean you shouldn't try to help your baby to feel comfortable in water – an important first step in water safety training. Before you take the plunge with your baby, however, do acquaint yourself throughly with the following points. Keep them in mind, too, if you plan on enrolling your baby in a swim class.

- A baby should not be taken into a pool or other large body of water until good head control is achieved – that is, when the head can be lifted to a 90° angle routinely. Before this skill is mastered, usually by four or five months of age, the head might accidentally bob under the water.

- A baby with any kind of chronic medical problem, including frequent ear infections, should have the doctor's okay before you allow him to play in water. A baby with a cold or other illness should be temporarily barred from water activities, other than in the bathtub, until recovery is complete.

- The baby who likes and is used to water is probably less safe near it than one who is afraid of it. So don't leave a child, even one who has had 'swimming' lessons, unattended near water (a pool, hot tub, bathtub, lake, ocean, puddle) for *any* period of time. Drowning can occur in less time than it takes to answer the phone – in *less than 2.5 cm (an inch)* of water. If you must leave the waterside, even for a second, take baby with you.

- All infant water activity should be on a one-to-one basis with a responsible adult. The adult should not be fearful of the water because such fear could be passed on to the infant.

- Infant swim instructors should be qualified to teach swimming to babies and should be certified in infant CPR.

- A baby who is fearful of the water or resistant to being dunked should not be forced to participate in water play.

- Water in which an infant plays should be comfortably warm. In general, babies like

Drownproofing your Family

The best way to 'drownproof' your family is to:

1. Teach your children never to enter the water without an adult present and never to horseplay near the water. Even children who can swim well should never enter the water without a friend around.

2. Be sure that children are *always* supervised by a responsible adult when they are around water, even a small wading pool with barely 2.5 cm (an inch) of water in it.

3. Always drain paddling pools when not in use, and turn them over so they won't fill with rainwater.

4. Make certain any pool areas (yours and your neighbours') that are accessible to your children are enclosed with high fencing they can't scale and locked securely with a self-latching lock they can't reach.

5. Insist that children playing around pools or natural bodies of water, or on boats, wear life vests (not flotation toys) until they can swim on their own and are old enough to be responsible in the water.

6. Install a pool alarm, if you have a pool, but recognize that it doesn't provide absolute security.

7. Never use a pool with the cover partly in place – children can become entrapped in it.

8. Remember that pool covers can fill with water and become as dangerous as the pool itself.

9. Teach your children to float and to doggie-paddle in the water when they are three or four years old.

---

water between 28.9° and 30.5°C (84° and 87°F). Infants under six months should never be dunked in water cooler than this. Air temperature should be a least 1°C (3°F) warmer than water temperature, and water play should be limited to thirty-minute sessions to avoid chilling. Also, to reduce the risk of infection, pool water should be properly chlorinated and natural bodies of water should be unpolluted.

- Infants in nappies should wear waterproof pants that have snug elastic around the leg, but undue concern about leakage is unnecessary. Since babies have tiny bladders, the amount of urine passed is negligible; the chlorine should take care of any stray germs.

- An infant's face should not be submerged. Though babies instinctively hold their breath under water, they continue to swallow. Swallowing large quantities of water, which many babies do during water play, can dilute the blood, leading to water intoxication. This watering down of the blood can dangerously reduce the levels of sodium.

The resultant swelling of the brain can cause restlessness, weakness, nausea, muscle twitching, stupor, convulsions and even coma. Babies are much more susceptible than adults to water intoxication because of a smaller blood volume (it doesn't take a huge quantity of water to dilute it) and because they tend to swallow anything in their mouths. Water intoxication is a devious condition. Since a baby doesn't show any signs of trouble while in the water, and symptoms don't appear until three to eight hours after its ingestion, the illness is often not connected with swimming.

Submersion also increases the risk of infection, particularly of the ears and sinuses, as well as of hypothermia (dangerously low body temperatures).

- Tubes, water wings, mattresses, or other flotation devices lend a false sense of security to a baby and the parent. It takes but a moment for a little one to slip from a tube or tumble off a float. CE approved vests should be worn around the water by babies and young children, but even these should never replace constant adult supervision.

- A toy bobbing in a pool can become a fatal attraction: keep all objects out of the pool when not in use.

- A pool, wading pool, or spray with a missing drain cover should not be used until the drain is repaired. A baby or young child could be seriously injured by the force of the suction.

- Adults supervising babies or children near water should be familiar with resuscitation techniques (see page 441), preferably through a hands-on course. Rescue equipment, such as life preservers, and a CPR-technique poster should be posted near any swimming area. A phone should be readily available for emergency calls.

Weaning in Summer

Though old wives (or young mothers who've consulted with their elders) may tell tales to the contrary, there's no reason to hurry babies into giving up the breast or bottle before summer starts or to postpone weaning until autumn. The best time for weaning is the time that's best for you and your baby – it needn't be planned by the season or dictated by the weather report.

That fable foiled, it is true that babies need more fluids in the warm-weather months (and year-round in warm climates) than when the mercury plummets. So just make sure your baby gets enough fluids –

whether from breast, bottle, cup, or foods high in water.

Food Spoilage

Food is much more likely to spoil when the sun shines and temperatures rise, so take special precautions with your baby's food in warm weather. Follow the tips on page 224 to reduce the chances of food poisoning. On outings, use an ice pack to keep formula, milk, opened jars of juice or baby food, or table foods chilled (keep several small ice packs in the freezer, ready to go), or tote beverages in a thermos or in a jar with added ice cubes (for juice only, since formula or milk shouldn't be diluted). A soft-sided six-pack cooler gives extra protection on longer outings and is easy to carry. Don't use food or drink once it's no longer cool to the touch – at warmer temperatures bacteria might have had some time to multiply.

Swollen Cheeks

Every once in a while, both mother and doctor are confounded in the summer by the unexplained swelling of a baby's cheeks, sometimes accompanied by redness. The problem usually turns out to be 'popsicle panniculitis', a seasonal diagnostic oddity caused by tissue damage from sucking on ice pops. The cure is simple: switching to another, less-chilling snack. The swelling subsides quickly and the colouration fades within a few weeks.

What You May Be Concerned About In Winter Or Wintry Weather

Keeping Baby Warm

Baby, it's cold outside. And, just as when it's warm outside, your own comfort can be your guide to dressing older babies and children. But infants under six months –

because they have a greater ratio of body surface to body weight and because they can't yet shiver to generate heat – need a little more protection than you do.

Even when the weather is only slightly cool, a young baby should wear a hat to help retain heat (25% of body heat is lost via the head). When the temperature is near freezing, the hat should cover baby's ears, mittens the hands, warm socks and booties the feet, a scarf or neck warmer the neck. When the wind is biting or temperatures are very low, a scarf can be wrapped around the face or a knitted mask hat slipped over it, but be careful not to block the nose. A raincover will keep wind and snow out of a pushchair or pram, and warmth in. But even a well-bundled baby shouldn't be out in very cold weather for long periods.

In cold weather, a lot of lightweight layers are more effective and less restrictive than a couple of heavy garments. If at least one layer is wool, baby will be warmer. Down or imitation down makes for a warm snowsuit or bunting.

The following cold weather tips will also help to keep your baby cozy and comfortable:

- Be sure your baby has recently had a meal or snack before going out – it takes a lot of calories to maintain body heat in cold weather. A hot meal is comforting, but its warming effects don't last long.

- If any of your baby's clothes should become wet, change them immediately.

- A toddler should wear waterproof, lined boots when walking in wintry weather; the boots should be roomy enough to let in air, which will offer some extra insulation, to circulate around stockinged feet.

- In a car, remove your baby's hat and one or more layers of clothing, if possible, to prevent overheating; if not, take care to keep the car cool. Also remove some clothing on a warm bus or train.

- In windy weather, use a mild moisturizing lotion or cream on exposed skin to keep it from chapping.

- Don't worry if your baby's nose runs when outdoors in cold weather. The cilia, or little hairs, that ordinarily move nasal secretions to the back of the nose instead of letting them drip out are temporarily paralyzed by the cold; once indoors, the running should stop. A little cream or Vaseline under the nose (not in it) will help prevent chapping.

Frostbite

While you needn't worry about your baby's nose running, you'd better be concerned if

---

Changeable Weather

If there's any kind of weather that puzzles even those who top best-dressed lists, it's that neither-here-nor-there weather so common in the spring and autumn. For the inexperienced mother of a young baby, the puzzle is even more complex. How do you piece together an outfit from baby's closet when the day dawns like a lamb but is expected to roar like a lion by sundown (or vice versa)?

In general, the layered look is the key to dressing for success in changeable weather. Most practical are lightweight layers, which can be easily added or subtracted as the weather unpredictably zigzags from warm to cool and back again. An extra jumper or blanket is always a sensible take-along in case the mercury takes a sudden sharp dip. A hat is a good idea for a young baby in almost any weather – a very light one with a sunshade when it's balmy, a warmer one on blustery days. An older baby can go hatless when temperatures are in the 15s or 20s°C (60s or 70s°F) and sun or wind isn't excessively strong. And remember, once your baby's thermostat becomes well regulated (at about six months), let your own comfort be your baby-dressing guide. A quick check of baby's arms, thighs, or nape of the neck (but not the hands or feet, which are almost always cool in young babies) will tell you if baby's comfortable. If you find these body parts are cool and/or if baby is fretful, he or she may be chilly.

the nose (or ears, cheeks, fingers, or toes) becomes very cold and turns white or yellowish grey. This indicates frostbite, which can cause very serious injury. Frostbitten body parts must be rewarmed immediately. See page 434 for how to do this.

After prolonged exposure to cold weather, a baby's body temperature may drop to below normal levels. This is a medical emergency – no time should be wasted in getting a baby who seems unusually cold to the touch to the nearest emergency room.

Prevent such cold weather emergencies by dressing your baby adequately, protecting exposed areas of skin, and limiting the time your baby spends outdoors in extreme weather.

Snow Burn

It isn't just the baby tagging along to tropical beaches for the winter holidays who is in danger of suffering a sunburn in winter – a baby enjoying a white Christmas or Hanukkah is, too. Since snow reflects up to 85% of the sun's ultraviolet rays, even a weak winter's sun can burn a baby's sensitive skin if it bounces off a snowy landscape first. So be sure to protect your baby's skin with clothing, a brimmed hat and sunscreen whenever you'll be spending a lot of time in sun and snow.

Keeping Baby Warm Indoors

In cold weather, baby's room should be kept at between 20° and 22.2°C (68° and 72°F) by day, and between 15.5°C and 18.3°C (60° and 65°F) by night. If indoor temperatures are higher than this, the arid heated air can dry the mucous membranes of the nose, making them more vulnerable to cold germs, and also the skin, making it itchy. You can prewarm your baby's sheets with a heating pad or hot-water bottle, but be sure the sheets aren't too hot at bedtime. Or use flannel sheets, which tend to stay comfortable to the touch even on cold nights. Layer light blan-

kets for warmth and comfort. If your baby regularly kicks the blankets off, use a sleeping bag or a blanket sleeper. Keep in mind that your baby's room is cooler at night than during the day (at least it should be), and that extra covering is needed during sleep, when metabolism slows. But try not to make the common mistake of overdressing your baby for bed. And if he or she awakens in the night in a pool of perspiration, remove a layer or two of covering.

Dry Skin

Few people, of any age, are exempt from the dry, itchy skin of winter. Though most people assume that merely protecting babies from the cruel assaults of wind and cold outdoors will keep their skin soft and supple, this isn't so. The major cause of winter dry skin is found indoors, not out. In most homes, once the heating season begins, the indoor air becomes hot and dry. And it's this hot, dry air that is a major contributor to skin dryness in winter. You can help counteract this effect in these ways:

Up the moisture in your home. Get a humidifier for your heating system, or at least a cold-mist unit (see page 616) for your baby's room. If this isn't possible, put pans of hot water on radiators (safely out of baby's reach); as the water evaporates, room air will be moisturized.

Up the moisture inside your baby. Babies (and all of us) get moisture for their skin from inside as well as out. Be sure your baby is getting enough fluids.

Up the moisture on baby's skin. Smoothing a good-quality baby lotion on baby's damp skin right after the bath will help retain the moisture. Ask the doctor to recommend a particular product, or select one that is hypoallergenic at the pharmacy.

Reduce the soap. Soap is drying. It rarely needs to be used on tiny infants – except once a day in the nappy area. Crawlers may need a sudsing on knees, feet and hands. But in general, use very little soap; particularly avoid using bubble bath or liquid soap to make bubbles in baby's bath, since soapy water is more drying than clear water. And use a gentle soap – ask your doctor for a recommendation.

Turn down the heat. The hotter the house, the drier the air (assuming no humidity is being returned to the air as the house is heated). For babies more than a few weeks old, the home need not be warmer than 20°C (68°F). If baby seems chilly at this temperature, it's better to add layers of clothing rather than degrees of heat.

Fireplace Fires

Before there were televisions, there were fireplaces to draw families together on a cold winter's evening. And even today, a roaring fire can rival whatever prime time has to offer, bringing warmth to both body and spirit. The trick, however, when babies and young children are part of the family circle, is to keep them safe when around the fire. Keep the fireplace covered, even once the fire's out (embers can stay hot for hours), with a screen that's too heavy for even strong and persistent little hands to move. For added protection, teach your baby early on that fire is 'hot!' and that touching it can cause pain. Be sure, too, that the flue is clear so fumes don't fill the room.

Holiday Hazards

Nothing is more wondrous to a young child than a home that's been decked out for the holidays. But if proper precautions aren't taken, nothing can turn out to be more dangerous. Concealed in many idyllic living-room scenes are a host of hazards. All of the following are potential threats to your baby. Some should be used with care, others shouldn't be used at all – at least until your child is older, wiser and less vulnerable.

Mistletoe and Jerusalem cherry. Both of these can be deadly if eaten. Do not bring them into your home or let your baby play near them when visiting.

Holly. This plant is only slightly poisonous (large quantities must be consumed for a baby to suffer serious consequences), but it's wise to keep it out of baby's reach. Christmas cactus is safe, however.

Poinsettia. This holiday beauty can cause local irritation to the mouth, and more serious poisoning if large quantities are ingested. Keep out of reach.

Evergreen trees and branches. These may aggravate asthma or similar disorders and can also be a fire hazard if not handled with care. If anyone in your home has such allergies, perhaps you should consider an artificial tree.

Pine needles. These can cause a persistent croupy cough if they lodge in the trachea (they can usually be dislodged by turning the child over and slapping the mid-back). Sweep them up regularly and, if possible, keep pine trees, wreaths and branches out of reach of babies and toddlers.

Snow-scene paperweights. Despite long-circulated rumours to the contrary, the liquid inside these is not poisonous. But once broken, it can become contaminated with germs; discard if the paperweight becomes cracked.

Angel hair. This is spun glass, which can irritate skin and eyes and cause internal bleeding if swallowed; use high up and out of baby's reach, if at all.

Artificial snow spray or flocking. These can aggravate a respiratory problem; don't use if anyone in your family has one.

Tree lights. Because young children may bite these enticing ornaments and suffer internal cuts, hang them high out of reach. Be particularly careful with small blinking lights, which contain a chemical that is hazardous if ingested.

Hanukkah or other candles. Light them and keep them completely out of baby's reach – and, of course, away from curtains or other flammable materials. If you display them in a window, be sure curtains are securely tied back.

Mini decorations. Very small tree ornaments, tree lights, dreidels, any items smaller than the diameter of baby's first (or with parts that can be pulled or broken off) can cause choking. Don't use these, or use them only where you're sure baby can't get to them.

Tinsel, glass or plastic ornaments and Styrofoam. All of these decorative items are alluring choking hazards. If a piece is bitten off, it can become stuck in the throat.

Tree preservatives. If you use one, check to see that it doesn't contain nitrates, which can cause a blood disorder if consumed. A curious baby may dip into the tree container for an unusual snack.

Gifts. These present numerous dangers. Perfumes, colognes, and cosmetics can cause poisoning; button batteries and toys with small pieces can cause choking. And throw away wrappings and ribbons. They are also easy for babies to choke on.

Food and drink. It isn't just the things that set the scene that can be dangerous; those that set the table can be, too. Every year, hundreds of young children are rushed to hospital emergency rooms after downing a martini, beer, or cupful of eggnog or spiked punch left carelessly within their reach. Thousands more do mischief to their teeth, appetites and eating habits with sugary holiday foods, which are too often passed into their tiny hands. So be sure that alcoholic drinks aren't left around, even briefly, on coffee or end tables where even moderately active crawlers can get to them. And indulge your baby (and your holiday guests, as well) with baked goods sweetened with fruit juice concentrates; a wide variety of such biscuits and cakes are commercially available, and many more can be baked at home.

While you're adorning your home for the holidays, keep decorations where baby can't get at them, or do your decorating while baby's asleep. Just in case a mishap should occur in spite of all your precautions, prepare for the holidays by becoming familiar with first-aid and CPR techniques, if you aren't already, and by posting the number of your doctor and/or local poison control centre where it will be handy.

Safe Gift Giving

First on any parent's list when doing holiday toy shopping should be safety. As tempting as toy stores are at this time of year, resist them until you've completely familiarized yourself with the tips for buying safe and worthwhile playings for your baby, starting on page 207. Remember, manufacturers can't always be counted on to produce what's best for your baby – particularly during the holiday season you, the buyer, must beware.

WHAT IT'S IMPORTANT TO KNOW:
The Season for Travel

In the days before parenthood, any season was the season for a trip. Summer excursions to a friend's beach house, winter holidays with parents in the whirlwind ski weekends squeezed in between busy work weeks, leisurely tours of Paris in the spring, escapes to the Caribbean when the streets back home were covered with ice, or to the mountains when they were steaming with heat and humidity.

But now what? Considering the effort involved in taking your baby across town on a simple shopping expedition – the hours of planning, the exacting execution and the enormous weight of baby, equipment and supplies lugged on your aching shoulders – the logistics of a two-week holiday, or even a two-day trip to grandmother, might seem too mind-boggling to consider attempting.

Yet you needn't wait until your children are old enough to carry their own luggage or are off on their own to satisfy your wanderlust or grandmother's pleas for a visit. Though holidays with baby will rarely be restful and will always be a challenge, they can be both feasible and enjoyable.

Planning Ahead

The days of spur-of-the-moment weekend getaways, when a restless spirit and a few garments and toiletries flung into an overnight bag took you where you wanted to go, ended abruptly with your baby's arrival. Now you can expect to spend more time planning a trip than taking one. Sensible preparatory steps for any trip with baby include:

Underschedule yourself. Forget itineraries that will take you through six scintillating cities in five whirlwind days. Instead, set a modest pace with plenty of unscheduled time – for an extra day on the road should you end up needing it, an extra afternoon at the beach or morning by the pool should you end up wanting it.

Update passports. If you haven't added your child's name to your passport you won't be able to take him with you.

Take medical precautions. If you're going abroad, check with the doctor to be sure baby's immunizations are up to date. If you're heading for exotic destinations, all of you may need specific immunizations (against typhoid, for example) or prophylactic treatments (to prevent malaria or hepatitis A).

Before taking an extended trip, schedule a well-child checkup if it's been a while since the last one. In addition to providing assurance that your baby's in good health, the visit will give you an opportunity to discuss your proposed trip with the doctor and ask any questions that might otherwise plague you while you're away – when it may be impossible, or at least impractical, to pick up the phone and call the surgery. If your baby has had a checkup within the previous month, a telephone consultation may be all that's needed.

If your baby takes medication, be sure you have enough for the trip, plus a prescription in case the supply is lost, spilled, or otherwise meets with calamity. If a medication needs to be refrigerated, keeping it on ice continuously may be difficult, so ask the doctor if it's possible to substitute another medication that needn't be kept cold. Since a stuffy nose can make a baby miserable, interfere with sleep and cause ear pain when flying, also ask the doctor to recommend a decongestant in case your child should come down with a cold. If you are going to a place where 'traveller's stomach' might be a problem, ask for a prescription for diarrhoea, too. For any medication you are taking along, be sure you know the safe dosage for a child your baby's age, as well as the conditions under which it should be administered and the possible side effects. Also useful, especially for extended trips: the name of a doctor at your destination or destinations.

Time your trip. What hour of the day or night you begin your journey will depend on, among other things, baby's schedule and how he or she reacts to changes in it, your mode of travel, your destination and how long it will take to get there. Assuming a nap has been taken en route, the excitement and chaos of arrival will probably make it possible to keep baby awake a couple of hours past the usual bedtime. (Of course, you will also have to pray trains and planes will be on schedule.)

Consider the advantages of travelling at off-peak times, when there are more likely to be empty seats for your baby to crawl over and fewer fellow passengers who might be disturbed.

If your baby habitually falls asleep in the car and you're planning a long-distance car trip, plan, if possible, to do most of your driving when he or she would ordinarily be asleep – during nap times or at night. Otherwise, you may arrive at your destination with a baby who's slept all day and is ready to play all night. If your baby sleeps well on trains or planes but is fussy when awake in such confined quarters, coordinate nap time with travel time. But if your baby is always too excited to sleep in such environments, plan to travel after nap time to avoid crankiness during the trip.

It may seem that getting to your destination as quickly as possible makes the most sense. But it doesn't always. For an active baby, for example, a connecting flight with some time to let off steam between legs of the trip may be better than a long nonstop.

Order ahead. When flying, don't plan on feeding even an older baby from a standard airline tray; entrées are astronomically high in sodium, bread is invariably of the refined variety, desserts are routinely sugary and nutritionally worthless. Instead, plan on sharing a special order, such as a cottage cheese and fruit platter and wholemeal bread, with your older baby. Special orders are usually just a 24-hour-in-advance phone call away, and you can often arrange for one when confirming your tickets. Even once you've put in your order, however, plan to take along a substantial stash of snacks. When flights are delayed or special orders go astray (neither unheard of these days), long waits between meals can make baby, and everyone else in the vicinity, miserable.

Some airlines, particularly on overseas flights, offer baby foods, bottles, nappies and 'sky-cots'. Ask about these when you make your reservations.

Arrange for suitable seating. If you're travelling by air, try to reserve bulkhead seats, which will give you extra room to move around and allow baby to sleep or play at your feet. If they're not available, request seats on the aisle – you may spend a lot of time pacing up and down it. Whatever you do, don't accept seats in the middle of a wide centre section, not just for your sake, but for the sake of those seated around you.

When reserving, also ask if it's possible to get a seat with an empty next to it – at least unless and until the plane is fully booked.

Though you can, and should, reserve space on many trains, you can't always reserve specific seats. But you can reserve sleeper compartments on some long-distance runs. Such compartments give you a measure of privacy, something you may really appreciate when spending long hours or days on a train with a baby.

Book in advance. You may assume that when travelling by road in off-peak seasons, hotel reservations won't be necessary. But many roadside establishments, especially those with lower rates, hang out 'no vacancy' signs nightly. So plan ahead where you will be stopping overnight, allowing more time to get there than you could ever possibly imagine needing, and reserve a room with a cot.

Choose a helpful hostelry. Whenever possible, look for a hotel that caters to the needs of families; many do not. One clue to what you can expect is whether or not cots (or cribs as they're called in the USA and Canada) and baby-sitters are available. You will probably have an uncomfortable stay at a hotel without such amenities. And you will probably feel unwelcome, too.

Equip yourself. Getting around, especially if you're travelling without another adult or with more than one child, will be easier if you have the right equipment:

- A baby sling, if baby is small. It will free your hands to juggle luggage – important when boarding and disembarking.

- A lightweight and very compact umbrella pushchair, for an older baby. You can hang totes from the handles, but be careful not to let the pushchair tip backwards.

- A wrist-to-wrist 'leash', for an active toddler. This may seem barbaric, but may be the only way to keep your child in tow.

- A portable baby seat – a cloth one adds almost no weight to your luggage.

- A car seat. On aeroplanes, if there is an empty seat next to you it can double as a safety seat, or it can be stored overhead.[2] Or if you plan on renting a car at your destination, you can rent a car seat with it – but be sure to reserve the seat at the time you reserve the car.

You can also rent or borrow other equipment, such as cots, playpens, high chairs and feeding seats, at the other end. Try to make these arrangements in advance.

Don't rock the boat before you set sail. To avoid unnecessary problems on your trip, avoid unnecessary changes just before it. Don't try weaning your baby, for instance, just prior to departure – the unfamiliar surroundings and changes in routine will be hard enough to deal with without adding other stresses. Besides, no other way of feeding baby on the road is as easy for you or as comforting for baby as breastfeeding. Don't introduce solids close to departure, either – beginning to spoonfeed is enough of a challenge (for both of you) at home. If your baby is ready for finger foods, however, consider introducing them a few weeks in advance. Portable nibbles are great for keeping babies occupied and happy en route.

If your baby isn't sleeping through the night, now is not the time to try to remedy the situation. There's likely to be some regression into night waking during a trip (and for a while, upon return), and letting baby cry it out in a hotel room or at grandmother's will enhance neither your holiday nor your welcome.

Don't be defensive or diffident. If you're met with less than total cooperation when

making your advance requests, keep your cool. Avoid becoming demanding or unpleasant yourself, but don't buckle under unnecessarily, either. The mixed reviews you get on these calls will continue throughout your trip: some flight attendants and hotel managers won't be able to do enough for you, others won't look your way except to glare.

Confirm. The day before your departure, confirm all your reservations if they haven't already been confirmed, and call to check departure times before leaving home. You don't want to arrive at the airport to find your flight's been cancelled or delayed four hours. Or at the train station to find the train is going to be late.

Packing Wisely

While virtually everything, including the kitchen sink (for rinsing off dropped bottles and dousing stains), might come in handy on your trip, packing it all would obviously not be advisable. Neither, however, would be starting out perilously underpacked. Instead, strive for a happy (albeit heavy) medium, taking only what you absolutely need, being as efficient as possible in your selection: sample sizes of liquid baby soap, paracetamol, toothpaste and the like; the extra-thin and extra-absorbent variety of disposable nappies; mix-and-match clothes in bright patterns that conceal stains well and thus hold out longer between launderings, and in lightweight fabrics that will dry fast if you need to rinse them out.

You can pack less if you'll be someplace where you can fill in the blanks, particularly if filling them in will be part of the fun – buying a couple of tiny shorts and T-shirt sets in Bermuda, for example, or a bottle of *bébé* shampoo in Paris. But if you'll be hiking in the Dales or camping in Scotland, all that you could conceivably end up needing should end up in your backpack. For the typical trip, you will probably want to pack these bags, filled as follows:

---

2. But be sure the seat is CE approved – the product label will probably so specify.

A changing bag. It should be lightweight, plastic lined, have outside compartments for storing tissues, wipes, bottles and other needed-in-a-hurry items, and a shoulder strap so you won't need to tie up a free hand carrying it. The items you'll want to keep handy in the bag include:

- A light jacket (waterproof nylon with a hood is best, since it doubles as a raincoat) or sweater in case the car, train, plane, or bus is chilly.

- Enough disposable, extra-thin, extra-absorbent nappies for the first leg of your journey, and then some, in case of a delay or an attack of traveller's tummy. Plan on buying nappies as you go rather than carrying packs with you from home, unless you're travelling by car and have the room, or unless you won't be able to purchase them at your destination.

- Wipes for your hands (and baby's) as well as the obvious. They can also serve to sanitize the arm of the plane seat that baby seems intent on chewing or the train window that he or she is set on licking clean and to outsmart spills on clothing or upholstery before they become stains.

- Nappy rash ointment, since unfamiliar foods, infrequent nappy changes and warm weather can all prompt an outbreak of nappy rash.

- A large waterproof bib, or a pack of disposable ones, to protect clothing. Just in case you accidentally leave the plastic bib in a restaurant or run out of throwaways, bring along a saftety pin or a nappy pin with which to fasten a restaurant napkin over baby's clothes.

- Some reclosable plastic bags to hold leaky bottles, dirty bibs or clothing and soiled nappies when a rubbish bin isn't immediately available.

- Sunscreen, if your destination will be sunny or snowy and your baby is six months or older.

- A light blanket or quilt for baby to nap on or play on en route, in restaurants and in homes that you visit. Or take along a shawl you can wear on your shoulders and use for baby when necessary.

- A small waterproof lap pad or changing pad to protect hotel beds and other surfaces when baby needs a change.

- A square metre (yard) of clear, heavy-duty plastic to protect hotel furniture and rugs during feedings, and to serve as inobtrusive protection under baby's high chair in restaurants.

- A comfort object, if your baby has one.

- A pair of socks or booties for a barefoot baby, in case you run into some heavy air-conditioning.

- Plastic outlet covers if your baby is a crawler or walker, to babyproof hotel rooms or homes you're visiting. You may also want to take a toilet lock if your baby is into water play.

- A generous supply of snacks and beverages. Don't rely on being able to find appropriate food for your baby on the road, in the air, or on the rails. Bring along enough food and drink for one or two more meals than you anticipate feeding, just in case. Depending on baby's culinary repertoire, take along baby food (dehydrated, if you must travel light); whole-grain crackers; small containers of bite-size dry cereal for nibbling; a small container of wheat germ for enriching white breads, cereals, pastas and rices; ready-to-use formula for the bottle baby in disposable bottles (preferably of light and unbreakable plastic); juice in a small bottle or thermos with a cup with a lid or small paper cups for cup-drinkers. Carry the small baby food jars to provide variety and avoid waste.

- A dozen plastic spoons in a plastic bag, for feeding baby en route. If there are no facilities for washing them, they can be dumped.

- Paper towels, unrolled, which are more practical, stronger and more absorbent than napkins.

- Something old and something new to entertain your baby – the old for comfort and reliability; the new for excitement and challenge. A small activity board and a brightly illustrated board book are good choices for an older baby; a mirror, rattle and a musical stuffed animal for a younger one. Leave home toys with a lot of pieces that can get lost or which are too bulky for easy packing and use in tight spaces. For a teether, be sure to take a couple of items to gnaw on.

- A small wallet. Since you have a limited number of hands, carrying a separate handbag will be virtually impossible as well as a little risky (you'll most likely look distracted and disorganized enough to qualify as easy prey for a pickpocket). Instead, keep personal items, plane, train, or bus tickets, and your wallet, with money, credit cards and copies of medication prescriptions, as well as baby's doctor's phone number and the names of recommended doctors at your destination, in a small, easy-to-identify-by-feel wallet in the changing bag. Or, as an alternative, keep your wallet handy in your pocket (if all of your travel outfits have safely deep pockets, you'll find life much easier).

A bag for baby's clothing. Ideal for baby's travel wardrobe is a small, lightweight, soft-sided carry-on with a shoulder or backpack strap. Since it can be kept handy in car, plane, or train, you'll be able to get at a fresh outfit without any fuss and without rummaging through your own suitcase in public. If you choose to pack baby's clothes in your suitcase, however, and that bag won't be available while you're travelling (because it's going to be either checked through on the plane, train, or bus, or buried in the car trunk), make sure you keep an extra outfit or two for baby in the changing bag.

A medical and toiletry bag. This bag should be inaccessible to a curious baby at all times (in overhead compartments on trains and planes, for example), and should preferably have a lock or be difficult to open. Ideally, it should also be waterproof and easy to clean, and again, a shoulder strap is a plus. Keep this bag with you as you go so that medications will be available, if needed, and to protect liquids from damage by freezing in the cargo compartment of planes. It can contain:

- Any prescription medicines and vitamins to last your trip; baby paracetamol; an anti-emetic for vomiting; an antiperistaltic for diarrhoea (Lomotil is not recommended for children under two); a decongestant, if recommended by the doctor.

- All medical insurance information.

- For outdoor trips, insect repellent, yellow soap for poison ivy, calamine lotion, bugbite medicine and a bee-sting kit if baby is allergic.

- A first-aid kit containing syrup of ipecac for accidental poisoning (but do not administer it without medical advice); bandaids and self-adhesive gauze pads; antibacterial cream (such as Neosporin); elastic bandages for sprains; thermometer; tweezers; baby nail clipper.

- Liquid baby soap, which serves as a cleanser for both hair and skin. The soaps found in hotel rooms aren't usually gentle enough for babies.

- Baby's toothbrush, or gauze pads for tooth wiping if teeth are in.

- Multi-purpose pocketknife, with can opener and scissors.

- A night light, if your baby likes to sleep with one.

Getting There is Half the Fun

Whether you will be going by land, air, or rail, there are several ways of making your trip easier.

If you're flying. Planes have the advantage for family travel of usually being the fastest commercial way of getting from one point to another. You can make a flying trip pleasant (at least relatively so) as well as comfortable, if you:

- Arrive early enough to take care of preboarding details like luggage and seats, but not so early that you have an uncomfortably long wait in the air terminal.

- Request bulkhead seats, if you didn't reserve them. If they aren't available, try to arrange a switch after boarding.

- Preboarding is an advantage offered to those travelling with children, allowing them to settle in and stow luggage in overhead compartments before the rush. However, if you have a baby who you expect will be fidgety in close quarters (remember, you won't be able to walk the aisles while they're being used for boarding), you may want to wait and board last. If you're travelling with another adult, ask if one of you can preboard with the luggage while the other spends some extra time with baby in the open spaces of the waiting area.

- Coordinate feedings with takeoff and landing. Children (especially babies) are even more prone than adults to the ear pressure, and sometimes pain, caused by cabin air pressure changes during ascent and descent. Nursing or bottle feeding at these times (or giving finger foods or a dummy) encourages frequent swallowing, which helps prevent the painful pressure buildup and the fussing and crying that usually accompany it.

- If your baby does do a lot of loud complaining, accept a kind hand from friendly fellow passengers if offered, and disregard those who are ignorant and uncompassionate enough to give you dirty looks.

- Give your baby a lot to drink during the flight; air travel is dehydrating. If you're nursing, be sure you, too, take extra fluids – but remember, beverages with caffeine or alcohol don't count.

- If your baby demands warmed feedings, ask flight attendants to warm bottles and baby food for you (without their tops). But remember to shake or stir thoroughly and to carefully double-check the temperature before serving to prevent scalding accidents, since microwaves can heat unevenly.

- If you're travelling alone, feel free to ask an attendant to hold baby while you use the lavatory.

- Deplane last, to avoid the squeeze and to be sure you have time to gather up all your belongings. (Let anyone who is meeting you know that you will be last off the plane.)

High Altitudes

If you're heading to an area high above sea level, there are certain precautions that need to be taken. Because the sun's rays are more intense at higher altitudes, you need to be particularly conscientious about using sunscreens and limiting sun exposure. And because fluid requirements are increased, your baby will need several additional millilitres/fl ounces of fruit juice or water daily while you remain at the higher altitude. In a baby who is anaemic, the reduced level of oxygen in the air may increase heart and respiratory rates and cause fatigue. This is nothing to be concerned about unless your baby has an infection or other medical condition, such as a heart ailment – in which case you should consult the doctor before making the trip. But do schedule frequent rest stops.

If you're going by train. Travelling by train, though slower than by plane, allows children a little more mobility. Your family train trip will be easier if you remember to:

- Ask a conductor to direct you to a non-smoking car, if appropriate.

- Board as early as possible to find a plum seat. If a wheelchair-bound passenger (who has first call) is not positioned in front of the first seat in a car, that's a good one for a family to take because of the open space in front of it where baby can nap or play. Also a good choice is a four-seater unit with a table, which allows families to spread out comfortably. If you have only one seat, it's a toss-up whether to favour the window seat (so baby can watch the scenery go by) or the aisle (so you can get up frequently for walks if baby is fidgety).

- Be sure to have a baby sling if you're travelling alone and baby can still ride in one; without it you may find it impossible to go to the lavatory. (Don't park your baby even briefly with anyone, no matter how friendly, particularly as the train nears a stop.)

- Accept help with the baggage when you board or detrain, if anyone offers, but don't let someone you don't know carry baby.

- If your train ride will be a long one, have a varied collection of toys so you can pull out a new one when your baby tires of the old. Or do some sightseeing. Looking out the window, pointing out cars, horses, cows, dogs, people, houses, sky, clouds, is an onboard activity that has saved many a mum at the bottom of her bag of tricks.

- Be sure to have plenty of snacks on hand. Lines for food on trains are often long and it would not be unusual to finally reach the counter only to find that the tuna sandwich you were counting on was sold out.

If you're driving. Driving is slower than other forms of transport, more taxing on you if you're the driver, and most confining to baby. But it does give you the luxury of going at your own pace, stopping when and where you'd like, and having ready transport at your destination. Make family car travel safer, more pleasant and more comfortable in these ways:

- Be sure that there are seat belts for all adults and older children, car seats for younger ones, and that the car never moves until all are safely secured and all doors locked. In hot weather, cover vinyl-seated car seats with soft cloths, towels, or mock lamb's wool. A rolled-up towel or a store-bought headrest will keep a young baby's head from slipping down in the car seat; a blanket folded under the thighs will increase comfort and endurance.

- Take frequent breaks (every two hours or so is ideal), since babies become restless sitting in car seats for very long stretches. When you do stop, take baby out for some fresh air, and if he or she's mobile, a crawl or walk. Use rest stops for nursing, too.

- Alternate roles. For a change of pace and companionship for everyone, alternate driving with sitting in the back entertaining baby.

- Attach playthings to baby's car seat with plastic links (or strings no longer than 13 cm/5 inches) so that you won't have to unbelt repeatedly to retrieve tossed toys.

- If you're driving in cold weather, especially if a storm is predicted, bring along extra clothing and blankets in case you get stranded. A car can quickly turn into a deadly icebox in subfreezing temperatures.

- Never leave a baby in a parked car in hot or very warm weather. Even with the windows open, the car can rapidly become a deadly oven.

At Hotels or Other Homes away from Home

The first overnighter away from home with your baby can be a little unnerving. But you can survive it if you take the following precautions:

- Upon arrival at your destination, do a safety check of the room you'll be staying in – especially if your baby is mobile. Check the cot to be sure slats are no more than 11 cm (4⅜ inches) apart. If they are, take baby to bed with you. Be sure open windows, electrical cords, glasses and so on aren't accessible. Cap exposed outlets.

- If you put baby on the bed for a nappy change or play, use a waterproof pad – to protect the bed from baby and baby from a possibly unsanitary bedspread.

- When you're feeding baby in the room, spread newspaper or a plastic square on the floor to protect carpeting – for courtesy's sake and so you won't be stuck for damages.

- Don't confine an active baby. Crawling under your supervision is okay unless the carpet is visibly dirty; exploratory toddling is fine, too, but again under a watchful adult eye.

- Arrange for baby-sitters through the hotel. Meet them at the bell captain's or concierge's desk, so you'll be sure you've got the right person.

Restaurant Survival

At one time babies were rarely seen in public eating places. Today, many babies spend as much time in restaurants as at the playground. If yours hasn't yet had the pleasure, however, the following tips should make restaurant hopping easier on your trip or anytime:

- Plan on eating early and quickly. When you're eating out with baby, you'll have to dine on baby's schedule not yours – even if that means being the earliest bird to catch the Early Bird Special. Choose fairly fast-paced eateries, too, so that baby will spend more time eating than waiting. And when your baby is finished eating, it's probably time to leave. Lingering over dessert and coffee is a pleasure of the past for most parents of young children.

- Call ahead to make sure the restaurant is equipped with high chairs or baby dining seats (a booster seat won't do until after baby's a year old), unless you plan to bring a portable one. The reception you get when you call, as well as whether or not such seating is available, will give you some indication of how welcome your baby will be.

- Request a table in the back or in a quiet corner of the restaurant, where your group is least likely to offend other diners or get in the way of restaurant personnel. It will also give you more privacy if you have to spend part of the dinner hour nursing. (Be discreet.)

- Bring along a bib and, in case the restaurant is carpeted, that square of clear plastic to spread on the carpet under baby's chair.

- Bring along some toys and books for diversion between courses or when baby's finished eating. Don't take them out, however, until they're needed, and then one at a time so they won't lose their novelty before the first course arrives. Baby will probably be content to play with a spoon, flirt with a waiter and point at the light fixtures for the first few minutes.

- Bring along some snacks (particularly finger foods that keep baby occupied) in case the food's a long time in coming or there's nothing that baby can or will eat. Again, keep these in reserve until they're needed. If your baby isn't on table foods yet, bring a jar or two of baby food and serve it up while the adults are waiting for their meal.

- Never let a child walk or crawl around a restaurant. Such exploration could result in serious injury and damage should a waiter bearing a heavy tray of food or drink, hot or cold, be tripped up.

- Order promptly and ask that baby's food be brought as soon as possible. If you're with your spouse or another adult, one of you can order while the other keeps baby busy out of doors or in the lobby until some food arrives.

- If you don't see it on the menu, ask for it. Most restaurants have a full supply of staples in the kitchen from which you can choose a meal for baby. Good choices include: cottage cheese, whole-meal bread, cheese, hamburger (not ordered rare, because of the danger of bacteria in undercooked meat), roast or grilled chicken, soft fish (check carefully for bones), mashed or boiled potato, peas (mash them), well-cooked carrots and string beans, pasta, melon.

- In areas where the safety of the water is questionable and sanitation a problem, avoid tap water (use carbonated bottled water and bottled juice for baby), raw vegetables, ice, dairy products that are not pasteurized and/or refrigerated, and restaurants where flies flit about and glasses look grimy.

- Be sensitive to other diners. If your baby is crying loudly or otherwise disturbing people around you, it's time for a stroll.

- You may find that occasionally you and your travelling companion (if you're lucky enough to have one) have to alternate shifts, eating and walking.

Having Fun

Be realistic about the itinerary. You just won't be able to keep up the same pace with a baby in tow as you would on a trip for adults only. Overschedule, and you'll end up underenjoying.

- Be flexible about the itinerary. If you'd planned to drive straight through from Calais to Nice, but baby's had it with the car seat by Paris, consider adding an overnight stop. If you've scheduled two days of sightseeing in Athens, but baby's crankiness is ruining the ruins for all of you by the first morning, postpone the Parthenon until another day or, perhaps, another trip.

- Stick to sites where baby won't be confined or required to be silent for long periods of time. Outdoor ruins, parks, zoos, and even some museums can be interesting to babies and young children – even if they spend most of their time just looking at other people. Hire a baby-sitter, if possible, when you want to go to the opera, a concert or the theatre.

- Remember whose needs must come first – if anyone's going to have a good time. If baby doesn't nap or eat on time, or is repeatedly subjected to uncustomarily late bedtimes, everyone will suffer the consequences. Do what the Romans do, by all means, but only if your baby can adjust easily.

SEVENTEEN

When Baby Is Ill

◆

There's nothing quite as pathetic, vulnerable and helpless-looking as an ill baby. With the exception of a sick baby's parents.

An infant's illness, even a mild one, usually hits mummy and daddy harder than baby, especially when it's a first illness in a first child. There's the anxiety when the initial symptoms appear, the alarm when they seem to worsen or others develop, the indecision over whether or not to call the doctor and when (children almost invariably get sick in the middle of the night or on weekends, outside of the usual surgery hours), the pacing while waiting for the doctor's call back (interminable even if it's only fifteen minutes), the ordeal of administering medicine and the worry, worry, worry.

Believe it or not, things do get better. With experience, parents learn to handle a feverish infant or a vomiting toddler with less panic and more self-assurance. To reach that point more quickly, it will help to learn how to evaluate symptoms, how to take and interpret a baby's temperature, what to feed a sick child, what the most common childhood illnesses are, and how to recognize and handle a real emergency

Before Calling the Doctor

Most baby doctors want to hear from you – no matter what the time of day or night – if you think your baby is really sick. But before you dial that probably already familiar number, be sure you're armed with a written list of all the information your baby's doctor might need to know in order to accurately assess the situation. To be an effective partner in your baby's health care, you should be ready and able to provide any or all of the following information should it prove pertinent. In most simple illnesses, only two or three symptoms will be present, but running down the list will ensure you haven't missed anything. Be prepared to tell the doctor when symptoms first appeared; what, if anything, triggered them; what exacerbates or alleviates them (sitting up reduces the coughing, for example, or eating increases vomiting); and which home remedies or over-the-counter medications you've tried treating them with. It will also be helpful to let the doctor know if your baby has been exposed to a cousin with chicken pox, a sibling with diarrhoea, or anyone else with a communicable illness, or if he or she has recently been injured, as in a fall. And remind the doctor of baby's age and any chronic medical problems.

Have handy the name and phone number of an open chemist, in case the doctor needs to phone in a prescription, and a pad and pencil for jotting down any instructions you receive.

Temperature. First test for temperature with your lips on your baby's forehead. If it feels warm to the touch, get a more accurate reading with a thermometer (see page 421). Remember that in addition to illness, readings can be affected by such factors as room or air temperature (a baby's temperature is likely to be higher after playing in an overheated house than after coming in on a snowy day); level of activity (exercise, energetic play and vigorous crying can all raise temperature); and time of day (temperatures tend to be higher later in the day). If baby's forehead is cool, assume there's no significant fever.

Heart rate. In some cases, knowing what your baby's heart rate is may be useful to the doctor. If your baby seems very lethargic or has a fever, take the upper arm (or brachial) pulse as shown above. The normal range in infants is between 100 and 130 beats per minute during sleep, 140 to 160 when awake and 160 to 200 while crying. The heart rate gets progressively slower as a child gets older and by age two is usually between 100 and 140.

Respiration. If your baby has difficulty breathing, is coughing, or seems to be breathing rapidly or irregularly, check respirations by counting how many times in a minute his or her chest rises and falls. Breathing is more rapid during activity (including crying) than during sleep, and may be speeded up or slowed down by illness. Newborns normally take about 40 to 60 breaths per minute; one-year-olds only 25 to 35. If your baby's chest doesn't seem to rise and fall with each breath, or if breathing appears laboured or raspy (unrelated to a stuffy nose), report that information to the doctor, too.

Respiratory symptoms. Is your baby's nose runny? Stuffy? Is the discharge watery or thick? Clear, white, yellow, or green? Is there a cough? Does it seem dry, hacking, heavy, crowing? Does the cough bring up any mucus? (Sometimes mucus will be vomited up with a forceful cough.)

Behaviour. Is there any change from the norm in your baby's behaviour? Would you describe your child as tired and lethargic, cranky and irritable, inconsolable or unresponsive? Can you elicit a smile?

Sleeping. Is baby sleeping much more than usual, or seeming to be unusually drowsy? Or is he or she having trouble sleeping?

Crying. Is baby crying more than usual?

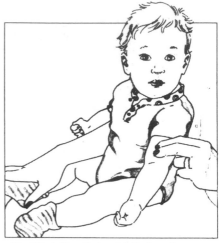

Practice taking the brachial pulse when your baby is healthy and calm.

Does the cry have a different sound or intensity – is it high pitched, for instance?

Appetite. Is baby eating as usual? Refusing the bottle or breast and/or turning down solids? Or eating everything in sight?

Skin. Does baby's skin appear different in any way? Is it red and flushed? White and pale? Bluish or grey? Is it moist and warm (sweaty) or moist and cool (clammy)? Or unusually dry? Are lips, nostrils, or cheeks excessively dry or cracking? Are there spots or lesions anywhere on baby's skin – under the arms, behind the ears, on limbs or trunk, or elsewhere? How would you describe their colour, shape, size, texture? Does baby seem to be trying to scratch them?

Mouth. Is there swelling on the gums where teeth might be trying to break through? Any red or white spots or patches visible on the gums, inside the cheeks, or on the palate or tongue?

Throat. Is the arch framing the throat reddened? Are there white or red spots or patches?

Fontanel. If the soft spot on top of your baby's head is still open, is it either sunken or bulging?

Eyes. Do baby's eyes look different than usual? Are they glassy, vacant, sunken, dull, watery, or reddened? Do they have dark circles under them, or seem partially closed? If there is a discharge, how would you describe colour, consistency and quantity?

Ears. Is baby pulling or poking at one or both ears? Is there a discharge from either ear?

Lymph glands. Do the lymph glands in the neck appear swollen?

Digestive system. Has baby been vomiting? How often? Is there a lot of material being vomited, or are baby's heaves mostly dry? How would you describe the vomitus (like curdled milk, mucus-streaked, pinkish, bloody?) Is the vomiting forcible? Does it seem to project a long distance? Does anything seem to trigger the vomiting – eating for example? Has there been any change in baby's bowel movements? Is there diarrhoea with loose, watery mucus, or bloody stools? Are movements more frequent, sudden and forceful? Or does baby seem constipated? Is there an increase or decrease in saliva? Or any apparent difficulty swallowing?

Urinary system. Are baby's nappies less wet than usual? Or do they seem wetter? Is there any noticeable change in odour or colour (dark yellow, for example, or pink)?

Abdomen. Does your baby's tummy seem different in any way – flatter, rounder, more bulging? When you press it gently, or when you bend either knee to the abdomen, does baby seem to be in pain? Where does the pain seem to be – right side or left, upper or lower abdomen?

Motor symptoms. Has your baby had, or is he or she having, chills, trembling, stiffness, or convulsions? Does the neck seem to be stiff or difficult to move – can the chin be bent to the chest? Does there seem to be any difficulty in moving any other part of the body?

How Much Rest for an Ill Baby?

In spite of well-meant advice you may get to the contrary from grandmothers, great-aunts and neighbours a sick baby needn't be confined to the cot or 'kept quiet'. You can trust your baby to listen to his or her own body and to comply with its commands. A very sick infant will relinquish the usual daily pursuits in favour of needed rest, whereas one who is just mildly ill or on the way to

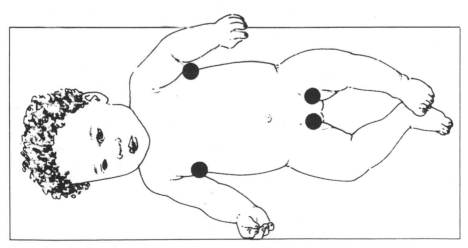

Lymph glands (locations are circled) are part of the immune system. Enlargement anywhere in the body may signal infection and should be reported to the doctor.

Mother's Intuition

Sometimes you can't put your finger on any specific symptom, but your baby just doesn't seem 'right' to you. Put a call in to the doctor. Most likely you'll be reassured, but it's also possible that you will have picked up something subtle that needs treatment.

recovery will be active and playful. In either case, there's no need to impose restrictions of your own. Just follow baby's lead. (If anyone does need a rest when a baby's sick, it's mother.)

Feeding an Ill Baby

Loss of appetite often accompanies illness. Sometimes, as in the case of digestive upsets, this is good since not eating gives the stomach and intestines a needed rest while they recover. Sometimes, as when there's a fever, it's not so good since the additional calories needed to fuel the fever that fights the infection may be lacking.

For most minor illnesses that don't affect the digestive system, no special diet is necessary except as noted under specific illnesses. But several general rules apply when feeding any sick baby:

Stress fluids. If your baby has a fever, a respiratory infection (such as a cold, influenza, or bronchitis), or a gastrointestinal illness with diarrhoea, clear fluids and foods with high water contents (juices, juicy fruits, soups, Best-Odds gels and frozen-juice desserts) or rehydration fluids (if necessary) will help prevent dehydration and should take precedence over solids. Offer them frequently throughout the day, even if baby takes no more than a sip at a time. Babies on formula or breast milk should suckle as often as they like, unless the doctor recommends otherwise.

Emphasize quality. Though the temptation may be to let your baby eat anything he or she will take – even if it isn't very nutritious and is loaded with sugar or salt – don't. Foods that offer little but calories are likely to sabotage your child's appetite for anything worthwhile. Since a child (like an adult) needs a lot of vitamins and minerals to help the immune system fight back, you should be sure that the little your baby is eating goes a long way nutritionally. (When digestive disorders limit dietary intake, see page 415). And continue baby's vitamin supplement, too, unless the doctor tells you otherwise.

Play favourites. Although you don't want a sick baby to subsist on a diet of junk foods, it's okay – if baby's appetite is ailing and diet isn't restricted – to allow carte blanche with healthy favourite foods. If that means nothing but formula or breast milk and bananas for four days (or cereal three times a day, or Pumpkin Muffins, orange juice and milk exclusively), that's okay. Try also, to stimulate an interest in eating in an older baby with 'fun' foods that look as good as they taste, such as Pancake Faces or Cottage Cheese Sundaes (all these recipes can be found in the Ready Reference).

Don't force. Even if your baby hasn't taken a bite in 24 hours, don't force. Forcing could set up a feeding problem baby might not recover from as spontaneously as he or she will from the illness. And don't worry if a few days of semi-starvation have your baby looking gaunt; babies tend to make up for lost meals after an illness, eating ravenously until lost weight is regained. Do let the doctor know about this loss of appetite.

When Medication is Needed

Sometime during the first year, it is very likely that medication will be recommended or prescribed for your baby. Starting with the very first time, make it a habit to ask the right questions about the medication and then to use it correctly.

WHAT YOU SHOULD KNOW ABOUT THE MEDICATION

Either the doctor or the chemist will be able to answer the following questions. Be sure to jot down the responses in a note-book (or better still, in a permanent 'health history') so you will have a record for ready reference now and in the future. Don't rely on your memory.

- What is the generic name of the drug? the brand name, if any?
- What is it supposed to do?
- What is the appropriate dose for your baby? (Be ready with your baby's approximate weight so that, if necessary, the doctor can calculate the dose accordingly.)
- How often should the medication be given; should baby be awakened in the middle of the night for it?
- Should it be taken before, with, or after meals?
- Should it be washed down only with certain liquids and not with others?
- What common side effects may be expected?
- What possible adverse reactions could occur? Which should be reported to the doctor? (Remind the doctor of previous reactions.)
- If your child has a chronic medical condition, might the drug have an undesirable effect on it? (Be sure to remind the prescribing doctor of the condition, since he or she may not have your baby's chart in hand.)
- If your child is taking any other medication, could there be any adverse interaction?
- How soon can you expect to see an improvement?

- When should you contact the doctor if there is no improvement?
- When can the medication be discontinued?

GIVING MEDICATION CORRECTLY

Medicines are meant to cure, but when used improperly, they often do more harm than good. Always observe these rules when giving medication:

- Don't give a baby under three months of age any medication not prescribed for him or her by a doctor, not even an over-the-counter one. Since infants tend to keep drugs in their systems longer than older children or adults, they can quickly build up to an overdose level.
- Always make sure the medicine you're giving your child is fresh. Don't use a drug if its expiration date has passed, or if it has changed in texture, colour, or odour. Pour expired medicines down the toilet.
- Measure medications meticulously according to the directions the baby's doctor has given you, or according to label directions on over-the-counter products. Use a calibrated spoon, dropper, or cup (all are usually available from your chemist) to get precise measurements (kitchen spoons are variable). To prevent spillage when using a calibrated spoon, pour the measured amount into a larger spoon before administering.
- Keep a record of the time each dose is given (tape a sheet of paper on the refrigerator or over the changing table, or use your baby record book) so you will always know when you gave the last dose. This will minimize the risk of missing a dose or doubling up accidentally. But don't worry about being a little late with a dose; get back on schedule with the next dose.
- Check the bottle label for care and storage directions and follow them. Some medicines need to be stored in the re-

frigerator or at cool temperatures and some must be shaken before use.

● If directions on the label conflict with the doctor's instructions and/or those received from the chemist, call the chemist or doctor to resolve the conflict *before* giving the medication.

● Always read the label before giving a medication, even when you're sure you have the right bottle. When administering medicine in the dark, check the label in the light first.

● Don't give medicines prescribed for someone else (even a sibling) to your baby without the doctor's approval. Don't even use a medicine previously prescribed for your baby without the doctor's okay.

● Don't administer medication to a baby who is lying down; this could cause choking.

● Always give antibiotics for the prescribed length of time, unless the doctor advises otherwise, even if your baby seems completely recovered.

● If your baby is having an adverse reaction to a medication, stop it temporarily and check with the doctor before resuming use.

● Don't continue giving a medicine beyond the time specified by the doctor; don't start giving one again after discontinuing it without checking with the doctor first.

● Record any medication you give your baby, the illness it was given for, the length of time it was taken, and any side or adverse effects in your baby's health history for future reference (see page 417).

HELPING THE MEDICINE GO DOWN

Learning how to give medication correctly is only the first step for parents, and usually the easiest. As far as many children are concerned, the cure is almost always worse than the disease; getting the medicine to go down often seems a hopeless task. And even when it does go down, it often comes right back up – all over baby, parent, furniture and floor.

If you're lucky, your baby will be one of those who actually delights in the medicine-giving ritual and even in the taste of strange liquids – whether they are vitamins, antibiotics, or pain relievers – and who opens up like a little sparrow at the first sight of a medicine dropper. If you're not so lucky, you've got an infant who is staunchly resistant, either from the start or after becoming wiser in the ways of resistance with advancing age. There is probably nothing that will make administering medicine to such a baby a pleasure, but these tips will help get more medicine down with less trouble:

● Chill the medication if this won't affect its potency (ask your pharmacist); the taste may be less pronounced when it's cold.

● Use a spoon that is gently rounded rather than deep, so it can more easily be wiped clean by baby. (If it doesn't come clean during the first pass, turn it over and pull it back over baby's tongue to clean off the dregs.) If your baby doesn't take kindly to a spoon, and a dropper isn't large enough for the prescribed dose, ask the pharmacist for a medicine spoon or plastic syringe, which will allow you to squirt the medicine deep into baby's mouth; but don't squirt more than a baby can swallow at one time. If your baby rejects medication from a dropper, spoon, or syringe and likes a teat instead, try putting the dose in a hand-held nursing-bottle teat so baby can suck it out. Follow this with water from the same teat so any medication remaining in the teat can be taken.

● Aim a spoon towards the back of the mouth, a dropper or syringe between molars or rear gum and cheek, since the taste buds are concentrated front and centre on the tongue. But avoid letting the dropper or spoon touch the back of the tongue, where it could set off a gagging reflex.

Use a medicine spoon or dropper to ease medications into baby's mouth.

- Unless you're instructed to give the medication with or after meals, plan on serving it up just before feeding. First because baby is more likely to accept it when hungry, and second because if baby does vomit it right back up, less food will be lost.

- Enlist help when you can. Holding a wriggly, uncooperative baby while trying to bring a spoon filled to the brim with medicine to an unwilling mouth without spilling would be a challenge even for a mother octopus, and can sometimes be next to impossible for the two-armed

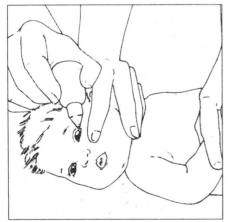

Keeping baby's head steady when using eye drops will help ensure that at least some of the medicine will hit its mark.

mum. If dad (or another assistant) isn't around to hold baby, try using an infant seat or a high chair as your extra pair of hands; but be sure to strap your baby in before you begin. If you have to go it alone with no seat to hold baby, try this procedure with a young medicine resister. First, premeasure the medicine and have it ready to use on a table within reach in a dropper, syringe, medicine cup, or spoon (which shouldn't be filled to the brim). Sit in a straight chair and position baby on your lap, facing forward. Put your left arm across baby's body, holding his or her arms securely. Take hold of his or her jaw with your left hand, your thumb on one cheek, your index finger on the other. Tilt baby's head backwards slightly and depress cheeks gently to open the mouth. With your right hand (reverse hands if you're left-handed), administer the medicine. Keep baby's cheeks slightly depressed until the medicine is swallowed. This entire procedure should take only a few seconds; longer and your baby will begin to fight being held down.

- Approach your baby confidently with medicine – even if past experience has taught you to expect the worst. If baby knows you're anticipating a battle, you're sure to get one. You may get one anyway, of course, but a confident approach could swing the odds in your favour.

- As a last resort, mix the medication with a small amount (1 or 2 teaspoons) of strained fruit or fruit juice – but only if the doctor hasn't ruled out such a mix. But don't dilute the medicine in a larger quantity of food or juice since then your baby may not finish it all. Unless your baby is generally tentative about new foods, use an unfamiliar fruit or juice for mixing since the medicine may impart an unpleasant taste to a familiar one, causing baby to reject it in the future.

- Paracetamol that comes in 'sprinkle caps' is tasteless and can be emptied into a spoonful of juice or fruit to make giving this medicine much easier.

The Chicken Soup Cure

It turns out that old wives (and old grandmothers) weren't telling tales when they claimed their chicken soup was as curative as anything their sons the doctors could prescribe. Medical research backs up what the apron set has told us all along: a bowl of hot chicken soup, besides making us feel loved, can help combat the symptoms of colds, coughs and flu. But when dosing your baby with this penicillin-in-a-pot, don't use commercial bouillons and broths from cubes or cans, which are astronomically high in salt and could cause serious chemical imbalances and an overload on the kidneys. Instead, don an apron and put up a pot from scratch, using chicken parts or a chicken or turkey carcass and plenty of parsley, parsnips, carrots, celery, leeks, onions and a couple of garlic cloves. Simmer the brew until the skin falls from the bones, skimming the foam and fat as they appear on top. Strain, and feed to baby at a comfortably warm temperature in a spoon, from a cup, or in a bottle if he or she takes one. (Don't purée the carrots for baby food, unless you're planning to serve them along with the soup they were cooked in, since most of the vitamins have cooked out into the stock.)

The Most Common Infant Health Problems

Infants in their first year of life are generally healthy and most of the illnesses to which they are susceptible are one-time affairs (see the chart starting on page 618 for details on these). But there are some illnesses that are so common, or that tend to recur so frequently in some babies, that parents need to know as much as possible about them. They include allergies, the common cold, constipation, ear infections and gastrointestinal illnesses with diarrhoea and vomiting.

Allergies

Symptoms: Depend on the organ or system inflamed by the hypersensitivity. The following are common body systems affected, and the related symptoms:

- The upper respiratory tract: runny nose (allergic rhinitis), sinusitis (though not in infants), earache (otitis media), sore throat (as much the result of mouth-breathing of dry air as from allergy), postnasal discharge (a dripping of mucus at the back of the nose into the throat that can trigger a chronic cough), spasmodic croup.

- The lower respiratory tract: allergic bronchitis, asthma.

- The digestive tract: watery, sometimes bloody, diarrhoea; vomiting; wind.

- The skin: atopic dermatitis, including such itchy rashes as eczema (see page 220), hives (blotchy, itchy, raised red rash, also called urticaria), and angioneurotic oedema (facial swelling, particularly around eyes and mouth, which is not as itchy as urticaria). When swelling occurs in the throat, breathing can be hampered.

- The eyes: itching, redness, watering and other signs of conjunctivitis.

Season: Any time of year for most allergies; spring, summer, or autumn for those related to pollens.

Cause: The release of histamine and other substances by the immune system in response to exposure to an allergen in persons who are hypersensitive to the allergen or a similar one (the sensitization occurs at an earlier exposure). The tendency towards allergy runs in families. The way allergy is manifested is often different in different members of the family – one has hay fever, another asthma and a third breaks out in hives upon eating strawberries.

Method of transmission: Inhalation (of pollen or animal dander, for example), ingestion (of milk or egg whites), or injection (penicillin shot or insect sting) of the allergen.

Duration: Variable. The duration of a single allergic episode may vary from a few minutes to several hours or several days. Some allergies, such as an allergy to cow's milk, are outgrown; others change, as children get older, from one kind of allergy to another. Many allergic people have allergies of one kind or another all their lives.

Treatment: The most successful treatment for allergy, though also often the most difficult, is to remove the offending allergen

from the sufferer's life. Here are some ways in which you can remove allergens from your child's environment, whether your child is definitely allergic (difficult to determine since skin tests are not very accurate in children under eighteen months) or only possibly so:

- Food allergens. See *Dietary changes.*
- Pollens. If you suspect pollen allergy (the clue is the persistence of symptoms as long as pollen is in the air, and their disappearance when it is gone), keep your child indoors most of the time when the pollen count is high or when it is particularly windy during pollen season (spring, late summer, or autumn, depending on the type of pollen), give daily baths and shampoos (to remove pollen), and use an air-conditioner in warm weather rather than opening the windows and admitting the pollen. If you have a pet, the animal can also pick up

---

Respiratory Sounds you Don't have to Worry About

Somewhere between four and eight weeks of age, many babies develop what might best be described as a 'snurgle'. These are sounds produced as the infant inhales through loose mucus in the nose and throat, which probably is a product of an increased functioning by the mucus-producing glands located in the normal lining of the respiratory tract. Often these sounds are accompanied by a rattling in baby's chest that can be felt with the hand. The snurgle doesn't interfere with breathing and the infants have no problem inhaling with their mouths closed – something they can't do when they have a cold. The condition is more noticeable in babies who have high arched palates or narrower-than-usual nasal passages. This noisy breathing is not a cause for concern and usually disappears within a few weeks as baby matures.

Some babies have a 'gurgle' that is noticeable when they feed and breathe

in. The gurgle originates in or below the larynx, or voice box. It is often associated with tracheomalacia, a condition that is the result of an unusually soft and flexible trachea, common in many infants. There is usually no associated cough, although there may be a liquidy sounding stridor, or vibrating sound. These gurgles may continue well into the second year, but should not interfere with growth and development and require no remedial treatmeat. The condition resolves as the rings of cartilage in the airway become more rigid.

If you note a snurgle or gurgle in your newborn or very young infant, ask the doctor about it. Most likely it is completely normal. If, on the other hand, an older baby suddenly develops strange breathing sounds, call the doctor at once. A raspy noise on breathing out – usually called a wheeze – should also be reported to the doctor.

Treating Baby's Symptoms

Symptom	Appropriate Treatment
Cough	Humidified air*
	Increased fluids*
	Reduction of dairy products, for babies over six months in whom milk seems to increase mucus production
	Cough medication, only if prescribed
	Postural drainage, if recommended and taught to you by the doctor
Croupy cough	Abundant steam*
	A trip out of doors
Diarrhoea	Increased fluids, oral rehydration (see page 414)
	Possible dietary changes (see page 414)
	Antidiarrhoeal medicine, only if prescribed
	Upright position*
Ear pain	Pain reliever, such as paracetamol or aspirin**
	Local dry heat to ear (hot water bottle)
	Decongestant, only if prescribed
	Antibiotics, only if prescribed for infection
	Ear drops, only if prescribed
Fever	Increased fluids (see page 424)
	Adequate calorie intake
	Antipyretic medication, such as paracetamol or aspirin,** only as recommended by the doctor
	Tepid bath or sponging, if medication is inappropriate or ineffective (see page 425)
	Light clothing and cool room temperature (see page 424)
Itching	Calamine lotion (*not* Caladryl or other antihistaminic preparation)
	Comfortably hot bath (test with your elbow or wrist; not for babies under six months)
	Soothing tepid bath*
	Colloidal oatmeal bath

Symptom	Appropriate Treatment
Itching (con't)	Prevention of scratching and infection (keep fingernails short and wash with antibacterial soap; cover hands with socks or mittens during sleep) Pain reliever, such as paracetamol (but *not* aspirin if chicken pox is a possibility)** Oral antihistamine, only if prescribed (but *not* topical antihistamines or anaesthetics)
Nasal congestion	Humidified air* Salt-water irrigation* Nasal aspiration* Head elevation* Increased fluids* Decongestant, only if prescribed Nose drops, only if prescribed
Pain or discomfort from minor injury	Comfort (cuddling) Distraction (see page 434) Pain reliever, such as paracetamol or aspirin** Local heat or cold, as appropriate
Sore throat	Soothing, non-acid foods and beverages Pain reliever, such as paracetamol or aspirin** Fever treatment, if needed (see facing page) Saltwater gargle, for older children
Teething pain	Comfort (cuddling) Local cold, applied to gums (see page 218) Pressure on gums (see page 218) Pain reliever, such as paracetamol or aspirin,** only if recommended by the doctor
Vomiting	Increased fluids, in small sips (see page 414) Restricted diet (see page 414)

* See Ready Reference for practical tips on carrying out this treatment.
**See precautions on page 426 before giving aspirin to an infant or child.

pollen when out of doors, so you should bathe him or her frequently, too. Such allergy is rare in infants.

- Pet dander. Sometimes pets themselves cause an allergy. If this is the case, or might be, try to keep your animal and your baby in different rooms, or keep the animal in the basement, garage, or garden. (In severe cases, the only solution may be to find the pet another home.) Since horsehair can also trigger allergy, don't buy a horsehair mattress for your baby's cot.

- Household dust. These particles fill the air in your home and are breathed in, unseen, by everyone in your family. That's no problem for most people, but for someone with a hypersensitivity to these substances, it can mean misery. Limit your baby's exposure, even if you just suspect this allergy, by keeping the rooms he or she lives in as dust-free as possible. Dust daily with a damp cloth or furniture spray when baby is not in the room; vacuum rugs and upholstered furniture and damp-mop floors often; avoid chenille bedspreads, carpeting, curtains, and other dust catchers where baby sleeps and plays; wash stuffed toys frequently; keep clothing in plastic garment bags; sheathe mattresses and pillows in airtight coverings (infant mattresses usually have airtight covers); put filters over hot-air vents; install an air filter. Any curtains, throw rugs, or other such items you do have should be washed at least twice a month, or packed away. Keep humidity low.

- Moulds. Control moisture in your home by using a well-maintained dehumidifier, providing adequate ventilation, and by exhausting steam in kitchen, laundry, and baths. Areas where moulds are likely to grow (rubbish bins, refrigerators, shower curtains, bathroom tiles, damp corners) should be cleaned meticulously with an anti-mould agent. Houseplants should be limited and firewood should not be stored in the house. Out of doors, be sure drainage around your home is

good, that leaves and other plant debris are not allowed to pile up, and that plenty of sun hits the garden and house to prevent damp areas from spawning mould. Keep baby's sand-pit covered in the rain.

- Bee venom. Anyone allergic to bee venom should avoid outdoor areas known to have bee or wasp populations. Carrying a beesting kit is mandatory for such individuals.

- Miscellaneous allergens. Many other potential allergens can also be removed from your child's world: wool blankets (cover them or use cotton or synthetic blankets); down or feather pillows (use foam or hypoallergenic polyester-filled ones) when baby's old enough to use one; tobacco smoke (no smoking in the house at all, or near baby in other locations); perfumes (use unscented wipes, sprays and so on); soaps (use only hypoallergenic types); detergents (you may have to switch detergents).

Since an allergy is a hypersensitive (or oversensitive) reaction of the immune system to a foreign substance, desensitizing (usually via gradually increased injected doses of the offending allergen) is sometimes successful in eliminating allergies – particularly pollen, dust and animal dander. Except in severe cases, however, desensitization is not usually started until a child is four years old. Antihistamines and steroids may be used to counteract the allergic response and bring down the swelling of mucous membranes in both infants and children.

Dietary changes:

- Elimination of possible dietary allergens, always using nutritionally equivalent substitutes (see The Infant Daily Dozen on page 214). Remove a suspected food allergen (cow's milk, wheat, egg whites, and citrus are among the possibilities) from your baby's diet under medical supervision; if symptoms disappear within a few weeks, you probably have discovered the culprit. You get further confirmation if the symptoms recur when the food is returned to the diet. Substitute oat, rice and barley flours for wheat; soya or hydrolysate formula[1] for cow's milk formula; egg yolks for whole eggs; and mangoes, cantaloupe, broccoli, cauliflower and sweet red peppers for orange juice to ensure vitamin C intake.

- Adequate fluid intake with respiratory allergies. Most nursing and bottle-fed infants get enough fluids, but many weaned babies do not.

Prevention:

- Breastfeeding, particularly when there is a family history of allergies, for at least six months, preferably for a year may help.
- Late introduction of solids, usually not until six months, and then with caution (see page 210). Even later introduction of the most serious offenders (cow's milk, egg whites, wheat, chocolate, citrus). Careful observation for reactions when food is introduced.

Complications:

- Asthma
- Anaphylactic shock, which can be fatal without treatment (but is rare).

When to call the doctor: Soon after you suspect an allergy. Call again whenever your child has new symptoms. Call immediately if there are any signs of asthma (wheezing), difficulty breathing, or signs of shock (disorientation, panting, rapid pulse rate, pale, cold, moist skin, drowsiness, loss of consciousness).

Chance of recurrence: Some allergies disappear in adulthood never to return; others return under different guises.

1. About 40% of babies allergic to cow's milk are also allergic to soya, so hydrolysate formula is usually a safer bet. *Do not* use so-called soya milks, since they do not provide adequate nutrition for infants. If you switch to goat's milk, vitamin supplementation will be needed because goat's milk is deficient in certain nutrients.

Diseases with similar symptoms:

- Bronchitis (but a child who seems to have repeated bouts of this disease probably has bronchial asthma).
- The common cold (like allergic rhinitis).
- Gastrointestinal illnesses (similar to digestive tract symptoms).

The Common Cold or Upper Respiratory Infection (URI)

Colds are very common among babies and young children because they have not had the chance to build up immunities against the many different cold viruses.

Symptoms:

- Runny nose (discharge is watery at first, then thicker and yellowish).
- Sneezing
- Nasal congestion

Sometimes:

- Dry cough, which may be worse when baby is lying down.
- Fever
- Itchy throat
- Fatigue
- Loss of appetite

Season: All year round.

Cause: More than 100 different viruses are known to cause colds.

Method of transmission: Usually spread from hand to hand.

Incubation period: One to four days.

Duration: Usually three to ten days, but in small children colds can linger longer.

Treatment: No known cure, but symptoms can be treated, as necessary:

- Suctioning of mucus with a suction bulb (see page 412). If mucus is hardened,

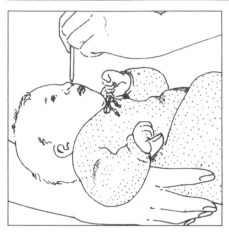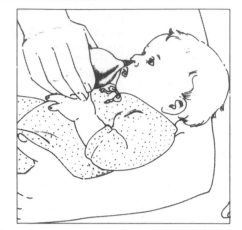

For a baby who's having trouble breathing through a stuffy nose, saline drops (left) to soften the mucus and aspiration (right) to suction it out will bring welcome relief.

before suctioning soften with over-the-counter saline nose drops. This may be necessary to help baby to feed as well as to sleep.

- Humidification (see page 616) to help moisten the air, reduce congestion and make breathing easier for baby.

- Letting baby sleep on belly rather than back, with head elevated (by raising the head of the cot or pram mattress with a couple of pillows or other supports *under* the mattress) to ease breathing.

- Decongestants, if needed to make it easier for baby to eat and sleep, but *only* with the doctor's okay.

- Commercial nose drops, if recommended by the doctor, to ease congestion. But follow directions carefully; use for more than a few days can cause a rebound reaction and make baby feel worse.

- Petroleum jelly (Vaseline) or similar ointment applied lightly to outside of, and under, nose to help prevent chapping and reddening of skin. But be careful to not let it get into the nostrils, where it could be inhaled or block breathing.

- Cough medicine, but only to ease a dry cough that interferes with sleep, and only if it is prescribed by the doctor. A cough

suppressant is not usually prescribed for a baby otherwise. *Antibiotics will not help* and should not be used unless there is bacterial secondary infection.

- Isolation, keeping the baby in the house and away from others for the first three days – which won't hasten recovery but will minimize spreading the cold to others.

Dietary changes: Baby can continue a normal diet (though many have a loss of appetite), with the following exceptions:

- Reduce intake of milk and other dairy products, since it is possible they may thicken secretions; infants exclusively on breast milk or formula can continue on them, unless the doctor advises otherwise.

- Increased intake of fluids to help replace those lost through fever or runny nose. If baby is old enough, drinking from a cup may be more comfortable than trying to nurse or bottle feed with a stuffy nose.

- Adequate intake of vitamin C foods. Whether or not vitamin C will prevent a cold is controversial, but some studies do show it can reduce the severity of symptoms. So including extra citrus or other juices high in vitamin C in your baby's fluid intake is a good idea.

The Sudden Cough

If your baby or young child suddenly begins coughing uncontrollably and does not seem to have a cold or other illness, consider the possibility that an inhaled object could be the cause. See page 447.

Prevention: Careful hand washing for all the family, especially when someone has a cold, and particularly before handling baby or baby's things. Coughs and sneezes should be covered; disposable tissues rather than handkerchiefs should be used; eating utensils and towels should not be shared. If possible, no one with a cold should handle baby's toys or feeding utensils.

Complications: Colds sometimes progress to ear infections or bronchitis, and less often to pneumonia or sinusitis.

When to call the doctor: If this is a first cold; if your baby is under three months old, or under four months and has a fever over 38.3°C (101°F); if the temperature goes up suddenly or a fever continues for more than two days; if a dry cough lasts more than two weeks, is interfering with baby's sleep, causes choking or vomiting, becomes thick and productive or wheezy, or if breathing difficulties develop; if a thick greenish yellow nasal discharge develops and lasts more than a day, or if the discharge is streaked with blood; if there is an unusual amount of crying (with or without tugging at the ears) or a complete loss of appetite; or if baby seems really out of sorts. A cough that lasts more than three weeks in an infant or six in an older baby may require consultation with a specialist.

Chance of recurrence: Since having a cold caused by one virus doesn't make baby immune to a cold caused by another, babies, who haven't had the chance to build up immunities to many viruses, can have one cold right after another.

Diseases with similar symptoms:

- Rubella, chicken pox and German measles begin with cold-like symptoms; check those diseases (see table starting on page 617) for additional symptoms.
- Respiratory allergies
- Influenza

Constipation

This problem is rare in breastfed babies (even if they move their bowels rarely and their movements seem difficult to expel) because their movements are never hard. Constipation does, however, occur in formula-fed infants.

Symptoms:
- Infrequent bowel movements with stools that are hard (often small pellets) and hard to pass; infrequency alone, however, is not a sign of constipation and may be your baby's normal pattern.
- Stool streaked with blood, if there are anal fissures (cracks in the anus caused by the passage of hard stool).
- Gastric distress and abdominal pain.
- Irritability

Season: Any time, but may be more frequent in winter when less fruit is consumed.

Cause: A sluggish digestive tract, illness, insufficient fibre in diet, insufficient activity, or an anal fissure that makes defecation painful; occasionally, a serious medical condition.

Duration: May be chronic or occur just occasionally.

Treatment: Though constipation is not unusual in bottle-fed infants, symptoms should always be reported to the doctor, who can, when necessary, check for any abnormalities that might be causing it. Occasional constipation or mild chronic constipation is usually treated with dietary changes (see below); an increase in exercise may help (in infants, try moving the legs in a bicycle fashion when you see your baby having difficulty with a movement). Do not give laxatives, enemas, or any medication without the doctor's instructions.

Dietary changes: Make these only after consultation with baby's doctor:

- Give 30 to 50 ml (a fl ounce or two) of prune or apple juice by bottle, cup, or spoon.
- For a baby on solids, add a teaspoonful of bran to morning cereal; increase intake of fruits (other than banana) and vegetables.
- In older babies, cut back on milk if daily intake exceeds three cups.

Prevention: When solids are added to baby's diet, be sure to include only whole grains plus plenty of fruits and vegetables. Move to chunkier textures as soon as baby seems ready for them, rather than sticking to strained foods for the entire first year. Also be sure baby's fluid intake is adequate and that baby has plenty of opportunity for physical activity.

Complications:

- Fissures
- Difficulty with toilet training.
- Impacted stool (stool that is not passed naturally and may be painful to remove manually).

When to call the doctor: If your baby seems to be constipated often or regularly; if the problem suddenly arises when it has not been noted before; or if there is blood in the stool.

Chance of recurrence: The problem can become a 'habit' if it isn't dealt with when it first occurs.

Diseases with similar symptoms:

- Intestinal obstructions or abnormalities

Diarrhoea

This problem, too, is unusual in breastfed babies because there appear to be certain substances in breast milk that destroy many of the microorganisms that cause diarrhoea.

Symptoms:

- Liquidy, runny stools

Sometimes:

- Increased frequency
- Increased volume
- Mucus
- Vomiting

Season: Any time, but may be more common in summer, when more fruit is consumed and food spoilage is common. Rotovirus infection is more common in winter.

Cause: Very varied:

- Illness
- Teething
- Sensitivity to a food in the diet.
- Too much fruit, juice (particularly apple or grape), or other laxative-type foods.
- Gastrointestinal infection (viral, bacterial, or parasitic).
- Antibiotic medication (feeding yogurt with live cultures to a baby on antibiotics may prevent this type of diarrhoea).

Method of transmission: Infectious cases can be transmitted via the faeces-to-hand-to-mouth route. Also transmitted by contaminated foods.

Incubation period: Depends on the causative organism.

Duration: Usually anywhere from a few

hours to several days, but some cases can become chronic if the cause is not discovered and corrected.

Treatment: Depends on the cause, but most common approaches are dietary. Sometimes medication may be prescribed. Do not give anti-diarrhoeal medication to an infant without the doctor's approval – some can be harmful to young children. Protect baby's bottom from irritation by changing nappies as soon as possible after they're soiled and by spreading on a thick ointment after each change. If nappy rash develops, see page 174.

A very sick baby may need hospitalization to stabilize body fluids.

Dietary changes:

Continuing formula or breast feedings in most cases is best. Since a baby with diarrhoea may develop a temporary lactose intolerance, a switch to a soya-based, lactose-free formula may be recommended if the diarrhoea doesn't improve on baby's regular formula.

- High fluid intake (at least 50 ml/2 fl ounces an hour) to replace fluids lost through diarrhoea. To augment breast milk or formula, a rehydration mixture (such as Dioralyte, Rehydrat or Rapolyte), available from a chemist, is usually recommended. Offer a few sips by spoon, cup, or bottle every two or three minutes, working up to 250 ml (8 fl ounces) between loose bowel movements. Do not give sweetened drinks (such as colas), undiluted fruit juices, athletic drinks, glucose water, or homemade salt-and-sugar mixtures.
- Continuation of solids, if baby takes them regularly. The theory that it is beneficial to 'rest the bowel' by withholding food in cases of diarrhoea is no longer widely accepted. The sooner a baby is fed, the less severe the diarrhoea will be. Starchy foods such as mashed banana, white rice or rice cereal, potatoes, pasta, or dry white toast can, depending on baby's usual diet, all be good choices. Small amounts of protein foods

(chicken, cottage cheese) are also appropriate.

- If there is vomiting, solid feeding is usually not resumed until vomiting has stopped. But do offer sips of clear fluids (diluted juices or oral rehydration fluid, if prescribed), or for an older baby, ice pops made with diluted fruit juice. Offering small amounts (no more than a tablespoon or two at a time, less for a very young infant) will greatly increase the chance that it will be held down. Once vomiting has ceased, foods can be added as above.
- When stool begins to return to normal, usually after two or three days, the doctor will recommend that you begin to return your baby to a regular diet but continue limiting milk and other dairy products (other than breast milk and formula) for another day or two.
- In diarrhoea that lasts for two weeks or more in a bottle-fed infant, the doctor may recommend a change in formula.

Prevention: Diarrhoea can't always be prevented, but risks can be reduced:

- Attention to sanitary preparation of foods (see page 224).
- Careful hand washing by baby's caretakers after handling nappies and going to the lavatory.
- The dilution of fruit juices taken by babies; limiting total intake. (Babies and young children have been known to have chronic diarrhoea as a result of drinking 1.1 litres (2 pints) or less of apple or grape juice a day.)

Complications:

- Nappy rash
- Dehydration, which if severe, could lead to coma and even death.

When to call the doctor: One or two loose stools is not a cause for concern. But the following indicate diarrhoea that may need medical attention:

- You suspect baby may have consumed spoiled food or formula.
- Baby has had loose, watery stools for 24 hours.
- Baby is vomiting (more than the usual spitup) repeatedly, or has been vomiting for 24 hours.
- There is blood in baby's stools.
- Baby is running a fever or seems ill.

Call *immediately* if baby shows signs of dehydration: decreased urine output (nappies aren't as wet as usual and/or urine is yellow); tearless and sunken eyes; a sunken fontanel; dry skin; scanty saliva.

Chance of recurrence: Likely if cause has not been eliminated; some babies are more prone to diarrhoea.

Diseases with similar symptoms:
- Food allergies
- Food poisoning
- Enzyme deficiencies

Middle-ear Inflammation (Otitis Media)

Babies are very susceptible to ear infections because their eustachian tubes are short and narrow. Most eventually outgrow this susceptibility.

Symptoms: In acute otitis media

Usually:
- Ear pain, often worse at night (babies sometimes pull or rub or hold their ears, but often give no indication of pain except for crying, and sometimes not even that; crying when sucking on breast or bottle may indicate ear pain that has radiated to the jaw).
- Fever, which may be slight or very high.
- Fatigue and irritability.

Sometimes:
- Nausea and/or vomiting
- Loss of appetite

Occasionally:
- No obvious symptoms at all.

On examination the eardrum appears pink at first, then red and bulging (though an eardrum may also appear red if baby's been crying or because of the light being used); without treatment pressure can burst the drum, releasing pus into the ear canal and relieving the pain; the eardrum heals eventually, but treatment helps to prevent further damage.

In serous otitis media (or fluid in the middle ear)

Usually:
- Hearing loss (which is temporary but can become permanent if condition persists for many months untreated).

Sometimes:
- Clicking or popping sounds on swallowing or sucking.
- No symptoms at all, other than the fluid in the ear.

Season: All year round, but much more common in winter.

Cause: Usually bacteria or viruses, though allergy can also cause middle-ear inflammation. Babies and young children may be most susceptible because of the shape of their eustachian tubes; because they are more likely to get respiratory infections, which usually precede ear infections; because they have immature immune response; or because they are often fed while lying on their backs. The eustachian tubes, which drain fluids and mucus from the ears down the back of the nose and the throat, are shorter in a baby than in an adult, so germs can easily travel through them into the middle ear. And because the tubes are horizontal rather than vertical (as in adults), drainage is poor, especially in infants who

Your Baby's Health History

If there isn't adequate space in your new arrival's baby book, buy a notebook to use as a permanent health history. Record all your baby's birth statistics, as well as information about each illness, medications given, immunizations, doctors and so on. What follows is a sampling of the kinds of things to include.

At Birth

Weight: Length: Head circumference:

Condition at birth:

APGAR at one and five minutes:

Results of Brazelton or other tests:

Any problems or abnormalities:

Infant Illnesses

Date: Recovered:

Symptoms:

Doctor called:

Diagnosis:

Instructions:

Medications given: How long:

Side effects:

Immunizations

                Date: Reactions:

DTP:

Boosters:

Polio:

MMR:

Other:

spend a lot of time on their backs. The short length also makes the tubes more subject to blockage (by swelling from allergy or from an infection, such as a cold, by a malformation, or by large adenoids). When the fluid can't drain normally, it builds up in the middle ear, causing serous otitis media. Fluid can also build up when the tube collapses because of pressure changes when travelling by plane. This fluid makes an excellent breeding place for infection-causing bacteria (usually streptococci or haemophilus influenzae).

Method of transmission: Not direct, but children in day care may be more vulnerable. There may be a family disposition to ear infections.

Incubation period: Often follows a cold or the flu.

Duration: Varies from as little as a few days but can become chronic.

Treatment: Ear infections require consultation with a doctor; do not try to treat on your own. Treatment may include:

- Antibiotics, when deemed necessary. Always give for the full time prescribed – usually 5 or 10 days – to avoid reinfection, chronic infection, or antibiotic resistance. Sometimes, an anti-inflammatory (corticosteroid) may be given, too. Decongestants are not usually helpful.

- Watchful waiting in situations that do not require immediate antibiotic treatment.

- Ear drops, only if doctor recommended.

- Baby paracetamol or ibuprofen, sometimes with codeine, for pain and/or fever.

- Heat applied to the ear in the form of a heating pad set on low, a hot-water bottle filled with warm water, or warm compresses (see page 616) – any of which can be used while you are trying to reach the doctor.

- Myringotomy (minor surgery to drain infected fluid from the ear through a tiny incision in the eardrum) if the eardrum appears about to burst; the incision will heal in about ten days, but may require special care until then.

- Insertion of a tiny tube to drain remaining fluids when a chronic infection doesn't respond to antibiotic therapy. This is done under general anaesthesia and is a last resort for cases that don't respond to other treatments. Usually a tube is tried if fluid has remained in one ear for six months – or in both ears for four months – with no improvement. The tube falls out after nine to twelve months, sometimes sooner. Risks must be weighed against benefits before resorting to tubes, the long-term benefits of which are unclear.

- Periodic ear exams until the ear (or ears) is back to normal to be sure the condition has not become chronic.

- Elimination or treatment of allergies related to repeated ear infections.

Dietary changes: Extra fluids for fever.

Prevention: A sure way to prevent otitis media is not yet known. Recent research, however, suggests that the following may reduce the risk of a baby's falling victim:

- Overall good health through adequate nutrition, plenty of rest and regular medical care.

- Breastfeeding for at least three months.

- An upright feeding position, especially when a baby has a respiratory infection.

- An elevated sleeping position when a baby has a cold (put a few pillows *under* the head of the mattress, not under baby's head.)

- Decongestants for children with colds or allergies, particularly before an air flight, and having baby suck on breast or bottle during takeoffs and especially landings, when most ear problems occur.

- Low-dose antibiotics for children with frequent ear infections during the height of the otitis media season, or just when the child comes down with a cold (the antibiotics don't cure the cold, but they can prevent a secondary infection such as otitis media).

- Smoke-free living space.
- Home child care rather than group day-care situations, where children are more likely to come down with otitis media.

Complications:
Among others:

- Chronic otitis media with hearing loss
- Mastoid infection
- Meningitis, bacteremia, pneumonia
- Brain abscess
- Facial paralysis

When to call the doctor: Initially, as soon as you suspect your baby may have an earache. Again if symptoms do not seem to begin clearing within two days, or if baby seems worse. Even if no ear infection is suspected, call if baby suddenly doesn't seem to be hearing as well as usual.

Chance of recurrence: Some babies never have an ear infection, others have one or two in infancy and then no repeats, and still others have them repeatedly on into toddlerhood and the preschool years.

Diseases with similar symptoms: foreign object in the ear, swimmer's ear and referred pain from respiratory infection can mimic an earache.

WHAT IT'S IMPORTANT TO KNOW:
All About Fever

Though you may remember your mother standing over you, thermometer in hand, concern in her voice, announcing, 'You've got a fever – I'd better call the doctor', fever hasn't always been cause for alarm. The ancients welcomed fevers because they believed they burned out bad 'humours'. In the Middle Ages, fever was actually induced on occasion to fight syphilis and certain other infections. And in fact, fever was considered so beneficial that it wasn't even treated until about 100 years ago, when aspirin, with its fever-reducing capabilities, came on the scene. By the time your generation was growing up, even the slightest rise in temperature was a cause for worry, and a high fever for all-out panic.

Oddly enough, as it turns out, Hippocrates had a better notion of what fever is all about than did the modern medical community of a generation ago. Recent research has confirmed that, as Hippocrates speculated, most fevers actually do more good than harm – that they do in a sense burn out, if not the bad humours, at least the bad germs that invade and threaten the body.

Instead of being a symptom to be feared and fought, fever is now recognized to be an important part of the body's immune response to infection.

Here's how scientists now believe fever plays its role. In response to such invaders as viruses, bacteria and fungi, white blood cells in the body produce a hormone now called interleukin, which then travels to the brain to instruct the hypothalamus to turn up the body thermostat. It appears that at higher body temperatures, the rest of the immune system is better able to fight infection. Fever may also lower iron levels while increasing the invaders' need for that mineral – in effect starving them. And when it's a virus that has launched the attack, fever helps enhance the production of interferon and other antiviral substances in the body.

When an individual's body temperature suddenly rises a couple of degrees above normal $(36.9°C/98.6°F)$[2] he or she often

---

2. All temperature readings referred to in this chapter are oral, the standard for temperature readings, unless otherwise noted.

feels paradoxically, chilled. The chilling serves to encourage a further rise in temperature in several ways. The involuntary shivering that usually occurs signals the body to turn its thermostat up still another notch and prompts the fever sufferer to take other measures that raise the body temperature, drink hot drinks, throw on another blanket, put on a jumper. At the same time, outlying blood vessels constrict to reduce heat loss, and body tissues – such as stored fat – are broken down to produce heat (which is why it is important to take extra calories during a fever).

A very high fever occasionally causes convulsions in infants and young children, usually at the very onset of the fever. Though they are frightening for parents, doctors now believe febrile convulsions are not dangerous. (See page 425 for safe handling of convulsions.) Studies have shown that children who have febrile convulsions show no neurological or mental impairment later on, though they are very slightly more apt to have an increased risk of epilepsy in the future (but the convulsions, it is suspected, are more likely to be a result of the tendency toward the disorder than the cause of it). Babies who have had convulsions with a fever once have a 30 to 40% greater chance of a repeat episode, and medical treatment doesn't affect that risk. Nor does treatment of a fever during the illness seem to reduce the incidence of seizures in these predisposed children, probably because the convulsions almost always occur just as the fever rises at the outset of an illness, before treatment can be given.

An estimated 80 to 90% of all fevers in babies are related to self-limiting viral infections (they get better without treatment). Most doctors today don't recommend trying to reduce such fever in babies over six months unless it is 38.9°C (102°F) or more, and some wait for significantly higher temperatures before they advise parents to get out the medicine dropper. They may, however, suggest the use of baby paracetamol even with lower temperatures to relieve aches and pains, make a baby more comfortable, improve sleep and, sometimes, to make a nervous mother feel better. On the other hand, illnesses caused by bacteria must be treated. Antibiotics lower temperatures indirectly by wiping out the infection. Depending on the illness, the antibiotic selected, the child's level of comfort, and the height of the fever, antibiotics and fever reducers may or may not be prescribed simultaneously.

Unlike most other infection-related fever, fever related to shock from a generalized bacterial invasion of the body, as in septicemia (blood poisoning), requires immediate medical treatment to lower the body temperature.

Normally, body temperature is at its lowest (as low as 35.8°C/96.5°F taken orally) between 2:00 and 4:00 in the morning, is still relatively low (as low as 36.1°C/97°F) when we get up, then slowly rises over the day until it peaks between 6:00 and 10:00 in the evening at about 37.2°C (99°F). It tends to be slightly higher in hot weather, lower in cold, higher during exercise than at rest. It's more volatile and subject to greater variation in babies and young children than in adults.

Fevers behave differently in different illnesses. In some, a fever may remain persistently elevated until a baby is well; in others it will be consistently lower in the morning and higher in the evening, spike (shoot up) periodically, or come and go with no obvious pattern. The pattern sometimes helps the doctor to make a diagnosis.

When fever is part of the body's response to illness, temperatures above 41.1°C (106°F) are rare, and those beyond 42.2°C (108°F) unheard of. But when fever is the result of the failure of the body's heat-regulation mechanism, as in heat illness, temperatures can soar as high as 45.5°C (114°F). Such temperatures can occur when the body produces too much heat or can't cool itself effectively, either through an internal abnormality or, more commonly, through overheating caused by an external heat source, such as a sauna or a hot tub, for example, or the inside of a parked car in warm weather (air temperatures inside the car can quickly shoot up to 45.5°C/113°F even with the windows open 5 cm/2 inches and the temperature outside a moderate

29.4°C/85°F). Overheating can also result from strenuous physical activity in hot or humid weather, or from being overdressed in warm weather. Infants and the elderly are most susceptible to heat illnesses because their temperature-regulation mechanisms are less dependable. Fever due to the failure of heat regulation is an illness in itself; and not only is it apparently not beneficial, it is dangerous and requires immediate treatment. Extremely high temperatures (over 41.1°C/106°F) that are illness related also require immediate treatment. It's believed that when a fever is that high it ceases to be beneficial, and its positive effects on the immune response may be reversed.

Taking Baby's Temperature

Because the touch of lips (or back of hand) against the side of the forehead can accurately detect a fever 9 out of 10 times (except where overdressing raises skin but not rectal temperature), and because temperature taking often provokes a battle, a few doctors recommend abandoning temperature taking after a baby is six months old. Most, however, prefer a more accurate indicator of a baby's condition than a parent's kiss. Taking the temperature during the course of an illness can answer such questions as 'Has the treatment effectively lowered the temperature?' or 'Has the fever risen, meaning a turn for the worse?' But though temperature readings can be useful, they needn't be taken every hour on the hour, as an anxious and inexperienced mum is often wont to do. In most cases, once in the morning and once in the evening is adequate. Take it in between only if baby suddenly seems sicker. If baby seems better, and your lips testify that the fever is down, you don't really need a second opinion from the thermometer.

The three parts of the body that can most accurately reflect core body temperature are the mouth, the rectum, and the axillary (armpit). Since putting a thermometer in the mouth of a baby is dangerous (most doctors don't re-

commend taking temperatures orally until a child is four or five), you'll be going the rectal or axillary route for quite a while.

Before you start. Try to keep your baby calm for half an hour before temperature taking, since crying or screaming could turn a slightly elevated temperature into a high one. (Though it's necessary to withhold hot or cold drinks or foods before taking an oral temperature, as they too could affect temperature readings, this precaution isn't necessary when taking rectal or axillary temperatures).

Preparing the thermometer. Wash thermometer with cold soapy water (warm or hot water can cause the mercury to expand and burst or crack the glass), rinse, then swab it with absorbent cotton wool dipped in rubbing alcohol. Check the mercury reading, and if it's above 35.5°C (96°F), shake it down carefully by holding the end of the thermometer opposite the bulb firmly between your thumb and forefinger and shaking with repeated downward snaps of the wrist. If possible, do the shaking over a bed or sofa and away from hard surfaces, such the lavatory bowl, in case you lose your grip and the instrument slips from your hand. Give yourself enough room so that the thermometer won't accidentally hit something and break. Lubricate the bulb end of a rectal thermometer with petroleum jelly (Vaseline) before inserting it. Rinse an oral thermometer thoroughly in cool water to remove the taste of alcohol.

Taking the temperature. *Rectal:* Prepare the thermometer and bare baby's bottom, speaking reassuringly as you do. Then turn baby onto his or her tummy on your lap (which gives you more control and allows the legs to hang at a 90° angle, making insertion easier) or on a bed or changing table (where a small pillow or folded towel under the hips will raise the baby's bottom slightly for easier insertion). To distract baby, try singing a couple of favourite songs or putting a favourite book or toy in baby's line of vision. Spread the buttocks with one hand, exposing the anus (the rectal opening). With the other, slip about 2.5 cm (an inch) of the bulb end of the thermometer into the rectum, being careful not to force it. Hold the thermometer in place for two minutes between your index and middle fingers, using your other fingers to press the buttocks together to keep the thermometer from sliding out and to keep baby from wriggling. Remove the thermometer immediately, however, if baby begins to show very active resistance. Even if the thermometer has been in for only half a minute or so, it will have registered to within a degree of the actual temperature and you will have a rough figure to report to the doctor. Wipe the thermometer with a piece of tissue before reading. (If you're a novice, you may want to put the thermometer down – the temperature won't change – while you redress and safely deposit baby, then pick it up again for reading.)

Rarely, a thermometer breaks while inserted. If this happens and you can't find all the pieces, call the doctor. But don't worry; the risk of more than a scratch is slight, and since the mercury is in a non-toxic form, it should do no harm to your baby (though it can damage precious metals).

Tympanic: This thermometer reads the temperature in the ear but using it takes some skill. If you buy one (prices are coming down), have your doctor show you how to use it.

Axillary, or underarm: An axillary reading is useful when a baby has

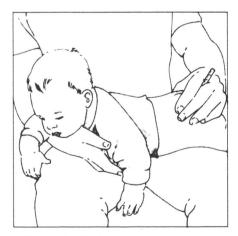

The rectal method.

The underarm method.

diarrhoea or won't lie still for a rectal or if only an oral thermometer (which should *never* be used rectally) is available. You can get an underarm reading with a rectal or oral thermometer in four to eight minutes or with the very new infrared model (similar to tympanic) in seconds. For either model, remove baby's shirt so it won't come between the thermometer and baby's skin and be sure the armpit is dry. Place the bulb end of the thermometer well up into the armpit, hold the arm snugly over it, gently pressing the elbow against baby's side. Distract baby as needed.

Oral: You can begin taking oral temperatures when your child can hold the thermometer securely under the tongue with lips closed and can understand directions not to bite down on it, usually at about age four or five, occasionally earlier. For a good oral reading, the thermometer should be tucked all the way into the pocket under the tongue and held there for two to four minutes (if there is mouth breathing, it will take longer for the thermometer to register).

Reading the thermometer. A rectal temperature is the most accurate since it picks up temperatures from the body's core, but the oral reading is considered the standard. Temperatures obtained rectally, as they are most frequently in infants, are usually one-half to a full degree higher than those determined orally; axillary readings are about one degree lower. On an oral thermometer, 36.9°C (98.6°F) is normal; 37.5°C (99.6°F) is the norm rectally; and 36.5°C (97.6°F) is normal for an axillary reading. A fever of 39°C (102.2°F) taken rectally is the equivalent of 38.4°C (101.2°F) taken orally and 37.9°C (100.2°F) by an armpit reading.

To read a mercury thermometer, hold it in a good light and rotate it until you see the silver column of mercury. Line up the mercury between the column calibrations and the numbers, which are marked in full degrees as well as every two-tenths degree. The point where the mercury ends indicates the temperature. Write it down, along with the time it was taken. When you report the temperature to the doctor, be sure to include whether it's a rectal, axillary, or oral reading.

Storing the thermometer. After use, wash the thermometer once again with cold soapy water, rinse and swab with alcohol. Then store it, in the case, away from such sources of heat as a sunny window, a radiator, a fireplace mantel, a tumble dryer and the kitchen stove (heat could cause expansion of the mercury and cracking of the glass).

Evaluating a Fever

Behaviour is a better gauge of how sick an infant is than body temperature. A baby can be seriously ill, with pneumonia or meningitis for example, and have no fever at all, or have a high fever with a mild cold.

Under the following conditions a baby with a fever requires immediate medical attention (call the doctor even in the middle of the night or go to the emergency room if the doctor can't be reached):

- The baby is under two months old.
- The fever is over 40.5°C (105°F) rectally.
- The baby has a convulsion for the first time (the body stiffens, eyes roll, limbs flail).
- The baby is crying inconsolably (and it clearly isn't colic), cries as if in pain when

touched or moved, or is whimpering, non-responsive, or limp.
- The baby has purple spots anywhere on the skin.
- The baby is having difficulty breathing once you've cleared the nasal passages.
- The baby's neck seems stiff; baby resists having the head pulled forward towards the chest.
- The onset of fever follows a period of exposure to an external heat source, such as the sun on a hot day or the closed interior of a car in hot weather. Heatstroke is a possibility (see page 378), and immediate emergency medical attention is indicated.
- A sudden increase in temperature occurs in a baby with a moderate fever who has been overdressed or bundled in blankets. This should be treated as heat illness.
- The doctor has instructed you to call immediately should your baby run a fever.
- You feel something's very wrong, but you just don't know what.

Under the following conditions a baby with fever needs medical attention as soon as practical:

- The baby is two to six months old (younger babies need *immediate* attention).
- The baby has a chronic illness, such as heart, kidney, or neurological disease, or sickle-cell or other chronic anaemia.
- The baby has had convulsions with a fever in the past.
- The baby exhibits signs of dehydration: infrequent urination, dark yellow urine, scant saliva and tears, dry lips and skin, sunken eyes and fontanel.
- The baby's behaviour seems uncharacteristic: he or she is excessively cranky, lethargic or excessively sleepy; unable to sleep; sensitive to light; crying more than usual; refusing to eat; pulling at ears.

- A fever that has been low grade for a couple of days spikes suddenly; or a baby who has been sick with a cold for several days suddenly begins to run a fever (this may indicate a secondary infection, such as otitis media or strep throat).

- The fever is over 38.9°C (102°F) rectally (or whatever temperature your baby's doctor recommends you call at). Though such a temperature is not in itself an indicator of a baby's being very sick (babies can run fevers of 40.5°C/105°F or 41.1°C/106°F with minor illness), check with the doctor, just in case.

- A fever isn't brought down by medication.

- A low-grade fever (under 102° rectally) with mild cold or flu symptoms lasts for more than three days.

- A fever lasts more than 24 hours when there are no other detectable signs of illness.

Treating a Fever

If your baby has a fever, take these measures as needed, unless the doctor has recommended a different course of action.

Keep baby cool. Contrary to popular belief, keeping a feverish baby warm with blankets, heavy clothing, or an overheated room is not a safe practice. These measures can actually lead to heatstroke by raising body temperature to dangerous levels. Dress your baby lightly to allow body heat to escape (no more than a nappy is needed in hot weather) and maintain room temperature at 20° to 22.2°C (68° to 70°F) (when necessary, use an air conditioner or fan if you have one, to keep the air cool, but keep baby out of the path of the air flow).

Increase fluid intake. Because fever increases the loss of water through the skin, it's important to be sure a feverish baby gets an adequate intake of fluids. For older

Aspirin or Non-Aspirin

Both aspirin and paracetamol (Calpol, Tempra, Panadol, Liquiprin) are antipyretics (fever reducers) and lower fever equally well, but aspirin is more effective in reducing inflammation (the heat, swelling, redness and pain of localized infection) and, possibly, in relieving pain. Given together, aspirin and paracetamol are statistically more effective at reducing fever longer (usually about six hours). It's not clear whether or not there are any benefits if they are given alternately.

Aspirin, though a powerful and valuable drug, is associated with a wide range of common side effects. It can diminish the immune response, cause inflammation and bleeding in the gastrointestinal tract, impair platelet function (increasing the risk of all types of bleeding) and induce an attack of asthma in susceptible people. Giving aspirin to children with such viral diseases as chicken pox and influenza (flu) has been linked to the development of Reye's syndrome, and it

is therefore never recommended for a baby or child who has, or is suspected of having, such an illness.

In comparison, paracetamol, although it has been known to cause liver damage in rare cases and may occasionally trigger an allergic reaction, is remarkably free of side effects. For this reason, doctors are much more likely to recommend paracetamol rather than aspirin for fever reduction in children. It comes in liquid form for infants as well as rectal suppositories for babies who can't or won't keep the liquid down.

Ibuprofen, which also lowers fever and relieves pain, is presently available for infants only by prescription.

Since all these medications can be dangerous in large doses, never give more than the doctor recommends; and when you're not using them, keep them (like all medications) safely locked away, out of the reach of babies and children.

Handling Febrile Convulsions

Convulsions due to fever usually last only a minute or two. Should your baby have one, keep calm (remember such convulsions are not dangerous) and take the following steps. Keep baby unrestrained in your arms or on a bed or another soft surface, lying on one side, with head lower than body if possible. Don't try to feed or put anything into baby's mouth, and remove anything (like a dummy) that might be in it. Babies often lose consciousness during a seizure, but they usually revive quickly without help. Any seizure that lasts five minutes or more requires immediate emergency help – dial 999 or your local emergency number.

When a seizure has ended, the baby often wants to sleep. If yours does, prop him or her in a side-sleeping position with blankets or a pillow. Then call the doctor. If you don't reach help immediately, you can give baby a sponge bath and, if he or she is more than six months old, paracetamol to try to lower the temperature while you're waiting. But don't put baby in the tub to try to reduce the fever since another seizure could occur and water could be inhaled.

babies, offer good sources of fluids often. These include diluted juices and juicy fruits (such as citrus and melons); water; clear soups; gelatin desserts (see page 604); and ice pops made from fruit juice. Give young infants frequent feedings of breast milk or formula. Encourage frequent sipping but don't force. If baby refuses to take any fluids for several hours during the day, inform the doctor.

Give fever-reducing medication, if necessary. If your baby is under six months old, wait until you've reached the doctor before administering any medication. If fever is over 39.4°C (103°F) rectally and/or your baby seems very uncomfortable, and you can't reach your doctor immediately, try to lower fever with a tepid sponging (see below). With older babies, the decision to give medication should be based on the doctor's prior recommendations. Ask the doctor in advance what you should do if your baby wakes up feverish in the middle of the night. At what temperature would he or she like you to administer a fever-reducing medication, give a sponging, or call? If you don't have this information in advance and if your baby is over six months old and has a middle of the night fever of over 38.9°C (102°F) with no other indications of needing immediate medical attention (see Evaluating a Fever), give the appropriate dosage of baby paracetamol (see page 615). If the temperature does not go down, or if it goes up, or if baby seems very uncomfortable, call the doctor. Until you are able to reach the doctor, try a tepid sponge or tub bath.

Sponging. Once a routine treatment for fever, sponging is now recommended only under certain circumstances, such as when fever-reducing medication isn't working (the temperature isn't down an hour after it is given); when trying to lower the body temperature of a baby under six months old without medication; or when trying to make a very feverish baby more comfortable.

Only tepid or lukewarm water (body temperature, neither warm nor cool to the touch) should be used for sponging. Using cool or cold water, or alcohol (once a popular fever-reducing rub), can raise rather than lower temperatures by inducing shivering, which prompts the confused body to turn up its thermostat. In addition, the alcohol fumes can be harmful if inhaled. Using hot water will also raise body temperatures and could, like overdressing, lead to heatstroke. You can sponge a feverish baby in the tub or out, but in either case the room should be comfortably warm and draught free.

● Sponging out of the tub. Have three flannels in a tub or basin of tepid water ready before you begin. Spread a waterproof sheet or pad, or a plastic tablecloth, on the bed or on your lap; place a thick towel over it and place baby, face up, on top of the towel. Undress baby and cover with a light receiving blanket or towel. Wring out one flannel so it won't drip, fold it, and place it on baby's forehead (remoisten if it begins to dry at any point during the sponging). Take another flannel and begin lightly rubbing baby's skin, exposing one area of the body at a time and keeping the rest lightly covered. Concentrate on the neck, face, stomach, inside of the elbows and knees, but also include the area under the arms and around the groin. The blood brought to the surface by rubbing will be cooled as the tepid water evaporates on the skin. When the rubbing flannel begins to dry out, switch it with the third one. Continue rubbing and sponging your baby, alternating flannels as needed, for at least twenty minutes to half an hour (it takes this long to lower body temperature). If at any time the water in the basin cools to below body temperature, add enough warm water to raise it again.

- Sponging in the tub. For many babies, baths are soothing and comforting,

especially when they are sick. If yours is one of these, do the sponging in the tub. Again, the water should be body temperature, and you should sponge and rub for at least twenty minutes to half an hour to bring the temperature down. Do not put a baby who has had a febrile convulsion in a tub for sponging.

What not to do. As important as knowing what to do when your baby has a fever is knowing what not to do:

- Do not force rest. A really sick baby will want to rest, in or out of the cot. If yours wants out, moderate activity is okay, but discourage strenuous activity as this could raise body temperature further.

- Do not give an enema, except under a doctor's directions.

- Do not overdress or bundle a baby warmly.

- Do not cover baby with a wet towel or wet sheet, since this could prevent heat from escaping through the skin.

- Do not 'starve a fever'. Fever raises the caloric requirement and sick babies, in fact, need more calories, not fewer.

- Do not give aspirin or paracetamol when heatstroke is suspected.

Know Your Baby

Babies, like other people, vary in their response to pain. Some can tolerate a great deal of it (the curious crawler who falls off the sofa, gets up without a whimper, and climbs right back on) and some very little (the fledgling toddler who screeches with every tumble, even when it's on a plush carpet). It's a good idea to take such differences into account when deciding how sick a baby is. For example, if your feverish baby, who is ordinarily a stoic, is pulling at one or both ears but doesn't seem to be uncomfortable, consider an ear infection and call the doctor. On the other

hand, if you've got a pain-sensitive baby, you might be wise not to fly to the phone every time he whimpers in discomfort.

Fever as a signal. Fever in a young infant, especially when there are no other symptoms of illness, suggests the possibility of a urinary tract infection (UTI). The diagnosis can be confirmed through a urinalysis. If a UTI is found, further tests may be done to determine if there is a urinary tract abnormality at the root of the infection. If there is, simple surgery can usually remedy it.

EIGHTEEN

First Aid Do's And Don'ts

♦

Accidents will happen. Even the most conscientious parents and caretakers can't avert them all. What they can do, however, is prevent serious damage by knowing what to do when an accident occurs. This section can help you do that. It will be even more helpful if reinforced with a live first-aid course. But don't wait until baby tumbles down the stairs or chews on a rhododendron leaf to look up what to do in an emergency. Now – before calamity strikes – become as familiar with the procedures for treating common injuries as you are with those for bathing baby or changing a nappy, and review less common ones when appropriate (snake bites, for example, when you are going on a camping trip). See that anyone else who cares for your baby does, too.

Below are the most common injuries, what you should know about them, how to treat (and not treat) them, and when to seek medical care for them. Types of injuries are listed alphabetically (abdominal injuries, bites, broken bones, etc.), with individual injuries numbered for easy cross-reference.

A grey bar has been added to the side of these pages, making the chapter easy to locate in an emergency.

ABDOMINAL INJURIES

1. Internal bleeding. A blow to your baby's abdomen could result in internal damage. The signs of such injury would include: bruising or other discolouration of the abdomen; vomited or coughed-up blood that is dark or bright red and has the consistency of coffee grounds (this could also be a sign of baby's having swallowed a caustic substance); blood (it may be dark or bright red) in the stool or urine; shock (cold, clammy, pale skin; weak, rapid pulse; chills; confusion; and, possibly, nausea, vomiting, and/or shallow breathing). Seek emergency medical assistance. If baby appears to be in shock (#44), treat immediately. Do not give food or drink.

2. Cuts or lacerations of the abdomen. Treat as for other cuts (#47, #48). With a major laceration, intestines may protrude. Don't try to put them back into the abdomen. Instead, cover them with a clean moistened flannel or nappy and get emergency medical assistance immediately.

BITES

3. Animal bites. Try to avoid moving the affected part. Call doctor immediately. Wash wound gently with soap and water for 15 minutes. Do not apply antiseptic or anything else. Control bleeding (#47, #48, #49), and apply a sterile bandage. Try to restrain animal for testing, but avoid getting bitten. Dogs, cats, bats, skunks and raccoons may be rabid, especially if they attacked unprovoked. Infection (redness, tenderness, swelling) is common with cat bites and may require antibiotics.

4. Insect bites. Treat insect stings or bites as follows:

- Scrape off the honeybee's stinger with the blunt edge of a knife or with your fingernail. Don't try to grasp the stinger with your nails or a tweezer – this could force more of the remaining venom into the skin.

- Remove ticks *promptly*, using blunt tweezers or your fingertips protected by a tissue, paper towel, or rubber glove. Grasp the bug as close to baby's skin as possible and pull upward, steadily and evenly. Don't twist, jerk, squeeze, crush, or puncture the tick. *Don't* use such folk remedies as vaseline, petrol, or a hot match – they can make matters worse. Save the tick for medical examination. If you suspect Lyme disease (page 626), call the doctor.

- Wash the site of a minor bee, wasp, ant, spider, or tick bite with soap and water. Then apply ice or cold compresses (page 614) if there appears to be swelling or pain. Follow with an application of bug-bite medication.

- Apply calamine lotion to itchy bites, such as those caused by mosquitoes.

- If there seems to be extreme pain after a spider bite, apply ice or cold compresses and call for emergency help. Try to find the spider and take it to the hospital with you, or at least be able to describe it; it might be poisonous. If you know the spider was poisonous – a black widow, brown recluse spider, tarantula, or scorpion, for example – get emergency treatment immediately, even before symptoms appear.

- Watch for signs of hypersensitivity, such as severe pain or swelling or any degree of shortness of breath, following any bee, wasp, or hornet sting. Individuals who exhibit such symptoms with a first sting usually develop hypersensitivities, or allergies, to the venom, in which case a subsequent sting could be fatal if immediate emergency treatment is not administered. Should your baby's reaction to a sting be anything more than slight pain or a bit of swelling, report this to the doctor, who is likely to recommend allergy testing. If allergy is diagnosed, it will probably be necessary for you carry a bee-sting emergency kit with you on outings during bee season.

- It's possible, of course, for sensitization to bee venom to occur without a previously noticed reaction, especially in a baby. So should a sting victim break out in hives all over the body, experience difficulty breathing, hoarseness, coughing, wheezing, severe headache, nausea, vomiting, thickened tongue, facial swelling, weakness, dizziness, or fainting, get immediate emergency medical attention.

5. Snake bites. It's rare that a baby is bitten by a poisonous snake, but such a bite is very dangerous. Because of an infant's small size, even a tiny amount of venom can be fatal. Following such a bite, it is important to keep baby and the affected part as still as possible. If the bite is on a limb, immobilize it with a splint if necessary, and keep it below the level of the heart. Use a cool compress if available to relieve pain, but *do not* apply ice or give any medication without medical advice. Sucking out the venom by mouth (and spitting it out) may be helpful if done immediately, but *do not* make an incision of any kind, unless you are 4 or 5 hours from help and severe symptoms occur. If baby is not breathing, give CPR (page 441). Treat for shock (#44), if necessary. *Get prompt medical help*; and be ready to identify the variety of snake if possible. If you won't be able to get medical help within an hour, apply a loose constricting band (a belt, tie, or hair ribbon loose enough for you to slip a finger under) 5 cm/2 inches above the bite to slow circulation. (Do not tie such a tourniquet around a finger or toe, or around the neck, head, or trunk.) Check pulse (see page 400) beneath the tourniquet frequently to be sure circulation is not cut off, and loosen it if the limb begins to swell. Make a note of the time it was tied.

Treat nonpoisonous snake bites as puncture wounds (#50), and notify baby's doctor.

6. Marine stings. Such stings are usually not serious, but an occasional baby or child will have a severe reaction. Medical treatment should be sought immediately as a precaution. First-aid treatment varies with the type of marine animal involved, but in general, any clinging fragments of the stinger should be gingerly brushed away with a nappy or piece of clothing (to protect your own fingers). Treatment for heavy bleeding (#49), shock (#44), or cessation of breathing (see page 441), if needed, should be begun immediately. (Don't worry about light bleeding; it may help purge toxins). The sting of a stingray, lionfish, catfish, stonefish, or sea urchin should be soaked in hot water, if available, for 30 minutes, or until medical help arrives. The toxins from the sting of a jellyfish or Portuguese man-of-war can be counteracted by applying alcohol or diluted ammonia. (Pack a couple of alcohol pads in your beach bag, just in case.)

BLEEDING

see #47, #48, #49

BLEEDING, INTERNAL

see #1

BROKEN BONES OR FRACTURES

7. Possible broken arms, legs, collar bones, or fingers. Signs of a break include a snapping sound at the time of the accident deformity (although this could also indicate a dislocation, #16); inability to move or bear weight on the part; severe pain (persistent crying could be a clue); numbness and/or tingling (neither of which a baby would be able to tell you about); swelling and discolouration. If a fractured limb is suspected, don't move the child without checking with the doctor first – unless necessary for safety. If you must move baby immediately, first try to immobilize the injured part (limb, head, neck) by splinting it in the position it's in with a ruler, a magazine, a book, or other firm object, padded with a soft cloth to protect the skin. Or use a small, firm pillow as a splint. Fasten the splint securely at the break and above and below it with bandages, strips of cloth, scarves, or neckties, but not so tightly that circulation is hampered. If no potential splint is handy, try to splint the injured limb with your arm. Check regularly to be sure the splint doesn't cut off circulation. Apply an ice pack to reduce swelling until medical attention is given. Though fractures in small children usually mend quickly, medical treatment is necessary to ensure proper healing. Take your child to the doctor or hospital even if you only suspect a break.

8. Compound fractures. If bone protrudes through the skin, don't touch the bone. Cover the injury, if possible, with sterile gauze or with a clean terry nappy; control bleeding, if necessary, with pressure (#49); and get emergency medical assistance.

9. Possible neck or back injury. If neck or back injury is suspected, don't move baby at all. Call for emergency medical assistance. Cover and keep child comfortable while waiting for help and, if possible, put some heavy objects (such as books) around the head to help immobilize it. Don't give food or drink. If there is severe bleeding (#49), shock (#44), or absence of breathing (see page 441), treat these immediately.

BRUISES, SKIN

see #45

BURNS AND SCALDS

Important: If a child's clothing is on fire, use a coat, blanket, rug, bedspread, or your own body (you won't be burned) to smother the flames.

10. Limited thermal (heat) burns. Immerse the burned extremity in cool water or apply cool (10° to 15.5°C/50° to 60°F) compresses to burns of the trunk or face. Continue until baby doesn't seem to be in pain any more, usually about half an hour. Don't apply ice, which could compound the skin damage, and don't break any blisters that form. After soaking, gently pat burned

Be Prepared

- Discuss with your baby's doctor what the best plan of action would be in case of injury – calling the surgery, going to the hospital, or following some other protocol. Recommendations may vary, depending upon the seriousness of the injury, the day of the week, and the time of day.

- Keep your first aid supplies (see page 39) in a childproof, easily manageable kit or box so it can be moved as a whole to an accident site. And, if possible, make the next phone you buy a portable, so that it can be taken to the site of any accident in or around your home.

- Near each telephone in your home, post the numbers of the doctors your family uses, the Poison Control Centre, the nearest hospital emergency room (or the one you plan on using), your chemist, the Emergency Service (999), as well as the number of a close friend or neighbour you can call on in an emergency. Keep a card with the same listings in your changing bag.

- Know the quickest route to the hospital or other emergency medical facility.

- Take a course in baby CPR, and keep your skills current and ready to use with periodic refresher courses and regular home practice on a doll. Also become familiar with first-aid procedures for common injuries.

- Keep some cash reserved in a safe place in case you need a cab fare to get to the hospital or a doctor's surgery in an emergency.

- Learn to handle minor accidents calmly, which will help you keep your cool should a serious one ever occur. Your manner and tone of voice (or those of another caretaker) will affect how your baby responds to an injury. Panic or worry on your part could upset your baby. And a baby who is upset is less likely to cooperate in an emergency and will be harder to treat.

- Remember that TLC (tender loving care) is often the best treatment for minor injuries. But tailor your comfort to the degree of seriousness of the hurt. A smile, a kiss and a little reassurance ('You're all right') are all a little bump on the knee may need. But a painful pinched finger will probably warrant a heavy dose of kisses and probably some distraction. In most cases, you will need to calm a baby before giving first aid. Only in life-threatening situations (which are fortunately rare, and in which babies are not usually up to being obstreperous) will taking some time to quiet baby interfere with the outcome of treatment.

area dry and cover with nonadhesive material (such as a non-stick bandage, or in an emergency, aluminium foil). Burns on the face, hands, feet, or genitals should be seen by a doctor immediately. Any burn, even a minor one, on a child under a year old warrants a call to the doctor.

11. Extensive thermal (heat) burns. Keep baby lying flat. Remove any clothing from the burn area that does not adhere to the wound. Apply cool wet compresses to the injured area (but not to more than 25% of the body at one time). Keep the baby comfortably warm, with legs higher than heart if they are burned. Do not apply pressure, ointments, butter or other fats, powder, or boric acid soaks to the burn. If baby is conscious and doesn't have severe mouth burns, nurse or give water or another fluid. Transport the child to the doctor's office or hospital at once or call for emergency medical assistance.

12. Chemical burns. Caustic substances (such as lye and acids) can cause serious burns. Gently brush off dry chemical matter from the skin and remove any contaminated clothing. Immediately wash the skin with large amounts of water, using the antidote, if any, recommended on the chemical container or using soap if available. Call a doctor or Poison Control Centre, for further advice. Get immediate medical assistance if there is difficult or painful breathing, which could indicate lung injury from inhalation of caustic fumes. (If a chemical has been swallowed, see #41.)

13. Electrical burns. Immediately disconnect the power source, if possible. Or pull victim away from the source using a dry non-metallic object such as a broom, wooden ladder, rope, cushion, chair, or even a large book – but not your bare hands. Initiate CPR (page 441) if baby is not breathing. All electrical burns should be evaluated by a doctor, so call your baby's doctor or go to the hospital at once.

14. Sunburn. If your baby (or anyone else in the family) gets a sunburn, treat it by applying cool tap-water compresses (see page 614) for 10 to 15 minutes, three or four times a day, until the redness subsides; the evaporating water helps to cool the skin. In between these treatments, apply Nutraderm, Lubriderm, or a similar bland moisturizing cream, or calamine liniment, which has the added benefit of drying out blisters. Don't use petroleum jelly (Vaseline) on a burn because it seals out air, which is needed for healing. And don't give antihistamines unless they are prescribed by the doctor. For severe burns, steroid ointments or creams may be prescribed, and large blisters may be drained and dressed. Though there have been some claims to the contrary, aspirin won't prevent damage to the skin; but a baby pain reliever, such as paracetamol, may reduce the discomfort.

CHEMICAL BURNS

see #12

CONVULSIONS

15. Symptoms of a seizure or convulsion include: collapse, eyes rolling upward, foaming at the mouth, stiffening of the body followed by uncontrolled jerking movements and, in the most serious cases, breathing difficulty. Brief convulsions are not uncommon with high fevers (see page 420). Deal with a seizure this way: clear the area around baby, but don't restrain except if necessary to prevent injury. Loosen clothing around the neck and middle, and lay baby on one side with head lower than hips. Don't put anything in the mouth, including food or drink, breast or bottle. Call the doctor. When the convulsion has passed, sponge with cool water if fever is present, but don't put baby into a bath or throw water in his or her face. If baby isn't breathing, begin CPR (see page 441) immediately.

CUTS

see #47, #48

DISLOCATIONS

16. Shoulder and elbow dislocations are common among toddlers – mostly because they are often tugged along by the arm by adults in a hurry. A deformity of the arm or the inability of the child to move it, usually combined with persistent crying because of pain, are typical indications. A quick trip to the doctor's surgery or the hospital, where an experienced professional will reposition the dislocated part, will provide virtually instant relief. Apply an ice pack and splint before leaving, if pain seems severe.

DOG BITES

see #3

DROWNING

17. Even a child who quickly revives after being taken from the water unconscious should get medical evaluation. For the child who remains unconscious, have someone else call for emergency medical assistance, if possible, while you begin CPR (see page 441). Even if no one is available to phone for help, begin CPR immediately and call later. Don't stop CPR until the child revives or help arrives, no matter how long that takes. If there is vomiting, turn baby to one side to avoid choking. If you suspect a blow to the head or a neck injury, immobilize these parts.

EAR INJURIES

18. Foreign object in the ear. Try to shake the object out by turning the baby so the ear faces down and shaking the head very gently. If that doesn't work, try these techniques.

- For an insect, use a torch to try to lure it out.

- For a metal object, try a magnet to draw it out.

- For a plastic or wooden object, dab a drop of quick-drying glue (don't use one that might bond to the skin) on a straightened paper clip and touch it to the object if it is visible. Do not probe into the inner ear. Wait for the glue to dry, then pull the clip out, hopefully with the object attached. Don't attempt this if there's no one around to help hold baby still.

If the above techniques fail, don't try to dig the object out with your fingers or an instrument. Instead, take baby to the doctor's surgery or the hospital.

19. Damage to the ear. If a pointed object has been pushed into the ear or if your baby shows signs of ear injury (bleeding from the ear canal, sudden difficulty hearing, swollen earlobe), call the doctor.

ELECTRIC SHOCK

20. Break contact with the electrical source by turning off the power, if possible, or separate the child from the current by using a dry non-metallic object such as a broom, wooden ladder, robe, cushion, chair, or even a large book. Call for emergency medical assistance and, if baby isn't breathing, begin CPR (see page 441).

EYE INJURY

Important: Don't apply pressure to an injured eye, touch the eye with your fingers, or instill medications without a doctor's advice. Keep baby from rubbing the eye by holding a small cup or glass (or an eyebath) over it or by restraining both hands, if necessary.

21. Foreign object in the eye. If you can see the object (lash or grain of sand, for example), wash your hands and use a moist cotton swab to gently attempt to remove it from baby's eye. You can also try to wash the object out by pouring a stream of tepid (body temperature) water into the eye while someone holds baby still, if necessary. If this is unsuccessful, try pulling the upper lid down over the lower for a few seconds.

If after these attempts you can still see the object in the eye or if baby still seems uncomfortable, proceed to the doctor's surgery or the hospital since the object may become embedded or may have scratched the eye. Don't try to remove an embedded object yourself. Cover the eye with a sterile gauze pad taped loosely in place, or with a few clean tissues or a clean handkerchief to alleviate some of the discomfort en route.

22. Corrosive substance in the eye. Flush the eye immediately and thoroughly with plain lukewarm water (poured from a jug, cup, or bottle) for 15 minutes, holding the eye open with your fingers. If just one eye is involved, keep baby's head turned so that the unaffected eye is higher than the affected one and the chemical run-off doesn't drip into it. Don't use drops or ointments, and don't permit baby to rub the eye or eyes. Call the doctor or the Poison Control Centre for further instructions.

Baby won't enjoy an eye bath, but it's crucial for washing away a corrosive substance.

23. Injury to the eye with a pointed or sharp object. Keep baby in a semi-reclining position while you seek help. If the object is still in the eye, do not try to remove it. If it isn't, cover the eye lightly with a gauze pad, clean flannel, or facial tissue; do not apply pressure. In either case, get emergency medical assistance immediately. Though such injuries often look worse than they are, it's wise to consult an ophthalmologist any time the eye is scratched or punctured, even slightly.

24. Injury to the eye with a blunt object. Keep baby lying face up. Cover the injured eye with an ice pack or cold compress (page 614). If the eye blackens, if baby seems to be having difficulty seeing or keeps rubbing the eye a lot, or if an object hit the eye at high speed, consult the doctor.

FAINTING

25. Check for breathing, and if it is absent begin CPR *immediately* (see page 441). If you detect breathing, keep baby lying flat, lightly covered for warmth if necessary. Loosen clothing around the neck. Turn baby's head to one side and clear the mouth of any food or objects. Don't give anything to eat or drink. Call the doctor immediately.

FINGER AND TOE INJURIES

26. Bruises. Babies, ever curious, are particularly prone to painful bruises from catching fingers in drawers and doors. For such a bruise, soak the finger in ice water. As much as an hour of soaking is recommended, with a break every 15 minutes (long enough for the finger to rewarm) to avoid frostbite. Unfortunately, few babies will sit still for this long, though you may be able to treat for a few minutes by using distraction or force. A stubbed toe will also benefit from soaking, but again it often isn't practical with an infant who won't cooperate. The bruised fingers and toes will swell less if kept elevated.

If the injured finger or toe becomes very swollen very quickly, is misshapen, or can't be straightened, suspect a break (#7). Call the doctor immediately if the bruise is from a wringer-type injury or from catching a hand or foot in the spokes of a moving wheel.

27. Bleeding under the nail. When a finger or toe is badly bruised, a blood clot may form under the nail, causing painful pressure. If blood oozes out from under the nail, press on it to encourage the flow, which will help to relieve the pressure. Soak the injury in ice water if baby will tolerate it. If the pain continues, a hole may have to be made in the nail to relieve the pressure. Your doctor can do the job or may tell you how to do it yourself.

28. Torn nail. For a small tear, secure with a piece of adhesive tape or a band-aid until the torn nail grows to a point where it can be trimmed. For a tear that is almost complete, trim away along the tear line and cover with a band-aid until the nail is long enough to protect the fingertip once again.

29. Detached nail. Completely remove the nail if it is still partly attached. Soak the finger or toe for 20 minutes in cold water, if possible, then apply antibiotic ointment and cover with a nonstick band-aid. For the next three days, soak once a day in

Treating a Young Patient

Babies are rarely cooperative patients. No matter how uncomfortable the symptoms of their illness or how painful their injuries, they are likely to consider the cure worse. It won't help to tell them that the calamine lotion will make chicken pox itch less or that the ice pack will keep a bruised finger from swelling. Even older children, who are capable of understanding such reasoning, are almost certain to resist it. But it may help to use distraction while trying to treat a baby or young child's illness or injury. Entertainment (begun before the treatment and, hopefully, before the tears have started) in the form of a favourite music box, video, or audio tape; a toy dog that yaps and wags its tail; a choo-choo train that can travel across the coffee table; or a parent or sibling who can dance, jump up and down, or sing silly songs can help make the difference between a successful treatment session and a disastrous one. Or try sailing some boats in the soaking water; taking a teddy's temperature; giving a doll a dose of medicine; putting an ice pack on doggie's 'boo-boo'.

How forceful you are about treatment will depend on the severity of the illness or injury. With a mild stuffy nose, aspirating the mucus may not be worth the battle. But if the stuffy nose is interfering with baby's sleep or eating, then the battle may be necessary. A slight bruise may not warrant upsetting yourself and a baby who's rejecting the ice pack. A severe burn, however, will certainly merit the cold soaks, even if baby screams during the entire treatment. In most cases, try to treat at least briefly – even a few minutes of ice on a bruise will reduce the bleeding under the skin and even thirty seconds of temperature taking will give a fairly good idea of baby's condition. And when baby's upset outweighs the benefits of the treatment, abandon it.

warm salt water (½ teaspoon salt to 575 ml/ 1 pint water) for about 15 minutes. Apply antibiotic ointment and cover with a fresh band-aid after each soaking. By the fourth day dispense with the ointment as long as healing continues, but continue the daily soakings for the rest of the week. Keep the nail bed covered with a band-aid until the nail is completely grown in. If the redness, heat and swelling of infection occur at any point, call the doctor.

FROSTBITE

30. Babies are extremely susceptible to frostbite, particularly on fingers and toes, ears, nose and cheeks. In frostbite, the affected part becomes very cold and turns white or yellowish grey. Should you note such signs in your baby, immediately try to warm the frosty parts against your body – open your coat and shirt and tuck baby inside next to your skin. As soon as possible, get to a doctor or hospital. If that isn't feasible immediately, get baby indoors and begin a gradual rewarming process. Don't put a baby with frostbite right next to a radiator, stove, open fire, or heat lamp, because the damaged skin may burn; don't try to quick-thaw in hot water, which can also add to the damage. Instead, soak affected fingers and toes directly in water that is about 38.9°C (102°F) – just a little warmer than normal body temperature and just slightly warm to the touch. For unsoakable parts, such as nose, ears and cheeks, use compresses (wet flannels or towels) of the same temperature, but don't apply pressure. Continue the soaks until colour returns to the skin, usually in 30 to 60 minutes (add warm water as needed), nursing baby or giving warm (not hot) fluids by bottle or cup as you do. As frostbitten skin rewarms it becomes red and slightly swollen, and it may blister. If baby's injury hasn't been seen by a doctor up to this point, it is important to get medical attention now.

If, once the injured parts have been warmed, you have to go out again to take baby to the doctor (or anywhere else), be especially careful to keep the affected areas warm en route, as refreezing of thawed tissues can cause additional damage.

After prolonged exposure to cold, a baby's body temperature may drop to below normal levels. This is a medical emergency known as hypothermia – no time should be wasted in getting a baby who seems unusually cold to the touch to the nearest emergency room. Keep baby warm next to your body en route.

HEAD INJURIES

31. Cuts and bruises to the scalp. Because of the profusion of blood vessels in the scalp, heavy bleeding is common with cuts to the head, even tiny ones, and bruises there tend to swell to egg size very quickly. Treat as you would any cut (#47, #48) or bruise (#45). Check with the doctor for all but very minor scalp wounds.

32. Possibly serious head trauma. Most babies experience several minor bumps on the head during the first year. Usually these require no more than a few make-it-better kisses from mummy, but it's wise to observe

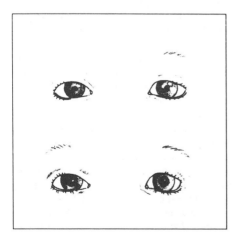

Pupils should become smaller in response to light (above) and larger once the light is removed (below).

a baby carefully for 6 hours following a severe blow to the head. Call the doctor or summon emergency medical assistance immediately if your baby shows any of these signs after a head injury.

- Loss of consciousness (a brief period of drowsiness – no more than two or three hours – is common and nothing to worry about).

- Convulsions

- Difficulty being roused (check every hour or two during daytime naps, two or three times during the night for the first 6 hours following the injury to be sure baby is responsive; if you can't rouse a sleeping baby, check for breathing; see page 441).

- More than one or two episodes of vomiting.

- A depression or indentation in the skull.

- Inability to move an arm or leg.

- Oozing of blood or watery fluid from the ears or nose.

- Black-and-blue areas appearing around the eyes or behind the ears.

- Apparent pain for more than an hour that interferes with normal activity and/or sleep.

- Dizziness that persists beyond one hour after the injury (baby's balance seems off).

- Unequal pupil size, or pupils that don't respond to the light of a penlight by shrinking (see illustration) or the removal of the light by growing larger.

- Unusual paleness that persists for more than a short time.

While waiting for help, keep your baby lying quietly with head turned to one side. Treat for shock (#44), if necessary. Begin CPR (page 441) if baby stops breathing. Don't offer any food or drink until you talk to the doctor.

HEAT INJURIES

33. Heatstroke typically comes on suddenly. Signs to watch for include hot and dry (or occasionally, moist) skin, very high fever, diarrhoea, agitation or lethargy, confusion, convulsions and loss of consciousness. If you suspect heatstroke, wrap your baby in a large towel that has been soaked in ice water (dump ice cubes in the sink while it's filling with cold tap water, than add the towel) and summon immediate emergency medical help, or rush baby to the nearest hospital. If the towel becomes warm, repeat with a freshly chilled one.

HYPOTHERMIA

see #30

INSECT BITES

see #4

LIP, SPLIT OR CUT

see #34, #35

MOUTH INJURIES

34. Split lip. Few babies escape the first year without at least one cut on the lip. Fortunately, these cuts usually heal very quickly. To ease pain and control bleeding, apply an ice pack. Or let an older baby suck on an ice pop or a large ice cube under adult supervision (switch to a fresh ice cube when the first has become small enough to choke on). If the cut gapes open, or if bleeding doesn't stop in 10 or 15 minutes, call the doctor. Occasionally a lip injury is caused by baby chewing on an electrical cord. If this is suspected, call the doctor.

35. Cuts inside the lip or mouth. Such injuries, too, are common in young children. An ice pack for young infants, or an ice pop or a large ice cube for older children to suck on under adult supervision (switch to a fresh ice cube when the first has become small enough to choke on), will relieve pain and control bleeding inside the lip or cheek.

Applying pressure to a cut lip with a piece of gauze held between thumb and forefinger will stop the bleeding.

To stop bleeding of the tongue if it doesn't stop spontaneously, squeeze the sides of the cut together with a piece of gauze or clean cloth. If the injury is in the back of the throat or on the soft palate (the rear of the upper mouth), if there is a puncture wound from a sharp object (such as a pencil or a stick), or if bleeding doesn't stop within 10 to 15 minutes, call the doctor.

36. Knocked-out tooth. If a permanent tooth is dislodged, it should be rinsed gently under running water while being held by the crown (not the root). It can then be reinserted into the gum, if possible, or held in the mouth or in tap water or milk en route to the dentist, who may be able to reimplant it if no more than 30 to 45 minutes have elapsed since the accident. There is little chance that the dentist will try to reimplant a dislodged baby tooth (such implantations often abscess and rarely hold), so precautions to preserve the tooth aren't necessary. But the dentist will want to see the tooth to be sure it's whole. Fragments left in the gum could be expelled and then inhaled or choked on by the baby. So take the tooth along to the dentist or to the hospital if you are unable to reach a dentist.

37. Broken tooth. Clean dirt or debris carefully from the mouth with warm water and gauze or a clean cloth. Be sure the broken parts of the tooth are not still in baby's mouth – they could cause choking. Place cold compresses (see page 614) on the face in the area of the injured tooth to minimize swelling. Call the dentist immediately for further instructions.

NOSE INJURIES

38. Nosebleeds. Keeping baby in an upright position or leaning slightly forward, pinch both nostrils gently between your thumb and index finger for 5 to 10 minutes. (Baby will automatically switch to mouth breathing.) Try to calm baby, because crying will increase the blood flow. If bleeding persists, try packing the bleeding nostril with a wad of absorbent cotton and pinch for 10 minutes more and/or apply cold compresses. If this doesn't work and bleeding continues, call the doctor – keeping baby upright while you do. Frequent nosebleeds, even if easily stopped, should be reported to baby's doctor.

39. Foreign object in the nose. Difficulty breathing through the nose and/or a foul-smelling, sometimes bloody, nasal discharge may be a sign that something has been pushed up the nose. Keep baby calm and encourage mouth breathing. Remove the

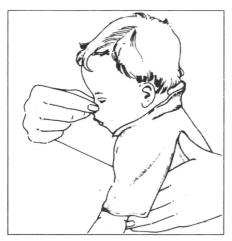

Pinching the nostrils stems the flow of a bloody nose.

object with your fingers if you can reach it easily, but don't probe or use tweezers or anything else that could injure the nose if baby moves unexpectedly or that could push the object farther into the nasal canal. If you can't remove the object, blow through your nose and try to get baby to imitate your action. If this fails, take baby to the doctor or emergency room.

40. Blows to the nose. If there is bleeding, keep baby upright and leaning forward to reduce the swallowing of blood and the risk of choking on it (#38). Use an ice pack or cold compresses (page 614) to reduce swelling. Check with the doctor to be sure there is no break.

POISONING

41. Swallowed poisons. Any nonfood substance is a potential poison. If your baby becomes unconscious, and you know of or suspect the ingestion of a dangerous substance, begin emergency treatment immediately. Place baby face up on a table and check for respiration (see page 441). If there is no sign of breathing, begin CPR promptly. Call for emergency medical assistance after 2 minutes, then continue CPR until baby revives or until help arrives.

The more common symptoms of poisoning include: lethargy, agitation, or other behaviour that deviates from the norm; racing, irregular pulse and/or rapid breathing; diarrhoea or vomiting (baby should be turned on one side to avoid choking on vomitus); excessive watering of the eyes, sweating, drooling; hot, dry skin and mouth; dilated (wide open) or constricted (pinpoint) pupils; flickering, sideways eye movements; tremors or convulsions.

If your baby has several of these symptoms (and they cannot be explained in any other way), or if you have evidence that your baby has definitely or possibly ingested a questionable substance, do not try to treat it on your own. Do not give your baby anything by mouth (including food or drink; the activated charcoal blend known as universal antidote; or anything to induce vomiting, such as syrup of ipecac, salt water, or egg whites). Instead, call the doctor, the local Poison Control Centre or the hospital emergency room *immediately* for instructions. Call even if there are no symptoms – they may not appear for hours. Take with you to the phone the container the suspected substance came in, label intact, as well as any of the remaining contents. Report the name of the substance (or of the plant if your baby ingested greenery) and how much of it you know or believe baby took, if it's possible to determine that. Also be prepared to supply your baby's age, size, weight and symptoms.

With many poisons, you will be advised to induce vomiting with syrup of ipecac in order to empty the stomach of as much of the poison as possible.[1] Give the dose recommended by the Poison Control Centre or the doctor. (If you have no ipecac available, ask medical personnel about using liquid washing-up – *not* dishwasher – detergent to induce vomiting.) If vomiting does not occur within 20 minutes, repeat the dose – but only once. If you succeed in inducing vomiting, collect the vomited material in a deep pan or bowl. If you are instructed to go to the emergency room or doctor's surgery, take the vomitus along for analysis. (It may be easier to carry it in a jar with a lid or a heavy zip-lock-type plastic bag, but bring along a clean bowl or bucket in case baby heaves again.) Also be sure to take the suspect substance (bottle of pills, container of cleaning fluid, branch of philodendron).

Vomiting is not usually induced in babies under six months of age because of the greater risk of choking in young infants. In babies six months to one year of age, it should be induced only under medical supervision. Vomiting should not be induced at any age when a corrosive substance (such as bleach, ammonia, or drain cleaner) or anything with a kerosene, benzene, or petroleum base (furniture polishes, cleaning fluid, turpentine) has been ingested. Nor when the victim is unconscious, drowsy, or having convulsions or tremors. In some cases, liquid charcoal, which absorbs the poison, is the preferred treatment.

42. Noxious fumes or gases. Fumes from petrol, car exhaust and some poisonous chemicals and dense smoke from fires can all be toxic. Get a baby who has been exposed to any such hazards to fresh air (open windows or take the child outside) promptly. If baby is not breathing, begin CPR (see page 441) *immediately* and continue until breathing is well established or help arrives. If possible, have someone else call the Poison Control Centre or an emergency medical service while you continue CPR. If no one else is around, take a moment to call for help yourself after 2 minutes of resuscitation efforts – and then return immediately to CPR. Unless an emergency vehicle is on its way, transport baby to a medical facility promptly, but not if doing so means discontinuing CPR or if you were also exposed and your judgment is impaired. Have someone else drive. Even if you should succeed in establishing breathing, immediate medical attention will be necessary.

PUNCTURE WOUNDS

see #50

SCRAPES

see #46

SEVERED LIMB OR DIGIT

43. Such serious accidents are rare, but knowing what to do when one occurs can mean the difference between saving and losing a limb or digit. Take these steps as needed immediately:

- Try to control bleeding. With several sterile gauze pads, a clean nappy, a sanitary towel, or a clean flannel apply heavy pressure to the wound. If bleeding continues, increase pressure. Don't worry about doing damage by pressing too hard. Do not apply a tourniquet without medical advice.

---

1. If you use up your ipecac, be sure to replace it.

- Treat shock if present. If baby's skin seems pale, cold and clammy, pulse is weak and rapid, and respiration is shallow, treat for shock by loosening clothing, covering baby lightly to prevent loss of body heat, and elevating legs on a pillow (or folded garment) to force blood to the brain. If breathing seems laboured, raise baby's head and shoulders slightly.

- Re-establish breathing, if necessary. Begin CPR immediately if baby isn't breathing (see page 441).

- Preserve the severed limb or digit. As soon as possible, wrap it in a wet clean cloth or sponge, and place in a plastic bag. Pack the bag with ice and tie it shut. Do not place part directly on ice, don't use dry ice, and don't immerse it in water or antiseptics.

- Get help. Call or have someone else call for immediate emergency medical assistance or rush to the hospital, calling ahead so they can prepare for your arrival. Be sure to take along the ice-packed limb; surgeons may be able to reattach it. During transport, keep pressure on the wound and continue other lifesaving procedures, if necessary.

SHOCK

44. Shock can develop in severe injuries or illnesses. Signs include cold, clammy, pale skin; rapid, weak pulse; chills; convulsions; and frequently, nausea or vomiting, excessive thirst and/or shallow breathing. To treat, position baby on back. Loosen restrictive clothing, elevate legs on a pillow or folded garment to force blood to the brain, and cover baby lightly to prevent chilling or loss of body heat. If breathing seems laboured, raise baby's head and shoulders very slightly. Get emergency medical assistance.

SKIN WOUNDS

Important: Exposure to tetanus is a possibility whenever the skin is broken. Should your child incur an open skin wound, check to be sure tetanus immunization is up-to-date. Also be alert for signs of possible infection (swelling, warmth, tenderness, reddening of surrounding area, oozing of pus from the wound), and call the doctor if they develop.

45. Bruises or black-and-blue marks. Encourage quiet play to rest the injured part, if possible. Apply cold compresses, an ice pack, or cloth-wrapped ice for half an hour. (Do not apply ice directly to the skin.) If the skin is broken, treat the bruise as you would a cut (#47, #48). Call the doctor immediately if the bruise is from a wringer-type injury or if it resulted from catching a hand or foot in the spokes of a moving wheel. Bruises that seem to appear out of nowhere or that coincide with a fever should also be seen by a doctor.

46. Scrapes or abrasions. In such injuries (most common on knees and elbows) the top layer (or layers) of skin is abraded, or scraped off, leaving the area raw and tender. There is usually slight bleeding from the more deeply abraded areas. Using sterile gauze or cotton or a clean flannel, gently sponge off the wound with soap and water to remove dirt and other foreign matter. If baby strenuously objects to this, try soaking the scrape in the bathtub. Apply pressure if the bleeding doesn't stop on its own. Cover with a sterile nonstick bandage. Most scrapes heal quickly.

47. Small cuts. Wash the area with clean water and soap, then hold the cut under running water to flush out dirt and foreign matter. Apply a sterile nonstick band-aid. A butterfly bandage (see illustration overleaf) will keep a small cut closed while it heals. Check with the doctor about any cuts on a baby's face.

48. Large cuts. With a sterile gauze pad, a fresh nappy, a sanitary towel, a clean flannel, or if necessary, your bare finger, apply pressure to try to stop the bleeding, elevating the injured part above the level of the heart, if

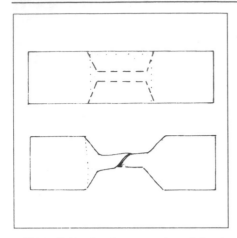

A butterfly bandage keeps a gaping cut closed so it can heal. Trim down a regular band-aid and make one complete twist to form a strong butterfly.

possible, at the same time. If bleeding persists after 15 minutes of pressure, add more gauze pads or cloth and increase the pressure. (Don't worry about doing damage with too much pressure.) If necessary, keep the pressure on until help arrives or you get baby to the doctor or hospital. If there are other injuries, try to tie or bandage the pressure pack in place so that your hands can be free to attend to them. Apply a sterile nonstick bandage to the wound when the bleeding stops, loose enough so that it doesn't interfere with circulation. Do not use iodine or other antiseptic without medical advice. Take baby to the doctor's surgery (call first) or the hospital for wounds that gape, appear deep, or don't stop bleeding within half an hour.

49. Massive bleeding. Get emergency medical attention by calling an ambulance or rushing to the nearest hospital if a limb is severed and/or blood is gushing or pumping out. In the meantime, apply pressure on the wound with gauze pads, a fresh nappy, a sanitary towel, or a clean flannel or towel. Increase the packing and pressure if bleeding doesn't stop. Do not resort to a tourniquet without medical advice as it can sometimes do more harm than good. Maintain pressure until help arrives.

50. Puncture wounds. Soak the injury in comfortably hot, soapy water for 15 minutes. Consult the baby's doctor or go to the hospital. Do not remove any object (such as a knife or stick) that protrudes from the wound, as this could lead to increased bleeding. Pad it, if necessary, to keep it from moving around. Keep baby as calm and still as possible to avoid thrashing and making the injury worse.

51. Splinters or slivers. Wash the area with clean water and soap, then numb it with an ice pack (see page 615). If the sliver is completely embedded, try to work it loose with a sewing needle that has been sterilized with alcohol or the flame of a match. If one end of the sliver is clearly visible, try to remove it with tweezers (also sterilized by flame or alcohol). Don't try to remove it with your fingernails, which might be dirty. Wash the site again after you have removed the splinter. If the splinter is not easily removed, try soaking in warm, soapy water for 15 minutes, three times a day for a couple of days, which may help it work its way out. If it doesn't, or if the area becomes infected (indicated by redness, heat, swelling), consult the doctor. Also call the doctor if the splinter was deep and your baby's tetanus shots are not up to date.

SPLINTERS OR SLIVERS

see #51

SUNBURN

see #14

TEETH, INJURY TO

see #36, #37

TOE INJURIES

see #26, #27, #28, #29

TONGUE, INJURY TO

see #35

Label Your Ipecac

Though it's a good idea to keep a bottle of syrup of ipecac among your first-aid supplies, this emetic (vomiting inducer) should never be administered without medical advice. To be certain that it isn't, tape a wide piece of adhesive with the warning 'DO NOT USE WITHOUT INSTRUCTIONS FROM THE DOCTOR' across the face of the bottle. Add the telephone number of the the baby's doctor, which should also be posted next to all the phones in your home.

And don't be afraid to use ipecac that is out of date. It is known to be 100% effective and safe up to four years after its expiration date. Keep a spare bottle, similarly labelled, in your changing bag for visiting and travel.

Some recent studies indicate that liquid charcoal may be a preferable treatment in some cases of poisoning. Check with your doctor to see if he or she recommends stocking liquid charcoal in your medicine chest.

Resuscitation Techniques For Babies

The instructions that follow should be used only as reinforcement. You must, for your child's sake, take a course in baby CPR (check with baby's doctor, a local hospital, or the Red Cross for the location of a class in your community) in order to be sure you can carry out these life support procedures correctly. Periodically, reread these guidelines or those you receive at the course and run through them step by step on a doll (*never* on your baby or any other person, or even on a pet) at least once a month so you will be able to perform them automatically should an emergency occur. Take a refresher course now and then – both to brush up on your skills and to learn the latest techniques.

The protocol below should be begun only on a baby who has stopped breathing, or on one who is struggling to breathe and turning blue (check around the lips and fingertips).

If a baby is struggling to breathe but hasn't turned blue, call for emergency medical assistance immediately or rush to the nearest emergency room. Meanwhile, keep baby warm and as quiet as possible, and in the position he or she seems most comfortable in.

If resuscitation seems necessary, survey baby's condition with Steps 1-2-3:[2]

1. Check for Unresponsiveness

Try to rouse a baby who appears to be unconscious by calling by name loudly, 'Annie, Annie, are you okay?' several times. If that doesn't work, try tapping the soles of baby's feet. As a last resort, try gently shaking or tapping baby's shoulder – do not shake vigorously and don't shake at all if there is any possibility of broken bones, or of head, neck, or back injury.

2. Seek Help

If you get no response, have anyone else present call for emergency medical assistance while you continue to Step 3. If you are alone with baby and feel sure of your CPR skills, proceed without delay, periodically calling loudly to attract help from neighbours or passersby. If, however, you are unfamiliar with CPR and/or feel paralyzed by panic, go the nearest phone immediately with the baby (assuming there are no signs of head, neck, or back injuries) or better still

---

2. This protocol is based on the latest rescue procedures of the American Red Cross and the American Heart Association, and was prepared with the assistance of Barbara Hogan of the Emergency Care Institute of Bellevue Hospital in New York. The training you receive may be somewhat different and should be the basis for your action.

bring a portable phone to baby's side and call 999 and ask for an ambulance. The dispatcher will be able to guide you as to the best course of action.

> *Important:* The person calling for emergency medical assistance should be certain to stay on the phone as long as necessary to give complete information and until the dispatcher has concluded questioning. The following should be included: name and age of baby; present location (address, cross streets, apartment number, best route if there is more than one route); condition (is baby conscious? breathing? bleeding? in shock? is there a heartbeat?); cause of condition (poison, drowning, fall, etc.), if known; phone number, if there is a phone at the site. Tell the person calling for help to report back to you after calling.

3. Position Baby

Move baby as a unit, carefully supporting head, neck and back as you do, to a firm, flat surface (a table is good because you won't have to kneel, but the floor will do). Quickly position baby face up, head level with heart, and use A-B-C[3] to survey his or her condition.

A: Clear the Airway

Use the following head-tilt/chin-lift technique to try to open the airway, unless there is a possibility of a head, neck, or back injury. If such an injury is suspected, use the jaw-thrust technique (below) instead.

> *Important:* The airway of an unconscious baby may be blocked by a relaxed tongue or epiglottis or by a foreign object. It must be cleared before baby can resume breathing.

---

3. If you suspect a head, neck, or back injury, go to step B to look, listen and feel for breathing before moving baby. If breathing is present, don't move baby unless there is immediate danger (as from fire or explosion) at the present site. If breathing is absent, and rescue breathing cannot be accomplished in the position baby is in, roll baby to a face up position as a unit so that head, neck, and body move as one without twisting.

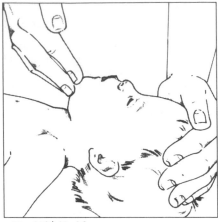

Head tilt/chin lift.

Head tilt/chin lift. Place the hand nearest baby's head on the forehead and one or two fingers (not the thumb) of the other hand under the bony part of the lower jaw at the chin. Gently tilt baby's head back slightly by applying pressure on the forehead and lifting the chin. Do not press on the soft tissues of the underchin or let the mouth close completely (keep your thumb in it if necessary to keep the lips apart). Baby's head should be facing the ceiling in what is called the neutral position, with the chin neither down on the chest nor pointing up in the air. The head tilt necessary to open the airway in a child over one year may be somewhat greater (the neutral-plus position). If the airway does not open in a neutral position, move on to check for breathing (B).

Jaw thrust, for use when neck or back injury is suspected: With your elbows resting on the surface where baby is lying, place two or three fingers under each side of the lower jaw, at the angle where the upper and lower jaw meet, and gently lift the jaw upward to a neutral position (see head tilt, above).

> *Important:* Even if baby resumes breathing immediately, get medical help. Any baby who has been unconscious, stopped breathing, or nearly drowned requires medical evaluation.

B: Check for Breathing

1. After performing either the head tilt or the jaw thrust, look, listen and feel for 3 to 5 seconds to see if baby is breathing: can you hear or feel the passage of air when you place your ear near baby's nose and mouth? Does a mirror placed in front of baby's face cloud up? Can you see baby's chest and abdomen rising and falling (this alone isn't proof of breathing, since it could mean baby is trying to breathe but isn't succeeding)?

If normal breathing has resumed, maintain an open airway with head tilt or jaw thrust. If baby regains consciousness as well (and has no injuries that make moving inadvisable), turn him or her to one side. Call for an ambulance now if someone else hasn't already called. If baby starts to breathe independently, and also starts to cough forcefully, this may be the body's attempt to expel an obstruction. *Don't interfere with the coughing.*

If breathing is absent, *or* if baby is struggling to breathe and has bluish lips and/or a weak, muffled cry, you must get air into the lungs immediately. Continue below. If an ambulance has not been summoned and you are alone, continue trying to attract neighbours or passersby.

2. Maintain an open airway by keeping baby's head in a neutral position (or neutral-plus position, if needed, with a baby over a year) with your hand on the forehead. With a finger of the other hand, clear baby's mouth of any *visible* vomitus, dirt, or other foreign matter. Do not attempt a sweep if nothing is visible.

> *Important:* If vomiting should occur at any point, immediately turn baby to one side, clear mouth of vomitus with a finger, reposition baby on back, and quickly resume rescue procedures.

3. Take a breath through your mouth and place your mouth over baby's mouth and nose, forming a tight seal (see illustration). With a baby over a year old, cover just the mouth, and pinch the nostrils closed with the fingers of the hand that is keeping the head tilted back.

4. Blow two *light, slow* breaths of 1 to 1½ seconds each into baby's mouth, pausing between them to turn your head slightly and take a breath. Observe baby's chest with each breath. Stop blowing when the chest rises, and wait for the chest to fall before beginning another breath. In addition listen and feel for air being exhaled.

> *Important:* Remember, a small baby needs only a small amount of air to fill the lungs. Though blowing too lightly may

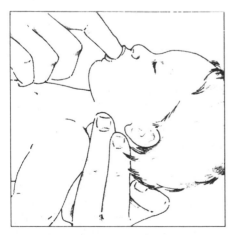

Clearing the baby's mouth of vomitus or foreign matter.

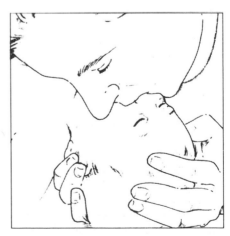

In rescue breathing for infants, both mouth and nose must be covered.

not expand the lungs fully, blowing too hard or too fast can force air into the stomach, causing distension. If at any point during rescue breathing baby's abdomen becomes distended, don't try to push it down – this might cause vomiting, which could present the risk of vomitus being aspirated, or inhaled, into the lungs. If the distension seems to be interfering with chest expansion, turn baby to one side, head down if possible, and apply gentle pressure to the abdomen for a second or two.

5. If the chest does not rise and fall with each breath, readjust the head-tilt/chin-lift (or jaw-thrust) position and try two more breaths. Blow a bit harder if necessary. If the chest still does not rise, it is possible that the airway is obstructed by food or a foreign object – in which case move quickly to dislodge it, using the procedure in 'When Baby Is Choking' on page 447.

For a baby over a year, and sometimes for a large younger baby, it may be necessary to tilt the jaw a bit more to the neutral-plus position in order to open the airway and ventilate (get air into) baby; retilt and try two more breaths. If that doesn't work, extend the chin further and try again; repeat until the chin is pointing straight up. If the chest still does not rise, proceed to 'When Baby Is Choking'.

C: Check Circulation

1. As soon as you've determined with two successful breaths that the airway is clear, check for a pulse. With an infant under a year, try to find the brachial pulse in the arm closest to you: keeping one hand on baby's head to maintain an open airway, use the other to pull baby's arm away from the body and turn it palm up. Use your index and middle fingers to try to locate the pulse between the two muscles on the inside of the middle arm, between the shoulder and elbow; see page 400. (With an older baby, take the carotid pulse in the neck). Since it's dangerous to give CPR to a baby whose heart is beating, do a thorough search; be

sure to give yourself a full 5 to 10 seconds to locate the pulse. (Parents should practise finding their baby's pulse under non-emergency conditions so they can find it in a hurry under stress.)

2. If you find no pulse, begin CPR (see page 446) immediately. If you find a pulse, baby's heart is beating. Begin rescue breathing immediately (below) if breathing has not resumed spontaneously.

Call the Ambulance

If the ambulance has not yet been called and there is someone available to make the call, have them do so now. If a call was made before baby's condition was assessed, have the caller contact the dispatcher again to give further information on baby's condition: whether or not baby is conscious, is breathing and has a pulse. Do not take time to call yourself if baby requires rescue breathing or CPR. Proceed without delay, periodically calling loudly to attract help from neighbours or passersby.

Resuscitation: Rescue Breathing

1. Blow into baby's mouth as described above at a rate of roughly one breath every 3 seconds (20 breaths per minute) for a baby under a year old (breathe, one and two and three and breathe), and once every 4 seconds (15 breaths per minute) for a baby older than a year. Watch to be sure baby's chest rises and falls with each breath.

2. Check for baby's pulse after a minute of rescue breathing to be sure the heart has not stopped. If it has, go to CPR. If it hasn't, look, listen and feel for spontaneous breathing (see page 443) for 3 to 5 seconds. If baby has begun breathing independently, continue to maintain an open airway and check breathing and pulse frequently while waiting for help to arrive; keep baby warm and as quiet as possible. If there is no spontaneous breathing, continue rescue breathing, checking for the pulse and breathing once every minute.

Important: The airway must be kept open for rescue breathing to be effective. Be sure to maintain baby's head in the neutral position during rescue breathing.

3. If you're alone and emergency medical help has not yet been summoned, call as soon as independent breathing has been established. If within a few minutes baby hasn't starting breathing independently, carry the child in the side hold to a phone, continuing rescue breathing as you go. On the phone, simply report, 'My baby isn't breathing', and quickly but clearly give all pertinent information (see above). Don't hang up until the dispatcher does; if possible, continue rescue breathing while the dispatcher is speaking; then get back to rescue breathing immediately.

Important: Do not discontinue rescue breathing until the baby is breathing independently or until medical professionals arrive to take over.

Cardiopulmonary Resuscitation (CPR): Babies Under One Year[4]

Important: In CPR, rescue breaths which force oxygen into the lungs where it is picked up by the bloodstream, must be alternated with chest compressions which artificially pump the oxygen laden blood to the vital organs and the rest of the body.

1. Continue with baby face up on a firm, flat surface. Baby's head should level with the heart.
2. Continue to maintain baby's head in a neutral position with one hand on the forehead. Place a small rolled towel, nappy, or other support under baby's shoulders and lift them just a bit, which will also help

---

4. One year is the arbitrary cutoff chosen by the Red Cross for switching from infant to child resuscitation procedures. The child's size may be a factor in some cases, but experts say that a slight error either way is not critical.

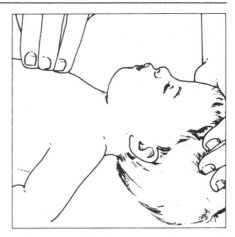

Compressions on infants can be done with two or three fingers.

maintain an open airway. Do not cause head to dip back more than slightly (see illustration page 442).

3. Position the three middle fingers of your free hand on baby's chest: imagine a horizontal line from nipple to nipple; place the pad of the index finger just under the intersection of this line with the breastbone, or sternum (the flat bone running midline down baby's chest between the ribs); the area to compress is one finger's width below this point of intersection.

4. Using two or three fingers, compress the sternum straight down to a depth of 1 to 2.5 cm (½ to 1 inch) (your elbow should be bent). At the end of each compression, release the pressure without removing your fingers from the sternum and allow it to return to its normal position. Develop a smooth compression-relaxation rhythm that allots equal time to each phase and avoids jerky movements.

After every fifth compression, pause with your fingers still in position on the sternum and deliver one slow rescue breath of 1 to 1½ seconds. Watch for the chest to rise. (If it doesn't, remove your fingers from the breastbone and lift the chin and blow again.) Aim for a rate of 100 compressions per minute, with a rescue breath after every five compressions. Count at a more rapid rate than you would if counting seconds: one, two, three, four, five – breathe.

6. After about a minute, take 5 seconds to check for the brachial pulse. If there is no pulse, give one slow rescue breath, then continue the compression/ventilation cycles of CPR, checking every few minutes for a pulse. If a pulse if found, discontinue chest compressions. Look, listen and feel for 3 to 5 seconds for spontaneous respiration. If breathing is present, keep airway open and baby warm and quiet, and continue to monitor baby's breathing. If baby is still not breathing, continue with rescue breathing alone as described above.

7. After one minute of CPR, if you are alone and have not been able to attract anyone who could call for emergency medical assistance up until now, go quickly to a phone (carrying baby with you, if possible, or bringing the phone to where baby is) and summon help; then immediately return to rescue procedures as needed.

Important: Do not discontinue CPR until breathing and heartbeat are re-established or until medical relief arrives.

Cardiopulmonary Resuscitation (CPR): Babies Over One Year

1. Continue with the child face up on a firm, flat surface. There should be no pillow under the child's head; the head should be level with the heart. The child's head should be in the neutral-plus position (pages 443 to 444) to keep the airway clear.

2. Position your hands: with your middle and index fingers, locate the lower margin of the rib cage on the side nearest you; follow the margin of the rib cage down to the notch where the ribs and the breastbone, or sternum (the flat bone running down baby's chest between the ribs), meet; place the middle finger of the hand nearest baby's feet on this notch and the index finger down next to it; place the heel of your other hand just above the index finger with the long axis of the heel lengthways, so that the two

fingers and your hand line up along the sternum.

Important: Do not apply pressure to the tip of the sternum (called the xiphoid process). Doing so could cause severe internal damage.

3. Compress the chest with the heel of your hand to a depth of 2.5 to 4 cm (1 to 1½ inches). The only contact should be between the heel of your hand and the flat lower half of the sternum – do not press on the ribs during compressions. Allow the chest to return to its resting position after each compression without lifting your hand from the chest. Develop a compression-relaxation rhythm that allots equal time to each phase and avoids jerky movements.

4. At the end of every fifth compression, pause, and with baby's nostrils pinched closed, deliver a slow breath of 1 to 1½ seconds. Chest compressions must always be accompanied by rescue breathing to ensure a steady supply of oxygen to the brain (a child without a heartbeat is not breathing and is not getting oxygen). Aim for a rate of 80 to 100 compressions a minute, with a breath after every five compressions. Count at a more rapid rate than you would if counting seconds: one, two, three, four, five – breathe.

5. After about a minute, take 5 seconds to check for a pulse. If there is no pulse, give one slow breath with the nostrils pinched closed, then continue compression/ventilation cycles of CPR, checking periodically for a pulse. If a pulse is found, discontinue chest compressions. But if baby is still not breathing, continue with rescue breathing alone.

6. If you have not been able to attract help by calling, and emergency medical assistance has not been summoned, take a moment to go to a phone and call now; then immediately return to rescue procedures as needed. If possible, carry baby with you to the phone in a side hold and continue rescue breathing as you go.

Important: Do not discontinue CPR until breathing and heartbeat are re-established or until medical relief arrives.

When Baby is Choking

Coughing is nature's way of trying to dislodge an obstruction in the airway. A baby (or anyone else) who is choking on food or some foreign object and who can breathe, cry and cough forcefully should not be interefered with. But if after two or three minutes baby continues to cough, call for emergency medical assistance. And when the choking victim is struggling for breath can't cough effectively, is making high-pitched crowing sounds, and/or is turning blue (usually starting around the lips), the following rescue procedures should be pursued. They should also be pursued *immediately* if the baby is unconscious and not breathing *and* if attempts to open the air way and breathe air into the lungs (see Steps A and B, pages 442 to 443) are unsuccessful.

> *Important:* An airway obstruction may also occur because of such infections as croup or epiglottitis. A choking baby who seems ill needs immediate attention at an emergency care facility. *Do not* waste time in a dangerous and futile attempt to try to relieve the problem.

For Babies Under One Year (Conscious or Unconscious)

1. Get help. If someone else is present ask them to phone for emergency medical assistance. If you're alone and unfamiliar with rescue procedures, or if you panic and forget them, take the baby to a phone or take a portable phone to where the child is and call for emergency medical assistance *immediately*. It's also usually recommended that even if you're familiar with rescue procedures, you take the time to call yourself before the situation worsens.

2. Position baby. Straddle baby face down along your forearm, head lower than trunk (at about a 60° angle; see illustration). Cradle baby's chin in the curve between your thumb and forefinger. If you are seated, rest your forearm on your thigh for support. If baby is too big for you to comfortably support on your forearm, sit in

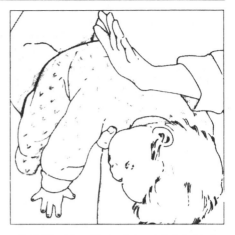

Back blows can often expel an inhaled object.

a chair or on your knees on the floor and place baby face down across your lap in the same head-lower-than-body position.

3. Administer back blows. Give four consecutive forceful blows between baby's shoulder blades with the heel of your free hand.

4. Administer chest thrusts. If there is no indication that the obstruction has been dislodged or loosened (forceful coughing, normal breathing, the object shooting out), place the flat of your free hand on the back, and supporting the head, neck and chest with the other hand turn the child over, again with the head lower than the trunk. Support the head and neck with your hand, and rest your forearm on your thigh for support. (A baby who is too large to hold in this position can be placed face up on your lap.) To position your hand, imagine a horizontal line from nipple to nipple. Place the pad of your index finger just under the intersection of this line with the sternum (the flat breastbone running midline down baby's chest between the ribs). The area to compress is one finger's width below this point of intersection. Position two fingers (three, if you aren't achieving effective compression with two – but be careful to stay within the area from one finger's width below the nipple line to above the end of

The Unsuspected Inhaled Object

If your baby seems to choke on something and then with or without emergency treatment seems better, watch carefully for any signs of continued problems such as an unusual tone when crying or talking; decreased breathing sounds; wheezing; unexplained coughing; or blueness around the lips or fingernails, or of the skin generally. If any of these signs is apparent, take baby immediately to the emergency room. It's possible an object has lodged in the lower respiratory tract.

the sternum) along the sternum on baby's chest. Deliver four chest thrusts, compressing the sternum to a depth of 1 to 2.5 cm (½ to 1 inch) with each, and allowing the sternum to return to its normal position in between compressions without removing your fingers. These are similiar to chest compressions but are performed at a slower rate – about 1 to 1½ seconds apart (one and, two and, three and, four).

If baby is conscious, keep repeating the back blows and chest thrusts until the airway is cleared or the baby becomes unconscious. If baby is unconscious, continue below.

5. Do a foreign body check. If there is no indication that the obstruction has been dislodged or loosened (forceful coughing, normal breathing, the object shooting out), check for a visible obstruction. Open the mouth, by placing your thumb in baby's mouth, and grasp the tongue and lower jaw between your thumb and forefinger. Depress the tongue with your thumb as you lift the jaw up and away from the back of the throat. If you see a foreign object, attempt to remove it with a sweep of a finger. Do not sweep the mouth if you do not see an obstruction, and do not try to remove a visible obstruction with a pincer grasp, as you might force the object farther into the airway.

6. Do an airway check. If baby is still not breathing normally, open the airway with a head-tilt/chin-lift manoeuvre and attempt to administer two slow breaths with your mouth sealed over baby's nose and mouth, as on page 443. If the chest rises

and falls with each breath, the airway is clear. Check for spontaneous breathing, Step B, and continue procedure as necessary.

7. Repeat sequence. If the airway remains blocked, keep repeating the sequence above until the airway is cleared and baby is conscious and breathing normally, or until emergency help has arrived. Don't give up, since the longer the baby goes without oxygen, the more the muscles of the throat will relax, and the more likely the obstruction can be dislodged.

For Children Over One Year (Unconscious)

1. Position baby. Place child face up on a firm, flat surface (floor or table). Stand or kneel at the child's feet (don't sit astride a small child) and place the heel of one hand on the abdomen in the midline between the navel and the rib cage, fingers facing towards the child's face. Place the second hand on top of the first.

2. Administer abdominal thrusts. With the upper hand pressing against the lower, use a series of 6 to 10 rapid, inward-and-upward abdominal thrusts to dislodge the foreign object. These thrusts should be gentler than they would be for an adult or older child. And be careful not to apply pressure to the tip of the sternum or to the ribs.

3. Do an airway check. If the child is still not breathing spontaneously, tilt the head and administer two slow mouth-to-mouth breaths, while pinching the nostrils closed. If the chest rises and falls with each breath, the airway is clear. Check for spontaneous breathing, Step B (see page 443), and continue the procedure as necessary.

4. Repeat sequence. If the airway remains blocked, continue repeating the sequence above until the airway is cleared and baby is conscious and breathing normally, or until emergency help has arrived. Don't give up, since the longer the child goes without oxygen, the more the muscles of the throat will relax, and the more likely the obstruction can be dislodged.

Important: Even if your baby recovers quickly from a choking episode, medical attention will be required. Call baby's doctor or the hospital.

For Children Over One Year (Conscious)

1. Position yourself. Stand behind the child and wrap your arms around his or her waist.

2. Position your hands. The thumb side of one fist should rest against the child's abdomen in the midline, slightly above the naval and well below the tip of the breastbone.

3. Administer abdominal thrusts. Grasp the positioned fist with your other hand and press it into the child's abdomen with a quick upward thrust (the pressure should be less than you would use on an adult). Repeat until you see the object ejected or the baby begins breathing normally.

NINETEEN

The Low-Birthweight Baby

♦

Most parents-to-be expect their babies to arrive right around the due date, give or take a couple of days or weeks. And indeed, the majority of babies do arrive on schedule – allowing them sufficient time to prepare for life outside the uterus, and their parents sufficient time to prepare for life with a baby.

But that vital preparatory time is cut unexpectedly – and sometimes perilously – short when baby is born prematurely and/or too small. Some of these babies weigh in just a few grams/ounces under the 2,500 gram (5-pound 8-ounce) low-birthweight cutoff, and are able to quickly and easily catch up with their full-term peers. But others, robbed of many weeks of uterine development, arrive so small that they can fit in the palm of a hand; and it can take months of intensive medical care to help them do the growing they were supposed to have done in the womb.

Many parents, too, are far from ready when birth comes too early. For them, the first postpartum days, sometimes weeks or months, are filled not with writing thank you notes, learning to change nappies and getting adjusted to having a baby in the house, but with reading hospital charts, learning to insert nasogastric tubes and getting adjusted to *not* having a baby in the house.

Though the low-birthweight baby (whether born early or not) is still at higher risk than larger babies, rapid advances in medical care for tiny infants have made it possible for the great majority of them to grow into normal, healthy children. But before they are carried proudly home from the hospital, their parents often experience many agonizing days and sleepless nights.

Feeding Baby: Nutrition for the Preterm or Low-Birthweight Infant

The feeding of the preterm infant is a science that itself hasn't reached term; there is still much to be learned about the nutritional needs of babies who arrive before their expected due date. But what is known, or suspected, grows each year, as neonatologists and neonatal intensive care nurses try to devise and perfect the best methods for nourishing babies who must be fed outside the uterus at a time when they should still be getting fed inside it.

One of the still unclear areas of knowledge – and one critical to the rest of the picture – is how much weight a preterm baby should gain each week. There are many variables that affect weight gain, in-

Portrait of a Premie

The parents of full-term newborns may be surprised when they first see their babies. The parents of preterm infants are often shocked. The typical premie weighs between 1,600 grams (about 3½ pounds) and 1,900 grams (about 4 pounds 3 ounces) at birth, and some weigh considerably less. The smallest can fit in the palm of an adult hand and have such tiny wrists and hands that a wedding ring could be slipped over them. The premie's skin is translucent, leaving veins and arteries visible. It seems to fit loosely because it lacks a fat layer beneath it, and often it is covered with a fine layer of body hair, or lanugo. Skin colouring changes when the infant is handled or fed. Because brown fat (the fat layer that keeps us warm) is absent, the baby is unable to keep itself warm. The premie's ears may be flat, folded, or floppy because the cartilage

that will give them shape is lacking.

Sexual characteristics are usually not fully developed – testicles may be undescended, the foreskin in boys and the inner folds of the labia in girls may be immature, and there may be no areola around the nipples. Because neither muscular nor nerve development is complete, many reflexes (such as grasping, sucking, startle, rooting) may be absent. And because of lack of strength and wind, the baby may cry little or not at all. He or she may also be subject to periods of breathing cessation, known as apnea of prematurity.

But being a premie is only a temporary condition. Once preterm newborns reach forty weeks of gestation, the time when, according to the calendar, they should have been born, they very much resemble the typical newborn in size and development.

cluding birth size, hereditary factors (babies of Asian women may be smaller and grow more slowly than those with a Nordic heritage, for example), atmospheric conditions (growth is slower at high altitudes than at sea level), and overall health. Some experts now believe that the growth potential of premature infants has been underestimated in the past, possibly because inadequate feeding led to inadequate weight gain, and inadequate weight gain became the accepted norm. As nutritional understanding has increased, and along with it average weight gains, the expectations have been upped. The 70- to 140-gram (2½- to 5-ounce) weekly gain once considered an appropriate goal for premies is rapidly being replaced by a suggested 90 to 210 grams (3¼ to 7½-plus ounces). Whatever the projected weight gain, it's unlikely to begin until the premature infant's condition has stabilized. You can expect your premature infant, like the full-term baby, to lose some weight before beginning to gain.

It's also now recognized that the nutritional requirements of a preterm infant differ

considerably from those of a baby born at term. Neither full-term breast milk nor ordinary baby formula – both of which term babies thrive on – are adequate for premies. These tiny babies need a diet closer to that they would have received if they were still in the uterus, including more protein, calcium, phosphorus, zinc, sodium and possibly other nutrients. And they need to obtain these nutrients in as concentrated a form as possible because they are able to take only very small amounts of food at a time – partly because their stomachs are small and partly because their immature digestive systems are sluggish, making the passage of food a very slow process.

When a very small neonate (newborn) is rushed to the intensive care nursery, an intravenous solution of water, sugar and certain electrolytes is usually given to prevent dehydration and electrolyte depletion. After that initial feeding, very premature babies (those who arrived earlier than 30 to 33 weeks of gestation) will be fed by a method not dependent on sucking (such as via a nasogastric tube going through the

Expressing Milk for a Premature Baby

The decision to breastfeed a preterm baby is not always an easy one, even for women who planned on nursing at term. A major attraction of breastfeeding, close mother-child contact, is usually absent, at least at first, and is replaced by a mother-machine-child affair that is difficult as well as lacking in satisfaction. But though almost all women find pumping their breasts exhausting and time-consuming, most hang in there knowing that this is the one way in which they can contribute to the well-being of the baby from whose care they otherwise feel excluded.

The following tips can make the effort to feed a preterm baby in the best possible way more efficient and less tedious:

- Keep in mind that if you were given magnesium sulfate for toxaemia, you may not have milk for as long as two weeks.

- See page 92 for tips on expressing breast milk. Ask about in-hospital facilities for expressing. If your hospital does not have a special room (with comfortable chairs, a breast pump and sterilization unit) set aside for mothers to use, ask if one can be set up, or for information on borrowing or renting a breast pump. Your local NCT or La Leche counsellor should be able to help you if the hospital can't.

- Begin expressing milk as soon after delivery as possible, even if your baby isn't ready to take it. Express every two to three hours (about as often as a newborn nurses) if your baby is going to use the milk immediately; every four hours or so if the milk is going to be frozen for later use. You may find getting up to pump once in the middle of the night helps build your milk supply; or you may value a full night's sleep more.

- It's likely you will eventually be able to express more milk than your tiny baby can use. Don't cut back, however, figuring you're wasting too much. Regular pumping now will help to establish a plentiful milk supply for the time when your baby takes over where the machine leaves off. In the meantime, the excess milk can be dated and frozen – in the hospital or at home – for later use.

- Don't be discouraged by day-to-day or hour-to-hour variations in supply. Such variations are normal, although you wouldn't be aware of them if you were nursing directly. Also normal when milk is expressed mechanically are an apparently inadequate milk supply and/or a drop in production after several weeks. Your baby will be a much more efficient stimulator of your milk supply than even the most efficient pump. When actual suckling begins, your supply is almost certain to increase quickly.

- When baby is ready for feeding by mouth (usually not until at least 1,300 grams, or 2 pounds 14 ounces, and 30 weeks are reached), ask if you can try to breastfeed rather than have baby put to the bottle, since new studies show that low-birthweight babies take to the former more easily than to the latter. But don't worry if yours does better on the bottle – use it while your baby gets used to breastfeeding.

nose and into the stomach) since such babies usually have not yet developed this reflex. Larger premies (at least 1,300 grams, or 2 pounds 14 ounces) who arrive at 30 weeks of gestation or later may be able to skip such gavage feedings and can often be put right to the breast, though they usually have to wait longer if they are to go to bottle feeding.

Since small premies can't self-regulate yet, feeding is very carefully monitored: How much fluid, protein, calcium and so on is the baby taking? How much is being excreted in urine and stool? How much is left in the stomach? How are blood gases (oxygen, for example) affected by feedings? The calculations, once done exclusively by hand, are now often turned over to a computer for very rapid and accurate processing so that the diet of each infant can be individually programmed. The baby's condition can provide clues to nutritional deficiencies: white streaks or white hair is a sign of protein malnutrition; poor skin integrity and cracking of the lips are signs of zinc deficiency; loss of pigmentation and chronic anaemia are signs of inadequate copper.

Many experts favour breast milk over formula for the premature baby, just as they do for the full-term infant. One reason is the presence of many important substances not found in cow's milk, including maternal antibodies, hormones and enzymes, particularly lipase, which dramatically improves a baby's ability to absorb much-needed fat. But not just any breast milk will do. It's been found that the milk produced by mothers who've just delivered premature babies has, thanks to the body's infinite wisdom, more of the things these babies need (protein, nitrogen, sodium, lactose and chloride) than does the breast milk of a woman who's delivered at term. So while your own milk (or that of another mother of a premature infant) will be good for your baby, term milk won't be. And if it comes from a milk bank, where milk is routinely heat-sterilized, it will

have the added disadvantage of having had the critically important lipase destroyed. Thus, if it's at all possible, nursing should be considered even if you weren't planning to breastfeed.

Sometimes, however, even the milk of a premie's mother isn't adequate for the baby. Since some of them, particularly very tiny ones, need even more concentrated nutrition – including more calories, protein, calcium and phosphorus and, possibly, more of such other nutrients as zinc, magnesium, copper and vitamin B^6 – the breast milk being fed through a tube or a bottle may be fortified as needed. If a baby is nursing directly, fortification may be given via intravenous or gavage feeding, or by a supplemental nutrition system, which allows simultaneous nursing and supplementation (see page 100). When possible, it's preferable not to give it to nursing infants via a bottle since this could lead to nipple confusion.

When a mother can't or doesn't wish to nurse, the highly concentrated formulas designed especially for premature babies (but not regular formulas) are a very good substitute. The intake of formula must, however, be very carefully monitored. Too much formula would be hard for the immature system to handle; too little would not support adequate growth. Soya formulas (because their calcium and phosphorus are not as well absorbed) are not ordinarily used for premature babies.

What You May Be Concerned About

Getting Optimum Care

'How do I know that our premature baby – she's only a little more than 1,125 g (2½ pounds) – is getting the best possible care?'

Small community hospitals provide care for noncomplicated cases of all types, including low-risk deliveries and normal newborns, but do not have neonatal intensive care units for very premature, low-birthweight, or sick

newborns. Second-level hospitals have somewhat more sophisticated facilities, can care for more complicated cases including many high-risk deliveries, and do have neonatal intensive care units that can care for most babies in trouble. Tertiary or teaching hospitals boast the most highly trained specialists, the most sophisticated facilities, and state-of-the-art Special Care Baby Units (SCBUs) ready to care for the tiniest and sickest of newborns.

Though healthy babies, including premies

The Special Care Baby Unit or Intensive Care Nursery

A first look at a Special Care Baby Unit can be frightening, especially if your baby is one of the tiny, helpless patients in it. (That's why it's a good idea for all expectant parents to routinely take that look during their antenatal tour of the hospital.) Knowing what you're looking at, however, can keep your fears from overwhelming you. Here's what you're likely to see in a typical Special Care Baby Unit or intensive care nursery:

- Babies naked or clad in nappies; in many hospitals they will be wearing little knit stocking caps to prevent heat loss through the head.

- Babies on 'warming beds', adjustable mattresses set under warming lights. Very sick babies are often cared for on these to allow easy access for carrying out procedures, such as insertion of feeding tubes.

- Babies in isolettes, see-through bassinets that are totally closed except for four portholes, two on either side. In some hospitals, isolettes will be fitted with water mattresses, which simulate floating in the amniotic fluid in the uterus and may improve breathing, or even with miniature hammocks.

- Tubes and wires and lines – from babies to monitors, to IV bottles, or to other apparatus that supply nourishment, clear respiratory secretions, monitor temperatures, breathing, heart rate and oxygen consumption, draw blood samples at regular intervals and carry out many other important functions.

- Monitors to record vital signs and to warn, by setting off an alarm, of any ominous changes. These monitors pick up information via leads that are either stuck on the skin with gel or inserted by needle just under the skin.

- Plastic hoods or ventilators for the administration of oxygen and to assist breathing.

- Suction setups at each cotside for removing excess respiratory secretions.

- Lights for phototherapy (bili lights) for babies with jaundice. The babies undergoing this treatment will be naked except for eye patches to protect their eyes from the light.

---

who weigh in at more than 2,250 grams (close to five pounds), do equally well at most hospitals; very small babies (those who are at the highest risk) do best at major teaching hospitals. Having your baby at such a facility is the best guarantee you can get of good care. If your baby is not in a tertiary hospital, discuss the possibility of having her transferred to one with her paediatrician, the present SCBU staff, and the staff at the hospital you are considering.

Wherever your baby is, your input will be important in ensuring optimum care. Become knowledgeable about low-birthweight babies in general, and about any special problems your baby has, by reading books and by asking questions. Whenever you're uncomfortable or unhappy about the course your baby's treatment is taking, raise your concerns with her paediatrician and/or the hospital nurses or neonatologists. You may be satisfied with their explanation, or perhaps things can be done differently. If you aren't satisfied, ask for a consultation with another neonatologist. If you feel uncomfortable challenging doctors, find a friend or relative to act as advocate.

Lack of Bonding

'We'd expected to bond with our baby right after birth. But since she arrived six weeks early and weighed only 1,500 g (3½ pounds), she was whisked away before we had a chance to even touch her. We're worried about the effect this will have on her – and on our relationship with her.'

During this stressful time, the last thing you need is another worry. And the last thing you need to worry about is bonding at birth. Love and attachment between parent and child develops over many months, even years, blossoming over a lifetime rather than bursting miraculously into full bloom during the first few moments of life. So instead of regretting the past and those first few moments (or even days) you've lost, start making the most of the present and of the months of parenthood that lie ahead. Though it isn't necessary to begin bonding at birth, you may be able to initiate the process while your baby is still in the hospital. Here's how:

Ask for a picture, along with a thousand words. If your baby has been moved from the hospital you delivered in to another hospital for upgraded intensive care (possibly essential to her survival), and you are not yet able to be discharged, ask that pictures of her be brought to you. Your husband or the hospital staff can take them and you can enjoy looking at them until you're able to look at the real thing. Even if more tubing and gadgetry is visible than baby, what you see will likely be less frightening and more reassuring than what you might have imagined. As helpful as a picture may be, you'll still want those thousand words – from your husband, and later the medical staff – describing every detail of what your baby is like and how she's getting along.

Relinquish daddy. While you're unable to visit your baby, your partner can spend extra time with her rather than visiting exclusively with you. You'll be more lonely, but at least you'll know that someone who loves your child will be with her. As soon as you're out of the hospital, you should each spend as much time as possible with the baby. But be certain not to neglect any older children at home since they will need you more than ever – neglect housework, business and everything else first.

Feast with your eyes. Just watching her in her isolette or warming mattress may help bring you closer.

Lay on the hands. Though it may seem that such a tiny and vulnerable infant is better off not being touched, studies have shown that premature infants who are stroked and lightly massaged while they are in intensive care grow better and are more alert, active and behaviourally mature than babies who are handled very little. The nurses in the SCBU will show you how to scrub (washing hands and arms up to the elbows) and don a hospital gown before reaching through the isolette portholes to get acquainted with your baby. Start with her arms and legs, since they are less sensitive at first than the trunk. Try to work up to at least twenty minutes of gentle stroking a day.

Carry on a conversation. To be sure, it will be a one-way conversation at first – your baby won't be doing much talking, or even crying, while she's in the SCBU. She may not even appear to be listening. But she will recognize your voice – and her daddy's. They will be the only familiar voices in the SCBU at first (she's heard them for months from the uterus), and hearing them will be comforting to her.

See eye to eye. If your baby's eyes are shielded because she's getting phototherapy for the treatment of jaundice, ask to have the bili lights turned off and her eyes uncovered for at least a few minutes during your visit so that you can make eye-to-eye contact, an important part of parent-child bonding.

Take over for the nurses. As soon as your baby's out of immediate danger, the nurses will probably be happy to show you how to change nappies, feed and bathe her, and even do some simple medical procedures for her. Caring for her during your visits will help make you more comfortable with the role of mother, while giving you some valuable experience for the months ahead.

Don't hold back. Many parents remain detached from their premature babies for fear of loving and losing. But that's a mistake. First, because the odds are very much with your preterm baby; the great majority survive to be healthy and normal. And second, because if you do hold back and the unthinkable happens, you'll always regret the moments you lost. The loss would be harder, not easier, to take.

Intrauterine Growth Retardation

'My baby wasn't premature, but she was just under 2,300 g (five pounds). The doctor said it was because of intrauterine growth retardation. Does this means she will be mentally retarded?'

As ominous as it may sound, intrauterine growth retardation, often shortened to IUGR, has nothing to do with any kind of mental or physical retardation after birth, only with growth retardation while in the uterus. The vast majority of infants with IUGR end up having normal IQs and neurological function. IUGR appears to be nature's way of ensuring a foetus's survival in a uterus where, for some reason, she is not getting an adequate supply of nutrients through the placenta. The reduction in size allows a baby to get along well on the reduced intake of nutrients. Doctors surmise that this protective mechanism is called into action when the placenta isn't functioning at optimal efficiency, limiting the passage of nutrients to the foetus, or when the mother's nutrition is inadequate, because of poor diet, smoking, illness, or other, unknown factors.

The baby's brain also appears to be protected by this survival mechanism, usually continuing to grow normally by taking more than its share of nourishment from what is available. That's why most babies with IUGR have heads that are even larger in relation to their bodies than are those of full-size newborns.

Though a low-birthweight baby is at high risk for many complications during the early days of life, most will do well with proper neonatal care. With good nutrition, preferably beginning with breast milk, you can

expect your baby to start thriving; and by the end of her first year she'll probably have caught up on many, or even on all, fronts with her peers. But should you decide to become pregnant again, try to determine first, with the aid of your doctor, what might have been responsible for the poor growing environment in your uterus so that your next baby won't have to struggle with the same problems antenatally.

Long Hospitalization

'The first time I saw our baby in the intensive care nursery I was devastated. It's horrible to think that our baby will spend the first weeks— maybe months— of his life in a sterile hospital room.'

Walking into an intensive care nursery may be an upsetting experience, but it's likely you'd be much more upset if there were no such facility available for your baby.

Someday we may have a better way of dealing with premature infants who experience no medical problems. In Bogota Colombia, for example, a system of kangaroo-style newborn care has evolved which eliminates sterile hospital nurseries and allows a mother to go home shortly after delivery. But instead of transferring her new baby to a cat or cradle, she carries him in a sling at her breast, where he can nurse on demand around the clock for the next few weeks of life. Even small preterm infants with no complications seem to thrive in this warm, cozy, nourishing environment. But unless and until such a system or a similar one is deemed safe and approved for use here, parents of premies will have to wait until their babies reach 1,800 to 2,300 g (four or five pounds) and a gestational age of 37 to 40 weeks before taking them home – or about as long as they would have had to wait if the babies had been carried to term.

Feeling anxious in such a situation is not only normal but healthy. Mothers who are anxious after the birth of a premature baby go on to be better at mothering than those who aren't. But the anxiety needs to be channelled into productive activities:

Hit the shops. Since your baby arrived ahead of time, you may not have had time to order baby furniture, layette items, a nappy service and the like. If so, now's the time to get that shopping done. If you feel superstitious about filling your home with baby things before baby is discharged from the hospital, put in your orders pending his homecoming. You'll not only have taken care of some necessary chores, you'll also have filled some of the interminable hours of baby's hospitalization and made a statement (at least to yourself) that you are confident of bringing him home.

Strike up a partnership. Parents of a premie often begin to feel that their baby belongs to the doctors and nurses, who seem so competent and do so much for him, rather than to them. Instead of trying to compete with the staff, try working together with them. Get to know the nurses (which will be easier if your baby has a 'primary' nurse in charge of his care at each shift), the neonatologist, the residents. Let them know you'll be happy to do little chores or errands for your baby – which can save them time and help you feel useful.

Get a medical education. Learn the jargon and terminology used in the SCBU. Ask a staff member (when he or she has a free moment) to show you how to read your baby's chart; ask the neonatologist for details about your baby's condition – and for clarification when you don't understand. Parents of premies often become experts in neonatal medicine, throwing around terms like 'RDS' and 'intubation' with the aplomb of a neonatologist.

Be a fixture at your baby's side. Some hospitals may let you move in, but even if you can't, you should spend as much time as possible with your baby, alternating shifts with your husband. This way you will not only get to know your baby's medical problems, but your baby as well. (If you have other children at home, however, they'll also need you now. Be certain that they get a substantial piece of mum and dad's time, too.)

Make your baby feel at home. Even though the isolette's only a temporary stop for your baby, try to make it as much like home as possible. Ask permission to put friendly looking stuffed animals around your baby and tape pictures (perhaps including stimulating black-and-white enlargements of snapshots of mummy and daddy) to the sides of the isolette for his viewing pleasure. And tuck in a baby music box for a little night and day music. Remember, however, that anything you put in the baby's isolette will have to be sterilized first, and that nothing should interfere with life-sustaining equipment.

Ready your milk supply. Your milk is the perfect food for your premature baby (see page 453). Until he's able to nurse pump your breasts for indirect feedings and in order to keep up your milk supply. Pumping will also give you a welcome feeling of usefulness.

Siblings

'We have a three-year-old daughter, and we don't know what to tell her about her new premature sister.'

Children, even children as young as yours, are able to understand and handle a lot more than we adults usually give them credit for. Trying to protect your daughter by keeping her in the dark about the condition of her new sibling will only make her anxious and insecure – particularly when you and your husband suddenly, and to her, inexplicably, start spending so much of your time away from home. Instead, enlighten her fully. Explain that the baby came out of mummy too soon, before she had grown enough, and has to stay in a special cot in the hospital until she's big enough to come home. With the hospital's okay, take your older daughter for an initial visit, and if it goes well and she seems eager, take her regularly. Children are just as likely to be fascinated by the wires and tubes as they are to be scared, particularly if their parents set the right tone – confident and cheerful rather than nervous and sombre. Have her bring a present for the baby, to be placed in the isolette, which will help her feel that she's a part of the team caring for her new sibling. If she would like to, and if you have the staff's permission, let her scrub and then touch the baby through the portholes. Like you, she will feel closer to the baby when she finally comes home if she has some contact now. (Read about sibling relationships in Chapter 26.)

Breastfeeding

'I've always been determined to breastfeed my baby and since she was born prematurely, I've been pumping milk to be fed to her through a tube. Will she have trouble switching to nursing later?'

So far, so good. From birth your baby has been provided with the best possible food for a premature newborn – her mummy's milk – in the only way such a tiny baby is able to take nourishment, through a tube. Naturally, you're concerned that she be able to continue to get this perfect food once she graduates to suckling.

A recent study, however, indicates you have little to worry about. It showed that premature infants weighing as little as 1,300 grams, or nearly 3 pounds, were not only able to suckle at the breast, but were more successful at it than they were with the bottle. It took these infants between one and four weeks longer to become proficient at sucking from the bottle than at suckling from the breast. In addition, their bodies responded better to breastfeeding. When they nursed their oxygen levels fluctuated little, while during bottle feeding they showed significant drops in oxygen levels, with these levels staying down for varying periods after feed-

ing. And they were comfortably warmer when being breastfed than when getting the bottle, which is important because premies, whose thermostats aren't operative, have trouble keeping themselves warm. This study and others like it show that the small preterm infant has the sucking reflex at 30 weeks, rather than at the 33- to 36-week point previously believed, and suggest that the prevalent practice of waiting until a preterm infant nurses well on a bottle before putting her to breast should be reconsidered.[2]

Once you do put your baby to the breast, you'll want to make conditions as conducive to success as possible:

- Read all about breastfeeding, beginning on page 49, before getting started.

- Be patient if the neonatologist or nurse wants your baby monitored for temperature and/or $TCPO_2$ (oxygen) changes during breastfeeding. This won't interfere with the breastfeeding itself and it will protect your baby by sounding an alarm in case she is not responding well to the feeding.

- Be sure you're relaxed, and that your baby is awake and alert but not crying frantically with hunger. A nurse will probably see to it that she is dressed warmly for this momentous event.

- Ask the staff if there is a special nursing area for premie mums, or at least a private corner with an armchair for you and your baby.

- Get comfortable, propping your baby on pillows, supporting her head. Many women find a side hold comfortable (see page 50) as well as easy on the nipples.

- If your baby doesn't yet have a rooting reflex (she probably doesn't), help her get started by placing your nipple, with the areola, into her mouth. Compress it

---

1. If the SCBU staff at your baby's hospital is not familiar with the study, refer them to the *Journal of Maternal Child Nursing*, April 1987. The study was done by Paula Meier, D.N.Sc., RN, at Michael Reese Hospital in Chicago.

with your fingers to make it easier for her to latch on to, and keep trying until she succeeds.

- Use your finger to press the breast away from her nose so your baby can breathe.

- Watch to be sure your baby is getting milk. The first few minutes of sucking may be very rapid, a non-nutritive sucking aimed at stimulating let-down. Your breasts are used to mechanical pumping and will take a while to adjust to the different motions of your baby's mouth, but soon you will notice that the suckling has slowed and that your baby is swallowing. This lets you know that let-down has occurred.

- If your baby doesn't seem interested in your breast, try expressing a few drops of milk into her mouth to give her a taste of what's in store.

- If it's okay with the hospital staff, nurse your baby for as long a period as she's willing to stay at the breast. Experts who've studied breastfeeding of premature babies recommend letting them remain at the breast until they've stopped active sucking for at least two minutes. Small premies have been known to nurse for close to an hour before being satisfied.

- Don't be discouraged if the first session, or even the first several sessions, seem unproductive. Many full-term babies take a while to catch on, and pretermers deserve the same chance.

- Ask that any feedings at which you cannot nurse be given by gavage rather than by bottle. If your baby is given bottle feedings while you're trying to establish breastfeeding, nipple confusion could interfere with your efforts. If human milk fortifier or other fortification is given to your baby to supplement the breast milk, ask that it, too, be given by gavage or by the supplementary nutrition system (see page 100).

You'll be able to tell how well your baby is doing on the breast by following her daily weigh-in. If she continues gaining about 1 to 2% of her body weight (about 15 to 30 grams for a 1,500-gram, or 3⅓-pound, baby) daily, or about 100 to 210 g (3½ to 7½ ounces) a week, she'll be doing fine. By the time she reaches her original due date, she should be approaching the weight of a full-termer – somewhere around 2,700 to 3,509 g (6 to 8 pounds).

Catching Up

'Our son, who was born nearly two months early, seems very far behind compared with other three-month-olds. Will he ever catch up?'

He's probably not 'behind' at all. In fact, he's probably just where a baby conceived when he was should be. Traditionally, in our culture, a baby's age is calculated from the day he was born. But this system is misleading when assessing the growth and development of premature infants since it fails to take into account that at birth they have not yet reached term. Your baby, for example, was just a little more than *minus* two months old at birth. At two months of age he was, in terms of gestational age (calculated according to his *original* due date), equivalent to a newborn; and now, at three months, he's more like a one-month-old. Keep this in mind when you compare him to other children his age or to averages on development charts. For example, though the average baby may sit well at seven months, your child may not do so until he's nine months old, when he reaches his seventh month corrected age. If he was very small or very ill in the neonatal period, he's likely to sit even later. In general, you can expect motor development to lag more than the development of the senses (vision and hearing, for example).

Experts use the gestational age, usually called 'corrected age', in evaluating a premature child's developmental progress up until he's two or two and a half. After that point, the two months or so differential tends to lose its significance – there isn't, after all, much developmental difference between a child who is four years old and one who is two months shy of four. And as your baby gets older, the behaviour gap between his corrected age and his birth age will diminish and finally disappear, as will any developmental differences between him and his peers (though occasionally, extra nurturing may be needed to bring a premie to that point). In the meantime, if you feel more comfortable using his corrected age with strangers, do so. Certainly do so when assessing your baby's developmental progress.

Instead of looking for specific behaviours from your baby at specific times, relax and enjoy his progress as it comes, providing support as needed. If he's smiling and cooing, smile and coo back at him. If he's starting to reach for things, give him the opportunity to practise that skill, too. When he can sit propped up, prop him in different surroundings for a while each day But always keep his corrected age in mind, and don't rush him. Pushing too hard too soon could have negative repercussions. For one, your baby could begin to feel inadequate if he can't do what you expect of him when you expect it. For another, you may use up so much enthusiasm pushing him when he isn't ready that when he is ready, you may have run out of baby-stimulating steam.

Use the infant stimulation tips in this book (pages 159, 256, 371), gearing them to your baby's behaviour rather than his age, and be careful to stop when he signals that he's had enough. You can, additionally, encourage motor development by placing your baby on his abdomen, facing outwards towards the room rather than towards the wall, as often and for as long as he'll tolerate it. Since premies and low-birthweight babies spend most of their early weeks, sometimes months, on their backs in isolettes, they often resist this position, but it's a necessary one for building arm and neck strength.

If, of course, your baby is far behind developmentally even after making allowances for his prematurity, and if he seems to stay that way, read page 310 and check with his doctor.

Handling Baby

'So far I've only handled our baby through the portholes of her isolette. But I'm worried about how well I'll be able to handle her when she finally comes home. She's so tiny and fragile.'

When your baby finally makes that long-anticipated trip home, she may actually seem pudgy and sturdy to you, rather than tiny and fragile. Like many premies, she'll probably have doubled her birthweight before hitting the requisite 1,800 to 2,300 g (4 or 5 pounds) necessary for discharge. And chances are you won't have any more trouble caring for her than most new mothers have caring for their full-term babies. In fact, if you have a chance to do some baby care at the hospital (something you should insist on) in the weeks before your baby's homecoming you'll actually be ahead of the game. Which is not to say it will be easy – rare is the new mother who finds it so.

If you're wondering how well you and your baby will do without a nurse or neonatologist looking over your shoulder, ready to step in if anything goes wrong, be assured that hospitals don't send home babies who are still in need of full-time professional care. Still, some mothers, particularly those who come home with such extra paraphernalia as breathing monitors or oxygen hoods, find it comforting to hire a baby nurse who has had experience with premies and their medical care to help them through the first week or two. Consider this option if you're anxious about going it alone.

Guilt

'I know that I wasn't as careful during my pregnancy as I should have been and I feel it was my fault that our son came so early.'

There's probably not one mother of a premature baby who doesn't look back and regret something she did during pregnancy that she might have done better – something that might have contributed to her baby's early arrival. Such feelings of remorse are normal, but not productive. It's almost impossible to be sure just what factor or factors are responsible for your baby's early arrival, and even if you are sure, assigning blame is not going to help your baby. What your baby needs now is a mother who is strong, loving and supportive, not one who is floundering in guilt. Read Chapter 20, which concerns newborns with medical problems, for some suggestions on how to deal with your feelings of guilt, anger and frustration. It may also help to talk to other parents of premies; you will find they share many of your feelings. Some hospitals have parent support groups; others feel parents do better consulting with the staff than with other parents. Do what seems to help you most.

Of course, next to taking the best possible care of your baby who's already been born, the most productive thing you can do is to make sure you take the best possible care of your next baby (if you decide to have one) before birth. Though not all cases of prematurity can be prevented, a great many can be. Consult with your obstetrician before becoming pregnant again to discuss your medical history, and follow a pre-pregnancy plan for getting your body and your eating and lifestyle habits into optimum shape (see *What to Expect When You're Expecting* and *What to Eat When You're Expecting*).

Permanent Problems

'Though the doctor says our baby is doing well, I'm still afraid that he'll come through this with some kind of permanent damage.'

One of the greatest miracles of modern medicine is the rapidly increasing survival rate for premature infants. At one time, a baby weighing in at 1,000 grams (about 2 pounds 3 ounces) had no chance of making it. Now, thanks to the advances in neonatology, many babies who are born even smaller than that can be expected to survive.

Of course, along with this increased survival rate has come an increase in the number of babies with moderate to severe handicaps. Still, the odds of your baby's coming home from his hospital stay both alive *and* well are very much in his favour. Only an estimated 10% of all premies and 20% of those between 675 and 1,500 g (1½ and 3½ pounds) end up with major handicaps. Better than 2 out of 3 babies born prematurely will turn out to be perfectly normal, and most of the others will have only mild to moderate handicaps. IQ will most often be normal, though preterm infants do have an increased risk of learning problems.

For a couple of years, even if your baby is absolutely normal, you can expect him to lag behind others of the same birth age. His progress is likely to follow more closely that of children of his corrected age. And if he was very small, or had serious complications during the neonatal period, he is very likely to lag behind his corrected age-mates too, particularly in motor development.

Premature infants may also display one or more neuromuscular abnormalities. They may not lose such newborn reflexes as the Moro, tonic neck, or grasp reflexes as early as term infants, even taking corrected age into account. Or their muscle tone may be abnormal, in some cases causing the head to droop excessively, in other cases causing the legs to be stiff and the toes to point. Though such signs may be worrisome in full-term babies, they usually aren't in pretermers. (Still, they should be evaluated by the doctor, and physical therapy should be begun if necessary).

Slow developmental progress in a premie is not only *not* cause for alarm, it is to be expected. If, however, your baby seems not to be making *any* progress week to week, month to month, or if he seems unresponsive (when he's not ill), speak to his doctor. If the doctor doesn't share your concerns, but doesn't allay them either, ask for a second opinion. Occasionally a mother, who sees her baby day in and day out, catches something the doctor misses. If there turns out to be no problem, which will most often be the case, the second opinion will help to erase your fears. And if a problem is discovered, the early diagnosis could lead to treatment as well as ongoing training and care, which may make a tremendous difference in the ultimate quality of your baby's life.

Car Seats

'My baby seems lost in the car seat we borrowed. Wouldn't she be safer in my arms?

It is extremely unsafe (and in many countries illegal) for a baby (premature or full term) to ride in mummy's (or anyone else's) arms rather than in a car seat. This presents a serious problem, however, to parents of low-birthweight babies. Not only are their small bodies often lost in a regular car seat, but they may also have trouble breathing in the semi-propped position the seat requires. One study has shown that some preterm infants show a decreased oxygen supply while riding in a car seat, and that this deficit may last for as long as thirty minutes or more afterwards. Some may also experience short periods of apnea (breathing cessation) in car seats. Much better for such infants is a new crash-tested infant car bed, in which the infant is prone rather than propped and which protects her in case of accident without compromising breathing. Check with your local nursery furnishings store to see if one is available locally. If for any reason you can't obtain such a bed or a seat designed for a premie, you may want to limit the amount of car travel you do with your baby for the first month or two at home, especially if she has had spells of apnea previously. Or ask her doctor about monitoring her breathing when she's in an ordinary car seat, at least for a while, to see if she is experiencing any problems.

To help your baby ride more comfortably in a car seat, roll a towel or small blanket and arrange it so that it cradles her head, or buy a ready-to-use head roll designed for infant car seats. If there's a big space between your baby's body and the harness (or anywhere else in the seat), use another folded towel or blanket to fill it in.

The same breathing problems may occur in young premature babies in infant seats and baby swings, so don't use either without the doctor's approval.

A Repeat with the Next Baby

'Will the fact that our first son was premature make it more likely that our second baby will be?'

Whether or not you're at high risk for a repeat premature delivery depends primarily on just what the cause of the first one was. If the suspected cause was something that is within your control – if such risk factors as smoking, heavy drinking, drug use, poor nutrition, inadequate weight gain and/or physical stress (a job requiring constant standing or heavy physical labour, for example) were part of your pregnancy profile – then you simply (or maybe not so simply) have to change your lifestyle to protect any future babies. If your doctor believes you are one of the small percentage of women in whom sexual intercourse seems to trigger labour prematurely, your lovemaking may have to be restricted during part or all of your pregnancy. If diagnostic tests point to hormonal imbalance as the reason for your premature labour, hormone replacement therapy may help you carry to term.

Other risk factors linked to prematurity are less easily controlled or eliminated, but they can often be modified. These include:

Infection. If an acute infection led to your first preterm delivery, you aren't likely to experience a repeat; but be sure you're clear of venereal disease (including chlamydia) and urinary tract and vaginal infections, and are immune to rubella, before conceiving again. If you do contract an infection

Special Care Tips for Preterm Babies

- Read the month-by-month chapters in this book; they apply to your preterm baby as well as to full-termers. But remember to adjust for your baby's corrected age.

- Keep your home warmer than usual, about 22.2°C (72°F) or so, for the first few weeks that your baby is at home. The temperature regulating mechanism is usually functioning in premature infants by the time they go home, but because of their small size and greater skin surface in relation to fat, they may have difficulty keeping comfortable without a little help. In addition, having to expend a great many calories to keep warm could interfere with weight gain. If your baby seems unusually fussy, check the room temperature to see if it's warm enough, and feel baby's arms, legs, or the nape of the neck to be sure it isn't too cool. (Don't, however, overheat the room.)

- Buy nappies made for premies, if necessary. You can also buy baby clothes in premie sizes, but don't buy too many – before you know it, your baby will have outgrown them.

- Sterilize bottles, if you're giving them. Though it may be an unnecessary precaution for a term baby, it's a good one to take for premies, who are more susceptible to infection. Continue for a few months, or until baby's doctor gives you the okay to pack away the sterilizer.

- Feed your baby frequently, even though this may mean spending most of your time nursing or bottle feeding. Premies have very small stomachs, and may need to eat as often as every two

or three hours. They also may not be able to suckle as efficiently or effectively as full-termers, and so they may take longer – as long as an hour – to drink their fill. Don't rush feedings.

- Unless your baby is getting formula containing all the required nutrients, give a baby multivitamin supplement as prescribed by the doctor. Preterm babies are at greater risk of becoming vitamin deficient than full-termers and need this extra insurance.

- Don't start solids until your doctor gives the go-ahead. Generally, solids are introduced to a preterm infant when weight reaches 5.9 to 6.8 kg (13 to 15 pounds), when more than 900 ml (32 ounces) of formula is consumed daily for at least a week, and/or when the corrected age is six months. Occasionally, when a baby is not satisfied with just formula or breast milk, solids may be started as early as three months, corrected age, or five or six months, chronological age.

- Treat your baby just as you would a full-term infant. Parents of babies who were born prematurely tend to think of their children as particularly fragile. They are often overly cautious (they worry that baby's too warm or too cold, or isn't eating enough or sleeping enough); overly indulgent (baby always gets his or her way); and overly attached (mothers often have difficulty separating from their premies). No limits are set and the baby, rather than the parents, is usually in charge. Such an atmosphere can interfere with normal development and turn out a dependent, demanding, unhappy child.

during pregnancy, have it treated medically as soon as possible. (But be sure the treating doctor knows you are expecting.)

Incompetent cervix. If your cervix dilated

prematurely under the weight of the growing foetus (probably because of muscular weakness), stitching it closed early on in a new pregnancy should prevent a recurrence.

Structural abnormalities of the uterus. Once diagnosed, these abnormalities can often be surgically corrected.

Placenta praevia. If your placenta was too low in the uterus, close to, partially covering, or fully covering the cervix, and is again next time (though it won't necessarily be), complete bed rest may ward off early labour.

Chronic maternal illness. If you have diabetes, heart disease, hypertension, or some other chronic illness, good medical care, sometimes including bed rest, can often prevent premature delivery; consult your doctor.

Stress. If physical or emotional stress contributed to your baby's early arrival, try to reduce it next time around. Get professional help if necessary.

Age. This is a prematurity risk factor you can't change – if you were over 35 the first time, you will be even older the next time.

But you can improve your chances of carrying to term by being sure you get optimum medical care not only from your doctor, but from yourself as well. Eliminating or modifying every alterable risk factor above can reduce your excess risk almost to that of a younger woman.

Whether or not the reason for your previous premature delivery is known, see your doctor before becoming pregnant again. Discuss what you can do to reduce the risk of your delivering prematurely again. Follow doctor's orders religiously – even if that means cutting back on your lovemaking, work and other activities. Also discuss the possibility of monitoring contractions at home with a device that can be hooked up by phone to the doctor's surgery or hospital. Since the monitor can usually spot contractions before you can, it often allows medical action – in the form of tocolytic drugs that stop contractions, bed rest, or other steps – to be taken early enough to forestall labour.

WHAT IT'S IMPORTANT TO KNOW:
Health Problems Common in Low-Birthweight Babies

Prematurity is risky business. Tiny bodies are not fully mature, many systems (heat regulatory, respiratory and digestive, for example) aren't yet fully operative and, not surprisingly, the risk of neonatal illness is greatly increased. As the technology for keeping such babies alive improves, more attention is being given to these conditions, most of which are rare or unknown among full-term babies, and successful treatment is becoming more and more the norm for many of them. New treatments are being developed almost daily and so may not be detailed here – but do ask your neonatologist or paediatrician about recent advances. The medical problems that most frequently complicate the lives of preterm infants include:

Respiratory distress syndrome (RDS). Because of immaturity, the premature lung often lacks pulmonary surfactant, a detergent-like substance that gives the lung surfaces their elastic properties. Without surfactant the tiny alveoli, or air sacs, of the lungs collapse like deflating balloons with each expiration, forcing the tiny baby to work harder and harder to breathe. Babies who have undergone severe stress in the uterus, usually during labour and delivery, are less likely to lack surfactant as the stress appears to speed lung maturation.

RDS was once frequently fatal, but nearly 80% of babies who develop RDS today survive, thanks to an increased understanding of the syndrome and new ways of treatment such as continuous positive air-way pressure (CPAP), which is administered through tubes in the nose or mouth, or via a plastic oxygen hood. The continuous pressure keeps the lungs from collapsing until the body begins producing sufficient surfactant, usually in three to five days. Sometimes, when lung immaturity is detected before delivery and delivery can safely be delayed, RDS can be prevented entirely by the administration, prior to birth, of a hormone to speed lung maturation and production of surfactant. Also promising as a way of preventing or reducing the severity of RDS is the instillation of artificial or human surfactant into a premature infant's lungs before the first breath is taken. For children in respiratory distress, extra-corporeal membrane oxygenation (ECMO), which employs a type of heart-lung machine, gives temporary support to the failing heart and lungs and provides a healing rest. (ECMO is used for many types of respiratory failure, not just that associated with RDS.)

Bronchopulmonary dysplasia (BPD). In some babies, particularly those with low birthweight, long-term oxygen administration and mechanical ventilation appear to combine with lung immaturity to cause BPD, or chronic lung disease. The condition is usually diagnosed when a newborn requires increased oxygen after the twenty-eighth day of life. Specific lung changes are generally seen on X-ray, and these babies frequently gain weight slowly and are subject to apnea. A few continue to require oxygen when they go home, others have fluids restricted or are put on diuretics or bronchodilators to prevent complications, and all require a high caloric intake to improve growth. Often the condition is outgrown as the lungs mature.

Hypoglycaemia. Low blood sugar can make an adult feel dizzy, jittery, or irritable, but in a newborn it can be much more serious, causing brain damage and retardation if left untreated. It's most commonly a problem in babies born of multiple births in which the smaller or smallest weighs less than 2,000 g (4½ pounds) and in babies of

diabetic mums (who usually have high, rather than low, birthweights). Hypoglycae-mia is routinely screened for during the first 24 to 48 hours, and if it's found, treatment to normalize sugar levels is begun immediately.

Patent ductus arteriosus. In the foetal circulatory system there is a duct connecting the aorta (the artery through which blood from the heart is sent to the rest of the body) and the left pulmonary artery (the one leading to the lungs) called the ductus arteriosus. This duct shunts blood away from the non-functioning lungs and is kept open during gestation by high levels of prostaglandin E (one of a group of fatty acids produced by the body) in the blood. Normally, levels of prostaglandin E fall at delivery and the ductus begins to close within a few hours. But in about half of very small premature babies (those weighing under 1,500 grams, or 3 pounds 5 ounces), and in some larger babies, levels of prostaglandin E don't drop and the ductus remains open, or 'patent'. In many cases there are no symptoms, except perhaps a little shortness of breath on exertion and/or blueness of the lips, and the duct closes by itself in the neonatal period. Occasionally, however, severe complications occur. Treatment with an antiprostaglandin drug (indomethacin) is often successful in closing the duct; when it isn't, simple surgery generally does the job.

Retinopathy of prematurity (ROP). This condition, also called retrolental fibroplasia, can lead to significant scarring and distortion of the retina of the eye, increased risk of myopia (nearsightedness), amblyopia (wandering eye), nystagmus (involuntary rhythmic movements of the eye), and even blindness. ROP is extremely common among very small babies – it afflicts 4 out of 5 babies who weigh under 750 grams (about 1 pound 10 ounces) as compared to only 3 in 100 of those who weigh 1,500 to 1,750 grams (3 pounds 5 ounces to 3 pounds 14 ounces). It was once thought to be caused by excessive oxygen administration, but it is now believed that the problem in many cases is an imbalance of oxygen in the baby's blood and that a variety of other factors (possibly including bright light in the nursery, maternal diabetes, or maternal antihistamine use during the last two weeks of pregnancy) probably also contribute to the condition. A newborn with ROP should be seen by a paediatric ophthalmologist. Close monitoring of blood gases in the infant when oxygen therapy is given is now routine and does seem to help minimize damage. Vitamin E given orally or intramuscularly also seems to help,[2] but blood levels need to be monitored regularly so the dosage can be changed as the baby grows. Aggressive therapy with cryosurgery (freezing to destroy the excess growth of blood vessels in the eye and to prevent further detachment of the retina) may be effective in preventing blindness. (Iron supplements are not usually given to infants with ROP who do not have iron deficiency anaemia until the retinas are mature or the condition has resolved, so don't give a supplement without the doctor's approval.)

Intraventricular haemorrhage. The immature brain of a foetus contains the germinal matrix, a gelatinous structure filled with veins, arteries and capillaries, which disappears at about 38 weeks. Infants born before it disappears are at high risk of haemorrhage because of the fragility of these vessels and the great amount of blood flow through them. Intraventricular haemorrhage is extremely common among preterm infants, striking 30 to 40%, most often within the first 72 hours of life. Haemorrhages are graded on a four-step scale, with grade I the least severe and grade IV the most severe. Grade IV requires close observation to correct any further problems that develop – for example, hydrocephalus. Regular follow-up cranial ultrasounds are usually ordered for grades III and IV until the haemorrhage is resolved. Babies with the more severe-grade haemorrhages are also at greater risk for seizures immediately and handicaps later on. Treatments are being developed to pre-

vent and/or treat the condition, including one in which temporary muscle paralysis is induced to reduce the fluctuation of blood flow in the brain.

Necrotizing enterocolitis. The symptoms of this bowel disease, in which tissue in the intestine becomes damaged and dies, usually appear between the second and twentieth day, almost always in low-birthweight babies. They include abdominal distention, bilious vomiting, apnea and blood in the stool. A great many theories have been advanced in an attempt to pinpoint the cause, none totally satisfactory. It seems most likely that a combination of factors, possibly including the use of formula (breastfed babies are less likely to be stricken), are involved. A baby with necrotizing enterocolitis is usually put on intravenous feedings, and treatment will depend on symptoms. If there is serious deterioration of the intestine, surgery is usually performed to remove the damaged portion.

Apnea of prematurity. Though apnea, periods of breathing cessation, can occur in any newborn, this problem is much more common among premature infants. Apnea of prematurity is diagnosed when a baby has such periods that last more than fifteen seconds or that are shorter but are associated with bradycardia, a slowing of the heart rate. When apnea is observed, testing is often done to determine if the infant needs monitoring (see page 179). Monitoring for apnea of prematurity is usually unnecessary past six months, but during that time the monitor has to be adjusted as the baby's heart rate goes through the normal slowing down that comes with growth (if it isn't, there may be a lot of false alarms for slow heart rate). This type of apnea, if it doesn't recur after a baby has reached his or her original due date, is not related to SIDS (sudden infant death syndrome).

Jaundice. Premature babies are much more likely to develop jaundice than are full-term infants. Read about the condition and its treatment on page 70.

2. Vitamin E is no longer given intravenously to newborns because it causes serious complications.

TWENTY

The Baby With Problems

◆

After nine months of hoping for a healthy, perfect baby, it is devastating to give birth to a child who is anything less than that. And no one who hasn't been dealt such a blow can possibly understand the pain involved. Still, the vast majority of parents do recover from their initial feelings of helplessness, hopelessness and despair. As they learn to cope with the complexities of having a baby with birth defects, they begin to see past the problems to the child underneath, a child who, above all, needs what all children need: love, attention and discipline.

Some find that the problem, which at first seemed so frightening, is easily corrected or at least alleviated with surgery, medication, or other treatment. Others learn that there is little or nothing that can be done to make their baby perfect. But even these families often find that raising a handicapped baby adds another dimension to their lives, that they achieve a sense of fulfillment they might never have experienced otherwise. They find that though they often must work long and hard to stimulate their child physically and intellectually, the rewards are all the more gratifying, and well worth the extra effort involved. And as time passes they often discover that their child, in addition to teaching them something about pain, has taught them a lot about love.

While much of the general information in this book is useful to parents of a child born with birth defects, this chapter deals with some of the adjustments and decisions that are unique to their situation. It may also be helpful to read Chapter 19 for other concerns, such as long-term hospitalization.

Feeding Baby:
Can Diet Make a Difference?

All parents want their offspring, disabled or not, to be the best they can be. And ensuring optimum nutrition – from birth on – is one way to help children develop to their greatest potential, whatever that potential might be. While a good diet can't change the fact that a child has a birth defect, or may not even improve his or her condition, it can have an impact on general health and can affect behaviour, learning ability and development. There's no evidence, however, that dietary manipulation (feeding a special diet, for example, or giving vitamin megadoses) can significantly improve the medical condition of a child born with a birth defect, except in cases where the defect is diet related.

For the child with no such unusual dietary needs, the best in nutrition begins with breast milk, when possible, or commercial infant formula, and then the Best-Odds Diet, page 214.

What You May Be Concerned About

Feeling Responsible

'Our doctor just told us that our baby isn't completely normal. I can't help feeling that I'm somehow responsible – that I could have done something to prevent his problem.'

Parents often feel responsible for the bad things that happen to their children; even a tumble precipitated by a toddler's own clumsiness can elicit a parental 'What did I do wrong?' When a child is born with a birth defect, the guilt can be overwhelming and debilitating. Parents may feel that it was something they did that was responsible for the child's condition, even though most often the cause was out of their control. Guilt can be particularly strong when one or both parents felt ambivalent about having a baby, as most parents-to-be do at some point. They may conclude that their unspoken thoughts were to blame for the child's condition – that it must be their punishment for not really wanting the baby. And as untrue as this may be, such parents often need repeated reassurance to convince them that they are not to blame.

Occasionally, as in the case of foetal alcohol syndrome, the development of a birth defect can be traced to a mother's actions, making the guilt all the more difficult to handle. It's important to remember, however, that alcoholism is as much a disease as is diabetes – that an alcoholic mother didn't drink because she was immoral or wanted to hurt her baby, but because the disease was controlling her. Though she can't undo what's been done, she can seek professional help now to deal with her problem and to prevent any further negative impact on this baby and babies she may have in the future.

Whether it's founded or unfounded, guilt won't do you, your husband, or your baby any good – and it could do all of you a great deal of harm. Instead of wasting emotional energy on self-flagellation, concentrate on the positive steps that can be taken to make your baby's future, and your family's, the best it can be.

Feeling Angry

'Ever since I gave birth to my daughter, who has Down's syndrome, I've been angry at everyone – the doctors, my husband, my parents, other mothers with normal babies, even the baby.'

Why wouldn't you be angry? Your dreams of nine months, or maybe longer, have been shattered. You look around at friends, neighbours, relatives, strangers at the supermarket with their normal babies, and you think bitterly, 'Why not me?' The fact that asking this question yields no satisfying answers further fuels your frustration. You may be angry at the doctor who delivered your baby (even if he or she wasn't at fault), at your spouse (even without logical reason), at your normal children (even though you know it's not their fault they're healthy and the new baby isn't).

Accept your anger as normal, but also recognize that, like guilt, it isn't a particularly productive emotion. Being angry takes a lot of energy – energy which really should be focused on your baby and her needs. You can't change the past, but you can make a difference in your child's future.

Not Loving the Baby

'It's been almost a month since our daughter was born with a birth defect, and I still don't feel close to her. I wonder if I ever will.'

Your feelings aren't at all unusual. Even parents with normal babies often take months to feel really close to their newborns. Initial rejection turns to ambivalence, then acceptance, and finally to love. For parents with handicapped infants, the process is, understandably, more gradual, with the first two reactions usually more exaggerated. Moving on to acceptance usually requires that a mother give up the idealized baby she carried in her mind's eye and open her heart to the child she does have. Interacting lovingly with your baby, singing lullabies, cuddling, stroking and kissing will help make the love grow and will help you to discover and focus on your baby's endearing qualities (all children have them).

If you don't feel closer to your baby as time passes, then seek counselling from someone experienced in working with parents of children with birth defects, or join a self-help group of such parents in your community. Your doctor or hospital should be able to direct you.

'Doctors tell us our little boy may not make it, so we're afraid to get too attached to him.'

Parents of babies whose lives are in jeopardy often share this fear of loving and losing, and consciously avoid bonding with their newborns. But in general, studies show, parents who allow themselves to get to know their critically ill babies (even if only through the portholes of an incubator) end up having an easier time coping if the child doesn't survive than do those who try to stay aloof. Perhaps this is because they are able to say, 'At least we loved him while we had him', and because they can truly grieve (you can't mourn for something you never had), a process necessary for them to resolve their feelings about their terrible loss. Showering love on your critically ill infant, in a sense providing him with a reason for living, can also have a significant impact on his will to survive, and might actually help to pull him through.

What to Tell Others

'Our son's birth defect is very obvious. People don't know what to say to me when they see him, and I don't know what to say to them.'

When people meet a child with a birth defect, their loss for words is often as obvious as the defect. They want to say the right thing, but they don't know what that is. They want to be kind and supportive, but they don't know how. They want to congratulate you on the birth of your baby, but feel almost as though condolences would be more appropriate. You can help them, and yourself, by acknowledging their discomfort, opening the way for them to express their feelings. If you're feeling able to, let them know you understand if they're uneasy, that most people are at first, and that it's perfectly natural. Beyond this, all that a casual friend need be told is that though your newborn is not the child you expected, he's yours, you love him, and you intend to treat him as normally as possible – and hope that they will do the same.

Of course, this is a rational approach to the question, and you may not feel rational at first. You may want to ignore strangers, and sometimes even friends and family, or to lash out if they are thoughtless or unkind. Don't feel bad if you're too upset to be able to put others at ease. With time and, if necessary, sensitive individual counselling or group therapy, you'll become better able to cope.

Friends and relatives who will be in closer, more frequent contact with your baby will need to know more. In addition to being encouraged to be open about their feelings, they will have to be educated about your child's problems and special needs. Provide them with reading material about your child's medical problems, ask the baby's doctor to speak with them, encourage them to talk informally to other family members of children with birth defects, or refer them to a support group. Include them in your baby's care – give them the opportunity to hold, change, bathe and play with him. In time they, too, will come to see him. as the lovable baby he is.

Sometimes close relatives, particularly grandparents, feel guilty ('Did I contribute a faulty gene?'), or angry ('Why couldn't you give us a healthy grandchild?'), or think they have all the answers ('Feed him this food,'

'Go to that doctor'). If your efforts to involve them in your baby's life and educate them about his problems don't help to overcome such attitudes, and if their negative input continues to threaten the delicate equilibrium of your nuclear family, keep lines of communication open, but don't let their problem become yours.

In spite of your best efforts, there will always be people who – probably because of their own insecurities – will make cruel and thoughtless comments, undervalue your child because he is different, and feel uncomfortable around him. There will be times when both you and he will be hurt by their intolerance. As much as you might like to educate the world, it isn't possible. You'll just have to learn to hold your head high and ignore the narrow-minded people you can't reach.

Be a Friend in Deed

Few people know what to do or say when they hear that a friend, relative, neighbour, or casual acquaintance has given birth to a child with a birth defect, a child who is seriously ill, or one who dies at or shortly after delivery. There are no pat answers; every individual and every situation is unique. But in general, these approaches are the ones likely to help the most:

- *Lend an ear*. Don't say 'I know how you feel'. You don't, and hopefully never will. Don't say 'You've got to be brave', or offer any other advice. The new parents in crisis will get plenty of advice from the professionals. What they need from you is love, support and a willing ear. Listen to what's on their minds and in their hearts without being judgmental or offering your viewpoints. Let them vent their feelings, whatever those feelings may be (you can expect them to be angry at times, despondent at others) and empathize with them – this will be the best therapy.

- *Become informed*. If the parents seem to want to talk about their baby's problems, listen. But if they've told the terrible tale too many times already, get your information second- or third-hand from a relative or friend so they needn't relive it again. To be better able to understand what they are going through, read this chapter (and if relevant, the previous one) and get further information, if you feel you need it, from an organization that deals with the baby's specific condition.

- *Use body language*. Often when words fail, the squeeze of a hand, a loving hug, a sympathetic look will get the message that you care across.

- *Keep in touch*. Because we don't know what to say or do, we often take the coward's way out and avoid the friend who is going through a crisis. Those who have been on the receiving end of such behaviour almost always say, 'I'd rather hear the wrong words than none at all'. Those phone calls, visits and invitations are more important now than at any other time and shouldn't be neglected. And though you shouldn't force your company on someone who would rather suffer their pain alone, don't give up after one 'We're not up to it yet'. Try again soon.

- *Help out*. There are innumerable tasks friends and family can take over when new parents are mourning the loss of an infant or are faced with one who is hospitalized or needs a great deal of attention. Cook a meal, baby-sit for older children, do the laundry, offer to vacuum, wield the dust cloth, or take over with the baby for an hour or two if possible. Any way in which you can lighten the burden will doubtless be appreciated.

Handling it All

'We love our new baby, even with all her problems and the special care she requires, but with another small child to care for and care about, I feel totally overwhelmed and unable to cope.'

Raising a child with a birth defect can be both physically and emotionally draining – particularly for the mother, on whom most of the responsibility usually falls, even if she's also employed outside the home. The pointers in Chapters 23 and 24, which can help any new mother, can also help you. But you'll need more:

More breaks. If you are a full-time mother (and many mothers of handicapped children are, choosing to postpone returning to their jobs), then you've got to find ways of getting out of the house, away from the stress of caring for your child day in and day out. Take off at least a few hours a week, leaving the baby with a relative, friend, trusted baby-sitter, or baby nurse. Have dinner with your husband, lunch with a friend, play a few sets of tennis, see a movie or a concert, or just browse at the shops – whatever will relax you most. Escaping for an hour or two every day – to go for a jog, get a facial or haircut (looking your best will give you a psychic boost), pick up a couple of books at the library – is even better if you can arrange it. If you have another child, then try to take some of your breaks with him or her; both of you will benefit.

More release. Don't bottle up your worries, fears, complaints – air them with your spouse, your mother or sister, your best friend, your doctor, other women in your situation, or a professional counsellor if necessary. You may not feel ready to face a self-help group for parents of children with similar problems at first, but you may find this helpful later on. Keeping a journal is another way to express your feelings and work out your anxieties. Record problems and progress, what you've done and what needs to be done. Seeing your life on paper may help make it seem more manageable.

More help. You can't do it alone. If you can't pay for help with household and child-care chores, you will need to rely on friends and family more than most. You needn't feel guilty about it, as long as you don't take the time and energy given by others for granted. Though you may feel like the sole beneficiary of their kindness, they also benefit – perhaps even more – by helping.

Getting the Right Diagnosis

'According to our family doctor, our son has a very serious congenital disorder. I just can't believe it – everyone in our family is so healthy.'

Serious illness, especially in our children, is difficult to accept. The first reaction is almost always denial: we cling to the hope that someone's made a mistake. The best way to resolve your nagging doubts is to double-check the diagnosis – no one, after all, is infallible. So if you haven't already, do have your child thoroughly examined by an experienced neonatologist, one familiar with the condition that's been diagnosed, and be sure that all appropriate tests are carried out, both to verify the diagnosis and to uncover any other problems that may exist. You can help ensure an accurate diagnosis by giving examining doctors as much information as possible about your family's medical history (including any familial genetic discorders) and your pregnancy history and behaviour (including tobacco use, alcohol or drug consumption, medications taken, illnesses, especially with accompanying fevers, use of hot tubs and so on). Your *candid* answers may, in fact, help a doctor to pinpoint an elusive diagnosis.

If the consulting doctor concurs with the first, you can be pretty sure their diagnosis is correct – and taking your child from doctor to doctor won't change the facts. Though there's always that one-in-a-million chance that even several doctors are wrong, the odds are much better that a problem does exist and that you, like most other parents of children with birth defects, are trying hard to deny it.

Be certain that you're completely clear about what the diagnosis is. The first time parents are told their newborn child has a birth defect, it's not unusual for most of the details to be washed away in a tide of overwhelming shock. What they hear is 'Your child isn't normal'; beyond that, everything's a blur. So request a second meeting with the doctor when your head is a little clearer (don't expect your thinking to be very focused for a while). In addition to the information you get from the doctors and/or nurses caring for your baby, seek out information in books, from parents in similar situations, and from organizations concerned with handicapped children and/or your baby's particular problem.[1] Don't rely, however, on advice from well-meaning but uninformed neighbours or family friends – it's likely to be based more on mythology than on medicine.

Before you take your baby home, ask his doctor exactly what your can expect (in terms of behaviour, development, medical problems) and what warning signs you need to be on the lookout for, as well as what you and the rest of your family can do to help your baby reach his potential. Take notes so that you'll have them to refer to when you go home.

Whether or not to Accept Treatment

'Our baby boy was born without part of his brain. The doctors say he has no chance of living, but they want to operate on him to keep him alive a little longer. We don't know what to do.'

While the issue of whether or not babies who have no hope of long-term survival

---

1. The following organizations may be able to help: Contact a Family, 16 Strutton Ground, London SW1P 2HP; Disabled Living Foundation (DLF), 380–384 Harrow Road, London W9 2HU; Royal Association for Disability and Rehabilitation, 25 Mortimer Street, London W1N 8AB; Voluntary Council for Handicapped Children, 8 Wakely Street, London EC1V 7QE.

should be treated and kept on life-support systems has become a major ethical one for society, it is now a painfully personal one for you. Your decision is one that, if at all possible, probably shouldn't be made without first talking it over with your family, a religious counsellor, the baby's doctors and the hospital ethicist, if there is one. In many cases there will be time for such reasoned decision making. Even when there isn't, and time is of the essence, there is usually a chance to talk with your baby's doctors and, possibly, a hospital chaplain. The doctors can usually tell you the quality of life you can expect your child to have if kept alive, and whether treatment will improve the quality of his life or only prolong his dying. The chaplain can explain the religious issues involved, and the ethicist, your legal rights and responsibilities as well as the ethical issues. When you make your decision, consider all the information and counsel you've received, but do what you believe in your heart to be right – because no matter what it is, that's the decision you will be able to live with best.

In some cases, parents of children for whom there is no hope have found some solace in being able to donate some of their baby's organs to save the life of another sick infant. This isn't always feasible – sometimes for medical reasons, sometimes for legal ones – but do ask your doctor and hospital authorities about the possibility of organ donation if it interests you.

Getting the Best Care and Treatment

'We're determined to give our baby, in spite of his handicaps, the best possible chance in life. But we're not sure how to do it.'

Your determination to help your child greatly increases his chances of enjoying a productive and satisfying life. But there's much more you can do, and the earlier you begin the better. Most babies with serious birth defects get the best start in a major teaching hospital, but occasionally a community hospital is equipped with an excellent Special Care Baby Unit (SCBU). A hospital near your home has the benefit of allowing you to visit regularly, which sometimes will compensate for a lack of scientific sophistication. To minimize the effects of a lengthy hospitalization, if that will be necessary, see pages 456 and 457.

Wherever your child is treated, you'll want to have him cared for by a doctor who specializes in dealing with his particular birth defect – though often day-to-day care can be provided by a local paediatrician or family doctor under the supervision of the specialist. With many birth defects, a team approach to treatment is best. The team may include doctors from various specialties, psychologists, physiotherapists, nutritionists, social workers, as well as a neonatologist and, usually, the baby's own doctor. If you aren't sure how to locate the appropriate specialist or specialists and the hospital staff can't help you, ask your health visitor about organizations specializing in your child's handicap.

Though excellent medical care and, often, early educational intervention will be crucial to your child's development, in most cases the home environment you create will be even more significant in determining how well he is prepared for life and whether or not he reaches his maximum potential. The primary need of most children born with birth defects is to be treated like other children – to be loved and nurtured, but also to be disciplined and expected to meet standards (which should, of course, take into account their individual limitations). And like other children, they need to feel good about themselves – to know that each step forward, no matter how small, is appreciated and applauded, and that they won't be expected to live up to the baby next door, only to their own possibilities.

A wide range of therapies, as well as high-tech aids – everything from adapted playground equipment and toys to special education software, laser canes (for sight-impaired children), cochlear implants (to aid hearing) and robotic devices – are now available to help you help your handicapped child grow, develop and enjoy. Ask a member of your child's care team about them, or check with the appropriate organization for information.

It should be reassuring to know that the majority of children with handicaps grow up psychologically sound, are well accepted by their peers and others, and have a risk of adjustment problems only slightly higher than that faced by children without handicaps.

Effect of Baby on Siblings

'We're planning to raise our Down's syndrome baby ourselves, but we're worried about how well our normal three-year-old daughter will handle the changes that she'll bring to her life.'

More and more parents are choosing to raise their handicapped child at home – a decision that often turns out to be good not only for the child and the parents, but for the rest of the family as well. Having a handicapped sibling at home can have a profoundly positive impact on the other siblings, making them, on average, more patient and understanding than other children and more adept at getting along with different kinds of people.

Your other child will need to have some special times with both parents (as impossible as this may sometimes seem, it's absolutely crucial). Children who feel neglected in such a situation often act up, manifest psychosomatic illnesses, and even play dumb in school to gain back parental attention. Most don't need counselling or therapy – just a little extra understanding. They need to be reassured that they aren't selfish or bad if they want their needs attended to, or if they sometimes feel resentful or ashamed of their sibling. They may also need reassurance that what has happened to her isn't going to happen to them, and may need extra support when they bring friends home.

An older sibling may also need special attention if the handicapped sibling is institutionalized. ('Why isn't my baby sister home with us?' 'Was she bad?' 'If I'm bad, will I be sent away, too?') Again, understanding and a reassuring explanation will be necessary. If a child continues to seem anxious about the situation, counselling is probably a good idea.

Many older siblings of handicapped children benefit from talking to others in their position. Many hospitals and organizations sponsor programmes for siblings; check into this possibility in your area. Such a programme gives children a chance to talk about their worries in a safe and supportive environment, and to learn that they're not alone.

Effects on Your Marriage

'My husband and I have cried a lot together since our son was born with a birth defect, but that's been the extent of our relationship. I'm afraid we'll never have emotional energy to spend on each other again.'

All new parents find that having a baby in the house restricts the amount of time they spend as a couple. Parents of babies born with a handicap discover the restrictions on romance and intimacy to be even greater, since caring for the baby saps not just physical strength, but emotional reserves as well. But the baby you came together to create is not inevitably going to tear you apart. Though it might seem that the cumulative effects of months and years of living with a handicapped child might weaken even the sturdiest marital relationships, they rarely do. Most marriages, it appears, not only hold up under the strain, they are strengthened by it. (Though there is a slightly increased risk of divorce when a child is chronically ill over a long period of time.) To help improve the chances that your marriage will become one of the happy statistics, make sure that:

The work is shared. No one can single-handedly care for a handicapped child and still have the energy left to be a loving partner to a spouse. If your husband works all day while you stay at home, let him take over some of the baby care responsibilities in the evening so you can have a break. If he's considering taking on a second job to ease the financial strain of your not working, it might be better for you to take a part-time job and to transfer more of the child-care load to him. Hired or volunteer relief child care, for at least a few hours a week, and/or household help can also ease the burden and free up some time and energy for each other.

Each partner gets enough support from the other. Both of you have hurts that need healing; both of you need to make adjustments in your lives. (Many people fail to realize that the father of a handicapped child may be as much in need of emotional support as the mother.) Facing the future as a team will be infinitely more productive and satisfying than facing it as individuals. Share your problems and concerns, and protect each other from outside assault (from overly critical grandparents, for example).

You make time for each other. All new parents need to make a concerted effort to make time alone for each other – or the time just doesn't happen. And as particularly difficult as it may be for you and your husband, you need to do the same. See page 570 for tips.

You give yourselves time. Romance may be the furthest thing from your minds right now, and it may take a few months before any desire returns. This is the rule among most newly delivered couples, and is even more likely in your situation. So instead of pressurizing yourselves to perform sexually when you're not emotionally ready, wait until you are. And remember, you don't have to make love to show love. Hugging and hand holding – sometimes even a good cry together – may be, more than anything, what both of you need right now.

A Repeat with the Next Baby

'We would like to have another baby within a year or so, but we're afraid that our daughter's birth defect might repeat in our next child.'

As common as this fear is among parents of children born with birth defects, it is in most cases unfounded; their chances of having a normal baby are often as good as those of other parents. But in order to predict the risk in your particular case, the cause of your baby's problem needs to be determined. There is a wide range of possibilities:

Genetic. If your baby's defect is determined to be genetic (passed on by genetic material from you and/or your husband), a genetic counsellor or, often, the baby's doctor will probably be able to give you precise odds on the likelihood of a repeat. In some instances, you will also be able to test future foetuses for the defect early in pregnancy, giving you the option to terminate should it turn up.

Environmental. If the birth defect was the result of a one-time event – such as an exposure during pregnancy to infection, chemicals, X-rays, medications, or other factors that interfered with normal foetal development – it is not likely to repeat unless the exact set of circumstances recur at the same critical point in pregnancy.

Lifestyle. If the defect can be traced to your smoking, alcohol consumption, drug abuse, or poor nutrition, for example, it is not likely to repeat in subsequent pregnancies unless the lifestyle mistakes are repeated.

Maternal factors. If your baby's problems seem related to your age, the shape or size of your uterus, or other unchangeable factors, they might repeat, though the risk can sometimes be reduced. For example, if you are past 35 and have a Down's syndrome baby, antenatal testing can diagnose the disorder in future pregnancies. Or if your uterus is misshapen, surgery may be able to reshape it.

Multifactorial. When a variety of factors are involved, predicting future outcomes may be more complicated, but the doctor or a genetic counsellor can still be helpful in such cases.

Unknown. Sometimes there is no apparent reason for a baby's birth defect. Usually such cases do not repeat. But if no one can say why your baby was not born completely normal, it would be a good idea to discuss the situation with a doctor familiar with genetic counselling before becoming pregnant again.

Before making a decision to become pregnant, be sure you are doing so for the right reasons. To deliver a healthy baby in order to compensate for one that wasn't healthy is not fair to the new child. Speak to your baby's doctor or to a family therapist if you feel in conflict.

If you do decide to become pregnant again, your obstetrician should be completely familiar with your previous history so that you can be monitored throughout pregnancy for any possible problems. But with good medical care and good self-care (you are your doctor's best partner), your odds of delivering a normal and healthy baby will be very good.

A Different Birth Defect Next Time

'I'm not so worried about having another child with the same birth defect – I can be tested for that. What I'm worried about is having one with a different defect.'

Even if the chances of a repeat of your first child's defect in your next baby may be somewhat higher than average (and this isn't always the case), the same would not be true of other unrelated defects. In fact, you and your husband have just as good a chance of producing a child free of other birth defects as any other set of parents.

As reassuring as these odds should be, it's normal to still harbour some nagging fears after what you've already gone through. To help ease them, talk to your doctor, consult a genetic counsellor, and follow the precautions listed above.

WHAT IT'S IMPORTANT TO KNOW:
The Most Common Birth Disorders

If your child hasn't been diagnosed as having a birth disorder but you've noticed symptoms associated with any of the following problems, don't panic – what you notice may indicate something far less serious than you're imagining. But do check with your baby's doctor. It may take more than a phone call to allay your fears; an examination or special testing may be necessary. If a problem does turn up, early recognition and prompt medical attention and therapy can often be beneficial. And many birth defects can be corrected entirely.

Common Birth Disorders

AIDS/HIV – PERINATAL

What is it? A serious disorder of the immune system.

How common is it? Rare, but becoming more common as more women are infected.

Who is susceptible? Babies born to infected mothers.

What causes it? The human immunodeficiency virus (HIV); most often passed on from mother to child during pregnancy, childbirth or breastfeeding.

Related problems. Pneumonia, cancers.

Treatment. Now life-prolonging.

Prognosis. In adults, believed to be always fatal, but some children have survived for several years.

ANENCEPHALY

What is it? A neural tube defect in which the failure of the neural groove to close normally early in pregnancy leads to lack of brain development and all or a major part of the brain is absent.

How common is it? Very rare in full-term babies, since 99% of foetuses with the defect are miscarried.

Who is susceptible? Not known.

What causes it? Not known at present. Heredity is probably involved in some way, along with adverse antenatal environment.

Related problems. All body systems are affected negatively.

Treatment. Antiviral drugs for HIV positive mother during pregnancy, for child after birth.

Prognosis. Now improving: many children have survived for several years.

AUTISM

What is it? An inability, that dates from birth or develops within the first two and a half years of life, to develop normal human relationships, even with parents. Babies don't smile or respond to parents or anyone else in any way and dislike being picked up or touched. There are usually extreme problems in speaking (including bizarre speed patterns such as echolalia, in which the child echoes the words just heard rather than replying), strange positions and mannerisms, erratic and inappropriate behaviour (compulsiveness and ritualism, screaming fit and arm flapping) and, sometimes, self-destructiveness. The child may have normal intelligence but appear to be retarded or deaf because of lack of responsiveness. Autism may sometimes be confused with childhood schizophrenia and occasionally may precede it.

How common is it? About 4/5 people in 10,000 will have classic autism; 15/20 in 10,000 will have autistic-like conditions.[2]

Who is susceptible? Male children are three to four times more likely to be autistic than females.

What causes it? Probably, according to a recent study, autosomal recessive inheritance: both parents must pass on recessive genes for the baby to be affected. There seem to be some differences in brain wave patterns in autistic children, which may be related to their condition. It is not related to parenting.

Related problems. Behaviour and developmental problems.

Treatment. At present there is no cure, but some children can be helped with behaviour modification therapy, stimulation, special training and, sometimes, drugs. When possible, the child remains at home, but sometimes the stress is more than a family can tolerate and institutionalization becomes necessary. Day-care programmes can sometimes help alleviate the stress while allowing the child to remain at home. Counselling is often helpful for the rest of the family.

---

2. Occasionally a child who seems to be autistic is helped by the elimination of foods to which he is allergic. See page 406.

Prognosis. At present, about a third of children recover sufficiently to function fairly normally, but most remain autistic and need special institutional care. Outlook is best when a child can be taught to use meaningful speech before age five.

CANCER

Rare in early infancy. Many infant cancers are highly curable today.

CEREBRAL PALSY

What is it? A neuromuscular disorder caused by damage to the brain. Motor impairment may be mild to disabling. The infant may have difficulty sucking or retaining the nipple; drool constantly; seldom move voluntarily; have arm or leg tremors with voluntarily movements; have legs that are hard to separate; have delayed motor development; and use only one hand or, later, use hands but not feet, crawl in a strange fashion, and walk on tiptoes. Muscle tone may be excessively stiff or floppy, but this may not be apparent until three months or so. Exact symptoms differ in each of the three different types of CP: spastic, athetoid and ataxic.

How common is it? Decreasing in frequency because of safer childbirth (except in the tiniest newborns) and better treatment of jaundice. About 15,000 cases a year.

Who is susceptible? Premature and low-birthweight babies, boys slightly more often than girls, white infants more often than blacks.

What causes it? Estimated 50% of cases are related to antenatal causes (including maternal infection or other illness, radiation, malnutrition); 33% related to the birth (including unusually prolonged or rapid labour, prolapsed cord, depressed maternal vital signs); 10% postnatal trauma (such as falls or other accidents), infection (of the brain), pathological jaundice and lack of oxygen (as when breathing is interrupted); 7% mixed causation.

Related problems. Sometimes, seizures; speech, vision and hearing disorders; dental defects; mental retardation.

Treatment. No cure, but treatment can help a child live up to potential. May include: physical therapy, braces, splints, or other orthopaedic appliances; special furniture and utensils; exercise; surgery, when needed; medication for seizures or to relax muscles if needed.

Prognosis. Varies with case. Child with a mild form, given proper treatment, may live a nearly normal life. Child with a severe form may be completely disabled. Disease does not get progressively worse.

CLEFT LIP AND/OR PALATE

What is it? A split, sometimes extensive, sometimes slight, occurs where parts of upper lip or palate (the roof of the mouth) fail to grow together. Some babies have only cleft lip, but more have only cleft palate. About 40% of affected babies have both.

How common is it? About 5,000 children a year, or approximately 1 in 700 births.

Who is susceptible? More common among Asians, less common among blacks. Also more common among premature babies and those with other defects.

What causes it? Heredity plays a role in about 1 in 4 cases; after having a baby with cleft, the odds of having another one increase slightly. But illness, certain medications, lack of essential nutrients (particularly folic acid) and other factors that adversely affect the prenatal environment may also interfere with normal development of lip and palate, possibly in combination with each other and/or heredity.

Related problems. Because sucking is usually difficult, feeding may be a serious problem, so special procedures are necessary (usually an upright position, small amounts, a teat with large holes or a special syringe). Ear infections are also common and need to be controlled.

Treatment. Usually a combination of surgery (sometimes in the first few months of life), speech therapy, dental adjustments (often including braces later in life), and psychological counselling.

Prognosis. Usually excellent with treatment.

CLUBFOOT

What is it? An ankle or foot deformity that occurs in three forms. In the most severe and least common, equinovarus, the foot twists inward and downward. If both feet are 'clubbed', the toes point towards each other. The most common type of club foot, calcaneal valgus, is milder. The foot is sharply angled at the heel and points upward and outward. In the mildest form of clubfoot, metatarsus varus, the front part of the foot is turned inward. This type may not be diagnosed until the baby is a few months old, though it is present at birth. Clubfoot is not painful and doesn't bother the baby until it's time to stand or walk.

How common is it? Affects 1 in 400 babies.

Who is susceptible? Boys are twice as likely to have clubfoot as girls.

What causes it? Not the position in the uterus, as was once believed (cases of this sort correct themselves after birth). Probably a combination of heredity and environmental factors, such as infection, drugs and disease, in most cases; but some cases are related to spina bifida, nerve diseases, or muscle diseases.

Related problems. The foot can't move up and down as it normally would in walking; the child walks as though on a peg leg. When both feet are affected, the child may walk on the sides or even tops of feet, leading to damage to this tissue and to abnormal leg development. Psychological problems may arise because of the abnormality. Occasionally there may be other defects as well.

Treatment. Mild cases may be treated by exercise alone. Plaster casts or surgery are used in more severe cases to force the twisted foot gradually and gently into place so that it can move up and down normally. Shoes connected with bars may also be used at night.

Prognosis. With expert early treatment, most grow up to wear regular shoes, take part in sports, lead active lives.

COELIAC DISEASE

What is it? Also called coeliac spruc or gluten-sensitive enteropathy (GSE), this is a condition in which there is sensitivity (not allergy) to gliadin, which is found in gluten (a component of wheat, rye, barley, oats and other grains), characterized by faulty food absorption and loss of appetite, poor growth, pot belly, consistently foul-smelling, fatty diarrhoea and sometimes anaemia, beginning after solid foods are introduced. May be mistaken for cystic fibrosis.

How common is it? An estimated 1 in 1,500 in the U.K. general population are affected. It is rare in blacks, Asians, Jews and those of Mediterranean descent.

Who is susceptible? Those with a genetic predisposition.

What causes it? Unclear, but most likely some combination of environmental factors and genetic disposition. Possibly linked to a defect in a gene that causes anti-gliadin antibodies to be produced; it is suspected that antibodies combine with gliadin to attack and flatten villi in the intestines, causing malabsorption and other symptoms.

Related problems. Symptoms of malnutrition such as developmental delay, fluid retention, late teething and rickets.

Treatment. Strict gluten-free diet, which usually begins to work within days and which must be adhered to for life. Nutritional supplements may also be prescribed.

Prognosis. Usually, a normal life on gluten-free diet.

CONGENITAL HEART DEFECT

What is it? Any heart defect, minor or major, that is present at birth. Though the defects can usually be diagnosed with a stethoscope, further tests such as X-rays, ultrasound and ECGs will be needed to verify abnormalities. Depending on the type of defect, one or more functions of the heart may be adversely affected. Symptoms may show up at birth, or not become apparent until adulthood. Cyanosis, or bluing of the skin, particularly around fingers, toes and lips, is the most common symptom.

How common is it? About 8 in every 1,000 babies in the U.K. is born with a heart abnormality, although about half of these require little or no medical treatment.

Who is susceptible? Children of mothers who had rubella during pregnancy, Down's syndrome children and those with affected siblings (though their increased risk is slight).

What causes it? In most cases, scientists just don't know. Certain infections (such as rubella, or German measles) and some chemicals (thalidomide, amphetamines, or alcohol, for example) are capable of causing heart abnormalities antenatally, but such abnormalities may sometimes be the result of a random genetic error.

Related problems. Sometimes, poor weight gain and growth, fatigue, weakness, difficulty breathing or sucking (because of weakness from heart failure).

Treatment. Surgery (either immediately or later in childhood), which varies according to the defect present, and sometimes drugs or a heart transplant can remedy heart defects. (Even a defect that causes no symptoms may require treatment to prevent problems later in life.) Sometimes a heart defect can be diagnosed before birth and medication given to correct it.

Prognosis. Most congenital heart defects are treatable, but some very serious ones may be disabling or even fatal. Most children with murmurs can lead normal lives with no restrictions on activities.

CYSTIC FIBROSIS (CF)

What is it? A condition in which there is a generalized dysfunction of the exocrine glands, the glands that discharge their secretions through an epithelial surface (such as the skin, the mucous membranes, the linings of the hollow organs). When sweat glands are affected, perspiration is salty and profuse, and excessive perspiration can lead to dehydration and shock. When the respiratory system is affected, thick secretions may fill the lungs, causing chronic coughing and increased risk of infection. With digestive system involvement, mucus secretions may make first bowel movements after birth difficult to pass, causing intestinal obstruction. The pancreatic ducts may also be obstructed, resulting in deficiencies of the pancreatic enzymes and inability to digest protein and fat. The stools, containing the undigested materials, are usually frequent, bulky, foul-smelling, pale and greasy. Weight gain is poor, appetite ravenous, abdomen distended, arms and legs thin and skin sallow. Sweat-test screening is available to pick out possible cases, but lack of meconium bowel movement after birth, salty skin and poor weight gain along with good appetite can be early indications.

How common is it? Relatively rare.

Who is susceptible? More common in those with central European ancestry (1 in 2,000–2,500 births) than in native Americans, or those of African, West Indian or Asian ancestry.

What causes it? Autosomal recessive inheritance: both parents must pass on recessive genes for a child to be affected.

Related problems. Pneumonia, because of respiratory secretions, is common. Also pancreatic insufficiency, insufficient insulin production, abnormal glucose tolerance, cirrhosis of the liver and hypertension, among others.

Treatment. The earlier the better, to prevent development of symptoms when possible. No cure exists, but treatment helps a child lead a more normal life. For sweat gland malfunction, generous salting of foods and salt supplements during hot weather. For digestive problems, pancreatic enzymes given by mouth with meals and snacks, limitation of fat, supplementation with fat-soluble vitamins (A, D, E and K). For various types of intestinal blockages (meconium ileus, rectal prolapse and so on associated with CF, both surgical and non surgical treatment is available and usually successful. For respiratory problems, copious fluid intake to thin secretions, usually daily respiratory physical therapy (including postural drainage, to help loosen and remove secretions) and oxygen therapy as needed. Room air is best kept cool and dry. Infections are treated with large doses of antibiotics. Initial studies indicate that treatment with anti-inflammatory agents (such as prednisone) may help reduce bouts of illness. If researchers find the gene (they have already located a genetic marker, a gene that seems to be inherited with CF), a cure may be possible.

Prognosis. Most cystic fibrosis babies once died in childhood, usually because of respiratory failure; today, with early diagnosis, aggressive treatment (particularly at one of the major CF centres) and strong family support, more than half live to the age of

21, and many are now reaching their 30s, 40s and 50s and have busy, active lives. Some have married, and though males with CF are sterile, several women have successfully borne children. The outlook for those born now is even better.

DEFORMATION

What is it? An abnormality in one or more organs or parts of the body.

How common is it? About 2 in every 100 babies has some deformity of this type.

Who is susceptible? An extra large foetus in a crowded uterus, or any foetus in a malformed or small uterus, or in a uterus with fibroids, an inadequate supply of amniotic fluid, or an unusual placental site; a foetus who shares the uterus with one or more siblings. Deformations are most common in babies of small and first-time mothers, and when there is an abnormal presentation such as a breech.

What causes it? Conditions in the uterus, such as those just mentioned, that put undue pressure on one or more developing parts of the foetus.

Related problems. Depends on abnormality.

Treatment. In most cases, none is necessary since the deformed part will gradually resume normal shape. Some conditions, however, such as scoliosis, clubfoot and hip dislocations do require treatment.

Prognosis. Good, for most conditions.

DOWN'S SYNDROME

What is it? A set of signs and symptoms that usually include mild to severe mental retardation, specific facial features (more obvious in some than in others), an oversized tongue and a short neck; they may also include a flat back of the head, small ears (sometimes folded at the tops) and a flat wide nose. Hearing and vision may be poor and various internal defects (particularly of heart or GI tract) may also exist. Down's syndrome children are often short and have loose muscle tone (responsible for some of the delayed development). They are also usually very sweet and lovable.

How common is it? Down's syndrome affects about 1,000 babies a year, or approximately 1 in 700 in the U.K.

Who is susceptible? Babies of parents who have already had a baby with the birth defect, or of a mother or father with a chromosome rearrangement, or of a mother over 35 (the risk increases with age). All ethnic groups and economic levels are affected.

What causes it? In 95% of the cases, an extra chromosome contributed by either the mother or the father, so that baby has 47 instead of 46 chromosomes. This cause of Down's syndrome is called Trisomy 21, because three number-21 chromosomes are present (normally there are two). About 4% of the time, certain other accidents affecting chromosome number 21 are responsible. For example, sometimes a piece of a normal chromosome 21 breaks off and attaches to another chromosome in the parent (this is called a translocation). The parent remains normal because he or she still has the right amount of genetic material. But if this augmented chromosome is passed on to a child, the child can have an excess of chromosome 21 material, resulting in Down's syndrome. Very rarely, an accident during cell division in the fertilized egg results in an extra chromosome in some but not all cells. This is called mosaicism and affected children may have only some Down's syndrome characteristics because only some of their cells carry the excess chromosome.

Related problems. Dental problems, poor eyesight and hearing, heart disease, gastrointestinal defects, thyroid dysfunction, early aging (including Alzheimer's disease), higher risk for respiratory illnessess, as well as leukaemia and other cancers.

Treatment. Antenatal tests can diagnose Down's syndrome in the foetus. Surgery, after birth, can correct heart and other serious medical abnormalities; in some countries, surgery is performed to make appearance more normal, but benefits are unclear. Early specialized education programs improve the IQs of Down's syndrome children who are mildly or moderately retarded.

Prognosis. Most children with Down's syndrome have greater capabilities than previously believed and early intervention can bring these abilities out, leaving fewer than 10% severely retarded. Many can be mainstreamed to a certain age in school, some even go to college. Most later find places in sheltered homes and workshops; some live and work independently; and some even marry. The average life span, once the hurdles of the first two to ten years are surmounted, is 55, more than twice what it was in the past.

FOETAL ALCOHOL SYNDROME (FAS)

What is it? A group of signs and symptoms that develop during gestation in a child whose mother drinks heavily during pregnancy. The most common are low birthweight, mental deficiency, deformities of the head and face, limbs and central nervous system; the neonatal mortality rate is high. Less obvious effects may occur in children of moderate drinkers.

How common is it? About 1 in 750 live births.

Who is susceptible? Babies of women who drink heavily. (It is estimated that 30 to 40% of women who drink heavily during pregnancy have babies with FAS.)

What causes it? Ingestion of alcohol – usually five or six drinks of beer, wine, or distilled spirits a day – during pregnancy.

Related problems. Developmental problems.

Treatment. Therapy for individual handicaps.

Prognosis. Depends on extent of problems.

HEART DEFECT – see Congenital Heart Defect

HYDROCEPHALUS (WATER ON THE BRAIN)

What is it? Absorption of the fluid that normally bathes the brain is blocked and the fluid collects. The pressure spreads apart the loosely connected parts of the skull, causing the head to become enlarged. This enlargement is often the first clue to the problem. Often occurs along with spina bifida, or following surgery to close an open spine. The scalp skin may be shiny and thin, neck muscles may be underdeveloped, eyes may look strange, cry may be high pitched and baby may suffer from irritability, lack of appetite and vomiting.

How common is it? Relatively rare.

Who is susceptible? Not clear, though infants with spina bifida are at increased risk.

What causes it? At birth, a defect in the membrane that is supposed to absorb cerebrospinal fluid; later, injury (sometimes from surgery to correct spina bifida) or a tumour.

Related problems. Retardation if fluid is not drained away regularly; complications with shunts, including infection and shunt malfunctions.

Treatment. Under anaesthesia, a special tube is inserted through a hole drilled in the skull into the brain to drain the excess fluid into either the abdominal cavity, the pleural cavity (surrounding the lung), or directly into a major blood vessel. The head gradually returns to normal size, but frequent checkups are necessary to be sure all is going well and the tube has not become blocked. Doctors are now trying to develop a treatment that doesn't require surgery.

Prognosis. Poor if the problem is well advanced by the time the baby is born. Good if treatment is begun early enough; this can usually prevent retardation. Complications can worsen the prognosis. Treatment before birth has not been successful.

MALFORMATION

What is it? An organ or part of the body appears abnormal. Sometimes several organs or body parts are affected, and grouped together, they form a syndrome that indicates a particular disease (such as Down's syndrome). Sometimes there is just one isolated malformation – such as a stunted limb.

How common is it? Probably fewer than 1 in 100 newborns is born with a noticeable malformation, usually a mild one.

Who is susceptible? Those with similar malformations in other family members; those whose parents, most often mothers, are exposed to certain dangerous environmental hazards before or after conception.

What causes it? Abnormal differentiation or organization during the development of the embryo, because of either a genetic or chromosomal abnormality or an environmental factor (such as X-ray or infection).

Related problems. Depends on the syndrome.

Treatment. Varies with the defect.

Prognosis. Depends on the malformation. (See individual conditions, such as spina bifida, Down's syndrome, etc.)

OPEN SPINE – see Spina Bifida

PKU – (PHENYLKETONURIA)

What is it? A metabolic disorder in which the individual is unable to metabolize a protein called phenylalanine. The buildup of phenylalanine in the bloodstream can interfere with brain development and cause serious retardation.

How common is it? 1 in 10,000 births in the U.K.

Who is susceptible? When both parents carry the trait, they have a 1 in 4 chance with each pregnancy of having a child with PKU. Low incidence among Finns, Ashkenazi Jews and blacks.

What causes it? Autosomal recessive inheritance: both parents must pass on recessive genes for a child to be affected.

How is it diagnosed? Because damage can occur during the first few months when babies appear normal, a blood test for PKU is routinely required within a few days of birth.

Related problems. Without treatment, children become irritable, restless and destructive; they may have a musty odour, dry skin or rashes and some have convulsions. They are usually physically well developed and frequently blonder than others in their families.

Treatment. A diet low in phenylalanine (which means low in such high-protein foods as breast milk, cow's milk, or regular cow's milk formula, and meat) begun immediately and continued for at least eight years to prevent retardation.[3] Though the sooner treatment begins the better, hope for a normal life is not entirely lost for children whose treatment may be delayed somewhat. Blood levels of phenylalanine are routinely monitored during treatment. Someday, medication to help with phenylalanine metabolism may be available.

Prognosis. Usually a normal life with special diet.

---

3. Some studies suggest it may be wise to maintain these dietary measures through the reproductive years, at least in women, and as long as feasible in males; it is certainly suggested for women who are pregnant or planning to be.

PYLORIC STENOSIS

What is it? A probably congenital condition in which thickening or overgrowth of the muscle at the exit of the stomach causes a blockage, leading to increasingly more severe and more forceful projectile vomiting (spewing 30 cm/a foot or more) usually starting at two or three weeks of age and accompanied by constipation. The thickening can usually be felt as a lump by the doctor; spasms of the muscle are often visible.

How common is it? 1 boy in 200; 1 girl in 1,000.

Who is susceptible? Males more often than females; sometimes tends to run in families.

What causes it? It isn't known what triggers

How Defects are Inherited

All the good and beautiful things a baby is are a result of the genes he or she inherited from both parents, as well as the environment in the uterus during the nine months of gestation. But the not-so-good things a baby is born with – a birth defect, for instance – are also a result of genes and/or environment. Usually the genes a parent passes on to a child are inherited from his or her own parents, but occasionally a gene changes (because of an environmental insult or some unknown factor) and this mutation is passed on.

There are several kinds of inherited disorders:

- Polygenic disorders (such as clubfoot and cleft lip) are believed to be inherited through the interaction of a number of different genes in much the same way that eye colour and height are determined.

- Multifactorial disorders (such as some forms of diabetes) involve the interaction of different genes and environmental conditions (either prior to birth or after it).

- Single-gene disorders can be passed on through either recessive or dominant inheritance. In recessive inheritance, two genes (one from each parent) must be passed on for the offspring to be affected. In dominant inheritance, just one gene is needed, and it is passed on by a parent who also has the disorder (by virtue of having the gene). Single-gene disorders can also be sex linked (haemophilia, for example). These disorders, carried in genes on the sex-determining chromosomes (females have two X-chromosomes and males one X and one Y), are most often passed from carrier mother to affected son. The male child, having only one X chromosome, has no opposite gene to counteract the one carrying the defect and is affected with the disorder. A female child receiving the gene on an X chromosome from her mother has also received a normal X chromosome from her father, which makes her a carrier but leaves her unaffected by the disorder.

development.

Related problems. Dehydration.

Treatment. Surgery, after baby's fluid levels have been normalized, is safe and almost always completely effective.

Prognosis. Excellent.

SICKLE-CELL ANAEMIA

What is it? An anaemia in which red blood cells (usually round) are abnormal (sickle shaped) and do a poor job of carrying oxygen to body cells, often getting stuck in and blocking blood vessels. Symptoms (such as fatigue, shortness of breath, joint swelling, especially in fingers and toes, and severe bone pain) don't usually appear until six months of age, but testing should diagnose immediately after birth.

How common is it? Approximately 1 in 200 black children in the U.K.; lower incidence in others. More research needed.

Who is susceptible? Primarily blacks of African descent, but also whites of Mediterranean/Middle Eastern heritage. Risk is 1 in 4 if both parents are carriers, 4 in 4 if both have the disease.

What causes it? Autosomal recessive inheritance: both parents must pass on recessive genes for child to be affected. Periodic crises can be triggered by infection, stress, dehydration and inadequate oxygen.

Related problems. Poor growth, delayed puberty, narrow body, curved spine and barrel chest; infection, particularly pneumococcal. Premature death common.

Treatment. Symptomatic, including pain relievers, blood transfusions, oxygen, fluids. Pneumococcal vaccine to prevent

infection. New treatment may stimulate body to manufacture normal blood cells.

Prognosis. Fair; some do not live past young adulthood, many don't reach middle age.

RH DISEASE

What is it? A condition in which a child inherits a blood type from the father that is incompatible with the mother's. If the mother has antibodies to the father's blood (from a previous pregnancy, an abortion, miscarriage, or blood transfusion), these antibodies attack the baby's blood.

How common is it? Much less common since the development of preventive techniques.

Who is susceptible? A baby who inherits Rh-positive blood from his or her father and has a mother with Rh-negative blood.

What causes it? Antibodies in mother's blood attack baby's blood cells, recognizing them as foreign.

Related problems. Blood disease, brain damage, or death before or shortly after birth.

Treatment. Often a complete blood transfusion of the baby with a blood incompatibility. Some babies may not need a transfusion immediately but do require one at 4 to 6 weeks because of severe anaemia. Prevention, with the injection of a vaccine called Rh immune globulin for Rh-negative mothers within 72 hours of the birth (or miscarriage or abortion) of a baby or foetus that is Rh-positive is the best treatment. This vaccine almost always prohibits the development of antibodies and protects future children. A dose of the vaccine may also be given about midway during pregnancy. Doctors are trying to develop a treatment for women who already have developed antibodies.

Prognosis. Usually good, with treatment.

When a Baby Dies

You've waited for this baby for nearly nine months. You've dreamed about it, felt it kick and hiccup, heard its heartbeat. You've picked out a cot, ordered a tiny layette, prepared your friends, family and life for the new arrival – and now you're going home empty-handed.

There's probably no greater pain than that inflicted by the loss of a child. And though nothing can banish the hurt you're feeling, there are steps you can take now to make the future more bearable, and to lessen the inevitable depression that follows such a tragedy.

- If death is near, consider organ donation.

- See your baby, hold your baby, name your baby. Grieving is a vital step in recovering from your loss. But you can't grieve for a nameless child you've never seen. Even if your child is malformed, experts advise that it is better to see him or her than not because what is imagined is usually worse than the reality. Holding and naming your baby will make the death more real to you and, ultimately, easier to deal with. So will arranging for a funeral and burial, which will also give you another opportunity to say goodbye. And the grave will provide a permanent site where you can visit your baby in future years.

- Discuss autopsy findings and other details with the doctor to harden the reality of what happened and to aid you in the grieving process. You may have been given details in the delivery room, but medications, your hormonal status and your sense of shock probably prevented you from fully understanding them.

- If possible, ask not to be sedated in the hours after you hear the news. Though it will ease your pain momentarily, it will tend to blur your recollections and the reality of what happened. Again, this makes it harder to get on with your grieving, as well as depriving you and your spouse of the chance to support one another.

- Save a photo (many hospitals take them) or other mementoes, so that you'll have some tangible objects to cherish when you think about your lost baby in the future. As morbid as this may sound, experts say it helps. Try to focus on positive attributes – big eyes and long lashes, beautiful hands and delicate fingers, a headful of hair.

- Ask friends or relatives not to remove all vestiges of the preparations you made for baby at home. Tell them you will do it yourself. As well-meaning as their gestures might be, coming home to a house that looks as though a baby was never expected will only add to your sense of unreality.

- Cry – for as long and as often as you feel you need to. Crying is part of the mourning process. If you don't cry now, it will remain unfinished business that you may find you have to attend to later.

- Expect a difficult time. For a while you may feel depressed; you'll probably have trouble sleeping, fight with your husband, neglect your other children. You will probably feel the need to be a child yourself, to be the one who is loved, coddled and cared for. All this is normal.

- Recognize that fathers grieve, too, but that their grief may in some cases be or appear to be shorter-lived and/or less intense, partly because, unlike mothers, they

SPINA BIFIDA (OPEN SPINE)

What is it? The bony spine, or backbone, that helps protect the spinal cord is normally open for the first few days of antenatal development but then closes. In spina bifida, the closing is incomplete. The resultant opening can be so slight that it causes no problems and is not noticed except through an X-ray taken later for other reasons, though a small dimple or tufts of hair may be visible on the covering skin. Or it can be large enough that part of the covering of the spinal cord (the meninges) protrudes haven't carried their baby inside them for so many months. And they often have different ways of dealing with their distress. They may, for example, try to bottle it up, to be strong for their partners. But then the pain often comes out in other ways: bad temper, irresponsibility, loss of interest in life – or they may use alcohol in an attempt to feel better. Unfortunately, a grieving father may not be much help to his wife, nor she to him, and both may need to seek support elsewhere.

- Don't face the world alone. If you're putting off getting back into circulation because you dread the friendly faces asking, 'Oh, what did you have?' take a friend who can field the questions for you on the first several trips to the supermarket, playground, bank and so on. Be sure that those at work, at church or synagogue, at other organizations in which you're active, are informed before you return so you don't have to do any difficult explaining.

- Expect your pain to lessen over time, but be prepared for the possibility that it will never go away entirely. The grieving process, with nightmares and intrusive recollections, is often not fully completed for as long as two years, but the worst is usually over in three to six months after the loss. If after six to nine months your grief remains the centre of your universe, if you lose interest in everything else and can't seem to function, seek help. Seek help, too, if from the beginning you haven't been able to grieve at all.

- Seek support. Like many other parents, you may derive strength from joining a self-help group for parents who have lost infants. But beware of letting such a group become a way of sustaining your rage or grief. If after a year (sooner, if you're having trouble functioning) you're still having problems coming to terms with your loss, you should seek individual therapy.

- Turn to religion, if you find it comforting. Some bereaved parents feel too angry with God to do this, but for many faith is a source of great solace.

- Don't expect that having another baby will resolve any unresolved grief. Do become pregnant again, if that's what you both want – first observing whatever waiting period the doctor recommends. But don't try to conceive in order to feel better, assuage guilt or anger, or gain peace of mind. It won't work and it could put an unfair burden on any new arrival. Any decision about your future fertility – either to have another baby or to undergo sterilization – should be postponed until the period of deepest sorrow has passed.

- Recognize that guilt can compound grief and make adjusting to a loss more difficult. If you felt ambivalent about having a baby (as many women do) and now feel your baby's death is your punishment, if your mother wasn't nurturing and you fear you aren't either and that's why you lost your baby, if you feel insecure about your womanhood and now believe your doubts have been confirmed (you couldn't produce a live baby), or if you feel you have failed your family and friends, seek professional support to help you understand that such feelings are in no way responsible for your loss. If you feel guilty even thinking about getting your life back to normal because you sense it is somehow disloyal to your dead baby, it may help to ask your baby, in spirit, for forgiveness or permission to enjoy life once again.

---

through, covered by a purplish red cyst or lump (a meningocele), which can range in size from 2.5 to 5 cm (an inch or two) in diameter to the size of a grapefruit. If this meningocele is low on the spinal column, it can cause weakness in the legs. In the most severe form of spina bifida, the spinal cord itself protrudes through the opening (a myelomeningocele). It often has little or no skin protecting it, allowing spinal fluid to leak out. The area is often covered with sores, the legs are paralyzed and bladder and bowel control become a problem later, though some children do attain this control.

How common it it? Affects 1 in 2,000 babies born in the U.S., though it has been estimated that 1 in 4 may have hidden spina bifida. The more severe form of the condition is fortunately the least common.

Who is susceptible? Children of mothers who already have an affected child have a 1 in 40 risk; with two affected children in the family, the risk rises to 1 in 5. Cousins of affected children have a two-fold increase in risk. It is three or four times more common among the poor than among the wealthy, is more frequent in Ireland and Wales, and is less common in Israel and among Jewish people in general.

What causes it? Not known at present. Heredity is probably involved in some way, along with adverse antenatal environment. Nutrition may be involved – recurrences have been reduced by the administration of vitamin supplements containing folic acid to mothers before conception and through the first two months of pregnancy.

Related problems. Infection when spine is visibly open. Also hydrocephalus (water on the brain) in about 70 to 90% of cases (see page 482). Impaired bladder and bowel control.

Treatment. None is needed for a slight defect. Cysts can be removed surgically and water on the brain drained. But though surgery can remove the most severe cysts, covering the opening with muscle and skin, the paralysis in the legs can't be cured. Physical therapy, and later leg braces and crutches or a wheelchair, will probably be needed. Casts may be applied to prevent or minimize deformity. Prior to surgery, it is important not to put pressure (even in the form of clothing) on the cyst. Team approach to treatment, with a range of specialists, is usually best.

Prognosis. Depends on severity of the condition. Most children with less severe conditions can have active and productive lives; most females will be able to bear children, but their pregnancies will be in the high-risk category. Quick treatment of hydrocephalus can generally prevent retardation.

TAY-SACHS DISEASE

What is it? Children with this lipid-storage disease, in which there is a congenital deficiency of an enzyme needed for breaking down fatty deposits in the brain and nerve cells, appear normal at birth. But about six months later, when the fatty deposits begin to clog cells, the nervous system stops working and children begin to regress – they stop smiling, crawling and turning over, lose the ability to grasp, gradually become blind, paralyzed and unaware of their surroundings. Most die by age three or four.

How common is it? Rare.

Who is susceptible? Mostly descendants of Central and Eastern European (Ashkenazi) Jews. Nearly 1 in 25 American Jews are carriers of the Tay-Sachs gene, and 1 in 3,600 Ashkenazi babies is affected.

What causes it? Autosomal recessive inheritance – one gene from each parent is necessary for child to be affected.

Related problems. Concern about future children; there is a 1 in 4 chance of an affected child with each pregnancy.

Treatment. None, though researchers are trying to find a way of replacing the missing enzyme. Those with Ashkenazi backgrounds should be tested for the gene before conception or during early pregnancy. If both parents have the gene, then amniocentesis can be performed to see if the foetus has inherited the disease. An option: therapeutic abortion.

Prognosis. Disease is invariably fatal.

THALASSAEMIA

What is it? An inherited form of anaemia in which there is a defect in the process necessary for the production of haemoglobin (the oxygen-carrying red blood cells). The most common form, Beta A thalassaemia, can range from the very serious form, called thalassaemia major to thalassaemia trait, which has no effect but shows up in blood or genetic testing. Even in serious cases, infants appear normal at birth, but gradually become listless, fussy and pale, lose their appetites and become very susceptible to infection. Growth and development are slow.

How common is it? About 12.5% of ethnic minorities in the U.K. have a haemoglobin disorder.

Who is susceptible? In the U.K., most frequently, those of Cypriot or Italian descent; also southern Asians and those from India, Pakistan and Bangladesh.

What causes it? Autosomal recessive inheritance: an affected gene must be inherited from each parent for the child to have the most serious form of the disease.

Related problems. Without treatment, the heart, spleen and liver all become enlarged and the risk of death from heart failure or infection multiplies. Eventually bones become brittle, distorting appearance.

Treatment. Frequent blood transfusions of young blood cells, and sometimes bone marrow transplants for children with the most severe form of the disease. Buildup of iron, which can lead to heart failure, can be treated with medication. Antenatal diagnosis is available to determine if a foetus is affected.

Prognosis. Excellent for those with minor forms of the disease; those with moderate disease also become normal adults, though puberty may be delayed. Of those with severe disease, more children are now living into

their teens and twenties, though the threat of heart failure and infection are still great.

TRACHEAL-OESOPHAGEAL FISTULA

What is it? A congenital condition in which the upper part of the oesophagus (the tube through which foods move from throat to stomach) ends in a blind pouch and the lower part, instead of connecting to the upper, runs from the trachea (windpipe) to the stomach. Since this makes taking food by mouth impossible, vomiting, choking and respiratory distress occur on feeding. Excessive drooling occurs since saliva can't be swallowed. Food getting into lungs can cause pneumonia and even death.[4]

How common is it? 1 in 4,000 live births.

Who is susceptible? Sometimes babies of women who had excessive amniotic fluid in pregnancy; one-third of victims are born prematurely.

What causes it? A defect in development, possibly due to hereditary or environmental causes.

Related problems. In a small percentage, heart, spine, kidney, and limb abnormalities also occur.

Treatment. Immediate surgery can usually correct condition.

Prognosis. If no other abnormalities, and surgery corrects the problem, outlook is very good.

WATER ON THE BRAIN – see Hydrocephalus

---

4. There are several other, much less common, deformities of the trachea and oesophagus.

TWENTY-ONE

The Adopted Baby

♦

This is it. You're about to become, or have just become, adoptive parents. You've been waiting for months – or, more likely, years – for this moment. But now that it's upon you, you're filled with trepidation. Along with joy, you feel uncertainty and a sense of inadequacy. Just like birth parents.

As an adopting parent, this chapter is for you. But so is most of the rest of this book. Your baby is like other babies, and you are like other mothers (except that you don't experience the physical symptoms of postpartum) and other fathers.

What You May Be Concerned About

Getting Ready

'My friends who are pregnant are involved in all kinds of preparations – childbirth classes, looking over hospitals, choosing paediatricians. But I don't know where to start in preparing for our adopted baby's arrival.'

Instead of surprising mothers with their babies without benefit of notice, Mother Nature wisely designed 'gestation'. This waiting period before birth (or hatching) was meant to give parents a chance to prepare for the arrival of their offspring. A chance for the mother bird to feather her nest, the expectant lioness to prepare her lair and, nowadays anyway, for the mother and father human to decorate a nursery, take classes, make key decisions about breastfeeding, child care and paediatricians, and generally prepare themselves emotionally, intellectually and physically for becoming a family.

For the couple about to adopt a baby, the waiting period is not usually a predictable

and manageable nine months, as it is for other expectant parents. For some, usually those who go the agency route, the entire process may drag on for years, but the big day itself arrives unexpectedly, not leaving enough time for reality to set in, much less for preparations to be made. It's much like the shock of being told you're pregnant one day and being delivered of a baby the next. For others, usually those who adopt privately, definite arrangements may be made to adopt a particular baby far in advance of the infant's due date, giving the adoptive parents-to-be the opportunity to go through pre-baby preparations that are not dissimilar in many ways to those of biological expectant parents. But no matter how much or how little time you have between learning you are going to become a parent and the actual arrival of your baby, there are some steps you can take to make the transition smoother:

Shop ahead. Read Chapter 2 of this book; most of the preparations for the arrival of a baby are the same whether you're adopting or birthing. If you are uncertain as to the date, scout around for the cot, pram, layette and so on in advance. Have everything picked out (brand names, style numbers, sizes) and listed along with the shop names and telephone numbers so that you can call for delivery the moment you hear from the adoption agency or lawyer. (Check in advance with the stores to be sure that your choices will be in stock.) If you are going the private adoption route and have an approximate arrival date, many shops will allow you to put your order in and then will hold delivery until you call. Should the adoption fall through, they will return your money. Such advance purchasing is a lot better than trying to do the shopping after the baby arrives, when you're busy trying to get acquainted and adjusted. But don't overbuy. Adoptive parents often wait so long for their babies that they end up with a drawerful of six-month sizes that go unworn.

Find out how adoptive parents feel. Talk to other couples who have adopted infants about their concerns, their problems and their solutions; and read some books on the subject. Find an adoptive parent support group and attend a few sessions – your clergyman, paediatrician, lawyer, or adoption agency may be able to direct you in locating individuals or groups.

Find out how newborns feel. Read up on childbirth so that you have some idea of what your baby has gone through when he or she finally does arrive. You'll learn that after a long, hard struggle to be born, babies may be tired – something that birth parents understand because they are tired, too. Adoptive parents, usually exhilarated and excited rather than exhausted by their baby's arrival, tend to overstimulate the newborn rather than allowing for needed rest.

Learn the tricks of the trade. Take a parenting class that gives instruction in such basics as bathing, changing, feeding and carrying baby. Or plan on hiring a baby nurse who is as good at teaching baby care as she is at practising it, for a day or two, or longer if you prefer, to help out with the basics (see page 14). But be sure to hire a nurse who helps rather than intimidates.

Take a good look at babies. Visit friends or acquaintances with young babies, or stop in at a hospital nursery at visiting time, so that a newborn won't seem such a foreign creature to you. Read about newborn characteristics in Chapter 3.

Pick your paediatrician. It's as important for you to have your doctor or paediatrician selected in advance as it is for the expectant couple (see page 25). You'll want someone who will be able to check your baby out on the very first day he or she is with you. A pre-baby interview will give you a chance to ask questions and voice concerns about becoming adoptive parents. And because the newborn's health is a special concern – unlike birth parents, adoptive parents can decide not to take a handicapped infant – you want the paediatrician to be available almost at a moment's notice to consult with doctors when the baby is born and to give you advice on the prognosis if there is a problem.

Consider breastfeeding. Some adoptive mothers are able to breastfeed their babies, at least partially. Check with your gynaecologist to discuss the possibility, and see page 493.

Not Feeling Like a Parent

'Not having gone through pregnancy and childbirth, holding a child born to someone else, I don't feel much like a mother to our adopted son and I'm afraid I never will.'

You don't have to be an adoptive mother to have trouble adapting to the role of mother. Most first-time birth mothers experience the very same self-doubts as they hold their newborns. Becoming a mother doesn't begin with conception and culminate in the moments directly after birth; motherhood evolves over the course of days, weeks, months and years of loving and caring. Though many women don't feel like mothers during those first challenging days, virtually all do eventually.

Still, while you are struggling to reach that point you may, like many adoptive parents, wish that you could somehow erase the fact of the adoption – that then hey presto! you would feel like a parent. But biological closeness doesn't guarantee emotional closeness, and though as an adoptive parent you may have a hard time accepting yourself as a mother, your baby will have no such difficulty. You – who love, shelter and provide for all his needs – are the real thing to him. And you'll know that long before you hear his first 'mama'.

Do keep in mind, however, that all babies are not created equally affectionate. Some tend not to be cuddly and don't enjoy being touched a lot (see page 154), but this has nothing to do with what their parents do or don't do. If you have such a baby, don't blame yourself or the fact that he's adopted.

Feeling Inadequate

'There must be some biological reason why I feel so inept as a mother. Ever since we got our little girl four days ago, I can't seem to do anything right – from changing a nappy to giving her a bath.'

Join the club – which, by the way, is by no means exclusive to adoptive mothers. How well a new mother or father handles the first few weeks on the parenting job has nothing to do with levels of hormones; more likely, it has to do with levels of experience and anxiety. If you've never held a tiny infant before your own, much less changed or bathed one, it's not surprising you're feeling all thumbs. Even for those who've confidently handled newborns as baby-sitters or big sisters (or even nurses or doctors), being suddenly charged with absolute, 24-hour-a-day responsibility for your own small and helpless human being can bring out

strong feelings of inadequacy and ineptitude.

For any new mother, hiring a baby nurse for a couple of days for a little on-the-job training (but make sure she's the kind who wants to teach rather than take over) can help instill confidence and speed transition from bumbling novice to self-assured pro. So will parenting classes and reading the first chapters of this book, particularly the Baby-Care Primer on page 72. And, of course, time.

Loving the Baby

'I've heard that birth mothers fall in love with their babies right in the delivery room. I'm afraid that because I didn't carry and deliver this baby, I'm never going to be able to love her in the same way.'

That all mother-baby love affairs begin in the delivery room is yet another motherhood myth. Your fears are shared by a large proportion of birth mothers who are surprised and disappointed to find they are not overcome by a great tide of love when they first hold their babies – and neither you nor they have anything to be concerned about. The seed of mother-baby (or father-baby) love doesn't sprout miraculously at first meeting, but takes time and nurturing to grow.

And it grows for adopting parents just as it does for birth parents. Studies show that adoptive families form good strong bonds, particularly when the child is adopted before the age of two. That the relationships are solid and loving is reflected in the fact that on psychological tests, adopted children often are shown to be more confident than non-adopted children, tend to view the world more positively, feel more in control of their lives, and see their parents as more nurturing than non-adopted children do.

Baby's Crying a Lot

'Our newly adopted baby girl seems to cry a lot. Are we doing something wrong?'

There aren't any healthy new babies who don't cry, and many of them happen to cry a lot – it is, after all, their only way of communicating. But sometimes, crying is increased by overstimulation. Many adoptive parents are so excited about the arrival of their new babies and so eager to show them off that they expose them to a steady stream of visitors. Just because you aren't exhausted from delivery doesn't mean your baby's not. Give her a chance to rest. Slow down, handle her gently, speak to her quietly. After a couple of weeks in a calm atmosphere, you may find she's crying less. If not, she may have colic, which is no reflection on you or your care, just a very common pattern of behaviour in the first three months of life.

Postadoption Blues

'If postpartum blues are supposed to be hormonal, how come I've been feeling depressed since we brought our adopted son home?'

If the baby blues were strictly hormonal adoptive parents and birth fathers wouldn't suffer from it. But many do. Actually a wide range of factors contribute to what a commonly called postpartum depression or the baby blues. And many of them have nothing to do with hormones or the stresses of delivery. Whether you adopt or deliver your life as a new mother is suddenly very different, much less orderly, much more out of your control. Perhaps you miss the stimulation of work, feel you have no time for yourself or your spouse, and are concerned about managing on one income, at least for a while. Or maybe you feel unsure of yourself as a mother. As an adoptive mother you may be worried about bonding with this new baby (can you love him as you would a biological child?), wonder if he'll turn out to

be healthy, if he'll grow up to be like you and your husband or like his biological parents. Or you may feel a tinge of disappointment that this baby, much as you're thrilled to have him, isn't biologically yours (this feeling will pass as the baby comes more and more to feel like your very own, and as you realize that, to him, you are the only parents he has).

You may also be worried that your baby's birth mother might change her mind during the waiting period. This can also lead to sleepless nights, anxious days and a heavy case of baby blues.[1]

But since it is likely that at least some of the causes of your depression are the same as for traditional postpartum depression, many of the cures may help you, too. See page 534 for tips to help you shake the blues and let you enjoy your new role more.

Not Being able to Breastfeed

'After years of trying to conceive, we've given up and are adopting. I've accepted that, but I am very disappointed that I won't be able to nurse when our baby arrives.'

Once a baby's born, there's just about nothing that a biological mother can do that an adoptive mother can't. And in this age of medical miracles, that even goes, to a certain extent, for breastfeeding. Though some mothers of adopted infants never succeed in inducing lactation at all, and most will never lactate enough to feed their babies exclusively from the breast, a few dedicated souls do manage to breastfeed their babies at least partially. And those adoptive mothers who attempt to induce lactation, even those who fail to produce milk, reap the benefits of the special intimacy nursing affords.

Breastfeeding will be possible only if the baby you are adopting is a newborn, not yet

---

1. When the waiting period is over, be sure to finalize the adoption in court. Some parents forget to do this and thus do not have legal custody of their children which could lead to serious complications later.

habituated to sucking on an artificial nipple, and if you have no medical condition (such as a history of breast surgery) that might prevent your producing milk.

Should you decide to try to breastfeed your baby, the following steps will increase your chances of success:

• Ask yourself why you're eager to breastfeed. If you're trying to prove your worth as a woman or to deny to yourself or to others, consciously or subconsciously, that your baby is adopted, you should reconsider. It's important for you to come to terms with the fact that you were unable to conceive and that your baby is adopted; if you don't, you and baby may run into problems later. If you simply want to give your baby the best nutritional start possible and to share the emotional pleasures of nursing with your new arrival, go ahead and give it a try.

• Ask yourself whether or not you are willing to put everything else in your life on hold while you try to establish lactation. You may have to nurse almost constantly and face weeks, even months, of trial, tribulation and frustration, with nothing to show for them but disappointment. Are you ready to accept the idea that you may not succeed? And that if you do, you may be able to supply only part of your baby's nourishment?

• Will your partner and other family members be understanding and supportive? Without such support, your chances of success are practically nil.

• See your obstetrician to discuss your hopes of trying to breastfeed your adopted baby, and to be sure that no condition exists that will make breastfeeding impossible or inadvisable in your case. If he or she doesn't seem to know anything about the subject (this wouldn't be unusual) or is not supportive, ask for a referral to a doctor who is familiar with lactation induction – possibly a paediatrician. If your doctor can't supply a referral, call the La Leche League in your community or in the nearest large city for the name of a doctor who can help you; they may also be able to recommend a lactation consultant.

• If you know in advance approximately when you will get your baby (as when you have arranged to adopt the child of a particular expectant mother), you should begin to try to stimulate lactation a month or so before the due date. To do this you will need a breast pump, preferably an electric one since a manually operated pump will take so much energy that you will almost certainly give up before you succeed.[2] (Some women enjoy enlisting their husbands in the effort to stimulate lactation.) See page 92 for information on expressing milk; if you successfully produce milk before your baby arrives, bottle and freeze it for future use or donate it to a milk bank.

Once you have your baby in your arms, try putting him to breast and see if he is satisfied with what you have to offer. Look for a sensation of let-down in your breasts and signs of adequate intake (such as contentment after feeding, wet nappies, frequent bowel movements). If he doesn't appear satisfied, hook up a supplemental nutrition system (see page 100), its bottle filled with formula recommended by baby's doctor, and let him take as much as he likes. (See page 97 for more tips on determining whether or not a baby is getting enough breast milk and on how to increase your milk supply.)

• If you won't know when you will be getting your baby until virtually the last minute, order a supplemental nutrition system (SNS) to be delivered when you get the word – or purchase one and keep it on hand. That way, when your baby arrives you will be able to try to stimulate milk production together via suckling

---

2. Call a local hospital or NCT group, your family doctor, an obstetrician, or the paediatrician you intend to use for your baby for information on the location of rental stations for electric pumps.

while he is nourished by formula. Divide baby's quota of formula (as recommended by his doctor) into at least eight (and preferably ten) feedings, so you can nurse every two or three hours. When baby is hungry, put the formula into the supplementary feeding bottle and put him to your breast. Let him suckle as long as he wishes to (assuming your nipples aren't too sore), even after he's emptied the bottle. Once your milk comes in, if it does, try to start each meal with breastfeeding, augmenting the breast milk with formula through the SNS if your baby still seems hungry.

- If you're having trouble with milk let-down, ask your doctor about prescribing an oxytocin nasal spray and/or a medication such as chlorpromazine or theophylline. One of these may stimulate the pituitary to produce prolactin (a hormone essential in milk production), but neither should be used for longer than a week or so.

- Get plenty of rest, relaxation and sleep; even a woman who has just given birth can't produce adequate milk if she's tense and overtired.

- Follow the Best-Odds Breastfeeding Diet (page 526), being particularly careful to get enough calories and fluids and to take a vitamin-mineral supplement.

- Don't give up too soon. A pregnant woman's body usually has nine months to prepare for lactation; give yours at least two or three months to get it going. If your baby was bottle fed at first, getting the hang of nursing may take even longer. Be persistent. If he doesn't feed at the breast a lot at first, supplement his stimulation of your nipples by expressing milk by hand or with a pump.

If in spite of all your hard work you don't succeed at producing milk, or don't produce enough to make you the sole supplier of your baby's nourishment (some biological mothers don't either), you should feel comfortable abandoning your efforts,

knowing you and your baby have already shared some of the important benefits of breastfeeding. Or you can continue nursing, supplementing your baby's intake of breast milk, if any, with formula, either through the supplemental nutrition system or with a bottle.

Grandparents' Attitudes

'My parents already have three grandchildren they dote on. And I'm very upset that they don't seem to be excited about the baby boy we've just adopted.'

It's easy for your parents to become attached to their biological grandchildren. They've borne their own children and slip easily into loving the children their children have borne. But they may be a little unsure whether they will be able to love an adopted grandchild as easily or as well – even as many adoptive parents are unsure – and may stay aloof for fear they will fail. Perhaps, too, they haven't yet resolved any feelings of disappointment (or guilt) they may have had about your not being able to conceive – they may even believe deep in their hearts that you still can – or anger if you're adopting by choice.

It's understandable that you feel hurt by your parents' seeming lack of interest in your baby, but don't be tempted to retaliate by excluding them from his life. The more you include them, the sooner they will grow to accept and love him.

Ideally, it's best to involve grandparents in preparing for the arrival of an adopted grandchild just as they would be, or have been, involved in preparing for a biological one. Enlist them in shopping for furniture and a layette, in picking out teddies and musical mobiles; consult with them on possible colours for the baby's room and on possible names for the baby. Choosing a family name for your child may make him feel more like 'real' family to them.

After you bring the baby home, seek your parents' advice on feeding and burping, bathing and changing, even if you don't really need it. If they live nearby, ask them to baby-sit when it's convenient. If you're planning a ritual circumcision, baby naming, or christening, invite them to play a major role in the planning and in the celebration themselves. If you're not having a religious ceremony, consider having a 'welcome baby' party for relatives and friends. Being able to show the baby off will make them feel more like grandparents.

If you feel comfortable doing so, talk to them about your perception of their feelings. Tell them that with this kind of new experience, uncertainties are natural – you've had some yourself. If they get a chance to vent their feelings, they may begin to feel more comfortable with them – and with you and the baby. If you can't raise the subject, perhaps a clergyman, doctor, respected relative, or family friend can do it for you.

Most of all, give your parents plenty of time to get to know your baby; to know a baby is usually to love him. Be sure that you're not being oversensitive or defensive, and just imagining that your baby is being treated differently. If in the end they still seem not to accept him fully, try to cover your hurt and keep family ties tied, with the hope that closeness will come gradually over the years.

Unknown Health Problems

'We've just adopted a beautiful little girl. She seems perfect, but I keep worrying that some unknown hereditary problem will surface.'

Adopted or not, the genetic makeup of every child is uncertain. And every parent worries occasionally about possible unknown defects. Fortunately, really serious genetic defects are rare and most parental worry unnecessary. It would be helpful to you, however, to get as complete a health history on both the baby's biological parents as possible, to give to the baby's doctor and in case of future illness. Also try to arrange, when drawing up adoption papers, for some way to trace the adoptive mother so that should an unlikely crisis arise and your baby needs help from the birth mother (a bone marrow transplant, for instance), you would be able to find her.

But while an adopted baby is not any more likely to have an inherited disorder than is one who isn't adopted, she is more subject to infection. Because she doesn't come equipped with the same germs as her adoptive mother and father, she is less likely than a biological child to have antibodies to infectious organisms in her new environment. Take some extra precautions for the first few weeks:

- Be sure feeding equipment is carefully sterilized (see page 56).

- Wash your hands before handling your baby, her bottle, or anything that may go into her mouth or come in contact with her hands.

- Limit visitors. Though the temptation to show her off is great, wait a few weeks before exposing her to large numbers of people. (She can use the rest, too.)

If your baby has come from abroad, particularly from Southeast Asia, she may also be harbouring an infection or parasites that would be rare here. Her paediatrician should know her country of origin and should check her for diseases indigenous to that area of the world upon her arrival here. Immediate treatment of any problems uncovered will not only assure your baby of a good start in life, unhampered by disease, but it will also protect the rest of your family and other contacts.

Dealing with Friends and Family

'A few close friends knew we were going to adopt a baby. But now that she's here we have to tell everyone we know. I'm not sure how to go about this.'

Whether they've adopted or delivered, the traditional way for new parents to spread their happy word is to send announcements to friends and family and, sometimes, to local papers. In your case, the announcement should make it clear that the baby is adopted ('We're delighted to announce the adoption of . . .'). Enclosing a picture of the baby will help make her seem more real to friends and family.

When talking to anyone about your baby, start right off saying 'our baby' or 'my baby'. In referring to the parents who conceived her, use the words 'birth' or 'biological' parents, rather than 'real' or 'natural'. *You* are baby's real parents, and the more you hear yourself say it, the more you – and everyone else – will come to accept it. If you have other biological children, don't call them 'my own' children or permit other people refer to them in that way.

Telling Baby

'Even though our son is still an infant I can't help worrying about how and when we're going to tell him that he's adopted.'

It's no longer a question, as it once was, of whether or not to tell a child that he's adopted. Today, experts agree that children need to know and have the right to know about their adoption, and should find out about it from their parents – not through inadvertent slips by relatives or taunts from neighbourhood kids. There's less agreement about when to tell, though support seems to be growing for the idea of gradually introducing a child to the fact that he's adopted from infancy on, so that the news doesn't come as a shock later.

You can start right now, while your baby is tiny and still doesn't really understand what you are saying. Just as a birth mother talks about the day her baby was born, you can talk about the day you brought your baby home: 'That was the best day of our lives!' And when you're gurgling and cooing at him, you can say, 'We're so happy we adopted you!' and 'We were so lucky to be able to adopt a baby as wonderful as you'. Though your baby won't be able to understand, even in the simplest terms, what 'adoption' means until he's three or four years old, early exposure to the concept will make it seem natural, and the eventual explanation of it less threatening and easier to cope with.

TWENTY-TWO

The First Postpartum Days

◆

What You May Be Feeling

You may experience all of these physical and emotional aftereffects of childbirth at one time or another during the first postpartum week, or you may note only a few of them. You may also have some less common symptoms. Report any unusual or severe symptoms to a hospital nurse or your doctor.

Physically:

- Chills, hunger and thirst in immediate minutes after delivery
- Bloody vaginal discharge (lochia) turning pink then brownish towards end of first week
- Cramping (afterpains) in abdomen even after first 24 hours
- Perineal discomfort and/or pain and numbness, if you had a vaginal delivery (especially if you had stitches)
- Exhaustion, particularly if labour was difficult or lengthy
- Incisional pain and, later, numbness in the area, if you had a caesarean delivery (especially if it was your first)
- Discomfort when sitting or walking if you had stitches
- General body soreness if you pushed for a long time
- Broken capillaries (in eyes, on face) if pushing was lengthy or difficult
- Difficulty urinating for a day or two
- Difficulty and discomfort with bowel movements for the first few days; constipation

- Haemorrhoids
- A slight fever just after delivery, perhaps because of dehydration
- Excessive sweating for the first few days; night sweats
- Hot flashes
- Chills for the first few days
- Breast discomfort and engorgement between the second and fifth (sometimes later) postpartum day
- Sore or cracked nipples if you are breastfeeding, after several days of nursing
- Fluid retention and swelling for the first few days of breastfeeding

Emotionally:

- Elation, depression, or both alternately
- Feelings of inadequacy and trepidation about mothering, about breastfeeding you're nursing
- Frustration, if you're still in the hospital but would like to leave
- Little interest in sex, or less commonly increased desire (but intercourse won't be okayed by your doctor until at least three weeks postpartum, more often six)

In the U.K., you will be visited at home by a Community Midwife for the first 10 days postpartum, and then by your Health Visitor. Both are trained to advise and respond to concerns about your health or your baby's health.

What To Expect At Your In-Hospital Checkups

The exact procedures will vary from hospital to hospital and doctor to doctor, but in general you can expect the following to be checked immediately after delivery:

- The placenta and amniotic membranes, to be certain they are intact

- The location and firmness of the fundus (the top of your uterus)

- Your level of anxiety, excitement and restlessness

- Your pulse and blood pressure (your pulse will initially be accelerated and your blood pressure elevated because of excitement and exertion, but should be back to normal within a few hours)

In the hours that follow delivery, and then less often during the rest of your hospital stay, the following will probably be checked periodically:

- Your pulse, blood pressure and respirations

- Your temperature (it may be elevated slightly during the first 24 postpartum hours, often due to dehydration)

- The location of the fundus (it rises above the level of your navel for a couple of days, then begins to descend; it should be in the centre of your abdomen – if it's to the right of centre, the bladder will be checked for distension)

- The firmness of the fundus (if it's soft, it may be massaged to help expel clots)

- Your perineum, for colour and condition of stitches, if any

- The lochia, for amount and rate of flow (if it's initially heavy it will be checked very frequently to be sure the rate slows; if it seems to spurt, the doctor will check for lacerations) and for colour

- Your bladder, for distension

- Your breasts, to determine if your milk has come in and to check the condition of the nipples

- Your legs, for signs of thrombosis (blood clots in the veins)

- Your incision, if you had a caesarean section

- The after-effects of medication, if any

You will also be asked:

- Whether you have urinated, and then if you are urinating regularly, and whether or not you have any burning or discomfort on urination

- Whether you have had a bowel movement if you're in the hospital more than a day or two, and whether regular bowel habits have been reestablished

- About discomfort or pain you may be experiencing

You will probably be instructed about:

- Care of the perineum

- Post-surgical care, including care of the incision if you had a caesarean

- Simple postpartum exercises

- Breastfeeding and breast care, if you are nursing

- Breast care, if you are not nursing

- Basic baby care

If necessary, medication may be prescribed for constipation, pain, or infection, or to dry up your milk if you're not nursing.

WHAT YOU SHOULD BE EATING
Surviving Hospital Food

There have been reports in medical journals about seriously ill patients, particularly those recovering from major surgery, starving to death on hospital food. Starvation isn't likely to be your problem in the postpartum ward, but in most hospitals it will be a challenge to put together a nutritious meal from the choices offered – a challenge that will require careful scrutiny of menus.

Depending on the time of day you deliver and on hospital policy, you may or may not be able to order your first hospital meals. If they are preselected for you, keep in mind that this may have been done without considering the fact that you are a newly delivered mother with special dietary needs, particularly if you are nursing. So prepare for the worst and pack a few nutritious postpartum snacks in your hospital bag. Good take-alongs include: whole-grain, juice-sweetened cakes or biscuits to appease your sweet tooth and provide some bulk to get you started on the road to regularity; some citrus or other fresh fruit, or raisins or other dried fruit, again for fibre, as well as for vitamins and minerals; a flask of wheat germ to sprinkle on pasta or pancakes or any other refined-grain food you find on your meal tray; a packet or two of nonfat dry milk to add to breakfast cereal or coffee to supplement your liquid milk intake; a small container of unprocessed bran in case your bowels need extra encouragement. Check with the hospital staff to see if there is a patients' refrigerator in which you can store items brought from home – and be sure to label them with your name and ward/room number.

Of course, your special dietary requirements shouldn't stand between you and the after-delivery celebration you've been looking forward to. Whatever that treat you've been craving – a hot fudge sundae, cream cheese and smoked salmon on a bagel, an ice cream cake, imported chocolate truffles – you'll have earned it. Special-request it from a family member or friend.

When you do get your meal order cards, spend some thoughtful time going over them and consider these points before you check off your selections:

You need milk (or another calcium source) to make milk. If you don't get five servings daily while you're nursing, the calcium needed for milk production is likely to be drawn from your own bones, making you a good candidate for osteoporosis years from now. Getting it while in the hospital shouldn't be too difficult. Order at least one container of milk with each meal (all hospitals will be able to provide you with skimmed or low-fat milk if you specify). Round out your requirement with more milk at snack time or with the equivalent in other calcium foods, such as cheese (35 g/1¼ ounces of Swiss, 45 g/1½ ounces of Cheddar, or 55 g/2 ounces of mozzarella equal 250 ml/8 fl ounces of milk), yogurt (150 g/5 ounces), dark green leafy vegetables (170 g/6 ounces of broccoli or 125 g/4½ ounces of kale), tofu coagulated with calcium (225 g/8 ounces). If you don't like drinking a lot of milk straight, fortify cereal (hot or cold), soups, or coffee with dried skimmed milk from home. Each 125 g/4½ ounces you sprinkle is one less cup of liquid milk you have to drink. If you don't use dairy products for any reason, use nondairy sources of calcium and take a calcium supplement for insurance. If you use goat's milk, be sure it's pasteurized and that you are taking a lactation vitamin formula.

You need plenty of fibre to activate your bowels. Not to mention plenty of vitamins and trace minerals to speed your general recovery. To make sure you get all of the above, pass your pencil by the white bread and rolls on the menu cards and place your x's beside the 'wholemeal' at all meals (or, if wholemeal isn't listed, write it in as a special request). Select whole-grain cereals (such as Weetabix or Shredded Wheat) for breakfast, opt for a bran muffin over the blueberry, dried prunes over prune Danish, a fresh apple over apple crumble. If the hospital's 'wholemeal' bread is clearly a commercial 'wheat' bread made partly or primarily with white flour, ask a visiting well-wisher to bring in a loaf of the real thing (for re-sandwiching tuna or accompanying scrambled eggs). If whole-grain cereals aren't on the menu, fortify what is with wheat germ and/or bran from your own private stash.[1] If dried prunes are stewed with sugar and fresh fruit isn't available, have some brought from home.

You need protein to regain and maintain your strength and to make milk. Getting enough should be easy. Even if you're nursing, a single serving of 85 g (3 ounces) of meat, poultry, or fish, 3 eggs, 125 g (4½ ounces) cottage cheese, or a complete vegetable-protein combination (grains and legumes, for example) at lunch and another at dinner – plus your milk – should easily cover your protein requirement, which will be down to three servings from the four you needed during pregnancy. If you're not nursing, you will need only two servings. Forgo dishes that are fried or heavily sauced if you want to get a head start taking off excess pregnancy weight and to have an easier time digesting your food.

You need vitamins and minerals, especially vitamin C, for healing. Order a salad and at least one cooked vegetable (preferable including a green leafy or yellow), plus fresh fruit and fruit juice every day. Be wary of syrupy compotes and canned fruits that are heavy with sugar but light on nutrients. For vitamin C, look for citrus, strawberries, melon, red or green peppers and cauliflower or broccoli that hasn't been boiled beyond nutritional recognition. If you can't find what you're looking for on hospital menus, request 'care packages' from home or the nearest fruit market.

---

1. If you do use bran, remember that it decreases the absorption of calcium taken with it and that it can't do its work without plenty of fluid to wash it down and out.

You need iron to replace what was lost with blood during and following delivery. Take your antenatal iron supplement or one that your doctor has just prescribed, but try to eat some iron-rich foods as well. Even if you normally eat red meat infrequently, order some beef or even liver for at least one meal and nibble on dried fruit between meals. If you prefer meatless sources of iron, scan the menu for chick peas or other beans or peas, spinach, or sardines. And continue taking your antenatal iron supplement.

You need fluids. An adequate fluid in-take will help you to urinate and move your bowels sooner and more easily, will aid in the production of milk and will replace body fluids lost through postpartum perspiration. In addition to milk (which is only two-thirds liquid), drink fruit and vegetable juices (if the ones the hospital offers don't excite you, request one that does – a bottle of sparkling cider, for instance, or strawberry-apple juice – from outside sources), order soups and ask for a jug of water to keep next to your bed.

You don't need empty calories. Much as you may be tempted to try every dessert on the hospital menu, keep in mind that every empty calorie now does one of two things: it replaces a nutrition-packed calorie that you need for recuperation (and milk production, if you're nursing) or, added to all nutrient-dense calories you need, it gives you more calories than you should be taking if you intend to start dropping pregnancy weight. Treat yourself to no more than one nutrition-empty dessert a day during your hospital stay, choosing those you feel you really can't live happily without. Opt, when given the choice, for ice cream, custards, or puddings (which at least contain some calcium and protein) over cakes, biscuits and pastries. (You'll probably be disappointed with the desserts, anyway; these aren't the desserts you get at your favourite restaurant or bake yourself.) In between splurges, especially if your stay is long, satisfy that ache in your sweet tooth with some juice-sweetened biscuits from the health-food store.

What You May Be Concerned About

Feelings of Failure

'For nine months I had an image of what my delivery would be like: natural, loving, peaceful. But it turned out to be none of these. My disappointment and sense of failure is so great that I've been crying on and off since my son was born two days ago.'

A century ago, when all deliveries were 'natural', women were grateful just to survive childbirth. Today, safe deliveries are so routine that they're almost taken for granted. And many women have come to expect, even demand, in addition to a good physical outcome, certain emotional rewards. When they don't end up getting them, they experience a sense of letdown and failure.

Part of the problem lies with those books and classes that prepare couples unrealistically for childbirth, emphasizing the 'experience' itself rather than the outcome. Though childbirth education can do a lot to help expectant couples participate in and cope with labour and delivery, it can sometimes give them the notion that childbirth is a test that one passes or fails. And then, if the big event doesn't turn out to be the glorious climax-to-pregnancy they've witnessed on film and read about in books – if they agreed to a pitocin drip to encourage contractions after twenty hours of fruitless labour, if they screamed obscenities instead of panting with Madonna-like serenity, if their wills as well as their bodies were violated by a scalpel in an episiotomy or a caesarean – these women (and often their partners) feel they've failed.

Yet they haven't. Because the ultimate criteria by which you can judge successful delivery are a healthy mother and a healthy baby. A woman's performance through the nine months of pregnancy – how she eats, drinks, cares for her body – is far more significant than what she does during the fourteen or so hours of labour and delivery.

And passing precious moments of new motherhood crying over what might have been is wasteful.

A labour that fulfills your greatest expectations is ideal, and perhaps you'll have it if there's a next time. But its importance is negligible when weighed against those 3,200 to 3,500 g (7 or 8 pounds) of healthy baby filling the bassinet beside your bed. Any delivery – or set of parents – that produced your very special newborn can't (and shouldn't) be called a failure.

Broken Tailbone

'I was really shocked when my doctor told me that my tailbone was broken during delivery. I've never heard of such an injury.'

You've probably never heard of a broken tailbone, or coccyx, because such an occurence is very rare. But as you now know, it does happen. More common is injury to the muscles of the pelvic floor, which can result in muscular spasm and tenderness in the area. Either can cause what is medically termed coccygodynia, or pain in the region of the coccyx at the base of the spine. Most women find the pain is most severe when they are sitting on a hard surface or straining (not just sitting) at the toilet. Lying down or sitting on a cushion or a rubber ring, or 'doughnut', usually offers relief.

Treatment may include heat applications and massage of the buttocks to relax the area, and, possibly, intrapelvic massage. With treatment, pain gradually lessens and is usually gone in a month or two.

Black and Bloodshot Eyes

'My eyes were bloodshot after delivery, and now I look like I'm getting two black eyes.'

Childbirth can not only leave a woman feeling as though she's been through the wringer, it can leave her looking as though she's been in the ring. The pushing during a long, hard second stage of labour can break small blood vessels in and around the eyes causing bloodshot and even black eyes. This is especially likely to occur when a woman holds her breath at the peak of a push and pressure builds up in her head. If your appearance makes you cringe every time you pass a mirror, or if you're concerned that visitors may be shocked when they see your shiners, go 'incognito' for a while with slightly tinted glasses.

Do, of course, discuss the condition and any treatment with your doctor. In most cases, cold compresses for ten minutes several times a day will be soothing and may even hasten healing; in extreme cases, a consultation with an ophthalmologist may be in order.

You should be able to pack the dark glasses away in a few days to a few weeks. Until then, don't feel self-conscious – all eyes will be on your baby, not on your eyes.

Abdominal Cramping

'I've been having cramplike pains in my abdomen, especially when I'm nursing.'

The last thing you want to feel after hours of labour is more contractions, but that's very likely what you're experiencing. These 'afterpains' are apparently caused by the normal postpartum contractions of the uterus as it goes about the important work of pinching off blood vessels torn by the separation of the placenta and of returning to prepregnancy size and location. After-pains are more likely to be felt by, and are more intense in, women whose uterine musculature is lacking in tone because of previous births or excessive stretching (as with twins); many first-time mothers aren't even aware of them. This cramping is likely to be more pronounced during nursing

because suckling releases the contraction-stimulating hormone oxytocin.

If the pain is severe enough to interfere with your sleep or if the tension it causes interferes with your nursing, a mild analgesic may be ordered for you. Don't hesitate to take it; such medication won't affect your baby because it doesn't pass into the colostrum in any significant amounts, and it may help you. The pain should subside naturally within two to seven days. If it doesn't, or if the analgesics don't relieve it, check with your doctor.

Chest Pain

'I delivered yesterday – after three hours of pushing – and today my chest hurts when I breathe. Is something wrong?'

You wouldn't expect to do three hours of pushups and not feel sore. And you can't expect to do three hours of baby pushing without feeling the effects of your workout. Which muscles will be sorest will depend on which you tensed and released most as you pushed; the aches and pains might be in the area of the rib cage, in the back, the legs, even in the shoulders.

Of course, such pain can occasionally indicate a more serious problem – such as a blood clot or internal bleeding – so it should be reported to the midwife promptly and to your doctor at the first opportunity. If the pain is indeed muscular, it should gradually diminish over the next several days. Heat (in the form of hot baths or showers or a heating pad) may be suggested to relieve the discomfort, or a pain medication may be prescribed.

Bleeding

'I knew I could expect a bloody discharge after delivery, but when I got out of bed the first time and saw the blood running down my legs, I was really frightened.'

Don't be alarmed. This discharge of left-over blood, mucus and tissue from your uterus, known as lochia (from the Greek for 'of childbirth'), is normally as heavy as (sometimes a little heavier than) a menstrual period for the first three postpartum days. It may total up to 500 ml (16 fl ounces) before it begins to taper off, but it often seems more copious than it really is. And a sudden gush upon getting out of bed in the first few days is common and no cause for concern. Since blood, primarily from torn vessels at the placental site, is the predominant ingredient of lochia during the immediate postpartum period, the discharge is quite red at first. Then as healing progresses and the bleeding slows, the discharge gradually turns to a watery pink, then to brown, and finally to a yellowish white over the next week or two.

Sanitary towels, *not* tampons (which could cause infection), should be used to absorb the flow, which may continue on and off for as little as two weeks or as long as six, and may occasionally be tinged with a bit of blood. Sometimes it seems to stop for a day or so and then resumes. Women who do too much too soon sometimes note a recurrence of actual bleeding after the first week – a clear sign to slow down because physical exertion is interfering with the healing process. Some women experience what seems to be a 'small period' about three weeks postpartum. This episode of painless bleeding is normal as long as it doesn't become profuse or prolonged, or repeat – in which case your doctor should be consulted.

Anything more than a slightly bloody discharge after the first week should be reported to your doctor since it could indicate that a small fragment of placenta may still be clinging to the wall of the uterus, or that the site at which the placenta was attached to the uterus hasn't healed completely. In either case a D and C (dilatation and curettage), in which the doctor dilates the cervix and scrapes away any remaining pieces of placenta from the uterine wall or dead tissue from a poorly healed placental site, usually stops the bleeding. Also inform your doctor if brownish or yellowish lochia persists longer than six weeks, since this could indicate infection, especially when associated with fever and/or abdominal pain or tenderness.

Breastfeeding and intramuscular or intravenous oxytocin (routinely ordered by some doctors following delivery) may both reduce the flow of lochia by stimulating uterine contractions and help to shrink the uterus back to normal size more quickly. Some doctors will massage the fundus (the top of the uterus) gently for a while after delivery to encourage uterine contractions. The shrinking of the uterus is vital because it pinches off exposed blood vessels at the site where the placenta separates from the uterus, preventing haemorrhage.

If the uterus is too relaxed and contractions weak, excessive bleeding may occur. This is most likely when the uterus has been overworked during a long or traumatic delivery or was overdistended because of multiple births, a large baby, or excess amniotic fluid; when the placenta was oddly placed or separated prematurely (abrupted); when fibroids prevented symmetrical contraction of the uterus; or when the mother was in a generally weakened condition at the time of delivery (due to anaemia, preeclampsia, or extreme fatigue, for example).

More uncommon is postpartum haemorrhage that occurs because of lacerations to the genital tract. Rarely, haemorrhage is due to a previously undetected bleeding disorder. Infection can also cause postpartum haemorrhage right after delivery or weeks later.

Most postpartum haemorrhages occur without any warning about seven to fourteen days after delivery. Since this relatively rare complication of childbirth can be life threatening, prompt diagnosis and treatment are vital. Any of the first six symptoms on the When to Call Your Doctor list on page 505 can be a sign of impending haemorrhage (or, in some cases, of postpartum infection) and should be reported immediately.

When to Call your Doctor

During the first six postpartum weeks, there remains the possibility of a post-childbirth complication. It could be signalled by one or more of the following, all of which require *immediate* consultation with your doctor:

- Bleeding that saturates more than one pad an hour for more than a few hours. Have someone take you to the emergency room or call 999 if you can't reach your doctor immediately. En route or while waiting for emergency help to arrive, lie down and keep an ice bag (or a securely tied plastic bag filled with ice cubes and a couple of paper towels to absorb the melting ice) on your lower abdomen (directly over your uterus, if you can locate it, or at the focus of the pain), if possible.

- Bright red bleeding any time after the fourth postpartum day. But don't worry about an occasional bloody tinge to your discharge, a brief episode of painless bleeding at about three weeks postpartum, or an increased flow that slows down when you do.

- Lochia that has a foul odour. It should smell like a normal menstrual flow.

- Large blood clots in the lochia. Occasional small clots in the first few days, however, are normal.

- An absence of lochia during the first two weeks postpartum.

- Pain or discomfort, with or without swelling, in the lower abdominal area beyond the first few days after delivery.

- After the first 24 hours, a temperature of over 37.8°C (100°F) for more than a day. Many women run temperatures as high as 38°C (100.4°F) right after delivery due to dehydration, and some run a low-grade fever when their milk comes in, but these fevers are of no concern.

- Sharp chest pain, which could indicate a blood clot. Call 999 or have someone take you to the hospital if you can't reach your doctor immediately.

- Localized pain, tenderness and warmth in your calf or thigh, with or without redness and pain when you flex your foot which could be signs of a blood clot in a leg vein. Rest, with your leg elevated, while you try to reach your doctor.

- A lump or hardened area in a breast once engorgement has subsided, which could indicate a clogged milk duct. Begin home treatment (see page 546) while waiting to reach the doctor.

- Localized pain, swelling, redness, heat and tenderness in a breast once engorgement has subsided, which could be signs of mastitis, or breast infection. Begin home treatment on page 546 while waiting to reach the doctor.

- Localized swelling and/or redness, heat and oozing at the site of a caesarian incision.

- Difficult urination; pain or burning when urinating; a frequent urge to urinate that yields little result; scanty and/or dark urine. Drink plenty of water while trying to reach the doctor.

- Depression that affects your ability to cope, or that doesn't subside after a few days; feelings of anger towards your baby, particularly if those feelings are accompanied by violent urges.

Thrombophlebitis

'I had a caesarean section and the doctor instructed me to put on elastic stockings first thing in the morning. Why?'

An ounce of prevention, even if it comes in the form of uncomfortable elastic stockings, is worth at least a pound of cure. Once in a great while, following a surgical delivery, a traumatic vaginal one, or a period of protracted bed rest (which makes circulation sluggish), a blood clot develops in a leg vein and the vein becomes inflamed. Women with varicose veins are more susceptible to the problem, and sometimes pressure from the stirrups during delivery seems to precipitate it. Called thrombophlebitis, this condition is a much less common postpartum problem today than it was forty years ago when women weren't even allowed to dangle their feet over the side of the bed until a week or more after delivery and when traumatic deliveries were more common.

Elastic stockings plus early ambulation (walking around as soon after delivery as is safe and practical) can usually prevent the problem. If for any reason (you were given a spinal anaesthetic, for instance) you are confined to bed after delivery for more than eight hours, doing simple leg exercises such as those on page 517 will help to improve the circulation of blood in your legs. If you feel a sharp pain on doing any exercise, particularly one in which you flex the foot (turning your toes up towards your body), stop exercising and notify the nurse.

There are basically two kinds of thrombophlebitis. When a clot forms in a superficial vein near the surface of the skin, the symptoms are tenderness and warmth right over the affected area and possibly a red line visible through the skin. Keeping the legs elevated and applying moist heat will usually resolve the problem quickly. When a deeper vein is involved, the area along the path of the vessel becomes painful, slightly swollen and exquisitely tender. Flexing the foot may cause pain in the calf, apparently because this movement stretches the inflamed vein. Occasionally, swelling of the leg may be extreme. Deep-vein thrombophlebitis is very serious, since the blood clot can break away and move to the lungs, and requires prompt treatment to dissolve the clot. Therapy usually includes: absolute bed rest with the affected leg elevated, warm heat, elastic stocking or bandage and anticoagulant medication to reduce the clotting ability of the blood. If such treatment is unsuccessful, which is rare, the vein may have to be tied off surgically.

Pain in the Perineal Area

'I didn't have an episiotomy and I didn't tear. Why am I so sore?'

You can't expect some 3,200 to 3,500 g (7 or 8 pounds) of baby to pass by the perineum without having some impact. Even if your perineum was left intact during the baby's arrival, the area has still been stretched, bruised and generally traumatized. Discomfort, ranging from mild to not-so-mild, is the very normal result. Time will be the best healer, but if discomfort is great, try some of the remedies on page 508.

'I'm afraid my episiotomy may be infected. It's very sore and really hurts when I laugh.'

The perineal soreness experienced by a vaginal deliverer is likely to be compounded if the perineum was torn or surgically cut in an episiotomy and then sutured. And though it won't hurt only when you laugh, it's likely to hurt more when you do – and when you cough or sneeze, as well. (Laughing, coughing and sneezing can't, however, cause your stitches to open up, nor can going to the bathroom.) Like any freshly repaired wound, the site of an episiotomy or laceration will take time to heal – usually seven to ten days. Pain alone during this time, unless it is severe, is not an indication that infection has developed.

While you're in the hospital (and later at home), a midwife will check your stitches periodically for inflammation or other indications of infection. But infection is very unlikely if good perineal hygiene has been practised.

Getting out of Bed

'I feel ready to be up and about, but the nurse said I can't get out of bed until eight hours after delivery.'

The six- to eight-hour bed rest rule is routine in many hospitals – partly because a woman's body has taken a beating and needs a rest, and partly because dizziness and even fainting, which can result in falls and serious injury, are common in those early postpartum hours.[2] So that you don't hurt yourself (or your baby, if you're carrying him or her), as well as for the hospital's protection, most hospitals insist on eight hours of bed rest postpartum. You may not even be allowed to go to the lavatory and may have to use a bedpan, instead. If you do get the okay for trips to the lavatory you will probably not be allowed to go alone.

It's easy for women who deliver at night or in the wee hours to obey this rule – by sleeping away the eight or so postpartum hours (not uninterrupted, of course, since they will be awakened for baby feedings). But to those who deliver by day, being confined to bed when they're raring to go can be trying. Still, doctor probably knows best: you will feel stronger when you do get up if you treat yourself to some well-deserved rest first. Your episiotomy or laceration repair, if any, will have begun to heal by the end of that eight-hour period, any soreness will interfere less with walking, and your vaginal discharge will have diminished somewhat.

And consider this: it may be a long time before you'll be enjoying the luxury of spending an entire eight-hour stretch in bed again. Savour the experience while you can.

Difficulty with Urination

'It's been several hours since I gave birth, and I haven't been able to urinate yet.'

During the first 24 postpartum hours, many women experience difficulty in passing urine. Some feel no urge at all; others feel the urge but are unable to fulfill it. Still others do urinate, but with accompanying pain and burning. There are a host of factors that may interfere with the return of normal bladder

function after delivery: the holding capacity of the bladder increases because, with the enlarged uterus out of the way, it suddenly has more room in which to expand – thus the need for urination may be less frequent.

- The bladder, bruised or otherwise traumatized during delivery due to pressures during childbirth, may have become temporarily paralyzed. Even when full, it may not send the usual voiding signals.

- Drugs or anaesthesia may decrease the sensitivity of the bladder or the alertness of the mother to its signals.

- Low fluid intake and fluid loss through perspiration during labour and delivery can combine with inadequate fluid consumption following childbirth to cause dehydration. The result – little urine to excrete.

- Pain in the perineal area may cause reflex spasms in the urethra (the tube that carries the urine from the bladder), making urination difficult. Swelling of the perineum may also interfere with urination.

- Urine may burn or sting the sensitive site of a fresh episiotomy or laceration repair, making a woman hesitant to urinate. This can be alleviated somewhat by standing astride the toilet while urinating so that the flow comes straight down, without touching sensitive tissue.

- Any number of psychological factors may also inhibit the ability to urinate – lack of privacy, fear that voiding may cause pain, embarrassment or discomfort over using a bedpan or needing assistance in the lavatory.

In spite of these impediments it's essential that the bladder be emptied within six to eight hours – to avoid urinary tract infection, loss of muscle tone in the bladder from overdistension and bleeding due to a distended bladder's interfering with the normal postpartum descent of the uterus. You can expect, therefore, that a nurse will ask you at least once a shift if you've urinated. You may be asked to void for the first time into a

2. This is due to a sudden drop in blood pressure, the kind you may have experienced during pregnancy when you got up too suddenly.

Perineal Care

Scrupulous attention to perineal care is necessary to prevent infection not only of the repair site when there's been an episiotomy or a laceration, but of the reproductive and urinary tracts in the woman who's recently delivered. The following steps are usually recommended:

- Wash your hands before *and* after going to the lavatory or changing a sanitary pad.

- Change sanitary pads at least every four to six hours. Secure them snugly so that they don't slide back and forth.

- Place and remove pads front to back to avoid dragging germs from the rectum to the vagina.

- Pour or squirt warm water (or an antiseptic solution, if one was recommended by your doctor) over the area after going to the lavatory. Pat dry with gauze pads, paper wipes, or medicated pads (which the hospital may supply), always from front to back.

- Keep your hands – and anyone else's – off the area until healing is complete.

Though discomfort is likely to be greater with a repair (with itchiness around the stitches possibly accompanying soreness), these suggestions are usually welcomed by all recently delivered mothers:

- Warm sitz baths, hot compresses, or heat lamp exposure. If you use the tub for a sitz bath, ring for the nurse immediately should you feel faint while in the bath. To avoid burns when using a heat lamp, use one in the hospital only under supervision; at home use only with instructions from your doctor.

- Chilled witch hazel on a sterile gauze pad or a rubber glove filled with crushed ice applied to the site of discomfort. Or line your sanitary towel with medicated pads at each change.

- Anaesthetic sprays, creams, or pads; mild pain medications, if prescribed by your doctor.

- No pressure positions. Lying on your side and avoiding long periods of standing or sitting can decrease strain on the area. Sitting on a pillow or a rubber ring (called a 'doughnut') may help, as may tightening your buttocks before sitting.

- Kegel exercises (see page 518). Do these as frequently as possible after delivery and right through the postpartum period to stimulate circulation to the area, which will promote healing. Don't be alarmed if you can't feel yourself doing them at first; the perineum will be numb right after delivery. Feeling will return to the area gradually over the next few weeks.

container, so that your output can be measured. And your bladder may be checked to be sure it's not distended with unpassed urine.

If you haven't urinated within eight hours or so of delivery, you may be catheterized (your bladder emptied of urine via a slim tube inserted into the urethra). But you can probably get the waterworks going more quickly and avoid catheterization (or if you have been catheterized following a caesarean, resume urinary function when the catheter has been removed) by trying the following:

Take a walk. Getting out of bed and going for a stroll as soon after delivery as you're allowed will help activate your bladder (*and* your bowels).

Take a drink. An adequate fluid intake will also help activate your bladder.

Go it alone. If you're self-conscious with an audience and feel you can manage on your own, ask the nurse to wait outside your room the first time you try to urinate. She can rejoin you when you've finished to give you a demonstration of perineal care and to help you back to bed if necessary.

Bed down with the bedpan. Dismiss your inhibitions and psych yourself into using the bedpan if you're too weak to walk to the bathroom, if hospital policy requires maternity patients to stay in bed for the first eight postpartum hours, or if your bladder seems intent on emptying drip-by-drip. Sitting on a bedpan (if it's metal, ask to have it warmed) can facilitate urination because it allows you to go the moment you feel the urge. It may help to arrange for privacy (have the curtain around your bed drawn if you're sharing a room), to pour a little warm water over the perineal area, to have a tap in your room turned on, and to sit rather than lie on the bedpan.

Go hot or cold. Warm the area up in a sitz bath or cool it down with ice packs, whichever seems to induce urgency for you.

Try that trickle trick. Running the water in the sink really does help encourage your own tap to flow. So does running warm water over the perineal area.

Having a Bowel Movement

'I delivered almost a week ago and I haven't had a bowel movement yet. I think fear of opening my episiotomy stitches is making me constipated.'

The passage of the first bowel movement after childbirth is a milestone of the postpartum period, one that doesn't come as soon as many women would like.

Several factors, both physical and psychological, may postpone the immediate return of normal bowel function after delivery. For one thing, the abdominal muscles that assist in elimination have been stretched during childbirth, making them less effective at this task. For another, like the bladder, the bowel itself may have been traumatized during labour and delivery, leaving it sluggish. In addition, it may be relatively empty thanks to increased activity (perhaps with

diarrhoea) in early labour, possibly an enema before delivery and some evacuation during it, decreased food intake through delivery, and perhaps little appetite in the immediate postpartum period because of excitement or exhaustion.

Perhaps the most potent inhibitors of postpartum bowel activity are psychological: the fear of splitting open the stitches; the embarrassment over lack of privacy in the hospital; and the pressure to perform.

Although reregulating your system is rarely either effortless or instantaneous, there are several steps you can take to make it easier and speedier:

Don't worry. Nothing will keep you from moving your bowels more effectively than worrying about moving your bowels. Don't worry about your stitches popping – they won't (though it may sometimes feel as though they will). And don't worry if it takes a few days to get your plumbing back into smooth working order – it just takes longer for some women than others.

Request roughage. Select whole grains, fresh fruits and vegetables and stewed prunes from the hospital menu, if possible. Supplement these with bowel-stimulating food brought in from outside. Apples, raisins, prunes and other dried fruit, nuts, bran muffins and wheat bran cereal or unprocessed wheat bran will help. Beware of chocolate, however. This classic gift for hospital patients tends to constipate.

Keep the liquids coming. To compensate for fluids lost during labour and delivery, and to help soften stool if you're constipated, you must increase your intake of fluids – especially water and fruit juices. But turn to prune juice only if all else fails since a glass of prune juice can be a very strong laxative.

Get off your bottom. You won't be running marathons the day after delivery, but you should be able to take short strolls through the corridors. An active body encourages active bowels. Kegel exercises, which can be done very soon after delivery, will help tone up the rectum.

Follow your urges. Try to answer immediately whenever nature calls, even if it's in mid-feeding (return baby to the bassinet) or if you have a roomful of company (ask them to leave for a few minutes if you'd like more privacy, or use the lavatory in the hall).

Don't strain. Straining on the toilet won't open your episiotomy or laceration repair, but it can lead to, or aggravate, haemorrhoids. Place your feet on a low stool or box to simulate the squatting position (the natural one for moving your bowels) and avoid straining.

The doctor may also recommend a stool softener to get things moving.

Once the first bowel movement has passed, you will probably breathe a great sigh of relief. But keep in mind that constipation may return if you become lax once you're back home and ignore these preventive measures. The first few bowel movements may pass with unaccustomed discomfort. But as stools soften and you become more regular, the discomfort will ease.

Haemorrhoids

'For nine months I escaped haemorrhoids. Now, postpartum, I suddenly have them.'

Haemorrhoids, also called piles (they resemble a pile of marbles or grapes), are actually varicose veins of the rectum or anus. They may be painful, itchy and/or burning, and they sometimes bleed. Internal hemorrhoids are found far up in the rectum, external ones right on the skin just beyond the anal sphincter.

Hemorrhoids often develop during pregnancy, particularly during the last trimester. Childbirth, because of the extreme pressure exerted on the rectum and anus during pushing, may make them worse or can even make them a problem for the first time. In new mothers who didn't have hemorrhoids before pregnancy, the bothersome symptoms usually lessen or disappear after the immediate postpartum period. In the meantime, taking the following steps can help minimize discomfort and may hasten that departure:

- Maintain regularity. Constipation aggravates haemorrhoids, so be sure to follow the tips on page 509 for avoiding it. In some cases your doctor may recommend a stool softener. (Do *not* take mineral oil, which can deplete your body of nutrients.)

- Apply heat or cold, whichever offers more relief. Warm sitz baths of about twenty minutes' duration are usually recommended, but some women find ice packs or chilled witch hazel soaks more soothing. Or you might try alternating hot and cold treatments.

- Keep the perineal area scrupulously clean. At first, rinse the area with water after each bowel movement, using a peri-bottle (a plastic squirt bottle, sometimes provided by the hospital, for keeping the perineal area clean) as directed. When you can begin wiping, use moistened, unscented white toilet tissue (which is less irritating than coloured) and wipe from front to back.

- Sleep or rest on your side, not on your back, and avoid long periods of standing (not a good idea right now, anyway) or sitting (when you do sit, use a rubber ring, or doughnut, if that makes you more comfortable).

- Do Kegel exercises (page 518) to improve circulation to the area.

- Use medicated suppositories or topical anaesthetics as recommended by your doctor.

- If haemorrhoids protrude, ask the nurse to show you how to tuck them back in.

If bleeding and/or discomfort continues in spite of your best efforts, check with your doctor to rule out any more serious condition and to see if more radical therapy might be needed to deal with your haemorrhoids.

Excessive Perspiration

'I've been waking up at night soaked with perspiration. Is this normal?'

What your doctor may sometimes refer to as diaphoresis, but is more commonly and less politely referred to as sweating, is one of the ways in which your body rids itself of pregnancy-accumulated fluids during the days following delivery (frequent urination is another). Sometimes perspiration continues to be a problem for several weeks – occasionally accompanied by hot flushes and/or chills – because of postpartum hormonal adjustments. Though you needn't worry about these symptoms, do make sure essential fluids lost through the skin are replaced, particularly if you're breastfeeding, by increasing your intake of liquids. An absorbent towel placed over your pillow may help make you more comfortable if you do most of your perspiring in bed.

Once you're back at home, it's a good idea to take your temperature if you're sweating excessively and, as a precaution, to report it to your doctor if it's over 37.8°C (100°F) orally.

Engorged Breasts

'My milk finally came in and my breasts are swollen to three times their normal size – and so hard, engorged, and painful that I can't bear to put on a bra. Is this what I have to look forward to until I wean my baby?'

If painfully tender, granite-hard breasts the size of an exotic dancer's were what mothers had to look forward to for the duration of the breastfeeding experience, most babies would be weaned before they entered their second week of life. The engorgement that arrives with a mother's milk can temporarily make nursing agonizing for her and, because the nipples are flattened by the swelling, frustrating for baby. The condition may be more severe when a baby isn't put to breast until 24 to 36 hours after birth.

Engorgement occurs rather suddenly, usually over a few hours, most often on the third or fourth postpartum day, but it can occur as early as the second day or as late as the seventh. It's more uncomfortable for some women than for others, is more severe with first babies, and also occurs later with first babies than with subsequent ones. Some lucky women get their milk without experiencing any discomfort or noticeable engorgement at all, especially if they are nursing regularly from the start.

Happily, engorgement and its distressing effects disappear within a matter of days. Until then, you can use heat or cold (some women find ice packs helpful, others hot showers or soaks) or a mild analgesic recommended by the doctor to reduce discomfort. A breast pump or manual expression of milk can help to get the flow started and ease engorgement enough to allow your baby to grasp the nipple for suckling. Using an oxytocin nasal spray prescribed by your doctor or applying warm soaks just before nursing to encourage milk let-down may also bring some relief.

Don't be tempted, however, to skip or skimp on feedings because of pain; the less your baby sucks, the more engorged you will become. The more you nurse your newborn, on the other hand, the more quickly engorgement will subside. If your baby doesn't nurse vigorously enough to relieve the engorgement in both breasts at each feeding, use a breast pump to do this yourself.

'I just had my second baby. My breasts are much less engorged than with my first. Does this mean I'm going to have less milk?'

It's common for the breasts to engorge less with second and subsequent pregnancies. Perhaps the breasts, having gone through all this before, have less difficulty adjusting to the influx of milk, or perhaps the experienced mother can get her baby started nursing more easily and more quickly, resulting in more efficient emptying of the engorged breast.

Very rarely, a lack of engorgement and of a sensation of milk let-down does indicate inadequate milk production, but only in first-time mothers. Many women, even first-timers, who don't experience engorgement turn out to have copious milk supplies nevertheless. There's no reason to worry that a milk supply might be inadequate unless a baby isn't gaining well (see page 97).

Drying up your Milk

'I'm not nursing. I understand that drying up the milk can be painful.'

Whether or not you're nursing, your breasts will become engorged (overfilled) with milk sometime between your second and seventh postpartum day, most often on the third or fourth. This can be an uncomfortable, even painful, experience – but it is blessedly temporary.

Medications to suppress lactation are no longer on the market. Such medications didn't always relieve engorgement, and if they did, the engorgement often returned a week or two after they were discontinued. They also occasionally caused serious side effects. So it is now recommended that non-nursing mothers take nature's course, letting the body take care of suppressing milk production. The breasts are designed to produce milk only as needed – if you don't nurse, production eventually ceases. Though sporadic leaking may occur for several days or even weeks, the worst of the engorgement shouldn't last more than 12 to 48 hours. During this time, ice packs, mild pain relievers and possibly squeezing a few drops of milk from the breasts may be helpful. Hot showers and soaks, however, though soothing, may stimulate milk production and aren't a good idea. Wearing a well-fitting, supportive bra is important until your breasts return to normal prepregnancy size, at about six weeks postpartum.

Hospital Confusion

'My doctor told me to stay in bed until noon today. At nine in the morning, a midwife came in and said I should get up and she would take me for a walk. Who do I listen to?'

In a hospital, as in any other institution, mistakes can be made. That's why it's important for you to take some responsibility for your own care. If something doesn't make sense – you're getting conflicting messages, a treatment is painful or uncomfortable, someone wants to give you a medication you think you already took or said you didn't want – speak up. If your nurse can't clear up the problem, ask to see the head midwife. If you're still not satisfied, call your doctor or midwife, or ask for a consultation. For non-medical issues, find out if the hospital has a patient advocate on staff – and turn there for help.

Going Home

'I had a relatively easy labour, my son is doing fine, and I feel terrific. I'd like to go home early, but everyone tells me I should stay in the hospital and rest.'

This is one case in which listening to 'everyone' might be a good idea. Childbirth takes its toll no matter how effortless and rapid the labour and delivery. And though in your present state of euphoria you may not feel that you need to rest, you'll find out otherwise very quickly if you do too much too soon. Your attitude is likely to change from 'Why should I rest?' to 'What's rest?' before the month is out.

So the question isn't whether or not you need rest – you do – but where you'll be most likely to get it. For the woman who's coming home to relatives, friends and/or hired help who will make it possible for her to take it easy, early discharge can bring welcome relief from the regimentation and relatively impersonal atmosphere of hospital life. On the other hand, for a woman who's returning with babe in arms to a home full of other children and devoid of help, the hospital stay, though brief and imperfect, often represents an idyllic, peaceful calm before the storm.

Also relevant to your decision is how much your personality will allow you to rest if you do go home, even if you're going home to lots of help. If you're not the kind of person who can lie idly by for a couple of days watching other people do your laundry, cook your meals and tidy your home, you're better off with the enforced vacation from household responsibilities that a post-partum hospital stay brings.

Of course, while a hospital stay some-times isn't medically necessary for you, it may be for your baby. And unless you don't mind being separated, you'll have to remain in the hospital for as long as your baby's doctor requires him to, unless that stay is prolonged.

'I was surprised to be told by my doctor that I was expected to go home only 24 hours after my baby was born. What's the big rush?'

With health-care costs spiralling, medical economists are looking in every hospital nook and cranny for ways to cut them. Thus the 24-hour discharge. It can also be argued that after an uncomplicated vaginal delivery, the very best place for a mother and her baby is at home. There are familiar sur-roundings and favourite foods (at least for mum), loving family and no exposure to hospital germs.

Of course, something could go wrong at home. So if you are discharged early, faith-fully follow the medical instructions you are given for you and your infant (ask that they be put in writing). If you note any warning signs that a problem might be developing in you (see page 505) or in your baby (see page 69), contact the appropriate doctor immediately. To help you over some of the early hurdles, make the most of your home visits from the midwife and health visitor; do contact the local NCT or La Leche League for additional advice on breastfeeding; and

book an early visit to the doctor (most doctors schedule them). It's also a good idea to ask to have your infant's PKU test done between the third and fifth days of life (earlier tests may not be valid). And re-member, getting the okay to go home doesn't give you carte blanche to start going out on the town, scrubbing floors, or even dusting the living room. If you don't take it easy, you might end up back in the hospital – and there go those cost savings.

Recovery from a Caesarean

'I had a caesarean section. How different will my recuperation be from that of a woman with a vaginal delivery?'

Recovery from a caesarean section is similar to recovery from any major abdominal surgery – with a delightful difference: instead of losing an old gall bladder or appendix, you gain a brand new baby.

Of course, there's another difference slightly less delightful. In addition to re-covering from the surgery itself, you'll also be recovering from childbirth. Except for a neatly intact perineum, you'll experience all the same postpartum discomforts you would have if you'd delivered vaginally – afterpains, lochia, breast engorgement, fati-gue, hair loss, excessive perspiration, the baby blues and, if you had a longish period of labour, the exhaustion and other after-effects of that as well.

As for your surgical recovery, you can expect the following in the recovery room:

Careful monitoring until anaesthesia wears off. If you had general anaesthesia, your memory of the time in the recovery room may be fuzzy or totally absent. Since everyone responds differently to drugs and each drug is different, whether you are clear-headed and alert in a few hours or not for a day or two will depend upon your body and upon the medications you were given. If you feel disoriented or if you have hallucinations or bad dreams, your husband or an understanding nurse can help you return to reality quickly.

It takes longer to shake the effects of a spinal or an epidural block than those of general anaesthesia. Numbness will wear off from the toes up, and you will be encouraged to wiggle your toes and move your feet as soon as you can. If you had a spinal block, you will have to remain flat on your back for eight to twelve hours. You may be allowed to have both your husband and your baby visit with you in the recovery room.

In some cases your doctor may elect to continue your epidural for several hours or more postpartum, extending the effects of the anaesthesia, but easing your pain.

Incisional pain. Once the anaesthesia wears off, your incision is going to hurt – though just how much depends on many factors, including your personal pain threshold and whether or not you've had a previous caesarean (subsequent recoveries are less uncomfortable than the first one). You will probably be given pain medication as needed, which may leave you with a woozy or drugged feeling. It will also allow you to get some needed sleep. You needn't be concerned if you're nursing: the medication won't pass into your colostrum in any meaningful amount, and by the time your milk comes in you probably won't need any more pain relief medication.

Possibly, nausea. If you do experience nausea, you may be given an antiemetic preparation to try to prevent vomiting. If you vomit easily, you might want to talk to your doctor about giving you such a medication before you even begin to feel queasy.

Encouragement to do breathing and coughing exercises. These help rid your system of any leftover general anaesthetic, and help to expand your lungs and keep them clear to prevent the complication of pneumonia. Done correctly, they may cause discomfort, but you may be able to minimize it by holding a pillow against your incision while performing them.

Regular evaluations of your condition. A nurse will check your vital signs (temperature, blood pressure, pulse, respiration), your urinary output and vaginal discharge, the dressing over your incision and the firmness and location of your uterus. She will also check your IV and urinary catheter.

Once you have been moved to your hospital room, you can expect:

Continued evaluation of your condition. Your vital signs, dressing, urinary output and vaginal discharge and your uterus, as well as your IV and catheter (while they remain in place), will be checked regularly.

Removal of the catheter after 24 hours. Urinating on your own may be difficult at this point, so try the tips on page 507. If you can't urinate on your own, the catheter may be reinserted until you can.

Afterpains. Like the woman who's gone through a vaginal delivery, you can expect to begin feeling afterpains about 12 to 24 hours after delivery. See page 503 for more about these contractions, which help bring your uterus back to prepregnancy shape.

A gradual return to a normal diet. About 24 hours after surgery, or soon after your bowels begin to show signs of activity (by moving or passing wind), your IV will be discontinued and you will be allowed fluids by mouth. Over the next few days, you will gradually return to your usual diet. Even if you're famished, don't try to circumvent doctor's orders by having someone sneak in a Big Mac. Take it slow getting back to your usual fare, or you may find yourself with unnecessary digestive discomfort. If you are breastfeeding, be sure to get plenty of fluids.

Referred shoulder pain. Irritation of the diaphragm from air in the abdomen following surgery can cause a few hours of sharp pain referred to the shoulder. An analgesic may help and it won't get into your colostrum.

Possible constipation. Like the mum who went through a vaginal delivery, you may have difficulty having a bowel movement for a few days. That's not a reason for concern, especially since you haven't eaten very much that can come out, anyway. Once you are eating, a stool softener and/or a laxative may be prescribed to help move things along. You could also try the tips on page 509, but don't introduce the roughage until you get the doctor's okay. If you haven't had a movement by the fourth or fifth or sixth postpartum day, you may be given a suppository or an enema.

Encouragement to get physical. Even before you are out of bed, you will probably be urged to start wiggling your toes, flexing your feet and pressing them against the end of the bed, and turning from side to side. You can also try these simple exercises: (1) Lie flat on your back, one leg bent at the knee, the other extended, while tightening your abdomen slightly. Slide the bent leg slowly down on the bed; repeat, reversing legs. (2) Lie flat on your back, both knees pulled up, feet flat on the bed, and raise your head a few centimetres/inches for about 30 seconds. (3) On your back, knees bent, tighten your abdomen and reach with one arm across your body to the other side of the bed, at about waist level; reverse. These exercises will improve circulation, especially in your legs, reducing the chance of developing a blood clot. But be prepared to find some quite painful, at least for the first 24 hours or so.

To get out of bed between 8 and 24 hours after surgery. You will first be helped to a sitting position, supported by the raised head of the bed. When you're ready to stand up, the process will be gradual, probably like this: using your hands for support, you will slide your legs over the side of the bed and dangle them for a few minutes. Then, slowly, you'll be helped to step down on to the floor. If you feel dizzy, which is normal, sit back down. Steady yourself for a few more minutes before trying again. Once standing, take a couple of steps. These may be extremely painful (though not everyone finds them so). Stand as straight as you can, and fight any temptation to hunch over to ease the discomfort. This difficulty in getting around is only temporary. In fact, you may soon find yourself more mobile than the vaginal deliverer next door – and you will certainly have the edge in sitting.

To wear elastic stockings. These improve circulation and are intended to prevent blood clots in the legs.

Wind pain. As your digestive tract (temporarily put out of business by surgery) begins to function again, trapped wind can cause considerable pain, especially if it presses against your incision line. Discomfort may be worse when you laugh, cough, or sneeze. Tell your nurse or doctor about your problem. You may be advised to walk up and down the corridor, or to try lying on your left side or on your back, with your knees drawn up and taking deep breaths while holding a pillow against your incision. If these tactics don't work, you may be given an enema or a suppository to help evacuate the gas. Narcotics are not usually recommended for gas pain because they can prolong the difficulties, which ordinarily last just a day or two. If pain remains severe, however, a tube inserted in your rectum to help the wind escape may spell relief.

Time with your baby. You can't lift your baby yet, but you can cuddle and feed him or her. (Place the baby on a pillow over your incision for feeding.) Depending on how you feel, and on hospital regulations, you may be able to have modified rooming-in. Some hospitals even allow full rooming-in following caesareans, which will be easier if your partner or mother or a friend can be with you a good deal of the time.

Sponge baths. Until your stitches or clips are removed (or absorbed), you probably won't be allowed a tub bath or shower. So enjoy the spongings.

Removal of stitches or clips. If your stitches aren't absorbable or if you have clips, they will be removed four to six days after delivery. And although the procedure isn't very painful, you may find it uncomfortable. When the dressing is removed, look at the incision with the nurse or doctor (even if you're squeamish) so you'll know what it looks like. Ask how soon you can expect the area to heal completely, what changes in appearance to expect with healing, and what kinds of changes might indicate a need for medical attention.

You can expect to go home about four to seven days after delivery.

WHAT IT'S IMPORTANT TO KNOW

Getting Back Into Shape

Back when you were pregnant, looking the part was part of the fun. Remember the thrill of buying your first pair of maternity jeans? The elation of watching your belly swell from a scarcely noticeable bulge to a larger-than-life watermelon? And the momentous day when you could finally walk down the street confident that everyone you passed could see that you were pregnant and not just unpleasingly plump?

Once delivery day has come and gone, however, looking pregnant quickly loses its appeal. No woman wants to look as though she's still toting a baby in her belly once she's started toting a newborn in her arms.

For many women it's not pregnancy pounds that keep them looking pregnant; most are shed without much effort in the first six weeks postpartum. Rather, it's stretched-out abdominal muscles that stand between those new mothers and their old prepregnancy silhouettes.

Unfortunately, simply waiting it out won't work. Pregnancy-stretched muscles regain some of their tone as time goes by, but won't ever return to their prepregnancy condition without a concerted exercise effort. Leave your tummy muscles to their own devices, and you'll find that their sagging increases as the years pass, and with each baby you deliver.

And exercise postpartum will do more than help you pull your tummy in. Abdominal routines will improve general circulation and reduce the risk of back problems, varicose veins, leg cramps, swelling of ankles and feet and the formation of clots in blood vessels. Perineal exercises will help you avoid stress incontinence (leaking of urine), which sometimes occurs after child-birth; dropping, or prolapse, of the pelvic organs; and will tighten your perineum so that making love, once you resume it, will be as good or better than ever. Regular exercise will also promote healing of your battered uterine, abdominal and pelvic muscles, hastening their return to normal and preventing further weakening from inactivity, as well as help your pregnancy-and-delivery-loosened joints return to normal (or nearly so). If excess weight is a problem, exercise will help you shed it (you can burn the 100 calories of a baked potato in just twenty minutes of brisk walking). And finally, exercise can provide psychological benefits, improving your ability to handle stress and to relax, while minimizing the possibility of postpartum depression.

If you have the time, opportunity and inclination, sign up for a postpartum exercise class, or buy a postpartum exercise book or video and fit an at-home programme into your schedule. If the idea of an intense exercise programme seems unappealing, regularly doing just a few simple exercises aimed at your particular problem areas (such as tummy, thighs, buttocks) can also get you back into shape. Add a daily brisk walk or other aerobic activity to your agenda and you will have put together an adequate exercise programme. Before you begin any exercise programme, of course, be sure you have your doctor's okay.

Guidelines for Safe and Sane Postpartum Exercise

- If you've had an uncomplicated delivery and are in good health, you can follow the simple exercise programme beginning on page 518. If you had a surgical or difficult delivery, or if you have medical problems, consult your doctor about when you can start exercising and which exercises would be appropriate.

- Stick to a schedule. Exercise done only sporadically is useless and thus a waste of your precious time. Muscle-toning exercises (leg lifts, sit-ups and pelvic tilts, for example) are best done daily in short takes; two or three 5-minute sessions a day will tone you up better than one 20-minute workout. Once you begin doing aerobic exercises (brisk walking, jogging, bicycling and swimming, for example), aim for at least three 20-minute sessions of sustained activity a week – though 40 minutes four or five times weekly may be a better goal for strengthening bones and preventing osteoporosis later in life.[3]

- Don't rush. Muscle-toning exercises are most effective when done slowly and deliberately, with adequate recovery time between repetitions. It's during the recovery periods that muscle buildup occurs.

- Start slowly if you haven't exercised recently or are doing unfamiliar exercises. Do only a few repetitions the first day, and increase the number gradually over the next week or two. Don't do more than the recommended amount, even if you feel great. Stop your workout as soon as you begin to tire.

- Avoid competitive sports until you get your doctor's okay to participate.

- Because your joints are still unstable and your connective tissue lax, avoid jumping; rapid changes of direction; jerky, bouncy, or jarring motions; and deep flexion or extension of joints. Also avoid knee-chest exercises, full sit-ups and double leg lifts during the first six weeks postpartum.

- Do muscle-toning exercises on a wood floor or tightly carpeted surface to reduce shock and provide sure footing.

- Do five minutes of warm-ups (very light stretching exercises, slow walking, or stationary biking against low resistance) before you begin exercising. Cool down at the end of each session with some gentle stretching exercises, but to avoid damaging loose joints, don't stretch to the maximum for the first six weeks.

- Get up slowly to avoid dizziness from a sudden drop in blood pressure and to equalize circulation, keep your legs moving for a few moments (by walking, for example) when you stand up.

- Once you begin doing aerobic exercises, be careful not to exceed your target heart rate. Ask your doctor what that is or find it in the table on page 518.

- Avoid vigorous exercise in hot weather or when you have a fever. Once the six-week postpartum period is over, you can begin exercising in warm weather by dropping back to less than half your usual level of activity and working back up gradually. Try to exercise early in the morning or in the evening – when the heat is generally less intense. Wear light-coloured, lightweight clothing and an open mesh hat or cap when exercising in the sun.

- Drink plenty of fluids before and after exercising, and if the weather is very hot or you are perspiring a great deal, have something to drink as you go, as well. Water is best; avoid sugar-sweetened drinks, including those marketed especially for athletes.

---

3. It's generally agreed that an exercise that is extremely strenuous, such as jogging, is best not done daily. The body needs a day of recovery in between to help prevent injury.

Heart Rate Guidelines for Postpartum Exercise

Your Age	Limit Yourself to This Heart Rate* (beats per minute)	Maximum Heart Rate for Your Age (beats per minute)
20	150	200
25	146	195
30	142	190
35	138	185
40	135	180
45	131	175

* Figures represent 75% of the maximum heart rate for each age group. Under proper medical supervision, more strenuous activity yielding heart rates that exceed these limits may be okay.

Source: ACOG Home Exercise Programs, 1985

- Stop exercising immediately and notify your doctor if you experience any of the following symptoms: pain, faintness, dizziness, blurred vision, shortness of breath, palpitations (your heart seems to tremble, flutter, or race), back pain, pubic pain, nausea, difficulty walking, or a sudden increase in vaginal bleeding (if brown or pink lochia turns red after exercise, you are overdoing).

- Don't use your baby as an excuse for not exercising. Most babies love lying on mummy's chest during a calisthenics session; snuggling in a baby carrier while she pedals a stationary bike, works a rowing machine, skiing machine, or treadmill; and being pushed in the pram or carriage while mummy walks or jogs. But don't bounce an infant around in a baby carrier while you jog or prop up on your bike a baby who can't sit independently.

A Postpartum Exercise Programme

All the following exercises are done in the basic position – lying on your back with your knees bent – though Kegels can be done in any position at all. Phase One exercises can be done while you're in your bed – in the hospital or at home; the others are best done on a hard surface, such as the floor. (If you invest in an exercise mat, it can do double duty as a play mat for baby.) Remember, this exercise programme is appropriate only for women who've had uncomplicated vaginal deliveries and are in good health. Others need to consult their doctors.

Phase One: Twenty-four Hours After Delivery

Kegel exercises. You may have been doing these all during pregnancy and you can resume them almost immediately after delivery. (If you've never done them, see below for directions.) At first, with your perineum still numb from the beating it took during delivery, you won't be able to feel yourself doing the Kegels. You can Kegel in bed, while reading or nursing. And you can Kegel while urinating – contract to stop, then relax to release the flow of urine, repeating several times at each visit to the bathroom. As muscle tone improves, you'll be able to restrict the flow to just a few

Kegel Exercises

Firmly tense the muscles around your vagina and anus. Hold for as long as you can, up to eight or ten seconds, then slowly release the muscles and relax for several seconds. Repeat. Do at least 25 repetitions at various times during the day, while sitting, standing, lying on your back, or urinating.

drops between each Kegel repetition. Both you and your sex life can benefit from your continuing to perform Kegels even beyond the postpartum period; and doing them during sexual intercourse is one of the best ways to combine your body's business with its pleasure.

Deep diaphragmatic breathing. Start in the basic position (see page 520). Place your hands on your abdomen so you can feel it rise as you inhale slowly through your nose; tighten the abdominal muscles as you exhale slowly through your mouth. Repeat just a couple of times at first to avoid hyperventilation. (If you feel dizzy, faint, experience tingling or numbness of fingers and toes, or blurred vision, breathe in and out into a paper bag or into your cupped hands.) Increase the number of breaths by two each day until you're up to ten. The exercise can be repeated several times during the day.

Phase Two: Three Days After Delivery

Now that your body is beginning to recover from some of the more immediate effects of childbirth, you can begin doing some more serious exercising. Before you begin, however, be certain that the recti abdominis (the pair of vertical muscles that run down the centre of your abdominal wall) didn't separate during pregnancy. This separation, called 'diastasis', is fairly common, especially in women who have had several children, and it will get worse if you do even mildly strenuous exercise before it closes up. Ask your doctor about the condition of your recti abdominis muscles, or perform this self-examination: as you lie in the basic position, raise your head slightly with your arms extended; then feel for a soft lump below your navel. Such a lump would probably indicate recti abdominis separation. You can help correct it with this routine: assume the basic position; inhale, cross your hands over your abdomen, then use your fingers to draw the separated halves of your rectus muscles together as you breathe out, raising your head slowly. Repeat three or four times, twice daily. Once the separation has closed, or if you didn't have one to start with, you can progress to the exercises that follow.

Note to Adoptive Mothers

Being a new mother is exhausting and stressful, whether you personally went through childbirth or not. Exercise is a wonderful way to reduce tension, keep your figure, improve your health and have fun with your baby. And it sets a good example for your child. So an exercise programme such as this one is important for you, too, though you needn't worry about the caveats for the mother going through postpartum. If you don't already exercise regularly, consider beginning now.

Phase Two: The Exercises

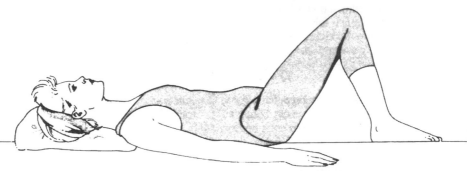

The basic position. *Lie on your back with your arms at your sides, palms down. Your knees should be bent, feet placed about 30 cm (12 inches) apart, and flat on the floor.*

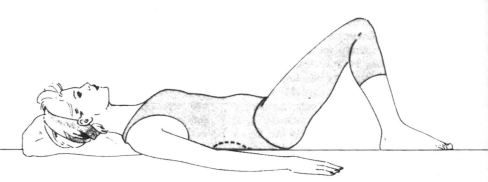

The pelvic tilt. *Assume the basic position. Inhale as you press the small of your back against the floor. Then exhale and relax, allowing your back to arch normally. Repeat three or four times to start, gradually increasing to 24.*

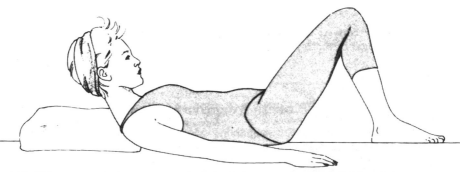

Head lifts. *Assume the basic position Inhale deeply. Raise your head very slightly, exhaling as you do. Lower your head slowly, while inhaling. Raise your head a little higher each day, gradually working up to lifting your shoulders slightly off the floor. Don't do full sit-ups for three or four weeks, and then only if you have very good abdominal muscle tone.*

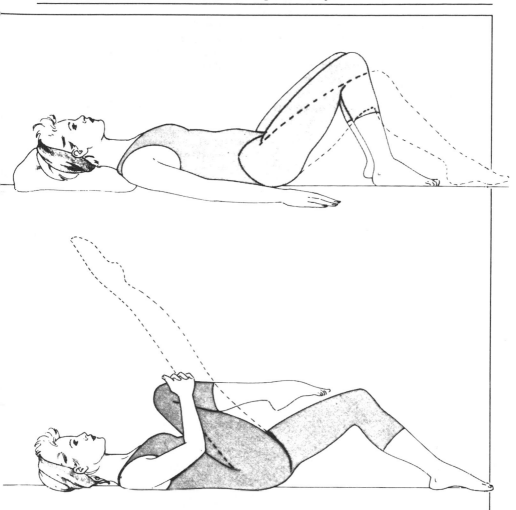

Leg slides. *Assume the basic position. Slide your right foot, sole flat on the floor and knee bending as you go, back towards your buttocks while pressing the small of your back against the floor. Slide your leg back down. Repeat with your left leg. Start with three or four slides per side and increase gradually until you can do twelve or more comfortably. After three weeks, try modified leg lifts: keeping the opposite leg bent, slowly lift one leg at a time slightly off the floor, then slowly lower it. If you can do these comfortably, start with three or four lifts per leg, gradually increasing the number to twelve each. Once you have this down, bring the lifted leg into your chest, straighten it up as far as it will go, then lower it slowly back to the ground. Repeat this twelve times with each leg.*

Phase Three: Four to Six Weeks Postpartum – Exercise for Life

Starting yourself on an aerobic exercise programme after the first four to six weeks – and staying with it as your baby grows – is important not only for your good health and longevity, but for your baby's; a mother who exercises regularly is likely to have children who will follow in her sneakersteps. But get your doctor's okay to proceed, especially if you had a difficult delivery. You can choose to exercise to a videotape or in an aerobics class, or you may decide to embark on a running, bicycling, rowing, skiing, or swimming programme of your own.[4]

---

4. Though swimming provides excellent aerobic exercise, improving cardiorespiratory fitness as well as jogging or walking does, it does not provide weight-bearing exercise, which research is beginning to show can help strengthen bones and ward off osteoporosis later in life. It may also be less useful in weight reduction.

TWENTY-THREE

Surviving the First Six Weeks

◆

What You May Be Feeling

During the first six weeks postpartum, you will be recovering from childbirth and delivery. You will probably experience many of the following to some degree at one time or another.

Physically:

- Continuing vaginal discharge (lochia), turning pink, then brownish, then yellowish white
- Fatigue, sometimes bordering on exhaustion
- Some pain, discomfort and numbness in the perineum, if you had a vaginal delivery (especially if you had stitches)
- Diminishing incisional pain, continuing numbness, if you had a caesarean section (especially if it was your first)
- Continuing bouts of constipation (although it should be easing up)
- Gradual flattening of your abdomen as your uterus returns to prepregnancy location in the pelvis (but only exercise

will bring you completely back to pre-pregnancy shape)
- Gradual loss of weight (you may lose all your pregnancy gain by the end of two months, or not until the end of the first year)
- Breast discomfort and nipple soreness, if you're nursing, until breastfeeding is well established
- Achiness in arms and neck; backache (from carrying and feeding baby)
- Noticeable hair loss
- Swollen neck glands; throat dryness and constriction

Emotionally:

- Elation, depression, or both alternately
- Either a sense of being overwhelmed or a growing feeling of confidence, or both alternately
- Decreased sexual desire (even if your doctor has given you the okay to resume) or increased desire (more rare)

What You Can Expect At Your Six-Week Checkup

Your doctor will probably schedule you for a checkup four to six weeks after delivery; if you had a caesarean, you may also see the

doctor at one to three weeks postpartum for a check of your incision. At six weeks you can expect the following to be checked, though the exact content of the visit will vary depending upon your particular needs and your doctor's philosophy:

- Blood pressure
- Weight, which will probably be down by 7.5 to 9 kg (17 to 20 pounds) or more from predelivery weight
- Shape, size and location of your uterus, to see if it has returned to its prepregnancy state
- Cervix, which will be on its way back to its prepregnancy condition, but will still be somewhat engorged; the surface may possibly be eroded

- Vagina, which will have contracted and regained much of its muscle tone
- Episiotomy or laceration repair site, if any; or, if you had a surgical delivery, the site of your incision
- Breasts, for any abnormalities
- Haemorrhoids or varicose veins, if you have had either during pregnancy or postpartum
- Your plans for birth control; if appropriate, a diaphragm will be fitted or birth control pills prescribed (see page 557)

Have any questions about your recovery or general health ready (bring a list, so you won't forget anything).

What You Should Be Eating: The Best-Odds Postpartum Diet

If you worked hard to revamp your eating habits during pregnancy, now isn't the time to abandon them, temporarily or permanently. And if you didn't eat right during pregnancy, you couldn't pick a better time to start good habits than now. Though a nutritious diet plan can include a few more perks postpartum than it did during pregnancy, careful eating will be essential if you're going to keep up your energy level, gradually take off that extra weight put on during the nine months of pregnancy and, if you're nursing, produce enough milk.

Nine Basic Diet Principles for New Mothers

Good nutrition is vital for a speedy recovery from childbirth and for the maintenance of the abundant energy, optimum health and vibrant spirits necessary for top-notch mothering. It is also crucial to successful nursing. While neglecting nutrition essentials when you're breastfeeding won't necessarily reduce your milk supply, at least not for a couple of months (even women who are

severely undernourished can often produce milk for a while), it may affect the nutritive value of your milk and shortchange your own body nutritionally. Whether you decide to nurse or not, these nine basic principles can serve as a guide to eating well during the postpartum period:

Make most bites count. Though each bite isn't as vital now as it was when you were sharing every one with your gestating baby, it's still important to make as many of them as possible count towards nutrition. Careful food selection will help ensure a plentiful supply of quality breast milk, enough energy to survive sleepless nights and endless days and a speedier return to prepregnancy shape. And don't waste bites when you're cheating, either; splurge only on those empty-calorie foods that provide optimum gastronomic pleasure.

All calories are not created equal. No matter who in the family you're feeding, the 1,500 calories (derived mostly from nutritionless, even dangerous, saturated fats and sugar) in *one* typical fast-food meal aren't nutritionally equal to the 1,500 calories (from protein and complex carbohydrates, laden with vitamins and minerals) in *three* well-balanced meals. Also compare: the 235 calories in a slice of frosted devil's food cake with the 235 calories in half a cantaloupe mounded with 100 ml (4 fl ounces) of ice milk or the 160 calories in ten french fries with the 160 calories in a baked potato topped with 2 tablespoons of yogurt and chives and 55 g (2 ounces) of broccoli flowerets.

Starve yourself, cheat your baby. Missing meals now is not as hazardous as missing them when you're pregnant, but a consistently irregular eating schedule can cut into your own reserves, giving you less energy for mothering. If you're nursing, severely inadequate nutrition – such as might develop on certain fad diets – could in time seriously reduce your milk supply.

Stay an efficiency expert. To keep your postpartum weight going down and your nutrition up, it's still important to select foods dense in nutrition in relation to their calorie content – tuna fish over sausage for lunch, pasta primavera over fettuccine Alfredo for dinner. If your problem is losing too much weight, look for foods high in both nutrition and calories but low in bulk, such as avocado and nuts, but stay away from foods like popcorn that fill you up without filling you, or your nutritional requirements, out.

Carbohydrates are a complex issue. And complex carbohydrates, unrefined, are just the kind you want to concentrate on postpartum (actually for ever – for a lifetime of good nutrition for yourself and your family). Whole-grain breads, cereals and cakes, brown rice, dried beans, peas and other legumes provide fibre (as important now as during pregnancy to ensure regularity) and plenty of vitamins and minerals – most of which are absent from refined grains even when they're enriched.

Sweet nothings – nothing but trouble. The average Briton consumes about 67.5 kg (150 pounds) of sugar in its various disguises a year. Some of this comes right from the sugar bowl and is sprinkled on cereals and fruits or stirred into coffee or tea. A fair amount is taken, not unexpectedly, in cakes, biscuits, sweets, pastries and pies. But a surprising proportion comes from such unlikely sources as soups, salad dressings, breakfast cereals, breads, hot dogs, luncheon meats and processed, canned, or frozen main courses and side dishes (hidden in the form of sucrose, dextrose, honey, fructose, corn syrup and so on).

If your sugar intake is just average, you're consuming over 800 nutritionless or empty calories a day. For a new mother who wants to make sure she gets her Daily Dozen without gaining a dozen (or more) kg/ pounds in the process, an occasional sugary treat won't create nutritional havoc, but consuming a great many empty calories a day will.

Eat foods that remember where they came from. Foods that are highly processed lose a lot of their nutrition in the process and people who consume them frequently, in turn, become nutritional losers. Often processed foods also contain unhealthy excesses of saturated fat, sodium and sugar, as well as artificial colours and other chemical additives, none of which enhance the diet and the last of which can occasionally contaminate breast milk (see page 542). The closer the food you eat is to its natural state, the better for your baby – and for you.

Make good eating a family affair. Include the whole household in your Best-Odds eating and your baby will grow up in a home where good nutrition is natural. You will extend not only your child's (or children's) lifespan, but those of your husband and yourself as well.

Don't sabotage your diet. Though you can go back to a morning cup of caffeinated coffee and an occasional alcoholic beverage even if you're nursing, much more caffeine or alcohol can definitely affect you and your baby adversely, as can any amount of tobacco or illicit drug use (see page 529).

The Best-Odds Daily Dozen for Postpartum and Breastfeeding

If you're familiar with the Best-Odds Diet, you already know that you needn't sit down with a ledger, a calculator and volumes of nutritive value tables before each meal in order to be sure you're getting the nutrients you need (to produce milk and stay healthy yourself if you're breastfeeding, or just to stay healthy if you're not). All you have to do is get your Daily Dozen.[1]

Calories. You'll need enough of these to keep up your energy levels (as a new mother, you will need more energy than ever before) and, if you're nursing, your milk supply. But not so many that you won't continue to gradually lose those pregnancy kg/pounds. If you're breastfeeding, you'll need about 400 to 500 extra calories a day above what you would need to maintain your prepregnancy weight (double that if you're nursing twins, triple for triplets). You can reduce that number a little after the first six postpartum weeks if you don't seem to be losing weight, but you shouldn't cut calories drastically because your body could start producing ketones, metabolic byproducts that (by passing into your milk) could be harmful to your nursing baby.[2] In addition, melting body fat quickly releases any toxic chemicals stored in the fat into your bloodstream and then into your breast milk.

If you're not nursing, you should be able to lose that unwanted pregnancy weight and fuel your recovery by eating the approximate

number of calories you would need to maintain your prepregnancy weight.[3] After the first six weeks postpartum, when recovery is complete and dieting is safer, you can reduce that number by 200 to 500 calories a day, but don't go on a stringent diet without medical supervision.

Nursing or not, weighing yourself regularly is the best way of determining whether your calorie intake is high, low, or just right. As long as you are losing pregnancy kg/pounds gradually and stop losing once your desired weight is reached, you're on target. Adjust your calories up or down if you're not. Keep in mind, too, that it's always wiser to increase exercise than to dramatically decrease calories. If you can't brake a too rapid weight loss, see your doctor.

Protein – three servings daily if you're nursing, two if you're not. One serving equals any of the following: 2½ to 3 glasses skimmed or low-fat milk; 400 ml/14 fl ounces evaporated skimmed milk; 250 ml/8 fl ounces low-fat yogurt; 125 g/4½ ounces low-fat cottage cheese; 85g/3 ounces Swiss cheese; 2 large eggs plus two whites; 5 egg whites; 85 to 100 g/3 to 3½ ounces fish, meat, or poultry; 140 to 170 g/5 to 6 ounces tofu; 5 to 6 tablespoons peanut butter; 1 protein combination of legumes and grains (see page 352).[4] Nursing mothers of twins or triplets need an extra serving for each additional baby. Vegans, those vegetarians who eat no animal protein, should add an extra protein serving daily since the quality of vegetable protein is not as high as that of animal protein.

Vitamin C foods – two servings daily if you're nursing, at least one if you're not. One serving equals any of the following: 85 g/3 ounces strawberries; ¼ small cantaloupe; ½ grapefruit; 1 small orange; 100 to 175 ml/4 to 6 fl ounces citrus juice; ½ large kiwi, mango, or guava; 45 g/1½ ounces

---

1. Note that some foods can provide more than one Daily Dozen serving. Broccoli, for example, can provide a green leafy, a vitamin C and, in somewhat greater quantity, a calcium serving. Many dairy products provide both protein and calcium servings, and some fruits and vegetables supply both yellow or green leafy and vitamin C servings.

2. Some recent research indicates that nursing mothers, especially in later months, may need fewer than the usually quoted 400 to 500 extra calories daily. Your weight should be your guide.

3. To find out how many calories it takes to sustain your prepregnancy weight, multiply your prepregnancy weight by 12 if you're sedentary, 15 if you're moderately active, and up to 22 if you're very active.

4. The portion sizes of these combinations are for toddlers. An adult serving would be about four times as large.

broccoli or cauliflower, 75 g/2½ ounces cabbage or kale; ½ medium green pepper or ⅓ medium red pepper; 2 small tomatoes or 250 ml/8 fl ounces tomato juice.

Calcium – five servings daily if you're nursing, three plus if you're not. One serving equals any of the following: 30 g/1¼ ounces Parmesan cheese; 30 to 45 g/1¼ to 1½ ounces most other hard cheeses (such as Swiss or Cheddar); 250 ml/8 fl ounces skimmed or low-fat milk; 100 ml/4 fl ounces evaporated skimmed milk; 15 g/½ ounces dried skimmed milk; 300 g/10½ ounces low-fat cottage cheese; 100 to 125 g/3½ to 4½ ounces broccoli, collards, or kale; 3 tablespoons treacle; 115 g/4 ounces canned salmon or 85 g/3 ounces sardines, with bones; 255 g/9 ounces tofu prepared with calcium. Mothers nursing twins, triplets, or more will need an extra calcium serving for each additional baby, and may want to use calcium-enriched dairy products or calcium supplements to get their quota. Vegetarians who don't use dairy products may find it difficult to meet the requirement from purely vegetable sources unless they are fortified with calcium (orange juice, for example) and may need calcium supplements. Though lack of calcium when nursing isn't likely to affect breast milk composition, the calcium drawn from a mother's bones to produce breast milk may make her more susceptible to osteoporosis later in life.

Green leafy and yellow vegetables and yellow fruits – at least three servings daily if you're nursing, two or more, if you're not. One serving equals any of the following: 4 apricot halves; ⅛ cantaloupe; ¼ large mango; 1 large yellow (not white) peach; 55 g/2 ounces broccoli; ½ small carrot; 15 to 25 g/½ to 1 ounce cooked greens; 45 to 85 g/1½ to 3 ounces winter squash, or 20 g/¾ ounce sweet potato, or 1 tablespoon unsweetened canned pumpkin; 1 large tomato; ½ red or chilli pepper.

Other fruits and vegetables – two or more servings daily. One serving equals any of the following: 1 apple, pear, banana, or white peach; 115 g/4 ounces cherries or grapes; 115 g /4 ounces cranberries; 1 slice pineapple; 350 g/12 ounces water-melon; 5 dates; 3 figs; 45 g/1½ ounces raisins; 5 or 6 asparagus spears; 15 g/2½ ounces bean sprouts or onions; 115 g/ 4 ounces parsnip, mangetout or green peas; 1 small potato; ¼ head iceberg lettuce; 45 g/1½ ounces mushrooms or summer squash.

Whole grains and other concentrated complex carbohydrates – six or more servings daily whether you're nursing or not. One serving equals any of the following: 45 g/1½ ounces cooked brown rice, wild rice, millet, kasha (buckwheat groats), unpearled barley, bulgar, or triticale; 45 g/1½ ounces whole cornmeal (before cooking); 1 serving cooked or ready-to-eat whole-grain cereal; 2 tablespoons wheat germ; 25 g/1 ounce unprocessed bran; 1 slice wholemeal bread; ½ wholemeal bagel or English muffin; 1 small or ½ large wholemeal pitta; 2 to 6 whole-grain crackers; 2 brown rice cakes; 85 g/3 ounces lentils, beans, or split peas; 115 g/4 ounces butter beans or black-eyed peas; 25 g/1 ounce wholemeal or high-protein pasta; 45 g/1½ ounces airpopped popcorn. Vegetarians should not count a carbohydrate serving as filling both a protein and a carbohydrate requirement. Keep in mind, especially if you have trouble keeping weight on, that you can have up to 11 servings a day of grain foods.

Iron-rich foods – one or more daily. Iron is found in varying amounts in beef, blackstrap molasses, carob, chick-peas and other dried legumes, dried fruit, Jerusalem artichokes, oysters (but don't eat them raw), sardines, soyabeans and soya products, spinach, and liver.[5] It is also found in wheat germ, whole grains and cereals that are iron-fortified.

High-fat foods – small amounts daily. While an adequate fat intake was essential during pregnancy, and your body was able to handle even those foods high in choles-

---

5. Eat liver only rarely in spite of its great nutritive value because of its very high cholesterol content and because it is a storehouse for the chemicals, including questionable ones, to which an animal is exposed.

terol with impunity, it is now once again necessary for you to consider limiting fat in your diet and carefully selecting the type of fat you do consume. It is generally agreed that the average adult should get no more than 30% of his or her total calories from fat; those at high risk for heart disease should limit their intake even more rigidly. This means that if your ideal weight is 56 kg (9 stone), you need 1,875 calories daily, no more than 30% of those, or 62 grams, from fat. That's the equivalent of 4½ fat servings (at 14 grams per) a day. If you're lighter, you will need fewer servings; if you're heavier, more. You can expect that you will get roughly one serving from drips and drabs in low-fat foods. The rest can come from fatty foods. One half fat serving equals: 25 g/1 ounce of hard cheese (Swiss, Cheddar, etc.); 45 g/1½ ounces mozzarella, provolone; 2 tablespoons grated Parmesan; 1½ tablespoons single cream, pecans, peanuts, or walnuts; 2 tablespoons whipped cream; 1 tablespoon cream cheese; 250 ml/8 fl ounces whole milk or whole-milk yogurt; 100 ml/4 fl ounces regular ice cream; 170 g/6 ounces tofu; ¼ small avocado; 1 tablespoon peanut butter; 100 g/3½ ounces dark meat or 200 g/7 ounces light meat turkey or chicken (no skin); 115 g/4 ounces fatty fish (such as salmon); 9 french fries; 1 egg yolk; 2 small biscuits or 1 average muffin; 1 slice of cake or 3 biscuits (these vary with recipes). Full servings equal: 1 tablespoon olive, safflower, corn, canola, or other vegetable oils or regular mayonnaise; 15 g/½ ounce butter or margarine; 2 tablespoons regular salad dressing; 85 to 170 g/3 to 6 ounces lean meat or 25 to 45 g/1 to 1½ ounces fattier cuts; 115 g/4 ounces tuna salad.

Salty foods – limited quantities. While salt restriction wasn't necessary in pregnancy, you may need to begin limiting it now. As a rule, avoid highly salted foods such as salted peanuts, crisps and pickles. Look for low-sodium cheeses, snack foods and prepared foods. Unless someone in your family is on a sodium-restricted diet, salting lightly to taste when cooking is okay. But remember that any family food you're planning to also feed to your baby or young child should go unsalted to the table –

because infants can't handle a great deal of sodium and because exposing them to salt will help give them a taste for it.

Fluids – at least 1.8 litres/3¼ pints daily if you're nursing, 1.3 to 1.8 litres/2¼ to 3¼ pints if you're not. You will need to add 900 ml/1⅔ pints if you're nursing twins. Water (preferably fluoridated), fruit and vegetable juices, milk, soups, and seltzer are all good fluid choices. But beware of too much of a good thing: excessive fluids (more than 2.7 litres/4¾ pints a day if you're nursing one child) can inhibit breast milk production.

Vitamin supplements. Take a pregnancy/lactation formula daily if you're breastfeeding – not as a replacement for a good diet, but as insurance because nobody's diet is perfect. The supplement should contain zinc and vitamin K. If you eat no animal products (not even milk and eggs), you should also be certain your supplement contains at least 4 micrograms of vitamin B_{12} (which is found naturally only in animal foods), 0.5 milligrams of folic acid and, if you don't get at least half an hour's dose of sunshine daily, 400 milligrams of vitamin D (the amount fortifying 1.1 litres/2 pints of milk).

Even if you're not breastfeeding, you should continue taking your pregnancy vitamins for at least the first six weeks postpartum. After that, a standard multiple vitamin/mineral supplement will fill in the nutritional gaps if you find you don't always have the time or opportunity to eat as well as you'd like. A supplement designed for women in the child-bearing years will provide the extra iron needed to replace iron that might have been depleted with pregnancy and/or postpartum bleeding and will again be lost when menstruation resumes.

If You're not Breastfeeding

Though good nutrition is important for all mothers postpartum, there are some basic differences in dietary needs between bottle-feeding and breastfeeding mums that you should be aware of. For one, if you're not breastfeeding, you can't continue eating for two. (If you did, you would soon end up looking like two.) For another, because what you eat and drink will no longer have a direct effect on your baby (unless it tampers with your temperament or energy level), you'll be able to be somewhat less rigid when it comes to sugar, caffeine, diet soft drinks and alcohol. Be aware, however, that caution and moderation are still necessary. Consider the following:

- Excess sugar in the diet can cause tooth decay, obesity and/or malnourishment, and once a 'sugar high' has ended, deep lows in energy and spirit often follow.

- Excess caffeine can lead to jitteriness, emotional instability and, at doses of 10 cups of coffee or more, ringing in the ears, delirium, irregular heartbeat, muscle tension and trembling.

- Saccharin is suspected of being a weak carcinogen and though moderate intakes of aspartame (Equal, Nutrasweet) have not been shown to be hazardous, the effects of excessive amounts over long periods are as yet unknown.

- Excesses of alcohol can impair your ability to cope sanely and safely with the tasks of mothering and can aggravate postpartum depression – not to mention the potential physical and emotional damage to the entire family over the long haul. A mother who drinks more than lightly (one to two drinks daily) puts her child at risk.

- Excesses of any or all nutritionally empty foods (such as sugar) or beverages (such as wine, beer, spirits, or soft drinks) can interfere with your intake of necessary nutrients.

- Any amount of tobacco use by you can increase your child's risk of a variety of illnesses as well as deprive him or her of a parent prematurely.

- The use of any illegal drug (cocaine, marijuana, heroin, crack and so on) or the abuse of legal drugs (uppers, downers) be damaging to your relationship with your child, threaten your child's health and safety (as well as your own) and be catastrophic to any future pregnancies.

What You May Be Concerned About

Getting Everything Done

'I've been home with my new daughter for only two days and I'm already falling behind on everything: cleaning, laundry, dishes, literally everything. My once immaculate house is now a mess. I've always considered myself a competent person – till now.'

Take the responsibility of caring for a newborn baby for the first time. Days and nights that seem like one endless feeding. Add a few too many visitors. A generous helping of postpartum hormonal upheaval. Possibly, a fair amount of clutter accumulated during your stay in the hospital. And the inevitable mountain of gifts, boxes, wrapping paper and cards to keep track of.

It's only natural to feel that as your new life with your baby is beginning, your old life – with its order and cleanliness – is crumbling around you.

Don't despair. Your inability to keep up with both baby and house during the first days at home in no way predicts your future success at mothering. (You can't, after all, judge an inexperienced employee's future performance on the basis of her first two days at a demanding new job.) Things are bound to get better as you regain your strength, become familiar with the basic baby-care tasks and learn to be a little less rigid. It will also help to:

Get hold of yourself. Dwelling anxiously on what you have to do makes facing it twice as difficult. Relax. Focus on what's really important: getting to know and enjoy your newborn. Banish thoughts of household chores while you're with her (relaxation techniques learned in childbirth class may help you to do this). When you look around you later on, the clutter and chaos will still be there, but you'll be better able to deal with it.

Get rest. Paradoxically, the best way to start getting things done is to start getting more rest. Give yourself a chance to recuperate fully from childbirth and you will be better able to tackle your new responsibilities.

Get help. If you haven't already arranged for household help – paid or unpaid – and taken steps to streamline housekeeping and cooking chores, now's the time to do so (see page 16). If necessary, remind your spouse that yours is a two-parent home (but gently, especially if he's not yet used to the idea; see page 533). Think of ways that he (or someone else you can rely on) can help ease your load – by calling you before leaving work in the evening for a list of last-minute items to pick up at the store, or dropping off the drycleaning on the way to work, or vacuuming and/or picking up where needed while you give the baby the last feeding of the evening (waking in the morning to at least a semblance of neatness can give your spirits a real boost).

Get your priorities straight. What's most important? The condition of your house or your new baby? Is it more important to get the vacuuming done while baby's napping or to put your feet up and relax so you can be refreshed when she awakens? Is it really essential to touch up those wash-and-wear shirts, or would taking the baby out for a walk in the pram be a better use of your time? Keep in mind that doing too much too soon can rob you of the energy to accomplish anything well, and that while your house will someday be clean again, your baby will never be two days (or two weeks, or two months) old again.

Get organized. Lists are a new mother's best friend. First thing every morning, while you're nursing (if you can manage it) or while your husband is giving baby her bottle or playing with her, jot down a list of what needs to be done. Divide your priorities into three categories: chores that must be taken care of as soon as possible, those that can wait until later in the day, and those that can be put off until tomorrow – or next week, or indefinitely. Assign approximate times to each activity, taking into account your personal biological clock (are you useless first thing in the morning, or do you do your best work at the crack of dawn?) as well as your baby's (as best as you can determine it at this point).

Though organizing your day on paper doesn't always mean that everything will get done on schedule (in fact, for new mothers it rarely does), it will give you a sense of control over what may now seem like a largely uncontrollable situation; plans on paper are always more manageable than plans whirling frenetically through your head. You may even find, once you've made your list, that you actually have less to do than you'd thought. Don't forget to cross off completed tasks for a satisfying feeling of accomplishment. And don't worry about what's not crossed off – just move those items to the next day's list.

Another good organizational trick of the new mother trade: keep a running list of baby gifts and their givers as they're received. You think you'll remember that Cousin Doris sent that darling blue-and-yellow sweater set, but after the seventeenth sweater set has arrived, that memory may be dimmed. And check off each as the thank-you is sent so you don't have to ponder, 'Did I or didn't I thank Aunt Jane?'

Get simplified. Use a one-step product on the kitchen floor, paper plates at the dinner table, frozen vegetables instead of fresh; order in pizza one night, pick up a selection from the local salad bar the next; take whatever steps are practical to cut down the time it takes to do necessary chores. Keep supplies and equipment close to where you will be using them to reduce the number of trips you have to make from room to room. Pack away for now knick-knacks and other items that take special care (they'll have to go once baby begins to crawl, anyway).

Get a jump on tomorrow tonight. Once you've bedded baby down each night, and before you collapse onto the sofa for that well-deserved rest, summon up the strength to take care of a few chores so that you'll have a head start on the next morning. Restock the nappy bag. Prepare formula and fill the bottles. Measure out the coffee for the coffee pot. Sort the laundry. Lay out clothes for yourself and the baby. In ten minutes or so, you'll accomplish what would take you three times as long – at least – with baby awake. And you'll be able to sleep better (when she lets you) knowing that you'll have less to do in the morning.

Get good at doubling up. Learn to do two things at once. Wash the dishes or grate carrots for the meat loaf while you're on the phone. Balance your chequebook or fold the laundry while you catch the news on TV. Read a book or tell an older child a story while you nurse a sleepy baby (an alert one needs more attention). There still won't be enough hours in the day, but this way you may only crave 36 instead of 48.

Get out. Unless the weather's inclement, plan an outing every day. This won't help you get the dusting done or the floors washed, but it will make these tasks seem less urgent.

Get to expect the unexpected. The best laid plans of mothers often (actually *very* often) go astray. Baby's all bundled up for an outing, the nappy bag is ready, your coat is on, and suddenly the distinct gurglings of a bowel movement can be heard from under all baby's gear. Off comes coat, bunting, nappy – ten minutes lost and a tight schedule is knocked totally out of kilter. To allow for such unexpected turns of events, build extra time into your daily schedules.

Get the joke. If you can laugh at your predicament, you're less likely to cry. So keep your sense of humour – even in the face of total disorder and utter clutter. Not only will this help you to keep your sanity, it will save your child from being one of those adults who looks back on a childhood where nobody smiled – because everyone was too busy maintaining order.

Get used to it. Living with a baby means living with a certain amount of mayhem most of the time. And as baby grows, so will the difficulty of keeping the mayhem in check. No sooner will you scoop the blocks back into their canister than she will dump them back out again. As fast as you can wipe mashed peas off the wall behind her high chair, she can redecorate with strained peaches. You'll put safety latches on the kitchen cabinets, and she'll figure out how to open them, covering the linoleum with your pots and pans.

And remember, when you finally pack your last child off to college, your house will be immaculate once again – and so lonely that you'll be ready to welcome the pandemonium they bring home on holidays.

Not Being in Control

'For the last ten years I've run my business, my household and every other aspect of my life quite effectively. But ever since I came home with my little boy I can't seem to get control of anything.'

There's been a coup in your home – as there is in the homes of all new parents. And the man who would be king in your castle isn't a man at all, but a newborn baby boy. As powerless as he may seem, he is quite capable of disrupting your life and usurping the control you once had over it. He won't care if you customarily take your shower at 7:15 and your coffee at 8:05, if you favour a leisurely cocktail at 6:30 and dinner promptly at 7:00, if you enjoy dancing into the wee hours on Saturday night and sleeping luxuriously late the morning after. He'll demand feedings and attention when he wants them, without first checking your schedule to see if it's convenient. Which means your routine and many of your old, comfortable ways may have to be abandoned for several months, if not several years. The only schedule that will matter, particularly in these early weeks, is his. And that schedule, at first, may have no discernible pattern you can latch on. Days, and especially nights, may pass a blur. You may often feel more like an automaton (and if you're nursing, a milk cow) than a person, more servant than master, wielding not the slightest measure of power over your life.

What to do? Hand the sceptre over graciously – at least for now. With the passage of time, as you grow more competent, confident and comfortable in your new role, and as your baby becomes more capable and less dependent, you will regain some of the control you've lost. Don't, however, expect to regain absolute power.

You might as well accept the fact that your life will never be quite the same, but then, would you really want it to be?

Regaining your Figure

'I knew I wouldn't be ready for a bikini right after delivery, but I still look six months pregnant a week later.'

Though childbirth produces more rapid initial weight loss than the Scarsdale, Stillman and Mayo Clinic diets combined (an average of 5,400 g/12 pounds at delivery), few women are satisfied with the results. Particularly after they catch a glimpse of their postpartum silhouettes in a mirror and see that they still look distressingly pregnant. The good news is that most are able to pack away their pregnancy jeans within the month. The bad news: the old jeans may not fit the way they used to for a while longer.

How quickly you return to your prepregnant shape and weight will depend on how many kg and cm/pounds and inches

you put on during pregnancy – and where they settled. Women who gained between 9,000 and 13,500 g/20 and 30 pounds on a good diet and at a gradual and steady pace may be able to shed it all, without dieting, by the end of the second month or so. On the other hand, those who overindulged and gained more than was necessary to produce a healthy, good-size baby – particularly if the weight was gained in uneven spurts on junk food – may find the return to postpartum shape more challenging.

No matter what your weight gain, sticking to the Best-Odds Postpartum and Breastfeeding Diet now should lead to slow, steady weight loss – with no loss of energy. Non-nursers can, once the six-week postpartum recovery period has passed, go on a sensible, well-balanced reducing diet with exercise to drop whatever weight remains. Nursing mothers who aren't losing weight can reduce calorie intake by a couple of hundred a day and increase activity to encourage weight loss without cutting into milk production. They will usually take off any remaining excess poundage when they wean their babies.[6]

But there are several reasons for that postpartum pregnant look that have nothing to do with weight gain. One is 2,300 g (5 pounds) or so leftover fluids, which will bloat your belly for the first few days after delivery but will flush out naturally, on their own, within the week. Another is the still-enlarged uterus, which continues to give the abdomen a pregnant appearance until it is finally reduced to prepregnancy size and has slipped back into the pelvis, usually by the end of the sixth postpartum week. But the major and most persistent reason most women continue to look a little pregnant well after delivery is stretched out abdominal muscles and skin. For most women, even after weight loss is accomplished, returning the abdomen to prepregnancy tone will require more than waiting for time and nature to take their

---

6. A nursing mother should never reduce her caloric intake drastically, however, since excessive burning of her own body fat could result in the release of ketones (byproducts of fat metabolism) and of toxic chemicals or drugs stored in the fat into her milk, which could be harmful to her baby.

course. In fact, it will sag for a lifetime unless a concerted exercise effort is made (see Getting Back into Shape on page 516).

There are, alas, some body changes that will stay with you no matter how many sit-ups and leg lifts you do and how carefully you monitor your diet – though you may not even be aware of them. Most common is a change in body configuration due to the loosening of the joints during pregnancy (to facilitate delivery) and their tightening up again postpartum. The changes may be either imperceptible or significant enough to increase a shoe or dress size. Women who have had caesarean sections may also note a slight alteration in the shape of the abdomen that won't yield to exercise.

Sharing Baby Care

'I feel guilty asking my husband for help with our new baby, especially at night – after all, he works all day and has to get up early in the morning. Yet I'm exhausted handling her all by myself.'

There's no more demanding job than the one you now hold; you'll need and deserve all the help you can get from your partner-in-parenthood. Having a job outside the home – even a particularly gruelling one – doesn't automatically exempt a man from taking on work inside the home, especially when that work is created by the arrival of a new baby that's half his doing. And when you're tempted to feel guilty about asking for help, remind yourself that you've been working all day, too, at a job that is almost undoubtedly more tiring and stressful (as much because of the newness as the nature of the work) than your mate's. And unless he's a professional baby nurse, helping you out with baby care will be a refreshing and satisfying break from the demands of his day, rather than an exhausting and tedious extension of them. And even if he is a professional baby nurse – or a paediatrician, or a school teacher, or if he works with little ones in some other capacity –

taking care of his own child will still be uniquely rewarding.

Of course, you may have to do some persuading to gain his full cooperation, and some initial labour negotiations may have to take place to work out a baby-and-housecare programme that is mutually acceptable. Ideally it is one that takes some of the burden off you without placing too much on him. (The initial deal can be renegotiated should you return to work.) Begin with these steps:

Speak up. Perhaps your husband isn't even aware that you need his help – maybe you're working too hard at making it look effortless. Or that you want his help – maybe he's got the impression you'd rather do it yourself, or that you think he's not competent to care for a baby. Sit down with him at a quiet time, when the baby's asleep and you're both fairly relaxed, and explain your needs calmly and rationally. You might find that your doing all the baby care is bothering him as much as it is you.

Teach him a thing or two. If lack of confidence and experience are keeping your husband from trying his hand at baby care, he will benefit from a few lessons. First demonstrate, then talk him through, several nappy changes. Have him observe and assist at bath time and in dressing the baby. Teach him a basic lullaby and share your most successful rocking technique with him (but remember, daddies generally hold babies differently than mummies do, and his own method may be even more successful than yours). Be a patient instructor and don't give up (or let him give up) if he takes ten minutes to change his first dirty nappy, if baby comes out of the first bath still soapy, or if he puts her dress on back-to-front. Keep in mind (and remind him) that fathers (like mothers) are made, not born, and that he has the innate capacity for mastering the fine art of baby care. At first, it may seem easier to change a nappy yourself than to watch him struggle through it. But eventually your efforts will pay off – as he becomes a thoroughly capable parenting partner.

Leave him alone. That is, with the baby. Occasionally devise (deviously, if need be) reasons why daddy and baby must be left alone together. Start with short periods of time – say fifteen or twenty minutes – and build up from there. Forced to perform in a sink-or-swim situation, most new fathers surprise themselves and their partners by staying afloat. This will build his self-confidence and give him a chance to get to know the baby, which will in turn make him feel better disposed towards helping out.

Overlook his mistakes. Unless something he's doing might endanger the baby (throwing her up in the air, for instance), don't be quick to comment on your husband's flubs. He's more likely to learn from his own mistakes (or your good example) than from your criticism. When you do need to show him the error of his ways, do so gently, to avoid undermining his self-confidence and creating hostility. And be ready to learn from him.

Set up a standard operating policy. For some people, drawing up and keeping to a schedule (Monday, Wednesday and Friday nights you change the nappies and he gives the bath, Tuesday and Thursday nights you bathe, he changes, nappies and so on) is the only way to ensure all the jobs will get done and the work will be divided fairly. For others, particularly those who see no need to keep score, divvying up responsibilities as they come along 'Could you change her nappy while I finish the dishes?') is a workable system. For still others, assigning duties according to personal strengths works best. If your husband's a four-star chef but you burn water, let him take over the kitchen. If baby seems to think dad's got more rhythm than you, let him do the rocking. But if he's hopelessly inept at holding a squirming, wet baby – even after repeated practice – you take over the bath chore.

Share the nights. Even if you're nursing, there's no reason why your husband should sleep through every night when you and baby don't. There's more to the middle-of-the-night routine than feeding. Dad can pick baby up, change her nappy if that's necessary, then bring her to bed for you to breastfeed. Depending on who's got more strength, either of you can return the little darling to her cot or cradle when feeding is done. But baby will probably be less likely to waken if the deed is done by dad, since the closeness of your breasts might prompt her to ask for seconds. If you're bottle feeding, either partially or totally, nighttime feedings can be divided between the two of you according to a mutually agreeable schedule. Maybe he takes all the feedings before 2 A.M. and you take all that follow. Or you alternate nights.

In spite of the best of intentions and the greatest goodwill, you may still end up doing the lioness' share of the child-rearing work. Many men, even if they believe intellectually in equality of the sexes (and especially if they don't) and were eager to participate in labour and delivery (and especially if they weren't), are just not ready to accept a full share of child-care tasks. Some may equate being a good father with being a good provider and feel that they are more than pulling their weight in the family by working longer hours. Others, because they have no role models on which to build (they were fatherless, or their own fathers steered clear of child-rearing duties), are uncomfortable and uncertain when confronted with parenting responsibilities. Old attitudes die hard.

If your husband, for whatever reason, fails to share the load with you, try to understand why this is so and to communicate clearly where you stand. Don't expect him to change overnight, and don't let your resentment when he doesn't trigger arguments and stress. Instead explain, educate, entice; in time, he'll meet you – partway, if not all the way.

Depression

'I have everything I've always wanted: a wonderful husband, a beautiful new baby girl – why do I feel so miserable?'

Roughly one-half (some estimates go as high as 90%) of all new mothers ask the same question, complaining of weepiness, unhappiness, anxiety and mood swings during the first week or so after delivery. This bout of 'baby blues' is probably related to the precipitous drop in oestrogen and progesterone after childbirth, and usually clears up within a few days, though some women find it comes and goes over the first six weeks.

Less common (it probably affects 25% of first-time mothers and 20% in subsequent pregnancies) and longer lasting (it often begins during the first six weeks and can persist for months) is true postpartum depression. Hormone variations offer one explanation for this depression. The fact that sensitivity to hormonal fluctuations varies from woman to woman is believed to explain, at least partially, why it is that although all women experience the same shift in hormonal levels after delivery, not all suffer mood changes. Depression can also be triggered by the hormonal changes related to weaning.

But there are a host of other factors that are believed to contribute to postpartum depression. Some of these non-hormonal factors may explain why fathers and adoptive mothers, who have no postpartum hormone changes to blame, are also subject to such depression:

The end of the pregnancy. For women who passed the nine months in relative misery – with morning sickness, varicose veins, backaches and indigestion – the end of pregnancy is something to celebrate. But if you thoroughly enjoyed pregnancy, its conclusion may be something to mourn, particularly if more children are not on your agenda. You may feel a sense of loss and emptiness, and miss the uniquely intimate sensation of carrying your baby inside you. You may even regret the disappearance of your bulging belly, to which you'd grown fondly accustomed.

A feeling of anticlimax. Childbirth – the big event you'd trained for and anticipated for so long – is over.

The shift from centre stage to backstage. Your baby is now the star of the show. Visitors flock to admire the baby at your bedside rather than enquiring after your health. Your husband, who may have kept you on a pedestal for nine months, may now be so busy doting on his newborn child that, however unintentionally, he ends up ignoring you when you need his adoration most. With a wave of the obstetrician's wand, you've done a reverse Cinderella – the pregnant princess has become the postpartum peasant. This change in status will accompany you home. When you go out with the baby now, people may be less quick to offer assistance – as you struggle to fold a pushchair, juggle a baby and a nappy bag, and hail a taxi – than when you were pregnant and were carrying the baby almost effortlessly inside of you. Strangers won't glance at your tummy and beam any more, friends won't comment on your radiance; all eyes will be on the baby and all compliments and smiles directed at her.

Hospitalization. Eager to get home and begin mothering, you may be frustrated by the lack of control you have over your life and your baby's in the hospital, and a prolonged stay may compound your frustration. If this is not your first baby, you may miss your older child or children, feel guilty about being away from them, and worry about how they're doing – particularly if this is the first time you've been separated.

Going home. It's not unusual to feel overwhelmed and overworked by the responsibilities that greet you ('What do I do first?'), especially if you have no help and if dishes, dust and dirty clothes have been allowed to pile up while you've been away. Returning to a house that's now crowded with baby things (your home has been taken over by this tiny invader) may also be unsettling.

Disappointment. In your newborn: she is so small, so red, so puffy, so unresponsive – not the cuddly, all-smiles model baby you pictured. About the birth and/or in yourself:

if unrealistic expectations of an idealized childbirth experience weren't realized, you may feel (unnecessarily) that you're a failure. About motherhood: it isn't at all what you expected, and the letdown is depressing.

Exhaustion. Fatigue following childbirth, compounded by the rigours of caring for a newborn, can make you feel unable to meet the multiple challenges you face.

Lack of sleep. People deprived of sleep, whether they are airline pilots, prisoners of war, or doctors in training, can experience severe mood changes. New mothers are no exception.

Physical discomfort or pain. Your episiotomy or caesarean incision burns, your breasts are uncomfortably engorged, your haemorrhoids are excruciating and those afterpains are a pain. It's not easy to be cheerful when you hurt so much.

Feelings of inadequacy. Virtually every new mother doubts her ability to handle the role. If you're a total novice, you may wonder 'Why did I have a baby if I can't take care of it?' If you're a veteran who had reached the point of handling one child with aplomb but are now overwhelmed by two, you may wonder 'Why did I have another?' If you seem to get less respect in the role of mother than you did when you held a paying job, you may feel like less of a person. And it's disheartening not to feel good about yourself.

Feelings of guilt. Maybe you really didn't want this baby when you became pregnant, and even though you do now, you feel guilty. Or you feel guilty about not loving her at first sight, or not thinking she's beautiful, or not enjoying the tedium of motherhood. Or about having to go back to work in the near future, or not bringing in income if you're planning to stay home. Guilt, no matter what the cause, can be very depressing.

Mourning for the old you. Your carefree, possibly career-oriented self has passed (at least temporarily) with your baby's birth. So has your self-and/or couple-oriented way of life – time-consuming hobbies, frequent dining out, classes, or movies may realistically have to take a back burner for a while.

Unhappiness over your appearance. Before you were fat and pregnant; now, to your over-critical eyes, you're just plain fat. You can't stand wearing maternity clothes any more, but nothing else fits.

Lack of support. If you don't have enough support – from family and friends, but especially from your spouse – facing the job of new mother may be overwhelming and depressing.

Nonbaby-related stress. Problems – family, job, financial – that aren't related to your new baby can nevertheless induce postpartum depression.

Though there's no sure cure for postpartum depression other than the passage of time, there are ways of minimizing it (some doctors are using gradually decreasing doses of hormones successfully) and of fading those baby blues:

- If the blues arrive at the hospital, ask your husband to bring in a romantic dinner for two; limit visitors if their chattering grates on your nerves, invite more of them if they cheer you up. If it's the hospital environment that's getting you down, enquire about early discharge (see page 512).

- Fight fatigue by accepting help from others, by being less compulsive about doing things now that can wait until later, and by trying to grab a nap or rest period when your baby is napping. Use baby feeding times as your rest periods – nurse or bottle feed in bed or in a comfortable chair with your feet up.

- Follow the Best-Odds Nursing or Postpartum Diet (page 524) to keep your strength up. Avoid sugar (especially in combination with chocolate), which can act as a depressant in some people.

- If you enjoy a drink, unwind with your husband over a cocktail during the baby's dinner hour or enjoy a glass of wine during your own, but be careful not to overdo – even moderate amounts of alcohol can exacerbate your depression and, if you're nursing, intoxicate your baby.

- Treat yourselves to dinner out, if possible. If not, make believe. Order dinner in (or maybe your husband will cook), dress up, create a five-star-restaurant ambience with candlelight and soft music. And keep your sense of humour handy, in case baby decides to interrupt your romantic interlude.

- Communicate to your husband any feelings of under-appreciation you may be experiencing. He may not realize that you need him as much as the baby does.

- Ask for help with the house, the baby, other children – from your husband, your mother, your neighbours, your friends, or whoever's willing, able and available. If you can't get all the help you need for free, and if you can afford it, consider hiring someone (a teenager, an elderly neighbour) to free you up for an hour or two a day – so you can freshen up, take a bath or a nap, prepare dinner, or do whatever else you need to do.

- If your problem is coping with the new baby plus a toddler, or more – the depression usually increases geometrically with each baby – see the tips in Chapter 26.

- Look your best so you'll feel your best. Walking around, hair unkempt, in a robe all day would depress anyone. Shower before your husband leaves in the morning (you may not get a chance later); comb your hair; put on makeup if you ordinarily wear it.

- Get out of the house. Meet a friend for lunch, window shop, traipse through a museum – with the baby, or if you can enlist a volunteer to stay home with her, without.

- Get active. Exercise can help chase away the baby blues and, at the same time, get rid of any postpartum flab that might be compounding your depression. (See page 525.)

- Make some time for yourself. Set aside half an hour or so a day just for you and pretend you're a lady of leisure. While your baby naps or someone else watches her, read the newspaper (unless current events depress you), make a dent in that novel, watch a video movie, do an exercise routine, catch up on your letter writing, pamper yourself with a facial, a manicure, or a bubble bath.

- If you think your misery might like some company, get together with any new mothers you know and compare frustrations. If you don't know any, find some. Ask your doctor for names of new mothers in your neighbourhood and start a new-mothers group. Contact women who were in your childbirth class and organize a weekly reunion. Take a postpartum exercise or parenting class (most welcome babies).

- If yours is the kind of misery that wants to be alone, indulge in some solitude. Through ordinary depression generally feeds on itself, some experts believe that this is not true of the postpartum variety. If spending time with cheerful people only makes your mood worse, avoid socializing for a while. Don't, however, leave your husband out in the cold. Husbands, too, are susceptible to postpartum depression, and yours may need your support as much as you need his.

- *Seek professional help immediately* if your depression persists for more than one week and is accompanied by sleeplessness (you can't sleep even when the baby does); lack of appetite; loss of interest in yourself and your family; a feeling of hopelessness, helplessness, and lack of control; suicidal urges; the wish that the baby were gone or had never come; thoughts of harming the baby; other weird thoughts or fears, hallucinations or delusions.

At least 10% of all new mothers in the U.K. suffer from some form of postnatal depression – and numbers outside of those who actually seek counselling are thought to be higher. On the chance that you could be one of them, get a professional diagnosis in a hurry if you have the symptoms of severe depression described here. Don't allow yourself to be put off by 'Oh, it's the baby blues – you'll get over it' or 'Just buck up and you'll be fine'. Prolonged maternal depression can interfere with mother-child bonding and interaction, and is often detrimental to an infant.

If you are unsure of where to turn, ask your obstetrician, nurse-midwife, family doctor, cleric, or a friend who has had a good counselling experience to refer you, or call a community mental health centre. Contact a postpartum depression support group if there's one in your community, or find out about starting one.[7] If you see a non-medical therapist, you should also have a medical doctor involved in your treatment, because postpartum depression has a hormonal component.

If at any time you feel a strong urge to hurt your baby, whether you think you're depressed or not, go immediately to a neighbour's house, call a doctor (yours or your baby's) or someone who can get to where you are in a hurry (a friend, your husband, your mother), or dial 999. You can be helped.

'I feel terrific, and have since the moment I delivered three weeks ago. Is all this good feeling leading up to one terrific case of the blues?'

Unfortunately, feeling good isn't nearly as newsworthy as feeling bad. You'll find no

shortage of coverage in magazines, newspapers, or books of the roughly 50% of newly delivered women who are affected to some degree by postpartum depression; but you'll see little or nothing written about the other 50% who aren't, and who feel terrific after giving birth.

Baby blues are common, but they're by no means inevitable. And there's no reason to believe that if you've been feeling buoyant, you're in for an emotional dunking. Since most cases of postpartum depression occur within the first week after birth, the odds are pretty good that you've escaped them. If you'd like to improve the odds even further, see the tips for fading those baby blues (page 536). They can prevent as well as cure.

Some women have mild mood swings postpartum as they did during pregnancy – they feel overwhelmed and inadequate one day (baby didn't sleep at all, spit up all over a new blouse, and leaked a bowel movement on the sofa), euphoric and competent the next (baby took three three-hour naps, got rave reviews in the supermarket and smiled a first smile). Such mood swings are both normal and temporary.

Very occasionally a woman does develop a delayed case of postpartum blues, sometimes at the time of weaning her baby from the breast. Anyone who at any time develops the symptoms of severe depression described on page 537 should seek immediate professional help.

Feeling Inadequate

'I really thought I could handle it. But the moment our little boy was handed to me, all my confidence dissolved. I feel as though I'm a total flop as a mother.'

Though the ultimate rewards of motherhood are greater than those of any other occupation, the stresses and challenges are greater, too – particularly at the beginning. After all, there's no other job in the world that thrusts you, without previous training

---

7. For information, contact: The Association for Postnatal Illness, 25 Jerdan Place, London SW6 1BE; (0171) 386–0868.

or experience and without supervisory guidance, into fully responsible eighteen-to twenty-hour shifts. What's more, there's no other job that offers as little feedback during the first weeks to let you know how you're doing. The only person who could possibly give you a job evaluation is a largely unresponsive, unpredictable and uncooperative newborn who doesn't smile when he's satisfied, doesn't hug you when he's grateful, sleeps when he should be eating, cries when he should be sleeping, hardly even looks at you for more than a couple of minutes and doesn't seem to know you from the next-door neighbour. A sense of satisfaction in a job completed seems totally absent. Virtually every job you do – changing nappies, making formula, washing baby clothes, feeding baby – is quickly undone and/or needs redoing almost immediately. It's not surprising that you feel like a failure at your new profession.

Even for a seasoned pro the postpartum period is no picnic; for a novice, it can seem like a never-ending series of blunders, bumbles, mishaps and misadventures. And yet there are better times in sight (though you may have trouble envisioning them); competence at mothering is closer than you'd now imagine. In the meantime, keep these points in mind:

You're unique. And so is your baby. What works for another mother and baby may not work for you, and vice versa. Avoid making comparisons.

You're not the only one. More first-time mothers than ever before have had no previous experience with newborns. And even among those who've had some, very few manage to glide through those first weeks as though they'd been doing it all their lives. Remember, mothers are not born, they are made on the job. Hormones do not magically transform newly delivered women into able mothers; time, trial and error and experience do. If you have the opportunity of sharing your worries with other new mothers, you will be reminded

that though you are unique, your concerns as a new mother aren't.

You need to be babied. In order to be an effective mother, you've got to baby yourself a little. Tell yourself, as your own mother would, that you need to eat right and get enough rest, particularly in the postpartum period, and that moderate exercise to keep your energy level up and a bit of relaxation now and then to elevate your spirits are important, too.

You're both only human. You shouldn't expect or demand perfection from either yourself or your baby – now, or at any point in your relationship.

Your instincts can be trusted. Give them a chance instead of self-doubting them away. In many cases, even the greenest mother knows more about what's right for her baby than more experienced friends and relatives or baby books.

You needn't go it alone. While you should trust your own instincts and shouldn't make comparisons, there's a lot of good advice and comforting support out there you can benefit from. Seeking it from grandmothers, sisters, or friends, or in books or magazines doesn't brand you as incompetent, but as open-minded and willing to learn. Judiciously sift through information acquired from others, test out what seems right for you and your baby, discard what doesn't.

Your mistakes can help you grow, and they won't count against you. Nobody's going to fire you (though on a particularly bad day you may wish that you could quit) if you make mistakes. Mistakes are an important part of learning to be a mother. You can expect to continue making them at least until your children are off to college. And if at first you don't succeed, just try, try something else (the baby only screams louder when you rock him in your arms side to side, so try holding him over your shoulder and swaying back and forth).

Your love won't always come easy. It's sometimes difficult to relate lovingly to a newborn – a basically unresponsive creature who takes greedily but doesn't offer much in return (except dirty nappies). And it may be some time before you stop feeling like a fool, babbling in baby talk and crooning off-key lullabies, and before you can hug and kiss this tiny bundle naturally and unselfconsciously. (See page 158 for tips on talking to baby.)

Your baby is forgiving. Forget to change his nappy before a feeding. Let soap drip into his eye during his shampoo. Get a turtleneck stuck halfway over his head. Your baby will forgive and forget these and a multitude of other minor sins – as long as he gets the message that you love him loud and clear. If he does, he will even forgive you when you're too frazzled to smile at him or when you let him cry for an extra few minutes because you're in the lavatory or a pot is boiling over on the stove.

The ultimate rewards are fantastic. Think of motherhood as a long-term project, with results that will be unfolding in the months and years ahead. When you see your baby's first smile, watch him reach for a toy, laugh out loud, pull himself up, say 'Mummy, I love you', you will know that you've done a good job, that you have indeed accomplished something very special.

Visitors

'I feel like a real heel, but I'm tired of the steady stream of visitors at our door since our son was born.'

Short of hanging a 'quarantine' or 'gone fishing' sign on your front door, there's little you can do to keep your baby's admirers away entirely. There's no more powerful magnet to friends, family and neighbours, after all, than a newborn. But there are ways of minimizing the number of visits, and of making those that are unavoidable less burdensome:

- Limit visitors the first week or two to immediate family and close friends. You can put the blame on 'doctor's orders', since most agree that visitors should be limited during the first few postpartum weeks.

- Buy or borrow a telephone answering machine and tape a message that gives all the pertinent baby data to callers – date of birth, weight, name – as well as the information that visitors are limited. Return the calls at your convenience, inviting close friends and family to visit at specific times.

- Ask visitors to call ahead; don't be afraid to say that a suggested stop-in time is not convenient, but do propose an alternative when possible.

- Be the hostess with the leastest, for now. Put a bowl of fruit on the coffee table and some paper cups next to the kitchen sink if that makes you feel any better, but don't offer more elaborate refreshments – save your energy for feeding the baby.

- Don't be shy about letting guests know when they've overstayed their welcome. A not so subtle hint, such as 'I've got to grab a nap while baby's napping', should get the point across. Of course, for those who don't take hints, there's nothing wrong with a candid request to leave.

- Consider 'showing' your baby at a single event – perhaps a baptism, a ritual circumcision, a baby naming, or a welcome-baby party – and let friends know they will have a chance to see him then. Get grandmother or other relatives or close friends to help set up the party so that you won't overwork. Keep it simple (unless you can afford a catered affair), sticking to a limited menu of cheese, crackers and wine, or coffee, tea and cake.

Whatever you do, don't feel guilty because you aren't eager for visitors. You are going through a very complex adjustment period and you have a right to want – and to have – some peace, quiet, and privacy.

Doing Things Right

'I'm so worried that I'm going to make a wrong move that I spend hours researching every little decision I make about my baby. I want to make sure I do everything right for her, but I'm driving myself and my husband crazy.'

No one can do *everything* right – not even a mother. We all make mistakes – mostly little ones, occasionally bigger ones – in raising our children and most of the time they make it to adulthood just fine. (In fact, it's through making a few mistakes and learning from them that we become more effective parents.) In addition, it's not always possible to know what's 'right' in a particular situation; what's right for one mother and baby may in some cases be wrong for another.[8]

Even reading all the literature and consulting experts won't always give you all the answers. Getting to know your baby and yourself, and learning to trust your instincts and good sense, is often a better route to making decisions you both can live with. It's true, for example, that some babies love to be snugly swaddled, but if yours cries whenever she's wrapped up tightly in a receiving blanket, consider that she would rather be free to kick up her heels. And the experts may tell you young babies like to listen to high-pitched sounds, but if yours clearly responds more positively to a deep voice, come down an octave. Trust yourself and your baby – you may not always be right, but you won't go too far wrong.

---

8. There are exceptions, however. In matters of safety, for example. It is *always* right to strap an infant in a car seat, even for short rides, and *always* right to keep poisonous substances locked out of a baby's reach. And in matters of health, no medical decision should be made without consultation with your baby's doctor.

Postpartum Tub Baths

'I seem to be getting a lot of contradictory advice about whether or not tub baths are safe in the postpartum period. Are they?'

At one time new mothers weren't permitted to set foot in a tub until at least one month after delivery because it was believed that bacteria from the bath water would cause postpartum infection. Today, it's known that still bath water does not enter the vagina, and infection from bathing is no longer considered a threat. Some doctors, in fact, recommend tub baths in the hospital (when available) on the theory that bathing removes lochia from the perineum and from between the folds of the labia more efficiently than showering. In addition, the warm water is comforting to the sore episiotomy site, relieves swelling in the area and soothes haemorrhoids.

Still, your doctor may prefer that you hold off on bathing at least until you go home, sometimes even later. If you're eager to bathe (which may be especially true if you have no shower at home), discuss the question with him or her; you may be able to get a dispensation. If you do bathe during the first week or two following delivery, be sure the tub is well scrubbed before its filled. (But be sure you're not the one who does the scrubbing.) And get help getting into and out of the tub during the first few postpartum days, when you still may be shaky. Whether you are using the shower or tub, be certain to always use a clean flannel and towel, washing your breasts nipples first (with water only), and then the perineum (with mild soap and water), before going on to the rest of you. Don't be afraid of opening any stitches as you wash; you won't.

Time Spent Breastfeeding

'Why didn't somebody tell me I'd be nursing my baby 24 hours a day?'

Maybe because you wouldn't have believed it. Or because nobody wanted to discourage you. Either way, now you know. Nursing is; for many mothers, a nearly round-the-clock job in the early weeks. But take heart; as time passes, you'll spend less of it as a captive of your baby's eager sucking. As breastfeeding becomes solidly established, the number of feedings will begin to tail off. By the time your baby's sleeping through the night, you'll probably be down to five or six feedings, taking a total of only three or four hours out of your day.

In the meantime, put everything else that's clamouring to be done out of your mind; relax and savour these special moments that only you can share with your baby. Make double use of them by keeping a baby journal, reading a book, or scheduling your day on paper. Chances are that once your baby is weaned, you'll look back and think how much you miss nursing.

Contamination of Breast Milk

'Does everything I eat or drink get into my breast milk? Could any of it harm my daughter?'

Feeding your baby outside the womb doesn't require quite the degree of careful monitoring of your own diet that feeding her inside the womb did. But for as long as you're breastfeeding, a certain amount of restraint is needed in what goes into you in order to ensure that everything that goes into your baby is safe.

The basic fat-protein-carbohydrate composition of human milk isn't dependent on what a mother eats. If a mother doesn't consume enough calories and protein to produce milk, her body will tap its own stores for milk production until the stores are depleted. Certain vitamin deficiencies in a mother's diet, however, can alter the vitamin content of her breast milk. So can excesses of certain vitamins. A wide variety of substances, from seasonings to medications, can also show up in breast milk, with varying implications for the newborn.

To keep breast milk safe and healthy, and up to your baby's taste specifications:

- Follow the Best-Odds Nursing Diet (page 526).

- Avoid foods to which your baby seems sensitive. Garlic, onions, cabbage and chocolate are common offenders, provoking bothersome wind in some, though by no means all, babies. Some, particularly those with very discriminating palates, will simply reject the breast after you've eaten a food that imparts a strong or unfamiliar flavour to their accustomed beverage.

- Take a vitamin supplement especially formulated for pregnant and/or lactating mothers. With the exception of vitamin C, which appears to enter the breast milk in only tiny amounts, *do not* take any other vitamins without the advice of your doctor.

- Do not smoke. Many of the toxic substances in tobacco enter the bloodstream, and eventually your milk. Though the long-term effects of these poisons on your baby aren't known for sure, one can safely speculate that they aren't positive. On top of that, it is known that second-hand smoke from parental smoking can cause a variety of health problems in their offspring.

- Do not use any recreational drugs (other than an occasional single alcoholic beverage). Take medicines only with medical approval. Most drugs pass into breast milk to some extent – some appearing to have no effect on a nursing baby at all, others a mild transient effect, and still others a significant detrimental effect. But not enough is known about the long-term effects of medications on the nursing infant to recommend that a mother take any drug without first weighing the risks against benefits.

All medications which pose even a theoretical risk to the nursing baby carry a warning – on either the label, the package, or both. When the benefits outweigh the possible risks, your doctor will probably okay the occasional use of certain of these (cold medications or mild pain relievers, for example) without medical consultation and prescribe others when your health requires it. Like an expectant mother, a nursing mother does neither herself nor her baby a favour by refusing prescribed medication under such circumstances. Do be sure, of course, that any doctor who prescribes a medication for you is aware that you are breastfeeding.

For the most up-to-date information on which drugs are believed safe and which aren't, check with your child's doctor. The most recent research indicates that most medicines (including paracetamol, ibuprofen, most sedatives, antihistamines, decongestants, antihypertensives, antibiotics and antithyroid drugs) are compatible with nursing. Some, however, including anticancer drugs, lithium and ergots are clearly harmful. Others, including aspirin, many tranquillizers, antidepressants and antipsychotics are suspect.

In some cases, a medication can safely be discontinued for the duration of nursing; in others, it is possible to find a safer substitute. When medication is needed short term, nursing can be interrupted temporarily (with breasts pumped and milk discarded). Or dosing can be timed for just after nursing or before baby's longest sleep period. Often non-drug treatments (see page 567) can be used.

- Drink alcoholic beverages only rarely. Until recently, it was believed that one or two drinks a day would be harmless to the nursing infant, but a recent study suggests that as little as one glass of wine a day could slow both large and small motor development in the baby. More study needs to be done, but to be safe rather than sorry, limit alcohol intake. Alcohol has other drawbacks as well. It dehydrates, causing the loss of fluids needed for milk production. In large doses, it can make baby sleepy, sluggish, unresponsive and unable to suck well. In very large doses, it can interfere with

breathing. Alcohol can also impair your own functioning (whether you're nursing or not), making you more susceptible to depression, fatigue and lapses in judgment, weakening your let-down reflex and making you less able to care for, protect and nourish your baby. And like any nutritionally vacant food or beverage, too much alcohol can add excess calories (and thus weight) or divert your appetite from necessary nutrients. So drink only rarely. And then limit your intake to one or two drinks (one drink equals 350 ml/12 fl ounces of beer, 150 ml/5 ounces of wine, or 40 ml/1½-ounces of distilled spirit). If you can't limit your drinking, or stop at two, you have a problem. Seek help from a doctor or Alcoholics Anonymous.

- Restrict your intake of caffeine. One or two cups of caffeinated coffee, tea, or cola a day won't affect your baby or you. More probably will, making one or both of you jittery, irritable and sleepless. The caffeine also acts as a diuretic, drawing valuable fluids out of your body. And too many nutritionless beverages, caffeinated or not, can spoil your appetite for nutritious beverages and foods.

- Don't take laxatives; some will have a laxative effect on your baby. To combat constipation, step up your fibre and fluid intake and exercise more.

- Take aspirin or paracetamol only with your doctor's approval, and never exceed the prescribed dose or frequency. Since ibuprofen is excreted into the breast milk in only tiny amounts, ibuprofen medications may be considered a safer choice for the nursing mother.

- Avoid excessive quantities of chemicals in the foods you eat. An occasional diet soda won't hurt, but frequent consumption of those containing saccharin isn't a good idea. Aspartame-sweetened soft drinks appear to be a better choice since aspartame is secreted into the breast milk in only tiny amounts. Whether you're nursing or not, however, heavy use of aspartame isn't wise because all of its long-term effects are not yet known. Do not use it at all if either you or your baby has PKU. And though no food additive currently in general use has been proven toxic to a baby who gets it via mother's milk, several are suspect. So it is prudent to limit your total intake of foods containing long lists of additives, including preservatives, artificial colours and flavours and stabilizers.

- Don't drink herbal teas. Some of the herbs found in true herbal teas (unlike those in flavoured decaffeinated teas) are powerful drugs, possibly harmful to a nursing infant. So stay away from any unprescribed herbs or herbal teas that contain any ingredient not ordinarily found in your diet (orange rind and dried apples, for instance, should be okay).

- Minimize the incidental pesticides in your diet. A certain amount of pesticide residue in your diet (from produce, for example), and thus in your milk, is virtually unavoidable and not likely to be harmful. But it's wise to try to keep such residues to a minimum by purchasing, when possible, produce that is certified organically grown; peeling or scrubbing other vegetable and fruit skins with washing-up liquid and water and rinsing well; choosing low-fat milk products, lean meats, white-meat poultry with the skin removed; and eating organ meats rarely (the pesticides and other chemicals ingested by animals are stored in fat, fatty skin and such organs as the liver and brain).

- Avoid eating freshwater fish (such as trout, perch, whitefish, salmon and bass) that might have been contaminated by industrial wastes in lakes and rivers. Exceptions can be made if you know that they've come from safe waters (farm-raised trout, for instance, should be okay). Most deep-water ocean fish are considered safe to eat, but swordfish and tuna, which can contain high levels of methylmercury, should be eaten less frequently. Peri-

odically, fish from certain off-shore areas are found to be unsafe. If you're unsure about a particular fish, contact your local health department.[9]

Sore Nipples

'Breastfeeding is something I always wanted to do. But my nipples have become so excruciatingly sore that I'm not sure I can continue nursing my son.'

At first you wonder if your newborn will ever catch on; then before you know it, he's suckling so vigorously your nipples become sore, even painful. The problem is not uncommon, and in fact most women suffer at least a little nipple soreness before breastfeeding becomes well established. But in the vast majority of these women, soreness peaks at about the twentieth feeding, nipples start to toughen up, and nursing becomes more comfortable. For some women, however, particularly those with delicate or fair skin or whose babies are very vigorous nursers, the nipples get worse before they get better, cracking, becoming exquisitely tender, and sometimes bleeding. Nursing sessions can become torture.

Fortunately, there is relief at the end of the tunnel even for these women, though sometimes not for a month or six weeks. In the meantime, these precautions will help alleviate the discomfort:

- Be certain your baby has the entire areola (the dark area around the nipple) in his mouth when nursing and not just the nipple. Not only will his sucking on the nipple alone make you sore, but he won't get much milk. If engorgement makes it difficult for him to grasp the full areola, express a little milk manually or with a

---

9. If you believe you have had extensive exposure to PCBs (through your work, eating a lot of contaminated fish, or some other source), have your breast milk tested before you decide to breastfeed your baby. If you have high levels of PCBs in your breast milk, you may be advised not to nurse.

breast pump before nursing to reduce the engorgement and make it easier for him to get a good grip.

- Expose nipples to air whenever possible, but especially after nursing. Just lower the blinds and leave the flaps of your nursing bra down as you go about your business at home.

- Remove any waterproof lining from your bra (again, to encourage air circulation), and don't insert waterproof pads.

- If only one nipple is sore, don't favour it by nursing more on the other one. But do nurse first on the less sore one, since your baby's sucking will be most vigorous at the beginning of a feeding session. If both nipples are sore, alternate the breast you start with at each feeding. If possible, reduce nursing periods to five minutes on each side and nurse more often.

- Let nature – not cosmetic companies – take care of your nipples. Nipples are naturally protected and lubricated by skin oils; commercial preparations should be used only when nipple cracking is severe, and then should be as pure as possible. Unmedicated lanolin and A & D ointment are effective; petroleum-based ointments and petroleum jelly itself (Vaseline) are not. Clean the nipples only with water – never with soap, alcohol, tincture of benzoin, or premoistened towelettes – whether they are sore or not. Your baby is protected from your germs by antibodies in your milk, and the milk itself is clean.

Rotate nursing positions so a different part of the nipple will be compressed at each feeding; but always keep baby facing your breast.

Relax for fifteen minutes or so before feedings – listen to music, watch TV, catnap, do relaxation exercises – to banish the tension that could inhibit milk let-down. Or try a glass of wine or beer occasionally to enhance let-down. Or encourage it with an oxytocin nasal spray prescribed by your doctor, or with warm breast soaks or a warm

shower prior to nursing sessions. If let-down doesn't occur, your baby will have to suckle desperately to get milk, adding to nipple soreness.

Leaking and Spraying

'My breasts leak a lot. Sometimes I even spray milk across the room. It's messy and embarrassing.'

The good news is that leaky breasts are full of milk; the bad news is there isn't a great deal you can do to stem the flow, though it will probably ease up sometime in the second month, once your baby's demands and your supply equalize. In the meantime, there are a few tricks you can try:

- Wear breast pads in your bra to absorb any leaking milk; but be sure to change them frequently to avoid setting up conditions of warmth and moisture in which bacteria can breed.

- Wear clothes that camouflage the milk stains – dark prints do this best – and that are washable.

- Try crossing your arms tightly across your breasts when you feel let-down occurring in public; the pressure may curb let-down.

- Try not to go very long between feedings, but if you must, express some milk when your breasts become too full.

Mastitis

'My little boy is an enthusiastic nurser, and though my nipples were a little cracked and sore, I thought everything was going pretty well. Now, all of a sudden, one breast is very tender and hard – worse than when my milk first came in.'

For most women the course of breast-feeding, after a shaky initial startup, is relatively smooth. But for about 1 in 20 – and it sounds like you're one of them – mastitis (an inflammation of the breast) comes along to complicate matters. This infection can occur anytime during lactation, but is most common between the tenth and twenty-eighth postpartum days.

Mastitis is usually caused by the entry of germs, often from the baby's mouth, into a milk duct through a crack or fissure in the skin of the nipple. Since cracked nipples are more common among first-time breastfeeders, whose nipples are not used to the rigours of infant sucking, mastitis strikes these women more often. The symptoms of mastitis include severe soreness, hardness, redness, heat and swelling over the affected duct, with generalized chills and usually fever of about 38.3 to 38.9°C (101° to 102°F) – though occasionally the only symptoms are fever and fatigue. Prompt medical treatment is important, so report any such symptoms to your doctor immediately. Prescribed therapy may include bed rest, antibiotics, pain relievers and ice or heat applications.

Though nursing from the affected breast will be painful, you should not avoid it. In fact, you should let your baby nurse frequently to keep the milk flowing and avoid clogging. Empty the breast thoroughly by hand or with a pump after each feeding if your baby doesn't do a thorough job himself. Don't worry about transmitting the infection to your baby; the germs that caused the infection probably came from his mouth in the first place.

Delay in treating mastitis could lead to the development of a breast abscess, the symptoms of which are excruciating, throbbing pain; swelling, tenderness and heat in the area of the abscess; and temperature swings between 37.8° and 39.4°C (100° and 103°F). Treatment generally includes antibiotics and, frequently, surgical drainage under local anaesthesia. If you develop an abscess, breast-feeding on the affected breast must be halted temporarily, though you should continue to empty it with a pump until healing is complete and nursing can resume. In the meantime, your baby can continue nursing on the healthy breast.

Lump in Breast

'I've suddenly discovered a lump in my breast. It's tender and a little red. Could it be related to nursing – or something worse?'

Finding a lump in a breast strikes fear in any woman. But fortunately, what you describe is almost certainly related to nursing – a milk duct has probably become clogged, causing milk to back up. The clogged area usually appears as a lump that is red and tender. Though not serious in itself, a clogged duct can lead to breast infection, so it shouldn't be neglected. The basis of treatment is to keep milk flowing:

- Empty the affected breast thoroughly at each feeding. Offer it first and encourage baby to take as much milk as possible. If there still seems to be a significant amount of milk left after nursing (if you can express a stream, rather than just a few drops), express the remaining milk by hand or with a breast pump.

- Keep pressure off the clogged duct. Be sure your bra isn't too tight or your clothes too constricting. Rotate your nursing positions to put pressure on different ducts at each nursing.

- Be sure that dried milk isn't blocking the nipple. Clean any away with sterile cotton wool dipped in cooled boiled water.

- Don't stop nursing, if at all possible. Now is not the time to wean your baby, or to cut back on nursing. This would compound the problem.

Occasionally, in spite of your best efforts, infection develops. If the tender area becomes increasingly painful, hard and red, and/or if you develop a fever, call your doctor (see page 547).

Hair Loss

'My hair, which was really luxuriant during pregnancy, now seems to be falling out in handfuls.'

Don't panic, and don't order a hairpiece. This fallout is normal and can be quite heavy, but it will stop well in advance of baldness – though an occasional new mum may begin to wonder if it will. Ordinarily, the average person sheds 100 head hairs a day, each of which is replaced by new growth. When a woman is pregnant (or taking oral contraceptives), hormonal changes slow normal hair loss considerably, making the hair thicker and more luxuriant than ever before. But this reprieve from normal hair loss lasts only as long as the pregnancy. During the first three to six months after delivery (or after one stops taking the pill), all the hairs that were scheduled to have fallen out during pregnancy are shed. Regrowth can't keep up with the loss at first, and so hair looks much thinner than usual.

By the end of your baby's first year, your hair should be back to prepregnancy thickness. In the meantime, a good haircut may minimize the problem.

Renewed Bleeding

'My discharge turned to pink towards the end of my first postpartum week and got even lighter the next. Now, after fourteen days, all of a sudden it's red again, and heavier.'

If you find your discharge is either reddish or a little heavier than it has been recently, it may mean nothing more than that you are more active than you should be. In which case a slower pace, with self-enforced, feet-up rest periods, should return your lochia to normal. On the other hand, if menstrual-like bleeding either continues beyond the first week or suddenly recurs later in the postpartum period, you should immediately call your doctor or midwife. If you can't reach him or her right away and bleeding is heavy, saturating a sanitary pad in one hour or less for a few hours, go to the nearest hospital. If it's not that heavy, be certain to make contact with your doctor within a few hours (or, if it's the middle of the night, first thing in the morning) so that you can be ex-

amined – either vaginally or via a sonogram – to determine the source of your bleeding.[10]

Abnormal vaginal bleeding after the first week postpartum suggests the possibility that the placental site is not healing (involuting) properly or that a fragment of placenta remains in your uterus (this can happen even if the placenta seemed whole when checked at the time of delivery). Either condition could result in life-threatening haemorrhage if not treated promptly. Lack of involution usually responds to a treatment including rest, antibiotics and sometimes medication to help the uterus contract. Retained placental fragments often requires hospitalization, with surgery, careful curettage (scraping) of the lining of the uterus, antibiotic therapy and possible blood transfusions. Recovery is usually rapid and hospital discharge is frequently permitted as soon as 24 hours after admission. In most instances, arrangements can be made for a nursing baby to be brought to the mother for feedings during hospitalization. If this isn't possible, a temporary alternative feeding plan can be implemented (see page 90).

Postpartum Infection/Fever

'I've just returned home from the hospital and I'm running a fever of about 38.3°C (101°F). Could it be related to childbirth?'

Thanks to Dr. Ignaz Semmelweis, the chances of a new mother's developing childbirth (or puerperal) fever today are extremely slight. It was in Vienna in 1847 that this young Hungarian doctor discovered that if birth attendants washed their hands before delivering a baby, the risk of childbirth-related infection was greatly reduced. (At the time, his theory was considered so outlandish that he was driven from his post,

10. Some women experience a mini-period about three weeks postpartum, but it is brief and not as heavy as that described above. Even if you suspect that this is the reason for your bleeding, report it to your doctor.

ostracized and later died a broken man.) And thanks to Sir Alexander Fleming, the British scientist who developed the first infection-fighting antibiotics, the occasional case that does occur is easily cured.

The most severe cases of postpartum infection usually begin within 24 hours of delivery. While a fever on the third or fourth day could indicate postpartum infection, it could also be caused by a cold or flu virus or some other minor problem. Occasionally a low-grade fever of about 37.8°C (100°F) accompanies engorgement when your milk first comes in.

There are several types of postpartum infection and the symptoms vary according to the site at which the infection took hold. A slight fever, vague lower-abdominal pain and sometimes a foul-smelling vaginal discharge characterize endometritis, an infection of the lining of the uterus (the endometrium), which is particularly vulnerable after childbirth until the site where the placenta detached has healed. Endometritis is most likely to occur if a fragment of the placenta remains in the uterus; it can spread from the endometrium to the uterus and even into the bloodstream. When a laceration to the cervix, vagina, or vulva becomes infected, there will usually be pain and tenderness in the area and sometimes a foul-smelling thick discharge, abdominal or flank pain, or difficult urination. With certain types of postpartum infection, fever spikes as high as 40.5°C (105°F) and is accompanied by chills, headache and malaise. Sometimes there is no obvious symptom but fever.

Treatment with antibiotics is very effective, but it should begin promptly. You should therefore report any fever during the first three postpartum weeks to the doctor – even if you also have cold or flu symptoms – so that its cause can be determined and treatment started, if necessary.

Long-Term Caesarean Recovery

'I am just now going home, a week after a caesarean. What next?'

The process of recovery is a bit more extended if you've had a surgical delivery rather than a vaginal one. Over the next several weeks, you can expect:

To need plenty of help. Reliable paid help – a baby nurse and/or a housekeeper – is ideal for at least the first week, when your strength and energy levels will be at low tide. If hiring is not financially possible, you'll need extra help from your husband, supplemented when he's not home by rotating shifts of relatives and friends. It's best not to do any lifting (including the baby) or any housework for at least the first week back home. If you must lift the baby, have the cot mattress set at waist level and lift so as to put the strain on your arms rather than your abdomen. If you have to bend, bend at the knees, not at the waist.

To have little or no pain. But if you do hurt, a mild pain reliever should help. Don't take any medication, however, if you are breastfeeding, unless you've got an okay from your baby's doctor.

To note progressive improvement at the incision site. Your incision will be sore and sensitive for a few weeks, but this will gradually lessen as it heals. A light bandage and loose clothing will help protect it from irritation. Occasional pulling and twitching sensations, other transient pains and eventually itching can be expected with healing. All will subside over the course of the next few weeks. Numbness of the abdomen around the scar can last longer, possibly several months. Lumpiness of the scar tissue will diminish (unless you are prone to keloids, or thick scar tissue) and the scar may turn pink or purplish before it finally fades. If pain returns or worsens, if the area around the incision turns an angry red or becomes swollen, or if you notice a brown, grey, green, or yellow discharge coming from the wound, the incision may have become infected. Report such symptoms to your doctor promptly. A clear fluid discharge should also be reported, though it may be perfectly normal.

To wait at least four weeks before resuming sexual intercourse. Your doctor may recommend that you wait anywhere from four to six weeks before engaging in intercourse (though other kinds of lovemaking are certainly permissible). When you get the green light will depend on how your incision is healing and when your cervix returns to normal. (See page 550 for tips on making postpartum lovemaking more successful. Also see Postpartum Contraception, page 557.) You are, incidentally, much more likely to find early postpartum intercourse comfortable than are women who delivered vaginally.

To be allowed to start exercising once you are free of pain. Since the muscle tone of your perineum probably hasn't been compromised much, you may not need to do Kegel exercises (though they're a good pelvic toner for anyone). When your doctor gives the go-ahead, concentrate instead on those abdominal muscles (see page 518). Make 'slow and steady' your motto; get into an exercise programme gradually and continue it daily. Expect it to take several months before you're back to your previous level of fitness.

Resuming Sexual Relations

'My doctor says I have to wait six weeks before having sex again. A friend tells me this isn't necessary.'

It's fairly safe to assume that your doctor is more familiar with your medical condition than your friend is. Though a doctor may in some instances okay intercourse as early as two weeks postpartum, your doctor's restriction is probably based on what he or she believes is best for you, taking into consideration the kind of labour and delivery you had, whether or not you had an episiotomy or a laceration repair and the speed of your healing and recovery. Some doctors, however, apply the six-week prohibition routinely to all their postpartum patients, regardless of individual circumstances. If you think this may be the case with your doctor, and you're feeling up to making love, ask if he or she will consider bending the rules for you. This will be possible only if your cervix has healed and the lochia has stopped completely. If you do get the go-ahead, you may still decide to postpone intercourse if it causes severe pain in your perineal area.

Should your request be denied, however, it's wise to follow doctor's orders. Waiting the full six weeks couldn't hurt (at least not physically), while not waiting might.

WHAT IT'S IMPORTANT TO KNOW:
Making Love Again

Is the honeymoon over? Has the romance faded now that there's a little fledgling sharing your love nest? Will you ever feel that heady rush of abandon in bed again? For that matter, will you ever stop feeling tired long enough to feel anything else at all?

For most women, even those who lived highly memorable love lives before delivery, doubts that any kind of sexual relationship with their husband will ever resume, at least on a regular basis, are nagging and numerous. Though a very few women do find themselves amorous in the immediate postpartum period (alas, even before they have been given the okay to consummate their desires and sometimes before their mates feel ready) because of genital engorgement, most women find the postpartum period (and sometimes a several-month stretch following it) a sexual wasteland.

Why the Lack of Interest?

There's no shortage of reasons why you may not feel like making love now, among them:

- Readjusting hormones can zap sexual desire during the postpartum period, and later if you're breastfeeding.

- Temporary physiologic changes can cause a reduction in both the rapidity and the intensity of sexual response.

- Your libidos (yours and your spouse's) usually lose when they compete with sleepless nights, exhausting days, dirty nappies and the endless needs of a demanding newborn.

- Fear of pain, of doing some internal damage, of your vagina being stretched out, or of becoming pregnant again too soon may nip any romantic buds before they blossom.

- A painful first intercourse postpartum can make the thought of further attempts unappealing. Pain on subsequent tries can make lovemaking extremely awkard and uncomfortable. Such pain may continue for a while even after the perineum is healed.

- Discomfort because of decreased vaginal lubrication, a result of hormonal changes during the postpartum period and during lactation in women who are breastfeeding, can also dull desire. The problem usually lasts longer in nursing mothers, but can continue for as long as six months even in those who aren't breastfeeding.

- Uneasiness because of lack of privacy, particularly if your baby is sharing a room with you, can quench desire. Your head believes what you've heard – that your baby will be oblivious to and unaffected by your lovemaking – but your body balks at the idea.

- Mothering may be taking all the loving and nurturing you have to give right now and you may sometimes be unable to summon any up for anyone else, even your husband.

Easing Back into Sex

To help you overcome some of the most common postpartum sexual difficulties:

Lubricate. Altered hormone levels during the postpartum period (which may not normalize in the nursing mother until her baby is partially or totally weaned) can make the vagina uncomfortably dry. Use a lubricating product (like K-Y Jelly) or lubricating vaginal suppositories until your own natural secretions return.

Medicate. If necessary, ask your doctor to prescribe a topical oestrogen cream to lessen pain and tenderness.

Take a nip. Don't get drunk, of course (since overindulgence, as Shakespeare pointed out, 'provokes the desire, but it takes away the performance'), but if you drink, do indulge in a glass of wine with your husband before making love, to help both of you relax physically and emotionally. The alcohol will also numb some of your pain, lessen your fear of it and lessen his fear of causing it. If you don't drink, try relaxation or meditation techniques instead.

Exercise. Kegel exercises (see page 518) will help to tone the pelvic muscles, which are associated with vaginal sensation and response during intercourse.

Vary positions. Side-to-side or woman-on-top positions allow more control of depth of penetration and put less pressure on a sore perineum. Experiment to find what works best for you.

- Breastfeeding may be satisfying your sexual needs (without your realizing it), making you less receptive to your husband's overtures. (Though nursing mothers are often interested in sex earlier than women who don't breastfeed.)

- Leaking of breast milk, stimulated by sexual foreplay, may make either you or your husband uncomfortable, physically as well as psychologically. Or you may not want to have your breasts touched by your mate at all, seeing them as nurturing rather than sexual right now and finding such foreplay annoying.

- There are so many other things that you feel you need or want to do that sex may seem less important now – if you have a spare half hour, lovemaking may not be at the top of the list.

What can you do About it?

In spite of the bleak outlook for lovemaking at present, there's promise for the future. You will surely live to love again, with as much pleasure and passion as ever – and maybe, because you have been brought closer by sharing parenthood, even more. In the meantime, there are many steps you can take to improve both interest and performance right now:

Don't rush it. It takes at least six weeks for your body to recover completely, and sometimes much longer – especially if you had a difficult vaginal delivery or a caesarean section. Your hormonal balance may not return to normal until you resume menstruating, which, if you are breastfeeding, may not be for several months or more. Don't feel obligated to jump into bed the minute your doctor gives you permission. If you don't feel up to it – mentally, emotionally, or physically – wait a while.

Express love in other ways. Intercourse isn't the only way for a couple to love. If you're not ready to go all the way, try cuddling and caressing in front of the TV,

backrubs in bed and hand holding while strolling in the park with baby. As for any couple getting acquainted (and you, after all, are becoming reacquainted physically), romance en route to the bed is an important first step. If you're not too pooped to pop, you can even try mutual masturbation. But some evenings, there may be nothing more satisfying than the intimacy that is shared lying in each other's arms.

Expect some discomfort. Many women are surprised and disheartened to find that postpartum intercourse can really hurt. If you've had an episiotomy or a laceration that required stitching, you may indeed experience some degree of pain or discomfort (ranging from mild to severe) for weeks, even months, after the tissues have outwardly healed. You may have pain with intercourse, though probably less of it, if you delivered vaginally, perineum intact – and even if you had a caesarean. To minimize pain, try the tips in Easing Back into Sex, page 550.

Don't expect perfection. Don't count on perfectly orchestrated orgasms at your very first return engagement. Many women don't have orgasms for several weeks or even longer when they start making love again. But with time, caring and patience, the thrill does return and sex becomes as satisfying as ever.

If you can't beat baby's schedule, work around it. Falling into each other's arms when and where the spirit moves may no longer be possible. Instead, you may have to make time by that spirited little alarm clock in the cot. Baby is napping at 3 o'clock on Saturday afternoon; drop everything and head for the bedroom. Or if the little angel has been predictably sleeping from 7 to 10 every evening, plan ahead for a romantic interlude. If he or she wakes up crying just as your evening is reaching a climax, try to see the humour in your plight. You can, incidentally, if you can concentrate, keep your baby waiting for a couple of minutes if need be. Should sexual encounters with your spouse continue to be less frequent for a while (sometimes for a long while), strive for quality rather than quantity.

Keep your priorities straight. If making love is important to you, reserve for it by cutting corners elsewhere (in areas that won't affect your family's physical or emotional well-being). Go an extra day before running the vacuum, use frozen vegetables instead of fresh, keep the family in easy-care clothes. If you spend your entire day at full throttle, trying to be Supermum, homemaker and perhaps career woman as well, you won't have the strength left to do anything in bed but close your eyes.

Talk about it. A good sexual relationship is built on trust, understanding and communication. If, for instance, you're too exhausted one night from 24-hour baby care to feel sexy, don't beg off with a headache.

Instead, be honest. If your husband has been sharing baby-care responsibilities from the beginning, he's very likely to understand (he may, in fact, be too fathered-out some nights himself). If he hasn't, and he doesn't understand your exhaustion, this may be the time to explain that your handling all the baby and house care yourself is wearing you out and that if he would help out, even a little, you might be left with more energy at night.

Communicate, too, about problems like a dry vagina or pain during intercourse. Tell your spouse what hurts, what feels good, what you'd rather put off until next time.

Don't worry about it. The more you worry about a lack of libido, the less libido you're likely to have. So face the facts of postpartum life, relax and take your sexual relationship one night at a time, confident that the romance will return to your life.

TWENTY-FOUR

Enjoying the First Year

◆

What You May Be Feeling

By the end of the first six weeks postpartum, your body should have recovered from the traumas of pregnancy, labour and delivery. You may, however, expect to experience one or more of the following during the first year.

Physically:

- Further loss of weight, until you reach your prepregnancy weight or another goal

- Further flattening of your abdomen, particularly if you exercise

- Extreme fatigue, at least until your baby sleeps through the night

- A return of menstruation if you are not breastfeeding, or if you have reduced the number of nursings or weaned your baby

- Backache and other aches and pains from toting baby

Emotionally:

- Reduced sexual desire, at least at first

- Exhilaration, frustration, boredom

- A gradual increase in confidence and a lessening of the feeling of being overwhelmed

What You Should Be Eating: The Best-Odds for a Healthy Future

Eating regularly during your baby's first year is difficult enough, but eating well often seems impossible. Yet good diet is imperative if you are to keep up your energy, maintain good health and, if you're nursing, produce quality breast milk. So it's important to continue to get your Postpartum Daily Dozen (see page 524) and to follow the Nine Basic Principles of a Healthy Diet.

If you're nursing, your diet will have to change as your baby's does. As baby takes more and more nourishment from other sources – formula, cow's milk, solid foods – and less and less breast milk, you will have to reduce your caloric intake. But this doesn't require counting calories, just keeping a close eye on the scale. If it shows your weight going up when it should go down or stay level, then you are taking in too many calories. If you are losing when you shouldn't be, or losing very rapidly, then you're not eating enough. Adjust accordingly.

Once you've weaned your baby from the breast, or if you've never nursed at all, the Best-Odds Postpartum Diet can continue to be a blueprint for healthy eating in the years to come. Follow it, not only to feel better and live longer, but to set a good example for that new little baby of yours.

What You May Be Concerned About

Finding Outside Interests

'As much as I'm committed to being a full-time mother, I'm starting to feel suffocated by staying home with my new daughter. There's got to be more to life than changing nappies.'

In the first few months of a baby's life, when the demands of feeding and caring for her are round-the-clock and seemingly endless, about all a new mother has the time or inclination to crave is sleep. But once baby has settled into a routine and mother into a manageable rhythm, the dreary doldrums may settle over the frenetic fog of earlier weeks. Instead of finding yourself with too much to do and not enough time in which to do it, you may find yourself with too much time and not enough to do with it. The challenge gone from getting through a day's baby-care chores, you may well begin to feel like a wind-up mother going mechanically through the motions, and to crave the stimulations and satisfactions of life beyond the four walls of home. And particularly if you were involved in many activities before – a career, hobbies, school, athletics, community work – you may start to feel those four walls closing in, and start doubting your self-worth as well as your decision to stay home with your baby.

Yet a rich, full, satisfying lifestyle and life with baby are not, as they may seem now, mutually exclusive. The important first step toward achieving such a lifestyle is to recognize that woman (or man) cannot live by baby alone – though your mother, or others of her generation, may have taken twenty years to find that out. Even if you adore every moment with your baby, you still need intellectual stimulation and the chance to communicate with someone who can say more than ah-goo, ah-goo (cute as that may be). There are a variety of ways of achieving these goals, and of reclaiming the sense of self you feel you've lost:

Through Your Baby

You can look upon your baby as an obstacle to entry into the grownup world – or as a ticket to it. The following will give you a shot at finding adult interaction through your baby:

Mother and baby groups. Locate an existing group or seek out mothers interested in joining you to set up a new one up by putting up a notice at the baby's doctor's office, at your church or synagogue, on your building complex, supermarket, or community bulletin board. Try for a group with mothers whose interests match yours.

Baby classes. Classes designed for babies are often more valuable for their mothers. By signing up for such a class (first making sure it's appropriate and safe for your baby; see page 205), you'll have the weekly opportunity to meet and talk with other women, many of whom have chosen to stay home with their babies.

Mothers' discussion groups. Join an established one, or become involved in setting up a new one. Invite guest speakers (a local paediatrician, a nurse, a librarian, an author and others who can address your needs as mothers and/or as women); jointly hire a baby-sitter or sitters for the children. Meet in homes, a church, synagogue, school – or wherever there's space available – weekly, every other week, or monthly.

The local playground or play area. Where babies play, mothers can't be far behind. The playground is not only a great place for infants (even when too young to be mobile, they find watching the children and the activity fascinating) and older babies (when they can sit well, they usually love the swings, and many can tackle the slide and climbing areas before they are a year old), it is also an ideal place for mothers to meet other mothers and set up 'play dates'.

These dates, too, are more for the benefit of the mothers at this point than they are for their babies, who aren't yet capable of 'playing together'.

Through Personal Enrichment Activities

Being a full-time mother doesn't mean you can't be anything else. Continue to pursue old interests, or find new ones, through any of the following:

A course at a local college. Take it for credit, or just for fun or intellectual enrichment.

An adult education class. They are proliferating all over the country and offer everything from aerobics to Zen.

A study group or class at your church or synagogue. While you were working you might not have found time to take a course in biblical criticism or comparative religion. Now's your chance.

An exercise class. Challenging the body activates the mind. In addition, an exercise programme, particularly one that offers child care or combines mother exercise with baby exercise, is a good place to meet other women with similar interests.

Active sports. Playing tennis or golf or another favourite sport regularly will help keep both body and mind well toned, as well as provide companionship.

A museum or art gallery. Become a member of a local museum and you can visit regularly, studying one exhibit each time. (It will be even more fun if you go with another parent.) Added benefits for baby: early exposure to art and artifacts is visually and intellectually stimulating (infants are often fascinated by paintings and sculpture) and will help keep young minds open to them later.

Educational video or audio tapes. Watch videos while doing household chores or nursing, listen to audios while driving; keep up with an old interest or explore a new one (learn a foreign language via a Walkman, for instance). Educational tapes are often available at no charge at the public library.

Books. They can take you anywhere, anytime. They can teach, challenge and entertain. Take a book you're reading everywhere you go – read while you nurse, on a stationary bike, while baby naps, before bed.

Through Good Works

The crisis in volunteerism grows as more and more women work at paying jobs full-time and as society continues to further downgrade work that isn't paid. If you're not in the paid work force, then your local charities and community service organizations need you. Choose an organization you already belong to or join a new one, and offer your services. If you don't know where to start, you can contact a central clearinghouse for volunteers if there is one in your city, or you can ask at your local school, hospital, house of worship, or poverty centre where volunteers are needed. The possibilities are endless: tutoring a child or adult in English or other subjects; visiting the elderly (they'll doubly appreciate your visit if you bring your baby along) or shut-ins; cheering patients at hospitals; serving meals at a soup kitchen; and so on.

Or use volunteer work to keep your professional skills from becoming rusty. Teach a course in your area of expertise at your local church, synagogue, or adult learning centre; write a newsletter; design a direct-mail campaign; or provide medical care or legal counsel *pro bono*.

Through Paid Work

Being a full-time mother doesn't mean you can't be a part-time worker. A few hours a week at work related to your present field or a field you'd like to break into can keep you in touch, provide adult contacts and offer escape from your daily routine. See page 576 for suggestions on how to find or create such work options, particularly those you can pursue from your home.

Making Baby Fit In

Though baby may be the cause of the lack of stimulation in your life, she doesn't have to stand in the way of a cure. In virtually every situation, her needs can be attended to at the same time yours are.

Take her along. In a baby carrier or push-chair, she will enjoy (or sleep through) short visits to museums or galleries. She'll also, in some cases, be able to accompany you on your volunteer assignments (such positions are often far more flexible than paid ones) and to less formal courses, such as those given at community centres (try to time baby's feeding and/or nap to coordinate with the lecture to reduce the risk of her distracting you or others; bring quiet toys for an older baby).

Leave her with someone. Accept offers of assistance from relatives and friends. Or consider the possibility of co-op baby-sitting with another mother of a young child (you baby-sit for both babies on Mondays while the other mother goes out, then she reciprocates on Thursdays).

Hire a baby-sitter. If you can afford it, this is usually the most reliable source of relief.

Depend on dad. Schedule your outside activities when your husband will be at home (play tennis or go to an aerobics class on the weekend, take French literature in the evening). Though this will cut down on the amount of time you spend together as a family, it will give daddy more time alone with baby, something he might not ordinarily have if he works full-time – and a wonderful plus for their relationship.

Use child care. Some colleges offer nursery facilities for children of students, some exercise programmes offer baby-sitting, a very few workplaces offer day care for children of employees. If there are other mothers of infants or young children in a class or course you're taking, ask if they'd like to chip in for a communal baby-sitter! The advantage of having on-site care is greatest if you're breastfeeding exclusively.

Leaving Baby with a Baby-Sitter

'I don't work outside the home, but I do occasionally leave my nine-month-old son with a baby-sitter– and always feel guilty when I do.'

As every employer knows, no worker can stay on the job round the clock and round the calendar and still be effective. And as a self-employed mother, you'll have to recognize this fact, too. No matter how much you enjoy your child and how much he enjoys you, you'll both benefit from some time apart. Take it – and don't feel guilty.

Stretched Vagina

'Now that our son is sleeping through the night, my husband and I have finally resumed a fairly active sex life. The problem is that I seem roomier than before I delivered and making love is less satisfying for both of us.'

Most women come out of vaginal deliveries more roomy than when they went in. Often, the change isn't significant enough to be noticed by either partner. Sometimes, as when conditions were previously too cramped for comfort, it's welcomed. Occasionally, however, a vaginal delivery – particularly when no episiotomy was performed – can leave a woman who was 'just right' before stretched out enough to markedly decrease the pleasure she and her husband experience during intercourse.

The passing of time may help tighten things up a bit, and so can keeping up with your Kegels. (If you haven't been doing Kegel exercises throughout pregnancy and postpartum, it's not too late to start now; see page 518.) Repeat these muscle toners as many times as you can during the day; get into the habit of doing them while you're cooking, watching TV, nursing, or reading – even during intercourse.

Very rarely, the muscles don't tighten up. If six months have passed since delivery and you still feel that you're too slack, it may be useful to discuss with your doctor the possibility of surgical repair to snug things up. The procedure is a minor one, but it can make a major difference in your love life.

Return of Menstruation

'I weaned my daughter two months ago and I still haven't had a period. Could something be wrong?'

The resumption of the menstrual cycle in women who've been nursing can vary widely. Some women, especially those with substantial fat reserves, produce enough oestrogen while they're nursing to start menstruating again before weaning, sometimes as early as six weeks to three months postpartum. But others, particularly those who have nursed for a long time, nursed exclusively, or had irregular menstrual periods before pregnancy, may not menstruate until several months after they've weaned their babies. Be sure, however, that you're eating enough and haven't been losing weight too quickly; strenuous dieting, especially when combined with strenuous exercise, can temporarily stall the return of the menstrual cycle. And mention the situation to your doctor at your next checkup, which will probably be scheduled some time after the sixth month postpartum.

In women who aren't nursing their babies, the cycle can resume anywhere between four weeks and three months postpartum. Again, a delay in the start of menstruation could be the result of undernutrition due to overzealous dieting.

If you haven't yet had a period, don't count on this to prevent your becoming pregnant. See overleaf for information on more reliable means of contraception.

Getting Pregnant Again

'I want to wait at least two years before having another baby. A friend of mine said not to worry about birth control because she heard you can't get pregnant if you're nursing.'

Your friend is only a little bit right, which means that if you depend on nursing as a contraceptive, you could end up a little bit pregnant. Some women who breastfeed find their menstrual periods don't return at all while they are nursing, and sometimes not for months past weaning; this usually means they aren't ovulating and can't conceive. The factors that seem to boost the ovulation-suppressing effects of breastfeeding include: low levels of body fat (hormones produced by body fat can stimulate menstruation); frequent nursings (more than three times a day may keep menstruation away); late weaning (often, the longer weaning is postponed, the longer ovulation is delayed); and delayed introduction of supplementation to breastfeeding (formula, solids, even water can all reduce breast milk intake, signalling the body that it's time to resume menstruating).

Many nursing mothers, however, particularly those who have excess fat stores or whose babies are only partially breastfed, do resume menstruating and can become pregnant. The catch: it's impossible to predict who will or won't menstruate while nursing. That wouldn't be a problem if everyone had a 'sterile' menstrual period before ovulating again for the first time. Then the arrival of menstruation would warn that it's time to resume using contraception. But this is just not the case. Some women ovulate and conceive again before their periods return and they can go from pregnancy to pregnancy without ever menstruating in between.

If you would be devastated by another pregnancy now (your body might be, even if your mind could accept it), you should use a more reliable form of contraception than nursing. The following all have advantages and disadvantages, and the choice is a personal and individual one that should be based on your physical condition, your lifestyle, your doctor's recommendation and your own feelings and circumstances. All are effective when used correctly and consistently, but only sterilization is 100% certain to prevent conception.

Oral contraceptives. Today's low-dose oral contraceptives work basically by suppressing ovulation and are very effective at preventing conception. But many women are confused about their safety. And it's no wonder. Scientific evidence seems to careen crazily back and forth. The following is what is known as this book goes to press. Check with your doctor to learn the latest.

The risk of heart attack, stroke and blood clots is increased in OC users, so they aren't recommended for women at high risk for these cardiovascular problems (see below). The risks increase with extended use – longer than five years.

Though OCs appear to protect against certain forms of cancer (ovarian and endometrial, for example), some recent studies point to a connection between the Pill and breast cancer in some women (those who went on the Pill early, before a pregnancy, and took it for more than three years). On the plus side, OCs appear to protect against nonmalignant breast disease, ectopic pregnancy, ovarian cysts and iron-deficiency anaemia (due to less bleeding with the menses), and reduce the risk of arthritis and the incidence of menstrual cramping. Other benefits, for some women, are diminished premenstrual tension and very regular periods.

If you're breastfeeding, the Pill is probably not the birth control method for you since the hormones in it can suppress lactation. (Your doctor may, however, okay the use of a progestin-only pill after breast-feeding is well established.) It's also not usually recommended for women over 45, women over 35 who smoke (some say 35 should be the cutoff even for women who don't smoke), those who have a history of blood clots (thromboses), heart attack, stroke, angina, known or suspected breast

or endometrial cancer, liver tumours, undiagnosed vaginal bleeding (which could indicate a malignancy), or jaundice during pregnancy. The Pill may also be unsuitable for women with a history of fibroids in the uterus, diabetes, high blood-cholesterol levels, high blood pressure (or a history of it during pregnancy), obesity, depression, gall bladder disease, or exposure to DES prenatally. Women with a history of migraines, asthma, epilepsy, or kidney or heart disease may find the Pill worsens their condition; if they elect to take it, very close medical monitoring is needed.

Oral contraceptives provide the most effective nonpermanent method of birth control (most failure is due to a user's missing a day or taking pills in the wrong order) and they allow for spontaneity in lovemaking. But some women report side effects, most commonly fluid retention; weight changes; nausea and vomiting; breast tenderness; abdominal cramps; skin discolouration; an increase in bladder and vaginal infections; an increase or decrease in sex drive; hair loss; intolerance to contact lenses (because of fluid retention); and menstrual irregularities (spotting, breakthrough bleeding, or rarely, amenorrhoea, or total cessation of menstruation). Less common are reports of depression, listlessness, or tenseness. Many of these side effects are less severe or less common with the new low-dose combination pills and the progestin-only minipills, though menstrual irregularities are more common with these. Side effects often diminish or disappear completely after the first few cycles of pill use.

If you're planning to have another baby, fertility may take longer to return if you're using OCs than if you're using a barrier contraceptive. Ideally, you should switch to a condom or diaphragm about three months prior to the time you plan to try to conceive. About 80% of women ovulate within the first three months after stopping the Pill, 95% within a year – though you should check with your doctor after six months if you still aren't pregnant.

If you decide to try the Pill, your doctor

will help you determine which type is best for you based on your menstrual cycle, weight, age and medical history, and will select the lowest possible dose compatible with your needs (most women do best on less than 50 micrograms of oestrogen). Then it's up to you to use this birth control method intelligently. Take it regularly; if you miss even one pill, or if you have diarrhoea or vomiting (which can interfere with absorption of the pill by your body), use backup protection (such as a condom and spermicide) until your next period. See your doctor every six months to one year for monitoring of your health; report any problems or signs of complications that show up between visits, and be sure to inform anyone prescribing medication of any kind that you are on oral contraceptives (some drugs interact adversely with the Pill). Limit caffeine intake, *do not smoke* and because oral contraceptives increase the need for certain nutrients (though they decrease the need for others), take a daily vitamin supplement that contains the RDA of vitamins B_6, B_{12}, C, riboflavin, zinc, and folic acid.

If you have trouble remembering to take pills, ask your doctor about the new 5-year hormonal implant that suppresses ovulation and builds up cervical mucus to block sperm. Implanted in the arm, it's effective and can be removed anytime you want to conceive.

IUD, or intrauterine device. This type of birth control (it is not strictly speaking a contraceptive, since it interferes with implantation rather than conception) was out of favour for several years because of suspected risks and legal battles.

Today, however, the IUD is making a comeback. But to protect users and themselves, some companies in the U.S. are marketing exclusively to doctors and clinics who agree to supply IUDs only to women who are 25 years of age or older, who have at least one child and who are in a mutually monogamous relationship. Your doctor should inform you fully of the risks of IUD use.

For many women, particularly those who don't plan to have more children, these risks are outweighed by the benefits. The major one: once it is inserted, it can be forgotten about for at least a year (often up to four, depending upon the device), except to check regularly (monthly is a good idea) for the string attached to it. This allows for a spontaneous sex life with no pausing to find and insert a diaphragm or put on a condom, and no need to remember to take a daily pill. In addition, the IUD does not interfere with breastfeeding nor does it affect the nursing infant.

The IUD should not be used by a woman who is exposed to multiple partners, or has a partner who is. Nor should it be used by

---

Oral Contraceptive Warning Signs

If you are taking an oral contraceptive and experience any of the following symptoms, call your doctor *immediately*. If your doctor can't be reached, go to the nearest emergency room.

- Sharp pains in the chest

- Coughing up of blood

- Sudden shortness of breath

- Pain or tenderness in the calf or thigh

- Severe headache

- Dizziness or faintness

- Muscle weakness or numbness

- Disturbed speech

- Sudden partial or complete loss of vision, blurred vision, flashing lights

- Severe depression

- Yellowing of the skin

- Severe abdominal pain

IUD Warning Signs

A woman wearing an IUD should call her doctor *immediately* if she experiences any of the following:

- A missed or delayed period, followed by spotty, scanty, or irregular bleeding
- Cramping, tenderness, sharp pain in the pelvis or lower abdomen (after the discomfort of the initial insertion has passed)
- Fainting or an urge to have a bowel movement associated with such pain
- Such pain that radiates down the legs, or pain in the shoulder
- Unusual or abnormal vaginal bleeding, with or without pain (other than the not abnormal spotting or staining following the initial insertion)
- Unexplained chills and fever
- Painful intercourse
- Genital sores or vaginal discharge

a woman with a history of PID (pelvic inflammatory disease) or ectopic pregnancy; known or suspected uterine or cervical malignancy or premalignancy (or even an unexplained abnormal Pap smear); abnormalities of the uterus or an unusually small uterus; menstrual or other bleeding irregularities (the IUD can increase menstrual flow and cramping); postpartum or postabortion infection within the past three months; or by a woman who recently delivered a baby, or experienced a miscarriage or abortion. Allergy or suspected allergy to copper rules out the use of a copper IUD.

Possible complications include cramping (which can be severe) during insertion and, rarely, for a few hours or even days following; uterine perforation; accidental expulsion (it might go unnoticed and leave you unprotected); and tubal or pelvic infections. The intrauterine device is extremely effective in preventing pregnancy, although when pregnancy does occur while one is still in place, it can cause complications.

Diaphragm. The diaphragm is a dome-shaped rubber cap that is placed over the cervix, the mouth of the uterus, to block the entry of sperm. It is an effective birth control method when used properly with a spermicidal gel to inactivate any sperm that might get past the barrier. Aside from possible increases in the risk of toxic shock syndrome (TSS) from leaving the diaphragm in for prolonged periods (contrary to directions) or of urinary tract infections and an occasional allergic reaction triggered by either the spermicide or the rubber, the diaphragm is safe. In fact, used with a spermicide, it appears to reduce the risk of pelvic infections that can lead to infertility. And it in no way interferes with lactation or affects a nursing baby.

The diaphragm must be prescribed and fitted by a medical professional. *Refitting is essential after childbirth*, as the size and shape of the vagina may have changed. The diaphragm has the disadvantage of having to be inserted before each intercourse, left in for six to eight hours, and removed within 24 hours. (Some experts suggest it's prudent to remove it within twelve to eighteen hours, and some recommend women insert their diaphragms nightly when they brush their teeth to avoid neglecting to use it in a moment of passion). And since the diaphragm is inserted through the vagina, this method is unappealing to some women.

The cervical cap. The cervical cap is similar to the diaphragm in many ways. It must be fitted by a doctor, must be used with a spermicide, and does its job by preventing the entry of sperm into the uterus. Its success at preventing pregnancy is about the same as the diaphragm, though theoretically the diaphragm's figures are better. The cap offers a couple of additional advantages. Shaped like a large thimble, the pliable rubber cap, whose firm rim fits snugly around the cervix, is only about half the size of the diaphragm; and it can be left in place for 48 hours rather than the 24-hour outside limit recommended for the diaphragm. Odour and difficulty inserting the cap may, however, present problems for some women.

The vaginal sponge. A more recent addition to the birth control arsenal, the sponge, like the diaphragm, the cervical cap and the condom, is considered a barrier method of contraception, one that blocks the entrance to the uterus, keeping sperm from swimming up to meet an ovum. But its major contraceptive effect is probably through the spermicide it releases. It seems somewhat less effective than the diaphragm, but when it contains nonoxynol-9, it appears to reduce the risk of contracting such sexually transmitted diseases as gonorrhoea and chlamydia. It can, however, increase the risk of the less serious vaginal infection candida. Fears that use of the sponge might cause birth defects, cancer, or TSS haven't proved out, and in fact, there is some evidence that the sponge may inhibit the development of TSS. But some people are allergic to the spermicide used. And some women are uncomfortable inserting the sponge into the vagina.

The sponge is growing in popularity because it requires neither a visit to the doctor nor a prescription, it is relatively easy to use (you insert it yourself, like a diaphragm), it allows for greater spontaneity than other barrier methods (providing continuous protection for a full 24 hours after insertion), and it is believed to have no effect on the nursing infant. It should not be left in longer than recommended and great care should be taken to remove the entire sponge (a piece left in could cause odour and infection). And it should not be used during the six-week postpartum period or shortly after a miscarriage, abortion, or D and C, without a doctor's approval.

Condom. A sheath for the penis made of latex or natural skin (from the intestines of a sheep) and often called a rubber, the condom is a very effective if used conscientiously, though it is somewhat less foolproof than the Pill. Its effectiveness, as well as its ability to combat pelvic infection, is enhanced if it is used with a spermicidal agent or jelly, and if care is taken to see that it is undamaged before use. The condom is totally harmless, though the latex or any spermicide used with it may spark an allergic reaction in some people. It has the advantage of not requiring a doctor's visit or prescription, of being easily available and easy to carry, and of reducing the risk of transmitting infections, such as gonorrhoea, chlamydia and AIDS (the latex variety is better at preventing passage of the AIDs virus). Because it in no way interferes with breastfeeding or affects the nursing infant, and because it doesn't require postpartum refitting (as does the diaphragm), it is an ideal 'transitional' method for many women. Some find, however, that because it must be put on before intercourse (and not until erection), it interferes with spontaneity. Others find that putting on the condom can be part of the lovemaking. Care should be taken when sheathing the penis to leave a small reservoir at the tip of the condom (some have one built in) to hold the semen. The penis should be withdrawn before the erection is totally lost and while the condom is held on. The use of a lubricating cream (or a lubricated condom) will help make insertion more comfortable when the vagina is dry after pregnancy and during lactation.

Spermicide foams, creams, jellies, suppositories and contraceptive films. Used alone, these antisperm agents are fairly effective at preventing pregnancies. They are easy to obtain without a prescription and don't interfere appreciably with lovemaking, but they can be messy.

Calendar-rhythm method. This approach, which depends on keeping careful records of when one menstruates and avoiding intercourse during the middle of the cycle when ovulation usually takes place,

Calculating the Calendar Rhythm Method

The calendar method A woman keeps a record of her monthly menstrual cycles for three to six months. She then calculates:

- Day A = the number of days in her shortest cycle minus 18

- Day Z = the number of days in her longest cycle minus 11

Thus if her longest cycle is 30 days and her shortest 28, she figures:

- Day A = 28–18 = 10

- Day Z = 30–11 = 19

Her fertile period (unsafe for intercourse if she does not want to become pregnant) runs from A to Z, days 10 to 19 of her menstrual cycle, counting the first day of her menstrual period as 1.

---

is impossible to use before periods have resumed. Because of the irregularity of the menstrual cycle in many women, it has been the least effective of the various popular birth control methods. For this reason, and because of the much greater effectiveness of Natural Family Planning (NFP; see below), women who wish to use a form of contraceptive that is natural and doesn't contradict religious teachings, prefer NFP.

Natural family planning. A refinement of the calendar-rhythm method, NFP depends on using one or more body signs or symptoms to determine the time of ovulation. The more factors a couple takes into considera-

tion, the better the success rate. These factors include mucus changes in the vagina (the mucus is clear and can be pulled into strings at ovulation); basal body temperature changes (the baseline temperature, measured first thing in the morning, drops slightly just before ovulation, reaches its lowest point at ovulation, and then immediately rises to a high point before returning to the baseline for the rest of the cycle; see diagram); and cervical changes (the normally pink cervix becomes bluish). Intercourse is avoided from the first sign that ovulation is about to occur until three days after.

Though it's possible to use natural family planning without the help of a doctor, learning

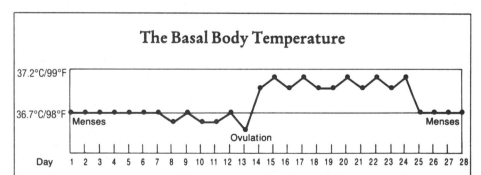

The Basal Body Temperature

37.2°C/99°F

36.7°C/98°F   Menses   Menses

Ovulation

Day   1 2 3 4 5 6 7 8 9 10 11 12 13 14 15 16 17 18 19 20 21 22 23 24 25 26 27 28

The basal body temperature The BBT can help to pinpoint more accurately the unsafe period of ovulation. To get the BBT, the woman takes her temperature every morning *immediately* on awakening, be-

fore speaking, sitting up, etc. In most women the temperature will drop and then rise abruptly at the time of ovulation as seen above. Three full days after ovulation, intercourse can be resumed.

the latest techniques from an informed professional can increase the effectiveness of this (or any) type of birth control.

Because NFP is much more effective at preventing pregnancy than the calendar-rhythm method, and because it, too, is sanctioned by religious groups that find other forms of birth control objectionable, NFP has largely replaced the older method.

Surgical sterilization. Tubal ligation (the tying of the fallopian tubes) for women and vasectomy (the tying or cutting of the *vasa deferentia*, the tubes that transport sperm from testicles to penis) for men must be considered permanent, though occasionally it is possible to reverse them (newer techniques may be easier to reverse). Sterilization is also increasingly safe, with no known long-term health effects, and virtually foolproof. The occasional failure one hears of generally is due not to a failure of the method, but rather to a slipup in the surgery or carelessness on the part of a man who fails to use other birth control methods until all viable sperm have been ejaculated.

Sterilization is frequently the choice of couples who feel their family units are complete. Some women opt to have their tubes tied immediately after delivering their last child.

Diagnosing a New Pregnancy

'I had a baby about ten weeks ago and started feeling a little queasy yesterday. How soon can you get pregnant again and, if you're nursing, how can you tell if you are?'

A new pregnancy at ten weeks postpartum is unusual, particularly in a nursing mother (who isn't likely to ovulate until breast-feedings begin to be supplemented), but it's not unheard of. Unless you or your partner have been sterilized, you run the risk of conceiving any time you have intercourse, even if you use birth control and especially if you don't. A postpartum pregnancy, however, may be difficult to recognize. This is particularly true if you haven't resumed menstruating, since the first tip-off most women get that they might be pregnant is a missed period. If you're nursing, another pregnancy clue many women rely on – tender and enlarged breasts with increased vascularization – may be obscured. However, you may begin to notice other clues that you may have conceived once a new pregnancy is established: a diminished milk supply because different sets of hormones operate in pregnancy and lactation (but such a drop in production may also be due to exhaustion, not nursing enough, or other factors); morning sickness or queasiness (which could also result from something you ate or a gastrointestinal virus); or frequent urination (this could instead be due to a urinary tract infection).

If you have any reason to suspect you are pregnant, or even if you're just unreasonably nervous about the possibility, use a home pregnancy test or go to your doctor or a clinic for a blood test. In the unlikely event that you turn out to be pregnant, see an obstetrician, midwife, or your family doctor as soon as possible. A new pregnancy within a year of childbirth puts a tremendous strain on the body, and you'll need close medical supervision, extra rest and plenty of good nutrition. Because it is virtually impossible to properly nourish a breastfeeding infant and a developing foetus at the same time, it's advisable to wean your infant to formula. If you feel very strongly about continuing to nurse, discuss your feelings with your doctor; you may be able to partially breastfeed and to supplement with formula. If you do, it will be extremely important to consume enough extra calories (about 300 for the foetus and another 200 to 500 for milk production), protein (five servings a day), and calcium for both baby making and milk making (the equivalent of six servings a day), as well as to get plenty of rest.

Exhaustion

'I expected to feel rundown during the postpartum period, but it's been three

*months since I had my baby and I'm
still exhausted. Could something be
wrong?'*

Many a new mother has dragged herself to
her doctor's office complaining of overwhelming chronic fatigue – convinced she's
fallen victim to some fatal malady. The nearly
invariable diagnosis? A classic case of new
motherhood.

Rare is the woman (or man, if he's a full-
time parent) who escapes this parental fatigue syndrome, characterized by physical
exhaustion that never seems to ease up and
an almost total lack of energy. And it's not
surprising. There's no other job as emotionally and physically taxing as mothering in
the first year. The strain and pressure are not
limited to eight hours a day or five days a
week, and there are no lunch hours or coffee
breaks to allow relief. For the first-time
mother, there is also the stress inherent in
any new job: mistakes to be made, problems
to solve, a lot to learn. If all this isn't enough
to produce exhaustion, the new mother may
also have her strength sapped by breastfeeding, by toting around the load of rapidly
growing infant and accompanying paraphernalia, and by night after night of broken
sleep.

The new mother who goes back to an
outside job may also suffer from fatigue and
exhaustion – from trying to do two jobs
well. She gets up early to attend to several
mummying jobs, often including nursing,
before she even leaves for her job away from
home. That job may or may not be a respite,
depending on how stressful it is, but when
she returns home, unless she has a full-time
housekeeper or a particularly helpful and
competent spouse, she will still have
cooking, cleaning, laundry and baby care to
contend with. To top it all off, she can be up
with the baby half the night and still be
expected to be alert and cheerful in the
morning. Exhaustion would be inevitable
for Supermum herself.

Of course, it's a good idea see your doctor
to be sure there is no medical cause for your
exhaustion. If you get a clean bill of health,
be assured that in time, as you gain ex-

perience, as your routine becomes routine,
and as your baby begins sleeping through
the night, the unrelenting fatigue will gradually disappear (though you may not feel
totally 'caught up' on your rest until your
children are all in school). And your energy
level should pick up a bit, too, once your
body adjusts to the new demands. In the
meantime, be sure to eat well, get some
exercise and try the tips for relieving postpartum depression, many of which may also
help reduce fatigue.

Aches and Pains

*'I've been having backaches and a
nagging pain in my neck, arm and
shoulder ever since our son was born.'*

Nothing quite compares to carrying a baby
and an overstuffed nappy bag around all day.
And this weighty burden almost always explains those aches and pains in the neck,
arms, wrists, fingers, shoulders and backs of
new mums – and increasingly, as they share
more of the load, of new dads.

Recognizing the cause of your afflictions is
the first step towards relieving them. (Often,
mothers and the doctors they consult fail to
make this connection, with batteries of
unnecessary tests the common result.) The
next step is to try to alleviate the problem
with a combination of preventive and
curative measures:

- If you haven't yet taken off all of your
  pregnancy weight, gradually do so now.
  Excess weight puts unnecessary strain on
  your back.

- Exercise regularly, concentrating on
  those exercises that strengthen the abdominal muscles, since they support the
  back, and those that strengthen the arms
  (see page 518 for a basic postpartum
  exercise programme).

- Assume a comfortable position for
  feeding baby. Don't slouch, and be sure
  your back is supported – if you can't slide
  all the way to the back of the chair, tuck a

pillow behind you. Use pillows or armrests, as needed, to support your arms as you hold baby and direct breast or bottle. And don't cross your knees.

- Learn to bend and lift correctly. Place feet shoulder-width apart and bend at the knees, not at the waist. When lifting baby or anything else, put the weight on your arms and legs rather than on your back.

- Don't stretch to reach high places; stand on a footstool instead.

- Be conscious of your posture. Walk, sit and lie with your buttocks tucked under and abdomen tilted inward (this is called a 'pelvic tilt').

- Sleep on a firm mattress, or put a board under an overly soft one. A mattress that sags in the middle will have you sagging, too. Lie on your back or side (but not your stomach) with your knees bent.

- If you push a pram or pushchair, be sure the handles are at a comfortable height for you. If they aren't, see if you can have them adjusted, or if they're too short, buy extenders.

- If shoulder pain is a problem, carry the nappy bag in the crook of your arm rather than on your shoulder, or use a backpack.

- Use a heating pad or warm bath to temporarily relieve muscle discomfort and spasm.

- Try not to stand for long periods of time; if you must, keep one foot on a low stool with your knee bent. If you're on a hard-surfaced floor, use a small rug as a cushion underfoot.

- Instead of walking the floor night after night with a colicky infant in your arms, try using a swing (once he's six weeks old) or a rocker to comfort him.

Urinary Incontinence

'Ever since my second child was born, I find that I leak a bit of urine when I cough or laugh or strain to lift something.'

Your problem is probably stress incontinence, which is fairly common in women after childbirth, particularly in those who've had several children. The usual cause is weak muscle tone in the vaginal wall that supports the urethra and bladder. The bladder may push through the weakened musculature, causing a cystocele, or bulge, which is actually a hernia. A small cystocele may not even be noticed, but a large one may droop down to or even through the vaginal opening and can cause some discomfort in addition to the incontinence. Doing two or three hundred Kegel exercises spread out over the course of a day every day for a couple of months (see page 518) may help to strengthen the muscles in the vaginal wall and eliminate the problem. In severe cases, surgery may be recommended to remedy the condition. Unfortunately, unless the uterus is also removed, the cystocele may recur because of the weight of the uterus, especially a pregnant one, pressing down on the bladder and pushing it once again into the vaginal wall.

Friendships

'I feel uncomfortable with my friends who don't have children, but I don't know any women with young babies and feel very lonely.'

Major changes in one's life – a new school, a new job, a new marriage, a move to a new community, a divorce, children leaving the nest, retirement, widowhood – almost always have some effect on relationships. The arrival of a baby is no different. Yet somehow, many women seem more uncertain about how to deal with the changing balance of friendships when they become mothers than at almost any other time. Perhaps that's because nothing quite changes the way you see yourself and the way others see you as much (though for some women, a divorce or widowhood also has the effect of redefining them as people).

Many factors can contribute to changes in your social life post-baby. For one, you undoubtedly have a lot less time and energy for socializing. For another, until you go back to paid employment – whether that's six weeks or six years after your baby is born – you'll feel somewhat removed emotionally as well as physically from the circle of friends that revolved around your job or career. For still another, your interests, if they haven't already, will begin to change. As much as you still might enjoy a conversation centred around foreign policy, films, literature, or gossip, you've probably recently developed an interest in discussing the merits of baby exercise classes or the efficacy of various nappy rash preparations, sharing thoughts on how to quiet a crying baby or how to get more sleep, bragging about baby's first successful attempt at turning over or cutting a first tooth. Yet another factor upsetting your social life: some single friends seem less comfortable with you. This may be partly because you share less in common and partly because some of them, consciously or unconsciously, are envious of your new family. And finally, friendships that are only job-deep (or partying- or tennis-deep) often don't have what it takes to survive change.

What most women are searching for is a way to integrate the women they were with the mothers they've become – without diminishing either. That isn't easy. Trying to stay completely within the old circle denies that you're a mother now. Abandoning old friends and spending time only with other new mothers denies the old you. Making new friends while keeping some of the old will probably be the happiest and most fulfilling of compromises, one which satisfies all the women you are.

See your old friends socially on occasion – for lunch, the ballet, a seminar. They'll want to hear about your baby and your new lifestyle (but not exclusively) and you'll want to hear what's new and what's the same, at work and with their relationships. Try to stick to subjects you have in common, whatever brought you together in the first place. You may find yourself feeling a little uncomfortable at first, but pretty soon you'll know which friendships are going to continue and which it makes sense to put on hold, except perhaps for birthdays and holidays. You may be surprised to find that one or more old friends become very involved in your new life and offer a great source of support. And those old friends you lose touch with may suddenly seek you out again when they begin to have families of their own.

Making new friends among the new mothers in your community is relatively easy. It only requires your turning up at places where mothers of babies congregate (at playgrounds, exercise classes, mothers' groups, play groups, your church or synagogue). Seek out those who share not only your interest in babies but also some of your other interests, so that these friendships can be multi-dimensional and so that you'll have more to talk about than nappies and day care – though you'll find babies will often be the subject of choice.

Different Mothering Styles

'My closest friend is relaxed and disorganized, doesn't worry if her seven-month-old doesn't get his lunch until dinnertime, drags him to parties until all hours – and is in no hurry to return to work. I'm compulsive about everything – bedtimes, meals, clean laundry – and I went back to work part-time when my son was three months old. Who's doing something wrong?'

Nobody. Each mother has to mother in the way that's most comfortable for her. You would probably have a nervous breakdown trying your friend's laissez-faire mothering style, and she would do likewise trying yours. The only time you need fear you're doing something wrong is when your baby tells you – by fussing or crying a lot, by seeming depressed and unresponsive, or by not thriving physically – that he's not satisfied with your approach to mothering. If that happens you've got to make some adjustments – because babies, like mothers, are individuals, with different styles.

A baby who is happy and healthy is saying to his mother, no matter what her style, 'You're doing a great job!'

Breastfeeding During Illness

'I've just come down with the flu. Can I still breastfeed my baby without her getting sick?'

Breastfeeding your baby is the best way to strengthen her resistance to your germs (and other germs around her) and to keep her healthy. She can't catch cold or flu germs through your breast milk, though she can become infected through other contact with you. To minimize the spread of infection, always wash your hands before handling your baby or her belongings and also before feedings; if she ends up getting sick in spite of your precautions, see the treatment tips on page 414. To speed your own recovery as well as keep up your milk supply and your strength while you have a cold or flu, drink extra fluids (a cup of water, juice, soup, or decaffeinated tea every hour while you're awake), be sure to take your vitamin supplement, try to get your Daily Dozen (being particularly certain to meet your vitamin C requirements), and rest when you can. If you have a lot of congestion, drinking juices instead of milk for a couple of days may help reduce it (though this theory is controversial). Check with your doctor if you need medication – *don't* take any without medical approval.

If you come down with a 'stomach virus', or gastroenteritis, you should again take precautions against infecting your baby – though the risk is small, since breastfed babies appear to be protected against most such infections. Wash your hands, especially after you've gone to the bathroom, before touching your baby or anything that she might put into her mouth. Take plenty of fluids (particularly diluted fruit juices or decaffeinated teas[1]) to replace those lost through diarrhoea or vomiting, but limit solids to such bland items as white toast, converted rice, boiled or baked potatoes without the skin, cream of wheat or cream of rice, bananas, apple purée, and Best-Odds gelatin desserts (see page 604).

Though common colds and flus can't be transmitted through breast milk, some forms of hepatitis can. If you come down with this disease, discuss with your baby's doctor the advisability of discontinuing nursing. AIDS may also be transmitted through breast milk; an infected mother should discuss the advisability of nursing with a paediatrician familiar with AIDS.

'I have a cold sore; can my baby boy catch it?'

The cold sore, or fever blister, which usually develops on the lip or around the mouth, is caused by a herpes virus, but a different strain from the one that causes genital herpes. Most people are first infected as children, with the initial episode often including fever as well as sores in the mouth. After the acute phase passes, the virus usually lies dormant in the body for months or even years. During times of physical or emotional stress, it may be reactivated. The most obvious symptom of the flare-up is a blister that oozes and later scabs over. It's only during the blister phase that the virus is transmissible, but it appears that not everyone is susceptible.

To avoid passing the infection on to your baby, wash your hands very thoroughly before handling him or anything that goes into his mouth (including his hands, bottle, or dummy and your nipples) – and no kissing or drinking from the same cup! Lactobacillus (the bacterial culture used to make yogurt), available in tablet form at your chemist and taken as directed, often helps to ward off a threatening cold sore at the first tingle or at least to stop one from becoming

---

1. The once popular diarrhoea cure of cola, ginger ale, or other carbonated beverages is no longer recommended because sugar appears to increase diarrhoea.

full blown. Try that treatment or ask your doctor to suggest another.

If you have an active genital herpes infection, you should be careful to wash your hands thoroughly after using the lavatory and before you feed your baby; use condoms to protect your spouse unless he's already infected. To keep baby away from the sores and from any clothing that touches them, slip into a clean robe or cover your lap with a fresh towel before feeding or handling him. Since herpes can be very risky for a newborn, be especially careful if the infection flares shortly after you deliver.

Persistent Depression

'I can't seem to shake my postpartum depression. My son's already four months old, but I have no energy. I don't feel like doing anything or seeing anybody or even leaving the house. My husband says I need help, but I keep hoping I'll come out of it on my own.'

Maybe you will come out of it on your own, and maybe you won't. In about one in a thousand cases, postpartum depression is so severe and so persistent that expert treatment is needed to bring the new mother to emotional equilibrium. Your prolonged depression suggests that you may be that one in a thousand. There's no point in suffering (or making your family suffer) any longer on the chance that you may beat the blues yourself – get help now. Talk to your obstetrician or family doctor first. He or she may be able to help you; if not, you will be referred to a specialist. Because your problem is more likely to be physical (caused by a hormone imbalance) than emotional, a medical doctor is likely to be able to help more quickly and more satisfactorily than a nonmedical therapist. Hormone therapy may be helpful in some cases.

Whomever you turn to for help, do it quickly. The sooner you shed the baby blues, the sooner you can start enjoying your baby and your new life as a mother.

Finding Time for Yourself

'I'm so busy seeing to my new daughter's needs that I never have time to see to my own. Sometimes I don't even have a chance to take a shower.'

Little things can mean a lot to the mother of a young baby. And often these little things that others take for granted – going to the bathroom when you feel the urge, having a cup of coffee while it's still hot, sitting down for lunch – become luxuries she can no longer afford.

Still, it's important to *make* time you can call your own. Not only so that you (and your husband) will remember that your needs count, but so that your baby, as she grows in awareness, will recognize this, too. 'Mother' needn't be synonymous with 'martyr'. You don't have to suffer frequent urinary tract infections from infrequent trips to the bathroom, or indigestion from eating on the go, or chronically and depressingly greasy hair from postponing showers. Though it will, indeed, take a lot of judicious juggling to meet your own needs without neglecting your baby's, it will be well worth it for both of you. After all, a happier mother is a better mother.

How to best make time for yourself will depend on such factors as your schedule, your priorities and just what it is you want to find time for. But the following tips can help put a little more personal time in your life:

Let baby cry. Not for half an hour, but certainly it won't hurt if you put her safely in her cot and let her fuss while you brush your teeth or put on some mascara and lipstick.

Include baby. Sit down to lunch with your baby. If she's not yet on solids, put her in a baby seat on the table and chat with her as you eat. Or take your lunch to the park if she's more content in her pushchair and if weather permits. Place her in her baby seat on the bathroom floor while you attend to personal needs – she'll be getting early potty training while you get relief. Or play peekaboo with her from behind the curtain while you shower.

Depend on daddy. Shower while he breakfasts with her in the morning, or give yourself a facial while he takes her for a walk on Saturday afternoon. Don't feel guilty about turning baby over to him in his spare time; a mother's work (whether full-or part-time) is more consuming and demanding than any paid job.

Exchange favours. Trade baby-sitting services with other mothers who also need to free up some time. Sit for a friend's baby and your own one afternoon or morning a week while she does whatever it is she needs to get done; she reciprocates another day.

Hire help. You may not be able to afford even a part-time baby-sitter, but you probably can afford a young teenager to entertain your baby while you prepare dinner or attend to other chores at home.

Baby Forgetting You

'I'm going to be starting back to work in a couple of weeks. What worries me most is that my baby won't know me when I get home at night.'

This concern is at the top of the worry list of virtually every mother who has to leave her baby – even briefly – for any reason. But it's a worry that can quickly be crossed off the list. Babies know their mothers very early, recognize their voices almost at birth, and don't forget them even if they are away for the day.

Quality Time

'I hear a lot about the importance of spending quality time with your children. Well, even though I spend virtually all my time with my son, I'm so busy that I'm not sure there's any quality to it.'

Along with the proliferation of the working mother (a misnomer, since *all* mothers work) came the popularization of the concept of 'quality time': if a mother couldn't spend a lot of time with her child, the least she could do was make the best of the time she did spend with him. The theory seemed to imply that quantity was no longer important. But there's quality in quantity, too. You don't have to drop everything, sit down on the floor and play with your baby all day long to provide him with quality care. You give quality time every time you change his nappy and smile at him, every time you feed him and talk to him, every time you bathe him and splash around with bath toys. You do it even when you chat with him from the kitchen as he races around in his walker, sing to him while you're driving in the car, lean over to tickle him in his playpen as you vacuum by, or sit him down with some blocks while you sit down with the bills.

Quality parenting time is time spent relating to your child in passive as well as active ways, and something that a loving and responsive mother who spends a lot of time with her child can hardly avoid providing. You'll know if you're succeeding just by watching your baby – does he smile, laugh, respond, seem basically content? If the answers are yes, he's getting quality time.

'As a mother who works outside the house full-time, I worry that I don't spend enough quality time with my daughter.'

An employed mother is under enough pressure without having the added pressure of worrying about whether the time she spends with her child or children is of the proper quality (which, incidentally, isn't the kind of pressure that enhances performance). If you do have limited time with your baby, the impulse is to make every minute count. Accepting the impossibility of this (there will be moments when you'll need to do things other than child care, moments when she'll want to turn her interests elsewhere; days when you'll be in a lousy mood, days when she'll be) will, ironically, be the first step in ensuring your time with her is well spent. The following are other steps you can take:

Act natural. No need to don your Supermum cape before you walk through the door. All your daughter wants is *you*. And no need to fill every minute you have with her with stimulating activities. Instead, be spontaneous and take your cues from your baby (she may be too pooped at day's end for active play). Quality time is time spent together, whether it's eating together, cuddling together, or just being together in the same room (even if you're not doing the same thing).

Involve your baby. Take her with you into the bedroom while you change from your work clothes, and otherwise include her in your routine when you get home from work. She can play with the empty envelopes while you open the mail, empty the carrier bags while you put away groceries, or bang on pots and pans while you prepare dinner.

Tell her about your day. This will serve two purposes. One, it will ensure that you're communicating with her (she loves to listen to you talk, even if she doesn't understand what you're saying). Two, unloading your day's experiences will help you unwind and make a faster transition from your job to your homelife.

Give your house short shrift. With time at a premium, devote less of it to matters that matter less (cleaning, cooking and clothes care for instance). Take shortcuts in dinner preparation wherever possible (cook double quantities, freeze half to reheat another night; use frozen vegetables; get your green leafies from the local salad bar). Let the dust accumulate all week, and wait until the weekend to tackle it all at once with your husband. Or if you can afford it, hire someone to clean once a week. Use no-iron clothes, skipping the touch-ups, and send out your shirts if they have to be perfect.

Keep your dinner on the back burner. Or don't put it on at all until your baby's gone to bed. Late meals may not be best for digestion, but they'll give you more time to spend with your baby while she's awake (give her your undivided attention while she dines) and more time to spend with your husband when she's asleep (when he can be the centre of attention). Though family dinnertimes are important later on, they're not really necessary now. At this age, in fact, meals with baby can be so stressful that instead of enhancing togetherness, they can give it a bad name.

Tune out distractions. You can't give your baby quality time while you're catching the six o'clock news. Save television watching, radio listening and phone-call making for after your baby's gone to bed. Turn on the answering machine to postpone talking to incoming callers until after her bedtime, too.

Don't shut out your husband. In your quest for quality time with your baby, don't forget time spent as a family. Include your husband in whatever you're doing with the baby, from bathing to tickling. Also keep in mind that time he spends with her alone is important, too, for several reasons. It allows him to enjoy the pleasures of participatory parenting, something many fathers of generations past missed. It gives your baby the benefits of closeness with two unique individuals. And it doubles her quality time.

Finding Time for Romance

'My husband and I are both so busy – with our jobs, our new son, the house – that we rarely find any time for each other. And when we do, we're too tired to make the most of it.'

The three that baby makes isn't necessarily a crowd, but he can crowd your days and nights so much that you have no time left for the company of two. The period of new parenthood is actually one during which it is very easy for couples to grow apart instead of closer. Yet your relationship with your husband is the most significant in your life – more important even than the relationship with your child (children grow up and leave the nest, but hopefully your mate will be yours into old age). It was your love for each other that created your family in the first place, and it's that love that can best nurture and sustain it.

Nevertheless, the husband-wife relationship is the most easily taken for granted. If either of you neglected your jobs or your baby, the consequences would be clear and swift. Even the results of neglecting such home chores as cleaning and cooking would quickly become evident. But the results of neglecting a marriage often are not apparent at first; still; they can erode a relationship before the partners even realize it.

So give your relationship its due now and make a conscious effort to keep the love-lights glowing or, if they seem to have flickered out, to rekindle them. Rethink your priorities and reorganize your time in any way you have to, but free some up to spend alone together. One way is to put your baby on a reasonably early-to-bed schedule (see page 169 for tips on how) and settle back for some quality time with each other. Share a leisurely late dinner (no TV, no phone calls, no reading the daily paper and, hopefully, no crying baby allowed). A glass of wine may help you unwind (unless it leads to three or four, which may unravel you completely); candlelight and soft background music will help set the romantic mood.

Every such evening need not culminate in coitus. Indeed, intercourse may turn out to be a relatively rare treat in the exhausting early months – it may even be a treat you won't be very interested in for a while. Right now, verbal intercourse can be even more beneficial to your relationship than the sexual variety. But resist the temptation to talk exclusively about the baby; that would defeat the purpose of your interlude.

Try to wangle a romantic night out on the town at least once a month; more often would be even better. Have dinner, see a movie, visit with friends, or do whatever it is you enjoy doing together most. Also try to arrange for a baby-free hour or two on weekends to pursue a shared interest. Hire a baby-sitter, swap sitting time with a neighbour, or enlist a grandparent (this is a great deal for everyone concerned).

If you can't seem to squeeze a regular rendezvous into your current schedule, a reevaluation of that schedule is in order. Perhaps you're trying to do too much. One or both of you may have to cut back working hours, drop a class, miss a football game or bowling night, or reduce TV watching.

Jealousy of Daddy's Attention to Baby

'As terrible as this sounds, I'm finding that I'm jealous of the time my husband spends with our daughter. I sometimes wish he'd devote half as much attention to me.'

As harmless – even as heartwarming – as a budding romance between father and infant may seem to an outsider, it can be genuinely threatening to a woman who's not used to sharing her husband's affection, particularly if she's enjoyed his solicitous attention during nine months of pregnancy.

Although your feelings of jealousy will probably subside on their own once the family dynamics have had some time to work themselves out, there are several steps you can take to deal with them in the meantime:

Be assured. The first thing you need to do to overcome the feelings you're experiencing is to recognize that they're normal and common – not petty, evil, selfish, immoral, or otherwise shameful. Dump that guilt.

Be grateful. Consider how lucky you are to be married to the kind of man who's eager to spend time with his baby. Though active participation from the male partner in parenting is increasingly common, it's by no means standard. Take advantage of the time they spend together to catch up on chores or personal needs. Watch with appreciation the love that's blossoming between the two of them, and try to support it; the bonds they're building now will last a lifetime, through the terrible twos and even the turbulent teens, and will make your daughter a better woman (or make your son a better man).

Be a part of it. Father and baby should certainly share some time alone together, but sometimes a third player will be welcome. Join that tickle fest (he gets the ribcage, you get the toes), flop down on the bed beside them as they read a book, sit down and make their two-way game of 'catch' on the rug three-way.

Be honest and open. Don't just sulk from the sidelines when daddy and baby leave you out of the loving action. In the excitement of discovering a new best buddy, your husband may not realize that he's been shutting out his (relatively) old one; he may even believe he's helping you out. Tell him, without being offensive or putting him on the defensive, how you feel and exactly what he can do about it (for example, tell *both* of you how pretty you look, give *both* of you a kiss and hug when he comes and goes, snuggle spontaneously with *both* of you). He can't fulfill your needs unless he knows what they are.

Be there for him. Remember, a relationship that works, works two ways. You can't ask your husband to devote more attention to you without your reciprocating. Make sure you, too, haven't been spending all your time, energy and affection on the baby, unwittingly leaving none of the above for him. Dote on him, and you're bound to find him doting back.

Be there for baby, too. Maybe your husband is consciously or subconsciously trying to compensate for attention he feels your baby isn't getting from you. Perhaps you're so busy with other responsibilities (a job, housework, volunteer work, sports, or whatever) that you have little time left for your child. If that's the case, be grateful she's getting parental attention somewhere, and consider reassessing your priorities to make certain that she gets more of it from you.

Jealousy of Daddy's Parenting Skills

'I thought that mothers were supposed to be naturally better at parenting than fathers. But my husband has a way with our son – making him laugh, calming him down, rocking him to sleep – that I don't. And that makes me feel inadequate and insecure.'

Every parent enters parenthood with something to offer his or her baby, with no one contribution more valuable or desirable than another, at least not as far as the little beneficiary is concerned. Some parents are better at the fun-and-games aspects of baby raising (roughhousing, getting a good giggle going, playing peekaboo), some at the nuts-and-bolts tasks (feeding, bathing, getting baby dressed without a struggle). Some, like your husband, display a knack for building rapport with baby.

Still, it isn't surprising for one parent to be a little envious of the other's talents. But it's possible to shake such feelings:

Consider yourself lucky. The father who's able and willing to participate so fully and successfully in baby care is a precious commodity and can take a lot of the pressure off mum. Let him practise his baby magic whenever possible. For any partnership to be productive each partner should contribute what he or she knows and can do best.

Don't be a female chauvinist. Sexual stereotypes that depict women as naturally better at parenting than men are inaccurate and, ultimately, destructive to all concerned. There is no child-care responsibility other than breastfeeding that all mothers are more naturally suited to than all fathers, or vice versa. Some parents (no matter what gender) have a natural knack for parenting skills, some have to work hard at mastering infant care. Given the opportunity, any parent of either sex can overcome a lack of natural aptitude in time.

Give yourself more credit. You may not realize how much you do for your baby and how well you do it – though your baby almost certainly does, and he couldn't do without you.

And give yourself a chance. Just because certain parenting skills don't come as easily to you as they do to your husband doesn't mean they'll always be elusive. If you're breastfeeding, you may find that once you've weaned your baby and the distraction of breast milk is past, you'll be able to calm him on your chest as well as your husband does. With practice and a lessening of self-consciousness, you will also learn to sing the lullabies and silly songs your baby loves, to play finger games and make funny faces, and to rock him with a comforting rhythm.

Instead of mimicking what seems to work for your husband, start doing what comes naturally to you. Your odds for success will be better if you don't start out with a defeatist attitude, which your smarter-than-you-think baby is sure to sense. Also make sure you get the chance to give yourself a chance. If your baby-care assignments all seem to be the more tedious, less rewarding ones (changing nappies or giving the dreaded shampoo, for instance), negotiate some changes in the duty roster with your husband. When he takes over some of the less glamorous tasks, you will be freed up for some of the fun ones.

And remember, no matter how good a relationship dad and baby develop, there will always be times when no one else will do for your child but you, and you'll hear those soon to be familiar words: 'I want my mummy.'

Feeling Unappreciated as a Woman

'Ever since our son was born, I've felt that my husband sees me only as the mother of his child, not as the woman he loves.'

A man doesn't usually grow up thinking of his own mother as a sexual being, or if he

does, he quickly learns to sublimate such thoughts. When the woman he loves, and who is the sexual being in his life, becomes a mother, his feelings about her often become confused. She frequently adds to his dilemma by acting more like a mother than a partner as she busily tries to master the new and challenging role of mother.

Though this is a common problem in new families, it isn't an insolvable one and resolving it is one of the most significant steps you can take to ensure your baby will grow up in a happy, intact home. You *can* be both mother to your child and wife and lover to your spouse; it only takes a little extra effort.

Make yourself feel like a woman. Caring for your looks is a good place to begin. Clean and well-groomed hair (an easy-care haircut will help), simple makeup (if you customarily wear it, or if you feel you need it now that you're getting less sleep), and fresh clothes (a shirt baby has spit up on isn't going to inspire romance) will not only make you feel more attractive, they will help your husband to see you as a desirable woman. Hoping to start the day that way every day would, for most new mothers, be unrealistic; but attaining that state before a husband's key turns in the door in the evening may not be. Even on the worst of days, when a shampoo is impossible, when you feel lucky to find a sweatshirt that doesn't clash with your leggings, you can take five minutes for a quick face wash and mini-makeover: put on some mascara and blusher, run a brush through your hair, dab on some of your favourite scent. You'll feel better and your efforts won't be lost on your spouse.

Make him feel like a man. Most new mothers transfer their focus from their husband to their baby, at least initially. That's good for the perpetuation of the species, but not so good for the perpetuation of the marriage. Make it a point to romance your husband as you would like to be romanced. Hug him unexpectedly from behind while he's washing the dishes, squeeze his hand when he passes the baby shampoo, lavish him with compliments when he comes home with a new haircut, kiss him anytime (and anywhere) at all. Cook his favourite meal, give him an unbirthday present, ask him how his day went instead of just complaining about yours.

Share the baby. Making your husband feel more comfortable as a father may help him feel more like a man, reduce any resentment about sharing you with the baby and make him more a part of your new life, which in turn may help rekindle the romantic flame for both of you. Encourage him to participate in baby care without nagging him to do so, making it seem more like a privilege and a pleasure than a chore. And be sure to praise, not criticize, his efforts – even if they're clumsy at first.

Thinking about the Next Baby

'I'm nearly forty and had my first baby nearly a year ago. I know it's early to be thinking about another, but I don't have many fertile years left.'

Today, decisions about spacing offspring often have less to do with the latest psychological literature on what's best for baby than on the exigencies of time. Many women are trying to squeeze in a second or third baby before they reach forty, or soon thereafter.

It's best to wait at least a year after the birth of one child before becoming pregnant with the next. Many mums and babies have, it's true, come through closer spacings with no problems, but a year's hiatus gives a mother's body adequate time to heal and recover strength (particularly important if the first baby was delivered by caesarean section). It also allows for nursing the first child for a full year if desired. What it doesn't allow for, unfortunately, is optimum time for that child to be the baby of the family. It's probably not ideal to be displaced by a younger sibling when you're barely out of nappies yourself; and today, most babies still aren't even at 21 months. The experts are divided on what is ideal, though most suggest a two- to four-year wait, which some (but not all) studies indicate gives children a slight edge. But generalities don't work for every family, and the best time for you to have another baby is when you and your spouse feel your family is ready.

Since waiting longer than a year is not always an acceptable option, you should also know that close spacing of children can work well. It offers some pluses that two- to four-year spacing doesn't, particularly once the first few years of chaos, sleepless nights and endless nappies are over: the siblings may be closer chums; and the same toys, movies, activities and holidays may interest both. With plenty of love, attention, and preparation your oldest can make the transition from baby to older sibling with a minimum of trauma (see page 588).

If you are seriously thinking about becoming pregnant again soon, see your doctor for a complete checkup now; take care of any dental problems, too. Then, in the two or three months before you start trying to conceive, start preparing your body:[2]

- Wean your baby, if you haven't already. Or in the competition for nutrients, someone's bound to lose – and it's most likely to be the unborn baby. Setting up such a sibling rivalry isn't healthy or recommended. You, too, may suffer if your stores are drained of calcium and other essential nutrients.

- Follow the Best-Odds Prepregnancy Diet (see footnote number 2), and encourage your husband to improve his diet, too. Continue taking a pregnancy vitamin supplement.

- Get or stay in shape with exercise and try to bring or keep your weight as close to ideal as possible. Do not diet strenuously, however, in the few months before conception, and *don't* try to lose weight once you've become pregnant.

---

2. For a more detailed prepregnancy plan, see our book *What to Expect When You're Expecting*.

- Discontinue using birth control pills or spermicides at least two months (or better still, three) before the time you plan to begin trying to conceive. Switch to condoms until you're ready to begin trying.

- Avoid excesses in alcohol during the pre-pregnancy stage; stop drinking altogether once you start trying to conceive. If you smoke or use other 'recreational' drugs, quit before you try to conceive. Your husband, too, should abstain from alcohol and drugs while you are trying to conceive. If either of you can't quit, get help.

- Once you've begun trying to conceive, limit prescription and over-the-counter drugs to those your doctor approves for use during pregnancy.

- Also once you begin trying, avoid exposure to X-rays or potentially hazardous chemicals.

- Relax. Excess stress in your life can prevent your conceiving and too much tension during pregnancy isn't good for your foetus, your older baby, or you.

WHAT IT'S IMPORTANT TO KNOW:
To Work or Not to Work

Many women, because of a variety of pressures – societal, career, financial – don't have the option of staying at home after their babies are born. However, for those who have a choice, the process of decision making is often agonizing. Child-care experts – because they are in disagreement – offer these mothers little guidance. Some believe there is no harm and possibly some benefit when a mother takes a job and leaves her baby in a child-care situation. Others believe just as strongly that there is the potential for more than a little damage to the infant in a two-paycheque family and urge that one parent (for practical reasons it's usually the mother) stay at home, at least part-time, until the baby is three years old.

Research is no more helpful. Study results are contradictory. Primarily this is because such research is both difficult to do and difficult to evaluate. (How do you judge the effects on her offspring when a mother holds a paying job. Or doesn't hold one? Which effects are important to evaluate? Which are difficult to quantify? Are there some we can't even predict? Will problems show up early or not until adulthood?) In addition, the research is often coloured by the bias of the researcher.

With no clear-cut evidence on the long-term risks or benefits of a mother's working outside the home to go on, the full weight of making this decision falls entirely on the parents. If you're pondering the quesiton, asking yourself the following questions may help you sort out the best way to go.

What are your priorities? Consider carefully what is most important in your life. List your priorities in order on paper. They may include your baby, your family, your career, financial security, the luxuries of life, holidays, study – and may be vastly different from those of the woman next door or the woman at the next desk. After charting your priorities, consider whether returning to employment or staying at home will best meet the most important of them.

Which full-time role suits your personality best? Are you at your best at home with the baby? Or does staying home make you impatient and tense? Will you be able to leave worries about your baby at home when you go to your job, and worries about your job at the office when you're home with the baby? Or will an inability to compartmentalize your life keep you from doing your best at either job?

Would you feel comfortable having someone else take care of your baby? Do you feel no one else can do the job as well as you can? Or do you feel secure that you can find (or have found) a person (or group situation) that can substitute well for you during your hours away from home?

How do you feel about missing the major milestones? The first time your baby laughs, sits alone, gets up on all fours and crawls, or takes a step – will you mind hearing about it secondhand? Will you feel saddened and slighted if the nanny is the one your baby runs to when hurt? Do you feel you can learn to tune in to your baby's unspoken needs and feelings by just spending evenings and weekends together?

How much energy do you have? You'll need plenty of emotional and physical stamina to rise with a baby, get yourself ready for work, put in a full day on the job, then return to the demands of your baby, home and husband once again. Often, what suffers most when energy is lacking in the two-paycheque family with young children is the relationship between husband and wife.

How stressful are your job and your baby? If your job is low stress and your baby's a piece of cake to care for, the duo may be relatively easy to handle. If your job is high pressure and your baby is, too, will you find yourself unable to cope with both, day in and day out?

If you do return to employment, will you get adequate support from your spouse or from some other source? Even a mother from the planet Krypton couldn't do it all alone. Will your husband be willing to do his share of baby care, shopping, cooking, cleaning and laundry? Or are you able to afford outside help to take up the slack?

What is your financial situation? Will your not working threaten your family's economic survival, or just necessitate cutting down on the extras you've been enjoying? Are there ways of cutting back so that the loss of your income won't hurt so much? If you go back to work, how much of a dent will job-related costs (clothes, commutation, child care) make in your income?

How flexible is your job? Will you be able to take time off if your baby or your nanny is sick? Or come in late or leave early if there's an emergency at home? Does your job require long hours, weekends and/or travel? Are you willing to spend extended time away from the baby?

How will not returning to your job affect your career? Putting a career on hold can sometimes set you back when you return to the working world. If you suspect this will happen to you (though many women discover, when they return, that their fears haven't materialized), are you willing to make this sacrifice? Are there ways to keep yourself in touch professionally during your at-home years without making a full-time commitment?

Is there a compromise position? Maybe you can't have it all and remain sane, but you may be able to have the the best of both worlds by looking for a creative compromise. The possibilities are endless and depend on your skills and work experience. If your skills are valuable to someone full-time, then you should be able to sell them part-time. It's possible a current or previous employer, or somebody new, will hire you on a flexible, reduced, or job-sharing schedule. Or maybe you can be a freelance consultant rather than a full-time employee. Perhaps you can do some or all of your work at home, or bring your baby to the office part-time (some women have done this successfully full-time). Or take your baby with you to see clients and on assignments (again, something a few determined women have managed to pull off). When you have the choice, it's usually better to work four or five half-days than two or three full ones – that way you won't be apart from your baby for long stretches.

If are an estate agent, show houses twice a week; tutor two or three afternoons for pay if you're a teacher; see clients a couple of nights a week if you're a therapist; teach some self-help health classes if you're a nurse; take in typing if you're a secretary; or work part-time for a group or in a clinic if you're a doctor. If you enjoy teaching, start a class in your area of expertise (anything from cooking to creative writing, from aerobic exercise to exercising rights in housing court, from how to fix a car to how to prepare tax returns) at your local church or synagogue, or an adult learning centre.

Or run a part-time business out of your home. If you're an accountant or an advertising copywriter, find a few clients whose accounts you can handle from your den; if you're a writer, editor, or graphic designer, look for freelance assignments. If you've a knack for knitting, design sweaters to sell to baby boutiques; if you make an incomparable carrot cake, package your creations for a local gourmet shop.

If you decide to work out of your home, for yourself or someone else, you may still need a baby-sitter for at least part of your working hours. But you can also plan to work while baby naps and after he or she's in bed for the night, and to do pickups and deliveries with baby in tow. Getting help with the household chores is important so that you won't have to give up too much of your time with the baby.

Whatever choice you make, it's likely to require some measure of sacrifice. As committed as you might be to staying home, you may nevertheless feel a pang or two (or more) of regret when you talk to friends who are still pursuing their careers. Or as committed as you might be to returning to your job, you may experience regret when you pass mothers and their babies on their way to the park while you're on your way to the office.

Such misgivings are normal, and since few perfect situations exist in our imperfect world, they're something you'll have to learn to live with. If, however, they begin to

multiply and you find dissatisfaction outweighing satisfaction, it's time to reassess the choice you've made. A decision that seemed right in theory when you made it may seem all wrong in practice now – in which case you shouldn't hesitate to reverse or alter it, if at all possible.

And when everything isn't as idyllic as you'd like, remember that children who get plenty of love are very resilient. Even the wrong decision, if there is such a thing, isn't likely to leave permanent scars.

When to Return to your Job

There's no predictably perfect point at which someone can say, 'Okay, now you can go back to your job. Your baby will be fine and so will you.' If you decide to go back to work during the first year, when you pick up that briefcase or lunchbox will depend in part on your job and the amount of maternity leave you were able to wangle and in part on when you and your baby are ready. And that's highly personal and highly individual.

If you have the choice, experts suggest you wait at least until you've 'attached' or 'bonded' with your baby and feel competent as a mother. Bonding can take three months (though if your baby has had colic, you will probably just be starting to become friends at this point), or it can take five or six. Unfortunately many women with difficult babies hurry back to their jobs, assuming someone else can do a better job with the baby than they can. With the task of bonding incomplete, some of these women never do reach the point of feeling competent at mothering – which could be detrimental to the mother-child relationship.

Maternity leave and benefit arrangements in the U.K. lag behind much of the Western world. Canadian workers are guaranteed up to 41 weeks of leave with job security and 60% pay, Italians get up to five months with 80% pay, and West Germans 18 weeks at full pay. We should be able to do at least as well.

TWENTY-FIVE

Becoming A Father

◆

For the nine months of your partner's pregnancy, the direct care of your baby was pretty much out of your hands – not by choice, but thanks to the quirks of reproductive biology. You could stand by, offering love and support, but you couldn't take over the responsibility of nurturing your baby even for a moment.

Now that the cord's been cut, the rules of the game have changed. No longer do you need special biological equipment for the job of child care. You don't even need experience. All you need is the will to chip in and parent. Not as your partner's chief assistant and bottle washer, but as her partner in the wonderful, unpredictable, exhausting, exhilarating, enlightening, ever-challenging business of parenting.

What You May Be Concerned About

Your Diet and Your Baby

'I gave up a lot of my favourite foods when my wife was pregnant so I could support her efforts to eat right for our baby. But enough's enough. Now that our son's here, shouldn't I be able to eat what I like?'

Your baby's nutritional dependence doesn't end with the cutting of the umbilical cord. Until he's grown and has moved out of your home, your child will likely be what you (and the rest of the family) eat. Elect to breakfast on doughnuts or Danish pastries, snack between meals on crisps or biscuits, wash down your lunchtime sandwich with Coke, leave your carrots and courgettes at dinner, and you're setting a dietary example that he's sure to follow.

Another significant reason to take your diet seriously, even while your child is a young infant, is to increase the odds that you'll be around when he's older, and that you'll be a healthy, productive father to

him as he grows. The diseases that are most likely to take your life, or the lives of other Western males, prematurely – cancer, heart disease, stroke, diabetes – can all be prevented to some degree by eating right.

Continue to eat a diet high in fibre-rich complex carbohydrates (such as whole-grain cereals and breads, high-protein or whole-grain pastas, dried peas and beans, fruits and vegetables), low in sugar, salt, fat (especially hardened or saturated fats) and cholesterol, and moderate in protein – for baby's sake as well as your own.

And don't sabotage the benefits you give your baby through good diet by smoking. Children of smoking parents have considerably more illness than children of non-smokers, and they are more likely to smoke themselves. They are also more likely to be colicky. If you're a smoker and have had difficulty quitting, seek help from your doctor or join a smoking cessation programme or group.

A Disappointing Delivery

'My wife and I had our hearts set on a natural childbirth. But delivery didn't go as we'd hoped and she ended up needing medication. I was upset then, and I still feel a sense of disappointment.'

Like many women experiencing childbirth today, many husbands have come to believe that the labour and delivery experience is a test to be passed or failed. If medication, an episiotomy, or even a caesarean proves necessary, these husbands consider the birth a failure and often end up feeling not only disappointed but angry. These attitudes are usually born in childbirth education classes and in pregnancy books that emphasize the joy of the birth experience over a safe outcome, and that pressurize couples to 'go natural' under almost any circumstance. The implication is that when a woman asks for medication it's because she's inexcusably weak, not because the pain is unbearably strong. Descriptions of the birthing process can be more idealistic than realistic, often calling the pain of childbirth 'discomfort' in spite of the fact that research has shown it to be the most severe pain experienced by humans.

That's not to say that the birth experience never turns out to be a perfect and perfectly natural one, just that more often it doesn't. And in the long run, it really doesn't matter whether it does or not. As long as both mother and child come out of the birthing or delivery room healthy, childbirth was a success and both parents have every reason to be happy. By making your wife feel that you're dissatisfied with her 'performance' (even indirectly) if medical intervention proved necessary, you may heighten her own feelings of inadequacy and intensify her disappointment – both of which can put her at increased risk for postpartum depression. Instead, let her know how proud you are of her, how you admire her courage, how happy you are that both she and the baby came through the ordeal in good shape and how much both of them mean to you.

Bonding

'I expected to be overwhelmed with affection for my baby the first time I held her in the birthing room, but I wasn't. She's so unresponsive, so red and puffy, so unlike what I'd imagined she'd be.'

To a first-time parent who's never even seen a minutes-old newborn before, disappointment and dismay are as likely to be first reactions to the just-delivered offspring as love and affection. As with any romance, your love affair with your baby will require plenty of time and nurturing to develop and deepen. Even those new parents who seem to fall in love with their babies 'at first sight' find their relationships growing richer as the months pass.

Relax. As your baby becomes more responsive, so will you. And what you'll feel once you've had a chance to get to know her will have far more impact on your future than what you feel at your first meeting.

If, however, you don't begin to feel any love towards your baby in the weeks ahead, and especially if you feel anger, hostility, or violent urges, seek immediate psychological counselling from your family doctor, a family therapist, a psychiatrist, or another mental health professional.

'My wife had an emergency caesarean and I wasn't allowed to be with her. I didn't hold our son until 24 hours later and I'm afraid bonding will suffer.'

Until the 1970s, fathers rarely witnessed the birth of their children and none had even heard of the concept of 'bonding'. Nevertheless, most developed loving relationships with their sons and daughters. And though in recent years, witnessing the birth of their offspring has enriched the lives of many men, it hasn't guaranteed a lifetime of father-child closeness.

Being able to share the moment of delivery with your wife is certainly ideal, and being deprived of that opportunity is reason for disappointment – particularly if you spent months training together for child-birth. But it's no reason for a less than loving relationship with your baby. What really bonds you with your baby is day-to-day contact – changing nappies, bathing, feeding, cuddling, lullabying, playing. He will never care that you didn't share in the moment of birth or the first hours after it, but he will surely miss you if you aren't there when he needs you from then on.

Wife's Postpartum Depression

'We have a beautiful and healthy baby girl, just what my wife has always wanted. Still, she's been weepy and unhappy ever since she came home from the hospital.'

A number of factors – from a sense of let-down over not being pregnant any more to frustration over still looking as if she is – combine with hormonal upheaval to trigger postpartum depression in about half (some estimates go as high as 90%) of all newly or recently delivered women. Fortunately for the vast majority (about 999 in 1,000), the depression is neither severe nor long lasting, and usually resolves within the first couple of weeks postpartum.

Though hormonal changes may contribute to postpartum depression, you don't have to be an endocrinologist – only a loving and attentive husband – to help banish it. Try to:

Lighten her load. Fatigue, a major contributor to depression, is an inevitable component of the postpartum period. Be sure that your wife has all the help she needs – from you when you're around and from others when you're not.

Brighten her day – and night. When the new arrival becomes the centre of everyone's attention, the new mother often feels neglected. She may also feel inadequate (having much to learn about the care and feeding of an infant) as well as unattractive

(having several pregnancy kg/pounds still to shed). Here, too, you can make a difference. Compliment her at unexpected moments on how good she is with the baby, how radiant she looks, how slim she's getting, how motherhood becomes her. Cheer her up with little gifts – flowers, a new book, a pretty nightgown – but not chocolates, which will only feed the depression and the extra weight.

Take her away from it all. Time alone together is critical not only for her sake but also for the sake of your relationship. Make some time daily for the two of you (see page 570 for help).

If your wife's depression lasts more than two weeks, is accompanied by sleeplessness, lack of appetite, expressions of hopelessness and helplessness, or suicidal or violent urges, don't wait any longer for it to pass. Insist that she seek help – from either her obstetrician, the family doctor, or a skilled therapist. A very occasional new mother needs psychiatric care to clear the hurdles of the first few months of motherhood.

Once in a while, the depression holds off until the new mother weans her breastfed baby. As with any depression, it should be treated if it persists.

Your Depression

'How come my wife feels terrific since our son was born, and I'm the one with postpartum depression?'

Today's fathers are becoming more involved in pregnancy, childbirth and child care than ever before. Short of carrying the foetus and nursing the baby, there's virtually nothing they're not getting into – including postpartum depression. In fact, a full 62% of dads in one study were found to be suffering from the 'baby blues'. Though there's been some speculation that hormones are somehow the cause, there's been no evidence to support the theory. It's much more likely that any number of the following contributing factors are combining to bring you down at what you may have expected would be one of the highest points of your life:

Financial stress. Rare is the father who is exempt from financial concerns once there's another mouth to feed, body to clothe, mind to educate and future to plan for. The stress can be compounded when one paycheque in a two-paycheque family suddenly disappears, even temporarily.

Feeling like a third wheel. A father who's become accustomed to being the centre of his wife's life may be chagrined to suddenly discover himself on the sidelines, watching her attention being lavished on a noisy newcomer.

A love life lost. Many men find their sex lives are curtailed, at least temporarily, which is depressing enough. But on top of that they fear that the romantic relationship they once enjoyed with their wives will never be completely revived.

Changed relationships. A husband who had been dependent on his wife for the fulfillment of a variety of needs may be upset to find she's suddenly unavailable because she's busy filling someone else's needs. Conversely, a husband used to having his wife depend on him may be unnerved to find that she, having found a dependent of her own, no longer is. Until he adjusts to the changing family dynamics, a new father can feel emotionally out of kilter.

Altered life style. You needn't have had a full social calendar before baby's arrival to be depressed about not having any social life at all now that he's here. At least for a while, even a film or a dinner with friends may be elusive, and staying home night after night can certainly spark a dark mood in anyone but the most naturally reclusive new father.

Sleep deprivation. Though the father who routinely answers his baby's calls is likely to be most worn out by middle-of-the-night wakings, even the father who doesn't is bound to feel the effects of night after night of disturbed sleep. The physical exhaustion soon takes an emotional toll, often in the form of depression.

Being aware of the possible causes of your 'baby blues' may help you to escape, or at least manage, them – particularly if you take steps to modify their effects (see tips throughout this chapter). Then again, it's possible that your depression will linger for a few weeks no matter what you do and then disappear as unexpectedly as it arrived. If it doesn't, and if it starts to interfere with your functioning and/or with your relationship with your wife and/or your child, speak to your family doctor or contact a therapist.

Feeling Unsexy

'The delivery of our new daughter was miraculous to watch. But seeing her emerge from my wife's vagina seems to have turned me off to sex.'

Human sexual response, compared to that of other animals, is an extremely delicate mechanism. It's at the mercy not only of the body, but of the mind as well. And the mind can, at times, play merciless havoc with it. One of those times, as you probably already know, is pregnancy. Another, as you are now discovering, is the postpartum period.

It's very possible that your sudden disinterest in sex has nothing to do with having seen your baby born. Most brand-new fathers, whether they've viewed delivery or not, find both the spirit and the flesh somewhat less than willing for a while – although there's certainly nothing abnormal about those who don't. There are many very understandable reasons: fatigue, especially if the baby is waking frequently at night; uneasiness over loss of privacy, especially if your baby is sharing your room; fear that she will awake crying at the most inopportune moment; concern that intercourse may hurt your wife, even though the doctor has given you a green light; and finally, general physical and mental preoccupation with your newborn, to whom your energies are sensibly directed at this stage in her life.

In other words, it's probably just as well that you aren't feeling sexually motivated, particularly if your wife, like many women in the early months of motherhood, isn't either. Just how long it will take for your interest (and hers) to return is impossible to predict. As with all matters sexual, there's a wide range of normal. For some couples, the urge will precede even the doctor's go-ahead. For others, six months or more may pass before l'amour and le bébé begin to coexist harmoniously. (Some women find desire lacking until they stop breastfeeding, although on the average, breastfeeding mothers find passion rekindled earlier than non-breastfeeders.)

Some fathers, however, even if they've been prepared for the experience in class, do emerge from childbirth feeling that their 'territory' has been 'violated', that the special place that had been reserved for loving has suddenly taken on an all-too-functional purpose. If that's actually the case with you, you will need to – first intellectually and then emotionally – begin to accept the idea that the vagina's sexual and reproductive functions are equally important and equally miraculous. Neither excludes the other and, in fact, they are very much interconnected. Most importantly, the vagina is a vehicle for childbirth only briefly, but it is a source of pleasure for you and your wife for a lifetime.

'Fondling my wife's breasts used to be an important part of our sexual foreplay. Now that she's breastfeeding, that's becoming a big problem.'

Like the vagina, breasts were designed for both fun and function. And although these purposes are not only not mutually exclusive, but are actually interdependent in the grand scheme of things (if sex weren't fun, there wouldn't be as many babies to nurse), they can conflict temporarily during lactation.

Many couples, either for aesthetic reasons (leaking milk, for instance) or because they feel uncomfortable using their baby's source of nourishment for their own sexual pleasure, find breastfeeding a very definite turnoff. Others, however, find it a sexual turn-on, possibly because of its inherently sensual nature. Either reaction is perfectly normal.

If you feel that your wife's breasts are too functional to be sexy now, if leaking occurs on stimulation and you find that to be unpleasant, or if your touching them dampens your wife's ardour, simply leave them out of sexual foreplay until baby is weaned. And don't worry – all uneasiness will pass once breastfeeding ceases.

Be sure, however, to be open and honest with your wife now; taking a sudden, unexplained, hands-off approach to her breasts could leave her feeling that motherhood has somehow made her unappealing. Be sure, too, that you're not harbouring resentment against the baby for using 'your' breasts; as strange as it may seem, many men do.

'The first time we had sex after the baby was born my wife had a lot of pain. Now I'm so afraid of hurting her again that I've been avoiding sex.'

You may hurt your wife more by avoiding sex than by initiating it. More than ever before, your wife needs to feel attractive, desirable and wanted – even if she herself is hesitant to engage in intercourse because of fear of pain or lack of desire. Although your intentions are certainly noble, your steering away from lovemaking may lead to the development of beneath-the-surface anger and resentment in either or both of you, which could jeopardize your relationship.

But before you approach her again sexually, approach her verbally. Tell her your concerns, and find out what hers are. Decide together whether you want to wait a little longer before trying again, or whether you want to make love despite the discomfort. Keep in mind that you needn't worry about causing physical harm if your wife's doctor has examined her and given the go-ahead. Whatever you decide, the tips on page 549 will help minimize the pain and maximize the pleasure when lovemaking resumes. And remember, too, that postponing intercourse doesn't mean banishing romance from your lives. Intercourse is by no means the only way two people can enjoy each other and show their love. Right now, you may find just as much fulfillment lying in each other's arms.

Exclusion from Breastfeeding

'My wife is breastfeeding our son. There's a closeness between them I can't seem to share and I feel left out.'

There are certain immutable biological aspects of parenting that undeniably exclude you, the father: you can't be pregnant, you can't labour and deliver (which many would consider a definite plus) and you can't breastfeed. But as millions of new fathers discover each year, your natural anatomical limitations don't have to relegate you to spectator status. You can share in nearly all the joy, anticipation, trials and tribulations of your wife's pregnancy, labour and delivery – from the first kick to the last push – as an active, supportive partner. And though you'll never be able to put your baby to breast (at least not with the kind of results your baby's looking for), you *can* share in the feeding process:

Be your baby's supplementary feeder. There's more than one way to feed a baby. And though you can't nurse, you can be the one to give any supplementary bottles. It will not only give your wife a break (whether in the middle of the night or in the middle of dinner), it will give you extra time for closeness with your baby. Don't waste an opportunity by propping the bottle in the baby's mouth. Strike a nursing pose, with your baby snuggled close to your chest.

Don't sleep through the night. Sharing the joys of feeding also entitles you to share the sleepless nights. Even if your baby's not

getting supplementary bottles, you can be a part of nighttime feeding rituals by rising to get baby out of the cot, doing any necessary nappy changing and bringing him to his mummy for nursing. Should he still be awake after the feeding, you can rock and soothe him to sleep before putting him back to bed. Here, your not being the nursing parent works in your favour; since your baby doesn't feel or smell breasts filled with milk, he is much more likely to be calmed by you than by his mother.

Watch in wonder and appreciate. Enormous satisfaction can be had in simply observing the wondrous miracle that is breastfeeding. Next time you feel left out, take a few minutes to sit with your wife and baby and witness the love that passes between them as they nurse – it's bound to make you feel closer to both of them.

Participate in all the other daily rituals. Nursing is the *only* daily child-care activity limited to mothers. And chances are if you make at least one, or better still several, of these chores (such as bathing, dressing, feeding solids, changing nappies) your responsibility, you'll be too busy building your own relationship with your baby to be envious of your wife's.

Jealousy of Mother's Attention to Baby

'I love my new daughter, but I also love my wife – and as much as I hate to admit it, I'm jealous of all the time she spends with her. She doesn't seem to have any energy left for me.'

There may be a companionable new twosome in your family, but it shouldn't leave you feeling as though three's a crowd. Though it's natural that your wife should be somewhat preoccupied with the baby, it shouldn't be at the expense of your relationship as a couple – a relationship that is vital to your future as a family and that needs nurturing to survive the assaults of parenthood, now and in the future. To help deal with your feelings (which, though normal and common, can become destructive if allowed to fester) and to preserve and improve your own twosome, take these steps:

Make your feelings known. Perhaps your wife isn't aware that as she's getting to know your baby she's losing touch with you. Tell her how you feel, but in a constructive discussion, rather than a destructive tirade. Let her know you appreciate the terrific job she's doing as a mother, but remind her that full-grown men, too, need regular doses of tender loving care – though they may not always be as vocal as babies in demonstrating that need.

Make a threesome. Since you can't (and wouldn't want to) beat them, join them. As time alone with each other becomes a more and more precious and elusive commodity, concentrate on spending more time together as a family – stretching that mother-baby twosome into a cozy threesome – which you may find will strengthen the bonds between you as a couple. Pitching in with baby care will give your wife more time to devote to you, while giving you less inclination (and energy) to feel jealous.

Make a deal. Negotiate for some private time with your wife. Try to arrange to set aside an hour each night (after the baby's asleep and before the television goes on) for the two of you to spend together eating dinner (if it isn't too late), sipping wine or tea, unwinding, chatting (hopefully not just about the baby), getting to know each other again. And bargain to reserve at least one night a month (more, if possible) for a special and romantic evening out. But be understanding when she falls asleep at a movie or while you're trying to have an adult conversation – her exhaustion can't be willed away by either of you.

Make a little whoopee. Romance is a two-way street. And it's possible that your wife is feeling as neglected by you since the baby's been born as you are by her. So go out of your way to cast that romantic spell: be spontaneous (flowers for no reason), flirtatious (hug her from behind as she bends over to pick up that nappy), lavish her with compliments (especially when she needs them most). Play a determined Romeo and it won't be long before she's your Juliet again.

In spite of all your efforts, and even your wife's good intentions, you may find that she still seems distant. That's not unusual in women for anywhere between six weeks to six months after the birth of a baby. This attitude may be part of a built-in protective mechanism that keeps a new mother from cohabiting too soon after delivery, prevents her from conceiving too quickly and ensures that her attention and energies are focused on the newborn. It isn't a reflection on her husband or a barometer of her love for him. Be patient and it will pass. If, however, the estrangement lasts well into the second half of the year, and talking about it doesn't help, professional counselling may be needed.

Feeling Inadequate as a Father

'I want to be involved with caring for the baby and I want to help my wife out. But I've never had any experience with an infant and I'm feeling completely useless.'

You're a pioneer, treading where the vast majority of past generations of fathers either dared not or cared not to tread. Like any pioneer, you probably have neither hands-on nor passed-on (if your own father didn't participate in baby care) experience to count on. Little wonder, then, that you're feeling a little insecure at the outset.

It's a feeling, however, that's bound to be short-lived. The willingness to try and a lot of love to offer are the only qualifications needed to succeed at parenting. Though those with some baby care under their belts may get off to a faster start, even a novice like you will be running (and rocking and bathing and changing) neck-and-neck with them within a couple of months. In the meantime, you needn't worry about your baby's suffering because of your in-experience. First of all, he can tolerate a lot more manhandling than you'd think – and he won't 'break' if your touch is tentative or awkward. Second, he'll be a good sport as you learn. He has no frame of reference, no 'perfect' father to measure you against. As long as his immediate needs are attended to, even in a bumbling way, and he senses your good intentions, he's bound to accept you – imperfections, inexperience and all.

Studies show that fathers exhibit the same physiological responses to a baby's crying as mothers and they can be just as sensitive to a baby's cues (although because they're less likely to spend as much time around baby as a mother, they're less likely to sharpen this sensitivity and respond accordingly). Some fathers, in fact, once the initial trepidation has worn off, demonstrate even greater natural ability for parenting than their female partners. And babies aren't blind to this: by their first birthdays, babies are as likely to object to being separated from father as from mother, and a full 25% are more likely to go to their dads than their mums when given the choice.

If your wife has had previous experience caring for babies, or is taking to the job more readily than you, have her show you the ropes. If she's as green as you, learn as you go, together (the tips in the Baby-Care Primer will help). You'll both be pros the next time around.

Handling Baby

'I'm afraid I'm not gentle enough when I handle my new daughter.'

One of the benefits of a baby's having two parents is that she has the opportunity to experience the love and attention of two different people. Often the mother is more gentle and slower paced, sings to her baby in a high, soft voice and has a soft body to snuggle up against; she's usually the one that a baby comes crying to for comfort. The father is often a little rougher, more lively and fast paced in his handling; his voice is deeper and his body harder; he's the one baby most frequently turns to for fun and games. A baby quickly comes not only to accept the differences between parents, but to enjoy them. (The degrees of gentleness and roughness vary from person to person, of course. Working mothers are more likely to resemble fathers in the way they relate to their children, and in an occasional family the ways mother and father treat their baby may even be totally reversed.)

While it's all right to handle your baby a little more energetically, real roughhousing is dangerous; see page 281.

Baby's Crying

'Our little boy is colicky and it's so bad that sometimes I just don't want to come home.'

The sound of a screaming baby isn't a pleasure to come home to – even for the most loving father. And it isn't a pleasure to stay home with, either – even for the most dedicated mother. Your wife undoubtedly harbours some secret fantasies of sneaking out of the house when your baby starts his daily wailing marathon, and not returning until he's screamed himself to sleep. Unless you've got regular help, however, it isn't likely that either of you will be able to escape. But you can reduce the agony somewhat and retain your sanity by following the tips on surviving colic on page 125. And happily, as bad as things are, you can be pretty sure they will soon get better. Most colic disappears miraculously when baby reaches three months.

If, in the meantime, the crying makes you angry, try some strenuous exercise or a punching bag to release your hostilities. If at any time it makes you feel angry enough that you fear you might hurt the baby, speak to a doctor, cleric, or therapist immediately, or telephone the local Child-Abuse Hotline.

Unfair Burden

'I work a long day at the office while my wife stays home with our daughter. I don't mind helping out a little on the weekend, but I resent her pressurizing me to give her a hand on week nights – particularly in the middle of the night.'

Caring for your baby when you come home from work, a time when you used to relax and unwind from the pressures of the day, may seen an unfair burden; it does to many husbands of women who don't work outside the home. But it's actually an incomparable opportunity in disguise. In previous generations, few fathers were given a chance to spend significant amounts of time with their babies, which was a shame. As a member of a more enlightened generation, you're getting the chance to get to know your daughter as you couldn't otherwise. You may miss the evening news or a before-dinner nap, but you'll find that an even better way to relax and unwind is with your baby. Nothing can make you forget a personnel problem, a botched job, or a lost deal faster than conversing in coos with your baby as you change her nappies, watching her splash and giggle in the tub, or rocking her gently to sleep. And while you're forgetting your workaday cares, you'll also be building a collection of moments to remember.

Which is not to say that every moment you spend with your little one, particularly in the middle of the night, will be one you'll want to remember (some will pass in such a thick, sleepy fog that you wouldn't be able to remember them even if you wanted to). Like any job, baby care has its quota of anxiety and drudgery.

And this job – with its pluses and minuses – is the one your wife does all day while you're at work. Her workday is at least as physically and emotionally demanding as yours (more so if she's nursing). She needs relief in the evening more than you need the rest you'll be giving up by helping her. Sure, you'll have to rise in the early light of morning to start another day at work, but so

will she – and unlike you, she won't be able to take lunch hours, coffee breaks and, often, not even lavatory breaks.

And next time you walk the floor with your colicky baby while your wife prepares dinner, remember that soon the rewards of your involvement in baby care will begin to outweigh the stresses. At first, it will be the smiles and gurgles meant just for you, then a breathless 'da-da' when you come through the door, then a finger raised for your kiss to make a boo-boo better. Later, and for years to come, compensation will come in the form of a closer relationship with your child that will not only bring joy, but will also make the more difficult times a little easier.

Of course, sometimes both your wife *and* you will need a break from child care, so be sure that once in a while there's a night out for just the two of you.

Not Enough Time to Spend with Baby

'I work long hours, often staying late at the office. I want to spend more time with my new son, but I don't seem to have any.'

If there was ever something worth making time for, that little baby of yours is it. As terrific a job of parenting as one parent can do, two can do it twice as well. Baby boys who get lots of attention from their fathers are brighter and happier by the time their half-year birthday rolls around than boys who don't. So it's not just you who stands to lose if you don't spend time with your son. (Little girls, too, grow up more confident when they are close to their dads.)

Make more time for your baby, even if it means taking time from other important activities in your life. Organization may help. Try to dovetail your working hours and your baby's waking ones. If you don't have to be in the office until ten, spend the early morning with him; if you don't get home until eight, see if your wife can arrange his schedule so that he naps early in the evening, then is up for a visit with you before bedtime (of course, this will cut into time alone with her). If a lot of extracurricular activities (whether nighttime meetings or weekend sports) keep you from your baby's side, cut back on them. The organizations and teams will still be there when your baby is a little older – at which point his schedule will be more regular and easier to work around.

Especially if you're not able to make a great deal of time for your baby, it's important to make the most of the time you do have. Don't read the paper at the breakfast table, sit glued to the six o'clock news before dinner, or sleep until noon on Saturday.

Instead, wield the baby spoon at breakfast, give the bath at six o'clock, take the baby to the playground on Saturday morning.

You can also make time for your baby by including him, when feasible, in your other activities. If you've got a few errands to run, strap him in a baby sling and take him along. If jogging is on your schedule, tuck him in a pram or pushchair and increase your aerobic effort by pushing as you go (but *don't* jog with him in a baby sling). And if you've got some chores to do, prop him securely in a baby seat and let him watch as you provide a blow-by-blow description of what you're doing.

TWENTY-SIX

From Only Child To Older Child

◆

When you brought your first child home from the hospital, you and your husband were novices at parenting, with lessons to be learned, adjustments to be made and the challenge of forming an attachment to a new member of the family waiting to be faced. When you bring a second child home, you'll already be seasoned pros when it comes to parenting; instead of you, it will be your older child who will need to do most of the learning, make most of the adjustments and work the hardest at forming an attachment to the newborn. It won't be any easier for your older child than it was for you and, considering age and level of maturity, it may be considerably more difficult. Following the suggestions and tips in this chapter won't make the transition from only child to older child effortless for your firstborn (or for you), but it can help to make it smoother.

The best tip of all? Relax. Children take their cues from the adults around them. If you're anxious about how your child is going to react to having a new sibling, your child will be anxious, too.

What You May Be Concerned About

Preparing an Older Child

'We have a two-and-a-half-year-old and we're expecting another baby. How can we best prepare our first child so she won't feel threatened?'

Pregnancy and childbirth have become a family affair. Like fathers in the 70s, siblings in the 80s are no longer excluded from the nine months of preparation and excitement that will culminate in the arrival of a new brother or sister. Instead of trying to piece together what is about to happen from hushed whispers among adults and mysterious talk about cabbage patches and storks, today's firstborns are often involved in the pregnancy from the early months on.

Preparation of a sibling is at least as complicated as the preparation of the expectant parents. The first step, of course, is to tell the older child that her mother is pregnant. Just when this should be done has generated some controversy among child-care experts. For a long while, the prevailing belief was that young children should not be told very early in a pregnancy because an early announcement would leave too much 'waiting' time – and waiting is something that children are usually not very good at. More recently, however, it's been suggested that children begin to sense something is 'going on' very early. Perhaps they overhear serious or excited grownup conversations, see their mother not feeling well or being distracted, note other changes around the house – and they wonder 'What are they keeping from me? What is going to happen?' And often the fears born of ignorance are far worse than the reality – and worse, too, than a long and sometimes boring wait. Letting a child know early also gives you more time to help her adjust to the idea of a sibling and to work out her feelings ahead of time. It may make sense to wait until test results are obtained if you're having amniocentesis, or until the danger period is over if you have a history of miscarriages – although your child may be more upset if you're confined to bed and she hasn't been told why.

Once the kitten's out of the bag, there are a number of steps that parents can take to make the expected arrival less threatening to the child already in residence – and perhaps even eagerly anticipated:

- Make any planned major changes in your child's life early in the pregnancy if you haven't had a chance to make them before conception. For example, get her enrolled and settled in a preschool or play group so that she'll have an out-of-home experience to escape to once the baby's arrived and won't feel she's being put out because of the baby. Begin toilet training her or weaning her from the bottle now, rather than just after your new baby's birth. Any significant changes not made within a month or two of the baby's due date should probably be postponed until a couple of months after the birth, if possible.

- Get your child used to spending a little less time alone with you. If you never have before and will need to after the baby arrives, start leaving her with a baby-sitter for short periods during the day. If daddy hasn't been very involved in caring for her up till now, ease him into the feeding, bathing and bedding down routines so that he will make a skillful stand-in for you when you're in the hospital and when you're busy with the new baby. Initiate some regular father-firstborn fun activities (Sunday morning breakfast out, Saturday afternoon at the playground, an after-dinner story hour), rituals that can continue to be enjoyed far into your new addition's first year. Be careful, though, not to withdraw too far from your firstborn; she needs to be reassured (through loving actions, not in so many words) that the arrival of a baby won't mean the loss of her mummy.

- Be honest and open about the physical changes you're undergoing. Explain that you're tired or grumpy because 'making a baby' is hard work, not because you're tired of her or sick. But don't use the pregnancy as an excuse for not picking her up as much as you used to; picking up a child is not in any way threatening to your pregnancy unless your doctor has for some reason, such as premature dilatation of your cervix, forbidden it. If you can't pick her up because your back is killing you, blame your back, not the baby – and give her extra hugs from a sitting position. If you need to lie down more often, suggest she lie down with you and nap, read her a story, or watch TV together.

- Introduce your child to the new baby while it's still in the uterus. Show her month-by-month pictures of foetal development that seem appropriate for her age, explaining that as the baby grows so will mummy's tummy, and that when the baby is big enough it will be ready to come out. As soon as kicks are easily seen and felt by outsiders, let her experience the baby's movements herself. Encourage her (but don't push her if she resists) to kiss, hug and talk to the baby. When referring to the baby, call it 'our baby' or 'your baby' to give her a sense that it belongs to her as well as to you. Explain that there's no way to tell whether it's a brother or a sister (unless, of course, you've learned the sex in advance through amniocentesis) and make a game out of guessing.

- Take your child to at least one or two antenatal visits (and if she seems interested and isn't disruptive, take her to all of them) so she will feel like more than a player in the unfolding pregnancy drama. Hearing the heartbeat will help make the baby more of a reality for her. If a sonogram photograph has been taken, show her that, too. But be sure to bring a snack and a book or favourite toy to the doctor's or hospital in case of a long wait or a waning attention span. And if she decides she doesn't care for a return visit, abide by her wishes without pressurizing her to change her mind.

- Involve your child in any baby preparations she shows interest in. Let her 'help' you pick out furnishings, a layette, toys – and even let her select an inexpensive monstrosity or two herself. Go through her old baby clothes and toys together to select items which might be recyclable – but don't push her to hand down anything until she wants to. Let her open any baby gifts that arrive before the baby.

- Familiarize your child with babies in general. Show her photos of herself as a baby and tell her what she was like (be sure to include some stories that will show her how much she's grown up since then). If possible, take her to a hospital nursery to look at the newborns (so she will know they aren't as 'pretty' as older babies). If you have friends with small babies, arrange for the two of you to spend some time with them. Point out babies everywhere – in supermarkets, in the park, in picture books. So that she'll be prepared for reality, explain that babies do very little besides eat, sleep and cry (which they do a lot of), and that they don't make good playmates for quite a while. If you're planning to nurse, explain that baby will drink milk from mummy's breasts (just as she did, if she did), and if you have a friend who is nursing, arrange a casual visit at feeding time.

- In trying to prepare your child, don't raise issues that may never materialize. For instance, don't tell her 'Don't worry,

we'll love you just as much as the new baby', or 'We'll still have plenty of time for you'. Such statements, although well intentioned, can set your child up for worries about how well she'll be able to compete with her new sibling for your love and attention.

- If you're planning to have your older child vacate a cot for her expected sibling, do it several months in advance of your due date. If she's not ready for a bed, buy her another cot – preferably one that can convert to a junior bed. If you'll be moving her to a different room, do this, too, well in advance, and have her help with the decor and furnishings. Put the emphasis on her graduating to a new bed or new room because she is growing up, rather than on her being displaced from the old by the baby.

- If you have a car, get your older child accustomed to sitting in the back seat if she isn't already used to sitting there; a new toddler seat (or newly handed-down one) may make the transition easier. Put a car seat for the baby in the front, perhaps with a doll in it, for a few weeks prior to your due date.

- Try out names you're considering on your child, involving her in the selection process. 'Naming' the baby will help make her feel closer to him or her. (Of course, it would be courting disaster to give your preschooler complete creative control over the process; you'll have to make the final determination, unless you want your second child named Pingu.)

- If there's a sibling class available in your neighbourhood – some hospitals offer them – enroll your child. It's important for her to know that there are other children in the same spot she's in – about to have a new sibling. Even if she's taking a class, and especially if she isn't, prepare her further by reading her books on the subject – there are many 'new baby' books geared to her age group on the market.

- As your due date draws near, prepare your child for your spending some time at the hospital when the baby arrives. Have her help you pack your suitcase and encourage her to add something of hers that she would like you to take along to keep you company – a teddy bear, a picture of her, or a picture she's drawn, for instance. Be sure that whoever is going to be caring for her is fully familiar with her routines, so there won't be any break from them at this sensitive time. Tell her in advance who the caretaker will be (best mummy substitutes are daddy, grandma, grandpa, another familiar relative, a regular baby-sitter or nanny, or a close family friend), and assure her you will come home in a few days. If the hospital permits sibling visits (many do), tell her when she will be able to visit you and the baby. Whether she will be able to visit or not, a prebirth tour of the hospital, if one can be arranged, will make her feel more comfortable about your going away.

- Don't suddenly shower her with gifts or special outings in the weeks before delivery. Instead of placating her, such unaccustomed overindulgence may well give your child the sense that something terrible is about to happen and that you're trying to soften the blow. It may also give her the idea that baby's impending arrival is bestowing her with valuable bartering power and lead her to attempt to trade good behaviour for presents and favours in the future. Buy just a couple of small but thoughtful gifts to give her after the baby arrives – perhaps one to give at the hospital and one for when you get home, for her being such a big help while mummy was away. For a fairly young child, a batheable baby doll that's just the right size for her arms is often a good gift; later she can bathe, 'nurse', or change her baby doll while mummy takes care of the real thing. Shop with her for (and let her wrap) a small gift for the baby 'from her' that she can bring to the hospital on the occasion of their first meeting.

- In your efforts to prepare your first child for the birth of your second, don't overdo it. Don't let your pregnancy and the expected family addition become the primary focus of your household, or the dominant topic of conversation. Remember that there are, and should be, other concerns and interests in your toddler's life – and that they deserve your attention, too.

Siblings at the Birth

'With second baby, we have the option of having our three-year-old son attend the birth. But we're not sure how healthy it would be for him.'

When your generation was being delivered, childbirth was for mothers only. Fathers paced the floors of hospital waiting rooms and siblings never made it to the hospital at all, passing their mothers' labours at grandmother's house watching The Woodentops and being indulged with chocolate cake, only vaguely aware, if at all, of what was going on. Today, fathers are usually present at the big event (they sometimes even 'deliver' their babies and cut the cords themselves) and children have moved into the waiting rooms. The next logical step, according to some, is to allow the children to join the rest of the family in the delivery room. And indeed, a few hospitals have opened their birthing room doors to brothers and sisters of all ages.

While virtually everyone agrees that the father's move into the delivery room has been a positive one, there has been a great deal of controversy over the wisdom of letting siblings follow in their father's footsteps. Though theoretical benefits are suggested (less rivalry or better attachment between siblings; less trauma for the child, who doesn't feel deserted when the mother goes off to pick up his 'replacement'), the major reason children attend sibling births seems to be that their parents want them there. And the possible negative results appear to outweigh any positive ones. For one thing, childbirth can be an unsettling and difficult experience for a child to understand – with the blood, grunts, groans and sometimes screams from mother and the unbaby-like look of the emerging newborn. (At least one study shows, however, that not all children are distressed by viewing a birth; some are merely bored, especially during a long labour, and some actually become actively involved.) For another, though complications are uncommon in the typical low-risk labour and delivery, there is no way of predicting whether all will go smoothly. Should an emergency caesarean become necessary or should something be seriously wrong with the newborn, the resultant flurry of activity and change in atmosphere – probably necessitating the child's unceremonious eviction – could be truly frightening, possibly with long-term impact. In addition, having a child in the room during active labour or pushing can be distracting and inhibiting to the mother (she may want to cry out, but feel hesitant in front of him). And as mother and dad focus on the work of delivering the new child and then express wonder and excitement at its arrival, the older child may feel left out.

On the other hand, most experts concur that under normal circumstances, having an older sibling greet his new brother or sister immediately *after* the actual birth offers all of the benefits of attending the birth but presents none of the risks. And if your hospital allows this option or if you have a home birth; it's a good one to pick up. If it doesn't, speak to your doctor about trying to effect a change in policy or at least wangling an exception. If that fails, remember that a delay in meeting will not doom sibling harmony – there are plenty of other ways to build a loving relationship between your children.

If you do decide to have your child present at the birth, be certain he is very well prepared (he should see films and pictures of births, watch you practise your breathing exercises and, if possible, attend a sibling class on childbirth), and that you have food, books, toys and other diversions to keep him occupied when your contractions don't.

If at any point he wants to leave, let him – without showing any disappointment. Be sure another familiar adult is waiting outside to stay with him or to take him home or to grandmother's case of such a change of heart.

Separation and Hospital Visits

'Will visiting me in the hospital make my older child miss me more than if she doesn't see me at all?'

Quite the contrary. Being out of your child's sight doesn't mean you'll be out of her mind. Seeing you at the hospital will assure her that you're all right, that you haven't gone off and left her for another child, and that she's still important in your life. And studies show that children who don't visit their mothers are more likely to show hostility to them upon homecoming. 'I don't like you, mummy – you left me all alone.' In most hospitals, she will also be allowed to see, sometimes even touch and 'hold', her new baby brother or sister, which will give her a sense of reality about this new sibling and make her feel an important part of the new baby excitement.

You can make the hospital visits – and the separation – go more smoothly if you do the following:

- Be sure your child is prepared in advance for the visit. She should know how long she's going to stay and that she's going to have to go home without you and the baby. And tell her if regulations will limit her to seeing the baby through the nursery window.

- Be sure you're prepared for your child's visit. If you're expecting her to rush headlong into your arms and fall in love at first sight with her new sibling, you may be disappointed. It's very possible that she'll give either you or the baby or both of you the cold shoulder, that she'll seem tentative or out of sorts, that she'll burst into angry or sorrowful tears upon leaving. Such negative or neutral reactions are common, are not a cause for concern and are better than no visit at all. Keep your expectations realistic and you'll be pleasantly surprised if all goes smoothly – and you won't be unduly upset if they don't.

- If you leave for the hospital in the middle of the night, or when your older child is in nursery school or otherwise away from home, leave her a note that can be read to her when she wakes up or returns. Tell her that 'our' baby is ready to come out, that you love her and that you'll see her or speak to her soon. If it's practical (grandmother or someone else can come along to stay with her) and possible (the hospital allows it), take her along to the hospital to await baby's arrival. Have a bag for her, as you do for yourself. It should include a change of clothing, nappies (if she wears them), play things and snacks you know she will enjoy. If labour is lengthy (it is less likely to be the second time around) and you are confined to the labour room, have daddy come out and deliver regular bulletins, possibly even have lunch with her in the cafeteria. Of course, if her bedtime comes up before the baby comes out, you will probably want to have her taken home so she can sleep in her own bed; if she is still around when the baby arrives, try to arrange for her to visit – at least with you, and possibly with her new sibling.

- Make sure to place a picture of your older child on your bedstand, so she'll know that you've been thinking of her when she comes to visit.

- If it's possible, have whoever is bringing your child to visit you stop at a store on the way so that she can buy you and her new sibling small presents. Exchanging gifts (this is the time to give her that little something you picked up for her before delivery) will help break the ice and make her feel important. The practice of giving a gift 'from the baby' is common, but most kids see right through the ploy, and it's not a good idea to start this re-lationship with a deception, however innocent.

- Hold a little 'birth-day' party for the new enlarged family in your hospital room. Have a cake (the older child will probably be pleased that she can have a piece and her new sibling can't), candles (she can blow them out), and a few decorations (let her choose them).

- Have the same person who brings your child to visit take her home. If daddy takes her and then stays on for an extended visit while she's sent home with a grandparent or friend, she may feel doubly deserted.

- Between visits, or if she can't visit, keep in touch by phone (avoiding sensitive times such as right before bed, if you feel that the sound of your voice may upset her) and by writing notes that daddy can read to her. She may feel good, too, about making a drawing or two for you to display in your hospital room. Have daddy or a favourite relative take her out to dinner or on some other special outing so that it will be clear that the new baby isn't the only thing everyone is interested in these days – and make sure that conversation during the outing doesn't centre around the baby unless she wants it to.

- Arrange to go home early, if you want to and can, so that your older child can begin sharing in the new baby experience sooner and so that the separation time is reduced.

Easing the Homecoming

'How can I make coming home with the baby less traumatic for my older son?'

An older sibling usually has mixed feelings when it comes to the homecoming. He knows that he wants his mother to come home, but he's not quite as sure about the baby she's planning to bring with her. In a way he likes the idea – having a new baby in the house is exciting and different and, if he's old enough, it's something to boast to his friends about. But he's probably at least a little nervous when he ponders how his life is going to change once that baby's carried through his front door and deposited in what used to be his cot.

How you handle the homecoming will influence, at least initially, whether your child's greatest expectations or worst fears about the new baby are realized. Here's how to accentuate the positive and minimize the negative:

• Consider giving your child an active role in the homecoming, having him come to the hospital with his daddy to take you and the new baby home. This will work only if grandma or another familiar adult is along (so that daddy can be free to take care of the paperwork and such) and if hospital policy permits.

• Or have him help with preparations for the baby at home (he can lay out nappies and cotton wool balls and so on for the baby, for example) while daddy goes to pick you up. Try to come into the house first (perhaps daddy can wait in the car with the baby) so that you can greet your older child privately for just a few minutes.

• Start right off using the baby's name, rather than always referring to the new sibling as 'the baby'. This will give your older child a sense that this baby is really a person, not just an object.

• Limit visitors for the first few days at home – for your own health and sanity, and for your older child's sake. Even the most well-meaning of visitors tend to go on endlessly about a new baby, all but ignoring the older child. Those visitors you can't deny immediate access to (such as grandparents, aunts and uncles and close friends) should be briefed in advance not to be overly and obviously effusive toward the baby, and to give plenty of attention to the older sibling. You can also suggest that visitors come when he's in school or after he's gone to

bed. Limiting visitors for the first week or so has other benefits – more time for you to regain your strength and more opportunity for the bonding of your expanding family.

• Focus much of your attention on your older child, particularly in the early days, when the baby will probably be sleeping a good deal of the time. Hang his drawings on the refrigerator, applaud toileting if he's newly trained, tell him how proud you are about his being such a good big brother, be quick with praise and slow with anger. Avoid the mistake of parents who worship at the new baby's cot ('Oh, look at those tiny fingers!' or 'Isn't she beautiful!' or 'See, she's smiling!'), leaving the older child feeling very much an unnecessary and unappreciated appendage. But don't go to the extreme of never kissing, hugging, or showing affection for the baby in front of the sibling, either. If you do, the child will be confused ('I thought we were supposed to love this baby. Is it possible my parents will soon stop loving me, too?') or see right through your plan or beyond it ('They're pretending not to like the baby so I won't know that they really like her more than me'). Instead, bring the older child into the talk about the baby: 'Look at those tiny fingers; do you believe yours were once so small?' or 'Isn't she beautiful? I think she looks just like you' or 'See, she's smiling at you; I think she loves you already.' Your child will feel more comfortable if you freely display natural affection for the new baby (without overdoing it), as well as for him.

• Allow your older child to open all the baby gifts and (assuming they aren't breakable or dangerous) to play with them for a bit if he wishes, even if they're clearly 'baby' toys, pointing out that they're the baby's presents but that he can play with them until she's old enough to appreciate them. Some wise visitors remember to bring a small gift for the older child; but should several days pass and truckloads of baby gifts come in with nothing for the older sibling, have grandmother or daddy bring home something special just for him. You can also show him some of the gifts he received as a newborn, explaining that now it's his new baby's turn to get gifts. And if the influx of gifts really seems excessive, put away those that don't come to his attention. Eventually, those cards and gifts will stop coming.

- If your older child decides he wants to stay home from nursery school for a few days, let him. This will assure him that you aren't pushing him out of the house so you can enjoy the baby, and it will give him some opportunity to bond with the baby. (But decide in advance, with his consultation, just how long his holiday will be so that he doesn't get the idea that he can stay home permanently.) Don't, however, force your child to stay home if he would rather go to school. He may feel the need to be in a place where there is no baby and where there are other centres of interest.

Open Resentment

'My toddler is openly resentful of the new baby. He tells me he wants him to go back to the hospital.'

You obviously can't carry out your child's wishes, but you can – and should – let him express them. Though his feelings may seem very negative, the fact that he is able to vent them is very positive. Every older sibling feels a certain measure of resentment towards the new intruder (or to his mother for bringing the intruder in); some just express it more overtly than others. Instead of implying to your older child that he's bad to feel that way ('Oh, that's a terrible thing to say about the baby!'), tell him that you understand that it isn't always fun to have a new baby in the house – for him or you. Let him talk out his resentment if he wants to, but don't dwell on the subject. Move on quickly to something upbeat ('How about if we bundle the baby up and go to the play-ground together?').

Some children don't feel free to express negative feelings towards a new baby and it's a good idea to encourage them to talk about how they feel. One way to do that is to confide your own mixed feelings: 'I love the baby, but sometimes I hate having to get up in the middle of the night to feed him' or 'Boy, with our new baby I hardly ever have a free moment for myself'. Another is to tell and/or read stories about older siblings with mixed feelings about new arrivals. If you are an older sibling yourself, you can talk about how you felt when a new baby came along.

'My daughter shows no hostility towards her new brother. But she's been acting very moody and disagreeable with me.'

Some older siblings don't see any point in confronting a newborn (after all, you can't get a rise out of him no matter what you do) or feel too inhibited to show their hostilities towards him (they've been told too often that they're supposed to be loving and affectionate). The next best target, one they feel they can torment with less guilt and more satisfying results, is mummy. It is, after all, mother who is spending hours feeding the baby, changing the baby, rocking and cuddling the baby, and spending much less time than she used to with her. A firstborn may vent her feelings towards her mother by throwing tantrums, exhibiting regressive behaviour, refusing to eat, or rejecting her mother entirely and turning to her father or someone else (a baby-sitter, for instance) as a 'favourite'. This type of behaviour is a common and normal part of the period of adjustment to the new baby.

As at any developmental stage, it's important to deal with disagreeableness calmly and to not take it personally. Try to respond with patience, understanding, reassurance and extra attention. And remember, this too will pass – usually within a few months.

Your Own Resentment

'Since our second child arrived, I've felt pulled in all directions and often find myself resenting the demands for time and attention from my older son, which makes me feel very guilty.'

You're overtired and overpressured – it's not surprising that you have hostile feelings that need venting. And it's also not surprising that you're tempted to vent them on your older child (though some women choose their husbands as the would-be targets) rather than your newborn. Like an older sibling who redirects his anger at his mother, you probably recognize that an infant isn't an acceptable object of disaffection. You probably also believe, at least subconsciously, that now that your firstborn is an older child he should be more mature – if only he would 'act his age', you probably reason, everything else would be so much easier. An unrealistic and unjust, but common, belief. (Besides, your child probably is acting his age.)

Though such feelings aren't unusual among second-time mothers, they often do come as a surprise to those mothers who spent their second pregnancies worrying that they wouldn't be able to love their new child as much as their first. They're shocked to see how easily and quickly the new baby creeps into their hearts, and feel fickle and guilt-ridden when they find themselves begrudging their older child his requests for time and attention.

Recognizing your negative feelings and accepting the reasons for them is an important step in overcoming them. This may be the first time in your life that you feel anger or resentment towards your children, but it won't be the last. Such feelings occur even in the best of human relationships. But as you settle into a comfortable rhythm as a mother of two, more adroit at sharing yourself with both your children, you'll find the feelings will dissipate. (If they don't, or if they become more severe, talk to your doctor or see a counsellor who can help you work them out.)

Explaining Genital Differences

'My three-year-old daughter is obsessed with her new brother's penis. She wants to know what it is and why she doesn't have one. I don't know what to tell her.'

Try the truth. As young as your daughter is, if she's old enough to ask questions about her body and her brother's, she's old enough to get some honest answers. It can be quite a shock for a little girl to see something on her baby brother that she doesn't have (or for a little boy to note the absence of a penis on his baby sister; is it possible that he'll lose it, too? he wonders). The simple explanation that boys (and men, like daddy) have penises and girls (and women, like mummy) have vaginas is probably all that is needed, and will help your child understand one fundamental difference between males and females. Be sure to use the proper names for these body parts just as you would for the eyes, nose, or mouth, and add more information only if it's requested – though you may want to let her know that girls have vaginas so that when they grow up they can have babies and boys have penises so they can be fathers. If your child asks to know more than you can comfortably impart, look for a book for parents that can help you with the task, and/or for one written and illustrated at your child's level that you can read to her.

Nursing in Front of an Older Child

'I'm planning to nurse my second baby, but I'm worried about doing so in front of my four-year-old son.'

Though there's speculation that seeing the parent of the opposite sex fully undressed may be harmful to a child preschool-age and older, there's no reason to believe any damage can be done if a boy watches his mother nurse. In fact, it's more likely to be harmful if you go out of your way to keep your son away from you while you nurse – considering how much time is spent nursing a newborn, you'd be seeing very little of your older child. And besides baby's nap time, there'll no more undivided time you can give your son than when you're nursing. Almost any quiet activity, from reading a story to playing a game, can be pursued during feeding sessions.

If you're uncomfortable about your son's seeing your breasts (although they're almost certain not to be stimulating to him, particularly in that context), nurse discreetly. But don't overreact if he does catch a glimpse or if he reaches a curious hand over for a squeeze. Many experts agree that both prudery, which could give a child the idea that there's something bad or unclean about the human body and its functions, and blatant exhibitionism, which dampens respect for personal privacy and could lead to unwanted stimulation, probably help to build unhealthy attitudes towards sexuality.

The Older Child who Wants to Nurse

'My two-and-a-half-year-old son, watching me nurse the baby, has been saying he wants some milk, too. I thought the interest would pass if I ignored it, but it hasn't.'

The best way to cure an older sibling (up to three or four years old) of the desire to nurse is to let him know that he can. (A child more than four years old should understand that nursing is for babies.) Often, just your okay will be enough and he won't feel the need to pursue the issue further. If he does, let him. You may feel uncomfortable, but he'll feel that he's being given access to this mysterious and special relationship the baby has with you. Chances are one nip is all he'll need to make him realize that babies don't have it so good after all. The warm, watery, unfamiliar, poor-excuse-for-milk fluid he extracts almost certainly won't be worth the effort involved (and he may well give up before the milk ever makes it to his mouth).

His feelings of curiosity satisfied, he'll probably never ask to nurse again and he'll likely feel more sympathy for the baby (who's stuck drinking that stuff when he's guzzling apple juice and 'real' milk and gobbling raisins and peanut butter sandwiches) than jealousy.

If he continues to show an interest in nursing, or if he objects to baby's indulging, it's probably not a breast to suck on that he's after, but a breast (and a mummy) to snuggle up against and some of the attention he feels the baby's always getting when nursing. Including your older child in the nursing sessions may be all that's necessary to quell his interest in taking to the breast. There are several simple ways to do this. Before you sit down to nurse, for example, say 'I'm going to give the baby some milk now. Would you like some juice?' or 'Would you like your lunch now, while baby is eating?' Or take the quiet opportunity offered by nursing to read him a story, help him do a puzzle, or listen to records with him (good because you don't have to use your hands), steadfastly resisting the temptation to watch TV or catch up on phone calls instead. And be sure, too, that your firstborn gets plenty of hugging and cuddling when you're not feeding the baby.

Regressive Behaviour

'Ever since her sister was born, my three-year-old daughter has started acting like a baby herself. She talks in baby jargon, wants to be picked up all the time, and even has toileting accidents.'

Even fully grown adults can't help sometimes envying a newborn her undemanding existence ('Oh, that's the life!' they'll sigh as a sleeping baby is wheeled by them in a cushy carriage). It's not surprising that a youngster, barely out of the carriage herself and just beginning to master some of the myriad of responsibilities that come with growing up, would yearn for a return to babyhood when confronted with an infant sibling. Especially when she sees that acting like a baby works very well for her new sister, who is allowed to lie in the lap of luxurious leisure (not to mention the lap of her mummy), who is carried everywhere, catered to endlessly, opens her mouth to whimper and receives precisely what she wants when she wants it (instead of receiving a sharp 'Stop that whining!').

Rather than pressurizing your older daughter to 'be a big girl' at this sensitive time, baby her when she wants to be babied – even if it means caring for two 'babies' at once. Give her the attention she is craving (rock her in your arms when she's tired, carry her up the stairs once in a while, feed her when she demands it) and don't chide her when she regresses to one-word sentences (even if it grates on your nerves), wants to take her milk from a bottle (even if she never has before), or if her toilet habits take a sudden turn for the infantile. At the same time, encourage her to act her age by being especially lavish with praise when she is particularly grown up – when she cleans up after herself, is a big help to mummy, or goes on the potty. Offering such praise in front of others will reinforce its benefits. Remind her that she was your first baby and now she's your big girl. Point out, too, the special things that she can do that her sister can't, such as enjoying ice cream at a birthday party, zooming down the slide at the playground, or having pizza out with mummy and daddy. Bake with her while baby is napping, enlist her help when food shopping, send her on a picnic with daddy, take her to see a film while the baby stays with a baby-sitter. In her own time, she will figure out for herself the advantages of being the older child and will decide to leave her baby past behind.

The Older Sibling Hurting the New Baby

'I left the room for a minute and was horrified when I returned to find my older son jabbing his baby sister with a toy. She wasn't hurt this time, but it

seemed as though he was trying to make her cry on purpose.'

Although such an assault would seem, on the surface, nothing more than a sadistic attempt to harm an unwanted newcomer, this isn't usually the case. Though there may be an element of hostility involved (and this is only natural, considering the upheaval a newborn causes in an older sibling's life), these seemingly malicious attacks are often merely innocent investigations. Your son may have been trying to make his sister cry not out of malevolence, but out of curiosity to find out how this strange little creature you've brought home works (just as he is constantly examining and probing everything else in his environment). The trick is to react to such a situation without overreacting. Impress upon your older child, by example and by involving him in baby care when you're around, the importance of being gentle with the baby. When he gets rough, react calmly and rationally, avoiding angry, guilt-provoking recriminations for him (if he's into tormenting you, he will enjoy having triggered your outburst) and hysterical protectiveness for her (which can reinforce any feelings of jealousy). Avoiding the explosive response is even more vital if the baby has actually been hurt; making an older child feel guilty about what he has done, whether it was intentional or not, can leave permanent emotional scars and serves little positive purpose.

When it comes to older sibling hurting younger, prevention is preferable to punishment. No matter how well you believe your older child has got the message, don't leave the two of them alone together again until your older child is of an age – probably around five years old – to understand what damage he can do. Younger children do not really have a sense of the extent of injury they can inflict with their actions, and they can inflict serious harm unintentionally.

Avoiding Jealousy

'I'm wondering how I can divide myself fairly so that both my four-year-old son and his new baby brother get the attention they need, and so the older child won't be jealous.'

As much as a second you (or at least a second pair of arms) would prove helpful at this time in your life, that isn't possible. There will be only one of you to go around and that fact leaves you divided at least two ways for many years to come. The question is how to make the division in a way that will be best for your four-year-old as well as for his new brother.

Later on in your child-rearing years, the split will have to be pretty much equal; the amount of time you spend with one child will have to be matched fairly evenly by the amount of time you spend with the other (just as every apple or slab of cake will have to be divided precisely to satisfy both children). Now, however, a little lopsidedness in favour of your older child is not only acceptable, it's best. Consider, first, that your older child is used to being an only child, and to not sharing your attention (save with your husband), and that your baby, happily unaware of who's getting more of you, will be basically content as long as his fundamental needs are being met. In addition, for a while, the baby will be getting a considerable amount of attention from significant and nonsignificant others, while your older child, looking on from the sidelines, will be largely ignored. Consider, too, that unlike your firstborn, who came home from the hospital to a relatively quiet home, your new baby has been born into a very active household, with plenty of parent-children interaction to keep his senses occupied and stimulated. If he sits on your lap while you're building a block city or fitting together puzzle pieces with your older son, or nestles in a baby sling while you push your older son's swing, he's receiving as much stimulation as if you were playing with him directly. Finally, remember that there's another 'caretaker' in your home now – your older son – who will be giving lively attention to your baby.

And though doing 'double duty' will no doubt prove tricky, increasingly so as your baby nears demanding toddlerhood, you will soon become very adept at it. You'll learn to share your attention with your older child without cutting into your time with the younger not only by taking care of the needs of both at once (nursing or bottle feeding the one while reading a story to or doing a puzzle with the other, for instance), but also by appointing your firstborn as your chief assistant. He can fetch nappies for the baby when he's wet, sing and dance for the baby when he's cranky and help you fold and put away the baby's laundry – matching those little socks is a chore for you, but a challenge and a learning experience for a child. Feeling useful will help keep him from feeling neglected.

But the older sibling needs more than shared time – he needs an unbroken span of time alone with you every day. If you don't have household help, finding such time may be difficult, but it's nevertheless essential. Baby's nap time (assuming your baby naps well during the day) is ideal if you can resist the urge to do the laundry, tidy up the house, or read the daily paper (these may have to wait until both children are in bed). So is early evening when daddy is home and can entertain the baby for a while. (Don't forget your older child will appreciate time alone with his father, too.)

In addition to seeing that your older child gets his fair share of attention, there are other steps you can take to modify the jealousy factor. For one, you should always refer to the infant either by his name or as 'yours' or 'yours' – never 'mine'. For another, try to avoid making the older child's life revolve around the younger's: 'Keep quiet – baby's sleeping' or 'You can't sit on my lap – baby's nursing' or 'Stop poking the baby – you'll hurt him!' You can get the same (or even a better) result by keeping 'don't' directives to a minimum and rephrasing them more positively: 'Baby's sleeping. Let's see if we can whisper so he won't wake up.' Or 'How about sitting on this chair right next to me so we can be close together while I'm nursing?' Or 'Baby really loves it when you stroke him gently like this.'

Though you should limit the times you say you can't play with him or get something for him because you're busy with the baby, it's unrealistic to attempt to never use the baby as an excuse; that's a part of life with a sibling that your older child will just have to learn to accept. It will be easier for him if you continue to remind him of the benefits of being the older child and if sometimes you turn the tables. Say to the baby (even if your child may have doubts about baby's comprehension), 'You're going to have to wait a minute for your nappy change because I have to give your brother his snack', or 'I can't pick you up now because I have to tuck your big brother in'.

Since you can spread yourself only so thin, you'll probably have to engage in some benign neglect of home and hearth in order to avoid neglecting your children. It will be more important to sit down and watch 'Playdays' with your preschooler than to run the vacuum over the living room rug, more important to take the family to the park than to spend the day slicing and chopping foods for dinner. Limit housekeeping chores to the very essential (and/or, if you can't live with the lived-in look and if you can afford it, get someone else to help with them), keep the baby in disposable nappies (or use a nappy service) and the rest of the family in no-iron clothes, use frozen vegetables (they're at least as nutritious as fresh) when necessary and keep meals simple (including those for baby; see page 241 for the merits of commercial baby food). Enlist your older child to help with such chores as dusting, opening vegetable packages, or setting the table; at first his help may seem more a hindrance, but with a little practice, you'll be surprised to find that he'll become more of a help.

Lack of Jealousy

'I was all prepared for sibling rivalry when we decided to have another baby.

But throughout the pregnancy and in the four months since her brother's arrival, my daughter hasn't shown any jealousy. Is that healthy?'

As you already know, your daughter has a personality all her own. Her reactions to the arrival of a new sibling may be completely different from those of a peer and yet be just as normal and healthy. Though many children do show hostility towards a new baby in the family, such feelings aren't inevitable, or necessary for the development of a strong sibling relationship. A child who seems delighted with a new sibling isn't necessarily hiding feelings of jealousy; she may just be secure enough to feel unthreatened by the new arrival. She may, however, once the helpless little newcomer takes to the floors as a crawler, find some solid ground for resentment as he tears up her books, scatters her blocks on the floor and chews the fingers off her favourite doll.

Still, in the meantime, you should be sure that she gets as much time and attention as her new sibling, even if she isn't demanding it. If you unintentionally begin to take her for granted because she's being such a good sport about the new baby, she may start to feel neglected and eventually become resentful.

And because almost every child feels some negative feelings towards a sibling somewhere along the way, make sure she knows it's okay to have such feelings and give her ample opportunity to express them.

Sibling Attachment

'I wonder how I can help my older child to feel more connected to his new baby brother.'

Mothers and fathers bond with their new babies by interacting with them while taking care of them. And there's no good reason why siblings can't do the same. With close adult supervision, even the youngest of older siblings can share in baby's care and begin to feel a sense of attachment to the baby – and an easing of postpartum jealousy. Depending on the age of the older child, he can participate in a variety of ways, including the following:

Nappy-changing. A school-age child can actually change a wet nappy with mum standing nearby; a toddler can help by fetching a clean one, handing mum a wipe, patting down the adhesive tape on a disposable, or entertaining the wriggling baby during the process.

Feeding. If your baby is bottle fed, or takes a relief bottle occasionally, even a fairly young child can hold it for him. If your baby is on the breast exclusively, your older child can't actually do the feeding, but he can snuggle next to you with a book while you nurse his sibling.

Burping. Even a toddler can pat baby's back to bring on an after-meal burp – and they usually delight in the results.

Bathing. Bath time can be a fun time for the whole family. An older sibling can pass the soap, flannel, or towel, pour rinse water (temperature-tested by an adult) over baby's body and entertain baby with his own bath toys or with singing. But don't let a sibling under twelve be baby's only chaperone at bath time – not even for a moment.

Baby-sitting. While an older sibling can't take total responsibility for a younger one until he's a teen (never allow a preschooler to mind a baby alone for even a minute), he can be dubbed 'baby-sitter' when you're close by. Babies find no one quite as amusing as their older siblings and finding that they have the ability to entertain baby is ego-boosting to senior sibs.

Escalating Warfare

'My daughter was very loving towards her little brother from the time he was born. But now that he's crawling and able to get into her toys, she's suddenly turned on him.'

For many older siblings, a newborn doesn't pose much of a threat. He's helpless, basically immobile, incapable of grabbing away books or breaking up dolly tea parties. Give him several months to develop reaching, crawling, cruising and other motor skills, and the picture takes a turn from the idyllic. Even older children who have been loving (at least most of the time) to a younger sibling up to this point may suddenly begin to display hostility. And you can hardly blame them – a miniature barbarian has just invaded their turf. Their crayon boxes have been looted, their books violated, their dolls plundered.

To defend her turf, an older sibling (tension is usually greatest if the age difference between the two siblings is three years or less) often begins screaming at, hitting, pushing and knocking down the baby. Sometimes there is a mix of affection and aggression in the actions: what begins as a hug ends up with baby on the floor crying. The action often accurately reflects the child's conflicting inner feelings. As the parent, you have to walk a narrow tightrope in such a situation – protecting the younger sibling without punishing the older. Though you should make it clear to your older child that it's not permissible to hurt her younger brother intentionally, you should also make it clear that you understand and sympathize with her plight and her frustrations. Try to give her the chance to play without him around part of the time (while he naps, is in the playpen, or is otherwise occupied). Particularly when she has guests over, respect her privacy and property and be sure that her younger sibling does, too. Spend some extra time with her and intervene on her behalf whenever the baby takes away or tries to destroy her belongings, instead of always urging her to 'let him – he's only a baby'. But do give her plenty of praise on occasions when she comes to this mature realization on her own.

Fairly soon, the tables will turn. Little brother, tired of being pushed around and strong enough to do some intentional pushing (and hair pulling and biting) of his own, will start fighting back. This usually occurs near the end of the first year, and is followed by a couple of years or more of mixed feelings between sib-lings – a confusing combination of love and hate. And you can expect these years, when you'll often feel more like a referee than a parent, to be a constant challenge to your patience and your ingenuity – as well as a joy.

PART THREE

Ready Reference

Best-Odds Recipes

For the First Year and Beyond

◆

They don't know a bisque from a brioche or a pâté from a pot-au-feu, but babies and toddlers are some of the most discriminating eaters on the gastronomic scene. And discriminate they do – against vegetables, protein foods and just about everything their parents would like them to eat. At mealtimes, pleasing them is a long shot, displeasing them a cinch, and getting them to take in their quota of the Daily Dozen a near impossibility – or so it too often seems.

But there is hope – and help – on the next few pages. Though the recipe hasn't been created that will make every baby 'open wide for the choo choo', those that follow stand a good chance of making it through a majority of young tunnels. All will go a long way in nourishing your little food critic and in satisfying, in most cases, several nutritional requirements at once.

Super Cereal

One bowl of this powerhouse cereal and your toddler will be leaping tall block buildings in a single bound.

Makes 1 toddler portion
55 g (2 oz) oat circles or other unsweetened whole-grain dry cereal
1 tablespoon wheat germ
2 tablespoons instant dried skimmed milk
2 dried apricots, finely chopped
100 ml (4 fl oz) whole milk

Mound the first four ingredients in a small cereal bowl in the order given, pour the milk over all, and serve immediately.

Best-Odds Toddler Servings per portion: 1 Protein; 1½ Whole Grain; 1 Calcium; 1 Yellow Fruit; some Iron

Fruited Cheese Bread

Even a baby determined to live on bread alone can't help but thrive when the bread is packed with protein, calcium and minerals. Bake ahead, slice and freeze for fussy mornings or afternoon snacks.

Makes 2 loaves, 24 x 14 x 7.5 cm (9½ x 5½ x 3 inches)

535–590 g (19–21 oz) wholemeal flour
45 g (1½ oz) wheat germ
1 teaspoon salt
2 sachets active dry yeast
250 ml (8 fl oz) water
100 ml (4 fl oz) apple juice concentrate
4 tablespoons vegetable oil
225g (8 oz) unsalted low-fat cottage cheese
1 whole egg
2 egg whites
45 g (1½ oz) rolled oats
170 g (6 oz) shredded low-sodium Swiss cheese
225 g (8 oz) chopped dried currants, raisins, or dates

1. Combine 170 g (6 oz) of the flour, the wheat germ, and the salt in the bowl of an electric mixer. Remove 210g (7½ oz) of the mixture and combine with the yeast. Make a well in centre of remaining flour and return yeast mixture to the well.

Low-Sodium Baking Powder

Ordinary double-acting baking powder is very high in sodium and is a major source of sodium in the Western diet. Since excess sodium is not good for babies (or anyone else), we suggest using low-sodium baking powder, available in health food stores, for baking these Best-Odds recipes. If you use ordinary baking powder, use ⅔ as much (2 teaspoons for every 3 called for).

2. Combine the water, juice concentrate, oil and cottage cheese in a saucepan and heat over medium heat until very warm. Gradually add this mixture to the yeast mixture in the well, stirring as you do. Beat together at medium speed, scraping the sides of the bowl as needed, for 2 minutes.

3. Add the egg, egg whites and 115 g (4 oz) flour to the dough; beat the dough again, scraping sides of bowl as needed, for 2 minutes. Blend in the rolled oats.

4. Turn out the dough onto a lightly floured board. Knead until smooth and elastic, about 8 to 10 minutes (or knead in mixer or processor, following appliance directions). If the dough remains too sticky, add the remaining flour, 2 tablespoons at a time, as needed. Place in a large bowl oiled with a little more vegetable oil turning to grease on all sides. Cover tightly with foil. Set bowl in a warm place until dough has doubled in bulk, about 1 hour.

5. Punch down the dough. Turn it out onto a lightly floured board. Knead in the Swiss cheese and the fruit. Divide the dough in half. Shape each half into a loaf and place each loaf in a 24 x 14 x 7.5 cm (9½ x 5½ x 3-inch) loaf tin that has been well greased with additional vegetable oil. Brush the top of each loaf lightly with oil, cover with a tea towel and let rise in a warm place until doubled, about 1 hour.

6. Fifteen minutes before baking the loaves, preheat the oven to 190°C (375°F) or gas mark 5.

7. Bake until the loaves are nicely browned and the bottoms sound hollow when tapped, about 35 to 40 minutes.

Best-Odds Toddler Servings in 1 slice or ⅒ loaf: 2 Grain; 1½ Protein; ½ Other Fruit; ½ Calcium; some Iron

Pumpkin Muffins

Yellow-vegetable nutrition in a delectable disguise. Keep frozen for days when baby won't take vegetables straight.

Makes about 24 muffins

Vegetable cooking spray
350 ml (12 fl oz) apple juice concentrate
4 tablespoons vegetable oil
2 whole eggs
4 egg whites
350 g (12 oz) canned, unsweetened, solid-pack pumpkin
285 g (10 oz) raisins
210 g (7½ oz) wholemeal flour
25 g (1 oz) wheat germ
4½ teaspoons low-sodium baking powder
2 teaspoons ground cinnamon

1. Preheat the oven to 200°C (400°F) or gas mark 6. Coat 24 muffin tin cups with vegetable cooking spray or line each with a cake case. Set aside.

2. Combine the juice concentrate, oil, eggs, egg whites, pumpkin and raisins in a blender. Purée until the raisins are chopped.

3. Mix together the flour, wheat germ, baking powder and cinnamon in a large

mixing bowl. Gradually add the pumpkin mixture, blending with an electric mixer set on low, or mix slowly by hand, just until well combined.

4. Pour the batter into the prepared muffin tins, filling each cup two-thirds full. Bake for 15 to 20 minutes. The muffins are done when a toothpick inserted into the centre of one comes out clean (or with just a crumb or two attached).

Best-Odds Toddler Servings in 1 muffin: 2 Yellow; 1+ Whole Grain; 1 Other Fruit; ½ Protein

Pancake Faces

Smiles on the pancakes are bound to bring smiles to the high chair. Serve them plain or with fruit-only preserves, yogurt blended with fruit-only preserves, sliced bananas, sautéed apples or pears, or unsweetened apple purée. Freeze leftover pancakes for easy and nutritious finger food anytime.

Makes about 24 small pancakes

250 ml (8 fl oz) whole milk
4 tablespoons dried skimmed milk
2 tablespoons apple juice concentrate
15 g (½ oz) butter or margarine, melted
1 whole egg
2 egg whites
100 g (3½ oz) wholemeal flour
45 g (1½ oz) wheat germ
1½ teaspoons low-sodium baking powder
Vegetable cooking spray
Chopped raisins
Dried apricots cut into thin strips

1. Combine all the ingredients up to and including the baking powder in a blender, and process just until smooth. Let the mixture stand for 15 minutes.

2. Spray a nonstick frying pan or griddle with vegetable cooking spray. Heat over medium-high heat until very hot. Reduce the heat to medium, stir the batter and spoon it onto the griddle to make 7.5-cm (3-inch) pancakes.

3. Using bits of raisin and strips of apricot, add facial features to the pancakes. When the surface of the pancakes begins to bubble and the bottoms are nicely browned, about 2 minutes, turn and brown the other side, about 1 minute more.

4. Serve the pancakes face side up with any of the suggested accompaniments.

Best-Odds Toddler Servings in three 7.5-cm (3-inch) pancakes: 1 Protein; 1 Whole Grain; ¼ Calcium; some Iron

Golden-Nugget Oatmeal Flapjacks

The whole family will flip for these fruity pancakes. Serve them with yogurt, unsweetened apple purée, fresh berries, juice-sweetened apricot preserves, or Dried Apricot Purée (see page 610).

Makes about 48 silver-dollar-size pancakes

250 ml (8 fl oz) whole milk
4 tablespoons apple juice concentrate
25 g (1 oz) butter or margarine, melted
1 whole egg
2 egg whites
140 g (5 oz) wholemeal flour
25 g (1 oz) rolled oats
25 g (1 oz) wheat germ
2½ teaspoons low-sodium baking powder
4 tablespoons dried skimmed milk
1½ teaspoons vanilla extract
1 teaspoon ground cinnamon (optional)
115 g (4 oz) dried apricots, finely chopped
Vegetable cooking spray

1. Beat the whole milk, juice concentrate, butter, egg and egg whites together in a large bowl. Add in the remaining ingredients through to the vanilla (or cinna-

mon, if using) and beat just until smooth. Fold in the chopped apricots.

2. Spray a frying pan or griddle with vegetable cooking spray. Heat over medium-high heat until very hot. Reduce the heat to medium and spoon batter to make 5-cm (2-inch) pancakes. When the surface of the pancakes begins to bubble and the bottoms are nicely browned, about 2 minutes, turn and brown the other side, about 1 minute more.

Best-Odds Toddler Servings in four 5-cm (2-inch) pancakes: ⅔ Whole Grain; ½ Protein; some Calcium; ¼ Fat

Croque Bebe

Your baby doesn't have to speak a word of French (or English, for that matter) to enjoy the intriguing taste and bountiful nutrition of these French toast-style grilled cheese sandwiches.

Makes 1 sandwich

1 egg
50 ml (2 fl oz) milk
2 slices (about 55 g/2 oz) low-sodium Swiss or Cheddar cheese
2 slices low-sodium whole-grain bread
Vegetable cooking spray

1. Beat the egg and milk together lightly in a bowl large enough to hold the bread.

2. Layer the cheese between the bread slices. Soak the sandwich in the egg mixture, turning it until the liquid is absorbed.

3. Spray a nonstick frying pan with vegetable cooking spray. Heat over medium-high heat until hot. Reduce the heat to medium and brown the sandwich on both sides.

Best-Odds Toddler Servings in ½ sandwich: 2 Whole Grain; 1 Calcium; 1 Protein

Banana French Toast

One of baby's favourite flavours – banana – enhances the appeal of this French toast; nonfat dry milk adds a jolt of protein and calcium. It makes a nutritious breakfast, lunch, or supper as well.

Makes 4 slices

1 egg
2 tablespoons banana-orange juice concentrate
2 tablespoons apple juice concentrate
½ small banana
4 tablespoons dried skimmed milk
4 slices low-sodium whole-grain bread
Vegetable cooking spray

1. Combine the ingredients through to the milk in a blender and process until smooth. Transfer the mixture to a bowl large enough to hold the bread.

2. Soak the bread in the concentrate mixture, turning the slices until all the liquid is absorbed.

3. Spray a nonstick frying pan with vegetable cooking spray. Heat over medium-high heat until hot. Reduce the heat to medium-low. Add the bread and cook until the bottoms are nicely browned, about 3 minutes. Turn and cook the second side, about 2 minutes. Serve warm.

Best-Odds Toddler Servings in 1 slice: 2 Whole Grain; ¾ Protein; ½ Other Fruit; ¼ Calcium

Variation: Omit banana and banana-orange juice concentrate and use 4 tablespoons apple juice concentrate.

Cottage Cheese Sundae

Hold the hot fudge and the ice cream. A baby with unspoiled taste buds will be just as happy with this naturally sweet, naturally nutritious version. Serve any time of the day, and vary according to seasonal availability of fruit.

Makes 1 toddler portion

4 tablespoons sliced fresh fruit (bananas, cantaloupe, peaches, strawberries)
4 tablespoons unsalted low-fat cottage cheese
1 tablespoon sour cream (omit for children older than two)
2 tablespoons juice-sweetened preserves
1 tablespoon wheat germ

Arrange fruit in a ring on a small plate. Fill the centre of the ring with cottage cheese. Top with the remaining ingredients.

Best-Odds Toddler Servings per portion: 1½ Protein; 1 Whole Grain; 1 Other Fruit (if bananas or white peaches are used); 1 Vitamin C (if strawberries or cantaloupe is used); 1 Yellow Fruit (if cantaloupe or yellow peaches are used); ½ Fat

Funny Fingers

The protein of your choice will become baby's choice under this crispy coating. Serve Funny Fingers as finger food, of course.

Makes 1 toddler portion

25 g (1 oz) fresh fish fillet, such as sole, flounder, or haddock, or boneless chicken breast; or 45 g (1½ oz) tofu
4 tablespoons fine wholemeal breadcrumbs (see Note)
1 tablespoon grated Parmesan cheese (optional)
Dash garlic powder
½ teaspoon mayonnaise
Vegetable cooking spray

1. Preheat the oven to 180°C (350°F) or gas mark 4.

2. Cut the fish (checking carefully for bones), chicken, or tofu into 1-cm (½-inch) strips.

3. Combine the breadcrumbs, grated cheese, if using, and the garlic powder in a small bowl, stirring until well blended.

4. Spread the mayonnaise on the fish, chicken, or tofu strips, then roll them in the crumb mixture. Arrange the strips in a shallow pan sprayed with vegetable cooking spray. Bake for 5 minutes; turn, and bake 5 minutes more.

Best-Odds Toddler Servings per portion: 1½ Protein; 1 Whole Grain; ⅓ Calcium

Note: You can make your own breadcrumbs in a blender or food processor, using cubes of your favourite bread that has gone slightly stale. Store unused crumbs in the freezer until needed.

Baby's First Cake

Even if the doctor's red light on eggs hasn't been lifted yet, you can let 'em eat cake – if it's this fruit-studded but eggless wonder.

Makes 1 single-layer 20-cm (8-inch) square cake

Vegetable cooking spray
280 ml (9 fl oz) plus 2 tablespoons apple juice concentrate
8 tablespoons whole raisins
8 tablespoons chopped raisins
8 tablespoons chopped dates
55 g (2 oz) butter or margarine
1½ teaspoons ground cinnamon
100 g (3½ oz) wholemeal flour
25 g (1 oz) wheat germ
4½ teaspoons low-sodium baking powder

1. Preheat the oven to 160°C (325°F) or gas mark 3. Coat a 20-cm (8-inch) square nonstick baking tin with vegetable cooking spray. Set aside.

2. Combine the juice concentrate, dried fruits, butter and cinnamon in a small saucepan. Simmer over low heat until the butter is melted. Remove from the stove and let cool.

3. Combine the flour, wheat germ and baking powder in a mixing bowl. Gradually blend in the fruit mixture, stirring just until mixed. Do not overmix.

4. Pour the batter into the prepared baking tin. Bake about 30 minutes. The cake is done when a toothpick inserted into the centre comes out dry. Cover loosely with foil during baking if the cake starts to brown.

5. To keep the cake from becoming dry and too hard for baby to gum, cover with aluminium foil or store in a plastic bag as soon as it has cooled slightly.

Best-Odds Toddler Servings in ⅛ cake: 1½ Other Fruit; 1 + Whole Grain; ⅓ Protein

Golden Cake

Vitamin A finds its way into another unexpectedly delicious place; this time, a light but homely cake, scented with cinnamon. Freeze in squares for convenient serving.

Makes 1 single-layer 23-cm (9-inch) square cake

225 g (8 oz) dried apricots, finely chopped
350 ml (12 fl oz) apple juice concentrate, or more if needed
140 g (5 oz) wholemeal flour
25 g (1 oz) wheat germ
3 teaspoons low-sodium baking powder
1½ teaspoons ground cinnamon
2 egg whites, lightly beaten
4 tablespoons vegetable oil
Vegetable cooking spray
125 g (4½ oz) juice-sweetened apricot preserves or Dried Apricot Purée (recipe follows)

1. Preheat the oven to 180°C (350°F) or gas mark 4.

2. Combine the apricots with ⅔ of the juice concentrate in a small saucepan. Bring to a boil, then lower the heat and simmer, uncovered, until the apricots are soft, 5 to 15 minutes. Drain, reserving juice in a liquid measuring cup and setting apricots aside.

3. Blend the flour, wheat germ, baking soda and cinnamon together in a large mixing bowl. Add the egg whites and the remaining juice concentrate; stir to blend.

4. If necessary, add enough juice concentrate to the reserved juice to make 100ml (4 fl oz) liquid. Stir in the oil and heat just until hot. Add the liquid and the reserved apricots to the flour mixture. Stir just until smooth.

5. Pour the batter into a nonstick 23-cm (9-inch) square tin coated with vegetable cooking spray. Bake until the top springs back when lightly touched and the sides have begun to pull away from the tin, about 35 minutes. While still warm, spread with apricot preserves or purée. Cool, and serve.

Best-Odds Toddler Servings in one 5-cm (2-inch) square: 1 Whole Grain; ½ Protein; ½ Yellow Fruit; Iron

Dried Apricot Purée

A quick and easy homemade fruit spread, rich in vitamin A and iron.

Makes about 350 ml (12 oz) purée

225 g (8 oz) dried apricots
250 ml (8 fl oz) apple juice concentrate

Combine the ingredients in a saucepan and simmer, uncovered, until the fruit is soft, 5 to 15 minutes. Purée in a blender or food processor until smooth. Use as a spread on cake or bread, or as a topping for yogurt or cottage cheese.

Best-Odds Toddler Servings in 2 tablespoons: ½ Yellow Fruit; 1 Other Fruit; some Iron

First Birthday Cake

Carrots disappear magically from a toddler's plate when they come in a cake. Frost for birthdays and other special occasions, but also keep a supply of plain squares in the freezer for snacking and daily desserts.

Makes 1 double-layer 23-cm (9-inch) square cake

400 g (14 oz) thinly sliced carrots (5 medium)
600 ml (21 fl oz) apple juice concentrate (you will use slightly less than this)
225 g (8 oz) raisins
Vegetable cooking spray
285 g (10 oz) wholemeal flour
25 g (1 oz) wheat germ
2 tablespoons low-sodium baking powder
1 tablespoon ground cinnamon
4 tablespoons vegetable oil
2 whole eggs
4 egg whites
1 tablespoon vanilla extract
175 ml (6 fl oz) unsweetened apple purée
Cream Cheese Frosting (recipe follows)

1. Combine the carrots with 280 ml (9 fl oz) of the juice concentrate in a medium-size saucepan. Bring to a boil, then lower the heat and simmer, covered, until carrots are tender, 15 to 20 minutes. Purée in a blender or food processor until smooth. Add the raisins and process until finely chopped. Let mixture cool.

2. Preheat the oven to 180°C (350°F) or gas mark 4. Line two 23-cm (9-inch) square cake tins with waxed paper and spray the paper with vegetable cooking spray.

3. Combine the flour, wheat germ, baking

powder and cinnamon in a large mixing bowl. Add half the juice concentrate, the oil, eggs, egg whites and vanilla; beat just until well mixed. Fold in the carrot purée and apple purée. Pour the batter into the prepared cake pans.

4. Bake until a knife inserted in the centre comes out clean, 35 to 40 minutes. Cool briefly in the tins, then turn out onto wire racks to cool completely. When cool, frost with Cream Cheese Frosting.

Best-Odds Toddler Servings in one 5-cm (2-inch) frosted square: 3 Yellow Vegetable; ½ + Other Fruits; 1½ Whole Grain; 1 + Protein; some Iron; 1 Fat

Cream Cheese Frosting

The traditional foil for carrot cake – but without the sugar.

Frosts one 2-layer cake

100 ml (4 fl oz) apple juice concentrate
450 g (16 oz) light cream cheese
2 teaspoons vanilla extract
115 g (4 oz) finely chopped raisins
1½ teaspoons unflavoured gelatin

1. Set aside 2 tablespoons of the juice concentrate.

2. Process the remaining juice concentrate, the cream cheese, vanilla and raisins in a blender or food processor until smooth. Transfer to a mixing bowl.

3. Stir the gelatin into the 2 tablespoons juice concentrate in a small saucepan; let stand 1 minute to soften. Heat to boiling and stir to dissolve gelatin.

4. Beat the gelatin mixture into the cream cheese mixture until well blended. Refrigerate just until the frosting begins to set, about 30 to 60 minutes. Frost the cake.

Oatmeal Raisin Cookies

Even the baby who hasn't yet sprouted a sweet tooth can gum these cakey treats.

Makes 3 to 4 dozen cookies

Vegetable cooking spray
140 g (5 oz) wholemeal flour
45 g (1½ oz) wheat germ
30 g (1 oz) rolled oats
1 tablespoon low-sodium baking powder
2 teaspoons ground cinnamon
250 ml (8 fl oz) apple juice concentrate
4 tablespoons vegetable oil
2 egg whites or 1 whole egg
115 g (4 oz) raisins

1. Preheat the oven to 190°C (375°F) or gas mark 5. Coat 2 baking trays with vegetable cooking spray. Set aside.

2. Mix the flour, wheat germ, oats, baking powder, and cinnamon in a large mixing bowl.

3. Combine the juice concentrate, oil, egg and raisins in a blender. Blend at medium speed until the raisins are chopped. Pour the mixture into the dry ingredients and stir together.

4. Drop the batter by heaped teaspoons onto the prepared trays, about 2.5 cm (1 inch) apart. Flatten each mound with the back of a fork. Bake, being careful not to let the cookies brown and become crispy, about 8 to 10 minutes. Let the cookies cool slightly on the trays before removing to a plastic bag. (This will prevent the cookies from becoming hard). Wait until cookies are completely cool before closing the plastic bag. Continue baking cookies until the batter is finished. Cookies can be frozen.

Best-Odds Toddler Servings in 2 to 3 cookies: 1 + Whole Grain; ¾ Other Fruit; ½ Protein; some Iron

Apple-Cranberry Cubes

They wiggle, they jiggle, they shake and they shiver – and these cubes of fruit gel haven't a drop of sugar in them to spoil the fun. The perfect answer, too, when a sick baby won't, or shouldn't, eat anything solid and refuses liquids.

Makes 4 toddler portions

1 tablespoon unflavoured gelatin
4 tablespoons water
350 ml (12 fl oz) unsweetened apple-cranberry juice
4 tablespoons apple juice concentrate

1. Mix together the gelatin and the water in a medium-size bowl; let stand to soften, 1 minute.

2. Meanwhile, in a small saucepan, bring the apple-cranberry juice to a boil. Add the juice to the gelatin mixture and stir until the gelatin is thoroughly dissolved. Add the juice concentrate. Pour the mixture into a 20-cm (8-inch) square baking tin and chill until firm. Cut into cubes and mound in a pretty dessert dish.

Best-Odds Toddler Servings in ¼ recipe: 1 Other Fruit

Variation: Use apple juice instead of apple-cranberry for babies or children with gastrointestinal viruses.

Banana-Orange Jelly

Same wiggle, with a little more kick.

Makes 4 toddler portions

1 tablespoon unflavoured gelatin
100 ml (4 fl oz) water
250 ml (8 fl oz) fresh orange juice
100 ml (4 fl oz) banana-orange juice concentrate
1 small banana, sliced

1. In a small saucepan, stir the gelatin into the water; let stand to soften, 1 minute. Heat over medium-high heat just to boiling.

2. Stir in the juice and juice concentrate until the gelatin is thoroughly dissolved.

3. Pour half the mixture into an 20-cm (8-inch) square baking tin and freeze until thickened, about 10 minutes. Add a layer of sliced banana and cover with the remaining gel mixture. Refrigerate until firm.

4. To serve, cut into four squares.

Best-Odds Toddler Servings in one portion: 1 Other Fruit

Peachy Yogurt

Commercial frozen yogurts have as much sugar in them as ice cream – some even more. This one only tastes as though it does.

Makes 4 toddler portions

500 ml (16 fl oz) whole-milk plain yogurt
85 g/3 oz peeled, sliced fresh yellow peaches
4 tablespoons apple juice concentrate

1. Combine all ingredients in a blender and process until smooth.

2. Prepare according to the directions for your ice-cream maker. Or, pour into a 20-cm (8-inch) square baking tin and freeze until mushy. Scrape mixture into a large mixing bowl and beat until fluffy. Repeat the freezing-heating process once or twice more. Then freeze until desired texture is reached. If the dessert freezes too hard, let it defrost until spoonable.

Best-Odds Toddler Servings in ¼ recipe: + Yellow Fruit; 1 Protein; 1 Calcium

Common Home Remedies

The doctor recommends suctioning baby's nose to ease the congestion of a cold. Cold compresses, you hear, are the best way to treat a burn. And steam is ideal for treating a baby with the croup. But just how do you suction a baby's nose? What is a cold compress? And how do you build up enough steam to ease the croup? This guide to home remedies will give you the answers.

Cold Compresses

Fill a basin (a styrofoam bucket or cooler is best) with cold tap water and a tray or two of ice cubes. Dip a clean flannel into the water, wring it out, and place it over the affected part. Re-chill the cloth when the cold dissipates.

Cold Soaks

Fill a basin (a styrofoam bucket or cooler is best) with cold water and a tray or two of ice cubes. Immerse the injured part for 30 minutes, if possible. Repeat in 30 minutes, if necessary. Do not apply ice directly to baby's skin.

Cool Compresses

Fill a basin with cool water from the tap. Dip a flannel or towel into the water, squeeze it out, and apply to injured part. Re-dip when the cloth no longer seems wet and cool.

Eye Soaks

For eyes, dip a clean flannel in warm, not hot, water (test it for comfort on your inner wrist or forearm), and apply to baby's eye for 5 to 10 minutes every 3 hours.

Heating Pad

A hot-water bottle, which has no cords or heating element, is usually safer to use with an infant. If you use a heating pad, re-read directions before each use, be sure the pad and cord are in good condition, and cover entirely with a terry nappy if the pad doesn't have a cloth covering. Keep the temperature low, do not leave baby and use no more than 15 minutes at a time.

Hot Compresses

See 'Warm compresses'. Never use hot compresses on a baby.

Hot Soaks

Fill a basin with water that feels comfortably hot on your inner wrist or arm (not to your fingers). Never use water you haven't tested first. Immerse injured part in basin.

Hot-Water Bottle

Fill a hot-water bottle with water that is just warm to the touch. Wrap the bottle in a

Dosage Chart for Common Infant-Fever Medication*

Tempra	Drops	Syrup
Under 3 months 5.8 kg/13 lb**	½ dropper	¼ teaspoon
3 to 9 months 5.8 to 9 kg/13 to 20 lb**	1 dropper	½ teaspoon
10 to 24 months 9.4 to 11.7 kg/21 to 26 lb	1½ droppers	¾ teaspoon
2 to 3 years 12 to 15.7 kg/27 to 35 lb	2 droppers	1 teaspoon

Calpol or Panadol	Drops	Elixir
Under 3 months 2.7 to 5 kg/6 to 11 lb**	½ dropper	none
4 to 11 months 5.4 to 7.7 kg/12 to 17 lb**	1 dropper	½ teaspoon
12 to 23 months 8.1 to 10.4 kg/18 to 23 lb	1½ droppers	¾ teaspoon
2 to 3 years 10.4 to 15.7kg/23 to 35 lb	2 droppers	1 teaspoon

* These are paracetamol preparations; aspirin should not be given without a doctor's recommendation. Always read packaging instructions carefully.

** *Do not* give medication to babies under six months old without the doctor's recommendation. Give medication every four hours as needed, but no more than 5 times daily. If weight range and age don't correlate, use the dosage appropriate for baby's weight.

towel or terry nappy before applying to baby's skin.

Humidifier

See 'Steam'.

Ice Pack

Use a commercial ice pack you keep in the freezer or a plastic bag filled with ice cubes (and a couple of paper towels to absorb the melting ice) and closed with a twist tie or rubber band. Also usable: an unopened tin of frozen juice concentrate; an unopened package of frozen food. Do not apply ice directly to a baby's skin.

Increased Fluids

Frequently nurse the baby who is solely breastfed. Give formula to a bottle baby, unless the doctor says not to. Give water between feedings, and when baby is taking juice dilute half-and-half with water. But do not force fluids unless the doctor tells you to. When baby is vomiting, tiny sips of fluids spaced out stay down better than larger quantities. (See specific illnesses for preferred fluids.)

Nasal Aspiration

With baby held upright, squeeze bulb of aspirator (see illustration, page 412) and place tip carefully in one nostril. Slowly release bulb to draw mucus into it. Repeat with second nostril. If mucus is dried and caked, irrigate with salt water (see below) and aspirate again.

Salt-Water Irrigation

Though it's possible to use a homemade salt solution (add ⅛ teaspoon salt to 100 ml (4 fl oz) cooled boiled water), commercial saline solutions are safer. Put two drops in each nostril using a clean small dropper to soften crusts and clear congestion. Wait 5 to 10 minutes and suction with a nasal aspirator. Do not use irrigation or commercial nose drops for more than three days, because such use can worsen congestion.

Steam

Use a cold-mist humidifier or a steam vaporizer placed out of baby's reach to moisten the air; or place a bowl of hot water on a hot radiator (out of baby's reach) or a kettle or pot of hot water on the stove in the same room as baby.[1] For quick and abundant steam for a baby with croup (see page 620), close the bathroom door, turn on the hot water in the shower full blast, and fill the room with steam. Remain with baby in the bathroom until the croupy cough stops. If cough has not improved in ten minutes, check with the doctor.

Warm Compresses

Fill a basin (a styrofoam bucket or cooler is best) with warm (it should not feel uncomfortable on your upper arm), not hot, water. Dip a clean flannel in the water, wring it out, and place it over affected part as directed by baby's doctor.

---

1. Since germs and moulds can multiply in a cold-mist humidifier, wash yours daily according to manufacturer's instructions when it's in use. It's generally recommended that the tank be cleaned with washing-up liquid and water, then rinsed with a mild solution of chlorine bleach and water. At each use it should be refilled with fresh water. Cold mist vaporizers are most likely to send germs and mould into the air; steam vaporizers are less likely to, but present a burn hazard. Best are ultrasonic units, which eject no live moulds and very few bacteria into the air. But because the ultrasonic units pulverize not only bacteria and mould but minerals in the water, straight tap water, with its normal mineral content, should not be used in them. The mineral particles emitted by the humidifier are fine enough to be breathed into the deepest parts of the lungs and could increase risk of colds and flu, and aggravate chronic respiratory illnesses. Use distilled water or filter tap water to remove the minerals.

Common Childhood Illnesses

◆

Though the doctor will usually be the one to diagnose your baby's illnesses, you may find the basic information in this chart helpful as you try to sort out the possibilities and prepare to seek medical help. Keep in mind that not every child has a textbook case of every illness. Your child's symptoms, duration of disease and so on may vary from those listed here.

The details of how to treat specific symptoms (such as a cough, diarrhoea, or an itch, for example) or of how to handle a fever are omitted from the chart to avoid repetition. For information on treating symptoms, see page 408; for treating a fever, see page 424.

To aid in diagnosis, symptoms are numbered if they can be expected to appear at different times in the course of the illness. Rashes are listed separately for quick and easy comparison.

Scientists aren't always certain how disease is transmitted. But most frequently germs seem to be passed to a healthy person through droplets from the sneezes or coughs of an infected individual; on bits of dust in the air (airborne); via direct contact (touching the infected individual, most often hand-to-hand); via indirect contact (touching an object contaminated by the infected person); via respiratory secretions (mucus, phlegm) either directly or indirectly; via faeces, directly or indirectly; via body fluids (tears, saliva, blood, pus, urine) by direct or indirect contact; via sexual activity or contact with sexual fluids; through contaminated food; or through animal or insect vectors, or carriers. Depending on the infectious organism, a person may be more susceptible to infection when general health is poor, when there is an open wound, sore, or other break in the skin, or when there has been no immunity developed.

The risk of contracting most diseases can be reduced by keeping your baby in general good health (immunizations, regular medical checkups, good nutrition, adequate rest), practising good hygiene (washing hands after using the toilet or changing nappies and before handling baby or food, disposing of soiled nappies and tissues in a sanitary fashion), and isolating anyone with an infectious disease in your home as best you can (separate linens, dishes, utensils).

Even if this chart tells you everything you want to know about a particular childhood illness, it is no substitute for medical advice. Consult your baby's doctor as recommended.

DISEASE/SEASON/ SUSCEPTIBILITY	SYMPTOMS
	NON-RASH (numbers indicate order of appearance) RASH

	NON-RASH	RASH
BRONCHIOLITIS (inflammation of the smaller branches of the bronchial tree) **Season:** Respiratory synctial viruses (RSV), winter and spring; parainfluenzae viruses (PIV), summer and autumn. **Susceptibility:** Greatest in those under 2 years, especially under 6 months, or with a family history of allergy.	1. Cold symptoms. 2. *A few days later:* Rapid, shallow breathing; wheezing on breathing out; low-grade fever for about 3 days. *Sometimes:* Chest does not seem to expand with breathing in; pale or bluish colour.	
BRONCHITIS (inflammation of the bronchial tree and often the windpipe, or trachea) **Season**: Varies with causative microorganism. **Susceptibility**: Greatest in children under 4 years.	1.*Usually*: Cold symptoms. 2. *Abrupt onset of*: Fever, about 38.9°C (102°F); harsh cough, worse at night, sometimes paroxysmal, with vomiting; greenish or yellow sputum; wheezing or whistling on breathing out, especially with a family history of respiratory allergy; lips and fingernails tinged blue.	
CHICKEN POX (Varicella) **Season**: Late winter and spring in temperate zones. **Susceptibility**: Most people are infected as children.	Slight fever; malaise; loss of appetite.	Flat red spots turn into pimples, then blister, crust and scrab; new crops continue to develop for 3 to 4 days, mostly on the body.

CAUSE/TRANSMISSION/ INCUBATION/DURATION	CALL THE DOCTOR/ TREATMENT/DIET	PREVENTION/RECURRENCE/ COMPLICATIONS
Cause: Various viruses, most often RSV or PIV; rarely, bacteria. **Transmission:** Usually via respiratory secretions by direct contact or on household objects. **Incubation:** Varies with causative organism; usually 2 to 8 days. **Duration:** Acute phase may last only 3 days; cough from 1 to 3 weeks or more.	**Call the doctor immediately or go to A&E** if doctor can't be reached. **Treatment:** Hospitalization; possibly, antiviral drug. **Diet:** If food can be taken by mouth, frequent small meals.	**Prevention:** No vaccine available; avoid exposure of infants with a family history of respiratory allergy. **Recurrence:** Can recur, but symptoms may be milder. **Complications:** Heart failure; bronchial asthma.
	Cause: Usually a virus; less often, bacteria, but secondary bacterial infection is common. Cough made worse by tobacco smoke. **Transmission**: Usually via respiratory secretions. **Incubation**: Varies with causative organism. **Duration**: Fever lasts 2 or 3 days; cough 1 or 2 weeks or more.	**Call the doctor** if cough is severe, or lasts more than 3 days. **Treatment**: Symptomatic, for cough, if needed; in some cases, antibiotics. **Diet**: Increase in clear fluids.
Cause: Varicella-zoster virus. **Transmission**: Person-to-person via droplets, and airborne; very contagious from 1 to 2 days before onset until all lesions are scabbed. **Incubation**: Usually 14 to 16 days, but can be as short as 11 or as long as 20. **Duration**: First vesicles crust in 6 to 8 hours, scab in 24 to 48; scabs last 5 to 20 days.	**Call the doctor** to confirm diagnosis; **call immediately** for high-risk children; **call again** if symptoms of encephalitis appear. **Treatment**: for itching (page 408) and fever (page 424). DO NOT GIVE ASPIRIN.	**Prevention**: Avoid exposure for high-risk children and non-immune expectant mothers. **Recurrence**: Extremely rare; but dormant virus may flare up as shingles later in life. **Complications**: Rarely, encephalitis; anyone on steroids or those who are immunocompromised can become seriously ill. **In expectant mothers**, possible risk to foetus; contact doctor if exposure occurs.

DISEASE/SEASON/ SUSCEPTIBILITY	SYMPTOMS NON-RASH (numbers indicate order of appearance) RASH
CONJUNCTIVITIS (**Pinkeye**; inflammation of the conjunctiva, or lining of the eye)	*Depending on cause, may include:* Bloodshot eyes; tearing; discharge; burning; itching; light sensitivity. Usually begins in one eye, but may spread to the other.
CROUP (Acute Laryngotrachetis) **Season**: Varies; usually occurs at night. **Susceptibility**: Young children.	Hoarseness; sharp, barking cough; crowing, wheezing, or grunting sound on breathing in. *Sometimes:* Difficulty breathing.
EAR INFECTION (**Otitis media**)	See page 416.

CAUSE/TRANSMISSION/ INCUBATION/DURATION	CALL THE DOCTOR/ TREATMENT/DIET	PREVENTION/RECURRENCE/ COMPLICATIONS
Cause: Many, including viruses, bacteria, chlamydia, allergens, parasites, fungi, environmental irritants, blocked tear duct (see page 106) and silver nitrate drops at birth. **Transmission**: For infective organisms, eye-hand-eye. **Incubation**: Usually brief. **Duration**: Varies: silver nitrate, 3 to 5 days; virus, 2 days to 3 weeks (can become chronic); bacteria, about 2 weeks; others, until allergen, irritant, or duct blockage is removed.	**Call the doctor** to confirm diagnosis; **call again** if condition worsens or does not start to improve. **Treatment**: Eye soaks; separate bed linens and towels to prevent spread of infection; elimination of irritants, such as tobacco smoke, when possible; drops or ointment prescribed for bacterial and herpes infections, possibly for viral conjunctivitis (to prevent secondary infection), and to relieve discomfort of allergic reaction.	**Prevention**: Good hygiene (separate towels when family member is infected); avoidance of allergens and other irritants. **Recurrence**: Some people are more susceptible and more likely to have recurrences. **Complications**: Blindness (rare, except with gonorrhoeal infection); chronic eye inflammation; eye damage from repeated attacks.
Cause: Usually, virus (most often parainfluenzae or adenovirus; occasionally, bacteria or inhaled object. **Transmission**: Probably, person-to-person; contaminated objects; droplet spray. **Incubation**: 2 days (usually follows cold or flu). **Duration**: 12 hour; may recur over several days.	**Call the doctor immediately** if steam doesn't bring relief; if baby looks blue, has blue lips, or is drooling excessively; or if you suspect an inhaled object. **Initial treatment**: Steam (see page 616). **Follow-up**: Humidifier. **Diet**: Reduce intake of dairy products, especially if mucus is heavy. Sleep in same room as baby to reassure and to be handy for treating another attack.	**Prevention**: Supply humidified air to baby with cold or flu. **Recurrence**: Tends to repeat in some children. **Complications**: Breathing problems; pneumonia; ear infection about 5 days after recovery.

DISEASE/SEASON/ SUSCEPTIBILITY	SYMPTOMS
	NON-RASH (numbers indicate order of appearance) RASH

ENCEPHALITIS
(inflammation of the brain)
Season: Depends on cause.
Susceptibility: Varies with
cause.

Fever; drowsiness;
headache.
Sometimes: Neurological
impairment; coma at a late
stage.

EPIGLOTTITIS
(inflammation of the
epiglottis)
Season: Winter months in
temperate climates.
Susceptibility: Not
common in children
under 2.

Low-pitched cough; muffled
voice; difficulty breathing
and swallowing; drooling.
Sometimes: Protruding
tongue; fever.
Child seems ill.

FIFTH DISEASE
(**Erythema Infectiosum**)
Season: Early spring.
Susceptibility: Greatest in
children 2 to 12 years old.

Rarely: Joint pain.

1. Intense flush on face
(slapped-cheek look).
2. *Next day*: Lacy rash on
arms and legs.
3. *3 days later*: Rash on
inner surfaces, fingers, toes,
trunk and/or buttocks.
4. Rash may reappear on and
off with exposure to heat
(bath water, sun) for 2 or 3
weeks.

**GASTROINTESTINAL
UPSET**

See Diarrhoea, page 414.

GERMAN MEASLES
(**Rubella**)
Season: Late winter and
early spring.
Susceptibility: Any
unimmunized person.

None in 25% to 50% of
cases.
1. *Sometimes*: Slight fever;
swollen neck glands.

2. Small (2mm/$\frac{1}{10}$-inch), flat,
reddish pink spots on face.
3. Rash spreads to body and,
sometimes, to roof of
mouth.

CAUSE/TRANSMISSION/ INCUBATION/DURATION	CALL THE DOCTOR/ TREATMENT/DIET	PREVENTION/RECURRENCE/ COMPLICATIONS
Cause: Bacteria or viruses (often a complication of another disease). **Transmission**: Depends on cause; some viruses transmitted via insects. **Incubation**: Depends on cause. **Duration**: Varies.	**Call the doctor immediately or go to A&E** if you suspect encephalitis. **Treatment**: Hospitalization is required.	**Prevention**: Immunization against diseases for which this is a complication, for example measles. **Recurrence**: Unlikely. **Complications**: Neurological damage; can be fatal.
Cause: Bacteria, most often haemophilus influenzae (Hib). **Transmission**: Probably, person-to-person, or inhalation of droplets. **Incubation**: Less than 10 days. **Duration**: 4 to 7 days or longer.	**Call 999 immediately or go to A&E**. While waiting for help, keep baby upright, leaning forward, with mouth open and tongue out. **Treatment**: Hospitalization; establishment of airway; antibiotics.	**Prevention**: Hib immunization. **Recurrence**: Slight possibility. **Complications**: Can be fatal without prompt medical attention.
Cause: Possibly, human parvovirus. **Transmission**: Probably person-to-person. **Incubation**: 4 to 14 days; usually 12 to 14. **Duration:** 3 to 10 days, but rash may reappear on and off for up to 3 weeks.	**Call the doctor** only if you need confirmation of diagnosis or if other symptoms occur. **Treatment**: None. **Diet**: No changes.	**Prevention**: None. **Recurrence**: Possible. **Complications**: Only in those who are immune deficient or pregnant (can cause miscarriage, though most women are immune by the time they conceive).
Cause: Rubella virus. **Transmission**: 7 to 10 days before rash appears until possibly 7 days after rash appears; via direct or droplet contact. **Incubation**: 14 to 21 days; usually 16 to 18. **Duration:** A few hours to 4 or 5 days.	**Call the doctor** if a non-immune pregnant woman is exposed. **Treatment**: None. **Diet**: No changes.	**Prevention**: Immunization (MMR). **Recurrence**: None; one case confers immunity. **Complications**: Very rarely, thrombocytopenia or encephalitis.

DISEASE/SEASON/ SUSCEPTIBILITY	SYMPTOMS NON-RASH (numbers indicate order of appearance) RASH	
HAND-FOOT-MOUTH DISEASE (Vesicular Stomatitis) Season: Summer and autumn in temperate climates. Susceptibility: Greatest in babies and young children.	1. Fever; loss of appetite. *Often:* Sore throat and mouth (discomfort nursing); difficulty swallowing.	2. *In 2 or 3 days:* Lesions in mouth; then fingers, maybe feet, buttocks, sometimes arms, legs and, less often, face. Mouth lesions usually blister.
HERPANGINA Season: Mostly, summer and autumn in temperate climates. Susceptibility: Greatest in babies and young children. Occurs alone or with other diseases.	1. Fever (37.8° to 40°C/100° to 104°F, even 41.1°C/106°F); sore throat. 1. or 3. Painful swallowing. *Sometimes:* Vomiting; loss of appetite; diarrhoea; abdominal pain; lethargy.	2. Distinct greyish white papules in back of mouth or throat that blister and ulcerate (5 to 20 in number).
HERPES SIMPLEX (Cold Sores, Fever, Blisters) Season: Any, but sunshine can precipitate flare-up of virus. Susceptibility: Most primary infections occur in childhood.	*Primary infection:* Fever (can be 41.1°C/106°F); sore throat; swollen glands; drooling; bad breath; loss of appetite. *Often:* No symptoms. *Subsequent flare-ups: Possibly:* headache. Infection can also occur in the eye.	*Primary infection:* Sores in mucous membranes of mouth. *Subsequent flare-ups:* Welt forms on or near lip, tingles and itches, then blisters and oozes (painful stage), finally crusts and scabs (may itch).
HYDROPHOBIA	See **Rabies**.	

CAUSE/TRANSMISSION/ INCUBATION/DURATION	CALL THE DOCTOR/ TREATMENT/DIET	PREVENTION/RECURRENCE/ COMPLICATIONS
Cause: Coxsackie virus. **Transmission**: Mouth-to-mouth; faeces-to-hand-to-mouth. **Incubation**: 3 to 6 days. **Duration**: About 1 week.	**Call the doctor** to confirm diagnosis. **Treatment**: Symptomatic (page 408). **Diet**: Soft foods will be more comfortable.	**Prevention**: None. **Recurrence**: Possible. **Complications**: None.
Cause: Coxsackie virus. **Transmission**: Mouth-to-mouth; faeces-to-hand-to-mouth. **Incubation**: 3 to 6 days. **Duration**: 4 to 7 days, but healing can take 2 to 3 weeks.	**Call the doctor** to confirm diagnosis; **Call immediately** if convulsions or other symptoms occur. **Treatment**: Symptomatic. **Diet**: Soft foods will be more comfortable.	**Prevention**: None. **Recurrence**: Possible. **Complications**: None.
Cause: Herpes simplex virus (HSV) remains in body and can be reactivated by sun, stress, teething, a cold, fever. **Transmission**: Direct contact with lesion, saliva, stool, urine, or eye discharge; or with household articles within hours of contamination. **Incubation**: Possibly, 2 to 12 days. **Duration**: Scab falls off within 3 weeks.	**Call the doctor** only if baby seems ill. **Treatment**: Over-the-counter ointment may help; antiviral drugs in high-risk children. **Diet**: For primary infection, soft, non-acid foods; during subsequent flare-up, plain yogurt with live cultures may help. (A crushed lactobacillus tablet added to the yogurt will increase effectiveness.)	**Prevention**: Avoid triggering factors when possible. **Recurrence**: Latent infection can flare up anytime. **Complications**: Eye involvement.

DISEASE/SEASON/ SUSCEPTIBILITY	SYMPTOMS NON-RASH (numbers indicate order of appearance)	RASH

INFLUENZA (Flu; upper respiratory infection, or URI)
Season: More often in cold months; often in epidemics.
Susceptibility: Anyone, but very old and very young can become more ill.

Sometimes: None noted.
1. *Usually, abrupt onset of:* Fever (38° to 40°C/100.4° to 104°F); shivering; malaise; dry, unproductive cough; diarrhoea/vomiting; achiness (adults).
2. *Often, 3 or 4 days after onset*: Cold symptoms.
3. *Sometimes, for next 1 or 2 weeks*: Productive cough; fatigue.

LYME DISEASE
Season: May 1 to Nov. 30, with most cases in June and July.
Susceptibility: Everyone; heaviest concentration of cases in Northeastern areas of the U.S.; disease is rare but present in parts of Scotland.

1. or 2. *Often*: intermittent or variable fever, malaise, headache, mild neck stiffness and achiness.
Sometimes, as disease spreads: Headache, fatigue, aches and pains, nervous system involvement.
3. *Late disease, if untreated*: Chronic arthritis, especially in knees; further central nervous system involvement; *rarely*: heart damage.

1. *Usually*: An often bull's-eye shaped red rash (*erythema migrans*) at the site of tick bite, which usually expands over days to form a larger red rash.

2. *Sometimes*: If disease spreads, multiple rashes develop, similar to, but often smaller than, the primary lesion.

MEASLES (Rubeola)
Season: Winter and spring.
Susceptibility: Anyone not already immune.

1. *For 1 or 2 days*: Fever; runny nose; red, watery eyes; dry cough.
Sometimes: Diarrhoea; swollen glands.

2. Tiny white spots like grains of sand appear inside of cheeks (Koplik spots); may bleed.
3. Dull, red, slightly raised rash begins on forehead, behind ears, then spreads downwards giving a red-allover look.

CAUSE/TRANSMISSION/ INCUBATION/DURATION	CALL THE DOCTOR/ TREATMENT/DIET	PREVENTION/RECURRENCE/ COMPLICATIONS
Cause: A variety of influenza viruses. **Transmission**: Inhalation of respiratory droplets; use of contaminated articles. Communicable from 5 days before symptoms appear. **Incubation**: 1 to 2 days. **Duration**: Acute phase, a few days; convalescent phase, 1 to 2 weeks.	**Call the doctor** if baby is under 6 months, if symptoms are severe or continue 3 days, or if fever is over 38.9°C (102°F). **Treatment**: Symptomatic; in severe cases antiviral drugs may be prescribed. DO NOT GIVE ASPIRIN. **Diet**: Extra fluids.	**Prevention**: Annual immunization for certain high-risk infants; antivirals for others (ask the doctor and see page 150); avoiding crowds in flu season. **Recurrence**: Common. **Complications**: Secondary bacterial infections: otitis media, bronchitis, croup, pneumonia. Also Reye's syndrome.
Cause: A spirochete. **Transmission**: Spread by bite of the pinhead-size deer tick (which is carried by deer, mice and other animals, and can jump from them to humans) and possibly, other ticks. Since ticks take a long time to inject bacteria, prompt removal may prevent infection. **Incubation**: 3 to 32 days. **Duration**: Without treatment, possibly years.	**Call the doctor** if you suspect anyone in your family may have been bitten by a tick. **Treatment**: Antibiotics appear essential to defeat disease; effective even at late stages. **Diet**: No changes.	**Prevention**: Protective coverup clothing when out of doors in infested areas; removal of ticks; alertness to possible tick bites; *prompt* removal of ticks. **Recurrence**: Possible; there is no lasting immunity. **Complications**: Neurological, cardiac, motor abnormalities.
Cause: Measles virus. **Transmission**: Direct contact with droplets from 2 days before to 4 days after rash appears. **Incubation**: 8 to 12 days. **Duration**: About a week.	**Call the doctor** for diagnosis; **recall immediately** if cough becomes severe, if convulsions or symptoms of pneumonia, encephalitis, or otitis media occur, or if fever goes up after going down. **Treatment**: Symptomatic; warm soaks, dim lights if eyes are sensitive (but bright light not harmful). **Diet**: Extra fluids for fever.	**Prevention**: Immunization (MMR); strict isolation of infected persons. **Recurrence**: None. **Complications**: Otitis media, pneumonia, encephalitis; can be fatal.

DISEASE/SEASON/ SUSCEPTIBILITY	SYMPTOMS NON-RASH (numbers indicate order of appearance) RASH	
MENINGITIS (inflammation of the membranes around the brain and/or the spinal cord). **Season**: Varies with causative organism; for Hib, winter. **Susceptibility**: Depends on causative organism; for Hib, greatest for infants and young children.	Fever; high-pitched cry; drowsiness; irritability; loss of appetite; vomiting; bulging fontanel. *In older children, also*: stiff neck; sensitivity to light; blurred vision and other signs of neurological ills.	
MENINGO-ENCEPHALITIS (a combination of meningitis and encephalitis)	See **Meningitis** and **Encephalitis**.	
MUMPS **Season**: Late winter and spring. **Susceptibility**: Anyone not immune.	1. *Sometimes*: Vague pain; fever; loss of appetite. 2. *Usually*: Swelling of salivary (parotid) glands on one or both sides of jaw, below and in front of ear; ear pain; pain on chewing, or on taking acid or sour food or drink; swelling of other salivary glands. No symptoms at all in about 30% of cases.	
NONSPECIFIC VIRAL ILLNESSES **Season**: Mostly summer. **Susceptibility**: Mostly young children.	*Vary, but may include*: Fever; loss of appetite; diarrhoea.	Various types of rashes are seen with NSV.
OTITIS MEDIA	See page 416.	

CAUSE/TRANSMISSION/ INCUBATION/DURATION	CALL THE DOCTOR/ TREATMENT/DIET	PREVENTION/RECURRENCE/ COMPLICATIONS
Cause: Most often, bacteria, such as Hib; also viruses, which cause less serious disease. **Transmission**: Depends on organism. **Incubation**: Varies with organism; for Hib, probably less than 10 days. **Duration**: Varies.	**Call the doctor immediately** if you suspect meningitis, **or go to A&E** if doctor can't be reached. **Treatment**: For viral meningitis, symptomatic; for bacterial, hospitalization required. **Diet**: Extra fluids for fever.	**Prevention**: Hib immunization for Hib infections; stringent health-care rules in day-care centres. **Recurrence**: None with Hib; one attack confers immunity. **Complications**: Hib and other bacterial forms can do lasting neurological damage, and can be fatal; viral forms usually do no long-term damage.
Cause: Mumps virus. **Transmission**: Usually 1 or 2 days (but could be as long as 7 days) prior to onset until 9 days after onset via direct contact with respiratory secretions. **Incubation**: Usually 16 to 18 days, but can be 12 to 25. **Duration**: 5 to 7 days.	**Call the doctor** for diagnosis; **call back immediately** if there is vomiting, drowsiness, possible headache, back or neck stiffness, or other signs of meningoencephalitis either along with or following the mumps. **Treatment**: Symptomatic for fever and pain; cool compresses applied to cheeks. **Diet**: Non-acid, non-sour soft diet.	**Prevention**: Immunization. **Recurrence**: Very slight chance of recurrence if only one side was affected. **Complications**: Meningoencephalitis; other complications rare in infants, but can be serious in adult males.
Cause: Various enteroviruses. **Transmission**: Faeces-to-hand-to-mouth; possibly mouth-to-mouth. **Incubation**: 3 to 6 days. **Duration**: Usually a few days.	**Call the doctor** to confirm diagnosis; **call again** if baby seems worse or if new symptoms appear. **Treatment**: Symptomatic. **Diet**: Extra fluids for diarrhoea, fever (see pages 414, 424).	**Prevention**: None. **Recurrence**: Common. **Complications**: Very rare.

DISEASE/SEASON/ SUSCEPTIBILITY	SYMPTOMS NON-RASH (numbers indicate order of appearance) RASH
PERTUSSIS **(Whooping Cough)** **Season**: Late winter/early spring. **Susceptibility**: Half of all cases occur in babies under 1 year.	1. *Catarrhal stage*: Cold symptoms with dry cough; low-grade fever; irritability. 2. *Paroxysmal stage, 1 or 2 weeks later*: Coughing in explosive bursts with no breaths between; thick mucus expelled. *Often*: Bulging eyes and protruding tongue; pale or red skin; vomiting; profuse sweating; exhaustion. *Sometimes*: Apnea, in infants; hernia, from cough. 3. *Convalescent stage*: Cessation of whooping and vomiting; reduced coughing; improved appetite and mood. Mild in immunized children.
PHARYNGITIS	See **Sore Throat**
PNEUMONIA (Inflammation of the lung) **Season**: Varies with causative factor. **Susceptibility**: Anyone, but especially the very young, very old and those with chronic illnesses.	*Commonly, after cold or other illness, baby seems suddenly worse, with*: Increased fever; productive cough; rapid breathing; blueness; wheezy, raspy, and/or difficult breathing; abdominal bloating and pain.

CAUSE/TRANSMISSION/ INCUBATION/DURATION	CALL THE DOCTOR/ TREATMENT/DIET	PREVENTION/RECURRENCE/ COMPLICATIONS
Cause: Bordetella pertussis bacteria. **Transmission**: Direct contact via droplets; most communicable during catarrhal stage, less so later; antibiotics reduce period of communicability. **Incubation**: 7 to 10 days; rarely more than 2 weeks. **Duration**: Usually 6 weeks, but can last much longer.	**Call the doctor promptly** for persistent coughing. **Treatment**: Hospitalization for infants; antibiotics (may help reduce symptoms in first stage, communicability later); oxygen; mucus suctioning; humidification. **Diet**: Frequent small feedings; fluid replacement; intravenous feeding if necessary.	**Prevention**: Immunization (DTP) **Recurrence**: None; one attack confers immunity. **Complications**: Many, including: otitis media; pneumonia; convulsions. Can be fatal, especially in infants.
Cause: Various organisms, including bacteria, mycoplasma, fungi, viruses and protozoa, as well as insult by chemical or other irritant or inhaled object. **Transmission**: Varies with cause. **Incubation**: Varies with cause. **Duration**: Varies with cause.	**Call the doctor** for productive or persistent cough; or if a slightly sick baby seems worse or has increased fever or cough; **call immediately or go to A&E** if baby has difficulty breathing, turns a bluish colour, or seems very sick. **Treatment**: Symptomatic. Most cases can be treated at home. Antibiotics, if needed. **Diet**: Fluids; adequate nutrition.	**Prevention**: Hib immunization for Hib infections; protection of susceptible infants against illness. **Recurrence**: Many types can recur. **Complications**: Riskiest for those infants weakened by other illnesses or low birthweight.

DISEASE/SEASON/ SUSCEPTIBILITY	SYMPTOMS NON-RASH (numbers indicate order of appearance) RASH

RABIES (Hydrophobia)
Season: Anytime, but more rabid dogs in summer.
Susceptibility: Anyone.

1. Local or radiating pain, burning, sensation of cold, itching, tingling at bite site.
2. Slight fever (38.3° to 38.9°C/ 101° to 102°F); lethargy; headache; loss of appetite; nausea; sore throat; loose cough; irritability; sensitivity to light and noise; dilated pupils; rapid heart-beat; shallow breathing; excessive drooling, tearing, sweating.
3. *2 to 10 days later*: Increased anxiety and restlessness; vision problems; facial weakness; fever up to 39.4°C (103°F). *Often*: Fear of water, with liquids expelled; frothy drooling.
4. *About 3 days later*: Paralysis.

RESPIRATORY SYNCYTIAL VIRUS (RSV)
Season: Winter and early spring in temperate climates; rainy season in tropics.
Susceptibility: Anyone, at any age, but about 66% contract by age 1, most by age 3.

Range from mild cold-like symptoms to bronchiolitis and bronchopneumonia, with: cough, wheezing; sore throat; painful breathing; malaise; inflamed mucous membranes of nose and throat.
Sometimes: Apnea (especially in premies).

REYE'S SYNDROME
Season: Anytime.
Susceptibility: Mostly children who are given aspirin during a viral illness such as chicken pox or influenza.

1 to 7 days following a viral infection: Persistent vomiting; lethargy; rapidly deteriorating mental state (irritability, confusion, delirium); rapid heartbeat and respiration.
May progress to: Coma.

CAUSE/TRANSMISSION/ INCUBATION/DURATION	CALL THE DOCTOR/ TREATMENT/DIET	PREVENTION/RECURRENCE/ COMPLICATIONS
Cause: Rabies virus. **Transmission**: From an infected animal, via a bite *rarely*: licking of an open wound, scratches or abrasions; *possibly*: close exposure to a rabid bat or other animals. **Incubation**: 9 days to 1 year, but 2 months is average. **Duration**: About 2 weeks to point of paralysis.	**Call the doctor** following a bite by any animal you do not know for certain has been vaccinated against rabies. **Treatment**: Restrain animal; see first aid instructions for animal bites (page 427); postexposure prophylaxis (PEP) with human rabies immune globulin (HRIG) and human diploid cell vaccine (HDCV) will be given if animal can't be found or turns out to be rabid; tetanus booster will be given as needed. Hospitalization if disease is not headed off. **Diet**: No dietary changes.	**Prevention**: Immunization of pets and individuals at high risk; teaching babies caution with strange animals; community effort to keep strays off street and wild animal population rabies-free. **Recurrence**: None. **Complications**: Disease if left to natural course, untreated, is fatal. Once symptoms occur, mortality rate high, even with treatment.
Cause: Respiratory syncytial virus (RSV). **Transmission**: Via eyes or nose through contact with infected person or contaminated articles from 3 days to 4 weeks from onset. **Incubation**: Usually 5 to 8 days. **Duration**: Varies with illness caused.	**Call the doctor** if baby with cold symptoms has difficulty breathing (nostrils flare), is wheezing, has a raspy cough, or has very rapid respiration (see page 400). **Treatment**: Symptomatic; may also include antiviral drug and hospitalization, if needed. **Diet**: For symptoms only.	**Prevention**: Isolation, careful handwashing, avoidance of exposure to smoke; RSV immune globulin in high-risk infants; no vaccine as yet. **Recurrence**: Possible, but usually as upper respiratory infection after age 3. **Complications**: Lower respiratory disease in 33% of infants (2.5% require hospitalization); otitis media.
Cause: Unknown, but appears to be related to such viral illnesses as chicken pox and influenza, and to aspirin use during them. **Transmission**: Unknown. **Incubation**: Unknown, but seems to occur within days of onset of viral infection. **Duration**: Varies.	**Call the doctor immediately** if you suspect Reye's Syndrome, **or go to A&E.** **Treatment**: Hospital treatment is vital.	**Prevention**: Avoid giving aspirin with viral diseases such as chicken pox or influenza. **Recurrence**: None. **Complications**: Can be fatal, but survivors usually have no lasting problems.

DISEASE/SEASON/ SUSCEPTIBILITY	SYMPTOMS NON-RASH (numbers indicate order of appearance)	RASH
ROSEOLA INFANTUM **Season**: Year-round, but more common in spring and autumn. **Susceptibility**: Greatest in babies and young children.	1. Irritability; loss of appetite; fever (38.9° to 40.5°C/102° to 105°F). *Sometimes*: Runny nose; swollen glands; convulsions. 2. *On 3rd or 4th day*. Fever drops and baby seems better.	3. Faint pink spots that turn white upon pressure on body, neck, upper arms and, sometimes, face and legs. In some cases, there may be no rash.
SCARLET FEVER **(Scarlatina)** **Season**: Year-round, but more common in cold months. **Susceptibility**: Greatest among school-age children; less common in those under 3 and in adults.	Similar to strep throat, but often heralded by vomiting and characterized by rash.	Bright red rash on face, groin and under arms; spreads to rest of body and limbs; leaves skin rough, peeling.
SORE THROAT, VIRAL **(Tonsillitis; Pharyngitis)** **Season**: Autumn, winter and spring. **Susceptibility**: More often, older children.	Moderate fever (38.3° to 39.4°C/101° to 103°F); fatigue; throat pain or discomfort; some difficulty swallowing; irritability and fussiness. Throat appears red and tonsils may be swollen. *Sometimes*: Hoarseness; coughing.	

CAUSE/TRANSMISSION/ INCUBATION/DURATION	CALL THE DOCTOR/ TREATMENT/DIET	PREVENTION/RECURRENCE/ COMPLICATIONS
Cause: Probably virus. **Transmission**: Unknown; not highly contagious. **Incubation**: 5 to 15 days. **Duration**: 3 to 6 days.	**Call the doctor** to confirm diagnosis; **call back** if fever persists for 4 or 5 days, if baby develops convulsions or seems ill. **Treatment**: Symptomatic. **Diet**: Increased fluids for fever.	**Prevention**: None known. **Recurrence**: Apparently. **Complications**: Very rare.
Cause: Streptococcus bacteria. **Transmission**: Direct contact with infected person. **Incubation**: 2 to 5 days. **Duration**: About 1 week in infants under 6 months, but runny nose and general crankiness can last 6 weeks; about 1 to 2 weeks in older babies.	See **Strep Throat**.	**Prevention**: Isolation of infected persons and good preventive hygiene. **Recurrence**: Can occur. **Complications**: See **Strep Throat**.
Cause: Various viruses, most often adenovirus; also enterovirus. (Chronic sore throat may be due to allergy; tobacco smoke; hot, dry air, or other factors.) **Transmission**: Depends on causative virus; probably respiratory route with adenovirus. **Incubation**: Depends on causative virus; 2 to 14 days with adenovirus. **Duration**: 1 to 10 days.	**Call the doctor** if you suspect baby has a sore throat, so throat culture can be taken to rule out strep. **Treatment**: Symptomatic. Paracetamol for pain. (Babies are too young for gargling or sucking on lozenges.) DO NOT GIVE ASPIRIN. **Diet**: Soft cold foods may be easier for a baby on solids to tolerate. Fluids.	**Prevention**: Isolation of infected person and good hygiene. In chronic sore throat, the removal of the cause. **Recurrence**: Possible. **Complications**: Unlikely, except in children with suppressed immunity.

DISEASE/SEASON/ SUSCEPTIBILITY	SYMPTOMS
	NON-RASH (numbers indicate order of appearance) RASH

STREP THROAT (Streptococcal Pharyngitis)
Season: October through April.
Susceptibility: Most common in school-age children.

In infants under 6 months: Fever; moderate inflammation of the throat.
In older babies: Low-grade fever; mild sore throat.
Sometimes: No symptoms noted.
In chronic strep: Runny nose; fluctuating temperature; crankiness; loss of appetite; pallor.
In older children: High fever; red pussy throat; trouble swallowing; swollen tonsils and glands; abdominal pain.

TETANUS (Lockjaw)
Season: When more time is spent out of doors.
Susceptibility: Anyone not immunized.

Localized: Spasm and increased muscle tone near the wound.
Generalized: Involuntary muscle contractions that can arch back, lock jaw, twist neck; convulsions; rapid heartbeat; profuse sweating; low-grade fever; difficult sucking, in infants.

TONSILLITIS

See **Sore Throat**.

UPPER RESPIRATORY INFECTION (URI)

See **Common Cold** (page 411) and **Influenza**.

CAUSE/TRANSMISSION/ INCUBATION/DURATION	CALL THE DOCTOR/ TREATMENT/DIET	PREVENTION/RECURRENCE/ COMPLICATIONS
Cause: Streptococcus pyogenes, a group of Group A streptococcus bacteria. **Transmission**: By direct contact with infected individual from 1 day before onset to 6 days after, but antibiotics reduce communicability to 24 hours. Highly contagious. **Incubation**: 2 to 5 days. **Duration**: About 1 week in infants under 6 months, but runny nose and general crankiness can last 6 weeks About 1 to 2 weeks in older babies.	**Call the doctor** initially for diagnosis (throat culture will confirm); **call again** if fever doesn't drop in 2 days, or if new symptoms appear. **Treatment**: Symptomatic. Antibiotics to prevent complications. **Diet**: Soft cold foods may be easier for a baby on solids to tolerate. Fluids.	**Prevention**: Isolation of infected persons and good hygiene. **Recurrence**: Possible. **Complications**: Infection can spread to ears, mastoids, sinuses, lungs, brain, kidneys, skin (impetigo). Rheumatic fever less common but does occur in infants; also joint pain and rashes.
Cause: Toxin produced by bacteria called Clostridium tetani, which spreads through the body. **Transmission**: Transmitted via contamination by the bacteria of a puncture wound, a burn, a deep scrape, or an unhealed umbilical cord. **Incubation**: 3 days to 3 weeks, but an average of 8 days. **Duration**: Several weeks.	**Call the doctor immediately or go to the A&E** if unvaccinated baby incurs susceptible wound. **Treatment**: Medical treatment essential: tetanus toxoid to prevent development of disease; tetanus antitoxins; muscle relaxants; antibiotics; respirator.	**Prevention**: Immunization (DTP); sanitary care of umbilicus; avoidance of outdoor injuries when possible. **Recurrence**: None. **Complications**: Many, including: ulcers; pneumonia; abnormal heart rate; blood clot in lung. Can be fatal.

Height and Weight Charts

Record your baby's weight and length at birth in a permanent health record and update his or her progress at each visit to the doctor. To chart measurements on these graphs, find baby's age along the bottom of the page and weight (in kilograms and pounds) or length (in centimetres and inches) along the side. Put a colour dot at the point where the two

GIRLS HEIGHT CHART

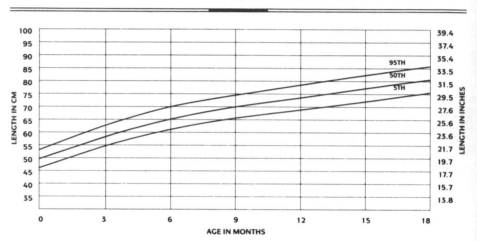

GIRLS WEIGHT CHART

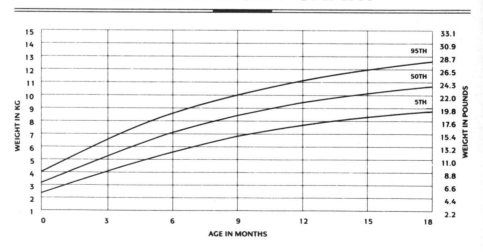

come together. To see your baby's progress, connect the dots as they are added. Ninety out of every one hundred children fall within the fifth and ninety-fifth percentiles. Though those in the top and bottom five per cent may come by their size genetically and be doing well, some may be growing too slowly or gaining too quickly. If your baby falls into either of these groups, discuss your concern with the doctor. Check with the doctor, too, about any sudden variation from the typical pattern (in height or weight or both), though such a variation may be perfectly normal for your baby.

BOYS HEIGHT CHART

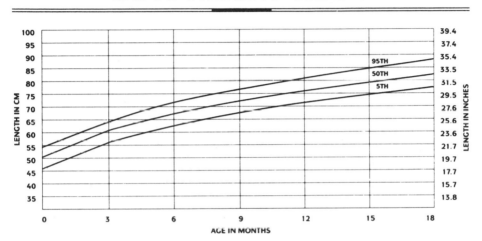

BOYS WEIGHT CHART

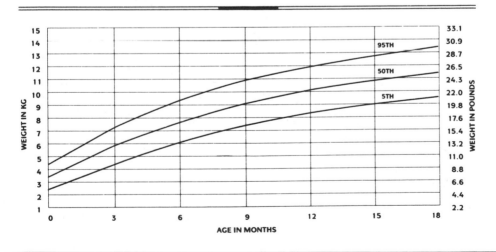

Index

♦

A

Abscess, breast, 546
Abdomen
  cramping in, postpartum, 503
  in sick baby, 401
  injuries to, 427
  lump in, postpartum, 519
  muscles of, postpartum, 519
  pain in, postpartum, 503, 547
  shape of, postpartum, 532
Abrasions, first aid for, 439
Accidents to baby
  falls, 338
  parental reaction to, 338
  prevention of, 285
Accidents caused by baby handling of, 329
Acne, infant, 94
Acquired Immune Deficiency Syndrome, 476
Active baby, 154
Adaptability, poor, 155
ADD (Attention Deficit Disorder), 370
Additives in food, 235
Advenovirus, 621
Adopted baby, 490
  and friends and family, 496
  breastfeeding and, 493
  grandparents and, 495
  health problems in, 496
  hiring baby nurse for, 492
  loving, 492
  of foreign birth, 496
  picking doctor for, 491

  preparing for, 490
  telling baby, 497
Adoption
  and baby blues, 493
  and breastfeeding, 9, 493
  and loving baby, 492
  and not feeling like a mother, 491
  and parental insecurity, 491, 492
Adoptive mother and exercise, 519
Adoptive parents, 491
Advice, unasked for, 222
Afterpains, 503, 414
Aggressiveness in older child, 598
  hitting, 360
AIDS, 476
  and breastfeeding, 9
Air, indoor
  pollution of, 232
Airway
  clearing of, in CPR, 441
  suctioning of, at birth, 45
Alar, 238
Alcohol, 350, 525
  and making love, 551
  baby-sitter, use by, 188
  in breast milk, 543
  in mother's diet, 525
Allergy(ies), 406
  and breast milk, 3
  causes of, 410
  food, 214, 223, 226, 411
  prevention of, 411
  symptoms of, 406
  to cow's milk, 112, 140

  treatment of, 410
Altitudes, high, 395
Aluminium pots, 242
Anaemia, 249
Anaesthesia and breastfeeding, 51
Anencephaly, 476
Angel hair, 388
Anger, parental
  because of crying baby, 126
  handling, 331, 333
  over abnormal baby, 468
  toward baby, in severe depression, 537
  toward older child, 596
Animal bites, 427
Antenatal interview, 34
Anterior fontanel, 104
Anti-cancer foods, 236
Antiseptic cream, 39
Apgar test, 47, 48
Apnea, 180
  and car seats, 462
  of prematurity, 181, 466
Appearance of newborn, 65
Appetite
  changes in, 97, 361
  decrease in, 361
  erratic, 306
  in newborn, 64
  in sick baby, 400
  increase in, 363
  loss of, 308
  loss of, and teething, 152
  poor, 362
Apple-cranberry cubes, 612
Apples, chemicals in, 238

WHAT TO EXPECT
THE TODDLER YEARS
Arlene Eisenberg, Heidi E. Murkoff & Sandee E. Hathaway

'How can I get my toddler talking?'

'My daughter's nearly three and still not potty trained. What can I do?'

'Is there any way to avoid my toddler's tantrums?'

'My toddler is a fussy eater - how can I be sure he's eating what he should?'

Overflowing with intelligence and good common sense, this comprehensive guide provides clear explanations and useful guidelines on everything a parent might want to know about the second and third years of their child's life. On a month-by-month basis, *What to Expect the Toddler Years* explains what a toddler will be able to do at that age, and what to expect in the months ahead. Featuring topics from potty-training to sleeping problems, disciplining to how to encourage learning and thinking, this book covers it all - including invaluable advice on how parents can make time for themselves in the midst of it all.

What to Expect the Toddler Years is an essential guide to keeping a toddler safe, healthy and - above all - happy.

0 684 81677 6

£12.99

WHAT TO EXPECT
WHEN YOU'RE EXPECTING
Arlene Eisenberg, Heidi E. Murkoff & Sandee E. Hathaway

'Is it safe to have a baby after 35?'

'Will the drinks I had before I knew I was pregnant harm my baby?'

'I haven't had morning sickness. Can I still be pregnant?'

The world's bestselling pregnancy manual answers the concerns of parents-to-be in a clear, comprehensive, month-by-month format. It explains what it is important for you to know, and gives advice and information on what you may be concerned about, at every stage of your pregnancy from planning to post-natal. Covering everything from amniocentesis to sex, maternity clothes to breastfeeding, and with a special section for fathers, this is the pregnancy guide to reassure you month after month.

0 684 81787 X

£10.99

BABIES!

A Parent's Guide to Surviving (and Enjoying!) Baby's First Year
Dr Christopher Green
Author of *Toddler Taming*

The arrival of a baby is one of the most memorable events in a parent's life. It is an exciting time yet many parents feel uncertain and confused and are not sure what to do. Well, don't despair. *BABIES!* brings back fun to childcare. It's a practical, commonsense, up-to-date guide to the everyday concerns of parents facing the first year of their baby's life. Dr Christopher Green's irresistible style of light-hearted yet authoritative advice aims to reassure parents to trust their own instincts and do what feels right and works for them.

'A "survival" guide to the first year with a difference. A light-hearted, humorous look at the pleasure and pitfalls of parenthood distilled from years of listening to thousands of mothers and fathers and finding out what worked for them. I fell in love with Dr Green's book at the bonding chapter' *Daily Express*

'The key to *Babies!* is to help instil parental confidence and bring a bit of distance and humour to the whole business . . . good, upbeat stuff' *Sunday Telegraph*

0 671-69673-4

£10.99